MAJOR PRINCIPLES
OF MEDIA LAW

2013 EDITION

Genelle Belmas

California State University, Fullerton

Wayne Overbeck

California State University, Fullerton
Member of the California Bar

WADSWORTH
CENGAGE Learning™

Australia • Brazil • Japan • Korea • Mexico • Singapore • Spain • United Kingdom • United States

**Major Principles of Media Law:
2013 Edition**
Genelle Belmas and Wayne Overbeck

Editor-in-Chief: Lyn Uhl

Publisher: Michael Rosenberg

Assistant Editor: Erin Bosco

Editorial Assistant: Rebecca Donahue

Media Editor: Jessica Badiner

Marketing Brand Manager: Ben Rivera

Marketing Coordinator: Brittany Blais

Senior Market Development Manager:
Kara Kindstrom

Print Buyer: Doug Bertke

Production Service: PreMediaGlobal

Senior Rights Acquisitions Specialist:
Mandy Groszko

Cover Designer: Paul Neff

Cover Image: © Paul Pantazezscu

Compositor: PreMediaGlobal

For product information and technology assistance, contact us at
Cengage Learning Customer & Sales Support, 1-800-354-9706

For permission to use material from this text or product,
submit all requests online at **www.cengage.com/permissions**
Further permissions questions can be emailed to
permissionrequest@cengage.com

Library of Congress Control Number: 2012944591

ISBN-13: 978-1-111-83684-9

ISBN-10: 1-111-83684-1

Wadsworth
20 Channel Center Street
Boston, MA 02210
USA

Cengage Learning is a leading provider of customized learning solutions with office locations around the globe, including Singapore, the United Kingdom, Australia, Mexico, Brazil, and Japan. Locate your local office at
www.cengage.com/global

Cengage Learning products are represented in Canada by
Nelson Education, Ltd.

To learn more about Wadsworth, visit **www.cengage.com/wadsworth**

Purchase any of our products at your local college store or at our preferred online store **www.cengagebrain.com**

Printed in the United States of America
1 2 3 4 5 6 7 16 15 14 13 12

Table of Contents

Preface

This is the 24th edition of *Major Principles of Media Law,* and the 22nd published on an annual revision cycle. This edition includes new developments through the end of the Supreme Court's 2011-2012 term and will be in print in time for fall 2012 classes; it sports glossary terms, sidebars and pictures (most either public domain, U.S. Government work, out of copyright, or licensed by their owners under the Creative Commons attribution license), and additional elements like "Focus On" sidebars and recommendations about what students should learn about their state law.

Hundreds of changes take place in media law every year. This year, most Court watchers were entranced by the decisions in the Obamacare and Arizona immigration policy lawsuits. The Court, surprisingly to some, upheld most of both laws. At least some commentators thought that Chief Justice John Roberts exercised masterful control over both these cases. Editorialist David Savage wrote in a June 30 *Los Angeles Times* editorial, "The message from Roberts was that the high court, even in a heated election year, was an independent institution and an enforcer of the Constitution—not a friendly forum for just one party or one side of the ideological divide."

And that ideological divide is getting deeper. Perhaps illustrative of the tensions between the parties (as well as the genders) in June 2012 was the silencing of two female Democratic lawmakers in Michigan by a male Republican House Speaker in response to their discussion of a Michigan abortion bill. Reps. Barb Byrum and Lisa Brown introduced an amendment to the bill that would limit access to vasectomies, and when debate became heated and Rep. Brown said, "I'm flattered that you're all so interested in my vagina, but no means no," she was gaveled down, and the women were told they would not be recognized to speak on the floor the day after. The issue was inflamed when the Republican Speaker of the House called Brown's comments on the floor a "temper tantrum." Moreover, Justice Antonin Scalia's often vitriolic and pointed dissents—and political comments from the bench—have been criticized by some as harmful to the Supreme Court and the judiciary as a whole.

Yet, even in a year dominated by non-First Amendment cases, the Court still gave us some new rulings, including a narrowing of the public domain (*Golan v. Holder*), a striking down of the Stolen Valor Act (*U.S. v. Alvarez*), and a Privacy Act case (*FAA v. Cooper*). As well, there were developments in filesharing, net neutrality, tobacco advertising, fair use, cable television technologies, and antitrust actions, including against Google and Apple.

The 24th edition of *Major Principles* also notes many other changes in the law. Here are just a few of the highlights of what is new in this edition.

Chapter One (The Legal System) discusses:
- Updates on vacancies in the federal judiciary
- Updates on calls for more judicial ethics monitoring

Chapter Two (The Legacy of Freedom) discusses:
- The WikiLeaks saga: the release of confidential documents and its repercussions
- Administrative efforts to combat information leaks

Chapter Three (Prior Restraints) discusses:
- The Supreme Court's opinions in *Reichle v. Howards*, in which it upheld the rights of

Secret Service agents to act to protect lives, and *U.S. v. Alvarez*, in which the Court struck down the Stolen Valor Act as an undue burden on the First Amendment
- More developments in funeral protest law
- Abortion speech laws and their limitations
- Additional developments in online anonymous speech

Chapter Four (Libel and Slander) discusses:
- Developments in Section 230 protections, including a controversial Washington law combating child sex trafficking
- Defamation in political campaign literature

Chapter Five (Privacy) discusses:
- The Supreme Court's decision in *U.S. v. Jones*, saying that GPS tracking counts as a search under the Fourth Amendment
- Developments in DOMA legislation and abortion protest laws
- The FTC's revisiting and updating of COPPA and a new privacy report

Chapter Six (Copyrights and Trademarks) discusses:
- SOPA and PIPA fallout and the Internet blackout
- The Supreme Court's decision in *Golan v. Holder*, upholding Congress' jurisdiction over the public domain and URAA's constitutionality
- The Court's grant of *cert* in *John Wiley & Sons, Inc. v. Kirtsaeng*, another look at the first-sale doctrine
- New generic top-level domains to be approved
- A *South Park* episode and parody

Chapter Seven (Fair Trial-Free Press) discusses:
- Continuing social media issues in the courtroom
- Gag orders—yes, they still show up!
- Update on the pilot project in cameras in federal courtrooms
- Unsealing of Boy Scout "perversion files"

Chapter Eight (Newsgatherer's Privilege) discusses:
- The Oregon's Supreme Court's refusal to extend its shield law to bloggers
- Developments in the Risen privilege case

Chapter Nine (Freedom of Information) discusses:
- The Supreme Court's holding in *FAA v. Cooper* that Privacy Act plaintiffs may recover for only financial damages
- FOIA lawsuits on waterboarding, bank bailouts, and the death of bin Laden

Chapter Ten (Obscenity and Pornography) discusses:
- Age records for sex workers
- Bans on library access for sex offenders
- Standing for a dancer to challenge an injunction against her venue denied

Chapter Eleven (Regulation of the Electronic Media) discusses:

- The Supreme Court's decision in *FCC v. Fox*, dodging the First Amendment implications of the FCC indecency policy, and the Janet Jackson "wardrobe malfunction" case, finally over
- A new section on the Computer Fraud and Abuse Act
- The ongoing net neutrality debate, including impending lawsuits
- New cases dealing with the definition of a cable company

Chapter Twelve (Ownership and Antitrust Issues) discusses:

- The Supreme Court's granting of *cert* in *Behrend v. Comcast Corp.* to determine whether cable customers could be granted class status
- The FTC's antitrust investigation of Google
- Justice's investigation of eBook pricing by Apple and several book publishers

Chapter Thirteen (Advertising Regulation) discusses:

- Continuing developments in campaign finance, including the Supreme Court's defense of *Citizens United* against the Montana Supreme Court
- Several cases questioning the validity of the Family Smoking Prevention and Tobacco Control Act, including the dramatic cigarette packaging rules
- Stephen Colbert's SuperPAC

Chapter Fourteen (Student Press Law) discusses:

- A test of the Illinois student free press act and an application of the *Christian Legal Society* case
- Continuing developments in schools' attempts to regulate student social media use off-campus
- New developments in boobie bracelet litigation

* * *

All this and much more happened in one year. As has been true ever since these annual revisions began, *Major Principles of Media Law* will be the first media law textbook in print with many of the year's new developments.

As Wayne Overbeck has written in this *Preface* in previous years, having a textbook this current is possible only because of the emergence of desktop publishing technology—and because there are publishers willing to throw out traditional schedules for textbooks. A media law textbook produced on the old timetable is at least a year out of date when it arrives in college bookstores for the first time and may be four or five years out of date before it is replaced by a new edition. I share Wayne's belief that an up-to-date textbook makes teaching (and learning) this challenging and always-changing subject much easier.

Although much of the material is new, *Major Principles of Media Law* retains the primary goal it has had through 20+ editions: to present a clear and concise summary of the law for mass communications students.

Additional resources for instructors can be found on the book's password-protected companion website. These resources include a test bank and chapter-specific PowerPoint slides that are available for download at www.cengagebrain.com.

If this book succeeds, much of the credit should go to the 60 reviewers who have offered so many helpful suggestions since the first edition was written years ago. Special thanks should go to the most recent reviewers, including Andy Alali, California State University, Bakersfield; Ron Allman, Indiana University Southeast; Jodi Bromley, Old Dominion University; Christopher Burnett, California State University, Long Beach; Michael Cavanagh, State University of New York at Brockport; Tom Dickson, Missouri State University; Thomas Gardner, Westfield State College; Thomas Gladney, University of Wyoming; Dale Grossman, Cornell University; Jake Highton, University of Nevada, Reno; James Landers, Colorado State University; Carole McNall, St. Bonaventure University; Fritz Messere, State University of New York at Oswego; Donald Mohr, Purdue University; Henry Ruminsky, Wright State University; Jeff Stein, Wartburg College; and Omar Swartz, University of Colorado at Denver. I offer separate thanks to Tom Gardner and Robert Humphrey who have taken the time to point out typos, clarity issues and the like over the past few years. These comments are most helpful in my continued quest to make the content accessible as well as accurate. I welcome students and faculty alike to contact me with suggestions and corrections.

I offer my continued gratitude to Wayne Overbeck, who has trusted me with this work that he so ably shepherded through so many editions, and to Rick Pullen of California State University, Fullerton (now also retired!), who was co-author of the first two editions of this book. I offer tons of thanks to my CSUF colleague in media law, Jason Shepard, for always forwarding me new information for the book. Our intellectual collaborations are one of the best parts of the job.

I add a few names to the list of individuals to whom I'm indebted, for whom a mere "thanks" seems hardly enough: xtine burrough's design continues to be a critical part of this book's success, and I'm lucky to have her talent and friendship. Thanks again to Christine Amarantus for allowing me to reprint in Chapter Three her excellent picture of the Westboro Baptist protestors and counter-protestors that originally appeared in the *Daily Titan*, to Michelle A. Scott for her wonderful photo of the Supreme Court building in all its glory in Chapter Seven, and to Lourdes Cueva Chacón for the great image of old license plates that graces the "law of licence plates" sidebar in Chapter Three. And cheers and lattes to all the students who found typographical and other errors in past editions. They are my best proofreaders.

To Gene and Ginner Belmas, my biggest cheerleaders—thanks, Mom and Dad, as always. My mom reads parts of this book every year! How cool is that? And I don't even have to threaten to test her on it. To Nero, for keeping me honest in many ways. And last but never least, to Douglas Bornemann, Ph.D., J.D., for being willing to have an overstressed wife and a houseful of paper for several months each year. A million "thank yous" can never, ever suffice for all you do for me. This one is truly blessed, every moment of every day.

Genelle Belmas, Ph.D.
July 1, 2012

for Mike C. (a.k.a. Corinthalas/Grizzmo), because being awesome is even better in print.

For updates during the academic year, access to archives of material not published in this year's print edition, and contact information, please visit my website:

www.genellebelmas.com

Table of Cases

1   *The American Legal System*

A merica has become a nation of laws, lawyers and lawsuits. Both the number of lawsuits being filed and the number of lawyers have doubled since the 1970s. California has about four times as many lawyers today as it had in 1975. Nationwide, there are more than a million attorneys. For good or ill, more people with grievances are suing somebody.

The media have not escaped this flood of litigation. The nation's broadcasters, cable and satellite television providers, newspapers, magazines, wire services, Internet services and advertising agencies are constantly fighting legal battles. Today few media executives can do their jobs without consulting lawyers regularly. Moreover, legal problems are not just head-aches for top executives. Working media professionals run afoul of the law regularly, facing lawsuits and even jail sentences.

Million-dollar verdicts against the media are no longer unusual, and the big national media are by no means the only targets. For example, in 1980 one medium-size newspaper in Idaho was ordered to pay $1.9 million in a libel case—not because the newspaper published a horribly libelous falsehood but merely because the paper refused to say who told a reporter where to find public records about wrongdoing by an insurance company. A higher court eventually set aside that ruling, but by then the paper had spent thousands of dollars on legal expenses to defend itself (*Sierra Life v. Magic Valley Newspapers*, 6 Media L. Rep. 1769). Likewise, those who do video production work, prepare advertising copy or post messages on the Internet may risk lawsuits and threats of lawsuits for anything from libel to copyright infringement. More than ever before, a knowledge of media law is essential for a successful career in mass communications.

This textbook was written for communications students and media professionals, not for lawyers or law students. Perhaps we should begin by explaining how the American legal system works.

▪ THE KEY ROLE OF THE COURTS

Mass media law is largely based on court decisions. Even though Congress and the 50 state legislatures have enacted many laws affecting the media, the courts play the decisive role in interpreting those laws. For that matter, the courts also have the final say in interpret-ing the meaning of our most important legal document, the U.S. Constitution. The courts have the power to modify or even overturn laws passed by state legislatures and Congress, particularly when a law conflicts with the Constitution. In so doing, the courts have the power to establish legal precedent, handing down rules that other courts must ordinarily follow in deciding similar cases.

But not all court decisions establish legal *precedents*, and not all legal precedents are equally important as guidelines for later decisions. The Supreme Court of the United States is the highest court in the country; its rulings are generally binding on all lower courts. On matters of state law the highest court in each of the 50 states (usually called the state supreme court) has the final say—unless one of its rulings somehow violates the U.S. Consti-tution. On federal matters the U.S. Courts of Appeals rank just below the U.S. Supreme Court. All of these courts are *appellate* courts; cases are appealed to them from trial courts.

There is an important difference between trial and appellate courts. While appellate courts make precedent-setting decisions that interpret the meaning of law, trial courts are

precedent:
a case that other courts rely on when deciding future cases with similar facts or issues.

appellate court:
a court to which a finding from a lower court may be appealed.

questions of fact:
resolutions of factual disputes that are decided by a jury.

remand:
to send back to a lower court for evaluation based on new legal rules.

responsible for deciding factual issues such as the guilt or innocence of a person accused of a crime. This fact-finding process does not normally establish legal precedents. The way a judge or jury decides a given murder trial, for instance, sets no precedent at all for the next murder trial. The fact that one alleged murderer may be guilty doesn't prove the guilt of the next murder suspect.

In civil (i.e., non-criminal) lawsuits, this is also true. A trial court may have to decide whether a newspaper or broadcaster libeled the local mayor by falsely accusing the mayor of wrongdoing. Even if the media did—and if the mayor wins his or her lawsuit—that doesn't prove the next news story about a mayoral scandal is also libelous. Each person suing for libel—like each person charged with a crime—is entitled to his or her own day in court.

The trial courts usually have the final say about these *questions of fact*. An appellate court might rule that a trial court misapplied the law to a given factual situation, but the appellate court doesn't ordinarily reevaluate the facts on its own. Instead, it sends the case back (*remands*) to the trial court with instructions to reassess the facts under new legal rules written by the appellate court. For instance, an appellate court might decide that a certain piece of evidence was illegally obtained and cannot be used in a murder trial. It will order the trial court to reevaluate the factual issue of guilt or innocence, this time completely disregarding the illegally obtained evidence. The appellate court's ruling may well affect the outcome of the case, but it is still the job of the trial court to decide the factual question of guilt or innocence, just as it is the job of the appellate court to set down rules on such legal issues as the admissibility of evidence.

This is not to say trial courts never make legal (as opposed to fact-finding) decisions: they do so every time they apply the law to a factual situation. But when a trial court issues an opinion on a legal issue, that opinion usually carries little weight as legal precedent.

Sometimes there is high drama in the trial courtroom, and that may result in extensive media coverage. One trial verdict may even inspire (or discourage) more lawsuits of the same kind. Still, the outcome of a trial rarely has long-term legal significance. On the other hand, a little-noticed appellate court decision may fundamentally alter the way we live. That is why law textbooks such as this one concentrate on appellate court decisions, especially U.S. Supreme Court decisions.

■ STRUCTURE OF THE U.S. COURT SYSTEM

Because the courts play such an important role in shaping the law, the structure of the court system itself deserves some explanation.

Fig. 1 shows how the state and federal courts are organized. In the federal system, there is a nationwide network of trial courts at the bottom of the structure. Next higher are 12 intermediate appellate courts serving various regions of the country, with the Supreme Court at the top of the system.

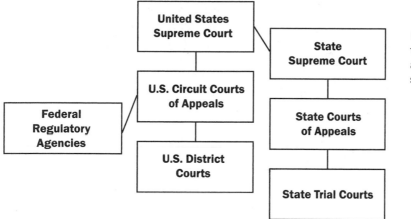

FIG. 1. Organization of the federal courts and a typical state court system.

U.S. District Courts

In the federal system there is at least one trial court called the U.S. District Court in each of the 50 states and the District of Columbia. Some of the more populous states have more than one federal judicial district, and each district has its own trial court or courts. As trial courts, the U.S. District Courts have limited precedent-setting authority. Nevertheless, a U.S. District Court decision occasionally sets an important precedent. The primary duty of these courts, however, is to serve as trial courts of general jurisdiction in the federal system; that is, they handle a variety of federal civil and criminal matters, ranging from civil disputes over copyrights to criminal trials of persons accused of acts of terrorism against the United States.

U.S. Courts of Appeals

At the next level up in the federal court system, there are U.S. Courts of Appeals, often called the *circuit courts* because the nation is divided into geographic *circuits* (see Fig. 2). That term, incidentally, originated in an era when all federal judges (including the justices of the Supreme Court) were required to be "circuit riders." They traveled from town to town, holding court sessions wherever there were federal cases to be heard.

Each circuit court today serves a specific region of the country, and most of these courts still hear cases in various cities within their regions. There are 11 regional circuit courts. Fig. 2 shows how the United States is divided into judicial circuits. In addition, a separate circuit court (the U.S. Court of Appeals for the D.C. circuit) exists solely to serve Washington, D.C.; it often hears appeals of decisions by federal agencies, many of them involving high-profile issues. Many "D.C. circuit" judges are promoted to the Supreme Court. There is also a U.S. Court of Appeals for the Federal Circuit. Unlike the other circuit courts, this one serves no single geographic area. Instead, it has nationwide jurisdiction over certain special kinds of cases, including patent and customs appeals and some claims against the federal government.

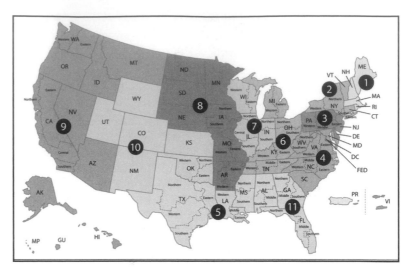

FIG. 2. Geographic Boundaries of United States Courts of Appeals and United States District Courts.

U.S. Library of Congress, http://www.uscourts. gov/uscourts/images/ CircuitMap.pdf

This court is the product of a merger of the old Court of Claims and the Court of Customs and Patent Appeals. This book will generally refer to these courts by their numbers (e.g., First Circuit, Ninth Circuit).

Some of the circuits have been divided over the years as the population grew. Until 1981, the Fifth Circuit included Alabama, Georgia and Florida, the states that now comprise the Eleventh Circuit. Legislation has been proposed repeatedly to divide the far-flung Ninth Circuit, which serves Alaska, Hawaii and the entire west coast (nine states with a total population of about 60 million people). Although critics say it is too large and too California-oriented because California's huge population has resulted in many of the Ninth Circuit's judges coming from one state, Congress has never agreed upon a plan to divide it. Attorney General Eric Holder told a Senate committee in 2010 that he is open to investigating a "reconfiguring" of the Ninth Circuit due to its geographic size and its workload. The Ninth Circuit has 29 active judges (one was added in 2009), by far the largest number of any circuit. The second largest circuit is the Fifth, which has 17 active judges. Each court also has *senior judges* who are officially retired but volunteer to continue hearing cases.

The losing party in most U.S. District Court trials may appeal the decision to the circuit court serving that region of the country. The decisions of the circuit courts produce many important legal precedents; on federal questions the rulings of these courts are second in importance only to U.S. Supreme Court decisions. Although each circuit court has a large number of judges, most cases are heard by panels of three judges. Two of the three constitute a majority and may issue the *majority opinion*, which sets forth the court's legal reasoning that led to the decision. Sometimes a case is considered so important or controversial that a larger panel of judges decides the case, usually reconsidering an earlier decision by a three-judge panel. When that happens, it is called deciding a case *en banc*. Ordinarily, an *en banc* panel consists of all of the judges serving on a particular circuit court. As the circuit courts grew larger, Congress authorized smaller *en banc* panels in some instances. The Ninth Circuit used panels of 15 judges to hear cases *en banc* for a time and now uses panels of 11.

Since these appellate courts decide only matters of law, there are no juries in these courts. Juries serve only in trial courts, and even there juries only decide factual issues (such as the guilt or innocence of a criminal defendant), not legal issues. Appellate cases are decided by judges alone, unassisted by a jury—both in the federal and state court systems.

One point should be explained about the significance of the legal precedents established by the U.S. circuit courts. As long as the decision does not conflict with any U.S. Supreme Court ruling, each circuit court is free to arrive at its own conclusions on issues of law, which are then binding on lower courts in that circuit. A circuit court is not required to follow precedents established by other circuit courts around the country, although precedents from other circuits usually carry considerable weight and are often followed.

Occasionally two different circuit courts will rule differently on the same legal issue. When that happens, the trial courts in each region have no choice but to follow the local circuit court's ruling. Trial courts located in other circuits may choose to follow either of the two conflicting precedents, or they may follow neither. Since this kind of uncertainty about the law is obviously bad for everyone, the U.S. Supreme Court often intervenes, establishing a uniform rule of law all over the country.

As well as hearing appeals of federal trial court decisions, the circuit courts also hear appeals from special-purpose courts and federal administrative agencies. For instance, decisions of both the Federal Trade Commission and the Federal Communications Commission may be appealed to the federal circuit courts. Such cases are often heard by the U.S. Court of Appeals for the D.C. circuit, giving that court a major role in communications law.

It bears noting that even though there are many judges serving in federal courts below the Supreme Court, there are empty judicial seats that go unfilled for months. Sometimes appointments to these seats are politically charged. A snapshot of the current state of vacancies in the federal judiciary, on June 13, 2012, showed 75 vacancies in the federal system, with 34 pending nominees. This information is tracked by the Administrative Office of the U.S. Courts (www.uscourts.gov).

The U.S. Supreme Court

The U.S. Supreme Court is the highest court in the country. Its nine justices are the highest-ranking judges in the nation, and its decisions represent the most influential legal precedents, binding on all lower courts.

Because of this court's vast authority, it is common for people involved in a lawsuit to threaten to "fight this all the way to the Supreme Court." However, very few cases have any real chance to make it that far. The U.S. Supreme Court is, after all, only one court, and it can decide only a limited number of cases each year. The Supreme Court accepts at most a few hundred cases annually

ride circuit:
the historic practice in which judges rode from place to place to hear appeals in person.

en banc:
Latin/French for "in the bench," a session where all judges on a court participate in the hearing and resolution of a case, rather than just a small panel. Pronounced "on bonk."

for review—out of about 10,000 petitions for a hearing. In the end, the court issues formal signed opinions in no more than about 100 cases each year. In recent years the Court has produced even fewer: often only 80 or 90 per term. Obviously, some screening is required to determine which cases will get that far.

In doing the screening, the Supreme Court tries to hear those cases that raise the most significant legal issues, those where the lower courts have flagrantly erred, and those where conflicting lower court decisions must be reconciled. However, the fact that the Supreme Court declines to hear a given case does not mean the high court necessarily agrees with the decision of a lower court. To the contrary, the Supreme Court may disagree with it, but it may choose to leave the decision undisturbed because it has a heavy caseload of more important matters.

The fact that the Supreme Court declines to review a lower court decision establishes no precedent: for the Supreme Court to refuse to hear a case is not the same as the Supreme Court taking up the case and then affirming the lower court's ruling. When the Supreme Court declines to take a case, the lower court ruling on that case remains in force—but it is still just the decision of a lower court. There are occasions, however, when the Supreme Court accepts a case and then affirms the opinion of a lower court instead of issuing its own opinion, giving the lower court's opinion the legal weight of a Supreme Court decision.

The nine justices vote to decide which cases they will hear of the many appealed to them. Under the Supreme Court's rules of procedure, it takes four votes to get a case on the high court's calendar.

Cases reach the U.S. Supreme Court by several routes. For one, the Constitution gives the Supreme Court *original jurisdiction* over a few types of cases (the first court to hear those cases). Disputes between two states and cases involving ambassadors of foreign countries are examples of cases in which the Supreme Court has original jurisdiction. Even these cases may sometimes be heard in lower courts instead—with the blessing of the Supreme Court's nine overworked justices. In disputes between states, the Court may appoint Special Masters to hear evidence and prepare factual findings prior to oral argument.

Then there are a few cases in which the losing party in the lower courts has an automatic right to appeal to the Supreme Court. For example, when a lower federal court or the

FIG. 3. The Supreme Court of the United States, 2010.

Steve Petteway, Collection of the Supreme Court of the United States.

Front, L-R: Justice Clarence Thomas, Justice Antonin Scalia, Chief Justice John Roberts, Jr., Justice Anthony Kennedy, Justice Ruth Bader Ginsburg.
Back, L-R: Justice Sonia Sotomayor, Justice Stephen Breyer, Justice Samuel Alito, Justice Elena Kagan.

highest court in a state rules an Act of Congress unconstitutional, the U.S. Supreme Court must hear an appeal if asked to do so by the government. The Supreme Court is required to accept these cases for review.

Finally, there are a vast number of cases that the Supreme Court may or may not choose to review; it is not required to hear these cases, but some raise very important questions. In these cases the losing party in a lower court asks the Supreme Court to issue a *writ of certiorari* (often abbreviated *cert*). Technically, a writ of *certiorari* is an order from the Supreme Court to a lower court to send up the records of the case. *Certiorari granted* means the Court has agreed to hear an appeal, while *certiorari denied* means the Court has decided not to hear the case. (This book will use the terms "*cert* granted" or "*cert* denied.") For the Court to grant *cert*, four of the nine justices must vote to hear the case. This is called the *rule of four.*

This *certiorari* procedure is by far the most common way cases reach the Supreme Court, although many more petitions for *cert* are denied than granted. Cases may reach the Supreme Court in such appeals from both lower federal courts and from state courts. The U.S. Supreme Court often hears cases that originated in a state court, but only when an important federal question, such as the First Amendment's guarantee of freedom of the press, is involved. Most of the Supreme Court decisions on libel and invasion of privacy that will be discussed later reached the high court in this way.

The Supreme Court will consider an appeal of a state case only when the case has gone as far as possible in the state court system. That normally means the state's highest court must have either ruled on the case or refused to hear it.

It would be difficult to overstate the importance of the nine justices of the U.S. Supreme Court in shaping American law. That is why bitter battles are so often fought in the U.S. Senate over the confirmation of those nominated to be Supreme Court justices. The makeup of the Court can determine the scope of First Amendment freedoms, what due process rights are afforded to those accused of crimes, whether abortions remain legal and a thousand other major issues. As Chapter Five explains, in 1992 the Supreme Court upheld the basic principle of *Roe v. Wade,* the landmark abortion decision, by a 5-4 vote. Three justices appointed by presidents who opposed abortions (Anthony M. Kennedy and Sandra Day O'Connor, appointed by Ronald Reagan, and David H. Souter, appointed by George H.W. Bush) formed the nucleus of the majority that upheld *Roe v. Wade.* Had any of them voted as the president who nominated them probably expected, *Roe v. Wade* would have been overturned. But no one can predict how a jurist will vote once on the high court. Souter, considered a conservative

original jurisdiction:
the first court with jurisdiction to hear a case; in the case of the Supreme Court, its findings in original jurisdiction cases are final.

writ of certiorari:
the order issued by the Supreme Court when it agrees to hear a case.

rule of four:
four justices must agree to grant *certiorari* to hear a case before the case is permitted to be argued before the Court.

when he replaced the liberal William Brennan, has written some surprisingly liberal opinions, including a stirring defense of the free press (see Chapter Eight). In contrast, Clarence Thomas, who replaced Thurgood Marshall (the first African-American ever to serve on the Supreme Court and an avowed liberal), has taken a decidedly more conservative course as a jurist than his predecessor.

With the retirement of Justice Byron White in 1993, a Democratic president had the opportunity to appoint a Supreme Court justice for the first time since the 1960s, and Bill Clinton nominated longtime federal appellate judge Ruth Bader Ginsburg to replace White. A year later, Justice Harry A. Blackmun, who was perhaps best known for writing the Court's main opinion in *Roe v. Wade,* also retired. Clinton then made Stephen G. Breyer, another federal appellate judge, his second nominee for the Supreme Court. Both Ginsburg and Breyer were viewed as moderates.

Another decade passed before there were other changes in the makeup of the Supreme Court. George W. Bush appointed John G. Roberts Jr. to replace William Rehnquist as chief justice when Rehnquist died in 2005. Bush then named Samuel A. Alito to replace Sandra Day O'Connor, who retired in 2006. Although both new justices were considered judicial conservatives, Roberts' record during his first years as chief justice seemed to mark him more as a consensus builder than a doctrinaire conservative, while Alito's early voting record was more conservative than O'Connor's. O'Connor wielded great influence as a centrist, frequently providing the decisive fifth vote on a philosophically divided court.

In 2009, President Barack Obama got his first chance to appoint a justice to the Supreme Court when Justice David Souter announced his retirement after 19 years on the Court. He appointed Judge Sonia Sotomayor, a federal judge from the Second Circuit, who is the first Hispanic justice and the third woman to serve on the Supreme Court. Obama also made history with his appointment of Elena Kagan, dean of Harvard Law School, as *solicitor general,* the first woman to hold that office. The solicitor general argues for the government of the United States before the Supreme Court. When Justice John Paul Stevens announced his retirement in 2010, after nearly 35 years on the Court, Obama chose Kagan as his second Supreme Court appointment. In June 2011, Donald B. Verrilli, Jr. (a former clerk to Justice Brennan) was approved by the Senate and sworn in to succeed Kagan as solicitor general.

The Supreme Court is sometimes closely identified with its chief justice, who may set the tone for the entire court. For example, the "Warren Court," named for Earl Warren, who served as chief justice from 1953 to 1969, had an enormous influence on the modern interpretation of the First Amendment. Later in this chapter and in Chapter Four there are references to the Warren Court's major role in reshaping American libel law. But the Warren Court did far more than that: it also rewrote American obscenity law and greatly expanded the rights of those who are accused of crimes, to cite just two examples. In the decades since the era of the liberal Warren Court ended, more conservative justices have dominated the Supreme Court. Under Chief Justice William Rehnquist, the court began to overturn some of the precedents established by the Warren Court, particularly in such fields as criminal law. And yet, many of the Warren Court's landmark decisions still stand, a tribute to the influence wielded by Warren and his judicial colleagues. An interesting footnote: although the term "the Warren Court" is synonymous with *judicial liberalism,* Warren had been a Republican governor of California and he was appointed to the Supreme Court by Dwight D. Eisenhower, a Republican president.

FIG. 4. The four female Justices in the Justices' Conference Room prior to Elena Kagan's investiture, Aug. 7, 2010.

Steve Petteway, Collection of the Supreme Court of the United States.

L-R: Justice Sandra Day O'Connor (Ret.), Justice Sonia Sotomayor, Justice Ruth Bader Ginsburg and Justice Elena Kagan.

The State Courts

Each of the 50 states has its own court system, as already indicated. Larger states such as California, New York, Ohio, Pennsylvania, Texas, Illinois and Michigan have two levels of state appellate courts plus various trial courts, duplicating the federal structure.

In these states, the intermediate appellate courts (usually called simply "courts of appeal") handle cases that the state supreme court has no time to consider. The state supreme court reviews only the most important cases. Worth special note is the New York system, which is structurally similar to the systems in other populous states, but with opposite nomenclature. In New York, the "supreme court" is a trial court that also has intermediate appellate jurisdiction; there are many such courts in the state. New York's highest court is called the Court of Appeals. Maryland also calls its highest court the Court of Appeals.

In smaller states, the trial courts send cases directly to the state supreme court, which may have from three to nine or more justices to hear all appeals in the state. As both the population and the volume of lawsuits increase, more and more states are adding intermediate appellate courts.

The states tend to have a much greater variety of trial courts than does the federal government, since the state courts must handle many minor legal matters that are of no concern to the federal courts. A typical state court system includes some kind of local court that handles minor traffic and civil matters and perhaps minor crimes. Such courts are sometimes called municipal courts, county or city courts, justice courts, or the like.

In some states the highest trial courts not only hear the most important trials but also perform some appellate functions, reviewing the verdicts of the lower trial courts.

State and Federal Jurisdiction

It may seem inefficient to have two complete judicial systems operating side by side. Wouldn't it be simpler and less expensive to consolidate the state and federal courts that operate in each state? Perhaps it would, but one of our strongest traditions is power sharing between the federal government and the states. We'll have separate state and federal laws—and separate court systems—throughout the foreseeable future.

residual jurisdiction:
the Tenth Amendment gives all powers to the states that are not granted to the federal government or prohibited to the states by the Constitution.

federal question:
an area in which the federal government has subject jurisdiction, including interpretation of the Constitution and acts of Congress and international treaties.

diversity of citizenship/ diversity jurisdiction:
when one party to a lawsuit is from one state and the other is from another state; diversity jurisdiction gives the federal courts jurisdiction over such lawsuits.

complete diversity:
no plaintiff in a case can be from the same state as any defendant in the same case.

federal preemption:
when the federal government has sole jurisdiction over a subject area.

concurrent jurisdiction:
when the federal government and the states share jurisdiction.

How then is authority divided between the federal and state courts? State jurisdiction and federal jurisdiction sometimes overlap, but basically the state courts are courts of *residual jurisdiction*; that is, they have authority over all legal matters that are not specifically placed under federal control. Anything that isn't a *federal question* automatically falls within the jurisdiction of the state courts. In addition, the state courts may also rule on some issues that are federal questions (for instance, First Amendment rights).

What makes an issue a federal question? The Constitution declares that certain areas of law are inherently federal questions. For instance, the Constitution specifically authorized Congress to make copyright law a federal question. And Congress, acting under the authority of the Constitution, has declared copyrights and many other matters to be federal questions. Congress has used its constitutional power to regulate interstate commerce as a basis for federal regulation of broadcasting, for instance. Legal issues such as copyrights and broadcast regulation are inherently federal questions because of their subject matter.

In addition, federal courts may intervene in state cases if a state court ruling conflicts with the U.S. Constitution. Much of mass communications law is based on cases of this type. In almost every area of state law discussed in this textbook, the U.S. Supreme Court has intervened at one time or another, interposing federal constitutional requirements on the states. Most often, of course, the constitutional issue is freedom of expression as protected by the First Amendment; the Supreme Court has often overruled state laws and court decisions that violated the First Amendment.

In addition to these federal questions, there is another reason the federal courts will sometimes agree to hear a case: *diversity of citizenship.* This principle applies only when a citizen of one state sues a citizen of another state. For example, if a New Yorker and a Pennsylvanian are involved in a serious auto accident, each may be able to avoid a lawsuit in the other's state courts under the diversity principle. If there is a lawsuit, it may well be removed to a federal court instead of being heard in a state court.

The framers of the Constitution felt it would be unfair to force anyone to fight a lawsuit on someone else's "home turf," so they ordered the federal courts to provide a neutral forum to hear these disputes involving citizens of two different states. The theory is that a state court might be biased in favor of its own citizens and against outsiders. When a federal court hears a case that would be a state matter if it involved two citizens of the same state, the federal court's right to hear the case is based on *diversity jurisdiction* rather than *federal question jurisdiction.* In diversity lawsuits, the trial may still occur in the home state of one of the litigants, but in a federal rather than a state court.

There are limits on diversity jurisdiction. If there were not, the federal courts might be overwhelmed by minor cases. To avoid that problem, federal courts accept diversity-of-citizenship cases only when the dispute involves more than $75,000. This jurisdictional threshold has been increased repeatedly over the years. Until it was raised from $10,000 to $50,000 in 1988, the federal courts had to handle many relatively minor civil lawsuits—cases that federal judges felt should rightfully be left to the state courts.

Another limitation on diversity jurisdiction is the requirement of *complete diversity*. That is, all of the parties on one side of a lawsuit must come from a different state than anyone on the other side. That means, for instance, that a lawsuit by a New Yorker against both an individual from Pennsylvania and an insurance company in New York would not usually qualify as a diversity case.

Sometimes there is considerable legal maneuvering when a case does qualify for federal jurisdiction, either because a federal question is involved or because there is diversity of citizenship. One side may want the case kept in state court, while the other prefers a federal court. Such a case may be filed in a state court, removed to federal court, and eventually sent back to a state court.

One more point about federal-state relationships bears explaining. Certain legal matters are exclusively federal concerns, either under the Constitution or an act of Congress. In those areas, the federal government is said to have *preempted the field*. That is, no state law in this area is valid; the federal government has exclusive jurisdiction. Copyright law is one such area.

In certain other areas of law, Congress has enacted some federal laws without preempting the field. The states may also enact laws in these areas, providing that the state laws do not conflict with any federal laws. These are called areas of *concurrent jurisdiction*. Examples in media law include the regulation of advertising, antitrust law and trademark regulation. A typical dividing line in such an area of law is the one that exists in trademark regulation, where the federal Lanham Act protects trademarks of businesses engaged in interstate commerce, while many states have laws to protect the trademarks of local businesses.

In addition to the areas of law preempted by the federal government and areas of concurrent jurisdiction, of course, a large number of legal matters are left to the states—unless a state should violate some federal principle in the exercise of that authority. Libel and invasion of privacy are two areas of media law that are essentially state matters. Recently the U.S. Supreme Court has been refining the concept of federalism by limiting the power of Congress to curtail the traditional authority of the states, a trend that is discussed later.

Judicial Behavior

Questions about whether judges should *recuse* (remove) themselves from cases in which they or their families have financial or social interests have been in the news in the late 2000s. For example, about three-quarters of the states choose their judges by election. Campaign donations to judicial elections are on the rise, and in 2009 the Supreme Court said that a judge's failure to recuse himself from a case in which he received significant campaign donations from one of the litigants violated the due process rights of the other litigant.

At issue in *Caperton v. A.T. Massey Coal Company Inc.* (556 U.S. 868) was the decision of West Virginia Supreme Court of Appeals chief justice Brent Benjamin not to recuse himself in a case in which one of the litigants, Massey Coal, had given him $3 million in campaign donations. Justice Benjamin had refused several times to remove himself from the case, and his court reversed a $50 million award against Massey Coal.

In a 5-4 decision, the Supreme Court said that the due process clause of the Fourteenth Amendment was violated by Justice Benjamin's participation in this case. Justice Anthony Kennedy wrote, "We conclude that there is a serious risk of actual bias—based on objective and reasonable perceptions—when a person with a personal stake in a particular case had a significant and disproportionate influence in placing the judge on the case by raising funds or directing the judge's election campaign when the case was pending or imminent." Kennedy also pointed out that the extreme facts in this case would likely limit any potential of increased recusal demands or interference with judicial elections.

Several Supreme Court justices made the news in 2011 regarding their participation in social or financial arrangements, raising questions about whether such participation should require the justices to recuse themselves from certain cases. For 13 years Clarence Thomas failed to disclose income his wife had received from conservative groups, and Samuel Alito held Disney stock during the time that he decided an indecency case involving ABC, a Disney subsidiary (he admitted he should have recused himself). Thomas and Antonin Scalia are also alleged to have connections to Koch Industries, whose owners fund conservative causes. Judges decide for themselves whether to recuse from cases or not.

Should the Supreme Court be held to the same ethical guidelines for recusal that bind lower courts? In February 2011, over 100 law professors signed onto a letter drafted by Alliance for Justice that was sent to the Senate and House Judiciary Committees. The letter called on the committees to apply the standard code of ethics for U.S. judges to the Supreme Court and establish procedures to enforce that code, require a written opinion when a justice denies a motion to recuse him/herself, and develop a procedure to review a denial of recusal. Rep. Chris Murphy (D-CT) introduced a bill, the Supreme Court Transparency and Disclosure Act of 2011, to codify these calls for action into law. However, the bill did not make it out of committee, and there has been no further action.

■ TYPES OF LAW

Although the courts play a major role in shaping the law, the other branches of government also have the power to make laws in various ways. In fact, the term law refers to several different types of rules and regulations, ranging from the bureaucratic edicts of administrative agencies to the unwritten legal principles we call the *common law*. This section explains how the courts interact with other agencies of government in shaping the various kinds of law that exist side by side in America.

The Constitution
The most important foundation of modern American law is the U.S. Constitution. No law that conflicts with the Constitution is valid. The U.S. Constitution is the basis for our legal system: it sets up the structure of the federal government and defines federal-state relationships. It divides authority among the three branches of the federal government and limits their powers, reserving a great many powers for the states and their subdivisions (such as cities and counties).

The First Amendment to the Constitution is vital to the media. In just 45 words, it sets forth the principles of freedom of the press, freedom of speech and freedom of religion in America. The First Amendment says:

Congress shall make no law respecting an establishment of religion, or prohibiting the free exercise thereof; or abridging the freedom of speech, or of the press; or the right of the people peaceably to assemble, and to petition the government for a redress of grievances.

What do those words mean? The job of interpreting what they mean has fallen to the appellate courts, which have written millions of words in attempting to explain those 45 words. For instance, the First Amendment sounds absolute when it says "Congress shall make no law...." However, the courts have repeatedly ruled that those words are not absolute, and that freedom of expression must be balanced against other rights. In practice, the First Amendment should really be read more like this: "Congress shall make *almost* no laws..." or "Congress shall make *as few laws as possible*...abridging freedom of speech, or of the press...." The chapters to follow will discuss the many other rights that the courts have had to balance against the First Amendment.

Another point about the First Amendment is that it originally applied only to Congress and to no one else. It was written that way because its authors did not think it was their place to tell the state governments not to deny basic civil liberties; their purpose was to reassure those citizens who feared that the new federal government might deny basic liberties. They felt that many basic liberties were so firmly rooted in the common law that no written declaration was needed to assure that the states would safeguard these liberties. However, it became clear over the years that state and local governments, like the federal government, may violate the rights of their citizens from time to time. Hence, the Supreme Court eventually ruled that the First Amendment's safeguards should apply to state and local governments as well.

The U.S. Constitution plays the central role in American law. No law may be enacted or enforced if it violates the Constitution. The courts—particularly the U.S. Supreme Court—play the central role in interpreting what the Constitution means, often in practical situations that the founders never dreamed of when they wrote the document more than 200 years ago. Perhaps the Constitution has survived for so long because the courts do adapt it to meet changing needs, and because it can be amended when there is strong support for this step. The Sixteenth Amendment, for example, was approved in 1913, authorizing the federal income tax at a time when the federal government needed to find a way to bring in more revenue. And the Twenty-first Amendment, approved in 1933, abolished prohibition (thus ending an era that began when the Eighteenth Amendment was enacted to ban alcoholic beverages). The normal procedure for amending the Constitution is for each house of Congress to approve a proposed amendment by a two-thirds vote, after which it must be ratified by three-fourths of the states.

In addition to the federal Constitution, each state has its own constitution, and that document is the basic legal charter for the state. No state law may conflict with either the state's own constitution or the federal Constitution. Each state's courts must interpret the state constitution, overturning laws that conflict with it.

Likewise, many cities and counties have *home rule charters* that establish the fundamental structure and powers of local government. Like the state and federal constitutions (which local governments must also obey), local charters are basic sources of legal authority. On the other hand, many local governments operate under the general laws enacted by state legislatures instead of having their own local charters.

In these circumstances, the courts must decide when a government action—be it an act of Congress or the behavior of the local police department—violates one of these basic government documents. When that happens, it is the job of the courts to halt the violation.

The Common Law

The common law, which began to develop out of English court decisions hundreds of years ago, is our oldest form of law. It is an amorphous collection of legal principles based on thousands of court decisions handed down over the centuries. It is *unwritten* law in the sense that you cannot sit down and read it all in one place as you can with the statutory laws enacted by Congress. Starting nearly 1,000 years ago, English judges began to follow *legal precedents* from previous cases. Each new decision added a little bit to this accumulated body of law. As it grew, the common law came to include rules concerning everything from crimes such as murder and robbery to non-criminal matters such as breach of contract.

When the American government took its present form with the ratification of the Constitution in 1789, the entire English common law as it then existed became the basis for the American common law. Since then, thousands of additional decisions of American courts have expanded and modified the common law in each state.

It should be emphasized that the common law is mainly state law and not federal law; an important U.S. Supreme Court decision so ruled years ago. Each state's courts have developed their own judicial traditions, and those traditions form the basis for that state's common law, which may vary from the common law of other states.

Several controversial U.S. Supreme Court decisions in recent years underscored the continuing power of the common law as a force that even Congress cannot ignore. In *Alden v. Maine* (527 U.S. 706, 1999) and several other cases, the high court looked back to the status of the common law before the Constitution was ratified in 1789 and concluded that a concept called *sovereign immunity* was firmly entrenched in the law then—and was not abrogated by the Constitution. Sovereign immunity exempts the "sovereign" from being sued in the courts. In eighteenth-century England, the sovereign was the king or queen. In the pre-constitutional United States, the individual states had sovereign immunity.

How does sovereign immunity affect modern America? In these recent decisions, a 5-4 majority of the Supreme Court said the states still enjoy sovereign immunity, and Congress does not have the right to authorize lawsuits against the states either in federal courts or in state courts. The result: the Court held that states are largely exempt from various federal laws that purport to allow private parties (such as individuals and corporations) to sue a state. The court said the states (but not private parties) are exempt from many patent and copyright infringement lawsuits, for example. In 2002, the Court held that the states are immune not only to many lawsuits but also to some actions brought by federal regulatory agencies (*Federal Maritime Commission v. South Carolina State Ports Authority*, 535 U.S. 743).

These decisions were widely criticized in the media. They are based on an expansive view of common law concepts that are routinely taught in law school and that still apply today—in the opinion of the Supreme Court majority. Of course, the states have all *voluntarily* agreed to set limits on their own sovereign immunity over the years by enacting laws to allow lawsuits against themselves under various circumstances.

Like federal constitutional law, the common law can grow and change without any formal act of a legislative body precisely because it is based on court decisions. When a new situation arises, the appellate courts may establish new legal rights, acting on their own authority.

A good example of the way the common law develops a little at a time through court decisions is the emergence of the right of privacy. As Chapter Five explains, there was no legal right of privacy until the twentieth century. But as governments and the media (and eventually, the Internet) became more powerful and pervasive, the need for such a right became apparent. The courts in a number of states responded by allowing those whose privacy had been invaded to sue the invader, establishing precedents for other courts to follow.

In addition to privacy law, several other major areas of mass media law had their beginnings in the common law tradition, among them libel, slander and the earliest forms of copyright protection.

If this all happens through judicial precedent, with the courts expected to follow the example set by earlier decisions, how can the common law correct earlier errors?

The common law system has survived for nearly a thousand years precisely because there are mechanisms to allow the law to change as the times change. Courts don't always follow legal precedent; they have other options.

When a court does adhere to a previous decision, it is said to be observing the rule of *stare decisis*. That Latin term, roughly translated, means "Let the precedent stand." However, courts need not always adhere to the rule of *stare decisis*. Instead, a court faced with a new factual situation may decide that an old rule of the common law should not apply to the new facts. The new case may be sufficiently different from previous ones to justify a different result. When a court declines to follow a precedent on the ground that the new case is a little different, that is called *distinguishing* the previous case. When an appellate court does that, the common law grows and keeps up with changing times.

Another option, of course, is for a court to decline to follow precedent altogether, even though the factual circumstances and issues of law may be virtually identical. That is called *reversing* or *overruling* a precedent; it is considered appropriate when changing times or changing conditions have made it clear that the precedent is unfair or unworkable.

A good example of the way this process works is provided by the 1954 ruling of the U.S. Supreme Court in the famous school desegregation case, *Brown v. Board of Education* (347 U.S. 483). Although this case is based on an interpretation of the Constitution and is therefore an example of the development of constitutional law rather than the common law, it provides a good illustration of just how the law develops over the years. When the high court took up the *Brown* case, there was a judicial precedent, an 1896 Supreme Court decision called *Plessy v. Ferguson* (163 U.S. 537). In that earlier case, racial segregation had been ruled constitutionally permissible

statute:
any law that is adopted by a legislature of a federal, state or local governmental body.

sovereign immunity:
the ability of a government to limit lawsuits against it.

stare decisis:
Latin for "let the law or the decision stand," the policy of courts to rely on precedents.

distinguishing a case:
declining to follow a precedent based on the precedential case differing from the case being decided.

reversing/overruling a precedent:
choosing not to follow precedent even if the facts of the case being decided are very similar.

as long as the facilities provided for different races were "separate but equal." But in 1954 the Supreme Court pointed out that more than half a century's experience under the *Plessy* rule proved that the "separate but equal" approach didn't work. The Court noted that segregated facilities were almost always unequal—and ruled that the public schools of America had to be desegregated. As a result of that new decision, the precedent from the 1896 case was no longer binding, and a new precedent replaced it. In the end, the *Brown* case became one of the most important court decisions of the twentieth century.

Statutory Law

The third major type of law in America is the one most people think of when they hear the word *law*. It is statutory law, a sweeping term that encompasses acts of Congress, laws enacted by state legislatures and even ordinances adopted by city and county governments.

If constitutional and common law are largely unwritten (or at least uncodified) forms of law because they are the result of accumulated court decisions, statutory law is just the opposite. It is law written down in a systematic way. Statutory laws are often organized into *codes*. A *code* is a collection of laws on similar subjects, indexed and arranged by subject matter. Much federal law is found in the *United States Code*. Each title of the U.S. Code deals with a particular subject or group of related subjects. Title 17, for example, deals with copyright law, discussed in Chapter Six. On the state level, statutory law is similarly organized, although not all states refer to their compilations of statutory laws as codes.

Although statutory law is created by legislative bodies, the courts have an important place in statutory lawmaking just as they do in other areas of law. That is true because the courts have the power to interpret the meaning of statutory laws and apply them to practical situations. For this reason, law books containing statutory laws are often *annotated*. This means each section of the statutory law is followed by brief summaries of the appellate court decisions interpreting it. Thus, one can quickly learn whether a given statutory law has been upheld or if it has been partially or totally invalidated by the courts. Annotated codes also contain cross-references to other relevant analyses of the statutory law, such as attorney general's opinions or articles in law reviews.

Why would a court invalidate a statutory law? It can happen for several reasons. First, of course, if the statute conflicts with any provision of the appropriate state or federal constitution, it is invalid. In addition, there are sometimes conflicts between two statutory laws enacted by the same state legislature or by Congress. When that happens, the differences must be reconciled, and that may mean reinterpreting or even invalidating one of the laws. In addition, courts may void laws that conflict with well-established (but unwritten) common law principles. For instance, Chapter Eight explains that a number of state legislatures have enacted *shield laws* to protect journalists' news sources. But several courts have overruled these shield laws on the ground that they infringe on judicial prerogatives guaranteed by constitutional or common law principles.

There is considerable interplay between the courts and legislative bodies in the development of statutory law. As already indicated, often a new legal concept is recognized first by the courts, whose decisions will make it a part of the common law. At some point, a legislature may take note of what the courts have been doing and formally codify the law by enacting a statute. The courts may then reinterpret the statute, but the legislature may respond by passing yet another statute intended to override the court decision.

We will see precisely this sort of interplay between a legislative body and the courts in several areas of media law, particularly in such areas as copyright, shield laws and broadcasting. For example, the Supreme Court once ruled that most private, at-home videotaping of television shows is legal under the U.S. Copyright Act, explained in Chapter Six. Congress then considered legislation that would have revised the Copyright Act to overturn that decision and outlaw home videotaping. That legislation was rejected because most members of Congress believed public opinion supported the court's interpretation of the law.

On the other hand, if the Supreme Court had said a constitutional principle (such as the First Amendment) protected the right to make home videotapes of TV shows for personal use, the only way to reverse that ruling would have been by amending the Constitution—or waiting for the court to reverse its own earlier decision. Congress cannot pass a statutory law to overrule a Supreme Court decision *interpreting the meaning of the Constitution.* Congress can, of course, propose a constitutional amendment and submit it to the states for ratification. Short of that, the most Congress can do when a statutory law is ruled unconstitutional is to revise it to bring it into compliance with the Constitution.

Administrative Law

Another important kind of law in America is administrative law. Within the vast bureaucracies operated by the federal government and by the states, there are numerous agencies with the power to adopt and enforce administrative regulations, and these regulations have the force of law. The term "administrative law" may seem contradictory, but these agencies do have law-making powers.

In fact, agencies often have so much authority that it would seem to violate the traditional concept of separation of powers. They may write and enforce rules and try alleged violators, handing out *de facto* criminal penalties to those convicted. The Federal Communications Commission is a regulatory body with that kind of authority over the electronic media. The Federal Trade Commission exercises similar authority over the advertising industry.

While these agencies have considerable power, there are important checks and balances that limit their authority. For example, their decisions may be appealed to the courts, and that gives the appellate courts a veto power over the rules adopted by these agencies.

In addition, many of these agencies were created by legislation, and in recent years Congress and the various state legislatures have proven that they can take back some of the authority they handed out, either directly by rewriting the enabling legislation or indirectly by making budget cuts. A notable example of this is the limitations imposed on the Federal Trade Commission by Congress in 1980 (see Chapter Thirteen). Also, while the policy-making boards and commissions of these agencies are rarely elected, the commissioners are usually appointed by the president or the governor of a state, who is elected. Their appointments must usually be confirmed by a legislative body.

Among the thousands of agencies with administrative rule-making powers, some of the most important (in addition to the FCC and FTC) are the Interstate Commerce Commission, the Federal Aviation Administration and the Nuclear Regulatory Commission on the federal level, and the state regulatory bodies that determine rates charged by public utilities.

Actions in Equity

One final kind of "law" that should be mentioned here is not really a form of law at all but an alternative to the law: a remedy for legal wrongs called *equity*.

Hundreds of years ago in England, it became obvious that courts sometimes caused injustices while acting in the name of justice. There are some circumstances in which faithfully applying the law simply does not result in a fair decision. For example, the common law has always held that *damages* (money) would right a wrong, and that the courts should not act until an injury actually occurred—and even then they could do nothing except to order a payment of money to compensate the injured party. Obviously there are times when letting a court sit back and wait for an injury to occur just isn't satisfactory. The harm might be so severe that no amount of money would make matters right. In those situations, courts have the power to act in equity: they can issue an *injunction* to prevent a wrong from occurring.

A good example of an occasion when an action in *equity* would be appropriate is when highway builders are about to excavate and thus destroy an important archeological site. Those seeking to preserve the site cannot wait until after an injury occurs and sue for damages. The artifacts that would be destroyed might be priceless.

The concept of equity is an old one: it developed in medieval times. In English common law, people facing irreparable injuries began to appeal to the king, since he was above the law and could mete out justice when the courts could or would not. As the volume of requests for this sort of special consideration increased, kings began to appoint special officers to hear appeals from those who could not get justice in the courts of law. Such officers came to be known as *chancellors* and their court became known as the *court of the chancery*. As time went on, this brand of justice based on the dictates of someone's conscience came to be known simply as equity.

Equity works in much the same way today, but in America the same courts that apply the law usually entertain actions in equity, too. Unlike the law, which has elaborate and detailed rules, equity is still a system that seeks to offer fairness based on the dictates of the judge's conscience. Equity is only available in situations where there is no adequate remedy under the law, and only then if the person seeking *equitable relief* is being fair to the other parties.

There are legal actions that are based on equity rather than law. Probably the most important for our purposes are injunctions, which are court orders requiring people to do something they are supposed to do (or to refrain from doing something that would cause irreparable harm). Chapter Three discusses several attempts by the federal government to prevent the publication of information that government officials felt would cause irreparable harm to national security. When a court orders an editor not to publish something, that is ordinarily an example of an action in equity.

■ CRIMINAL LAW AND CIVIL LAW

Another major distinction in the law is between criminal and civil law. Although criminal and civil law are not categories comparable to statutory law, the common law or administrative law, there are important differences between civil and criminal cases.

In a criminal case, someone is accused of committing an act that is considered to be an offense against society as a whole—a crime such as murder, rape or robbery. Therefore, society as a whole ("the people," if you will) brings charges against this individual, with the taxpayers paying the bill for the people's lawyer, often called the district attorney (or U.S. attorney in federal cases). If the person accused of the crime *(the defendant)* is impoverished, the taxpayers will also pay for his or her defense by providing a lawyer from the local (or federal) public defender's office. Defendants who are more financially secure will hire their own defense lawyers, but the basic point to remember is that the legal dispute is between the defendant and "the people"—society as a whole. Moreover, because the defendant's life or liberty may be at stake, the prosecution must prove *guilt beyond a reasonable doubt.* That is a difficult standard of proof.

In a civil case, it is a different matter. Here, one party claims another party injured him or her individually, without necessarily doing something so bad it is considered a crime against society as a whole. It's just a dispute between two individuals (or two corporations, or two government agencies, etc.). The courts simply provide a neutral forum to hear a private dispute. The burden of proof is correspondingly lower in civil cases: to win, a litigant must usually prove his or her case by the *preponderance of the evidence,* but not necessarily *beyond a reasonable doubt,* as in criminal cases.

Don't assume that all legal matters are either criminal or civil matters—some are both. The same series of events may lead to both civil and criminal litigation. For instance, someone who has an auto accident while intoxicated may face criminal prosecution for drunk driving as well as civil lawsuits by the victims for personal injuries and property damage, among other things.

burden of proof:
the party who has this burden must present evidence to support his/her claim.

beyond a reasonable doubt:
the level of certainty required for a criminal conviction and the highest level of proof; does not mean absolute certainty but only a remote possibility of another reasonable explanation.

preponderance of the evidence:
the level of certainty required for a civil decision, a lower burden than for criminal cases; means that the facts support one side more than the other.

tort:
a civil wrong creating a right for a victim to sue a perpetrator.

tortfeasor:
person who commits a wrong.

defendant:
the tortfeasor in a civil lawsuit or accused in a criminal lawsuit.

plaintiff:
person who brings a lawsuit.

types of damages:

general: compensation for non-monetary loss.

special: compensation that requires proof of monetary losses.

actual/compensatory: can include both general and special damages.

presumed: awarded without any proof.

statutory: damages set by statute.

treble: three times the actual damages.

punitive: damage award, often high, intended to punish a wrongdoer.

■ TORTS AND DAMAGES

Two other legal concepts that should be explained here are the concepts of *torts and damages.* Most civil lawsuits not based on a breach of contract are tort actions. A *tort* is any civil wrong that creates a right for the victim to sue the perpetrator. Almost any time one party injures another, the resulting lawsuit is a tort action.

For example, if you are walking across the street and you're struck by a car driven by a careless driver, you have a right to sue for your personal injuries in a tort action for *negligence.* Suppose you need surgery as a result of the accident. If the doctor at the hospital should forget to remove a sponge from your body after the emergency surgery, you could sue for the tort of *medical malpractice.*

On the other hand, if you could prove that the car struck you not because the driver was careless but because a manufacturing defect caused the steering to fail, you could sue the manufacturer for the tort of *products liability.*

Finally, you could sue for *libel* if the local newspaper falsely reported that you had just committed a crime and were fleeing from the crime scene when you were hit by the car.

All of these legal actions and dozens of others fall into the broad category called torts. The person who commits the wrong is called the *tortfeasor;* he or she becomes the *defendant* in the lawsuit while the victim is the *plaintiff.*

Several of the important legal actions affecting the media are tort actions. Examples include libel and slander, invasion of privacy and unfair competition.

To win a tort lawsuit the plaintiff generally has to show that there was some sort of wrongful act on the part of the tortfeasor, often either negligence or a malicious intent. The plaintiff also has to show that he suffered some kind of *damages,* although courts are sometimes permitted to presume damages when certain kinds of wrongful acts have occurred.

This brings us to the definition of damages, which is a central point in this introduction to media law. In many states, there are three basic kinds of damages: general damages, special damages and punitive damages.

General damages are monetary compensation for losses incurred under circumstances in which the injured party cannot place a specific dollar amount on the loss. In an auto accident where you suffer personal injuries, for instance, you may win general damages to compensate you for your pain and suffering, which are obviously intangible. In a libel suit, the plaintiff seeks general damages for embarrassment or loss of prestige in the community.

Special damages are a little different. Here, the plaintiff must prove out-of-pocket monetary losses to win compensation. In the auto accident we've been using as an example, you can show that your doctor and hospital bills came to a certain amount of money. Maybe you can also show that you were unable to work for several months or years, or maybe you needed in-home nursing care or rehabilitation. These are all things for which courts can establish specific dollar values. Special damages are intended to compensate for these kinds of provable losses.

Sometimes other terms are used to describe the various types of damages. *Actual damages* or *compensatory damages* means provable losses, including out-of-pocket losses (special damages) and, in some instances, some intangible but none-the-less real losses (i.e., general damages). *Presumed damages* are damages that a court assumes occurred without any proof. For many years, libel plaintiffs were awarded presumed damages without having to prove the defamation actually caused any injury. In some kinds of lawsuits such as copyright infringement cases, *statutory damages* may be awarded by a court without proof of a tangible or intangible loss. Instead, the damage award is based on legal rules set forth in a statutory law such as the Copyright Act. In some areas of law, *treble damages* (three times the actual damages) are awarded as a means of discouraging improper behavior. For example, federal antitrust and advertising fraud laws allow treble damages.

In contrast to general and special damages, *punitive damages* are not based on any tangible or intangible loss. Instead, they are intended as a punishment for a person (or company) that commits a maliciously wrongful act. For the victim, they constitute a windfall profit—and the Internal Revenue Service taxes them as such. For the wrongdoer, they're a form of non-criminal punishment, imposed by the court to deter such wrongful actions.

Punitive damages are only awarded in those tort actions where the victim can prove there was malice on the part of the tortfeasor. As we'll see in Chapter Four, the term *malice* has more than one meaning in law. For the purpose of winning punitive damages in most tort actions, it means ill will or evil intentions toward the victim. In libel cases, it usually has a different meaning, but either way, it is difficult to show malice—unless the tortfeasor actually set out to injure someone deliberately.

In recent years, juries have awarded millions (or billions) of dollars in punitive damages to victims of alleged corporate misconduct who could only prove that they were entitled to modest general and special damage awards. The U.S. Supreme Court has responded to this trend by overturning large punitive damage awards as a violation of the corporate defendant's due process rights. In a 2003 decision, the Court ruled that punitive damages should not ordinarily exceed 10 times the general and special damages. For example, if a plaintiff is entitled to $100,000 in compensatory damages, the Court was saying a jury should not ordinarily award more than $1 million in punitive damages. Often the punitive damage award, if any, should be far less than that, the Court held (*State Farm v. Campbell*, 538 U.S. 408).

This decision is likely to benefit the media by reducing the tendency of jurors to impose very large punitive damage awards in libel cases. It also brings U.S. law closer to the law in other countries. Even in countries with a common law heritage, such as England, courts generally limit punitive damages to relatively small sums. In many other countries, punitive damages are not allowed at all. The highest courts in Italy and Germany, for example, have refused to enforce judgments of American courts that involved a punitive damage award.

As we'll see later, keeping track of the various kinds of damages is important in several areas of media law. Sometimes one type of damages is available but not another. It is not unusual for a plaintiff in a libel suit, for example, to be denied a right to sue for anything but special damages because a newspaper has printed a retraction.

■ THE STORY OF A LAWSUIT

Perhaps the best way to illustrate how the legal system works is to follow a lawsuit through the courts, step by step. We'll trace a civil case called *New York Times v. Sullivan* (376 U.S. 254), a libel suit that is usually remembered for the very important legal precedent it established. Its effect on libel law is discussed in Chapter Four. However, it is also an excellent case to illustrate court procedures, since the case was carried through almost every step that occurs in civil lawsuits.

Anyone who thinks a newspaper story has injured his/her reputation has a right to sue the newspaper for monetary damages. This case involved a lawsuit between an individual named L. B. Sullivan and the company that publishes the *New York Times*.

The case began after the *New York Times* published an advertisement from a group of African-American civil rights leaders that described instances of alleged police brutality in the South. Some of the incidents occurred in Montgomery, Alabama. The ad was accurate for the most part, but it did contain several errors of fact. It did not name any individual as responsible for the alleged police misconduct. Nevertheless, Sullivan, who was one of three elected commissioners in Montgomery and the man in charge of police and fire services there, contended that his reputation had been damaged by the ad, so he hired a lawyer and sued the *New York Times* for libel. He contended that to criticize the police was to criticize the city commissioner who oversees the police department. The result was a lawsuit that went all the way to the U.S. Supreme Court after a variety of intermediate steps.

Initiating the Lawsuit

When Sullivan's lawyer filed the papers required to initiate the lawsuit (a document called the *complaint*), the clerk of the trial court assigned the case a number for record-keeping purposes, and the case became known as *Sullivan v. New York Times*. In our legal system, court cases are identified by the names of the parties to the dispute, with a little "v." (for versus) between the two names. When there are multiple parties on either side, the case is popularly identified by the name of the first person listed on each side. The name of the party bringing the lawsuit (the *plaintiff*) appears first, followed by the name of the party defending (the *defendant*). When the defendant loses the case in the trial court and then appeals, the two names are sometimes reversed. Hence, this case later became known as *New York Times v. Sullivan*.

As the plaintiff, Sullivan was seeking an award of monetary damages. The *New York Times*, of course, wanted to convince the court it had done nothing to injure Sullivan and that damages should therefore not be awarded.

Sullivan could have chosen to sue the *New York Times* in the New York state courts or even in the federal courts (based on diversity of citizenship). However, at that point in history many southerners bitterly resented northern efforts to promote the civil rights of African-Americans in the South. To many in Alabama, the *New York Times* symbolized all that they disliked. Thus, Sullivan's lawyer knew his client would have a much more sympathetic jury in Alabama than in New York. Besides, it would certainly be more convenient for them (but not for the *Times*) to try the case there.

Having filed the complaint in the proper Alabama trial court, the next step was to *serve* the *New York Times*. That is, a *process server* had to deliver a copy of the papers announcing the lawsuit to an appropriate representative of the newspaper. Some states permit the plaintiff to simply mail a copy to the defendant, depending on the nature of the case.

Serving the *New York Times* was a bit of a problem for Sullivan, since the paper didn't have any offices or regular employees in Alabama. Shortly after Sullivan initiated his lawsuit, a *Times* reporter visited the state to cover a civil rights demonstration, but *Times* lawyers in New York advised the reporter to leave the state before Sullivan's process servers could catch up with him, and he did so.

Sullivan ultimately served the papers on an Alabama resident who was a "stringer" (a part-time correspondent) for the *New York Times*. The *Times* immediately filed a motion in the Alabama courts to *quash* (invalidate) the service of process. Anxious to gain jurisdiction over the *Times*, the Alabama court denied the motion—and then found a technicality in the *Times'* legal petition that enabled the Alabama courts to hear the case.

Given the sentiments of many Alabama residents toward the *New York Times*, this would seem to have been an ideal case to be tried in federal court on a diversity of citizenship basis. However, the Alabama courts ruled that the *Times* had voluntarily consented to Alabama jurisdiction by the manner in which the motion to quash the process service was worded.

Although it had a daily circulation of only 390 in the entire state and about 35 in the Montgomery area, the *New York Times* was forced to submit to the jurisdiction of the Alabama state courts due to a legal technicality.

Once the Alabama court established jurisdiction, the paper was obliged to respond to the lawsuit. The *Times* filed a reply (called the *answer*), denying Sullivan's claims. If no answer had been filed, the *New York Times* would have *defaulted*. That means the court would have been free to award Sullivan whatever he asked for, without the paper having any say in the matter. But the *Times* did file an answer, denying any *liability* (responsibility for the alleged wrong).

Pretrial Motions

The *Times* also initiated a series of legal motions designed to get the case thrown out of court before trial by saying, in effect, "Look, this is nothing but a harassment lawsuit, and we shouldn't be put to the expense of a full trial."

Two kinds of pretrial motions can lead to a dismissal of the case before trial. One is called a *demurrer* (or simply a *motion to dismiss*) and it contends that there is no *legal basis* for a lawsuit, even if every fact the plaintiff alleges is true. The other kind is a motion for *summary judgment,* and it is often based on the defendant's contention that there is no *factual basis* for the lawsuit to proceed further even if all the facts that the plaintiff alleges are completely true. A summary judgment motion may also be made when either side

complaint:
the document that initiates a lawsuit.

answer:
the defendant's response to the complaint; no answer results in *default,* where the court rules for the other side.

serve:
to deliver a copy of the complaint to the appropriate party.

quash:
to invalidate or void.

liability:
responsibility for an alleged wrong.

demurrer/motion to dismiss:
a pretrial motion that requests that the case be dismissed based on the lack of legal basis to support it.

summary judgment:
a pretrial motion in which the parties agree on the facts and one party is entitled to a judgment as a matter of law.

discovery:
the pretrial process by which the parties share information and evidence, including *depositions* and *interrogatories.*

contends that there is no real disagreement between the parties about the facts, and that the judge should simply decide the case without further proceedings.

The *Times* filed a series of demurrers to argue that, among other things, the ad in no way referred to Sullivan and thus there was no legal basis for Sullivan to sue. (Someone must be identified and defamed before he/she can sue for libel, as Chapter Four explains.)

Demurrers and motions for summary judgment are particularly important for the media, because the media are often sued by people who may be embittered over unfriendly news coverage but who have no valid basis for a lawsuit. In such cases, the media may be entitled to a dismissal without the expense of a full trial. However, pretrial dismissals deny plaintiffs their day in court. Thus, a court reviewing such a request must give the plaintiff the benefit of every doubt. A pretrial dismissal is improper if there is any reasonable possibility the plaintiff could win at a trial.

This point is important because a number of Supreme Court decisions affecting the media have come on appeals of motions to dismiss a case before trial. When a newspaper or television station, for instance, is denied a pretrial dismissal and the U.S. Supreme Court affirms the denial, that does not mean the Court thinks the plaintiff will eventually win the lawsuit. Rather, it merely says that the plaintiff might have some slight chance to win and, in our system of justice, has a right to try. If you keep that point about court procedures in mind, some of the seemingly anti-media decisions we discuss later may not appear so harsh.

Returning to the *Sullivan* case, the Alabama court denied all of the *Times'* motions to dismiss the case before trial, and a trial was eventually scheduled.

Discovery

After the legal maneuvering over motions for summary judgment and demurrers, there is another very important pretrial procedure: the process of *discovery*. It is a process that allows each side to find out a great deal about the strengths and weaknesses of the other side's case. *Subpoenas*, or court orders compelling testimony or information, can be part of this process. Each *litigant* (party to the lawsuit) is permitted to ask the opposition a variety of oral questions (at *depositions)* and written questions *(interrogatories)*. During depositions, each side is permitted to meet and question hostile witnesses who are under oath (i.e., the witness has taken an oath promising to tell the truth).

As a result of discovery, a defendant might find out how substantial the plaintiff's losses really were, for instance. A plaintiff who says the wrong thing during a deposition can devastate his or her own case. And each litigant can size up the other's witnesses to see whether they will be credible in court. Much important information is revealed during discovery.

Why do courts allow discovery? Experience has shown that allowing discovery encourages many out-of-court settlements of lawsuits that would otherwise clog up the courts. If you find out that your opponent has a good case against you, you'll be much more likely to make a generous settlement offer. Taking a case to trial costs time and money, so it is in everybody's interest to see cases settled out of court whenever possible. The more each side knows about the other's case, the more likely they are to reach an agreement on their own.

However, Sullivan and the *New York Times* were hopelessly far apart; no settlement was possible. Sullivan was suing for half a million dollars, and the *Times* was contending that this was ridiculous. With a circulation of only 35 in Sullivan's county, and with him never mentioned either by name or title, the *Times* felt there was simply no way the ad could have done $500,000 worth of damage to the man's reputation.

The Trial

Sullivan and the *New York Times* faced off in a courtroom for trial. The first step in the trial was the selection of a jury, a process that raises another interesting point about civil cases.

Jury rights in civil cases differ somewhat from those in criminal cases. A defendant's right to a trial by a jury is one of the cornerstones of our criminal justice system, but no such stringent constitutional safeguards are involved in civil cases. There is a growing trend toward reducing the size of civil juries from the traditional panel of 12 to as few as six persons, and to allow verdicts to be rendered by nonunanimous civil juries. Only a few states allow nonunanimous juries or juries of fewer than 12 persons to decide major criminal cases.

In fact, many civil cases are tried without any jury because the losing side could be stuck with a bill for the jury, a risk neither side wishes to take. (By contrast, the defendant never has to pay for asserting his constitutional right to a jury trial in a criminal case.) Moreover, some civil litigants avoid jury trials because they feel they will fare better if a judge decides the facts as well as the law. But on the other hand, there are instances where a civil plaintiff may insist on a jury trial in the hope that the jurors will become emotional and award a big judgment. That happened in the Sullivan case.

Sullivan's lawyers were not unaware of the hostility many white southerners felt toward both the civil rights movement and the *New York Times* in the early 1960s when this case was tried. Blacks were still rare on Alabama juries at that point. The lawyers felt—correctly—that their client would do well before a jury.

Thus, the trial began. Sullivan, as the plaintiff, presented his evidence first, and then the *New York Times* responded. The plaintiff always goes first, the defendant last. A variety of witnesses testified for each side, with Sullivan's witnesses saying that they indeed associated him with the actions of the Montgomery police, and that they would think less of him if they believed the charges in the *New York Times* advertisement. Other witnesses testified about what they claimed were inaccuracies in the ad.

In its response, the *Times* contended that publishing the ad was protected by the First Amendment and that the ad in no way referred to Sullivan. The significance of these arguments will become more clear in Chapter Four, which discusses what one must prove to win a libel suit and what the media must prove to defend such a lawsuit.

After all of the evidence was in, the judge instructed the jury on the law. He told the jurors the material was libelous as a matter of law. Thus, their job was to decide only whether the *Times* was responsible for the publication and whether, in fact, the ad referred to Sullivan. The judge ruled that Sullivan did not need to prove any

appellant:
party that appeals a case to a higher court.

respondent:
party on the other side of an appealed case.

subpoena:
Latin for "under penalty;" an order to an individual to appear before a body at a particular time to give testimony.

majority opinion:
the opinion of the court that gets the most votes and carries the weight of legal precedent.

dissenting opinion:
an opinion written by a judge disagreeing with part or all of the majority or another judge's opinion.

concurring opinion:
an opinion written by a judge agreeing with part or all of the majority or another judge's opinion.

actual monetary losses due to the ad, since damages could be presumed from any libelous statement under Alabama law.

Eventually the jurors adjourned to a private room and arrived at a verdict: a judgment of half a million dollars (the full amount requested) for Sullivan. They would see to it that the *Times* would pay for its decision to publish an ad alleging police brutality in Montgomery, Alabama. After that verdict was rendered, the *New York Times* took two important procedural steps. The first was to file a motion for a new trial, citing what it claimed were errors and irregularities in the original trial. That motion was promptly denied in this case, but that doesn't always happen.

If a trial court judge feels the jury improperly weighed the evidence or was not impartial, or if improper evidence was presented at the trial, or if various other procedural errors occurred during the trial, the losing side may be entitled to a new trial. In this case, the motion for a new trial was denied. Then the *Times* exercised its other option, appealing the verdict to the Alabama Supreme Court.

The Appeal

When a case is appealed, the nomenclature changes a little. The party that appeals the case becomes the *appellant,* while the other party becomes the *respondent.* When the losing side at the trial level appeals, the names may be reversed, as we already suggested would happen in this case. Hence, the *New York Times* became the appellant and Sullivan the respondent: the case became known as *New York Times v. Sullivan.*

The Alabama Supreme Court agreed to hear the *New York Times v. Sullivan* case. When an appellate court grants an appeal such as this one, several things occur. First, each side submits a *brief* which is an elaborate argument of the legal issues involved in the case: a brief is not always brief. The appellant's brief must argue that the trial court erred in applying the law to the facts at hand, while the respondent must defend the trial court's decision.

After the briefs are filed and read by the appellate justices, oral arguments are usually scheduled. At oral arguments the lawyers for each side are given a short period of time to highlight their main points. The justices may ask them questions, sometimes on obscure points, perhaps forcing the lawyers to use up their time allotment without ever getting to their most important arguments. Sometimes the lawyers (and knowledgeable spectators such as journalists who regularly cover the court) can guess which side will win from the kind of questions the justices are asking. Appellate court justices sometimes reveal their own sympathies by the nature of their questions.

After the oral arguments, the justices informally vote on the case to see how they will rule. Once the positions of the various justices are clear, one justice will be assigned to write the *majority opinion*—the opinion that will prevail and become a legal precedent. If other justices disagree with this opinion, they may write *dissenting opinions* in which they argue that the majority is in error. Or a justice may agree with the result reached by the majority but disagree with some of the reasoning. When that happens, the result is a *concurring opinion.* A justice may also concur with another's concurring or dissenting opinion.

Dissenting and concurring opinions are important, because as times change it is not unusual for a new majority to coalesce around what was once a minority viewpoint. A dissenting opinion may become the foundation for a later majority opinion.

When the appellate opinion is then published—that is, printed in a law book that provides a verbatim record of all published decisions of the particular court—that decision officially becomes a legal precedent, adding a little more to the ever-growing body of law.

Not all appellate opinions are published in law books. Many courts publish only their most important opinions. For many years the unpublished ones had little or no weight as legal precedents. But because appellate court opinions are usually accessible via computer databases today, more and more appellate courts are allowing all of their decisions to be treated as legal precedents, largely eliminating the legal distinction between published and unpublished decisions. In 2006, the Supreme Court approved a proposal from the Judicial Conference of the United States to allow all new decisions of the federal appellate courts to be cited as legal precedents after Jan. 1, 2007. However, state appellate courts in California and a few other states still allow only their officially published decisions to be treated as legal precedents. The California Supreme Court and the highest courts in a few other states still set aside some lower appellate court rulings as legal precedents by simply ordering them *decertified for publication.* A decertified decision may still appear in law books, but officially it no longer exists as a legal precedent.

There are other occasions when an appellate court decision will lose its significance as a legal precedent. For instance, that occurs when a higher court decides to review the decision and issue its own ruling on the case.

In *New York Times v. Sullivan,* the Alabama Supreme Court affirmed the judgment of the trial court in full, upholding the half-million-dollar libel award to Sullivan. In an elaborate legal opinion, the Alabama Supreme Court defended the trial court's finding that it had jurisdiction over the *New York Times.* Then the court upheld the trial judge's controversial jury instructions, in which he told the jurors Sullivan didn't need to prove any actual losses to win his case. Finally, the state supreme court affirmed all other aspects of the decision, including the large award of damages.

After this setback, the *New York Times* had one hope left: the chance that the U.S. Supreme Court might agree to hear the case in spite of the fact that civil libel had traditionally been purely a matter of state law. The *Times* petitioned for a *writ of certiorari,* contending that this kind of a libel judgment violated the First Amendment because it would inhibit public discussion of controversial issues such as civil rights.

To the amazement of some legal experts, the Supreme Court agreed to hear the case.

The U.S. Supreme Court Ruling

When the *New York Times v. Sullivan* case reached the U.S. Supreme Court, all of the steps just described happened again. Elaborate briefs were filed by both sides, and oral arguments were heard by the nine Supreme Court justices. Then the justices conferred privately and Justice William J. Brennan was selected to write a majority opinion in what was destined to become the most famous court decision of all time on libel law.

Chapter Four describes the legal reasoning of the Supreme Court in this landmark decision. At this point, we'll simply say the *New York Times* won. The decisions of the Alabama courts were *reversed and remanded.* That means the Supreme Court invalidated the lower court decisions and ordered the Alabama trial court to reconsider the facts of the case under new legal rules set down by the Supreme Court.

As a practical matter, sometimes a decision like this one terminates the case. Sullivan's lawyers knew they could not win a trial conducted under the new legal ground rules. When the U.S. Supreme Court reversed and remanded the Alabama court's decision, this case was terminated—in fact if not in legal theory.

Other Options

In addition to reversing and/or remanding a lower court ruling, there are several other options open to an appellate court. The decision can be upheld (*affirmed*) or it can be affirmed in part and reversed in part. Then a new trial may be scheduled later. But whatever the ultimate outcome of the case at trial, often the most important aspect is the precedent-setting ruling of an appellate court. In the study of media law, you will encounter cases where the discussion centers on a major legal issue—and the final disposition of the lawsuit isn't discussed at all. After a landmark appellate ruling, it may take many more years to complete all of the various legal maneuvers at the trial court level and conclude a lawsuit—or the matter may be terminated as soon as a high appellate court rules.

Certainly a valid criticism of the American legal system is the length of time it takes to get a case to trial, up through the appellate courts and then back to trial again if necessary. If "justice delayed is justice denied," as critics of the system have suggested, the route through the American court system often includes enough detours to deny justice to many.

Another ethical issue raised by all of this, of course, is the prohibitive cost of justice. By the time a case reaches the U.S. Supreme Court, each side will typically have spent several hundred thousand dollars in legal fees, court costs and even printing bills.

■ HOW TO FIND THE LAW

Once you understand the various kinds of law and how the American legal system fits together, it isn't difficult to learn the law on any given subject. Legal research (i.e., the process of finding out what the law is on a subject) involves nothing more than knowing how to use some basic online reference tools or books that every well-stocked law library keeps on its shelves. Most larger county courthouses either have a law library or are located near one since judges who must make legal decisions every day need ready access to the laws on which to base their decisions. Also, every accredited law school has an extensive law library. Most of these law libraries are open to the public. You can go in and look up the law for yourself.

More than ever before, it is also possible to use the Internet, or a computer database such as Lexis-Nexis or Westlaw, to do legal research. These computer databases, once so costly that only the best-heeled law firms could afford them, are now accessible online via many university libraries, although the academic version of Lexis-Nexis lacks some features used in legal research.

The amount of legal information available on the Internet is enormous and growing daily—a trend that is revolutionizing legal research. In the absence of a specialized legal database, the Internet itself has become a powerful legal research tool, as a growing number of state and federal courts, as well as many other government agencies, have begun posting the full text of their decisions, regulations and other documents on their websites. For example, there is a wealth of regulatory information about advertising on the Federal Trade Commission's website (**www.ftc.gov**) and about the electronic media on the Federal Communications Commission's website (**www.fcc.gov**). Among more general online legal resources, some of the most popular include Thomas (**thomas.loc.gov**), the Library of Congress legislative information website; FindLaw (**www.findlaw.com**), a comprehensive privately maintained website; the Cornell Legal Information Institute site (**www.law.cornell.edu**), widely regarded as one of the best law sites; and Oyez (**www.oyez.org**), Northwestern University's multimedia U.S. Supreme Court site that has audio of oral arguments before the court, among other things. The official website of the federal court system (**www.uscourts.gov**) also has the full text of most recent federal court decisions, including those of the Supreme Court and the U.S. Courts of Appeals.

Court Decisions

Precedent-setting appellate court decisions are not difficult to look up, because there's a citation system that will tell you where to find each case. Throughout each chapter in this book you'll find citations to important court decisions in that area of media law. After the names of the two parties in the case, you'll see the case citation (a series of numbers and letters). We've already discussed the landmark libel decision *New York Times v. Sullivan*. When you look up that case in this or any other law-oriented book, you'll see this legal citation after the name of the case: 376 U.S. 254. The letters and numbers tell you exactly where to find the full text of the Supreme Court's ruling in a law book.

The "U.S." in the middle tells you which court ruled on the case because it stands for *United States Reports*, a series of books carrying the official text of Supreme Court decisions. Thus, to find the decision in print, you'd ask the law librarian where the "U.S. Supreme Court Reports" are kept. When you find this large collection of identical-looking volumes, the rest is simple. The first number in the citation (376) refers to the volume number of the law book in which the *New York Times v. Sullivan* case appears. You would look down the row, find the volume labeled "376" on the binding and pull it out.

Now you're there. The number after the "U.S." is the page number where the text of the case begins. Turn to page 254 in volume 376 of the *United States Reports*, and there's *New York Times v. Sullivan*. Before the actual text, there are introductory notes explaining the decision, designed to facilitate a quick review of the case highlights. Some citations end with the year of the decision. For example, *New York Times v. Sullivan* is cited as 376 U.S. 254, 1964.

When doing online research using Lexis-Nexis or Westlaw, for example, it's possible to search by the case name, the citation, or both—or to search for key words in the text of the case. Most researchers find that to be much faster than tracking down cases on a law library's bookshelves. Many case citations have letters in the middle such as "F.2d" or "F.3d." "F.2d" means *Federal Reporter, second series,* which is a set of law books containing decisions of the various U.S. Courts of Appeals. Why *second series?* The publisher of these books began producing them many years ago, and after a time the original editorial treatment and even the style of the binding seemed old-fashioned. Thus, the publisher modernized the book and started a second series, beginning again with volume number one in the new series. In 1993, the publisher launched a *third series,* once again starting with volume number one. If you see a citation to "F.3d," the case is a 1993 or later decision of a U.S. Court of Appeals.

In this textbook you will see a variety of legal citations to court decisions, and in each instance the letters in the middle tell you which court decided the case. Those decisions of the federal district courts that are published as legal precedents (many are not) appear in the *Federal Supplement* (abbreviated "F.Supp." in citations).

The citation system works much the same way in the state courts. In Chapter Five there's a reference to a privacy case called *Briscoe v. Reader's Digest,* 4 C.3d 529. That is a decision of the California Supreme Court, and the case appears in the *California Supreme Court Reports, third series*. To find the case, you would find volume 4 of that series and turn to page 529. Chapter Eight cites a case on reporter's privilege named *Zelenka v. Wisconsin,* 266 N.W.2d 279. It's a decision of the Wisconsin Supreme Court, but the citation refers to the *Northwestern Reporter, second series*. That series carries important court decisions from a number of midwestern states. It is a part of the *National Reporter System,* one publishing house's collection of regional reports that cover all 50 states. Most larger law libraries have the National Reporter system and perhaps other sets of volumes reporting the major cases of the state appellate courts around the country. Lexis-Nexis and Westlaw both have the full text of cases from all 50 states.

In many instances, law libraries have more than one set of law books reporting the most important court decisions. This is true in part because there are competing legal publishing houses, each seeking to offer a full set of reports of the major appellate cases. To illustrate by returning once again to *New York Times v. Sullivan,* here is a more complete set of citations to that case: 376 U.S. 254, 84 S. Ct. 710, 11 L.Ed.2d 686 (1964). Don't be intimidated by all those numbers: let's take it a step at a time. You already know what "376 U.S. 254" means. But suppose that volume is unavailable when you visit the law library. No problem. Just go to the next citation. "S. Ct." means *Supreme Court Reporter,* and if you pull down volume 84 and look on page 710, there's your case. Or you could go to "L.Ed.2d", which means *Lawyer's Edition, U.S. Supreme Court Reports, second series,* and pull down volume 11 and look on page 686. In each of these law books, the text of the Supreme Court decisions is exactly the same, but the introductory matter and editorial treatment may vary somewhat in these privately published books. Many law libraries keep all three of these sets of Supreme Court rulings in their collections, at least partly because the privately published versions are usually in print long before the official *U.S. Reports* become available.

Some very recent cases are shown with citations to a computer database such as Lexis-Nexis. In fact, the growing use of computer databases may soon lead to wholesale changes in the legal citation system described here. The page numbering system used in traditional citations has been based on *book pages,* of course. However, the pagination of a case is quite different on a computer screen, which typically consists of about 24 lines per "page." Colorado, Louisiana and Wisconsin have adopted new citation systems more compatible with computerized research methods. Several other states and the federal government are considering similar changes.

In the mass communications field, another convenient way to look up court decisions is to check the *Media Law Reporter.* One volume is published each year, and it carries the full text of most precedent-setting court decisions on media law, including Supreme Court decisions, lower federal court rulings and state cases. In this book there are several citations to the Media Law Reporter (abbreviated in citations as Media L. Rep.).

When doing legal research online, you have a major advantage: you can search for key words in the opinion (words such as *actual malice,* to note just one of many examples). In addition, you can quickly find later cases in which a particular case is mentioned.

Legal Encyclopedias

What happens if you don't know the names of any court decisions and you want to learn something about the law on a particular topic? One place you might look is a legal encyclopedia. These are just like regular encyclopedias—except that they discuss only legal subjects. There are two leading legal encyclopedias in America, produced by different publishing houses: *American Jurisprudence,* or "Am. Jur." for short, and *Corpus Juris Secundum,* or "CJS."

Legal encyclopedias are not difficult to use. The many legal topics they treat are listed in alphabetical order with brief summaries of the major legal principles in each area. The only trick is knowing where to look for a particular subject, and for that there's a comprehensive index at the end of each set. If you want to know more about libel law, for instance, you would look up the word "libel," and you would be told where to go for more information. It's not always that straightforward, because the name you have in mind may not be the key word under which that subject is indexed; you may have to think of some synonyms. Once you find the right word in the index, it will lead you directly to a summary of the law, whether it's bankruptcy or crimes, unfair competition or medical malpractice.

As well as these national legal encyclopedias—which try to summarize the general rules of law around the country—there are legal encyclopedias that specifically summarize the laws of one state. Most of the populous states have such encyclopedias, bearing names such as *Florida Jurisprudence, California Jurisprudence, Texas Jurisprudence* or *New York Jurisprudence.*

One thing you need to be aware of when you consult a physical legal encyclopedia is the existence of *pocket parts.* The law changes every year, often drastically. What a legal encyclopedia says in its main text is supplemented by annual updates that are tucked into a pocket at the back of each volume. Make it a habit to check the pocket part first, lest you waste time learning something that is no longer valid law.

Because there have been thousands of important court decisions, and because many of them have reached seemingly inconsistent conclusions, the American Law Institute has commissioned groups of legal scholars to write summaries of the law as it has developed over the years through court decisions. These are called *Restatements* of the law, and the courts give them considerable weight. The *Restatement of Torts* summarizes libel, privacy and other areas of tort law, and is an important reference work in these fields. The *Restatements* carry far more legal weight than any legal encyclopedia, although they might seem less user-friendly to newcomers doing their first legal research.

Annotated Codes

Once you have read a survey of your subject in a legal encyclopedia, you might want to learn more about the subject by actually reading some of the court decisions and statutory laws summarized in the encyclopedia. We've already described the method of finding court decisions by working from the case citations found in any law book. Looking up the text of a statutory law is often even easier.

Many of the important state and federal laws are organized by subject matter. To look up a statutory law, you locate the appropriate book of state or federal statutes: a legal encyclopedia will refer you to statutory laws as well as court decisions that pertain to your subject. If you wanted to read the federal Copyright Act, for instance, you would use its legal citation, which is "17 U.S.C. § 100 *et seq.*" That means Title 17 of the *United States Code,* Section 100 and following sections. To find the text of the Copyright Act, you would ask the law librarian where the U.S. Code volumes are kept, and then look up Section 100 in Title 17. The number before the name of a state or federal code is always the title, book or volume number, and the number after the name will lead you to the correct chapter and section. The nomenclature varies somewhat from state to state, but the principles are the same.

There are two things to remember in looking up statutory laws in this fashion. One is that the most complete sets are annotated; they contain brief summaries of court decisions interpreting the statutory laws as well as the text of the laws themselves. It's important to make sure the law you're learning has not been overruled by a court decision. And be sure to check the pocket parts if you're using physical volumes of the law.

Like encyclopedias, the annotated collections of statutory laws are extensively indexed. If you want to learn what the law of libel is in West Virginia, for instance, you can simply look up libel in the index to the *West Virginia Code* and then turn to the appropriate sections to find both statutes and summaries of cases mentioned in the annotations.

In some chapters of this book, there are suggestions for simple legal research you can do to learn exactly what the laws are on the particular topic in your state. No comprehensive national survey textbook can hope to summarize the law in each state in great detail, but you can fill in those details for your own state. If you are doing legal research online, many websites and databases offer statutory laws as well as regulatory information, searchable by key words.

Administrative Regulations

Administrative law is such a vast and amorphous thing that we will not devote much space to the problems of researching it here. However, students with a special interest in broadcasting, for instance, should be aware that the regulations of the Federal Communications Commission are organized to facilitate research.

Title 47 of a legal work called *The Code of Federal Regulations,* or "CFR" for short, contains the FCC's rules and regulations. Working from the table of contents, you can quickly look up the FCC's rules on a particular point of broadcast regulation in CFR. CFR is updated frequently, since the administrative agencies whose regulations appear in it are constantly changing their rules.

There are also privately published summaries of the actions taken by major administrative agencies. In the case of the FCC, a company named Pike and Fischer has provided information about the agency's actions since the 1930s. Many major law libraries keep complete sets of specialized legal reference materials such as *Pike and Fischer's Communications Regulation.* And, of course, many regulatory agencies such as the FCC have their own websites that include compilations of their regulations, news releases and reports.

"Shepardizing" Cases

The courts frequently interpret and reinterpret previous decisions. Anyone conducting legal research should make sure the key cases in any given topic are still *good law* and have not been reversed by a higher court or a later decision of the same court. A good way to do that is to consult a cross-reference index called *Shepard's Citator.* Most law libraries have *Shepard's* covering all state and federal appellate courts, and many online databases let you perform this function with a few clicks. By "Shepardizing" cases before citing them, you can avoid the mistake of writing 10 pages about a court decision that has been overturned.

WHAT SHOULD I KNOW ABOUT MY STATE?	• What federal circuit is my state in? • Where is my closest federal district court? • How is my state judicial system structured? • Where is my closest state trial court? • How are my state's judges chosen (elected, appointed)? • What does my state constitution say about free speech and press rights? • What should I know about how criminal and civil procedures work in my state?

2 *The Legacy of Freedom*

Americans are sometimes accused of taking freedom for granted. It is easy to talk about the First Amendment almost as if it were a universal law of nature, a principle that always existed and always will.

That, of course, is not the case. The kind of freedom of expression that is permitted today in the United States and a few dozen other democracies is unique in world history. Our freedoms were won through centuries of struggle, and they could easily be lost. Even today, fewer than half of the world's people live in countries that fully recognize such basic freedoms as freedom of speech, freedom of the press and freedom of religion. Government leaders in many countries consider "national security" (or their own personal security in office) more important than their people's freedoms. Many leaders see the media only as tools of propaganda or national development—weapons to be used against their rivals, both foreign and domestic. But as the 2011 use of Facebook and Twitter to create governmental and societal change by Egyptian protesters vividly demonstrated, the "mass media" is less easy to control in the age of the Internet than it was in the age of newspapers. Moreover, as information can easily be manipulated in digital format, what challenges will sites like WikiLeaks offer to those who wish to keep certain information secret?

As we will see in a review of the history of freedom of speech and press in the United States to the present day, some of the same issues, albeit using different technologies, face Americans in the 21st century as faced those Americans who experienced its founding.

■ CENSORSHIP IN ENGLAND

This summary of the evolution of freedom of expression could begin in the ancient world, were this chapter a survey of the philosophical underpinnings of modern civilization. Powerful arguments for freedom of expression were made thousands of years ago in ancient Greece and several other places around the globe. But our tradition of freedom of expression traces its roots most directly to England about 400 years ago.

In the 1600s, England was caught up in a battle that mixed politics and religion. The monarchy and the government-sponsored Church of England were determined to silence dissenters, many of them Puritans. Moreover, the religious and political struggle was closely linked with an economic battle between the aristocracy and the rising middle class.

Leaders on both sides of this ideological battle understood the importance of the printing press and sometimes resorted to heavy-handed efforts to censor ideas they considered dangerous. In those days more than one Englishman was jailed, tortured and eventually executed for expressing ideas unacceptable to those in power. Brutality that would be shocking to Americans—or Britons—today was fairly commonplace in England in that period.

Official censorship was enforced through a licensing system for printers that had been introduced as early as 1530. The licensing denied access to printing presses to people with unacceptable ideas, but it also enabled government representatives to preview and pre-censor materials before publication. Moreover, by making the possession of a license to print a coveted privilege, the government was often able to control underground printing. The licensed printers themselves helped to ferret out bootleg presses to protect their own self-interests.

Milton and the Puritans

By the early 1600s censorship was being used to suppress all sorts of ideas that threatened the established order. This inspired some of the leading political philosophers of the day to write eloquent appeals for freedom of expression as a vital adjunct to the broader freedom from religious and political oppression they sought. An early apostle of freedom of expression was John Milton, who in 1644 wrote his famous argument against government censorship, *Areopagitica*. Milton's appeal for freedom contained this statement:

> Though all the winds of doctrine were let loose to play upon the earth, so Truth
> be in the field, we do injuriously by licensing and prohibiting to misdoubt her
> strength. Let her and Falsehood grapple; who ever knew Truth put to the worse
> in a free and open encounter?

Out of this passage several modern ideas emerged, including the concept that a *self-righting* process would occur through open debate of controversial issues. In effect, Milton said censorship was unnecessary because true ideas would prevail over false ones anyway. Milton advocated something of a *marketplace of ideas*. That was a revolutionary idea: almost no one in Milton's time believed that freedom of expression should be universal. But even to Milton, this freedom had its limits. Although he favored far more freedom than most of his contemporaries, Milton did not think free expression rights should be extended to persons who advocated ideas that he considered dangerously false or subversive. His appeal for freedom specifically excluded "popery (support for the Roman Catholic Church) and open superstition" and ideas that were "impious or evil."

In fact, after the Puritan movement led by Oliver Cromwell gained control of England and executed King Charles I in 1649, Milton accepted a government appointment that required him to act as something of a government censor. One of his duties was to license and oversee the content of an official newssheet, *Mercurius Politicus*. By 1651—only seven years after he appealed to the government to allow true and false ideas to struggle for popular acceptance—Milton was engaged in the prior censorship of ideas. And he was serving in a government that imposed strict Puritan beliefs on England and showed little tolerance for the beliefs of other religious groups.

Was Milton's later employment inconsistent with the spirit of *Areopagitica?* Perhaps it was, but even today scholars disagree about the role Milton actually played in Cromwell's government. Some doubt that Milton really did much censoring. Whatever Milton later did—or did not do—to earn a living, his *Areopagitica* was an eloquent appeal for freedom of expression and an important influence on later English political thought.

In fairness to Cromwell's followers, we should also point out that there were some who went further than Milton did in advocating freedom of expression. For instance Roger Williams, a onetime Puritan minister in the Massachusetts Bay colony who was exiled to Rhode Island for his controversial religious ideas, later returned to England and wrote *Bloudy Tenent of Persecution for Cause of Conscience* in the same year as Milton's *Areopagitica*. Williams urged freedom of expression even for Catholics, Jews and Muslims—people Milton would not have included in his marketplace of ideas.

Perhaps even more emphatic in their arguments for freedom from censorship in the 1640s were the Levellers, a radical Puritan group. Their tracts consistently contained passages condemning censorship and the licensing system. In their view, free expression was essential to the religious freedom and limited government authority they so fervently sought.

In a 1648 petition to Parliament, the Levellers appealed for a free press. When "truth was suppressed" and the people ignorant, this ignorance "fitted only to serve the unjust ends of tyrants and oppressors." For a government to be just "in its constitution" and "equal in its distributions," it must "hear all voices and judgments, which they can never do, but by giving freedom to the press."

Despite the Puritans' rhetoric, England restored the monarchy in 1660 and the licensing of printers continued (although Parliament by then had a much larger say in the process). Although the post-1660 Restoration period was marked by unprecedented freedom—and even bawdiness—in English literature, it was also a time of religious repression. A 1662 act of Parliament, for instance, limited the number of printing presses and prohibited the printing of books contrary to the Christian faith as well as seditious or antigovernment works.

John Locke and Natural Rights

As the struggle between the monarchy and Parliament became more intense in the late 1600s, new philosophers of free expression emerged. Perhaps chief among them was John Locke. His ideas were not necessarily original, but he presented them so eloquently that he is remembered as one of the most important political theorists of his time. Locke's famous *social contract theory* said that governments were the servants of the people, not the other way around. Locke believed men were endowed with certain natural rights, among them the right to life, liberty and property ownership. In effect, Locke said the people make a deal with a government, giving it the authority to govern in return for the government's promise to safeguard these natural rights.

Central to these natural rights, Locke felt, was freedom of expression. Thus, when the English licensing system came up for review in 1694, Locke listed 18 reasons why the act should be terminated. The act was allowed to expire, primarily because of "the practical reason arising from the difficulties of administration and the restraints on trade."

Other forces in English society were also providing impetus for freedom of expression. For one, Parliament gained a major victory over the monarchy in the Glorious Revolution of 1688. James II, an avowedly Catholic king so offensive that several warring factions united against him, fled the country that year. Then in 1689 Parliament enacted a Bill of Rights and invited William of Orange and his consort, Mary, James' Protestant daughter, to assume the throne with limited powers. In the Declaration of Rights, William and Mary

marketplace of ideas: the notion that there should be freedom of speech so that all ideas would have a chance to be heard, considered and compete for attention and believers.

social contract theory: a theory of government where the people give up some rights to enjoy other rights, moving from a state of nature to a state of cooperation for self-governance; Locke's version of the social contract said that people have natural rights such as life, liberty and property rights.

sedition: incitement of resistance to or revolt against the government.

accepted these conditions, ending England's century-long struggle between Parliament and the monarchy.

In addition, a two-party system was emerging in England; the times were ready for open, robust political debate. The two parties, the Whigs and Tories, both relied extensively on the printing press in taking their views to the people.

Seditious Libel as a Crime

If official censorship by licensing the press was a thing of the past as England moved into the 1700s, the crime of seditious libel (i.e., the crime of criticizing the government or government officials) remained a viable deterrent to those who publish defamatory tracts.

A good illustration of this problem was the 1704 case of John Tuchin, who was tried for "writing, composing and publishing a certain false, malicious, seditious and scandalous libel, entitled, *The Observator*" (see *Rex v. Tuchin,* 14 Howell's State Trials 1095). Tuchin was convicted, and in the process the judge defined the common law on seditious libel:

> If people would not be called to account for possessing the people with an ill
> opinion of the government, no government can subsist. For it is very neces-
> sary for all governments that the people should have a good opinion of it. And
> nothing can be worse to any government, than to endeavor to procure animosi-
> ties, as to the management of it; this has been always looked upon as a crime,
> and no government can be safe without it be punished.

This common law rule did not go unchallenged for long. Free press advocates, perhaps strengthened by their success in abolishing licensing, opened the 18th century with a flurry of writings advocating greater freedom. Nevertheless, criticism of the government remained a crime throughout the century, with the truthfulness of the criticism not a defense against the charge. The prevailing legal maxim was "the greater the truth, the greater the libel."

How could this be? The assumption underlying this philosophy was reminiscent of Milton: if a printer publishes a false attack on the government, it will be disregarded by the people; if, on the other hand, a truthful attack is published, the people are likely to lend it credence and perhaps revolt, causing disorder and anarchy.

Parliament itself recognized the abuses possible under the common law of seditious libel, and in 1792 the Fox Libel Act was passed. That act permitted juries, rather than judges, to decide whether a statement was libelous. Prior to that time, the law allowed the jury to determine only whether the defendant was guilty of printing the libelous publication. The judge ruled on the legal question of whether the material was actually libelous. This legal reform did not eliminate seditious libel prosecutions, but it did make it more difficult for a government to punish its critics because a jury, whose members might well sympathize with the defendant's allegedly libelous statements, could decide if the statements were libelous.

An additional reform came in 1843, further strengthening the rights of those who would criticize the government in England. In that year, Parliament passed Lord Campbell's Act, establishing truth as a defense in all seditious libel cases. Thus, the old maxim, "the greater the truth, the greater the libel," was at last abolished.

While the struggle for freedom of expression was being fought in England, a parallel battle was under way in the American colonies.

■ FREEDOM IN A NEW NATION

Although many of the early colonists in North America left England or the European continent to escape religious or political oppression, they found (or created) an atmosphere of less than total freedom in some of the colonies here. As the Puritans gained control in New England, they established close church-state ties, and persons with unpopular religious or political ideas were hardly more welcome here than they had been in England.

In fact, the first laws that restricted freedom of the press in North America preceded the first newspaper here by some 30 years. Even without any specific authority, colonial rulers often simply assumed they had the right to censor dissenting publications because the authorities had that right in England. Even after licensing was abolished in England, colonial leaders continued to act as if they had licensing powers, and several colonial newspapers carried the phrase "published by authority" in their mastheads years after the right to publish without government permission was won in England.

Moreover, in North America as in England, seditious libel prosecutions were used to control the press, as were laws that placed special tax burdens on newspapers. The Stamp Act of 1765, for instance, taxed newspapers by forcing publishers to purchase revenue stamps to attach to each copy. The result was such blatant defiance of British authority by colonial publishers that it helped inspire the eventual revolution against the mother country.

The Zenger Libel Trial

Early in the colonial publishing experience there was a seditious libel case that became a *cause célèbre* on both sides of the Atlantic: the trial of John Peter Zenger in 1735 (*Attorney General v. John Peter Zenger*, 17 Howell's State Trials 675).

Zenger, a German immigrant, was the publisher and printer of the *New York Weekly Journal*. His paper became a leading voice for the opposition to a particularly unpopular royal governor, William Cosby. After some legal maneuvering, the governor was able to have Zenger jailed and charged with "printing and publishing a false, scandalous and seditious libel, in which...the governor...is greatly and unjustly scandalized, as a person that has no regard to law nor justice."

Zenger was fortunate enough to have Andrew Hamilton of Philadelphia, one of the most respected lawyers in the colonies, make the trip to New York for his defense. And Hamilton, ignoring the orders of Cosby's hand-picked judge, appealed directly to the jury. He urged the jurors to ignore the maxim of "the greater the truth, the greater the libel" and to decide for themselves whether the statements in question were actually true, finding them libelous only if they were false.

"Nature and the laws of our country have given us a right—and the liberty—both of exposing and opposing arbitrary power ...by speaking and writing truth," Hamilton said.

In urging the jurors to ignore the judge's instructions and acquit Zenger if they decided the statements were true, Hamilton was clearly overstepping the bounds of the law. A less prestigious lawyer might have been punished for an action so clearly in contempt of the court's authority. However, Hamilton was not cited, and his eloquent appeal to the jury worked: the jury returned a not-guilty verdict even though there was little question that Zenger was the publisher of the challenged statements.

It would be difficult to overstate the importance of the Zenger trial in terms of its psychological impact on royal governors in America. Still, its direct effect on the common law was minimal in America and England itself. Even in those days, a criminal trial verdict established no binding legal precedent. English courts continued to punish truthful publications that were critical of government authority. For instance, the trial of John Wilkes for publishing a "wicked and seditious libel," a 1763 English case, made it clear that the common law had not been changed by the Zenger trial.

Nevertheless, the argument was made again and again that mere words critical of the government—and especially truthful words—should not be a crime. In 1773 the Rev. Philip Furneaux wrote that only overt acts against a government should be punished:

> The tendency of principles, tho' it be unfavourable, is not prejudicial to society,
> till it issues in some overt acts against the public peace and order; and when
> it does, then the magistrate's authority to punish commences; that is, he may
> punish the overt acts, but not the tendency which is not actually harmful; and
> therefore his penal laws should be directed against overt acts only.

■ THE FIRST AMENDMENT

When a series of incidents strained relations between England and the colonies past the breaking point, the colonists declared their independence in 1776. Yet even in breaking with England, the Americans borrowed heavily from the mother country. Thomas Jefferson's ideas and even some of his language in the Declaration of Independence were borrowed from English political philosophers, notably John Locke. Locke's natural rights and social contract ideas appear repeatedly in the declaration.

After independence was won on the battlefield, the new nation briefly experimented with a weak central government under the Articles of Confederation and then became a unified nation under the Constitution, ratified by the states in 1788. Despite its ratification, many Americans feared the new federal government, particularly because the Constitution had no guarantees that basic civil liberties would be respected. Although the defenders of the Constitution argued that these civil liberties were firmly entrenched in the common law we had inherited from England, many were wary. Some states ratified the Constitution only after they received assurances that it would be amended quickly to add a Bill of Rights.

That promise was kept. In the first session of Congress, the Bill of Rights was drawn up and submitted to the states to ratify. It was declared in force late in 1791. Of paramount concern to the media, of course, is the First Amendment. Taken literally, it is almost everything that a free press advocate might hope for, but phrases such as "Congress shall make no law" have not always been taken literally. In fact, the exact meaning of the First Amendment has been vigorously debated for more than 200 years.

Early First Amendment Questions

The record of the Congressional discussions when the Bill of Rights was drafted is sketchy: it is impossible to be certain what Congress had in mind. Constitutional scholars have advanced various theories, but most doubt that the majority of the framers of the Constitution intended the First Amendment to be an absolute prohibition on all government actions that might in any way curtail freedom of the press.

The crucial question, then, and the one that is the focus of the rest of this chapter, is this: which restrictions on freedom of expression are constitutionally permissible and which ones are not? Many scholarly works have been published attempting to answer this question; several historians have dedicated much of their lives to examining records, debates and documents of the period in an attempt to find the answers. Some of their conclusions will be presented shortly.

Whatever the first Congress intended in drafting those words, it was only a few years later that Congress passed laws that seemed to be a flagrant violation of the First Amendment. In 1798 Congress hurriedly approved the *Alien and Sedition Acts*, a group of laws designed to silence political dissent in preparation for a war with France, a war that was never declared. The Sedition Act made it a federal crime to speak or publish seditious ideas. The law had one important safeguard: truth was recognized as a defense. Nevertheless, a fine of up to $2,000 or two years' imprisonment was prescribed for any person who dared to:

> ...(W)rite, print, utter or publish, or ...knowingly and willingly assist or aid in writing, printing, uttering or publishing any false, scandalous and malicious writing or writings against the government of the United States, or either house of the Congress of the United States, or the President of the United States, with intent to defame the said government, or either house of said Congress, or the said President, or to bring them, or either of them, into contempt or disrepute; or to excite against them, or either or any of them, the hatred of the good people of the United States, or to stir up sedition within the United States.

There were about 25 arrests and 15 indictments under the act. All were aimed at opponents of President John Adams and the Federalist Party, which then controlled Congress and had enacted the law over the opposition of Jefferson and his followers. Even though the Federalist press was often guilty of vicious attacks on Thomas Jefferson and other non-Federalist government officials, no Federalist was ever prosecuted under the Sedition Act. A two-party system was emerging, and the Jeffersonian, or anti-Federalist, opposition party was the real target of the Sedition Act.

Jefferson, by then vice president, strenuously opposed the Alien and Sedition Acts. The Kentucky and Virginia legislatures passed resolutions, backed by Jefferson, that purported

Focus on...
Monitoring international press freedom

The Daniel Pearl Freedom of the Press Act was named for *Wall Street Journal* reporter Daniel Pearl, who was killed by terrorists in Pakistan in 2002 while investigating the war on terrorism. President Obama signed this Act in 2010, requiring that the State Department look into possible violations of press freedoms when compiling its Annual Country Reports on Human Rights Practices series.

"What this act does is it sends a strong message from the United States government and from the State Department that we are paying attention to how other governments are operating when it comes to the press," said Obama at the signing ceremony.

FIG. 6. President Barack Obama talks with Adam Pearl, son of murdered journalist Daniel Pearl, before signing the Daniel Pearl Freedom of Press Act in the Oval Office.

Official White House Photo by Pete Souza.

to "nullify" these laws, thus raising questions about states' rights that would not be resolved until the Civil War. James Madison, later to be Jefferson's secretary of state and then the fourth president, made it clear in drafting the Virginia Resolution that he felt the Sedition Act was a violation of the First Amendment. Madison believed the First Amendment was supposed to be an absolute prohibition on all actions of the federal government that restricted freedom of the press. Jefferson probably agreed. In one letter to a friend, he wrote: "I am...for freedom of the press and against all violations of the Constitution to silence by force and not by reason the complaints or criticisms, just or unjust, of our citizens against the conduct of their agents." When Jefferson ran for president in 1800, he made the Alien and Sedition Acts a major issue; public discontent over these laws was certainly an important factor in his victory. Immediately after his inauguration, Jefferson ordered the pardon of those who had been convicted under the Sedition Act.

Jefferson's record as a champion of a free press was not entirely unblemished. During his presidency he was subjected to harsh personal attacks by some opposition newspapers. Although he usually defended the right of his foes to express their views, he eventually became so annoyed that he encouraged his backers to prosecute some of his critics in state courts.

■ THE FIRST AMENDMENT: SCHOLARS' VIEWS

The Sedition Act expired in 1801, and it was more than 100 years before Congress again attempted to make criticism of the government a federal crime.

However, this does not prove the First Amendment was intended to eliminate seditious libel as a crime, and the debate over that issue continued well into the 20th century. Historian Leonard Levy, a leading constitutional scholar, once wrote, "What is clear is that there exists no evidence to suggest an understanding that a constitutional guarantee of free speech or press meant the impossibility of future prosecutions of seditious utterances...."

Levy argued that most likely the framers of the First Amendment weren't certain what its full implications were, but that most of the framers believed future prosecutions for seditious utterances were possible. However, later in his life Levy rethought that conclusion based on extensive additional research into the content of early American newspapers. He ultimately decided that the framers must have intended for the First Amendment to provide "a right to engage in rasping, corrosive, and offensive discussions on all topics of public interest." His earlier, more narrow view of the First Amendment was presented in a 1960 book, *Legacy of Suppression: Freedom of Speech and Press in Early American History*. In 1985, he published a revised and enlarged edition of the book retitled *Emergence of a Free Press*. In the preface, Levy wrote: "Some states gave written constitutional protection to freedom of the press after Independence; others did not. Whether they did or not, their presses operated as if the law of seditious libel did not exist."

In revising his views, Levy came much closer to agreeing with several other noted legal historians. For example, Harvard Professor Zechariah Chafee wrote that the First Amendment was indeed intended to eliminate the common law crime of seditious libel "and make further prosecutions for criticism of the government, without any incitement to law-breaking, forever impossible in the United States."

Chafee, in his 1941 work, argued that freedom of expression is essential to the emergence of truth and advancement of knowledge. The quest for truth "is possible only through absolutely unlimited discussion," Chafee said. Yet, he noted that there are other purposes of government, such as order, the training of the young, and protection against external aggression. Those purposes, he said, must be protected too, but when open discussion interferes with those purposes, there must be a balancing against freedom of speech, "but freedom of speech ought to weigh heavily on that scale."

Chafee argued against prior restraint of expression unless it was very clear that such expression imperiled the nation. He wrote:

> The true boundary line of the First Amendment can be fixed only when
> Congress and the courts realize that the principle on which speech is classi-
> fied as lawful or unlawful involves the balancing against each other of two very
> important social interests, in public safety and in the search for truth. Every
> reasonable attempt should be made to maintain both interests unimpaired, and
> the great interest in free speech should be sacrificed only when the interest in
> public safety is really imperiled, and not, as most men believe, when it is barely
> conceivable that it may be slightly affected.

Chafee's boundary line, then, is that point where words will incite unlawful acts. As we'll see later, that is precisely the point at which the Supreme Court has drawn the line in recent decisions on the meaning of the First Amendment.

A third noted constitutional scholar, Alexander Meiklejohn, agreed for the most part with Chafee's interpretation of the First Amendment. He said that only expression that incites unlawful acts should be punishable. Further, he said, incitement does not occur unless an illegal act is actually performed and the prior words can be directly connected to the act. Then, and only then, can words be punished in spite of the First Amendment.

Meiklejohn said that the First Amendment was written during a time when large sections of the population were hostile to the form of government then being adopted. Thus, the framers knew full well that a program of political freedom was a dangerous thing. Yet, Meiklejohn said, the framers chose to write the First Amendment as it is and not the way the courts have rewritten it during the twentieth century. He said that if the framers had wanted the federal government to control expression, the First Amendment could have read: "Only when, in the judgment of the legislature, the interests of order and security render such action advisable shall Congress abridge the freedom of speech."

Both Chafee and Meiklejohn felt that the voters must be well informed to make wise decisions. Both endorsed Milton's "marketplace of ideas" concept, and Meiklejohn supported Milton's view that truth will prevail in this clash of ideas:

> No one can deny that the winning of the truth is important for the purposes of
> self-government. But that is not our deepest need. Far more essential, if men are
> to be their own rulers, is the demand that whatever truth may become available
> shall be placed at the disposal of all the citizens of the community.

Much of what we have just discussed is quite theoretical, but the views of scholars such as Chafee, Meiklejohn and Levy have often influenced the U.S. Supreme Court when it was forced to make difficult decisions about the scope and meaning of the First Amendment in the real world.

■ NINETEENTH-CENTURY PRESS FREEDOM

Whatever the framers of the Constitution and Bill of Rights intended, the question
received little attention in the 1800s. The nineteenth century was a time when Americans
were preoccupied with such overriding issues as national expansion and slavery. There was
surprisingly little attention given to the meaning of the First Amendment during most of
that century. Instead, the country and the courts were looking at other issues.

The Supreme Court and Judicial Review

In 1803, the Supreme Court gained the power to declare acts of Congress unconstitutional and thereby invalidate them. In the landmark case of *Marbury v. Madison* (1 Cranch
137), what the court really did was simply to declare that it had the power to overturn acts
of Congress. Perhaps the court got away with it mainly because President Jefferson and his
followers were happy with the outcome of the case.

Just before his term expired, John Adams, the lame-duck Federalist president, had
appointed a number of federal judges. Because of their belated appointments, they came
to be called "midnight judges." The new judges were Federalists, and the Jeffersonians
were anxious to keep them from taking office. James Madison, Jefferson's secretary of state,
refused to give William Marbury, one of the would-be judges, his signed commission (the
document appointing him to office). Marbury sued to get the commission. The Jeffersonians were not displeased when the Court, under its famous chief justice, John Marshall,
dismissed Marbury's claim by overturning the Judicial Act of 1789, on which the would-be
judge had based his lawsuit. In the convoluted politics of the day, Marshall—a Federalist—
had sided with the Jeffersonians on a small matter (Marbury's commission), but in so doing
Marshall had prevailed on the larger issue: the right of the courts to review actions of other
branches of government for compliance with the Constitution.

Ironically, Chief Justice Marshall had himself been appointed by John Adams during
the final year of his presidency. Although the Federalist Party faded away, never winning
another national election, Marshall served as chief justice for 34 years, allowing the Federalist philosophy to have an ongoing impact on American law long after the Federalist Party

disappeared from the scene. Marshall's Supreme Court asserted its authority in many other areas, attempting to define the scope and limits of federal power. In 1812, the Court ruled that the federal courts had no authority to entertain actions involving common law crimes such as criminal libel. In *U.S. v. Hudson and Goodwin* (7 Cranch 32), the Court said this area of law fell within the exclusive domain of the states, a philosophy that has remained largely unchanged ever since. On the other hand, in *McCulloch v. Maryland* (4 Wheat. 316), an 1819 decision that is among Marshall's most famous, the Court upheld the right of Congress to create a national bank and regulate the economy even though a narrow, literal reading of the Constitution might not permit it. Having so ruled, Marshall then declared once and for all that the states may not tax agencies of the federal government.

When the Bill of Rights was added to the U.S. Constitution, its authors wanted to be certain that the federal government's powers would be strictly limited so as to avoid usurping the powers of the states. The Tenth Amendment reads, "The powers not delegated to the United States by the Constitution, nor prohibited by it to the states, are reserved to the states respectively, or to the people." To the amazement of many Americans, the Supreme Court reasserted the principle of a strictly limited federal government in a series of decisions 200 years later. For example, in 2000, the Supreme Court overturned the Violence against Women Act of 1994, holding that Congress had invaded an area reserved for the states (i.e., the prosecution of crimes such as rape) by passing this law *(U.S. v. Morrison,* 529 U.S. 598).

While the federal government stayed out of mass communications law during much of the nineteenth century, the states filled that void. Throughout the century, the states were expanding the common law and adopting statutory laws in such areas as libel and slander.

One of the best-known state cases was the 1804 libel trial of Harry Croswell in New York (*People v. Croswell*, 3 Johnson's Cases 336). Croswell attacked President Jefferson in print and was prosecuted for criminal libel. He was convicted and appealed to a higher state court. His defense attorney, Federalist leader Alexander Hamilton, argued that truth plus "good motives for justifiable ends" should be a defense in such cases.

Although Croswell lost when the appellate panel of four judges deadlocked 2-2, the concept that truth should be a libel defense was sometimes called the *Hamilton Doctrine* and was adopted in a number of states during that era. For instance, the New York legislature recognized the truth defense by statute in 1805—and added a provision empowering the jury to determine whether the statement in question was actually libelous. Some states had recognized truth as a libel defense even before that time and, of course, the 1798 Sedition Act had recognized it on the federal level. Nevertheless, what Andrew Hamilton, the distinguished Philadelphia lawyer, had argued for in the Zenger trial 70 years earlier gained general acceptance in American law only after another distinguished lawyer named Hamilton made it his cause as well.

Alexander Hamilton, of course, didn't live long enough to enjoy whatever recognition the Hamilton Doctrine might have brought him: a newspaper account of something he purportedly said during the Croswell trial led to the infamous duel in which he was killed by Aaron Burr, then the vice president of the United States.*6*

Slavery and Free Expression

Aside from the gradual evolution of libel law, probably the most significant conflict over American freedom of expression in the 1800s resulted from the struggle over slavery and the War Between the States.

As the national debate over slavery intensified in the early 1800s, a number of southern states enacted "gag laws" that prohibited the circulation of newspapers and other materials advocating the abolition of slavery. Although these laws were clearly acts of prior censorship and violated the spirit of the First Amendment, the First Amendment had not yet been made applicable to the states, and these laws were never tested for their constitutionality.

Some northern states also attempted to curb abolitionist literature through various laws; these laws too escaped constitutional scrutiny because the Bill of Rights did not yet apply to the states. Even Congress adopted rules to suppress debate about slavery that violated the spirit and probably the letter of the First Amendment. When anti-slavery groups began submitting petitions to Congress asking that the slave trade in Washington, D.C. be abolished, the House of Representatives adopted internal "gag rules" to prevent these petitions from being introduced and considered. These rules not only censored anti-slavery members of Congress but also took direct aim at the First Amendment's provision guaranteeing the right to petition the government. Rep. John Quincy Adams of Massachusetts, who returned to Congress after serving as the nation's sixth president, led the fight against these gag rules. At one point he arrived in Washington with anti-slavery petitions signed by more than 50,000 persons. When he was barred from presenting them formally, he left the petitions stacked high on his desk in the House of Representatives as a silent protest against the gag rules. In 1844, Adams—by then 77 years old—finally garnered enough support to have the Congressional gag rules eliminated.

During the Civil War itself, a vigorous antiwar movement emerged in the North, and antiwar editors came to be known as Copperheads. Some of them tested freedom of the press in wartime to the limit, openly advocating a southern victory.

The Copperheads' rhetoric often hindered recruiting for the Union Army. On several occasions, military commanders in the North acted against Copperheads, creating a difficult dilemma for President Lincoln, who was deeply committed to the First Amendment but also wanted to end the war quickly. He is generally credited with exercising great restraint in the face of vicious criticism from the Copperhead editors. On one occasion he actually countermanded a general's decision to occupy the offices of the *Chicago Times* to halt that paper's attacks on the war effort.

However, in 1864 Lincoln reached his breaking point when two New York newspapers published a false story claiming there was to be a massive new draft call—an announcement sure to stir violent anti-draft riots. The president allowed the editors to be arrested and their papers occupied by the military until it was learned the newspapers got the story from a forged Associated Press dispatch that they had every reason to believe was authentic. As it turned out, the story was fabricated by an unscrupulous journalist who hoped to reap large profits in the stock market during the panic he expected the story to produce.

After the end of the Civil War, the Fourteenth Amendment was approved, requiring the states to safeguard the basic civil liberties of all of their residents. The relevant part of the Fourteenth Amendment reads as follows:

> No state shall make or enforce any law which shall abridge the privileges or immunities of citizens of the United States; nor shall any State deprive any person of life, liberty or property, without due process of law; nor deny to any person within its jurisdiction the equal protection of the laws.

Like the First Amendment, this amendment had far-reaching consequences that were not fully understood when it was adopted. Its immediate impetus came from the desire to protect the former slaves from oppressive legislation in southern states. But during the twentieth century the "liberty" clause of the Fourteenth Amendment was relied upon repeatedly to make the various federal rights guaranteed in the Bill of Rights—including the First Amendment—applicable to the states. Under a modern understanding of constitutional law, no state could enforce a gag law of the sort adopted by many states before the Civil War.

John Stuart Mill's Philosophy

While the United States was preoccupied with the struggle over slavery, John Stuart Mill, an English political philosopher, was refining theoretical concepts of freedom of expression.

Mill's *On Liberty*, first published in 1859, defined the limits of freedom and authority in the modern state. He said that by the mid-1800s the important role of the press as one of "the securities against corrupt or tyrannical government" was well recognized—at least in such countries as England and the United States. He stressed that any attempt to silence expression, even that of a one-person minority, deprives the people of something important. He said that "if the opinion is right, they (the people) are deprived of the opportunity of exchanging error for truth; if wrong, they lose what is almost as great a benefit, the clearer perception and livelier impression of truth, produced by its collision with error."

Mill presented four basic propositions in defense of freedom of expression. First, he said an opinion may contain truth, and if one silences the opinion, the truth may be lost. Second, there may be a particle of truth within a wrong opinion; if the wrong opinion is suppressed, that particle of truth may be lost. Third, even if an accepted opinion is the truth, the public tends to hold it not on rational grounds but as a prejudice unless forced to defend it. And fourth, a commonly held opinion loses its vitality and its effect on conduct and character if it is not contested from time to time.

In these terms, Mill expanded upon Milton's "marketplace of ideas" concept. The impact of these ideas on the evolution of free expression became evident in the twentieth century.

■ SEDITION IN THE TWENTIETH CENTURY

Wars and the threat of wars tend to make lawmakers worry more about national security and less about such ideals as freedom of speech. The Alien and Sedition Acts of 1798 were passed at a time when war with France seemed imminent, and the Civil War created pressures for censorship of those who opposed that war effort.

Early in the twentieth century, this nation became involved in what many Americans thought would be the war to end all wars: World War I. In preparing the country for this all-out war, Congress again decided that domestic freedom would have to be curtailed. The result was the Espionage Act in 1917, which was expanded by the Sedition Act in 1918.

In passing these laws, Congress was not merely expressing its own collective desire to suppress unpopular views. In fact, there was a growing worldwide movement for fundamental social change, a movement many Americans found threatening. Already, Marxist revolutionaries were on the move in Russia, and socialists, anarchists and Marxists were also highly visible in this country. Moreover, we were about to undertake a war against Germany, and yet there were millions of persons of German descent living in America. In addition, labor unions such as the Industrial Workers of the World (the "Wobblies") were gaining wide support and calling for basic changes in the capitalist system.

The Espionage Act was passed shortly after the United States entered World War I. It prohibited seditious expression that might hurt the war effort. This federal law was particularly aimed at those who might hamper armed forces recruiting, and it was written so broadly that it was once used to prosecute a grandmother who wrote a letter urging her grandson not to join the army.

Unlike the 1798 Sedition Act, which resulted in only a handful of prosecutions, the 1918 Sedition Act was vigorously enforced. About 2,000 persons were arrested for violating the Espionage and Sedition acts and nearly 1,000 were convicted. Several of the convictions were appealed to the U.S. Supreme Court, which upheld every conviction it reviewed.

Early Free Expression Decisions

The first Espionage Act or Sedition Act case to reach the Supreme Court was *Schenck v. U.S.* (249 U.S. 47) in 1919. Charles T. Schenck, general secretary of the Socialist Party, and another socialist were convicted under the Espionage Act and state anarchy and sedition laws for circulating about 15,000 leaflets to military recruits and draftees. The tracts denounced the draft as an unconstitutional form of involuntary servitude, banned by the Thirteenth Amendment. They urged the draftees not to serve and called the war a cold-blooded venture for the profit of big business.

When their conviction was reviewed by the Supreme Court, the socialists argued that their speech and leaflets were protected by the First Amendment. The Court was thus compelled to rule on the scope and meaning of the First Amendment. In a famous opinion written by Justice Oliver Wendell Holmes Jr., the Court rejected the socialists' argument:

> We admit that in many places and in ordinary times the defendants in saying all that was said in the circular would have been within their constitutional rights. But the character of every act depends upon the circumstances in which it is done. The question in every case is whether the words used are used in such circumstances and are of such a nature as to create *a clear and present danger* that they will bring about the substantive evils that Congress has a right to prevent (emphasis added).

In short, the Supreme Court said the First Amendment is not absolute. Congress may abridge freedom of speech whenever that speech presents a "clear and present danger" to some other national interest that is more important than freedom of speech at the moment.

In reaching this conclusion, Holmes made his famous analogy: "free speech would not protect a man in falsely shouting fire in a theatre and causing a panic." Thus, he wrote, free speech can never be considered absolute. Instead, each abridgment of freedom must be weighed against its purpose to decide if it is an appropriate or inappropriate one.

Although the *clear and present danger* test has proved to be vague and difficult to administer, it replaced a common law test for allegedly dangerous speech that was even more difficult to administer without unduly inhibiting freedom. The old common law test, known as the *reasonable tendency* or *bad tendency test,* was established in England in the 1700s and adopted as American common law along with the rest of the English common law. This test could be used to forbid any speech that might tend to create a low opinion of public officials,

(L) FIG. 8. John Locke
(1632-1704).

*Library of Congress, Prints
and Photographs Division,
[LC-USZ62-59655].*

(R) FIG. 9. John Stuart
Mill (1806-1873).

*Library of Congress, Prints
and Photographs Division,
[LC-USZ62-76491].*

institutions or laws. It gave prosecutors wide latitude to prosecute anyone charged with seditious libel. Whatever its limitations, the clear and present danger test was more precise and offered more protection for unpopular speech than the old reasonable tendency test.

Following *Schenck,* the Supreme Court quickly upheld the convictions of two other persons charged with violating the Espionage Act: Jacob Frohwerk, a German language newspaper editor, and Eugene V. Debs, the famous leader of the American Socialist Party who later received nearly a million votes for president of the United States while in jail.

Eight months after the *Schenck, Frohwerk v. U.S.* (249 U.S. 204) and *Debs v. U.S.* (249 U.S. 211) decisions, the Supreme Court ruled on another Espionage Act case, *Abrams v. U.S.* (250 U.S. 616). The convictions of Jacob Abrams and four others who had published antiwar leaflets were upheld, but this time the Court had a new dissenter: Justice Holmes had rethought his position and wrote an eloquent defense of freedom of expression that was joined by Justice Louis Brandeis.

In the majority opinion that affirmed the convictions, Justice John Clarke said the primary goal of Abrams and his co-defendants was to aid the enemy. That constituted a clear and present danger to national interests. But Holmes and Brandeis replied:

> It is only the present danger of immediate evil or an intent to bring it about
> that warrants Congress in setting a limit to the expression of opinion where
> private rights are not concerned. Congress certainly cannot forbid all effort to
> change the mind of the country. Now nobody can suppose that the surreptitious
> publishing of a silly leaflet by an unknown man, without more, would present
> any immediate danger that its opinions would hinder the success of the govern-
> ment aims or have any appreciable tendency to do so.

This opinion was very influential in later years, but at the time it was a minority view. Neither the country nor the Supreme Court was in a mood to be tolerant toward political radicals.

In the last Espionage Act case it reviewed, the Supreme Court affirmed a lower court ruling that denied second-class mailing privileges to the *Milwaukee Leader,* the best known Socialist paper in the country. The high court found that articles in the *Leader* "sought to convince readers... that soldiers could not be legally sent outside the country," and thus the sanctions were appropriate (*U.S. ex rel. Milwaukee Social Democratic Publishing Co. v. Burleson,* 255 U.S. 407, 1921).

By today's standards, these Supreme Court decisions seem repressive. The expression of views that would have been considered well within the protection of the First Amendment in more recent times led to criminal prosecutions during World War I. Obviously, First Amendment law was in its infancy at that point. The courts felt little obligation to observe the niceties of constitutional law at a time when leftists seemed threatening to many Americans.

■ THE FIRST AMENDMENT AND THE STATES

During the first part of the twentieth century, at least 20 states enacted their own laws against various kinds of political radicalism. The common element in these laws was a fear of groups that sought to change the American political and social system and advocated force as a means of accomplishing their goals. The constitutionality of these laws was soon challenged by those convicted under them, and it wasn't long before some of these cases reached the U.S. Supreme Court.

Probably the most important of these state sedition cases was *Gitlow v. New York* (268 U.S. 652), which reached the Supreme Court in 1925. Benjamin Gitlow, a New York socialist, and three others were convicted of violating a state criminal anarchy law by writing a document called the "Left Wing Manifesto." They were also convicted of distributing a paper called *The Revolutionary Age.*

Gitlow argued that the New York law violated his freedom of expression, as guaranteed under the First Amendment. In so doing, he was asking the high court to reverse an 1833 decision that said the Bill of Rights only applied to the federal government (*Barron v. Baltimore,* 7 Peters 243). Gitlow contended that the Fourteenth Amendment's requirement that

FIG. 10. Supreme Court of the United States, 1924.

Library of Congress, Prints and Photographs Division, [LC-USZ62-91090].

Front, L-R: Justice Willis Van Devanter, Justice Joseph McKenna, Chief Justice William Howard Taft, Justice Oliver Wendell Holmes, Justice James McReynolds.
Back, L-R: Justice Pierce Butler, Justice Louis Dembitz Brandeis, Justice George Sutherland, Justice Edward Sanford.

the states safeguard the "liberty" of their residents meant the civil liberties guaranteed in the Bill of Rights could no longer be violated by the states.

Enacted after the Civil War and intended to safeguard the civil rights of the former slaves, the Fourteenth Amendment applies specifically to the states. Among other things, it has a provision known as the *due process clause,* which says, "...nor shall any state deprive any person of life, liberty or property, without due process of law...." Gitlow argued that "liberty," as the term is used in the Fourteenth Amendment, includes all of the freedoms guaranteed in the First Amendment.

By making this argument, Gitlow won a tremendous long-term victory for freedom of expression, but he lost his own appeal. In an amazingly brief passage, the Supreme Court completely rewrote the rules on constitutional law, acknowledging that the Fourteenth Amendment had indeed made the First Amendment applicable to the states (known as the *incorporation doctrine*). But then the Court said the First Amendment did not protect Gitlow's activities, thus upholding the New York conviction: "A state in the exercise of its police power may punish those who abuse this freedom by utterances inimical to the public welfare, tending to corrupt public morals, incite to crime, or disturb the public peace."

Although Gitlow's conviction was affirmed, the Supreme Court had almost offhandedly rewritten the basic rules governing free expression rights at the state and local level. By requiring the states (and their political subdivisions such as city and county governments) to respect freedom of speech, press and religion, the Supreme Court had vastly expanded the rights of Americans. In 2010 the Supreme Court by a 5-4 vote incorporated the Second Amendment, the right to keep and bear arms (*McDonald v. City of Chicago*, 130 S. Ct. 3020).

Two years after *Gitlow,* the Supreme Court affirmed another state conviction in a case that produced a famous opinion defending freedom of expression. In that case (*Whitney v. California,* 274 U.S. 357), Charlotte Anita Whitney was prosecuted for violating a California criminal syndicalism law, a law that made it a felony to belong to a group that advocated forcible change. Whitney was a member of the Communist Labor Party, but she had argued against its militant policies at a meeting just before her prosecution.

Despite these mitigating circumstances, the Supreme Court affirmed her conviction. For technical reasons, Justice Brandeis concurred in the Court's decision, but his concurring opinion (which Justice Holmes joined) was a powerful appeal for freedom:

> Those who won our independence by revolution were not cowards. They did not fear political change. They did not exalt order at the cost of liberty. To courageous self-reliant men, with confidence in the power of free and fearless reasoning applied through the processes of popular government, no danger flowing from speech can be deemed clear and present, unless the incidence of the evil apprehended is so imminent that it may befall before there is opportunity for full discussion. If there be time to expose through discussion the false-hood and fallacies, to avert the evil by the processes of education, the remedy to be applied is more speech, not enforced silence.

Brandeis said he believed that free speech should be suppressed only in times of emergency and that it was always "open to Americans to challenge a law abridging free speech and assembly by showing that there was no emergency justifying it."

clear and present danger:
a judicial test to determine whether speech should be suppressed; only when speech poses a clear and present danger should it be stopped.

due process:
a constitutional guarantee, contained in the Fifth and Fourteenth Amendments, that the government may not take away anyone's life, liberty or property arbitrarily or unfairly, and that legal proceedings will be fair and include notice to those affected.

incorporation doctrine:
a constitutional doctrine by which many of the rights contained in the first eight amendments of the Bill of Rights are applied to the states using the due process clause of the Fourteenth Amendment; the First, Second, Fourth, and Sixth Amendments, as well as parts of the Fifth and Eighth Amendments, have been incorporated.

The Supreme Court finally reversed a conviction for expressing radical ideas for the first time in another 1927 case, *Fiske v. Kansas* (274 U.S. 380). In that case, a defendant was prosecuted merely for belonging to the Industrial Workers of the World, the "Wobblies"—and the primary evidence against him was the preamble to the Wobblies' constitution. There was no evidence that he had advocated or engaged in any violent or otherwise unlawful acts. The Court said the preamble simply didn't present sufficient evidence of unlawful goals to justify the conviction.

■ POSTWAR SEDITION AND DISSENT

The 1918 Sedition Act, like its 1798 predecessor, was only in force a short time: most of its provisions were repealed in 1921. Major portions of the 1917 Espionage Act were not repealed, but that law was specifically written so that it only applied in wartime. Thus, for nearly two decades after 1921, there was no federal law prohibiting seditious speech. But as World War II approached, those who felt the need to curtail freedom in the interest of national security again gained support in Congress. Finally, a sedition law was attached to the Alien Registration Act of 1940, popularly known as the Smith Act because one of its sponsors was Congressman Howard Smith of Virginia.

Among other things, the new sedition law made it a crime to advocate the violent overthrow of the government or even to belong to a group that advocated overthrowing the government by force. In addition, there were provisions making it a crime to proselytize for groups having such goals. The law did not require proof that the group might actually carry out any of those goals before its members could be prosecuted; mere advocacy was sufficient. Nor did this law apply only during wartime.

The 1940 law was rarely used at first. In fact, compared to other wars, World War II elicited little domestic opposition, perhaps because of the manner in which the United States became involved in that war as well as the widely publicized atrocities of the Nazis. However, during the tense "cold war" era that followed World War II, the Smith Act was used to prosecute numerous members of the American Communist Party.

The Smith Act's constitutionality was first tested before the U.S. Supreme Court in a 1951 case involving 12 alleged Communists, *Dennis v. U.S.* (341 U.S. 494). Eugene Dennis and the others were tried on charges of willfully and knowingly conspiring to overthrow the U.S. government by force. After a controversial nine-month trial, they were convicted and the Supreme Court eventually upheld the convictions.

Chief Justice Fred Vinson's opinion, in which three other justices joined, didn't specifically apply the clear and present danger test to the defendants' activities. Instead, the Court adopted a test formulated by Learned Hand, a famous appellate court judge who heard the case before it reached the Supreme Court. Hand's test is this: "In each case (courts) must ask whether the gravity of the "evil," discounted by its improbability, justifies such invasion of free speech as is necessary to avoid the danger." By using Judge Hand's *modified version of the clear and present danger test*, it was possible for the Supreme Court to sustain the convictions without any evidence that there was a real danger that the Communists could achieve their stated goals. Justice Vinson ruled that the American Communist movement, tiny though it was, constituted a sufficient "evil" to justify the limitations on freedom of speech inherent in the Smith Act. For the moment, it would be unlawful even to belong to an organization that advocated the violent overthrow of the government. Chief Justice Vinson wrote, "Certainly an attempt to overthrow the Government by force, even though doomed from the outset because of inadequate numbers or power of the revolutionists, is sufficient evil for Congress to prevent."

After winning the *Dennis* case, the U.S. Justice Department began a new series of prosecutions under the Smith Act. During the early 1950s at least 121 persons were prosecuted under the act's conspiracy provisions, and others were prosecuted under the provisions outlawing mere membership in organizations advocating violent overthrow of the government.

This may seem to be an alarming violation of the American tradition of free speech, but it was in keeping with the mood of the times. The early 1950s were the heyday of McCarthyism, a time when prominent Americans were accused of pro-Communist sympathies, often with little or no proof. For example, a number of well-known writers and motion picture celebrities were blacklisted in the entertainment industry after undocumented charges were made against them. In Congress, the House Committee on Un-American Activities conducted investigations that its critics felt were little more than witch-hunts designed to harass those with unpopular ideas.

However, the times were changing, and so was the makeup of the Supreme Court. Senator Joseph McCarthy of Wisconsin, the man whose name is synonymous with the red scare, was censured by his Congressional colleagues, and public disapproval of his tactics increased notably by the time of his death in 1957. Meanwhile, the Court gained several new members, most notably Chief Justice Earl Warren, who led the Court into an unprecedented period of judicial liberalism. Warren was appointed in 1953 after the death of Chief Justice Vinson.

In 1957 the Supreme Court responded to these changes by modifying the *Dennis* rule in another case involving the prosecution of alleged Communists under the Smith Act, *Yates v. U.S.* (354 U.S. 298). In this case, the Supreme Court reversed convictions or ordered new trials for 14 people charged with Communist activities. In so ruling, the Court focused on the distinction between teaching the desirability of violently overthrowing the government as an abstract theory and actually advocating violent action. The Court said the convictions had to be invalidated because the jury instructions did not require a finding that there was any tendency of the advocacy to produce forcible action.

The Supreme Court said the Smith Act could only be used against "the advocacy and teaching of concrete action for the forcible overthrow of the Government, and not of principles divorced from action." The justices did not return to the clear and present danger test as such, and the Court insisted it was not abandoning the *Dennis* rule. But the new requirement of proof that the defendant was calling for action rather than teaching an abstract doctrine made it very difficult to convict anyone under the Smith Act. As a result, this controversial law was almost never used against political dissidents after that time.

Changing Times: the 1960s

Perhaps it was fortuitous timing that the Smith Act was rarely used against radicals after 1957, because in the 1960s there was a period of political dissent unprecedented in twentieth-century America. Thousands—and eventually millions—of Americans came to disagree with their government's handling of the Vietnam War, and countless numbers of them vociferously demanded changes in the political system that led to this unpopular war. Had that happened at a time when the government was prepared to vigorously enforce the Smith Act (and when the courts were willing to brush aside the First Amendment and let it happen) far more people than were jailed under the World War I Sedition Act might have been imprisoned for opposing the government during the Vietnam War.

The First Amendment protection for those accused of seditious speech was again expanded in a controversial 1969 Supreme Court decision involving a Ku Klux Klansman. In that case, *Brandenburg v. Ohio* (395 U.S. 444), a man convicted of violating an Ohio criminal syndicalism law contended that his conduct was protected under the First Amendment. Brandenburg spoke at a Klan rally that was filmed. Part of the film was later televised nationally. Much of what was said was incomprehensible, but the meaning of other remarks was quite clear. Brandenburg urged sending "niggers" back to Africa and Jews to Israel, and also talked of the need for "revengeance."

Was this a call for action that could be prosecuted under the *Yates* rule, or was it merely the teaching of abstract doctrine? The Supreme Court went beyond the constitutional protection it had given speech in the *Yates* decision. In *Brandenburg,* the court said the First Amendment even protects speech that is a call for action, as long as the speech is not likely to produce *imminent lawless action.* Thus, the point at which the First Amendment ceases to protect seditious speech is not when there is a call for action, but when that call for action is persuasive and effective enough that it is likely to produce imminent results. The Court said:

> ...(T)he constitutional guarantees of free speech do not permit (state regulation) ...except where the speech is directed to inciting or producing imminent lawless action, and is likely to incite or produce such action.

Brandenburg's criminal conviction was reversed, and the Supreme Court invalidated the Ohio criminal syndicalism law itself. In so doing, the Court reversed the 1927 *Whitney v. California* decision, in which a state law virtually identical to Ohio's had been upheld. This provides an interesting illustration of the way a dissenting or concurring opinion of one generation can inspire a majority opinion in another. Justice Brandeis' concurring opinion in *Whitney* argued for an imminent danger requirement: Brandeis said the First Amendment should not permit sanctions for political speech unless it threatens to provoke imminent lawless action. More than 40 years later, the Supreme Court adopted that view in the Brandenburg decision, repudiating the majority opinion in *Whitney.*

Even now—many years after the *Brandenburg* decision—millions of Americans feel passionately that the Supreme Court was wrong: the Ku Klux Klan and other racist organizations do not deserve First Amendment protection, they believe. During the 1980s and 1990s, there was national controversy about "hate speech." Many states passed laws forbidding that kind of speech, and the Supreme Court ultimately stepped into the debate by ruling on the issue twice, in 1992 and 1993 (see Chapter Three).

■ INTERPRETING THE CONSTITUTION

In tracing the development of First Amendment freedoms, we have noted several philosophies and "tests" that have been proposed to aid in interpreting what the First Amendment means. Because interpreting the Constitution is so central to the study of media law, we will summarize some basic principles of constitutional interpretation.

Almost every dispute about constitutional rights involves some kind of a *balancing* test. The courts must weigh conflicting rights and decide which is the most important. That means sometimes one constitutional principle must give way to another: there are few absolutes in constitutional law. That fact, of course, is unfortunate for the media. Were the First Amendment an absolute, many of the legal problems the media face would not exist. Given an absolute First Amendment, there would be no such thing as sedition or prior restraint, and it is doubtful the media could even be held accountable for libel, invasions of privacy, or copyright infringements. Certainly there would be no obscenity law and no limits on media coverage of the criminal justice system. But if that were the case, many of society's other interests would be forced to yield to freedom of speech and freedom of the press.

Fortunately or unfortunately, depending on your point of view, the *absolutist theory* of the First Amendment has never been the majority view on the U.S. Supreme Court. Some of the founding fathers, such as James Madison, may have considered the First Amendment something of an absolute safeguard for free speech, and two well-known Supreme Court justices who served during the 1950s and 1960s (Hugo Black and William O. Douglas) took an almost absolutist position. However, the majority view has always been that the First Amendment must be weighed in the balances against other rights and social needs. Thus, the courts' task over the years has been to develop guidelines to assist in this balancing process.

One of the best-known of these guidelines for balancing the First Amendment against other interests has been the clear and present danger test. As already noted, it was first cited by Justice Oliver Wendell Holmes in the 1919 *Schenck* decision. In the years since, it has sometimes been applied to political speech cases, although in recent years the Supreme Court has not mentioned it in the leading decisions on free speech. As Chapter Eight explains, the Court has also applied the clear and present danger test in resolving conflicts between the media and the courts, weighing the First Amendment guarantee of a free press against judges' rights to exercise their contempt of court powers.

Some constitutional scholars argue for a *preferred position test* as an alternative to balancing the First Amendment against other rights and social interests. In their view, the First Amendment should occupy a preeminent place in constitutional law and should rarely give way to other interests. Some believe that during the era when Earl Warren was chief justice, the Supreme Court leaned toward that view of the First Amendment. Indeed, many of the decisions most favorable to the media were handed down by the Warren Court.

In a more general way, the Supreme Court always uses a kind of preferred position test in weighing constitutionally protected interests against other values. In *U.S. v. C.I.O.* (335 U.S. 106), a 1948 case, Justice Wiley Rutledge articulated this view. The normal rule of judicial interpretation requires the courts to adopt a presumption in *favor* of the validity of legislative acts. However, he said, when a legislative act restricts First Amendment rights, the presumption must be reversed so that there is a presumption against the validity of the law rather than in favor of its validity. Thus, he advocated a "reverse presumption of constitutionality" when a statutory law is challenged on constitutional grounds.

imminent lawless action:
the current incarnation of the clear and present danger test; speech can be suppressed if it causes or results in immediate violence or other lawlessness.

absolutist theory:
a reading of the First Amendment which takes literally the phrase "Congress shall make no law," suggesting an absolute protection for speech.

preferred position theory:
a theory of the First Amendment which favors the rights of free speech and press over other rights when balanced against those rights.

rational relationship:
a theory that gives high deference to government regulation; if government provides a legitimate objective and the regulation is reasonably related to that objective, the regulation will stand.

compelling state interest:
a right that is fundamental to society, like voting or national security, receives the highest level of judicial review.

The concept that the rights protected by the Bill of Rights occupy a preferred position compared to other interests has been mentioned in a number of other Supreme Court decisions. However, on a practical level that bias in favor of constitutional rights does not necessarily translate into tangible results. What the Court still does is balance the competing interests—albeit with the scales tipped slightly toward constitutional rights.

The Supreme Court has also developed a series of more specific guidelines to use in evaluating claims that a statutory law or government action violates a constitutional right. When a statute (or a state's application of the common law) is challenged, the Court normally looks for nothing more than a *rational relationship* between the law and a legitimate government goal. When a state law is challenged, for instance, the state may try to defend it by showing that the law bears a rational relationship to its police power or its duty to promote the health and welfare of its citizens.

However, when the claim is that the statute violates a fundamental right protected by the Constitution, the state must show a *compelling state interest* to justify the statute. The state must, in effect, convince the court that its objective in enacting this statute is of such overriding importance that a fundamental right (such as freedom of expression) must give way.

A good example of this is described in Chapter Thirteen, where the Court's landmark decisions on commercial speech are discussed. Although advertising generally enjoys less First Amendment protection than most other forms of speech, in some cases the Court has required a state to show a *compelling* state interest to justify restrictions even on some types of advertising (see *Bigelow v. Virginia,* 421 U.S. 809, 1975). More often, though, governments must show only a *substantial government interest* rather than a compelling one to justify restrictions on advertising (see *Central Hudson Gas and Electric v. Public Service Commission of New York,* 447 U.S. 557). These tests are admittedly subjective, and not even all justices agree about when each should apply. Justice Clarence Thomas, for example, has often claimed that advertising should have no less First Amendment protection than other forms of speech.

Another way the courts, and particularly the Supreme Court, evaluate state and federal statutes is to decide whether they are *vague* or *overly broad.* If a law that limits constitutionally protected rights is so broad that it inhibits freedom more than is necessary to achieve a legitimate government purpose, or if it is so vague that it is difficult to know exactly what speech or conduct is prohibited, it may be invalidated for overbreadth or vagueness.

If a court is going to invalidate a statutory law, it has two options: (1) to find that the law is unconstitutional and thus void under all circumstances; or (2) to find that it is unconstitutional only as it has been applied to the person challenging the law. Moreover, given an ambiguous law, the courts have an obligation to resolve the ambiguity in such a way as to avoid a constitutional conflict if possible.

The U.S. Supreme Court has the final say in construing the language in federal statutes, but the *state* courts have the final say in interpreting *state* laws. The Court can only decide whether a state law is unconstitutional as interpreted by the state courts; it cannot reinterpret a state statute. This means the U.S. Supreme Court sometimes has to send a case back to a state court to find out what a state law means. Once the state court spells out the meaning, the nation's highest court can then decide whether the law—as interpreted by the state court—violates the U.S. Constitution. If it does, it is invalid, of course. But if the state court can interpret the law in a way to avoid a conflict with the U.S. Constitution, the law is valid.

Obviously, determining whether a given statute or government action violates the Constitution is a difficult and subjective job. The Supreme Court has a variety of guidelines that it may choose to follow (or choose to ignore) in any given situation.

Critics of the process suspect that whatever test is or isn't applied in a particular case, the ultimate outcome of the case depends more on the values and priorities of the nine justices than on how the facts measure up against one or another set of guidelines. In short, whatever other test may be applied, cases are decided on the basis of a rather subjective balancing process in which various competing values, interests and social objectives are weighed.

In his autobiography, former Justice William O. Douglas described a revealing conversation he had with then-Chief Justice Charles Evans Hughes soon after being appointed to the Court:

> Hughes made a statement to me which at the time was shattering but which over the years turned out to be true: "Justice Douglas, you must remember one thing. At the Constitutional level where we work, 90 percent of any decision is emotional. The rational part of us supplies the reasons for supporting our predilections."

In the end, most Supreme Court-watchers would probably agree. So much for theories that purport to reconcile the Court's seemingly inconsistent rulings on the meaning of the First Amendment...

Against this backdrop of historical and legal developments, we can argue that the more things change, the more they stay the same. That is, many of the issues facing American society today reflect similar concerns for the law of free speech and press as have been faced throughout the decades. Yet technological developments and new forms of war have put a new face on these issues.

■ THE FUTURE OF FREEDOM IN A TERRORIST ERA

In this chapter, we have traced nearly 400 years of struggles for freedom of expression. Of the total history of humanity, that is but a tiny portion. Where, then, is freedom going in the next 400 years? Perhaps more to the point, what will be the future of freedom in the near future—an era that may be dominated by the threat of terrorism in many parts of the world?

Obviously, no one can answer these questions. Freedom in America may depend on who runs the country—and the world. It also depends on who is appointed to the Supreme Court, the federal appellate courts and the appellate courts of the 50 states. And it depends on who is elected to national, state and local offices. It is those people who shape the law.

In a larger sense, the future of freedom is always decided by the changing mood of the times. As several later chapters explain, there has been a growing sentiment in America today in favor of more restrictions on free expression. Polls often show that large numbers of people think the First Amendment should not protect the work of artists, musicians and others whose choice of language or subject matter may be offensive. Many people think the broadcast media, including cable and satellite television, should be subject to tougher government restrictions to curb the use of offensive language and images. Some also believe the Internet should be more regulated to limit the kind of words and images that are allowed. How can such restrictions on free expression be reconciled with the First Amendment?

In much of the world the Internet has revolutionized the idea of free expression. Even in China, which by some estimates has at least 30,000 government workers policing the Internet for unacceptable content in a program that critics have called the "great firewall," the 'Net has brought new freedom. By 2008, an estimated 250 million Chinese were online, making the regulation of content a difficult challenge. Some American companies have drawn criticism for cooperating with the Chinese government by filtering out content of which the government disapproves. When Microsoft launched a new portal in China called MSN Spaces, some objected to the company's insertion of filters that cause a yellow warning to appear on the screen when someone uses words like "democracy," "capitalism," "liberty" or "human rights." Even "June 4th," a reference to the 1989 Tiananmen Square killings in Beijing, is filtered out. Microsoft's supporters point out that software companies have to comply with local laws in many countries. Other U.S. companies including Google and Yahoo.com have also modified their content to satisfy the Chinese government.

There is a no more dramatic illustration of the power of unfettered information than was demonstrated in the 2011 resignation of Egyptian president Hosni Mubarak. Mubarak, widely known to suppress dissent and political opponents, stepped down amid anti-government protests and civil unrest that was broadcast worldwide on Twitter and Facebook. Despite the government's shutdown of Internet access throughout the country for a time, images and statements posted online were reposted by sympathetic people around the world.

Was this the first "Twitter revolution," and can we expect more? Opinions vary. While it is clear that social media helped the revolt to gather momentum, some have suggested that once the Internet was shut down, Egyptians engaged in the kind of protest that has been going on for centuries: they went out on the streets with thousands of others. Yet it seems clear that social media has the power to create international buzz for social movements.

In the U.S., the threat of terrorism and the government's response to it has given rise to new developments in law and the spread of information in a free society—perhaps best demonstrated by a website called WikiLeaks.

The USA PATRIOT Act

In America, the threat of terrorism prompted new restrictions on civil liberties in the aftermath of the events of Sept. 11, 2001. The USA PATRIOT Act, passed shortly after the attacks, created a new crime of domestic terrorism, broadened the federal government's power to monitor telephone and Internet communications and authorized the attorney general to detain any foreigner believed to threaten national security, among other things. The law's name is an acronym for "Uniting and Strengthening America by Providing Appropriate Tools Required to Intercept and Obstruct Terrorism."

Despite growing concerns about the USA PATRIOT Act's implications for the civil liberties of Americans, Congress renewed the law in 2006. The new version made permanent many provisions of the act that had originally been temporary measures with a four-year sunset clause. The two most controversial provisions were renewed with some modifications and only for another four years. One is the "library provision" that allows government investigators to obtain records from libraries and businesses that would reveal an individual's financial or medical information or even private reading habits. A second controversial provision extends the authorization for "national security letters"—subpoenas issued by a government agency such as the FBI instead of a court.

In 2010, three controversial elements of the USA PATRIOT Act that were set to expire were extended by President Barack Obama: a "lone wolf" provision that allows the government to track a non-United States person who has no discernable affiliation to a foreign power; a "business records provision" that allows the government to compel third parties, such as financial services and travel and telephone companies, to turn over business records of a terrorism suspect without that suspect's knowledge; and a "roving wiretaps" provision which allows the government to monitor phone lines or Internet accounts of terrorism suspects, regardless of whether non-suspects regularly use those lines or accounts. In 2011, President Obama signed another extension of these provisions that will expire in 2015. (He created a bit of controversy by signing the law while in France with an "autopen," a machine that automatically signs a signature—the first president to sign a bill into law this way.)

The renewal of the USA PATRIOT Act does not resolve the questions raised by the *New York Times* in reporting that President George W. Bush had authorized the National Security Agency to conduct secret domestic surveillance without court authorization. A federal criminal investigation was launched to determine how word of that secret program was leaked to the news media, creating the potential for journalists to be subpoenaed to identify their sources. The investigation could also lead to the criminal prosecution of journalists for reporting this story, despite its newsworthiness. A similar controversy arose when *USA TODAY* reported that several major telephone companies had given the federal government telephone records for millions of Americans.

A federal judge ruled in 2004 that the USA PATRIOT Act violated fundamental constitutional safeguards by allowing federal agencies to gather information about U.S. citizens secretly under

vagueness:
unclear or subject to several interpretations by reasonable individuals; laws that are vague are often overturned on that basis.

overbreadth:
regulating too much protected speech in regulating unprotected speech; laws must be written so as not to proscribe protected speech.

national security letters without court approval. The same judge ruled in 2007 that the new version of the act still gives federal investigators unconstitutionally broad powers to spy on individuals. In 2008, the federal government appealed, contending that the USA PATRI-OT Act's sweeping authorization of domestic surveillance is needed to fight terrorism and does not violate the Constitution. In that case, *Doe v. Mukasey*, 549 F.3d 861, a three-judge panel of the Second Circuit upheld the lower court's decision that the "gag order" provisions imposed on recipients of National Security Letters (NSLs), forbidding them to talk to anyone about those letters. A NSL is a subpoena for information such as phone records and Internet activity used by the Federal Bureau of Investigation and other agencies. The burden of proof was also shifted in this case from the recipient of the letter to the government to initiate judicial review of the gag orders.

In 2010 the Supreme Court took up the question of whether some attempts to monitor terrorism activity conflict with the First Amendment. In *Holder v. Humanitarian Law Project* (130 S. Ct. 2705), the Court upheld the constitutionality of 18 U.S.C. §2339B, a "material support" statute that criminalizes the provision of material support or resources to any foreign terrorist organization designated by the Secretary of State, including "training," "expert advice and assistance," "service" and "personnel," even to support peaceful actions. Under the most stringent level of review applied to laws that regulate speech based on its content (*strict scrutiny*, discussed in Chapter Three), the government had met its burden.

Chief Justice John Roberts, writing for a 6-3 majority, limited the decision's breadth, noting that other applications of the statute might not be constitutional: "In particular, we in no way suggest that a regulation of independent speech would pass constitutional muster, even if the Government were to show that such speech benefits foreign terrorist organizations." But Justice Stephen Breyer, writing in dissent for himself and Justices Sonia Sotomayor and Ruth Bader Ginsburg, felt otherwise: "I believe the Court has failed to examine the Government's justifications with sufficient care. It has failed to insist upon specific evidence, rather than general assertion. It has failed to require tailoring of means to fit compelling ends. And ultimately it deprives the individuals before us of the protection that the First Amendment demands."

The Second Circuit ruled that §2339B was not unconstitutionally vague in 2011 in *U.S. v. Farhane* (634 F.3d 127). American citizen Rafiq Sabir, a medical doctor, had sworn allegiance to al-Qaeda and promised to treat its wounded members; he was convicted and sentenced to 25 years. The court rejected Sabir's claims, saying that the law clearly defined the various elements of material support and that Sabir's claim of a right to practice medicine was not more important than Congress' right to pass laws in the nation's defense.

The Fifth Circuit in 2011 also upheld the convictions of five individuals who served as officers of the Holy Land Foundation for Relief and Development under §2339B (*U.S. v. El-Mezain*, 664 F.3d 467). The foundation, the government alleged, was a front to funnel funds and assistance to Hamas, considered a foreign terrorist organization. The trials, the court concluded, were flawed in some ways but the five individuals were "fairly convicted."

WikiLeaks

Perhaps no media story of 2010 and 2011 garnered quite as much publicity, shock, and controversy as the release by WikiLeaks of thousands of confidential pages of sensitive or embarrassing government information. Touting itself on its website (wikileaks.org) as a publisher of "material of ethical, political and historical significance while keeping the

FIG. 11. WikiLeaks editor-in-chief Julian Assange, 2010.

Espen Moe, "IMG_4739," March 20, 2010 via Flickr, Creative Commons attribution license.

identity of our sources anonymous," WikiLeaks and its colorful (and controversial) spokesperson and editor-in-chief, Julian Assange, not only made government officials nervous but resulted in calls for new legislation to prevent such unauthorized releases of information.

On at least three occasions in 2010, WikiLeaks released classified information: a group of over 76,000 documents entitled "Afghan War Diary" about the war in Afghanistan; over 40,000 documents called "Iraq War Logs;" and most dramatically, over 250,000 United States embassy cables, some of which proved humiliating to U.S. diplomats (for example, one cable described current Russian president Dmitry Medvedev as playing Robin to previous president and prime minister Vladimir Putin's Batman).

International reactions to the leaks were varied, with some foreign officials laughing it off to others expressing concern about the information contained in the documents and about the matter of the leak in general. The White House issued a strong statement of condemnation: "The United States strongly condemns the disclosure of classified information by individuals and organizations which could put the lives of Americans and our partners at risk, and threaten our national security."

In the wake of the release of the embassy cables, both houses of Congress introduced versions of a bill named the SHIELD Act ("Securing Human Intelligence and Enforcing Lawful Dissemination Act"). The act would amend the Espionage Act of 1917 to make it a crime for any person to knowingly and willfully disseminate "in any manner prejudicial to the safety or interest of the United States" any classified information about "the human intelligence activities of the United States." The bill did not become law, but President Obama in 2011 issued Executive Order 13587, titled "Structural Reforms to Improve the Security of Classified Networks and the Responsible Sharing and Safeguarding of Classified Information" to avoid classified information leaks. The order stressed the dual goals of "responsible sharing and safeguarding of classified information on computer networks that shall be consistent with appropriate protections for privacy and civil liberties." WikiLeaks released over 700 files related to prisoner interrogations at Guantánamo Bay in April 2011. In the ongoing investigation of WikiLeaks, the Department of Justice subpoenaed Twitter account information of several key individuals. Two judges have granted access, rejecting both First and Fourth Amendment arguments to the contrary (*In re Application of the United States of America for an Order Pursuant to 18 U.S.C. §2703(d)*, 2011 WL 5508991).

Censorship in the 21st Century

In much of the world it is still commonplace for governments to censor the media directly. It was not long ago that those who advocated basic civil liberties were brutalized in many other countries that now permit free expression and free elections. The story of how earlier generations won the freedoms we enjoy today is an important part of this summary of mass communications law. Within the United States, however, the overriding factor in determining the status of freedom in the near future is likely to be the progress of the war against terrorism. Already, legal controversies have raged over issues such as the propriety of trying some of those accused of terrorist acts in military as opposed to civilian courts, as President George W. Bush decreed by executive order. Military courts lack some of the safeguards guaranteed by the U.S. Constitution in civilian courts.

Whenever a society feels threatened by subversive forces within or powerful enemies abroad, freedom suffers. Over the past 200 years, constitutional freedoms have been curtailed repeatedly in wartime. Former Chief Justice William Rehnquist wrote a book in 1998, several years before Sept. 11, summarizing some of that history. In *All the Laws but One: Civil Liberties in Wartime*, Rehnquist discussed Supreme Court decisions concerning the constitutionality of military trials for those accused of subversive activities. His conclusion was that the Supreme Court has often interpreted the law differently in wartime than in peacetime, but with each successive war, Americans became *more* protective of civil liberties and less willing to abandon constitutional rights in the name of national security.

Is that still true in this era of terrorism? Although the limits on First Amendment freedoms within the United States since Sept. 11 have been minimal compared to those imposed during World War I, for example, there have been growing concerns both in the U.S. and abroad about America's respect for human rights overseas. The United States was once something of a beacon to the world in advocating broader human rights. When the United Nations General Assembly approved the Universal Declaration of Human Rights in 1948, the United States was its most prominent advocate. The U.S. was a leading advocate of the 1975 Helsinki Accords, in which 35 mostly European countries pledged to respect basic human rights. The U.S. has also been a leading advocate of human rights within the Inter-American Commission on Human Rights, among other international bodies.

But in the 2000s, many human rights advocates in America and abroad expressed concerns about the way the U.S. government was pursuing the war on terrorism. Perhaps the most controversial practice was "extraterritorial rendition" in which U.S. agents kidnapped suspected terrorists and their supporters in foreign countries and took them to still other countries for questioning that involved torture, using methods not legal within the U.S. Many Americans and others asked whether these acts were necessary and appropriate ways to fight terrorism. The abuse and torture of Iraqi detainees by American military personnel in the Abu Ghraib prison is another uncomfortable element of this new war on terror.

Looking beyond the effect of terrorist threats on civil liberties, there are other issues that should not be ignored. The behavior of the media themselves may help determine how much freedom we have. Journalistic sensationalism, inaccuracy and arrogance—as well as monopolistic media business practices—invite punitive responses by governments. Perhaps one can point at WikiLeaks as well, as its bold releases of information are decried by some as espionage. If the media are to preserve their freedom, they must stand firm against abuses by governments at all levels, but they must also be responsible in exercising that freedom.

3   *Modern Prior Restraints*

Censorship. That word has a lot of emotional impact today, just as it has throughout American history. But its meaning has shifted over the years. Today, censorship in a legal sense usually means *prior restraint* of communications by an agency of government, not *subsequent punishment* for disseminating an unlawful form of communication. As Chapter Two explains, the First Amendment is not absolute: the courts have allowed a variety of limitations on freedom of expression. But most of those limitations would be classified as subsequent punishments, not prior restraints. For example, lawsuits that charge someone with libel or invasion of privacy involve the threat of subsequent punishments, not prior restraints. The media are free to disseminate defamatory communications or communications that invade someone's privacy, but they must be prepared to face the legal consequences—afterward.

However, there are some occasions when prior restraints are permitted—times when an agency of government actually engages in some form of prior censorship. And prior restraints are usually considered a far greater threat to freedom than subsequent punishments. If the media are free to publish controversial or unpopular facts and opinions without government interference beyond the threat of punishment afterward, at least a few courageous publishers and broadcasters (or bloggers) will take the risk and make the questionable material public. If the material turns out to be of social importance, the publisher may still be punished, but at least the people will have the information and a public dialogue can begin. However, if government authorities can prevent the publication from ever occurring, the public may never know about important facts or ideas, and the democratic process may be thwarted. A democratic society cannot long survive if prior censorship by government is commonplace.

Only a few forms of prior restraint are permitted in America today; many communications that are highly offensive to someone (or perhaps to almost everyone) are protected by the First Amendment and may not be censored. Nevertheless, there are times when prior censorship does occur, or is attempted, at least. The result may be a major controversy—and perhaps a landmark court decision. For example, sometimes government officials attempt to censor the news media to prevent the dissemination of information that they see as a threat to national security. And sometimes unpopular groups are denied the right to demonstrate or distribute literature in public places such as city sidewalks or parks, or to place their monuments in those parks.

Another form of prior restraint involves laws that have been enacted to forbid "hate speech" that expresses hostility on the basis of ethnicity, religion, gender or sexual orientation; as we will see, funerals have become a hot spot for picketing activity, with the Supreme Court agreeing to hear a funeral picketing case. Also, discriminatory taxation of the media can be a form of government censorship. And there are other examples of prior restraints: government censorship of controversial films, bureaucratic attempts to regulate stock market newsletters, issues of animal cruelty and rules that forbid the media to publish confidential information such as the names of juvenile offenders or rape victims. In all of these diverse situations, there is one common element: a government agency or official is attempting to censor some kind of communication that is considered unacceptable—and that action raises First Amendment questions. In this chapter, we look at these and a few other forms of prior restraint.

prior restraint:
government stopping speech before it has been published; also often called *censorship*.

vacate:
to set aside or void.

content-neutral regulation:
a regulation that regulates all speech the same, regardless of its content; receives a lower level of judicial scrutiny, called "ordinary scrutiny" or "relaxed scrutiny."

content-based regulation:
a regulation that regulates speech based on its content; receives a high level of judicial scrutiny, called "strict scrutiny."

time, place and manner regulation:
a content-neutral regulation that regulates the time, place and/or manner of speech acts; for example, noise regulations applied to all concerts equally, or parade permits that cost the same.

public forum:
a place like a park or sidewalk in which free speech activities traditionally take place.

■ NEAR V. MINNESOTA

A good place to begin any discussion of prior restraints is a landmark Supreme Court decision more than 85 years ago—a case that resolved some of the most basic issues in this field of law. In the 1931 case of *Near v. Minnesota ex rel. Olson* (283 U.S. 697), the U.S. Supreme Court made it clear that prior restraints are generally improper in America. The case resulted from a Minnesota state law that allowed government officials to treat a "malicious, scandalous and defamatory newspaper" as a public nuisance and forbid its publication. Under this law, a county attorney brought suit to shut down *The Saturday Press*, a small weekly newspaper produced by Howard Guilford and J. M. Near.

Guilford and Near had published several articles critical of certain public officials over a period of two months. In their attacks, they charged that a gangster controlled gambling, bootlegging and racketeering in Minneapolis. They claimed law enforcement agencies did little to stop this corruption. In particular, they accused the police chief of gross neglect of duty, illicit relations with gangsters and participation in corruption.

A trial court ruled the paper a public nuisance under the Minnesota law and banned its further publication. The Minnesota Supreme Court affirmed the ruling, and Near appealed to the U.S. Supreme Court. In a decision that made constitutional history, the Court overturned the lower courts and allowed Near to continue publishing. In a narrow 5-4 decision, the high court traced the history of prior restraints and concluded that a newspaper may not be censored before publication except under very exceptional circumstances. Chief Justice Charles Evans Hughes wrote:

> The fact that for approximately one hundred and fifty years there has been almost an entire absence of attempts to impose previous restraints upon publications relating to the malfeasance of public officers is significant of the deep-seated conviction that such restraints would violate constitutional rights. The general principle that the constitutional guaranty of the liberty of the press gives immunity from previous restraints has been approved in many decisions under the provisions of state constitutions.

The Court cited James Madison's interpretation of the First Amendment as well as the views of William Blackstone, a highly respected British jurist of the eighteenth century. Blackstone argued against prior restraints but in favor of punishments afterward for those whose publications turn out to be unlawful.

The Supreme Court also pointed to *Schenck v. U.S.* (discussed in Chapter Two) as an example of an exceptional circumstance in which prior restraint might be proper. Chief Justice Hughes said that, in addition to prior censorship in the interest of national security, prior restraints might be proper to control obscenity and incitements to acts of violence. The Court said, "The constitutional guaranty of free speech does not protect a man from an injunction against uttering words that may have all the effect of force."

In the decades since the landmark *Near v. Minnesota* decision, the closeness of the Supreme Court's vote against prior restraints has often been overlooked. The dissenters in *Near,* who needed just one more Supreme Court justice on their side to prevail, would have allowed prior restraints under many more circumstances. In fact, their reading of history led them to believe that the only form of prior restraint the First Amendment was actually intended to prohibit was licensing of the press by the executive branch of government.

Despite the decision's closeness, the *Near* case established a pattern that the Supreme Court has followed ever since. The Court has often invalidated prior restraints on the media, declaring that censorship would be possible under the right conditions but usually failing to find those conditions. But this doesn't mean there are no attempts at prior restraint; as recently as 2010 a judge enjoined a legal newspaper from publishing information obtained from court records in a story about POM Wonderful; this case is discussed in Chapter Seven.

■ NATIONAL SECURITY AND THE "PENTAGON PAPERS"

One of the most controversial forms of prior restraint has involved government efforts to censor the news media to prevent potential breaches of national security. In 1971 the Supreme Court decided a very significant case involving censorship in the name of national security, a case that pitted then-President Richard Nixon against two leading newspapers, the *New York Times* and the *Washington Post.* The case came to be known as the "Pentagon Papers" case, although its official name is *New York Times v. U.S.* (403 U.S. 713). For the first time in U.S. history, the federal government sought to censor major newspapers to prevent them from publishing secret documents that would allegedly endanger national security.

A secret Defense Department study of American policy during the Vietnam war was surreptitiously photocopied and portions of it given to several newspapers. It revealed questionable decisions by four presidents (Truman, Eisenhower, Kennedy and Johnson) that led the country into the war. Although the "Pentagon Papers" only covered the period through 1968, and thus did not cover Nixon's presidency (Nixon took office in 1969), the *Times'* and *Post's* editors knew Nixon would be outraged if these secret documents were published. Nonetheless, after consulting with First Amendment lawyers, the *Times* and *Post* went ahead.

When the first installment of a planned series based on the "Pentagon Papers" appeared in each newspaper, the Nixon administration demanded that the *Times* and *Post* halt all further stories on the subject. When they refused, the Justice Department secured a temporary order from a federal district judge forbidding the *Times* to publish any more articles on the "Pentagon Papers." The judge then changed his mind and *vacated* (set aside) the order, but a federal appellate court reinstated it. The case was immediately appealed to the U.S. Supreme Court. Meanwhile, another federal appellate court refused to stop the *Post* from publishing more stories about the "Pentagon Papers."

In view of the flagrant censorship inherent in the order against the *Times,* the Supreme Court decided the case only two weeks after the controversy arose, during what might otherwise have been its summer recess. The Nixon administration argued that publication of the "Pentagon Papers" would endanger national security and damage U.S. foreign relations.

The newspapers replied that this was a clear-cut First Amendment issue involving information of great importance to the American people. Further, the newspapers contended that the entire classification system under which these documents were declared secret should be revised. The system existed only by presidential order; it was not established by an act of Congress. And at least one Pentagon official had conceded in Congressional testimony that only a few of the millions of classified documents actually dealt with *bona fide* military secrets or other material affecting national security.

The Supreme Court voted 6-3 to set aside the prior restraint and allow the publication of articles based on the "Pentagon Papers." Journalists proclaimed the victory as if it were the outcome of the Super Bowl. *Newsweek*, for instance, put "Victory for the Press" in bold yellow type on its cover. But unfortunately, it wasn't that clear cut. In a brief opinion, the Court had simply said the government had failed to prove that the articles would endanger national security sufficiently to justify prior restraint of the nation's press. In the majority were Justices Black, Brennan, Douglas, Marshall, Stewart and White. The minority consisted of Justices Harlan and Blackmun and Chief Justice Burger.

In addition to the brief opinion by the Court, the nine justices wrote their own separate opinions explaining their views. When legal scholars began analyzing those opinions, they realized the decision was no decisive victory for the press.

Only two of the justices (Black and Douglas) took the absolutist position that prior restraints such as the government sought would never be constitutionally permissible. Justice Marshall said the courts should not do by injunction what Congress had refused to do by statute (i.e., authorize prior censorship). Justice Brennan said the government simply hadn't satisfied the very heavy burden of proof necessary to justify prior censorship in this case.

However, the other five made it clear they either favored censorship in this case or would at least condone criminal sanctions against the nation's leading newspapers after publication of the documents. At least two justices (Harlan and Blackmun) favored prior restraint in this case, while Chief Justice Burger voted to forbid publication at least until the lower courts had more time to consider the matter, although he didn't really address the substantive issue of prior restraint. Justice White, in an opinion joined by Justice Stewart, said the government had not justified prior censorship but also suggested (as did Burger) that the editors could face criminal prosecution after publication for revealing the secret documents.

Thus, the "Pentagon Papers" case was not a clear-cut victory for freedom of expression, but at least the nation's press was allowed to publish stories based on the documents. No journalist was ever prosecuted in connection with the "Pentagon Papers," although the government unsuccessfully prosecuted Dr. Daniel Ellsberg, the social scientist who copied the documents in the first place. In June 2011, the federal government finally released the entire 7,000-page report, 40 years after the *Times* published its stories.

The question of prior restraint in the interest of national security also arose in a controversial 1979 case, *U.S. v. The Progressive* (467 F. Supp. 990). This case was never given full consideration even by a court of appeals, let alone by the Supreme Court, so it has limited value as a legal precedent. Nevertheless, it did dramatize the conflict between freedom of the press and the need for national security.

The Progressive, a liberal magazine, was planning to publish an article entitled "The H-bomb Secret: How We Got It, Why We're Telling It." The author, Howard Morland, had assembled an apparently accurate description of a hydrogen bomb through library research. The magazine sent the article to the federal government prior to publication, requesting that its technical accuracy be verified. The U.S. Department of Energy responded by declaring that publication of the article would violate the secrecy provisions of the 1954 Atomic Energy Act. The U.S. Justice Department sought a court order prohibiting publication.

Federal Judge Robert Warren issued an order forbidding the magazine to publish the article. He said the article could "accelerate the membership of a candidate nation in the thermonuclear club." He distinguished this case from the "Pentagon Papers" case in that he said the H-bomb article posed a current threat to national security. Also, he ruled, a specific statute prohibited the article's publication, whereas there was no statutory authorization to censor the "Pentagon Papers."

Ultimately, however, Judge Warren offered a pragmatic rationale for censorship: "Faced with a stark choice between upholding the right to continued life and the right to freedom of the press, most jurists would have no difficulty in opting for the chance to continue to breathe and function as they work to achieve perfect freedom of expression."

Doubting that the issue was quite that black and white, *The Progressive* appealed Warren's ruling. However, before a federal appellate court could decide the case, articles describing an H-bomb in similar detail appeared in other publications, rendering the case *moot* (beyond the law's reach). Once the information was published elsewhere, the government dropped its attempt to censor the magazine article.

Therefore, the *Progressive* case left many important issues unresolved. One of the most troubling is that the information for the article was gleaned from non-classified sources, yet when it was put into an article questioning the classification system, the U.S. government tried to censor it. Also, Judge Warren's abandonment of the First Amendment invited appellate review. In reviewing Warren's order, a higher court might have clarified the extent to which the national security classification system overrides the First Amendment.

Censoring Present and Former Government Employees

Should government employees have the same First Amendment rights as other citizens? What about employees of agencies such as the Central Intelligence Agency (CIA), who have access to government secrets and are required to sign agreements that they will not disclose

FIG. 12. Daniel Ellsberg speaking at the 2008 American Library Association conference.

Terry Ballard, "Daniel Ellsberg," June 30, 2008 via Flickr, Creative Commons attribution license.

these secrets? What about other government employees—people who have no particular access to government secrets?

A major challenge to the national security classification system came from two former employees of the Central Intelligence Agency, both of whom published books on their CIA experiences. In both instances, the agency attempted to censor the ex-employees' writings under a provision of their employment contracts that prohibited them from publishing information they gained as CIA agents without the agency's prior approval. Both employees contended these contract provisions violated their First Amendment rights.

The first case, *U.S. v. Marchetti* (466 F.2d 1309, 1972), arose after Victor L. Marchetti left the CIA and published a book and a magazine article critical of CIA activities. When the agency learned he was about to publish another book, it got a court order temporarily halting the project. After a secret trial (much of the testimony was classified), the court ordered Marchetti to submit everything he might write about the CIA to the agency for approval. Marchetti appealed that decision, but it was largely affirmed by the U.S. Court of Appeals.

However, the appellate court said the CIA could only censor classified information, and after further legal maneuvering a district court allowed the agency to censor only 27 of 166 passages in the new book that the agency wanted to suppress.

Although the U.S. Supreme Court refused to review the *Marchetti* case, in 1980 it did rule on a similar case, *Snepp v. U.S.* (444 U.S. 507). Former CIA agent Frank Snepp resigned in 1976 and wrote a book alleging CIA ineptness in Vietnam. He did not submit it for prior CIA approval, as required by his employment contract. After its publication, the U.S. government filed a breach of contract suit against Snepp. Snepp contended the contract violated his First and Fifth Amendment rights.

A trial court ordered Snepp to turn over all his profits from the book to the government and submit any future manuscripts about the CIA to the agency for prior approval. An appellate court reversed that ruling in part, prompting the Supreme Court to hear the case.

The Supreme Court reinstated the trial court's order against Snepp without even hearing full arguments from both sides: the Court never let Snepp present his case. But the high court upheld the validity of the contract, ignoring the prior censorship implications of such contracts. The Court said: "He (Snepp) deliberately and surreptitiously violated his obligation to submit all material for prepublication review. Thus, he exposed the classified information with which he had been entrusted to the risk of disclosure."

The *Snepp* case, then, was decided according to the provisions of Snepp's employment contract and would not be applicable to persons who had not signed such contracts. However, thousands of present and former CIA employees are subject to such contracts—and the CIA has now reviewed and censored many other manuscripts written by former employees.

This issue arose again in 2007 when former CIA operative Valerie Plame Wilson and her publisher sued the CIA for forbidding her to publish such basic facts as the dates of her CIA employment in her memoir. Plame became newsworthy because the former top aide to Vice President Dick Cheney, I. Lewis "Scooter" Libby, was convicted of perjury for denying his role in revealing Plame's CIA status to the media after her husband wrote a newspaper column critical of the Bush administration. She lost, even though those dates had been reported online because the government had not declassified them. In 2009, the Second Circuit ruled that the CIA's refusal to allow Wilson to publish information about her possible pre-2002 CIA service, even though the information had been previously publicly disclosed, did not violate the First Amendment (*Wilson v. CIA*, 586 F.3d 171).

Another controversy over restrictions on the speech rights of government employees occurred in 1989 when Congress amended the Ethics in Government Act to bar not only members of Congress but virtually all federal workers from receiving "honoraria"—payments for writing articles or giving speeches—even if the subject has little to do with their official duties. Few would question the wisdom of telling federal officials they cannot be paid for giving talks about job-related subjects to special interest groups that they regulate. But the federal regulations written to implement the law did not stop there. One Internal Revenue Service worker pointed out that she had been supplementing her $22,000 annual salary by earning about $3,000 a year as a freelance writer. Her articles were about camping and the outdoors, a subject that had nothing to do with her job, but the new rules prohibited her from being paid for her writing. Other workers who wrote or gave talks about subjects such as African-American history, the Quaker religion and dance performances also objected to the rules. Several lawsuits were filed by government workers who had been paid for writing or speaking about subjects unrelated to their work, contending that they should have the same right as other citizens to be paid for writing and speaking.

In 1995, the Supreme Court ruled on this question in *U.S. v. National Treasury Employees Union* (513 U.S. 454). The Court said the ban on federal employees receiving pay for writing articles or giving speeches was excessively broad and a violation of the First Amendment. The Court's 6-3 majority held that Congress had gone too far by banning payments for speeches and articles not only by senior government officials but also by rank and file employees of the executive branch. The Court ruled that lower-level employees could not be barred from accepting payments for speeches and articles. Writing for the majority, Justice John Paul Stevens agreed that there is a legitimate basis for the ban on senior government officials being paid for speaking and writing about policy issues that relate to their official duties, but he said lower-level government employees should have the same First Amendment rights as other citizens, including the right to be paid for their articles and speeches. The high court overturned the ban entirely as it applied to lower-level government employees, although Stevens said Congress might be able to rewrite the ban so that it would be valid if it applied only to speeches and articles directly relating to an employee's official duties.

Meanwhile, in 1993 Congress expanded the free expression rights of federal workers in another way by amending the Hatch Act, which had prohibited most partisan political activities by federal employees for more than 50 years. Under the 1993 amendments, most federal workers may now work in political campaigns, do political fund-raising and hold positions in political parties—as long as they do it on their own time. Federal workers are still barred from holding partisan elective offices, however. About 85,000 workers in sensitive federal jobs, such as many law enforcement and national security-related positions, are not covered by the 1993 Hatch Act amendments. They are still barred from partisan political activities, even on their own time.

Although many public employees now have a right to speak publicly about controversial issues, the First Amendment does not necessarily protect their right to report alleged wrongdoing to superiors inside a government agency. In *Garcetti v. Ceballos* (547 U.S. 410), a 2006 decision, the Supreme Court ruled that the First Amendment does not protect a government attorney who allegedly faced retaliation after reporting suspicions of police misconduct to a supervisor. Writing for a 5-4 majority, Justice Anthony Kennedy said, "We hold that when public employees make statements pursuant to their official duties, the employees are not speaking as citizens for First Amendment purposes, and the Constitution does not insulate their communications from employer discipline." The First Amendment applies if certain conditions are met: the employee is speaking as a private citizen, not as a public employee, and the speech is a matter of public concern.

The Court was divided along liberal-conservative lines, with Samuel Alito providing the deciding vote. The Court was apparently deadlocked 4-4; the case was re-argued when Alito joined the Court, enabling him to participate—creating a 5-4 majority. (A newly appointed justice cannot vote in cases argued before he or she joined the Court.)

The Second Circuit in 2009 addressed when an employee's speech may be a matter of public concern in *Sousa v. Roque* (578 F.3d 164). Bryan Sousa, an engineer for the Connecticut Department of Environmental Protection, reported concerns about workplace violence in the department. He was put on leave and underwent several fitness-for-duty evaluations before ultimately being fired for unauthorized absences. He alleged that he had been punished for speaking out. The district court granted summary judgment for the department. The Second Circuit reversed and remanded, saying that while the speaker's motive may be considered as part of the determination, it is not the sole factor; the court added that "whether an employee's speech addresses a matter of public concern is a question of law for the court to decide, taking into account the content, form, and context of a given statement as revealed by the whole record."

Garcetti does not affect various federal and state laws that protect whistleblowers. However, if no such law protects an employee in a particular situation, the First Amendment does not fill the gap, according to this Supreme Court decision. On the other hand, if an employee's allegation of wrongdoing by superiors is not related to the employee's official duties, such speech is still protected by the First Amendment, according to a 2007 Ninth Circuit decision (*Marable v. Nitchman*, 511 F.3d 924). Ken Marable, an engineer for the Washington State Ferry system, complained that his superiors were engaged in corrupt practices that wasted public funds and endangered public safety. He said he faced disciplinary actions and sued, alleging his First Amendment rights had been violated. The court said Marable had a right to pursue his case because his speech had nothing to do with his official duties and had "all the hallmarks that we normally associate with constitutionally protected speech."

State law can also control whether an employee's speech is protected. In *Huppert v. City of Pittsburg* (574 F. 3d 696, 2009), the Ninth Circuit said that a police officer who talks to FBI agents about police corruption outside his normal job and is allegedly punished by the police department for doing so is actually pursuing his official duties, and therefore that speech is not protected. Relying on *Garcetti*, the court said that Ron Huppert's speech "owes its existence to [his] professional responsibilities" and was not protected—even though Huppert had been told by the FBI that his inquiries were not part of his official duties. The court added that police officers' official duties under California law include crime detection and prevention, so Huppert's conversations with the FBI were part of his job.

A related question that often arises among journalists and public relations practitioners is whether government employees can be forbidden to talk to a reporter without first seeking approval of a public affairs officer or other government official. The Second Circuit held that such a requirement violates the First Amendment in *Harman v. City of New York* (140 F.3d 111, 1998). A radio station interviewed a child-welfare worker about the death of a young child. When the interview was aired, the employee was suspended for speaking to the media without first getting approval from New York's Media Relations Office as required by city policy. The worker then sued, and the appellate court held that the city could not justify such censorship of government workers. Even though the city contended that the policy did not really prevent city employees from speaking to the media, the court rejected the policy because it allowed city officials to delay an employee until his/her comments were no longer newsworthy. Also, the policy was overly broad, the court held.

The U.S. Supreme Court handed down a pair of decisions in 2011 that provided additional guidance regarding the First Amendment's protections on speech or petition acts by government employees. The first case, *Nevada Comm'n on Ethics v. Carrigan* (131 S. Ct. 2343), saw the Court uphold a Nevada law that prohibited government employees from voting on or debating matters in which they have a conflict of interest. Sparks city council member Michael Carrigan was censured by the state for failing to recuse himself from a vote for a casino project whose developer retained a close friend of Carrigan's.

Writing for a unanimous Court, Justice Antonin Scalia wrote that voting by a lawmaker should not be considered a personal speech act. "[A] legislator's vote is the commitment of his apportioned share of the legislature's power to the passage or defeat of a particular proposal" and not his own speech act, unlike those of voters, which are their own symbolic speech acts, said Scalia. Moreover, he added, the United States has had a long history of conflict-of-interest rules that require recusal.

Justices Anthony Kennedy and Samuel Alito concurred in the outcome, with Kennedy warning that this interpretation has the potential for burdens on other protected speech, and Alito suggesting that legislative votes may have "expressive character."

In the second case, *Borough of Duryea v. Guarnieri* (131 S. Ct. 2488), the Court placed additional limits on government employees' First Amendment protections for workplace grievances. Charles Guarnieri filed a union grievance when he was fired as chief of police in Duryea, Penn., and when he was rehired, orders were issued that governed his return to the position. He argued that the grievance was a petition protected by the First Amendment (protected by the petition clause, not the free speech clause), and these orders were in retaliation for that protected grievance. The Third Circuit said that the public concern test does not limit public employees' petition clause claims, but the Supreme Court disagreed, ruling unanimously that government retaliation against an employee does not create liability under the First Amendment's petition clause unless the petition deals with a public concern.

Justice Anthony Kennedy wrote that Guarnieri could as easily have used the speech clause to bring his claim, and he used the free-speech cases (including *Garcetti*) as the basis for his opinion. He avoided creating a different rule for actions brought under the petition clause: "Unrestrained application of the Petition Clause in the context of government employment would subject a wide range of government operations to invasive judicial superintendence," adding, "Petitions, no less than speech, can interfere with the efficient and effective operation of government." Justices Clarence Thomas and Antonin Scalia concurred; Thomas expressed doubt that lawsuits should count as petitions under the First Amendment, and Scalia questioned whether the "public concern" test should apply in petition cases.

False Speech

In recent years there have been a number of cases dealing with false speech. Can a person be punished for publishing or saying things he or she knows to be false but that aren't defamatory? Several recent cases, including a Supreme Court case, dealt with a 2005 law called the Stolen Valor Act. This act criminalizes the false representation of having been awarded "any decoration or medal authorized by Congress for the Armed Forces of the

United States, any of the service medals or badges awarded to the members of such forces, the ribbon, button, or rosette of any such badge, decoration, or medal, or any colorable imitation of such item." Courts' reactions to the law have been mixed. A federal district court in Virginia upheld the law, stating, "The statute's purpose is not related to the suppression of free speech, and incidental restrictions on freedom are no greater than is essential for the furtherance of that purpose" (*U.S. v. Robbins*, 759 F. Supp. 2d 815).

The Ninth Circuit struck down the act by a 2-1 vote as overbroad, while the Tenth Circuit upheld it. The U.S. Supreme Court granted *cert* in the Ninth Circuit case and overturned the Stolen Valor Act by a 6-3 vote in 2012 (*U.S. v. Alvarez*, No. 11-210). Calling Xavier Alvarez's lies "but a pathetic attempt to gain respect that eluded him," Justice Anthony Kennedy wrote that there is no "general exception to the First Amendment for false statements." Quoting Justice Oliver Wendell Holmes' dissent in *Abrams v. U.S.* (see Chapter Two), that "the best test of truth is the power of the thought to get itself accepted in the competition of the market," Kennedy said that the power of the American people to ferret out and refute false claims like those covered in the Act was preferable. "Truth needs neither handcuffs nor a badge for its vindication," he added. Justice Samuel Alito, joined by Justices Antonin Scalia and Clarence Thomas, dissented. Alito accused the majority of a departure from "a long line of cases recognizing that the right to free speech does not protect false factual statements that inflict real harm and serve no legitimate interest."

The Stolen Valor Act is not the only instance of knowingly false speech to be punishable under state or federal law, and the outcomes are decidedly varied. For example, an Illinois state appeals court upheld a state law that criminalized false representation of someone as a parent, legal guardian or other relation of a minor child to any government official (*Illinois v. Farmer*, 949 N.E.2d 770), while a Minnesota state appeals court overturned a state statute that criminalized "knowingly making false statements that allege police misconduct, but not knowingly making false statements to absolve police" as an unconstitutional content-based restriction (*Minnesota v. Crawley*, 789 N.W.2d 899).

The Eighth Circuit relied on the Ninth Circuit's analysis in *Alvarez* to overturn a part of the Minnesota Fair Campaign Practices Act that criminalizes knowingly making a false statement about a proposed ballot initiative. The court applied strict scrutiny and said, "Prior decisions that have discussed the worthlessness of speech categorically excepted from the First Amendment are descriptive not prescriptive—they tell us something about the speech that is exempt but not about what other types of speech may be exempt from First Amendment scrutiny" (*281 Care Committee v. Arneson*, 638 F.3d 621, 2011).

In 2007, the Washington Supreme Court overturned a state law that allowed a government agency to punish political candidates for making what the agency deemed to be false statements in campaign materials. Marilyn Rickert, a Green Party candidate for state legislature, was fined $1,000 for making two statements that the Public Disclosure Commission determined to be false about State Sen. Tim Sheldon, who was re-elected despite the allegedly false campaign flier. She challenged the fine. In *Rickert v. Public Disclosure Commission* (168 P.3d 826, 2007), the 5-4 majority said, "The notion that the government, rather than the people, may be the final arbiter of truth in political debate is fundamentally at odds with the First Amendment." The dissenters said the court's decision was an "invitation to lie with impunity."

■ CENSORING "HATE SPEECH"

One of the most troubling First Amendment issues involves restrictions on what is called "hate speech." During the late 1980s and 1990s, several hundred colleges adopted rules forbidding hostile remarks toward persons of any racial or ethnic group, gender or sexual orientation. These rules are intended to foster a campus environment that is not perceived as hostile by members of any group. But because many of these rules were written so broadly that they could be used to prohibit expression of unfashionable viewpoints on social issues, critics charged that they really enforced "politically correct" speech. Meanwhile, more than 40 states adopted laws criminalizing "hate speech" in various forms. Like many of the campus rules, some laws banned the expression of ideas, rather than forbidding violent acts.

Because these rules and laws are intended to punish those who express bigoted ideas, they have staunch defenders, including many civil libertarians. But do they really square with the First Amendment? Their defenders say that they do, and they cite the *fighting words doctrine* expounded by the U.S. Supreme Court in a famous case more than 60 years ago: *Chaplinsky v. New Hampshire* (315 U.S. 568, 1942). In that case, the high court upheld the criminal conviction of a man who used words likely to produce an immediate violent response—a breach of the peace. Thus, speech likely to cause a fight, such as calling someone a "damned fascist" during the heyday of Hitlerism (as happened in *Chaplinsky*), may be prohibited, the Court ruled. Like calling someone a fascist then, "hate speech" can be banned today under the fighting words rationale, the defenders of these laws and rules say.

However, in 1992 the Supreme Court revisited this controversial issue and ruled that "hate speech" cannot be banned on the basis of its content—although violent action can, of course, be prohibited. Ruling in the case of *R.A.V. v. St. Paul* (505 U.S. 377), the high court overturned a St. Paul, Minn. ordinance intended to punish those who burn crosses, display swastikas or express racial or religious hatred in other ways. The case involved a Caucasian youth who burned a homemade cross in the front yard of an African-American family's home. He could have been prosecuted for a variety of other offenses, including arson and trespassing, but city officials chose to prosecute him under the "hate speech" law. Because he was a juvenile, "R.A.V." was originally identified only by his initials. Later he was widely identified in the media as Robert A. Viktora.

In ruling against the St. Paul law, Justice Antonin Scalia said:

> Let there be no mistake about our belief that burning a cross in someone's yard is reprehensible. But St. Paul has sufficient means at its disposal to prevent such behavior without adding the First Amendment to the fire.

In an opinion that was a wide-ranging defense of the First Amendment right to express unpopular and offensive ideas, Scalia said that governments may not punish those who "communicate messages of racial, gender or religious intolerance" merely because those ideas are offensive and emotionally painful to those in the targeted group.

The Supreme Court was unanimous in overturning the St. Paul "hate speech" ordinance, but the justices disagreed about the legal rationale for doing so. Four justices (Byron White, Harry Blackmun, Sandra Day O'Connor and John Paul Stevens) argued that the ordinance was unconstitutional only because it was overly broad—not limited to expressions that could lead to violence under the fighting words doctrine.

The other five joined in a majority opinion taking a much broader view of the First Amendment rights of those who engage in "hate speech." They said that any law is unconstitutional if it singles out expressions of "bias-motivated hatred" for special punishment. While the majority did not specifically overturn *Chaplinsky*, they made it clear that the fighting words doctrine cannot be used to suppress the expression of racial, religious or gender-based hostilities. That kind of viewpoint discrimination violates the First Amendment.

The *R.A.V. v. St. Paul* decision stirred a new national controversy about the meaning of the First Amendment—and it created deep rifts among traditional allies. The St. Paul youth was represented by the American Civil Liberties Union, which argued that St. Paul's "hate speech" law violates the First Amendment. But other traditionally liberal, pro-civil-liberties groups such as People for the American Way criticized the Supreme Court ruling.

The *R.A.V.* ruling raised serious doubts about the constitutionality of many other "hate speech" laws as well as many of the campus speech codes adopted in recent years. However, this was by no means the first time the courts had held that "hate speech" is protected by the First Amendment. Several universities' speech codes had been overturned by lower courts prior to the Supreme Court's ruling in the *R.A.V.* case.

The Supreme Court's 1992 decision on "hate speech" was reminiscent of *Brandenburg v. Ohio*, the Court's 1969 decision upholding the First Amendment rights of a Ku Klux Klan member. As Chapter Two explains, that case represented an expansion of the scope of the First Amendment in that the Court upheld the Klansman's right to make an offensive (and bigoted) speech at a Klan rally, as long as the speech did not create an imminent danger of violent action.

On the other hand, when an act of violence is motivated by hatred based on race, religion, national origin, gender or sexual orientation, the First Amendment does *not* protect the violent act. Indeed, a state may impose harsher penalties for violent acts motivated by hatred than it would otherwise for the same violent acts. The Supreme Court so held in a unanimous 1993 decision, *Wisconsin v. Mitchell* (508 U.S. 476). The case arose when several African-American youths watched the movie *Mississippi Burning* and then attacked a white youth. After seeing the movie, Todd Mitchell, then 19, asked his friends, "Do you feel all hyped up to move on some white people?" Then Mitchell saw a 14-year-old youth across the street and said, "There goes a white boy. Go get him." The victim spent several days in a coma, but survived. Mitchell was convicted of aggravated battery, and his sentence was increased under a state hate-crime law. Writing for a unanimous Court, Chief Justice William Rehnquist said, "A physical assault is not by any stretch of the imagination expressive conduct protected by the First Amendment."

In so ruling, the Court upheld the law in Wisconsin—and similar laws in many other states—that treat hate crimes as more serious offenses than crimes in which hate cannot be proven to be the motivation. In 2000, the Supreme Court added a proviso to this: if there is a sentence enhancement for a hate crime (i.e., a crime is punished more severely if motivated by hate), that extra sentence must be imposed by the jury—not added later by the judge (*Apprendi v. New Jersey*, 530 U.S. 466).

In 2003, the Supreme Court once again addressed the conflict between the First Amendment and legislative attempts to curb expressions of hate such as cross-burning.

The Court again said cross-burning is protected by the First Amendment—but not when the act is an attempt to intimidate someone rather than an expression of symbolic speech. In *Virginia v. Black* (538 U.S. 343, 2003), the Court reviewed Virginia's across-the-board ban

Focus on...
The law of flags

The flag is a revered symbol in America. For many, there is no more precious symbol of democracy and freedom. So when it's burned or there are issues with its display, lawmakers get involved.

FIG. 13. American flag.

Author's collection.

Burning the flag is an acceptable way to dispose of a damaged or old flag, and it is currently constitutional to burn one in protest. Interestingly, even after flag desecration laws were struck down in 1989 in *Texas v. Johnson*, legal blogger and First Amendment scholar Eugene Volokh found at least a dozen flag desecration prosecutions since 1992 (post-*R.A.V.*) in Florida, North Carolina, Pennsylvania, Texas, and Washington state (he reported that most were dismissed but two led to convictions).

In 2006, President Bush signed the Freedom to Display the American Flag Act, which prohibits condominium associations from denying their members the ability to display the flag. Associations can put reasonable time, place and manner restrictions on the display, such as size and flag pole placement, but cannot ban American flag display altogether. Several states have similar laws.

on cross-burning. The Court upheld its use to prosecute those who burn a cross on a neighbor's property with the intent to intimidate those who live there—or the intent to intimidate anyone else. But a majority of the Court also held that burning a cross in an open field at a political rally is protected by the First Amendment as symbolic speech unless the specific intent to intimidate can be proven.

Writing for the Court, Justice Sandra Day O'Connor said that the Ku Klux Klan's history of using burning crosses to intimidate African-Americans, Jews and others justified Virginia's law against cross-burning that is intended to intimidate someone. "Threats of violence are outside the First Amendment," she wrote, adding, "The burning cross often serves as a message of intimidation, designed to inspire in the victim a fear of bodily harm." She said this history justifies Virginia's decision (and that of many other states) to ban cross-burning as a "signal of impending violence."

However, the Court overturned the conviction of the lead defendant in the case, Barry Elton Black, a Klansman who led a rally in an open field at a farm in Virginia. The Court held that there was insufficient proof that this political rally, which featured a verbal attack on "the blacks and Mexicans" by one speaker and an attack on former President Bill Clinton and his wife, Hillary Rodham Clinton, by another, was specifically intended to intimidate anyone. Instead, the Court saw it as a form of protected symbolic speech. The rally concluded with the singing of a hymn, "Amazing Grace," and the symbolic burning of a 30-foot cross. The Court also said two other defendants who had burned a cross in an African-American neighbor's yard could be prosecuted for that.

Justice O'Connor reconciled the case with *R.A.V. v. St. Paul* by interpreting that decision narrowly to protect only symbolic speech but not cross-burning intended to intimidate someone. "A ban on cross-burning carried out with the intent to intimidate is fully consistent with our holding in *R.A.V.* and is proscribable under the First Amendment," she explained.

The 2003 decision led several justices to issue separate concurring or dissenting opinions. Perhaps most notable was Justice Clarence Thomas' opinion. Thomas, the Court's only African-American justice, said he would uphold the Virginia law and other anti-cross-burning laws in full. During oral arguments in this case, Thomas had called cross-burning "a symbol of a reign of terror." In his separate opinion when the case was decided, he said cross-burning should never be regarded as symbolic speech protected by the First Amendment.

On the other hand, Justices David Souter, Ruth Bader Ginsburg and Anthony Kennedy said they would not uphold any law forbidding cross-burning. In an opinion joined by Ginsburg and Kennedy, Souter said any ban on cross burning is a "content-based" ban on a symbolic message and could not survive First Amendment scrutiny.

One irony in *Virginia v. Black* is that Virginia rewrote its cross-burning law after a lower Court invalidated the version of the law under review by the Supreme Court. The new law requires proof of specific intent to intimidate and would probably be upheld in full under the Supreme Court majority's rationale.

Some years earlier the Supreme Court ruled that still another form of inflammatory and offensive speech is protected by the First Amendment in *Cohen v. California* (403 U.S. 15, 1971). In that case, Paul R. Cohen was criminally prosecuted for appearing in a Los Angeles courthouse wearing a leather jacket emblazoned with the motto "Fuck the Draft." At the time, several people who had demonstrated against the Vietnam-era military draft were standing trial. The Supreme Court ultimately held that this was a constitutionally protected expression of opinion, despite the offensiveness of the word. Writing for the Court, Justice John Marshall Harlan said:

> While the particular four-letter word being litigated here is perhaps more distasteful than most others of its genre, it is nevertheless often true that one man's vulgarity is another's lyric. Indeed, we think it is largely because governmental officials cannot make principled distinctions in this area that the Constitution leaves matters of taste and style so largely to the individual.

Perhaps the main point of all of these cases is that the First Amendment protects the expression of opinions in many forms, however unenlightened or vulgar the speaker's ideas (or choice of words or symbols) may seem to be.

The First Amendment does not protect unlawful conduct such as acts of intimidation, violence, arson or trespass. But the line is not bright: the Ninth Circuit in 2010 overturned a city council's expulsion of a man who gave the Nazi salute at a council meeting. Robert Norse, a homeless advocate, performed the salute at two Santa Cruz city council meetings and was ejected. A panel of the Ninth Circuit originally found that the ejections did not violate Norse's rights because his salutes were not "on account of any permissible expression of a point of view" but rather in response to the council enforcing its own rules.

The Ninth Circuit reheard the case *en banc* and ruled for Norse on procedural grounds. The court said that the district court had not provided Norse enough time for him to build his case, nor did it rule on his objections to evidence (*Norse v. City of Santa Cruz*, 629 F.3d 966). Concurring, the redoubtable Chief Judge Alex Kozinski noted that Norse's salute might not have even been noticed had not one council member gotten offended and ordered Norse ejected. The council member, Kozinski said, "clearly wants Norse expelled because the 'Nazi salute' is 'against the dignity of this body and the decorum of this body' and not because of any disruption. But, unlike der Führer, government officials in America occasionally must tolerate offensive or irritating speech." The city has appealed the case to the Supreme Court.

What about speech that federal authorities feel is "not quite right" but isn't an outright threat, or bumper stickers with a contrary political message at a president's public speech? Steven Howards and his son were at a Colorado mall when then-Vice President Richard Cheney was making a public appearance there. Secret Service agents heard Howards tell someone on his cell phone, "I'm going to ask him [the Vice President] how many kids he's killed today." The agents watched as Howards approached Cheney, asked him a question, and then laid a hand on his shoulder. The agents arrested Howard for assaulting the vice president and turned him over to state law enforcement; those charges were dropped but Howard sued the agents under the First and Fourth Amendments. The Tenth Circuit said that two agents violated Howard's First Amendment rights by retaliating against him for his speech act: "when Mr. Howards was arrested it was clearly established that an arrest made in retaliation of an individual's First Amendment rights is unlawful, even if the arrest is supported by probable cause." One agent admitted that Howards' comment "disturbed" him, and the other became angry when Howards told him how he felt about the Iraq war.

But the Supreme Court in 2012 unanimously said that the Secret Service agents did not violate Howards' First Amendment rights (*Reichle v. Howards*, No. 11-262). Justice Clarence Thomas wrote that the question was not one of First Amendment retaliation, but rather the "right to be free from a retaliatory arrest that is otherwise supported by probable cause"— and there is no such right, he said. Justice Ruth Bader Ginsburg, concurring in the result, added that the agents "were duty bound to take the content of Howards' statements into account in determining whether he posed an immediate threat to the Vice President's physical security."

In a case that drew two Supreme Court justices' dissent from denial of *cert*, a divided panel of the Tenth Circuit affirmed qualified immunity for Secret Service agents who refused to allow two individuals to attend a 2005 speech given by President George W. Bush at a Colorado museum because the bumper sticker on their car read "No More Blood For Oil" (*Weise v. Casper*, 593 F.3d 1163). Leslie Weise and Alex Young were removed from the event in accordance with a White House Advance Office policy of excluding those who disagree with the President from his official public appearances. The court said that the law regarding was not clearly established at the time of the event, and "no specific authority instructs this court … how to treat the ejection of a silent attendee from an official speech based on the attendee's protected expression outside the speech area." The dissent pointed out that the speech in question "is unquestionably protected, or more accurately, entitled to be protected under the First Amendment. It is severely distressing that such protection is not forthcoming from this court."

Weise and Young appealed to the Supreme Court, which declined to hear the case. However, Justice Ruth Bader Ginsburg, joined by Justice Sonia Sotomayor, took the unusual step of issuing a dissent from the denial of *cert*: "I cannot see how reasonable public officials, or any staff or volunteers under their direction, could have viewed the bumper sticker as a permissible reason for depriving Weise and Young of access to the event."

In 2009, President Barack Obama signed the Matthew Shepard and James Byrd, Jr. Hate Crimes Prevention Act after over a decade of advocacy by human rights groups. The act gives the Department of Justice jurisdiction over violent crimes where a victim has been chosen due to his/her race, color, religion, gender, sexual orientation or disability. The department can also help state and local jurisdictions with investigation of hate crimes.

Sadly, the election of the first African-American president resulted in several threats against the life of President Barack Obama and his family. The first arose against then-candidate Obama by Walter Bagdasarian, described by the Ninth Circuit as "an especially unpleasant fellow." Bagdasarian posted on a Yahoo! message board various comments such as "Obama fk the niggar, he will have a 50 cal in the head soon." He was charged under a law that makes it a felony to threaten to kill or do bodily harm to a major presidential candidate. Under *Virginia v. Black* (discussed earlier), the court said, the question that must be asked is "Did the speaker subjectively intend the speech as a threat?" In this case, the court said no, and thus there is no true threat (*U.S. v. Bagdasarian*, 652 F.3d 1113, 2011).

However, the Eighth Circuit (*U.S. v. Christenson*, 653 F.3d 697, 2011) said that Chane Christenson's lengthy e-mails sent to the White House were threats; they included such verbiage as "WHATS SO HARD ABOUT A BIRTH RECORD? ... I HOPE SOMEONE KILLS YOU AND YOUR FAMILY REAL SOON. TO WARN THE NEXT ILLEGAL ALIEN WHO TRIES TO TAKE YOUR PLACE. I WASNT RACISET UNTILL 2008 ... kill obama MRS OBAMA AND THE 2 LITTLE NIGGER BRAT KIDS!" Christenson pled guilty, and then said that he suffered from mental illness and alcohol and drug dependence and that there was an insufficient factual basis to convict him. He argued his messages were political hyperbole. But the court did not agree: "That correspondence containing threatening language is phrased in outrageous terms does not make the correspondence any less threatening."

But an e-mail written to a bankruptcy court by a man asking for permission to pay for antidepressant medication was *not* considered a threat, even if it threatens that the man may become "homicidal." In *U.S. v. O'Dwyer* (443 Fed. Appx. 18), the Fifth Circuit said that Sean O'Dwyer's statements in the e-mail were conditional and hypothetical and did not threaten harm to any named individual. Given O'Dwyer's history of using "coarse and hyperbolic language in prior court proceedings," this e-mail was not a true threat, said the court.

Flag-Burning and the First Amendment

While the constitutional ramifications of laws forbidding "hate speech" were being debated at colleges, in the media and in the nation's courtrooms, there has also been much debate concerning a related free-expression issue: flag desecration. Americans have been bitterly divided over two Supreme Court decisions holding that flag-burning is a protected form of expression. Like cross-burning, the act of burning the American flag stirs strong feelings in many people—and they find it hard to see the value of permitting this kind of symbolic "speech." When this issue gained national attention, it became clear that many Americans believed the American flag was a national symbol that deserved special protection. But like Ku Klux Klan members, those who desecrate the flag were given First Amendment protection by the Supreme Court. The Court concluded that there is a higher principle involved in these cases, and that a truly democratic society must extend free expression rights even to those whose ideas or political activities are reprehensible to most people.

In 1989 and 1990, the Supreme Court handed down two separate decisions on flag-burning as symbolic speech protected by the First Amendment. In 1989, *Texas v. Johnson* (491 U.S. 397), the Court declared that Gregory Lee Johnson could not be punished for burning an American flag during the 1984 Republican National Convention to protest then-President Reagan's policies. In a decision that produced strong dissenting opinions by four justices, the majority ruled that flag desecration is a protected form of symbolic speech, particularly when it occurs in a clearly political context (as it did in this case).

Like the Ku Klux Klan decision of 1969 and the "hate speech" decision in 1992, the flag desecration ruling brought vehement objections from many people. President George H.W.

Bush, for example, called for a constitutional amendment to overturn the Johnson ruling and restore flag desecration as a crime. On the other hand, many civil libertarians feared that such a constitutional amendment would end up including restrictions on other First Amendment freedoms such as the right to express controversial views on racial issues and the right of consenting adults to possess erotic but non-obscene literature.

After a major public debate over this question, Congress enacted the Flag Protection Act of 1989, a federal law that carried penalties of up to a year in jail and a $1,000 fine for flag desecration. President Bush allowed this act to go into effect without his signature, declaring that he still favored a constitutional amendment instead of a statutory law that could be overturned by the courts. Predictably, the new law was challenged in court as soon as it went into effect. Recognizing the importance of this question, the Supreme Court agreed to hear this new case on an expedited schedule. In 1990—just a year after its first decision on this issue—the Court declared the new flag protection law to be unconstitutional.

Ruling in the case of *U.S. v. Eichman* (496 U.S. 310), the same 5-4 majority reaffirmed its earlier holding that flag desecration is a form of symbolic political speech protected by the First Amendment. While the four dissenting justices again advanced legal arguments to explain why they felt that the First Amendment should *not* protect those who desecrate the flag—as they did a year earlier—in the later decision they also took the unusual step of criticizing public officials who exploited the popular emotions on this issue for their own partisan gain. Writing for the four dissenters, Justice John Paul Stevens said the integrity of the flag is tarnished "by those leaders who seem to advocate compulsory worship of the flag even by individuals it offends, or who seem to manipulate the symbol of national purpose into a pretext for partisan disputes about meaner ends."

Nevertheless, the *Eichman* decision triggered a new campaign for a constitutional amendment that would modify the First Amendment to exclude flag desecration from its scope. Congress took up the issue immediately. But this time, much of the debate centered on the question of whether it was wise to amend the First Amendment for the first time in American history. In June, 1990, only days after the *Eichman* ruling, the proposed anti-flag-burning amendment was killed when the House of Representatives failed to give it the two-thirds majority required for constitutional amendments. As the debate reached its conclusion, many members of Congress argued that the flag is a symbol of American freedom—including even the freedom to burn the flag itself as a political protest.

More recently, new proposals for a flag protection amendment cleared the House several times but failed to gain a two-thirds majority in the Senate. Most recently, the House approved a flag protection amendment in 2005, this time by a 286-130 vote. But in 2006 the Senate fell one vote short of the needed two-thirds majority, voting 66-34 in favor of the measure. It would have taken 67 yes votes to approve the measure and send it to the states for ratification. Because the legislatures of all 50 states have already endorsed such a constitutional amendment, it could well be ratified by the necessary three-fourths (38) of the states if it ever clears both houses of Congress. The most recent version of the proposed constitutional amendment said only this: *"The Congress shall have power to prohibit the physical desecration of the flag of the United States."*

Does the *R.A.V.* decision—upholding the First Amendment rights of racial or religious bigots—and the *Johnson* and *Eichman* rulings—which upheld the First Amendment rights of flag-burners—mean that the First Amendment *never* allows speech or symbolic speech to be made a crime unless there is a call for action that may actually lead to unlawful acts or

FIG. 14. Protesters
outside the Lloyd
Center Mall, August
2007.

*Lisa Norwood, "Wars are
barbaric slaughter,"
August 28, 2007 via Flickr,
Creative Commons
attribution license.*

intimidate someone? Generally, the answer has been yes—even if the speech is highly offensive. But if unlawful acts of violence *do* occur, the violent acts are not protected by the First Amendment, as the Supreme Court pointed out in *Wisconsin v. Mitchell.*

In addition, the Supreme Court has also ruled that in some circumstances speech itself may be censored. For example, the high court has often ruled that the First Amendment does not protect speech or writings that are legally *obscene.* The problem in that area, of course, is deciding whether a particular work is obscene or merely pornographic but not legally obscene. That task has fallen to the Supreme Court, which has sometimes had to decide on a case-by-case basis whether specific films, books, images or performances are obscene. Chapter Ten discusses the problems of obscenity, pornography and the First Amendment. Another category of speech that has not always been given full First Amendment protection is *commercial speech* (including commercial advertising), although that appears to be changing now (see Chapter Thirteen). In addition, *broadcasting* does not enjoy the same First Amendment protection as other media. The courts have sometimes upheld government controls on broadcast content when similar controls would be unconstitutional if applied to other media (see Chapter Eleven).

■ CONTROLS ON LITERATURE DISTRIBUTION

If the First Amendment does not permit the direct censorship of such offensive forms of expression as "hate speech" or flag-burning, are there other ways governments can control those who want to engage in these forms of expression? Could a local government simply refuse to let a group like the Ku Klux Klan or the American Nazi Party hold rallies or distribute literature on public property? What about other groups whose views are controversial, such as Operation Rescue, an anti-abortion group known for large and sometimes confrontational demonstrations?

Over the years, there have been hundreds of court decisions about questions such as these. The basic answer is that federal, state and local governments may adopt *content-neutral time, place and manner restrictions* on First Amendment activities—but groups wishing to express controversial views cannot be censored through the use of laws governing public assemblies or literature distribution. For example, a government agency may require that all groups obtain a permit before holding a parade on the public streets or a large rally in a public park. And the permit could impose reasonable time limits or noise limits for such events. Similarly, a government agency may set reasonable limits on the places where groups hand out their literature or collect signatures on petitions. However, no government may issue permits for rallies, parades and literature distribution to groups with which it agrees, while denying permits to groups with which it disagrees unless there is a *compelling state interest that justifies such a content-based restriction* on First Amendment activities. The Supreme Court has repeatedly ruled on cases involving these issues, holding that governments may not arbitrarily deny controversial or unpopular groups the right to distribute literature or hold rallies or demonstrations in a *public forum*—a public place where First Amendment activities are regularly permitted.

Governments can also declare certain areas to be *nonpublic forums* and control literature distribution in that way. For example, in 2010 the Seventh Circuit rejected a non-profit group's argument that a display rack in a state park was a public forum and said the park could refuse to display the group's "scary" pamphlet that provided tips on avoiding asbestos contamination at the park (*Illinois Dunesland Preservation Society v. Illinois Department of Natural Resources*, 584 F.3d 719). The Supreme Court declined to review the case.

Jehovah's Witness Cases

The Supreme Court first ruled on the constitutionality of restrictions on literature distribution in cases involving the proselytizing activities of the Jehovah's Witness movement. Since this religious group engages in door-to-door and street-corner soliciting that is unpopular with many Americans, its efforts led to restrictive ordinances in a number of cities by the late 1930s. The Witnesses challenged these limits on their First Amendment rights in a series of lawsuits, several of which reached the U.S. Supreme Court and established new free-expression safeguards that benefitted not only Jehovah's Witnesses but also the advocates of many other religious and political causes. In 2002, the Supreme Court revisited these issues again in still another Jehovah's Witness case, illustrating the timelessness of these issues.

The first of these Jehovah's Witness cases was *Lovell v. City of Griffin* (303 U.S. 444), decided in 1938. Alma Lovell, a Witness, circulated pamphlets in Griffin, Ga., without the city manager's permission, something a local law required. She was fined $50, but she took her case all the way to the Supreme Court and won.

The Supreme Court found the ordinance invalid, saying it "strikes at the very foundation of the freedom of the press by subjecting it to license and censorship." The city claimed the First Amendment applied only to newspapers and magazines and not to Lovell's pamphlets. The Supreme Court disagreed: "The liberty of the press is not confined to newspapers and periodicals. It necessarily embraces pamphlets and leaflets. These indeed have been historic weapons in the defense of liberty, as the pamphlets of Thomas Paine and others in our own history abundantly attest." Moreover, the Court emphasized that the First Amendment protects the right to distribute literature as well as the right to publish it.

Elsewhere, a number of communities attempted to curb Jehovah's Witnesses by using anti-littering ordinances against them. Several of these laws were considered by the Supreme Court in a 1939 case, *Schneider v. State of New Jersey* (308 U.S. 147).

The Court said a city indeed has the right to prevent littering, but it must do so by punishing the person who actually does the littering, not by punishing someone who hands literature to willing recipients. The person handing out a pamphlet cannot be punished even if the recipient later throws it away, the high court said.

In *Schneider*, the Supreme Court also invalidated a city ordinance that required anyone seeking to distribute literature door-to-door to get police permission first. The Court said giving the police discretion to decide which ideas may and may not be advanced by neighborhood canvassing is a violation of the First Amendment. A city may limit the hours of door-to-door soliciting, but requiring an advance permit is unconstitutional when the permit system gives police discretion to approve or deny permits for causes they like or don't like.

In 1942, the Supreme Court first approved and then invalidated another city ordinance that had been used against a Jehovah's Witness, this one simply requiring a $10 "book agent" license for all solicitors. In this case (*Jones v. Opelika*, 316 U.S. 584), the high court initially upheld the license requirement. But some 11 months later, the Court vacated its decision and adopted what had been a dissenting opinion as the majority view. The court's final decision was based on the fact that the ordinance gave city officials discretion to grant or revoke these licenses without explaining why the action was taken.

To the amazement of many, 60 years later the same kind of questions were addressed again in still another Supreme Court decision involving Jehovah's Witnesses, *Watchtower Bible and Tract Society v. Village of Stratton* (536 U.S. 150, 2002). Stratton, a small town in Ohio, adopted an ordinance that made it a misdemeanor for door-to-door "canvassers" to promote "any cause" without first obtaining a permit from the mayor's office. The ordinance also made it a misdemeanor for anyone to go to a private home where a "no solicitors" sign was posted—a provision the Jehovah's Witnesses did not challenge.

After lower courts largely upheld the Stratton ordinance, the Supreme Court overturned its permit requirement on an 8-1 vote. Writing for the Court, Justice John Paul Stevens said extending such a permit requirement to religious and political advocates and other noncommercial canvassers violates the First Amendment. The Court did not rule out permit systems that apply only to commercial solicitors.

Stevens said the Stratton ordinance is overbroad and "offensive—not only to the values protected by the First Amendment, but to the very notion of a free society." He condemned laws that require citizens, "in the context of everyday public discourse," to first inform the government of their desire to speak "and then obtain a permit to do so."

Stevens emphasized the right, first recognized by the Court long after the earlier Jehovah's Witness cases, of religious and political advocates to engage in anonymous speech. Any permit system for these canvassers necessarily violates that constitutional right and also precludes spontaneous acts such as going across the street to talk to a neighbor about a cause. Stevens said some citizens might "prefer silence to speech licensed by a petty official."

As a result of these and other Jehovah's Witness cases, it is now a settled principle of constitutional law that government authorities may not arbitrarily grant solicitation permits to those advocating popular ideas while denying permits to advocates of unpopular ideas. Even a *content-neutral* permit system that merely controls the time, place and manner of free expression raises constitutional questions because it precludes anonymous religious or political speech and forces those who want to engage in this kind of activity to ask a government for prior permission. For example, the Witnesses won a remand in 2011 in the First Circuit against a Puerto Rican law intended to combat crime called the Controlled Access Law, which permits municipalities to grant permits to neighborhood homeowners' associations to control vehicular and pedestrian access. The First Circuit said the law, as applied to the Witnesses, unreasonably burdened them in their proselytizing. Applying intermediate scrutiny, the court said that the law was not facially unconstitutional but that some limits on access were acceptable. Calling the case "novel and difficult," the court noted that "the precedents on access to public places require fine tuning of the statute's local administration" and remanded the case for further consideration (*Watchtower Bible and Tract Society of New York, Inc. v. Sagardía de Jesús*, 638 F.3d 81).

What about access to prison inmates? The Ninth Circuit addressed the question in 2011 in *Hrdlicka v. Reniff* (631 F.3d 1044). Ray Hrdlicka wanted to distribute his magazine, *Crime, Justice & America,* free but unsolicited, to prison inmates in California county jails. Several jails had policies that did not allow the distribution. Relying on a test from an earlier Supreme Court case (*Turner v. Safley,* 482 U.S. 78, 1987), the district court had issued summary judgment for the jails. But a divided panel of the Ninth Circuit said that the *Turner* test was more nuanced than the district court had thought and reversed and remanded the case; the fact that the publication was not solicited by the prisoners did not, for the majority, matter: "A First Amendment interest in distributing and receiving information does not depend on a recipient's prior request for that information." The dissent claimed that Hrdlicka had no special right to demand that a prison distribute his magazine, stating, "A prison is not a public forum, and a ban on unrequested publications is a content neutral method for sheriffs to ensure efficient administration of their facilities."

However, these cases generally involve the acts of government agencies that attempted to control the dissemination of ideas in public forums or by door-to-door canvassing. Is the rule different if the activity occurs in a company-owned town or a private shopping center?

Private Property and Literature Distribution

The Supreme Court first addressed the question of literature distribution on private property in a 1946 case, *Marsh v. Alabama* (326 U.S. 501). The case arose in Chickasaw, Alabama, a company town owned by Gulf Shipbuilding. The distribution of literature without permission of the town's authorities was forbidden.

The case arose when a Jehovah's Witness tried to pass out tracts there. She was told that permission was required before solicitation was allowed, and she would not be given permission. She was ordered to leave, and when she refused she was prosecuted for trespassing.

Even though the entire town was privately owned, the high court stood by its earlier decisions in the *Marsh* case. Noting that for all practical purposes this company town was a city, the Court applied the same rules to it as had been applied to other cities. The Court pointed out that the town was in fact open to the public and was immediately adjacent to a four-lane public highway. Even though the streets were privately owned, the public used them as if they were public streets. The Court said:

> Ownership does not always mean absolute dominion. The more an owner, for his advantage, opens up his property for use by the public in general, the more do his rights become circumscribed by the statutory and constitutional rights of those who use it.

More than 20 years later, the Supreme Court applied the same kind of logic to a private shopping center in *Amalgamated Food Employees Local 590 v. Logan Valley Plaza* (391 U.S. 308, 1968). This case involved union picketing, which had been forbidden on shopping center premises. The union challenged this rule and won.

The Supreme Court compared the private shopping center to the private town in *Marsh* and said the same right to distribute literature existed here. However, the Court said a factor in its decision was that the case involved a labor dispute to which a merchant in the shopping center was a party. The Court did not say whether the First Amendment would have applied if there had not been this close relationship between the picketing and the merchant.

That question was addressed by the Supreme Court in 1972 in *Lloyd Corp. v. Tanner* (407 U.S. 551). In that case there was no relationship between the material being distributed and any merchant in a shopping center. This decision allowed a large shopping center in Portland, Oregon, to ban anti-Vietnam War protesters who wanted to pass out literature.

In the years between the *Logan Valley* and *Lloyd* decisions, four Supreme Court justices appointed by Richard Nixon had replaced key members of the liberal Warren Court, and those four justices helped create a new majority that backed away from the Court's previous rulings about literature distribution on private property. The Court said there was no constitutional right to distribute literature in this case, particularly because there was no relationship between the literature and the business being conducted at the shopping center. However, the majority did not specifically say it was overruling the *Logan Valley* decision.

In 1976 the Supreme Court came full circle, expressly reversing the *Logan Valley* decision as it decided another shopping center case, *Hudgens v. NLRB* (424 U.S. 507). This case involved warehouse employees of the Butler Shoe Company who were on strike. When they picketed a Butler store in an Atlanta shopping center, the center's management ordered them out of the mall. The National Labor Relations Board held this to be an unfair labor practice, and the shopping center owner appealed.

The *Hudgens* majority made it clear that there is no longer any constitutional right to distribute literature at a private shopping center, even if the literature specifically involves a labor dispute with a merchant doing business there. The Court said that, if First and Fourteenth Amendment rights are involved, the content of the material should be irrelevant; it shouldn't matter whether the literature has anything to do with the business being conducted at the shopping center or not. Whatever the subject matter of the literature, there is no constitutional right to distribute it at a private shopping center, the *Hudgens* majority ruled. However, this would not prevent the NLRB from ordering an employer to allow picketing on another legal basis; the Court merely ruled out any such right under the federal Constitution. The NLRB, for example, could rule that to deny picketing rights was an unfair labor practice, in violation of federal labor laws.

There were those who thought *Hudgens* settled the matter of literature distribution at private shopping centers, but they were wrong. In 1980, the Supreme Court made another sharp turn in its circuitous route through this area of law in the case of *PruneYard Shopping Center v. Robins* (447 U.S. 74). This case presented the conservative majority on the Supreme Court with a classic confrontation between private property rights and states' rights, two causes that have sometimes been rallying cries of conservatives. At a shopping center near San Jose, California, a group of high school students tried to distribute literature opposing a United Nations resolution against "Zionism." They were refused permission, and they sued in California's state courts. The state supreme court said that the California Constitution provides a broader guarantee of free expression than the federal Constitution. The California court said there is a right to distribute literature in private shopping centers in California, even if no such right is guaranteed by the federal Constitution.

The center's owners appealed to the U.S. Supreme Court, contending that this ruling denied their property and due process rights under the federal Constitution. The respondents replied, of course, in states' rights terms, asserting the right of a state to afford its citizens more free speech rights than the federal Constitution mandates.

In a 7-1 opinion, Justice William Rehnquist chose states' rights over property rights, ruling that the California Supreme Court decision violated no federal right of the shopping center owners that was as important as a state's right to define freedom for its citizens. Rehnquist said the U.S. Supreme Court's earlier rulings on access to shopping centers were not intended to "limit the authority of the state to exercise its police power or its sovereign right to adopt in its own Constitution individual liberties more expansive than those conferred by the Federal Constitution."

In short, the Supreme Court affirmed California's right to create broader rights than the federal Constitution requires. The effect of the *PruneYard* decision is to leave it up to other state legislatures and courts to decide whether to grant literature distribution rights in private places similar to those recognized in California.

In the years since the *PruneYard* decision, the highest courts in a few other states have recognized at least a limited right to engage in various forms of free expression at private shopping malls. These decisions have been based on several different legal grounds, including general free expression provisions in state constitutions and the right to circulate petitions for ballot measures, also recognized in some state constitutions.

States that have recognized free expression rights at large malls include Massachusetts (*Batchelder v. Allied Stores Int'l*, 445 N.E.2d 590), Colorado (*Bock v. Westminster Mall Co.*, 819 P.2d 55), Washington (*Alderwood Associates v. Washington Environmental Council*, 635 P.2d 108, but also note *Southcenter Joint Venture v. National Democratic Policy Committee*, 780 P.2d 1282, which curbed free expression other than petition-circulating at malls in Washington) and New Jersey (*New Jersey Coalition Against War in the Middle East v. J.M.B. Realty Corp.*, 650 A.2d 757, and *Green Party of New Jersey v. Hartz Mountain Industries*, 752 A.2d 315).

In New Jersey, for example, the state supreme court ruled in the *Coalition Against War* case that the owners of large regional shopping malls must permit leafletting and similar political speech, subject to reasonable time, place and manner restrictions. In the *Green Party* case, the New Jersey Supreme Court ruled that a mall could not require those who want to do leafletting to obtain a $1 million liability insurance policy. Such insurance is prohibitively expensive if it can be obtained at all, the court noted. Nor can mall managers limit groups that want to do leafletting to just one day a year. Those restrictions are not reasonable, the New Jersey Supreme Court ruled. However, the court also emphasized that it was authorizing only literature distribution, not bullhorns, megaphones, placards, picket signs, parades or similarly intrusive actions. And the court emphasized that it was authorizing free-expression activities only at large regional malls, not at smaller shopping centers, football stadiums, theaters or other private places that may attract crowds.

The New Jersey cases closely parallel post-*PruneYard* decisions of the California courts in allowing leafletting only at large shopping malls. In 1999, for example, a California appellate court held that there is no right to circulate petitions outside a stand-alone store—as opposed to a mall with many stores (*Trader Joe's Co. v. Progressive Campaigns Inc.*, 73 C.A.4th 425). In 2001, the California Supreme Court went a step further, rejecting any right to circulate literature inside a large, gated apartment complex (*Golden Gateway Center v. Golden Gateway Tenants Association*, 26 C.4th 1013). In this case, the court ruled 4-3 that the California Constitution does not protect free speech on private property unless it is "freely and openly accessible to the public," carving out an exception to the *PruneYard* rule for places that are not the functional equivalent of downtown sidewalks—places where there is no state action, the court said. However, Justice Janice Rogers Brown, writing for the majority, said the decision "does not give apartment owners *carte blanche* to stifle tenant speech." She said tenants may communicate with one another in many ways without leaving unsolicited newsletters at doorways, which is what the tenants association wanted to do.

After that ruling, some thought the California Supreme Court might abandon the *Prune-Yard* principle and allow shopping malls to ban controversial speech, but the court reaffirmed *PruneYard* instead. Ruling on Christmas Eve, 2007, the California Supreme Court gave a major victory to labor unions and others who want to picket at private shopping malls, reaffirming their right to do so even if they urge shoppers to boycott a store in the mall.

In *Fashion Valley Mall v. National Labor Relations Board* (42 C.4th 850), a closely contested 4-3 decision, the court said the free-expression rights of protesters still outweigh the property rights of the mall's proprietors.

Writing for the majority, Justice Carlos R. Moreno said, "The mall's purpose to maximize the profits of its merchants is not compelling compared to the union's right to free expression." That produced a surprisingly strong dissenting opinion by Justice Ming W. Chin, in which he attacked "the bankruptcy of the majority's position," noting how few other states' courts have followed the *PruneYard* precedent since it was decided nearly 30 years earlier.

The *Fashion Valley* case involved picketing by unionists outside a department store, urging customers not to shop there because the store was a major advertiser in the *San Diego Union-Tribune*, which was involved in a labor dispute with the union.

In Nevada, a major legal controversy has involved literature distribution and picketing on the heavily-used sidewalks along the Las Vegas Strip. When the street was widened in the early 1990s, local authorities allowed several large hotels to retain ownership of the new sidewalks as their private property.

Hotel owners then banned leafletting on the new sidewalks for "erotic" entertainment, arguing that as private property, the sidewalks are not a public forum. The county also restricted commercial leafletting along the Strip in general. In 2001, a divided Nevada Supreme Court upheld the right of the casinos to ban leafletting for outcall services and similar businesses. Three justices joined in an opinion saying the sidewalks are not a public forum. Two others said that even if the sidewalks are a public forum, the leafletting in question is not protected by the First Amendment because it represents a commercial message for an apparently illegal activity (*S.O.C. v. The Mirage*, 23 P.3d 243, 2001).

However, the hotel owners quickly learned that it wouldn't be that easy to control the privatized, once-public sidewalks. Two months later the Ninth Circuit held that the sidewalks along the Strip are in fact a public forum to which the First Amendment applies (*Venetian Casino Resort v. Local Joint Executive Board of Las Vegas*, 257 F.3d 937). In a case involving picketing by a labor union, the federal court rejected The Venetian's attempt to render the sidewalks off limits to free expression. The U.S. Supreme Court declined to hear the hotel's appeal in 2002, leaving the Ninth Circuit decision as a binding precedent and protecting the right to engage in traditional First Amendment activities such as union picketing along the Strip. Later the U.S. Court of Appeals in Washington, D.C. also ruled in favor of the unions, holding that the hotel violated labor law by trying to halt picketing on the sidewalks (*Venetian Casino Resort v. NLRB*, 484 F.3d 601, 2007).

For a time the police and casino security personnel ignored these court decisions, prompting new threats of litigation by the American Civil Liberties Union. In 2004 local officials, casinos owners and civil libertarians reached an agreement that would allow many forms of free expression on Las Vegas Strip sidewalks, including the privatized ones in front of leading hotels on the Strip.

A similar dispute arose a few miles away in downtown Las Vegas when the city closed five blocks of Fremont Street, creating a pedestrian mall on which all forms of solicitation and leafletting were banned. In 2003 the Ninth Circuit held that the downtown mall was still a traditional public forum where any government restriction on free expression would have to be justified under a rigorous strict scrutiny test (*City of Las Vegas v. ACLU*, 333 F.3d 1092). In 2006, the same court ruled that the city's restrictions on solicitation on Fremont Street were unconstitutional because they were *not* content-neutral: some kinds of soliciting were allowed but others were not (*ACLU v. City of Las Vegas*, 466 F.3d 784).

The Ninth Circuit also ruled in 2008 that a private business could not exclude a group from petition signature-gathering on public sidewalks. John Ascuaga's Nugget, a private company, had obtained a permit from Sparks, Nev., to hold a rib cook-off in a public area. When a group of individuals tried to gather signatures on a petition there, they were told that the area was now private because of the permit, and law enforcement escorted them out. The court said that the group had been completely excluded "for no reason other than the asserted right of the permittees to exclude anyone expressing a political message," and this is a First Amendment violation (*Dietrich v. John Ascuaga's Nugget*, 548 F.3d 892).

Another controversy concerning privatized once-public sidewalks arose in Salt Lake City. In 2002, the Tenth Circuit held that the sidewalks along a recently-closed portion of Main Street in Salt Lake between the Mormon Temple Square and the church's administrative complex are still a public forum. Ruling in *First Unitarian Church et al. v. Salt Lake City Corp.* (308 F.3d 1114), the court held that the Church of Jesus Christ of Latter-day Saints could not ban expressive activities on the sidewalks even though the city sold the street to the church. After buying that block of Main Street, the church converted it into an "ecclesiastical park." The city retained a pedestrian easement to assure that the sidewalks would remain open to the public. The church left the sidewalks open but banned traditional free expression activities such as leafletting, soliciting, picketing and demonstrating for various causes.

The ban was challenged by several local organizations, backed by the ACLU. They argued that a city cannot terminate the public-forum status of downtown sidewalks by selling the street and sidewalks to a church. The court agreed, concluding that the area within the public sidewalk easement retained its status as a free-speech zone. "The city cannot create a 'First Amendment-free zone.' Their attempt to do so must fail," the court held.

Later the city and the church reached an agreement under which the city abandoned the public sidewalk easement altogether, allowing the church to control or forbid expressive activities there, while the city received two acres of land elsewhere in return. The church agreed to build a $5 million recreation center on the two acres. That arrangement was upheld by the Tenth Circuit (*Utah Gospel Mission v. Salt Lake City Corp.*, 425 F.3d 1249, 2005).

Still another aspect of the problem of First Amendment rights on private property led to an important Supreme Court decision in 1994: the question of local ordinances that forbid property owners to place signs containing political messages on their own property. In *City of Ladue v. Gilleo* (512 U.S. 43), the Supreme Court overturned an ordinance in Ladue, Mo. (a suburb of St. Louis) that barred almost all signs in the front yards of private homes.

The case arose when a Ladue woman, Margaret Gilleo, put up a sign in her yard protesting the Persian Gulf War in 1990. It was stolen, so she put up another sign. Someone knocked

Focus on...
The law of license plates

You might not think that license plates would generate much First Amendment law, but perhaps surprisingly, there have been several cases in the appeals courts, and one that made it all the way to the Supreme Court. In *Wooley v. Maynard* (430 U.S. 705, 1977) the Court said that New Hampshire could not require its citizens to display the state motto, "Live Free or Die," on their license plates if they have moral objections to that sentiment.

FIG. 15. License plates, Ardovino's Desert Crossing, New Mexico.

Photo by Lourdes Cueva Chacón. Used with permission.

In 2008, the Seventh Circuit held in *Choose Life Illinois v. White* (547 F.3d 853) that Illinois could constitutionally exclude *all* points of view on abortion from its plates, and in 2004, the Fourth Circuit in *Rose v. Planned Parenthood of South Carolina* (361 F.3d 786) said that South Carolina could not issue "Choose Life" plates without allowing the other side of the debate a similar forum. A federal district court in South Carolina said that a state law requiring the issuing of "I Believe" license plates violated the constitutional separation of church and state (*Summers v. Adams*, 669 F. Supp. 2d 637, 2009).

But in other venues, the outcome was different. The Eighth Circuit said in 2009 in *Roach v. Stouffer* (560 F.3d 860) that Missouri could not discriminate based on the viewpoint of the speaker when approving applications for specialty plates. The Ninth Circuit agreed in 2008 and said that Arizona had created a public forum in its plates and could not discriminate in that forum in *Arizona Life Coalition v. Stanton* (515 F.3d 956). The Sixth Circuit also said in 2006 that Tennessee would have to issue plates in *ACLU of Tennessee v. Bredesen* (441 F.3d 370). The Third Circuit said in 2010 that New Jersey's rejection of the plates may be unconstitutional viewpoint discrimination in *Children First Foundation Inc. v. Legreide* (373 Fed. Appx. 156) and remanded the case. In 2010, the Second Circuit overturned Vermont's ban on plates that referred to religion or deities as unconstitutional viewpoint discrimination (*Byrne v. Rutledge*, 623 F.3d 46). The Supreme Court has so far declined to review any of these decisions.

But there is a lighter side to license plate law. In 2009, a Colorado vegan woman was blocked from displaying a plate announcing her love of a certain soybean product: "ILVTOFU." And the Nevada Supreme Court allowed the vanity plate "HOE," stating that the online Urban Dictionary's definition of the word as slang for "prostitute" was an insufficient reason to deny the plate, which the driver claimed was short for "Tahoe" (*Nev. Dept. of Motor Vehicles v. Junge*, No. 49350, 2009).

that sign down, and she reported this vandalism to police. She was then told her signs were illegal and she sued, alleging that the city was violating her First Amendment rights. After a lower court ordered the city not to enforce its sign ordinance, Gilleo placed a sheet of paper in a window that read, "For Peace in the Gulf." That, too, was probably a violation of Ladue's rules, but it didn't matter: the Supreme Court ruled that the town's strict sign ordinance was unconstitutional. The court said this ban on almost all yard signs precluded an entire category of speech, thereby violating the First Amendment. The court conceded that Ladue could ban most commercial signs in front yards (but not "for sale" signs: see Chapter Thirteen for a discussion of that issue). However, this ordinance went too far by censoring all political and religious messages that might be conveyed in yard signs.

But a St. Louis sign ordinance failed a constitutional challenge in 2011. The Eighth Circuit said in *Neighborhood Enters., Inc. v. City of St. Louis* (644 F.3d 728) that the ordinance was content-based and could not be justified under strict scrutiny. The ordinance, said the court, makes "impermissible distinctions based *solely* on the content or message conveyed by the sign." Thus, a strict scrutiny standard of review applies, and the ordinance failed the test because it was not narrowly tailored nor are the city's goals of promoting traffic safety and aesthetics sufficiently compelling.

■ PRIOR RESTRAINTS AND ABORTION PROTESTS

Between the 1980s and the 2000s, the controversy over abortion led to new conflicts concerning the scope and meaning of the First Amendment. The abortion debate continues to rage; in June 2010, the *New York Times* reported that at least 11 states had passed laws regulating or restricting abortion so far that year. Congress, the courts and state and local governments have all become involved in the emotion-charged debate not only about abortion itself but also about the methods used by demonstrators who oppose abortions. There are several related questions involved. Under what circumstances may demonstrations near medical clinics be restricted? When may demonstrations that target the homes of doctors and other clinic workers be restricted? When does the First Amendment protect the fiery rhetoric of abortion foes? And may the federal anti-racketeering law be used against a group that espouses a cause such as the idea that abortion is morally wrong?

The Supreme Court first addressed the question of whether a town may ban demonstrations near the homes of doctors and other abortion workers in a 1988 case, *Frisby v. Schultz* (487 U.S. 474). In this case the town of Brookfield, Wisc., a suburb of Milwaukee, banned demonstrations near private homes after anti-abortion protesters picketed several times in front of a doctor's home. Sandra Schultz and other anti-abortion demonstrators sued Russell Frisby and other town officials, charging that the ordinance violated their First Amendment rights. The Court affirmed Brookfield's right to ban targeted picketing at a specific private home. In essence, the majority held that while residential streets in general are a public forum, the space in front of a specific home is not. That means a city must allow protesters to walk down residential streets carrying signs, but if they stop and linger too long near one particular residence, that conduct is not protected by the First Amendment. If a local government wishes to do so, then, it may forbid targeted picketing at someone's home. The Court based its decision largely on the idea that a person is entitled to a certain amount of privacy and freedom from harassment in his or her own home. Writing for the Court, Justice Sandra Day O'Connor said:

> The First Amendment permits the government to prohibit offensive speech as intrusive when the "captive" audience cannot avoid the objectionable speech.... The target of the focused picketing banned by the Brookfield ordinance is just such a "captive." The resident is figuratively, and perhaps literally, trapped within the home, and because of the unique and subtle impact of such picketing is left with no ready means of avoiding the unwanted speech.

In the years since *Frisby v. Schultz* was decided, the controversy over abortion demonstrations has become even more heated. Some anti-abortion groups have launched major campaigns targeting the homes of doctors and others who work at clinics that perform abortions. By 2006, many cities had adopted restrictions on picketing individual homes patterned after the Brookfield ordinance, and the courts, including the Supreme Court, ruled on anti-abortion protest questions in many new cases.

During the 1990s many cities and states—and eventually Congress—passed laws to curtail demonstrations not only near clinic workers' homes but also near clinics where abortions are performed. In 1994, Congress enacted the Freedom of Access to Clinic Entrances (FACE) Act, which prohibits protesters from blocking access to abortion clinics or intimidating patients and employees. First offenses carry fines of up to six months in prison and $10,000 fines. Those convicted of repeated violations of the law could face life imprisonment and fines of up to $250,000.

Almost as soon as the new federal law went into effect, anti-abortion demonstrators challenged it in court. Among other things, they contended that it unduly restricts their First Amendment freedoms and violates the ban on cruel and unusual punishments in the Eighth Amendment by imposing such severe sentences on persons who are doing nothing more than civil rights and antiwar demonstrators did in the 1960s: engaging in civil disobedience as an act of conscience. In 1995, those arguments were rejected in two federal appellate court decisions, *Woodall v. Reno* (47 F.3d 656) and *American Life League v. Reno* (47 F.3d 642). Deciding the two cases together, the Fourth Circuit ruled that the FACE Act does *not* violate the First Amendment because it targets only unprotected acts such as obstructing doorways, not activities protected by the First Amendment such as peaceful picketing.

But in 2008, the Ninth Circuit held that the First Amendment rights of anti-abortion activists were infringed when they were ordered to leave the site of a middle school they were circling with a truck emblazoned with enlarged images of aborted fetuses. In *Center for Bio-Ethical Reform v. Los Angeles County Sheriff Dept.* (533 F.3d 780), the court said that police violated the First Amendment when they required the activists to remove their truck from an area adjacent to the middle school. There was some disruption to normal school activities, but the court said that it was not acceptable to remove the speakers just when they started to get reactions from their intended audience. The Supreme Court denied *cert.*

The Center, however, lost in the Sixth Circuit in 2011 on a challenge to a "Rightwing Extremist" policy they allege was part of a report from the Department of Homeland Security. The plaintiffs claimed that the government engaged in a "policy of targeting certain individuals and groups…for disfavored treatment based on their viewpoint on controversial political issues[.]" A federal district court denied the claim, and the Sixth Circuit affirmed, saying that, in addition to not having established that such a policy even exists, the plaintiffs had not shown injury "that would deter a person of ordinary firmness from further participation in constitutionally protected activity" (*Center for Bio-Ethical Reform, Inc. v. Napolitano*, 648 F.3d 365). Both an *en banc* review by the Ninth Circuit and *cert* at the Supreme Court were denied.

Censoring "The Nuremburg Files"

The FACE Act was also the basis for a controversial appellate court decision in 2002 that upheld part of a large monetary judgment against anti-abortion activists and also affirmed a judge's order censoring a website that allegedly advocated violence against abortion workers.

Ruling in *Planned Parenthood of the Columbia/Willamette v. American Coalition of Life Activists* (290 F.3d 1058), the Ninth Circuit ruled on a 6-5 vote that the judgment did not violate the First Amendment rights of anti-abortion activists. The case involved a website named

"The Nuremburg Files" that called abortion doctors "baby butchers" and included names, home addresses and license plate numbers as well as names of spouses and children of some doctors who performed abortions. If such a doctor was killed, as three who were depicted in "wanted" posters on the website had been, the site showed a line through the doctor's name.

When a group of abortion providers sued under the FACE Act, a federal jury awarded $107 million in actual and punitive damages. Over the objections of five dissenters, the six-judge majority on the Ninth Circuit upheld the actual damages but ordered the trial court to reconsider the amount of the punitive damages. The majority also upheld an injunction by the trial judge ordering some of the "wanted" posters taken down, an order that was undisputedly a prior restraint of communications on a controversial public issue.

Eleven judges participated instead of the usual panel of three because the court was reconsidering the case *en banc.* Earlier, a three-judge panel of the Ninth Circuit had upheld the website and posters as protected speech in a ruling that was set aside by the *en banc* decision. The majority ruled that the language of the website constituted "true threats" to health care workers even though there were no explicit threats on the site. Writing for the majority, Judge Pamela Rymer said a true threat is one "where a reasonable person would foresee that the listener will believe he will be subjected to physical violence upon his person, (and) is unprotected by the First Amendment." She added, "It is not necessary that the defendant intend to, or be able to carry out the threat; the only requirement for a true threat is that the defendant intentionally or knowingly communicate the threat."

In three separate opinions, the dissenters said the majority was weakening the First Amendment by its dismissal of the free expression rights of abortion foes. Judge Alex Kozinski, joined by four judges, wrote: "While today it is abortion protesters who are singled out for punitive treatment, the precedent set by this court... will haunt dissidents of all political stripes for many years to come." In another dissenting opinion, Judge Marsha Berzon said the abortion foes who faced this large monetary penalty "have not murdered anyone." She added, "neither their advocacy of doing so nor the posters and website they published crossed the line into unprotected speech.... If we are not willing to provide stringent First Amendment protection and a fair trial to those with whom we as a society disagree as well as those with whom we agree...the First Amendment would become a dead letter."

Supreme Court Rulings on Abortion Protests

Prior to the "Nuremburg Files" decision, the activities of abortion protesters near clinics led to three U.S. Supreme Court decisions, all of which required the Court to balance the rights of protesters against those of clinic patrons and staff. The Supreme Court handed down a fourth decision on the rights of abortion protesters in 2003.

In a 1994 case, the Supreme Court upheld a Florida court's injunction ordering demonstrators to stay 36 feet away from the entrances to an abortion clinic (*Madsen v. Women's Health Center,* 512 U.S. 753). In that case, the Supreme Court's 6-3 majority, in an opinion by Chief Justice William Rehnquist, said the 36-foot buffer zone was not an undue restriction on demonstrators' First Amendment rights.

However, in *Madsen* the Supreme Court overturned several other parts of the Florida court order, including a provision that barred demonstrators from approaching patients anywhere within 300 feet of the clinic. The Court also overturned a portion of the Florida order that banned demonstrations within 300 feet of the residences of clinic workers. Rehnquist said that was too broad a restriction on the First Amendment rights of anti-abortion demonstrators, although a smaller buffer zone around workers' homes, coupled with limits on the time and duration of residential demonstrations, might be acceptable. The Supreme Court also overturned a portion of the Florida court order that prohibited demonstrators from displaying "images observable" by patients in the clinic. Rehnquist said the complete ban on signs was overly broad, although a ban on signs carrying threats might be acceptable. On the other hand, Rehnquist's opinion upheld a part of the Florida order that banned excessive noise during abortion protests.

In 1997, the Supreme Court went further to protect the First Amendment rights of anti-abortion demonstrators, overturning a New York judge's order that required them to stay 15 feet away from clinic patrons and workers. Ruling in *Schenck v. Pro-Choice Network* (519 U.S. 357), an 8-1 majority of the Court held that demonstrators have a right to approach patrons on public sidewalks. The Court overruled the judge's order establishing a 15-foot "floating bubble" around patrons that abortion protesters could not enter. But the Court upheld another part of the judge's order that created a 15-foot no-demonstration zone around clinic entrances. Again writing for the Court, Chief Justice Rehnquist emphasized that picketing, leafletting and even loud protesting are "classic forms of speech that lie at the heart of the First Amendment." Rehnquist noted that sidewalk protesters have no right to grab, push or stand in the way of persons going to abortion clinics, but he also said the New York judge's ban on approaching patrons or workers was overly broad: "We strike down the floating buffer zones around people entering and leaving clinics because they burden more speech than is necessary" to protect the free flow of traffic and public safety.

In ruling on all of these specific restrictions on demonstrations, the Supreme Court held that they were *content neutral* (that is, they would apply to everyone, regardless of the issue addressed by demonstrators). Therefore, the restrictions were valid unless they imposed a greater burden on First Amendment freedoms than was necessary to serve a *significant government interest*. The Court's majority concluded that there was a significant government interest in protecting the safety of clinic workers and patients, and in assuring that they could enter and leave the clinic freely. The Court held that small buffer zones around clinic entrances are sufficient to accomplish those goals, and that larger buffer zones or floating buffer zones around clinic patrons or workers create an undue burden on free expression.

Lower federal courts applied these principles similarly in cases decided after *Schenck v. Pro-Choice Network*. For example, in 1997 the Ninth Circuit overturned several provisions of a Phoenix city ordinance in *Sabelko v. City of Phoenix* (120 F.3d 161), including a requirement that protesters step back eight feet from clinic patients and workers even when they were much farther than 15 feet from a clinic entrance. The court ruled similarly in overturning a Santa Barbara, Calif. ordinance that established an eight-foot floating buffer zone around clinic workers and patients (*Edwards v. City of Santa Barbara*, 150 F.3d 1213, 1999).

In 2000, however, the Supreme Court *upheld* a Colorado state law that included an eight-foot floating buffer zone. Ruling in *Hill v. Colorado* (530 U.S. 703), the Court's 6-3 majority said the Colorado law was narrowly tailored enough to pass constitutional muster. The law established a 100-foot zone around every health care facility's entrance. Inside that perimeter, no one could distribute leaflets, display signs or engage in sidewalk counseling within eight feet of another person unless that person consented to being approached. Displaying signs within the perimeter, but not within eight feet of any person, was legal.

After first ruling that the Colorado law was content neutral, the Court held that it was a valid time, place and manner regulation of speech. The Court noted that protest signs can be read, and normal conversations can occur, at a distance of eight feet. The Court called that distance a "normal conversational distance." The Court said the ban on approaching people does not prevent leafletting because a protester can stand in one place and hand out leaflets as people approach the person doing the leafletting.

"This statute simply empowers private citizens entering a health care facility with the ability to prevent a speaker, who is within eight feet and advancing, from communicating a message they do not wish to hear," Justice John Paul Stevens wrote for the Court. In short, the majority in *Hill* said this floating buffer zone is sufficiently different from the one over-turned in *Schenck* to be constitutional.

Buffer zones were before the circuit courts several times in 2009. The First Circuit left intact a 35-foot buffer zone as a valid time, place and manner regulation in *McCullen v. Coakley* (571 F.3d 167), saying that it was content-neutral, sufficiently narrowly tailored, and left open ample alternative channels of communication. However, the Third Circuit struck down a two-layer protest zone scheme in *Brown v. City of Pittsburgh* (586 F.3d 263). That court said that the two zones together, a buffer zone of 15 feet from facility entrances and a "bubble zone" of 100 feet in which protestors could not come closer than eight feet to an individual, made it impossible for those who wished to hand out leaflets to reach their audiences: "With the Ordinance's multi-zone restrictions, not only are leafletters unable to stand within fifteen feet of clinic entrances, but they are constrained from moving freely even outside of that protective zone." The Third Circuit said in *McTernan v. City of York* (577 F.3d 521) that a handicapped ramp leading to a Planned Parenthood clinic was off-limits to anti-abortion protestors. Because the protestors were able to gather on the sidewalk next to the ramp and access all clinic visitors, the state had a public interest in keeping the ramp safe for handicapped patrons, and the ramp was a non-public forum, the court rejected the plaintiffs' claims that their freedom of speech and religion were chilled.

An Oakland ordinance modeled after the Colorado one survived part of a challenge in 2011 in *Hoye v. City of Oakland* (653 F.3d 835). The Ninth Circuit upheld the "bubble ordinance" itself but said that the way in which it was enforced violated the First Amendment because it affected the anti-abortion speakers but not the escorts walking with clients to the clinics. And, the court said, the ordinance had been applied "only to efforts to persuade women approaching reproductive health clinics *not* to receive abortions or other reproductive health services, and *not* to communications seeking to encourage entry into the clinic for the purpose of undergoing treatment." This discriminatory enforcement is content-based, so the court sent the case back to fashion a remedy to ensure equal enforcement.

In 2003, the Supreme Court ruled, in *Scheidler v. National Organization for Women* (537 U.S. 393), that the federal Racketeer Influenced and Corrupt Organizations (RICO) Act cannot ordinarily be used by abortion providers to win treble damages and nationwide injunctions against abortion foes.

Those who demonstrate near clinics that perform abortions can still be sued under the Freedom of Access to Clinic Entrances (FACE) Act. However, that law lacks a treble damage provision and requires abortion foes to be sued state by state.

The high court ruled 8-1 that abortion protesters, even if they block clinic entrances with the ultimate goal of shutting down a clinic, are not normally guilty of the kind of "predicate offense" such as extortion that is required to bring a case under RICO. The decision effectively ends nearly 20 years of litigation by NOW and other abortion backers against the Pro-Life Action League and Operation Rescue, two anti-abortion groups, under RICO.

Several other groups that have demonstrated for various causes, including People for the Ethical Treatment of Animals (PETA), supported the anti-abortion groups, fearing that they, too, could be sued under the treble damages provisions of RICO.

Chief Justice William H. Rehnquist wrote the Court's majority opinion in *Scheidler*, saying that the holding should not affect the usefulness of RICO as a weapon to fight organized crime. In a concurring opinion, Justice Ruth Bader Ginsburg, joined by Stephen Breyer, said RICO could have also been used against civil rights demonstrators during the 1960s under the broad reading of RICO urged by abortion supporters.

Some years earlier, the Supreme Court ruled on another right-to-demonstrate question: the right to picket near a foreign government's embassy in Washington, D.C. In *Boos v. Barry* (485 U.S. 312, 1988), the Court overturned some provisions of a Washington, D.C. local ordinance aimed at preventing embarrassing demonstrations outside foreign embassies.

The Court held that Congress, in passing local ordinances to govern Washington, could not forbid picket signs that might say embarrassing things. Writing for the majority, Justice Sandra Day O'Connor said, "The display clause of (the ordinance) is unconstitutional on its face. It is a content-based restriction on political speech in a political forum, and it is not narrowly tailored to serve a compelling state interest." However, the Court affirmed another part of the ordinance requiring protesters to stay 500 feet away from the embassy that is the target of the picketing if police believe they pose a threat to the security of the embassy.

■ OTHER PICKETING AND RELATED ISSUES

If picketing in front of a private home can be banned to avoid disrupting the lives of the occupants, is it possible to ban other First Amendment activities that might be disruptive, inconvenient or embarrassing to an unwilling audience? The U.S. Supreme Court has addressed that kind of question several times.

In 1971 the Supreme Court was confronted with such a prior restraint issue in the case of *Organization for a Better Austin v. Keefe* (402 U.S. 415). Jerome Keefe was a real estate broker who allegedly engaged in "blockbusting" tactics in the community of Austin, near Chicago, Ill. That is, he was accused of attempting to panic white residents into selling at low prices to escape an influx of blacks that he claimed were moving into their neighborhoods. The Organization for a Better Austin (OBA), trying to halt this white flight, began circulating fliers attacking Keefe for his "panic peddling" tactics. Keefe got a court order that prohibited the OBA from distributing its fliers or picketing. The order was affirmed by an Illinois appellate court, and OBA appealed to the U.S. Supreme Court. The Supreme Court invalidated the injunction, noting that peaceful pamphleteering is protected by the First Amendment, and its prohibition is a prior restraint.

The Supreme Court has dealt with somewhat more difficult First Amendment problems in a series of cases involving the Hare Krishna movement, cases reminiscent of the early Jehovah's Witness cases.

In a 1981 case, *Heffron v. International Society for Krishna Consciousness* (452 U.S. 640), the Court had to decide how much access to a state fair Hare Krishna believers should have.

Like members of the Jehovah's Witness movement, Hare Krishna adherents believe their faith requires them to distribute literature and solicit donations from the public. Krishna members have attempted to promote their faith and solicit funds in many public places where people gather, often citing the earlier Jehovah's Witness cases to support their right to do so. The *Heffron* case arose when Krishna members were refused permission to distribute literature and solicit funds freely at the Minnesota State Fair. They were told they could only do so at a single booth. Under the fair's rules, booths were available to all groups on a non-discriminatory first-come, first-served basis.

The Krishna movement challenged the rules as a violation of the First Amendment, and the case eventually reached the U.S. Supreme Court. Krishna followers argued that distributing literature and soliciting funds are actually part of the movement's religious ritual, required of all members. To limit these activities is a violation of the First Amendment as interpreted in the *Schneider* and *Lovell* cases (discussed earlier), they contended. Minnesota fair officials conceded that Krishna followers, like Jehovah's Witnesses or anyone else, have a constitutional right to propagate their views at the state fair. However, they said it was necessary to restrict all such groups to booths to keep the fair orderly.

The Supreme Court majority agreed. The Court said it is not a violation of the First Amendment to require Krishna followers to practice their religion at a booth rather than at large throughout the state fair. The majority opinion pointed out that Krishna members remained free to mingle with the crowd and orally present their views, but it upheld the rule limiting solicitations and literature distribution to individual booths at the fair. The Court explained that if the Krishnas were allowed to proselytize throughout the fairgrounds, all other groups would have to be given the same privilege.

Access to Public Airports

If religious pamphleteering can be curtailed at government-sponsored events such as a state fair, can it also be restricted at other government-owned facilities where it might be disruptive, such as major airports?

The Supreme Court has addressed that issue in two cases inspired by the activities of Hare Krishna believers. In a 1987 case, *Board of Airport Commissioners v. Jews for Jesus* (482 U.S. 569), the Court overturned a rule adopted by the government agency in charge of Los Angeles International Airport that flatly prohibited all First Amendment activities at this government-owned facility.

After lower courts overruled several earlier attempts by the airport commissioners to ban literature distribution by Hare Krishna believers, the board adopted a complete ban on all First Amendment activities at the airport. Under this rule a clergyman associated with Jews for Jesus, an evangelical Christian organization, was barred from distributing leaflets there. The Jews for Jesus organization decided to challenge the validity of the ban on First Amendment grounds.

The high court unanimously held that the regulation was so sweeping as to be unconstitutional on its face. Writing for the Court, Justice Sandra Day O'Connor said almost any traveler might violate such an all-encompassing ban on First Amendment activities—by doing something as commonplace as talking to a friend or reading a newspaper, for instance. However, the Court did not rule out the possibility that more narrowly drawn regulations limiting the time, place and manner of literature distribution might pass constitutional muster. Nonetheless, federal judges repeatedly rejected later ordinances intended to regulate soliciting at Los Angeles International Airport. After Sept. 11, 2001, however, very little space at the airport was left open to the general public, and in 2006 a federal judge upheld post-Sept. 11 regulations that limited soliciting to only a few areas. In 2010 the California

Supreme Court declined to say whether the Los Angeles airport was a public forum (*International Society for Krishna Consciousness of California, Inc. v. City of Los Angeles*, 48 Cal. 4th 446).

In 1992 the Supreme Court had ruled on another case resulting from Hare Krishna members' First Amendment activities at airports. This time the Court ruled that soliciting donations can be banned, although handing out literature must be permitted at appropriate places in public airports. Ruling in *Lee v. International Society for Krishna Consciousness* (505 U.S. 830), a 6-3 majority of the Court held that Hare Krishna members could be barred from fund-raising at the New York area's public airports. Five of the justices also agreed that unlike city streets and parks, airports are not traditional public forums for First Amendment activities. However, in a separate opinion the Court ruled by a 5-4 vote that airports must still be open for First Amendment activities that are less intrusive than soliciting money (for example, handing out free literature).

By holding that distributing literature, but not soliciting money, at airports is protected by the First Amendment, the Court was following the pattern set two years earlier in a case involving U.S. Post Offices: *U.S. v. Kokinda* (497 U.S. 720, 1990). In that case, the Court upheld regulations of the Postal Service that prohibit all soliciting at post offices. The case began when several representatives of the National Democratic Policy Committee were criminally prosecuted for setting up a table to distribute literature and solicit contributions at the Bowie, Md. post office.

In a 5-4 decision that produced a strongly worded dissent by Justices Brennan, Marshall, Blackmun and Stevens, the Court upheld regulations that banned soliciting (but not all First Amendment activities) at post offices. Writing for the Court, Justice O'Connor said Postal Service regulations forbidding soliciting were justified because soliciting at post offices had often caused disruptions that interfered with the mail service. Post offices had never been First Amendment forums, she concluded, adding: "Whether or not the Service permits other forms of speech, it is not unreasonable for it to prohibit solicitation on the ground that it inherently disrupts business by impeding the normal flow of traffic."

Justice Anthony Kennedy concurred in the outcome of the case, but on a different rationale. He said post offices may well be public forums, but he also said the ban on soliciting was a reasonable time, place and manner restriction on free expression—and therefore valid. The four dissenting justices said they thought post offices were public forums and that in their view the ban on soliciting was *not* a reasonable time, place and manner restriction.

As a result of these cases, fund-raising can be prohibited not just at airports and post offices but also at many other government-owned facilities that are open to the public but are not traditional public forums. However, governments must allow other First Amendment activities such as literature distribution at many of these same places. And there is still a First Amendment right to solicit donations at places that *are* traditional public forums—subject only to the authorities' right to impose reasonable restrictions on the time, place, and manner of free expression activities.

On the other hand, purely private facilities such as shopping centers are not ordinarily First Amendment forums. First Amendment activities may usually be banned in such places whenever the owners choose to do so. Of course, if the owners wish to allow free expression activities—or if a state chooses to require the owners to allow such activities—they can occur on private property even though the United States Constitution does not guarantee literature distribution rights on private property.

FIG. 16. Shirley Phelps-Roper of the Westboro Baptist Church surrounded by counter-protesters in Long Beach, Calif., Feb. 2010.

*Photo by
Christine Amarantus.
Used with permission.*

The Supreme Court has ruled on one other aspect of literature distribution rights that should be noted here: the right to distribute unsigned political literature. In an important 1995 case, *McIntyre v. Ohio Elections Commission* (514 U.S. 334), the high court overturned laws in almost every state that banned the distribution of anonymous political handbills. Based on the idea that anonymous political "hit pieces" are unfair, inaccurate and often libelous, most states have had laws requiring that political literature carry the originator's name and address. But in the 1995 decision, the Court held that the concern about possible fraud and libel in unsigned political literature did not justify such a sweeping restriction on First Amendment rights. Ohio's ban on unsigned leaflets applied even to those that were completely truthful, the Court noted. Under the *McIntyre* decision, there is now a constitutional right to distribute unsigned political literature. In 2002, the high court concluded that this right also undergirds the right to do door-to-door non-commercial soliciting without first obtaining a city permit. Any permit requirement compels canvassers to give up their constitutionally protected anonymity, as the Court noted in *Watchtower Bible and Tract Society v. Village of Stratton*, discussed earlier.

Access to Parades, Public Places and Organizations

Another issue that stirred controversy in recent years has been the question of whether privately sponsored parades and fairs that are held on public property are First Amendment forums open to all viewpoints, or whether the sponsors have a First Amendment right to decide who will participate. A focal point of this debate has been the efforts of homosexual groups to participate in St. Patrick's Day parades. In New York, the Ancient Order of Hibernians, a Roman Catholic fraternal organization, sponsors the nation's oldest formal St. Patrick's Day parade: it was first held in 1762. Based on their religious beliefs, the Hibernians have refused to allow gay and lesbian groups to join the parade, which annually attracts as many as 150,000 participants and two million spectators. In 1993, a federal judge ruled that the Hibernians have a First Amendment right to exclude groups with whom they disagree.

On the other hand, the largest St. Patrick's Day parade in Boston has been sponsored by veterans' groups rather than a religious group, and in 1994 the veterans were ordered by a Massachusetts court to include a gay and lesbian group in the parade under a state law guaranteeing gay men and lesbians equal access to public facilities. The veterans' groups decided to cancel the parade instead. In 1995, they replaced the St. Patrick's Day Parade, in which marchers traditionally have carried green banners, with a protest march in which the marchers carried black flags to protest the court order. Meanwhile, the veterans also appealed to higher courts. The Massachusetts Supreme Court upheld the lower court's order, but in 1995 the U.S. Supreme Court disagreed and ruled in favor of the veterans.

In *Hurley v. Irish-American Gay, Lesbian and Bisexual Group of Boston* (515 U.S. 557), the Supreme Court ruled unanimously that the veterans' groups have a First Amendment right to choose which other groups they will include in their parade. Writing for the Court, Justice David Souter said the state could not use its public accommodations law to force a private group to admit anyone with whom it disagreed to a parade. He said that a parade by nature is an expressive activity and noted, "One important manifestation of the principle of free speech is that one who chooses to speak may also decide what not to say."

Souter noted the "enlightened purpose" of the public accommodations law (to prevent discrimination against gay men and lesbians), but said the state cannot force a private organization to alter its own message. Souter also added that individual gay men and lesbians are entitled to march in the parade as members of any group that is admitted to the parade, and that gay men and lesbians are certainly free to conduct their own parade on city streets (and presumably, to exclude veterans' groups if they wish).

A related issue has arisen concerning groups such as the Boy Scouts of America, an organization that has traditionally barred homosexuals from being scoutmasters. Do state laws guaranteeing equal access to public facilities or forbidding discrimination against homosexuals by business enterprises apply to private organizations? How can those laws be reconciled with a private organization's First Amendment freedom of association rights? Also, do these laws require the Boy Scouts to admit members who are unwilling to take the Scouts' oath affirming a belief in God?

The U.S. Supreme Court ruled on this issue in a widely anticipated 2000 decision, *Boy Scouts of America v. Dale* (530 U.S. 640). The Court's 5-4 majority ruled that the Boy Scouts may exclude gays as troop leaders, declaring that a private organization has the right to set its own moral code and espouse a viewpoint. In so ruling, the high court overturned a New Jersey Supreme Court decision that said the Boy Scouts had to allow gay scoutmasters under that state's law banning discrimination in public accommodations.

Writing for the Court, Chief Justice William Rehnquist said the Boy Scouts have a First Amendment right to freedom of association, including the right to include or exclude persons based on their beliefs or their sexual orientation. Thus, the Scouts could exclude James Dale, a one-time Eagle Scout and assistant scoutmaster who was dismissed after Scout leaders learned he was gay. "It appears that homosexuality has gained greater societal acceptance. But this is scarcely an argument for denying First Amendment protection to those who refuse to accept those views," Rehnquist wrote.

In 1996, the U.S. Supreme Court addressed another issue that touched upon the constitutional rights of gay men and lesbians and their critics. Although it is not a First Amendment case as such, it should be noted here. In *Romer v. Evans* (517 U.S. 620), the Court overturned a Colorado ballot initiative banning state and local laws giving legal protection to the rights of gay men and lesbians. The initiative was approved by a majority of Colorado voters in 1992. In a 6-3 ruling, the Court said a state cannot single out a group for "disfavored treatment" based on "animosity." Writing for the majority, Justice Anthony Kennedy said that the ballot initiative "classifies homosexuals not to further a proper legislative end but to make them unequal to everyone else. This Colorado cannot do." This decision does not necessarily guarantee gay men and lesbians equal rights in all areas of the law. But it was the first time the Court overturned a law intended to legalize discrimination against them.

On the other hand, in 1998 the Supreme Court declined to review a decision of the Sixth Circuit *upholding* a Cincinnati, Ohio, city charter provision that eliminated special protections for gay men and lesbians. The Cincinnati charter provision ruled out "any claim of minority or protected status, quota preference or other preferential treatment" for gay men and lesbians (*Equality Foundation of Greater Cincinnati v. City of Cincinnati,* 128 F.3d 289).

The Respect for America's Fallen Heroes Act was passed in 2006 and prohibits protests within 300 feet of the entrance of any cemetery under the control of the National Cemetery Administration from an hour before to an hour after a funeral. Many states have similar laws, passed in response to protests by the Westboro Baptist Church (WBC). The church, based in Topeka, Kansas, made headlines when it picketed the funerals of those who are gay or have gay affiliations, or those of soldiers who served in the armed forces under the theory that the Lord is punishing America for its evils. When Missouri passed its law banning protests at funerals, members of the church filed suit, claiming that their First Amendment rights were infringed. In 2008, the Eighth Circuit found that the church was likely to be able to prove that even though the Missouri law was content neutral, it was also likely to be overbroad, and enjoined the enforcement of the law, permitting the church's funeral pickets to continue until the law is fully evaluated. In *Phelps-Roper v. Nixon* (545 F.3d 685), the court said that the church "presents a viable argument that those who protest or picket at or near a military funeral wish to reach an audience that can only be addressed at such occasion and to convey to and through such an audience a particular message."

The Eighth Circuit's decision conflicts with the Sixth Circuit's 2008 conclusion in *Phelps-Roper v. Strickland* (529 F.3d 356), where that court said that a similar Ohio funeral protest law was content neutral, sufficiently narrowly tailored and served an important governmental interest; the Supreme Court declined to hear an appeal in *Nixon*.

The church continues to appear in court to challenge funeral protest ordinances. Two 2011 Eighth Circuit decisions struck down funeral protest laws, one a local ordinance in Manchester, Mo. (*Phelps-Roper v. City of Manchester,* 658 F.3d 813) and the other the Nebraska state law (*Phelps-Roper v. Troutman,* 662 F.3d 485). The court relied in both cases on its precedent in *Nixon.* Judge Diana Murphy, concurring in both decisions, nonetheless suggested in *Troutman* that "resolution of the competing legal interests arising in [*Nixon*] should be reconsidered by the full court."

The Supreme Court stepped into the fray in 2011, agreeing 8-1 with the Fourth Circuit that the WBC's funeral picketing activities and website (www.godhatesfags.com) were protected under the First Amendment. Albert Snyder's son, Marine Lance Cpl. Matthew A. Snyder, was killed in Iraq in the line of duty, and the members of the church picketed his Maryland funeral. The picketers complied with regulations and police directions, and Snyder did not see the protest until after the funeral when it was shown on local television.

In *Snyder v. Phelps* (131 S. Ct. 1207), Chief Justice John Roberts wrote that the content of the signs displayed by WBC protestors related to matters of public, rather than private, interest, as those signs focused on political and moral questions, and the protest was not intended as a private assault on the Snyder family, as WBC had been protesting funerals for some time. Because the WBC members followed all police rules as to where they protested and did not interfere with the funeral itself, the distress felt by the family was a result of the content of the signs. "What Westboro said, in the whole context of how and where it chose to say it, is entitled to 'special protection' under the First Amendment, and that protection cannot be overcome by a jury finding that the picketing was outrageous," wrote Chief Justice Roberts.

Justice Samuel Alito, writing in dissent, pointed out that the WBC could have chosen anywhere in Maryland or Washington, D.C. in which to protest, and the fact that they chose Snyder's funeral made the protest personal and was done to increase publicity. He concluded, "In order to have a society in which public issues can be openly and vigorously debated, it is not necessary to allow the brutalization of innocent victims like [the Snyder family]."

While there are federal and state funeral protest laws on the books, in the wake of Snyder, at least one bill was proposed to revise a federal law: the Safe Haven for Heroes Act would prohibit protests for five hours before and five hours after a military funeral and will limit protests to 2,500 feet from the funeral facility. However, this law may be too broad to pass constitutional muster, given that several months prior to the Supreme Court's decision, a federal judge in Missouri struck down that state's funeral protest law, which called for no protests for one hour before and one hour after the funeral and limited protests to 300 feet from ceremonies and processions (*Phelps-Roper v. Koster*, 734 F. Supp. 2d 870).

The Supreme Court has also addressed the question of when government regulations concerning the use of a public place such as a park become a form of censorship. In *Thomas v. Chicago Park District* (534 U.S. 316), the high court in 2002 upheld the reasonableness of Chicago's rules for deciding whether to grant permits to demonstrators seeking to stage an event in a public park. The Court ruled unanimously that the city's 13-point guidelines,

FIG. 17. A Ten Commandments monument at the Texas Capitol Building, similar to the one in Pleasant Grove City, Utah.

Geoff Nelson / Shutterstock. com

which require groups of more than 50 people to prove they have insurance, among other requirements, does not violate the First Amendment because it applies equally to all groups regardless of their viewpoint. Chicago officials defended the policy as necessary to assure fair access to local parks by individuals as well as large groups.

Writing for the Court, Justice Antonin Scalia said, "The licensing scheme at issue here is not subject-matter censorship but content-neutral time, place and manner regulation of the use of a public forum." He added, "The picnicker and soccer player, no less than the political activist or parade marshal, must apply for a permit if the 50-person limit is to be exceeded." The case was initiated by advocates of legalizing marijuana who frequently applied for permits to demonstrate in Chicago parks, sometimes gaining permission but sometimes being denied a permit.

The Supreme Court ruled on another access issue in 2006, upholding the Solomon Amendment, a federal law requiring colleges and universities to allow military recruiting if they receive federal funds and allow other recruiters. On many campuses, military recruiters had been barred because of the military's "don't ask, don't tell" policy toward homosexual service personnel. A coalition of law schools and law professors argued that they have a First Amendment right to decide who recruits on campus, and to bar recruiters who will not sign a non-discrimination pledge.

In *Rumsfeld v. Forum for Academic and Institutional Rights* (547 U.S. 47), Chief Justice John Roberts offered a three-part analysis of the First Amendment question. Writing for a unanimous Court, he said the Solomon Amendment does not require law schools or their faculties to speak in favor of military service. Nor does it prevent them from speaking against military service. Also, Roberts said there is little likelihood that students would mistakenly assume a college or university endorses any particular recruiter's policies merely because that recruiter is allowed on campus along with many others.

Roberts wrote: "Nothing about recruiting suggests that law schools agree with any speech by recruiters, and nothing in the Solomon Amendment restricts what the law schools may say about the military's policies. We have held that high school students can appreciate the difference between speech a school sponsors and speech the school permits because legally required to do so, pursuant to an equal access policy... Surely students have not lost that ability by the time they get to law school." (In *Board of Education of Westside Community Schools v. Mergens*, 496 U.S. 226, a 1990 case, the Court upheld the right of a Bible study group to meet on campus if other extra-curricular groups are granted that right.)

A different kind of access issue is presented by the permanent installation of monuments in public parks. The Supreme Court entered the controversy in a 2009 case called *Pleasant Grove City v. Summum* (555 U.S. 460). At issue was whether Corky Ra, founder of Summum, a religion whose goal it is "to help you liberate and emancipate you from yourself," could force Pleasant Grove City, Utah, to display a monument containing the "Seven Aphorisms of Summum" because the city had already accepted other monuments, including one of the Ten Commandments. The Supreme Court said that the city did not have to display the Summum monument because the placement of a permanent monument in a city park was a form of *government speech* and not subject to the First Amendment.

Relying on cases involving government-sponsored speech like *Johanns v. Livestock Marketing Association* (discussed in Chapter Thirteen), Justice Samuel Alito, speaking for a unanimous Court, said, "Permanent monuments displayed on public property typically represent government speech." Government need not maintain neutrality when it speaks, and government speech does not receive First Amendment scrutiny. Even if the monuments that Pleasant Grove City accepted were funded privately, the city engaged in selectivity in the choice of those monuments and did not open the park in which they were installed to all monuments. A federal judge in 2010 dismissed a followup lawsuit against Pleasant Grove alleging an establishment clause violation by the city for allowing the Ten Commandments monument.

Access to National Landmarks

In the 2000s, court have been asked whether government restrictions on speech around national monuments or in national parks unduly restrict speech. In 2010, the Third Circuit threw out the conviction of religious protester Michael Marcavage after he refused to move away from the Liberty Bell at a National Park Service ranger's request. Applying strict scrutiny, the court found that the government had not narrowly tailored its response to him, particularly given that there were other groups gathered at the Bell, and did not exercise the least restrictive means of dealing with his speech (*U.S. v. Marcavage*, 609 F.3d 264).

Marcavage made an appearance in the Seventh Circuit in 2011 as well, as part of a protest he organized in Chicago during the 2006 Gay Games (*Marcavage v. City of Chicago*, 659 F.3d 626). He alleged that he was restricted from entering three areas during the Games because he did not obtain a permit. The court threw out two of the three complaints and remanded the third back to the lower court to evaluate whether Marcavage's First Amendment rights had been violated. The court said that because of the location of the third area, Gateway Park near the Navy Pier, it may be that "the imposition of burdensome restrictions for small groups…might be overreaching."

Similarly, the D.C. Circuit struck down as overbroad the rules governing protests in national parks in 2010 (*Boardley v. U.S. Dept. of the Interior*, 615 F.3d 508). Michael Boardley and his group distributed free religious tracts in a "free speech zone" in Mount Rushmore National Park, and they were told by a ranger that they needed a permit; they left and applied for one but never received a response. When he filed suit, he then received the permit, but continued the suit on the grounds that the speech rules were too broad. The appellate court agreed: "The Constitution does not tolerate regulations that, while serving their purported aims, prohibit a wide range of activities that do not interfere with the Government's objectives," the court wrote. The court listed a number of speech acts, ranging from Girl Scout meetings to teachers taking students on field trips, that would require permits even though they do not interfere with government interests.

On the other hand, a regulation prohibiting chalking messages on the street in front of the White House was found to be constitutional because it was intended to prohibit defacement of public and private property in a content-neutral way, said the D.C. Circuit in 2011 (*Mahoney v. Doe*, 642 F.3d 1112). Rev. Patrick Mahoney requested permission for a chalk demonstration against abortion in 2008. He was allowed to bring banners and signs but was prohibited from chalking 1600 Pennsylvania Avenue NW, in front of the White House. The appellate court said that the chalking ban was a reasonable time, place and manner restriction because it was content neutral and served an important government interest in preserving the aesthetics of public property. Judge Brett Kavanaugh, concurring in the judgment, further noted, "No one has a First Amendment right to deface government property. No one has a First Amendment right, for example, to spray-paint the Washington Monument or smash the windows of a police car."

How about silent dancing in the Jefferson Memorial rotunda? No, said the D.C. Circuit in 2011. Mary Brooke Oberwetter and her friends refused to stop "silent expressive dancing" inside the Jefferson Memorial, saying she was observing Thomas Jefferson's birthday. She was arrested under National Park Service regulations that prohibit demonstrations without a permit, defined as "picketing, speechmaking, marching, holding vigils or religious services and all other like forms of conduct … which has the effect, intent or propensity to draw a crowd or onlookers."

The court pointed out that "there is no question that [Oberwetter] had the right to dance in order to express her admiration for Mr. Jefferson. Of course she did. But the question this case presents is whether she had the right to perform her dance inside the Jefferson Memorial." The court said she did not, because the Jefferson Memorial is "a space with a solemn commemorative purpose that is incompatible with the full range of free expression that is permitted in public forums" (*Oberwetter v. Hilliard*, 639 F.3d 545).

In 2012 President Obama signed the Federal Restricted Buildings and Grounds Improvement Act of 2011. The law criminalizes impeding or disrupting the conduct of government business or official functions in or near "any restricted buildings or grounds"—including the White House and vice president's residence, anywhere the president or others protected by Secret Service are or will be temporarily visiting, or an event of national significance. Critics call it the "anti-Occupy law" and allege that the breadth and vagueness of the law may well render it unconstitutional.

Newsrack Ordinances

Another difficult First Amendment issue concerns newsracks on public property. Many states and cities have adopted laws regulating the size and placement of newsstands on sidewalks, for instance. Some have banned newsracks altogether. This has produced a variety of conflicting court rulings. In 1988, the Supreme Court squarely addressed this issue for the first time, and in so doing handed the news media a significant victory.

In *City of Lakewood v. Plain Dealer Publishing Co.* (486 U.S. 750), the Court voted 4-3 to overturn a Lakewood, Ohio, ordinance that gave the town's mayor broad discretion to grant or deny publishers' requests to place newsstands on public sidewalks. The Court ruled that newsracks are a legitimate form of expression in a public forum protected by the First Amendment, and a city may not base decisions to grant or deny newsrack space on the content of the publication. The mayor of Lakewood, a suburb of Cleveland, rejected the *Cleveland Plain Dealer's* request to place newsracks at 18 locations in the town. The newspaper argued that the decision was arbitrary and violated the First Amendment.

Focus on…
True threats

In June 2009, the FBI arrested Internet radio host and blogger Hal Turner for threats against three Seventh Circuit judges for their decision upholding handgun bans.

According to a DOJ press release, Turner wrote on his blog, "Let me be the first to say this plainly: These Judges deserve to be killed." He posted their photographs, phone numbers, work address and room numbers, and information about the building in Chicago in which they work.

Turner also noted that another judge who had decided a case against a white supremacist found her husband and mother murdered in their home, saying, "Apparently, the 7th U.S. Circuit court didn't get the hint after those killings. It appears another lesson is needed."

Turner claimed he was trained as an agent provocateur by the FBI. Two trials ended in deadlock, and he was convicted in a third in August 2010.

Writing for the majority, Justice William Brennan acknowledged that a city could flatly prohibit all newsracks, but he said a city may not ban some while permitting others based on arbitrary decisions about their content. The Supreme Court remanded the case to determine if the Lakewood ordinance would be valid if the provisions allowing discrimination based on content were deleted.

Justice Byron White and two others joined in a vigorous dissenting opinion that compared newsracks to soft-drink vending machines and questioned their right to enjoy First Amend-

Focus on...
Is it protected? 2012 edition

Courts have construed many activities to have expressive components and thus to be under the First Amendment's purview. Here are a few of the odder freedom of expression questions that courts have been asked to address.

FIG. 18. Scenes of open gambling in Reno, Nevada casinos: game of faro, Oct. 8, 1910.

Library of Congress, Prints and Photographs Division, [LC-USZ62-64634].

Horn-honking: Helen Immelt parked outside a neighbor's house at 6:00 a.m. and honked her horn for 10 minutes in protest of her homeowners' association's order not to raise chickens in her yard. The Washington Supreme Court (*State v. Immelt,* 173 Wn.2d 1, 2011) overturned the ordinance as overbroad, saying that "it prohibits a wide swath of expressive conduct in order to protect against a narrow category of public disturbances." Dissenters said that the horn-honking was not really expressive speech, but merely "noise—loud noise."

Texas hold-em poker: The Second Circuit said that at least in the case of *AK Tournament Play v. Town of Wallkill* (444 Fed. Appx. 475, 2011), the plaintiffs had not made a sufficient case to extend First Amendment protection to a poker club. "Even assuming *arguendo* that there might be *some* circumstances under which a poker club's activities could involve sufficiently expressive or political content to merit protection under the First Amendment," said the court, the plaintiffs had not established them here.

Weddings on Hawaiian beaches: In *Kaahumanu v. Hawaii* (2012 U.S. App. LEXIS 11391), a wedding planner alleged that certain regulations governing weddings on public Hawaiian beaches were unconstitutional. The Ninth Circuit said that although wedding ceremonies clearly have First Amendment protection, most regulations were acceptable. The court did say that the state agency's power to modify or rescind a permit at any time for any reason was unconstitutional.

Access to federal horse roundups: Photojournalist Laura Leigh brought suit against the Bureau of Land Management for restrictions on her access to a horse gather in Nevada (*Leigh v. Salazar,* 668 F.3d 1126, 2012). The Ninth Circuit remanded the case to the lower court to determine whether the public has a First Amendment right of access to such roundups and if the regulations Leigh cited were appropriate. The lower court had not engaged in sufficient scrutiny of the facts.

Bonus! Are motorcycle burnouts free speech? Suck Bang Blow, a Myrtle Beach, S.C. biker bar, says yes and has brought the matter to federal court over an ordinance banning burnouts, which will hear arguments in May 2013.

ment protection. White said the majority's reasoning would, in effect, force many cities to allow private companies to do business on the public sidewalks.

In 1993, the Supreme Court went even further in upholding the right to distribute literature in newsracks on public property. In *Cincinnati v. Discovery Network* (507 U.S. 410), the Court said the city of Cincinnati could not flatly ban newsracks for commercial literature while allowing newspaper vending machines. City officials ordered Discovery (the publisher of a free magazine describing adult educational and recreational courses) and the publishers of a free real estate magazine to remove 62 newsracks from city property. Meanwhile, the city allowed more than 2,000 newspaper vending machines to remain on public property.

Voting 6-3, the Court rejected the city's contention that the free flyers could be banned because they were merely commercial speech. The Court ruled that commercial speech enjoys considerable First Amendment protection, and cannot be banned by a government agency unless the agency has a reasonable basis for doing so.

The Court rejected Cincinnati's argument that banning the 62 commercial newsracks would enhance the appearance of the city at a time when the city was not acting to remove 2,000 newspaper stands. The commercial speech aspects of this case are discussed in Chapter Thirteen.

Numerous lower courts have addressed these issues. In 2002, for instance, the Ninth Circuit upheld Honolulu's right to limit the number of newsracks and to award newsrack space by lottery. The court said the city's system was content neutral and a valid time, place and manner restriction—justified by the city's desire to avoid visual clutter while providing alternate channels of communication (*Honolulu Weekly v. Harris*, 298 F.3d 1037). The Fourth Circuit came to the same conclusion in 2010, finding a public airport's total ban on newsracks to be a significant harm to newspaper publishers' protected expression (*News and Observer v. Raleigh-Durham Airport Auth.*, 597 F.3d 570).

In 2012, the Fifth Circuit upheld the city of Houston's newsrack ordinance against a First Amendment challenge, saying it was content-neutral and carefully tailored to meet city aesthetic concerns (*Lauder, Inc. v. City of Houston*, 670 F.3d 664).

■ ANONYMOUS SPEECH

Increasing numbers of litigants have been willing to go to court to protect their anonymity—or to discover others' identities to sue them for libel or copyright infringement. In the 1990s and beyond, courts, including the Supreme Court, have been asked to wrestle with whether and when to unmask anonymous speakers.

As noted earlier, the Supreme Court's lead case in anonymous speech is *McIntyre v. Ohio Elections Commission*, in 1995, in which the Court struck down laws that prohibited the dissemination of anonymous campaign literature. But how does this endorsement of the right to remain anonymous apply to the online environment, particularly when there is a lawsuit at stake? Recent cases address anonymity in several online and offline contexts.

Online Anonymity

The case that is often considered to be the lead case in whether to require an online anonymous speaker to be revealed is the 2001 case of *Dendrite International, Inc. v. Doe* (775 A.2d 756). Dendrite, a pharmaceutical sales and support company, wanted the identity of an anonymous online poster to a Yahoo! message board so that the company could sue the person for libel. The New Jersey court denied Dendrite's claim and provided a five-part test for revealing the identity of an anonymous entity: First, the plaintiff must attempt to notify the anonymous poster, including by posting on the original message board. Second, the plaintiff must identify allegedly actionable statements made by the defendant. Third, the plaintiff must provide a basis on which to bring suit, such as libel. Fourth, the plaintiff must provide evidence for that claim, and finally, the court should "balance the defendant's First Amendment right of anonymous free speech against the strength of the *prima facie* case presented and the necessity for the disclosure of the anonymous defendant's identity to allow the plaintiff to properly proceed." (*Prima facie* is Latin for "at first sight," and it means obvious or self-evident.) In this case, the court said there was no evidence to suggest that Dendrite had been harmed or its stock prices reduced due to the false anonymous postings.

In the first such ruling by a state's highest court, the Delaware Supreme Court in 2005 upheld the right of Internet bloggers to speak anonymously. In *John Doe No. 1 v. Cahill* (884 A.2d 451), the court, using a modified version of the *Dendrite* test, said bloggers have a First Amendment right to anonymity unless someone suing a blogger has a clearly valid case, rejecting a local official's attempt to identify bloggers who criticized him on a newspaper-sponsored blog site. The Delaware court likened bloggers to the political pamphleteers who won Supreme Court decisions protecting their anonymity. Other courts are adopting or adapting this approach; for example, in 2008, a Maryland appeals court found that a plaintiff had not made a strong enough defamation case against five anonymous bloggers to compel their identification (*Independent Newspapers Inc. v. Brodie*, 966 A.2d 432).

In the late 2000s, the number of cases dealing with anonymous online speech exploded, with courts adapting elements from tests in cases like *Dendrite* and *Cahill*. A few cases are offered here, but there are many more. In 2009, the District of Columbia appeals court added a requirement that plaintiffs make the case that the information they are seeking is truly important for their cases in *Solers, Inc. v. Doe* (977 A.2d 941). A software industry association investigated Solers, a defense industry software company, in response to an anonymous tip to determine whether it was using pirated software. Although the industry association found no wrongdoing, Solers filed a complaint against the anonymous tipster. The court dismissed Solers' claim and said that the plaintiff must "determine that the information sought is important to enable the plaintiff to proceed with his lawsuit." Also in 2009, model Liskula Cohen was able to discover the identity of an anonymous blogger whom she wanted to sue for defamation for writing about her on a blog entitled "Skanks of NYC" (*Cohen v. Google, Inc.*, 887 N.Y.S.2d 424). The New York court said that to unmask an anonymous defendant, the plaintiff must make a *prima facie* showing of a "meritorious cause of action." (This case's libel actions will be discussed in Chapter Four.)

In 2010, the New Hampshire Supreme Court also explicitly endorsed the *Dendrite* test in a case involving an online service that gathers and posts online information about mortgage lenders, saying that it did not have to reveal the identity of an anonymous poster. The court said in *Mortgage Specialists Inc. v. Implode-Explode Heavy Industries Inc.* (999 A.2d 184), "We hold that the qualified privilege to speak anonymously requires the trial court to 'balanc[e]...the equities and rights at issue,' thus ensuring that a plaintiff alleging defamation has a valid reason for piercing the speaker's anonymity." The court remanded the case to the trial court to apply the *Dendrite* standard.

But courts differ in their willingness to apply these emerging tests. In 2010, a divided Illinois appeals court reversed a lower court's dismissal of a plaintiff's petition to reveal an anonymous source, ordering a news organization to reveal the anonymous poster. In *Maxon v. Ottawa Publishing Co.* (929 N.E.2d 666), the majority said that an Illinois rule made the application of the *Dendrite/Cahill* test unnecessary. The dissent claimed that the *Dendrite/Cahill* test "adds a crucial extra layer of protection to anonymous speech" and is "designed to protect the identity of those participating in non-actionable anonymous speech." And the Second Circuit adopted a test from a New York federal district court in determining whether to reveal the identity of an anonymous filesharer: "(1) [the] concrete[ness of the plaintiff's] showing of a prima facie claim of actionable harm... (2) [the] specificity of the discovery request... (3) the absence of alternative means to obtain the subpoenaed information... (4) [the] need for the subpoenaed information to advance the claim, ...and (5) the [objecting] party's expectation of privacy" (*Arista Records LLC v. Doe 3*, 604 F.3d 110, 2010).

But what if a news organization decides to *reveal* the identity of an anonymous online commenter? A Cleveland newspaper settled with an Ohio judge after it revealed her identity in 2010. Cuyahoga County Court of Common Pleas Judge Shirley Strickland-Saffold and her daughter, Sydney, sued the *Cleveland Plain Dealer* for defamation, breach of contract, and invasion of privacy after the *Plain Dealer* divulged that the pseudonym "lawmiss" connected to the judge's e-mail address was the source of comments about cases currently before her court (the Ohio Supreme Court removed the judge from one of those, a serial murder case). The judge claimed that her daughter and ex-husband were the authors of those comments.

However, the Ninth Circuit applied a reduced level of protection to anonymous commercial communication in 2011. In what was primarily a procedural case between Amway (formerly Quixtar) and Signature Management TEAM, a company that provides support materials like books and motivational speaker appearances to those who sell Amway products, the court said that the district court's application of the strict standard established in *Cahill* (a political speech case) went too far in protecting anonymous commercial speech. "[W]e suggest that the nature of the speech should be a driving force in choosing a standard by which to balance the rights of anonymous speakers in discovery disputes," the court said (*In re Anonymous Online Speakers*, 661 F.3d 1168).

Could this be the start of a trend in which courts evaluate different types of online anonymous speech differently? If so, the anonymity of participants on sites like Yelp and Urbanspoon, in which users review restaurants and shops, could be in danger. At least one district court in the Ninth Circuit has applied the distinction (*Cornelius v. DeLuca*, 39 Media L. Rep. 1660) but protected the anonymity of an online poster, saying that the post "is deserving of more protection than mere commercial speech but less than speech that lies at the heart of First Amendment values, such as religious or political speech."

Not every court follows the *Dendrite/Cahill* standard, believing it to be an unnecessary addition to the law. In considering whether clothing company Façonnable could obtain the identities of anonymous editors of a Wikipedia site that alleged that Façonnable was a supporter of militant group Hezbollah, a federal district court in Colorado said instead that "existing procedures, applied with a heightened sensitivity to any First Amendment implications, is the correct approach" to determine when anonymous speakers can be unmasked. The court ordered online service provider Skybeam to provide the identities; however, Skybeam was granted an emergency stay to avoid the disclosure. Then Façonnable voluntarily dismissed the case. The court later vacated the original order so as not to prejudice Skybeam in other cases (*Façonnable USA Corp. v. John Does 1-10*, 799 F. Supp. 2d 1202).

Twitter and Facebook have both been subpoenaed to turn over identifying information on some of their users (Twitter in a Boston case dealing with an Occupy Boston protest case; Facebook in Great Britain having to do with abusive messages posted about a woman's support of an X Factor candidate). Some states are considering bills to combat anonymous online posting. In New York, such a bill, introduced in 2012, would mandate that website administrators, if asked, "shall remove any comments posted on his or her web site by an anonymous poster unless such anonymous poster agrees to attach his or her name to the post and confirms that his or her IP address, legal name, and home address are accurate."

Offline Anonymity

While offline anonymity is not nearly as hot a legal topic as its online counterpart, the Supreme Court in 2010 again stepped into the debate in *Doe v. Reed* (130 S. Ct. 2811). At issue was whether the First Amendment is violated when a state compels public release of identifying information about petition signers—in this case, those who had signed an anti-gay rights petition in Washington state.

The Court said that as a general rule, disclosure of names under the Washington public records act is not a free speech violation, but disclosure could be problematic in some cases based on their facts. The plaintiffs in this case will be able to bring their case to the lower court again. The case is discussed in more depth in Chapter Nine.

■ DISCRIMINATORY TAXATION AS CENSORSHIP

One of the oldest forms of government control over the media is discriminatory taxation. Authorities in seventeenth- and eighteenth-century England used taxes to control the press. One of the major grievances of the colonists before the revolutionary war was the Stamp Act, which singled out newspapers and legal documents for heavy taxation. Taxes may be burdensome for everyone, but if governments can levy high taxes on the news media and exempt other kinds of businesses, governments can force crusading news organizations into bankruptcy—or force them to become docile to avoid punitive taxation.

For many years after independence, attempts to single out newspapers for special taxes were rare in America, but a classic example of such a tax cropped up in the 1930s. And during the 1980s and 1990s, there were repeated lawsuits charging that various tax schemes singled out the media for unfair treatment in violation of the First Amendment.

In 1936, just five years after its landmark *Near v. Minnesota* decision, the Supreme Court decided *Grosjean v. American Press* (297 U.S. 233). This case arose because Louisiana, dominated by Governor Huey "Kingfish" Long's political machine, had imposed a special tax on the 13 largest papers in the state, 12 of which opposed Long. The tax applied to total advertising receipts of all papers and magazines with a circulation over 20,000 copies per week.

The newspapers challenged the tax and a federal court issued an order barring the tax as a violation of the First Amendment. The Supreme Court heard the case on appeal and unanimously affirmed the lower court. In an opinion by Justice George Sutherland, the Court said the First Amendment was intended to prevent prior restraints in the form of discriminatory taxes. Sutherland noted that the license tax acted as a prior restraint in two ways. First, it would curtail advertising revenue, and second, it was designed to restrict circulation. The Louisiana tax, Justice Sutherland said, was "not an ordinary form of tax, but one single in kind, with a long history of hostile misuse against the freedom of the press."

The Supreme Court has overturned three other state tax systems that improperly singled out the media for unconstitutional taxation. In 1983, the Court overturned a Minnesota plan that taxed some—but not all—newspapers.

Minnesota created a "use" tax on the ink and newsprint used by newspapers in 1971. But after some of the smaller papers complained of the economic hardship the tax caused, the legislature rewrote the law to exempt the first $100,000 in newsprint and ink each newspaper purchased annually. Thus, the law in effect exempted small newspapers or, to put it another way, singled out large newspapers for a special tax. By 1974, one newspaper company—the *Minneapolis Star & Tribune*—was paying about two-thirds of the total amount the state collected from all Minnesota newspapers through this tax. Citing the *Grosjean* precedent, the *Star & Tribune* company challenged the constitutionality of the tax.

In *Minneapolis Star & Tribune v. Minnesota Commissioner of Revenue* (460 U.S. 575, 1983), the Supreme Court voted 8-1 to overturn Minnesota's tax on ink and newsprint. Justice Sandra Day O'Connor, writing for the Court, warned that because such a tax "targets a small group of newspapers," it "presents such a potential for abuse that no interest suggested by Minnesota can justify the scheme." Justice William Rehnquist dissented, arguing that the use tax in question was less of a burden than the normal sales tax paid by other businesses. (Minnesota had exempted newspapers from the state sales tax, a practice that was then common in other states as well.) Rehnquist said the state was actually conferring a benefit on the press, something the states may do without violating the First Amendment.

In 1987 the Supreme Court overturned another state taxation scheme that singled out some media for taxes not paid by others. This case involved an Arkansas sales tax that applied to general interest magazines but not to newspapers or to specialized magazines (e.g., religious, professional, trade and sports publications). In *Arkansas Writers' Project v. Ragland* (481 U.S. 221), the Supreme Court ruled the tax unconstitutional, relying on much the same rationale as in the *Minneapolis Star & Tribune* case.

In fact, the Court said the Arkansas tax was even more flagrantly unconstitutional than the one in Minnesota because it required government officials to base a tax break on the *content of the media.* "[O]fficial scrutiny of the content of publications as the basis for imposing a tax is entirely incompatible with the First Amendment's guarantee of freedom of the press," Justice Thurgood Marshall wrote for the majority. Thus, any tax giving some media favorable treatment while not extending the benefit across the board is unconstitutional. However, the Court did not rule out the possibility that a state could impose a tax on *entire categories of media,* taxing all newspapers while exempting all magazines, for instance.

The ruling produced a strong dissent from Justices Antonin Scalia and William Rehnquist (by then the Chief Justice). Scalia said that instead of promoting press freedom, the ruling would actually undermine other government tax breaks based on content, such as subsidies of public broadcasting, educational publications and the arts in general.

In 1989, the Supreme Court continued in this pattern by overturning a Texas tax system that granted sales tax exemptions to religious books, magazines and newspapers but not to secular publications. In *Texas Monthly v. Bullock* (489 U.S. 1), the majority ruled that the Texas tax scheme was unconstitutional because it violated the First Amendment's requirement of separation of church and state. In effect, the tax break was an unconstitutional state action to subsidize religion, they ruled. In a separate opinion, Justice Byron White said the tax scheme was invalid because it violated the First Amendment's free-press guarantees.

On the other hand, in 1991 the Supreme Court again made it clear that the media are subject to the same taxes as other businesses—as long as the tax does not improperly single out the media. Ruling in *Leathers v. Medlock* (499 U.S. 439), the Court voted 7-2 to uphold an

Arkansas sales tax that applied to cable and satellite television services—as well as to utilities, hotels and other businesses. Writing for the Court, Justice Sandra Day O'Connor said this tax was not like the taxes on the media that the Court had previously overturned: "There is no indication in this case that Arkansas has targeted cable television in a purposeful attempt to interfere with its First Amendment activities." Justices Thurgood Marshall and Harry Blackmun dissented, arguing that this kind of sales tax could be used to inhibit freedom of expression. They were especially troubled by the fact that the tax applied to pay-TV services but not to newspaper and magazine subscriptions.

A week after it upheld the Arkansas cable tax, the Supreme Court disposed of three other cases involving taxes on the media. The Court declined to review state court decisions on media taxes in Tennessee and Iowa. But in the third case, *Miami Herald v. Dep't of Revenue* (499 U.S. 972), the high court issued an order directing the Florida Supreme Court to reconsider the validity of a sales tax on magazines but not newspapers. The state court complied with the U.S. Supreme Court's order—and again ruled that the state cannot tax just magazines. Such a tax is improper because it is based on the content, the court ruled in 1992 (*Dep't of Revenue v. Magazine Publishers of America*, 604 So.2d 459).

To summarize, these Supreme Court decisions on media taxation basically say that the media may not be taxed in a discriminatory fashion. If some media must pay a tax that does not apply to others based on their content or their size, the tax is unconstitutional. But if the tax applies across the board to similar media—and especially if it applies to other businesses—it is valid.

■ OTHER PRIOR RESTRAINT QUESTIONS

The twentieth century was a time of government regulation, an era when many forms of activity were brought under government supervision for the first time. When the targeted activity involved the communication of ideas or information, however, the regulation has often been challenged as a violation of the First Amendment. This has forced the nation's courts—and ultimately the Supreme Court—to look at government control of expressive activities of many kinds. This section summarizes some key questions.

Censorship and Financial Information

Does the federal government have the right to prohibit the publication of newsletters offering advice to stock market investors by people with questionable backgrounds, or does the First Amendment protect the right to publish such newsletters? How about lawyers giving bankruptcy advice to clients; can that be regulated?

The newsletter question was raised in a 1985 Supreme Court decision, *Lowe v. Securities and Exchange Commission* (472 U.S. 181). Under the federal Investment Advisers Act, the SEC is empowered to regulate the dissemination of investment advice, even when the advice is in the form of a publication that would seem to be protected by the First Amendment. The act exempts "*bona fide*" newspapers and magazines. Christopher Lowe was convicted of mishandling a client's funds, and the SEC canceled his registration as an investment adviser. However, he continued to publish a financial newsletter. When the SEC tried to stop him from publishing his newsletter, he argued that he had a First Amendment right to publish it.

The Court ruled that Lowe's newsletter was in fact a *bona fide* publication and therefore exempt from regulation by the SEC. But writing for the majority, Justice John Paul

Stevens noted that Lowe's newsletter contained disinterested investment advice intended for numerous readers, not personalized advice for specific individual clients. The Court said the SEC *could* regulate those who give individualized advice, as opposed to publishers who offer their analyses of various investments to a general audience. Thus, Lowe qualified as a *bona fide* publisher, not as an investment adviser.

In short, the Court liberally interpreted the Investment Advisers Act's exemption for *bona fide* publications, and thereby avoided the First Amendment implications of the act's restrictions on giving investment advice. The Court did not resolve the question of when the right to communicate opinions about the stock market is protected by the First Amendment.

However, a year after it lost *Lowe* at the Supreme Court, the SEC abandoned many of its efforts to regulate publications and broadcasts that give investment advice or discuss economic issues. Nevertheless, the SEC continued to act against financial publications that allegedly published misleading information that might affect the stock market. In 1988, the SEC lost such a case in the U.S. Court of Appeals, *SEC v. Wall Street Publishing Institute Inc.* (851 F.2d 365). That firm, the publisher of *Stock Market Magazine,* was accused of publishing articles that were little more than corporate "flackery" (as a federal judge put it)— uniformly flattering articles that were written by the companies or their public relations agencies.

The SEC wanted a court order requiring *Stock Market Magazine* to disclose the origin of these articles. The appellate court ruled that neither the SEC nor the courts can delve into the sources or origins of magazine articles without violating the First Amendment. However, the appellate court did send the case back to a trial judge to determine whether some of the articles might have been paid advertising disguised as news. The court said that if the magazine was accepting payment for publishing the articles, the SEC might have the authority to force the magazine to disclose that fact. Accepting payment to publish an article would make the article a form of advertising; it should be identified as such.

In contrast, the government can constitutionally put limitations on bankruptcy advice. In 2010 the Supreme Court decided *Milavetz, Gallop & Milavetz v. U.S.* (130 S. Ct. 1324), holding that prohibitions on bankruptcy advisers giving certain types of advice to their clients contained in the Bankruptcy Abuse Prevention and Consumer Protection Act (BAPCPA) did not run afoul of the First Amendment. At issue was BAPCPA's provision barring debt relief services from advising clients to incur more debt for filing for bankruptcy; a law firm filed a pre-enforcement suit to request that the court say that it was not a debt relief agency and could advise its clients to incur additional debt.

Justice Sonia Sotomayor, writing for the Court, said that attorneys who provide bankruptcy advice are considered debt relief agencies for the purpose of BAPCA. Moreover, the law does not overburden speech, as it regulates only one form of legal advice: recommending that clients incur more debt in advance of filing for bankruptcy. She added, "[I]t is hard to see how a rule that narrowly prohibits an attorney from affirmatively advising a client to commit this type of abusive prefiling conduct could chill attorney speech or inhibit the attorney-client relationship."

Rock Concerts and the First Amendment

If motion pictures are protected from direct government censorship by the First Amendment, what about rock concerts? May a city restrict the sound levels at rock concerts in a city park without violating the First Amendment? In 1989, the Supreme Court ruled on this question in *Ward v. Rock Against Racism* (491 U.S. 781). For a number of years a group called Rock Against Racism sponsored annual concerts at a bandshell in New York City's Central Park. The group drew repeated complaints from other park-goers and nearby residents about the sound level at RAR concerts. Eventually the city set limits on the sound level and placed monitors to measure the sound. When the prescribed volume was repeatedly exceeded during a RAR concert, city officials ordered the sound turned down. The concert promoters refused and were cited for excessive noise several times as the concert continued. The city finally cut off power to the bandshell to halt the concert—and refused to allow RAR to hold future concerts in Central Park. RAR sued the city.

The Supreme Court acknowledged that rock music is a form of expression protected by the First Amendment. However, the city's limits on sound level were a reasonable time, place and manner restriction. The majority said the city's policy has "no material impact on any performer's ability to exercise complete artistic control over sound quality." The Court conceded that the city's use of its own technician to control sound levels was not the least intrusive means of achieving the goal (i.e., keeping the volume down). The city could have continued to monitor sound levels, issue citations, and halt concerts if the sound level remained too high. In earlier cases, governments had been required to use the least intrusive means of regulating time, place and manner. However, the Court dropped that requirement and said that it is no longer necessary that time, place and manner restrictions on First Amendment freedoms be as non-intrusive as possible.

Dissenting, Justices Marshall, Brennan and Stevens objected to the broad sweep of the Court's decision: "Until today, a key safeguard of free speech has been government's obligation to adopt the least intrusive restriction necessary to achieve its goals. By abandoning the requirement that time, place and manner regulations must be narrowly tailored, the majority replaces constitutional scrutiny with mandatory deference (to local officials' decisions)."

The Court's decision settled the question of regulation of sound levels at rock concerts: the sound level may be limited—and government employees may be placed in charge of the equipment to make sure the limits are observed—without that violating the First Amendment. However, that does not mean government officials are free to control other aspects of performances at government-owned amphitheaters and arenas. For example, when officials in Burbank, Calif., banned all rock concerts while allowing other kinds of performances at a city-owned amphitheater, the Ninth Circuit overturned that action as a First Amendment violation (*Cinevision Corp. v. City of Burbank*, 745 F.2d 560, 1984).

Censoring Computer Encryption Software

Another prior restraint controversy involves government restrictions on the distribution and especially the export of computer encryption software—software that allows computer messages to be encoded so unauthorized persons cannot read them. The federal government imposed these restrictions out of fear that terrorists or others who might threaten national security could use the encryption technology to engage in secret communications that could not be intercepted and monitored by law enforcement authorities.

Eventually these export restrictions were undermined by two federal appellate court decisions—and dropped by the federal government itself—in a series of legal actions that extended First Amendment protection to *computer source code* (i.e., the basic computer instructions built into software). Nevertheless, in the aftermath of Sept. 11, 2001, new proposals to restrict encryption technology have been considered by the Justice Department.

In 1999, the Ninth Circuit overturned the original export restrictions in *Bernstein v. U.S. Department of Justice* (176 F.3d 1132). The court rejected the government's concerns that the unregulated spread of encoded messages would aid criminals and terrorists, ruling 2-1 that the restrictions constituted an impermissible prior restraint. The court said the regulations gave virtual veto power to federal bureaucrats to prevent the free distribution of source code needed by cryptography academicians and scientists to exchange ideas about encryption.

Shortly after the original *Bernstein* decision, the Ninth Circuit voted to withdraw the ruling and reconsider the case *en banc*. But then the federal government liberalized the rules concerning the overseas distribution of encryption software. Under the new rules, most limitations on the export of encryption software were dropped, leaving Americans free to export even the most powerful data-scrambling software without an export license. That also left Americans free to post encryption software online—something the federal government had opposed on the ground that it would make encryption software accessible overseas.

Meanwhile, in 2000 another federal appellate court ruled decisively that computer source code, including code used for encryption, is fully protected by the First Amendment. In *Junger v. Daley* (209 F.3d 481), the Sixth Circuit upheld law professor Peter Junger's right to place encryption software on his website, even though that would make it readily accessible to Internet users overseas. Ironically, the federal government had allowed Junger to export his computer law textbook, which contained the same encryption software. But the government refused to authorize him to put the software on his website.

Seizing Criminals' Royalties

Is it an unlawful form of censorship for a state to seize profits or royalties a criminal receives for telling or writing about his/her crimes? Many states and the federal government have laws allowing the authorities to take criminals' publishing profits and give them to the victims of their crimes. These laws are often called *"Son of Sam"* laws because New York's pioneering law of this type was enacted after serial killer David Berkowitz, who called himself by that name, received lucrative offers to tell his story.

The Supreme Court addressed this issue in 1991. The Court held that New York's "Son of Sam" law was unconstitutional because it imposed a special financial burden on communications—based on the content of the message. In *Simon & Schuster v. New York State Crime Victims Board* (502 U.S. 105), the Court said New York would have to show a compelling state interest to justify a law that burdened First Amendment activities in this way—and that the state had failed to do so.

Writing for the Court, Justice Sandra Day O'Connor said the law was "overinclusive" and therefore unconstitutional because it would apply to many legitimate literary works. Had it been in effect in an earlier era, the law would have allowed the state to seize the profits from works such as Henry David Thoreau's *Civil Disobedience*, O'Connor wrote. She added that some other laws of this type might be sufficiently different from New York's law to be valid.

Under the New York law, criminals were required to give up the royalties and profits from books, movies and other communications that in any way concerned their crimes. The money was then placed in a fund to compensate crime victims.

The law was challenged by the publishing house of Simon & Schuster, which paid Henry Hill, a former mafia figure, nearly $100,000 for his story about his life as a mobster who became a government informant. The resulting book, *Wiseguy*, became a best seller and was made into the movie *Goodfellas*. Simon & Schuster was holding another $27,000 that it owed to him when the Crime Victims Board demanded the money. Instead of complying, the publisher challenged the "Son of Sam" law—and prevailed when the Supreme Court declared the law to be unconstitutional.

In the years since the *Simon & Schuster* Supreme Court decision, several states have enacted narrower laws to give crime victims any money earned by convicted felons for telling the stories of their crimes. These laws generally apply only to persons convicted of a crime and are limited to money earned for a specific, detailed account of the crime.

While some of these laws have survived legal challenges, in 2002 the California Supreme Court overturned one in *Keenan v. Superior Court* (27 C. 4th 413). Barry Keenan, who kidnapped Frank Sinatra, Jr., son of the famous vocalist, in 1963, earned a reported $1 million for the movie rights to his story three decades later. The court rejected Sinatra's attempt to seize Keenan's earnings under the California "Son of Sam" law, holding that the law was so broad that it could be used to interfere with the right of authors to profit from works that happen to discuss a crime in detail.

The California legislature responded to the *Keenan* decision by enacting a new law under which victims of violent crimes may sue for damages for *up to 10 years after a felon is discharged from parole*. Previously, victims could only sue for one year from the time a crime was committed. The California law was designed to allow victims to sue criminals without violating the First Amendment right of criminals to sell their stories.

Liability for Inspiring Crimes

Another troubling First Amendment question involves holding the media accountable for crimes committed by readers or viewers who were allegedly inspired by a movie, website, television show, book, news story, magazine article or an advertisement. Although such cases may involve subsequent punishments rather than prior restraints, the issues they raise should be discussed here.

In 1998, the Supreme Court refused to intervene in a case where a book allegedly facilitated a crime: *Rice v. Paladin Enterprises* (128 F.3d 233, 1997). In this case, the publisher of a book called *Hit Man: A Technical Manual for Independent Contractors* was sued by the families of three people who were killed by a man who followed the detailed instructions in *Hit Man*. The publisher sought to have the lawsuit dismissed on First Amendment grounds, but a federal appellate court held that this book, with its "extraordinary comprehensiveness, detail and clarity" in describing how to commit murder, is not exempted from civil lawsuits by the First Amendment. The court held that a publisher can be sued by those who are injured (or the families of those who are killed) in this situation.

The Fourth Circuit called the 130-page book a "step-by-step murder manual, a training book for assassins." Because it was intended to train potential murderers and not merely to entertain, it falls outside the scope of the First Amendment, the court ruled.

After the Supreme Court refused to hear an appeal, Paladin settled. However, the case caused alarm among media organizations. Publishers, broadcasters and filmmakers, among others, had urged the Supreme Court to hear the case, arguing that the same rationale could be used in lawsuits alleging that books, magazines, scientific and military manuals, movies and other media might have inspired or assisted someone who committed a crime.

Similar issues were also raised in several other widely publicized recent cases, including one in which an Oakland, Mich. jury ordered the producers of the *Jenny Jones* television talk show to pay almost $30 million in damages to the family of a man who was killed by another man who had appeared with him on the show. The victim said (on camera) that he had a gay interest in the man who later shot and killed him. In 2002, a Michigan appellate court overturned the jury verdict, holding that the show's producers "had no duty to anticipate and prevent the act of murder committed by (a guest) three days after leaving defendants' studio and hundreds of miles away" (*Graves v. Warner Bros.*, 656 N.W.2d 195).

In 1999, the U.S. Supreme Court declined to intervene in a similar case where a Louisiana appellate court held that the family of a shooting victim could sue the producers of the movie *Natural Born Killers* if they could prove that the producers intended to inspire others to commit violent acts. In *Byers v. Edmonson* (712 So.2d 681), the Supreme Court refused to hear an appeal of the Louisiana court's ruling, which cleared the way for a lawsuit by the family of Patsy Byers, a convenience store clerk who was seriously wounded by a couple who had repeatedly watched *Natural Born Killers* and then went on a crime spree.

The Byers family never proved that filmmaker Oliver Stone and others involved in producing this movie actually *intended* to inspire violent acts by viewers, and a Louisiana judge eventually dismissed the case, ruling that Stone and the movie's distributor were protected by the First Amendment. However, this legal victory, coming only after lengthy (and costly) litigation, does little to protect the media from other lawsuits by crime victims or their families when a crime is committed by someone who watched a movie or television program—or read a book, a news story or a magazine article—about a similar crime.

Although lawsuits alleging that the media inspired a crime are becoming commonplace, this is not a new phenomenon. Nearly a decade before these cases arose, a family sued *Soldier of Fortune* magazine and won a large award because the magazine published an advertisement that led to a murder for hire.

The Eleventh Circuit eventually upheld the award and dismissed the magazine's First Amendment arguments (*Braun v. Soldier of Fortune Magazine*, 968 F.2d 1110, 1992). In 1985, the magazine carried an ad from an unemployed Vietnam veteran who described himself as a "37-year-old professional mercenary (who) is discrete (sic) and very private. Body guard, courier and other special skills. All jobs considered." He accepted an assignment to kill a man in Atlanta and was later caught and convicted of the crime. The family sued the magazine for wrongful death; a jury awarded the family $4.3 million. Publishers and industry groups asked the Supreme Court to grant *cert*, arguing that the case could have a serious chilling effect on First Amendment freedoms, but to no effect.

Animal Cruelty

As the success of organizations like People for the Ethical Treatment of Animals (PETA) demonstrates, the issue of cruelty to animals is a hot political and social topic. In 1992, Congress passed the Animal Enterprise Protection Act (AEPA). The act was intended to punish interference with commerce or commercial activities involving animals for research or testing. In 2009, the Third Circuit in *U.S. v. Fullmer* (584 F.3d 132) upheld its constitutionality. The plaintiffs, a group of animal-cruelty activists, argued that AEPA criminalized the speech on their website. The court said that at least some of the speech on the website was not protected under the *Brandenburg* standard (see Chapter Two), and some of the speech was reasonably considered to be "true threats" because, as the court pointed out, "given the success of the campaign in the past, including the destruction of private property and the telecommunication attacks on various companies, the implied threats were not conditional, and this speech rightly instilled fear in the listeners."

It is rare when an entire category of speech is excluded from First Amendment protection. The Supreme Court declined to do that in 2010 in *U.S. v. Stevens* (130 S. Ct. 1577), in a case involving the sale of videos depicting animal cruelty. Robert Stevens sold videos of pit bulls engaged in dogfighting to law enforcement and was charged under a 1999 federal animal cruelty law, the first person to be so charged. A divided *en banc* Third Circuit struck down the law, saying that it did not advance the government's interest in reducing animal cruelty but merely punished its depiction. Nor could the government demonstrate a compelling interest in regulating the speech.

The Court overturned the law as overbroad. Chief Justice John Roberts, writing for an 8-1 majority, rejected the notion that animal cruelty speech should be outside the protection of the First Amendment based on "an *ad hoc* balancing of relative social costs and benefits." However, Roberts did leave open the notion that a more carefully crafted animal cruelty law might be constitutional. Justice Samuel Alito dissented, saying that he did not think the law overbroad; it contains "a substantial core of constitutionally permissible applications."

At the end of 2010, President Barack Obama signed a law specifically banning at crush videos. Called the Animal Crush Video Prohibition Act of 2010, it criminalizes the creation, sale, and marketing of these videos. The law labels the videos "obscene," which may result in challenges because no sexual acts usually take place in these videos.

Censoring the Arts

As will be discussed in Chapter Ten, the Supreme Court upheld the requirement that National Endowment of the Arts recipients sign anti-obscenity pledges and that grantors of federal funding for artistic endeavors take into account "general standards of decency" in *National Endowment for the Arts v. Finley*. Several recent appellate decisions have addressed other issues of artistic freedom.

The Ninth Circuit, sitting *en banc* in *Berger v. City of Seattle* (569 F.3d 1029, 2009), overturned Seattle's street performance rules for the Seattle Center as prior restraints. "Magic Mike" Berger, a balloon artist and street performer, alleged that the rules requiring all performers to get permits, wear badges, perform only in certain areas and not verbally solicit donations violated the First Amendment because they applied only to performers. A three-judge panel of the Ninth Circuit upheld the rules. However, the court reheard the case *en banc* and found that the rules were not the least restrictive means of achieving the city's desired goals of ensuring public and performer safety and reducing territorial conflicts among performers. The majority said that the rules require "single individuals to inform the government of their intent to engage in expressive activity in a public forum, a requirement that neither we nor the Supreme Court has *ever* countenanced." The ever-quotable chief judge, Alex Kozinski, dissented for himself and two other judges, saying that the majority demanded not just rule workability, but perfection, and "perfection is hard to find in rules written and applied by mortals." He called the rules "measured and reasonable" and added, "There are times when the best thing judges can do is to butt out; this is surely one of them."

Art may be many things to many people, but in San Marcos, Tex., it is *not* a sledgehammer-wrecked car filled with dirt and planted with flowers. The Fifth Circuit upheld the city's "junked vehicle" ordinance designed to eliminate public eyesores against a First Amendment challenge brought by a novelty gift store chain that celebrated the opening of a new store by inviting the public to sledgehammer a car which is then planted and displayed. Pointing out that the ordinance was never intended as a speech regulation, the court said that it was reasonably tailored to achieve the city's goal of public aesthetics and had only an incidental burden on speech (*Kleinman v. City of San Marcos*, 597 F.3d 323, 2010).

Censoring Confidential Information

Another form of prior restraint results from laws and court orders forbidding the media to publish confidential information, often concerning crimes and court proceedings. This creates legal problems that fall into several areas, including fair trial-free press (discussed in Chapter Seven) and the privacy of crime victims (discussed in Chapter Five). This chapter discusses Supreme Court decisions concerning the censorship questions in these laws.

One of the most difficult problems in this area involves laws forbidding the media to reveal the names of crime victims, particularly sex crime victims. Although a good case can be made for protecting the privacy of crime victims, the Supreme Court has held that the media have a right to publish their identities if the information was lawfully obtained from court records. The Court so ruled in 1975, overturning a Georgia privacy judgment against a broadcaster who published a rape victim's name. In that case (*Cox Broadcasting v. Cohn*, 420 U.S. 469), a television reporter had obtained the victim's name from a court record, and the station later faced a civil invasion of privacy suit for broadcasting it. (No criminal charges were filed against the station, although publishing the name was illegal.) The Court said the First and Fourteenth Amendments do not permit either criminal sanctions or civil invasion of privacy lawsuits for the publication of truthful information lawfully obtained from court records. However, the states can keep victims' names secret if they wish.

Two years later the Court overturned an Oklahoma court order that banned publication of the name of an 11-year-old boy allegedly involved in a fatal shooting, in *Oklahoma Publishing v. District Court* (430 U.S. 377, 1977). Reporters attended the boy's initial hearing and learned his name there. Local media carried the name, but a judge ordered them not to publish the boy's name or picture again. The Oklahoma Publishing Company appealed the order to the state supreme court, which upheld it. The U.S. Supreme Court reversed, ruling that the order amounted to prior censorship in violation of the First and Fourteenth Amendments. The Court relied on *Cox Broadcasting* and said there was no evidence that the press got the information unlawfully or even without the state's permission.

In 1979, the Court overturned a West Virginia law that imposed criminal sanctions on newspapers for publishing the names of juvenile offenders. In this case (*Smith v. Daily Mail*, 443 U.S. 97), a newspaper published the name of a youth who killed another student at a

junior high school. Reporters learned his name by monitoring police radio broadcasts and talking
eyewitnesses. The Supreme Court again ruled that the media cannot be punished for publishing truth
information that was lawfully obtained. One aspect of the law that amazed Justice William Rehnqui
who wrote a concurring opinion, was that it prohibited newspaper publication of juvenile names but r
a broadcast of the same information.

The publication of another kind of confidential information produced a 1978 U.S. Supreme Co
decision, *Landmark Communications v. Virginia* (435 U.S. 829). The case involved the *Virginian Pil*
coverage of the proceedings of a state commission reviewing a judge's performance in office. The pap
published the name of the judge, among other information. Virginia had a law making these procee
ings confidential. The paper was criminally prosecuted and fined for publishing this information, a
the state supreme court upheld the judgment. But the Supreme Court ruled that the law violated t
First Amendment. The Court said judges have no greater immunity from criticism than other perso
or institutions. When a newspaper lawfully obtains information about a proceeding such as the one
question, the paper may not be criminally punished for publishing what it learns.

In 1989, the Supreme Court again addressed this kind of issue in *Florida Star v. B.J.F.* (491 U.S. 52
Under Florida law in effect then the media were forbidden to publish the names of sex crime victin
However, a reporter for the *Florida Star* copied the name of a rape victim from a police report that v
posted on the Jacksonville Sheriff's pressroom wall. The name was published, and the crime victim su
She won a $97,000 judgment from the newspaper, but the Supreme Court overturned the verdict, rul
that the newspaper could not be penalized for publishing the name when it was lawfully obtained fr
a police record—even though the police may have violated the Florida law by making the informati
available to a reporter. However, the 6-3 majority declined to rule that the media are *always* exempt fr
liability for publishing information that they lawfully obtain. The Court said that *Cox Broadcasting* a
other earlier cases had stopped short of ruling out all liability for the truthful publication of lawf
obtained information. But when judicial records are involved, the Court seemed to say that the me
are free to publish information they lawfully obtain.

An interesting footnote to the *Florida Star* case is that the state law forbidding the media to publ
the names of sex crime victims was eventually ruled unconstitutional by the Florida Supreme Court.
Florida v. Globe Communications Corp. (648 So.2d 110, 1994), the state court ruled that the Florida law v
too broad because it banned the publication of victims' names without any consideration of the circu
stances—and also too narrow because it applied only to the media. This case arose when the *Glob*
tabloid newspaper, published the name of the woman who accused William Kennedy Smith, a nephew
former President John F. Kennedy and Sen. Edward Kennedy, of rape. As was true in the *Florida Star* ca
the *Globe* lawfully obtained the alleged victim's name, and the woman eventually agreed to the release
her name—even appearing on national television after Smith was acquitted. When the *Globe* was cri
nally prosecuted for publishing the name, a trial court, a state appellate court and the Florida Supre
Court all agreed that the state law was unconstitutional.

The Supreme Court ruled on another Florida case involving the right to publish lawfully obtain
information in *Butterworth v. Smith* (494 U.S. 624, 1990). A reporter who had testified before a grand j
wanted to write about the things he told the grand jury—including alleged wrongdoing by a local pu
official. But under Florida law, it was illegal for a grand jury witness to disclose his/her testimony e
In overturning the Florida law, the Court ruled that it is an unconstitutional prior restraint to proh
a witness from publicly disclosing his own testimony even after the grand jury investigation ends. Cl
Justice William Rehnquist said that this case did not involve the reporter disclosing *anything he lear*
from a secret grand jury investigation. Instead, it was merely a journalist being forbidden to publish infor
tion already in his possession before he testified. That violates the First Amendment.

One noteworthy limitation on the media's right to publish lawfully obtained information involves the pretrial discovery process when a news organization is involved in a lawsuit. The Supreme Court has held that a judge can forbid a newspaper to publish information it obtains during discovery. In *Seattle Times v. Rhinehart* (467 U.S. 20, 1984), the Court said the *Seattle Times* and another paper *could* be forbidden to publish information they learned while defending a libel suit against a religious group. During discovery, the plaintiff was ordered to provide his organization's membership lists, tax returns and other financial information. The Court upheld the trial judge's order forbidding the newspapers to publish this material, saying they would be free to publish the information if they learned of it independently, but when a plaintiff is compelled to hand it over in a libel case, the judge may require that it remain confidential. This may be a prior restraint, but the Court said that it was legitimate.

The question of judicial censorship arose again in 1995 in a widely noted case involving *Business Week* magazine, which obtained 300 pages of documents that Procter & Gamble had filed in a complex lawsuit against Banker's Trust Co. In the lawsuit, P&G alleged that it suffered large losses on its investments because of the misdeeds of Banker's Trust. The documents, like many others filed with the court during the pretrial discovery process, were sealed—not open for public inspection. *Business Week* obtained them from one of the lawyers involved in the case, but a federal judge ordered *Business Week* not to publish information from the documents. After a series of legal maneuvers, the order was lifted. Later, the Sixth Circuit ruled that it was improper for the judge to censor the magazine in the first place. In *Procter & Gamble Co. v. Banker's Trust Co.* (78 F.3d 219), a 2-1 majority ruled that the judge did not have the very compelling legal reasons needed to justify an act of prior restraint of the press. The majority noted that the documents were nothing more than routine filings; their publication would not endanger any fundamental government interest. The case raised new questions about the routine practice of sealing documents filed during lawsuits.

Why was this case decided differently than *Seattle Times*, where the Court upheld a judge's right to order a newspaper not to publish court documents? The *Seattle Times* was a party to a lawsuit, and the opposing side was compelled by a court order to hand over confidential information. *Business Week* was not a party to the underlying lawsuit and obtained the court documents independently and lawfully. Thus, there was a far less compelling justification for a judge to impose a prior restraint. The *Seattle Times* case is a rare exception to the rule that the media may not be forbidden to publish court documents that they lawfully obtain.

WHAT SHOULD I KNOW ABOUT MY STATE?

- Does my state have hate crime or penalty enhancement laws? If so, what do they cover?
- Does my state have a "Son of Sam" law?
- What regulations do my state, city or municipality put on newsracks, billboards, and public transportation shelter signs?
- Are there ordinances that regulate how and where protests may take place? What do they specify? Are there fees?
- What noise regulations are there in my area?
- What has my state and federal circuit said about anonymity?

A SUMMARY OF PRIOR RESTRAINTS

What Is a Prior Restraint, and Is It Permitted in America?

A prior restraint is an act of government censorship to prevent facts or ideas that the government considers unacceptable from being disseminated. It is a far greater abridgment of freedom of expression than a subsequent punishment system, which allows publication but punishes the publisher afterward for any harm. Prior restraints are permitted only under extremely compelling circumstances, with the government agency that wishes to censor required to carry a very heavy burden of proof to justify it.

When Would a Direct Prior Restraint Be Constitutional?

In the "Pentagon Papers" case, the Supreme Court ruled that prior censorship of the news media would be permissible if the government could prove that irreparable harm to national security would otherwise occur. However, the government was unable to prove national security was sufficiently endangered to justify prior restraint in that case.

What is a Time, Place and Manner Regulation?

Governments may lawfully regulate the *time, place and manner* in which First Amendment activities occur, provided the rules are *content neutral*. Rules are content neutral if they treat all speech the same, regardless of its content. Rules that are content based, that treat different content of speech differently, must undergo increased judicial scrutiny. They may be found constitutional but the burden on the government is much higher to justify them.

Are There Other Rules Concerning Prior Restraints Today?

Laws that unduly restrict literature distribution or other free expression activities on public property may be prior restraints. Private property owners, on the other hand, may usually prohibit First Amendment activities on their property, although some states recognize limited free expression rights at *quasi*-public places such as large shopping malls. Discriminatory taxes that single out some media have also been declared unconstitutional. Laws forbidding racial and religious "hate speech" have been overturned on First Amendment grounds. However, material that is found to be a threat to individuals is not protected. Laws or court orders forbidding the media to publish information they lawfully obtain are usually unconstitutional, even if the information is legally confidential (e.g., some crime victims' names). While the media may not have a right of access to this kind of news, governments cannot ordinarily prevent its publication once the media have it—particularly if obtained from a public record. The law on anonymous speech, particularly online, is still developing.

4   *Libel and Slander*

Ever since American journalists won their basic First Amendment freedoms, their most serious ongoing legal problem has been the danger of being sued for *defamation—* libel or slander. Other threats to journalistic freedom arise from time to time, but over the past two centuries libel has been a continuing legal problem, with thousands of lawsuits resolved by the courts—and thousands more settled out of court. Even the fear of libel suits often leads journalists to suppress newsworthy stories they would otherwise publish, thus engaging in a form of self-censorship that may not be in the public interest.

A libel is a *written defamatory statement;* a slander is a *spoken* one. Libel and slander laws exist to protect people whose reputations have been *wrongfully* damaged. Clearly, there is a need for that kind of protection. However, many libel suits are filed by persons who were not actually libeled, but who are angry about unfavorable but true (and thus non-libelous) publicity. And hostile juries sometimes hand out enormous punitive damage awards against the media without worrying much about the validity of the libel claim itself.

A single libel suit can be financially devastating even to a powerful media corporation. Multimillion-dollar libel judgments have become commonplace in recent years. Although most of the large libel judgments are eventually overturned by appellate courts, the cost of defending such a lawsuit often runs into millions of dollars. For a small-market broadcaster or newspaper publisher, the cost of one libel suit—even one that is eventually won in court—can put the company on the brink of bankruptcy. For example, the *Alton Telegraph,* a small Illinois newspaper, filed for bankruptcy court protection after losing a $9.2 million libel judgment in the 1980s. The plaintiffs in the case eventually agreed to accept a $1.4 million settlement, and the paper managed to borrow enough money to stay in business— but just barely (see *Green v. Alton Telegraph,* 438 N.E.2d 203, 1982).

If small local newspapers are targets in libel suits, well-known national media are even bigger targets for angry jurors. A jury once awarded a former "Miss Wyoming" beauty contest winner $26.5 million for a *Penthouse* magazine article about a fictitious "Miss Wyoming" who resembled her. An appellate court eventually set aside the verdict and dismissed the case, but by then *Penthouse* had spent more than a million dollars on legal fees (*Pring v. Penthouse,* 695 F.2d 438, 1983). And $26.5 million is not the all-time record for a libel judgment: there have been several larger verdicts.

These judgments seem small compared to a 1997 verdict in which a Houston jury ordered the *Wall Street Journal* to pay *$222.7 million* (including $200 million in punitive damages) to an investment brokerage that went out of business shortly after the *Journal* reported on the firm's alleged difficulties. However, the judge later threw out the $200 million punitive damage award and eventually set aside the rest of the judgment as well, ruling that the brokerage withheld crucial evidence that would have corroborated the *Journal* story. But by then the *Journal* had spent several years and several million dollars defending itself in court.

One of the most controversial judgments against a news organization in many years was $5.5 million in punitive damages that a jury awarded to the Food Lion grocery chain in 1997 because ABC's PrimeTime Live had two of its staff members obtain jobs at Food Lion under false pretenses. The ABC staffers used hidden cameras to document the mishandling of foods. Although Food Lion did not even allege that ABC's report was libelous, the jury found ABC guilty of trespass, fraud and other wrongs in connection with its undercover newsgathering. The trial judge later reduced the punitive damage award to $315,000. In

defamation:
a false intentional written or spoken communication that injures a person's reputation.

libel:
a written defamation.

slander:
a spoken defamation.

actual malice:
in libel, a statement made with knowing falsity or reckless disregard for the truth; a high burden of proof for fault that falls on plaintiffs who are public officials or public figures.

negligence:
in libel, a statement made carelessly or without exercise of normal care in verification; a lower burden of proof for fault that falls on plaintiffs who are private figures.

1999, the Fourth Circuit overturned that award, upholding only $2 (yes, two dollars) in damages against ABC for trespass and a breach of the duty of loyalty to an employer by the two ABC staffers who took jobs at Food Lion only to get the story (see *Food Lion v. Capital Cities/ABC,* 194 F.3d 505).

From the outset, ABC's defenders saw Food Lion's lawsuit as an end run around libel laws by a company that could not prove the ABC report was false but wanted to sue anyway. The appellate court verdict largely vindicated ABC, but only after years of litigation and enormous legal bills for the network.

Although appellate courts often overturn or reduce these multi-million-dollar judgments against the media, that does not always happen. In 1987 the U.S. Court of Appeals in Chicago affirmed a $3.05 million libel judgment against CBS and a television journalist in *Brown & Williamson Tobacco Co. v. Jacobson* (827 F.2d 1119). The Supreme Court refused to hear an appeal in 1988, rendering the U.S. Court of Appeals decision final. The case resulted from broadcasts by Chicago news anchor Walter Jacobson accusing tobacco companies of targeting young people in their advertising. He cited as an example an ad that was never actually used.

While these are extreme examples, libel lawsuits are a daily concern of the media. And this fear can have a serious chilling effect on First Amendment freedoms: it causes some organizations to avoid controversial stories to minimize the risk of being sued.

This point has never been better illustrated than by the continuing campaign of the tobacco industry against media reporting of the alleged misdeeds of tobacco companies. It turned out that Brown & Williamson's libel victory in 1987 was only the beginning. In 1994, ABC reported on its *Day One* program that tobacco companies were regulating the amount of nicotine in their products, in effect spiking cigarettes to keep smokers hooked. Philip Morris filed a $10 *billion* libel suit, and in 1995 ABC paid Philip Morris $15 million to drop the case. ABC also apologized twice in prime time—even though the journalists who produced the award-winning program insisted that they could document their charges. How does all of this affect smaller media organizations—the ones that couldn't begin to write a $15 million check to get out of a lawsuit? Libel insurance is available, but it can be prohibitively expensive. Not even bloggers are safe—in 2009 a South Carolina judge awarded $1.8 million to the owner of an advertising agency who claimed that he had been libeled in a post on a Myrtle Beach blog; the alleged author of the blog said he was unaware of the proceedings and did not appear in court. A settlement was negotiated, and the appeal was dropped. Clearly those who prepare content for the media need to be aware of the legal hazards of libel and slander.

■ LIBEL DEFINED

Just what are libel and slander?

They are legal actions to compensate the victims of defamatory communications—communications that tend to injure someone's reputation. The legal distinction between a libel—a *written* defamatory statement—and slander—a *spoken* defamation—is perhaps less important today than it once was as a result of the convergence of the media as well as several important Supreme Court decisions. Often this chapter refers to all kinds of lawsuits for defamation under the term libel. In many (but not all) states, broadcast defamation is treated as libel rather than slander.

Libel and slander suits are almost as old as the English common law from which they emerged. Even before this country was colonized, libel and slander were recognized legal actions in much of the world. In fact, the concept that a person's good name is something of value, and that anyone who damages it has committed a wrong, can be traced back to the time of the ancient Romans—and on back to the Ten Commandments.

Most libel cases today are handled as civil tort actions, private disputes between two parties in which the courts merely provide a neutral forum. In earlier times, libel was often treated as a criminal matter: the prevailing view was that defamatory words might lead to a breach of the peace, and should be regarded as a crime. This was especially true in the case of *seditious libel* (the crime of criticizing the government), for reasons explained in Chapter Two. While some states still have criminal libel laws on their books, these laws are rarely enforced today. Some have been ruled unconstitutional. Thus, the bulk of this chapter will be devoted to civil rather than criminal libel.

Libel suits are ordinarily state cases, not federal ones. The U.S. Supreme Court has intervened in some state libel cases, reminding the states that their libel laws can have a chilling effect on freedom of the press. But aside from the Supreme Court's role in setting constitutional limits for libel suits, this remains a field of law reserved for the *states*.

However, that does not mean that libel suits are never tried in federal courts. State libel cases are sometimes heard in federal courts when the two parties live in different states, but even then, the federal courts apply state law rather than federal law.

Although libel is a matter of state law, its basic principles are much the same all over the United States, as is true of many kinds of law that grew out of the English common law. Moreover, the Supreme Court's rulings have tended to make libel law more uniform in the various states. Nevertheless, there are still important state-to-state variations; you may wish to supplement this national overview by reading your own state's libel statute. The state codes section of Lexis-Nexis and other online research services can be searched by keywords such as defamation, libel or slander.

■ AN OVERVIEW OF LIBEL

In studying a complex legal subject such as libel, it is easy to get lost in the details, overlooking some of the major principles. This section summarizes the basics of libel law.

Technically, a libel occurs whenever the *elements* of libel are present. As you look at the list of these elements, you will realize that many libelous statements are published and broadcast every day. But that doesn't mean numerous libel suits are filed against the media every day. Instead, most libelous publications and broadcasts are unlikely to produce lawsuits because they are covered by one or more of the legal *defenses* that apply in libel law. There's a difference between a libel and an *actionable* libel—one that's likely to get someone sued. To decide whether a given item is likely to produce a libel suit, you have to determine not only whether the elements of libel are present but also whether there is a viable defense.

For a libel to occur, at least four elements must be present—with a fifth one required in most cases. The elements are: (1) *defamation* (a message that tends to hurt someone's reputation); (2) *identification* of a victim (and potential plaintiff), either by name or some other designation that is understood by someone other than the victim and the perpetrator; (3) *publication, communication* **or** *dissemination* of the defamatory message to someone other than the victim and perpetrator; (4) an element of *fault* on the part of the communicator, usually by communicating a provably *false* message with *actual malice* or *negligence;* and (5) usually *damages* (tangible or intangible losses that may be compensated in money).

Once these elements are present, a libel has occurred. It doesn't matter whether the defamatory statement is in a direct quote, a letter to the editor, an advertisement, a broadcast interview, or whatever. With few exceptions, anyone who contributes to the libel's dissemination may be sued for it, even if the libel was originated by someone else. That means the reporter who writes a story, the editor who reviews it, and everyone else in the production process may be named as a defendant in a libel suit. Of course, the normal legal strategy is to go after the "deep pocket"—the person with enough money to make it worthwhile. Therefore, the prime defendant is usually a corporate owner or publisher, not the hired hands who actually processed the libelous material. If you were defamed in a letter to the editor, you might want to sue the letter writer and the editor who chose to print it, but your prime defendant would probably be the parent company.

Internet services that do not edit materials placed on their servers are generally exempt from liability for postings by bloggers and others, even though those who actually post libelous messages (and ARE liable) may be anything but "deep pockets." Section 230 of the federal Communications Decency Act generally exempts Internet services from liability for content created by others. But that is not true for the traditional media.

After you determine whether the elements of libel are present in a given communication, the next crucial question is whether any of the defenses apply. Three major defenses developed under common law and have been recognized for many years. In addition, defenses of lesser importance are also recognized in some instances; they will be noted later. The major defenses are: (1) *truth* that can be proven in court; this classic common law defense is stronger than ever because plaintiffs usually have the *burden of proving falsity* now; (2) *privilege,* which protects fair and accurate accounts of what occurs during many government proceedings or appears in many public records; (3) *fair comment,* a statement of *opinion* as opposed to provably false facts.

If one or more of these defenses is present, the media may publish libelous material without fear of losing a libel suit. However, many lawsuits are filed by people who know they have little chance of ultimately winning. The mere opportunity to force the media into court may seem inviting to someone who feels he or she has been subjected to unfair publicity. Thus, the cost of defending a libel suit is itself a deterrent to publishing some controversial stories, no matter how strong the defenses are. This is especially true in states that do not have a procedure for dismissing frivolous libel suits quickly (see anti-SLAPP laws later in this chapter). In addition to the *elements of libel and defenses*, there are other factors to consider in deciding if a particular defamatory statement is risky.

Who May Sue for Libel

The first step in analyzing any potentially libelous item is to determine whether there is a *plaintiff*—a party who may sue for libel. Generally, the rule is that any living person or other private legal entity (such as a corporation or an unincorporated business) may sue for libel. The right to sue for libel is what is called *a personal right, not a property right.* This means that the right dies with the individual: most states follow the common law rule that the heirs cannot sue on behalf of a deceased person unless they were also personally libeled. New Jersey and Pennsylvania do allow a libel victim's heirs to sue under certain circumstances, but that is the exception. However, a number of states allow the heirs to *continue an existing lawsuit* if a libel victim dies before the case is resolved.

On the other hand, corporations are not limited by the life span or tenure in office of any individual. They may pursue a lawsuit for decades, regardless of the departure of individual officers. But for a corporation to sue for libel, the organization itself must have been defamed, not just an individual officer.

It may seem surprising that a big company can sue for libel. Nevertheless, courts have often ruled that a corporation has the same right as an individual to sue for libel when its reputation is besmirched. However, special rules may apply when the defamation is directed at a product rather than the company itself. Many states allow a special legal action called *product disparagement* or *trade libel*. In a trade libel suit, the company usually has to prove that the libelous statement actually damaged its business, sometimes difficult to prove. These laws were rarely used for many years, but they enjoyed a new surge in popularity during the 1990s, when at least 13 states passed laws to protect perishable food products from negative publicity. These "veggie libel" laws are discussed later.

If companies can sue for libel, what about nonprofit associations and other unincorporated organizations? They, too, may sue for libel in some states, but the rule on this point varies somewhat around the country. And what about government agencies? On this question, the law does not vary: governments may not sue for libel anywhere. However, government officials may sue *as individuals* if their personal reputations are damaged by a libel.

Group Libel

What about a libel of a group of people? May the individuals sue? A long-recognized rule of law is that individuals may sue for libel when a group to which they belong has been defamed, but only if one of two conditions is met: (1) the group must be small enough that the libel affects the reputations of the individual members; or (2) the libelous statement must refer particularly to the individual who is suing.

Elements of libel:

defamation: false intentional communication that injures a person's reputation.

identification: can be accomplished by a name or any other information that sufficiently identifies a person.

publication/communication: to someone other than the perpetrator or the victim.

fault: includes falsity and is measured as *actual malice* or *negligence.*

damages: tangible or intangible losses that can be financially compensated.

Defenses to libel:

truth: a strong defense because the burden of proof is on the plaintiff to prove falsity.

privilege: also known as *qualified privilege,* given to accurate accounts of proceedings of public meetings or materials in public records.

fair comment: a statement of actual opinion (not provably false facts).

A libel of a five-member city council could very well hurt the reputations of all the individual members. But what about a libel directed against a big organization, such as the United States Army? Would it be legally safe to say something like "all soldiers are criminals"?

The courts settled that sort of group libel question long ago. No individual may sue for libel when the libelous statement is directed toward such a large group. The cutoff seems to be somewhere between five and 100 people, depending on which court you listen to. A court once allowed individual football players to sue when the University of Oklahoma football team was libeled. But other courts have refused to allow individuals to sue when groups considerably smaller than a college football team were libeled. In general, the bigger the group is, the less the chance an individual may be able to sue for libel.

To summarize: any living individual may sue if he or she is libeled, as may a corporation. Unincorporated organizations may sue in some states but not in others. Government agencies may not sue for libel, although government officials may if they are personally libeled. Individuals may sue for libel if they belong to a sufficiently small group that has been libeled.

In analyzing an item for possible libel, the next step after deciding there is a potential plaintiff is to check off the elements of libel and see if all are present. If so, then you should check off the defenses and see if any will protect you. That kind of analysis requires a more detailed summary of the elements of libel and the defenses.

■ THE ELEMENTS OF LIBEL

Defamation

Of the various elements of a libel case, the one that is sometimes the hardest to remember is the most obvious: the requirement that a statement actually *be* libelous (i.e., defamatory). Without defamation there is no libel, so the first step in analyzing a statement for potential libel is to decide whether there really is a defamation.

Over the years the courts have recognized a wide variety of statements as defamatory, dividing them into two categories: libel *per se* and libel *per quod*. Libel *per se* is the classic kind of defamation where the words themselves will hurt a person's reputation. Words such as "murderer," "rapist," "racist" and "extortionist" are obvious examples, but there are thousands of others. Any word or phrase is likely to be libelous if it falsely accuses a person of a heinous crime, public or private immorality, insanity or infection by some loathsome disease (e.g., AIDS), or professional incompetence. Even words that don't fall into any of these categories may be ruled libelous if they cause other people to shun and avoid the person.

When the words themselves communicate the defamation with no additional explanation needed (as the words would in the examples), you have libel *per se*. But when, on the other hand, it is not immediately apparent that the words are libelous, or when one must know additional facts to understand that there is defamation, it is called libel *per quod*.

A classic example of libel *per quod* arose in a case called *Fellows v. National Enquirer* (42 C.3d 234, 1986). The *Enquirer* reported that television director Arthur Fellows was "steady dating" a famous actress. That statement would not ordinarily be libelous—except for the fact that he had been married to someone else for many years. The paper didn't mention that he was married, and few readers knew this additional fact that made the statement libelous *per quod*. If the *Enquirer* had said he was committing adultery, that would probably qualify as libel *per se*. But merely to say he was dating an actress without mentioning his marriage would only be libel *per quod* (unless the fact that he was married was widely known).

When Fellows sued, he presented evidence that he was not dating the famous actress or anyone else besides his wife, but he lost because he could not prove *special damages* (any provable monetary loss). Many states require a showing of special damages in libel *per quod* cases, whereas only general damages (pain and suffering or merely embarrassment due to the loss of reputation) are typically required in cases of libel *per se.* Fellows may have been embarrassed by the article in the *Enquirer,* but he didn't suffer any significant financial losses (if anything, the libelous story might have helped his career).

The distinction between libel *per se* and libel *per quod* is becoming less important today. For many years, courts generally ruled that libel *per se* was automatically actionable; that is, the plaintiff didn't even have to prove general damages. Instead, courts would presume damages merely because a libelous statement had been published. But on the other hand, if it was only a matter of libel *per quod,* the plaintiff had to prove special damages.

However, the *Gertz v. Welch* (418 U.S. 323) Supreme Court decision, a landmark 1974 decision that we will return to later, prohibited presumed damages in many libel suits against the media. The plaintiff today must be prepared to prove that he or she suffered at least general damages whether the defamatory statement was libel *per se* or libel *per quod.* The only time damages may be *presumed* in cases involving the media is when the plaintiff proves *actual malice* (i.e., that a falsehood was published knowingly or with reckless disregard for the truth). Some states have even eliminated presumed damages in non-media cases.

As a result, there is not usually much difference between libel *per se* and libel *per quod* today when the media are involved. If a statement is libelous (either on its face or only because of unique circumstances in the context of the statement) the media may have to defend a libel suit, provided the victim of the libel can prove the rest of the elements of libel.

Several types of subject matter result in disproportionate numbers of libel suits. For instance, the reporting of crime news has probably produced more libel suits than any other kind of journalism. In the American system of justice, a person is presumed innocent until proven guilty: stories that label people as "rapists" or "murderers" before they are convicted by a court are particularly dangerous. The best way to avoid lawsuits is to be as accurate and specific as possible in reporting the news. If someone has been detained for questioning in connection with a certain crime, say that much and nothing more. If the person has been formally charged, report that but don't go beyond what the facts will support. If the person has been arraigned, indicted, bound over for trial, released on bail, or whatever, be careful to report only what has *actually happened* and no more. If the police are seeking someone for questioning, be wary of a story that identifies him/her as a "suspect" prematurely.

Several other areas of journalism also produce more than their share of libel suits. A number of libel suits have resulted from stories accusing someone of having "Mafia" or organized crime connections. Another dangerous area—because of the ease with which special damages can be proven—is any statement that reflects upon a professional person's competence. Professionals such as physicians, psychologists and attorneys rely on public confidence for their continued livelihood to a greater extent than most other persons. Should the local paper publish a story questioning a doctor's or lawyer's integrity or competence and his/her business thereafter declines, special damages can often be proven. A false or misleading statement (or even an innuendo) about a professional person invites a libel suit.

Those seeking public office are another group of people who generate a lot of libel suits. Although the media now have strong constitutional safeguards when sued by a public official or public figure, public officials are frequently inclined to file libel suits as a means

libel per se:
a statement that is defamatory on its face, such as calling someone a murderer, rapist or racist; a false accusation of a heinous crime, public or private immorality, insanity or infection by loathsome disease, or professional incompetence (*per se* is Latin for "in itself").

libel per quod:
a statement that requires additional background knowledge to understand that defamation has taken place (*per quod* is Latin for "whereby").

qualified privilege:
a defense for libel which covers truthful reports of what was said or done in a public government meeting or what is contained in public records; also called fair reporting.

strict liability:
liability without fault; a standard that puts responsibility on the perpetrator of an event regardless of the party who was actually responsible.

of saving face if nothing else. Even if there is little chance that the politician will ultimately win in court, the cost of defending a libel suit may force some publishers and broadcasters to think twice about carrying a story that reflects upon the character or competence of a politician.

For example, in 2012, a Maine state senate candidate filed suit against several opponents, alleging that a number of statements in campaign flyers were defamatory. The First Circuit, in a case replete with reflections on the "contact sport" nature of political campaigns, affirmed the lower court's dismissal of the case. After tracing the long Supreme Court history protecting political speech, the court said, "All this makes it quite obvious that defamation law does not require that combatants for public office act like war-time neutrals, treating everyone evenhandedly and always taking the high road. Quite the contrary. Provided that they do not act with actual malice, they can badmouth their opponents, hammering them with unfair and one-sided attacks…" (*Schatz v. Repub. State Leadership Comm.*, 669 F. 3d 50).

Another problem area is gossip about the private lives of the famous. Some publications that deal in this sort of "news" as their basic commodity expect (and are prepared for) frequent libel suits as a result. Of course, many celebrities would prefer to let the matter drop and thus avoid the cost and additional publicity a libel suit would bring, rather than sue a supermarket scandal sheet. But those who do sue may have a good chance of success: tales about the private lives of celebrities that a publisher knew or should have known to be false are beyond the First Amendment's protection.

What counts as defamation today? While this determination is fact-dependent, here are a few recent answers from the courts. A New Jersey appeals court said in 2009 that one candidate's truthfully reporting another's criminal background in campaign flyers, even when that conviction had been *expunged* (removed) from the record, was not libelous, as the expunging didn't make the information false. On appeal, the New Jersey Supreme Court agreed: the expungement statute didn't protect the private facts in the libel case, and "the breadth of the expungement statute—on its face—is limited to those government agencies that are statutorily required to be served with the expungement order" (*G.D. v. Kenny*, 15 A.3d 300, 2011). Defendants may raise truth as a defense, the court said.

Neither is it libelous, said the Second Circuit, to truthfully report that an individual is cooperating with law enforcement, even if that individual is in a prison population that might find that information unsavory (*Michtavi v. New York Daily News*, 587 F. 3d 551, 2009).

What about calling someone "gay"? The trend seems to be that this is not defamatory. A New York trial court ruled that the law of New York indicated that calling somone gay is libel *per se*. But the

New York appeals court overturned: "Given this state's well-defined public policy of protection and respect for the civil rights of people who are lesbian, gay or bisexual, we now overrule our prior case to the contrary and hold that such statements are not defamatory *per se*" (*Yonaty v. Mincolla*, 2012 NY Slip Op 04248, 2012). Calling someone gay during a talk show where the use of hyperbole and insults is common is also *not* defamatory, according to a New Jersey federal court in 2010; the court said that "it appears unlikely that the New Jersey Supreme Court would legitimize discrimination against gays and lesbians by concluding that referring to someone as homosexual 'tends so to harm the reputation of that person as to lower him in the estimation of the community as to deter third persons from associating or dealing with him'" (*Murphy v. Millennium Radio Group LLC*, 38 Media L. Rep. 2338). The Third Circuit on appeal did not address this issue; it did rule on copyright issues, discussed in Chapter Six.

Is the Internet changing what kinds of words are defamatory? Not just yet. In *Cohen v. Google, Inc.* (887 N.Y.S.2d 424) the anonymity elements of which were discussed in Chapter Two, an anonymous blogger writing on a blog called "Skanks of NYC" claimed that using the words "skank," "skanky," "ho" and "whoring" in reference to model Liskula Cohen was merely opinion. Moreover, the blogger (later revealed to be fashion student Rosemary Port) said that those words were no longer really defamatory; they "have become a popular form of 'trash talk' ubiquitous across the Internet as well as network television and should be treated no differently than 'jerk' or any other form of loose and vague insults that the Constitution protects." The court disagreed and said the words could reasonably be interpreted to suggest that Cohen was sexually promiscuous.

The Identification Element

Another element the plaintiff must prove in a libel suit is *identification*: at least some of the readers or listeners must understand to whom the defamatory statement refers.

Where a person's name is used, there is usually little difficulty in proving identification. However, there are a great many ways a person may be identified other than by name. Any reference—no matter how oblique—is sufficient if the plaintiff can produce witnesses who testify convincingly that they understand the libelous statement to refer to him or her.

Perhaps the classic example of an oblique reference producing a libel suit is the situation that led to the famous *New York Times v. Sullivan* (376 U.S. 254) decision of the Supreme Court. As Chapter One indicated, the plaintiff in that case was a city commissioner in Montgomery, Ala. What prompted the lawsuit was a *New York Times* ad that alleged police misconduct in the South (including Montgomery) but never mentioned Sullivan either by name or as a city commissioner. He was able to convince a jury that the criticism of the conduct of the local police injured his reputation because many people knew that one of his responsibilities as a city commissioner was to oversee the police. In reversing the judgment years later, the Supreme Court expressed doubt that the ad really referred to Sullivan. But the case had gone all the way up through the American legal system at a cost of thousands of dollars.

In short, don't expect to escape a libel suit by using a vague identification. If even a few people understand whom you are talking about, the identification requirement for a libel suit has been met.

Another problem that leads to many libel suits is an identification so vague that it can refer to more than one person. A famous libel case nearly a century ago proved this point. Two lawyers in the Washington, D.C., area were named Harry Kennedy. One used his middle initials; the other did not. The one who normally used his middle initials was arrested for a serious crime. The *Washington Post* reported the fact, but omitted the middle initials. The other Harry Kennedy sued for libel, claiming that his reputation had been damaged, and he won (*Washington Post v. Kennedy*, 3 F.2d 207, 1924).

The moral of this story is obvious: when you publish or broadcast a defamatory but true statement, be sure to identify the person or persons involved as completely as possible, lest you inadvertently also identify an innocent party. It is good journalistic practice to identify people by full name, address and occupation whenever the story involves potential libel.

Some publishers go so far as to make a special note of who is *not* involved in a libelous story. When news broke of the 1978 Jonestown massacre, in which several hundred followers of the Rev. Jim Jones were murdered or committed suicide in a South American jungle, one of the persons implicated was a young man named Larry Layton. Thousands of miles away in Los Angeles another man named Larry Layton was a prominent lawyer. One Los Angeles newspaper published a separate news story to tell its readers that the Larry Layton involved in Jonestown was not the same person as the attorney—even though none of the news stories about Jonestown had suggested otherwise.

Beyond the dangers inherent in publishing a story with libelous content when more than one person has the same name, there are pitfalls to avoid when two people have similar names, given that journalists do make errors. A notable example is the case of Ralph A. Behrend and R. Allen Behrendt, two medical doctors who had worked at the same hospital in Banning, Calif. The *Los Angeles Times* reported that Dr. Behrendt had been arrested for theft and using narcotics. Sure enough, it was really Dr. Behrend who was arrested—and Dr. Behrendt had a great libel suit against the *Times* as a result of this copy desk error (*Behrendt v. Times Mirror Co.*, 30 C.A.2d 77, 1939). If newspapers of the stature of the *Los Angeles Times* and the *Washington Post* have identification problems and face libel suits as a result, you can see why this sort of thing is a serious problem.

The Communication Element

A defamatory statement has to be *communicated (published* or *disseminated)* for it to be libelous. The rules in this area are quite liberal: any time someone besides the party making the defamatory statement and the victim sees or hears it, this requirement is met. Actually, the plaintiff in a lawsuit may have a tough time proving damages if only a few people saw or heard the defamatory statement. Nevertheless, there have been cases where communicating a libel to only a handful of people resulted in a lawsuit for the perpetrator of the libel.

In most instances, of course, libel suits against the media result from statements that were *actually* published or broadcast; proving the dissemination element is not difficult.

It should be reiterated that everyone who furthers the dissemination of a libel can be sued. Even though the defamation first appeared in a letter to the editor, in a public speech, or even in a wire service dispatch, with few exceptions every publisher or broadcaster who further disseminates it can be sued (as can the originator of the libel or slander). Unless one of the defenses is available, *the media are at risk even when they accurately report what someone else said.* The speaker may be sued—but in many instances so may everyone who further disseminates the libelous statement. You need not be the originator of a libel to be sued for it in the traditional media. As noted earlier, Internet services are generally exempt from liability for content provided by someone else.

In 2010, a Texas bankruptcy court was among the first courts to find that sending someone an e-mail with a link to an allegedly defamatory site counts as publication for purposes of libel: "An e-mail, just like a letter or a note, is a means for a statement to be published so that third parties are capable of understanding the defamatory nature of the statement" (*In re Perry*, 423 B.R. 215). The e-mail was also part of the context necessary to establish actual malice, said the court.

The Element of Fault

Until 1964, our summary of the things a plaintiff must prove to win a libel suit would have been basically complete at this point. However, in that year the U.S. Supreme Court handed down its landmark *New York Times v. Sullivan* decision. A decade later, the Supreme Court announced another very important libel decision, *Gertz v. Welch*. Both cases are discussed in depth in the section entitled "Libel and the Constitution," but in the interest of offering a logical presentation of the elements of libel, their basic provisions are summarized here.

In *New York Times v. Sullivan*, the Supreme Court ruled that public officials who sue for libel or slander must prove *actual malice*, which the court defined as publishing a falsehood with *knowledge of its falsity, or with reckless disregard for the truth*. In the *Gertz* case, the Supreme Court extended this principle by ruling that in all libel cases involving matters of public concern, the plaintiff must prove some degree of *fault*. No longer would the media face libel suits under a legal doctrine called *strict liability*, a doctrine assuming that whenever a wrong occurs its perpetrator will be held strictly responsible (no matter whose fault it was). Without this protection, the Supreme Court ruled, the fear of libel suits would unduly inhibit the media in covering controversial stories that should be reported in a free society. Therefore, these safeguards were required to protect First Amendment freedoms.

The Supreme Court in the *Gertz* case set up two levels of fault for the media: *negligence* and *actual malice*. The Court said the states could not allow libel suits by public figures and public officials unless they could prove actual malice, something the Court had already said in *New York Times v. Sullivan* and several other cases before *Gertz*. But the Court also said (for the first time) that private citizens as well as public figures had to prove some fault on the part of the media to win libel cases. The Court ruled that the states could allow private citizens to sue by showing a lower level of fault than actual malice, perhaps just negligence. Alternately, any state that wished to do so could also impose the tough actual malice requirement on private citizens as well as public figures who sue the media for libel. The *Gertz* case raised two legal problems:

1. What is *negligence*, and how does it differ from *actual malice*?
2. Who is a *public figure*, and who is a *private person*?

Negligence is a term that has a long legal history in other kinds of tort actions, but it had not previously been used in libel cases. It refers to a party's failure to do something that he/she has a duty to do, and that a reasonable person would do. In libel cases, it has come to mean failing to adhere to the standards of good journalism by doing such things as checking the facts. Courts in several states have ruled that private persons must prove something more than negligence—but less than actual malice—in most libel cases against the media.

Plaintiffs cannot simply claim they informed a media organization about information they think could change coverage about them; they must prove that the media organization did not follow up on that information to demonstrate negligence, according to the Fifth Circuit in *Henry v. Lake Charles American Press LLC* (566 F.3d 164, 2009). Mark Henry, the owner of Chennault Jet Center, sued the Lake Charles *American Press* for libel for articles about a government investigation of alleged sales of contaminated fuel for military aircraft. Henry said his attorney had told the *American Press* that some of the information in the stories was wrong and gave the paper contact information for an Air Force official who could clarify the facts, and the newspaper had failed to act on this information. The Fifth Circuit reversed the lower court's denial of a motion under the Louisiana anti-SLAPP statute and found for the newspaper, saying Henry had provided no evidence that the newspaper had not followed up on the information provided by Henry's attorney. Simply proving that the attorney had contacted the newspaper did not prove that the paper had not followed up, and the burden was on Henry to demonstrate that the paper had been negligent.

Malice is another old legal term, but the Supreme Court gave it a special meaning in connection with libel suits in *New York Times v. Sullivan* by saying that it meant publishing a falsehood knowingly or with reckless disregard for the truth. "Reckless disregard" generally means publishing a false story when you strongly suspect it to be false—or should entertain such suspicions. That is very hard to prove in a libel case. But, as will be discussed, some states have common law definitions of "malice" that mean ill will or malicious intent, and one federal appeals court used such a state law to award a win in a libel suit to a plaintiff.

Since it is harder to prove actual malice than negligence, the *Gertz* decision made it important to determine who is a private person (and therefore required to prove only negligence in most states) and who is a public figure (and required to prove actual malice).

Why should it be harder for public figures to win libel cases? The court's rationale for this approach was twofold. First, public officials and public figures have much greater access to the media to reply to libelous charges than do private persons. Second, those who place themselves in the limelight have to expect some adverse publicity, while private persons should not be unduly subjected to publicity they do not seek.

Because winning a libel suit is usually much easier for a private person than a public figure, almost everyone who files a libel suit wants to be classified as a private person. The media, of course, want most plaintiffs classified as public figures. Several Supreme Court decisions since *Gertz* have helped to clarify who is and is not a public figure for libel purposes.

Proving Damages

Another way in which the Supreme Court's Gertz decision changed libel law was that, as mentioned earlier, it abolished what were called *presumed* damages except in those cases where the plaintiff was able to prove actual malice.

Under the old presumed damage rules, many states allowed plaintiffs in libel suits to simply skip the difficult matter of proving that they were really injured by the libelous publication or broadcast. If there was a libel, the courts would simply presume there were damages, without any proof. The Supreme Court's *Gertz* decision changed all that. Now all plaintiffs who cannot prove the media guilty of actual malice—even private persons—must prove damages to win their cases. Plaintiffs can win *special damages* by proving their out-of-pocket losses, of course. But in addition, the Court ruled that plaintiffs may also collect *general damages* for such intangibles as embarrassment and loss of reputation. Obviously, no dollar amount can be placed on such losses, but if the plaintiff can prove he or she was injured, the court (i.e., the judge or a jury) may then decide how many dollars the plaintiff should be given as compensation.

How is this different from presumed damages? It's subtle, but the difference is this: under the old presumed damages doctrine, plaintiffs didn't even have to offer *any* proof of their loss of reputation in the community. The court would just *assume* the bad publicity must have had a bad effect. Now plaintiffs must prove their was harm to their reputation. How can this be done? For example, a plaintiff may bring in witnesses to testify about the effect the defamatory statement had on his/her reputation. Often plaintiffs themselves testify that their former friends shunned them after a libel occurred.

For example, in an interesting turn of the tables in 2011, the Second Circuit determined that a newspaper publisher was unable to show that *per se* defamation by a mayor actually chilled his speech and resulted in damages (*Zherka v. Amicone*, 634 F.3d 642). Selim Zherka was the publisher of the *Westchester Guardian* in Yonkers, New York, and in 2007 the paper was critical of Yonkers mayor Philip Amicone's administration, alleging corruption and financial mismanagement. But Zherka sued Amicone, claiming that the mayor had retaliated against him by allegedly calling Zherka a "convicted drug dealer" and a "thug" at a public campaign event. The district court dismissed Zherka's claims, and the Second Circuit agreed. Saying that Zherka had failed to demonstrate "actual chilling" of his speech, the court said that simply alleging that the defamation was libel *per se* was not enough to establish that chilling had taken place. The court added, "Public officials must expect that their decisions will be subjected to withering scrutiny from the populace. A public official's response to that criticism is subject to limits, but the injury inflicted by that response must be real."

Similarly, to allege that a company had been defamed, a New York appeals court said that Sandals resorts would have to demonstrate that even an allegation of per se defamation "injured its business reputation or its credit standing" (*Sandals Resorts Int'l Ltd. v. Google, Inc.*, 2011 NY Slip Op 4179). Sandals claimed that defamatory messages were sent by unknown Google Gmail account holders containing accusations that Sandals resorts were subsidized by Jamaica, but the company only hires Jamaican citizens for menial jobs. The court said that the e-mails contained no real statements of fact (it called them "an exercise in rhetoric"), but included links to supporting evidence for recipients to draw their own conclusions. Sandals had not shown sufficient injury to satisfy the damages element of a libel claim.

In the *Gertz* decision, the Supreme Court went a step further in placing limits on damages in libel suits: it also held that punitive damages should *not* be awarded—even to private persons—without *proof* of actual malice (i.e., knowing or reckless publication of a falsehood) by the media. Previously, the courts in some states allowed punitive damage awards (which can involve huge amounts of money) on proof of a different sort of malice. That kind of malice involved showing that the publisher or broadcaster harbored ill will or evil intentions toward the plaintiff. Under that rule, a publisher could face a massive punitive damage award without being guilty of actual malice as the Court defined the term for libel cases.

As indicated earlier, punitive damage awards by no means disappeared in libel cases since the *Gertz* decision, but at least plaintiffs now must prove actual malice under the new definition to win punitive damages.

■ LIBEL DEFENSES

In analyzing a given news item (or advertisement, press release or whatever) for libel, the next step after determining if the elements are present is to decide whether any of the recognized libel defenses apply. At this point, however, the analysis must be approached a little differently. In order to win a libel case, the plaintiff must convince the court that the elements of libel are present; that is not the defendant's task. The plaintiff bears the burden of proof in that part of the case. But when it comes to building an affirmative defense against a libel suit, it's often the other way around: the defense bears the *burden of proof*. Thus, in many cases it isn't enough for publishers or broadcasters to believe they have a libel defense: they may have to prove it under a court's rules of evidence.

That can be a problem. The rules of evidence make it difficult to prove many things that are discovered through investigative journalism. A reporter may be absolutely convinced of the correctness of a story: the sources may be completely reliable and the reporter may have extensively double-checked the facts. But that doesn't mean the facts can be proven in court. For example, under a court's rules of evidence, hearsay (statements made by one person to another, with the second person testifying about what he was told) is often inadmissible. A good deal of the information a reporter gathers would be considered hearsay.

Another problem arises when journalists promise to keep the identities of sources confidential. Many important stories could not be developed without the use of such sources, but in a libel suit journalists may have to choose between identifying their sources and losing the case. A judge won't take their word that the source exists; the source may have to be identified during the discovery process, or may even have to testify. If the source cannot be produced without compromising journalistic ethics, the case may be forfeited.

Focus on...

Defamation by implication: diluting the truth defense

In 2006 a construction crane collapsed in Bellevue, Wash., and a man was killed. The *Seattle Post-Intelligencer*, in its coverage of the accident, featured a story on the crane's operator, Warren Yeakey, and his past battles with drugs and criminal activity. An investigation later revealed that mechanical problems had caused the accident, but Yeakey claimed though all the facts in the article about him were true, he had still been defamed—under a theory called *defamation by implication*.

Yeakey claimed the article didn't just discuss his past, but it "juxtapose[d] that history against the front page headline, the large photo of the collapsed crane...and all the other statements within the article so as to imply a defamatory connection between all these elements."

FIG. 19. Crane used in construction of railway bridge, circa 1910-1930.

Library of Congress, Prints and Photographs Division, [LC-DIG-ppmsc-01769]

Yeakey relied on a 2005 Washington Supreme Court case, *Mohr v. Grant* (153 Wash.2d 812), where the court said that defamation by implication happens when "the defendant juxtaposes a series of facts so as to imply a defamatory connection between them, or creates a defamatory implication by omitting facts." Other states (Florida, Iowa) have recognized this approach. The state court of appeals, however, found for the *Post-Intelligencer*, saying that Yeakey had "the mistaken belief that *Mohr* expanded the defamation tort to include defamation by implication through juxtaposition of truthful statements" (*Yeakey v. Hearst Communications, Inc.*, 234 P. 3d 332, 2010).

Is this part of a troubling trend, echoed in *Noonan v. Staples* from the First Circuit discussed in this chapter, of attempts by libel plaintiffs to water down the truth defense?

With these problems in mind, you should check off the defenses that might apply to a potentially libelous item. Only if there is a defense—and it could be proved in court—should the item be considered safe. There may be times when it is necessary to take a chance and publish an important story without certainty that it could be defended in court, but the decision to gamble in that way should only be made intelligently, after calculating the risks.

Truth

The oldest of all libel defenses—and certainly the most obvious—is *truth* (sometimes called *justification*). Since the early days of American independence, courts have been allowing publishers to prove the truth of what they printed as a means of defending against civil libel suits. For many years, there was a catch: in some states the proof of truth had to be accompanied by proof that the publisher's motives were not improper. For instance, a publisher sometimes could be sued for engaging in character assassination of an enemy (often a rival publisher), even if all of the charges were true.

And, of course, there was the additional catch that only those truthful facts that could be proved under a court's rules of evidence would be considered true in deciding the case. As just suggested, that has been a serious problem for journalists.

However, the U.S. Supreme Court revised the rules on truth as a libel defense, particularly by shifting the burden of proof from the media to the plaintiff. As indicated earlier, in its *Gertz* decision the Supreme Court said it was not constitutionally permissible to allow a libel judgment against the media unless the plaintiff could prove fault, with fault meaning the publication of a false statement of fact due to negligence or malice.

The Supreme Court reinforced this in a 1986 decision, *Philadelphia Newspapers v. Hepps* (475 U.S. 767). In that case, the *Philadelphia Inquirer* had published several articles linking beverage distributor Maurice Hepps to organized crime. When he sued for libel, he was unable to prove the charges false, but neither could the reporters fully document the charges to prove them true.

Pointing out that conclusively proving that type of charge can be difficult, the Supreme Court said that to prevent self-censorship of important stories by journalists, those who sue for libel must now bear the burden of proving the story false, at least when issues of public concern are involved. In such cases, *no* state may require the media to prove that a statement is true; the person suing must prove that it is false. Justice Sandra Day O'Connor explained:

> To ensure that true speech on matters of public concern is not deterred, we
> hold that the common-law presumption that defamatory speech is false cannot
> stand when a plaintiff seeks damages against a media defendant for speech of
> public concern.... There will always be instances when the factfinding process
> will be unable to resolve conclusively whether the speech is true or false. It is in
> those instances that the burden of proof is dispositive.

Thus, the rule today is that to win a libel case resulting from the media's coverage of any issue of public concern, the plaintiff always bears the burden of proving that the libelous statement is false. But what about libel cases *not* involving issues of public concern? The Supreme Court left that up to the states: the states are constitutionally required to place the burden of proof on plaintiffs only in cases involving public issues. However, some states have completely abandoned the common law rule that presumed all libelous statements to be false and now require all plaintiffs to prove the falsity of every allegedly libelous statement. Also, in most cases the old requirement of truth plus good intentions is no longer valid.

As a general rule, there can be no successful libel suit against the media unless the material is proven false—period. If it cannot be proven false, the publisher's motives no longer matter in most libel suits. However, one appeals court revisited this notion in 2009 and said that truthful statements may be actionable if the state statute uses a common law definition of malice, which does examine the motivations of the publisher.

If the publisher's motives are now irrelevant when a publication is truthful, they are very relevant if a publication turns out to be false. In that circumstance, the key issue may be whether the publisher or broadcaster knew or should have known that the libelous statement was false. If so, a court may find that there was actual malice, which means that even a public official or public figure may win a libel case against the media. And in cases involving private persons rather than public figures, publishing a false statement negligently but unknowingly—because of sloppy fact-checking—may be enough to lose a libel suit.

Also, in flatly stating that the First Amendment does not permit libel judgments against the media for truthful publications about public issues, we should emphasize that libel is not the only potential legal problem for the media. For example, a publisher or broadcaster may also be sued for invasion of privacy. As Chapter Five explains, truth is not always a defense in a privacy suit. The fact that a statement is truthful may preclude a successful libel suit, but not necessarily an invasion of privacy lawsuit.

Privilege

The legal concept of *privilege* is an old one, and it creates a strong libel defense for the media. A privilege is an immunity from legal liability, and the term is used in a variety of legal contexts. Chapter Eight discusses *reporter's privilege,* the concept that a journalist should be exempt from being forced to testify about his sources of information and unpublished notes. Other privileges excuse lawyers and doctors from testifying about much of what their clients and patients tell them in confidence.

As the term is used in libel and slander law, privilege means an immunity from a lawsuit. The concept was recognized in Article I, Section 6 of the U.S. Constitution, which created an absolute privilege for members of Congress engaged in debates on the floor of Congress. They may never be sued for anything they say there; they have absolute freedom of speech during Congressional debates.

Over the years, this absolute privilege has been broadened to encompass many other government officials, government proceedings and government documents. Today, there is a broad privilege for local, state and national legislative bodies, and it extends to major officials in the executive branch of government and to court proceedings. When performing their official duties, many government officials now have an absolute privilege; they cannot be sued for libel or slander as a result of what they do while conducting their official duties.

As this privilege for government officials was developing, the courts also recognized that in a democracy the news media need to be free to report to the public on what their elected leaders are doing and saying. This led to the concept of *qualified privilege,* sometimes called *conditional privilege,* or the *fair report privilege.*

Qualified privilege is a libel defense that allows the media to report on government proceedings and records without fear of a libel suit, provided they give a fair and accurate account. A biased account or one that pulls a libelous quote out of context may not be protected by the qualified privilege defense. However, this defense is broad enough to allow the media to publish many stories based on government documents or statements by government officials—without worrying about whether the statements themselves are true. If a charge of wrongdoing is contained in a government document such as a court record, for example, the media may publish it even if it later turns out to be false. Nevertheless, this defense raises at least two major legal questions:

1. What officials and records are within its scope?
2. Under what circumstances does it apply—when are officials conducting official business, and when are they doing something else?

It would take a detailed state-by-state summary to describe which officials and what records are covered by the qualified privilege defense, but some general rules have developed over the years. First, this defense clearly applies to official legislative proceedings from the local level to Congress, but not necessarily to informal and unofficial functions. What a local government official says during a meeting of a city council or commission is privileged, but what the same official says at a service club meeting or a campaign appearance (or writes in a press release, as will be explained shortly) may sometimes be a different matter.

In the executive branch of government, most states apply the privilege to the official conduct of senior elected officials, but not necessarily to lesser officials or appointees. The state attorney general's remarks on an official occasion may be privileged, for example, but not necessarily the statements of his deputies. In general, the less official the occasion and the lower the status of the person making the statement, the less likely it is to be privileged. However, many courts recognize the privilege defense even in situations involving unofficial public events where matters of public concern are discussed. On the other hand, in some states the courts are moving in the opposite direction, declining to extend the privilege defense beyond government officials. In New York, for instance, the Court of Appeals held that an allegedly libelous statement by a private citizen at a New York City Community Board meeting is *not* privileged (*600 West 115th Street Corp. v. Von Gutfeld*, 80 N.Y.2d 130, 1992).

In the judiciary, the privilege applies to public court proceedings and official records. It may not apply to proceedings and records that are not open to the public, however. If a particular type of proceeding is routinely closed to the public (as divorce and juvenile proceedings are in some states), the reporter who surreptitiously covers such a proceeding or publishes information taken from the secret records of the proceeding may not be protected by the privilege defense. Also particularly dangerous are false charges appearing in non-public documents that are "leaked" to the press.

Even if a document is obtained from court files open to the public, there are pitfalls for journalists. The *Pittsburgh Post-Gazette* had to pay nearly $3 million in damages and interest for publishing information that was obtained from a deposition in an old lawsuit in the case of *DiSalle v. P.G. Publishing Co.* (544 A.2d 1345, 1988). The *Post-Gazette* published a story saying an attorney who later became a judge had helped prepare a false will as a favor to a woman with whom he was having an affair. The accusation was made—or at least implied—in a deposition (a sworn pretrial statement) by the woman's brother, who was then challenging the validity of the will. The story was published *after* a court had ruled that the will was *not* fraudulent. The Supreme Court declined to hear an appeal, leaving intact a Pennsylvania court's ruling that the newspaper acted with actual malice in publishing the story.

Focus on...
Teddy Roosevelt's libel cases

Do American presidents ever sue for libel? Most do not. However, President Theodore Roosevelt filed at least one libel suit during his presidency (1901-1909) and participated in at least two thereafter. In the first case, TR sued famous publisher Joseph Pulitzer for libel over coverage of financial improprieties in the building of the Panama Canal; in February 1909 a grand jury indicted Pulitzer and some of his editors. The case was eventually dismissed.

FIG. 20. Theodore Roosevelt, c. 1904.

Library of Congress, Prints and Photographs Division, [LC-USZ62-13026]

After his presidency, in 1912, TR sued the publisher of the *Ishpeming Iron Ore* in the upper peninsula of Michigan for a mean-spirited editorial. Publisher George Newitt wrote, "Roosevelt lies, and curses in a most disgusting way, he gets drunk too, and that not infrequently, and all of his intimates know about it." Roosevelt brought all his power to bear on the case, and Newitt, outmaneuvered, eventually apologized and paid the president the damages he asked for: six cents.

Finally, in 1925, the former president found himself the defendant in a libel case brought by the publisher of the *Albany Times-Union* for a comment carried by many newspapers that in New York, "we see at its worst the development of bipartisan boss rule." Publisher William Barnes, Jr. was the Republican "boss," said TR. The trial was moved to Syracuse to avoid bias toward Barnes in Albany. Roosevelt won based on his counterclaims: Barnes was guilty of corruption, and probably also of collusion with the Democrats.

Another problem in reporting court news involves documents that have been filed but have not yet received any review by a judge. A number of states recognize a rule that court documents are not privileged (even though they may be available to the public) until they are in some way acted upon by a judge. An additional complication is that a lawyer who sends court documents to the media may not be protected from liability even if the document itself is privileged. In 2004, for example, the Pennsylvania Supreme Court held that the state's judicial privilege does not protect a lawyer who faxes court documents to reporters (*Bochette v. Gibson*, 860 A.2d 67). In essence, the court said it's okay if a reporter discovers public court records on his/her own and publishes them, but if a document is libelous, a lawyer can be sued for giving the document to a reporter.

A serious privilege problem involves reporting the police beat. Law enforcement officials sometimes let journalists see files that are not public records. A story based on such reports may not be protected by the qualified privilege defense: if the police privately suspect someone of a crime and they're wrong (i.e., guilt isn't proven in court), there is a danger of libel. Beware of undocumented charges leveled against a potential suspect, charges that may never be substantiated or placed in a public record. Stories about a person's arrest and booking are almost always privileged; stories quoting police hunches usually are not.

This is not to suggest that journalists should never report the progress of a law enforcement investigation aimed at someone suspected of a serious crime until *charges are formally filed or an arrest is made*. There are occasions when such a story is important news. At times, it may be necessary to report information not protected by the qualified privilege defense. But when that step is taken, it should be done with a full awareness of the potential for libel that may exist. At that point, the precise wording of the story may be crucial. To qualify a story by saying someone is only an "alleged" murderer probably will not help if he has not been charged with the crime, but to say he was "detained for questioning in connection with" a crime may—if that is really what has happened.

Equally troubling is the problem of government officials who engage in activities beyond the scope of their official duties. A 1979 U.S. Supreme Court decision provided a classic example of a United States senator engaged in a thoroughly newsworthy activity in which he was not—the court ruled—protected by privilege. The case, *Hutchinson v. Proxmire* (443 U.S. 11), involved the "Golden Fleece of the Month Awards," presented to various individuals and organizations by Sen. William Proxmire (D-Wis.) because he felt they were wasting the taxpayers' money in a conspicuous way. One of the winners of this tongue-in-cheek award was Dr. Ronald Hutchinson, a mental health researcher who had received nearly a half million dollars in government grants to study such things as the teeth-clenching habits of monkeys under stress. Dr. Hutchinson sued, claiming this satirical award damaged his professional reputation. Inasmuch as Senator Proxmire regularly issued press releases publicizing his selections for the "Golden Fleece" award, Hutchinson was able to show the elements of libel, including a publication beyond the limits of Proxmire's absolute privilege as a senator. The Court said this privilege covered the senator's remarks in the *Congressional Record* but didn't cover the press release even though it was almost a verbatim copy of those remarks. The Court ruled that the privilege defense did *not* protect Proxmire. The senator had gone beyond his official capacity in issuing a press release, even if it said the same thing he had said on the floor of Congress.

If a U.S. senator who pokes fun at what he considers wasteful government spending is not protected by the privilege defense, it should be apparent that this libel defense has its limitations. However, it should be noted that the libel suit was against the senator, and not against the media that reported the award. Probably no state would entertain (nor would the First Amendment allow) a libel suit against a news medium that accurately reported the contents of the Congressional speech in which Proxmire announced the award. The senator's mistake was republishing his own remarks off the floor of Congress.

The *Proxmire* decision troubled many journalists, because the "Golden Fleece" awards were not only newsworthy but also dealt with a matter of great public concern (wasteful government spending). For better or worse, the Supreme Court chose to restrict the scope of the constitutional absolute privilege of members of Congress. But that had little effect on the qualified privilege of the media to report on issues of public concern; that privilege has been expanding in recent years. Nor did it affect the right of other public officials to issue press releases: at least two other court decisions have extended public officials' common law privilege to their press releases. All *Proxmire* really did was to limit the constitutional privilege of those who serve in Congress.

As a means of protecting the media when they fairly and accurately report public records and public proceedings, qualified privilege represents an important safeguard. When a public official engages in slander during a government proceeding, or when an official public document carries a libelous charge, the privilege defense enables the media to report this newsworthy item to the public.

The breadth of the privilege defense was illustrated by a 1991 federal appeals court decision upholding the *National Enquirer's* right to reveal that entertainer Engelbert Humperdinck had been accused of having the AIDS virus—even though the newspaper staff was told the charge was false. In *Dorsey v. National Enquirer* (952 F.2d 250), the court reaffirmed that the

Focus on...
Fact vs. Opinion

How can you tell the difference between fact and opinion under *Milkovich v. Lorain Journal?*

As Chief Justice Rehnquist put it, "expressions of 'opinion' may often imply an assertion of objective fact." A statement like "I think my teacher gives men better grades than she gives women" is NOT really an opinion under *Milkovich.* Why? Because it could be proven true or false, if one had access to the teacher's grades. Someone who heard the statement might think that the speaker had knowledge to support that assertion. Simply prefacing this statement with "I think" does not make it an opinion under *Milkovich.*

On the other hand, a statement like "I think my teacher is a bad teacher" is truly opinion, because there is no way to prove "badness" one way or another. It may be up to a jury to determine whether a statement is fact or opinion.

privilege defense covered a court document filed by a woman who had a daughter by Arnold Dorsey (Humperdinck's real name) and who was seeking additional support payments on the ground that Dorsey was HIV-positive. The *Enquirer* said in a page-one headline, "Mother of His Child Claims in Court...Engelbert has AIDS virus." A photo caption contained Humperdinck's denial that he was HIV-positive. Although the *Enquirer* escaped liability in this case, photos and captions can create libel problems. For instance, in 2006 a federal appeals court refused to dismiss a libel suit against *Boston Magazine* for an article that implied Boston teenagers were promiscuous, illustrated by photos of local teenagers. A caption in small type said, "the photos... were from a... project on teen sexuality... of individuals unrelated to the people or events described in this story." One young woman who was recognizable in a photo sued, claiming that the article and photo created the impression she was sexually active, despite the disclaimer (*Stanton v. Metro Corp.*, 438 F.3d 119).

In addition to the qualified privilege defense, there is one circumstance under which the media are afforded an absolute privilege defense. Under Section 315 of the Communications Act, broadcasters are required to provide equal opportunities for air time to all candidates for a given public office. And the act denies the broadcaster any control over the content of a candidate's remarks made on the air under this provision. Thus, the broadcaster has no way to prevent a politician from defaming someone during such a broadcast.

In a 1959 decision (*Farmers Educational and Cooperative Union v. WDAY*, 360 U.S. 525), the U.S. Supreme Court afforded broadcasters an absolute immunity from libel and slander suits under these circumstances. Since they are forbidden to censor or otherwise control the content of political speeches required under Section 315, broadcasters are powerless to prevent a defamation and should not be held accountable if one occurs, the Court ruled.

Some states carry this logic a step further: they exempt broadcasters from liability for defamatory statements made as a part of network programming they are not allowed to edit locally (although the network remains liable).

The fair report privilege remained alive and well as two state supreme courts in 2010 supported it. The Supreme Judicial Court of Massachusetts in *Howell v. Enterprise Publishing Co.* (455 Mass. 641) said that a Brockton, Mass. newspaper was protected for its reports on the firing of James Howell, the superintendent of a sewer department, after inappropriate sexual materials were found on his work computer. The *Enterprise* used anonymous sources in some of its stories, and the court said that even those were protected under the fair reporting privilege, because those sources generally accurately reported government actions (even though there were a few errors). Noting that there might sometimes be a concern that anonymous reports will distort the truth of official actions, the court said that the information in this case provided by anonymous sources was accurate, adding, "The privilege to report official actions would mean very little, however, if to qualify for its protection, the media were limited to reporting such actions solely on the basis of on-the-record statements by high-ranking (authorized to speak) officials or published official documents."

In *Salzano v. North Jersey Media Group* (993 A.2d 778) the New Jersey Supreme Court upheld the fair report privilege after a state appellate court had narrowed it by applying it only to journalists' use of final judgments, not pretrial filings. Thomas Salzano had sued two New Jersey newspapers for libel after they reported on his bankruptcy case using information filed in court. The court said initial pleadings "fall squarely within the protective sweep of the privilege," and described the privilege as a hybrid: "It is conditional insofar as it attaches only to full, fair, and accurate reports of government proceedings. It becomes absolute once those prerequisites are met." The U.S. Supreme Court denied *cert.*

States may recognize other forms of qualified privilege. For example, in 2011, the Second Circuit affirmed a lower court's dismissal of a defamation suit against a Cornell scientist by his post-doctoral research associate on state qualified privilege grounds (*Chandok v. Klessig*, 632 F.3d 803). Meena Chandok sued her laboratory supervisor, Daniel Klessig, for defamation for claiming that her research in his lab was falsified, as no one in the lab after she left could replicate her research findings (a critical part of the scientific method). She declined his repeated invitations for her assistance in helping to replicate her findings. Klessig then reported to a federal funding agency his allegations of scientific misconduct and wrote letters to two journals in which Chandok's research had been published, retracting the articles and alleging that his investigation "strongly suggests that she falsified" her data.

A federal district court granted summary judgment to Klessig. On appeal, the Second Circuit agreed. In New York, there exists "a qualified privilege when [a statement] is fairly made by a person in the discharge of some public or private duty, legal or moral." Thus, the court said, in this case Klessig's reports of Chandok's alleged scientific misconduct were made as a result of his duty to report his findings to professional journals, government agencies, and his own institution, and were thus privileged.

Fair Comment and Criticism

Another of the classic common law libel defenses is called *fair comment*. Although it has been partially superseded by the constitutional protection for the media created by the Supreme Court in recent years, it remains important in many states.

The fair comment defense protects expressions of opinion about the public performances of persons such as entertainers and politicians who voluntarily place themselves before the public. The courts recognized long ago that reviewing public figures' performances is a legitimate function of the press and should be protected, even if it sometimes means excusing defamation.

As this defense was expanded by the courts, it came to protect even hostile expressions of opinion as long as two qualifications were met: the expression had to be based on facts that were correct and accurate, and it had to be a critique of the person's public performance rather than his/her private life.

In recent years, many states eliminated these requirements, extending libel protection to all expressions of opinion that are clearly labeled as such, while allowing libel suits only for *false statements of fact.* This trend was greatly encouraged by the majority opinion in the Supreme Court's *Gertz* decision, which said, "Under the First Amendment there is no such thing as a false idea. However pernicious an opinion may seem, we depend for its correction not on the conscience of judges and juries but on the competition of other ideas." That language seemed to rule out libel suits for expressions of opinion.

However, in 1990 the Supreme Court added an important qualification to this in the case of *Milkovich v. Lorain Journal Co.* (497 U.S. 1). In *Milkovich,* the court allowed a high school wrestling coach to sue a sports columnist who accused him of lying under oath during an investigation of a melee that broke out at a campus wrestling match. A lower court ruled that the entire sports column was an expression of opinion and therefore not libelous.

The Supreme Court held that expressions of opinion enjoy no *separate* Constitutional protection in libel suits. However, the court reaffirmed its holding in *Philadelphia Newspapers v. Hepps,* discussed earlier. The *Hepps* **case** held that libel plaintiffs must prove the falsity of any allegedly libelous statement, at least in cases involving matters of public concern. And because opinions by their nature cannot be proven true or false, expressions of opinion cannot be the basis for a successful libel suit. However, in *Milkovich* there was more than an expression of opinion: there were *potentially false factual allegations.* For example, to accuse a coach of lying under oath is to accuse him of a crime. This was a column of opinion—but it also contained factual allegations that might be proven false. The Supreme Court ruled that the states may allow libel suits in such situations. Chief Justice William Rehnquist, writing for the Court, used an example to explain the difference between fact and opinion:

> [U]nlike the statement, "In my opinion Mayor Jones is a liar," the statement, "in my opinion Mayor Jones shows his abysmal ignorance by accepting the teaching of Marx and Lenin," would not be actionable.

While a pure expression of opinion cannot be the basis for a libel suit, an opinion that carries a false factual implication (like the charge that "Mayor Jones is a liar") is not constitutionally protected. If the writer or speaker cannot prove that Mayor Jones actually told a lie on at least one specific occasion, the statement may be an actionable libel, not a protected expression of opinion. To say that someone told a lie is a factual allegation that may be proved or disproved; to say a person is "abysmally ignorant" is just someone's opinion.

The distinction between a fact and an opinion is often a very subtle one. As a result, it may be necessary to have a full libel trial in which a jury determines whether a given statement is a protected expression of opinion or a false and libelous factual allegation.

Nevertheless, the fair comment defense offers excellent protection for those who disseminate pure opinions. Fair comment often protects the media from liability even for vitriolic political rhetoric, social commentary and criticism of the arts. This defense allows the media to use intemperate language and get away with it, as long as a statement is clearly an expression of opinion. It has been said that the fair comment defense protects *rhetorical hyperbole.* For instance, during a single year various courts allowed the media to: accuse a church of "Nazi-style anti-Semitism," call someone the "worst" sports announcer in town, and refer to a newspaper publisher as a "near-Neanderthal" whose paper is published "by paranoids for paranoids." (See *Holy Spirit Assn. v. Sequoia Elsevier,* 426 N.Y.S.2d 759, 1980; *Myers v. Boston Magazine,* 403 N.E.2d 376, 1980; and *Loeb v. New Times,* 497 F.Supp. 85, 1980.)

Two federal court decisions may help to explain the difference between a statement of fact (which could lead to a successful libel suit if false) and an expression of opinion (which could not). In a 1985 case, *Ollman v. Evans* (750 F.2d 970), and a 1986 case, *Janklow v. Newsweek* (788 F.2d 1300), two different federal circuit courts faced the problem of separating fact from opinion. The first case arose when syndicated columnists Rowland Evans and Robert Novak accused Bertell Ollman, a political science professor at New York University, of not only being an avowed Marxist but also of wanting to use his teaching position as a platform for political indoctrination. He sued the columnists for libel.

In the second case, William Janklow, the governor of South Dakota, was described in a *Newsweek* magazine article as having had a long-running feud with Native American activist Dennis Banks. *Newsweek* implied that as South Dakota's attorney general, Janklow had prosecuted Banks to get revenge after Banks falsely accused him of raping an Indian girl. Janklow sued *Newsweek* for libel.

In both cases, the federal courts had to distinguish facts from opinion. In both, the courts found the statements to be opinions and thus not the proper basis for a libel suit. Both decisions are especially significant because they are *en banc* decisions—rulings by all judges of the particular circuit court instead of the usual panel of three judges.

Adapting and slightly modifying the guidelines developed in the *Ollman* case, the *Janklow* decision listed the following four criteria to be used in determining whether a statement is a potentially libelous fact or a protected expression of opinion:

1. *The precision and specificity of the disputed statement.* Calling someone a "fascist" is indefinite and therefore an opinion; charging someone with a specific wrongful act would be a statement of fact.
2. *The verifiability of the statement.* "If a statement cannot plausibly be verified, it cannot be seen as 'fact,'" the court said.
3. *The literary context in which the statement is made.* A court may look at the type of publication, its style of writing and intended audience to determine whether a statement is fact or opinion.
4. *The "public context" of the statement.* A statement made in "a public, political arena" or which "implicates core values of the First Amendment" is much more likely to be an expression of opinion than a statement of fact.

Concluding its analysis of the context of the *Newsweek* article, the *Janklow* ruling added: "Here we have criticism of the conduct of a state attorney general who now serves as governor, as well as questions about the actions of three other governors of two other states, all involving an issue of national importance, the treatment of Indian people. Few other discussions of public concern could make a greater claim for First Amendment protection."

While this four-part test may not be accepted by all courts dealing with fact-or-opinion questions, it has now been adopted by several federal circuit courts.

In 1994, a prominent federal court caused near panic among book reviewers and others who write critical reviews by holding that a book reviewer could be sued for expressing the opinion that a book contains "too much sloppy journalism." However, the court changed its mind and reversed itself a few months later, causing widespread relief among reviewers. In *Moldea v. New York Times Co.* (15 F.3d 1137, and 22 F.3d 310, 1994), the U.S. Court of Appeals in Washington, D.C. issued this surprising pair of opinions.

The case began when *New York Times* sports writer Gerald Eskenazi did a review of *Interference: How Organized Crime Influences Professional Football,* a book by Dan E. Moldea. The review, published in the *New York Times Book Review,* offered a number of examples from Moldea's book to back up the charge that it contained "sloppy journalism."

Moldea sued for libel, charging that the *New York Times* book review destroyed his career as an author. A trial court dismissed the lawsuit almost immediately and Moldea appealed. At first, the appellate court reinstated the lawsuit, but then the three-judge panel that ruled on the case took the unusual step of reversing itself. In the second ruling, the court held that to escape libel, a book reviewer's criticism must be "rationally supportable by reference to the actual text he or she is evaluating." In short, what a book review says about a book need not be more than a *supportable interpretation* of the book. The appellate court made it clear that in the context of a book review, a charge such as "sloppy journalism" is not libelous as long as it is backed up with valid examples from the book.

To summarize the fact-versus-opinion distinction, a false charge that someone committed a crime is likely to be ruled a libelous statement of fact, even if it appears on an "opinion" page of a newspaper, in a direct quote or in a letter to the editor or an advertisement. However, if the charge is made by a public official or during a government proceeding, the *privilege* defense may apply even though the charge is a false statement of fact and not a protected expression of opinion.

On the other hand, a clearly labeled column or editorial accusing a public figure of incompetence is likely to be ruled an opinion, protected by the fair comment defense. But between the extremes of falsely calling someone a murderer (almost certainly a statement of fact) and accusing a celebrity of lacking talent or accusing a politician of incompetence (which would usually qualify as an expression of opinion), there is a large gray area. In this ill-defined middle ground between fact and opinion, the courts must often decide on a case-by-case basis whether a statement is fact or opinion. If anything, the gray area is a little bigger as a result of the Supreme Court's 1990 decision in the *Milkovich* case.

However, one thing has become clear about the *Milkovich* decision: most states are continuing to dismiss libel cases based on statements that are clearly expressions of opinion as opposed to verifiably true or false statements of fact. When the *Milkovich* case was decided, many journalists feared an avalanche of lawsuits by persons criticized in columns, reviews, editorials and op-ed pieces. Except where an opinion piece also contains an allegedly false factual statement, that has simply not happened.

In the years since the *Milkovich* decision, most courts have continued to interpret the fair comment defense liberally, extending broad protection to expressions of opinion. Perhaps a 1998 decision of the Ninth Circuit illustrates the degree to which the courts are refusing to allow libel suits based on expressions of opinion. In *Dodds v. American Broadcasting Company* (145 F.3d 1053), the court dismissed a lawsuit filed by a judge after ABC's *PrimeTime Live* depicted him as incompetent. Writing for the court, Judge Stephen Reinhardt said, "Part of our American heritage is the right of all citizens to express their views about politicians, officeholders and umpires, frequently in highly unfavorable terms." He added that the First Amendment protects "statements of opinion concerning whether a person who holds high public office is fit for that office or is competent to serve... whether or not those statements are supportable, verifiable or based on facts or premises that are disclosed." In 1999, the Supreme Court declined to hear an appeal of this ruling.

These principles apply not only to "politicians, officeholders and umpires" but also to many other people who may be newsworthy, allowing the media to criticize them as well. For example, after the O.J. Simpson murder trial, *New York Post* columnist Andrea Peyser wrote that Johnnie Cochran, Simpson's lead attorney, "will say or do just about anything to win, typically at the expense of the truth." Peyser also said Cochran was part of a team of "legal scoundrels" who "dazzled a Los Angeles jury into buying his fantasy tale of a citywide police conspiracy in order to set free a celebrity who slaughtered his ex-wife."

In 2000, a federal appellate court upheld a trial judge's decision to dismiss Cochran's libel suit. The court said Peyser was merely exercising her constitutionally protected right to criticize Cochran's defense strategy, not accusing him of unethical conduct, lying or anything else that would be actionable as a libel (*Cochran v. NYP Holdings*, 210 F.3d 1036).

One court has extended the opinion defense to a radio host known for his confrontational style. The Ninth Circuit interpreted the distinction between fact and opinion in 2009 in *Gardner v. Martino* (563 F.3d 981) to be one of public expectations. Plaintiffs John and Susan Gardner brought suit against a talk show host, Tom Martino, for comments made on his nationally syndicated radio show about their personal watercraft business. A caller had complaints about the Gardners' handling of a defective craft, and Martino called the Gardners liars and made other negative comments about their business.

The court, in finding against the Gardners, said, in effect, that no one really expects bombastic talk show hosts like Martino to be purveyors of fact: "*The Tom Martino Show* is a radio talk show program that contains many of the elements that would reduce the audience's expectation of learning an objective fact: drama, hyperbolic language, an opinionated and arrogant host, and heated controversy." Martino reasonably relied on what the caller told him about her problems, and "it would be understood that the contested statements were the type of obvious exaggeration generally employed on Martino's program." Thus, said the court, Martino's statements were opinion rather than objective statements of fact.

The Sixth Circuit extended the opinion defense to an article in a weekly magazine called *Cleveland Scene*, in a defamation suit brought by the mayor of Seven Hills, Ohio (*Bentkowski v. Scene Magazine*, 637 F.3d 689). Entitled "The Bizarre Boy Mayor," the article began with this paragraph: "In his latest attempt to prove how super-duper cool his city is, Seven Hills Mayor David Bentkowski recently sent a bizarre letter to the suburb's 'young residents.' The three-page missive, mailed to residents '18-40ish,' explains that 'Seven Hills is actually starting to become "hip..."' The article also suggested that the mayor limited feedback at meetings and discouraged city employees from running for office.

The district court awarded summary judgment to the magazine, and the Sixth Circuit agreed, saying that the words in context were clearly protected opinion: "Here, the statements at issue were clearly made in the general context of opinion. The article uses words and phrases such as 'super-duper cool,' 'sweet,' 'rad,' 'killer,' 'Autistic Village,' 'student-council campaign speech,' and 'political IQ of Quiznos' lettuce.' It uses simile, hyperbole, and other figurative language to express ideas, and it is ridden with humor and sarcasm." No one would assume that the writer was trying to be unbiased.

The opinion defense has been extended in New York to even pointed, hurtful posts on a private Facebook page. In *Finkel v. Dauber* (906 N.Y.S.2d 697), a New York state court said that statements on such a page were opinion. Denise Finkel asserted that even though she was never named on the "Ninety Cents" Facebook page maintained by people she knew, she was the "11th cent" in posts such as "I heard that the 11th cent got aids when she hired a male prostitute who came dressed as a sexy fireman." The court called this opinion: "Taken together, the statements can only be read as puerile attempts by adolescents to outdo each other. While the posts display an utter lack of taste and propriety, they do not constitute statements of fact." The suggestion that the page constituted cyberbullying was rejected because the court could find no case law recognizing cyberbullying as a tort in the jurisdiction.

Minor Defenses

In addition to the generally recognized libel defenses, other defenses have been recognized by some courts. Also, two purely technical defenses should be noted here.

Perhaps the most interesting of the less-recognized defenses is one called *neutral reportage*. It got its main impetus from a 1977 Second Circuit decision in *Edwards v. National Audubon Society* (556 F.2d 113). That case involved a *New York Times* story reporting a heated dispute between the National Audubon Society and a group of scientists the society had accused of being "paid to lie" by pesticide companies. The paper attempted to cover both sides on this controversy and was sued by some of the scientists for reporting the charge against them, even though the reporter attempted to present their side of the story too. The Second Circuit recognized a special defense for this situation, pointing out that the paper was attempting to be neutral in reporting both sides of a controversial issue.

Although the idea of a neutral reportage defense is appealing to those who believe the media should be able to cover all sides of a controversy without risking a libel suit, the concept has not been widely accepted by other courts. For instance, shortly after the *Edwards* decision another federal appellate court declined to follow the precedent and refused to recognize the defense in a seemingly similar situation. Some state courts (in Florida, for instance) have recognized neutral reportage, while others (in Kentucky, Michigan, New York and Pennsylvania, for example) have not. In Illinois, one appellate court recognized neutral reportage but another appellate court rejected the concept.

In 1998, the California Supreme Court rejected neutral reportage in a case where a tabloid, *The Globe*, republished charges made in an obscure book that a farmer who had once been a photojournalist was the real assassin of Sen. Robert F. Kennedy. The California court held that the defense could be used by the media to escape liability for republishing known falsehoods about private persons who have little access to the media and therefore little opportunity to reply to the charges (*Khawar v. Globe Communications*, 19 C.4th 254). In 2004, the Pennsylvania Supreme Court ruled that neither the U.S. Constitution nor the Pennsylvania Constitution provides a neutral reportage defense. In *Norton v. Glenn* (860 A.2d 48), the court allowed a lawsuit where one borough council member engaged in heated exchanges with another. When a local newspaper reported charges and countercharges that the feuding local officials made *outside* of a council meeting, the result was a libel suit. (The reporting of charges made *during* the meeting would have been protected by the privilege defense.) The U.S. Supreme Court declined to hear appeals of either of these decisions.

In short, while neutral reportage has been accepted as a new libel defense in some jurisdictions, it has not yet gained the broad acceptance that many journalists hoped it would.

Among the technical (as opposed to substantive) libel defenses, two should be mentioned here: *consent* and the *statute of limitations*. Where it can be proved that a plaintiff gave an actual consent to a libelous publication, he or she cannot thereafter sue for libel. If the consent was voluntarily and intelligently given, it precludes a libel suit. Likewise, where the statute of limitations (the time limit during which a law suit must be filed) has run, the defendant is entitled to an easy dismissal without the trouble and expense of a trial.

FIG. 21. Justice
William J. Brennan, Jr.,
official Supreme Court
portrait, 1976.

*Library of Congress, Prints
and Photographs Division,
[LC-USZ62-60138].*

■ LIBEL AND THE FIRST AMENDMENT

The extent to which the U.S. Supreme Court has reshaped American libel law in recent years is probably best shown by the number of times we have already mentioned the Supreme Court in this chapter.

Until 1964 we could have concluded our discussion of libel law with almost no mention of the Supreme Court. For nearly 200 years of American jurisprudence, the nation's highest court took the position that civil libel suits were purely a state matter and none of its business. But in 1964 the historic *New York Times v. Sullivan* decision was handed down, establishing that there are constitutional limits to what states may do in awarding libel judgments.

What prompted this landmark Supreme Court decision was a half-million-dollar libel judgment against the *New York Times*. In making this award, an Alabama jury was allowed to presume that a massive injury had occurred simply because it found the wording of an advertisement libelous to L. B. Sullivan, a Montgomery city commissioner. The ad never mentioned Sullivan, and in fact only a few copies of that issue of the *Times* were ever distributed in Sullivan's community.

What did the advertisement say to produce such a large libel judgment? It said, among other things, that the Montgomery police had taken certain actions against civil rights demonstrators that they in fact had not. We could devote several pages of this chapter to the charges contained in the ad and the means by which Sullivan's lawyers convinced a jury that the ad defamed him even though he wasn't mentioned. However, Chapter One discussed this case to illustrate court procedures, so we'll not repeat the details here. But Sullivan won at the trial level, and the Alabama Supreme Court affirmed the judgment in its full amount.

Meanwhile, other Montgomery public officials filed additional libel suits against the *New York Times*, seeking total damages of $3 million. The *Times* was going to pay dearly for publishing a pro-civil rights advertisement that contained some factual errors and then distributing a few dozen copies of the paper in Montgomery, Ala.

Had the U.S. Supreme Court not chosen to review the case—instead maintaining its long tradition of leaving civil libel law completely up to the states—the threat of censorship

FIG. 22. The March 1960 New York Times advertisement that gave rise to the case of New York Times v. Sullivan in 1964.

National Archives at Atlanta, made available on Flickr as part of the U.S. National Archives' Documented Rights Exhibit.

via libel suits would have been a serious one. The Supreme Court broke with tradition and agreed to hear the case precisely because lawsuits such as this one were a serious threat to First Amendment freedoms.

Writing for a unanimous Court, Justice William Brennan ruled that the huge libel judgment against the *Times* could not stand—for three reasons. He said to allow such a judgment would in effect sanction a new form of government censorship of the press via civil libel suits. To avoid lawsuits by local officials in various communities to which the nation's major newspapers are mailed, the major papers would have to steer clear of controversial subjects. Moreover, Brennan wrote, the media need some "breathing space" in their handling of controversial issues—including some protection when errors inevitably occur during the "robust" debate of these issues.

Finally, Brennan pointed out that public officials voluntarily move into the public arena when they seek office, subjecting themselves to much more scrutiny than private citizens should have to face. Criticism is something they must expect. In return, public officials gain more access to the media to present their side of the story than a private citizen enjoys. Thus, public officials need less libel protection than other citizens.

Under this rationale, the Supreme Court ruled that public officials could no longer win libel judgments against the media unless they could prove *actual malice*:

> The constitutional guarantees require, we think, a federal rule that prohibits a public official from recovering damages for a defamatory falsehood relating to his official conduct unless he proves that a statement was made with "actual malice"—that is, with knowledge that it was false or with reckless disregard of whether it was false or not.

This language is among the most important ever written on mass media law in America. If you remember any single concept from this discussion, you should remember that public officials must prove actual malice to win libel suits, and you should remember how actual malice is defined. First, actual malice means *publishing a falsehood*. Second, it means publishing that falsehood either with *knowledge* that it was false, or with *reckless disregard* for whether it was false or not.

Malice is a legal term that has other meanings in other contexts, often referring to bad intentions. But in libel law it was given a special meaning in the *New York Times v. Sullivan* decision. But as we will see, a 2009 development in the First Circuit calls this traditional meaning of "malice" in libel cases into question.

When a landmark Supreme Court decision is handed down, there are often unanswered questions—issues that must be clarified by additional Supreme Court rulings. The *New York Times* case had exactly that result. First of all, what public officials are included in its coverage? Does it apply only to elected officials or does it also apply to public figures who hold no office? And does it apply to all public servants or just to certain prominent ones? And equally important, exactly what does "reckless disregard for the truth" mean?

Post-Sullivan Rulings

In the years that followed the New York Times decision, the Supreme Court attempted to resolve these ongoing questions by handing down a series of additional libel rulings. First, in a 1966 case (*Rosenblatt v. Baer*, 383 U.S. 75) the Court said the actual malice requirement would apply to minor public officials. A. D. Rosenblatt, a New Hampshire newspaper columnist, had accused the former supervisor of a county skiing and recreation area of mishandling public funds. The Court said even a public employee of that rank would henceforth have to prove actual malice to win a libel suit. The "public official" designation would apply to all who have "substantial responsibility for...the conduct of governmental affairs," the Court ruled. More recent rulings have cast doubts on the applicability of the actual malice requirement to minor public employees, but for the moment the rule was that almost anybody on the public payroll who made policy decisions would have to prove actual malice.

Then in 1967 the Court applied the actual malice rule to public figures who held no office and offered guidance on the meaning of the "reckless disregard" concept in two cases decided together, *Curtis Publishing Co. v. Butts* and *Associated Press v. Walker* (388 U.S. 130).

The *Curtis* case arose when the *Saturday Evening Post*, published by Curtis, carried an article entitled, "The Story of a College Football Fix." The article claimed that Wally Butts, athletic director at the University of Georgia, had given Alabama coach Paul "Bear" Bryant information in advance about Georgia's game plans for an upcoming football game between the two schools. The story was based on information provided by an insurance agent in Atlanta who said he had overheard a telephone conversation between Butts and Bryant through an electronic error.

Although there was no deadline pressure and the article was published some time after the game, the *Post* did not double-check the story with anyone knowledgeable about football to see whether the information the insurance man claimed he overheard would in fact have helped Alabama or hurt Georgia.

The *Walker* case differed in several respects. It resulted from an AP dispatch detailing the activities of former U.S. Army General Edwin Walker, who resigned his command and engaged in conservative political activities, often speaking out against school desegregation.

Walker was present at the University of Mississippi during the initial desegregation of the campus. A group of whites attacked the federal marshals who were protecting the first black student enrolled at the university. Walker had addressed the crowd of whites. The AP dispatch, moved over the wires within minutes after the fast-breaking events occurred, said ex-General Walker led the charge of the whites. Walker claimed he called for a peaceful protest, counseled against violence, and denied leading the charge.

Butts and Walker each won a libel judgment of about half a million dollars; both Curtis Publishing and the Associated Press appealed to the U.S. Supreme Court. The Supreme Court voted 5-4 to affirm Butts' libel judgment against the *Saturday Evening Post,* but unanimously overruled Walker's judgment against the AP. The Court took the occasion to compare the two situations as a way of illustrating what reckless disregard for the truth means.

But first, a majority of the Supreme Court justices agreed that both men were public figures and should be subject to the *New York Times v. Sullivan* rule, although neither was a public official at the time of the respective libel suits. Walker was no longer an officer in the U.S. Army, and Butts received his salary from the Georgia Athletic Association, a private corporation, not from the state.

However, both men were involved in issues "in which the public has a justified and important interest." Although the court was not unanimous in deciding that the *New York Times* rule as such should apply to public figures as well as public officials, the precedent has held up in the years since and is now settled law. Thus, both men had to show reckless disregard for the truth to win their libel suits.

Why, then, did Butts win while Walker lost? The Court pointed out that there was a big difference between the types of reporting that went into the two stories. The AP was under intense deadline pressure and had no time to double-check its information; the Post was not. The AP had a reporter with a good reputation for accuracy on the scene; the Post relied on the uncorroborated statements of a non-journalist, a man who was in fact an ex-convict, and the magazine's staff never checked the story with anyone who had special expertise in football. Further, the conduct AP's reporter attributed to Walker was consistent with Walker's previous statements on the issue of school desegregation. In short, because the Court found a substantial difference between the *Saturday Evening Post's* reporting practices and AP's, the libel judgment against the *Post* was affirmed while the one against AP was reversed.

The Supreme Court continued its trend of reversing libel judgments against the media with three cases it handed down on the same day in 1971, *Monitor-Patriot Co. v. Roy* (401 U.S. 265), *Ocala Star-Banner v. Damron* (401 U.S. 295) and *Time Inc. v. Pape* (401 U.S. 279). The *Monitor-Patriot* case stemmed from a syndicated column that branded a candidate for the U.S. Senate as a "small time bootlegger" because of a conviction in the 1920s. The plaintiff contended the publisher was vulnerable to a libel judgment because the conviction involved his private life long ago and had nothing to do with his public performance. The Supreme Court ruled the actual malice requirement had not been met, and the libel case could not be sustained, to no one's surprise. After all, the accusation was basically true.

In *Ocala,* the Supreme Court overruled a libel judgment where a newspaper had confused two brothers, identifying a candidate for office as having been convicted of perjury when in fact it was his brother who had been convicted. The Supreme Court said there was no reckless disregard for the truth in this copy desk error. At the time, this seemed to free the media from liability when a public official or public figure is the victim of an accidental misidentification problem such as those discussed earlier in this chapter.

The *Pape* case involved a libel contained in a U.S. Commission on Civil Rights report, disseminated in a *Time* magazine article. *Time* had changed the reported information somewhat, but the Supreme Court found no reckless disregard for the truth in *Time's* reporting of a statement charging a Chicago police officer with brutality—even though the story did not make it clear these were mere allegations. *Time's* imprecise reporting was forgiven in large part because the report itself was ambiguous and subject to more than one interpretation.

The theme in all three of these 1971 cases seemed clear: the traditional rules of libel must give way when a public official is the plaintiff, lest the threat of libel suits unduly inhibit the reporting of public affairs.

Almost Abolishing Libel: The Rosenbloom Case

Moreover, later in 1971 the Supreme Court handed down a decision that was heralded by some as the ultimate victory for the media over the threat of libel: *Rosenbloom v. Metromedia* (403 U.S. 29). Although there was no majority opinion, the three-justice plurality opinion seemed to foreclose libel judgments against the media whenever the plaintiff was involved in an issue of public interest, no matter how private a citizen he or she might be.

George Rosenbloom, a Philadelphia magazine dealer, was arrested during a police campaign against obscenity, and he was called a "smut distributor" and a "girlie-book peddler" on radio station WIP, owned by Metromedia. He was never convicted, and a court granted an injunction ordering the police to leave him alone, since the books were not legally obscene. Rosenbloom sued the station and won a $275,000 libel judgment. An appellate court reversed, although Rosenbloom contended that he was a private citizen rather than a public figure and should not be required to prove actual malice to win a libel suit.

The U.S. Supreme Court agreed on a 5-3 vote that he should not win a libel judgment, but only three justices (Brennan, Burger and Blackmun) joined in the plurality opinion. Justices Black and White concurred in the result, but on a different rationale. What made *Rosenbloom* memorable was the sweep of the language in that plurality opinion. Justice Brennan, writing for the court, said the distinction between public officials and public figures on the one hand and private citizens on the other "makes no sense." He said that in the future the criterion for applying the actual malice requirement should be whether the plaintiff was involved in a matter of "public or general interest." Thus, the court seemed to be saying the media could bootstrap themselves out of libel suits by publicizing a private person's activities so as to generate public interest and then avoid a lawsuit because of that public interest.

After *Rosenbloom*, it seemed that virtually everyone whose name appeared in a newspaper or in a radio or television newscast might have to prove actual malice. And because proving actual malice turned out to be so difficult, it appeared for a time in the early 1970s that the media were at last virtually free from their most troubling legal problem, the libel suit.

Malice, Negligence and Gertz

However, three years later the hope that libel was being abolished vanished when the Supreme Court handed down its famous *Gertz v. Welch* decision in 1974. Much has already been said of this decision, which profoundly changed the law of libel in all 50 states—and thus laid the foundation for modern libel law when private persons are involved.

Elmer Gertz, a Chicago lawyer, represented the family of a young black man who had been killed by a Chicago police officer (the officer was later prosecuted for the act). With Gertz's help, the family was seeking civil damages in a suit for *wrongful death* in the late 1960s.

An article appeared in *American Opinion,* the magazine of the ultraconservative John Birch Society, claiming that Gertz was part of a communist conspiracy to discredit law enforcement. Gertz was called a "communist-fronter" and a "Leninist." The article also falsely accused Gertz of various subversive activities.

Gertz sued Robert Welch Inc., publisher of *American Opinion,* and initially won a $50,000 jury verdict against Welch. However, the trial judge set aside the verdict and ruled that Gertz was a public figure who could not win a libel judgment without proving actual malice, something he had not proved during the original trial. Then the Supreme Court's *Rosenbloom* decision was announced, and an appellate court upheld the trial judge's decision that Gertz would have to prove actual malice to win a libel judgment against Welch. Gertz asked the Supreme Court to review the determination that he was a public figure.

In a narrow 5-4 decision that Justice Blackmun said he joined only because the country needed a clear-cut majority opinion on an issue as important as libel law, the Supreme Court backed away from the *Rosenbloom* decision and reinstated the distinction between private persons and public figures. The Court said that Gertz, although he was a prominent Chicago lawyer, had done nothing to seek public figure status in this context. Thus, he should not be constitutionally required to prove actual malice to win a libel suit.

The Supreme Court said the states should feel free to allow private persons such as Elmer Gertz to win libel suits against the media by proving a level of fault short of actual malice. However, in no case could the media be held on the "strict liability" (or "liability without fault") basis that had been the prevailing rule of law for at least 200 years. The Court said the media had to be guilty of something beyond merely publishing a falsehood—there had to be some level of fault. Still, the Court didn't say every state had to allow private persons to prove mere negligence, just that the states could allow this lesser standard of proof for private plaintiffs if they wished. But the Court also said any state that wished to could still require private persons to prove actual malice.

As a result, in all 50 states public figures still have to prove actual malice. But in most states that is not required of private persons. Most states accepted the Supreme Court's invitation and adopted rules under which private persons must prove only some level of negligence to win a libel case against the media. However, some state courts have chosen to require all libel plaintiffs—private persons as well as public figures—to prove actual malice in any libel case involving an issue of public or general concern (see, e.g., a 1999 Indiana Supreme Court decision that so held: *Journal-Gazette Co. v. Bandido's,* 712 N.E.2d 446).

Now both of these terms—*actual malice* and *negligence*—have special meanings in law. There is no way we can define them in a way that would be applicable in all states. We already indicated that negligence is a less serious breach of the standards of good journalism than reckless disregard for the truth. Negligence may well mean nothing more than publishing a falsehood as a result of sloppy reporting, or perhaps even because an innocent error slipped past the copy desk. Some states say it means failing to do the kind of checking a "reasonable man" would do under the circumstances.

In addition to ruling that private persons could be allowed to sue for libel without proving actual malice, *Gertz* had an important effect on damage awards in libel suits, as already noted: the ruling required most private libel plaintiffs to prove at least *general damages* (sometimes called *actual damages*). The Court said that in the absence of a showing of actual malice, there could be no punitive or presumed damages. Instead, plaintiffs who could only prove negligence and not actual malice could win only such damages as they could prove, although those damages would not be limited to just out-of-pocket losses (special damages).

As a result of these sweeping changes in American libel law, a new period of reassessment occurred, as the courts and legislatures tried to adapt their rules to the new constitutional boundaries. It quickly became apparent that the crucial issue in future libel suits would often be whether the plaintiff was a public figure or a private person. To assist in resolving this question, the *Gertz* ruling offered this observation about public figures and private persons:

> For the most part those who attain this status [public figure] have assumed roles of especial prominence in the affairs of society. Some occupy positions of such persuasive power and influence that they are deemed public figures for all purposes. More commonly, those classed as public figures have thrust themselves to the forefront of particular public controversies in order to influence the resolution of the issues involved. In either event, they invite attention and comment.

Thus, the Supreme Court was saying that many public figures are so classified only because they have thrust themselves into the vortex of a particular controversy. These people might be called *vortex public figures*, and the courts were to look mainly to a libel plaintiff's own conduct in deciding whether the definition applied.

There is one ironic footnote to the *Gertz* case: after the landmark Supreme Court decision, Elmer Gertz patiently waited as his case meandered through pretrial procedures and finally went to trial again. Although the Supreme Court decision emphasized that non-public figures such as Gertz didn't necessarily have to prove actual malice, during the second trial a jury agreed that he did prove actual malice and awarded him $400,000 in damages (including $300,000 in punitive damages). The new judgment was affirmed by a federal appellate court in 1982 —eight years after the Supreme Court decision and 14 years after the police shooting that led to the original libel (*Gertz v. Welch*, 680 F.2d 527).

Private Persons and Public Figures

In the aftermath of the *Gertz* decision, the Supreme Court repeatedly had to decide whether libel plaintiffs were public figures (who had to prove actual malice to win their lawsuits) or private persons (who could win by proving just negligence). The first of these cases, *Time Inc. v. Firestone* (424 U.S. 448, 1976), involved a divorce in a wealthy and socially prominent Florida family. Russell Firestone, an heir to the tire company fortune, sued his wife Mary Alice for divorce on the grounds of extreme cruelty and adultery, and the case received extensive publicity. When the divorce was granted after a trial in which there was considerable evidence of marital infidelity on both sides (enough evidence "to make Dr. Freud's hair curl," the judge said), *Time* magazine reported that one of the grounds for the divorce was adultery.

However, the judge was vague about the legal grounds for the divorce, and in fact an obscure provision of Florida law would have prohibited the award of alimony if adultery had been a ground for a divorce. Since Firestone had been granted alimony, her alleged adultery couldn't have been one of the legal grounds on which the divorce was granted. This obscure point of Florida law escaped the *Time* correspondent—but that could hardly be called publishing a falsehood with reckless disregard for the truth. (Was it even negligent reporting?) Obviously, if Firestone were ruled a public figure she would have less chance to win a libel judgment. There was evidence that she was indeed a public figure and even sought publicity: she held two press conferences to discuss the divorce and subscribed to a clipping service. The story was covered in no fewer than 45 articles in one local newspaper.

However, the Supreme Court ruled that Firestone was *not* a public figure. She had not voluntarily thrust herself into any public controversy. The Court said: "Dissolution of marriage through judicial proceedings is not the sort of 'public controversy' referred to in *Gertz,* even though the marital difficulties of extremely wealthy individuals may be of interest to some portion of the reading public." The Court said Firestone had really done nothing more than she was required to do—avail herself of the courts to terminate a marriage.

The Supreme Court seemed to be saying this: while some celebrities and politicians are so pervasively famous that they are all-purpose public figures, most people do not become public figures unless they voluntarily inject themselves into a public debate on a controversial issue. As a result, some relatively well-known persons may not be considered public figures should they sue for libel based on a reference to their personal lives. And when it comes to persons involved in a crime, the Court's *Firestone* ruling made it clear they will *not* ordinarily be classified as public figures: "There appears little reason why these individuals should substantially forfeit that degree of protection which the law of defamation would otherwise afford them simply by virtue of their being drawn into a courtroom."

After the Supreme Court ruled that Firestone was not a public figure, she chose not to pursue her lawsuit further, and the case was eventually dismissed.

It would be difficult to overemphasize the extent to which the thinking in the *Firestone* case is a retrenchment from the libel protection the media enjoyed in the late 1960s and early 1970s. However, the Supreme Court continued the same trend away from classifying newsworthy persons as public figures in a pair of 1979 decisions, *Hutchinson v. Proxmire* (443 U.S. 111) and *Wolston v. Reader's Digest Association* (443 U.S. 157).

The *Hutchinson* case (involving Senator Proxmire's Golden Fleece Award) was discussed earlier in connection with its adverse effect on the privilege defense. At this point, we will simply add that it offered the media little comfort on the issue of who is a public figure, either. The Court said that Dr. Hutchinson was *not* a public figure, despite the fact that he was the research director of a major state-controlled mental health facility—and had won large grants from tax monies. The *Wolston* case followed the same policy of narrowing the definition of a public figure, thus freeing more individuals to sue for libel without proving actual malice. Ilya Wolston had an aunt and uncle who had pleaded guilty to charges of spying for the former Soviet Union, and he had been cited for contempt himself when he failed to comply with a Congressional subpoena. Other than that contempt citation, he was never convicted of any offense. Many years later, a *Reader's Digest* publication included his name in a list of "Soviet agents" in the United States. He sued for libel and a lower court dismissed his case, ruling that he was a public figure who could not prove actual malice. The Supreme Court reversed, finding that he had done nothing to inject himself into a public controversy.

Once again, a libel plaintiff was ruled to be a private person who did not need to prove actual malice to win his case, thereby reducing the media's First Amendment protection and making it much easier for the plaintiff to win.

The definition of a public figure or public official was changing. If some of the Court's early libel rulings were decided under the new standards, would Athletic Director Butts be a public figure—or a public official? What about Pape, the Chicago policeman?

In the decades since the *Firestone, Hutchinson* and *Wolston* decisions, the public figure-private person question has been addressed in literally thousands of lower court cases. If there is a general rule today, it is that many people whose names are in the news are *not* public figures—unless they inject themselves into a public controversy or take other actions likely to place them in the limelight. Even people who hold newsworthy but non-elective government positions may not necessarily be classified as public figures or public officials. For example, in a surprising 1999 decision, the Ohio Supreme Court held that a public high school *principal* was neither a public official nor a public figure for libel purposes and therefore did not have to prove actual malice (*East Canton Education Association v. McIntosh,* 709 N.E.2d 468). In contrast, the Ohio Supreme Court had previously ruled that a public school superintendent *was* a public official (*Scott v. The News-Herald,* 496 N.E.2d 699, 1986), while courts in some other states have found principals to be public officials. So who is a public figure or public official today? The answer depends on which court decides the question.

■ REFINING THE ACTUAL MALICE RULE

Once someone is ruled to be a public official or public figure, he/she faces the difficult challenge of proving actual malice—as defined by the Supreme Court—to win a libel case. During the 1980s and 1990s, the high court clarified the scope of the actual malice rule, applying it in several difficult fact situations.

One of the most important of these cases to the media was *Bose v. Consumers Union* (466 U.S. 485). This 1984 case was a strong reaffirmation of the constitutional safeguards journalists enjoy under *New York Times v. Sullivan,* a decision handed down almost exactly 20 years before the *Bose* ruling. The case began when the Bose Corporation, a manufacturer of high-fidelity speakers, sued *Consumer Reports* magazine for a product review that commented negatively and hyperbolically about the performance of Bose speakers. In a 1970 article, the magazine said that with these speakers music "tended to wander about the room." A Consumers Union engineer had written a report that said the speakers made violins seem "about 10 feet wide."

The manufacturer sued for product disparagement and won a six-figure damage award. During the trial, the judge concluded that the engineer should have said Bose speakers made music sound as if it wandered "along the wall," not "about the room." This, he said, was evidence of actual malice. On appeal, the First Circuit reversed that judgment, ruling that the magazine was *not*

Focus on...
Bose v. Consumers Union, 466 U.S. 485 (1984)

The *Bose* case may be confusing without understanding the roles of different courts. Generally, trial courts with juries are triers of fact (establishing the record of facts to be used in an appeal), and appeals courts are arbiters of law. But these roles are not exclusive in libel cases.

Justice John Paul Stevens wrote, "Judges, as expositors of the Constitution, must independently decide whether the evidence in the record is sufficient to cross the constitutional threshold that bars the entry of any judgment that is not supported by clear and convincing proof of 'actual malice.'"

This means that appeals courts must exercise their own judgments, determining for themselves whether there was actual malice or not. A finding of actual malice, then, is a matter of law, not a finding of fact.

guilty of actual malice in its product review even if some of the engineer's words and conclusions were debatable.

Normally, appellate courts are not supposed to second-guess a trial court's assessment of the evidence in deciding factual issues (such as whether there was actual malice in this *Consumer Reports* article), but that is exactly what the First Circuit did in this case. The Supreme Court upheld that decision, ruling that the media need the additional protection of being able to appeal a trial court's determination of actual malice. To rule otherwise, the court said, would unduly erode First Amendment freedoms by denying the media the right to challenge some libel judgments that are improperly awarded by trial judges or juries.

In finding a lack of actual malice, Justice John Paul Stevens wrote for the majority, "We agree with the Court of Appeals that the difference between hearing violin sounds move around the room and hearing them wander back and forth fits easily within the breathing space that gives life to the First Amendment." Moreover, "an appellate court has an obligation to 'make an independent examination of the whole record' in order to make sure that the judgment does not constitute a forbidden intrusion on the field of free expression."

The *Bose* case represents a significant expansion of the protection the media enjoy under the *New York Times v. Sullivan* rule. When a judge or a jury finds actual malice in a publication or broadcast with little or no evidence of "reckless disregard for the truth," the media now have a second shot at that verdict.

Having the appellate courts empowered to re-evaluate the evidence in libel cases can be vital to the news media, as a 1990 decision involving entertainer Wayne Newton illustrated. Newton sued NBC after the network alleged that he had engaged in questionable business dealings and was in contact with persons involved in organized crime, among other things. A federal jury in Las Vegas—where Newton was a popular celebrity—ruled that he was libeled and awarded him $5.3 million in damages. But the Ninth Circuit overturned the verdict and ordered the case dismissed, ruling that Newton did not prove actual malice and that NBC's statements were basically correct (*Newton v. NBC*, 930 F.2d 662).

Narrowing Gertz

In 1985, the Supreme Court took a major step to narrow the scope of the *Gertz* case: it ruled that *Gertz* applies only to issues of public concern, not to libel cases arising from discussions of purely private matters. That happened in the case of *Dun & Bradstreet v. Greenmoss Builders* (472 U.S. 749).

This case began after Dun & Bradstreet, a credit reporting agency, falsely in-formed several of its clients that Greenmoss, a Vermont construction company, had filed for bankruptcy. The false credit report resulted from a young worker's negligent (but nonmalicious) error in record-checking. Although Greenmoss could not prove actual malice, it won a $350,000 libel judgment against Dun & Bradstreet. The award included punitive damages, despite the *Gertz* case's holding that even non-public figures must prove actual malice to win punitive damages. The judgment was eventually upheld by the Supreme Court.

Affirming the libel verdict, a three-justice plurality ruled that credit rating reports are not a matter of public concern and therefore should not be subject to the actual malice requirement as set forth in *New York Times v. Sullivan* and expanded in *Gertz v. Welch*. This represented a new distinction in libel law: the plurality said the actual malice rule from *Gertz* should continue to apply to libel cases involving issues of public concern, but not to cases involving purely private matters.

While the three justices in the plurality (Lewis Powell, William Rehnquist and Sandra Day O'Connor) voted to create this new exception to the *Gertz* principle, two others (Chief Justice Warren Burger and Justice Byron White) filed concurring opinions in which they agreed that *Gertz* was inapplicable to this situation. But both also said they would overturn *Gertz* itself if given the opportunity. They were dissenters when the *Gertz* decision was handed down in 1974. The remaining four justices dissented in the *Greenmoss* decision, arguing that the *Gertz* principle should apply to this case. Justice William Brennan, who authored the majority opinion in *New York Times v. Sullivan* in 1964, joined Thurgood Marshall, Harry Blackmun and John Paul Stevens to argue that credit reporting is a legitimate matter of public concern and therefore should be subject to the actual malice requirements of *Gertz*.

Nevertheless, the plurality of three justices who carved out this exception to *Gertz*— together with the two justices who would overturn *Gertz* altogether—constituted a majority of the Supreme Court, a majority that said *Gertz* simply does not apply to libel cases involving non-public issues. In such cases, the states are free to allow libel plaintiffs to win without proving either actual malice or negligence. (However, some states have chosen to continue requiring proof of actual malice or negligence in all libel cases, despite this ruling. The five justices were merely saying that the *states are not constitutionally required* to make plaintiffs prove actual malice or negligence in libel cases involving purely private matters.)

Affirming an Actual Malice Ruling

Proving actual malice is usually so difficult that few libel cases are won by public officials or public figures, the people who must prove actual malice to win any libel case that involves an issue of public concern. It is perhaps ironic that in 1989—almost exactly 25 years after the actual malice rule was created by the *New York Times v. Sullivan* decision—the Supreme Court upheld a libel decision involving actual malice for the first time since the 1960s.

Ruling in *Harte-Hanks Communications v. Connaughton* (491 U.S. 657), the Supreme Court unanimously affirmed a lower court's finding that the *Hamilton* (Ohio) *Journal-Beacon* was guilty of actual malice. The newspaper falsely reported that Daniel Connaughton, who was running for a judgeship in an election, wrongfully tried to discredit an opponent.

The Court reaffirmed the guidelines it had set down in the 1984 *Bose* case (discussed earlier), requiring appellate courts to independently review the evidence in libel cases involving alleged actual malice. But the Court then affirmed the appellate court's conclusion that actual malice was present in this case. Justice John Paul Stevens noted the newspaper's failure to check its own news sources—and the fact that an editor declined an opportunity to listen to tape-recorded interviews that could have cast doubts on the accuracy of the story. Those newsroom practices constitute more than just a departure from normal professional standards of journalism; they create evidence of actual malice, the Court concluded.

A jury had awarded Connaughton $5,000 in compensatory damages and $195,000 in punitive damages. The Supreme Court affirmed that verdict.

Actual Malice and Direct Quotations

Is it possible to libel people by misquoting them? When a book, newspaper or magazine uses quotation marks, do readers assume the words inside the quotes are the speaker's exact words? Suppose a reporter knows that a quotation is not precisely what the speaker said. Does that mean the reporter has published a knowing or reckless falsehood—and is therefore guilty of actual malice if a libel suit results from the quotation?

In 1991, the Supreme Court ruled on a libel case that raised those questions, *Masson v. New Yorker Magazine* (501 U.S. 496). The court said a serious misquotation that hurts a person's reputation may be libelous. But at the same time, the court upheld the right of journalists to rephrase what a person says without risking a libel judgment, unless the rephrasing results in a "material change in the meaning."

The case began when Jeffrey Masson, a psychoanalyst who once was the archivist for Sigmund Freud's papers, sued freelance writer Janet Malcolm and *New Yorker* magazine, among others, for publishing a lengthy article about him containing at least six quoted statements that he denied making. Malcolm conducted 40 hours of tape-recorded interviews with Masson. She also claimed there were additional non-recorded interviews during which she took detailed notes; Masson disputed that claim. He said she took no notes during most of the non-recorded interviews, and Malcolm could not find her notes at the time.

Among other things, Malcolm quoted Masson as calling himself an "intellectual gigolo" and "the greatest analyst who ever lived." Those phrases were not in the taped interviews, but Malcolm claimed Masson did say those things during the non-recorded interviews. Masson flatly denied making those statements, charging that he was seriously misquoted—and that the resulting misrepresentation of his views injured his reputation.

Lower federal courts dismissed Masson's libel suit before trial, ruling that the quoted statements were "rational interpretations" of things Masson did say on the tape and therefore not actionable. But the Supreme Court reinstated the case and remanded it to a federal appellate court to determine if the case should go to trial or be dismissed.

Writing for the Court, Justice Anthony Kennedy said that journalists could not be expected to be absolutely precise in every direct quote. However, he said that the quoted statements in the article differed *significantly enough* from the taped statements that Masson was entitled to a jury trial (at which he would have to prove that Malcolm did misquote him, did so knowingly or recklessly, and thereby damaged his reputation). Justice Kennedy said:

> We reject the idea that any alteration beyond correction of grammar or syntax by itself proves falsity in the sense relevant to determining actual malice under the First Amendment.... In some sense, any alteration of a *verbatim* quotation is false, but writers and reporters by necessity alter what people say, at the very least to eliminate grammatical and syntactical infelicities. If every alteration constituted the falsity required to prove actual malice, the practice of journalism, which the First Amendment standard is designed to protect, would require a radical change, one inconsistent with our precedents and First Amendment principles.

Thus, journalists who make minor changes in quoted statements by public figures are protected by the actual malice rule. But if the meaning is knowingly or recklessly changed in a "material" way, and the change hurts the person's reputation, then the person may have a case. (Private persons would only need to prove that they were libeled by a *negligent* misquote rather than by a knowing or reckless one under the libel law of most states.) In short, the *Masson* decision gives journalists some leeway in handling direct quotes, while holding them accountable for changing the meaning of a quote in a way that harms the quoted person's reputation.

When he wrote the Court's opinion in *Masson,* Justice Kennedy also offered a suggestion concerning the actual malice rule itself—one that might have been drawn from his experience as a law professor before he joined the Supreme Court. He said the term "actual malice" is confusing and should not be used in jury instructions. Instead, he said judges should merely tell jurors to decide if a falsehood was published knowingly or with reckless disregard for the truth. The problem, of course, is that many people who have never read a media law textbook assume (with the encouragement of most dictionaries) that "actual malice" means ill will or evil intentions. In libel cases involving public figures or public officials, it doesn't usually mean that at all.

Armed with the Supreme Court's holding that he could win if he could prove he was misquoted in a way that materially changed the meaning and thereby defamed him, Masson got a federal appellate court to refer the matter back to a federal trial court. In a 1993 trial, the jury agreed that he was libeled but deadlocked on the amount of damages to award (if any), and a mistrial was declared. In a second jury trial a year later, the jury ruled against Masson, concluding that he failed to prove his case. Masson then appealed once more, and in 1996 a federal appellate court upheld the jury's verdict. This ended a complex and costly 12-year legal battle (*Masson v. New Yorker Magazine*, 85 F.3d 1394).

By 1996, Malcolm's legal expenses exceeded $2.5 million. Ironically, in 1995 Malcolm said she finally found her long-lost notes from the non-recorded interviews, and they included several key statements that Masson denied making, including the "intellectual gigolo" quote. She said her two-year-old granddaughter pulled a stack of old books and papers off a shelf, including a red notebook containing the missing notes from the Masson interviews. If she could have produced those notes in 1984, the case might have been disposed of much earlier, saving her and her publishers a fortune in legal expenses.

But what about statements actually made by public figures but presented in a context that changes the viewer's understanding of the speaker's statement? The Ninth Circuit in 2010 said that it didn't matter that the plaintiff's statement was actually spoken by him, because the context in which it was presented made it misleading. In *Price v. Stossel* (620 F.3d 992), Dr. Frederick Price, a televangelist, delivered a sermon in which he actually said, "I live in a 25-room mansion. I have my own $6 million yacht. I have my own private jet, and I have my own helicopter, and I have seven luxury automobiles." ABC's *20/20* program, featuring John Stossel as news correspondent, placed the clip in a context so it appeared as though Price was bragging about his own material wealth—when actually Price was speaking from the perspective of a hypothetical wealthy person who is unhappy despite that wealth. ABC did broadcast a retraction, but Price sued. The district court dismissed the case because Price did actually speak the words at issue.

But the Ninth Circuit reversed. Relying on *Masson*, the court said that "the proper comparison is between the meaning of the quotation as published and the meaning of the words as uttered," and thus, the court concluded, "the video quotation of Price's statement materially changed the meaning of Price's words." The court remanded the case for consideration of whether Price could meet the other elements of libel.

The *Price* case might foreshadow what could happen in the case of Shirley Sherrod's libel claims against conservative blogger Andrew Breitbart. In July 2010, Breitbart posted a video clip of a speech Sherrod made for an NAACP fundraising event while she was Georgia State Director of Rural Development for the U.S. Department of Agriculture. The clip contained quotes that made Sherrod, who is black, look as if she was discriminating against white farmers by stating that she might not have done all she could to help a white farmer who was acting superior to her. Sherrod was forced to resign from the Department of Agriculture under pressure from her superiors, and the NAACP and other groups decried her—until it was determined that Breitbart had selectively edited out the context of Sherrod's speech, in which the major point was that it was poverty, not race, that was key to rural development. She was offered a position in the department but turned it down.

In 2011, Sherrod filed suit against Breitbart, alleging libel, false light and infliction of emotional distress. Breitbart moved to use Washington, D.C.'s new anti-SLAPP law against Sherrod's suit, and she countered that anti-SLAPP laws don't apply in federal court—a position other states have taken, although several circuits have enforced state anti-SLAPP laws in federal cases (the Fifth in *Lake Charles American Press* discussed earlier, the Ninth in *Newsham* discussed below, and in 2010, the First Circuit applied the Maine statute in a case involving an elementary school principal, *Godin v. Schencks*, 629 F.3d 79). The Sherrod case is ongoing and will likely continue even after Breitbart's death in 2012.

State Statutes and "Malice" in Common Law

The First Circuit in 2009 sent shockwaves through media companies and attorneys with its decision in *Noonan v. Staples* (556 F.3d 20, *reh'g en banc denied*, 561 F.3d 4) by returning to a state's archaic interpretation of the "actual malice" standard in libel. Usually truth is considered to be an absolute defense against a libel claim, but the First Circuit interpreted Massachusetts state law to suggest that even truthful statements could give rise to a libel action if they were published with malicious intent.

Plaintiff Alan Noonan was fired from his sales position at office supply company Staples for padding his travel expense accounts, an allegation that the trial court found was true. A Staples executive vice president sent a mass e-mail to 1,500 Staples employees informing them that Noonan had been fired for violating the travel and expense policy and warning them that non-compliance would be taken seriously. Noonan sued for libel. The trial court found for Staples, as did the First Circuit initially. However, after a rehearing, the First Circuit reversed. In what some commentators have called the most dangerous libel decision in decades, the First Circuit applied a 1902 Massachusetts law that said that even true statements can result in libel if the defendant acted with ill will or malevolent intent—a common law interpretation of "actual malice." The court said the 1902 statute had been passed before the 1964 *New York Times v. Sullivan* decision that provided the modern interpretation of "actual malice" and dealt with defenses under traditional tort law.

> Since a given statement, even if libelous, must also be false to give rise to a cause of action, the defendant may assert the statement's truth as an absolute defense to a libel claim. ... Massachusetts law, however, recognizes a narrow exception to this defense: the truth or falsity of the statement is immaterial, and the libel action may proceed, if the plaintiff can show that the defendant acted with "actual malice" in publishing the statement. ... Since 1964, however, the term "actual malice" has taken on a new meaning in defamation cases involving public figures; in this context, a person acts with "actual malice" when he acts "with knowledge that [a defamatory statement] was false or with reckless disregard of whether it was false or not." But, the Supreme Court has explained that actual malice in the public-figure context is different than "common-law malice" or "ill will," which is sometimes required under state law.

After finding that the meaning of "malice" in the 1902 statute should mean publication with ill will, the court noted that the sending of an e-mail naming an employee and saying that the employee had been fired had never been done before, and that it may have been sent to draw attention away from Noonan's supervisor's malfeasance. Many of the Staples employees who received the e-mail did not travel and would have no reason to be informed of the policy's enforcement. These actions, said the court, could be interpreted by a jury to indicate that the vice president acted with ill will toward Noonan. The court remanded the libel case back to the trial court. The First Circuit declined to rehear the case *en banc*. However, on remand, the jury found for Staples, saying that the company did not act with malice in sending the truthful e-mail.

Does this case open the door to plaintiffs' attorneys encouraging courts to apply state statutes' common law definitions of malice as ill will in cases where the publication was true? Some commentators have suggested that Staples lost at the First Circuit because the plaintiff in this case was not a public official. In Massachusetts, at least, the precedent remains.

■ LIBEL AND PROCEDURAL RIGHTS

The details of courtroom procedure often seem to be arcane and irrelevant technicalities—certainly not issues that should concern journalists. However, on three occasions in recent years the Supreme Court has ruled against the media on procedural issues that can be vitally important in libel cases. On the other hand, the Supreme Court has ruled in favor of the media in several other libel cases that were decided on legal technicalities.

The Supreme Court held in 1979 that libel plaintiffs have the right to inquire into journalists' thought processes at the time when an allegedly libelous story was being prepared. Ruling in the case of *Herbert v. Lando* (441 U.S. 153), the Court said that since libel plaintiffs often have to prove actual malice or at least negligence on the part of journalists, they are entitled to use the *pretrial discovery* process (explained in Chapter One) to check on journalists' attitudes and thought processes.

The *Herbert* case caused considerable alarm among journalists when the Supreme Court ruled that the First Amendment does not excuse journalists from providing state-of-mind evidence to libel plaintiffs who are looking for proof of actual malice. Actually, though, the decision did little more than uphold a long-recognized principle of discovery: each party is permitted to use discovery to gather information about the other side's case. Where the plaintiff must prove actual malice to win his case, the rules have allowed plaintiffs to seek evidence of malice.

The *Herbert* case arose when a military officer sued the producers of the CBS television program *60 Minutes* for libel and then sought state-of-mind evidence during the discovery process. The show's producers refused to cooperate, citing the First Amendment, but the high court ruled that the First Amendment provides journalists with no special immunity from the normal rules of discovery.

Where does the *Herbert* case leave the media? Technically, it leaves the media in the same position they were in before this decision: required to cooperate in the discovery process even if it means responding to questions designed to determine whether there really was actual malice present when an allegedly libelous story was prepared. However, the decision appears to have had an important psychological impact on libel cases. The Supreme Court has in effect endorsed and encouraged the aggressive use of discovery procedures by libel plaintiffs as a means of ferreting out evidence of actual malice or negligence. Since *Herbert*, discovery has been an increasing burden for the media in libel cases. Ironically, Herbert eventually lost his libel suit when a federal appellate court dismissed the bulk of his case against CBS in 1986—12 years after the lawsuit began.

Discovery and News Sources

The discovery process has produced a new dilemma for the media in more and more libel suits. If a plaintiff must prove fault on the part of the media, that means he or she must inquire into a journalist's reporting methods to see if there was negligence or actual malice.

As a result, more and more libel plaintiffs are demanding to know where a reporter got the information that appeared in an allegedly libelous story. That means the plaintiff wants to identify the reporter's news sources so they can be interviewed and possibly called as witnesses in a libel trial. However, one of the strongest ethical standards of journalism is the principle of keeping confidential sources confidential (see Chapter Eight for further discussion of this point). In recent years a number of journalists facing libel suits have refused to reveal their sources during the discovery process.

This has sometimes caused problems for the media. Under the normal rules of discovery, if one party to a lawsuit refuses to cooperate in turning over requested evidence to the other side, that evidence may be presumed not to exist. Some judges have responded to a reporter's refusal to reveal his sources in a libel case by simply ruling that there were no sources. Consequently, the court may conclude that story was published with reckless disregard for the truth—no matter how reliable the sources actually were. The result is almost certain defeat in a libel suit.

Many states have shield laws that exempt reporters from having to reveal their sources. However, these laws often protect the reporter only from a contempt of court citation; such laws may not override the rules of discovery in civil litigation. In some instances, there is simply no way a publisher or broadcaster can defend a libel suit without revealing confidential sources, so he or she must choose between violating a promise to a news source and losing a big libel suit.

This problem is so severe that some libel insurance policies are invalid unless the publisher or broadcaster agrees to reveal confidential news sources if a libel suit is filed. It may cost a publisher thousands (or possibly millions) of dollars to maintain source confidentiality; the result could even be bankruptcy. This can create a serious ethical dilemma for journalists and their employers.

The Role of Retractions

In at least 33 states, publishing (or in some instances broadcasting) a retraction or correction of a libelous item reduces the likelihood of a successful lawsuit against the media or at least reduces the risk of a news organization facing a large damage award. One of the aspects of libel law that a communications professional should understand is his/her own state's rule on retractions.

In most states that have retraction laws, publishing a timely retraction of a libel (and placing the retraction in as prominent a place as the original libel) limits the damages that may be won. In many states, a retraction restricts the plaintiff to special damages (provable out-of-pocket monetary losses, which are often difficult to show). Therefore, publishing a retraction may effectively preclude a lawsuit in many instances.

The provisions of the retraction laws vary widely from state to state. Some of the strongest ones are found in midwestern and western states, such as Arizona, California, Idaho, Nebraska and Nevada. These states all have laws that require a potential plaintiff to demand a retraction within a fixed period of time (often 20 days after learning of the libel). After that, the media usually have another 21 days to publish or broadcast the retraction.

Under these retraction statutes, if the plaintiff fails to demand a retraction or if a suitable retraction is published or broadcast, the plaintiff is limited to special damages (provable out-of-pocket monetary losses). In these states a plaintiff may win other damages only if: (1) a retraction was demanded in a timely fashion; *and* (2) a legally adequate retraction was not published or broadcast in a timely fashion. To be legally adequate, a retraction usually must retract all of the libelous charges without further libeling the potential plaintiff. Also, the retraction must be as prominent as the original libel.

On the other hand, some states have retraction laws that simply say a libel defendant can show that a retraction was published as a way to "mitigate" damages, or perhaps to defend against charges of malice.

Not all retraction laws are equally comprehensive in their protection of the media, however. About half of the states that have retraction laws specifically include broadcasters within their coverage. Several other states have laws that cover "all libel suits" or "all media." But several states have retraction laws that apply only to the print media or, more specifically, only to newspapers. California's retraction law is unusual in that respect: it protects newspapers and radio and television stations but not magazines. That was a crucial factor in actress Carol Burnett's libel suit against the National Enquirer: the trial court ruled the *National Enquirer* a magazine and not a newspaper, thus denying it the protection of the retraction statute. An appellate court affirmed that ruling (*Burnett v. National Enquirer*, 144 C.A.3d 991, 1983). Montana's retraction law, on the other hand, was once so comprehensive that it was ruled unconstitutional. The Montana Supreme Court ruled that the law violated the state constitution because it in effect denied libel plaintiffs any reasonable remedy for the wrongs they might have suffered (*Madison v. Yunker*, 589 P.2d 126, 1978).

The Montana legislature responded to that decision by rewriting the state retraction law in 1979. As rewritten, the law was weaker than those in many neighboring states: it required a demand for a retraction prior to a libel suit only if the plaintiff was going to seek punitive damages. And publishing a retraction prevented only punitive damages. With or without a retraction, the media might still have to pay general as well as special damages.

Retraction statutes are obviously useful in situations where the media have made an honest error, but they do little good in many of the circumstances that produce lawsuits—situations in which the publisher does not feel he or she made an error and is in no mood to back down. Moreover, there is a natural human tendency to believe the original charge—not anyone's later denial. To accuse someone of a crime in print and then retract, saying it was all a mistake, is certain to leave some readers with a strong suspicion that it really wasn't a mistake. For this reason, some people question whether retraction statutes are really fair to libel victims. Nevertheless, many states have such laws, and they have an important impact on libel litigation in those states.

Because retraction laws vary so much from state to state, there has been a movement to standardize and strengthen these laws. In 1994, the American Bar Association approved a model retraction law called the *Uniform Correction or Clarification of Defamation Act*. While ABA approval does not necessarily lead to a model law being adopted in any particular state, it does increase the likelihood that various state legislatures will consider it. The model law, written by the National Conference of Commissioners on Uniform State Laws, gives libel victims 90 days after a defamatory statement is published to request a correction or clarification. Then the publisher has 45 days to publish a correction or clarification. The model law provides that no libel plaintiff may sue for damages without first seeking a correction or clarification, and limits plaintiffs to special damages (for provable monetary losses) if a suitable correction or clarification is published.

The uniform law's drafters said it was designed to give a libel victim a "quick and complete vindication of his or her reputation" while giving publishers a "quick and cost-effective means of correcting or clarifying alleged mistakes and avoiding costly litigation." Whether it will ever be widely adopted remains uncertain.

Long-Arm Jurisdiction

Another growing burden for the media—albeit once again not really a new burden—is the cost of defending libel suits in courts thousands of miles from home. The rise of online communication only adds to this issue for anyone who posts anything online.

For many years the law has said persons and companies that engage in interstate commerce may be sued in any state where they have *minimum contacts*. The Supreme Court so ruled in 1945, in a case called *International Shoe v. Washington* (326 U.S. 310).

However, some journalists have argued that they should not be forced to defend a libel suit in a faraway state merely because copies of their newspaper or magazine are distributed there or their material is broadcast there. That argument has gotten nowhere with the Supreme Court, which has ruled twice that the First Amendment should not be considered in such cases. Instead, the court said, lawsuits against journalists should have to meet only the same test of fairness as would a lawsuit against another kind of business. In short, if it would be fair for a company that makes cars or lawnmowers to be hauled into court in a distant state where its products are sold, it is also fair for the media to be sued in that state if their "product" is sold there.

In two cases decided on the same day in 1984—*Calder v. Jones* (465 U.S. 783) and *Keeton v. Hustler* (465 U.S. 770)—the high court unanimously rejected the argument that forcing journalists to defend themselves in faraway courts would have any chilling effect on freedom of the press. That means the national media and their employees may be sued in *any* state— and a libel plaintiff is entitled to engage in *forum shopping*. A plaintiff can select the state with the most favorable laws and file a libel suit there, regardless of where any of the prospective defendants live or maintain offices.

The *Calder v. Jones* case arose when the *National Enquirer* published a story claiming that producer Marty Ingels had driven his wife, actress Shirley Jones, to drink. "[B]y 3 o'clock in the afternoon she's a crying drunk," the *Enquirer* said. Jones and Ingels both sued the sensational tabloid in California, where they live. Although headquartered in Florida, the *Enquirer* itself did not challenge the California court's jurisdiction. However, John South, the writer of the story, and Iain Calder, editor of the *National Enquirer,* both argued that they should not have to defend themselves in a courtroom nearly 3,000 miles from home.

The Supreme Court unanimously ruled that the writer and editor were subject to California jurisdiction even though neither went to California to research or write the story. Justice William Rehnquist, who wrote the Court's opinion, pointed out that the *Enquirer* was selling about 600,000 copies of each issue in California—twice as many as in any other state.

"An individual injured in California need not go to Florida to seek redress from persons who, though remaining in Florida, knowingly cause the injury in California," Rehnquist wrote. Shortly after the Supreme Court's *Calder v. Jones* decision, Jones and Ingels reached a settlement with the *National Enquirer* to terminate the case. The paper agreed to print a retraction and an apology, and to pay a large cash settlement. Neither side would reveal the amount of the settlement, but Ingels released a statement that said the amount took into account the fact that he and his wife had spent $300,000 in attorney's fees by then.

Although the Supreme Court's decision in the Jones case was troubling to some journalists, the *Keeton v. Hustler* case seemed far more so. At least Jones and Ingels had filed suit in the state where they lived and worked; they could hardly be accused of "forum shopping." But in *Keeton*, neither plaintiff nor defendant seemed to have any particularly good reason for suing in New Hampshire. Rather, the choice of New Hampshire was clearly a matter of forum shopping: it was apparently the only state whose statute of limitations (i.e., the deadline) for filing libel suits was not past when the suit was filed.

Kathy Keeton, an executive at *Penthouse* magazine, sued for libel after *Hustler* ran a cartoon suggesting that she had contracted a venereal disease from *Penthouse* publisher Robert Guccione. She initially sued in Ohio (where *Hustler* was then headquartered), but her case was dismissed because she missed the Ohio filing deadline. By then, it was apparently too late to sue for libel anywhere but New Hampshire, which permitted libel suits as long as six years after publication (that deadline has since been shortened to three years).

When this case was filed, *Hustler* was selling about 10,000 copies of each issue in New Hampshire, but it had no other ties to the state. And Keeton had no ties to the state at all: she lived and worked in New York. Both the federal district court in New Hampshire and the First Circuit ruled that the jurisdictional requirements were not satisfied. The appellate court suggested that libel cases should be subject to tougher jurisdictional standards than other kinds of lawsuits in order to protect First Amendment freedoms.

The Supreme Court overturned that ruling and reinstated Keeton's lawsuit. "[T]here is no unfairness in calling (*Hustler*) to answer for the contents of that publication wherever a substantial number of copies are regularly sold and distributed," Justice Rehnquist wrote.

Long-Arm Jurisdiction, Libel and the Internet

Another question that has arisen is whether long-arm jurisdiction should apply when allegedly libelous material is posted on the Internet. Many American media lawyers were alarmed when the highest court in Australia held in 2002 that Australian mining magnate Joseph Gutnick could sue an American company, Dow Jones, publisher of *Barron's* and the *Wall Street Journal*, in the Australian state of Victoria, where he lives. The lawsuit was based on an alleged libel that appeared on the Barron's website, hosted in New Jersey. The High Court of Australia held that a person who is well-known in Australia can sue for libel there even if the libel appears on a website based in another country and the site owner has little contact with Australia beyond the fact that the site can be viewed there. Dow Jones argued unsuccessfully that it could be sued only in the U.S. (*Dow Jones v. Gutnick*, 2002 H.C.A. 56).

The risk of being sued overseas troubles many Internet publishers not only because of the cost and inconvenience of defending a lawsuit in a faraway country, but also because the law of libel is less favorable to media defendants in many other countries than it is in the U.S.

However, British libel law is now moving closer to U.S. law. The House of Lords, acting as the United Kingdom's highest court, ruled in 2006 that journalists may publish allegations about public figures without having to prove the truthfulness of the charges, as long as the reporting is responsible and in the public interest, in *Jameel v. Wall Street Journal Europe* ([2006] U.K.H.L. 44). A panel of Law Lords said the *Wall Street Journal* and its European edition could not—and should not have to—prove the truth of a story about the monitoring of bank accounts for links to terrorism by the Saudi Arabian government at the request of the United States. The article mentioned accounts of a company controlled by Muhammed Abdul Latif Jameel, but did *not* say Jameel was knowingly aiding terrorists. Nevertheless, Jameel sued for libel.

Without a change in British libel law, stories about international terrorism such as that one could not safely be published, the Law Lords noted, because a media defendant could never prove the truth in a case involving secret government surveillance. The Lords took note of the importance of such stories, expanding the media's rights under British libel law.

American courts are split on the issue. Some U.S. courts have held that libel cases cannot be filed in a distant court just because a news item appeared on the Internet. In *Young v. New Haven Advocate* (315 F.3d 256, 2002), the Fourth Circuit disagreed with the High Court of Australia's conclusion. In a decision three days after the Australian ruling, the Fourth Circuit held that the warden of a Virginia prison could not sue Connecticut newspapers in Virginia for posting material that allegedly libeled him on their Connecticut-based websites. The Fourth Circuit held that the articles were aimed at a Connecticut audience, denying Virginia jurisdiction over the Connecticut newspapers' websites. At about the same time, the California Supreme Court held that California cannot take jurisdiction over out-of-state residents merely because their websites are allegedly harmful to Hollywood or Silicon Valley businesses. In *Pavlovich v. Superior Court (DVD Copy Control Assn.)* (29 C.4th 262, 2002), the California court said a Texan could not be sued under California's long-arm jurisdiction law for posting computer code on the Internet that allows DVDs to be copied.

On the other hand, some courts have extended their long-arm jurisdiction laws to apply online. The Ohio Supreme Court in 2010 said that the state's long-arm statute applied to the Internet, making it possible for Ohio businesses to sue individuals from other states who defame them online (*Kauffman Racing Equipment LLC v. Roberts*, 930 N.E.2d 784). And the Tenth Circuit also allowed an online defamation case to proceed in New Mexico (*Silver v. Brown*, 382 Fed. Appx. 723, 2010). David Silver, a New Mexico investment banker, alleged that he had been defamed by Matthew Brown, the CEO of a Florida corporation, on Brown's site "DavidSilverSantaFe.com" after their business relationship soured. Brown additionally engaged in search engine optimization to try to ensure that his gripe site would appear in search results before Silver's site. Using reasoning from *Calder v. Jones*, the court said that the offending blog was intentionally posted and aimed at New Mexico with knowledge that the brunt of the injury would be felt there.

In some states, the long-arm statute has no history of application to an online setting. In 2009, the Eleventh Circuit asked the Florida Supreme Court to *certify a question* (a process by which the highest court in a state can answer a question that would affect the outcome of a case in which there is no controlling legal precedent in that state) on that state's long-arm statute. The Eleventh Circuit was asked to consider whether the dismissal of a case filed by Internet Solutions Corp., a Florida recruiting and advertising company, against Tabatha Marshall, owner of a website in which she commented on alleged phishing scams, was appropriate. Marshall had no connections to Florida other than the fact that her website could be accessed there, as it can anywhere else in the world.

The court asked the Florida Supreme Court whether posting of allegedly defamatory material about a Florida company on a non-commercial website owned and operated by a non-resident with no other connections to Florida would "constitute the commission of a tortious act within Florida" for purposes of the state's long-arm statute. The answer from the Florida Supreme Court? The mere posting would not be enough; "the material posted on the website about a Florida resident must not only be *accessible* in Florida, but also be *accessed* in Florida in order to constitute the commission of the tortious act of defamation within Florida" (*Internet Solutions Corp. v. Marshall*, 39 So. 3d 1201, 2010). This low standard will be satisfied in most cases. The Eleventh Circuit said Marshall was subject to the Florida long-arm statute and remanded the case (*Internet Solutions Corp. v. Marshall*, 611 F.3d 1368, 2010). Will other states and courts follow suit? If so, this extends the reach of online libel actions.

In August 2010, the SPEECH Act (Securing the Protection of our Enduring and Established Constitutional Heritage) was signed by President Barack Obama; this law, which applies to all courts, both state and federal, invalidates foreign libel judgments against Americans that would fail in the U.S. under First Amendment or due process protections.

At least one state has taken action in the area of international libel judgments. California passed a version of the Uniform Foreign-Country Money Judgments Recognition Act, an act that many other states have adopted that addresses the enforcement of foreign judgments in the U.S., that specifically includes defamation judgments: the judgment will not be accepted for a claim of defamation "unless the court determines that the defamation law applied by the foreign court provided at least as much protection for freedom of speech and the press as provided by both the United States and California Constitutions."

To combat libel tourism, the U.K. Ministry of Justice released a draft defamation bill in March 2011. Lax British libel laws have resulted in London becoming a place where celebrities can easily win libel suits. Some of the issues identified by the draft bill: a requirement that a statement must have caused substantial harm to be considered defamatory, statutory defenses for truth and "honest opinion," as well as other privilege defenses, introduction of a single publication rule, and an "action to address libel tourism by ensuring a court will not accept jurisdiction unless satisfied that England and Wales is clearly the most appropriate place to bring an action against someone who is not domiciled in the UK or an EU Member State." But there is little change in the placement of the burden of proof, which is generally on the defendant to prove truth (rather than the plaintiff, as is true in American law).

Section 230:
shorthand for Section 230 of the Communications Decency Act of the Telecommunications Act of 1996; gives online service providers strong protection from liability for libelous material posted by third-parties on their systems—as long as they do not act as publishers of that material.

common law republication rule:
rule that says that anyone who republishes libelous material can be sued, not just the original creator or publisher.

certify a question:
a process by which the highest court in a state can answer a question that would affect the outcome of a case in which there is no controlling legal precedent in that state.

Libel and Liability on the Internet

Traditionally, most libel and slander lawsuits have resulted from newspaper and magazine articles and radio or television broadcasts. However, recently many lawsuits have been filed by people who say they were defamed by something that appeared online.

Online communication has grown explosively: today there are millions of websites with even more millions of users who post literally billions of words of new material on the Internet every week. Inevitably, some of that material is libelous.

When a libelous message is posted on a website, a "blog," a "chat room" or a newsgroup, it is obviously disseminated: many persons are likely to see it. But is anyone other than the originator of the message legally responsible?

At first, the answer was yes. In 1995, a New York trial judge ruled that Prodigy, a commercial provider of computer communications, could be sued for libel because a subscriber posted a message accusing an investment firm of criminal conduct (*Stratton-Oakmont Inc. v. Prodigy Services Co.*, No. 11063/94). The judge ruled that Prodigy assumed *editorial control* and thus became the legal equivalent of a publisher by *attempting to monitor the content of incoming messages* with text-scanning software (i.e., software that checks for offensive words or phrases). Therefore, the online service could be sued for libel, the judge said. Although the ruling caused concern among online service providers, Prodigy eventually settled the case by doing nothing more than issuing an apology.

However, Section 230 of the Telecommunications Act of 1996 overruled the basic thrust of the *Prodigy* decision by declaring that Internet service providers are not to be treated as publishers and held liable for the content of the messages they carry, regardless of whether they employ a content filtering system to screen out objectionable material or merely deliver all messages without any review. Internet service providers are now free to screen out material they consider obscene or otherwise inappropriate without assuming liability for everything they *do not* screen out. Even if an Internet service provider is notified of an allegedly libelous posting and does not then delete it, the provider is exempt under this law, according to a 1997 decision of the Fourth Circuit (*Zeran v. America Online*, 129 F.3d 327). In sweeping terms, the appellate court held that online services are exempt from liability under state libel laws for any message posted by a third party. In 1998, the U.S. Supreme Court declined to review this decision, leaving it intact.

The Ninth Circuit later ruled that a provider is exempt even if it does minor editing before a libelous item is posted *(Batzel v. Smith*, 333 F.3d 1018, 2003).

In recent years dozens of other courts have dismissed libel suits against Internet providers based on Section 230, including several federal appellate courts and the highest state courts in California and Florida. In 2006, the California Supreme Court held that only those who create a libelous Internet message may be sued, not Internet providers or even users who post a message created by someone else. The California case, *Barrett v. Rosenthal* (40 C.4th 33), is so broad that it seems to exempt traditional newspaper publishers and broadcasters from libel suits for content generated by others on their websites, even when they could be held liable if the same material were disseminated in print or in a broadcast. The Florida Supreme Court ruled similarly, but not in such sweeping terms, in *Doe v. America Online* (783 So.2d 1010, 2001).

The 2006 California case arose when Ilena Rosenthal, a San Diego women's health activist, posted materials critical of two medical doctors, including an allegedly libelous e-mail written by another critic of the two doctors, on two Internet newsgroups. The doctors sued

Rosenthal for libel. The lawsuit was quickly dismissed because much of what Rosenthal posted was opinion, not provably false statements of fact. However, a California appellate court held that certain statements could be seen as false statements of fact and therefore actionable libels. The appellate court declined to apply the federal Section 230 exemption, triggering an appeal to the state Supreme Court.

The California Supreme Court reversed the appellate decision, ruling that Rosenthal was protected by Section 230 even though she was only an Internet user and not a provider. As long as she did not create the allegedly libelous content but merely posted materials created by others, her postings are exempt from liability.

This appears to leave Internet publishers with far broader protection than traditional media. Under the *common law republication rule*, recognized in most states, anyone who republishes libelous material may be sued, not merely the creator. Newspapers can be sued for libelous letters to the editor and for libels contained in direct quotations, among other things. Similarly, broadcasters can be sued for statements made by callers on talk shows. If the material is a defamatory, false, unprivileged statement of fact as opposed to opinion, the media are generally liable for republishing it, regardless of who originated the libel. But under *Barrett v. Rosenthal*, Internet providers and users are exempt from liability for republications. Under cases like this one, the Internet remains a wide-open forum where messages can be freely forwarded to others, regardless of whether they may be libelous. Only the creator—often someone who is "lawsuit-proof" because he or she has no assets—is liable.

Section 230 may not immunize online service providers from all claims, however. In *Barnes v. Yahoo! Inc.* (565 F.3d 560, 2009), the Ninth Circuit said that Section 230 did not insulate Yahoo from *promissory estoppel* claims (as will be discussed in Chapter Eight, *promissory estoppel* prevents someone from withdrawing from a promise if the other person has relied upon that promise and acted upon it to his/her detriment).

After Cecilia Barnes broke up with her boyfriend, he created a Yahoo profile under her name with her actual e-mail address, work address and phone number. He posted nude pictures of her on it and then impersonated her in Yahoo chat rooms and directed interested men to the profile—all without her permission. Barnes began getting contacted by men interested in sex. She followed Yahoo's instructions to have the profile removed but Yahoo did not act, even after repeated requests via postal mail, fax, and telephone—and after having spoken to a Yahoo director who promised to "walk over" the removal request personally. She then filed suit, alleging a *promissory estoppel* claim.

Judge Diarmuid O'Scannlain, writing for the Ninth Circuit, called the case "a dangerous, cruel, and highly indecent use of the internet for the apparent purpose of revenge." In finding that Barnes had a *promissory estoppel* claim against Yahoo, he noted that she was not framing Yahoo as a publisher "but rather as the counterparty to a contract as a promissory who has breached." Under these circumstances, Section 230 does not provide immunity. On remand, the district court refused to dismiss; Barnes "alleged sufficient facts to suggest her position substantially and detrimentally changed in reliance on defendant's promise."

Section 230 has also barred liability for online service providers when underage users are assaulted in person by adults they meet online. In *Doe v. MySpace Inc.* (528 F.3d 413, 2008) the Fifth Circuit found that Section 230 immunizes MySpace from liability for a minor's sexual assault by an adult she met on MySpace after lying about her age. Her case centered on the notion that "MySpace should have implemented safety technologies to prevent [her] and her attacker from meeting," and that MySpace was negligent for not having done so.

The Fifth Circuit did not agree, saying that the plaintiff's claim was simply a claim against MySpace as a publisher, against which Section 230 immunizes it. The Supreme Court declined to hear an appeal. A California appeals court came to the same conclusion as the Fifth Circuit in a very similar case in 2009; the court said that the plaintiff, a minor who had been sexually assaulted by someone she met on MySpace, wanted MySpace "to ensure that sexual predators do not gain access to (i.e., communicate with) minors on its Web site" and this activity is expressly covered by Section 230 (*Doe II v. MySpace Inc.*, 175 Cal.App.4th 561).

The Fourth Circuit indicated in 2009 that plaintiffs who want to circumvent a website's Section 230 protection by saying that it is a content provider rather than a distributor must provide sufficient evidence to demonstrate the claim (*Nemet Chevrolet v. Consumeraffairs.com*, 591 F. 3d 250). Nemet alleged that the consumer review website was actually an "information content provider" with respect to 20 complaints about it on the website. The court said that Nemet had not provided sufficient evidence to prove its claim, and Consumeraffairs. com's action of simply providing a forum was not enough: "Even accepting as true all of the facts Nemet pled as to Consumeraffairs.com's liability for the structure and design of its website, the amended complaint 'does not show, or even intimate,' that Consumeraffairs. com contributed to the allegedly fraudulent nature of the comments at issue."

Several appellate courts at the federal and state levels have recently ruled for the first time on Section 230. The Eighth Circuit's first opinion on Section 230 was in 2010 in *Johnson v. Arden* (614 F.3d 785). Susan and Robert Johnson owned Cozy Kittens Cattery in Missouri, and they sued a number of individuals and service providers after seeing negative comments about their cattery on ComplaintsBoard.com. The court said that ComplaintsBoard.com's online service provider, InMotion, could not be held liable due to Section 230 protection: "InMotion did not originate the material that the Johnsons deem damaging."

In *Shiamili v. The Real Estate Group of New York, Inc.* (17 N.Y.3d 281), the New York Court of Appeals (the state's highest court) by a 4-3 vote that Section 230 applied to comments by third parties on a blog site, even if the editorial role taken by the hosts was unusually active. Christakis Shiamili, CEO of Ardor Realty Corp., sued The Real Estate Group for allegedly defamatory comments made by a person calling him/herself "Ardor Realty Sucks" on a blog the group hosted. Despite the fact that The Real Estate Group moved the comments to their own stand-alone post and highlighted them as a story, the court ruled that Section 230 still barred liability. This broad interpretation was not without its critics on the court. Chief Judge Jonathan Lippman, while agreeing that such an interpretation was generally acceptable, lamented the fact that on its first Section 230 decision, the court "shielded defendants from the allegation that they abused their power as website publishers to promote and amplify defamation targeted at a business competitor." In his opinion, the court went too far in extending the protection in this case.

As courts continue to extend Section 230 protection in ever-increasing numbers of cases, some plaintiffs have tried creative ways to circumvent it. For example, in one California case, plaintiffs, a couple who owned several roofing companies, alleged that Google was liable for defamatory comments about those companies because Section 230 should not apply. Their reasoning? Google's *programming* made it possible for the defamatory comments to be published. Even the federal district judge seemed a bit puzzled: "Plaintiffs seem to be referring to the source code underlying the services offered on Defendant's website." The court rejected this argument (*Black v. Google, Inc.*, 2010 U.S. Dist. LEXIS 82905).

In a somewhat novel approach to circumvent Section 230 protections, the plaintiffs in *Blockowicz v. Williams* (630 F.3d 563, 2010) tried to use Rule 65(d), a federal rule governing injunctions. Essentially, the Blockowiczs argued that the operators of the Ripoff Report website, where the alleged defamatory content was posted, aided and abetted the publication of the defamation when the operators refused to remove the offending posts. The district court and the Seventh Circuit both rejected this claim, saying that the Ripoff Report's "mere inactivity is simply inadequate to render them aiders and abettors in violating the injunction." However, gossip website TheDirty.com was *denied* Section 230 protection because it *encouraged* offensive postings that were heavily moderated (the case, *Jones v. Dirty World Entm't Recordings, LLC*, 766 F. Supp. 2d 828, E.D. Ky. 2011, involved a teacher who was also a Cincinnati Bengals cheerleader allegedly sleeping with the team and her students).

However, those who *create* libelous online content remain liable. Many individuals have been sued for the content of their websites or even e-mail messages. In 2002, for example, a jury in California's Silicon Valley ordered two research scientists to pay $775,000 in punitive and compensatory damages to a high-tech company and two of its managers for posting thousands of defamatory messages on Internet message boards. Although an appellate court upheld the damage award, the California Supreme Court set it aside for reasons other than Section 230, ordering a trial court to reconsider the case (*Varian Medical Systems v. Delfino*, 35 C.4th 180, 2005).

In 2012, the state of Washington passed a controversial law intended to combat child sex trafficking. SB 6251 would punish the knowing publication, dissemination or display of (or being the direct or indirect cause of) "any advertisement for a commercial sex act, which is to take place in the state of Washington and that includes the depiction of a minor." However, several Internet organizations filed suit to enjoin the enforcement of the law, arguing that SB 6251, though well intended, conflicts directly with Section 230 protections.

A federal judge agreed and issued that injunction in June 2012 (*Backpage.com, LLC v. McKenna*, No. C12-954-RSM, W.D. Wash.). The case is ongoing.

Can one libel someone, or be libeled, in just 140 characters? The microblogging service Twitter has engendered for several lawsuits; none have generated written opinions. In 2009, Chicago resident Amanda Bonnen publicly "tweeted" a friend of hers, inviting a visit—despite the mold she alleged was in her apartment: "You should just come anyway. Who said sleeping in a moldy apartment was bad for you? Horizon realty thinks it's okay." Horizon Realty sued Bonnen for $50,000. A Cook county judge dismissed the case; media reports quoted the judge as saying in court that the tweet was "really too vague" to be actionable.

Also in 2009, singer Courtney Love was sued by fashion designer Dawn Simorangkir for statements Love made on her Twitter and MySpace accounts that allegedly threatened Simorangkir after she sent Love a bill for her Boudoir Queen fashions. According to the complain, among other tweets and posts, Love tweeted (complete with typos), "oi vey dont fuck with my wradrobe or you willend up in a circle of corched eaeth hunted til your dead." Simorangkir sued for defamation and invasion of privacy, among other actions.

In March 2011, Love agreed to pay $430,000 to Simorangkir to settle the case. However, it did not take long for the singer to make headlines for libelous tweets again: this time her target was attorney Rhonda Holmes in San Diego. The May 2011 tweet suggests Holmes was bribed not to represent Love again in a fraud case after Love fired her and then tried to hire her back: "i was fucking devastated when Rhonda J Holmes Esq of San Diego was bought off." Holmes said in her complaint that Love became angry when she refused to represent her. That case is pending. However, Love's daughter with Kurt Cobain, Frances Bean Cobain, has been subpoenaed to testify in the case for her response to allegations by Love on her Twitter account that Frances had been seduced by Foo Fighters front man Dave Grohl. In denying that allegation, Frances said, "Twitter should ban my mother."

Another question that has produced several court decisions is the extent to which Section 230 exempts Internet services from liability for *advertising* created and posted by others. That is discussed in Chapter Thirteen.

The same libel defenses that are recognized when other media are involved generally apply when an alleged libel is disseminated online. For instance, in 2003 the Sixth Circuit held that Michigan's "fair reporting" privilege protects the posting of court documents that are public records even if a company posts its own court filings on its website (*Amway Corp. v. Procter & Gamble Co.*, 346 F.3d 180).

Libel and Summary Judgment

Like several earlier Supreme Court decisions on libel, the *Calder* and *Keeton* cases involved attempts by the media to terminate libel suits before trial by means of a motion for summary judgment or a motion to dismiss on other procedural grounds. As explained in Chapter One, a summary judgment is a ruling in which the court decides the case without trial, saving the expense and trouble of a prolonged lawsuit.

However, because a pretrial dismissal denies the plaintiff his/her day in court, it is only supposed to be granted when it is absolutely certain the plaintiff could not win.

In recent years, some courts have recognized that many libel suits against the media are filed not in the hope of winning but as a means of harassment. Thus, libel suits have sometimes been thrown out of court under summary judgment proceedings. This procedure has been particularly applicable in situations where a public official or public figure is suing but is clearly unable to prove actual malice.

In 1986 the Supreme Court addressed this problem—and endorsed the idea that many of these questionable libel suits should be dismissed on summary judgment. Deciding the case of *Anderson v. Liberty Lobby* (477 U.S. 242), the court said that public figures must provide "clear and convincing" evidence that a jury could find actual malice on the part of the media—or have their lawsuits dismissed on motions for summary judgment.

The Anderson case involved three magazine articles written by syndicated columnist Jack Anderson concerning Willis Carto, founder of the Liberty Lobby (an ultraconservative political organization). Anderson called Carto a "neo-Nazi," a "racist" and "anti-Semitic," among other things. Carto sued but a trial judge dismissed the case, ruling that Carto was a public figure who could not prove that the statements were made with actual malice. The judge noted that there had been extensive research to document Anderson's articles, a fact that would have made it extremely difficult to prove Anderson guilty of "reckless disregard for the truth." Carto appealed the dismissal; his case eventually reached the Supreme Court.

The high court ruled by a 6-3 majority that if a libel plaintiff such as Carto cannot show by "clear and convincing" proof that he could win the case if it went to a full trial, the case should be dismissed without subjecting the media to the expense of a trial.

Both media lawyers and lawyers for libel plaintiffs agreed that this decision would have an enormous dollars-and-cents effect on libel law. Both sides agreed that it represented a clear invitation to trial judges to dismiss libel suits on summary judgment instead of letting them go to trial. Media attorneys generally predicted that the *Anderson* case would reduce the high cost of defending libel cases for the news media.

In the years since the *Anderson* decision, these predictions have generally come true. At least four different federal appeals courts have held that *Anderson* requires them to conduct an independent review of the record when they decide whether to allow summary judgment in a libel case, and to dismiss the case if the plaintiff is someone who must prove actual malice—but cannot do so by clear and convincing evidence.

However, in 2002 the Ninth Circuit disagreed in a case involving alleged fabrication of product testing results by *Consumer Reports* magazine. In *Suzuki Motor Corp. v. Consumers Union* (292 F.3d 1192, revised in 2003 at 330 F.3d 1110), the court declined to uphold a trial judge's grant of summary judgment. The appeals court said it would not conduct an independent review of the record and grant summary judgment but would instead allow a jury trial on the merits of the case.

Suzuki submitted evidence that the Suzuki Samurai, which *Consumer Reports* said rolls over too easily, in fact never tipped during 37 tests on the magazine's test course in 1988 and was rated highest of the SUVs tested, until a senior editor demanded changes to increase the likelihood of a roll. The National Highway Traffic Safety Administration later criticized Consumers Union's testing as unscientific.

Suzuki also alleged that Consumers Union was doing fund-raising at the time of the tests and needed a "blockbuster" story to bring it national attention. The appellate court held that the claim of financial motivation combined with evidence of rigged testing could allow a jury to find actual malice, something Suzuki would have to prove to win this case.

The court declined to reconsider the case *en banc* in 2003, and that produced an impassioned defense by Judge Alex Kozinski, who argued that it would be impossible for Suzuki to prove actual malice because Consumers Union described its original and revised testing procedures in detail, and then expressed constitutionally protected opinions about the results of the tests.

SLAPP suit:

shorthand for "strategic lawsuit against public participation," a suit that is an attempt by a corporation to stop the exercise of First Amendment rights such as petition, assembly, speech and press by threatening high-cost libel suits based on the content of those exercises.

Getting "SLAPP" Lawsuits Dismissed

A lawsuit can be an intimidating form of harassment, as journalists have sometimes discovered. The whole point of the *Anderson* case was to allow journalists to get harassment libel suits dismissed quickly on summary judgment. In recent years, it has also become commonplace for citizen activists to be sued for libel or slander by wealthy corporations when they speak against a corporate project at public hearings or circulate petitions to oppose a project. These lawsuits are often nothing more than a form of intimidation—an attempt to silence a corporation's critics. An acronym to describe these lawsuits has gained wide acceptance: *SLAPP (strategic lawsuits against public participation).*

Because it is costly to defend a lawsuit, citizens who oppose corporate activities in the public arena may have no choice but to back down in the face of a threatened lawsuit. Sometimes leaders of a citizens' group that opposes a project such as a large real estate development receive letters from the developer's lawyers telling them they will be sued for libel or slander if they don't stop criticizing the project. Such lawsuits have been given the SLAPP acronym because they take aim at the very foundation of democracy: the right to speak out on local issues at public hearings where the whole point is to solicit comments from citizens.

The SLAPP acronym was first used by Penelope Canan and George W. Pring, two Denver University professors who advocated legislation to curb these lawsuits in an article published by the *California Western University Law Review* in 1990. They published a book on the subject, *SLAPPs: Getting Sued for Speaking Out,* in 1996.

By 2012, anti-SLAPP laws had been enacted in various forms in at least the following states: Arizona, Arkansas, California, Delaware, Florida, Georgia, Hawaii, Illinois, Indiana, Louisiana, Maine, Maryland, Massachusetts, Minnesota, Missouri, Nebraska, Nevada, New Mexico, New York, Oklahoma, Oregon, Pennsylvania, Rhode Island, Tennessee, Texas, Utah, Vermont, and Washington, as well as the territory of Guam and Washington, D.C. There is no federal anti-SLAPP law but several have been considered.

In Colorado, the state Supreme Court recognized a right of citizen activists to get harassment lawsuits dismissed quickly under the common law even without an anti-SLAPP law (see *Protect Our Mountain Environment v. District Court,* 677 P.2d 136, 1984).

California is widely regarded as having the most sweeping anti-SLAPP law in the country. This law requires anyone who sues someone else because of his/her exercise of free speech in the public arena to show at the outset that there is a "probability" the lawsuit has a valid basis and is not a form of harassment. If a court determines there is not a "probability" that the plaintiff has a valid case, the lawsuit is to be dismissed quickly, sparing the defendant the expense of fighting a prolonged legal battle that could have a chilling effect on free speech.

Plaintiffs who file these harassment lawsuits must pay defendants' legal expenses if such a lawsuit is dismissed before trial. On the other hand, under California's anti-SLAPP law defendants must pay the plaintiff's legal expenses incurred in opposing the motion for dismissal if a court rules that the lawsuit is valid enough that it should not be dismissed before trial. Those who get a lawsuit dismissed under the anti-SLAPP law are allowed to countersue for malicious prosecution, among other things.

California's anti-SLAPP law not only protects individuals who face a harassment lawsuit from a corporation but also protects corporate defendants in some lawsuits filed by individuals. For example, it has been held to protect the media from meritless libel suits even if the plaintiff is an individual and the defendant is a corporation. Because corporations using the law against individual plaintiffs is the opposite of what its authors envisioned, the California anti-SLAPP law was amended in 2003 to curb its use by defendants in lawsuits filed solely in the public interest and lawsuits alleging false advertising. But it still allows the media to get groundless libel cases dismissed quickly.

Among hundreds of decisions interpreting the anti-SLAPP law, California appellate courts have held that a politician may use the anti-SLAPP law to dispose of a meritless lawsuit based on campaign literature (*Beilenson v. Superior Court*, 44 C.A.4th 944, 1996), government officials may use the law to halt lawsuits resulting from their statements about matters in the public record (*Bradbury v. Superior Court*, 49 C.A.4th 1108, 1996), and an attorney can use the law to protect his use of a company's name in an ad soliciting clients (*Simpson Strong-Tie Co. Inc. v. Gore*, 49 Cal. 4th 12, 2010). Courts have also reaffirmed that media corporations may use anti-SLAPP laws to dispose of meritless libel suits filed by individuals (*Braun v. Chronicle Publishing Co.*, 52 C.A.4th 1036, 1997). The Ninth Circuit has ruled that state anti-SLAPP laws may also be used to get meritless cases dismissed when they are filed in federal instead of state courts based on diversity of citizenship (see *Thomas v. Fry's Electronics*, 400 F.3d 1206, 2005; and *U.S. ex rel. Newsham v. Lockheed Missiles & Space Co.*, 190 F.3d 963, 1999).

Most other state anti-SLAPP laws are generally similar to California's but some are more narrowly drawn. Some do not include the provision requiring plaintiffs to pay a defendant's legal expenses in all cases. The New York law specifically applies only to those who speak out concerning land-use issues being considered by government bodies such as zoning boards. And the highest court in Massachusetts in 2010 declined to offer protection under the state's anti-SLAPP law to a reporter who is also an activist in a libel suit filed against her by a real estate developer (*Fustolo v. Hollander*, 455 Mass. 861). The Supreme Judicial Court said that the anti-SLAPP law did not apply, as "Hollander did not engage in petitioning activities 'on her own behalf as a citizen' because she wrote the articles in her capacity as a reporter, and also because she received compensation for doing so."

Perhaps typical of many of the SLAPP cases is one that arose in Minnesota. In this case, a retired wildlife biologist was sued shortly before his 80th birthday for speaking out against a developer's plans to build townhouses across Lake Amelia from his home of 40 years. The biologist contended that the townhouses would disrupt the breeding places of threatened species of birds near the lake. After running up more than $20,000 in legal expenses, he settled the lawsuit—under terms he was forbidden to discuss. Minnesota adopted its anti-SLAPP law amidst the public outcry about this case.

■ OTHER ISSUES IN DEFAMATION LAW

A number of other questions and problem areas in defamation law have arisen in recent years. This section discusses some of these issues.

Libel and Emotional Distress

Libel is only one of many legal theories on which a lawsuit may be based. When someone sues for libel, he or she may also sue on some other legal theory such as invasion of privacy. It is entirely possible to lose a libel case but win on a different legal basis—because the elements and defenses may be different under the two legal theories. A plaintiff may have a weak libel case (because of the truth defense, for example) but a strong invasion of privacy case (truth is not always a defense in those cases). In recent years it has become common for those who sue the media for libel to add other charges, often invasion of privacy or even the intentional infliction of emotional distress, a trend that is discussed in Chapter Five.

That trend led to a 1988 Supreme Court decision that presented about as clear a contrast between plaintiff and defendant as any lawsuit discussed in this book: *Hustler Magazine v. Falwell* (485 U.S. 46). Although widely reported as a libel case, it was primarily an emotional distress case. But in the end, the high court disposed of it by applying the classic *New York Times v. Sullivan* doctrine as if it had been a libel case.

The case began when *Hustler* magazine published a satirical purported advertisement suggesting that the Rev. Jerry Falwell, founder of the Moral Majority and arch-enemy of *Hustler* publisher Larry Flynt, had his first sexual experience in an outhouse with his mother. The Falwell pseudo-ad was a take-off on an advertising campaign for Campari liquor that used "the first time" as its theme. Falwell, whose Moral Majority movement vigorously opposed pornography, frequently attacked Flynt, whose magazine is widely regarded as an explicit erotic publication. The purported ad was Flynt's satirical reply. It was clearly labeled as fiction, not to be taken seriously. (Courts often hold that a satirical statement cannot be

FIG. 24. A historic political cartoon: "The 'rail splitter' at work repairing the union," depicting Vice President Andrew Johnson and President Abraham Lincoln, 1865.

Library of Congress, Prints and Photographs Division, [LC-DIG-ppmsca-17158].

THE 'RAIL SPLITTER' AT WORK REPAIRING THE UNION.

libelous even without a disclaimer, provided a reasonable reader would understand that it is satirical. In 2004 the Texas Supreme Court so ruled in *New Times v. Isaacks*, 146 S.W.3d 144.)

Nevertheless, Falwell sued *Hustler* on two grounds: libel and the intentional infliction of emotional distress. A jury awarded Falwell $200,000 on the emotional distress rationale and ruled against him in the libel case. Because Falwell was clearly a public figure, he would have had to prove actual malice to win his libel case. And the ad was obviously satirical; it could not be understood as presenting facts that the reader was supposed to take literally. Thus, Falwell could not prove actual malice. However, in affirming the jury verdict, a lower federal court had said Falwell did not need to prove actual malice to win an emotional distress case.

That verdict alarmed many journalists because it suggested that numerous other public figures who could not win libel cases could get around the protection provided by the actual malice rule by suing for intentional infliction of emotional distress instead of libel. However, the Supreme Court voted unanimously to overturn the verdict for Falwell. Writing for the Court, Chief Justice William Rehnquist said that public figures must henceforth prove actual malice to win damages for emotional distress, just as they must in libel cases. To rule otherwise would force political cartoonists, among others, to heavily censor their work. He wrote:

> The appeal of the political cartoon or caricature is often based on exploration of unfortunate physical traits or embarrassing events—an exploration often calculated to injure the feelings of the subject. Lincoln's tall, gangling posture, Teddy Roosevelt's glasses and teeth and Franklin D. Roosevelt's jutting jaw and cigarette holder have been memorialized by political cartoons ...and our political discourse would have been poorer without them. There is no doubt that the caricature of (Falwell) published in *Hustler* is at best a distant cousin of the political cartoons described above and a rather poor relation at that.... "Outrageousness" in the area of political and social discourse has an inherent subjectiveness about it which would allow a jury to impose liability on the basis of the jurors' tastes or views, or perhaps on the basis of their dislike of a particular expression.

What encouraged many journalists the most about the *Falwell* decision was that it was not only a strongly worded defense of freedom of the press, but that it was authored by Rehnquist, who rarely took a broad view of the First Amendment in his earlier decisions. Rehnquist often dissented when the court expanded First Amendment rights.

The media still face many emotional distress lawsuits. In fact, media lawyers sometimes call emotional distress a "tag-along tort" because plaintiffs' lawyers so often toss in this claim when they sue for libel. For example, the Kansas Supreme Court in 2010 reversed judgments against a news organization for outrage (the same thing as emotional distress in Kansas) and defamation in the reporting that a man had been detained in connection with the famous BTK murder investigation (*Valadez v. Emmis Communications*, 229 P.3d 389). In overturning the awards on appeal, the Kansas Supreme Court said that Valadez had not met the burden of proof for outrage. The media's conduct must be reasonably considered to be outrageous and the plaintiff must have suffered more than just discomfort. The court added, "Conduct that rises to the level of tortious outrage must transcend a certain amount of criticism, rough language, and occasional acts and words that are inconsiderate and unkind."

But in the years since the *Falwell* case, as the *Valadez* case shows, it has become clear that a plaintiff must prove that the media engaged in clearly *outrageous* conduct that was either *deliberate* or *reckless*, and caused *severe* emotional distress to win this kind of lawsuit. That is not often easy to do. And, of course, public-figure plaintiffs now have to prove actual malice as well if the lawsuit is based on the *content* of something that appeared in the media. (As Chapter Five explains, the media are often sued for *newsgathering torts* based on the *behavior* of media representatives instead of the content of what was published or broadcast.)

Product Disparagement and "Veggie Libel"

During the 1990s, a close relative of libel—*product disparagement*—became a newsworthy topic after many years of obscurity. Farmers and ranchers in some areas became alarmed about what they considered to be overly sensational media accounts of alleged health hazards associated with food products. They cited examples in which food producers suffered large losses when public demand for a perishable product suddenly dwindled after the media reported claims that the product might be unsafe. Food producers lobbied for state laws allowing them to sue in response; these laws are known as "veggie libel" or "trade libel" laws.

This trend began with a case in which Washington state apple growers sued CBS for a *60 Minutes* segment that said Alar, a chemical used by some growers to enhance the growth and appearance of apples, could cause cancer. There was a large decline in apple consumption, and growers claimed the CBS report was false or at least exaggerated—and cost them $130 million. Their lawsuit was eventually dismissed; a federal appellate court ruled that the growers could not prove the CBS report was false—as they must to win a product disparagement lawsuit (*Auvil v. CBS 60 Minutes*, 67 F.3d 816, 1995).

In response to the CBS story, a number of states passed new laws that were much tougher than traditional product disparagement laws, authorizing growers to sue whenever false information is published claiming that a perishable food product is unsafe. Such laws were passed in at least 13 states: Alabama, Arizona, Colorado, Florida, Georgia, Idaho, Louisiana, Mississippi, North Dakota, Ohio, Oklahoma, South Dakota and Texas. Most of these laws define false information as not based on "reliable scientific data." Allowing growers to sue under these circumstances raises First Amendment questions because growers, journalists and consumer groups are not likely to agree about what is "reliable" scientific data.

Such laws made national headlines in 1997 and 1998 when a group of Texas cattlemen sued talk show host Oprah Winfrey after a guest on her show discussed mad cow disease, an illness that had caused the death of at least 20 persons in Britain, and raised questions about whether this illness could spread to the United States. Cattle prices dropped sharply, and the cattlemen sued Winfrey under Texas' "veggie libel" law.

Amidst what many called a media circus, the case went to trial in Amarillo, Tex. Winfrey moved production of her show there during the trial. But the case went badly for the cattlemen almost from the beginning. With no written opinion, the trial judge dismissed the part of the lawsuit that was based on the "veggie libel" law, allowing the cattlemen to continue the case only under a general business defamation law. In the end, the plaintiffs were unable to persuade the jury that Winfrey or her guest intended to harm the Texas cattle industry by making knowingly false statements about it, as required by the business defamation law. The jury quickly ruled against the cattlemen—in a case far more newsworthy than legally significant. In 2000, the Fifth Circuit upheld the verdict (*Engler v. Winfrey*, 201 F.3d 680).

Nonetheless, many media attorneys expressed fears that future "veggie libel" lawsuits could seriously chill the First Amendment right of the media to report legitimate health questions about food products.

Libel and Fiction

The fundamental question in many libel cases is truth or falsity: only if a statement is false can it be the basis for a successful libel case. But what about libelous innuendoes in a work of fiction—which by its very nature is *intended* to be false? Most media organizations didn't worry about this problem until the 1980s, because courts rarely allowed libel suits based on works of fiction. A more serious legal problem was the threat of privacy suits by those who recognized themselves—or thought they did—in fictitious works.

However, in the 1970s and 1980s that began to change. Courts started finding sufficient identification in works of fiction to support libel judgments. The result for the media has become a vicious circle: to avoid identifying any real person, those who write novels, short stories and scripts carefully fictionalize their characters. However, if a real person nevertheless can convince a court he/she has been identified in the fictitious work, every respect in which the fictional character differs from the real person is a "falsehood" and thus exacerbates the libel. The *New York Times v. Sullivan* rule sometimes has been applied—some say misapplied—with disastrous results for the media. In a work of fiction, the characters necessarily differ from real people, but some courts have ruled fictionalization equals knowing or reckless falsehood, thus proving actual malice and opening the door to punitive damages.

The case that initiated this trend toward libel judgments for fictionalization was *Bindrim v. Mitchell* (92 C.A.3d 61, 1979), a California appellate court ruling. As a decision of an intermediate appeals court in a single state, it carries little weight as a precedent, but it encouraged other fiction based libel cases, including the Wyoming judgment against *Penthouse* in the introduction to this chapter (*Pring v. Penthouse*, 695 F.2d 438, 1983).

In *Bindrim*, novelist Gwen Davis Mitchell described a fictitious "nude encounter marathon" similar to therapy sessions conducted by Dr. Paul Bindrim, a psychologist. In fact, Mitchell had attended one of Bindrim's sessions and signed an agreement not to write about it. But in Mitchell's book, entitled *Touching*, the psychologist who conducted the sessions had a different name and did not physically resemble Bindrim. The main thing the real man and the fictional character had in common was that they both conducted nude encounters on the theory that nudity made the therapy sessions more effective. Nevertheless, a jury found that Bindrim was identified and libeled by the fictional account in the novel, and awarded Bindrim $75,000 in total damages against Mitchell and her publisher, Doubleday and Company. The award was later reduced to $50,000.

Both the California and U.S. Supreme Courts refused to review the lower appellate decision, which affirmed the judge's determination that Bindrim was sufficiently identified for a libel suit. "The test is whether a reasonable person, reading the book, would understand that the fictional character was, in actual fact, the plaintiff," the appellate majority wrote.

The *Bindrim* ruling was widely criticized by writers and publishers, but no higher court was willing to review it. This was not the first time a libel judgment had ever been based on a work of fiction: as early as 1920 the New York Court of Appeals had ruled similarly (*Corrigan v. Bobbs-Merrill*, 228 N.Y. 58). Other courts reached similar conclusions later, but none with quite the impact of *Bindrim*, which caused widespread alarm among writers and publishers.

However, fiction writers could take some comfort in the ultimate decision in the "Miss Wyoming" libel suit against *Penthouse*. The Tenth Circuit reversed the multimillion-dollar jury verdict, and the Supreme Court declined to hear a further appeal.

The case stemmed from a *Penthouse* article describing a fictitious "Miss Wyoming" who competed in the Miss America Pageant, a champion baton twirler who had an even more interesting talent: oral sex. The story said she performed an act of oral sex at the pageant before a national television audience, and the recipient of her favors was levitated—he rose up in the air in defiance of the laws of gravity. Kim Pring, a champion baton twirler who once represented Wyoming in the Miss America Pageant, sued, claiming the story was about her and damaged her reputation. A Wyoming jury agreed and awarded $26.5 million in damages ($25 million in punitive damages). The appellate court overturned the jury verdict because it found the story to be "physically impossible in an impossible setting," and thus not something readers could reasonably understand as describing actual events involving Pring.

The court called the story "gross, unpleasant, crude," but said the First Amendment is not limited to decent ideas. It also offered guidance on the murky issue of libel and fiction: "The test is not whether the story is or is not characterized as 'fiction,' 'humor,' or anything else in the publication, but whether the charged portions in context could be reasonably understood as describing actual facts about the plaintiff or actual events in which she participated." Thus, the court said the *Penthouse* story was too incredible and obviously false to be libelous to Kim Pring. However, this decision offers little comfort for serious fiction writers. If a story is an accurate portrayal of life, it may be a more powerful (and artistically sound) literary work—but also more likely to be the basis for a libel suit. In effect, the *Pring v. Penthouse* decision says fairy tales are immune to libel judgments, but realistic literature is not.

Libel and Broadcasting

So far this summary of the principles of libel law has made almost no distinction between the print and electronic media. That was done in the interest of clarity and simplicity—and because it is generally justified. There are, however, some special libel problems when the broadcast media are involved. Not the least of these problems is the question of whether a broadcast defamation is really a libel at all or is in fact a *slander*. Before broadcasting came along, slander (a spoken defamation) was a limited legal action for the obvious reason that an oral statement was a fleeting thing, while a printed one might be read by thousands of people over many years. In view of slander's limited nature, the courts generally ruled that one could only win a slander suit by proving special damages unless the slander fell into one of several particularly offensive categories that were sometimes called slander *per se*. Because of these restrictions, successful slander suits were relatively rare.

But when broadcasting developed, the potential for harm in a spoken defamation became at least as great as in a written one. Recognizing the pervasiveness of a broadcast defamation, some states simply declared that broadcast defamation would be regarded as libel, not slander. Other states such as California classified broadcast defamation as slander but liberalized the requirements for a successful slander suit so there was little difference between libel and slander. Some states even adopted the rule that a defamation contained in a script would be treated as a libel (since it was written down, after all), while an ad-libbed one would be treated as slander. Only a few states still adhere to that rule today.

These variations in broadcast defamation law may seem quaint—and perhaps they are today. Whatever its name, broadcast defamation is a viable legal action in all states. As noted earlier, some states exempt local broadcasters from liability for defamation occurring during network programs they have no power to edit, but even then the network remains liable. And, as already noted, the Supreme Court has exempted broadcasters from liability for defamation occurring during political advertising that broadcasters are forbidden to censor under Section 315 of the Communications Act.

Aside from these exceptions, a broadcast defamation is as actionable as a printed one, and perhaps more because of the massive audiences the electronic media attract. In evaluating defamation that was broadcast rather than published, the same rules normally apply.

However, there are other practical problems in broadcasting. If broadcasters are to be held accountable for slanders by various people whose voices are broadcast, how can broadcasters hope to protect themselves? Various solutions have been developed, among them the practice of putting as much programming as possible on tape or film to expedite pre-broadcast review. Call-in shows have produced problems in this respect; those who call in can hardly be expected to obey (or even know about) the rules of libel. One common solution is the use of a short time delay to allow the broadcaster to bleep out potentially offensive remarks. That means, of course, that the talk show host or producer must be able to recognize defamation—and delete it—quickly.

Criminal Libel

Although some states still have criminal libel laws on the books, they have rarely been enforced since two 1960s Supreme Court decisions. Criminal libel laws generally cover situations in which civil libel law is inapplicable. For instance, some states still make it a crime to libel a dead person—a form of libel rarely actionable in civil suits. In addition, some states forbid distributing literature so defamatory that it may cause a breach of the peace.

Shortly after handing down its landmark *New York Times v. Sullivan* civil libel ruling in 1964, the Supreme Court announced an important criminal libel decision: *Garrison v. Louisiana* (379 U.S. 64). That case arose when New Orleans prosecutor Jim Garrison severely criticized a group of judges, calling them sympathetic with "racketeer influences" and "vacation-minded." Prosecutor Garrison was himself prosecuted under a Louisiana law that made it a crime to defame public officials.

The Supreme Court said Garrison's prosecution was not permitted by the First Amendment unless it could be proved that he made false statements either knowingly or with reckless disregard for the truth. In short, the court said the same tough standards that apply in civil libel suits by public officials also apply in criminal prosecutions for defamation of public officials: actual malice must be shown.

The Supreme Court dealt another blow to criminal libel in the 1966 case of *Ashton v. Kentucky* (384 U.S. 195), a decision stemming from circulation of a pamphlet that attacked various local officials. The circulator was prosecuted for criminal libel because the pamphlet allegedly threatened to cause a breach of the peace. The Supreme Court unanimously reversed the conviction, ruling the law overbroad and in violation of the First Amendment.

As a result of these Supreme Court decisions and parallel rulings by a number of state courts, criminal libel prosecutions constitute a minimal legal threat to the media today. If the remaining criminal libel laws were vigorously enforced, few of them could withstand a constitutional challenge at this point in our history.

Prior Restraint to Prevent Libel

Normally, when someone sues for libel and wins, the court awards monetary damages. But may a court instead engage in prior restraint, ordering the defendant not to make any more defamatory statements about the plaintiff? The California Supreme Court ruled in 2007 that a woman who repeatedly made false statements about a restaurant adjacent to her home could be ordered not to do so in the future.

In *Balboa Island Village Inn v. Lemen* (40 C.4th 1141), the court said that Anne Lemen could be ordered not to make future statements falsely accusing the restaurant of serving tainted food and engaging in child pornography and prostitution. Lemen had run a long campaign against the restaurant, making those and other charges that were proven false when the restaurant owner sued her for libel and won. Justice Carlos Moreno wrote for a 5-2 court, "A properly limited injunction prohibiting defendant from repeating to third persons statements about the Village Inn that were determined at trial to be defamatory would not violate defendant's right to free speech." The dissenting justices were troubled by this nearly unique endorsement of prior restraint: "To forever gag the speaker—the remedy approved by the majority—goes beyond chilling speech; it freezes speech."

The Kentucky Supreme Court held in 2010, citing *Lemen*, that a lower court's "broad-sweeping and vaguely worded injunction against future expression, before final adjudication of its defamatory character, constitutes an improper prior restraint on speech" (*Hill v. Petrotech Resources Corp.*, 325 S.W.3d 302). An investor retained an agency owned by H.C. Hill to recover investments made in Petrotech. As the court put it, Hill's agency used "highly aggressive collection techniques," which included posting statements online claiming that Petrotech was "crooked" and in violation of various securities and criminal laws. The lower court enjoined Hill from making defamatory statements about Petrotech throughout the case or until further ordered by the court. The Kentucky high court adopted the following rule: "defamatory speech may be enjoined only after the trial court's final determination by a preponderance of the evidence that the speech at issue is, in fact, false, and only then upon the condition that the injunction be narrowly tailored to limit the prohibited speech to that which has been judicially determined to be false."

Libel As A Political Question

Courts may decline to decide cases that implicate issues best left to other branches of government—for example, questions dealing with national defense or presidential power. In 2010 the D.C. Circuit dismissed a libel suit filed by owners of a Sudanese pharmaceutical plant as a *political question*. The owners alleged that the Clinton administration had defamed them by saying they had ties to Osama bin Laden to justify a missile attack on the plant

In *El-Shifa Pharmaceutical Industries Co. v. U.S.* (607 F.3d 836), the court said that it could not verify the truth of what the government had said about the plant. The court added that "the political question doctrine bars our review of claims that, regardless of how they are styled, call into question the prudence of the political branches in matters of foreign policy or national security constitutionally committed to their discretion."

■ AN OVERVIEW OF MAJOR ISSUES

Through most of American history, the threat of being sued for libel has been the most serious continuing legal hazard for the media, and that threat has not disappeared. For a time, it appeared that the libel problem was subsiding. After *New York Times v. Sullivan,* the Supreme Court handed down several decisions in the 1960s and early 1970s that made it more difficult for plaintiffs to win. By the time of *Rosenbloom v. Metromedia* in 1971, even private persons involved in public issues were being required to prove actual malice (i.e., that a falsehood was published with knowledge or with reckless disregard for the truth).

However, the 1974 *Gertz v. Welch* decision reversed that trend. While *Gertz* rewrote the common law of libel in all 50 states by forcing even private plaintiffs to prove at least negligence in most cases (something not usually required before), it also reclassified many people as private persons when they were previously considered public figures.

The high cost of defending a libel suit grew even higher after the Supreme Court's *Keeton v. Hustler* and *Calder v. Jones* decisions, which permit *forum shopping* in libel cases. Few people would question the fairness of requiring a major corporation to defend a lawsuit in a state where it injures someone while doing business. Years ago the Supreme Court authorized states to exercise *long-arm jurisdiction* over companies having *minimum contacts* with a particular state. Some of today's most controversial questions involve long-arm jurisdiction on the Internet and related online issues. Does operating a website constitute *minimum contacts* sufficient to allow a libel plaintiff to sue anywhere the site can be viewed, including foreign countries? And is the exemption from liability for everyone except the creator of a defamatory online message, enshrined in Section 230, fair to those who are defamed online? Libel suits over Twitter will likely become more common.

Other issues remain controversial. The Supreme Court's *Milkovich v. Lorain Journal* decision sent a message to the states to give expressions of opinion less protection in libel cases. While statements of pure opinion are still exempt from libel suits, that is not necessarily true of mixed statements that include false factual allegations within an expression of opinion. Editorials, letters to the editor, columns, reviews and "op-ed" pieces often combine factual assertions with expressions of opinion; now they enjoy less protection from libel suits.

But the Court has given the media some help in libel cases. *Philadelphia Newspapers v. Hepps* declared the burden of proof in virtually all libel cases involving the media falls on the plaintiff. The media need not prove the truth of an allegedly defamation; the plaintiff must prove it is false. And *Bose v. Consumers Union* told appellate courts to review evidence in libel cases to be certain that actual malice was really shown when it was required to be.

The adoption of anti-SLAPP laws in many states to curb *strategic lawsuits against public participation* has been helpful to the media. Although these laws are intended primarily to protect citizen activists who speak out on controversial issues, in some states they also protect the media from harassment lawsuits. Even in states lacking an anti-SLAPP law, of course, media defendants can always seek to have nuisance libel suits dismissed before trial by seeking summary judgment, a tactic encouraged by the Court's *Anderson v. Liberty Lobby* decision. Unfortunately, a summary judgment motion cannot be made until later in a lawsuit than a dismissal motion under most anti-SLAPP laws, running up the legal expenses for both sides.

Another scary current development for media organizations is the First Circuit's determination in *Noonan v. Staples* that truth may not always be an absolute defense for libel cases.

Ultimately, the discussion of libel must end where it began: with the observation that the system is costly and cumbersome—and that libel is and will remain a serious legal problem for the media.

WHAT SHOULD I KNOW ABOUT MY STATE?	• What does my state's libel law say; how does it define terms like "actual malice" and "negligence"? • What is my state's statute of limitations for libel? • What defenses does my state recognize for libel? Does my state recognize the neutral reportage defense, for example? • Does my state have an anti-SLAPP law? If so, how has it been interpreted?

A SUMMARY OF LIBEL AND SLANDER

What Are Libel and Slander?

Libel and slander are legal actions to compensate someone whose reputation has been wrongfully damaged. Traditionally, a written defamation was called libel and a spoken defamation was called slander, but in many states the two are virtually identical.

Who May Sue or Be Sued for Libel?

Individuals and corporations—but not government agencies—may sue. Unincorporated associations may sue in some states but not in others. An individual may sue for group libel if the group is very small and the libel refers particularly to that individual. Usually anyone who contributes to the publication—or republication—of a libelous statement may be sued, even if the libel is in a direct quote, a live interview, an advertisement or a letter to the editor.

To Win a Libel Suit, What Must a Plaintiff Prove?

To win, the plaintiff (the person who initiates the lawsuit) must prove all of the elements of libel, which are: (1) *defamation*; (2) *identification*; (3) *publication/communication*; (4) in cases involving issues of public concern, *fault* on the part of the publisher or broadcaster (i.e., dissemination of a falsehood due to either negligence or actual malice); (5) in many instances, *actual damages*.

What Defenses Are There?

Even though all of the elements of libel may be present, the plaintiff will not prevail if the defendant can prove that any of the recognized defenses apply. The major ones are: (1) *truth*; (2) *fair comment and criticism*; (3) *privilege*. The Supreme Court has ruled that the plaintiff usually *bears the burden of proof*; he/she must prove the falsity of a libelous statement—the defendant does *not* have the burden of proving truth. In many states, publishing a timely retraction—as prominently as the original libel—limits the plaintiff to special damages (i.e., provable monetary losses).

Are There Different Rules for Public Figures and Private Persons?

The Supreme Court has ruled that public officials and public figures must prove actual malice, meaning the publication of a falsehood with knowledge of its falsity or with reckless disregard for the truth. With the Supreme Court's blessing, most states now permit private persons to win libel cases by proving merely negligence on the part of the media, not actual malice. In cases involving purely private matters rather than issues of public concern, the high court has held that the states may allow private persons to win libel cases without proving any fault at all.

5 *The Right of Privacy*

The legal concept called *the right of privacy* has much in common with libel and slander. Like libel, invasion of privacy is usually a tort action—a civil lawsuit in which an injured party sues for monetary compensation. Moreover, privacy, like libel, is basically a state legal matter, although the U.S. Supreme Court has sometimes stepped in to place constitutional limits on state actions in this area just as it has in libel law. In fact, some of the major Supreme Court decisions on libel are cited in privacy lawsuits—and Supreme Court decisions on invasion of privacy are sometimes cited in libel cases.

Invasion of privacy and libel are so similar that persons offended or embarrassed by media publicity often sue for both, hoping to win on at least one of the two legal theories. Libel and invasion of privacy overlap enough to invite this sort of double-lawsuit strategy, particularly because the two actions have slightly different defenses. It is possible to have an excellent libel defense in a situation, but a weak defense against an invasion of privacy suit.

However, there are important differences between libel and invasion of privacy, including their histories. Libel was incorporated into the English common law hundreds of years ago, but invasion of privacy is a relatively new legal action. It was not widely recognized by the courts or legislatures until the twentieth century.

The Supreme Court continues to delve into the implications of government violations of personal privacy, and some of the cases do not implicate the First Amendment. For example, in 2012, the Court addresses privacy issues raised by the Fourth Amendment. The Court ruled that attaching a global positioning system (GPS) device to a person's car without that person's knowledge counted as a "search" under the Fourth Amendment. Thus, the defendant's drug conviction must be reversed because the GPS evidence that was used against him was not lawfully obtained (*U.S. v. Jones*, No. 10-1259). Still, because privacy is a derived right, based in amendments other than the First Amendment, it is important to follow the Court's movements in these related areas. (The Court in 2012 also ruled on a Privacy Act case dealing with medical privacy, *FAA v. Cooper*, discussed in Chapter Nine.)

Although privacy law developed only recently, it has become one of the most important and controversial aspects of communications law. However, much of privacy law in the 2000s is concerning issues of data privacy rather than the four torts we'll discuss in this chapter. The ability of our technological gadgets to gather and transmit information, as well as our affection for online social networks, contribute to these new developments.

■ THE HISTORY OF PRIVACY LAW

The legal concept of a "right of privacy" developed only after the media, corporations and government agencies became powerful enough—and technically sophisticated enough—to threaten individual privacy. That happened early in the twentieth century.

By 1900, the biggest newspapers had achieved circulations of nearly a million copies a day, and they did it with a heavy emphasis on stories about crime and scandal, stories that were not always truthful and tasteful. It became obvious that the media could destroy someone's reputation, sometimes in a way that did not make a libel suit a good remedy. Suppose, for instance, that a sensational newspaper revealed intimate (but truthful) details of a person's private life. The truth defense would preclude a successful libel suit, but shouldn't there be some way for the injured party to win justice in court?

FIG. 25. Justice Louis
Dembitz Brandeis,
between 1905 and
1945.

*Library of Congress, Prints
and Photographs Division,
[LC-DIG-hec-16557].*

In one of the most widely quoted law review articles of all time, Samuel D. Warren and Louis D. Brandeis addressed this issue in 1890. (Brandeis later served on the U.S. Supreme Court and wrote several well-known opinions on freedom of expression in America.) Their essay in the *Harvard Law Review* contended that there should be a right of privacy either under the common law or state statutory law. Such a right, they felt, should protect prominent persons from gossipy reporting of their private affairs. The article was prompted at least in part by the experiences of Warren's family, which had occasionally found its name mentioned in unflattering ways in the Boston press.

"The press is overstepping in every direction the obvious bounds of propriety and of decency," they wrote. "Gossip is no longer the resource of the idle and of the vicious, but has become a trade, which is pursued with industry as well as effrontery."

Influential as that law review article became later, it did not create an overnight legal revolution. In fact, it was a dozen years later when a case based on the Warren-Brandeis theory finally reached a New York appellate court, and the court didn't buy the idea. The case (*Roberson v. Rochester Folding Box Co.*, 64 N.E. 442, 1902), was brought by Abigail Roberson, whose picture was used without her permission in a flour advertisement. She sued, but the court ruled that "the so-called 'right of privacy' has not yet found an abiding place in our jurisprudence...." However, Roberson's defeat in court quickly was turned into a victory in the New York legislature, which responded to a public outcry over the court decision by passing the nation's first statutory law on privacy. Acting in 1903, the legislature enacted what are now Sections 50 and 51 of the New York Civil Rights Law, which read in part: "[T]he name, portrait or picture of any living person cannot be used for advertising purposes or for purposes of trade, without first obtaining that person's written consent."

Obviously, this was not a sweeping law: it didn't address the sort of invasion of privacy Warren and Brandeis had in mind. All it did was outlaw commercial exploitation of a person's name or likeness without consent—a separate legal wrong we call *misappropriation* or invasion of the *right of publicity* today. It said nothing about situations in which the media reveal intimate details about a person's private life or engage in intrusive newsgathering.

Two years after the New York privacy law was enacted, a state supreme court judicially recognized a right of privacy in connection with the media for the first time. In that 1905 case (*Pavesich v. New England Life Insurance Co.*, 50 S.E. 68), the Georgia Supreme Court upheld the right of an artist named Paolo Pavesich to sue New England Life for using his likeness in an advertisement without permission. The ad included a photo of Pavesich and a testimonial implying that he endorsed the company's insurance.

Another famous early privacy case raised a different question, one that has plagued the courts (and journalists) ever since: can a public figure return to a private life and then sue for invasion of privacy if the press does a "where-is-he-now" story years later? In *Sidis v. F-R Publishing Co.* (113 F.2d 806, 1940), William J. Sidis sued the publisher of the *New Yorker* magazine for doing an article about him. He was a one-time mathematical genius who graduated from Harvard University at age 16. The article, published some 20 years later, revealed that he was living in a shabby rooming house and working as a low-salaried clerk. It ridiculed him and even included a cartoon with a caption calling him an "April fool."

Should someone like William Sidis be able to sue the *New Yorker* for invading his privacy? A federal appellate court ruled that the case should be dismissed, pointing to the newsworthiness of the story. The court said that someone who becomes a celebrity even involuntarily (as Sidis had) cannot completely avoid publicity later in life.

The *Sidis* case did not settle this issue, of course. Old-but-true-facts cases continue to arise, and the media defend coverage of such stories by citing the continued public interest in the subject and by pointing out that the coverage is often based on truthful reporting of public records. Publicity-shy plaintiffs, of course, argue that they should not be forced to have their past deeds revealed to people who have forgotten (or never knew) about them.

However, two legal concepts were emerging from these early privacy cases. First, there is the idea that the news media do not need anyone's consent to do stories about *newsworthy* subjects. But, on the other hand, when a person's name or likeness is used for commercial purposes (as in advertising), it must be with the person's permission. Most states have now recognized at least these aspects of the right of privacy, either by statute or court decision.

Meanwhile, the U.S. Supreme Court began to recognize that there is also a *constitutional* right of privacy, although none of the early Supreme Court decisions actually involved the media. Rather, the early cases all involved the right of individuals to be free of excessive *government* intrusions into their private lives. The high court acknowledged the right of privacy in a law enforcement context as long ago as 1886, in *Boyd v. U.S.* (116 U.S. 616). In that case, the Court said the Fourth and Fifth Amendments provide protection against governmental invasions of the "sanctity of a man's home and the privacies of life."

Then in 1928, Louis Brandeis—by then a Supreme Court justice—wrote a famous dissenting opinion in which he urged recognition of the right of privacy in *Olmstead v. U.S.* (277 U.S. 438). That case involved government eavesdropping to gain evidence against suspected bootleggers in the prohibition era, and the majority opinion held that there was no violation of any right of privacy unless the federal agents committed a physical trespass in order to listen in. But in his dissent, Brandeis called for a "right to be let alone." He said the framers of the Constitution intended "to protect Americans in their beliefs, their thoughts, their emotions and their sensations.... They conferred, as against government, the right to be let alone—the most comprehensive of rights and the right most valued by civilized man."

Since then, the Supreme Court has specifically recognized the right of privacy, both in media cases and in other areas. For instance, the *Olmstead* majority opinion, which allowed government eavesdropping as long as there was no physical trespass, was reversed some 40 years later in *Katz v. U.S.* (389 U.S. 347). In that 1967 case, federal agents had used monitoring devices atop a public telephone booth to gather evidence against alleged bookmakers (i.e., persons taking illegal bets on horse races). The Court said a person's right to privacy extends to all areas where there is a justifiable expectation of privacy. Unauthorized law enforcement surveillance activities need not involve a physical trespass to constitute a violation of the Fourth Amendment, the Court ruled.

In the decades since *Katz,* the Supreme Court has repeatedly ruled on the privacy issues raised by the use of other technologies by law enforcement investigators to conduct searches without a search warrant. In 2001, the court ruled against federal agents who used heat-sensing equipment to detect an indoor marijuana farm. In *Kyllo v. U.S.* (533 U.S. 27), a 5-4 majority declared that the use of thermal imaging equipment violated the right of privacy guaranteed by the Fourth Amendment even though there was no physical intrusion into the home. This was true even though the imaging equipment merely detected heat radiating out from the home, and did not involve looking into the house, the Court said.

Writing for the Court, Justice Antonin Scalia made a distinction between using a technology that is in widespread public use (such as binoculars, which the court had previously allowed police to use in surveillance of private homes), and an exotic technology such as this one—which detected heat from rooms where the resident was using heat-generating lights to grow marijuana plants. Scalia said there *is* an expectation in privacy in this instance.

The Supreme Court also relied largely on a privacy rationale in reaching its famous decisions on birth control, abortion and homosexual rights. In the 1965 ruling that overturned state laws against contraceptive devices (*Griswold v. Connecticut,* 381 U.S. 479), Justice William O. Douglas said the various rights listed in the Bill of Rights, taken together, add up to a right of privacy that bars the state from involving itself in individuals' sexual relations in marriage. Although some of the other justices based their decision on a different rationale, Douglas' view was widely quoted later in support of a limited constitutional right of privacy. A couple's decision to use contraceptives was a private matter and none of the state's business, Douglas was saying. Thus, the Connecticut law banning the use of contraceptives (even by married couples) was ruled unconstitutional.

In the landmark 1973 Supreme Court decision that overturned state laws against abortions (*Roe v. Wade,* 410 U.S. 113), the court focused on concepts related to personal privacy in reaching the decision that abortions were a private matter between a woman and her physician, at least during the early months of pregnancy.

In the years since 1973, *Roe* has become the most controversial Supreme Court decision of the twentieth century. Millions of Americans vehemently disagree with the ruling that a state cannot prohibit abortions during the first six months of pregnancy when the fetus is not viable outside the womb. Millions of others strongly support the court's holding that there is a right of privacy in this area. It was inevitable that the Supreme Court would have to revisit the abortion question again and again.

In 1989, a deeply divided Court stopped just short of overturning *Roe v. Wade* in a case called *Webster v. Human Reproductive Services* (492 U.S. 490). In that case, the Court did uphold some restrictions on abortions that had been adopted in Missouri. The Court affirmed Missouri's ban on abortions in public hospitals and abortion counseling by public employees as well as a law requiring doctors to test the fetus for viability before performing an abortion if the fetus appeared to be at least 20 weeks old.

By 1991, two liberal justices who were strong supporters of *Roe v. Wade* (William Brennan and Thurgood Marshall) had been replaced by more conservative justices (David Souter and

Clarence Thomas). Many on both sides of the abortion controversy expected the Supreme Court to overturn *Roe v. Wade* in a 1992 case. But to almost everyone's astonishment, a new coalition of moderate conservatives led the Court in a 5-4 vote to reaffirm the basic holding of *Roe* in *Planned Parenthood of Southeastern Pennsylvania v. Casey* (505 U.S. 833). Justice Sandra Day O'Connor formed a coalition with Justices Anthony Kennedy and David Souter to rule that the states may not place an *undue burden* on a woman's right to choose an abortion during the early months of pregnancy. When the decision was announced, O'Connor said she was personally very opposed to abortions, but she added, "Our obligation is to define the liberty of all, not to mandate our own moral code...."

The Court upheld Pennsylvania laws establishing a 24-hour waiting period for adult women who want an abortion and requiring teenagers to get a parent's or a judge's permission for an abortion. Those were *not* undue burdens, the court held. But the court overturned Pennsylvania's requirement that married women had to notify their husbands of their plans. That, they said, *was* an undue burden.

Justice Harry Blackmun, who wrote the court's opinion in *Roe v. Wade* 19 years earlier, concurred in the 1992 decision to reaffirm it, as did Justice John Paul Stevens. Chief Justice William Rehnquist and three other conservatives dissented, indicating that they would overturn *Roe v. Wade*. Blackmun, who had been widely quoted as predicting that the court would overturn *Roe*, was at least as surprised as anyone else. In what may be among his most memorable words as a Supreme Court justice, Blackmun wrote: "[N]ow, just when so many expected the darkness to fall, the flame has grown bright.... Make no mistake, the joint opinion of Justices O'Connor, Kennedy and Souter is an act of personal courage and constitutional principle." Blackmun also included a surprisingly candid and personal statement in his concurrence:

> I am 83 years old. I cannot remain on this court forever, and when I do step down, the confirmation process for my successor may well focus on the issue before us today. That, I regret, may be exactly where the choice between the two worlds will be made.

Of course, the confirmation battles involving Justices Kennedy, Souter and Thomas had all focused on this issue. All three were appointed by Republican presidents opposed to abortions, but two of them voted to uphold the basic tenets of *Roe v. Wade*. Ironically, when Blackmun did leave the court two years after the *Planned Parenthood* decision, the debate over the confirmation of his successor (Stephen Breyer) focused mainly on other issues. Nevertheless, no one—including the presidents who appoint Supreme Court justices—can predict which way the next Supreme Court decision on a volatile issue such as abortion will go.

In 2000, the Supreme Court ruled that a Nebraska law forbidding "partial birth abortions" placed an undue burden on a woman's constitutional right to terminate a pregnancy and was therefore unconstitutional (*Stenberg v. Carhart*, 530 U.S. 914). The Nebraska law defined partial birth abortion as a procedure in which a person "...intentionally delivers into the vagina a living unborn child, or a substantial portion thereof, for the purpose of performing a procedure" that the person knows "will kill the unborn child."

In essence, the Court said this law (and similar laws banning partial-birth abortions in about 30 other states) was too broad, precluding abortion methods that are safer for the mother than some alternative methods used in late-term abortions. Four justices dissented, writing four separate opinions. In essence, they argued that a state should be free to ban partial birth abortions for various reasons. Justice Antonin Scalia said, "The method of killing a human child...proscribed by this statute is so horrible that the most clinical description of it evokes a shudder of revulsion."

In 2003, Congress approved a federal Partial Birth Abortion Ban Act, forbidding certain partial-birth abortion procedures. This federal law is similar to the Nebraska state law overturned in the *Stenberg v. Carhart* decision, but legal challenges to it had a very different outcome: the Supreme Court eventually upheld the law. Initially, the federal law was overturned by three different federal appellate courts. The Second, Eighth and Ninth Circuits all declared it unconstitutional because it places an undue burden on the right of women to have abortions even when it is necessary for their health (see *National Abortion Federation v. Gonzales*, 437 F.3d 278, 2006; *Carhart v. Gonzales*, 413 F.3d 791, 2005; and *Planned Parenthood Federation v. Gonzales*, 435 F.3d 1163, 2006).

However, in 2007 the Supreme Court overturned all three appeals court decisions, voting 5-4 to uphold the constitutionality of the Partial Birth Abortion Act. Justice Samuel Alito provided the fifth vote to restrict abortion rights in the new decision, *Gonzales v. Carhart* (550 U.S. 124). A year earlier, he replaced Justice Sandra Day O'Connor, the architect of the undue burden test and frequently the fifth vote to uphold abortion rights on the Court.

Writing for the new majority, Justice Anthony Kennedy now took what appeared to be a different approach than he had in joining O'Connor's opinion in the 1992 *Planned Parenthood* case. This time, he wrote for the court, "The government has a legitimate and substantial interest in preserving and promoting fetal life." He said the government may regulate "the medical profession in order to promote respect for...the life of the unborn."

The 5-4 majority in the 2007 decision upheld the federal ban on essentially the same kind of procedure that was forbidden in Nebraska in the law *overturned* by a 5-4 majority in *Stenberg v. Carhart* seven years earlier. In the new ruling, Kennedy focused more on "the life of the unborn" and not on women's privacy rights or the right of doctors to choose the safest procedure for women. He wrote, "It is precisely this lack of information concerning the way the fetus will be killed that is of legitimate concern to the State.... The State has an interest in ensuring so grave a choice is well informed." Kennedy said he was not abandoning O'Connor's undue burden test, but he said it should apply only if a law creates a burden for "a significant fraction of women." If it's a burden for just a few women who need a relatively unusual procedure, their only recourse would be to sue to have the law ruled unconstitutional as applied to them—while waiting to get an abortion until a court can rule. That would leave the law intact for everyone else.

The Supreme Court's 2007 decision was applauded by abortion opponents, who launched a campaign to win restrictions on abortions state by state. It was condemned by abortion rights advocates and some doctors. The media quoted one doctor and professor of medicine as saying, "It is patronizing. And for them to tell us how to practice medicine is dangerous." This doctor, who delivers babies and performs abortions, added, "If I have a patient with a placental abruption, there can be life-threatening bleeding. The fastest way to deal with that is to empty the uterus. But I will have to stop and think: Could I go to jail for trying to stop this bleeding?"

The *Gonzales v. Carhart* case overshadowed a 2006 Supreme Court decision that unanimously but on narrow grounds ordered a lower court to reconsider a New Hampshire ban on abortions without parental consent because it lacked an exception for medical emergencies

(*Ayotte v. Planned Parenthood of Northern New England,* 546 U.S. 320). On the eve of her retirement, Justice O'Connor wrote her last decision on abortion—and the only one for a unanimous Court. But the Court did not overturn the New Hampshire law itself. Instead, the high court merely ordered the First Circuit to reconsider whether the law could be salvaged by judicially adding a medical emergency exception to the requirement of a 48-hour delay to allow for parental notification.

A year before its 1992 *Planned Parenthood* decision, the Supreme Court addressed a related issue: whether the federal government can order health care providers who receive federal funds not to mention abortions to their patients. In *Rust v. Sullivan* (500 U.S. 173), the Court upheld such federal regulations. In so ruling, the Court's 5-4 majority ruled that doctors do *not* have a First Amendment right to inform their patients about abortions. (However, the federal rules were later rewritten to eliminate this ban on federally-supported doctors mentioning abortions to their patients). Dissenting in the *Rust* case, Justice Harry Blackmun called the case a major retreat from previous decisions protecting First Amendment rights as well as the right of privacy. Blackmun wrote, "One must wonder what force the First Amendment retains if it is read to countenance the deliberate manipulation by the government of the dialogue between a woman and her physician."

The Second Circuit, however, found that a funding policy saying that "[n]o funds… may be used to provide assistance to any group or organization that does not have a policy explicitly opposing prostitution" was impermissible because it compelled recipients to take on the government viewpoint. In *Alliance for Open Soc'y Int'l, Inc. v. U.S. Agency for Int'l Dev.* (651 F.3d 218, 2011), the court said a provision of the U.S. Leadership Against HIV/AIDS, Tuberculosis, and Malaria Act of 2003 violated the "unconstitutional provisions" test, which says that "the government may not place a condition on the receipt of a benefit or subsidy that infringes upon the recipient's constitutionally protected rights, even if the government has no obligation to offer the benefit in the first instance." The case differs from *Rust*, the court said, because the recipients must "voice the government's viewpoint and to do so as if it were their own"—not just remain silent if they do not agree.

As of 2012, seven states (Alabama, Georgia, Idaho, Indiana, Kansas, Nebraska, and Oklahoma) have laws that forbid abortions after 20 weeks of gestation—even though these laws conflict with *Roe v. Wade*. (Louisiana is poised to become the eighth after the state House approved a similar bill in June 2012.) No cases have yet been filed against these laws, which are based on the notion that a fetus can feel pain at 20 weeks.

Courts continue to wrestle with state laws regulating abortion. In 2011 and 2012, courts examined abortion laws in North Dakota (*Planned Parenthood v. Rounds*, 653 F.3d 662) and Texas (*Texas Medical Providers Performing Abortion Services v. Lakey*, 667 F.3d 570). In North Dakota, the Eighth Circuit removed an injunction against the enforcement of the law, which includes provisions that mandate giving a woman seeking an abortion information in very emotionally charged terms, such as the language that to have an abortion would be to "terminate the life of a whole, separate, unique, living human being." In Texas, the Fifth Circuit upheld a "sonogram bill" that must be offered to women considering having abortions. Under the law, a woman could decline to listen to listen to the fetus' heartbeat or view images of the fetus in the sonogram, but under most circumstances she must listen to a doctor's explanation of that sonogram. Relying on *Casey*, the court said that "such laws are part of the state's reasonable regulation of medical practice and do not fall under the rubric of compelling 'ideological' speech that triggers First Amendment strict scrutiny."

While the Supreme Court was considering the constitutional right of privacy in connection with abortions, another privacy issue was looming in the background—the issue of gay rights. On a 5-4 vote, the Court ruled in 1986 that there was *no* constitutional right of privacy to protect even private, consensual homosexual acts by adults. But in 2003 the Court reversed itself and held that a law banning private homosexual acts by adults violated the constitutional right of privacy.

In 1986 the Supreme Court declined to recognize constitutional privacy rights for homosexuals in *Bowers v. Hardwick* (478 U.S. 186). In *Bowers,* the Court upheld a Georgia law forbidding sex acts such as sodomy even between consenting adults in private. The Georgia law, similar to laws then in effect in more than 20 other states, made sodomy a crime for everyone including heterosexual married couples, although it was primarily enforced against homosexuals. Georgia officials said there had been few modern prosecutions.

In refusing to overturn the Georgia law in 1986, the 5-4 majority said that the authors of the Constitution were surely not trying to protect the rights of homosexuals when they wrote the Bill of Rights. Although the Court earlier had held that the Constitution includes a right of privacy in connection with contraception and abortion, the majority in *Bowers* ruled that the same privacy rights do not exist when the private sex lives of homosexuals are concerned. Writing for the court, Justice Byron R. White said:

> We think it is evident that none of the rights announced in those cases (involving contraception, abortion, and similar questions) bears any resemblance to the claimed constitutional rights of homosexuals to engage in acts of sodomy.

The *Bowers* decision was controversial, particularly because Justice Lewis Powell, who said at the time that he had joined the five-member majority only reluctantly, later said he had changed his mind. Speaking to New York University law students in 1990 (after his retirement from the Court), Powell said of his vote in the *Bowers* case, "I think I probably made a mistake." With Powell's vote on the other side, of course, the 5-4 decision would have gone the other way, and the Court would have recognized a constitutional right of privacy for gay men and lesbians in 1986.

After the *Bowers* decision, a number of states recognized a right of privacy for homosexuals under their own *state* constitutions, ruling that these state constitutions provided a broader right of privacy than the U.S. Constitution. One of these states was Georgia. In a widely noted 1998 decision, the Georgia Supreme Court held that the sodomy law that led to *Bowers v. Hardwick* violates the privacy guarantees of the Georgia Constitution (*Powell v. State of Georgia,* 510 S.E.2d 18). And in 1996, the U.S. Supreme Court ruled that the voters of Colorado could not legalize discrimination against homosexuals by passing a ballot initiative to invalidate existing state and local laws protecting homosexuals' rights. That decision, *Romer v. Evans,* is discussed in Chapter Three.

In 2003, the U.S. Supreme Court revisited this issue, taking the highly unusual step of reversing one of its own prior decisions only 17 years later. In *Lawrence v. Texas* (539 U.S. 558), the Court voted 6-3 to overturn a Texas law similar to the Georgia law that it had upheld in *Bowers.* By a narrower 5-4 majority, the Court also voted to overturn *Bowers.*

The *Lawrence* case arose when Houston police entered John Lawrence's apartment to investigate what turned out to be a false report of a disturbance. But they found Lawrence and another man engaged in anal sex. The two men were arrested, jailed overnight and fined

FIG. 26. President Barack Obama signs the Don't Ask, Don't Tell Repeal Act of 2010 at the U.S. Department of Interior in Washington, D.C., Dec. 22, 2010.

Official White House photo by Chuck Kennedy.

$200 each for violating Texas' anti-sodomy law. They challenged the law's constitutionality.

Writing for the majority, Justice Anthony Kennedy said the two men "are entitled to respect for their private lives" in upholding their privacy. "The state cannot demean their existence or control their destiny by making their private sexual conduct a crime," he added. The decision overturned not only the Texas sodomy law but also laws in 12 other states that still prohibited acts of anal and oral sex. At the time of the *Lawrence* decision, four states (Texas, Oklahoma, Kansas and Missouri) banned sodomy only between homosexuals. Nine other states had laws banning such acts between heterosexual as well as gay couples. The *Lawrence* decision was widely hailed by gay-rights attorneys as the most important Supreme Court decision in many years.

Justices Antonin Scalia, Clarence Thomas and Chief Justice William H. Rehnquist dissented. Scalia said, "The court has taken sides in the culture war." He also criticized the majority for its willingness to overturn a prior decision after only 17 years, an action that violated the principle of *stare decisis*, in his view. Thomas said he would vote against the Texas sodomy law if he were a Texas legislator, but as a justice he could not vote to overturn it because he does not think the Constitution includes any general right of privacy.

By the time the Supreme Court recognized a constitutional right of privacy for gay men and lesbians in the *Lawrence* case, another question involving their constitutional rights had become a major issue: whether they have a right to marry. By 2010, 29 states enacted laws or constitutional amendments defining marriage as a union of a man and a woman. Several state supreme courts had upheld these amendments. On the other hand, the Massachusetts Supreme Judicial Court ruled in 2004 that gays in that state have a constitutional right to marry (*Opinions of the Justices to the Senate*, 802 N.E.2d 565).

In 2008, the California Supreme Court ruled that gay men and lesbians have broad constitutional rights under the state constitution, including the right to marry (*In re Marriage Cases*, 43 C.4th 757). However, Proposition 8, a measure to amend the California Constitution to define marriage as a union between a man and a woman, passed a November 2008 election and was promptly challenged in the courts. In 2009 in *Strauss v. Horton* (46 Cal. 4th 364), the California Supreme Court upheld Proposition 8, saying. "Proposition 8 must be understood as creating a limited exception to the state equal protection clause." The court did, however, say that the ruling could not be applied retroactively to annul the marriages of 18,000 gay marriages that took place in California prior to the passage of Proposition 8.

Justice Carlos Moreno, in dissent, wrote, "In my view, the aim of Proposition 8 and all similar initiative measures that seek to alter the California Constitution to deny a fundamental right to a group that has historically been subject to discrimination on the basis of a suspect classification, violates the essence of the equal protection clause of the California Constitution and fundamentally alters its scope and meaning."

But in August 2010, federal district judge Vaughn Walker struck down Proposition 8 as unconstitutional under the due process and equal protection clauses of the Fourteenth Amendment in *Perry v. Schwarzenegger* (704 F.Supp.2d 921). In a lengthy opinion, the judge noted that marriage is a fundamental right, and fundamental rights cannot be voted upon. Moreover, he said, Proposition 8 could not even survive rational basis scrutiny, much less the much stricter test that abridgments of fundamental rights must surmount. Thus, he wrote, "Proposition 8 fails to advance any rational basis in singling out gay men and lesbians for denial of a marriage license. Indeed, the evidence shows Proposition 8 does nothing more than enshrine in the California Constitution the notion that opposite-sex couples are superior to same-sex couples." He ordered a permanent injunction against Proposition 8.

Judge Walker's decision was promptly appealed, but there was a question as to whether the appellants (two pro-Proposition 8 organizations) had standing to bring the appeal; if they didn't, then only the named parties could appeal, and Schwarzenegger and Attorney General (now Governor) Jerry Brown both opposed Proposition 8. The California Supreme Court refused to force Schwarzenegger or Brown to defend the proposition, so the appellants asked the Ninth Circuit for a stay pending appeal. The Ninth Circuit granted the stay, heard oral arguments, and then *certified a question* (asked the highest state court an opinion on a question of that state's law) to the California Supreme Court: Under California law, do the pro-Proposition 8 organizations have the right to defend the proposition if the named parties do not? The California Supreme Court agreed to address the question and set an expedited schedule for the hearing "as early as September" 2011. Most legal commentators view this as a landmark case that will eventually reach the U.S. Supreme Court.

Several states either legalized gay marriage or planned to do so: Connecticut, Iowa, New Hampshire, Vermont, Washington, D.C. and New York have joined Massachusetts in allowing same-sex marriage. Maine's legislation legalizing gay marriage was overturned by referendum in 2009. Rhode Island, and Maryland recognize but do not perform same-sex marriages. The federal government is prohibited from allowing gay marriage by the 1996 Defense of Marriage Act, which says that no state must recognize a same-sex marriage even if it is recognized in other states and defines marriage as a legal union between a man and a woman for the federal government. In two Massachusetts cases in 2010, *Gill v. Office of Personnel Management* (699 F.Supp.2d 374) and *Commonwealth of Massachusetts v. U.S. Dep't of Health and Human Services* (698 F.Supp.2d 234), DOMA was found to be an unconstitutional infringement on the states' right to determine marital status, based on the Tenth Amendment. "This court has determined that it is clearly within the authority of the Commonwealth to recognize same-sex marriages among its residents, and to afford those individuals in same-sex marriages any benefits, rights, and privileges to which they are entitled by virtue of their marital status. The federal government, by enacting and enforcing DOMA, plainly encroaches upon the firmly entrenched province of the state, and, in doing so, offends the Tenth Amendment," the judge wrote in *Commonwealth of Massachusetts*.

In 2011, Attorney General Eric Holder notified House Speaker John Boehner that the Obama administration believed DOMA to be unconstitutional and so would no longer defend the statute in court. Twenty bankruptcy judges in Los Angeles signed a 2011 court opinion that stated that DOMA was unconstitutional because it forbids legally married same-sex couples from jointly filing for bankruptcy, again on equal protection grounds (*In re Balas and Morales*, No. 2:11-bk-17831).

Several courts have declared DOMA unconstitutional, including the First Circuit in *Commonwealth of Massachusetts v. U.S. Dep't of Health and Human Services* (2012 U.S. App. LEXIS 10950), in which the court pointed out the impact of DOMA on states like Massachusetts that permit same-sex marriage: "One virtue of federalism is that it permits this diversity of governance based on local choice, but this applies as well to the states that have chosen to legalize same-sex marriage. Under current Supreme Court authority, Congress' denial of federal benefits to same-sex couples lawfully married in Massachusetts has not been adequately supported by any permissible federal interest." The issue may finally reach the Supreme Court: a group of House Republicans have appealed the First Circuit opinion to the Supreme Court, formally filing a petition for cert at the end of June 2012. It remains to be seen whether the Court will take the case.

"Don't Ask, Don't Tell" (DADT) made the news in 2010 as President Obama signed an act repealing the policy, which prohibits the military from discriminating against closeted gay or bisexual service members or applicants, while forbidding openly gay or bisexual persons from serving. The DADT policy had been upheld in four circuit courts. But in 2010 a federal judge said that it violated the First and Fifth Amendments in a case filed by the Log Cabin Republicans, the largest Republican gay organization (*Log Cabin Republicans v. U.S.*, 716 F. Supp. 2d 884), saying that it did not further the government's interests in unit cohesion or military readiness and is a content-based regulation. Even subject to a relaxed scrutiny deferential to military needs, the policy could not stand. President Obama signed the Don't Ask, Don't Tell Repeal Act of 2010. DADT was no longer policy as of September 20, 2011. The Ninth Circuit mooted an appeal by the Log Cabin Republicans, saying "The repeal of Don't Ask, Don't Tell provides Log Cabin with all it sought and may have had standing to obtain" (*Log Cabin Republicans v. U.S.*, 658 F.3d 1162).

Despite all these advances, some are still disappointed in the Obama administration's commitment to gay rights. President Obama vacillated in his feelings about gay marriage; when he was a senator, he supported it, and then when running for president he backed off. In the wake of New York's legalization of same-sex marriage, he said his position on the issue was "evolving." But Obama in May 2012 said that he believed same-sex marriage should be valid, a reversal from some of his earlier comments.

The four privacy torts:

intrusion: a physical unauthorized entry into a person's private space.

private facts: publication of facts that are actually private that would be embarrassing to the victim.

false light: publication of distorted or fabricated information about a person that would cause others to believe things about that person that were not true.

appropriation: the unauthorized use of a person's name or likeness for some kind of gain, either financial or otherwise.

While the Supreme Court's decisions about privacy rights in these controversial areas have generated more headlines, the Court has also recognized a right of privacy in several areas that directly affect the media. The rest of this chapter concerns the purely media-related aspects of privacy law, including data privacy.

■ AN OVERVIEW OF PRIVACY LAW

While the Supreme Court was wrestling with constitutional questions concerning the right of privacy, the states were developing their own concept of privacy, often in cases involving the media.

In 1960 William L. Prosser, one of the greatest legal scholars of his era, published an analysis of privacy law in which he said the concept of invasion of privacy really breaks down into four different legal rights. His classification has been widely accepted and provided the basis for many of the court decisions in this field that have followed. Prosser wrote:

> The law of privacy comprises four distinct kinds of invasion of four different interests of the plaintiff, which are tied together by a common name, but otherwise have almost nothing in common except that each represents an interference with the right of the plaintiff ... "to be let alone." Without any attempt to (write an) exact definition, these four torts may be described as follows:
>
> 1. Intrusion upon the plaintiff's seclusion or solitude, or into his private affairs;
> 2. Public disclosure of embarrassing private facts about the plaintiff;
> 3. Publicity which places the plaintiff in a false light in the public eye;
> 4. Appropriation, for the defendant's advantage, of the plaintiff's name or likeness. (48 *Calif. Law Review* 383, 1960)

Courts in a number of states had recognized these four kinds of invasion of privacy before Prosser wrote his classic analysis; many others have done so in the years since. Even today, though, not all states recognize all four kinds of invasion of privacy as a legal wrong that may be remedied in a civil lawsuit. For example, about 10 states have declined to recognize Prosser's third kind of invasion of privacy, that of holding someone up before the public in a false light. The false light concept closely parallels libel, and some states have chosen not to recognize it as a separate action. But for the most part, Prosser's four-category breakdown of privacy law remains valid.

The *intrusion* concept is based on a journalist's conduct as a newsgatherer. Reporters—and especially photographers or video crews—who pursue someone too aggressively may face this kind of lawsuit. The late 1990s saw an explosion in litigation of this kind.

Private facts cases usually result from the dissemination of intimate or embarrassing information about a person's private life or past—information that may be factually correct, thus precluding a successful libel suit.

Lawsuits based on holding a person before the public in a *false light* resemble libel suits because there must be an element of falsity in the communication. The basic difference between libel and false light privacy is that the latter does not necessarily require proof that the false statement is defamatory.

The fourth kind of invasion of privacy occurs most often in advertising and entertainment-related communications. Alternately called *misappropriation* or an invasion of the *right of publicity*, it prohibits the unauthorized use of a person's name, likeness, voice or some other element of his/her public persona for someone else's commercial gain.

As in libel law, there are defenses that the media may assert to escape liability in lawsuits for invasion of privacy. The two most widely recognized ones are *newsworthiness* (also called the *public affairs* or *public interest* defense) and *consent*. If the media show that the subject matter of a news story or news broadcast is newsworthy, the plaintiff in a private facts lawsuit will normally lose in court. However, the newsworthiness defense is of little help when the alleged invasion of privacy involves an intrusion or holding someone before the public in a false light. Even celebrities have some right to be free of harassment by journalists, although that right is limited. And no amount of newsworthiness will excuse a story that holds someone up before the public in a false light. Newsworthiness is not helpful when the issue is an unauthorized commercial use of a person's name or likeness (in an advertisement, movie or poster, for instance). In fact, the more newsworthy a person is, the greater the potential injury is likely to be if his/her name or likeness is used commercially without consent.

The consent defense is most applicable in misappropriation cases: celebrities regularly give their consent to commercial uses of their names and likenesses, but for a fee. The consent defense could also be useful in other kinds of privacy lawsuits, provided it could be shown that the person suing actually gave consent.

In addition to these two common law defenses, the Supreme Court has created constitutional defenses in privacy cases, just as it has in libel cases. In fact, the *New York Times v. Sullivan* principle has been transplanted from libel to privacy law and applies in certain kinds of privacy cases. In addition, the Court has also recognized a constitutional right of the media to publish the contents of many public records that are lawfully obtained, notwithstanding anyone's claim that publishing the information is an invasion of privacy.

Although these defenses often enable the media to defeat invasion of privacy claims in court, the fact remains that serious legal hazards exist in this area. For that reason, the four major categories of invasion of privacy warrant a more detailed summary.

■ INTRUSION

The concept of *intrusion* is based more on the conduct of a reporter, photographer or video crew than on the content of the media. It is a legal action to compensate a person when a journalist unduly intrudes into his or her *physical solitude or seclusion* or *private affairs*. It often involves snooping, eavesdropping, using a hidden camera or simply being in the way when someone has a reasonable right to expect a little peace and quiet.

In general, journalists have a right to ask questions or take pictures in public places without risking a lawsuit for this kind of invasion of privacy. In fact, in this era of miniaturized electronic listening devices and long telephoto lenses, technology has created a variety of new newsgathering opportunities (or threats to personal privacy, depending on your point of view). While the law affords journalists a good deal of latitude in gathering the news, there are limits to this right: journalists are sometimes sued for stepping over the bounds of propriety in their pursuit of a story or visual image. The growing popularity of "tabloid television" shows led to a number of new controversies and lawsuits in this area, as video crews aggressively pursued their subjects—often into their own private homes during "ride-alongs" with law enforcement officers. This has led to a series of new court decisions holding

newsgathering tort:
torts that involve how news is gathered rather than what is published; can include wiretapping/phone recordings, ride-alongs, fraud, breach of duty of loyalty, trespass, and other torts.

ride-along:
when a media professional accompanies the police on official duties.

that the media may sometimes be sued for intrusive newsgathering, including two notable U.S. Supreme Court decisions in a two-year period.

Early Intrusion Cases

Long before cellphone eavesdropping and media ride-alongs with law enforcement officers became national issues and led to Supreme Court decisions, a number of individuals charged that intrusive newsgathering invaded their privacy. These early cases played a major role in shaping the modern concept of intrusion.

The pioneering case of *Dietemann v. Time Inc.* (449 F.2d 245, 9th cir., 1971) is a good example of an intrusion by journalists that violated someone's privacy. Two reporters for *Life* magazine investigated a man suspected of practicing medicine without a license by posing as a patient and her husband. They visited the man at his home—where he practiced his craft—and surreptitiously took photographs. They also carried a hidden transmitter so law enforcement personnel nearby could monitor and record the conversation. The result was a criminal prosecution and an article in *Life* called "Crackdown on Quackery."

The man accused of medical quackery sued for invasion of privacy and ultimately won $1,000 in general damages, but only after several years of litigation and an appeal to the U.S. Court of Appeals. In a 1971 decision the appellate court agreed that the pictures and story were newsworthy but said the reporters had intruded upon Dietemann's privacy in gathering the information. The magazine had a right to publish the story but it did not have the right to use hidden electronic devices in the man's home to get the information.

If the news media may not surreptitiously enter a private home to get a story, may journalists go into a private home that is the scene of a fire and take pictures at the invitation of a public official? The Florida Supreme Court addressed that question in a 1976 case, *Florida Publishing Co. v. Fletcher* (340 So.2d 914). A photographer took a picture of a silhouette left on the floor by a girl's body after a fire, and the girl's mother sued, claiming a trespass and an invasion of privacy, among other things.

The Florida Supreme Court found no actionable trespass or invasion of privacy in the photographer's actions. In fact, a fire marshal had asked the photographer to take the picture when the marshal's own camera ran out of film. The court said, "The fire was a disaster of great public interest and it is clear that the photographer and other members of the news media entered the burned home at the invitation of the investigating officers." The court noted that it was customary for journalists to accompany public officials to the scene of such disasters. In 1977 the U.S. Supreme

Court refused to review this case. However, as noted earlier, in 1999 the high court ruled that when *law enforcement* officials enter private property with a search warrant and allow the media to go along, they are violating the Fourth Amendment and inviting a lawsuit.

Long before this, there were circumstances in which journalists who went onto private property without permission of the owner or tenant could be sued successfully. In one early case of this type, *Le Mistral Inc. v. CBS* (402 N.Y.S.2d 815, 1978), a New York court partially affirmed a trespass judgment against WCBS-TV. The case arose because a news camera crew photographed the interior of a swanky French restaurant over management objections in covering a story on health code violations.

The *Fletcher* and *Le Mistral* cases raise questions about the rights of photographers under privacy law. It is difficult to generalize on this subject because the rules vary somewhat from state to state, but in most states photographers who trespass to get a picture may face both civil and criminal sanctions unless they have consent to be there from someone authorized to give it. On the other hand, photographers in public places may generally shoot any subject within view for news purposes—but not for commercial or advertising purposes, for reasons that will be explained later in this chapter. There are occasional exceptions, but the general rule is that anything within camera range of a public place may be photographed for journalistic purposes. If the picture has even a little newsworthiness, and if no false impression is created with a misleading caption, it is usually safe.

Nevertheless, even in public places a photographer may not lawfully be so offensive in taking pictures as to seriously interfere with the subject's right to be left alone. The classic example of harassment by a photographer is the case of *Galella v. Onassis* (487 F.2d 986, 2d cir., 1973). Ron Galella, a freelance photographer who made something of a career of photographing the late Jacqueline Kennedy Onassis and her children in the late 1960s and early 1970s, was ordered by a federal appellate court to stay 25 feet away from Onassis and even farther from her children. This was by no means a typical case: Galella's conduct prior to the court order had been outrageous. He had engaged in a variety of offensive activities, some of which actually endangered the safety of Onassis and her children. He followed her and her children, bumped into other people while taking pictures, spooked a horse her son was riding, and was generally underfoot at all hours.

In fact, a decade after the original lawsuit Onassis again hauled Galella into court for invading her privacy. She contended that he had repeatedly violated the original order by failing to stay far enough away, among other things. The court agreed and found Galella in contempt (*Galella v. Onassis*, 533 F.Supp. 1076, 1982). The court emphasized—again—that Galella had a right to photograph Onassis (or any other celebrity) in public places, or to write articles about her if he wished. But Galella's conduct was so outrageous as to justify some restrictions on his activities, the court said. This was, in short, an unusual situation.

In more typical circumstances, there is little that celebrities can do about those who photograph them in public places, except perhaps to surround themselves with bodyguards whose job is to make it impossible for anyone to get an unobstructed shot. Occasionally, in fact, those who try to photograph the famous actually encounter violence from bodyguards. In those cases, photographers may well have grounds for their own lawsuits—against the celebrity's protectors. But that does nothing to salvage the pictures that the guards may either destroy or prevent the photographer from taking.

In recent years, however, the ability of journalists using powerful microphones and tele-photo lenses to see and hear the activities of people in their own homes and other private places without trespassing has led many to rethink whether journalists should be free to report everything they can see or hear from a public place.

The Hazards of Intrusion: Ride-Alongs

Many lawsuits have been filed in state and federal courts charging journalists—particularly photographers, television crews and reporters with hidden cameras—with various wrongful acts while gathering the news. These lawsuits often alleged not only an invasion of privacy (intrusive newsgathering) but also an intentional infliction of emotional distress (see Chapter Four). The resulting court decisions have raised questions about the proper line between the First Amendment freedoms of journalists and the privacy rights of celebrities and others who are involved in newsworthy situations such as accidents.

In fact, this area of law has acquired a new name: *newsgathering torts*, a term that encompasses a variety of different legal theories advanced by those who want to sue because of journalists' *newsgathering behavior*—as opposed to suing because of the *content* of what appears in the media. Those who are angry about journalists' newsgathering activities may sue for intrusion, of course, and for the infliction of emotional distress. In addition, the media are being sued for trespass, fraud and "outrage," which some states recognize as a tort.

The U.S. Supreme Court's *Wilson v. Layne* (526 U.S. 603) decision in 1999 made it clear that the media—and law enforcement officers—risk liability for media ride-alongs that allow journalists to enter a private home, even if the officers have a search warrant. The court held that while a search warrant gives officers the right to enter a private home, it is nevertheless a violation of the Fourth Amendment's ban on illegal searches and seizures for journalists to go into a home without the consent of residents.

The Court reached this conclusion in considering appeals by several different persons whose homes (or in one case, a large ranch) were invaded by the news media during ride-alongs with officers. The *Wilson* case itself began when law enforcement officers, armed with an arrest warrant, entered the home of Charles and Geraldine Wilson at 6:45 a.m. to arrest their son, who turned out not to be living there. A *Washington Post* reporter and photographer entered the home with the officers and observed a scuffle between officers and Charles Wilson, who came out of his bedroom wearing only briefs to ask the officers why they were in his home. No photographs of the incident were ever published, but the Wilsons sued the officers for allowing journalists to enter their home.

The Supreme Court ruled that law enforcement officials are violating the Fourth Amendment in most instances when they allow the media to accompany them onto private property to conduct a search or make an arrest. Writing for the court, Chief Justice William Rehnquist said that the Fourth Amendment's protection against unreasonable searches and seizures "embodies centuries-old principles of respect for the privacy of the home.... It does not necessarily follow from the fact that the officers were entitled to enter (a suspect's) home that they (were) entitled to bring a reporter and a photographer with them."

The Court stopped short of ruling that the officers could be sued in *Wilson v. Layne*—as opposed to future cases. Rehnquist noted that the law on ride-alongs may not have been clear before this definitive Supreme Court ruling. But in the future, there can be no doubt that officers who allow the media to accompany them onto private property to conduct searches or make arrests are inviting lawsuits for violating the Fourth Amendment.

Another case that troubled many journalists (and contributed to the Supreme Court's decision to hear *Wilson v. Layne*) was *Berger v. Hanlon* (129 F.3d 505), a 1997 decision of the

Focus on...
"Big Brother is watching you"

If you've spent any time playing with Google Maps (maps.google.com), you know that by using Google's Street View, you can, as Google says, "zoom, rotate and pan through street level photos of cities around the world." Google creates these maps by sending cars through neighborhoods with panoramic cameras to take pictures from public streets. But what if the cameras capture something illegal or private? At least one image has been captured of a drug deal going down, for example. How have the courts responded to privacy claims?

Aaron and Christine Boring lived on a private road in Pittsburgh, Penn. In browsing Google Maps, they found color images of their home, car, and swimming pool that they had given no permission for Google to obtain or use. They sued for trespass, publication of private facts and intrusion upon seclusion. A lower court found for Google, and the Third Circuit agreed, at least on the privacy claims. The court, in an unpublished (non-precedential) opinion, agreed that the Borings were not entitled to recovery for private facts or intrusion, because Google's conduct "would not be highly offensive to a person of ordinary sensibilities." But the Borings were entitled to pursue the trespass claim, and the case was remanded to the lower court (*Boring v. Google, Inc.*, 38 Media L. Rep. 1306, 2010).

FIG. 27. A circa 1818 map of the city of Washington in the District of Columbia.

Library of Congress, Prints and Photographs Division, [LC-USZ62-15171].

Ninth Circuit. In the *Berger* case, Cable News Network (CNN) arranged to send a television crew with federal wildlife agents on a raid of a 75,000-acre ranch in Montana. The federal agents suspected that Paul Berger, the elderly owner of the ranch, had killed American bald eagles in violation of the Endangered Species Act. An agent wearing a hidden microphone searched the ranch and questioned Berger and his wife inside their home.

The court said that by agreeing to cooperate with CNN, the federal agents had "transformed the execution of a search warrant into television entertainment." Judge Mary Schroeder held that the federal agents and CNN could both be sued for an allegedly unlawful intrusion, adding, "Law enforcement authority was used to assist commercial television, not to assist law enforcement objectives."

Berger was later acquitted of charges of killing protected species and convicted only of a misdemeanor pesticide charge that carried a $1,000 fine. In turn, the Bergers sued the federal agents—and CNN—for $10 million for the alleged invasion of privacy.

Responding to the court ruling in the Bergers' favor, their attorney told the media, "Twenty armed agents carrying weapons in 10 trucks rolled onto my clients' property looking for something that didn't exist. What they were doing was performing for the cameras."

The *Berger* case was appealed to the U.S. Supreme Court. The high court considered it along with *Wilson v. Layne* and then sent the *Berger* case back to the U.S. Court of Appeals to reconsider the issue of law enforcement liability based on *Wilson v. Layne*. The high court said that the federal officers should be given *qualified immunity* for allowing the *Berger* ride-along because the law was not clear when the ride-along occurred. The appellate court then followed that reasoning, granting legal protection to the officers who authorized the ride-along, while holding that CNN itself was not entitled to qualified immunity, thereby leaving the network in a difficult legal position (*Hanlon v. Berger*, 526 U.S. 808).

Even before *Wilson v. Layne*, media attorneys were warning of the legal hazards of intrusive journalism based on earlier adverse court decisions. In 1998, the California Supreme Court alarmed many media lawyers by ruling that a television producer may be sued when a crew shoots video of an accident victim being freed from a car and receiving emergency medical care in a rescue helicopter. In *Shulman v. Group W Productions* (18 C.4th 200), the court ruled that Ruth Shulman, the accident victim, had a right to go to trial with her claim that the video crew's coverage of her auto accident was unduly intrusive. Although the state Supreme Court was deeply divided in its reasoning, five of the seven justices agreed that the media can be sued for intruding on an accident victim's privacy, even if the accident itself is newsworthy. On the other hand, the justices agreed that the media could *not* be sued for the revelation of private facts in a situation as newsworthy as an accident near a major highway.

Writing the court's lead opinion, Justice Kathryn Mickle Werdegar said, "The state may not intrude into the proper sphere of the news media to dictate what they should publish and broadcast, but neither may the media play tyrant to the people by unlawfully spying on them in the name of newsgathering.... A jury could reasonably believe that fundamental respect for human dignity requires the patient's anxious journey be taken only with those whose care is solely for them and out of sight of the prying eyes of others (via cameras)."

What appeared to trouble the justices most about the *Shulman* case was that the video crew secretly recorded Shulman's post-accident conversations with emergency workers at the scene and in the helicopter by using microphones hidden on paramedics.

The use of hidden cameras or microphones has been central to several other cases in which the courts have ruled that journalists could be sued for intrusive newsgathering. In the aftermath of these cases, most media attorneys are cautioning their clients that it is legally hazardous *ever* to do photographic or video coverage during a law enforcement ride-along in which journalists accompany officers onto private property, even if the photos are never published and the video is never aired. And now very few officers are willing to risk being sued by allowing ride-alongs that enter private property (unless someone with authority to do so gives consent for the media's presence).

The Hazards of Intrusion: Hidden Cameras and Secret Taping

The courts are also showing a growing impatience with the use of hidden cameras in private or semi-private places. In a widely noted 1999 decision, the California Supreme Court ruled that ABC could be sued for having reporter Stacy Lescht pose as a psychic and use a hidden camera to videotape the conversations of workers who were paid to give psychic advice via telephone. Ruling in *Sanders v. ABC* (20 C.4th 907), the high court ordered a lower court to consider reinstating $1.2 million in damages and attorney's fees that had been won by two employees of the telepsychic operation who were shown on ABC's *PrimeTime Live*.

Writing for a unanimous court, Justice Kathryn Mickle Werdegar said that even workers who talk openly to co-workers can have "a limited, but legitimate, expectation that their conversations and other interactions will not be secretly videotaped by undercover television reporters." However, she also said that the *Sanders* decision does not preclude all use of hidden cameras by journalists in the state. She said a violation of privacy only occurs if the intrusion is "highly offensive to a reasonable person," and that the determination of reasonableness should include consideration of the motives of newsgatherers. The media can still argue that the use of hidden cameras is justified in a specific situation by a legitimate need to gather news that could not be obtained in any other way.

In the *Sanders* case, the telepsychics worked in cubicles in a large room that was off limits to nonemployees. Lescht, the ABC reporter, sometimes stood on her chair and looked around the room. Unbeknownst to other employees, she had a camera hidden in a flower on her hat and a microphone attached to her brassiere. That, the court concluded, was unduly intrusive even though the resulting story revealed the newsworthy fact that the telepsychics did not always take the advice they were giving to 900-line callers very seriously.

The same ABC undercover investigation also led to a Ninth Circuit decision in 1999. In this case, the court ruled that the subjects of hidden-camera exposés cannot sue for federal wiretap violations unless they can show that a news organization *intended* to commit a crime or a civil wrong. This ruling came in *Sussman v. ABC* (186 F.3d 1200).

In *Sussman,* 12 employees of the telepsychic operation claimed that by surreptitiously recording their conversations and airing them on *PrimeTime Live,* ABC violated the federal anti-wiretapping statute, the Electronic Communications Privacy Act. By adopting this strategy, their attorneys hoped to establish a precedent that would permit lawsuits against the media even in states that do not follow the *Sanders* precedent. But it didn't work. Writing for a unanimous panel, Judge Alex Kozinski seemed to be saying that *Sanders* defines the outer limit of media liability for a hidden-camera exposé. He wrote: "Although the ABC taping may well have been a tortious invasion of privacy under state law, plaintiffs have provided no probative evidence that ABC had an illegal or tortious purpose when it made the tape."

The *Sanders* and *Sussman* cases are reminiscent of another case in which ABC was slapped with a $5.5 million jury verdict for having two *PrimeTime Live* staffers take jobs at the Food Lion grocery store chain in North and South Carolina—and use hidden cameras to record alleged health hazards. As noted in Chapter Four, that verdict was reduced to $315,000 by the trial judge and later reduced to a token amount ($2) by a federal appellate court. But ABC spent at least a million dollars by most estimates for its legal defense.

On the other hand, some recent court decisions have upheld the right of journalists to use hidden cameras and microphones. A notable example is *Deteresa v. ABC* (121 F.3d 460), a 1997 decision in which the Ninth Circuit interpreted California privacy law to allow a television network to secretly tape a conversation between a producer and a reluctant news source on her front porch and then use a small portion on the air. The court dismissed a lawsuit against ABC by Beverly Deteresa, a flight attendant who worked the flight

---

Focus on...
Blogger privacy

As noted in Chapter Three, American bloggers have some protections for their privacy. Some courts have said that for an anonymous blogger to be revealed, the plaintiff must make a case that he/she will prevail if the case is brought.

But British bloggers have no shield of anonymity, an English court ruled in 2009. In the first British case dealing with the privacy of Internet bloggers, Richard Horton, a Lancashire detective and author of a popular blog, "NightJack: An English Detective," had requested an injunction to prevent *The Times* (London) from revealing his name, which had been found out by a *Times* reporter.

Horton, said Mr Justice Eady of the High Court, had no "reasonable expectation" of anonymity because "blogging is essentially a public rather than a private activity" (*The Author of A Blog v Times Newspapers Ltd,* [2009] EWHC 1358 (QB)).

that carried O.J. Simpson to Chicago the night of the murders of Nicole Brown Simpson and Ron Goldman.

A week after the murders, an ABC producer went to Deteresa's condominium to ask her to appear on an ABC program and discuss the flight. She declined, but she also volunteered that she was "frustrated" to hear news reports about the flight that she knew were false. Among other things, she challenged news accounts that Simpson kept his hand in a bag of ice during the flight. After further conversation, she said she would "think about" appearing on ABC. The producer called Deteresa the next day and again asked her to appear. When she declined, the producer told her he had recorded their conversation the previous day on her porch, and that an ABC cameraperson had videotaped them talking from a public street nearby. She hung up on the producer; later her husband called the producer and demanded that the tape not be aired. ABC did air a five-second clip on *Day One*, with a summary of her recollections of Simpson's behavior during the flight.

The Ninth Circuit held that Deteresa had no reasonable expectation of privacy when she talked to a TV producer on her front porch, in plain view of a nearby street. The court said ABC did not violate California's wiretap law, which forbids surreptitious taping of any "confidential communication" because that law applies only when someone reasonably expects the *content* of a conversation to be confidential. Deteresa knew she was talking to a media representative and that others could see and hear the conversation, the court pointed out. And she continued to talk to him about what she saw on the flight. Based on these facts, there was no violation of the wiretap law. Nor was there an actionable invasion of privacy by intrusion, the federal appellate court concluded. The U.S. Supreme Court later declined to hear an appeal.

Illustrating the complexity of the rapidly evolving law of hidden-camera journalism, the same court that upheld ABC's right to air secretly-taped video of Beverly Deteresa on her doorstep later ruled against another news organization that did something similar. In 1999, the Ninth Circuit ruled in *Alpha Therapeutic Corp. v. Nippon Hoso Kyokai (NHK)* (199 F.3d 1078) that it may be an invasion of privacy for a broadcaster to secretly tape an interview on someone's doorstep and then air it without consent. This time the court said a medical director and his company could sue because NHK, Japan's government-backed television network, did the same thing that ABC did—but aired much more of the tape.

In the *Alpha Therapeutic* case, the appellate court said a jury could conclude that the surreptitious taping was an invasion of privacy because McAuley knew only that he was talking to a reporter—he did not know the conversation was being taped. The court said, "A person may reasonably expect privacy against the electronic recording of a communication, even though he or she had no reasonable expectation as to confidentiality of the communication's contents." The court held that a jury could find the taping to have been conducted in a private place, and to be "highly offensive" to a reasonable person—the two elements required for an actionable intrusion under California law. (Like *Deteresa*, this was a federal case based on diversity of citizenship, which requires the federal court to apply state law.) This court also cited California's wiretap law, which permits civil lawsuits by victims of surreptitious taping of any "confidential communication."

Unlike most state laws and the federal wiretap law, the wiretap laws in California and 12 other states require *all* parties to a "confidential communication" to consent to the taping or monitoring of a conversation by others. Most such laws require the consent of only *one* party, which means a company can record all of its incoming calls in those states. In 2006, the California Supreme Court ruled that a company in a one-party consent state may not secretly record incoming calls from California, where all parties must consent to recording (*Kearney v. Salomon Smith Barney*, 39 C.4th 95).

The California Supreme Court in 2002 adopted a very broad definition of the term "confidential communication," increasing the number of conversations that would be considered confidential and therefore off limits for secret taping or monitoring. The court disavowed the more narrow definition of "confidential communication" used by the federal court in the *Deteresa* case, underscoring the pitfalls for journalists who tape a conversation without the knowledge of all parties. In *Flanagan v. Flanagan* (27 C.4th 766, 2002), the court said a communication is confidential, and therefore cannot be secretly taped, whenever any party believes it is not being taped or monitored by anyone else. Under this definition, even a party who knows the *content* of a conversation is not confidential may have a reasonable expectation of privacy that precludes secret taping.

Again illustrating the complexity and contradictions on this area of law, another federal appellate court *upheld* the right of ABC to use hidden cameras for newsgathering in another part of the country in a 1995 decision, *Desnick v. American Broadcasting Company* (44 F.3d 1345). In this case, ABC's *PrimeTime Live* equipped seven persons with hidden cameras and had them pose as patients at clinics that did cataract procedures. The resulting story suggested that the Desnick Eye Centers, a chain of 25 eye clinics in Illinois, Indiana and Wisconsin, did unnecessary cataract surgeries for Medicare patients. The Seventh Circuit held that Desnick did not have a right to sue for intrusion even though ABC had people posing as patients enter the clinics with hidden cameras. The *Desnick* decision was particularly notable because the court's opinion was written by Richard A. Posner, one of America's best-known appellate judges and a widely quoted expert on privacy law.

ABC won another hidden-camera case in 2003, when the Ninth Circuit dismissed a lawsuit against the network for using hidden cameras to show questionable procedures in an Arizona medical lab that evaluated pap smear samples (*Medical Laboratory Management Consultants v. ABC*, 306 F.3d 806). The court said ABC did not violate anyone's reasonable expectation of privacy under Arizona state law in the 52-second video clip of the lab that was aired on *PrimeTime Live*. The video revealed only lab procedures and related business matters, not anyone's personal affairs.

The Hazards of Intrusion: A Supreme Court Ruling

The question of surreptitious monitoring and recording of telephone conversations—and then broadcasting them—resulted in a Supreme Court decision in 2001. In *Bartnicki v. Vopper* (532 U.S. 514), the high court ruled that a broadcaster had a First Amendment right to air a newsworthy but pirated tape recording of a private cellphone call. By a 6-3 vote, the Court rejected the argument that airing such a tape is a violation of the federal wiretap law.

In this case, a Pennsylvania broadcaster, Frederick Vopper, was given a tape of a conversation between two teacher's union officials. Whoever made the tape gave it anonymously to a local anti-tax crusader amidst a controversy over teachers' salaries. The anti-tax crusader then passed it on to Vopper, who broadcast it on his talk show several times. The tape included some fiery rhetoric aimed at local school leaders. At one point, one union official said to the other, "we're going to have to go to their homes...to blow off their front porches" if school board members resisted the union's demands for a pay raise. Gloria Bartnicki and another union leader sued Vopper for airing the tape of their conversation.

No one disputed the point that whoever monitored the phone call and made the tape violated the law. But the court ruled that when such a tape *concerns an issue of public concern and the media lawfully obtain it from a third party without participating in or encouraging the illegal taping*, the media have a First Amendment right to air the tape.

Justice John Paul Stevens relied heavily on the "Pentagon Papers" case (*New York Times v. U.S.*, discussed in Chapter Three), in which the Court allowed the *Times* to publish excerpts from the so-called Pentagon Papers even though they had been illegally copied and then given to the *Times*. "A stranger's illegal conduct does not suffice to remove the First Amendment shield about a matter of public concern," Stevens said.

However, two justices, Stephen Breyer and Sandra Day O'Connor, wrote a concurring opinion in which they took a narrower view of the media's rights in such cases. They said the media would not have the right to air a tape that reveals gossip about someone's private life, as opposed to a discussion of a major local issue such as teachers' salaries. And there were three dissenters, Chief Justice William Rehnquist and Justices Antonin Scalia and Clarence Thomas. They said the media should *not* be free of liability for airing a bootlegged tape of a private phone conversation even if it addresses an issue of public concern.

Thus, the result was a victory for the media, but a narrow one. The right to air a pirated tape extends only to a tape of a conversation about an issue of public concern—usually a political or social issue. Also, new telephone technologies have made the interception of private phone calls much more difficult in recent years. Media lawyers generally hailed the *Bartnicki* decision as good—while emphasizing that it may have little real impact on personal privacy because of improvements in telephone privacy protection in the digital age.

Significantly, shortly after deciding *Bartnicki* the Supreme Court refused to intervene in another case where a television station played a more active role in illegal taping: *Peavy v. WFAA-TV* (221 F.3d 158, 2000). In this case, the Fifth Circuit said the station could be held liable because a reporter cooperated with a family that illegally monitored and taped a neighbor's cordless telephone conversations. The neighbor, Carver Dan Peavy, was an elected Dallas, Tex., school trustee. The taped conversations led the TV reporter to believe that Peavy had taken kickbacks on school insurance purchases. The tapes were *not* aired, but they were used by WFAA-TV in preparing several stories about alleged wrongdoing by Peavy. Peavy sued, but a trial court dismissed the case on First Amendment grounds. The appellate court reinstated the case.

In 2007, the U.S. Court of Appeals in Washington, D.C. also declined to apply the *Bartnicki* decision to a case involving disclosure of an illegally intercepted cellphone conversation. In *Boehner v. McDermott* (484 F.3d 573), the court held that a member of Congress violated the law by giving to the media a recording of a cellphone conference call involving other members of Congress, even though he played no part in making the illegal recording. The tape, concerning an ethics probe of then-House Speaker Newt Gingrich, received wide publicity. On a 5-4 vote, the court said a public official has no First Amendment right to disclose even a newsworthy tape that was lawfully obtained from someone else (who recorded it illegally). Disclosing such a tape is a violation of the public trust, the court said.

But in a bright spot, several appellate courts have answered the question of whether openly recording a police officer in public is a form of wiretapping in the negative. Absolutely not, said the First Circuit in 2011 in *Glik v. Cunniffe* (655 F.3d 78). Simon Glik openly recorded three police arresting someone in Boston in 2007 with his cell phone, and he was charged with violating the Massachusetts wiretapping law, disturbing the peace and aiding the escape of a prisoner. The district court dismissed the charges, and the police appealed. The First Circuit unequivocally held that Glik was exercising his First Amendment rights to record the officers in a public place. "[A] citizen's right to film government officials, including law enforcement officers, in the discharge of their duties in a public space is a basic, vital, and well-established liberty safeguarded by the First Amendment," the court wrote. While the right to record may be regulated in such acceptable ways as time, place and manner restrictions, the court noted, Glik was well within his protected rights. Moreover, because Glik openly recorded the officers, the recording was not "secret" as targeted by the wiretapping statute. Thus, the court concluded, "Glik was exercising clearly-established First Amendment rights in filming the officers in a public space, and...his clearly-established Fourth Amendment rights were violated by his arrest without probable cause."

The Seventh Circuit agreed by a 2-1 vote in 2012 in *ACLU v. Alvarez* (679 F.3d 583). The ACLU sought to enjoin the enforcement of an Illinois wiretapping law that would make public recording "a class 1 felony—with a possible prison term of four to fifteen years—if one of the recorded individuals is performing duties as a law-enforcement officer" (it would be a class 4 felony otherwise). Video recording was acceptable, but audio recording was not. The Seventh Circuit first established that "[a]udio recording is entitled to First Amendment protection" and then went on to evaluate the law under intermediate scrutiny. In finding that the law was too broad, the majority said, "The ACLU wants to openly audio record police officers performing their duties in public places and speaking at a volume audible to bystanders. Communications of this sort lack any 'reasonable expectation of privacy' for purposes of the Fourth Amendment." The court then allowed the preliminary injunction. Judge Richard Posner dissented, saying, in effect, that the majority's interpretation of the First Amendment right to record "is likely to impair the ability of police both to extract information relevant to police duties and to communicate effectively with persons whom they speak with in the line of duty."

The Hazards of Intrusion: Other Problems

With only a few exceptions, the trend today is for the courts to take a narrow view of aggressive newsgathering methods that allegedly intrude upon one's physical solitude. After the death of Princess Diana in 1997, journalists began to face laws restricting their right to pursue newsworthy persons or use high-tech hardware to observe people in private places.

A pioneering anti-paparazzi law was enacted in 1998 in California. Under this law, it is a *constructive invasion of privacy* for journalists even to *attempt* to capture images or sounds of "personal or familial activities" on private property where there is a reasonable expectation of privacy if "enhancing devices" such as a boom microphone or telephoto lens are used to capture images or sounds that could not be obtained without these devices. And if journalists trespass to obtain such images or sounds, that is also an invasion of privacy—regardless of whether they use enhancing devices. In either case, victims may sue for *treble damages* (three times the actual damages). The law was expanded in 2005 to allow treble damages and the seizure of profits in lawsuits by celebrities who are assaulted by paparazzi. That provision was signed into law by Gov. Arnold Schwarzenegger—who with his wife, Maria Shriver, was once blocked in a car by paparazzi at their son's pre-school. Two photographers were convicted of false imprisonment in that incident. While the mainstream media try to distance themselves from paparazzi tactics, it doesn't foster journalistic freedom when a celebrity who ends up being the governor has firsthand experience with paparazzi who chase and trap him in a car.

Even in states without this kind of law, aggressive journalists may risk not only civil lawsuits but also criminal sanctions. At various times journalists have been charged with trespassing, assault and reckless driving, among other things.

Some journalists have also been accused of misrepresenting their identity to gain information from news sources. Sometimes they do just that (in violation of most media codes of ethics). But often a source has second thoughts about granting an interview and then claims to have been misled, misquoted or both. To the alarm of the news media, the California Supreme Court in 2007 allowed an intrusion lawsuit to go to trial where a news source accused a psychology professor and author of misrepresenting her identity, a charge she denied (*Taus v. Loftus*, 40 C.4th 683).

Many tabloid television cases have been litigated, but few are as notable—and troubling—as *Clift v. Narragansett Television* (688 A.2d 805), in which a news person spoke by phone with a man barricaded in his home, threatening to commit suicide. The man apparently watched the television news, which included a taped excerpt from the phone call, at 6:04 p.m. and then killed himself at 6:07—with his television still on and tuned to the station that aired the newscast. His widow sued the station on various grounds, and in late 1996 the Rhode Island Supreme Court denied the station's motion to have the case dismissed.

■ DISCLOSURE OF PRIVATE FACTS

The second widely recognized kind of invasion of privacy is the *public disclosure of private facts*. In many states, to win a private facts case, a plaintiff has to prove that there was a public disclosure of a private fact that is not newsworthy and in a manner that is offensive or objectionable to a reasonable person. A few states including Oregon allow private facts lawsuits only if the revelation is truly outrageous (*outrage* as a legal concept is discussed later in this chapter). And several states, including New York and North Carolina, do not recognize this form of invasion of privacy. In 1997, a plurality of the Indiana Supreme Court rejected private facts as a legal action in that state (*Doe v. Methodist Hospital*, 690 N.E.2d 681). On the other hand, in 1998 the Minnesota Supreme Court broke new legal ground by recognizing not only the private facts concept but also intrusion and misappropriation as actionable forms of invasion of privacy in that state (*Lake v. Wal-Mart Stores*, 582 N.W.2d 231).

A legal action for the revelation of private facts provides a remedy for a person who has been embarrassed by a publication but may have little chance to win a libel suit because the facts revealed are accurate. In many states this type of invasion of privacy causes problems for journalists, often because it is hard to anticipate which stories may lead to lawsuits. What may seem clearly newsworthy to journalists may seem to be a flagrant instance of revealing private facts to someone else. Perhaps a summary of some of the situations that have led to lawsuits will help illustrate the problem.

In some states, publishing or broadcasting information about a person's shady past has produced litigation, especially if the person later changed his/her way of life. For nearly 75 years California courts led the nation in this area, allowing those whose unsavory past was revealed to sue even if the information was true and in the public record. However, in 2004 the California Supreme Court joined courts in many other states (and the U.S. Supreme Court) in holding that accurate reports of public records are constitutionally protected, even many years later. The earliest—and perhaps still the best known—of these old-but-true-facts cases is a 1931 California Appellate Court ruling, *Melvin v. Reid* (112 C.A. 285). The case resulted from a motion picture that revealed the past activities of a former prostitute who had been charged with murder and acquitted. Her maiden name was used in the movie advertising. However, after the murder trial the woman had moved to another town, married and adopted a new lifestyle. She said her new friends were unaware of her past. The court ruled that she was entitled to sue for invasion of privacy. In so doing, the court created a *social utility* test to determine whether the newsworthiness defense should apply. In *Melvin* and some later California cases, courts held that if a communication had little social utility or social value, the newsworthiness defense might not apply.

Actually, the movie producer in the *Melvin* case may have committed two different kinds of invasion of privacy: revealing private facts and commercially exploiting the woman's name without permission. The latter type of invasion of privacy is discussed later.

In several cases after *Melvin*, California courts reiterated the principle that a person's privacy may sometimes be invaded by the republication of old news if the republication has little social utility. For example, in the 1971 case of *Briscoe v. Reader's Digest* (4 C.3d 529), the California Supreme Court allowed a lawsuit to proceed where the *Reader's Digest* had published the name of a man convicted of truck hijacking 11 years earlier. The man had been rehabilitated and started a family in another place. His new family and friends first learned of his past from the magazine article. Although the man ultimately lost his case, the state Supreme Court said there was a legal basis for a lawsuit under such circumstances.

California courts allowed several other old-but-true facts cases to go to trial; it was not until 2004—long after the U.S. Supreme Court had recognized a constitutional right to publish information lawfully obtained from public records, that California disavowed *Briscoe* and held that the media may publish truthful information obtained even from old public records. In the 2004 case, *Gates v. Discovery Communications* (34 C.4th 679), the California Supreme Court held that the news media and entertainment industry may now disseminate truthful information lawfully obtained from public records even when the information exposes a rehabilitated ex-convict to new hatred or ill will.

In this case, Steven Gates sued the Discovery Channel for airing a documentary about a San Diego murder in which Gates had been convicted as an accessory after the fact. The murder occurred 12 years before the television program was broadcast. By then Gates had served his time, moved to a new community, become a successful salesman and opened a business with his wife. Gates said that the program caused him to lose friends, quit his business and move, and contributed to his divorce.

The state Supreme Court rejected Gates' claims. "(C)ourts are not freed by the mere passage of time to impose sanctions on the publication of truthful information that is obtained from public official court records," Justice Kathryn Mickle Werdegar wrote for a unanimous court. She said that the media may do reenactments of historical events under this principle. "Any state interest in protecting, for rehabilitative purposes, the long-term anonymity of former convicts" does not justify abridging the First Amendment, she wrote.

The court said lawsuits based on the truthful publication of public records should be allowed unless there is a "need to further a state interest of the highest order." Gates' desire to keep his past confidential does not meet that test, the court held, ruling that the case should have been dismissed under California's anti-SLAPP law.

The U.S. Supreme Court made the Gates decision inevitable by upholding the constitutional right to publish truthful information lawfully obtained from most public records. In

Cox Broadcasting v. Cohn (420 U.S. 469), a 1975 case, and in several later cases, the high court rejected lawsuits against the media for publishing such information.

The *Cox* Supreme Court decision resulted from a news broadcast that identified a rape victim in Georgia. A Georgia law prohibited publishing or broadcasting the identity of rape victims, but a reporter was given a copy of the court records during criminal proceedings against several young men accused of the rape. The victim, Cynthia Cohn, was identified in these public records, and Cox Broadcasting used the name in its coverage of the trial. The victim's father, Martin Cohn, sued Cox Broadcasting, contending that the broadcasts identifying his daughter invaded his privacy.

The Georgia Supreme Court upheld the law against publishing rape victims' names and also ruled that the father could sue under common law invasion of privacy principles. However, the U.S. Supreme Court reversed that decision. Writing for an 8-1 majority, Justice Byron White ruled that a state may not impose sanctions against the media for accurately reporting the contents of open court records such as those involved in this case. Quoting an earlier opinion by Justice William O. Douglas, Justice White said: "A trial is a public event. What transpires in the courtroom is public property."

At the time, this decision was viewed as a victory for the media. As noted in Chapter Three, the Supreme Court has also applied this principle in some other circumstances. A later Supreme Court decision suggested that the *Cox* rule was *not* limited to court records: "Our holding there (in *Cox*) was that a civil action against a television station for breach of privacy could not be maintained consistently with the First Amendment when the station had broadcast only information which was already in the public domain" (*Landmark Communications v. Virginia*, 435 U.S. at 840, 1978).

However, in a 1989 decision, *Florida Star v. B.J.F.* (491 U.S. 524), the Supreme Court avoided more broadly interpreting the *Cox* rule, as Chapter Three explains. While the 1989 case also overturned an invasion of privacy judgment against a news organization for publishing a rape victim's name, this decision is more limited in scope. In fact, this time the court said that the media are not necessarily exempt from all lawsuits even when they accurately report information that they lawfully obtain. If the information is obtained lawfully from court records, it is safe to publish. But the Court stopped short of saying that the same thing is always true when the information is obtained elsewhere. On the other hand, state laws banning the publication or broadcast of sex crime victims' names have also faced constitutional challenges in state courts. As noted in Chapter Three, the Florida Supreme Court overturned such a law in 1994 in *Florida v. Globe Communications Corp.* (648 So.2d 110).

If the *Cox* and *Florida Star* cases give the media the right to publish information they lawfully obtain from court records, does that mean state laws against publishing the names of juvenile offenders are invalid? The U.S. Supreme Court has also addressed that issue.

Naming Juveniles and Other Ethical Issues

Obviously, there are ethical as well as legal issues involved in publishing the names of sex crime victims and juvenile offenders. But in both areas, many of the legal issues have now been resolved in favor of the media. The Supreme Court in 1979 ruled that no state may impose *criminal sanctions* where the media have disseminated the names of juvenile offenders, even if that information was secured from sources other than public records. The high court didn't rule out *civil* invasion of privacy lawsuits where such information is secured from unofficial sources, but at least criminal prosecution of journalists was forbidden.

The 1979 case (*Smith v. Daily Mail,* 443 U.S. 97) was a test of a West Virginia law making it a crime for a newspaper to publish the name of any young person involved in juvenile court proceedings. The case arose when two newspapers were indicted after they identified a 14-year-old boy charged with fatally shooting a schoolmate. The shooting occurred at a junior high school, and journalists learned the name from eyewitnesses. They also heard the name by monitoring a police band radio.

After the indictments, the West Virginia Supreme Court overturned both the indictments and the state law, and the U.S. Supreme Court agreed. Chief Justice Warren Burger wrote: "At issue is simply the power of a state to punish the truthful publication of an alleged juvenile delinquent's name lawfully obtained by a newspaper."

In voiding the law, the Court said that the magnitude of the state's interest in protecting the anonymity of juvenile crime suspects is not sufficient to justify imposition of criminal penalties on the newspapers. However, Burger warned that the Court might uphold a similar law if there were an issue of "unlawful press access to a confidential judicial proceeding" or an issue of "privacy or prejudicial pretrial publicity," or if the publication were false.

Still, this represented another instance when the Supreme Court felt it necessary to intervene to protect the right of the media to disseminate lawfully obtained information. The *Daily Mail* case did not create a new privacy defense, but it did make it clear that criminal prosecution of the media is not an appropriate way to prevent the dissemination of juvenile names (and presumably other kinds of information that could be embarrassing).

Another important point to remember about *Smith v. Daily Mail* is that it did not prohibit invasion of privacy lawsuits for publication of personal information that is not part of a public record; the Supreme Court only banned criminal sanctions. Moreover, the Supreme Court has not created any special right of access to the names of rape victims and juvenile offenders. It is still constitutionally permissible for a state to keep that kind of information secret—and many states do so. But if the media do obtain the information lawfully, it may be published without fear of criminal prosecution. And, as just explained, the *Cox* case and several later Supreme Court decisions generally protect the media from civil suits for invasion of privacy when they lawfully obtain the names of sex crime victims from public records. But there are several unresolved problems in this area—particularly where the media obtain the information from confidential sources instead of public records.

FIG. 28. The Wedge In Newport Beach, Calif., where Mike Virgil surfed.

YoTuT, "The Wedge, Newport Beach," July 25, 2009 via Flickr, Creative Commons attribution license.

Still another case that raised powerful ethical questions as well as legal ones is *M.G. v. Time Warner* (89 C.A.4th 623, 2001), in which a California appellate court allowed Little League parents to sue because *Sports Illustrated* published a photo of their children alongside their coach, who turned out to be a child molester. Although none of the children was named, they were identifiable. The appellate court refused to dismiss the lawsuit, ruling that the photo was not necessarily newsworthy and that publishing it could be an "intrusion" that "outweighs the values of journalistic impact and credibility." Time Warner attorneys assailed the decision, which cleared the way for a trial, as legally wrong, allowing a lawsuit for publication of "truthful, nonprivate information on a subject of legitimate importance."

There are still other limitations on the right of the media to publish truthful information that was lawfully obtained. For example, there was a troubling 1988 case about the naming of a woman who could identify a murderer: *Times Mirror Co. v. Superior Court of San Diego County* (198 C.A.3d 1420). In this case, a woman returned home just after her roommate had been raped and murdered. As she arrived, she saw the murderer leaving. The *Los Angeles Times* published her name and said she had discovered the body, but did not identify her as the person who also saw the fleeing suspect. Nonetheless, she sued, contending that publishing her name while the suspect was at large endangered her safety.

The *Times* argued that the use of the name was absolutely privileged because the name was in the official coroner's report, a public record. However, a California appellate court declined to order the case dismissed on a 2-1 vote. Although the dissenting judge said the ruling could have a chilling effect on First Amendment freedoms, the other two judges who heard the appeal concluded that the First Amendment does *not* necessarily apply here. They were clearly troubled by the facts of this case: a major newspaper published the name of someone who could identify a suspected murderer who was not in custody. When no higher court was willing to hear the *Times'* appeal, the newspaper settled the case by paying an undisclosed sum of money to the woman.

Given compelling facts such as these, courts are likely to continue creating exceptions to the principles upheld in Supreme Court decisions such as *Cox Broadcasting* and *Florida Star*. But as a general rule, the media may disseminate truthful information lawfully obtained from public records.

Private Facts: Other Contexts

In addition to the kinds of cases discussed so far, there are other situations that produce private facts lawsuits. Often the facts are contemporaneous and correct but simply embarrassing for some reason. In these cases, the crucial issue is usually whether the facts fall within the newsworthiness defense.

There have been many such cases litigated over the years, most of them ultimately won by the media. However, the litigation is often protracted and costly, and the threat of such a lawsuit is often a deterrent to publishing stories containing embarrassing personal information. A good example of is *Virgil v. Time Inc.* (527 F.2d 1122, 9th cir., 1975). This case involved Mike Virgil, a surfing enthusiast who was profiled in an article in *Sports Illustrated.* The writer of the article had interviewed Virgil at great length and had also received Virgil's permission to photograph him. Before the article was published, Virgil revoked all consent for publication of the article and photographs because he feared the article would focus on bizarre incidents in his life that were not directly related to surfing.

The fact that Virgil revoked his consent for the publication did not mean the article could not be published. The news media routinely publish and broadcast stories about people who don't want publicity. When an item is published or broadcast without the subject's consent, it merely means the publisher or broadcaster must be certain it is newsworthy enough to preclude a successful lawsuit for invasion of privacy.

The article about Virgil was published over his objections, and it contained this quotation:

> Every summer I'd work construction and dive off billboards to hurt myself or drop loads of lumber on myself to collect unemployment compensation so I could surf at The Wedge.

The article also said he had extinguished a cigarette in his mouth and had eaten spiders and insects. Virgil sued for invasion of privacy, and his lawsuit reached the Ninth Circuit on a motion to dismiss the case before trial. The court said that unless a subject is newsworthy, the publicizing of private facts is not protected by the First Amendment. The court said: "In determining what is a matter of legitimate public interest, account must be taken of the customs and conventions of the community, and what is proper becomes a matter of the community mores."

The U.S. Supreme Court refused to review the circuit court's ruling that Virgil had a right to take his case to trial. The case went back to a federal district court, which ruled that *Sports Illustrated* published a "newsworthy" article that in fact generally portrayed Virgil in a positive way in the context of prevailing social mores (424 F.Supp. 1286, 1976).

Thus, the magazine eventually won the *Virgil* case, but only after a protracted and expensive legal battle. Moreover, the appellate court's ruling left much room for uncertainty about which stories are protected by the newsworthy defense and which ones are not. Newsworthiness is a broad but vague privacy defense.

But suppose an ordinary citizen happens to be in the right place at the right time to do something heroic, and as a result the whole world learns intimate details of his or her life. Has that person's privacy been invaded? A good example of this problem is the case of Oliver Sipple, who may have saved former President Gerald Ford's life during an assassination attempt in 1975. When Sara Jane Moore, the would-be assassin, took aim at the president, Sipple struck her arm and caused her shot to miss. He was hailed as a hero, but soon the media also revealed the fact that he was a homosexual, an active member of the San Francisco gay community. He sued for invasion of privacy, but the California Court of Appeal ruled that the stories about his sexual preferences were newsworthy, given all of the circumstances (*Sipple v. Chronicle Publishing Co.*, 10 Media L. Rep. 1690, 1984).

However, the court ordered that its decision in the *Sipple* case not be published in the official reports of California appellate court decisions. Under California law, unpublished decisions may not be cited as legal precedents. This is, nonetheless, an interesting case that raises difficult ethical and legal issues.

Another case that raises troubling ethical as well as legal issues is *Diaz v. Oakland Tribune* (139 C.A.3d 118, 1983). Toni Ann Diaz was originally a male, but she underwent surgery to change her sex. Then she enrolled at a community college and was eventually elected student body president. Apparently no one on campus was aware of the sex change operation until it was revealed in a column in the *Oakland Tribune*. She sued for invasion of privacy and won a jury verdict of $775,000. But an appellate court overturned the verdict and ordered a new trial, ruling that the trial judge erred in requiring the newspaper to prove the story newsworthy. Instead, the burden should have been on Diaz to prove that the story was *not* newsworthy, the appellate court held. As student body president, Diaz had often been in the news; she dropped the case rather than go through a second trial at which she would have to prove that the story was not newsworthy. Nonetheless, the newspaper's decision to reveal the fact of Diaz' sex change raises ethical questions.

Perhaps equally troubling—and a good illustration of the legal hazards of journalistic sensationalism—is an Orlando, Florida case in which a television station showed a video of a police officer holding the skull of a six-year-old girl who was kidnapped and murdered. The girl's family—and thousands of other viewers—were shocked by the video, shown on the evening news without any warning, even to the family. In *Armstrong v. H & C Communications* (575 So. 2d 280), a Florida appellate court ruled that showing the skull was not an actionable invasion of privacy because of the public interest in the girl's abduction and the discovery of her remains. On the other hand, the court ruled that the family could sue the station on the legal theory that showing the video was an outrageous act.

Like a number of other states, Florida recognizes *outrage* as a separate basis for a lawsuit— a legal wrong somewhat akin to the *intentional infliction of emotional distress* (see Chapter Four). In states that recognize outrage as a legal wrong, a person may be sued for engaging in a course of conduct that would make a reasonable person angry enough to say, "that is outrageous," even though the wrongful act may not fit into any other category that is recognized as a basis for a lawsuit. In the *Armstrong* case, there was evidence not only that the video angered many viewers but also that it was shown over the objections of some members of the station's staff, and that the station later expressed regrets when it became clear that many viewers were offended. Those facts could form the basis for a lawsuit against the station, the Florida court held. A California appellate court reached a similar conclusion in a case where a television reporter confronted several children and told them two neighborhood children were killed by their mother, who then killed herself. The reporter asked the children for their reaction to this news. The court said the reporter and the television station could be sued for the intentional infliction of emotional distress under these circumstances (*KOVR-TV v. Superior Court of Sacramento County*, 31 C.A.4th 1023, 1995).

Do surviving family members of the dead have privacy rights in outrageous cases? In *Catsouras v. State of California Highway Patrol* (181 Cal. App. 4th 856, 2010), a California appeals court said that they do, at least in some cases. Nikki Catsouras was killed in a terrible car accident in which she was decapitated. Photos of the accident taken by the California Highway Patrol were leaked; those images went viral online, and cruel pranks were played on Catsouras' family (for example, the family received e-mails with the images with such captions as "Hey Daddy, I'm still alive"). The trial court dismissed the Catsouras' claim, and the appeals court overturned. Saying that there was no press freedom at issue here, the appeals court said, "The dissemination of death images can only affect the living. As cases from other jurisdictions make plain, family members have a common law privacy right in the death images of a decedent, subject to certain limitations." Petitions for rehearings were unsuccessful. Does this finding elevate the privacy rights of the dead over rights of the living, as some critics have suggested?

These cases involving outrage or emotional distress are often reminiscent of the situations that may lead to lawsuits for the *intrusion* form of invasion of privacy. There is clearly an overlap among the various areas of privacy law and some of the similar legal actions that have evolved in recent years.

To summarize, the private facts area of privacy law is by no means clearly defined. Usually the media win private facts lawsuits by asserting the newsworthiness defense, but even then, a court may allow the lawsuit to go to trial on some other legal basis. Also, no one—not the courts, not legal scholars, and indeed not even journalists—can precisely define newsworthiness. Another unresolved issue is when the media may be sued for revealing allegedly private facts contained in public records, given *Cox's* strong affirmation of the constitutional protection for news reports of information lawfully obtained from public records.

The conflict between the individual's right to keep private facts private and the media's right to report the news raises a number of other ethical questions, too. For instance, should the media be able to make a person a celebrity by intensive coverage and then defend against a privacy lawsuit by citing that celebrity status? Does mere publicity make a person newsworthy, or must one already be newsworthy before publicity is permitted? Moreover, when the media make the judgment that someone is newsworthy and publicize his or her activities, should the First Amendment permit the courts to second-guess that judgment?

■ FALSE LIGHT AND FICTIONALIZATION

The third area of privacy law that has produced litigation for the media is referred to as *false light* invasion of privacy. It involves publicity that places the plaintiff in a false light before the public. This kind of privacy case might be described as a libel case but without the defamation.

As noted earlier, false light is recognized in most states, but it has been rejected as a valid basis for a lawsuit in about 10 states. For example, in 1984 the North Carolina Supreme Court rejected the false light concept in that state (*Renwick v. News and Observer*, 312 S.E.2d 405). A decade later, the Texas Supreme Court ruled similarly, rejecting the false light concept in Texas (*Cain v. Hearst Corp.*, 878 S.W.2d 577). The Texas Supreme Court said it was rejecting the false light concept because it "substantially duplicates the tort of defamation (i.e., libel and slander) while lacking many of its procedural limitations." By 2000, appellate courts in Massachusetts, Minnesota, Mississippi, Missouri, Ohio, Virginia, Washington and Wisconsin had joined the Texas and North Carolina courts in refusing to recognize false light invasion of privacy. In 2002, the Colorado Supreme Court also rejected false light as a basis for a lawsuit (*Denver Publishing Co. v. Bueno*, 54 P.3d 893). But in 2007, the Ohio Supreme Court, which had previously rejected false light, recognized it as a valid legal action as long as the person suing can prove actual malice (*Welling v. Weinfeld*, 866 N.E.2d 1051).

Where it is recognized, a person may sue when portrayed falsely in a manner that would be highly offensive to a reasonable person. Photographers (and those who write captions for photographs) have been especially vulnerable to this kind of lawsuit, but other journalists should also be aware of the pitfalls in this area. Two false light privacy cases stemming from inaccurate reporting reached the U.S. Supreme Court many years ago.

The first of these false light Supreme Court decisions came in 1967. The case, *Time Inc. v. Hill* (385 U.S. 374), involved the James J. Hill family, which gained notoriety when it was taken hostage in its own home by three escaped convicts in 1952. The incident was clearly newsworthy, especially because two convicts were eventually killed in a shoot-out with police.

One year after the event, novelist Joseph Hayes published *The Desperate Hours*, a story about a family taken hostage by escaped convicts. Later the novel was made into a play and a motion picture. The story line differed in significant ways from the Hill family's experiences, although there were similarities. For example, the escaped convicts were not brutal to the Hill family during the real hostage situation, but in the book the escapees did commit acts of violence toward the fictional hostage family.

An invasion of privacy suit was filed by the Hill family in 1955 after an article was published in *Life* magazine reviewing the play based on Hayes' book. *Life* directly stated that the play was based on the Hill family incident. The Hills sought damages on grounds that the magazine article "was intended to, and did, give the impression that the play mirrored the Hill family's experience, which, to the knowledge of defendant …was false and untrue."

The Hill family won a $30,000 judgment in the New York state courts, but Time Inc., appealed the case to the U.S. Supreme Court, which in 1967 reversed the New York judgment.

Justice William Brennan, writing for a divided court, applied the *New York Times v. Sullivan* libel rule to this kind of privacy lawsuit. Brennan said persons involved in a *matter of public interest* could not win a false light privacy suit unless they could show that the falsehood was published either knowingly or with reckless disregard for the truth. Although some have suggested that the Hills could have proven reckless disregard for the truth if they had opted to pursue the case through a second trial, they dropped the case instead.

In transplanting the *New York Times v. Sullivan* rule into privacy law, Justice Brennan emphasized that it was to be applied only in the "discrete context of the facts of the Hill case." Nevertheless, Brennan's opinion has often been applied by state courts and was cited in a later U.S. Supreme Court ruling on false light invasion of privacy.

That later ruling, *Cantrell v. Forest City Publishing Co.* (419 U.S. 245, 1974), presented the U.S. Supreme Court with the chance to abandon the *Time Inc. v. Hill* requirement in privacy cases the same year the court limited application of the *New York Times* rule to public figures in libel cases, but the court didn't address that issue. Instead the court upheld an invasion of privacy judgment against a newspaper by saying the paper was guilty of "calculated falsehoods" and "reckless untruth." The court did not say what the outcome of the case would have been if the newspaper had been guilty of nothing more than negligence.

The *Cantrell* case resulted from newspaper coverage of the consequences of the collapse of a bridge across the Ohio River. A man named Melvin Cantrell was among 44 victims, and Joseph Eszterhas, a *Cleveland Plain Dealer* reporter, followed up the tragedy with a feature story about how the man's death affected his widow and children. Several months after the accident, Eszterhas and photographer Richard Conway visited the Cantrell residence to gather information for the follow-up. Margaret Cantrell, the widow, was not home, so Eszterhas talked to the children and Conway took many pictures. The resulting feature appeared as the lead story in the *Plain Dealer's* Sunday magazine. It stressed the family's abject poverty and contained a number of inaccuracies including a description of Margaret Cantrell's mood and attitude, with statements clearly implying that Eszterhas had talked to her.

Mrs. Cantrell brought an action for invasion of privacy against the publisher of the newspaper. When the U.S. Supreme Court reviewed the case in 1974, it upheld a $60,000 judgment in her favor. The Court said the evidence showed that the newspaper "had published knowing or reckless falsehoods about the Cantrells." The Court also said much of what was published consisted of "calculated falsehoods and the jury was plainly justified in finding that…the Cantrells were placed in a false light through knowing or reckless untruth."

Interestingly enough, the Supreme Court ruled that the photographer who took the pictures should not be held liable since there was no misrepresentation inherent in his pictures. In comparison, there was an obvious misrepresentation in the feature story itself.

The *Hill* and *Cantrell* cases are notable because they reached the U.S. Supreme Court—but they are not necessarily representative of all false light privacy suits. As indicated earlier, another common source of false light privacy lawsuits is misleading photo captions. Two California Supreme Court decisions in the 1950s nicely illustrate the problem in this area.

Both lawsuits were initiated by John and Sheila Gill, a couple who operated a candy and ice cream store at Farmer's Market, a tourist attraction in Los Angeles. Noted photographer Henri Cartier-Bresson caught the couple sitting side by side at the counter in their shop. John had his arm around Sheila, and they were leaning forward with their cheeks touching. The photo, taken without permission on private property open to the public, was published in both *Harper's Bazaar*, a Hearst publication, and *Ladies Home Journal*, a Curtis publication.

The Hearst publication used the photo to illustrate an article entitled, "And So the World Goes Round." The couple was described as "immortalized in a moment of tenderness." However, the Curtis publication used the photo in a different context. There, it illustrated an article on the dangers of "love at first sight," with statements such as this one: "Publicized as glamorous, love at first sight is a bad risk." Further, the article went on to condemn this sort of thing as love based on "instantaneous powerful sex attraction—the wrong kind of love."

The Gills sued both publishers, but the two lawsuits produced opposite results. In *Gill v. Hearst Corporation* (40 C.2d 224, 1953), the couple lost. The California Supreme Court found no misrepresentation of their status, and thus no basis for an invasion of privacy lawsuit. But in *Gill v. Curtis Publishing* (38 C.2d 273, 1952), the couple won: the court found that the Gills had been held up before the public in a false light, since there was no basis for saying their relationship was "love at first sight" or based merely on "instantaneous ...sex attraction."

The two *Gill* cases are typical of many others that have been filed since. If there is a general rule in these situations, it is that a photograph is reasonably safe if the caption is not misleading, provided it was taken in a public place and is used in a manner that falls within the newsworthiness defense. However, if the caption creates a false impression about the subjects, or if it is used for a commercial purpose such as advertising (as opposed to a journalistic purpose), the risk of a lawsuit for invasion of privacy is often much greater.

Perhaps one of the most memorable examples of a false light claim is Linda Duncan. Her face was shown in a Washington, D.C. television report on the spread of herpes with a voiceover saying, "for the 20 million Americans who have herpes, it's not a cure." She claimed that a reasonable person would believe she had herpes, and the court said she had a valid false light claim (*Duncan v. WJLA-TV*, 106 F.R.D. 4, DDC 1984).

■ MISAPPROPRIATION

The fourth type of invasion of privacy protects people from unauthorized commercial use of their names, photographs and other aspects of their "public personas." This concept has been given several names, including *misappropriation* or *commercial appropriation*. Today it is often referred to as a violation of the *right of publicity*. Perhaps it has more than one name because it is a very broad legal concept; no one term really describes all of the kinds of legal issues involved in this field. Whatever its name, this concept is quite different from the other three kinds of privacy law: it involves the economic rights of people whose names are well known, not the personal rights of private individuals who just want to be left alone.

Although right of publicity lawsuits are occasionally filed by private persons whose names or photographs were used for someone else's commercial gain, more often the plaintiffs in these lawsuits are celebrities, people whose names have great commercial value. Usually the problem isn't that the celebrity objects to publicity per se; what he or she objects to is not being adequately *paid*—or perhaps having his/her name or image used commercially in an objectionable way. An endorsement or an appearance by a celebrity may be worth thousands (or even millions) of dollars, and the celebrity's lawyers want to make sure their client collects. There are times, of course, when a celebrity doesn't want to endorse a particular product at all, regardless of what fee may be offered. And some celebrities simply refuse to do *any* endorsements.

The media have the right to do *news stories* and publish newsworthy photographs of celebrities as often as they wish—with or without permission. No celebrity has the right to keep his or her name or picture out of the news media. The newsworthiness or public affairs defense protects the right of the media to cover news about celebrities. What the right of publicity prevents is the unauthorized *commercial exploitation* of the celebrity's name or likeness (in advertising or product endorsements, for example).

The right of publicity is the oldest privacy right to be recognized by the law. The 1902 *Roberson* case, discussed in the section on the history of privacy, would be called a right of publicity case if it were decided today. The New York statutory privacy law that was enacted in response to the *Roberson* decision is fundamentally a right of publicity law—it protects a person's name and likeness from unauthorized commercial exploitation.

In the years since that pioneering New York case, most states have recognized the right of publicity in some form, either by statute or court decision. The concept was given its contemporary name in a 1953 Second Circuit decision, *Haelan Laboratories v. Topps Chewing Gum* (202 F.2d 866, 1953). The case involved the right of baseball players to control the commercial use of their names and photos on baseball trading cards, and the court said:

> We think that in addition to an independent right of privacy ...a man has a right
> in the publicity value of his photograph, i.e., the right to grant the exclusive privi-
> lege of publishing his picture.... This right might be called a "right of publicity."

A variety of state laws and court decisions have reiterated the point made in the *Haelan* case: no one may *commercially exploit* a person's name, public persona, or likeness without consent. Various courts have said the right protects sports figures, entertainment celebrities, and even people who would be classified as public figures only because of their involvement in controversial public issues.

Nor does the right of publicity just protect a person's name and likeness. A number of courts have ruled that the right extends to the commercial exploitation of other aspects of a celebrity's public persona. A memorable illustration of this point is the 1983 federal appellate court decision in a case called *Carson v. Here's Johnny Portable Toilets Inc.*, 698 F.2d 831).

The case arose after Here's Johnny Portable Toilets Inc. began marketing its products in 1976. Entertainer Johnny Carson, longtime host of NBC's *Tonight Show*, was introduced to viewers with the phrase "Here's Johnny" from the time he became the host in 1962 until he retired 30 years later. Carson was obviously not amused when the toilet company not only called its product "Here's Johnny" but also added the phrase, "the world's foremost commodian." Carson sued, alleging a violation of his right of publicity, among other things.

Overruling a trial judge who had dismissed Carson's lawsuit, the appellate court held that the use of "Here's Johnny" as a brand name did violate Carson's right of publicity. The court emphasized that a person's full name need not be used for his right of publicity to be violated, especially in a case involving a celebrity as well known as Johnny Carson. Clearly, the phrase "here's Johnny" was associated with Carson in the minds of millions of television viewers. In fact, at one point in the case the company had conceded that it was trying to capitalize on Carson's reputation.

In deciding the *Here's Johnny* case in this way, the appellate court cited another case it had ruled on about 10 years earlier: *Motschenbacher v. R. J. Reynolds Tobacco* (498 F.2d 821). In that case, the court held that a race car driver's right of publicity was violated by an advertisement in which R. J. Reynolds used a photo of his car, even though the driver's face was not visible. The car's markings were so distinctive that the car fell within the driver's public persona, the court ruled.

Thus, the right of publicity protects celebrities and others from the commercial use of far more than just their names and likenesses. Catch phrases and even tangible objects that are closely associated with a celebrity in the public mind may be off limits to advertisers (unless permission is negotiated and paid for).

However, there are limits to this rule. Another federal appellate court decision permitted a tire company ad to use actresses dressed in miniskirts and boots, a style that singer Nancy Sinatra had popularized, even though the advertisements also featured a revised version of "These Boots are Made for Walkin'," one of her popular songs. In *Sinatra v. Goodyear* (435 F.2d 711), the court said it was clear that Nancy Sinatra was neither singing the song nor appearing on camera in the ad, which promoted Goodyear's "Wide Boots" tires. The court said Sinatra's right of publicity had therefore not been violated. (Note that the use of the song itself was not an issue. The advertiser had made arrangements with the copyright owner for use of the song.)

A similar question arose in a 1988 right of publicity case much like the *Sinatra v. Goodyear* case—but with a different result. In *Midler v. Ford Motor Company* (849 F.2d 460), singer-actress Bette Midler sued Ford and Young & Rubicam, Ford's ad agency, for using a Midler sound-alike vocalist in advertising for the Mercury Sable. The ad agency asked Ula Hedwig, who was Midler's backup singer for a decade, to sing a Midler hit song, "Do You Wanna Dance," and to "sound as much as possible like the Bette Midler record." Before employing Hedwig to do the singing, the ad agency had asked Midler's agent to have Midler sing in the commercial—and was turned down.

Although the ad agency had obtained permission to use the copyrighted song, Midler contended that the recording sounded so much like her performance that many listeners would believe it was her. Citing *Motschenbacher* as a precedent, a federal appellate court said there were adequate grounds for Midler to pursue her lawsuit. Like the cigarette ad showing the race car driver's auto, this ad campaign might lead many people to conclude that Midler was endorsing the product, the court said. The case was sent back to a trial court to assess damages; in 1989, a jury awarded Midler $400,000. In 1992, the Supreme Court denied *cert.*

Why was this case decided differently than the *Sinatra* case? Perhaps the most significant reason was that there was more likelihood of the public being deceived into believing there was an endorsement by Midler. In reality, *Midler* was based on the idea that the impersonation itself was wrong; there was no actual misappropriation of Midler's name, likeness or voice. However, there was no impersonation in the *Sinatra* case: it was obvious in the Good-year ad that Nancy Sinatra was neither on camera nor doing the singing—although the Goodyear ad used a song closely identified with Sinatra, just as the Ford ad did with Midler.

The *Sinatra v. Goodyear* and *Midler v. Ford* cases raise the question of how far an advertiser can go in using celebrity impersonations. Traditionally, the rule has been that celebrity imitations do not violate a celebrity's right of publicity as long as the public is not deceived into thinking the celebrity is actually appearing in the ad or endorsing the product.

Advertisers have often relied on the phrase, "celebrity voice impersonated," for protection when they did sound-alike ads. However, the *Midler* decision led many advertising agency lawyers to believe that a disclaimer may not be enough. They are becoming especially wary of celebrity impersonations—with or without a disclaimer—in the aftermath of an even bigger damage award to a celebrity in an impersonation case: more than $2 million. In *Waits v. Frito-Lay* (978 F.2d 1093, 1992), the Ninth Circuit upheld almost all of a $2.5 million jury verdict against the manufacturer of Doritos brand corn chips for doing commercials featuring a song made popular by singer Tom Waits, using a close imitation of his vocal style. The Supreme Court declined to review that decision.

At about the same time as the *Waits* case, the same appellate court also ruled that game show hostess Vanna White had the right to sue Samsung Electronics and its advertising agency, David Deutsch, for ads featuring a blond robot wearing a gown and jewelry reminiscent of White's on-air style, and standing in front of a large game board. Although Judge Arthur Alarcon dissented, arguing that there was little likelihood of the public mistaking a mechanical robot for Vanna White, the 2-1 majority ruled that this could be a wrongful commercial exploitation of White's public persona—and allowed her to take her case to trial (*White v. Samsung*, 971 F.2d 1395, 1992).

Samsung asked the Ninth Circuit to rehear the case *en banc*. That request was denied, but it gave one of the nation's most quotable appellate judges, Alex Kozinski, a chance to issue a colorful opinion objecting to the court's decision not to rehear the case. Kozinski blasted the court for its expansion of the right of publicity. Among other things, he said:

> Something very dangerous is going on here....The panel's opinion is a classic case of overprotection. Concerned about what it sees as a wrong done to Vanna White, the panel majority erects a property right of remarkable and dangerous breadth: Under the majority's opinion, it's now a tort for advertisers to *remind* the public of a celebrity. Not to use a celebrity's name, voice, signature or likeness; not to imply the celebrity endorses a product; but simply to evoke the celebrity's image in the public's mind. This Orwellian notion withdraws far more from the public domain than prudence and common sense allow. It conflicts with the Copyright Act and the Copyright Clause. It raises serious First Amendment problems. It's bad law, and it deserves a long, hard second look.

Perhaps encouraged by Kozinski's passionate arguments, Samsung then appealed to the Supreme Court, but as in the *Midler* and *Waits* cases, the court refused to hear an appeal of this case. White then took her case to trial, and in 1994 a jury awarded her $403,000 in damages, which Samsung and its ad agency agreed to pay instead of appealing the case again. In return, White agreed not to appeal for a chance to seek an even larger judgment.

Another similar dispute led to *Wendt v. Host International* (125 F.3d 806, 1997). George

Wendt and John Ratzenberger, the actors who played Norm and Cliff in the "Cheers" television series, sued Host for placing animatronic robotic figures resembling them in airport bars modeled after the set of "Cheers." They contended that the robots resembled them sufficiently to be a possible misappropriation, and a federal appellate court agreed, ruling that they had a right to take their case to trial. In a series of rulings, various courts held again and again that Host could be sued for invading the two actors' right of publicity even though Host had purchased the right to depict the "Cheers" bar scene from Paramount Studios, the copyright owner. Eventually the U.S. Supreme Court refused to review this case, clearing the way for a trial. In 2001, Paramount and the actors settled under undisclosed terms.

In essence, the courts were saying in *Wendt* that a copyright and the right of publicity are separate legal rights: a copyright clearance does not give someone the right to depict the actors who appeared in the copyrighted show. To depict actual people without consent and for commercial gain is a violation of the right of publicity.

Although the *Midler, Waits, Wendt* and *White* cases were all federal cases, they were based primarily on California state law—either the statutory right of publicity in the California Civil Code or state common law principles.

However, the recent trend toward courts refusing to allow celebrity impersonations in advertising began in New York. In 1984 a New York judge ruled that the use of a celebrity look-alike in an ad violated Jackie Onassis' right of publicity, and he ordered an ad agency to stop using an Onassis look-alike to promote Christian Dior clothes. The judge issued this order without finding that anyone was actually deceived into thinking Onassis was appearing in the ad or endorsing the product.

These cases were all based on state law because the right of publicity is an area of state, not federal, law. There have been proposals for a federal right of publicity law, including one from the American Bar Association, but Congress has not acted on any of these proposals.

Misappropriation and the News

If celebrities have a right to prevent the unauthorized commercial use of their names and likenesses—and sometimes even the right to prevent advertisers from *reminding* the public of them (as Judge Kozinski put it)—where does that leave a journalist who wants to write news stories about the famous?

That is an important issue, and the answer is relatively clear: the right of publicity does not apply to news situations, even though the media are commercial enterprises. The print and broadcast media are free to use a person's name and likeness whenever the situation creates newsworthiness—and the courts have tended to be very liberal in defining newsworthiness for these purposes. Even if a news medium engages in advertising to promote itself and reproduces a photograph of someone famous that appeared in print or on the air, that advertisement does not usually fall within the right of publicity.

However, if a newspaper, magazine, or radio or TV station uses the name or photograph of a celebrity in a way that implies an endorsement, it is a different matter. Cher, the singer and actress, was involved in a case that illustrated this point in 1982.

In *Cher v. Forum International* (692 F.2d 634), Cher had granted an interview to a freelance writer who hoped to write an article for *Us* magazine. The article was rejected by *Us*, and the writer then sold it to the publishers of two other magazines, *Star* and *Forum*. Both published it. *Star* carried the article with a headline that offended Cher. The headline read, "Exclusive Series ...Cher: My life, my husbands, and my many, many men."

Cher disliked the idea that the interview ended up in *Star* instead of *Us*, and she disliked the headline even more. But what apparently offended Cher the most was that *Forum* not only ran the article but also used her name and likeness in advertising that implied she endorsed and read the magazine. One ad in the *New York Daily News* included Cher's photograph and the words, "There are certain things that Cher won't tell *People* and would never tell *Us*. She tells *Forum*.... So join Cher and *Forum's* hundreds of thousands of other adventurous readers today." What *Forum* did was to promote the article in a way that clearly implied an endorsement by Cher. Although *Forum's* publication of the article itself did not violate Cher's right of publicity, the advertising for it did, the court ruled in finding for Cher.

This case illustrates the principle that the media may freely publish stories about newsworthy people—but not advertisements that imply an endorsement—without violating their right of publicity. On the other hand, if the ad had promoted the story by saying something like "Read an interesting article about Cher in *Forum*," it would probably have been safe.

Former football star Joe Montana discovered a similar legal principle when he tried to prevent a newspaper from publishing promotional posters and a souvenir edition based on earlier news coverage of his football heroics. In *Montana v. Mercury News* (34 C.A. 4th 790, 1995), a California appellate court upheld the right of the *San Jose Mercury News* to publish materials celebrating the San Francisco 49ers four Super Bowl victories during the 1980s. Even though individual pages of the souvenir edition were sold—and the cover included an artist's drawing of Montana—the court held that the paper had the right to publish these items about newsworthy events such as Montana's triumphs in the Super Bowl.

The *Montana* and *Cher v. Forum* decisions were both based in part on the *Booth Rule*, an old principle of privacy law that says the media may use previously published newsworthy materials in later advertising of the publication itself as long as no endorsement is implied. This concept originated with *Booth v. Curtis Publishing* (182 N.E.2d 812), a 1962 New York Court of Appeals decision that allowed *Holiday* magazine to use a previously published photo of actress Shirley Booth in later advertising for the magazine.

A different legal issue was raised when the Coors brewery did advertising that included a drawing based on a news photograph of baseball star Don Newcombe pitching for the Brooklyn Dodgers in the 1949 World Series. A federal appellate court said Newcombe had the right to sue Coors and its ad agency for misappropriation (*Newcombe v. Adolf Coors*, 157 F.3d 686, 1998). A newspaper that published the photo in 1949 could republish it to advertise itself later, but others cannot. Newcombe particularly objected to the use of his image in beer advertising because of his own acknowledged problems with alcoholism.

Another case that raised questions about the boundary between public affairs or news and commercial exploitation of a celebrity's public persona arose soon after Arnold Schwarzenegger was elected California governor in 2003. An Ohio company that had made "bobblehead" dolls depicting various public officials, including George W. Bush, Bill Clinton, Hillary Rodham Clinton and John Kerry, started selling a doll featuring Schwarzenegger with a gun—an obvious reference to his most famous role in the *Terminator* movies. He sued, alleging a violation of his right of publicity. The product used his name and a photo from his days as an actor without consent. But the company's defenders pointed out that when an actor becomes a public official, the rules change. An actor can prevent someone from using his or her name or image on a product without consent; a politician probably cannot. In the end, the lawsuit was settled with an agreement under which the company could sell bobblehead dolls depicting the California governor, but without the gun.

May a magazine digitally alter a photo? Actor Dustin Hoffman won a $3 million jury verdict against *Los Angeles Magazine* in 1999 after the magazine used a digitally altered photo of Hoffman's head superimposed on a model in a designer dress. The jury concluded that the magazine's use of Hoffman's image was commercial misappropriation, not news coverage, even though it was one of a series of digitally altered photos depicting celebrities in modern, fashionable attire. In 2001 the Ninth Circuit reversed the jury verdict, holding that the magazine had a First Amendment right to publish the altered photograph of Hoffman as news, particularly because he made *Tootsie*, a movie in which his character cross-dresses (*Hoffman v. Capital Cities/ABC*, 255 F.3d 1180).

Although this is unusual, a celebrity won a lawsuit stemming from news coverage in a 1997 case, *Eastwood v. National Enquirer* (123 F.3d 1249): the Ninth Circuit *upheld* a large damage award won by actor Clint Eastwood against the *National Enquirer* for merely publishing an article about him when he had not submitted to an interview with that publication. On its face, this seemed very similar to the case Cher lost against the *Star*. The *National Enquirer* billed the story as "exclusive" when in fact it had appeared earlier in a British tabloid, but the *Enquirer* pointed out that it had purchased exclusive U.S. rights to the story from the British author. Eastwood objected to the implication that he would grant an exclusive interview to the *Enquirer* (just as Cher did when she sued the *Star*), but Eastwood won $150,000 in damages, plus at least $650,000 in attorney's fees. Eastwood claimed that the purported interview never occurred at all, and that his quotes were fabricated by a British journalist (and then reprinted in the *Enquirer*). Eastwood apparently prevailed because the court thought calling the story "exclusive" was a misappropriation of his name (an argument that the court did not accept in Cher's case). The only real difference between the Cher and Eastwood cases may be the fact that Cher admitted being interviewed by the writer of the article, while Eastwood denied even sitting for an interview. But both publications claimed they had an "exclusive" story when the celebrity never agreed to be interviewed by that publication.

Perhaps the best conclusion here is that anyone can write and publish an article about Cher or Clint Eastwood (or reprint someone else's article with permission of the copyright owner), but saying it's "exclusive" is dangerous—sometimes. And don't even consider using the celebrity's name in an advertisement that implies an endorsement of the publication—that goes beyond what the Booth Rule allows. Virtually every other form of commercial advertising (as opposed to news coverage) falls within the restrictions of the right of publicity. In most advertising, you cannot include photographs of recognizable people, be they famous or unknown,

right of publicity:
a form of the misappropriation tort that permits individuals to control the commercial aspects of their names and likenesses; protected differently state by state.

Booth rule:
the media may use previously published newsworthy materials in later advertising of the publication itself as long as no endorsement is implied.

unless you get their consent. This rule applies equally to advertising in the print and electronic media: you can be sued if you use a street scene in a television ad without getting the consent of everyone recognizable on the street.

The *right of publicity* also applies to the entertainment media. When someone produces a motion picture, all of the people appearing on the screen who are recognizable must give their consent—which is why producers commonly use "extras" who are on the payroll instead of just photographing anyone who happens to be walking past for use in scenes showing public places. These rules do not apply, of course, to most news and public affairs productions. Nor do they ordinarily prevent accurate portrayals of newsworthy persons in docudramas based on news events. But in movies produced for entertainment purposes, the unauthorized use of a person's likeness invites a lawsuit.

Nonetheless, major television networks routinely broadcast docudramas without obtaining the consent of every single person depicted. Where the story is based on facts that have already been reported by the news media, there is little risk of a successful right of publicity lawsuit by anyone who was involved in the story. This is especially true where the facts are in the public record (in court documents, for example).

A noteworthy 1994 federal court decision reaffirmed the right of authors and motion picture producers to tell a person's life story without violating that person's right of publicity. In *Matthews v. Wozencraft* (15 F.3d 432), the Fifth Circuit upheld the right of author Kim Wozencraft to use a character based on her ex-husband and fellow police officer Creig Matthews in her book, *Rush*. Their story received extensive media publicity: they served as undercover narcotics officers in Texas, became romantically involved, used marijuana and cocaine themselves (but later denied it under oath), and falsified evidence to win a drug conviction. They eventually served time in federal prison and were divorced.

Wozencraft later earned a master's degree at Columbia University and published *Rush*, which was based on their life stories. She eventually sold the movie rights to the book for $1 million and Matthews sued, alleging that she violated his right of publicity by using his life story without permission. The court held that a person's life story does not fall within Texas' right of publicity and affirmed a lower court decision to dismiss Matthews' lawsuit. In so ruling, the court noted that their story had already received extensive news coverage. The court also held that Wozencraft had a First Amendment right to publish a book about these events without Matthews' consent.

But, the Eleventh Circuit said, there must actually *be* a news story to qualify for protection. That court found that there was a right to privacy in old nude images of a dead woman. Professional wrestler Chris Benoit killed his wife, Nancy, and their son, and then killed himself in 2007. *Hustler* magazine published stills from a nude video that Nancy had made 20 years earlier, accompanying an article on the deaths. Nancy's mother, Maureen Toffoloni, brought a claim based on her daughter's right of publicity. The trial court dismissed the claim, saying that the images were newsworthy. The Eleventh Circuit disagreed (*Toffoloni v. LFP Publishing Group*, 572 F.3d 1201, 2009). Asking "whether a brief biographical piece can ratchet otherwise protected, personal photographs into the newsworthiness exception," the court answered no, saying the article was "incidental" to the photos. Moreover, the court added, "The Georgia courts have never held, nor do we believe that they would hold, that if one is the victim of an infamous murder, one's entire life is rendered the legitimate subject of public scrutiny." In 2011, a federal judge reduced *Hustler's* penalty to $375,000, down from nearly $20 million awarded by a jury.

On the other hand, even a news presentation may lead to a lawsuit for invasion of the right of publicity under some circumstances. An excellent example is a case that produced a U.S. Supreme Court decision—the only one to date dealing with the right of publicity.

The case was *Zacchini v. Scripps-Howard Broadcasting* (433 U.S. 562, 1977), and it involved Hugo Zacchini, who called himself "the human cannonball" and had an "act" in which he was shot from a cannon into a net at fairs and other exhibitions. His entire "act" was filmed and broadcast as news by Scripps-Howard Broadcasting despite his objections to the filming. He sued for invasion of his right of publicity under Ohio law, but the state Supreme Court said the First Amendment precluded any recovery by Zacchini because the newscast covered a matter of "legitimate public interest."

However, in 1977 the U.S. Supreme Court modified the Ohio ruling by declaring that the First Amendment did *not* protect a broadcaster who took a performer's entire act and showed it without consent as news. The Supreme Court didn't rule that Zacchini's rights had necessarily been invaded: that was a matter for Ohio state courts to decide. But the high court did say that Scripps-Howard was not constitutionally exempt from being sued if the state courts cared to entertain such a suit.

The case was returned to the Ohio courts, and Zacchini won. To deny him a right to sue when his entire act was broadcast without his consent would deny him the economic value of his performance, the state court said.

The *Zacchini* decision is troubling to many journalists, particularly because it seems to suggest that other people whose ability to earn money is somehow damaged by a news story could also sue. Also, the Court didn't really consider whether Scripps-Howard actually profited from the telecast at Zacchini's expense.

There is obviously a fine line between news coverage of a celebrity's activities and the commercial exploitation of the person's name and likeness. Normally the courts give the news media considerable leeway in this area, but the rule is different in a situation such as the *Zacchini* case where all or most of a performer's act is broadcast without consent.

The test of what is improper commercial exploitation and what is legitimate news coverage would seem to be somewhat like the test used to determine what is a fair use under copyright law (discussed in Chapter Six). Thus, a purported news story or news broadcast that seriously impairs a celebrity's ability to make a profit by exercising his or her right of publicity is less likely to be considered proper than one using only a small portion of a performance and having little effect on the celebrity's profit opportunities.

Even news coverage of people who aren't celebrities sometimes produces right of publicity lawsuits. A number of people whose photographs have been used in newspapers and news programs without their consent have sued for an alleged invasion of their right of publicity, but they have almost always lost in court if the photograph was taken in a public place and the use was even minimally newsworthy. The news media clearly have the right to use people's names and show their likenesses in covering the news—without violating anyone's right of publicity. Of course, there is still the danger that the combination of a photograph and text matter may place someone in a false light. If that happens, a false light invasion of privacy lawsuit may result, even though there may be no basis for a right of publicity lawsuit.

One more question that often arises is whether an artist may sell products featuring a rendering of a celebrity—on T-shirts, for example. In 2001 the California Supreme Court ruled against an artist who sold T-shirts bearing his sketch of the Three Stooges. The court unanimously ruled that the sketches were far more "imitative" than "creative," and therefore

Defenses to invasion of privacy:

newsworthiness: a claim that a story or image is newsworthy is excellent for private facts cases because judges interpret the defense broadly.

plain view: information gathered in plain view in a public place is usually protected from intrusion claims.

consent: permission for the publication of the material, best if written.

truth: may eliminate an actual malice finding in a false light claim.

a violation of the comedy trio's heirs' rights. Artist Gary Saderup's "undeniable skill is manifestly subordinated to the overall goal of creating literal, conventional depictions of The Three Stooges so as to exploit their fame," the court wrote, rejecting the artist's claim of a First Amendment right to draw (and sell) sketches of celebrities (*Comedy III Productions v. Gary Saderup Inc.,* 25 C.4th 387). On the other hand, the California Supreme Court reached the opposite conclusion in a 2003 case, upholding the right of a comic book publisher to do cartoons that were caricatures of musicians Johnny and Edgar Winter. The comic miniseries, published by DC Comics, featured characters named Johnny and Edgar Autumn. The court said these were "fanciful, creative characters, not pictures of the Winter brothers," ruling that the depictions had *transformative value* lacking in Saderup's depictions of the Three Stooges (*Winter v. DC Comics,* 30 C.4th 881). Thus, the commercial use of a photograph or other almost-literal image of a celebrity is more likely to be a violation of the right of publicity than a depiction that adds *transformative value* to the image.

A Personal or Property Right?

One unsettled point about the right of publicity is whether it is a *personal right* or an inheritable *property right*. Courts in various regions of the United States have taken conflicting positions on this question.

In a widely noted case involving Bela Lugosi, the star of the original *Dracula* film, the California Supreme Court ruled that the right is a personal right and dies with the person. In the 1979 case, *Lugosi v. Universal Pictures* (25 C.3d 813), the court had to mediate a long-standing dispute between Universal and the widow and son of the late actor. The Lugosis contended that Universal was violating their inherited publicity rights by marketing T-shirts and other "Dracula" souvenirs using the actor's likeness after his death. The state supreme court said they had no right to sue, because the right of publicity could not be inherited. Even if a person builds a business marketing his name or likeness during his lifetime, the court said the most his heirs could inherit would be monies from the use of his name or likeness during his lifetime—not the right to control the commercial exploitation of his right of publicity after his death. The California state legislature later passed the Celebrity Rights Act, a law giving the heirs of deceased celebrities the right to profit from the commercial use of their names and likenesses for 50 years (later extended to 70 years) after their deaths. That law effectively overturned *Lugosi* and made the right of publicity a fully inheritable property right in California.

The death of an even more famous celebrity, rock-n-roll musician Elvis Presley, produced conflicting federal appellate court decisions on this question. Almost as soon as Presley died, unauthorized commercial exploitation of his name and likeness began. In a 1978 decision *(Factors v. Pro Arts*, 579 F.2d 215), the Second Circuit ruled that Presley's right of publicity was a property right and survived his death. Moreover, the court said that the right could be transferred to a business, which could maintain its exclusive right to exploit Presley's name after his death.

However, two years later another federal circuit court ruled in just the opposite way regarding Elvis Presley. The Sixth Circuit ruled, in *Memphis Development Foundation v. Factors* (616 F.2d 956, 1980), that Presley's right of publicity did not survive his death. Thus, the court said Factors did not have an exclusive right to exploit the rock and roll star's name and likeness. At issue was the foundation's right to sell $25 pewter replicas of a statue of Presley it planned to erect in Memphis. The court said, "After death, the opportunity for gain shifts to the public domain, where it is equally open to all."

Further confusing matters, after the *Memphis Development Foundation* decision was published, the court that decided the case (the Second Circuit) reversed itself. In a 1981 ruling (*Factors v. Pro Arts*, 652 F.2d 278), the court followed the Sixth Circuit's lead, concluding that Presley's right of publicity did *not* survive his death. The Second Circuit made this abrupt switch because it felt obligated to follow the law of Tennessee, Presley's home state, as it had been interpreted by a court in that region (the Sixth Circuit).

The *Factors* decision did not settle the matter: Tennessee and several other states joined California in enacting statutory laws forbidding the unauthorized commercial exploitation of a deceased celebrity's name or likeness for 50 years or longer. In Indiana, celebrities' publicity rights are protected for 100 years. In Tennessee, the law has no cutoff date, giving the owners of Presley's right of publicity the exclusive right to exploit his name and likeness in perpetuity. New York, on the other hand, refused to recognize that the right of publicity extends beyond a celebrity's lifetime, although legislation that was proposed in 2007 would change that. California's right of publicity law was amended in 2007 to extend its coverage retroactively to celebrities who died as early as 1915, giving their heirs the right to control and profit from the use of their public personas for 70 years after their deaths.

The court decisions and laws governing the inheritability of the right of publicity do *not* affect the *copyright* on a celebrity's recordings or motion pictures. As the next chapter explains, copyrights are always property rights rather than personal rights, and they do *not* terminate at the artist's death. Only the inheritability of the right of publicity, not that of copyrights, is at issue here.

The boundary line between copyrights and the right of publicity was illustrated in a 1998 court decision resulting from the efforts of Robyn Astaire, the widow of Fred Astaire, to control and often to prevent the commercial exploitation of the celebrated actor's public persona. A federal appellate court held that she could not prevent a company from using stock public domain footage of Astaire in instructional videos, as opposed to commercial endorsements (*Astaire v. Best Film and Video*, 136 F.3d 1208).

Another difference between copyrights and the right of publicity is that the latter does not extend to non-residents, at least under the California law. That became clear when a charity trust fund established to control uses of the late Princess Diana's public persona tried to stop the Franklin Mint from selling a Princess Di commemorative doll. The Ninth Circuit held that the trust fund could not prevent the sale of the dolls, in part because the trust fund is based in Great Britain (*Cairns v. Franklin Mint*, 292 F.3d 1139, 2002).

■ PRIVACY DEFENSES

Throughout this chapter we have repeatedly talked about the legal defenses available to the media in various kinds of privacy cases, but in the interest of completeness we should separately reiterate them here.

In most cases where the media are defendants, the best defense is *newsworthiness,* often called *public affairs* or *public interest.* If it is possible to convince a court that a given story, broadcast, or photograph is newsworthy, the plaintiff will not win a private facts lawsuit. The trend just about everywhere is for the courts to define newsworthiness liberally, recognizing that even sensational reporting is permissible as long as it is not inaccurate. Therefore, the media do not often lose private facts cases, although the cost of defending a lawsuit alone may deter coverage of some kinds of stories.

However, if there are inaccuracies, it is a different matter. False light privacy cases against the media are more often successful, with the constitutional standards first established in libel cases sometimes used to evaluate the media's conduct. The Supreme Court created a limited First Amendment defense for false light privacy cases in its *Time Inc. v. Hill* decision. That defense protects the media from false light privacy suits for non-malicious but erroneous publications involving matters of public interest. If a journalist has not been guilty of actual malice, a person involved in a newsworthy event has little chance of winning a false light privacy suit. If, on the other hand, there has been wrongful conduct by the media, plaintiffs fare about as well in false light privacy cases as in libel cases.

In intrusion cases, the inquiry focuses on the conduct of the media when a court tries to decide if someone's right of privacy has been invaded. The newsworthiness of a story is not a defense for unscrupulous reporting methods. A journalist who resorts to unlawful acts in getting a story (or otherwise intrudes upon some-one's right to be let alone) may face a privacy lawsuit. The use of telephoto lenses, boom microphones and other enhancing technology can lead to intrusion lawsuits in some states. The fact that someone or something is in *plain view of a public place* is generally a valid defense, although sometimes the use of image or sound enhancement technology may offset that defense.

In areas other than news-editorial journalism, the best (and often the only) privacy defense is *consent.* Persons who consent to a use of their names or likenesses have no recourse when the use to which they consented occurs. But even then, there are a few legal technicalities about consent. First, the consent must be in a form that is legally enforceable, and that means there must be a contract that complies with the formalities of contract law. The person who enters the contract must be of age, and the contract must be supported by some form of consideration. Consideration is often thought of as another way of saying money, but it can be other things, even intangibles. Any time the person who is giving the right to use his or her likeness commercially gets something of value in return, that is consideration enough. For instance, photo release forms are one of the most common kinds of contracts granting consent, and they sometimes simply say that the person posing gives his or her consent for publication of a picture in return for the free publicity that may result. Publicity is a valid form of consideration.

To be valid, the consent must be voluntarily entered into. And it must be given in a manner that lends itself to proof in court, if necessary. For that reason, a written consent is much better than an oral one, and infinitely better than the implied consent a photographer tries to establish when he says, "...but he posed willingly."

Another caution is that the consent must be all-encompassing enough to apply to all situations in which a person's name or likeness is likely to be used. A consent for one commercial use may not imply any consent for subsequent uses of the same photograph, for example. And a consent to use a picture at one time may not be a consent to use it later. All of these kinds of problems are contract law problems, and the solution lies in writing a contract that leaves no loopholes.

In addition to the newsworthiness and consent defenses, the Supreme Court has, in effect, created another separate constitutional defense for publication of information lawfully obtained from court records. The *Cox Broadcasting v. Cohn* and *Florida Star v. B.J.F.* decisions included language assuring the media's right to report information lawfully obtained from court records and possibly other public records. That right may not include a right to report on rehabilitated criminals' past activities—additional decisions are needed to clarify that issue—but in other respects the right to report the contents of lawfully obtained court records appears to be firmly entrenched.

These, then, are the defenses in privacy law. Because they differ from the defenses in libel cases, it is possible to publish something that is safe from a libel standpoint but risky under privacy law (or vice versa). In evaluating stories that may defame or embarrass someone, you should keep that point in mind. Once you have analyzed any sort of material that you plan to publish or broadcast for potential libel and concluded it is safe, you must also run through the possible invasion of privacy problems.

■ THE INTERNET AND PRIVACY

Perhaps no technical advance of the twentieth and twenty-first centuries created greater concern about personal privacy than the explosive growth of personal computer technology—and especially the Internet. Internet privacy has become a major national issue, particularly privacy in social networking sites like MySpace. This led to legislation and calls for legislation in many places. Certain aspects of this question involve the privacy issues of the sort addressed in this chapter, including legislation to protect the public from unscrupulous data-gatherers and the legal questions surrounding the use of people's names and images on the Internet without consent.

Internet Privacy: MySpace, Facebook and Social Networking Sites

As the popularity of social networking sites like MySpace, Facebook, YouTube and Twitter continues to rise, the courts are being asked to address questions of how information on those sites is protected, managed, and used. These sites are facing privacy lawsuits and outrage from privacy advocates. A 2009 report by two computer scientists found that online social networks (OSNs) "leak" private information; the report said that "most users on OSNs are vulnerable to having their OSN identity information linked with tracking cookies. Unless an OSN user is aware of this leakage and has taken preventive measures, it is currently trivial to access the user's OSN page using the ID information."

In 2010, Facebook had two possible class-action lawsuits filed against it that allege that it discloses personal information like real names, schools and friends lists to its advertisers. Facebook has said that it has revised its code so that personal information in profile tags is no longer sent to advertisers. The social network had already revised its privacy rules once in May 2010 in response to complaints, providing new settings to control what information is seen by whom. The Federal Trade Commission has been very active in privacy issues in the past few years. In perhaps the highest profile of these cases, data broker Spokeo settled with the FTC for $800,000 for data privacy allegations (the case is discussed in Chapter Thirteen). In 2011, Facebook settled charges with the agency that it had made user information public that it had promised to keep private. Facebook agreed, among other things, to 20 years of privacy audits.

Are social networking sites private or public? In 2009, a California appeals court said that MySpace is more like a bulletin board than a private room, at least if the individual page is set to be public. College student Cynthia Moreno posted a hostile "ode" to her hometown of Coalinga, Calif., on her MySpace page. The high school principal in Coalinga saw the ode and sent it to the editor of the local paper, the *Coalinga Record*, who published it as a letter to the editor with Moreno's full name. Moreno's family, still living in Coalinga, received the brunt of the community's ire; their home was shot at and they had to close the 20-year-old family business. In *Moreno v. Hanford Sentinel Inc.* (172 Cal. App. 4th 1125), the court considered whether Moreno had a cause of action for publication of private facts and intentional infliction of emotional distress.

The court said that the posting on MySpace was not private; anyone could see it, and Moreno had her picture and first name on her profile, so her identity was not private, either. Nor did Moreno's family have a cause of action because privacy rights are personal rights. The court did say that a jury should decide whether there was intentional infliction of emotional distress and remanded the case for consideration.

The Stored Communications Act makes it a crime for anyone who "intentionally accesses without authorization a facility through which an electronic communication service is provided" or "intentionally exceeds an authorization to access that facility," and by doing so "obtains, alters, or prevents authorized access to a wire or electronic communication while it is in electronic storage in such system." Employees of a New Jersey restaurant who were fired after supervisors saw their MySpace "gripe group" page venting about the workplace brought suit in *Pietrylo v. Hillstone Restaurant Group* (29 I.E.R. Cas. 1438, 2009). The supervisor got the password to the group from another employee who said she gave it up because she was afraid of being fired. The fired employees alleged that their participation in the gripe group was private and that their employer violated the Stored Communications Act by accessing the invitation-only group. Hillstone's motion for summary judgment was denied. A jury found that Hillstone managers violated the Stored Communications Act by intentionally accessing the MySpace gripe group without authorization. But the managers prevailed on the privacy claims, as the jury said that the employees had no reasonable expectation of privacy in the MySpace group.

The Fourth Circuit said that a plaintiff must prove actual damages to be able to recover statutory damages under the Stored Communications Act. Bonnie Van Alstyne brought suit under the act after discovering that the president of her former employer, Electronic Scriptorium, Limited, had been accessing her personal e-mail account for more than a year after she left the company. The trial court awarded her both statutory and punitive damages, and the Fourth Circuit reversed those damages and remanded for reconsideration (*Van Alstyne v. Electronic Scriptorium Limited*, 560 F.3d 199, 2009).

In 2011, Twitter settled with the Federal Trade Commission a privacy complaint alleging that the micro-blogging site had lied to its users and put their privacy at risks by failures to protect their privacy personal information. The FTC claimed that lax e-mail and account security procedures at Twitter allowed hackers to break in and send out false tweets between January and May 2009. The settlement ordered Twitter to create and maintain a comprehensive security system that will be audited regularly. Google also settled with the FTC in 2011 over allegations that its social networking tool, Buzz, violated privacy policies by using information provided by users in their use of Gmail accounts for another purpose, social networking through Buzz, without getting permission to do so. Google must create and implement a privacy policy and be audited.

In 2012, Maryland became the first state to pass a law that forbids employers to demand the passwords for their employees' social network sites (Illinois will likely become the second, as both houses of its legislature have passed a similar bill). The Maryland law reads in part: "An employer may not request or require that an employee or applicant disclose any user name, password, or other means for accessing a personal account or service through an electronic communications device." Nor can an employer refuse to hire a potential employee because the applicant refuses to turn over passwords.

States are becoming more aggressive in pursuing sex offenders on social networks as well. Louisiana passed a law that will be effective in August 2012 that all sex offenders must post that status on their Facebook profiles (Facebook already forbids sex offenders to use the site in its Terms of Service). An earlier version of the law forbidding nearly all Internet access by sex offenders was struck down by a federal judge (*Doe v. Jindal*, 2012 U.S. Dist. LEXIS 19841, 2012). It remains to be seen whether this new version will be constitutional.

Internet Privacy: Protecting Children—and Adults

Responding to concerns expressed by many parents and community groups, Congress passed the 1998 *Children's Online Privacy Protection Act* (COPPA) to limit the collection of information from children under age 13 without parental consent. (This law should not be confused with the Child Online Protection Act (COPA), a different 1998 law intended to curtail access to adult materials by minors. That law is discussed in Chapter Ten.)

COPPA limits the ability of children under 13 to have e-mail accounts without parental consent, and it requires those who gather data to deal with parents before dealing with their children. A website cannot simply have children fill in personal information on an electronic form and then click "send" when they're finished. The act includes federal *preemption*: states may not enact conflicting laws governing the collection of information from children. Websites that collect personal information about children must post their privacy policies prominently. The law also includes provisions

---

Focus on...
E-mail privacy

People are starting to understand that e-mail is neither completely private nor secure. The Electronic Freedom Foundation, an organization that has advocated for free speech and privacy online since 1990, has a few recommendations to keep e-mail communications safe and clean.

* Use a secondary or "side" e-mail account for posting in chat rooms, mailing lists and newsgroups, and keep your "main" account for trusted contacts.

* Don't reply to spammers for any reason; this tells them that the e-mail is "live," and your address may well be sold to other spammers.

* Avoid sending highly personal e-mails to mailing lists, and keep your private business on your private home computer.

For more tips and other information about online security and e-mail, check out www.eff.org.

for self-regulation by industry groups that develop their own programs to protect children's privacy. The Federal Trade Commission is charged with supervising and approving these self-regulation programs. In 1999, the FTC adopted regulations to implement this law.

A company that operated virtual worlds for children agreed to pay a fine of $3 million to the FTC in 2011 to settle charges that they violated COPPA by illegally collecting information about children under 13 without parental consent—the largest penalty to date under COPPA. Playdom, Inc. operated a number of children's sites, including one called "Pony Stars" on which the FTC said 821,000 children registered to play.

In 2011, the FTC proposed updates to COPPA, including refining some of the law's definitions, streamlining the processes by which website operators obtain parental consent, adding new ways to obtain that consent, and strengthening requirements for security.

In 2005, Congress established new federal standards for issuing driver's licenses to make it more difficult to obtain a license under a false identity. However, this legislation would give more bureaucrats access to applicants' personal information, making crimes like identity theft easier, not more difficult, some privacy advocacy groups charged.

The FTC issued the final version of its new privacy report in March 2012. Titled "Protecting Consumer Privacy in an Era of Rapid Change," it includes a number of recommendations for both online and "brick-and-mortar" businesses. Some of the things the report recommends:

Focus on...
"Pulling plug on privacy"

That's the title of a 2011 essay by Alex Kozinski, chief judge of the Ninth Circuit, well known for his quotable decisions. He and one of his law clerks, Stephanie Grace, wrote a eulogy for privacy on *The Daily*, an iPad-only magazine.

The judge and his clerk blame all of us for the death of the Fourth Amendment, the amendment that guards against unreasonable searches and seizures, as we gave up little bits of our privacy for convenience and a few pennies saved: "It started with the supermarket loyalty programs. They seemed innocuous enough—you just scribble down your name, number and address in exchange for a plastic card and a discount on Oreos. The problem, at least constitutionally speaking, is that the Fourth Amendment protects only what we reasonably expect to keep private." Thus, say Kozinski and Grace, we've forfeited our expectations of privacy by giving away so much of it.

FIG. 29. Customer loyalty cards.

Public domain image by Mattes, via Wikimedia Commons.

The eulogy concludes: "With so little left private, the Fourth Amendment is all but obsolete. Where police officers once needed a warrant to search your bookshelf for 'Atlas Shrugged,' they can now simply ask Amazon.com if you bought it. Where police needed probable cause before seizing your day planner, they can now piece together your whereabouts from your purchases, cellphone data and car's GPS. Someday soon we'll realize that we've lost everything we once cherished as private. And as we grieve the loss of the Fourth Amendment, we'll be forced to look deep in our hearts—and at the little pieces of plastic dangling from our keychains—and ask ourselves if it was all worth it. R.I.P."

- regulations that extend to "all commercial entities that collect or use consumer data that can be reasonably linked to a specific consumer, computer, or other device;"
- "privacy by design," meaning that companies need to incorporate principles of privacy into all their baseline practices;
- companies should limit their gathering of information using mobile devices and geolocation data, regularly purging unnecessary information from their records and to give consumers a choice before collecting "sensitive data" (defined as data about children, health, finances, Social Security numbers, and some geolocation data);
- development of "Do Not Track" mechanisms to let consumers opt out of online tracking; and
- consumers' ability to affirmatively consent (or "opt in") to material changes to privacy regulations and transparency in companies' data practices.

In May 2012, the agency also held an open meeting to consider revisions and updates to its 2005 guidance document, "Dot Com Disclosures," on advertising and privacy issues online.

Although the United States has not enacted a comprehensive Internet privacy law, the European Union has done so—and placed U.S. corporations in the position of having to comply with European standards if they wish to do business in Europe. The EU law requires member countries to implement data-protection standards to prevent the inappropriate use of personal information obtained over the Internet. In 2008 an EU privacy panel decided search-engine providers, including Google, Yahoo and Microsoft, must reduce the time they keep search records to six months from 18 months in most cases.

In 2010, the Fourth Circuit held that someone posting child pornography has no reasonable expectation of privacy from the FBI seeking his personal information from his ISP (*U.S. v. Bynum*, 604 F.3d 161). Marques Bynum was observed by an FBI undercover agent to be uploading child pornography in an online chat group. The agent subpoenaed Yahoo! for Bynum's subscriber information and used that information to obtain a search warrant for his home, where more child pornography was found. Bynum sued, saying that the subpoena was unlawful. The Fourth Circuit said no; when he "voluntarily conveyed all this information to his internet and phone companies" he "assumed the risk that th[ose]e compan[ies] would reveal [that information] to police." The court added that "[e]very federal court to address this issue has held that subscriber information provided to an internet provider is not protected by the Fourth Amendment's privacy expectation."

Internet Privacy: E-mail and Text Messages

Other controversial aspects of Internet privacy concerns the interception and review of e-mail or other electronic communications and surreptitious monitoring of closed discussion groups, often by an employer. Employers have defeated challenges to the common practice of monitoring e-mail that passes through a corporate server, and in 2010 the Supreme Court said employees' text messages can be monitored for legitimate work purposes.

Both government and private employers often monitor e-mail, and there is little that employees can do about it, aside from using an outside e-mail server to avoid having their messages read by supervisors. Even if an employer provides a computer to an employee for *home* use, but with the provision that it is to be used for company business only, the employee has no reasonable expectation of privacy that would prevent the employer from getting a court order to examine files on that computer (*TBG Insurance Services v. Superior Court*, 96 C.A.4th 443, 2002).

In 2004, the Third Circuit ruled similarly in a Pennsylvania case, upholding an employer's right to search employee e-mail stored on the company's server. The court reasoned that the employer is the e-mail "provider" and therefore exempt from the Electronic Communications Privacy Act, which protects e-mail privacy under certain circumstances (*Fraser v. Nationwide Mutual Insurance Co.*, 352 F.3d 107). In 2005 the First Circuit essentially agreed, holding that an Internet service provider who stores and transmits e-mail violates the ECPA by accessing the messages (*U.S. v. Councilman*, decided *en banc*, 418 F.3d 67).

The Supreme Court in 2010 said that if an employer monitors employees' communications on company equipment pursuant to legitimate work-related concerns, those communications are not private. At issue were sexually explicit text messages sent by a SWAT team member on his city pager. The Ninth Circuit ruled that the Fourth Amendment's ban on unreasonable searches and seizures protects employees from searches of their e-mail and text messages that are handled by an outside provider, not an in-house system. That court declined to hear the case *en banc*, but the Supreme Court granted *cert*—and disagreed.

In *City of Ontario v. Quon* (130 S. Ct. 2619), the Court said that the search of the text messages was reasonable. Justice Anthony Kennedy, writing for the Court, said that the department's policy made it clear that the text messages were *not* private. Kennedy did, however, acknowledge that new technologies suggest the need for a new examination of how companies deal with unofficial uses.

> Cell phone and text message communications are so pervasive that some persons may consider them to be essential means or necessary instruments for self-expression, even self identification. That might strengthen the case for an expectation of privacy. On the other hand, the ubiquity of those devices has made them generally affordable, so one could counter that employees who need cell phones or similar devices for personal matters can purchase and pay for their own.

Justice Antonin Scalia concurred but took Kennedy to task for suggesting that new technologies require new legal interpretations: "The Court's implication...that where electronic privacy is concerned we should decide less than we otherwise would...or that we should hedge our bets by concocting case-specific standards or issuing opaque opinions—is in my view indefensible. The-times-they-are-a-changin' is a feeble excuse for disregard of duty."

The federal Electronic Communications Privacy Act was at the center of another controversy in 2006, when *USA TODAY* and other news media reported that several of the largest telephone companies had handed over telephone and e-mail records of millions of Americans to the National Security Agency, in violation of the ECPA's ban on such disclosures. Not only was calling information given to federal investigators, but the content of telephone calls and e-mail was apparently monitored by the federal government on a massive scale without court authorization. The Electronic Frontier Foundation and others sued over this controversial and seemingly unlawful government surveillance. Some defended the surveillance as necessary to fight terrorism—and said revealing that the monitoring program even existed was a crime by journalists. Others said domestic surveillance on this scale is a fundamental violation of American civil liberties. This issue is also discussed in Chapter Two.

The California Supreme Court in 2003 ruled that Intel Corp. could not use a trespass rationale to prevent a former employee from sending e-mail messages hostile to the company to current employees at work, upholding his free expression rights (*Intel. Corp. v. Hamidi*, 30 C.4th 1342). The court held that the company would have a case for trespassing only if the e-mail in some way damaged the company's computer system.

The Eleventh Circuit supported a very limited view of e-mail privacy when it held that e-mails sent to and received by a third party result in the expectation of privacy being lost (*Rehberg v. Paulk*, 598 F.3d 1268, 2010). Investigators used a state subpoena to an Internet service provider to access Charles Rehberg's e-mails. The court said that "Rehberg's voluntary delivery of emails to third parties constituted a voluntary relinquishment of the right to privacy in that information." In 2011, the U.S. Supreme Court granted *cert* to address a different question: whether a government official can be sued for causing someone to be wrongly prosecuted by giving false testimony to a grand jury. The Court unanimously ruled in 2012 that a witness in a grand jury proceeding is entitled to the same absolute immunity as a witness who testifies at a trial (*Rehburg v. Paulk*, No. 10-788).

Misappropriation and the Internet

As the Internet has become a pervasive medium of communication, many questions have arisen concerning the unauthorized use of the names and images of celebrities and sometimes others. This question has led to many lawsuits but few precedent-setting appellate court decisions. In one of the first cases to be resolved, television actress Alyssa Milano won a $238,000 default judgment against a Minnesota man and got several other website operators to pay undisclosed settlements for posting nude photographs of her. In a series of lawsuits, she accused website operators of violating her right of publicity. She contended that these website operators were making thousands of dollars a month in access fees paid by users to view their websites.

As explained earlier, the news media have a First Amendment right to use the name and image of anyone, including private persons as well as celebrities. This is true regardless of whether the news medium is delivered to the public at no charge, as is broadcast television, or sold, as are newspapers and magazines. The mere fact that a fee is charged for a newspaper or magazine (or access to a website) does not automatically make its use of someone's name or image a commercial misappropriation. But there have been many lawsuits that questioned where the boundary should be drawn between coverage of the news and commercial misappropriation.

At this point, the few courts that have addressed the unauthorized use of someone's name or likeness on the Internet have generally found the uses to be misappropriations, not journalistic uses. However, it remains clear that news coverage is not a form of misappropriation. Where a website is clearly engaged in covering the news, it can use celebrities' (and other people's) names and images without permission. If a website is not covering the news, its owner can be sued for the unauthorized use of peoples' names or images.

Still another factor that must be considered when images are posted on a website is *copyright ownership,* which is discussed in the next chapter. It may not be a misappropriation to publish someone's picture on the Internet in a journalistic context. But whoever owns the copyright to the picture may sue for copyright infringement even if the person in the picture has no recourse under privacy law.

■ DATA PRIVACY DEVELOPMENTS

Sometimes, as Chapter Nine suggests, the government wants to keep information private that the media wants to be public, but in many cases, individuals are fighting to retain their informational privacy from the government or from private companies. As we've noted earlier, the area that seems to be growing most quickly in the courts as well as in the minds of legislatures, government regulatory agencies and the public is data privacy. The Internet makes it all too easy for information to be gathered, stored, aggregated, and searched.

But is there an actual *constitutional* right to data privacy? Some justices on the U.S. Supreme Court would say no, as they did in a 2011 case. The Court ruled in favor of the National Aeronautics and Space Administration's (NASA) background checks for employees of companies working under contract in *NASA v. Nelson* (131 S. Ct. 746). Robert Nelson, a contract employee of Jet Propulsion Laboratory (JPL), objected to a background questionnaire intended to eliminate differences between contract employees who had worked at JPL for years without background checks and those newly hired. Two sections, one asking about treatment or counseling for recent illegal drug use and another with open-ended questions for references to answer, were under consideration. Justice Samuel Alito, writing for a unanimous Court, upheld the questions as not violating the constitutional rights of the employees. The government, he said, has "an interest in conducting basic employment background checks." But Alito did *not* address the major question in the case: is there a constitutional right to informational privacy? Alito assumed there was for purposes of the case (without actually ruling that there is) and said that if the right did exist, it was not violated here.

But Justices Clarence Thomas and Antonin Scalia in their concurring opinions made no secret of their position on the informational privacy right: there isn't one. Scalia wrote bluntly: "A federal constitutional right to 'informational privacy' does not exist." Thomas, going even further, quoted himself from *Lawrence v. Texas*: "I can find neither in the Bill of Rights nor any other part of the Constitution a general right of privacy."

These justices' opinions notwithstanding, following are a few major developments in data privacy from all three branches of government.

Medical Privacy

In 1996, with little fanfare, Congress enacted a privacy law governing medical records: the Health Insurance Portability and Accountability Act (HIPAA). That law, implemented by regulations adopted by the Clinton administration, imposed new restrictions on the release of medical information to protect the privacy of patients' medical records. Some portions of the rules were opposed by health insurers and others in the health care industry who said they were too restrictive and too costly to implement. Privacy advocates also lobbied for changes in the rules, as did media representatives who said information that has been reported for years will now be off limits to journalists. After hearing arguments from the industry, privacy advocates and journalists, the Bush administration amended the rules and allowed them to go into effect in 2003.

The regulations require that doctors and other health-care providers obtain written consent from patients before sharing their health records. The rules also allow patients to see their own files and request corrections of errors. Patients must also be told how their health information will be used when possible.

Of most concern to journalists are provisions of the regulations that restrict the release of once-public information such as the identity of well-known hospital patients and the medical condition of those admitted after an accident, natural disaster, crime or terrorist act. There are *criminal* penalties of up to 10 years in prison and fines of $250,000 for revealing confidential medical information, which may cause potential news sources to avoid taking a chance of revealing information to journalists even when it may not be restricted.

A number of states already had medical privacy laws that included some of these provisions, but HIPAA established *nationwide* standards for medical record privacy. However, HIPAA also has a loophole: it says health information can be disclosed "to the extent that such… disclosure is required by law." In 2006, the Ohio Supreme Court ruled that HIPAA does not preempt the Ohio Public Record Act's provisions requiring disclosure of some health information that HIPAA seemingly made secret (*State ex rel. Cincinnati Enquirer v. Daniels*, 844 N.E.2d 1181).

Does the type of medical condition suffered change the amount of privacy to which someone is entitled? Apparently it does in the Second Circuit. At issue before the court in *Matson v. Bd. of Educ. of the City Sch. Dist. of N.Y.* (631 F.3d 57) was this question: "[D]oes the Constitution protect Matson's right to maintain the confidentiality of her fibromyalgia?" (Note that this case was not brought under HIPAA.) Dorrit Matson, a music teacher, claimed that the board of education had violated her constitutional privacy rights by disclosing the fact that she suffered from fibromyalgia (chronic pain often brought on by anxiety or stress) in an online report. A divided appellate panel said that the interest in privacy varies with the medical condition; for example, HIV/AIDS would require the highest level of confidentiality. But, said the court, "although fibromyalgia is a serious medical condition, it does not carry with it the sort of opprobrium that confers upon those who suffer from it a constitutional right of privacy as to that medical condition."

Congressional Actions

Congress has been busy drafting laws to protect data privacy in 2011 and 2012. A few notable examples: Sen. Patrick Leahy (D-VT) announced the Personal Data Privacy and Security Act of 2011. The bill would require some data holders to disclose personal electronic records to individuals for a fee and to include information on how to correct errors in those records. Sen. Leahy also proposed the Electronic Communications Privacy Act Amendments Act of 2011 to update ECPA, a major federal online privacy law. Leahy's press release described the bill as "common-sense changes to existing law to improve privacy protections for consumers' electronic communications and to clarify the legal standards for the government to obtain this information."

Sens. John Kerry (D-MA) and John McCain (R-AZ) proposed the Commercial Privacy Bill of Rights Act of 2011, aimed at creating a privacy "bill of rights" to protect people from the increasingly invasive commercial data-collection industry.

Several online "do not track" bills were also announced: the Do Not Track Me Online Act of 2011, to make the FTC "prescribe regulations regarding the collection and use of information obtained by tracking the Internet activity of an individual, and for other purposes" and Do Not Track Kids Act of 2011, to "amend the Children's Online Privacy Protection Act of 1998 to extend, enhance, and revise the provisions relating to collection, use, and disclosure of personal information of children." It remains to be seen if any of these bills become law; none have yet made it out of Congressional committees.

Other Data Privacy Cases

Other pieces of personal data have had their days in court. In 2010, Amazon fought off an attempt by the North Carolina Department of Revenue to turn over names, addresses and transaction data of all North Carolina residents who purchased anything from Amazon between 2003 and 2010—50 million transactions, according to Amazon—in an investigation of Amazon's tax liability. Amazon argued that this would be a serious privacy violation under the First Amendment and the Video Privacy Protection Act (VPPA), a 1988 federal law that prohibits the "wrongful disclosure of video tape rental or sale records" (which also includes DVDs, CDs and other forms of media). Amazon had already turned over data to the state for purposes of determining tax liability and argued that the state did not need customer information. A federal judge agreed with Amazon: "The First Amendment protects a buyer from having the expressive content of her purchase of books, music, and audiovisual materials disclosed to the government. Citizens are entitled to receive information and ideas through books, films, and other expressive materials anonymously" (*Amazon.com LLC v. Lay*, 758 F. Supp. 2d 1154). The court also agreed that the VPPA also prohibited the release of the data.

In *Pineda v. Williams-Sonoma Stores, Inc.* (51 Cal. 4th 524, 2011), the California Supreme Court said that stores could no longer require customers to provide their ZIP codes when buying something with a credit card. Jessica Pineda gave her ZIP code to Williams-Sonoma and claimed that they stored it and then used it with her address to engage in marketing. Williams-Sonoma claimed that this practice did not abridge Pineda's privacy under state law because her ZIP code was not unique to her. Justice Carlos Moreno wrote, "The Legislature intended to provide robust consumer protections by prohibiting retailers from soliciting and recording information about the cardholder that is unnecessary to the credit card transaction."

ZIP code privacy was also at issue in *Tyler v. Michaels Stores* (2012 U.S. Dist. LEXIS 1569). The judge followed the reasoning from the California Supreme Court in saying that a ZIP code was personally identifiable information. But Melissa Tyler lost her claim because, the court said, she didn't show "an injury or loss" and "a causal connection between [Michaels'] deceptive act or practice and [her] injury."

The Fourth Circuit found that the First Amendment protected a blogger's right to post the Social Security numbers (SSNs) of public officials in Virginia as a protest to the state's postings of land records online without first *redacting* (removing) SSNs. In *Ostergren v. Cuccinelli* (615 F.3d 263, 2011), the court said that Virginia did pass a law ordering the redactions of SSNs, but did not appropriate enough funds to do the full job, and many records remained that contained SSNs. In protest, B.J. Ostergren, owner of "The Virginia Watchdog" website, started posting public records that contained SSNs she got while searching government records. The Virginia general assembly changed a statute so that Ostergren could be charged with knowingly disseminating SSNs online. She filed suit, alleging that she had a right to engage in protected government criticism.

The Fourth Circuit said the district court didn't go far enough to remedy the constitutional problems of Virginia's law. The court relied on the "Pentagon Papers" line of cases (*Cox Broadcasting, Florida Star, Daily Mail* and others), saying that "the First Amendment does not allow Virginia to punish Ostergren for posting its land records online without redacting SSNs when numerous clerks are doing precisely that." The court was essentially saying that Virginia had to clean up its own act first.

■ AN OVERVIEW OF MAJOR ISSUES

Privacy law is full of controversial questions. In the aftermath of *Lawrence v. Texas* in 2003, what is the scope of the right of personal privacy? Is there still a conflict between privacy rights and the power of governments to regulate an individual's choice of sexual partners? What about privacy rights in the abortion context? Was *Gonzales v. Carhart* correctly decided? Does it signal a major curtailment of a woman's constitutional right to choose to terminate or continue a pregnancy, in consultation with her doctor?

The media are often caught up in these questions but have their own privacy concerns. The trend toward "tabloid television" has produced new ethical and legal dilemmas. When is it acceptable for journalists to go undercover or use hidden cameras to get a story? Does it matter if the story is truthfully reported when the newsgathering is really intrusive?

What about law enforcement ride-alongs? The Supreme Court has now ruled that it violates the Fourth Amendment for officers to take journalists with them when they enter private property with a search warrant or arrest warrant. Was this decision right? Which should take priority—the right of privacy inside one's own home or the news value of showing people who are suspected of serious crimes at the moment of their arrest?

And what about paparazzi? There are media willing to buy these pictures because a large segment of the public wants to see candid pictures of celebrities—and is willing to pay for the privilege. Do celebrities abandon all privacy rights when they become famous?

What about the right of publicity? Where does a celebrity's right to profit from the use of his/her name or likeness end? Is there enough First Amendment protection for those who want to use some element of a celebrity's right of publicity? Where do the cases involving Bette Midler, Tom Waits and Vanna White leave advertisers? Is federal appellate Judge Alex Kozinski correct in saying that it is now illegal for advertisers to create an image or sound that merely *reminds* the public of a celebrity?

There are other contexts in which the rules on privacy remain unclear or controversial. When, for example, may a journalist report embarrassing but truthful private facts? Should the media be free to report any facts that they lawfully obtain? Do the Supreme Court's *Cox Broadcasting* and *Florida Star* decisions go too far, or perhaps not far enough? Should there be any private facts that are off-limits to the press?

The constitutional status of privacy is still up for grabs. Two justices on the Supreme Court are on record as staunchly opposing it. Finally, what about Internet privacy? Should the U.S. adopt something like the European Union's strict privacy standards to govern the collection of personal data? When should e-mail or other electronic communications be able to be monitored or obtained by employers or courts? And what precautions should social networking sites like Facebook take when dealing with information on their sites?

<table>
<tr><td>

WHAT SHOULD I KNOW ABOUT MY STATE?

</td><td>

- What privacy torts does my state recognize? (There are four: intrusion, private facts, false light, and misappropriation.)
- Does my state recognize the right of publicity?
- What are my state's rules about recording conversations on the phone or in person? Who has to know that the recording is taking place?

</td></tr>
</table>

A SUMMARY OF THE RIGHT OF PRIVACY

What Is Invasion of Privacy?

Invasion of privacy is a legal action to compensate persons whose right of privacy has been interfered with. There are four generally recognized types of invasion of privacy: (1) *intrusion* upon a person's physical solitude; (2) publication of *private facts*, causing embarrassment; (3) placing a person before the public in a *false light*; (4) *misappropriation*, or *unauthorized commercial exploitation* of a person's name or likeness.

Are These Rights Universally Recognized?

No. Some states have recognized all four kinds of invasion of privacy, while others allow lawsuits for only some of them. However, statutory laws or court decisions in virtually all states recognize that a person's name or likeness may not be exploited in commercial advertising without permission.

What Is the Right of Publicity?

Misappropriation and violation of the *right of publicity* are terms for the fourth type of invasion of privacy listed above (the commercial exploitation of a person's name or likeness). The right of publicity is fundamentally different from the other types of privacy in that it involves a *property right* that is inheritable in many states rather than a *personal right* that is extinguished when the victim of an invasion of privacy dies. Those who use a person's name, voice, photograph or any other element of his/her *public persona* for a commercial purpose must have consent.

What Defenses Are There?

The courts have recognized several defenses as applicable to one or more of the four kinds of invasion of privacy. The primary ones are: (1) *newsworthiness* or public interest (which applies mainly in private facts cases); (2) *consent*; and (3) a constitutional *public record defense* (which also applies mainly in private facts cases).

Is Invasion of Privacy a Serious Legal Problem for the Media?

Compared to libel, invasion of privacy was traditionally a less serious legal problem for the news media. While the media lose privacy lawsuits on occasion, courts have broadly interpreted the newsworthiness defense to protect the media from many types of privacy lawsuits. However, right of publicity lawsuits are an increasingly serious problem for advertisers, the entertainment industry and others who exploit celebrities' public personas for commercial gain. And "tabloid television" has created new controversies and lawsuits that raise difficult questions about hidden cameras and intrusive or undercover newsgathering.

6   *Copyrights and Trademarks*

Should anyone be able to own words, images, sounds or ideas? Shouldn't information and ideas belong to everyone in a free society? Why should copyright owners—rarely the actual creators of artistic, musical or literary works—be able to lock up someone else's creative endeavors and treat them as private property, denying their use to others? Specifically, why should record companies, publishing houses and Hollywood producers be able to buy other people's creative works and then profit from them, depriving even the creators of any say about the future use of their works? Should a television distribution company be able to purchase the rights to classic movies and then change them despite the objections of the people who made those movies into classics in the first place?

Should those creative works be locked as they are, without permission for others to transform them, to mix and "mash" them into new creative works? A recent example: The creator of the iconic "Obama Hope" and "Obama Progress" posters, Shepard Fairey, made headlines in 2009 when he brought suit against the Associated Press for declaratory judgment that the poster was a fair use of the original photograph. Fairey admitted using an AP image taken in 2006 by Manny Garcia at the National Press Club in Washington but said in his suit that his use was transformative:

> While the evident purpose of the Garcia Photograph is to document the events that took place at the National Press Club that day in April 2006, the evident purpose of both Obama Progress and Obama Hope is to inspire, convince and convey the power of Obama's ideals, as well as his potential as a leader, through graphic metaphor.

Fairey and the AP settled the dispute in 2011, with Fairey agreeing to share the rights to make merchandise from the "Obama Hope" image with the AP.

The growth of the Internet has created difficult new questions about copyright law. It has become easy for millions of Internet users around the world to share copyrighted materials. Even worse, in the view of some copyright owners, the Internet also makes it easy to share software that defeats the copy-protection schemes built into some digital audio and video products. There is potential for huge damage awards as well; in 2012, as will be discussed, a court reinstated a case against Google for a $1 billion (yes, *billion!*) infringement lawsuit filed by motion picture companies against its video-sharing site YouTube.

One of the big news stories of early 2012 was the online and public protest against two proposed anti-piracy bills, the Stop Online Piracy Act (SOPA) and the PROTECT IP Act (Preventing Real Online Threats to Economic Creativity and Theft of Intellectual Property Act, or PIPA, which was itself a rewrite of another failed 2010 bill, the Combating Online Infringement and Counterfeits Act (COICA)). These bills, ostensibly targeted toward combating international piracy and copyright infringement online, would have also affected American sites as contributory infringers, so that YouTube, Twitter and Facebook could be liable. In January 2012, the online community, including sites like Wikipedia, Wired, and the *Huffington Post*, responded with a daylong blackout called "American Censorship Day" in protest of the bills. Millions of Americans signed various petitions against the bills. The White House also weighed in: "Any effort to combat online piracy must guard against the risk of online censorship of lawful activity and must not inhibit innovation by our dynamic

FIG. 30. Shepard
Fairey's iconic "Obama
Hope" poster at the
National Portrait Gallery,
Washington, D.C.

*djLicious, "IMGP4761,"
February 14, 2009 via Flickr,
Creative Commons attribution
license.*

businesses large and small." Soon after the blackout, several of the bills' sponsored withdrew their support, and Congress announced that action on the bills would be postponed. While the Internet community may have breathed a sigh of relief, there can be little doubt that Congress will again attempt to legislate against piracy both here and abroad.

Still other copyright questions have arisen. Motion picture writers, actors and directors objected bitterly to the "colorization" of classic black and white movies by the distribution companies that own the copyrights. Authors chronically complain about the things publishers do to their manuscripts, including publishing them electronically after contracting only to publish in traditional printed formats.

And those who write and perform music sometimes see others gain control of their music—and profit from it. Much has been written about singer Michael Jackson's purchase of the copyrights to many of the Beatles' songs. Jackson bought the Beatles' copyrights about 1985, after Paul McCartney told him of the value of copyrights. Jackson later struck a deal with Sony Corp., merging his copyright portfolio with Sony's, thereby reducing his interest in the Beatles' songs to 50 percent, but also giving him part ownership of many other music copyrights, old and new. As Jackson's financial woes mounted in 2005, near the time of his acquittal on child molestation charges, some of his advisers predicted that he would eventually have to sell more of his copyright holdings to pay debts estimated at $300 million. Paul McCartney, who wrote many of the Beatles songs alone or in collaboration with John Lennon, has often expressed regrets over telling Jackson about investing in music copyrights in the first place. But McCartney has his own music publishing company that controls the copyrights not only to his post-Beatles music but also to the works of many others, including Buddy Holly. Industry sources place McCartney's net worth over $1 billion, much of it from his portfolio of music copyrights.

For years singer-composer John Fogerty refused to perform his biggest hits from his days with the Credence Clearwater Revival group to avoid encouraging his fans to buy those now-classic recordings. Why didn't he want people to buy his early recordings? Because his former manager and music publisher received some of the profits from those recordings—and Fogerty was locked in a bitter fight with the former manager for years. The ex-manager sued Fogerty for copyright infringement because Fogerty wrote new songs that allegedly sounded too much like his own older recordings. (A federal jury ruled in Fogerty's favor in that case, and eventually his ex-manager sold his interest in the record label, clearing the way for Fogerty to return to the label and re-release his old songs.)

Copyright law creates a maze of problems for the entire creative community. To make a video and distribute it legally, one must obtain copyright clearances from many sources, including the owner of the underlying story, the author of the script, music composers and publishers, recording artists and record companies, among others.

Clearly, these are difficult philosophical questions; there are no satisfactory answers to some of them. But the fact remains that creative works, like inventions and trademarks, are often treated as private property—property that can be bought and sold or even rented out, if you will. Collectively, the law governing this kind of property is called *intellectual property law*. It includes copyrights, trademarks, unfair competition and patent law. Mass communicators are primarily concerned with copyrights (which protect creative works such as books, periodicals, manuscripts, music, film and video productions, computer software and works of art) and trademarks (which protect words, phrases and symbols identifying products and services). Unfair competition, a legal concept that sometimes protects works not covered by copyright or trademark law, is also important to some communicators. Patents, on the other hand, typically protect inventions and scientific processes. They are usually more important to scientists and engineers than to mass communicators.

Intellectual property law exists to encourage creativity by protecting the creator's right to make a profit from the dissemination of his or her works. The basic rationale for it is that creative people are just as entitled to profit from their labors as are the people who make consumer goods. However, in practice the creators of copyrighted works frequently find it necessary to sell their works to others—often at low prices—just to make a living. As a result, by the time a creative work becomes highly profitable, someone other than the creator is often entitled to the bulk of the profits.

The fact that someone other than the creator often profits from copyrights is troubling to some people. Another troubling aspect of intellectual property law is that it creates monopolistic controls on knowledge. For that reason educators, librarians, scientific researchers and even newsgatherers sometimes find copyrights and patents to be a major annoyance.

Even antitrust lawyers for the U.S. government have been known to oppose copyright laws because of their monopolistic tendencies. For instance, during the Congressional debate over a comprehensive revision of the U.S. Copyright Act in the mid-1970s, the Justice Department lobbied to weaken the proposed amendments to minimize the restraints on competition inherent in copyright protection.

Though intellectual property law may be monopolistic and an abridgment of free expression, it has a long history in the United States. It is unlikely this form of monopoly will soon disappear, the First Amendment notwithstanding.

Intellectual property law originally evolved within the English common law, but the framers of the U.S. Constitution considered it so important that they specifically recognized it, making both copyrights and patents federal matters right from the time the Constitution was ratified. Article I, Section 8 of the Constitution includes this language:

> The Congress shall have the power to promote the progress of science and the useful arts, by securing for limited times to authors and inventors the exclusive right to their respective writings and discoveries.

Shortly after the Constitution was ratified, Congress accepted that invitation and enacted the first federal copyright law, the Copyright Act of 1790. That law has been revised several times since, as technology created new problems that could not have been anticipated by the framers of the Constitution. The 1976 Copyright Act—the most recent comprehensive revision of the law—attempted (not always successfully) to deal with such troublesome problems as photocopying, audio and video recording, satellite communications and cable television. More recently, even more difficult questions have arisen because of the growth of the Internet and digital filesharing, among other issues.

Critics of modern copyright law like to point out that the Constitution says copyrights and patents are supposed to be *for limited times*. The 1790 Copyright Act decreed that copyrights would last for 14 years, renewable for another 14—far less than today's 95-year term for corporate copyrights. Because copyright owners have done a better job of lobbying than consumers, librarians, educators, journalists and others who would often benefit from shorter copyright terms, Congress has repeatedly extended the duration of copyrights.

Whatever the unresolved problems in copyright law, the history of Congressional involvement makes copyright law fundamentally different from some of the other areas of media law: it is an area of federal statutory law, not primarily a form of state statutory or common law. If the problems of copyright law are to be solved at all, they must be resolved mainly by Congress, with help from the federal courts.

There is another way in which copyrights and other kinds of intellectual property law differ from such areas of law as libel and invasion of privacy. As Chapters Four and Five point out, the right to sue for libel, slander or most kinds of invasion of privacy is a purely personal right; it dies with the aggrieved party. That person's heirs usually have no basis for a lawsuit unless they were also personally injured. Copyrights and trademarks are entirely different in this respect. They create property rights rather than personal rights, rights that may be passed on to one's heirs. In fact, copyright law is specifically written to provide legal rights many years after the death of a work's creator.

■ AN OVERVIEW OF COPYRIGHT LAW

To summarize very briefly, the owner of a copyright has the *exclusive right* to *reproduce* the copyrighted work, to create *derivative works* based on it, and to *distribute* copies, *perform* the work or *display* it to the public. Anyone else who does these things without the copyright owner's permission is guilty of *copyright infringement* unless what that person does qualifies as a *fair use*. To prove an infringement, the copyright owner must show *substantial similarity* between the original work and the allegedly infringing work. The owner must also show that his/her copyright is *valid* and the infringer had *access* to the original work and violated one of the exclusive rights just listed. When the copyright eventually expires, the work then falls into the *public domain*; at that point, the once-exclusive rights belong to everyone.

What Copyright Law Covers

The Copyright Act of 1976 continued a tradition begun in earlier U.S. copyright laws, setting up a system under which people may protect their creative works from unauthorized copying. The 1976 law was a major rewrite of the 1909 Copyright Act, and the 1976 law has been amended a number of times since then.

What sorts of things may or may not be copyrighted under this law? Generally, all kinds of creative endeavors may be copyrighted. That includes literary (fiction and non-fiction, prose and poetry), musical (and any accompanying words), and dramatic works (including music), as well as choreographic works and panto-mimes, pictorial, graphic and sculptural works (both photographs and paintings), computer software, maps, architectural designs, recordings, motion pictures and radio or television productions (whether dramatic or news/documentary). Just about everything that is printed or broadcast may be copyrighted.

However, there are some very important exceptions to that rule. Probably the most important one for the media is that the news itself cannot be copyrighted, although a *description* of a news event can be. The first reporter to reach the scene of a plane crash, for instance, cannot prevent others from reporting the fact that the plane crashed or the details of how it happened. The most that this reporter can deny to others is his or her account of the event. Others may tell the story in their own words.

Thus, it is commonplace for journalists to rewrite each other's stories. When one reporter scores an important "scoop," others quickly pick up the story, carefully putting it in their own words and perhaps giving credit to the original source. Even though this is permissible under copyright law, it should be emphasized that one news medium cannot systematically purloin all of its news from a competitor to avoid having to employ its own news staff. To do that is called *unfair competition,* and courts have awarded damages for that kind of wrongdoing even though it may not be a copyright infringement. Systematic "news piracy," as it has been called, is not permissible. More will be said of unfair competition later.

There are several other important categories of material that cannot be copyrighted. Like news, other forms of factual informa-tion cannot be copyrighted. Historical or scientific information, for instance, is available to everyone. (However, remember that a particular description of the facts can be copyrighted, and that a scientific process may be patented.) And ideas, processes and inventions may not be copyrighted; usually they may be protected only by patent law. Copyright law protects the style of presentation, not the underlying factual information or ideas.

In an important 1991 case, the U.S. Supreme Court empha-sized the point that only an *original* arrangement of facts can be

derivative works:
a whole work based on parts of one or more other works; for example, making a movie from the story in a book.

public domain works:
works that can be freely used by the public because their creators no longer have an exclusive right to restrict or receive a royalty for their repro-duction or use.

unfair competition:
to "reap what one has not sown" by taking one's competitor's work and passing it off as one's own.

copyrighted, not the facts themselves. The court held that the information in a telephone directory lacks the requisite originality and creativity to be copyrightable (*Feist Publications v. Rural Telephone Service Co.*, 499 U.S. 340). In 1997, another widely noted court decision went against the compilers of databases: the Eleventh Circuit denied copyright protection to *The Television & Cable Factbook*, a large compilation of factual information. The Supreme Court declined to review that case (*Warren Publishing v. Microdos Data Corp.*, 115 F.3d 1509). However, the Copyright Act still protects a compilation of facts when it is an *original* selection and arrangement of facts, even if all of the underlying facts were obtained from public records that are available to all. Someone else could do another compilation, of course, using the same underlying facts. A mere listing of all of the facts (a printout of the information on every gravestone in a cemetery, for example) is not copyrightable.

In addition to facts, another thing that cannot be copyrighted is a word or short phrase, including the words that constitute *trademarks* and *service marks*. As will be explained later, they may be protected under state and federal trademark registration laws, but they cannot be copyrighted. You cannot be sued for copyright infringement for mentioning someone's trademark in a book or news story, for example. However, you may face a trademark infringement lawsuit if you wrongfully exploit a protected trademark as if it were your own. Within the limits of libel law, you can write anything you like about a product with a registered trademark such as Coca-Cola, but you cannot make soft drinks and call them Coca-Cola.

Securing a Copyright

Once you have a creative work that is eligible for copyright, obtaining copyright protection is easy. Basically, copyright protection is automatic: you don't have to do anything to copyright a work once it is *fixed in a tangible medium of expression*. You can *register* the copyright, and you should put a *copyright notice* in the work. However, the failure to do those things does not cause you to forfeit your copyright.

Although it is no longer mandatory, you normally announce to the world that your work is copyrighted by inserting a notice in a prominent place that says the work is copyrighted. The notice says something like this: "Copyright © 2011 by J.J. Author." The © is a standard symbol to indicate that a work is copyrighted.

The 1976 Copyright Act was amended in 1988 to make it far more flexible regarding the insertion of this copyright notice. Under the 1909 version of the Copyright Act, the failure to include the notice—or even putting it in the wrong place—generally meant forfeiture of copyright protection. Under the 1988 amendments to the 1976 Act, there was a complete liberalization of the rules on inserting copyright notices. Now even if you should fail to insert the notice, your copyright is valid, although innocent infringers (those who do not know the work is copyrighted) have some legal protection until they are notified of the copyright.

For full copyright protection, it is also desirable to register the copyright. You are still required to register the copyright before filing any lawsuit against an infringer, and if you register within 90 days of publishing the work—or at least *before* an infringement occurs—you have better legal protection than you would otherwise.

What happens to a work if you do not insert the copyright notice or register the copyright? You still have a valid copyright, but you must notify any infringer that the work is copyrighted. Of course, if you choose not to claim copyright protection, the work falls into the *public domain*. That means the work belongs to everyone, and anyone who wishes may reproduce or perform it as if he or she owned the copyright.

How do you register a copyright? First, you secure the proper forms from the U.S. Copyright Office from its website, www.copyright.gov. For most works that are primarily text, you will need Form TX. For serial publications (newspapers, magazines, etc.), use Form SE. For sound recordings, Form SR is required. For films, broadcast works and the like, request Form PA. For visual arts works, Form VA is required. The Copyright Office also has a free package of copyright information that will be sent on request or can be downloaded.

To complete registration, you fill out the forms (either electronically or in paper), pay the prescribed fee and send in one or in some cases two copies of the work to be deposited in the Library of Congress. There are some exceptions to this deposit requirement for bulky works such as motion pictures and certain works of art. Copyright registration fees changed in 2009. The Copyright Office implemented a three-tiered pricing system: $35 for registration of a basic claim to copyright filed electronically (no change in price); $50 for registration using Form CO, which is filled out online, printed with barcodes that contain application information, and then mailed in (up from $45); and $65 for registration with traditional paper forms without barcodes (up from $45).

You have to complete these steps for each edition you want to register. Some critics of the system have argued that the deposit requirement allows the Library of Congress to acquire most of the major works published in America—for free. Some have unsuccessfully challenged the validity of the deposit system in court.

Focus on...
Harry Potter goes to court!

The wildly popular Harry Potter series, by British author J.K. Rowling, has been the subject of several lawsuits.

In 2008, Steven Vander Ark's website, *Harry Potter Lexicon,* was held to have infringed Rowling's copyright. But many thought that Judge Robert Patterson correctly balanced the issues in the fair use arena. Specifically, Vander Ark's site copied *verbatim* large parts of Rowling's copyrighted work, so much that the work could not be said to be transformative. Had the *Lexicon* been more transformative, the judge said, Vander Ark might have won.

FIG. 31. Reading book 7 of the Harry Potter series.

retro_writer, "harry potter," August 4, 2007 via Flickr, Creative Commons attribution license.

In another case, Warner Bros. sued a Bollywood (the Hindi-language film industry in Mumbai, India) movie named *Hari Puttar: A Comedy of Terrors.* An Indian court threw out the case because it said the public would be able to differentiate between the two films (*Hari Puttar's* plot is more like *Home Alone*). And "Hari" is a popular Indian name and "puttar" means "son" in Punjabi.

In 2011, a federal district court dismissed a copyright claim by the estate of an author alleging that *Harry Potter and the Goblet of Fire,* the fourth book of the series, infringed on a 1987 book entitled *The Adventures of Willy the Wizard – No 1 Livid Land (Allen v. Scholastic Inc.,* 739 F. Supp. 2d 642). The court said no reasonable jury could find substantial similarity between the books (for example, Willy wears "a hoop earring, a floor length tunic, pointy Aladdin-type shoes, and a bent, cone-shaped hat" and Harry is a "'skinny boy of fourteen' with large round glasses, 'bright green eyes and untidy black hair'").

By dropping the mandatory registration requirement, the Copyright Act legalized a practice that had become commonplace: merely inserting the copyright notice without doing anything further unless an infringement occurs. The new law legitimized this practice by eliminating copyright registration as a precondition to the validity of a copyright. However, registering either within 90 days of publication or before an infringement occurs still gives you more legal remedies than you would have if you do not register until later, and you still must register before suing an infringer. Registering a copyright also has other advantages. For example, a copyright must be registered before U.S. Customs will stop infringing goods from being imported. Also, registration creates a rebuttable presumption that the facts in the registration statement are true (i.e, anyone who challenges the validity of a registered copyright bears the burden of proving that the facts are not true). Even if a copyright isn't registered, the *deposit* requirement still applies, with fines and other penalties awaiting those who fail to send the Copyright Office the required copies (usually two)—if they get caught.

In 2010, the Copyright Office issued an interim rule regarding mandatory deposit of electronic works published in the U.S. and available only online. These works are exempt from mandatory deposit until the Copyright Office issues a demand for them. Also in 2010, Congress passed, and President Obama signed, the Copyright Cleanup, Clarification, and Corrections Act, which increased the use of electronic communication at the Copyright Office and allowed Copyright Royalty Board decisions to be judicially reviewed. It also eliminated dated clauses in the Copyright Act and applied the phonorecord exemption to all pre-1978 records, amending the law to read "The distribution before January 1, 1978, of a phonorecord shall not for any purpose constitute a publication of *any musical work, dramatic work, or literary work* embodied therein."

Remedies for Infringements

Copyright protection would mean little if the law had no enforcement provisions. Thus, the Copyright Act provides a variety of legal remedies for copyright owners to use against infringers. When a copyright *is* registered, the remedies available include the right to seek an injunction (a court order to stop the infringement), a court order to impound all pirated copies, court-ordered payment of the copyright owner's attorney's fees by the infringer, and either actual or statutory damages. Owners of unregistered copyrights retain some (but not all) of these rights, as will be explained shortly.

In 1994, the Supreme Court ruled that the provision for attorney's fees cuts both ways: both plaintiffs (those who sue, claiming that someone infringed their copyright) and defendants (those sued for copyright infringement) can ask the court to order the other side to pay their attorney's fees if they win. That ruling came in *Fogerty v. Fantasy* (510 U.S. 517), the case in which singer John Fogerty was sued by his former manager and music publisher, who claimed that Fogerty's new songs were so similar to his older songs that they infringed the copyrights on the older songs (which were owned by the publisher). Fogerty won the case, and the Supreme Court said the trial court could order the publisher to pay Fogerty's attorney's fees. A trial court later awarded Fogerty over $1.3 million in attorney's fees, and that ruling was upheld by an appellate court in 1996 (*Fogerty v. Fantasy*, 94 F.3d 553).

Statutory damages are an arbitrary sum of money a court may award when actual damages (i.e., the infringer's net profits) are hard to prove or nominal (perhaps because the infringer made little or no profit). Congress increased the amount of statutory damages by 50 percent in 1999. Now the damages for each infringement may range from $750 to $30,000 at the judge's discretion, although awards as low as $300 are authorized for innocent infringements, with amounts as high as $150,000 permitted in a flagrantly intentional infringement.

In an important interpretation of the Copyright Act in 1998, the Supreme Court ruled that the defendant has a constitutional right to a jury trial in copyright infringement lawsuits seeking statutory as well as actual damages (*Feltner v. Columbia Pictures Television*, 523 U.S. 340). Previously, statutory damage cases were decided by judges without a jury.

Of course, if the infringer made a great deal of money, the copyright owner would seek actual damages rather than statutory damages.

When a copyright is unregistered at the time of an infringement, the copyright owner may still seek remedies. First, however, he/she must register the copyright, following the procedures described earlier. Only then may a lawsuit for copyright infringement be initiated. After registering the copyright, the owner may sue the infringer for actual damages—but not statutory damages. He or she may also seek an injunction or court-ordered impoundment of the pirated copies, but not attorney's fees.

Nevertheless, the viability of an unregistered copyright should not be overlooked. Actual damages alone can be a substantial deterrent because of the manner in which they are calculated. To collect actual damages, the copyright owner sues for both his or her losses and the infringer's gross profits. The infringer then must prove all of his or her expenses in order to get them deducted from that gross profit figure. Thus, actual damages are supposed to take away all of the net profit from an infringement.

However, this provision can be so harsh to an infringer that courts have been known to refuse to enforce it fully. For instance, there was a famous 1940 U.S. Supreme Court decision involving a pirated script that was made into a major-studio motion picture, complete with high-priced promotion and big-name stars.

After deducting all costs, the profits for the movie (*Letty Lynton*, starring Joan Crawford and Nils Asther) came to nearly $600,000—a very large sum for the time. A trial court complied with the Copyright Act and awarded that full amount to the author of the pirated script. However, the Supreme Court set aside the provisions of the Copyright Act and apportioned the profits, awarding the author only about $120,000. Much of the profit was attributable to factors other than the script, the high court held (*Sheldon v. MGM*, 309 U.S. 390).

Despite the *Sheldon* decision, large actual damage awards do occur. Moreover, the infringer could face criminal sanctions. The law was designed to make copyright infringements painful and expensive, whether the copyrighted work is registered or not.

Can a plaintiff bring a copyright infringement suit after he/she has submitted an application, or does the plaintiff have to wait until the Copyright Office issues a certificate of registration? The Ninth Circuit in 2010 said that submission is enough in *Cosmetic Ideas, Inc. v. IAC/Interactivecorp* (606 F.3d 612). Cosmetic Ideas submitted an application for a copyright for a necklace design and then brought suit against IAC/Interactive Corp. for infringement. The district court dismissed; the Ninth Circuit reversed. Noting that the circuits have split on this question (the Fifth and Seventh allow suits at application, while the Tenth and Eleventh say that the certificate must be issued), the court said that the statute mandates that registration is to be dated as of the date of application, not of approval. Thus the court held that the receipt by the Copyright Office of a complete application satisfies the registration requirement, agreeing with the Fifth and Seventh Circuits. The Supreme Court often grants *cert* in areas where the circuits are divided, so this issue is ripe for the Court to take.

protectible elements:
elements of a work that can be copyrighted; does not include elements like facts, common measures, and the like.

scènes à faire:
French for "scene to be done," scenes that are so customary in the genre of work that it is expected that they will be there; e.g., in a western, a saloon scene with a flirtatious female server.

Proving an Infringement

Suppose someone publishes a work that you feel was pirated from a similar work that you created. What can you do about it?

As already pointed out, there are many remedies available if you sue the infringer and win your lawsuit. But to win a copyright infringement lawsuit, there are several things you have to prove. One is that the alleged infringer had some access to your work. Another is that there is substantial similarity between the two works. And, of course, you have to prove that your copyright is valid in that it covers a legitimate, original work.

In the case of a *verbatim* copy of a copyrighted work, proving these things is usually not difficult, but what happens if the infringer was skillful enough to modify the original work? At that point, you must prove there is substantial similarity between your work and the allegedly infringing work—and that is not always easy. Where literary works are involved, authorities on literature are sometimes brought in as expert witnesses to testify about the subtle similarities of plot, character development and theme. For the substantial similarity test to be met, there must be similarity in the specific expressive elements of the two works (including plot, themes, dialogue, mood, setting, characters and sequence of events). The Ninth Circuit calls this the *extrinsic test* for similarity, an objective test. In addition, the Ninth Circuit has said the works must be substantially similar under a more subjective *intrinsic test*, which considers whether an ordinary, reasonable audience would find the works substantially similar in total concept and feel. In 2004, the Sixth Circuit used the extrinsic-intrinsic analysis in a Michigan case, *Murray Hill Publications v. Twentieth Century Fox Film Corp.* (361 F.3d 312). In a case involving singer Mariah Carey's 1999 song, "Thank God I Found You," the Ninth Circuit in 2004 ruled that in music, the extrinsic test for similarity involves analyzing such elements as chord progression, key, tempo, rhythm and genre, not just comparing melodies (*Swirsky v. Carey*, 376 F.3d 841). The court said there was enough similarity between the chorus of Carey's song and an earlier song by Seth Swirsky and Warryn Campbell that they could take their lawsuit against Carey to trial.

Some federal courts have taken a less specific approach in judging substantial similarity, following the lead of the Second Circuit, which has evaluated substantial similarity by determining "(a) that defendant copied from plaintiff's copyrighted work and (b) that the copying... went so far as to constitute improper appropriation" (*Arnstein v. Porter*, 154 F.2d 464, 1946).

Under either analysis of substantial similarity between two works, there must be proof of similarity of the *protectible elements*, not just the underlying historical facts—which cannot be copyrighted. For example, if someone made a new movie about the 1912 sinking of the ocean liner Titanic, it could include the same historical characters and events depicted in the James Cameron movie *Titanic*. It could *not* use characters and plot lines substantially similar to the fictitious aspects of the film, such as the story of the aristocratic Rose DeWitt Bukater falling in love with the free-spirited artist Jack Dawson and fleeing her arrogant, wealthy fiancé, Cal Hockley.

For example, the Ninth Circuit applied the extrinsic test for determining substantial similarity in *Benay v. Warner Bros. Entertainment* (607 F.3d 620), saying that Warner Bros. had not infringed the copyright of two brothers' screenplay in the movie *The Last Samurai*—despite the fact that the movie and the screenplay had the same title and shared many of the same plot elements. The court said that although the plot elements were similar, the stories were different, and generally plot ideas are not copyrightable; they "remain forever the common property of artistic mankind." Plot ideas, then, are not protectible elements.

Sometimes there is only one way to depict something, and then a copyright owner who claims an infringement may have to prove that a later work is not just similar but virtually identical. For example, in 2003 a federal appeals court ruled that a photograph of a vodka bottle that was used in an advertising campaign did not infringe the copyright on an earlier and obviously similar advertising photograph of the vodka bottle. The court applied the *merger* doctrine, which holds that a work will not be protected from infringement unless a later work is virtually identical when the underlying idea of the work can be expressed in only one way, resulting in a merger of the idea and the copyrighted work. The court also cited the *scènes à faire* doctrine, which holds that a work is not protected if the expression embodied in the work necessarily flows from a common idea—in this case an image of a vodka bottle for advertising (*Ets-Hokin v. Skyy Spirits Inc.*, 323 F.3d 763).

After all of this legal analysis of what constitutes substantial similarity is completed, the original copyright owner ultimately has to convince a judge or jury that the *average* person (not just an expert) would see the new work as similar enough to have been pirated from the original.

Not only is substantial similarity sometimes difficult to prove when a pirated work is not an exact copy of the original, but there can be problems in proving access to the original work. If someone who has never seen nor heard of your copyrighted work creates a similar work or even an identical one, that is not a copyright infringement. If you cannot prove the alleged infringer had some opportunity to learn of your work, you can't prove he or she copied it. If the second work is truly an independent creation by someone who had no access to your original work, he or she can copyright it and go into business reproducing and selling it, as far as copyright law is concerned. (However, he or she may have other legal problems in the unfair competition and trademark areas, to be discussed shortly).

Given the pervasiveness of the media and the Internet today, though, it is rare for creative persons to be able to prove that they had no access to any earlier published work that is substantially similar to theirs. For example, musician George Harrison spent several years in court trying to prove that his 1971 hit song, "My Sweet Lord," was not copied from "He's So Fine," a 1963 song that a group called the Chiffons made into a big hit on the charts (*Bright Tunes Music Corp. v. Harrisongs Music, Ltd.*, 420 F.Supp. 177, 1976). The two songs have virtually the same melody, but Harrison vehemently argued that he was not familiar with the earlier song and had no intention whatever to plagiarize it. In the end, a court ruled that he could not have avoided hearing the earlier song at some time or other, and that he must have been inspired by its catchy tune, *at least at the subconscious level*. (Ironically, during a contract dispute with Harrison, his former managers purchased the rights to "He's So Fine."

Because of his managers' resulting conflict of interest, a court later required Harrison to pay only a small penalty and then awarded him the ownership rights to both "My Sweet Lord" and "He's So Fine" in several countries!)

In 2008, Joe Satriani, a guitarist who played with Mick Jagger, filed suit against British group Coldplay for alleged copyright violations in Coldplay's song "Viva La Vida." Satriani claimed that "Viva La Vida" infringed on his 2004 song "If I Could Fly." He has asked for a jury trial and is requesting all profits from the alleged infringement—which could be significant, given the success of Coldplay's album *Viva La Vida or Death and All His Friends,* which was 2008's bestselling album, selling 6.8 million copies worldwide. Coldplay's response? They said Satriani didn't write the melody either and said that "If I Could Fly" "lacks originality" and should not be copyrighted. In 2009 the case was settled and dismissed *with prejudice,* which means that Satriani cannot bring the suit again.

How do you prove that your work is independently created and original when you plan to submit it to someone else for possible publication? How do you prevent an editor, for instance, from taking the work and using it without payment? There are various ways to amass evidence that could be used in court to prove your original authorship, should a lawsuit be necessary. The classic advice was to mail a copy to yourself before submitting the work to anyone else, retaining the copy in the sealed (and postmarked) envelope. However, the 1976 Copyright Act provided a much more dependable approach: you may now copyright the unpublished work under federal law and register it with the U.S. Copyright Office. Then your copyright is protected, prior to the work's submission to anyone who might be tempted to claim it as his or her own. It is far better to register the copyright than to merely mail yourself a copy and keep it in a sealed envelope.

The Fifth Circuit said that a defendant could not raise the "innocent infringer" defense, saying that copyright notices appear on CDs, and that the defendant's "reliance on her own understanding of copyright law—or lack thereof—is irrelevant" (*Maverick Recording Co. v. Harper,* 598 F.3d 193). Whitney Harper, who was 16 at the time of the infringement, testified that she thought that downloading files was just like listening to an Internet radio station. The court awarded the statutory damages of $750 per song (37 in total).

The Duration of Copyrights

The duration of copyright protection has been extended repeatedly. As noted earlier, U.S. copyrights were originally valid for 14 years and could be renewed for another 14. In 1831, Congress extended the term to 28 years, renewable for 14 more. Under the 1909 Copyright Act, copyrights were valid for 28 years and could be renewed for another 28 years. The 1976 Copyright Act extended the basic term of a copyright to the author's life plus 50 years. For works created anonymously or for hire, the term was extended to 75 years from the date of publication. For unpublished "works made for hire" and for unpublished anonymous or pseudonymous works, the term was set at 100 years from the year of creation by the 1976 act.

In 1998, Congress added 20 more years to all of these copyright terms in the Sonny Bono Copyright Term Extension Act. Therefore, the basic term now is the author's life plus 70 years, or 95 years for works created anonymously or for hire, which means most corporate copyrights are valid for 95 years. Unpublished works made for hire or created anonymously are now protected for 120 years from the year of creation. The 20-year extension applies retroactively to all works created after Jan. 1, 1978 as well as to new works. Copyrights now expire on Dec. 31 of the expiration year.

How do these extensions of copyright periods affect works copyrighted earlier? For pre-1978 works that still held a valid copyright when the 1998 law went into effect, the term was extended to 95 years from the original copyright date by granting automatic 67-year renewals to most of these works when their original 28-year term expires. The 1998 act did not restore copyright protection to many works that had fallen into the public domain.

The Congressional action to extend copyright terms once again in 1998 was surprisingly controversial. Although the extension brought U.S. law into line with that of many European countries, it was vigorously opposed by a coalition of law professors, librarians and others who felt it would unduly deny future generations of creative persons the right to adapt and expand upon established works by imposing an excessive delay before copyrighted works fall into the public domain. They questioned whether allowing a copyright to run for 70 years beyond the author's lifetime instead of 50 would really encourage authors to do more or better work. But on the other hand, they contended, the term extension had a serious downside, preventing others from doing *derivative works* (new works based on older works) for 20 more years. To buttress their argument, they pointed to the U.S. Constitution, which authorized Congress to establish copyright protection only for *limited times*. Is 120 years—or even 95 years—what the framers of the Constitution meant by limited times?

In response to these arguments, the recording industry and other copyright owners contended that creative works should not fall into the public domain while they are still popular. They pointed out that many songs had been falling into the public domain that were still widely performed. Foes of still longer copyright terms replied that even popular works *should* become everyone's property *someday*, and that the framers of the Constitution never intended for that "someday" to be 95 or 120 years later.

Eventually the coalition opposed to extending copyright terms challenged the constitutionality of the Sonny Bono Act. The Supreme Court upheld the Bono Act in *Eldred v. Ashcroft* (537 U.S. 186), a 2003 case. The Court's 7-2 majority declared that extending copyrights by another 20 years, so that many last 95 years or longer, did not violate either the First Amendment or the constitutional provision for limited copyright terms. The decision was a victory for movie studios, publishers, record labels and others who own the most valuable copyrights. It was a defeat for historians, journalists, and librarians who need access to older copyrighted works.

Writing for the majority, Justice Ruth Bader Ginsburg rejected the argument that the repeated extension of copyright terms by Congress violated the "limited times" provision of the Constitution by creating perpetual copyrights. "Those earlier acts did not create

Creative Commons licenses:

Attribution (by) lets others distribute, remix, tweak, and build upon your work, even commercially, as long as they credit you for the original creation.

Attribution Share Alike (by-sa) lets others remix, tweak, and build upon your work even for commercial reasons, as long as they credit you and license their new creations under the identical terms.

Attribution No Derivatives (by nd) allows for redistribution, commercial and non-commercial, as long as it is passed along unchanged and in whole, with credit to you.

Attribution Non-commercial (by-nc) lets others remix, tweak, and build upon your work non-commercially, and although their new works must also acknowledge you and be non-commercial, they don't have to license their derivative works on the same terms.

All definitions are from the Creative Commons website: creativecommons.org perpetual copyrights, and neither does the [Bono Act]," she wrote. Perhaps even more important, Ginsburg rejected the idea that the monopoly created by copyrights violates the First Amendment. She noted that the copyright clause and the First Amendment were written within a few years of each other and concluded that the framers of the Constitution did not intend for the free-expression provisions of the First Amendment to limit copyrights. In essence, Ginsburg said that copyright laws are generally exempt from First Amendment scrutiny.

Justices John Paul Stevens and Stephen Breyer dissented. Stevens criticized the majority for "failing to protect the public interest" and "ignoring the central purpose of the copyright/patent clause." Breyer said the term extension "will likely inhibit new forms of dissemination through the use of technology." He added, "I cannot find any constitutionally legitimate, copyright-related way in which the statute will benefit the public."

Many of those who challenged the extension of copyright terms in the *Eldred* case are affiliated with Creative Commons, a worldwide non-profit organization that is seeking to establish a large body of creative works for others to build upon and share. Its founding chair was Stanford Law School professor Lawrence Lessig, who argued the case against copyright term extensions at the Supreme Court (see www.creativecommons.org). Many of the images in this book are licensed with Creative Commons licenses via the image-sharing sites Flickr or Wikimedia Commons. Other images are from the U.S. government; these images are not entitled to copyright protection under the Copyright Act.

In 2007, the Ninth Circuit followed up the *Eldred* case by rejecting an appeal by librarians and archivists to roll back the copyright term extensions for out-of-print works and other older works whose copyright owners cannot be located (*Kahle v. Gonzales*, 487 F.3d 697). The Supreme Court declined to hear an appeal in 2008.

The Copyright Owner's Exclusive Rights

Once there is a copyright, the owner has a variety of property rights that are protected by federal law. First of all, the copyright owner has the exclusive right to reproduce the work and sell copies. In addition, the copyright owner may abridge, expand, revise or rearrange the copyrighted work. And the copyright owner has the right to perform or display the copyrighted work. The owner also has the exclusive right to create derivative works based on a previous copyrighted work (for instance, a novelization of a motion picture or a movie script based on a novel). The owner can sell (or give away) any or all of these rights. In practice, many creators of copyrighted works sell their rights to corporations that agree to publish or distribute a work and pay the creator a portion of the income from the work as *royalties*.

The creator of a work may also make arrangements that amount to renting out the work by allowing someone else to use the work temporarily in return for royalties. Granting first North American serial rights to a magazine allows the author to earn royalties for an article's initial publication while retaining ownership of the copyright. That allows the author to use the work in a later anthology, for instance. As explained later in this chapter, the republication of printed works in electronic form (by posting them on the Internet or an information service such as Lexis-Nexis, for example) has created new copyright questions. Many publishers routinely republished works in electronic form under contracts granting North American serial rights without paying additional royalties. By 2000, court decisions forced publishers to rewrite contracts to cover the republication of works in electronic form.

In some of the performing arts areas, it is also commonplace to give others the right to arrange and perform a work in return for the payment of royalties. In fact, the law requires those who own the copyrights to musical works to grant anyone permission to make *sound recordings* (i.e., CDs and tapes) of their music once it has been publicly performed. This is called *compulsory licensing*. The recording artist merely pays the prescribed royalties for each copy of the recording that is sold; the copyright owner cannot allow one performer to record a song while denying that right to others. The amount of these royalties is specified in the Copyright Act, although copyright owners sometimes agree to lower royalties to encourage well-known artists to record their songs. Those who record copyrighted music under the compulsory licensing provision of the Copyright Act must perform it essentially as written; they cannot normally make major changes without the consent of the copyright owner.

There is no similar compulsory licensing system for most other kinds of copyrighted works, such as written materials, audiovisual works and works of art. Nor does the compulsory license apply to *synchronization rights* (the process of combining music with the visual images in a movie or video). The producer must get specific permission to add music to a movie or video—if the copyright owner is willing to grant it. However, the 1976 Copyright Act did establish a compulsory licensing system in one area: cable television. The copyright problems of music and cable television will be discussed more fully later in this chapter.

In the motion picture, television and music industries, incredibly complex business arrangements have been developed to compensate the owners of the many copyrights that go into modern productions. Often there are separate arrangements with the authors of an underlying short story or novel, screenwriters who adapt the work, those who write, arrange and perform the music and lyrics, choreographers and many others. And these arrangements cover a variety of different rights. For example, the producer of a television show obtains (and pays for) the synchronization rights to include music in the show. However, the *performance rights* for the same music are another matter: ordinarily each television station must pay for the performance rights, because the producer does not purchase these rights. Broadcasters would prefer to have *source licensing*—in which the producer of the program obtains the performance rights—but that is not the usual arrangement. Most broadcasters obtain *blanket licenses* from music licensing agencies for all of the copyrighted music they put on the air. All-news and talk radio stations often obtain *per-program licenses*, which are less expensive for stations that air little music.

The case of *Stewart v. Abend* (495 U.S. 207), a 1990 Supreme Court decision, illustrates the great complexity of the copyright arrangements in the entertainment industry. This case involved the right of a group headed by actor Jimmy Stewart to re-release an old movie, *Rear Window*. The problem was that Sheldon Abend had purchased the rights to the short story on which the movie was based from the heirs of the story's author after the author died. The original 28-year term had expired, and the heirs had renewed the copyright (as permitted under the 1909 copyright law, which was in effect when this movie was made). The high court supported Abend's contention that Stewart's group had to negotiate again for the rights to the original story after the copyright renewal. The original sale of the rights to the story was valid only during the first copyright term, the court held.

Lawyers for the major Hollywood studios strenuously objected to this ruling, arguing that it would make it prohibitively expensive to re-release many old movies—or to use old story lines or music in new movies. The Copyright Act now deals with this issue by providing a *derivative works exception*. Under some circumstances, the original author regains ownership of an old copyright when it is renewed, but the owners of derivative works (such as a movie based on a copyrighted story) do not lose their rights when the copyright on the underlying work is renewed and reverts to the original author. However, under the 1976 Copyright Act and more recent laws, copyrights have longer but non-renewable terms.

Current law recognizes *termination rights* for non-renewable copyrights, allowing authors or their heirs to retrieve copyrights that an author might have signed over to a publisher early in life, when he or she had little bargaining power. Post-1978 copyrights may be terminated by authors or their heirs after 35 to 40 years. Copyrights on earlier works now may be retrieved by heirs at various times from 56 to 75 years after the original copyright term began. This aspect of copyright law was widely discussed in 2006 when the son and granddaughter of author John Steinbeck won a federal court ruling that they and not Steinbeck's publisher will eventually control the book publishing rights to novels such as *The Grapes of Wrath* and *Of Mice and Men*.

When a movie's copyright expires and it falls into the public domain, the underlying screenplay usually falls into the public domain as well, according to a federal appellate court decision (*Batjac Productions v. GoodTimes Home Video Corp.*, 160 F.3d 1223, 1998).

"Works Made for Hire"

There are many instances when those who create artistic and literary works sell some or all of their rights to others instead of retaining those rights themselves. Often the author or creator of a work cannot afford to publish it and promote it properly. Thus, he or she makes a deal with a publisher to get the work into print—and in return the publisher asks for an assignment of the copyright. That means the publisher and not the author then owns the copyright to the work.

That is a common arrangement. However, there are some potential hazards in copyright law that may trap unwary creators of copyrighted works. One is the Copyright Act's *works made for hire* provision. The law says that if a person creates a work within the scope of his or her employment, the copyright belongs to the employer, not to the creator of the work. For example, if you are a staff writer for a newspaper, the publisher owns the copyright on the stories you write on the job unless you can negotiate a contract that says otherwise. Any time you create something on the job, that principle applies.

FIG. 32. A selection of Bratz dolls.

Saffy, "Goodbye Girls!" June 15, 2009 via Flickr, Creative Commons attribution license.

Few people would question the fairness of that part of the "works made for hire" rule, but what about writers and others who do freelance work? What about the composer who accepts a commission to write the score for a new musical production? In many cases the law presumes that such a person is not creating a "work made for hire." However, there can be questions about whether a person is actually an employee or a freelancer. Also, contracts offered by publishers and others who buy creative works are often written to offset this presumption. If your contract says you are doing a "work made for hire," someone else may end up owning all rights to your creative efforts rather than just the first reprint or performance rights you intended.

In 1989 the Supreme Court ruled on the "works made for hire" provision of the Copyright Act in the case of *Community for Creative Non-Violence v. Reid* (490 U.S. 730). The court had to deal with a situation not uncommon among freelancers, including writers, photographers, artists and composers. In many instances freelancers agree to produce a work on assignment without having a clear arrangement for copyright ownership. Under the Copyright Act's "works made for hire" provision, such works are presumed to belong to the creator if he or she is truly *independent* but not if the person is more like an employee than an independent contractor. The Court ruled that if the creator of a work is an independent contractor as that term is normally defined in other areas of law, he or she is entitled to the copyright—unless the creator and whoever commissioned the work have a contract that says otherwise.

Some copyright experts considered the Supreme Court's test for independent contractor status to be so liberal that many media corporations reassessed their policies on copyright ownership. The court seemingly tipped the scales in favor of those who create works in freelance situations. Many freelance works that corporations assumed they owned may now legally belong to the original creator instead.

The *Reid* case involved a dispute between James Earl Reid and Community for Creative Non-Violence (CCNV), an organization that commissioned Reid to do a sculpture for display at a Christmas pageant in Washington, D.C. His sculpture, entitled "Third World America," depicted a homeless family sleeping on a grate in a street. CCNV contended that because it contracted with Reid to do the sculpture, supervised his work, and then paid him, he was really an employee and therefore CCNV owned the copyright to the sculpture. Reid contended that he owned the copyright—and therefore had the right to profit from reproductions of the sculpture.

The Court ruled that Reid retained the copyright. The language suggested that those not on an organization's regular payroll almost always retain the ownership of works they create unless there is a contract that spells out some other arrangement. The crucial factor in the entire "works made for hire" area of copyright law at this point appears to be the contract between the freelance creator and the person who commissions the work and pays for it. If the contract clearly says who owns the copyright, that contract is enforceable. If, however, the contract is vague or silent about copyright ownership, or if there isn't any contract, the law will presume that the freelance creator owns the copyright. This does not affect works created by employees rather than freelancers: an employer still owns an employee's job-related creative endeavors unless there is a contract that gives copyright ownership to the employee.

In 2000, a widely publicized dispute between recording artists and record labels illustrated some of the pitfalls and complexities of the "works made for hire" provision of the

Copyright Act. A member of Congress who had many recording industry executives among his constituents quietly inserted a provision into a federal budget bill adding sound recordings to the list of works that could be works made for hire. When several well-known recording artists found out about it, they cried foul. The Copyright Act says an "author" who transfers ownership of a copyright to someone else has the right to cancel that transfer after 35 to 40 years in many cases, thus retrieving ownership of the copyright. However, those termination rights do not apply to works made for hire.

Because recording artists, like authors, routinely sign contracts that transfer copyrights on their works to a publisher (or in this case, a record label), that provision gives them a chance to recover their copyrights much later in life, when they and their works may have become famous and their copyrights valuable assets. But the law said only the "author" of a work has the right to retrieve the copyright. Congress responded to the public outcry by quickly deleting sound recordings from the list of works that can be works made for hire.

Barbies or Bratz? In a hotly contested series of cases, Mattel initially won a large judgment ($100 million) against MGA Entertainment, the company that makes the pouty-lipped Bratz dolls. Mattel had successfully argued that Carter Bryant, the designer of the Bratz dolls, invented them while he was still working for Mattel. A federal court judge ordered MGA to stop selling, manufacturing, advertising or licensing the dolls or any other product with the Bratz name and banned MGA from using the Bratz name. The Ninth Circuit at the end of 2009 offered MGA a reprieve, staying the order and allowing the company to sell the dolls until it could rule on the appeal.

And when the court did rule, it gave the win to Bryant (*Mattel, Inc. v. MGA Entm't, Inc.*, 616 F.3d 904, 2010). "It is not equitable to transfer this billion dollar brand—the value of which is overwhelmingly the result of MGA's legitimate efforts—because it may have started with two misappropriated names," said the court, remanding the case to trial. In that 2011 trial, the jury awarded Bryant $88.4 million, saying that Mattel may have misappropriated trade secrets from MGA. Will Mattel appeal? It seems fair to think it will—stay tuned.

Federal Copyright Law Preemption

One of the most significant changes in copyright law that resulted from the passage of the 1976 Copyright Act is that now both published and unpublished works are protected under the federal system. Previously, the federal law protected only published works, leaving unpublished materials protected only by the varying state laws that developed from what was called *common law copyright.*

That meant there were different rules and sometimes two different copyright offices with which to deal because some states set up their own registration systems to protect the copyright on unpublished works.

That dual system of state and federal copyright protection also caused both state and federal courts to stretch their definitions of the word "published" to protect authors. If someone handed out 100 copies of a short story to friends or potential publishers, was it published? If the author remembered to put in the copyright notice, federal courts tended to rule that it was published so the federal copyright system could be used to protect the work from would-be infringers. But if, on the other hand, the author failed to insert the notice, the work would fall into the public domain if "published." Thus, state courts tended to bend the rules to find that such works were really unpublished so they could provide common law copyright protection to otherwise unprotected authors.

The 1976 law eliminated this double standard for new works. As soon as a work is *fixed in a tangible medium of expression*, it is protected by the federal law. This means that as soon as a work is written down on paper, saved on a computer disk, recorded on film or tape, or placed almost anywhere else outside the creator's mind, it can be copyrighted under the federal law. One need not wait until the work is published to secure protection—federal copyright protection is immediately available. To secure this protection, you merely include a copyright notice in the draft of the work—and you may register the unpublished work if you want the strongest possible protection. But even without the copyright notice, under 1988 amendments to the Copyright Act the author is protected from all but innocent infringers.

In short, the 1976 Copyright Act completely abolished the state common law copyright system for works published after January 1, 1978 (the effective date for the 1976 law). For new works, state laws relating to copyrights were *preempted*. That is, all such laws were superseded by the federal law and ceased to be valid for new works. Congress always had the authority to abolish state common law copyright protection and assume complete jurisdiction in this field; in the 1976 Copyright Act Congress finally did so, thus simplifying the American copyright system.

However, a 2005 decision of New York's highest court illustrated that common law copyright is still a powerful tool for controlling some earlier works. In *Capitol Records v. Naxos of America* (4 N.Y.3d 540), the New York Court of Appeals held that sound recordings made before federal copyright law was amended in 1972 to cover recordings are still protected by New York's common law copyright—and will be protected until the year 2067! The court said several performances by world-renowned classical musicians that were recorded in England in the 1930s are still protected by New York's common law, even though they have been in the public domain in England since the 1980s. Under English copyright law in effect then, recordings were protected for 50 years, a vastly shorter term than the 135-year term the New York seemingly established for one recording made in England in 1932. The New York court sent the case to a federal court to reconsider other issues, but the ruling was a major defeat for Naxos, a company that digitally re-masters and re-releases old classical works in the public domain. Naxos is free to sell these re-mastered classical works in England—or anywhere else where they are in the public domain, but apparently not in New York and other states that may follow New York's lead.

Can state law claims be preempted by federal copyright law if the rights asserted under them are equivalent to exclusive rights of copyright holders? The Ninth Circuit addressed that question in 2011 sitting *en banc* in the case of *Montz v. Pilgrim Films & Television* (649 F.3d 975). Plaintiffs Larry Montz and Daena Smoller approached NBC Universal and the Sci-Fi (now Syfy) Channel with an idea for a reality television show featuring "paranormal investigators." The companies were not interested but several years later Syfy came out with the show *Ghost Hunters*. Montz and Smoller sued in state court for breach of implied contract and breach of confidence.

A panel of the Ninth Circuit said that the state claims were equivalent to copyright claims, but the *en banc* court vacated that decision, saying that "copyright law does not preempt a contract claim where plaintiff alleges a bilateral expectation that he would be compensated for use of the idea." The Copyright Act preempts state claims where the work "come[s] within the subject matter of copyright" and the state law grants "legal or equitable rights that are equivalent to any of the exclusive rights within the general scope of copyright." The Supreme Court declined to grant *cert.*

■ THE FAIR USE DOCTRINE

If there were no exceptions to the hard and fast rules of copyright law, no journalist, historian or teacher could do his or her job very well. No one could quote even one sentence from a copyrighted work for the purposes of teaching, scholarly criticism or even reporting the news. Because of these problems, the *fair use doctrine* exists—and creates a major exception to the copyright rules.

Basically, the fair use doctrine is a legal concept that was originally created by the courts to allow some copying of copyrighted works in spite of the seemingly absolute rules against it in the 1909 Copyright Act. The courts recognized that such things as quoting brief passages for scholarly criticism or satire were reasonable and did not interfere with the copyright owner's financial return.

The 1976 Copyright Act specifically recognized the fair use doctrine and established guidelines for determining which uses of copyrighted works are fair ones. Congress even addressed the tough issue of photocopying and attempted to establish some basic rules in that area. To decide if a given use of a copyrighted work is a fair use, the Copyright Act says these four factors must be considered:

1. The *purpose and character of the use*, including whether it is for profit or for a nonprofit educational purpose;
2. The *nature of the copyrighted work*;
3. The *amount and substantiality of the use*;
4. The *effect the use will have on the value* or profit-making potential of the original work.

This four-part test is vague and general; it often takes a court decision to determine whether a given use of copyrighted material is an illegal copyright infringement or a legal fair use. To clarify some of the resulting uncertainties, there have been several voluntary agreements between representatives of copyright owners and various other interests (such as education) on what constitutes a fair use.

For instance, as Congress was completing its revision of copyright law in 1976, representatives of educators, authors and publishers met to decide what would constitute a fair use of a copyrighted work in a classroom. Under their agreement, teachers are permitted to photocopy as much as a chapter of a book, an article from a newspaper or magazine, a short story, an essay or poem, and charts, graphs, drawings or similar materials—but only for their own use. Showing a DVD that is only licensed for home use, much less a pirated copy, is not a fair use.

During the 1990s another issue involving classroom copying became controversial: the use of course packages in college classes. In 1991 a federal court ruled that Kinko's Graphics, a major producer of these course packets, had to pay royalties for virtually all of the copyrighted materials (such as magazine or journal articles and book chapters) included in these custom anthologies of previously published materials (*Basic Books v. Kinko's Graphics Corp.*, 758 F.Supp. 1522). The court held that such large-scale copying was *not* a fair use. The result is that companies and college bookstores charge higher prices for course packets so royalties can be paid to each copyright owner.

Focus on...
My Kindle ate my homework

Amazon.com's hot-selling e-book Kindle is perhaps the book of the future: you're able to download what you want immediately, read it on a non-glare screen, annotate it, and carry thousands of books with you to school, on a trip, or just to the park. And prices are coming down on e-book technology. What's not to like?

Well, if you're high school senior Justin Gawronski, you might not be so happy to turn on your Kindle one day and find that your annotated copies of George Orwell's classics *1984* and *Animal Farm* had been deleted by Amazon—along with your notes. Amazon had gotten a legal notice that it did not have a license to distribute particular editions of those books in the United States, so it simply wirelessly deleted copies on users' Kindles without telling them. In 2009 Gawronski settled with Amazon.com. The court awarded him attorney's fees and established a rule for Amazon's electronic works: customers have a "non-exclusive right to keep a permanent copy" of each work and to view it an unlimited number of times for personal, non-commercial use. Moreover, Amazon has new rules to deal with deletions: the company cannot remotely delete or modify books unless the user consents or requests a refund for the book, or if a judicial order mandates deletion, or if there is a virus or other harm posed by the book (*Gawronski v. Amazon.com, Inc.*, No. 09-CV-01084)

FIG. 33. Amazon's Kindle 2.

Larry Page, "My Kindle 2," Sept. 1, 2009 via Flickr, Creative Commons attribution license.

In 1996, the advocates of free copying for classroom use thought they had won a great victory when the Sixth Circuit refused to follow the *Kinko's* decision in *Princeton University Press v. Michigan Document Services* (74 F.3d 1528). In this case, the court's 2-1 majority seemingly gave teachers and copying services *carte blanche* to copy magazine and journal articles as well as large parts of books for inclusion in course packets by holding that such copying is a fair use, not a copyright infringement.

Armed with this decision, many copying services geared up for a bonanza of royalty-free copying. But then the celebration ended: the full panel of judges sitting on the Sixth Circuit voted to set aside the earlier ruling and rehear the case *en banc* (with all judges participating). The judges then voted 8-5 to overturn the earlier decision and ruled that large-scale copying for course packets is indeed an infringement, not a fair use (*Princeton University Press v. Michigan Document Services*, 99 F.3d 1381).

Another fair use question concerns photocopying by libraries. The Copyright Act is rather specific about this because an important court decision had allowed wholesale reproduction of copyrighted works by libraries—something Congress wished to curtail. That case (*Williams and Wilkins v. U.S.*, 487 F.2d 1345) was initiated by a publishing house whose medical journals were being photocopied on a massive scale by federally funded medical libraries so the libraries could avoid purchasing additional copies. The publishing house lost: in 1973 a federal court said the dissemination of medical knowledge was so important that this copying was a fair use. The case was appealed to the Supreme Court, but because the high court divided 4-4 (with one justice not participating), the judgment of the lower court stood.

Alarmed at the *Williams and Wilkins* case, publishers lobbied in Congress to win restrictions on library photocopying into the 1976 Copyright Act. The result was another compromise, with the rules for photocopying by libraries spelled out in considerable detail. Basically, the law now says it is a fair use for a librarian to make copies of damaged or deteriorating works that cannot be replaced at a reasonable cost, and to provide single copies to those who request them, provided the request is for only a small portion of a work. An entire work that cannot be purchased at a reasonable price may also be copied at a patron's request.

These rules contain other qualifications and restrictions that will not be summarized here. Significantly, however, they apply only to copying done by library staff members, not copying by members of the public who use coin-operated machines. The Copyright Act exempts librarians from liability for copyright infringements by unsupervised library patrons, as long as a warning about infringements is posted near the self-service copy machine.

Obviously, the law on photocopying was written in this fashion in tacit recognition that there is simply no way to prevent private individuals from engaging in coin-operated infringements—just as there is no way to prevent private audio or videotaping of copyrighted materials that are broadcast (a separate problem that is discussed later).

Fair use continues to be an issue with university reserves. In a whopping 350-page decision, a federal district court said that only five of 99 alleged infringements by Georgia State University in its electronic reserves did violate the plaintiffs' copyrights. The judge said in *Cambridge Univ. Press v. Becker* (U.S. Dist. LEXIS 78123, 2012) that the plaintiffs, Cambridge University Press, Oxford University Press, and SAGE Publications, had not demonstrated that they lost significant amounts of money from the electronic reserves after engaging in a case-by-case evaluation of all alleged infringements (hence, the length of the decision). It will take some time to determine what the impact of this case will be on university libraries' electronic reserves policies. "This is a less flexible standard than many libraries would like, I think, and it seems too rigid to be a good fit with the overall structure of fair use," Kevin Smith, scholarly communications officer at Duke University, wrote on his blog. But the court acknowledged what teachers, scholars, and others who wish to use copyrighted materials already know: "The truth is that fair use principles are notoriously difficult to apply."

Fair Use and Historical Events

Many problems have arisen as courts tried to apply the fair use doctrine. One of the most important involves the conflict between copyright law and the public's right to know. Several court decisions have addressed these questions.

One of the best-known tests of the fair use doctrine came in a 1966 federal appellate court decision, *Rosemont Enterprises v. Random House* (366 F.2d 303). In that case, Rosemont (a company set up by billionaire industrialist Howard Hughes) was trying to prevent publication of a biography about Hughes, who intensely disliked publicity.

Rosemont learned that the biographer was relying heavily on information gleaned from several old *Look* magazine articles about Hughes. The company quickly bought the copyright on those articles and then sought an injunction to prevent publication of the new biography as an infringement of the copyrighted articles.

A trial court ruled in Rosemont's favor, but the federal appellate court reversed that decision, holding that a copyright owner has no right to, in effect, copyright history. The appellate court noted that the magazine articles were only a fraction of the length of the book and that there had been extensive independent research for the book. The court brushed aside the argument that the book, like the original copyrighted magazine articles, was aimed at a popular market and was not merely an instance of scholarly criticism (something that earlier court decisions had recognized as a fair use).

Ultimately, the court ruled that there is a legitimate public interest in the doings of the rich and powerful, and that this interest outweighs the copyright consideration in a case such as this one. Random House was allowed to publish its book about Howard Hughes without incurring liability for a copyright infringement.

Another fair use case involving an issue of even greater public interest arose a few years later, *Time Inc. v. Bernard Geis Associates* (293 F.Supp. 130, 1968). That case involved amateur photographer Abraham Zapruder's film of the assassination of President John F. Kennedy in 1963. The highly unusual and revealing film was purchased by Time Inc., and published in *Life* magazine. Of course, it was copyrighted.

Later, author Thomas Thompson was publishing a book advocating a new theory about the assassination, *Six Seconds in Dallas*. Bernard Geis, the publisher, offered to pay *Life* a royalty equal to the entire net profits from the book in return for permission to use *Life's* still photographs made from the copyrighted film, which was central to Thompson's theory. *Life* refused. The book publisher then hired an artist to make charcoal sketches from the copyrighted photographs, and these appeared in the book. Time Inc. sued for copyright infringement. The federal court said the use of charcoal drawings instead of the photographs themselves did not eliminate the copyright infringement, but the court also pointed to the legitimate public interest in the assassination of a president and said this was a fair use of the copyrighted pictures. To rule otherwise would prevent a full public discussion of the controversial issues raised by President Kennedy's assassination.

More recently, the Assassination Records Review Board declared the Zapruder film to be U.S. government property and an arbitration panel ordered the government to pay Zapruder's heirs $16 million for the film. Critics said that sum was outrageous, especially since the government was buying only the physical film, not its copyright. The copyright eventually reverted to the Zapruder family, and the family has been criticized for charging those who need to use the images (documentary filmmakers, historians, journalists) high license fees.

A somewhat similar copyright dispute arose in the late 1990s, when the estate of Dr. Martin Luther King, Jr. sued CBS for using nine minutes of Dr. King's famous 16-minute-long "I Have a Dream" speech in a documentary history of the twentieth century. The estate contended that CBS was guilty of copyright infringement for including the segment. CBS responded by arguing that the speech, which was heard live by an enormous audience and has been quoted widely ever since it was delivered in 1963, is such an important public event that no one should be able to prevent others from using it for journalistic purposes. However, a federal appellate court overturned a judge's decision to dismiss the lawsuit and said the King estate could pursue its claim against the network (*Estate of Martin Luther King v. CBS*, 194 F.3d 1211). The network then settled the case by agreeing to make a donation to the Martin Luther King Center.

Fair Use and Unpublished Works

If President Kennedy's assassination was such an important issue that republishing photographs of it was a fair use, the same cannot be said of publishing previously unpublished excerpts from President Ford's memoirs about his decision to pardon Richard Nixon of all Watergate offenses.

In a case that pitted journalists against authors and book publishers, the Supreme Court ruled in 1986 that *The Nation* magazine was guilty of copyright infringement for *"scooping"*

Time magazine and a book publisher by publishing a preview article about former President Gerald Ford's memoirs. In *Harper & Row Publishers v. The Nation Enterprises* (471 U.S. 539), the Court said the unauthorized use of about 300 words of *verbatim* quotations from Ford's memoirs before they were published elsewhere constituted piracy, not a fair use.

Ford contracted with Harper & Row to publish his book, and *Time* magazine agreed to pay $25,000 for the right to publish excerpts in a magazine article. Shortly before the *Time* article was to appear, *The Nation* somehow obtained a copy of Ford's manuscript and published an article based on the memoirs. The article focused on Ford's explanation of his controversial decision to pardon former President Richard Nixon for his role in the Watergate scandal. *Time* then refused to publish (or fully pay for) its article about Ford's memoirs, since *Time* had been "scooped" by another magazine. Harper & Row then sued *The Nation* for copyright infringement.

Reversing a lower court, the Supreme Court ruled that *The Nation's* story went beyond news reporting and was not protected by the fair use doctrine. The court emphasized that journalists are free to publish summaries of copyrighted manuscripts, since neither facts nor ideas can be copyrighted. But publishing 300 words of *verbatim* quotations before the authorized publisher could get the memoirs into print was not a fair use.

The Court implied that a similar article—even one containing 300 words of direct quotations—would be a fair use rather than a copyright infringement once the author's original work was in print. However, by publishing the excerpts as news before the original work was published, *The Nation* excessively cut into the profit potential of the work, the Court held.

In ruling as it did, the high court had to strike a balance between the First Amendment right of the media to cover the news and the right of an author to profit from his copyrighted creative efforts. This conflict between freedom of expression and the right of an author to profit from his/her work has existed as long as there have been copyright laws. And this Supreme Court ruling will surely not settle the issue.

Writing for the Court, Justice Sandra Day O'Connor said, "The obvious benefit to author and public alike of assuring authors the leisure to develop their ideas free from fear of expropriation outweighs any short-term 'news value' to be gained from premature publication of the author's expression." Journalists generally viewed the *Harper & Row* decision as a serious defeat for their interests because it limited their right to quote extensively from the unpublished writings even of a former president. Although it does not prevent them from quoting a public official's writings *after* publication—or perhaps paraphrasing a person's unpublished works—much newsworthy (and historically important) information about the famous is locked up in their unpublished writings.

Journalists, historians and others with an interest in the unpublished works of the famous became even more alarmed when federal appellate courts began expanding on the *Harper & Row* rule to limit the right to quote from the unpublished works of famous people. Perhaps the most controversial of these cases involved the works of the late L. Ron Hubbard, founder of the Church of Scientology. In that case, *New Era Publications v. Henry Holt & Co.* (873 F.2d 576, 1989), the court allowed a firm affiliated with Scientology to prevent the use of 41 unpublished writings of Hubbard in Russell Miller's biography, *Bare-Faced Messiah*. The biography offended Scientologists by portraying their founder as a bizarre and sometimes dishonest messianic figure—and quoted his own correspondence with government agencies to back up those charges.

By ruling that those quotations were not protected by the fair use doctrine, the court in effect allowed Scientologists to censor an unflattering portrayal of Hubbard. While the court allowed the book itself to be published and allowed the use of a number of other quotations from Hubbard's writings, the passages that were ordered deleted were important to the author's thesis. And perhaps most troubling to journalists and historians, this allows those who control the unpublished works of celebrities to pick and choose—allowing authors of sympathetic biographies to quote from their works while denying the same privilege to those doing more objective biographies.

Organizations representing book publishers, historians and journalists began urging Congress to amend the Copyright Act to re-legalize the use of quotations from the unpublished works of important historical figures. After several years of discussion—and several more appellate court decisions—many journalists and scholars were even more uncertain of when they could and couldn't quote the unpublished writings of famous persons.

In 1992, Congress responded to this problem by adding this sentence to the Copyright Act: "The fact that a work is unpublished shall not itself bar a finding of fair use if such finding is made upon consideration of all the above factors" (i.e., the four-part test that is used to determine whether the fair use doctrine applies in a given situation). Six U.S. Senators issued a joint statement intended to further clarify the law, reaffirming that the purpose of the new language was to overcome the uncertainty among journalists and scholars. They said that the fair use doctrine does indeed apply to unpublished works when the four-part test is met. Given this message from Congress, courts have generally been more sympathetic to the use of quotations from the unpublished works of the famous by journalists and scholars in recent years.

The Supreme Court's *Harper & Row* decision—and the ongoing controversy it generated—was in the news again in 2003 when a strikingly similar new controversy arose. Just before *Living History*, the memoir by Sen. Hillary Rodham Clinton (D-N.Y.) of her eight years as First Lady, was officially released, the Associated Press somehow obtained a copy of the book and published juicy quotations. If Gerald Ford's revelations about his pardon of former President Nixon made headlines a generation ago, Sen. Clinton's revelations about her anger and angst over Bill Clinton's "serial philandering in the White House" (as some news media put it) made even bigger headlines. And once again, *Time*, which had purchased the right to reprint excerpts of Sen. Clinton's memoirs, found itself scooped.

However, this scoop was different, some media critics said. It generated such powerful headlines ("Hillary's Book Bombshell," for instance) that it surely increased sales of the book—which broke records when about a million hard-cover copies were sold within days of the book's release, allowing Simon & Schuster, the publisher, to quickly recoup the entire $8 million royalty advance the company had paid to Sen. Clinton. Also, the AP scoop did not lead to the cancellation of reprints or previously scheduled television interviews with Sen. Clinton—again in contrast to Harper & Row's experience when *The Nation* scooped everyone else with pre-publication quotes from Ford's memoirs.

Is the AP story quoting Clinton's memoirs a copyright infringement or a fair use? Copyright attorneys disagreed on that point, but the president of Simon & Schuster was widely quoted as downplaying the significance of the scoop, making a lawsuit akin to Harper & Row's lawsuit against *The Nation* unlikely.

If you have ever been asked to submit a paper to Turnitin.com for evaluation of plagiarism, the Fourth Circuit has said that you have no infringement claim against its owner, iParadigms, if your paper is kept and added to the anti-plagiarism database. In *A.V. v. iParadigms LLC* (562 F.3d 630, 2009), the court applied the four-part fair use test and said that iParadigm's use of students' work is transformative and unconnected to any creative elements in the work. Moreover, the fact that iParadigms makes money with this use does not affect the students' abilities to sell their unpublished works, even to so-called "paper mills" for resale, as iParadigms does not replace these paper mills, simply suppresses demand for them. Thus, iParadigms' use of the student work is a fair use.

Fair Use, Television News and Video Clipping Services

Another controversial application of the fair use doctrine has involved *video clipping services*—businesses that make videotapes of television news and public affairs programs for sale to individuals and organizations that are mentioned on television. The idea of a clipping service is nothing new: for years newspaper clipping services have monitored the print media for stories that mention their clients. Originally, these firms literally clipped stories from newspapers and sent them to public relations practitioners and others who needed to see what the media were saying about them or their clients. Modern clipping services often photocopy newspaper and magazine articles for their customers.

Video clipping firms do essentially the same thing for their customers—but with video-tape or DVDs. In addition to taping newscasts and providing copies to people and organizations that are mentioned on television, clipping services provide audio transcripts of television newscasts. Also, they prepare "photo boards"—still photographs taken from the video every few seconds, each with a transcript of the accompanying audio. During the 1980s, the video clipping business enjoyed enormous growth. Everyone from prominent politicians to the Library of Congress uses video clipping services to keep track of television news coverage. As a result, several video clipping services that started out as small businesses in some-body's basement mushroomed into million-dollar operations.

The growth of the video clipping industry led to lawsuits by television stations that objected to someone else taping their material, repackaging it, and selling it for a profit. In the early 1990s, several federal courts ruled that video clipping services are not protected by the fair use doctrine—they are guilty of copyright infringement. Perhaps most notable of these cases is *Georgia Television Company v. Television News Clips of Atlanta* (983 F.2d 238, 1993). In that case, the court rejected a clipping service's argument that it had a First Amendment right to provide video clippings even if the fair use doctrine does not apply to video clippings. Instead, the court said video clipping services were violating the Copyright Act.

After several defeats in court, video clipping services sought legislation to exempt them from copyright liability. Although many members of Congress use video clipping services themselves and were sympathetic, key Congressional leaders did what they often do when someone asks Congress to intervene in a dispute between two industries: they urged broadcasters and video clipping services to try to resolve their differences privately.

The major networks and local stations eventually authorized the clipping services to use their newscasts in return for relatively modest license fees.

A related controversy has arisen from the wholesale use of video news footage by competing news organizations. Whenever one station or network comes up with a particularly powerful video segment, everyone else rushes to get it on the air—and worries about copyright permissions later. The celebrated amateur video of the Rodney King beating by Los Angeles police officers is a prime example. George Holliday, the man who made the video, granted one Los Angeles television station (KTLA) permission to use the video—under terms that were later hotly disputed—but the video quickly appeared on stations and networks around the world. As a result, Holliday filed a copyright infringement lawsuit.

A federal judge dismissed Holliday's lawsuit in 1993, citing four grounds for doing so: (1) there was evidence that Holliday gave KTLA permission to use the tape and release it to other media outlets; (2) Holliday's consent should preclude his later claims of copyright infringement; (3) the use of his tape fell within the fair use doctrine; and (4) the First Amendment permits public airing of certain works "of great importance to democratic debate." In connection with the First Amendment and fair use arguments, the judge cited *Time Inc. v. Bernard Geis Associates*, the case mentioned earlier in which Time Inc. was not allowed to prevent the use of drawings based on an amateur photographer's movie in a book about President Kennedy's assassination.

However, the Ninth Circuit alarmed many broadcast journalists by ruling in 1997 that the fair use doctrine may *not* necessarily cover the use of another highly newsworthy video that was taken from a helicopter during the riots that occurred in Los Angeles after the first trial and acquittal of the officers who beat King. In *Los Angeles News Service v. KCAL-TV Channel 9* (108 F.3d 1119), the appellate court overturned a trial court's dismissal of a lawsuit stemming from the unauthorized use of video of the beating of Reginald Denny, a Caucasian truck driver, by African-American youths at the beginning of the riots.

The video was taken by Los Angeles News Service (LANS) and provided to several stations, but LANS refused to authorize KCAL-TV to broadcast the tape. KCAL then obtained the tape from another station and aired it without LANS' consent. When LANS sued for copyright infringement, KCAL argued that the riots were so newsworthy that the fair use doctrine would permit the use of the tape. However, the appellate court held that other fair use factors besides newsworthiness had to be considered, including the economic effect of KCAL's use of the tape. To weigh all of these factors, a full trial would be needed, the appellate court ruled.

Under the *KCAL* decision, broadcast journalists who use even highly newsworthy video footage on the air without first obtaining a copyright clearance may risk a lawsuit.

In a related decision a year later, the same federal appellate court held that LANS could recover damages from overseas use of the Reginald Denny video because it was copied illegally in the United States (*Los Angeles News Service v. Reuters Television*, 149 F.3d 987).

However, in 2002 the same court held that use of a few seconds of the Reginald Denny video by Court TV (now TruTV) *was* a fair use, noting the brevity of the segment used as well as the fact that Court TV used it not as news coverage of the beating in competition with the copyright owner but rather to promote its coverage of the later trial of those accused of the beating. However, the court said CBS, which passed the video along to Court TV, could be sued for other reasons (*Los Angeles News Service v. CBS Broadcasting*, 305 F.3d 924).

Parodies and Fair Use

When composers Marvin Fisher and Jack Segal wrote the song, "When Sunny Gets Blue," it probably never occurred to them that someone might rewrite the lyrics as "When Sonny Sniffs Glue." But the song, a big hit for vocalist Johnny Mathis in the 1950s, was a hit again with those new lyrics in the 1980s.

Radio personality Rick Dees included a 30-second excerpt of the tune—with his own lyrics—in a 1984 comedy album. In part, the lyrics went this way: "When Sonny sniffs glue, her eyes get red and bulgy, then her hair begins to fall."

Fisher and Segal weren't amused, and the resulting lawsuit, *Fisher v. Dees* (794 F.2d 432) produced a 1986 ruling by the Ninth Circuit that clarified the scope of the fair use doctrine.

Affirming a trial judge's decision to dismiss the lawsuit without a trial, the appellate court said the unauthorized revision of the lyrics was unmistakably a parody. It was not intended to tap the same market as the original song about a woman's depression after a love affair turned sour, the court ruled.

The composers had conceded that a brief excerpt—perhaps a single bar—would have been a fair use but argued that using most of the tune was excessive and therefore a copyright infringement. The court disagreed. Judge Joseph Sneed wrote, "Although we have no illusions of musical expertise, it was clear to us that Dees' version was intended to poke fun at the composers' song, and at Mr. Mathis' rather singular vocal range." The court reaffirmed that someone may do a parody of a copyrighted work without infringing the copyright.

However, a number of other courts have disagreed with that conclusion, especially where the parody yields large profits—and a literal reading of the *Fisher v. Dees* case would deny the copyright owner any share of the profits.

In 1994 the Supreme Court finally addressed this question, ruling that even a highly profitable parody may still be a fair use rather than a copyright infringement. The high court so ruled in a case involving a parody of a Roy Orbison song from the 1960s, "Oh, Pretty Woman," by the rap group 2 Live Crew.

In *Campbell v. Acuff-Rose Music Co.* (510 U.S. 569), the Supreme Court held that 2 Live Crew's commercial purpose in recording a parody did not necessarily make the new song (called "Pretty Woman") a copyright infringement rather than a fair use of the material borrowed from Orbison's original hit. The new song took the opening bass notes and the first line of the lyrics before launching into new material.

Writing for a unanimous Supreme Court, Justice David Souter declared that the 2 Live Crew song had sufficient "transformative value" to permit a trial court to find that it was a fair use rather than an infringement despite its commercial intent. Souter emphasized that the other parts of the fair use test must still be applied: the fact that a work is a parody with "transformative value" does not automatically make it a fair use.

The case was sent back to a trial court to consider the various fair-use factors, including the percentage of the original taken and whether the new work would hurt sales of the original by tapping the same market. Justice Souter noted that 2 Live Crew had originally sought permission to adapt Orbison's song—and was turned down. He said this fact does not necessarily resolve the question of whether the new song is a fair use or an infringement.

In short, the Supreme Court said that even a commercially successful parody of a copyrighted song may be a fair use rather than a copyright infringement, depending on how the other fair use criteria are weighed. And the court held that, as always in copyright infringement lawsuits, fair use questions must be decided on a case-by-case basis.

Another point that should be noted about "Pretty Woman" is that the 2 Live Crew recording was treated by the Supreme Court as a parody as opposed to a satire. A *parody* (borrowing from a copyrighted work *to poke fun at that particular work*) is more likely to be a fair use than a *satire* (borrowing from a copyrighted work *to lampoon someone or something else* rather than the copyrighted work itself). This distinction was illustrated by a 1997 federal appellate court ruling against the publishers of a rhyming summary of the O.J. Simpson murder trial, using a style obviously borrowed from the classic "Dr. Seuss" book, *The Cat in the Hat*. The court halted distribution of the new work, called *The Cat NOT in the Hat, A Parody by Dr. Juice (Dr. Seuss Enterprises v. Penguin Books*, 109 F.3d 1394). The court held that "Dr. Juice" mimics but does not parody Dr. Seuss' style.

The *Campbell v. Acuff-Rose* case did not address another troubling question about fair use and music copyrights: the use of *sampling*. In this era of digital technology, it has become increasingly commonplace for recording artists to sample the work of others and include it in their new recordings. In a 2003 decision involving the punk-rap group the Beastie Boys, the Ninth Circuit held that the group's use of a six-second, four-note excerpt did not infringe the copyright on a musical composition. The group paid a license fee to sample the six seconds of a *recording* by jazz flutist James Newton, but didn't pay to use the *underlying composition* (*Newton v. Diamond*, 349 F.3d 591, *amended at* 388 F.3d 1189). The Supreme Court declined to hear an appeal of this decision, although many in the music industry think the high court needs to clarify when it's okay to sample someone else's copyrighted work.

Why are parodies and sampling not permitted automatically under the compulsory licensing provision of the Copyright Act? That provision allows anyone who pays the prescribed royalties to record a copyrighted song; it does not permit major revisions and adaptations without the consent of the copyright owner.

Another widely publicized case involving a parody—this one of a famous novel and motion picture—arose in 2001. Author Alice Randall wrote a book for Houghton Mifflin that is an African-American retelling of *Gone With the Wind*. Entitled *The Wind Done Gone*, it includes characters who closely resemble those in the Civil War classic. But it also has new characters, including Scarlett O'Hara's half sister—the daughter of plantation owner Gerald O'Hara (simply called "Planter" in the new novel) and a slave, thus putting a new spin on the story of *Gone With the Wind*.

The estate of Margaret Mitchell, author of *Gone With the Wind*, sued to halt publication of the new work, contending that it was an unauthorized derivative work and therefore a copyright infringement. A federal judge issued an injunction to prevent the new work's publication, but the Eleventh Circuit issued an order to set aside the injunction, allowing the new work to be published. The appellate court said the injunction against publication was "an unlawful prior restraint in violation of the First Amendment." That left the Mitchell estate free to pursue its lawsuit for monetary damages. The dispute was settled in 2002 when the estate agreed to drop the lawsuit. In return, Randall's publisher agreed to make an unspecified donation to Morehouse College, a historically black men's college in Atlanta.

In 2009 J.D. Salinger got a temporary injunction against publication of an "unauthorized sequel" to his classic novel *The Catcher in the Rye*. The "sequel," *60 Years Later: Coming Through The Rye*, written by "John David California" (pen name of Fredrik Colting, living in Sweden) purports to tell the further story of Salinger's famous character, Holden Caulfield, at age 76, wandering around New York after having escaped a retirement home. Salinger alleged that the publication "is not a parody and it does not comment upon or criticize the original. It is a ripoff pure and simple." U.S. district judge Deborah Batts said that she was having difficulty seeing any criticism or comment at all in the sequel (unlike *The Wind Done Gone*). She enjoined the publication (*Salinger v. Colting*, 641 F. Supp. 2d 250) and said that Colting's work was not sufficiently transformative. However, in 2010 the Second Circuit said that the judge had erred in issuing the preliminary injunction (*Salinger v. Colting*, 607 F.3d 68). The appeals court, in sending the case back to Batts for reconsideration, said, "Because Salinger had established a *prima facie* case of copyright infringement, and in light of how the district court, understandably, viewed this court's precedents, the district court presumed irreparable harm without discussion." Such a misapplication was understandable, the court said, because the Second Circuit's rules in this area conflicted with the Supreme Court's rules, established in a 2006 case, *eBay, Inc. v. MercExchange* (547 U.S. 388). The *eBay* case dealt with patent law, but the Second Circuit said it applied equally to copyright law, and asked Batts to apply that standard. J.D. Salinger died in January 2010. He had fiercely defended the character of Holden Caulfield over the years and refused offers to make a movie based on his book. But in 2011, the Salinger estate settled with Colting, reluctantly permitting the sequel to be published in countries other than the U.S. and Canada, and there when the copyright on *The Catcher in the Rye* runs out.

Political candidates who use popular music in their campaigns without permission run the risk of lawsuits. In 2010, musician Don Henley, a founding member of the Eagles and longtime supporter of the Democratic Party, took issue when a California Republican assembly candidate adapted two of his songs in campaign advertisements. Charles DeVore used the tunes of "The Boys of Summer" and "All She Wants To Do Is Dance" from Henley's 1984 *Building the Perfect Beast* album and wrote different lyrics ("The Hope of November" and "All She Wants To Do Is Tax") intended to mock Democratic rivals. Henley alleged both copyright violation and false endorsement. DeVore argued the use was a fair use, but the judge did not agree, saying although "November" was a satire and "Tax" a parody, neither met the case for fair use (*Henley v. DeVore*, 733 F. Supp. 2d 1144). DeVore borrowed too much from the original songs, said the court, for the uses to be fair.

Can a court determine fair use *without* discovery and trial? The Seventh Circuit said yes in 2012, particularly when the work is a clear parody. The court took on a claim by Samwell, creator of the Internet viral video "What What (In The Butt)," against *South Park's* character Butters' parody of the video. In finding for Comedy Partners, the company behind *South Park*, the court said, "[T]his is an obvious case of fair use. When a defendant raises a fair use defense claiming his or her work is a parody, a court can often decide the merits of the claim without discovery or a trial. When the two works in this case are viewed side-by-side, the *South Park* episode is clearly a parody of the original WWITB video, providing commentary on the ridiculousness of the original video and the viral nature of certain YouTube videos" (*Brownmark Films, LLC v. Comedy Partners*, 2012 U.S. App. LEXIS 11454).

Moreover, since there is no "Internet money" for the original video on YouTube, there could be no monetary damages, said the court, adding that Brownmark had not provided evidence "that the *South Park* parody has cut into any real market (with real, non-Internet dollars) for derivative uses of the original WWITB video."

Fair Use and Advertising

May a company show a competitor's copyrighted material to do comparison advertising? Is that a fair use or a copyright infringement? By 2000, two different federal appellate courts had addressed this issue, and both held that a competitor's material may indeed be used in comparison advertising. In *Sony Computer Entertainment v. Bleem* (214 F.3d 1022), the Ninth Circuit held that Bleem, a video game software producer, could display frozen images ("screenshots") from games played on the Sony PlayStation video console in an attempt to show that its software is superior to Sony's.

The Fifth Circuit ruled similarly in *Triangle Publications v. Knight-Ridder Newspapers* (626 F.2d 1171, 1980). In that case, the court allowed a newspaper to display the cover of *TV Guide* to compare its own TV program magazine with the national publication.

In the *Sony* case, the court ruled that a competitor may use single-frame screenshots for comparative advertising. The court did not grant Bleem a free hand to use computer-generated simulations of the TV screen; the holding was limited to actual single-frame photographs of Sony's games taken from a TV screen.

Bleem's goal in its comparison advertising was to show that its games, which are played on a computer with a high-resolution monitor, have higher quality video than Sony's games, which use an ordinary, low-resolution TV set as a video display.

"Although Bleem is most certainly copying Sony's copyrighted material for the commercial purposes of increasing its own sales, such comparative advertising redounds greatly to the purchasing public's benefit with very little corresponding loss to the integrity of Sony's copyrighted material," Judge Diarmuid O'Scannlain wrote for the court.

In weighing the four factors that determine whether a particular use of a copyrighted work is a fair use or an infringement, O'Scannlain concluded that all four factors favored Bleem's use of Sony's screen images.

■ COPYRIGHTS AND MUSIC LICENSING

Mass communicators are finding themselves increasingly involved in the copyright problems of the music industry, whether they want to be or not. As indicated earlier, there is *compulsory licensing* in the music field, which means anyone can record copyrighted music by merely paying a specified royalty for each CD or tape sold. Also, once a song is recorded, anyone can play the recording without paying the recording artist for *performance rights*: the Copyright Act does not give recording artists the right to collect royalties for "performances" that consist of merely playing their *sound recordings* privately (with a notable exception, explained later) However, the law does recognize performance rights in the underlying music and lyrics that are used in a sound recording. The result: broadcasters have to pay for the right to play copyrighted music on the air, but the money goes only to composers and music publishers, not to recording artists and record companies (unless they also happen to hold the copyrights to the underlying music and lyrics). Business establishments that play music often must pay copyright royalties to composers and music publishers but not to recording artists for the same reason.

How can a composer or music publisher ever keep track of all the different radio stations and night clubs, for instance, that are using his or her copyrighted material? Wouldn't it be impossible to monitor every single radio station, let alone visit every club?

To solve that sort of practical problem, several music licensing organizations have been established to represent the interests of composers, lyricists and music publishers. The most important ones in the United States are the American Society of Composers, Authors and Publishers (ASCAP) and Broadcast Music Inc. (BMI). Using sampling techniques, both organizations keep track of whose music is being played on the air—and collect money for the copyright owners that they represent. Both ASCAP and BMI sell most broadcasters (and other users of copyrighted music) *blanket licenses* that allow them to use all of the music whose copyright owners are represented by ASCAP or BMI. (As noted earlier, some stations find it less expensive to purchase *per-program licenses* instead.) Altogether, ASCAP and BMI control the copyrights to some 10 million songs and collect more than $300 million a year from broadcasters for the right to *perform* these songs by playing them over the air. They collect millions more for non-broadcast uses of copyrighted music. While ASCAP and BMI dominate the music licensing business, a third licensing organization, the Society of European Stage Authors and Composers (SESAC), has been seeking to increase its small share of the American licensing business—and recently signed up several well-known copyright owners as clients. The International Confederation of Societies of Authors and

Composers, in France, coordinates international music licensing by members in about 100 countries.

ASCAP, BMI and SESAC grant licenses only for the *performance* of copyrighted music, including live performances and playing recorded music. Those who wish to make their own recordings or include copyrighted music in a video production must obtain separate *synchronization* or *mechanical* licenses from the Harry Fox Agency, which was established by the National Music Publishers Association to coordinate this kind of licensing. All of these organizations have websites that explain which uses of copyrighted music fall within the jurisdiction of each.

Given the large amount of money involved, there are recurring disputes (and lawsuits) over the collection and distribution of royalties for copyrighted music. But in the end, most broadcasters and other users of copyrighted music have little choice but to pay up: music is essential to their programming, and ASCAP and BMI between them control the performance rights to the vast majority of copyrighted music.

ASCAP and BMI send representatives out to collect royalties from the owners of night clubs and other business establishments where copyrighted music is played or performed. ASCAP and BMI have formulas based on such things as the size of the establishment and its business volume to determine the amount that each business has to pay for its *blanket license.* Even non-profit organizations such as schools and churches are required to pay royalties for certain uses of copyrighted music, although some uses of music in classrooms and at "services at a place of worship" are exempt under Section 110 of the Copyright Act. The National Association for Music Education maintains a website with more information about classroom uses of copyrighted music.

ASCAP and BMI both charge radio stations flat fees for blanket licenses. Music licensing costs most stations about three percent of their net revenues after deductions. Stations buying only per-program licenses pay a higher rate, but only for the times when music is played. There are separate fee schedules for bars and concert halls, among other venues.

Under some circumstances retail stores must pay royalties for the music that is heard in their establishments. One of the more controversial questions in copyright law is whether store owners should have to pay royalties for merely playing a radio in their establishments.

For many years, the legal rule was that all but the smallest stores had to pay royalties if a radio was turned on. The Supreme Court once ruled that very small stores that played a "homestyle" radio were exempt from royalties (that occurred in *Twentieth Century Music Corp. v. Aiken*, 422 U.S. 151, 1975, a case involving a fast-food chicken shop with 1,055 square feet of total floor space). But a federal appellate court later ruled that this exemption did not apply to a chain of large clothing stores that had radios hooked to commercial-quality sound systems (*Sailor Music v. The Gap Stores*, 668 F.2d 84, 1981). Based on that case, ASCAP and BMI demanded royalties from virtually all retail chains, as well as individual stores larger than 1,055 square feet of floor space.

In 1991, however, two federal appellate courts ruled that large chains of retail stores are exempt from paying royalties if each store has no more than one homestyle radio playing, with small home-type speakers placed nearby. One of the cases, *BMI v. Claire's Boutiques* (949 F.2d 1482), involved a chain of 749 stores, mostly smaller than 1,000 square feet. Each store had a small radio and two speakers purchased from the Radio Shack chain. BMI contended that all of the stores in the chain had to be counted together, and that Claire's was really playing 700 radios, not one radio as permitted by copyright law. The appellate court didn't buy that argument, and ruled that under existing law, each store should be counted separately. Even the larger stores in the Claire's Boutiques chain were ruled to be exempt from paying royalties as long as they had only one radio and two speakers, the court ruled.

Shortly later, another federal appellate court went even further. In *Edison Brothers Stores v. BMI* (954 F.2d 1419), the court ruled that the size of the store isn't a crucial factor. The court held that this major retail chain, whose stores average 2,000 square feet, is exempt from paying royalties as long as each store plays a homestyle radio with speakers in or near the radio (as opposed to a commercial sound system with many speakers in the ceiling).

Alarmed at the prospect of American retailers *en masse* turning off their commercial sound systems and buying radios for their stores at Radio Shack to get out of paying copyright royalties, BMI appealed both cases to the Supreme Court. But the high court declined to take up either case. The result: it was perfectly legal for a store owner to play a homestyle radio with a couple of speakers without paying royalties.

After years of debate about this issue, Congress passed the Fairness in Music Licensing Act in 1998. Expanding on the two *BMI court* decisions, this law exempted small retail establishments, restaurants and bars from paying royalties for playing copyrighted music on radio or television sets in their establishments. Under a compromise between the business community and copyright owners, retail businesses smaller than 2,000 square feet and restaurants and bars smaller than 3,750 square feet were exempted from paying royalties if all they do is play homestyle radio or TV sets. Even larger businesses can qualify for the exemption if they have no more than four TV sets or six speakers. However, these rules apply only to the reception of *broadcast music*. Business owners are not exempt from paying copyright royalties for the use of recorded or live music. To collect the royalties, ASCAP and BMI file numerous lawsuits against retail stores and club owners who are using copyrighted music but refuse to obtain licenses from ASCAP and BMI. Rather than pay royalties directly, many business establishments instead buy a canned music service, which provides music for a flat fee that includes the cost of royalty payments.

Once ASCAP, BMI and other licensing agencies have collected the royalties from broadcasters, owners of business establishments and others, the money is distributed to copyright owners on the basis of formulas that account for the amount of air time each owner's material has been receiving. It is assumed that each song's popularity in night clubs and other businesses like retail stores parallels the song's popularity on the nation's radio stations.

Are ringtones "public performances" and therefore subject to additional royalty payments? That was the question posed by ASCAP, who wanted to collect royalties on ring tones, despite the fact that the provider already paid fees. In 2009, a federal district court said no: "When a ringtone plays on a cellular telephone, even when that occurs in public, the user is exempt from copyright liability, and [the carrier] is not liable either secondarily or directly" (*Cellco P'ship v. Am. Soc'y of Composers*, 663 F. Supp. 2d 363). How much does the provider have to pay? The D.C. Circuit in 2010 confirmed the Copyright Royalty Board's assessment of 24 cents per ringtone (*Recording Industry Assn. of America v. Librarian of Congress*, 608 F.3d 861).

■ CABLE TELEVISION COPYRIGHT PROBLEMS

Another major feature of the 1976 Copyright Act is a section dealing with the special problems created by cable television systems. In fact, one of the major reasons Congress finally passed the 1976 Copyright Act after years of stalemated deliberations was a pair of U.S. Supreme Court decisions on cable television and copyright law.

In the 1968 case of *Fortnightly v. United Artists* (392 U.S. 390), the Supreme Court had ruled that a cable television system is really nothing more than a sophisticated receiving antenna. Thus, cable systems—or community antenna television (CATV) systems, as they were then called—were not "performing" the copyrighted programming they picked up off the air, amplified, and delivered to their subscribers' homes for a fee. In so ruling, the Supreme Court exempted CATV systems from any obligation to pay royalties.

Then in a 1974 decision, *Teleprompter v. CBS* (415 U.S. 394), the Supreme Court went even further. It held that CATV systems were still not performing the programming even if they retransmitted it over great distances via microwave relay. Only if they copied and replayed the material rather than delivering it "live" would they be liable to pay royalties to copyright owners, the court ruled.

Alarmed by these two Supreme Court decisions, motion picture and television producers, broadcasters and others with a stake in the protection of copyrighted works banded together and began lobbying Congress for legislation to establish copyright royalties for cable television systems. They prevailed, and the 1976 Copyright Act was written to require cable systems to pay royalties for all distant television stations they import. The 1976 law did not require cable systems to pay royalties for picking up local television and radio signals and delivering them to their subscribers' homes. However, as Chapter Eleven explains, the 1992 Cable Television Consumer Protection and Competition Act allows broadcasters to demand compensation from local cable operators for the use of their copyrighted programming.

The royalties that cable and satellite systems, and now Internet broadcasters, pay to copyright owners are determined by an entity within the U.S. Copyright Office, a Copyright Royalty Board. This board replaced the Copyright Arbitration Royalty Panels that were used to set royalty rates for many years.

Another broadcast copyright issue became highly controversial in the late 1990s—"white areas" where TV signals cannot be received over the air. The major television networks and local stations filed copyright infringement lawsuits against satellite providers for signing up customers for network programming in communities that were by no means "white areas" but rather places easily within range of local TV stations. Their objection: when someone gets network programming from a distant station, typically in New York or Los Angeles, that cuts into the potential audience for nearby stations. For a time, satellite subscribers had to go to their local stations seeking permission to receive network television via satellite—a request that was not often granted: most local stations didn't want to lose any more viewers.

Finally Congress intervened in this dispute in 1999, passing a new Satellite Television Home Viewers Act. This law authorized satellite television providers to deliver local television stations to subscribers in each station's service area if they paid royalties to the stations.

The Satellite TV Home Viewers Act enabled satellite services to compete on an equal basis with cable for the first time. Their inability to carry local TV stations had handicapped them in their competition with cable until this law was enacted. But this law created another kind of unfairness, broadcasters said. Most had not been able to negotiate cash payments from cable systems under retransmission consent (see Chapter Eleven). Armed with the new rules giving them royalties from satellite TV services, they attempted to win payments for the use of their signals from cable systems as well—with mixed success. See also discussions in Chapter Eleven on the government's attempts to define what a cable company is.

■ RECORDING TECHNOLOGIES AND COPYRIGHT LAW

While cable and satellite interests, broadcasters and program producers were battling in Congress, another equally intense battle over copyright protection has been waged on Capitol Hill: the fight over copyrights and new technologies, such as home video and audio tape recording and, more recently, the exchange of copyrighted materials on the Internet. And like the cable copyright dilemma, some of these battles over copyright protection were triggered by a controversial Supreme Court decision.

When video cassette recorders (VCRs) began to gain popularity in the late 1970s, motion picture and television producers became alarmed by the ease with which the public could tape programs off the air for later viewing. The producers saw the sale of home videotapes as a lucrative new market, and they felt that market would be jeopardized if consumers could simply tape movies and TV shows off the air for free.

In a landmark Supreme Court decision, the court ruled in 1984 that home videotaping is *not* necessarily a copyright infringement. In *Sony Corp. of America v. Universal City Studios* (464 U.S. 417), the Court split 5-4 in ruling in favor of the estimated 20 million Americans who had VCRs in their homes by then.

Writing for the Supreme Court's majority, Justice John Paul Stevens pointed out that nothing in the Copyright Act specifically prohibits consumers from taping TV shows for later viewing, a practice commonly called "time shifting." Instead, such noncommercial videotaping is a fair use of copyrighted programming, Stevens wrote in his majority opinion:

> One may search the Copyright Act in vain for any sign that the elected representatives of millions of people who watch television every day have made it unlawful to copy a program for later viewing at home, or have enacted a flat prohibition against the sale of machines that make such copying possible.

Forecasting the legislative battle that he knew would follow the Supreme Court's decision, Stevens conceded that Congress could "take a fresh look at this new technology just as it so often has examined other innovations in the past. But it is not our job to apply laws that have not yet been written," he added.

In so ruling, the Supreme Court reversed a federal appellate court decision that held private at-home videotaping to be a copyright infringement. The lower court suggested that a flat royalty fee could be added to the price of each blank tape and each video recorder to compensate the entertainment industry for the copying that consumers would do.

Critics of the lower court decision pointed out that not all VCRs and blank tapes were used to tape copyrighted TV shows. Thus, they said, a blanket royalty would force many VCR owners to pay for copyright infringements they do not commit. As a result, such a royalty should more accurately be called a "tax" to support the entertainment industry, not a royalty, some contended.

Program producers replied by pointing to the potential for the sale of videotapes that might not be realized if consumers could freely tape TV shows. The industry needs those revenues to produce new and better shows, they said.

The Supreme Court's majority was clearly influenced by the fact that some uses of VCRs are clearly *not* copyright infringements. In fact, Justice Stevens noted that the television production community itself was divided on home videotaping: children's television host

Fred Rogers had made it clear that he *wanted* those who could not view *Mr. Rogers' Neighborhood* at its scheduled time to tape it for later viewing!

In the end, the Supreme Court passed the buck to Congress by ruling that at-home videotaping was not a copyright infringement under existing law. Predictably, both sides launched major lobbying efforts in Congress after the Supreme Court's 1984 decision. But Congress was not anxious to get involved in this touchy dispute. Legislation was introduced to collect royalty fees on the sale of VCRs and blank tapes, but it was never approved by Congress. As a result, noncommercial use of VCRs for time shifting is still a legal fair use. However, this does not mean that copying rented movies and keeping them indefinitely is a fair use. Nor was any non-home use of off-air videotapes made a fair use by the *Sony* decision. The *Sony* ruling led to major legal battles between copyright owners and technology companies, with many of the same arguments being made again. Eventually the U.S. Supreme Court ruled that the *Sony* precedent does not protect some of the new digital technologies. That decision, *MGM v. Grokster*, is discussed later. In Chapter Eleven, *Cartoon Network and CNN v. CSC Holdings*, a case on copyrights and cable on-demand service, will be discussed.

■ COMPUTERS, THE INTERNET AND COPYRIGHT LAWS

The mushrooming growth of the personal computer business created many copyright dilemmas—problems involving both computer software and the Internet. When Congress enacted the 1976 Copyright Act, personal computers were primitive gadgets being built by a handful of hobbyists. Only a few years later, millions of personal computers had been sold to the general public and copyrighted computer software, music and movies were being traded openly at almost every high school in America.

At least five different legal questions have become controversial: (1) the protection of computer software copyrights, (2) the basic problems of digital copying and copy-protection, (3) the question of sharing copyrighted files over the Internet (particularly music and movies), (4) the problems of Internet broadcasting, and (5) problems that arose when publishers began placing their printed materials online.

Copyright Law and Computer Software

Like movies, music and TV shows, computer software has been copied by consumers on an enormous scale, prompting copyright owners to look for new ways to control what they see as a flagrant copyright infringement by the public. Moreover, several leading computer hardware and software companies waged a long—and ultimately unsuccessful—legal battle to keep competitors from making products that had a "look and feel" similar to theirs.

At first, it was not clear that certain types of computer software could even be copyrighted. A computer's "operating system," for example, is a complex pattern of binary numbers (ones and zeros) stored inside an electronic component known as a "read-only memory" (ROM) chip. Because these operating instructions for computers are readable only by the machines themselves and not by humans, some copyright experts questioned whether they could even be covered by copyright law (as opposed to patent law, which is normally what protects the designs of electronic and mechanical devices from infringement).

However, securing a patent is a difficult and time-consuming process, while registering a copyright is easy. Many computer manufacturers wanted to copyright their computer operating instructions rather than waiting and hoping to secure a patent eventually.

What brought this esoteric legal dilemma into focus was the appearance of the Apple II computer, an early personal computer for which thousands of programs were written. Few people questioned the rightness of extending copyright protection to these "application programs," programs that made it possible to play video games, do word processing, or solve complex mathematical problems on a personal computer. However, the Franklin Computer Company began making "Apple-compatible" computers, computers that used a basic operating system so similar to the Apple II operating system that the Franklin Ace computers would run programs written for the Apple.

Meanwhile, a number of companies in the Far East also began making Apple-compatible computers, some of them blatant copies of the Apple II's styling and electronic circuitry. Since some of these competing computers were sold for less than half the price of an Apple computer, the Apple corporation began an aggressive legal campaign to halt the sale of Apple-compatible computers.

The legal rationale for this campaign was that Apple's operating system was a legitimately copyrighted product that no one else could duplicate without permission. Franklin and others defended themselves by pointing out that copyright law had not previously covered "useful devices" like a ROM chip containing computer code. To apply the Copyright Act to such things would be about like letting General Motors copyright the designs of the parts in its cars so no one else could make tires or carburetors that would fit on GM cars. Such things should be patented if they are really novel inventions, but if they are not novel enough to be patented, competitors should be free to copy the designs without fear of a lawsuit, Franklin and other Apple-compatible computer makers argued.

The question of whether a computer's encoded "operating system" could be copyrighted was resolved in two federal appellate court decisions—both decisive victories for Apple. In *Apple Computer Inc. v. Franklin Computer Corp.* (714 F.2d. 1240), a 1983 ruling of the Third Circuit, the validity of Apple's copyright on its computer operating instructions was upheld. Writing for the court, Judge Dolores Sloviter rejected the argument that a pattern of ones and zeros embedded in a computer chip was not copyrightable. She said copyright protection "is not confined to literature in the nature of Hemingway's *For Whom the Bell Tolls.*" The Ninth Circuit agreed in a 1984 case, *Apple Computer Inc. v. Formula Internat'l* (725 F.2d 521).

Later, Apple took aggressive steps to keep others from making software that looked and operated like the software used on the Macintosh line of personal computers. In 1988, Apple sued Microsoft Corp. and Hewlett-Packard Co.—two major producers of competing computer software—for producing software using pull-down menus, icons and a "mouse" as a pointing device, all key features of the Macintosh system. Apple contended that these features are too close to the "look and feel" of the Macintosh.

A previous U.S. District Court decision, *Brøderbund v. Unison World* (648 F.Supp. 1127), had held that a new computer program with too much of the same "look and feel" as an existing one could be a copyright infringement. After that ruling, Lotus Development Corp., creator of the Lotus 1-2-3 spreadsheet program, sued the makers of two competing spreadsheet programs because their spreadsheets used many of the same commands and looked much the same on the screen as Lotus 1-2-3.

Lotus and Apple both drew immediate criticism for filing these lawsuits. In both cases, those suing did not originate the "look and feel" that they were trying to prevent others from using. Lotus 1-2-3 closely resembles VisiCalc, a spreadsheet program that was widely used on early Apple II computers. In fact, one of the people who developed VisiCalc later helped design Lotus 1-2-3. And Apple was not the first computer maker to use pull-down menus with a pointing device and icons: Xerox and others used these ideas first. Many critics felt Apple's desire to keep the Macintosh "look and feel" unique was like General Motors saying that other brands of cars could not have steering wheels—or a brake pedal to the left of the accelerator. If users are to be able to freely move back and forth among different brands of computers, all should operate in essentially the same way just as cars do.

In 1992, a federal judge dismissed the bulk of Apple's copyright infringement lawsuit against Microsoft and Hewlett-Packard, largely rejecting the idea that the "look and feel" of a computer program is something that can be protected under copyright law. The rest of Apple's lawsuit was dismissed in 1993—and Apple's appeals were not successful (see *Apple Computer Inc. v. Microsoft Corp.*, 35 F.3d 1435). In 1995, the Supreme Court refused to review the lower court decisions against Apple; the company had almost nothing to show for the 10 years and millions of dollars it spent trying to win a legal monopoly on the "look and feel" of the Macintosh. By then it was clear that Microsoft could continue to produce its popular Macintosh-like Windows software, with or without Apple's blessing—and the U.S. Justice Department was investigating Microsoft rather than Apple for engaging in allegedly monopolistic business practices in the computer industry—an investigation that led the Justice Department to file a series of widely publicized antitrust lawsuits against Microsoft (see Chapter Twelve).

Meanwhile, Lotus also failed in its attempt to keep competitors from making programs with command structures similar to the Lotus 1-2-3 command structure. In *Lotus Development Corp. v. Borland International* (49 F.3d 807, 1995), the First Circuit ruled that Lotus could not copyright its command structure. The court ruled that the words and commands used to operate a spreadsheet are an uncopyrightable "method of operation," not a copyrightable creative aspect of the program. Elaborating on the court's decision in a concurring opinion, Judge Michael Boudin likened the command structure to the standard QWERTY typewriter keyboard layout used by almost all typewriter makers.

In 1996, the Supreme Court took up the *Lotus* case, but the justices deadlocked 4-4 after hearing oral arguments. Justice John Paul Stevens disqualified himself from participating in the case. A tie vote affirms the lower court's decision but denies it the full precedent-setting power of a Supreme Court decision.

In general, the trend today appears to be for the courts to take a narrow view of software copyrights, thus allowing new competitors to enter the field with products similar to or compatible with the industry leaders' products. This is true in the video game field as well as the application software market. In 1992, two major federal court decisions expanded the right of independent companies to make cartridges that run on another company's video games in spite of the game-maker's copyright claims. First, a federal appellate court held that Nintendo could not prevent Galoob Toys from making a video game cartridge called "Game Genie," which plugs into Nintendo units and allows players to change the speed, mobility or number of "lives" of a video game character. The Game Genie is a fair use rather than an unlawful derivative work under copyright law, the court held *(Galoob Toys v. Nintendo of America*, 964 F.2d 965). If the Game Genie had been declared to be a derivative work, then the copyright owner (in this case, Nintendo) would have the exclusive right to produce it.

Another 1992 federal appellate court decision involving rival video game manufacturers further limited the right of any software producer to use the Copyright Act to avoid competition. In the case of *Sega Enterprises v. Accolade Inc.* (977 F.2d 1510), the court held that computer software companies may disassemble a competitor's computer code so they can determine how to make compatible products. The *Sega* case, which is widely regarded as a landmark case in the software industry, extended the fair use doctrine to cover this kind of "reverse engineering." If the court had ruled that it is a copyright infringement to dismantle a competitor's software and examine its inner workings in order to make a compatible product, competition in the software industry would have been severely curtailed.

In 2000, a federal appellate court again held that reverse engineering is a fair use and not a copyright infringement, allowing a company whose software emulates the functions of Sony's PlayStation game machines to disassemble Sony's copyrighted software in order to determine how to make compatible products (*Sony Computer Entertainment v. Connectix Corp.*, 203 F.3d 596). The court suggested that Sony could file for a patent and not a copyright to protect its PlayStation game machine—and Sony quickly did just that. However, the court also noted that it is more difficult to obtain a patent than a copyright, stating, "If Sony wishes to obtain a lawful monopoly on the functional concepts in its software, it must satisfy the more stringent standards of the patent laws."

In recent years, another software copyright-related controversy arose. Many software providers include "shrinkwrap" contracts in their packaging. By breaking the seal, the user agrees to the terms of a contract that may carry far greater restrictions than copyright law would allow, often completely overriding the fair use doctrine and also the *first sale doctrine*, a rule under which the original purchaser of a copyrighted work (such as a book) is free to resell it used without paying additional royalties. The first sale doctrine says that "the owner of a particular copy...lawfully made under this title, or any person authorized by such owner, is entitled, without the authority of the copyright owner, to sell or otherwise dispose of the possession of that copy." Many shrinkwrap contracts simply nullify fair use and first sale concepts. Are these shrinkwrap contracts valid? Generally, copyright owners and those they authorize to use a copyrighted work may enter into contracts that override copyright law. Some courts have upheld the restrictions imposed by shrinkwrap contracts (see *ProCD v. Zeidenberg*, 86 F.3d 1447, 1996). Some advocates of consumer rights see the *copyright misuse doctrine* as a possible remedy. Under that doctrine, it is a copyright misuse to secure an exclusive right or limited monopoly not granted by copyright law that is contrary to public policy. Some also say shrinkwrap contracts are not valid when they conflict with federal copyright law because of the federal preemption provision of the Copyright Act.

In 2010, the Supreme Court affirmed by a split vote a Ninth Circuit decision on the first sale doctrine, denying a discount store's right to buy consumer items overseas and bring them back for resale without the copyright holder's consent. Costco got Omega Swiss watches by buying them from a New York company who had bought them on the "gray market" overseas from authorized distributors. Omega had not given permission for the watches to be imported to the U.S. or sold by Costco.

The Ninth Circuit said that the first sale doctrine does not apply to foreign imports that are manufactured and first sold abroad. Why? The court said that to interpret the doctrine otherwise "would be to ascribe legality under the Copyright Act to conduct that occurs entirely outside the United States, notwithstanding the absence of a clear expression of congressional intent in favor of extraterritoriality." Thus foreign companies would get more protection than those in the U.S. The Supreme Court affirmed that decision by a split vote in *Costco Wholesale Corp. v. OMEGA, S.A.* (131 S. Ct. 565, 2010). This decision by the Court does not create national precedent.

The Court will again revisit the first-sale doctrine in 2012 or 2013; it granted cert in *John Wiley & Sons, Inc. v. Kirtsaeng*, (654 F.3d 210), a Second Circuit case in which that court found that Supap Kirtsaeng, a Thailand native, violated copyright law by importing foreign-made editions of U.S. textbooks into the United States to sell on eBay. The first-sale doctrine, said the court, does not apply to goods manufactured in a foreign country. There is a circuit split on the issue, which is likely why the Court took the case.

If you buy software, do you own, or just license, the copy of the software you bought? That question was addressed before the Ninth Circuit in three cases, one having to do with the hugely popular video game World of Warcraft (WoW).

In the first of these cases, the Ninth Circuit heard an appeal of a case in which Timothy Vernor sold used but legitimate versions of Autodesk computer-assisted design software on eBay; the software company said he was infringing copyright in doing so because the license was not a transfer of ownership. The district court pointed out that the Ninth Circuit had two views on who owns the software, and found in Vernor's favor using the older of the two precedents. The Ninth Circuit reversed, saying that "Autodesk retained title to the software and imposed significant transfer restrictions: it stated that the license is nontransferable, the software could not be transferred or leased without Autodesk's written consent, and the software could not be transferred outside the Western Hemisphere." Thus, because Vernor never owned the software, he could not sell it without permission, as he could under the first sale doctrine as an owner (*Vernor v. Autodesk*, 621 F.3d 1102, 2010).

In the second case, the makers of World of Warcraft, Blizzard Entertainment, won at the district court level against MDY Industries, maker of a program called a "bot," named Glider, that lets users play WoW unattended. The court said that WoW players do not own the physical copy of the game software but can only load a copy into their computers' memories, subject to Blizzard's license. The Ninth Circuit sided with the "bot" makers—but not completely (*MDY Industries v. Blizzard Entertainment*, 629 F.3d 928, 2010). "A Glider user violates the covenants with Blizzard, but does not thereby commit copyright infringement because Glider does not infringe any of Blizzard's exclusive rights. For instance, the use does not alter or copy WoW software," said the court. However, Blizzard's license for WoW did

FIG. 34. Filesharing defendant Joel Tenenbaum (L) and his attorney, Harvard law professor Charles Nesson (R).

Courtesy of the Joel Fights Back Legal Team, used with permission.

the same thing it did for Autodesk in the Vernor case: "a software user is a licensee rather than an owner of a copy where the copyright owner (1) specifies that the user is granted a license; (2) significantly restricts the user's ability to transfer the software; and (3) imposes notable use restrictions." Blizzard did all this, so it owns the copyright and simply licenses it to WoW players.

Finally, a federal district court said that the first sale doctrine protects the sale of promotional CDs, even though the CDs contained licenses that attempted to limit their resale and transfer. In *UMG Records, Inc. v. Augusto* (628 F.3d 1175, 2011), the Ninth Circuit agreed, saying that Troy Augusto could lawfully sell promo CDs on eBay, supporting the first sale doctrine, even if the CDs had "Promotion—Not for Sale" labels on them. The court said, "UMG's distribution of the promotional CDs under the circumstances effected a sale (transfer of title) of the CDs to the recipients. Further sale of those copies was therefore permissible without UMG's authorization."

Thus, at least in the Ninth Circuit, the first sale doctrine is a decidedly mixed bag of results for both copyright holders and the purchasers of their products. Given the complexity of the copyright and patent issues involved in these cases—and the enormous amount of money at stake—it is certain that these legal battles will continue, with unpredictable results.

Internet Problems: Basic Issues

Inevitably, questions of copyright ownership in cyberspace have become controversial as millions of people began accessing the Internet. The problems became even more complex and controversial when millions of people also began exchanging music and digital video—and posting their own content that includes copyrighted material—on the Internet, to the horror of copyright owners. Although there is much uncertainty in this newly developing area of the law, a few principles are clear.

The basic principle is that *a copyright is still a copyright*, regardless of the means by which a copyrighted work is published, performed or distributed (although those three legal terms are being redefined in the cyberspace age). Also, the fact that a document is posted online somewhere without a copyright notice does not prove that the document is in the public domain. Under current law, no recently created work falls into the public domain unless the creator or other copyright owner expressly places it in the public domain.

One of the fundamental issues that arose with the Internet is the question of holding Internet service providers liable for what their subscribers do. Congress included provisions in the 1996 Telecommunications Act under which Internet service providers (ISPs) and websites can escape liability for both libel and copyright infringements committed by their millions of customers and contributors if they act promptly to remove allegedly unlawful materials. In passing this law, Congress recognized that it is impossible for ISPs to monitor everything that every user does online. In 2004, a federal appeals court in Virginia reaffirmed that Internet service providers are not liable for copyright infringements by those who post materials on their systems, even if the provider reviews the materials (*CoStar Group v. LoopNet*, 373 F.3d 544).

In 1998, Congress passed the Digital Millennium Copyright Act (DMCA), a far-reaching new law that expanded on the Telecommunications Act, giving both copyright owners and ISPs extensive legal protection—but at the expense of those who post and use material on the Internet, including librarians, educators, website owners, the Internet-surfing public and even broadcasters.

The DMCA has many provisions. Among other things, it brought the United States into compliance with the provisions of two World Intellectual Property Organization (WIPO) treaties. Perhaps the most noteworthy of these provisions is a requirement that VCR manufacturers start adding circuitry that will make it impossible for consumers to copy rental videos and pay-per-view television programming. Another little-noticed provision gives copyright protection to "cookies," the small files that are quietly placed on computers when they are used to surf the Internet, enabling some Internet hosts to ascertain what sites a computer user has visited. Some attorneys said this provision makes it a copyright infringement for a computer user to delete these cookies from his or her own computer, even though they may have been placed there without the user's knowledge or consent.

The DMCA also established new rules governing digital copyrights, giving additional copyright protection to digital renderings of motion pictures, videos, sound recordings, photography and graphics. The act also banned many technologies that could circumvent encryption and copy-prevention schemes.

One of the DMCA's most controversial features concerns the handling of alleged copyright infringements on the Internet. The law exempted Internet service providers and services like YouTube from liability for what their subscribers or users may post if they act quickly to deny access to content containing alleged infringements. A copyright owner merely notifies the host that the material infringes a copyright, providing a statement that he/she has a "good faith belief" that the use of the disputed material is an infringement.

The Internet provider must then notify the poster of the material and promptly shut down access to it. The poster, in turn, can oppose the shutdown only by stating *under penalty of perjury* that the challenged material is being removed by mistake or was wrongly identified. In contrast, the copyright owner is *not* obligated to declare anything under penalty of perjury. Nor is the poster of the material allowed to make a fair use defense of the use of the challenged material.

In effect, this allows copyright owners to shut down websites or Internet postings without ever going to court to prove that an infringement has in fact occurred. Internet providers and hosts are exempt from copyright liability—if they act as copyright enforcers by responding quickly to "take-down" requests (valid or not). If they fail to play that role, they can be held liable for any infringement that may occur.

Critics of these provisions of the DMCA have pointed out that the act was the result of a compromise between copyright owners and Internet service providers. Website owners, educators, librarians and others who advocate a broad fair use doctrine were not at the bargaining table when this law was negotiated.

Another criticism of the act is that it made it easier for companies to use copyright law to seek a monopoly over products like garage door controls and ink cartridges for printers, to the detriment of consumers. In 2004, federal appeals courts ruled against a manufacturer who wanted to prevent a competitor from making compatible garage door remote controls (*Chamberlain Group v. Skylink Technologies*, 381 F.3d 1178) and a printer maker who wanted to prevent others from making ink cartridges that would work on its printers (*Lexmark International v. Static Control Components*, 387 F.3d 522).

Internet Problems: Filesharing

Filesharing became the major copyright issue in cyberspace in the 2000s. One Internet start-up company particularly incurred the wrath of the recording industry: Napster, an Internet-based peer-to-peer music sharing service. Napster enabled millions of users to share music—most of it copyrighted. The larger problem of filesharing—"piracy" according to copyright owners—produced numerous lawsuits, countersuits, proposals for legislation and technical "solutions" intended to make various kinds of copying more difficult. After the recording industry won a series of legal victories over Napster, it eventually went bankrupt (the name was later taken over by a for-pay music downloading service). The original Napster service was replaced by several others after it was shut down, and the recording industry responded with lawsuits against them and their users, too.

The recording industry's legal attack on Napster began with a request for an injunction in federal court to halt the filesharing. A federal judge granted an injunction in 2000, but the Ninth Circuit issued a stay, allowing Napster to continue for a few more months while an appeal was heard. In 2001, the appellate court upheld much of the recording industry's case. In *A&M Records et al. v. Napster* (239 F.3d 1004), the appellate court held that when computer music enthusiasts exchange digital music files via Napster, that is often a copyright infringement. The court rejected Napster's contention that music sharing should be a fair use, just as home video taping television programs for later viewing is a fair use.

At one time about 10 percent of the music being exchanged via Napster either was not covered by a current copyright or was exchanged with the copyright owner's permission. So Napster was allowed to continue operating for a time, but the copyrighted music had to be removed. In ruling that the non-infringing uses of Napster precluded a judicial decree to shut it down altogether, the appellate court was echoing its own earlier ruling when the recording industry tried to ban the sale of the Diamond Rio portable MP3 player (*Recording Industry Association of America v. Diamond Multimedia Systems*, 180 F.3d 1072). In that 1999 decision, the appellate court said it was inappropriate to ban the sale of a product that has *substantial non-infringing uses.*

Meanwhile, several record labels announced their own Internet music distribution systems, most of which charge subscribers a monthly fee for the privilege of downloading music. In 2003, Apple Computer Inc. launched iTunes, a fee-based music service, with the blessing of the recording industry, and introduced the iPod portable music player. By 2007, iTunes and the iPod were so popular that when Apple CEO Steve Jobs said he would drop all copying restrictions from music sold by iTunes "in a heartbeat" if he could, some industry analysts thought it might happen. Some iTunes songs can be downloaded in a non-protected format—at a higher price.

That would be a fundamental change in industry thinking about "digital rights management" (i.e., copy prevention). In 2005, the recording and motion picture industries won a major victory when the U.S. Supreme Court ruled in *MGM v. Grokster* (545 U.S. 913) that copyright owners can sue technology companies who encourage consumers to share copyrighted files. The unanimous decision held that modern filesharing is different from what was happening at the time of the *Sony* decision in 1984. Not only is copying of digital files easier and more widespread than home video copying was then, but companies like Grokster and StreamCast Networks (another defendant in this case) actively facilitate the process. These companies make no effort to prevent illegal filesharing, the Court said.

"We hold that one who distributes a device with the object of promoting its use to infringe copyright, as shown by the clear expression or other affirmative steps taken to foster infringement, is liable for the resulting acts of infringement by third parties," Justice David Souter wrote for the Court.

However, the *Grokster* decision also set up a balancing test to provide some protection to scientific innovators. The Court said it was unrealistic to force a company developing a new product to predict how consumers might use its product months or years later. If a company merely learns that consumers are using its product for an illegal purpose, that is not sufficient to make the company liable for the acts of others. This balancing is needed so as not to "compromise legitimate commerce or discourage innovation having a lawful purpose," the Court said.

The *Grokster* decision cleared the way for the recording and motion picture industries to go after companies that encourage filesharing as well as cracking down on individual users of filesharing networks like Grokster, as the industries did starting in 2003. Industry lawyers filed lawsuits against thousands of individuals who allegedly shared music or movies over the Internet. Two federal appeals courts ruled that Internet providers need not reveal their subscribers' names to recording industry attorneys without a judge's subpoena in each case (*RIAA v. Verizon*, 351 F.3d 1229, 2003; and *RIAA v. Charter Communications*, 393 F.3d 771, 2005), but the industry then began seeking individual subpoenas to identify targeted filesharers. Now armed with the *Grokster* decision, the industry went after software and hardware creators who facilitate copying within the jurisdiction of U.S. courts. The industry won a large monetary settlement from the Australia-based KaZaA network and then won a court judgment against the makers of the Morpheus filesharing software. In 2008, the six leading Hollywood studios won a verdict of $111 million from the TorrentSpy.com filesharing website. Its parent company filed for bankruptcy protection in the United Kingdom.

Peer-to-peer services are not faring well in the courts. As discussed in Chapter Three, the Second Circuit refused to overturn a district court's order to an ISP to disclose the identities of individuals alleged to be involved in filesharing (*Arista Records LLC v. Doe 3*, 604 F.3d 110, 2010). A federal district court also found in 2010 that LimeWire had induced its users to engage in infringing actions in *Arista Records LLC v. Lime Group* (715 F. Supp. 2d 481). Judge Kimba Wood said that LimeWire was aware of infringing activity by its users, attempted to attract infringing users and to enable them to commit infringements, depended on infringements for business success and did not try to reduce infringing activities. The RIAA received a permanent injunction against LimeWire, and LimeWire settled for $105 million in 2011.

isoHunt, a Canadian BitTorrent index and search engine, was permanently enjoined in 2010 (*Columbia Pictures v. Fung*, 2010 U.S. Dist. LEXIS 91169); the court said that isoHunt needed to be shut down permanently because the studios had suffered significant losses, and isoHunt owner Gary Fung said that he would not attempt to control infringement unless ordered by the court. Moreover, the court added that "a defendant who is liable for inducing infringement may be enjoined from *distributing* his products in the future, *even if* he no longer promotes an inducing message." Movie titles that isoHunt receives from studios can no longer be hosted, indexed, or linked to by the site, and isoHunt must bar certain search terms associated with infringement (such as "warez" and "DVD rips"). isoHunt continues to maintain that it is merely a search engine, similar to Google.

The most controversial thing the record industry did, though, is filing so many lawsuits against individuals who allegedly shared copyrighted music. By 2008, at least 30,000 such lawsuits had been filed—and some were going to trial when defendants refused to pay a settlement. Two very high-profile cases made the news in the late 2000s: Jammie Thomas-Rasset and Joel Tenenbaum.

FIG. 35. Stockholm protesters during a demonstration on June 3, 2006, protesting the police raid of the BitTorrent filesharing website "The Pirate Bay."

Gabriel Ehrnst Grundin via Wikimedia Commons.

In the largest verdict at the time, a federal jury in October 2007 ordered a Minnesota woman to pay a $222,000 fine ($9,250 for each of 24 copyrighted songs she allegedly shared via the Internet). Jammie Thomas, a 30-year-old single mother of two who earned $36,000 a year as an employee of an Native American reservation, was found by the jury to have shared songs via the KaZaA filesharing site, although she denied it. The jury could have awarded the record labels as much as $150,000 for *each instance* of filesharing.

In 2008 the trial judge said he would consider setting aside the monster verdict against Thomas and ordering a new trial. In 2009, Thomas, now Jammie Thomas-Rasset, was granted a new federal jury trial under the theory that merely the "making available" of songs for download was insufficient for infringement. She lost, however, and the jury *increased* the damage award to $1.92 million ($80,000 per song, up from $9,250 per song). Some have suggested that this huge award violates Congressional intent and due process guarantees and may cause a backlash against the recording industry.

In 2010, a court reduced Thomas-Rasset's fine from $80,000 per song to $2,250 per song, or $54,000 total, saying that "The need for deterrence cannot justify a $2 million verdict for stealing and illegally distributing 24 songs for the sole purpose of obtaining free music." The RIAA then gave Thomas-Rasset a settlement offer of $25,000, which she rejected. She lost for the *third* time in November 2010, with a jury awarding $1.5 million to the recording companies. Her attorneys have asked the judge to throw out all damages in the case.

At the end of 2008, the RIAA announced that it would no longer pursue lawsuits against filesharers but would form partnerships with Internet service providers to restrict online access of those sharing files. But filesharing issues continue to make the news. A Harvard law professor, Charles Nesson, is representing a Boston University doctoral student, Joel Tenenbaum, in federal court in a million-dollar counterclaim against the RIAA for Tenenbaum's sharing of 30 songs over filesharing application KaZaA. Tenenbaum's motion for dismissal of the case was denied and the case went to a jury (*Capitol Records Inc. v. Alaujan*, 626 F. Supp. 2d 152, 2009). Judge Nancy Gertner had allowed the hearing to be webcast but the RIAA objected, and her decision to allow the webcasting was overturned by the First Circuit; that issue is discussed in Chapter Seven.

webcast:
media content
delivered over the
Internet, either on
demand or live.

CSS:
Content Scramble
System, a digital
rights management
(copy protection)
scheme licensed by
the DVD Copy Control
Association.

Tenenbaum has fared no better in court than Thomas-Rasset. He and his attorney, Nesson, tried to convince the court to adopt a definition of fair use that would "excuse all file sharing for private enjoyment" and that the judge called "so broad that it would swallow the copyright protections that Congress created, defying both statute and precedent" (*Sony BMG Music Entertainment v. Tenenbaum*, 672 F. Supp. 2d 217). After Tenenbaum admitted on the stand that he did indeed download the files in question, the judge told the jury that they could no longer decide the issue of infringement, and instead would only be addressing willfulness and damages. The jury returned a verdict of $675,000—$22,500 per song. Judge Gertner then reduced the damages to $67,500, calling that award "significant and harsh," adding, "It adequately compensates the plaintiffs for the relatively minor harm that Tenenbaum caused them and, even more importantly, should serve as a strong deterrent against unlawful file-sharing" (*Sony BMG Music Entertainment v. Tenenbaum*, 721 F. Supp. 2d 85, 2010).

Thomas-Rasset's fine was lowered to $54,000 from that $1.5 million by a federal judge in 2011, who called the award "appalling." But the RIAA appealed that fine to the Eighth Circuit, saying that it was too low. The Supreme Court refused to hear an appeal of Tenenbaum's case, leaving the $675,000 jury verdict in place. Both cases are ongoing.

One of the most popular filesharing protocols is called BitTorrent, which distributes the download burden among many users. Torrent-tracking websites facilitate communication among "peers" sharing files. In Stockholm in 2009, the Swedish owners of the popular torrent-tracking website The Pirate Bay were found guilty of promoting copyright infringement and sentenced to serve one year in prison and pay a fine of 30 million Swedish kroner (about $3.5 million). A Swedish court denied the request for a retrial. After the Swedish Supreme Court refused to hear their appeal, two of the Pirate Bay's founders, in a last-ditch effort to avoid jail time, appealed to the European Court of Human Rights in June 2012— probably postponing the final outcome for several years.

Social networking and video sharing sites, especially MySpace and YouTube, became so popular that they attracted a series of high-profile lawsuits by copyright owners. Media conglomerate Viacom sued YouTube for more than $1 billion because YouTube users were posting thousands of videos containing copyrighted materials. While Viacom and YouTube privately negotiated, YouTube said in court that it should not be liable because it promptly takes down all infringing material and therefore falls within the copyright safe harbor of the Digital Millennium Copyright Act. YouTube and MySpace both installed their own internal filters in an attempt to prevent the posting of copyrighted content. Critics of these lawsuits argued that they ignore the fair use doctrine, under which many postings are perfectly legal even if they make some use of copyrighted material.

In a huge win for Google and YouTube, a federal district court in June 2010 agreed with Google and dismissed the billion-dollar infringement claim, saying that YouTube fully qualifies for DMCA "safe harbor" protection, and that YouTube promptly responded to Viacom's requests under DMCA to take down infringing material. The court pointed to the fact that in 2007, Viacom had gathered nearly 100,000 videos into one massive take-down notice—and YouTube had taken down virtually all of them by the following business day. Veoh, another video-hosting site, had won a summary judgment claim in 2009 against Universal Music Group under the DMCA's safe harbor. Veoh claimed that it had no actual knowledge of infringing materials being posted by their users, and the district court agreed. Both UMG and Viacom appealed.

In 2011, the Ninth Circuit affirmed in *UMG Recordings, Inc. v. Veoh Networks, Inc.* (667 F.3d 1022) that Veoh was protected under the DMCA's safe harbor, and UMG appealed. However, the Second Circuit in *Viacom Int'l, Inc. v. YouTube, Inc.* (676 F.3d 19, 2012) came to a different conclusion, *reversing* the lower court's decision to toss out the $1 billion lawsuit and reviving the lawsuit. "[A] reasonable jury could find that YouTube had actual knowledge or awareness of specific infringing activity on its website," said the court in vacating the summary judgment for YouTube. The Ninth Circuit, then, in response to UMG's appeal, asked for supplementary briefing (i.e., more information from the parties) on actual knowledge of infringement and on whether "a service provider [has] to be aware of the specific infringing material to have the 'right and ability to control' the infringing activity." It is possible that in light of the Second Circuit's opinion, the Ninth could follow suit and find that the safe harbor would not apply in Veoh's case.

Despite the fact that YouTube flashes a warning before allowing users to upload their videos that tells them not to post copyrighted material, plenty of unauthorized content reaches YouTube. Under the DMCA's rules, when copyright holders notify YouTube of infringing material, YouTube will take the content down. Still, several media companies sued YouTube for infringement. In the wake of these lawsuits, YouTube instituted a "Content ID" system that it says lets copyright owners "identify user-uploaded videos comprised entirely OR partially of their content, and choose, in advance, what they want to happen when those videos are found." Critics of this system say that it flags more than it should without regard to whether a use is a fair use.

In 2008, a federal district court ruled in favor of Stephanie Lenz, a Pennsylvania mother who had videotaped 29 seconds of her toddler dancing to Prince's hit "Let's Go Crazy" and posted it on YouTube. Universal Music Corp. informed YouTube that the video was infringing and ordered it to be removed. YouTube removed the video and informed Lenz that it had done so. Claiming that Universal removed the video just to satisfy Prince, who has not been shy about asserting his rights, Lenz said that Universal had no right to remove her video without considering that it might be a fair use. The court agreed with Lenz:

> As Lenz points out, the unnecessary removal of non-infringing material causes
> significant injury to the public where time-sensitive or controversial subjects
> are involved and the counter-notification remedy does not sufficiently address
> these harms. A good faith consideration of whether a particular use is fair use is
> consistent with the purpose of the statute.

The court also cleared the way for Lenz to bring suit against Universal for acting in bad faith (*Lenz v. Universal Music Corp.*, 572 F. Supp. 2d 1150). Lenz won a victory at the district court in 2010 when it granted her partial summary judgment against Universal's defenses in her counterclaim. The DMCA says that a copyright owner who makes false statements as part of a takedown notice "shall be liable for any damages, including costs and attorneys' fees, incurred by [the plaintiff] as the result of the service provider relying upon such misrepresentation in removing or disabling access to the material or activity claimed to be infringing." In other words, a company who falsely claims a use is copyrighted must pay damages to the user if the ISP uses that claim to take down the use. Universal raised defenses to this DMCA element, which the court rejected (*Lenz v. Universal Music Corp.*, 94 U.S.P.Q.2D (BNA) 1344).

Google was also sued by book publishers and authors for its digital book project, which was intended to allow keyword searches of millions of books, including many old and out-of-print books. Google defended itself by arguing once again that providing small samples of the material in larger works is a fair use, not an infringement. As noted, Google and the Authors Guild settled this case in 2008, with Google agreeing to compensate authors, but the settlement agreement is still up in the air: a judge said in 2011 that the settlement is not "fair, adequate, and reasonable" (*Authors Guild v. Google Inc.*, 770 F. Supp. 2d 666).

The international issues involved in Internet filesharing were central to the movie industry's fight against the DeCSS software, which defeats the CSS (Content Scramble System, licensed by the DVD Copy Control Association) encryption system used on DVD movies. As this controversy began, a federal judge ordered the 2600 Enterprises website to delete links that would help web surfers locate overseas websites offering the DeCSS software. The DeCSS software was written primarily by Jon Lech Johansen, a Norwegian youth, so he could view DVD movies on a Linux-based computer (as opposed to Windows). In 2003 a court in Oslo, Norway acquitted Johansen of violating Norway's anti-piracy laws because he owned the DVDs he wanted to copy. The court said a person has the right to copy his own DVDs in Norway. Many European countries have similar laws, allowing consumers to make copies of their DVDs and audio CDs for private use.

DeCSS overrides the copy-prevention features of DVDs, allowing them to be viewed and copied on Linux computers. In the 2600 case, the federal judge ruled that even linking to sites having the copying software is a *contributory copyright infringement* in violation of the DMCA. The defendants raised First Amendment questions and appealed the ruling—with the support of civil liberties and advocacy groups such as the Electronic Frontier Foundation.

Acting in late 2001, the Second Circuit rejected the First Amendment claims and upheld the bulk of the judge's order. Ruling in *Universal City Studios v. Corley* (273 F.3d 429), the court concluded that the DMCA does not violate the First Amendment by banning not only software that defeats copy-protection schemes but also information about such software. In essence, the appellate court said it is up to Congress to weigh the First Amendment against the claims of copyright owners.

In 2005, however, the DeCSS code was so widely circulated that a court said it could no longer be considered a trade secret, thus refusing to enjoin its posting on the Internet (*DVD Copy Control Association v. Bunner*, 116 C.A.4th 241). But copyright owners continued to press their case against DVD copying software under the DMCA and other legal grounds. In 2004 a federal judge banned the sale of two commercial DVD copying products. By then, millions of computer owners were copying DVD movies with little regard for its alleged illegality.

The DVD Copy Control Association litigated two other cases in 2009 involving the CSS technology. In *RealNetworks Inc. v. DVD Copy Control Assn.* (641 F. Supp. 2d 913), a federal district court ruled that RealNetwork's product RealDVD can no longer be sold; Judge Marilyn Hall Patel wrote, "RealDVD makes a permanent copy of copyrighted DVD content and by doing so breaches its CSS license agreement with DVD CCA and circumvents a technological measure that effectively control's access to or copying of [defendants'] copyrighted content on DVDs."

In *DVD Copy Control Assn. v. Kaleidescape* (176 Cal. App. 4th 697), the association alleged that Kaleidescape's system, which stores copies of DVDs and would allow a user to create a large library of DVDs without buying a single one, was a violation of the CSS license. A California district court disagreed, saying that the part of the license that Kaleidescape was purported to have violated was not part of the agreement that was actually executed. The appellate court reversed, saying the agreement did contain the contested part of the license, but also saying that it was unclear whether Kaleidescape had actually breached the license. The case was remanded to the trial court for that determination.

In 2005, Congress enacted the Family Entertainment and Copyright Act, making it a federal crime to record a movie in a theater or to offer online even one movie, song or software program before its official release date. Those provisions were passed at the behest of the entertainment industry, but the industry was not pleased when the bill also legalized products that enable consumers to filter out portions of DVDs that they may find offensive. Those provisions were backed by both conservatives and advocates of high-tech civil liberties such as the Electronic Frontier Foundation.

Still other controversies have arisen over alleged piracy. Many computer enthusiasts were horrified and outraged in 2001 when a group of researchers who devised a way to defeat music copy-protection technologies (something they were invited to do by the recording industry) got a stern letter from industry lawyers telling them to suppress their findings. The researchers (students and professors at Princeton and Rice Universities, among others) were on the verge of presenting a paper at a computer security conference when the industry threatened legal action unless they withdrew. The legal threat came from the Secure Digital Music Initiative (SDMI), a group formed by the world's biggest record labels to develop a way to distribute copy-protected digital music.

The researchers were led by professor Edward Felten of Princeton, an expert on encryption. He withdrew from the conference and then filed his own lawsuit, seeking a judicial declaration that the Digital Millennium Copyright Act, on which the industry based its threat, violates the First Amendment by preventing scholarly discussion of encryption and decryption technologies. His lawsuit was dismissed by a federal judge who ruled that Felten's rights were not violated because he did eventually publish his scholarly paper. Felten and his backers then asked a federal appellate court to reinstate the lawsuit.

By the mid-2000s, copyright owners were working on a number of fronts to curb unauthorized copying, over objections by consumer advocates and civil liberties groups. Hollywood and the broadcast industry eventually got the Federal Communications Commission to adopt a rule requiring that new digital television sets include *"broadcast flag"* technology to prevent unauthorized copying and retransmission of over-the-air TV programming. However, a federal appellate court overturned the broadcast flag requirement on the ground that the FCC exceeded its authority in adopting such a rule (*American Library Association v. FCC*, 406 F.3d 689, 2005). Unfortunately for consumers, manufacturers had already produced millions of digital TV sets containing broadcast flag technology before the court ruling.

Congress also considered new broadcast flag legislation and also legislation intended to close what industry advocates were calling the "analog hole." That term refers to the yellow, red and white video and audio output jacks on TV sets, which allow programs to be transferred to analog devices and ultimately to computers where the programs can be converted back to a digital format. Copyright owners want to ban analog output jacks to curb what they say is illegal copying. Consumer advocates argue that transferring content from one device to another (and most home video recording) is legal—and should remain so.

Meanwhile, record companies began marketing CDs in a copy-protected format without labeling them. Those CDs often would not play on computers. That led consumer advocates to sue the industry, seeking an order requiring that the copy-protected CDs at least be labeled and also seeking compensation to consumers for alleged damage to their equipment caused by the new CDs. And technology buffs in England reported that Sony's proprietary CD copy-protection system could be defeated by scribbling around the rim of the disk with a felt-tip marker. Sony and other record labels abandoned their CD copy-protection systems, at least temporarily.

The industry also began aggressively lobbying for state anti-piracy laws. About 20 states had enacted or were considering such laws by 2006.

The Electronic Frontier Foundation sued the major studios and TV networks in 2002 in an attempt to define consumers' TV-recording rights in the digital age. The online civil liberties group asked a federal judge to declare that consumers can use digital recorders to watch shows after they are broadcast, skip all commercials, transmit recordings to members of their households and send copies of free TV broadcasts to anyone on the Internet provided they receive no compensation. This was a countersuit filed in response to an industry lawsuit intended to halt the sale of digital video recorders (DVRs) that allow commercial-skipping. Eventually the lawsuits were dropped and the broadcast networks agreed on a new rating system that takes into account commercial-skipping with DVRs. Most TV advertising prices are based on measurements of the actual viewership of advertising, including DVR replays after the scheduled viewing time.

In 2004, the European Parliament approved new copyright rules for the European Union that are similar to the Digital Millennium Copyright Act, to the alarm of civil liberties and consumer groups in Europe. As a compromise, European regulators deleted a ban on devices that circumvent copy-protection measures and added protections for consumers "acting in good faith" who make copies for their own use. Each individual EU member country must approve the rules. In 2008, President George W. Bush signed the "Prioritizing Resources and Organization for Intellectual Property" (PRO-IP) Act of 2008, legislation toughening piracy penalties and creating an "intellectual property czar" who advises the president on strengthening copyrights domestically and internationally.

Webcasting and Copyrights

With little controversy, Congress quietly passed the Digital Performance Right in Sound Recordings Act of 1995, a law that ultimately forced many broadcasters to think twice about streaming their regular programming over the Internet. For the first time, this law gave record companies the right to receive royalties when their recordings are played over the air—but only on digital audio broadcast services, not ordinary AM and FM radio stations. As noted earlier, free, over-the-air broadcasters pay performance royalties only to the owners of music copyrights (via licensing agencies such as ASCAP and BMI), not to record companies and recording artists. In 2008, record companies were lobbying Congress for a change in the law to require AM and FM broadcasters to pay them royalties, just as digital broadcasters and webcasters must.

At first most broadcasters weren't alarmed by the 1995 law because it didn't seem to affect them, but it made music more costly for one of their competitors: satellite-based for-pay digital audio broadcasters. However, the law quickly became a huge problem once they started doing webcasting, streaming their over-the-air programming on the Internet.

In 2000, the U.S. Copyright Office issued rules explaining how the 1998 Digital Millennium Copyright Act and the 1995 Digital Performance Right law would apply to broadcasters. The new rules decreed that broadcasters, like other digital programmers, would pay separate royalties for streaming copyrighted music on their websites, and that for the first time they would pay royalties not only to music licensing agencies such as ASCAP and BMI but also to record companies for the use of sound recordings.

The Copyright Office also ruled that broadcasters who stream their regular programming over the Internet must follow a series of restrictions on digital broadcasts imposed by Congress in the 1995 law. That law forbids the streaming of more than three songs from one album or four songs by one artist in a three-hour period, and also forbids identifying a song before it is played. The result: many broadcasters could not put their over-the-air programming on the Internet without breaking the law because they routinely identify songs or recording artists before a song is played, and they often exceed the limitation on songs from one album or by one artist. (Broadcasters and the recording industry eventually agreed to modify some of these restrictions.)

In 2002, matters only got worse. A Copyright Arbitration Royalty Panel that had been established to set royalty rates proposed rates so high that most webcasters said they could not afford to pay them. The panel also said the rates would be *retroactive* to 1998. Many webcasters protested that the rates exceeded their total income. Eventually the Copyright Office modified the rates set by the panel but still left the rates prohibitively high for many webcasters. Later Congress also acted to reduce the rates temporarily for small and noncommercial webcasters, while broadcasters negotiated more favorable terms for webcasting.

In 2007 the newly established Copyright Royalty Board adopted still higher rates for webcasters with no discount for many small webcasters, prompting Congress to again consider reducing the rates. In response, SoundExchange, the entity that collects royalties for the recording industry, said it would negotiate with webcasters for possible temporary royalty rate reductions. Another problem

---

**Focus on...
Celeb suits**

Lindsay Lohan made headlines in 2010 when she sued financial company E*Trade for $100 million, alleging that a "milkaholic" baby in an E*Trade ad named Lindsay was modeled after her. But she's not the only celeb to sue.

In 2010 Paris Hilton, described by the Ninth Circuit as "a flamboyant heiress," won the right to pursue a trademark claim against Hallmark Cards for using her registered mark "That's hot" on a greeting card. The card showed Hilton serving a customer at a diner. She argued that the card was a rip-off of an episode of "The Simple Life" where she and Nicole Richie worked at a Sonic fast food restaurant.

Hallmark defended its use as a parody, but the court said Hilton had a good chance of demonstrating to a jury that it did not meet the legal standards (*Hilton v. Hallmark Cards*, 580 F.3d 874). The court remanded the case for a trial.

was that the Copyright Royalty Board also established a $500-a-year "administrative" fee that each webcaster would have to pay, regardless of its audience size or revenue, if any. For services like Live365.com, which in 2007 was hosting 10,000 webcasters (mostly individuals programming one or a few channels from their homes), that cost was impossibly high ($5 million a year in the case of Live365, a company that made a profit of $7,000 the previous year). Passing the cost along to the individual webcasters, many of whom had little or no revenue and were webcasting to express a viewpoint or as a hobby, would only force more webcasters to shut down.

In August 2007, a group representing online audio broadcasters reached a royalty agreement with SoundExchange. The deal temporarily reduced rates sufficiently that many Internet broadcasters could continue their programming. Online broadcasters were also negotiating separately with ASCAP and BMI to reduce the royalties they have to pay to the copyright owners of the underlying music as opposed to the recorded performances. By mid-2008, though, webcasters were seeking rate relief from Congress, pointing out that webcasters are still paying more per listener per song than satellite radio services. Traditional AM and FM radio stations still pay royalties only to music copyright owners, not to record labels. In 2009, SoundExchange and radio broadcasters had come to an agreement where SoundExchange would discount royalty rates for radio broadcasters who also simulcast online; this agreement does not extend to Internet-only radio stations, some of which were facing bankruptcy. Congress also passed the Webcaster Settlement Act of 2009, which would give webcasting groups and the recording industry 30 days to reach settlements on Internet radio music royalties.

Another obstacle to webcasting came from the Associated Press, which announced that it would charge broadcasters, newspapers and others an additional fee if they place AP stories and photos on their websites. AP has repeatedly threatened to sue website owners and bloggers who used even small excerpts from AP stories, despite the fair use doctrine. That leaves individuals and small website owners with the choice of taking down materials that are probably protected by fair use or fighting a legal battle against a well-funded entity. The AP launched one such crusade against the posting of brief excerpts of AP stories on the *Drudge Retort* (as opposed to the larger *Drudge Report*) in 2008.

Podcasting, which exploded on the scene in the 2000s, is subject to royalty payments if copyrighted material is used. Podcasting differs from webcasting in that the programming is designed to be downloaded for later playing on a portable player, like an iPod. Many podcasters deliver their files to their subscribers automatically, sometimes for a fee.

What is an interactive service? The Digital Millennium Copyright Act requires websites that stream music pay copyright owners individually if they are considered "interactive services"—meaning that they allow users to customize their experiences. At issue in the 2009 case of *Arista Records, LLC v. LAUNCHcast* (578 F.3d 148), was whether webcaster LAUNCHcast was an interactive service. If it was, then the company must pay individual licensing fees to copyright holders; if not, it would only have to pay a lower statutory licensing fee. LAUNCHcast allows users to create "stations" that play songs within a genre or similar to artists that users select. The Second Circuit said that that this was not sufficiently interactive to qualify LAUNCHcast as an interactive service. Users cannot request a particular song, and the webcaster "does not provide sufficient control to users such that playlists are so predictable that users will choose to listen to the webcast in lieu of purchasing music, thereby—in the aggregate—diminishing record sales."

Freelancers and Electronic Publishing

Until about 1995, most major publishers did not include a provision in the contracts signed by freelancers to cover electronic rights. The National Writers Union, an organization that represents about 3,000 freelance writers, sued the New York Times Co., other major publishers and the Lexis-Nexis computer database for using the writers' work electronically without specific permission. The publishers contended that these electronic databases were merely reproductions of the printed versions—and no separate copyright permission was required.

In 2001, the Supreme Court sided with the writers in *New York Times Co. v. Tasini* (533 U.S. 483). In this case, the Court ruled that Jonathan Tasini, former president of the National Writers Union, and other freelancers, own the electronic rights to their works unless they specifically assign those rights to a publisher.

The case involved only material produced by *freelancers* as opposed to staff writers. Under the "works made for hire" provision of the Copyright Act, employers automatically own the copyrights to works created by employees within the scope of their employment. It also does not involve most freelance works published since 1995, when major publishers began including specific provisions to authorize electronic republication in their standard contracts.

Responding to the Court's decision, representatives of the *New York Times* pointed out that between 1980 and 1995, the years covered by *Tasini*, the *Times* had published about 115,000 articles written by 27,000 different freelancers. Because of the difficulty of tracking down all of these authors and securing permission, *Times* publisher Arthur Sulzberger, Jr. said the *Times* "will now undertake the difficult and sad process of removing significant portions from its electronic historical archive." Some historians, including documentary filmmaker Ken Burns and historian Doris Kearns Goodwin, who filed an *amicus curiae* ("friend of the court") brief supporting the publishers, also lamented the gaps in the historical record that would result from the *Tasini* decision because publishers eventually removed so much freelance work from their databases.

Tasini said his union would be happy to work out a licensing system for freelancers similar to that used by ASCAP and BMI to compensate music copyright owners, with freelancers compensated each time someone accesses the electronic version of a story or other material that appeared in the major media. But by 2002, it was clear that the historians' worst fears were coming true. The *New York Times* removed more than 100,000 articles from its online archive and only restored about 15,000 of them after coming to terms with authors. Many of the other authors either could not be located or had not reached an agreement with the newspaper. And other newspapers that were not as concerned about being a newspaper of record as the *Times* simply deleted all pre-1995 freelance materials from their online archives and made no attempt to strike deals with freelance authors.

In joining Justice John Paul Stevens' dissenting opinion in the *Tasini* case, Justice Stephen Breyer said, "We may wipe out much of the history of the 20th century." The history isn't really gone. For those with the time and money to do research page by page, the full text of many newspapers remains intact on microfilm in some libraries. But for those who need the speed and global reach of online research, Justice Breyer's concern seems well-founded.

A New York federal district court approved an $18 million settlement in a class action suit brought by freelance writers whose publishers reproduced the works for electronic distribution without authorization in the wake of *Tasini*. Freelancer Irvin Muchnick and others brought suit in the Second Circuit, claiming the settlement was inadequate and problematic

Berne convention:
an international copyright agreement that requires all signatory countries to recognize the same rights for foreign creators as they do for their own citizens as well as adhere to certain minimum standards of protection.

because of its division of works into categories based on their times and statuses of copyright registration.

The Second Circuit overturned the settlement in 2007 (*Muchnick v. Thomson Corp. (In re Literary Works in Elec. Databases Copyright Litig.)*, 509 F.3d 116), saying the trial court could not rule on claims relating to unregistered works, as the Copyright Act grants federal district courts jurisdiction only over claims on registered works. Thus, the federal district court could not certify a class in the litigation. The Supreme Court in 2010 said the Second Circuit had erred. Writing for an 8-0 Court (Justice Sonia Sotomayor did not participate), Justice Clarence Thomas said that a copyright holder's failure to register a work does not restrict a federal court's jurisdiction over claims related to unregistered works. While most copyright holders are required by the Copyright Act to register their works prior to filing a federal lawsuit, the registration requirement "is a precondition to filing a claim that does not restrict a federal court's subject-matter jurisdiction," Thomas wrote (*Reed Elsevier, Inc. v. Muchnick*, 130 S. Ct. 1237).

In 2011, the Second Circuit said that the settlement did not represent the interests of most of the class. There was differential payment based on whether an article had been registered with the Copyright Office (registered articles were entitled to more money). Thus, the court concluded, "the district court abused its discretion in certifying the class and approving the settlement, because the named plaintiffs failed to adequately represent the interests of all class members"—one of the main requirements to certify a class (*In re Literary Works in Elect. Databases Copyright Litig.*, 654 F.3d 242).

Copyright Trolls

A new type of plaintiff made the news in 2010 and 2011, pejoratively labeled "copyright trolls." These copyright-holding companies approach copyright owners to purchase their rights and then aggressively sue those who allegedly infringe those works. Many users will just settle for statutory damages rather than fight the suit in court—an outcome that these companies count on. One judge disparaged the "business model" of these groups:

> Digiprotect acquires such rights from various copyright holders in order to—as Digiprotect's counsel described it—"educate consumers." This "education" of consumers consists primarily of bringing suit against such consumers and seeking "modest settlements" (*Digiprotect USA Corp. v. Does 1-266*, 2011 U.S. Dist. LEXIS 40679, 2011).

There are a number of such groups in action. For example, a group of attorneys calling themselves the U.S. Copyright Group

(USCG) made the news in 2010 by including nearly 5,000 anonymous defendants who downloaded the movie *The Hurt Locker* in one suit for one filing fee—what the EFF calls "spamigation." Such a move could be a money-maker for the USCG and copyright holders, as most defendants will likely pay $1,500-2,500 to escape the potential to have to shell out $150,000 or more. The judge in the case asked the USCG to explain why she should not remove 4,576 of the 4,577 anonymous defendants. The USCG said that all infringers "are both uploading and downloading portions of the file simultaneously." In 2011, USCG and Voltage Pictures, the studio behind *The Hurt Locker,* added 25,000 anonymous defendants to the list—making the case the largest one to date against filesharers. That case is pending.

One of the more notorious trolls, Righthaven LLC, bought rights for old news stories from the *Las Vegas Review-Journal* and brought over a hundred infringement suits in Nevada federal court. In one case against Democratic Underground, an online community for Democrats and progressives, the website (represented by Electronic Frontier Foundation (EFF) attorneys) claimed that the quote targeted by Righthaven (five sentences out of a 54-sentence article) was actually fair use—and filed a counterclaim against Righthaven.

Chief Judge Roger Hunt of the Nevada federal district court ruled for Democratic Underground. He said that Righthaven had never owned the copyright, and the actual owner was not named in the suit. Moreover, the judge called the claims of ownership "disingenuous, if not outright deceitful," and gave Righthaven two weeks to explain to him in writing "why it should not be sanctioned for this flagrant misrepresentation to the Court" (*Righthaven LLC v. Democratic Underground LLC,* 791 F. Supp. 2d 968, 2011).

EFF was jubilant after the win, saying in a press release: "In dismissing Righthaven's claim in its entirety, Chief Judge Hunt's ruling decisively rejected the Righthaven business model of conveying rights to sue, alone, as a means to enforce copyrights. The ruling speaks for itself." Does this spell the end of copyright trolling? Given the amount of money at stake in these kinds of cases, it's likely that groups like Digiprotect, Righthaven and USCG will try other legal techniques before the courts before they throw in the towel. Many such cases are dismissed, with the plaintiffs ordered to pay attorneys' fees (in one 2011 case, Righthaven was ordered to pay $120,000 in fees to Democratic Underground).

Other Internet Copyright Issues

Still other copyright problems have been created by cyberspace. A number of individual website owners have faced lawsuits because copyrighted materials were posted on their sites could be downloaded. Several cases involved copyrighted software or digitized images.

Playboy Enterprises has aggressively pursued the owners of Internet sites containing images owned by Playboy. In 1998, Playboy won what was then the largest statutory damage award in the history of American copyright law, a $3.74 million judgment against the owner of a site that allegedly distributed 7,475 Playboy-owned photographs over the Internet (*Playboy Enterprises v. Sanfilippo,* 1998 U.S. Dist. LEXIS 4773). In the late 1990s Playboy also won six-figure and seven-figure statutory damage awards against several other website operators.

Playboy also sued Terri Welles, the 1981 *Playboy* magazine "Playmate of the Year," in an attempt to keep her from identifying herself by that title on her website. However, a federal judge refused to grant a preliminary injunction in that case, holding that Playboy was unlikely to prevail in court even though "Playmate of the Year" is a registered trademark of Playboy. The judge said that a title such as "Playmate of the Year" becomes a part of a person's identity, like being an Academy Award winner, a former Miss America or a Heisman

Trophy winner. To indicate this status on a website is a fair use under trademark law. Playboy appealed and the Ninth Circuit affirmed the judge's ruling. In a later decision, the appellate court also held that Welles not only could identify herself as Playmate of the Year but that she could use words such as "playboy" and "playmate" in *metatags*—hidden keywords used by search engines. The court concluded that there were no suitable alternate words she could use in her metatags (*Playboy Enterprises v. Welles*, 162 F.3d 1169, 1998; 279 F.3d 796, 2002).

Search engines have also encountered other copyright and trademark problems. For one, Google.com and Yahoo.com have been sued by trademark owners for their lucrative practice of selling *sponsored links*—advertising tied to keyword searches. For example, if someone types the name of an insurance company or even a generic term like "car insurance," an ad for particular insurance company may appear along with the non-paid search results. Both Yahoo and Google now identify sponsored links, but they still sell advertising that pops up when a user types certain keywords, including brand names of competing products.

Google got in trouble for its keyword sales program in 2009. The Second Circuit found that Google's sale of keywords to trigger context-based advertising may be a use in commerce under the Lanham Act. When a user types in a word that Google has sold as an "AdWord," Google displays advertising on the search results screen that users can click on, and advertisers pay Google every time a user clicks on one of their ads. Advertisers could also buy their competitors' names as AdWords. Rescuecom, a computer-service franchising company, brought suit, saying that users may be confused because Google's labeling of "sponsored link" for keyword results is not clear.

Google's keyword ad sales may be use in commerce, said the court (*Rescuecom v. Google*, 562 F.3d 123): "Google's recommendation and sale of Rescuecom's mark to Google's advertisers, so as to trigger the appearance of their advertisements and links in a manner likely to cause consumer confusion when a Google user launches a search of Rescuecom's trademark, properly alleges a claim under the Lanham Act." The court said that it was not going to decide whether Google's use of Rescuecom's trademark in the AdWords program causes consumer confusion but it remanded the case to allow that question to be decided.

Keyword advertising continues to be litigated. In 2012, the Fourth Circuit said in *Rosetta Stone v. Google* (676 F.3d 144) that the district court's dismissal of the case was inappropriate. The case was the first time an appellate court established that a company can bring a trademark infringement suit on allegations that sponsored links confuse consumers. The court asked "whether there is sufficient evidence for a finder of fact to conclude that Google's 'use' of the mark in its AdWords program is 'likely to produce confusion in the minds of consumers about the origin of the goods or services in question.'" In answering yes, the court noted that it was possible to find that "Google intended to cause confusion in that it acted with the knowledge that confusion was very likely to result from its use of the marks."

The digital environment has created new issues in book publishing and access. In 2008, book authors and Google reached a settlement agreement for Google's "Library Project." Google had contracted with public and university libraries, including the University of Michigan, to create a digital archive of their holdings—many of which were still under copyright—for users to search for text online. The Authors Guild filed a class-action suit against Google. In the settlement, *Authors Guild v. Google* (No. 05 CV 8136, S.D.N.Y. 2008), the authors would receive $125 million in damages for those books scanned without permission, and a new not-for-profit organization controlled by authors and publishers will be created. Profits will be shared between Google and authors according to the terms of the settlement. Out-of-print books will be scanned and included by default, but books in print will have to be actively included. An amended settlement was filed in November 2009. The battle is ongoing. In 2012, Judge Denny Chin, who moved to the Second Circuit but still presides over this case, said that the authors would be granted class status to sue. Judge Chin wrote, "Class action is the superior method for resolving this litigation. It is, without question, more efficient and effective than requiring thousands of authors to sue individually" (*Authors Guild v. Google*, 2012 U.S. Dist. LEXIS 76080).

Still more perplexing copyright dilemmas have arisen online. One that may have no solution is "chain e-mail," the common practice of forwarding messages to large lists of friends, clients or customers. Someone will put a copyrighted work online, often dropping the original byline and copyright notice. He/she sends it to a few dozen friends, who then send it to others. Before long, thousands or millions of people have received the message.

How can any author protect his or her work from infringement by chain e-mail? This is only one of the dilemmas involving the Internet that must be resolved—if it can be resolved.

Federal law regulates "false copyright management information," punishing the publication or distribution of knowingly false copyright management information (17 U.S.C. § 1202). But what information is covered in copyright management information (CMI)? The Third Circuit reversed a DMCA claim based on CMI in *Murphy v. Millennium Radio Group LLC* (650 F.3d 295). Peter Murphy, a photographer, was hired by *New Jersey Monthly* magazine to photograph two New Jersey radio hosts for WKXW, owned by Millennium Radio Group; the image made it look like the hosts were nude, standing behind a WKXW sign. Then the radio station uploaded the image on its website without Murphy's permission and removed the identifying information, including the "gutter credit" identifying Murphy as the photographer. Moreover, visitors to the WKXW website were encouraged to manipulate the photo. The hosts made Murphy a subject of one of their shows, calling him "gay" (that part of the case is discussed in Chapter Four).

Murphy sued, saying that the federal CMI statute was violated when his credits were removed. He also said the use was not a fair use. The district court dismissed both claims, but the Third Circuit reversed: "the mere fact that Murphy's name appeared in a printed gutter credit near the Image rather than as data in an 'automated copyright protection or management system' does not prevent it from qualifying as CMI or remove it from the protection of § 1202." The court said that the posting of the photo on WKXW's website was not a fair use. This was among the first circuits to address what kind of information is included in CMI.

■ INTERNATIONAL COPYRIGHTS

So far, this discussion has concerned mostly domestic copyrights in the United States. But copyrights are becoming more and more an international matter. However, for more than 100 years the United States refused to become a participant in the *Berne Convention,* a major international copyright agreement. When the Berne Convention for the Protection of Literary and Artistic Works was established in 1886, the U.S. was probably the world's leading copyright pirate. American publishers freely republished European books without paying any royalties to the copyright owners. While most European nations agreed on a system of international copyright control, the U.S. simply refused to sign up.

How, then, have American works gained international copyright protection over the years? The U.S. has participated in another international copyright agreement called the *Universal Copyright Convention (UCC)* and also entered into reciprocal copyright agreements with individual countries. But perhaps more important, major U.S. publishers often arranged for the simultaneous publication of major works in Berne Convention member countries such as Canada to obtain full international copyright protection.

During the twentieth century the U.S. ceased to be a major copyright pirate and has instead become the world's leading *victim* of international copyright infringement. The result: U.S. copyright owners, including not only authors and movie-makers but computer software creators, began pressing Congress to join the Berne Convention. After 102 years of U.S. non-participation in the Berne Convention, Congress finally acted to allow this country to join—by approving the Berne Convention Implementation Act of 1988. On March 1, 1989, the United States officially joined the Berne Convention, becoming the 79th nation to do so. That gave American copyright owners protection in 24 countries with which the United States had no other copyright arrangement.

The Berne Convention offers far more copyright protection than the Universal Copyright Convention, of which the United States has long been a member. In essence, the UCC merely says copyright owners in any member country have whatever rights local citizens have in other member countries. If a country has little copyright protection, foreigners as well as that country's own citizens have little protection from piracy there. The Berne Convention, on the other hand, sets *minimum standards* for copyright protection, requiring each member country to provide at least that much protection.

The 1988 legislation made a number of revisions in U.S. copyright law to bring it into compliance with the requirements of the Berne Convention. For example, international copyrights are now protected under U.S. law *without registration.* But works published in the United States still must be registered before the owner can sue an infringer in U.S. courts.

Foreign copyright owners may sue for *actual damages* and other remedies (as opposed to statutory damages) without ever registering, although actual damages are often nonexistent in copyright cases (because the infringer often makes no profit). Domestic copyright owners may also sue for actual damages even if the copyright is unregistered when the infringement occurs—but they must still register before filing an infringement lawsuit, as explained earlier. Foreigners don't have to do that.

The complete elimination of copyright notice requirements was also required by the Berne Convention. Berne member countries must provide copyright protection *without any formalities.* However, compliance with the Berne Convention must comply with the First Amendment. A federal district court held a part of the Copyright Act violates the First Amendment in 2009. The case was remanded from the Tenth Circuit with orders to re-evaluate part of the Copyright Act, the Uruguay Round Agreement Act (URAA), which restores the U.S. copyrights of "foreign authors who lost those rights to the public domain for any reason other than the expiration of a copyright term." The plaintiffs, American performing artists who used works by foreign artists that had been in the public domain, such as Sergei Prokofiev's "Peter and the Wolf," claimed they were harmed by the higher licensing costs on the renewed copyrighted work. On remand, the judge said that although the Berne Convention does require some form of copyright restoration, URAA violates the First Amendment.

The Tenth Circuit reversed in 2010, saying that the URAA does *not* violate the First Amendment. Securing foreign copyrights for American works is a substantial interest. In 2011, the Supreme Court said that Section 514 of URAA did not exceed Congress' authority under the Copyright Act (*Golan v. Holder,* No. 10-545). Justice Ruth Bader Ginsburg, writing for a 6-2 majority (Justice Elena Kagan did not participate), said that no one gets any personal benefit to copy a work that is in the public domain, so returning works to copyright protection does not abridge anyone's rights. Moreover, she added, there is historical precedent that there is nothing sacred about the public domain: "The First Congress, it thus appears, did not view the public domain as inviolate." The implications are clear; the Court supported Congress' desire to have all works governed by the same legal policies, regardless of their circumstances of publication. The law, Ginsburg said, "continued the trend toward a harmonized copyright regime by placing foreign works in the position they would have occupied if the current regime had been in effect when those works were created and first published."

Justice Stephen Breyer, joined by Justice Samuel Alito, dissented. Breyer said that Congress did not, under the Copyright Act, have the authority to enact Section 514. Moreover, he said, since the Copyright Act is intended to encourage production of new works, this law should fail because it "provides no monetary incentive to produce anything new" as it affects only works already created.

American copyright owners gained even more international protection under the intellectual property provisions of the General Agreement on Tariffs and Trade (GATT), which was signed by 117 countries in 1994. GATT is a worldwide agreement covering many aspects of international business; its intellectual property provisions cover patents and trademarks as well as copyrights. In general, the GATT copyright provisions closely parallel the Berne Convention rules, setting minimum standards for international copyright protection. Perhaps the most important change is that the GATT provisions, once ratified by the signing countries, will apply in many countries that never joined the Berne Convention. The GATT provisions are administered by the World Trade Organization through the World Intellectual Property Organization (WIPO). Over time, GATT will have a major impact on U.S. copyrights, patents and trademarks. Perhaps GATT's major weakness is that, like many global agreements, it may be difficult to enforce in some signing countries.

Because the GATT agreement is so far-reaching, copyright lawyers spent years trying to sort out how it affects U.S. law. One of the first issues to arise was the question of *copyright restoration*. Under GATT, a large number of foreign works that had fallen into the public domain under U.S. law had their copyright protection restored. This is true because the copyrights of many pre-1978 works that had expired under U.S. law were restored under the longer copyright terms provided by other countries and recognized by the U.S. legislation to implement GATT. (See *Golan v. Holder*, in this chapter.) This particularly affects those who use footage from

---

Focus on...
Trademark genericide

When a trademark's owners allow others to use their marks in a generic way, they run the risk that they will lose those marks.

One of the more famous cases of trademark genericide is Bayer's loss of the trademark on Aspirin. Patented in 1900, the drug was quickly adopted for pain relief. German company Bayer allowed other companies to market their acetylsalicylic acid tablets under the Aspirin name, and it eventually lost the trademark (it was forced to give it up under the Treaty of Versailles after World War I).

The word Aspirin, according to a medical journal of the day, came from A for acetyl and "Spirsäure," an old German word for salicylic acid.

One can understand why the word "aspirin" caught on; somehow, asking for an "acetylsalicylic acid tablet" for your headache might just make your head hurt more!

old movies that were once in the public domain but may now be protected by copyright law again. A major concern is so-called *"orphan works:"* works whose copyright owners have vanished. Under the new rules, some of these old, formerly public-domain works again have valid copyrights—but there is no one available to grant permission for anyone to use these works. Companies that provide stock movie footage have been concerned that if they continue to use these ex-public-domain works without obtaining copyright clearances, owners of some of the reinstated copyrights may suddenly appear out of the blue and sue for copyright infringement. Because of extended copyright terms, millions of copyrighted works have also become orphan works.

The U.S. Copyright Office issued a lengthy report on the problem of orphan works in 2006, recommending new rules under which those who make a good-faith effort to find a work's owner would be liable only for modest fees and not the normal copyright infringement penalties if the owner later turns up.

In 2010 the U.S. was considering a new international intellectual property initiative called the Anti-Counterfeiting Trade Agreement (ACTA). The U.S. is one of several countries considering the act (including the European Union countries, Canada, Japan, Mexico, South Korea, Australia and New Zealand). According to the Office of the U.S. Trade Representative, ACTA is intended to "assist in the efforts of governments around the world to more effectively combat the proliferation of counterfeit and pirated goods, which undermines legitimate trade and the sustainable development of the world economy, and in some cases contributes to organized crime and exposes American families to dangerous fake products." Critics point out several problems with the act; for example, it contains fewer protections for online service providers, leaves out key definitions for "piracy" and "counterfeiting," and lacks many of the balancing elements that are currently part of U.S. intellectual property law. Concerns have been raised throughout the negotiation process about the secrecy surrounding the act; requests for information have been regularly denied, but a final version was released in 2010. In June 2012 the European Union parliament voted against ACTA, but the United States continues to support the act.

Despite the international agreements, Congress still has not fully addressed one major difference between U.S. law and the seemingly mandatory requirements of international copyright law: the recognition of *moral rights*.

Moral Rights and Other Issues

The debate over moral rights became heated when Congress voted to change U.S. copyright law to make it compatible with the requirements of the Berne Convention—more or less. In essence, moral rights give the creator of a copyrighted work some say over what happens to it later, even if the copyright is sold to someone else (such as a publishing house or a motion picture distributor).

Under American law, the copyright owner (who is often not the creator of the work) has the absolute right to change a literary or artistic work without the consent of the original author or artist. But under Article 6 of the Berne Convention, each member country must recognize moral rights, thereby giving the original artist the right to prevent the work from being changed without his or her consent.

The moral rights question has always been a major obstacle to American participation in the Berne Convention: U.S. copyright owners strongly oppose any recognition of moral rights, while groups of authors and artists want such rights. The moral rights issue received considerable publicity in connection with the colorization of older black and white motion pictures. Many of the actors and directors who made these movies view colorization as a sacrilege—like mutilating a classic painting. But the copyright owners see colorization as a way to make the films more appealing to a new generation of movie viewers. Cable entrepreneur Ted Turner was at the center of this controversy because his company colorized almost the entire MGM library of classic films. He purchased the copyrights to these films in the mid-1980s and then had them colorized, something he had every right to do, despite the bitter objections of many actors and directors.

For the most part, Congress sided with Turner and other copyright owners, refusing to recognize moral rights. When Congress voted to have the United States join the Berne Convention—still without recognizing moral rights—that action stirred a controversy among copyright lawyers. Some contended that signing the Berne Convention automatically gave legal recognition to moral rights in the United States, despite Congress' efforts to sidestep the issue. Others pointed out that the 1988 law specifically said joining the Berne Convention did not change American law on this point. And there was the question of how the U.S. could legally sign a treaty while steadfastly refusing to recognize one of its major provisions.

Some copyright owners argued that U.S. *trademark* laws now give adequate protection to moral rights, and that the U.S. could comply with the Berne Convention's moral rights provisions without changing American copyright law. To support that claim, they pointed to cases such as *Lamothe v. Atlantic Recording Corp.* (847 F.2d 1403), a 1988 decision of the Ninth Circuit. That case held that two rock musicians could use the Lanham Act, the federal trademark law, to sue a third musician who falsely claimed that he was the sole author of songs that they co-authored. They claimed that the third musician, Robinson Crosby of Ratt, falsely claimed sole credit for two songs on the album *Out of the Cellar*.

On the other hand, many in the creative community scoffed at the idea that U.S. trademark law provides adequate protection for moral rights. Trademark law only requires accurate labeling, not keeping the works true to the original artistic intent, they pointed out. For example, U.S. trademark law would allow a Picasso painting to be cut into pieces and sold as long as each piece is truthfully labeled as a Picasso. Under *Lamothe*, the copyright owner is still free to change a creative work without the creator's permission—as long as authorship credit is given. To the creators of copyrighted works, changing their artistic intent and still leaving their names on the work may be even worse than changing the work and dropping their names.

To address the issue of colorization, in 1988 Congress enacted a compromise law that pleased almost no one: the National Film Preservation Act. It created a National Film Preservation Board with representatives from 13 industry groups, including both the creative community and copyright owners. The board is authorized to nominate up to 25 films per year for inclusion in a National Film Registry. Each nominated film must be at least 10 years old, and only films that were released in theaters are eligible. The Librarian of Congress chooses some or all of the nominated films for inclusion in the registry. If a film is included, it can still be altered (or colorized) by the copyright owner, but there must be a conspicuous statement included in the altered version saying that the original film has been altered.

In 1990, Congress went a step further in protecting the rights of visual artists—but still stopped far short of giving full recognition to moral rights. The Visual Artists Rights Act of 1990 gives sculptors, painters and other visual artists the final say over whether their names

trade dress:
packaging or design
of a product that
promotes the product
and distinguishes it
from similar products;
e.g., the shape of a
Coca-Cola bottle.

secondary meaning:
a meaning that devel-
ops when the public
associates a trademark
with a particular
producer, rather
than the underlying
product.

are used on their works. Thus, artists can require that their names be kept on their works, and they can prevent their names from being used on works that have been altered without their permission. Also, the new law gives visual artists the right to sue those who mutilate or destroy their art works—even if they no longer own the copyright. However, it does not apply to many works created before this law went into effect. Nor does it apply to "works made for hire:" if the owner of a building commissions an artist to do a sculpture for the lobby, for example, a future owner of the building can ordinarily remove the sculpture without violating the law. A federal appellate court so ruled in a 1995 case, *Carter v. Helmsley-Spear Inc.* (71 F.3rd 77). The act also gives artists the right to "salvage" their works when they are about to be demolished—when a building with a mural on a wall is about to be torn down, for example. But the law says the artist has to pay for the removal process, which can be expensive. The Visual Artists Rights Act does not change the law concerning the colorization of motion pictures.

■ UNFAIR COMPETITION

Earlier in this chapter we pointed out that news, factual information and ideas cannot be copyrighted. However, there is another kind of law that may prevent one news medium from systematically pirating its news from another. That legal action is called *unfair competition* or *misappropriation,* and it has often been used as a supplement to copyright law. Unlike copyright, which is now exclusively governed by a federal statutory law, unfair competition is a tort action that has developed primarily through state court decisions. There is no federal unfair competition statute and few states have enacted statutory laws in this field even today.

Unfair competition was recognized as a separate legal action largely as a result of a 1918 U.S. Supreme Court decision that came to be regarded as a classic ruling: *International News Service v. Associated Press* (248 U.S. 215). The case arose because INS, owned by the Hearst newspaper chain, consistently appropriated AP stories (this was possible because some Hearst papers were also AP members) and distributed them to INS customers as if they were INS stories. The Supreme Court acknowledged that the news cannot be copyrighted, but it ruled that no business may purloin its basic commodity from a competitor, "reaping where it has not sown," to use the Court's language, a paraphrase of a passage from the Bible.

Following this Supreme Court precedent, a number of other courts have ruled similarly in similar situations, creating a new common law legal action for misappropriation. For instance, in 1963 the Pennsylvania Supreme Court decided a very similar case in the same way. In that case (*Pottstown Daily News Publishing Company v. Pottstown Broadcasting*, 192 A.2d 657), the court found unfair competition where a radio station had been pirating its news from the local newspaper on an ongoing basis.

However, some doubts were raised about unfair competition as an alternative to copyright law by two 1964 U.S. Supreme Court decisions, *Sears Roebuck and Co. v. Stiffel* (376 U.S. 225) and *Compco v. Day-Brite Lighting* (376 U.S. 234). These were unfair competition cases involving mechanical designs that could not be patented rather than news that could not be copyrighted, but the court's language was alarmingly sweeping.

The Supreme Court said the states simply could not create alternative forms of protection to fill in the gaps left by copyright and patent law. "When an article is unprotected by a patent or a copyright, *state* law may not forbid others to copy that article," the Supreme Court said (emphasis added). The Court seemed to be saying the entire field of patent and copyright law is federally preempted, thus denying the states any role in this area. And as already noted, even if the federal government did not preempt copyright law then, the new Copyright Act makes it clear that Congress intended to preempt copyright law in 1976.

However, a 1973 U.S. Supreme Court decision resurrected unfair competition as a viable legal action—if it was ever eliminated. In *Goldstein v. California* (412 U.S. 546), the court upheld a California law against record piracy at a time when copyright law did not cover sound recordings, despite the defendant's contention that the federal government had preempted the field under the *Sears* and *Compco* decisions.

In recent years there have been numerous unfair competition lawsuits in various states—and the courts have held that unfair competition still exists as a valid basis for a lawsuit, although it only covers a few activities that fall very close to the news piracy that led to the original *INS v. AP* case.

A New York federal judge allowed a lawsuit to go forward by the Associated Press against a competitor for copyright infringement and violation of the "hot news" tort. The "hot news" tort comes from *INS v. AP*, where the Court said that breaking news could be considered the "quasi property" of a news service.

In *Associated Press v. All Headline News Corp.* (37 Media L. Rep. 1403, 2009), the AP alleged that AHN rewrote and repackaged breaking news stories and infringed its copyright in doing so; AHN said that "hot news" is protected from copyright infringement. The judge disagreed with AHN, using the NBA pager case below as precedent, and allowed the infringement case to stand. The five elements to bring a "hot news" tort in New York were met, the judge said, quoting from the *NBA* case:

> (i) a plaintiff generates or gathers information at a cost; (ii) the information is time-sensitive; (iii) a defendant's use of the information constitutes free riding on the plaintiff's efforts; (iv) the defendant is in direct competition with a product or service offered by the plaintiffs; and (v) the ability of other parties to free-ride on the efforts of the plaintiff or others would so reduce the incentive to produce the product or service that its existence or quality would be substantially threatened.

The case settled in 2009 for an unspecified sum. A joint press release said that AHN "acknowledge[d] there were many instances in which AHN improperly used AP's content without AP's consent."

But "hot news" is still in the news: In *Barclays Capital Inc. v. TheFlyOnTheWall.com Inc.*, the Second Circuit overturned a New York federal court ruling against a financial news website for publishing stock recommendations of Wall Street banking firms, calling it a "hot news" misappropriation. But the appellate court reversed: "A firm's ability to make news—by issuing a recommendation that is likely to affect the market price of a security—does not give rise to a right for it to control who breaks that news and how" (650 F.3d 876). In addition, the court said, Fly's website, "which collects, summarizes, and disseminates the news of the firms' recommendations— is not the 'INS-like' product that could support a non-preempted cause of action for misappropriation"—rejecting *INS* as a precedent here.

A new controversy over the concept of unfair competition arose in the 1990s when various companies began providing sports scores and statistics *during actual sporting events.* For a fee, both computer and pager users could receive this information in real time. The National Basketball Association—backed by other sports leagues—eventually sued over this practice, alleging misappropriation under New York's unfair competition laws.

In *NBA v. Motorola* (105 F.3d 841), a 1997 decision, a federal appellate court held that providing sports information in this way is neither a copyright infringement nor unfair competition. The court noted that only the broadcast descriptions of the games (not the games themselves) can be copyrighted. And these services were not even copying the broadcast descriptions, the court held. Instead, they monitored the broadcasts and compiled their own statistics—using factual information that is available to all. In essence, the court said this was different from systematically taking someone else's news stories, rewriting them, and then selling them via a competing wire service. Even if the NBA develops its own real-time sports information service, others may monitor broadcasts to provide factual information to competing services, the court said.

Several companies offer "fantasy" sports in which participants use the names and statistics of actual players in their games. An estimated 13 million Americans were playing fantasy sports by 2008, mostly in arrangements licensed by the sports leagues. But C.B.C. Distribution and Marketing was sued by Major League Baseball in a contractual dispute. MLB contended that C.B.C.'s fantasy games violate its copyrights and the right of publicity of the players. C.B.C. contended that it has a First Amendment right to use the names and statistics of players whose names are in the news media daily—without paying licensing fees. The Eighth Circuit ruled that C.B.C.'s use of players' names and statistics is protected by the First Amendment, raising doubts about the validity of other fantasy sports license agreements that involve paying sports leagues for the use of players' names and stats (*C.B.C. Distribution and Marketing v. Major League Baseball*, 505 F.3d 818, 2007). The Supreme Court denied *cert.*

Fantasy sports league players won again in 2009. A federal district court in Minnesota said that the provider of a fantasy football game did not need a license from the NFL to use player names, statistics and other information for its game (*CBS Interactive Inc. v. National Football League Players Inc.*, 259 F.R.D. 398, 2009). The court relied on *C.B.C. Distribution*, the fantasy baseball case decided by the Eighth Circuit in 2008. In trying to differentiate the two cases, the NFL argued that perhaps the First Amendment implications of fantasy football may be less than those of fantasy baseball because there was no evidence presented about which sport had more public interest. The court wisely avoided getting into that debate:

> The Court doubts that the Eighth Circuit intended in *C.B.C. Distribution* to
> articulate some special application of First Amendment jurisprudence to cases

involving baseball only. Accordingly, the Court declines to indulge in a philosophical debate about whether the public is more fascinated with baseball or
football or the statistics generated by each. Suffice it to say that there is no
dispute that both professional baseball and professional football and the statistics
generated by both sports are closely followed by a large segment of the public.

A related controversy arose in 2007 when the National Collegiate Athletic Association
(NCAA) ordered the University of Louisville to expel a *Louisville Courier-Journal* reporter
from a baseball playoff game for blogging about the game while it was underway. In essence,
the NCAA claimed that it has an exclusive right to forbid the dissemination of factual information about a game in progress. The newspaper's lawyers, among others, said the NCAA
has the right to control television coverage of the game, but not the use of uncopyrightable
factual information.

■ TRADEMARKS

Another area of intellectual property law that fills a gap in copyright protection is trademark, tradename and service mark law. There is a federal trademark law, the Lanham Act
(officially, the Trademark Act of 1946). But unlike the Copyright Act, it is nonexclusive;
it does not preempt state trademark laws. In fact, many states have their own trademark
statutes, and all states recognize at least some kind of inherent right of a business to adopt
a name and prevent imitators from using it under the common law. A person who infringes someone else's trademark may be sued in federal court, in state court, or both. About
30 states have adopted all or most of the provisions of the Model State Trademark Bill,
proposed by the International Trademark Association.

These laws govern the slogans or other short phrases, logos and designs, symbols and
names under which businesses operate and market their products and services. An understanding of this area of law is especially important for a student planning a career in advertising or public relations.

The basic purpose of trademark laws is to prevent customer confusion. A new company
that adopts a logo or name that looks like or sounds like a famous trademark for a similar
product is likely to run afoul of the law, even if the logo or name is slightly different.

The Lanham Act established a nationwide registration system for trademarks and service
marks, which are basically a subcategory of trademarks. When a business wants to adopt a
trademark, the first step is to conduct a search to see if any competitor or potential competitor is using a similar name. Before seeking a federal trademark, most businesses (or their
lawyers) pay a commercial research firm to find out whether their chosen name is available
by searching the voluminous files of past trademark registrations (and other sources of
information on trademark usage, including the Internet). If no one else has registered the
name, the business follows a registration and filing procedure not unlike that set up by the
Copyright Act. As part of the registration process, proposed trademarks are published and
rival businesses may challenge the registration of a new trademark if they wish.

What sort of names may and may not be registered under the Lanham Act? Generally, any
name, phrase or symbol that distinguishes a firm's goods or services may be registered, but
there are some exceptions. Flags and symbols for cities, states and countries cannot be registered, for instance. Nor may the name, portrait or signature of a living person be registered

as a company's trademark—except under circumstances where the name or likeness has already become distinctively associated with a firm. However, well-known individual celebrities can register their names as trademarks for their own marketing purposes. A number of celebrities have done that since it became legally possible. (As Chapter Five explains, celebrities can also protect their names under right of publicity laws in many states.)

In addition, purely geographic names and descriptive terms (for instance "first rate," "high quality," "blue ribbon," and "A-1") are usually unregisterable. One reason for this rule is that most popular names, descriptive terms and geographic names are so widely used that no one may gain a monopoly on their use nationally in connection with trade. This is not to say you can't open a business and call it "A-1 Auto Repair" or "Blue Ribbon Trophy Company," but you'll have a tough time getting it registered nationally as your exclusive trademark.

Even if a name is so widely used that no one can register it as a national trademark, someone may gain the exclusive right to use it locally. For instance, if you start a business called "A-1 Auto Repair" when there is already a business in the area called "A-1 Car Repair Company," you may be sued in a state court.

Because there have been many businesses seeking distinctive trademarks for many years, the surest way to get a new trademark registered nationally is to come up with a new coined word. Many trademarks have been created this way: Exxon, Kodak and Lexus, for example.

Assuming a business gets its proposed trademark past the hurdles of registration, the firm may use the trademark in various ways. The name may appear on products, in advertising and on the corporate letterhead. The fact that the trademark is registered under the Lanham Act is indicated by the ® symbol after the word or phrase. However, trademarks may also be indicated in other ways. For instance, when registration has not yet been secured, a firm may indicate that it claims a word or phrase as a trademark by placing "TM" after the name (or "SM" for a service mark).

Once registered under the Lanham Act, a trademark is valid for 10 years but must be reaffirmed after the first five years. Thereafter, a renewal every 10 years is required. There is no limit to the number of times a trademark may be renewed, as long as the trademark owner can show that it is still being "used in commerce." Unlike a copyright, a trademark can be maintained as private property indefinitely.

However, a trademark may also be abandoned or lost. Under the Lanham Act, failure to use a trademark for two years creates a presumption that it has been abandoned. Acquiescence in allowing others to use your trademark in a generic way can also result in its loss, which explains why trademarks such as "Xerox" and "Coca-Cola" are so vigorously defended by their owners. Should those words be allowed to become generally descriptive of all photocopying or all cola-type beverages, the owners could lose their exclusive rights to these names, as did the owners of ex-trademarks such as "aspirin," "cellophane," "cornflakes," "yo-yo" and "linoleum."

Companies do various things to avoid losing their trademarks through widespread usage as generic words. Some companies advertise in magazines read by journalists to admonish writers and editors about the correct usage of their trademarks. The Xerox Corporation, for example, reminds journalists to capitalize "Xerox," and to use it as an adjective referring to a Xerox-brand product. Never use the word as a verb, the company insists. The company is outraged by statements such as, "Go xerox this for me."

Ideally, trademark owners want the news media to use their names as adjectives followed by a generic name for the product, such as "Dolby noise reduction system" or "Plexiglas

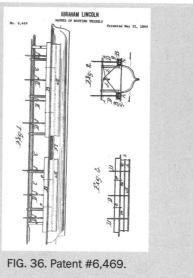

FIG. 36. Patent #6,469.

U.S. Patent and Trademark Office.

Focus on...
A presidential patent

The only president to have held a patent is Abraham Lincoln. On May 22, 1849, Lincoln was awarded Patent #6,469, "A Device for Buoying Vessels Over Shoals."

Lincoln's patent reads: "Be it known that I, Abraham Lincoln, of Springfield, in the County of Sangamon, in the State of Illinois, have invented a new and improved manner of combining adjustable buoyant air chambers with a steamboat or other vessel for the purpose of enabling their draught of water to be readily lessened to enable them to pass over bars, or through shallow water, without discharging their cargoes."

The U.S. Patent and Trademark Office reports that Lincoln whittled the model for his invention by hand, and the model is on display at the Smithsonian Institution National Museum of American History.

acrylic sheeting." The Dow Chemical Company has tried to prevent writers from using the term "Styrofoam cup" (Styrofoam is a trademark owned by Dow) because most Styrofoam brand plastic foam is used for other things, not for cups.

What happens to writers who misuse a trademark? Journalists who break the rules may receive pointed letters from a trademark owner's lawyers—all as part of the company's effort to demonstrate that it is not acquiescing to the generic use of its trademark. However, a company's lawyers can do little more than write angry letters when the news media use trademarks as if they were generic terms. In fact, courts sometimes regard the widespread generic use of a trademark in the news media as one form of proof that the word or phrase has lost its special meaning.

However, *non-journalistic* abuses of trademarks are another matter. News writers may get away with misusing trademarks, but when one company misuses another's trademark in its advertising or on a product, a lawsuit is likely to result. Even book authors must be careful to use trademarks correctly. It would be quite legal for someone not associated with Ford Motor Company to publish a book called, "How to Repair Fords," as long as it is made clear that Ford is a trademark, and that the author is not claiming it as his or her own trademark.

Although federal registration of a trademark is obviously desirable if it can be secured, a person or business that has used a name over a period of time acquires some special rights with or without federal registration. In fact, Lanham Act registration is unavailable to purely local businesses, although most states have their own registration systems under which local trademarks may be protected. State trademark protection varies widely. But whatever the specific rules are in a given state, the courts will step in to prevent a new business from creating public confusion by imitating the name or trademark of an old, established one.

Under the principles of common law and equity trademark protection (which protect trademarks regardless of whether they are registered at the state or federal level or unregistered), the key issue in a lawsuit is whether a word or phrase has acquired a *secondary meaning* in connection with a certain product or service. There is a secondary meaning if the words connote something more than their dictionary definition because of the commercial usage. For instance, the word "playboy" has one meaning in the dictionary, but when applied to a magazine, it has a special meaning beyond that.

If a word or phrase is found to have a secondary meaning to a substantial number of people, no one else may use the name for a similar kind of business in that locality without creating confusion and misleading the public. With or without a trademark registration under federal or state law, the mere use of a tradename over time gives the user certain ownership rights: no business is entitled to pass off its product or service as someone else's. Even if a newcomer registers the name as a trademark first, the original user of the name will often prevail in court. The goal is to prevent a newcomer from fraudulently trading on the goodwill of an established business. This is the overriding objective of the common law of trademarks, of state trademark laws and of the federal Lanham Act.

What sort of words can acquire a secondary meaning? A good illustration of how trademark law works was provided by two federal appellate court decisions that were handed down on the same day in 1993: *Pacific Telesis Group v. International Telesis Communications* (994 F.2d 1364) and *Fruit of the Loom v. Girouard* (994 F.2d 1359). Pacific Telesis, at one time a large regional telephone company, began using "Telesis" as part of its name in 1983. Two years later, a new firm adopted "International Telesis" as its name and entered the telecommunications consulting business. Pacific Telesis sued, and the Ninth Circuit eventually ruled that "telesis" (a Greek word meaning "event" or "fulfillment") is such a unique word when applied to the telephone industry that no one else in that line of business may use it without Pacific Telesis' permission. Ironically, Pacific Telesis was later acquired by SBC Communications and stopped using the name "telesis" for most purposes.

On the other hand, the same court refused to give Fruit of the Loom, a large clothing manufacturer, the exclusive right to use the word "fruit" in the apparel industry. The dispute arose when businessman Ken Girouard created a company called Two Left Feet and began making flip-flops called Fruit Flops and bustiers called Fruit Cups. The court agreed that the full name, "Fruit of the Loom," has a secondary meaning. It is, in fact, one of the oldest trademarks still in use: it was first registered in 1871! However, the court ruled that the use of the word "fruit" by itself is not enough to constitute a trademark infringement, even when used by another clothing manufacturer. The court said there was little likelihood that consumers would confuse the two names or the two product lines.

Trademark law also protects performing artists from unauthorized use of names so similar to theirs as to cause consumer confusion. In 2003, for instance, a federal appellate court ruled against the use of the name, "Beach Boys Family and Friends," by a group led by Al Jardine, the original lead guitarist with the famous Beach Boys group. Jardine did not have permission to use the name from Brother Records, owner of the Beach Boys name. Instead, Brother had licensed Mike Love, another member of the original Beach Boys, to use the name. In ruling against Jardine, the court focused on the risk of confusion, noting that Jardine's group promoted the name in ways that implied an endorsement by Brother. The court rejected Jardine's fair use arguments (*Brother Records Inc. v. Jardine*, 318 F.3d 900).

On the other hand, a 2002 federal appeals court decision held that the song, "Barbie Girl," in a 1997 album by the Danish band Aqua does not infringe Mattel's trademark rights in the name "Barbie" for dolls. The court cited the First Amendment in allowing this parody of a toy line that has become a cultural icon and said there was no danger of consumer confusion here (*Mattel Inc. v. MCA Records*, 296 F.3d 894). Note that this is one of several recent federal appeals court decisions concerning the scope of Mattel's rights to the Barbie name and image. In *Mattel Inc. v. Walking Mountain Productions* (353 F.3d 792), a 2003 case, an appellate court upheld Utah artist Tom Forsythe's right to make satirical use of Barbie dolls in a series of photographs he called "Food Chain Barbie." A judge later ordered Mattel to pay $1.8 million to the artist to cover his attorney's fees. On the other hand, in *Mattel Inc. v. Goldberger* (365 F.3d 133), a 2004 decision, an appellate court held that facial features of the Barbie doll such as the eyes, nose and mouth are protectible under copyright law.

Under certain circumstances not only a name or symbol but also a *color* may be protected as a trademark, according to a 1995 U.S. Supreme Court decision, *Qualitex Co. v. Jacobson Products Inc.* (514 U.S. 159). In essence, the Court said that if a company uses a distinctive color for its products for a long enough time, the color may become sufficiently associated with the product in consumers' minds that it has a secondary meaning.

Sometimes even a distinctive *sound* can qualify for trademark protection. A few sounds have gained trademark protection: for example, the roar of MGM's lion, the phrase "AT&T" spoken over a musical sound and NBC's three-note chime—famous since radio days. Harley-Davidson, the motorcycle manufacturer, stirred controversy in 1995 when it sought to register the sound of the V-twin engine on Harley bikes. Several other motorcycle manufacturers challenged that trademark application, arguing that their own V-twin engines made virtually the same sound. After running up legal bills for five years, Harley-Davidson dropped its attempt to obtain federal trademark protection for its engine sound in 2000.

Trademarks remain separate and distinct from copyrights. A 2003 U.S. Supreme Court decision underscored that principle in a case involving a new release on videotape of an old television series after the copyright expired. An Oregon company, Dastar Corp., released a video version of Twentieth Century Fox Film Corp.'s 1949 television series, "Crusade in Europe" about World War II. Fox tried to stop this by claiming a trademark infringement and false designation of origin of the new videotape series, named "Campaigns in Europe." The high court ruled unanimously that this was an improper use of trademark law to prevent the re-release of a television series that is now in the public domain under copyright law (*Dastar Corp. v. Twentieth Century Fox Film Corp.*, 539 U.S. 23).

Another aspect of trademark law has provoked enough controversy and uncertainty to produce two Supreme Court decisions: the question of whether a business can keep a competitor from imitating its *trade dress*. In *Two Pesos v. Taco Cabana* (505 U.S. 763, 1992), the high court upheld a federal court judgment in favor of Taco Cabana, a Mexican fast-food restaurant chain that claimed Two Pesos imitated the appearance and decor of its restaurants. The Supreme Court unanimously ruled that a store's *trade dress* can have "inherent distinctiveness," and if it does, that "look" can be protected under the Lanham Act. That may be true even if the trade dress has not acquired a *secondary meaning*, the court ruled. But the court didn't really define inherent distinctiveness, thus creating uncertainty about what is and is not protected as a part of a company's trade dress.

In 2000, the Supreme Court revisited the trade dress question, ruling unanimously that clothing designers may not ordinarily use federal trademark law to prevent others from making similar-looking apparel. Ruling in *Wal-Mart Stores v. Samara Brothers* (529 U.S. 205), the court held that designers may not gain trademark protection for their designs merely by claiming that the product is inherently distinctive. Instead, they must prove that the public so strongly associates the design with a designer that there is a secondary meaning. This is generally very difficult to prove. The Court said a product has a secondary meaning only when, "in the minds of the public, the primary significance of a (trademark) is to identify the source of the product rather than the product itself."

This decision leaves discounters such as Wal-Mart free to sell merchandise similar to high-end brand-name products as long as there is no actual counterfeiting or other deceptive marketing. Only if the public is deceived into believing they are buying the brand-name item is there likely to be a trademark infringement, the Court indicated. A product can resemble a brand-name item such as the children's clothing decorated with hearts and flowers that Samara designed and Wal-Mart's supplier imitated.

The *Wal-Mart* case limits the impact of the high court's earlier *Two Pesos* case. In *Two Pesos*, the court *upheld* a restaurant chain's right to protect the *trade dress* of its restaurants from imitators *without* proving the existence of a secondary meaning. But now the court has refused to protect the trade dress of products unless there is a secondary meaning.

In what could be an important development in trademark infringement, Gucci was permitted to bring suit against credit card processors for contributory infringement for processing payments for fake Gucci products (*Gucci America v. Frontline Processing Corp.*, 721 F. Supp. 2d 228, 2010). Gucci could proceed with the suit if it could show that the credit card processors "(1) intentionally induced the website to infringe through the sale of counterfeit goods or (2) knowingly supplied services to websites and had sufficient control over infringing activity to merit liability." Gucci was allowed to proceed at the trial court with the contributory liability element; the court said that a defendant may be liable for infringement "if it supplied services with knowledge or by willfully shutting its eyes to the infringing conduct, while it had sufficient control over the instrumentality used to infringe."

The years 2011 and 2012 saw a spate of designer companies filing trademark cases against alleged counterfeiters, including Louis Vuitton, Chanel, and Pernod. In perhaps the most notable of these, a court said it was acceptable for Chanel to, in effect, seize hundreds of domain names of counterfeiters of Chanel goods (*Chanel, Inc. v. Does*, 2011 U.S. Dist. LEXIS 131456).

Changes in Trademark Law

The Lanham Act was extensively revised by Congress in the Trademark Law Revision Act of 1988. Although many of the changes are highly technical, several have had an important effect on mass communications—particularly advertising.

Under the 1988 law, trademark owners may sue competitors who falsely malign their products or services for *treble damages* (i.e., three times the actual damages). However, in an effort to avoid undue restrictions on First Amendment freedoms, Congress limited this right to comparative brand name advertising by businesses, and not to political advertising or editorial commentary.

Most states have long recognized a right to sue for "trade libel" or "product disparagement." This law adds a *federal* legal right with a treble damage provision, making it easier for companies to deter false comparative advertising by competitors. Significantly, Congress rejected a proposed amendment to the new law that would have allowed *consumers* to sue for false advertising under the same provision of the law. Most states already allow consumers to sue false advertisers.

The revised version of the Lanham Act also has a provision allowing businesses to apply for trademark protection as much as three years before they actually put a product or service on the market by filing an "intent-to-use" application. This allows a company to reserve a name before launching the product or service. Under the old law, a product had to be in the marketplace before the application could be filed. This forced companies to make a token distribution of their new products and services in interstate commerce, but to do so quietly to avoid alerting potential competitors before the name or logo could be fully protected.

Eventually Congress passed the Federal Trademark Dilution Act of 1995, which made additional changes in the Lanham Act. Under this law, a trademark owner can sue an infringer for "lessening of the capacity of a famous mark to identify and distinguish goods or services, regardless of the presence or absence of competition between the parties or likelihood of confusion." Many trademark lawyers saw this as a major expansion of trademark law, allowing more lawsuits for "blurring" or "tarnishing" a trademark by someone who is not a competitor of the trademark owner. Blurring might occur when someone makes an unrelated product and uses a famous name, as Toyota did when it launched the Lexus, a car with virtually the same name as the pre-existing Lexis-Nexis computer data service (Toyota ultimately won the right to use the Lexus name after defending a lawsuit against Lexis-Nexis). *Tarnishment* involves the use of a word or phrase that creates a negative association with an established trademark. Under the concept, courts have halted such practices as the sale of "Enjoy Cocaine" posters using typefaces and colors similar to those in Coca-Cola's posters.

Many states already had anti-dilution laws; this law creates stronger *federal* protection from trademark dilution. Again, critics of the continuing growth of trademark and copyright law saw this as an example of the public domain shrinking. As intellectual property law grows, there are fewer and fewer words, phrases and creative materials left that the general public may use without risking a lawsuit—one of the major dilemmas in this area of law.

The question of trademark dilution led to a U.S. Supreme Court decision in 2003, followed by new federal legislation in 2006 and additional cases in the late 2000s. In *Moseley v. V Secret Catalogue Inc.* (537 U.S. 418), the Supreme Court made it more difficult for the owners of famous trademarks to prevent others from using similar names for their businesses. Interpreting the Federal Trademark Dilution Act, the Court unanimously overturned a lower court decision in favor of Victoria's Secret, which was trying to stop a Kentucky sex shop owned by Victor and Cathy Moseley from using "Victor's Little Secret" as its name.

Writing for the Court, Justice John Paul Stevens said trademark owners must show actual blurring or tarnishing of the trademark and not just the likelihood of dilution to enjoin a business from using a similar name. Stevens said it is not necessary to show an "actual loss of sales or profits," but a trademark owner must show "a lessening of the capacity of a famous mark to identify and distinguish goods or services." Stevens added that the mere fact that some customers make a "mental association" between a local business name and a nationally famous trademark is not enough to prove dilution. He said Victoria's Secret had not shown that the Kentucky store's name resulted in any real dilution of its trademark.

The high court remanded the case for reconsideration by a lower court, giving Victoria's Secret another shot at halting the Kentucky store's use of a similar name if Victoria's Secret can show actual *dilution* (lessening of uniqueness) of its trademark. The Court said a trademark owner does not necessarily have to show economic harm and might be able to use "circumstantial evidence" instead of consumer surveys to prove dilution.

In 2006, Congress responded to the Victoria's Secret case by passing the Trademark Dilution Revision Act (TDRA). Written primarily by trademark lawyers, it eliminated the Supreme Court's requirement that a trademark owner who sues for dilution must show that an actual dilution has occurred. Under the new law, a trademark owner has to prove only that a *likelihood* of harm exists. It also revised the definition of dilution and tarnishment to make it easier for trademark owners to sue without proving consumer confusion. The law retains fair-use protections to allow parodies, news commentary and comparison advertising that may use a famous trademark. But it also allows lawsuits for damages against those who "willfully intend to harm the reputation of a famous mark."

The 2006 TDRA was widely criticized by legal scholars and consumer advocates, who predicted that trademark owners could use it to stifle First Amendment freedoms. The Sixth Circuit interpreted the TDRA in 2010 in affirming a permanent injunction issued by a district court against the Moseleys (who had been operating their shop as "Cathy's Little Secret") from using "Victor's Little Secret." The court said that Victoria's Secret did have a valid dilution-by-tarnishment claim under the revised act, and added that "the creation of an 'association' between a famous mark and lewd or bawdy sexual activity disparages and defiles the famous mark and reduces the commercial value of its selling power" (*V Secret Catalogue v. Moseley*, 605 F.3d 382).

The TDRA does not require that a plaintiff prove "substantial similarity" between trademarks for a trademark owner to establish dilution by blurring, said the Second Circuit in 2009 (*Starbucks Corp. v. Wolfe's Borough Coffee, Inc.*, 588 F.3d 97). A family-owned coffee shop, Black Bear Micro Roastery, began selling dark-roasted coffee in 1997 under the name "Charbucks Blend" (later changed to "Mister Charbucks"). The national coffee company Starbucks brought suit and lost in the district court; as the appeal was pending, Congress passed the TDRA. The Second Circuit vacated and sent the case back to be determined under the new law, and Starbucks lost again.

On appeal, the Second Circuit said that Black Bear's logo was significantly different from Starbucks' logo, and their coffee products displayed the logo and name prominently. This, the district court said, was enough to defeat Starbucks' claim of dilution by blurring, and the Second Circuit said that this was incorrect and remanded the case. But Black Bear did not tarnish Starbucks' mark, the court said, because it was marketing the "Charbucks" brand in a positive way rather than using it to disparage Starbucks.

Trademarks and Internet Domain Names

With the surging growth of the Internet in the late 1990s, a difficult new legal dilemma arose for trademark owners and others who wanted to register *domain names*—the names used in website locators and e-mail addresses. To cite just a few examples, xerox.com is Xerox Corporation's domain name, just as ford.com is Ford Motor Company's domain name and harvard.edu is Harvard University's. Likewise, fcc.gov is the Federal Communications Commission's domain name. Adding "www." to any of these (or many thousands of other domain names) will take you to the organization's home page on the World Wide Web. The "Ford" or "Harvard" or "FCC" is the specific entity's domain name; the ".com" or ".edu" or ".gov" is called a *generic top-level domain name* shared by many organizations. Other currently recognized top-level domain names include ".mil" for military organizations, ".org" for non-commercial organizations and ".net" for entities loosely defined as computer networks. Many nations also have top-level domain names, such as ".us" for the United States.

Almost every large government agency, educational institution and corporation has a website—and wants it identified by the organization's popular name or trademark. Hundreds of lawsuits have been filed by trademark owners and others to contest the ownership of domain names. For many years Network Solutions Inc. (NSI), a Virginia-based company, had a government-sanctioned monopoly on registering domain names. (NSI's basic domain name registration business was later taken over by VeriSign, Inc.) By 2001 NSI had registered about 15 million domain names; the company received an annual fee directly or indirectly from each name registrant for maintaining the domain name database. NSI gained its unique status through a contract with the National Science Foundation—and quickly became embroiled in controversy over its domain name registration policies. NSI's contract expired in 1998. However, NSI won a two-year extension by promising to share its registration authority with other companies that would be selected by a nonprofit corporation.

The Internet Corp. for Assigned Names and Numbers (ICANN) was then established with the backing of the U.S. government and the World Intellectual Property Organization, among others. It was given the authority to designate new name registrars who would share that task with NSI. In 1999, ICANN began accrediting private companies to handle registrations for the .com, .org, and .net domains. As a result, NSI faced competition from other name registrars; its monopoly was over. In 2000 ICANN also approved seven new domain names to supplement .com, .org and .net (.xxx was approved in 2010). Private companies have created additional domain names and managed to get them recognized, at least informally by Internet service providers. ICANN also set up a global arbitration system so that disputes over domain names could be resolved quickly and without lawsuits. That system is widely used as an alternative to taking these disputes to court.

As NSI demonstrated when it had a monopoly, registering Internet names can be a lucrative business, but it also invites lawsuits: the company has been sued hundreds of times in disputes over domain names, which it has generally issued on a first-come, first served system. In some cases, individuals have registered hundreds of names with hopes of selling the names to trademark owners at a large profit. These people have been called "cybersquatters" and accused of "domain name hijacking." Instead of paying, many companies have sued—and usually prevailed based on proof that they hold a valid trademark in the name.

What happens when two companies use the same trade name—but for different products. Who gets to be "Dove.com?" The makers of Dove soap or Dove candy bars? What about two companies that use the same name as a trademark for similar products, but in different geographic areas? Each one may have a valid regional trademark, but the Internet crosses all regional boundaries. A federal appellate court had to deal with that kind of issue in a 1999 case, *Brookfield Communications v. West Coast Entertainment* (174 F.3d 1036). The case involved a dispute between two companies that had both used variations of the term, "movie buff," in their trademarks. Both wanted the domain name, "moviebuff.com." The court did a traditional trademark analysis and awarded the name to Brookfield because that company had used the name earlier, concluding that trademarks take priority over domain name registrations. Significantly, the court also held that Brookfield should have the exclusive right to use the "movie buff" name in *metatags* hidden in its web pages. The court held that it is a trademark infringement for a company to embed a competitor's trademark in metatags on its website so that search engines would lead net surfers to its site when they do a search keyed to the competitor's trademark. However, as noted earlier, another federal appellate court later upheld the right of former Playmate of the Year Terri Welles to use words such as "playboy" in the metatags on her personal website (*Playboy Enterprises v. Welles*).

Perhaps the best known cybersquatter was a man named Dennis Toeppen, who registered at least 240 different domain names and demanded payment for turning over the names to trademark owners. Among others, he had registered the names Delta Airlines,

Panavision, Neiman Marcus, Lufthansa and Eddie Bauer. When he demanded $13,000 from Panavision, that company sued and a federal court ordered Toeppen to hand over the names "Panavision" and "Panaflex" (*Panavision International v. Toeppen*, 141 F.3d 1316).

In 1999 Congress stepped into the ongoing disputes over domain names by enacting the Anticybersquatting Consumer Protection Act (ACPA), a law intended to ban (and criminalize) the practice of "*cybersquatting*"—registering someone else's trademark or a famous person's name as an Internet domain name in bad faith, hoping to make a profit by selling the name to its rightful owner. The law allows fines of up to $100,000 for cybersquatting. The law also authorizes courts to order the cancellation of Internet names that were registered in bad faith, and it applies to names that have already been registered as well as new registrations. In short, ACPA establishes civil and criminal remedies for cybersquatting, allowing those who choose to go to court with domain name disputes (as opposed to using ICANN's arbitration procedure) to do so under ground rules favoring trademark owners.

In an attempt to reduce "typosquatting" through the process of "domain tasting," ICANN revised its domain name registration policy in 2008. "Domain tasting" is the act of buying up domain names that are variations or spelling errors of trademarked corporate names and making money when users go to those websites and click on ads there. Because ICANN has a five-day grace period after which a domain name can be dropped and a refund from ICANN obtained, many squatters would register names, sit on them and make money until the grace period was up, then drop them at the end of the grace period and get the refund. An ICANN study demonstrated the breadth of the problem: in January 2007, 51 million domains were registered, but 48 million, or 94 percent, of those were dropped. ICANN no longer makes those refunds, which were about 20 cents per name, and it saw an 84 percent drop in domain name drops. The next phase of ICANN's plan may be to make registrars like Verisign and GoDaddy more accountable for their dropped domain names.

But the Ninth Circuit in 2011 said that re-registering a domain name was *not* the same as a "registration" under the ACPA. "We see no basis in ACPA to conclude that a right that belongs to an initial registrant of a currently registered domain name is lost when that name is transferred to another owner," the court said in overturning a lower court's award of $100,000 to GoPets Ltd. based on the re-registration of gopets.com by Edward Hise (*GoPets Ltd v. Hise*, 657 F.3d 1024).

While the battles over domain names continued, a separate trademark controversy arose over electronic *links*, which allow surfers to click on a highlighted word or phrase and move quickly to an entirely different site. Several companies objected to the use of their trademarks by others in links—and filed lawsuits. In the most famous of these cases, Ticketmaster, the electronic ticketing agency, sued Microsoft in 1997 for its inclusion of links to Ticketmaster in its web pages. Ticketmaster's main objection seemed to be that Microsoft routed surfers to Ticketmaster by way of other Microsoft-controlled sites that carried advertising (for Microsoft's profit, not Ticketmaster's). The case was settled in 1999 when Microsoft agreed not to link its Sidewalk city guides to pages within Ticketmaster's site. In several other cases, web businesses have objected when someone else links to a page deep inside their sites ("deep linking") instead of to the opening page, preventing customers from seeing their advertising. This issue is not resolved, although linking itself is perfectly legal.

However, linking can result in lawsuits. In *Kelly v. Arriba Soft Corp.* (336 F.3d 811), a federal appellate court ruled in 2002 and again in 2003 that the fair use doctrine permits a search engine to reproduce small "thumbnail" copies of images from a website, but not full-size images. The Ninth Circuit ruled against Perfect 10, an Internet purveyor of nude photographs, in a 2007 decision that essentially reaffirmed an earlier ruling saying the Google search engine could continue to use thumbnails of Perfect 10 images pending a full trial on the merits of a lawsuit by Perfect 10 against Google, Amazon.com and others. The appellate court said the burden of establishing that use of the thumbnails is a fair use and not a copyright infringement should be on Google, even at this preliminary stage of a lawsuit. But the appellate court also said Google had met this legal requirement. However, Google's links to other sites that display unauthorized full-size copies of Perfect 10's images may not be a fair use (*Perfect 10 v. Amazon.com*, 508 F.3d 1146). Perfect 10 sought a court order to force Google to remove the links to other websites and also to remove the thumbnails—before a full trial.

Google could face *secondary liability* for helping web surfers find other websites that display Perfect 10's full-size images in violation of Perfect 10's copyrights. That, like *deep linking* in which full-size images appear to be part of a website other the one where they are posted, may constitute copyright infringement. Deep linking is akin to *framing*, in which pages of one website appear to be part of another website.

But what about *embedding* a video? Is that a direct copyright infringement? Yes, said a federal district court in *Flava Works, Inc. v. Gunter* (2011 U.S. Dist. LEXIS 50067, 2011). Pornography company Flava Works found that Marques Gunter's company, myVidster, a video bookmarking site, had many embedded videos (but not hosted—the videos were hosted on other sites) that belonged to Flava. Flava demanded that myVidster remove those embeds, and myVidster complied, but Flava sued for infringement. The court, in finding for Flava, said that not only did myVidster not provide users warnings to not infringe others' copyrights, Gunter, in telling Flava that its videos were actually hosted on other sites, "pointed a finger at other websites while failing to acknowledge that his own website is perpetuating copyright infringement." The Seventh Circuit has been asked to review the decision.

Still other domain name and trademark disputes have arisen—and ended up in the courts. One is the use of a company's trademark on a website designed to *criticize* the company. Disenchanted former customers and former employees often set up websites to express their displeasure with companies. In one case, a website critical of the Bally Total Fitness Holdings Corp. was set up under the title "Bally Sucks." It displayed Bally's logo with the word "sucks" printed across it. When Bally sued for trademark infringement and dilution, a federal court held that sites such as this one are protected by the First Amendment. The court rejected Bally's attempt to use trademark law to shut down the site (*Bally Total Fitness v. Faber*, 29 F.Supp.2d 1161, 1998).

Another domain name problem involves renewals. Several domain name registrars immediately hand names over to domain name auction houses as soon as they expire, deriving a handsome profit from the resale of the name. There is little incentive for the registrar to make sure the name-holder renews on time, because the name may bring in far more than the renewal fee if it is re-sold at auction. Reputable registrars send out renewal notices, but if the name-holder misses the renewal deadline the name may be gone—short of litigation. By 2008, large companies were entering the domain name business, bidding huge sums for names that could be valuable. The name "porn.com" reportedly sold for $9.5 million—just for the name. But in 2010 ICANN announced that it gave its blessing to the .xxx generic top-level domain for pornography, ten years after it had first been suggested. No one seemed happy with the decision; some religious groups fear that the domain will lend legitimacy to pornography, while purveyors of sexual materials are concerned that it would be easy to censor the entire top-level domain.

In 2011, ICANN announced plans for a significant expansion in the number of generic top-level domains, or gTLDs (like .com and .gov). Companies will be able to choose whatever they'd like as their gTLD; for example, the Coca-Cola Co. could use .coke as its gTLD, and any address with .coke as the top-level domain would go to websites for Coca-Cola products. In June 2012, ICANN released a list of 1,930 gTLDs that private companies and others have registered to obtain. These include .aaa by the American Automobile Association, .dnb by Dunn & Bradstreet, and .weather by the Weather Channel. Not all gTLDs are uncontested: for example, seven entities want to register .web, and nine want to register .shop. ICM Registry, owner of the controversial .xxx domain, wants to add .sex and .porn to its holdings. .xxx registrations were open in September 2011. But not all holders of .xxx domains are necessarily pornographers—Conan O'Brien's site, conan.xxx, is decidedly *not* sexual.

■ PATENTS

Patent law, also addressed in the Constitution, provides protection for inventions. The U.S. Patent and Trademark Office is the government organization in charge of registration of patents. A patent gives the holder "the right to exclude others from making, using or selling the invention throughout the United States" for a certain amount of time in exchange for making information about the invention public by registering the patent. There are three types of patents: *utility patents*, for new and useful processes or machines (or improvements to them); *design patents*, for new, original and ornamental designs; and *plant patents*, for new varieties of plants.

As mentioned earlier, patent law usually is not of much concern to mass communicators, but in 2010 a high-profile Supreme Court case brought the issue to national attention. The Supreme Court in *Bilski v. Kappos* (130 S. Ct. 3218) took up a question regarding the patenting of methods claims, particularly business methods. The question before the Court was whether a "process" must be tied to a particular machine or transform a particular article into a different state or thing (called the "machine-or-transformation" test), to be eligible for patenting. The patent under consideration was a "procedure for instructing buyers and sellers how to protect against the risk of price fluctuations in a discrete section of the economy."

The Court rejected the patent on the financial method, and in so doing also rejected the "machine-or-transformation" test as the exclusive means of defining a patentable process. Justice Anthony Kennedy, writing for the Court, said, "It is true that patents for inventions that did not satisfy the machine-or-transformation test were rarely granted in earlier eras, especially in the Industrial Age... But times change. Technology and other innovations progress in unexpected ways." However, patents cannot be approved for abstract ideas. The Court declined to refine a definition of what would constitution a patentable process.

■ AN OVERVIEW OF MAJOR ISSUES

Intellectual property law is full of unresolved questions, many of them created by digital technologies. Some wonder whether *any* copyright can (or should) ever again be protected, given the ease with which digital images, music and movies can be exchanged worldwide— and the seeming ease with which copy protection schemes can be circumvented.

How can the movie and recording industries deal with the sharing of copyrighted materials when new laws, court decisions and technical "solutions" so often fail? Is it right for major corporations to sue millions of individual computer owners? Should the industry even try to catch every computer user who shares songs or movies with others? Don't some of the industry's anti-copying tactics violate the fair use doctrine, if not First Amendment?

Shouldn't American consumers have the right at least to make backup copies of CDs and DVDs for their own use, and to convert movies or music from one format to another? Consumers have that right in many European countries. Under recent industry proposals, even the right to copy free, over-the-air TV shows, long protected by the *Sony* Supreme Court decision, would be severely curtailed when broadcasts are digital. Now the industry wants to ban the ubiquitous yellow, red and white output jacks that allow old-fashioned analog video and audio to be transferred from one device to another. And in 2005, the Supreme Court ruled in *MGM v. Grokster* that technology manufacturers can be sued if they make products that they know will facilitate illegal copying.

Underlying all of this is a basic question. Corporate copyright owners are winning more and more rights at the expense of consumers with the passage of each new law that extends copyright terms or restricts what can be copied. The copyright lobby has won many battles over consumer advocates in Congress, but have copyright owners forfeited their chance to win the battle of public opinion? If the Copyright Office and industry-backed groups sponsor Copyright Awareness Weeks to educate the public (and especially students) about the importance of obeying the latest copyright restrictions, hasn't the battle already been lost?

The Internet has given us an entirely different kind of world where the old definitions of publishing, distribution and performance do not fit modern realities. It took nearly a year to circulate a book around the United States in 1790, and the duration of a copyright was 14 years. Now a book, movie or just about any other form of intellectual property can be circulated around the world in seconds—and corporate copyrights remain in effect for 95 years. Does that make sense? Apparently the Supreme Court thinks so. When the latest copyright term extension was challenged by legal scholars and others, the court ruled in the *Eldred* case that even copyrights lasting 120 years comply with the constitutional requirement that copyrights be for "limited times." Jack Valenti, longtime president of the Motion Picture Association of America (MPAA), was quoted—in Congress and elsewhere—as saying copyrights should last "forever less one day." That would comply with the U.S. Constitution by being a "limited time," right? Is there *ever* a time when creative works—let's take music and movies as an example—become part of the culture that should belong to *everyone* and not just to the corporations that bought the copyrights so long ago?

As copyright law becomes more unconscionable in the minds of millions, and damage awards rise higher and higher to totals that the average person could not pay, isn't it inevitable that many will come to see illegal copying as a legitimate form of civil disobedience?

WHAT SHOULD I KNOW ABOUT MY STATE?	• Both copyright and patent law are *federally preempted* (may be regulated only by the federal government), so there will not be much intellectual property state law here, other than state trademark litigation, registration and common law.

SUMMARY

A SUMMARY OF COPYRIGHT LAW

What May Be Copyrighted?

Many types of literary and artistic works may be copyrighted, including prose (fiction and non-fiction), poetry, scripts, musical scores and lyrics, photographs, films, videos, sound recordings, software, maps, paintings, sculptures and advertising layouts.

What May NOT Be Copyrighted?

Factual and historical information (including news) may not be copyrighted, although a *description* of a news event or a news production may. Ideas, processes, inventions and trademarks may not be copyrighted (inventions and processes may be patented and trademarks protected under state and federal trademark laws).

How Does One Secure a Copyright?

Copyright protection is automatic under U.S. law and international treaties. However, it is advisable to include a *copyright notice* in a prominent place in the work. Doing that notifies any would-be infringer of the copyright. Your copyright is valid without registration, but if you register before an infringement occurs, you have more legal rights than if you didn't, including the right to win statutory damages and lawyer's fees should a suit be filed. And you *must* register before filing a lawsuit. To do so, go to copyright.gov and follow the directions for online or traditional filing.

What Does a Copyright Give You?

The copyright owner has the right to reproduce, perform, revise or display the work for the duration of the copyright, which normally runs for the author's life plus 70 years or 95 years for corporate works. The owner may sell any or all of these rights. Under certain conditions copyrighted music may be recorded by anyone who pays the prescribed royalties (this is called *compulsory licensing*).

What Is the Fair Use Doctrine?

The Fair Use Doctrine allows anyone to make limited use of copyrighted works (e.g., quoting or photocopying a small portion of a work). Whether a use is a fair one is determined by weighing: whether the use is commercial or educational in character, the nature of the original work, the percentage of the original that is copied and the effect of the use on the owner's profits.

What is Creative Commons?

Creative Commons is an alternative to traditional copyright law. A creator may choose to license his/her work under a CC license, some of which grant more rights for others to lawfully use the work for remixing, mash-ups, or other transformations.

7 *Fair Trial-Free Press Conflicts*

One of the most troublesome conflicts inherent in the U.S. Constitution is a problem called *fair trial-free press*. The Sixth Amendment guarantees a person accused of a crime "the right to a speedy and public trial *before an impartial jury*." On the other hand, the First Amendment gives the media the right to report crime news, including information and visual images that could prejudice an entire community against someone who has not yet stood trial and is still presumed innocent by the law. Or, as illustrated by the celebrated O.J. Simpson murder trial in 1995, live coverage of a trial may leave a large segment of the population convinced that the defendant is guilty after a jury rules otherwise.

In recent years there have been many confrontations between the nation's courts and the media over this problem. In the 2000s, fair trial-free press issues were raised by the trials of celebrities (or people whose trials made them celebrities) like Robert Blake, Kobe Bryant, Michael Jackson, Scott Peterson and Martha Stewart—and, most recently, in 2011, Casey Anthony, in her trial (and acquittal) for the murder of her two-year-old daughter, Caylee, and former Illinois governor Rod Blagojevich's trial (and conviction) for corruption. In attempting to control prejudicial publicity and assure fair trials for defendants in sensational cases like these, the courts have taken a variety of steps to limit publicity and thereby protect the Sixth Amendment rights of defendants. However, some of these steps limit the media's First Amendment freedoms. There is no easy solution to this conflict between two constitutional rights: both freedom of the press and the right to trial before an impartial jury are central to the American ideal of a free society.

■ PREJUDICIAL PUBLICITY AND FAIR TRIALS

Many judges and attorneys contend there is an overabundance of crime news in the media. Many believe such news is so sensationalized that some celebrity defendants may be denied a fair trial by an impartial jury. Some also believe the media can make it impossible for the prosecution (*the people*, if you will) to get a fair trial. The jury is supposed to consider only the defendant's guilt or innocence in the specific case before the court, not whether he/she is of high moral character generally. A defendant's past record is not ordinarily considered relevant evidence, although there are notable exceptions. But sometimes the media report inflammatory information about a person's past, information that may not be admitted as evidence when the trial actually occurs. Moreover, the media may report unsubstantiated details of an arrest or unverified test results. Or they may reveal the existence of a "confession" that may not be admitted into evidence in court if it was given under duress. On the other hand, the media may also reveal details about the prosecution's case that the jury is not supposed to consider. As a result, it may be difficult to find unprejudiced jurors. Lawyers and judges may feel that drastic measures are necessary to control what they see as irresponsible journalism that interferes with criminal defendants' constitutional rights.

However, defenders of the press often cite the important role of the media in keeping the public informed about modern society—a society with a high crime rate. They point out that the press performs an important watchdog role in monitoring the administration of justice. Even most judges will concede that covering the criminal justice system is an important function of the media. And, of course, judges cannot ignore the fact that the media's right to cover the news is constitutionally protected.

FIG. 37. Oneida
County courthouse in
Rhinelander, Wisconsin.

Author's collection.

The O.J. Simpson Case and its Consequences

Perhaps no courtroom drama in American history better illustrates the problems of fair trial-free press than the criminal and civil trials of O.J. Simpson, the football legend and media celebrity. A criminal jury acquitted Simpson of killing his ex-wife and her friend Ronald Goldman in a brutal knife attack, while a jury in a later civil trial found him to be liable for the two deaths. The civil jury verdict, including a large punitive damage award, was later upheld on appeal (*Rufo v. Simpson*, 86 C.A.4th 573, 2001).

From the moment Simpson failed to surrender to police under a pre-arranged plan and was declared a fugitive, there was a worldwide media bonanza. At least 95 million viewers in the United States alone watched the two-hour pursuit leading to Simpson's arrest on live television. Within a few days, hundreds if not thousands of journalists were covering the story, and numerous incriminating details of the case were widely publicized. Almost all major American media outlets carried the tape or transcript of a 911 emergency call that Nicole Brown, Simpson's ex-wife, made a few months before she was killed, in which she said Simpson had broken down her door. Long before the trial almost everyone also knew that Simpson had entered a no-contest plea to misdemeanor wife-beating charges in 1989, and that Nicole had repeatedly called the police about earlier incidents in which Simpson allegedly beat her. The world even learned that in 1985 Simpson allegedly broke the windshield of Nicole's car with a baseball bat.

The publicity frenzy became so intense that in mid-1994 a judge took the extraordinary step of disqualifying the Los Angeles County Grand Jury from its normal role of hearing evidence and deciding whether to issue an indictment—on the ground that the grand jurors might be prejudiced by media publicity. Instead, the case proceeded to a preliminary hearing (which would not have been needed if there had been a grand jury indictment), with the major television networks providing gavel-to-gavel live coverage of the courtroom proceedings. And in another Los Angeles County courthouse a few miles away, a judge took the unheard-of step of postponing an *unrelated* murder trial, ruling that the Simpson publicity made it impossible for this other defendant to get a fair trial because the two cases were similar (like the Simpson case, this case involved a middle-aged African-American man accused of killing his younger, Caucasian ex-wife in a brutal knife attack that followed earlier incidents of domestic violence).

Once the Simpson trial began in 1995, the live television coverage repeatedly forced Judge Lance Ito to alter normal courtroom procedures. Time and again, millions of viewers got to see courtroom scenes on television that the jurors were not permitted to observe. As the trial increasingly focused on issues of race, police detective Mark Fuhrman was accused of using America's most inflammatory racial epithet more than 40 times. The jurors were not allowed to hear testimony about most of those times; Judge Ito ruled that its prejudicial effect would greatly outweigh its probative value as evidence. But Fuhrman's choice of words was a major story in the media for weeks. The jurors were sequestered—confined in a hotel and supervised to insulate them from the pervasive media publicity. However, they were allowed to have private conjugal visits. Can we ever know for sure that no visitor ever told any of the jurors the details of the Fuhrman controversy or other sensational developments in the case that occurred outside their presence but were shown on television?

Despite Judge Ito's efforts to assure that an impartial jury was selected, the news media carried many stories suggesting that some of the jurors were not impartial. When the jury rendered its not-guilty verdict, the event was viewed by the largest television audience in American history. Then the real controversy began—in the media and around the world.

Perhaps the one thing about Simpson's criminal trial that everyone on all sides agreed upon was that the media scrutiny was so intense that the American justice system may never be the same. Many believed that Simpson's real trial was in the media, and that the fair-trial, free-press issue was a more serious problem than it had ever been before.

The O.J. Simpson case prompted California and many other states to adopt new rules restricting what lawyers can say to the media before and during a trial. Another response to the Simpson trial was that judges from coast to coast had second thoughts about permitting television coverage of celebrated trials. Exercising powers they have in almost every state that allows cameras in trial courtrooms, judges have barred television coverage of many sensational trials since Simpson's criminal trial attracted an international television audience.

When the families of Ron Goldman and Nicole Brown Simpson sought monetary damages from O.J. Simpson in a civil lawsuit, cameras were barred from the trial. Of course, the civil trial was very different from the criminal trial for many reasons. In civil cases, courtroom procedures, the rules of evidence and the standard of proof are all different than in criminal cases. For instance, a civil jury may rule based on *the preponderance of the evidence* without being convinced *beyond a reasonable doubt* as is required for a conviction in a criminal case. And, of course, many trial lawyers saw the very different composition of the jury as a crucial difference between the criminal trial that led to Simpson's acquittal and the civil trial in which he was held liable for the deaths. Nonetheless, many observers also saw the absence of cameras as a significant factor in the dramatic reversal in the outcome of the case.

Almost every key player in the O.J. Simpson case (and several prominent authors who were not personally involved) wrote books about the trial. Several of these became best sellers, further swaying public opinion against Simpson, who found that he could no longer command top dollar as a television commentator or advertising spokesperson. Even Alan Dershowitz, a prominent law professor who was a member of Simpson's "dream team" of defense attorneys, defended the role of the "dream team" in his book (*Reasonable Doubts*) by saying, "A criminal trial is anything but a pure search for truth. When defense attorneys represent guilty clients—as most do, most of the time—their responsibility is to try, by all fair and ethical means, to *prevent* the truth about their client's guilt from emerging. Failure to do so...is malpractice." In 2004, a decade after the two murders, Simpson discussed his case in retrospect during a rare interview with the Associated Press. He blamed the media for the fact that so many people still consider him guilty long after he was acquitted by a jury. He eventually moved from California to Florida, but that did little to reduce media scrutiny of his case—and his still-newsworthy life, which became even more newsworthy after his arrest and conviction in a Las Vegas robbery scheme in 2008.

Lessons from Recent Celebrity Cases

The 2005 child molesting trial of singer Michael Jackson, the prosecution of basketball star Kobe Bryant in 2003 and 2004, and several other recent celebrity cases have again illustrated the fair trial-free press problem. Unfortunately for the news media, both the Jackson and Bryant trials had an effect that the Simpson case did not have: they led to precedent-setting appellate court decisions that could limit public access in future cases.

In the Jackson case, Judge Rodney S. Melville took many steps to reduce the possibility of prejudicial publicity. He not only barred television cameras from his courtroom and the courthouse itself but also ordered attorneys and others not to discuss a wide range of topics with the media. The judge also sealed such normally public records as an 82-page affidavit used to obtain a warrant to search Jackson's Neverland Ranch and a 1900-page transcript of grand jury proceedings in the case.

When the media appealed Judge Melville's sealing of documents, a California appellate court upheld most of his order. The court held that the danger of "public outrage" from prejudicial publicity was so great that these records had to be kept confidential until after the trial (*People v. Jackson (NBC Universal Inc.)*, 128 C.A.4th 1009, 2005). The appeals court noted that the most sensational portions of these documents had been leaked to the media and widely publicized—but upheld the secrecy order even though it seemed moot by then. When the Jackson case ended with an acquittal on all charges, several jurors said in interviews that they made it a point to decide the case *only* on evidence presented in the courtroom. At least two said they thought Jackson probably was a child molester—but the evidence presented was insufficient for them to find him *guilty beyond a reasonable doubt.*

In the Kobe Bryant case, a more fundamental First Amendment issue arose. Bryant was accused of sexually assaulting a woman who went to his hotel room in a Colorado resort area. The case was eventually dropped at the request of the alleged victim after she saw her name and details of her sexual history publicized in apparent violation of Colorado law.

The judge held a closed pretrial hearing at which the alleged victim's sexual history was discussed. A court clerk erroneously e-mailed the transcript of the hearing to seven news organizations. The trial judge quickly ordered the media not to publish information from the transcript, an order that was clearly a prior restraint. The Colorado Supreme Court heard an appeal by the media and on a 4-3 vote upheld much of the judge's order, ruling that protecting the privacy of an alleged rape victim is "a state interest of the highest order," and "sufficiently weighty to overcome the presumption in favor" of the media's right to publish (*People v. Bryant*, 94 P.3d 624, 2004). The media asked U.S. Supreme Court Justice Stephen G. Breyer to intervene, but he declined to act immediately. Instead, he said in a short opinion, "I recognize the importance of the constitutional issues at issue, but a brief delay will permit the state courts to clarify, perhaps avoid, the controversy at issue." The trial judge then released an edited version of the transcript, rendering the media's challenge moot. However, the Colorado Supreme Court decision remains a legal precedent that could limit the media's right to publish court documents in future cases.

A defendant's fame (or infamy) does not automatically mean that jurors will be biased against him/her, the Supreme Court ruled in 2010. *Skilling v. U.S.* (130 S. Ct. 2896) primarily addressed whether a fraud law was unconstitutional as applied to former Enron executive Jeffrey Skilling (it was), but a secondary question dealt with the impact of prejudicial publicity on Skilling's trial.

The Fifth Circuit had ruled that prejudice could arise simply from the fame of the defendant. Justice Ruth Bader Ginsburg, writing for the Court, disagreed, saying that Skilling had not shown that the *voir dire* process was insufficient to weed out biased jurors. She added, "Prominence does not necessarily produce prejudice, and juror *impartiality*, we have reiterated, does not require *ignorance.*" Justice Sonia Sotomayor dissented from this part of the opinion, saying that she believed that the *voir dire* was not sufficient to eliminate bias. "Under our relevant precedents, the more intense the public's antipathy toward a defendant, the more careful a court must be to prevent that sentiment from tainting the jury," she wrote.

Most recently, a panel of the Seventh Circuit reversed the order of a district court keeping the names of jurors secret until the end of the trial in the first Rod Blagojevich trial in 2010. The trial judge promised the jurors that their names would remain secret until the trial's end. But Chief Judge Frank Easterbrook said that the appellants (the Chicago Tribune Company, the New York Times Company, Illinois Press Association, and the Illinois Broadcasters Association) "seek access to the jurors' names not only to publish human-interest stories (though we don't denigrate that objective) but also because they want to learn whether the seated jurors are suitable decision-makers."

But Easterbrook said, the jurors' names would remain confidential until a hearing had taken place so that the district judge could offer "a better basis for understanding not only the risks of releasing the names before the trial's end, but also other options (and the risk that alternatives such as cautionary instructions will fail)" (*U.S. v. Blagojevich*, 612 F.3d 558).

A request was made to rehear the case *en banc*, which was denied. Judge Richard Posner and several other judges dissented from the denial, and Posner took the opportunity to strongly disagree with Easterbrook: "An experienced trial judge made a reasonable determination that the release of jurors' names before the end of the trial would expose the jurors to the widespread mischief that is a daily if not hourly occurrence on the Internet. ...Given the extremely high profile of this case nationwide as well as in Illinois, and the unusual attention-getting conduct of the principal defendant and his wife, there is no good argument for releasing the jurors' names before the trial ends." After the hearing, the trial judge declined the media's request for the names before the end of the trial.

In 2011, Blagojevich was found guilty of 18 of the 20 charges leveled against him in a second trial, including planning to sell the Senate seat that Barack Obama vacated when he became President (a deadlocked jury failed to convict on a number of counts in 2010).

Long before these cases forced this problem into the limelight, the Supreme Court had already dealt with fair trial-free press issues, and ruled that all defendants must be assured of a fair trial, media publicity notwithstanding. Although events of recent years may have dramatized the fair trial-free press problem as never before, the issues are by no means new.

Early Fair Trial-Free Press Cases

The Supreme Court has struggled with fair trial-free press questions for more than 50 years. The court first took the drastic step of reversing a state court's murder conviction on the grounds of prejudicial publicity in the 1961 case of *Irvin v. Dowd* (366 U.S. 717). Even before that, the Supreme Court had expressed concern about the effect of publicity on trials (in *Shepherd v. Florida*, 341 U.S. 50, and *Stroble v. California*, 343 U.S. 181) and it had reversed a federal conviction due to prejudicial publicity in the 1959 case of *Marshall v. U.S.* (360 U.S. 310), but *Irvin* is especially noteworthy because it was a murder case and because it was the first state conviction to be reversed mainly due to prejudicial publicity.

The case involved Leslie Irvin, who was convicted of murdering six people near Evansville, Ind. and in nearby Kentucky. Irvin had been arrested on suspicion of burglary and writing bad checks a month after the murders. However, the county prosecutor—under political pressure to come up with a suspect—issued press releases calling him a "mad dog" and saying he had confessed to the murders. Since the murders themselves had received extensive news media coverage, the "confession" (which Irvin denied) led to a barrage of publicity in which he was branded "the mad dog killer." Other stories focused on Irvin's criminal past, revealing information that would never be admitted into evidence at his trial.

The defense was granted a *change of venue* (a change in the location of the trial), but only to a nearby county where there had also been extensive publicity about the crimes and "confession." A second request for a change of venue was denied because Indiana law allowed only one change of venue. Subsequently, of 430 prospective jurors examined by the prosecution and defense attorneys, 370 admitted they had formed some opinion about Irvin's guilt. And of the 12 jurors finally seated to hear the case, eight admitted they believed Irvin was guilty before hearing any evidence in court but said they could be impartial anyway. Because they claimed they would be impartial, the defense could not show cause to have them discharged as jurors, and Irvin's lawyer had used up all *peremptory challenges* (requests to discharge prospective jurors without having to prove they would not be impartial).

The U.S. Supreme Court reviewed the case more than five years after Irvin was originally convicted and sentenced to death. (In the meantime he had escaped from Indiana's death row and been recaptured in San Francisco.) The Court found that Irvin had not received a fair trial and set aside his conviction. In 1962 Irvin was retried, convicted of one murder, and sentenced to life in prison, where he died in 1983.

"Trial by television" resulted in a U.S. Supreme Court reversing a murder conviction in 1963. Wilbert Rideau was arrested and charged with robbing a bank, kidnapping three bank employees, and killing one of them in 1961 in Louisiana. During jailhouse interrogation by the local sheriff, he confessed the crimes. The session was filmed and the film was shown on local television three times. The Supreme Court held that it was a denial of Rideau's right to a fair trial not to grant him a change of venue after the people "had been exposed repeatedly and in depth to the spectacle of Rideau personally confessing in detail to the crimes...." The court said his real trial occurred on television, not in the courtroom (*Rideau v. Louisiana*, 373 U.S. 723). Rideau was retried, convicted of murder and sentenced to life in prison. Later he was retried again for other legal reasons and again convicted of murder. He was eventually given a fourth trial on the ground that African-American jurors were excluded from his earlier trials. At that trial, he was convicted only of manslaughter. He was released in 2005 after 44 years in prison, during which he had become famous as a writer and speaker.

Contempt by Publication

Courts have broad power to hold others in contempt of court. In addition to *direct contempt* (an act that violates the decorum of the court or shows disrespect for the legal process) there is *indirect contempt* (sometimes called *constructive contempt* or *contempt by publication*), which involves a disrespectful act outside the courtroom. From the early 1800s until the 1940s, one of the major legal threats to journalists was indirect contempt. Journalists were frequently cited for contempt because of what they wrote about a judge or the justice system. Unlike other public officials, judges had the power to punish journalists—directly and immediately—for publishing things they did not like, and some judges used that power freely. Surprisingly, the First Amendment was not a constraint upon contempt powers until the 1941 Supreme Court decision *Bridges v. California* (314 U.S. 252), a landmark decision on contempt of court that stripped judges of their vast power to use indirect contempt against the media. The case resulted from two unrelated contempt citations, one against Longshoremen's Union leader Harry Bridges and another against the *Los Angeles Times*. Bridges sent a telegram to the secretary of labor threatening to call a massive West Coast dock strike if a court ruling unfavorable to him was enforced. Meanwhile, the Times published several editorials that judges disliked, including one entitled "Probation for Gorillas?" that admonished a judge to impose tough sentences on a group of Teamsters Union organizers.

Both Bridges and the *Times* were cited for indirect contempt, or contempt by publication. Deciding the two cases together, the Supreme Court ruled that these contempt citations violated the First Amendment. The Court prohibited contempt citations for public statements about pending cases in the future, unless it could be shown that the publication created a clear and present danger to the administration of justice. As a result, it became much harder for a judge to justify citing a journalist for indirect contempt of court.

A few years later, the Supreme Court overturned two more indirect contempt citations against newspapers in *Pennekamp v. Florida* (328 U.S. 331, 1946) and *Craig v. Harney* (331 U.S. 367, 1947). In *Pennekamp*, the Florida Supreme Court had upheld a contempt citation against the *Miami Herald* for publishing editorials accusing local judges of being soft on criminals. The *Craig* case arose when a Corpus Christi, Tex., newspaper criticized a judge for his handling of a minor landlord-tenant dispute. In both cases, the Court reversed, reiterating that the clear and present danger test applies to indirect contempt citations.

After those decisions, the use of indirect contempt against the media almost disappeared. For a time, about the only sort of contempt threat journalists faced was the kind that arises when a photographer is caught taking illicit courthouse pictures. To be cited for contempt, one almost had to advocate marching on the courthouse (see *Cox v. Louisiana*, 379 U.S. 559, 1965). In short, contempt of court citations stemming from what was published ceased to be a major legal problem for the media.

The Sheppard v. Maxwell Decision

In 1966 the U.S. Supreme Court handed down the ruling on prejudicial media publicity that has come to be regarded as the landmark decision in this area, *Sheppard v. Maxwell* (384 U.S. 333). Dr. Sam Sheppard, a socially prominent Cleveland, Ohio, osteopath, was involved in one of the most famous criminal trials of his generation, a case that was the subject of a television documentary, a long-running fictionalized television series and a motion picture (*The Fugitive*). At the time, many called it "the trial of the century."

protective order (gag order):
a court order preventing the media from publishing information about a case.

continuance:
a delay in a trial to allow publicity to die down.

sequester the jury:
to confine a jury in a way that the members will be unable to consume any media content about the case.

change of venue:
moving a court proceeding from one location to another to avoid prejudicial publicity.

Sheppard's pregnant wife, Marilyn Sheppard, was murdered at their home overlooking Lake Erie in 1954. "Dr. Sam" said he was asleep on a downstairs sofa when he was awakened by his wife screaming upstairs. On the way upstairs to investigate, he was accosted from behind by a "bushy-haired" intruder who knocked him unconscious and fled.

Within a few weeks, the local papers were editorially demanding Dr. Sam's trial and conviction. The media literally took over the courtroom during his trial, and at one point the jurors' home telephone numbers were published in a gesture certain to build pressure on them for a guilty verdict. The press reported all sorts of "evidence" that was not admitted at the trial. Some of the evidence that came out didn't help Dr. Sam. Although he initially denied it, at least one woman said she had an extramarital affair with him. And his account of what happened on the night of Marilyn Sheppard's murder was vague and confusing.

Sheppard was convicted and his conviction was affirmed by the Ohio courts. The U.S. Supreme Court declined to review the case at that point. However, when the high court took a new interest in the free press-fair trial problem in the 1960s, Sheppard's lawyers again asked the Supreme Court to review the case. This time the court did so, and in 1966—12 years after his original trial—Dr. Sam had his conviction reversed and was granted a new trial at which he was acquitted. (Ironically, Sheppard's defense attorney at the second trial was a young F. Lee Bailey. Almost 30 years later, Bailey was a member of the "dream team" of defense attorneys who helped get O.J. Simpson acquitted at the next "trial of the century.") But the Sam Sheppard story does not have a happy ending: four years after his acquittal, he died at age 46, after spending more than 10 prime years of his short life in prison.

In the mid-1990s, Cuyahoga County authorities reopened the case as new evidence emerged pointing to Richard Eberling, who said he had done handyman work at the Sheppard home just before the murder, as the real killer. Eberling, who was later convicted and sentenced to life in prison for the murder of another woman, publicly denied killing Marilyn Sheppard. When forced to submit new blood samples for comparison to blood stains found in the Sheppard home, Eberling volunteered that his blood might have been there because he suffered cuts while replacing a storm window at the home. Meanwhile, a supervisor at a home health care agency where Eberling once worked was widely quoted as saying Eberling told her in 1983 that he killed Marilyn Sheppard. She said she went to the police soon after Eberling confessed to her, but they showed no interest in reopening the case then.

After Eberling died in 1998, a fellow prison inmate gave a videotaped interview in which he said Eberling had told him he did kill Marilyn Sheppard—and did it because she cried for help and bit him while he was raping her. The same inmate also said Eberling had earlier told a different version of the story, claiming he was paid by Dr. Sheppard to kill Marilyn.

Later other evidence surfaced that might have helped to acquit Dr. Sam. Although the police knew there was evidence of a forced entry into the home, they did not reveal it at the time of the trial. Nor did they initially reveal that there was a trail of blood from the bedroom where Marilyn Sheppard died down to the cellar, and that two of her teeth were broken outward, suggesting that she bit her assailant and he left the blood trail while fleeing. (Dr. Sam had no cuts when police arrived to investigate the crime, but Eberling was later observed with a prominent scar on his left wrist.) In 1959, Eberling was arrested for unrelated crimes and a ring belonging to Marilyn Sheppard was found in his home. In later years, Eberling dropped tantalizing hints while still denying that he murdered Marilyn Sheppard. In one letter, he wrote, "Sam, yes, I do know the entire story." Another time he wrote, "The Sheppard answer is in front of the entire world. Nobody bothered to look."

In 1997, modern DNA testing of 43-year-old blood samples from the Sheppard home and tissue samples from Dr. Sam's body provided still more evidence that Dr. Sam's account was accurate and Eberling was the real killer. The DNA tests indicated that blood stains found around the home, including a stain on a wardrobe door two feet from Marilyn Sheppard's body, did not match Dr. Sam's blood, but they did match Eberling's.

In December of 1998, the Ohio Supreme Court allowed Sam Reese Sheppard, the Sheppards' son who has worked for many years to clear his father's name, to go to trial with a lawsuit alleging that Dr. Sam was wrongfully convicted and imprisoned.

In 1954, the Cleveland media had been anything but sympathetic to Dr. Sam's cause. By 1999, however, the media were taking a very different view of Sam Reese Sheppard's cause. Although the media may have sympathized with Sam Reese Sheppard, the same cannot be said of the jury that heard his civil lawsuit in 2000. The jury rejected Sam Reese Sheppard's attempt to clear his father's name and win damages for his alleged wrongful imprisonment. The eight-person jury declined to rule that Sheppard had proven his father's innocence by the preponderance of the evidence, as required in a civil case. But this verdict failed to end the controversy: the public debate about the original Sheppard trials continued.

Whatever the ultimate verdict of history may be about Dr. Sam Sheppard, his case prompted a landmark Supreme Court decision on fair trial-free press. In an 8-1 opinion written by Justice Tom Clark, the Court ruled that "the state trial judge had not fulfilled his duty to protect Sheppard from the inherently prejudicial publicity which saturated the community." The Supreme Court went on to instruct trial judges as to what they must do to ensure a fair trial. The Court warned that failure to follow these safeguards would result in more reversals of convictions.

The Supreme Court's *Sheppard* decision suggested a number of specific things the nation's trial judges could do to protect defendants from sensational media publicity. The court said judges should do some or all of the following things to control publicity and protect defendants' rights:

1. Adopt rules to *curtail in-court misconduct by reporters*;
2. Issue *protective orders* (sometimes called *gag orders*) to control out-of-court statements by trial participants such as lawyers;
3. Grant a *continuance* to postpone the trial until community prejudice has had time to subside;

4. Grant a *change of venue* to a place with less prejudicial publicity;
5. *Admonish the jury* to disregard the media publicity about the case; or
6. *Sequester the jury* (confine them in a place where they will not be able to read about the trial in newspapers or hear about it on radio or television).

Basically, Justice Clark was suggesting two different kinds of remedies: remedies that *compensate for* potentially prejudicial media publicity, and remedies intended to *eliminate* such publicity—but at the expense of First Amendment freedoms. In the years following *Sheppard*, judges tried all of these things to control publicity. Some also began to do things the Supreme Court didn't recommend in the *Sheppard* case, such as closing their courtrooms to the press and public and holding preliminary proceedings—or entire trials—in secret. These judicial actions raised new constitutional issues.

"Gag" Orders and the News Media

Of all these remedies for prejudicial publicity, the one that generated the most controversy involved the suppression of information about the trial. In the *Sheppard* decision Justice Clark wrote, "Neither prosecutors, counsel for defense, the accused, witnesses, court staff nor enforcement officers coming under the jurisdiction of the court should be permitted to frustrate its function."

Responding to this mandate, jurists all over the country began issuing orders that they call *protective orders* or *restrictive orders*; journalists tend to call them *gag orders*. Originally, these orders fell into two categories: those directed against only the participants in the trial, ordering them not to reveal prejudicial information to the media, and those directed against the media, ordering them not to publish prejudicial information even if they lawfully obtain it. The first category (orders intended to dry up the media's sources of prejudicial information) usually has been upheld when challenged on First Amendment grounds. But the second kind (those purporting to exercise prior restraint of the media) has not fared as well and they are rarely issued today—the Kobe Bryant case in 2004 being a rare exception.

In fact, in a television interview nine years after the *Sheppard* decision, Justice Clark said he did not mean that the media should be prohibited by judges from publishing information in their possession. Instead, gag orders were to be imposed only on those who might give prejudicial information to the press. More will be said of these orders shortly.

Other Remedies

The protective or gag order is just one of the remedies for prejudicial publicity recommended in the *Sheppard* decision, but it has surely been the most viable and controversial one. All of the others—which are really intended to compensate for prejudicial publicity instead of eliminating it—have limitations that sometimes render them impractical.

For example, a change of venue is expensive: it means all parties to the case, including witnesses, must travel a long distance for the trial, and it abridges the defendant's right to be tried in the place where the crime was committed, another constitutional right. Moreover, with today's pervasive media, the new community may be just as aroused about the case as was the community where the trial was originally scheduled.

Ordering a postponement of the trial also has major disadvantages. For one thing, it denies defendants their constitutional right to a speedy trial. For another, witnesses tend to become unavailable after a period of time. And finally, there is no assurance that the prejudicial publicity will not resume as the date of the long-delayed trial finally approaches. The community may harbor prejudices against a suspect for many years, and if anything a long delay may leave many persons more convinced than ever of the suspect's guilt.

Likewise, sequestering the jury has its drawbacks, although some states do sequester juries routinely in cases where the death sentence may be imposed. Nevertheless, many prospective jurors are unwilling to serve in a case where they will be isolated from the modern world for weeks or months. Moreover, sequestering a jury is expensive—the jurors must be provided food, lodging and entertainment.

And finally, it has become almost impossible to completely insulate jurors from the media. The celebrated trial of Charles Manson and his followers for the murder of actress Sharon Tate and her friends provides a good illustration of the problems involved with sequestration. In the Manson trial the jury was sequestered, but on various occasions newspapers containing prejudicial stories appeared in the courtroom, in the restrooms used by the jurors, and on newsracks the jurors saw during the bus ride from their hotel to the court. At one point, Manson himself held up a newspaper in court so that the jurors could see the main headline, which proclaimed, "Manson Guilty, Nixon Says." The judge immediately stopped the proceedings and asked the jurors if seeing that headline would influence their verdict and they all said it would not, but no one will ever know for sure if that was true.

Other ways to protect the defendant from prejudicial publicity are closing the trial or pretrial proceedings and directly questioning the jurors about their potential prejudices. The problems of closing the trial or pretrial hearings will be treated later in this chapter.

The difficulties of questioning the jurors about their prejudices (a procedure called *voir dire*) were already cited in connection with the *Irvin* case. Jurors may say they can be impartial when in fact they harbor strong prejudices based on the media publicity. Each side in a criminal trial is allowed to dismiss only a few jurors on peremptory challenges (i.e., without having to prove they are prejudiced). As the *Irvin* case illustrated, in a sensational case the defense may use all of its peremptory challenges and still be stuck with jurors who cannot be shown to be prejudiced but who are *not* impartial.

Furthermore, admonitions to the jury to disregard publicity they may see or read—another of the means of protecting the defendant's rights suggested in *Sheppard*—can hardly be expected to ensure that the jurors will not base their "guilty" or "not guilty" verdict on what they learn from the media as well as what they hear in court. Jurors being human, they will usually consider everything they know about the case in reaching a verdict, regardless of the source of that information. But the Supreme Court has said that *voir dire* proceedings should under most circumstances be open to the public.

This brings us back to protective (or "gag") orders, the most controversial but perhaps also the most practical means of protecting defendants from prejudicial publicity—these orders may actually eliminate the prejudicial publicity rather than merely compensate for it.

"Gag" Orders as Prior Restraints

Protective (or "gag") orders were in the center of a bitter debate between the media and the judiciary from the time of the *Sheppard* decision until the U.S. Supreme Court finally clarified the constitutional issues involved a decade later in a case called *Nebraska Press Association v. Stuart* (427 U.S. 53, 1976).

Gag orders were widely used all over the country in the early 1970s. A judge who believed an upcoming case might generate extensive publicity would almost routinely issue an order forbidding all parties in the case to make statements to the media. Such orders usually prohibited disclosing a defendant's prior criminal record, discussing the merits of the evidence in the case and revealing the presence or absence of any confession. In many instances, this kind of information would be excluded as evidence at the trial, which would do little good if the jurors already know about it from watching television or reading the newspapers. But some judges went beyond these restrictions and actually attempted to censor the media by ordering publishers and broadcasters not to disseminate information they already had.

After a number of state and lower federal court decisions on the validity of gag orders, the Supreme Court finally ruled on the issue in *Nebraska Press Association*. That ruling all but eliminated gag orders that directly restrained the press (as opposed to orders that prohibited trial participants from giving prejudicial information to reporters).

The case involved Erwin Charles Simants, an unemployed handyman with a purported IQ of 75. Simants borrowed his brother-in-law's rifle, walked to the house next door and murdered six members of the James Henry Kellie family. Simants turned himself in the day after the murders and confessed. However, there were legal questions about whether he had sufficient mental capacity to understand his rights; his confession was quickly challenged.

At the preliminary hearing, Lincoln County Judge Ronald Ruff ordered the media not to report any of the testimony. This gag order was appealed to District Court Judge Hugh Stuart by Nebraska news organizations. Stuart replaced Judge Ruff's order with his own.

Stuart's order prohibited the publication of certain kinds of prejudicial information. Later, the Nebraska Supreme Court modified the order to prohibit publishing only Simants' confession and any other facts "strongly implicative" of the suspect. The press was ordered not to even mention the existence of a confession.

The news organizations appealed the order to the Supreme Court. The high court ruled unanimously that this order was a violation of the First Amendment in that it imposed a prior restraint on publication. In striking down the order, Chief Justice Warren Burger, writing for the Court, referred to previous prior restraint cases and wrote, "A prior restraint, by contrast and by definition, has an immediate and irreversible sanction. If it can be said that a

FIG. 38. Chief Justice Warren E. Burger, official Supreme Court portrait, 1976.

Library of Congress, Prints and Photographs Division, [LC-USZ62-60136].

threat of criminal or civil sanctions after publication "chills" speech, prior restraint "freezes" it at least for the time."

But the Court did not totally rule out the possibility of protective orders being directed against the media in future cases. It said that in "extraordinary circumstances" such an order might be imposed. However, there must be sufficient evidence to reasonably conclude that:

1. There will be *intense and pervasive publicity* concerning the case;
2. *No other alternative measure*—such as a change of venue or continuance or extensive *voir dire* process—is likely to mitigate the effects of the pretrial publicity; and
3. The restrictive order *will in fact effectively prevent prejudicial material* from reaching potential jurors.

These guidelines from the *Nebraska Press Association* case were widely discussed again when a federal judge ordered Cable News Network (CNN) not to broadcast tape recordings of conversations between former Panamanian dictator Manuel Noriega and his lawyers. Noriega was in jail awaiting trial on drug trafficking charges at the time. The judge's order, a direct prior restraint, was quickly appealed by CNN, but the Supreme Court refused either to set aside the gag order or to take up the case at that point. The judge who had issued the order later reviewed the controversial tapes and concluded that their broadcast would not interfere with Noriega's right to a fair trial, so he decided not to make the order permanent. However, in 1994 the U.S. Attorney's office in Miami filed criminal contempt of court charges against CNN for broadcasting excerpts from the tapes while the order was in effect, and a federal judge fined CNN for the broadcast (*U.S. v. Cable News Network*, 865 F.Supp. 1549).

The Noriega case was unusual: in most instances gag orders targeting the media are overturned on appeal. Within weeks of CNN's contempt of court conviction, three state appellate courts overruled gag orders targeting the news media (see *Ohio ex rel. New World Communications v. Character*, 23 Media L. Rep. 1479, *Jacksonville Television Inc. v. Florida Dept. of Health and Rehabilitative Services*, 23 Media L. Rep. 1254 and *Kansas v. Alston*, 887 P.2d 681).

But not all gag orders are overturned on appeal. The Fifth Circuit in 2012 *upheld* a gag order that restricted access to individuals involved with the proceedings of a trial (e.g., attorneys) against Khalid Ali-M Aldawsari, a Saudi Arabian student accused of planning to create weapons of mass destruction. In denying the reporter's request to have the gag order overturned, the court noted that it was a narrow order and that news media had successfully been relying on information in the public record and public hearings to cover the case (*U.S. v. Aldawsari v. Clark*, 2012 U.S. App. LEXIS 11792).

In 2008, the *Orange County* (Calif.) *Register* was enjoined from reporting on trial testimony of witnesses in a case to which it was a party. Newspaper carriers had claimed that the *Register* had inappropriately classified them as independent contractors and denied them benefits they should receive as employees (like meal breaks, overtime pay, and minimum wage). The newspaper appealed the gag order, and the appeals court overturned it, saying that the gag order was a plain violation of the First Amendment because, in part, there were less restrictive means to accomplish the trial court's ends, particularly because the gag order applied only to the *Register* and no other news organizations (*Freedom Communications Inc. v. Superior Court of Orange County*, 167 Cal. App. 4th 150, Cal. App. 4th Dist., 2008). The carriers later settled with the *Register* for $22 million.

Gagging Trial Lawyers

Although the *Nebraska Press Association* case limited the power of judges to restrain the press, it had little effect on their power to impose gag orders on trial *participants*. By the 2000s, at least 40 states had rules regulating what lawyers may say publicly while they are handling a newsworthy case.

The American Bar Association has guidelines for professional conduct by lawyers. Among other things, these ABA "Model Rules" cover extrajudicial (out of court) statements. Although these rules are voluntary, many states' mandatory rules are based on them. The ABA rules were extensively revised in 1994. Under ABA Model Rule 3.6, lawyers are forbidden to make out-of-court statements that the lawyer "knows or reasonably should know... will have a substantial likelihood of materially prejudicing an adjudicative proceeding in the matter." This rule applies only while a case is pending and only to lawyers specifically involved in the case; it does not apply to other lawyers or law professors who may comment on a case in the media. Nor does it apply to lawyers who write books (or comment in other ways) after a case is over. There is a separate provision in ABA Model Rule 3.8 intended to prevent prosecutors from trying their cases in the media. Rule 3.8 directs prosecutors to "refrain from making extrajudicial comments that have substantial likelihood of heightening public condemnation of the accused." Rule 3.6 also allows lawyers to make "reasonable" statements to the extent necessary to mitigate "the substantial undue prejudicial effect of recent publicity not initiated by the lawyer or lawyer's client."

The ABA felt obliged to rewrite and in some ways liberalize its Model Rules because a Nevada state rule based on an earlier version of the ABA rules was declared unconstitutional in *Gentile v. State Bar of Nevada* (501 U.S. 1030, 1991). In that case, Nevada disciplined Dominic P. Gentile, a criminal defense lawyer, for making allegedly improper public comments after a client was indicted. Like the earlier ABA rule, the Nevada rule permitted attorneys to publicly describe the "general nature of the claim or defense," but only if it is done "without elaboration." Nevada Bar authorities punished Gentile for saying too much to the media. He appealed, and the Supreme Court held that Nevada's rules were too vague and therefore violated Gentile's First Amendment rights.

The *Gentile* case triggered a divisive controversy within the ABA. In the end, the ABA adopted new limits on what trial lawyers may say to the media about a pending case, but with the right-of-reply provision. After much debate, the ABA decided to retain a *substantial likelihood* test for public statements by lawyers: this forbids lawyers to say anything that would have a substantial likelihood of prejudicing a pending case. Some advocates of greater freedom for lawyers urged the ABA to adopt a *clear and present danger test* under which attorneys could only be punished if their out-of-court statements created a clear and present danger of prejudicing a pending case. Under that test, it would be much harder to prove that a lawyer's extrajudicial comments were improper—and lawyers would have greater freedom to make public statements about a pending case.

Many of the same issues have been raised concerning ethical rules and state laws forbidding candidates in judicial elections to announce their views on political and legal issues—issues that might come before them as judges. In *Republican Party of Minnesota v. White* (536 U.S. 765), the U.S. Supreme Court ruled in 2002 that Minnesota's restrictions on judicial candidates violated the First Amendment. The 5-4 majority rejected the argument that judges and prospective judges should always present the appearance of impartiality and instead ruled that judicial candidates, like other candidates for public office, have a right to speak about controversial issues, even if they might have to rule on some of those issues later. However, the Court did *not* decide whether judicial candidates have a right to pledge or promise that they will decide any particular case or issue a certain way. Many states have rules prohibiting such promises, and those rules are likely to be challenged on First Amendment grounds in future cases.

It has become routine for judges to order lawyers and other participants not to talk to the news media in sensational cases. Gag orders were imposed on lawyers in the Robert Blake, Kobe Bryant and Michael Jackson criminal cases, among others. That did not prevent the media from covering these and other sensational cases in ways that many judges considered improper and prejudicial. For example, a cable network aired a made-for-television movie about the Scott Peterson case before he could be put on trial for murdering his wife Laci (he was later convicted).

■ CLOSED COURTROOMS

Soon after the Supreme Court's *Nebraska Press Association* decision, a new conflict between judges and journalists assumed even greater proportions. Judges began to bar the press and the public from preliminary hearings, hearings on motions to suppress evidence and sometimes even from trials.

Although it has been customary for courtrooms to be open to the public throughout American history, there are a number of circumstances that may lead to a courtroom closure. Courtroom closures to protect a defendant's right to a fair trial are the primary subject of this chapter. However, courtrooms are also closed at times to protect an individual's privacy, to assure the secrecy of information affecting national security, or to keep the details of a police investigation confidential—to cite just three examples.

In the late 1970s there were increasingly frequent instances of preliminary criminal proceedings—and even trials—being closed to the press and the public in an effort to curtail prejudicial publicity. Gag orders directed against trial participants do not always stop the flow of prejudicial information to the press, and *Nebraska Press Association* imposed limits on judges' power to gag the press directly. Therefore, judges increasingly saw closed pretrial hearings as the best way to limit prejudicial publicity in sensational cases.

To understand the judges' viewpoint, we should explain why pretrial hearings occur and what happens at these proceedings. A *preliminary hearing* is intended as a check on law enforcement officers and prosecutors. It is a hearing where the case against the accused is reviewed by a judge, not to determine guilt or innocence but merely to decide whether there is enough evidence to justify a full trial. This is supposed to be a shortcut out of the criminal

Focus on...
The Nebraska Press Association test

The three-part test written by Chief Justice Burger for when gag orders are acceptable is a heavy burden for a court to reach.

The presumption that gag orders are generally invalid means the judge must gaze into a crystal ball and predict several things.

First, the court must show that there will be significant and pervasive publicity that will affect the defendant's right to a fair trial. If there hasn't been any yet, the judge must successfully argue that there will be.

Second, the court must make a case that nothing else he/she could do is likely to prevent or mitigate the damage that will be caused by this anticipated publicity.

Finally, the court must demonstrate—without actually trying it first—that a gag order will work to stop that anticipated prejudicial publicity.

justice system for defendants who should never have been charged in the first place. The purpose is *not* to decide if the accused is guilty beyond a reasonable doubt (the standard of proof required in a criminal trial) but to see if there is enough evidence to justify a trial.

As a result, only the prosecution presents evidence at most preliminary hearings. If there is enough evidence, a trial is scheduled, almost without regard to the strength of the defense's case. Thus, as a matter of strategy, the defense often waits until the full trial before presenting its side of the case. As a result, news coverage of a preliminary hearing is necessarily imbalanced in most instances since only one side has been heard. The defense does have the right to cross-examine prosecution witnesses, but even so, if the hearing is covered by the media, most of the news generated there is going to be unfavorable to the defendant, who may have to stand trial before jurors who read about the preliminary hearing in the papers.

Pretrial hearings on motions to suppress evidence are even more likely to produce prejudicial publicity. At these hearings, the defense asks a judge to throw out damaging evidence, often because it was obtained by an unlawful search or seizure. Or perhaps the challenged evidence is a confession that was secured through coercion. In any event, what good does it do to have the tainted evidence *suppressed* (i.e., ruled inadmissible at the trial) if prospective jurors learn about it on the evening news? For these reasons, many judges and lawyers feel that hearings on motions to suppress evidence should be closed to the press and public.

In addition to preventing jury prejudice, closing preliminary court proceedings protects the reputations of defendants who have been charged with a crime but are not held for trial because the hearing reveals that the prosecutor has little evidence.

Few journalists would deny that there are powerful arguments for secrecy at the pretrial stage in criminal proceedings, except for one thing: more than 80 percent of all criminal prosecutions in America are resolved without the case ever reaching a full trial. Because the judge's ruling on a motion to suppress crucial evidence is the decisive step in many criminal cases, serious plea bargaining usually occurs after these pretrial proceedings. If key evidence is barred, the prosecutor may be inclined to accept a guilty plea to a lesser charge or even drop the charges. If the evidence is ruled admissible, on the other hand, the defendant may plead guilty as charged at this stage, perhaps in return for a promise of a light sentence. In the vast majority of criminal proceedings, the last chance the public will have to monitor the justice system is at the pretrial hearing stage.

As a trend toward closed pretrial hearings developed, a constitutional challenge to this practice reached the Supreme Court in the 1979 case of *Gannett v. DePasquale* (443 U.S. 368). The Supreme Court upheld a judge's order barring a newspaper reporter from a pretrial evidentiary hearing in upstate New York. The case arose when two young men were charged with murdering a former New York policeman. They reportedly confessed the crime and were later indicted by a grand jury.

Because of the intense publicity surrounding the incident and the arrest, the defense and prosecution concurred in closing the pretrial hearing. When Judge Daniel DePasquale barred the press and public, the Gannett newspapers appealed the ruling. The state's highest court affirmed the order and Gannett asked the Supreme Court to hear the case.

In affirming the closure, Justice Potter Stewart, writing for a 5-4 Supreme Court majority, acknowledged that "there is a strong societal interest in public trials." His opinion also noted, "there is no question that the Sixth Amendment permits and even presumes open trials as a norm." However, Stewart continued, the Sixth Amendment right to a public trial belongs to the defendant and not the public, and it is a right the defendant may waive.

Justice Stewart agreed with the trial judge's decision that the press' right of access to this particular hearing "was outweighed by the defendant's right to a fair trial ...because an open proceeding would pose a reasonable probability of prejudice to these defendants."

Justice Stewart's opinion was joined by Justices John Paul Stevens, Lewis Powell, William Rehnquist and Chief Justice Burger. The latter three also wrote separate concurring opinions. Justices Marshall, Brennan, Blackmun and White joined in a dissent which said, "Secret hearings ...are suspect by nature. Unlike any other provision of the Sixth Amendment, the public trial interest cannot adequately be protected by the prosecutor and judge in conjunction or connivance with the defendant."

Justice Powell's concurring opinion was noteworthy in that it said the press and public should have a right to challenge proposed courtroom closures. In the years since *Gannett,* many journalists have done precisely that, sometimes successfully. Many reporters who regularly cover the courts carry a card with them containing the correct legal phrasing of a motion to object to a courtroom closure.

Nevertheless, the *Gannett* decision stood as a precedent permitting judges to close at least pretrial hearings when they felt the danger of prejudicial publicity would outweigh the public's right to observe the proceedings.

As a result, there was an avalanche of closed hearings—and even trials—in 1979 and 1980. The Reporters Committee for Freedom of the Press counted 21 courtroom closures ordered or upheld on appeal in the first 30 days after the *Gannett* ruling was announced. Within the year, there were at least 100 more such courtroom closures around the nation.

Open Trials: Richmond Newspapers v. Virginia

Apparently alarmed at the reaction to *Gannett* by trial judges, several Supreme Court justices made public statements condemning the trend toward courtroom closures. And the high court quickly agreed to review another related case, this one involving a closure of a full trial in Virginia. In this case (*Richmond Newspapers v. Virginia,* 448 U.S. 555, 1980), a county judge had cleared his courtroom of reporters and spectators before the fourth trial of a man who was charged with murdering a hotel manager. His first trial had been invalidated on a technicality, and the next two resulted in mistrials. Relying on a Virginia statute that allowed "the removal of any persons whose presence would impair the conduct of a fair trial," the judge simply closed the trial. The defendant was acquitted after a two-day closed trial because there were "too many holes" in the prosecution's case, the judge said.

Two jointly owned Richmond, Va., newspapers challenged the courtroom closure. Just a week after the *Gannett* ruling of the U.S. Supreme Court, the Virginia Supreme Court upheld the ruling closing this trial. Ruling in 1980—a year to the day after its controversial *Gannett* decision—the U.S. Supreme Court voted 7-1 to overrule this trial closing, a decision that was widely seen as a major victory for the media. Not only did the high court invalidate the closing of this particular trial, but Chief Justice Burger's opinion for the court recognized for the first time that there is a constitutional right of access to information inherent in the free press guarantees of the First Amendment:

> We hold that the right to attend criminal trials is implicit in the guarantees of
> the First Amendment; without the freedom to attend such trials, which people
> have exercised for centuries, important aspects of freedom of speech and of the
> press could be eviscerated.

preliminary hearing:
a hearing where the case against the accused is reviewed by a judge to decide whether there is enough evidence to justify a full trial.

Moreover, Burger's opinion went to some trouble to make it clear that this public right to attend trials, although only an implied right and not one specifically stated in the Constitution, was nonetheless legitimate. He pointed to a variety of other constitutional rights the Supreme Court has recognized over the years, although those rights too were only implied in the Constitution. Burger noted that the rights of association and privacy, the right to travel, and the right to be judged by the "beyond-a-reasonable-doubt" standard of proof in criminal cases were only implied and not stated in the Constitution.

Although this opinion was joined by only two other justices, at least two additional justices recognized a right of the public to attend trials in a separate opinion in the *Richmond* case. However, Justice Rehnquist (the only dissenter) said the states should be free to set their own standards on the administration of justice and found no provision in the federal Constitution that prohibited the Virginia judge from doing what he did.

In overturning the closure of a trial in the *Richmond* decision, the Supreme Court avoided reversing its year-old *Gannett* ruling, leaving judges free to close pretrial hearings in some instances where a closed trial might not be permitted. In fact, on the same day the Supreme Court handed down its *Richmond* decision, the court declined to review a lower court decision authorizing another closed pretrial hearing in New York.

Moreover, the Court did not even flatly forbid closed trials in the *Richmond* case. Instead, the high court said trials could still be closed under certain extraordinary circumstances. "Absent an overriding interest (in closing the trial) articulated in the (judge's) findings, the trial of a criminal case must be open to the public," Burger's opinion held. The Supreme Court did not give any guidelines for determining when a trial should be closed, but the Court did make it clear that a judge must pursue alternative means of ensuring the fairness of a trial before barring the press and public.

In short, *Richmond* limits a judge's discretion in barring the press and public from a trial, while permitting trial closures in extreme circumstances if the judge can set forth valid reasons for his action. This decision may not have gone quite as far as many journalists hoped it would, but it nonetheless sharply curtailed the nationwide trend toward closed courtrooms that had developed in the year between the *Gannett* and *Richmond* decisions.

Open Courtroom Cases After Richmond Newspapers

The *Richmond* decision was a vindication of the principle of open courtrooms in the United States. While there have been a number of controversial courtroom closures since that bellwether 1980 Supreme Court decision, the trend toward closed trials has been reversed. In fact, the Court has since handed down several more decisions overruling courtroom closures. In 1982, the Court invalidated a Massachusetts law that automatically closed the courtroom whenever a juvenile victim of a sex crime was to testify. In *Globe Newspaper Co. v. Superior Court* (457 U.S. 596), the Court said judges must evaluate each trial closure on a case-by-case basis rather than automatically closing a trial whenever a young sex crime victim is testifying. In a 6-3 decision, the high court found the Massachusetts law unconstitutional because it made the closure mandatory. The Court took pains to point out that judges could exclude the press and public in individual cases where they found that a minor's well-being would be in jeopardy if the trial were open.

Writing for the majority, Justice William Brennan took note of the court's ruling in *Richmond Newspapers* that the public has a constitutional right of access to criminal trials. However, Brennan pointed out that this right is not absolute: a trial may be closed if a state can show two things: (1) a "compelling governmental interest" that requires the closure and (2) that the law requiring closure is "narrowly tailored to serve that interest."

Weighing the Massachusetts statute—as interpreted by that state's highest court—the Supreme Court concluded that it failed this two-part test because a case-by-case determination of whether a criminal trial should be closed would be sufficient to protect young victims. The mandatory closure provision was overbroad, the Court held.

The case arose when a judge closed a rape trial in which the victims were three girls under age 18. The *Boston Globe* challenged the closure, and after several preliminary decisions the state Supreme Court upheld the mandatory closure provision of the Massachusetts law. The *Globe* appealed. The gist of the *Globe Newspaper* decision is nicely summarized by a footnote in the majority opinion:

> We emphasize that our holding is a narrow one: that a rule of mandatory
> closure respecting the testimony of minor sex victims is constitutionally infirm.
> In individual cases, and under appropriate circumstances, the First Amendment
> does not necessarily stand as a bar to the exclusion from the courtroom of the
> press and general public during the testimony of minor sex-offense victims.
> But a mandatory rule, requiring no particularized determinations in individual
> cases, is unconstitutional.

The ruling produced dissents from Chief Justice Warren Burger and Justice William Rehnquist, who felt the mandatory closure rule was not unconstitutional, and from Justice John Paul Stevens, who felt the case should not have been heard.

In 1984 the Supreme Court took another step to assure public access to the criminal justice system when it ruled that the jury selection process must also normally be open to the public. In the case of *Press-Enterprise Co. v. Superior Court (P-E I)* (464 U.S. 501), the court unanimously overturned a Riverside, Calif., judge's decision to close almost six weeks of jury selection procedures during a 1981 murder trial. The *Riverside* (Calif.) *Press-Enterprise* challenged the judge's actions.

The judge not only closed the jury selection process, but also refused to make a transcript of the proceeding public after the defendant was tried, convicted and sentenced to death for raping and killing a 13-year-old girl. The effect of the judge's decision was to ensure that the public would never know how the jury was selected for a trial that ended with a death sentence.

Writing for the Supreme Court, Chief Justice Warren Burger emphasized that the jury selection, like other aspects of criminal trials, has traditionally been open to the public—and should continue to be open in all but very unusual circumstances. He wrote, "Proceedings held in secret would ...frustrate the broad public interest; by contrast public proceedings vindicate the concerns of the victims and the community in knowing that offenders are being brought to account for their criminal conduct by jurors fairly and openly selected." However, Burger said there might be rare occasions when prospective jurors could be questioned in private in the judge's chambers to protect their privacy during discussions of "deeply personal matters." However, a transcript of the proceedings should be made available within a reasonable time unless that would further invade a juror's privacy. But to close the entire process for "an incredible six weeks" (as Burger put it) was going much too far.

Although the decision that the judge should not have closed the jury selection in this case was unanimous, three justices wrote separate opinions. Justice Thurgood Marshall said the jury selection and "all aspects of criminal trials" should be open, regardless of whether open jury selection might embarrass a prospective juror. Justices Harry Blackmun and John Paul Stevens wrote a separate opinion emphasizing the importance of jurors' privacy rights.

The importance of the 1984 *Press-Enterprise* decision was underscored 20 years later when a New York federal judge closed much of the jury selection process during the trial of home-lifestyle doyenne Martha Stewart. In a strong reaffirmation that jury selection must normally be open, the Second Circuit reversed the judge's order and said most of the jury selection process should have been open (*ABC Inc. v. Stewart*, 360 F.3d 90, 2004). Stewart was later convicted of lying to federal investigators during an inquiry into possible insider trading. She had sold nearly 4,000 shares of stock in a biotech company just before a public announcement of business reverses caused the stock price to plummet.

The Supreme Court may have settled the issue when it announced a constitutional right to an open *voir dire* in 2010. Eric Presley claimed that the exclusion of his uncle from *voir dire* proceedings in his drug trafficking trial abridged his Sixth Amendment right to a public trial. The Supreme Court agreed in a *per curiam* (unsigned) opinion in *Presley v. Georgia* (130 S. Ct. 721), saying, "Trial courts are obligated to take every reasonable measure to accommodate public attendance at criminal trials." Justices Clarence Thomas and Antonin Scalia dissented, noting that a public *voir dire* had never before been considered part of the Sixth Amendment's guarantee of a public trial and should not be simply assumed.

Also in 2010, the highest court in Massachusetts followed suit, saying that even a partial closure of jury selection proceedings could violate both the First and Sixth Amendments: "The public trial right applies to jury selection proceedings ... which are "a crucial part of any criminal case'" (*Commonwealth v. Cohen*, 921 N.E.2d 906).

A few months after the 1984 *Press-Enterprise* decision, the Supreme Court again reiterated that criminal proceedings *other than* the trial itself must normally be open. In *Waller v. Georgia* (467 U.S. 39, 1984), the high court overturned a judge's decision to close a lengthy pretrial evidence suppression hearing in a case where the police had searched numerous homes and conducted telephone wiretaps to gather evidence of gambling. The defendants argued that much of the evidence was unlawfully obtained, and they wanted it suppressed. Moreover, they demanded that the evidence suppression hearing be open to the public, but the judge refused to open the hearing. Then he admitted most of the evidence and convicted several defendants of various crimes.

The Court ruled that most of this evidence-suppression hearing, like the jury selection in the 1984 *Press-Enterprise* case, should have been open to the public. Only a little of the seven-day hearing involved material that might invade anyone's privacy, the Court noted. In *Waller,* the Court again emphasized the right of the public—as well as defendants—to have criminal trials and pretrial proceedings held in open court under most circumstances.

Two years after the original *Press-Enterprise* decision, the Supreme Court handed down another important decision with exactly the same name—and on a closely related aspect of the open-courtroom issue. In this 1986 case, *Press-Enterprise Co. v. Superior Court (P-E II)* (478 U.S. 1), the Court ruled that preliminary hearings and similar pretrial proceedings must be open unless there is a *substantial probability* that an open hearing will prejudice the defendant's right to a fair trial.

The 1986 case, commonly identified as *Press-Enterprise II* to distinguish it from the 1984 case, involved exactly the same two parties: the *Riverside* (Calif.) *Press-Enterprise* and the Riverside County Superior Court. This time, the newspaper protested the closing of a 41-day preliminary hearing for a male nurse accused of killing a dozen hospital patients with massive drug overdoses.

In California and many other states, a preliminary hearing is held in most major criminal cases. As explained earlier, these hearings are conducted by a judge to determine if there is sufficient evidence to hold the defendant for a full trial. The preliminary hearing is the only significant court proceeding in the great majority of criminal cases: less then 20 percent of major criminal cases actually go to trial. Therefore, the preliminary hearing is often the only opportunity the public will ever have to learn of the evidence against the accused. California law permitted the closing of a preliminary hearing whenever there was a *reasonable likelihood* that prejudicial publicity would result from an open hearing.

Writing for a 7-2 majority, Chief Justice Warren Burger objected to the almost-routine closing of preliminary hearings in California. Noting that they are often lengthy proceedings, he said they should be open to the public unless "there is a substantial probability that the defendant's right to a fair trial will be prejudiced by publicity that closure would prevent and ...(that) reasonable alternatives to closure cannot adequately protect the defendant's free trial rights." Burger also declared that if the courtroom is closed during a preliminary

FIG. 39. U.S. Supreme Court building, Washington, D.C., February 2011.

Photo by Michelle A. Scott. Used with permission.

hearing, it must be for as short a period of time as possible. He cautioned against closing a lengthy preliminary hearing: "Closure of an entire 41-day proceeding would rarely be warranted. The First Amendment right of access cannot be overcome by the conclusory assertion that publicity might deprive the defendant of (the right to a fair trial)."

In the aftermath of the Court's *Press-Enterprise II* decision, closed preliminary hearings have become rare—and judges are more reluctant to close other pretrial proceedings now. This ruling strengthens the growing body of constitutional law saying that the criminal justice system must be conducted openly, with the press and public invited to view the process.

In 1993, the Supreme Court reaffirmed the *Press-Enterprise II* decision, overturning a Puerto Rican law allowing closed preliminary hearings there. Puerto Rico, which has considerable local autonomy but must obey the U.S. Constitution, continued to hold closed preliminary hearings in felony cases when-ever a defendant requested it, in spite of the *Press-Enterprise II* decision. Ultimately, a journalist asked to be allowed to attend a closed preliminary hearing and was turned down. He then challenged the constitutionality of the Puerto Rican court rules and prevailed when the Supreme Court held that Puerto Rico, too, must allow public access to these proceedings (*El Vocero de Puerto Rico v. Puerto Rico*, 508 U.S. 147).

All of the cases summarized up to now involved *criminal* court proceedings. In 1999, the California Supreme Court ruled in a widely noted case that *civil* courtrooms should usually be open to the public. In *NBC Subsidiary v. Superior Court* (20 C.4th 1178), the court overturned a number of restrictions that a judge had imposed on the press and public during a trial pitting actor Clint Eastwood against his former lover, actress Sondra Locke.

The California Supreme Court recognized a broad constitutional right of the press and public to attend civil court proceedings as well as criminal proceedings. In a sweeping decision, the state supreme court unanimously ruled that the First Amendment protects the right to attend civil trials. Writing for the court, Chief Justice Ronald George traced the tradition of open courtrooms through history and relied heavily on the U.S. Supreme Court's landmark *Richmond Newspapers v. Virginia* decision in concluding that there is a constitutional right to attend civil court proceedings. Although *Richmond Newspapers* specifically affirmed the public's right to attend only criminal trials, George noted that there are strong public policy reasons to recognize a similar right in civil cases, marking the first time that any state's highest court had clearly recognized a constitutional right to attend civil court proceedings.

The media were successful in 2010 and 2011 in ultimately gaining access to various court proceedings after they had initially been denied. The Kentucky Supreme Court said that reporter Jason Riley and the *Louisville Courier-Journal* should have been granted access to a juror contempt hearing (the court decided the case even though it was moot because the situation is "capable of repetition, yet evading review"—thus appropriate for decision). The court said that "if it can be established that all defendants, or the public at large, have a stake in the process and outcome of such proceedings, then public access must be allowed" (*Riley v. Gibson*, 338 S.W.3d 230, 2011). Similarly, the Fifth Circuit said that "the press and public have a First Amendment right of access to sentencing hearings, and that the district court should have given the press and public notice and an opportunity to be heard before closing the sentencing proceeding" in the conviction of a drug cartel leader (*Hearst Newspapers, LLC v. Cardenas-Guillen*, 641 F.3d 168, 2011). The Second Circuit said that a lower court's closing of the *voir dire* proceedings in an immigration case was incorrect but did not result in the vacating of the defendant's sentence (*U.S. v. Gupta*, 650 F.3d 863, 2011).

Access to Courtroom Documents

If the nation's courtrooms are supposed to be open to the public under most circumstances, what about public access to *court documents*? In the aftermath of the Supreme Court's *Richmond Newspapers* decision and the cases that followed it, a number of lower courts have ruled that the press and public have a right to see and copy court documents even in sensational cases. Actually, court documents have normally been open for public inspection ever since colonial times: both the common law and many state constitutions require that court records generally be open. Recent decisions have reinforced that principle—and established that there is a *First Amendment* right of access to many court documents. No longer may a judge freely seal court records without considering the public's right to know.

A good example of a court decision affirming the right of access to court documents as well as the right to attend courtroom proceedings is *Associated Press v. District Court* (705 F.2d 114, 1983), a decision of the Ninth Circuit. This case arose when a federal judge closed some of the pretrial proceedings and also sealed many court documents in the celebrated federal drug case against automaker John DeLorean, who was accused of arranging a multimillion dollar cocaine deal to save his failing auto company.

The appellate court ruled that the judge's secrecy orders violated the public's First Amendment right of access to court documents and proceedings that have traditionally been open. The decision is noteworthy because of the court's specific recognition that the First Amendment includes a right of access to court documents.

However, the court said this right must be balanced against other rights, notably the defendant's right to a fair trial. Reiterating earlier decisions, the court said a three-part test should be used in deciding whether pretrial secrecy is justified. Before sealing documents or barring the public from the courtroom, the judge must determine that:

1. Allowing public access would cause "a substantial probability that irreparable damage to (a defendant's) fair trial right will result;"
2. There are no alternative ways to protect the defendant's right to a fair trial;
3. There is "a substantial probability" that the secrecy would actually prevent the defendant's rights from being violated.

In ordering the DeLorean records opened, the appellate court noted that there had been extensive publicity about the case in spite of the court records being sealed. The secrecy was not working and therefore could not be justified.

Focus on...
Court documents

In the online age, finding and obtaining court documents has become much easier. Although one can still go to the courthouse (and that may sometimes be easiest), most jurisdictions have electronic versions.

The PACER (Public Access to Court Electronic Records) system at pacer. gov) "allows users to obtain case and docket information from federal appellate, district and bankruptcy courts." Cost: eight cents a page. In 2009, a free Firefox extension called RECAP posts documents downloaded via PACER on a public website and suggests where free documents can be found.

Want decisions on your desktop right away? Many courts have free RSS (Real Simple Syndication) feeds to which you can subscribe that will send breaking decisions to your computer or cell phone. For a list of law-based RSS feeds, see www.findlaw. com/rss-index.

Also, in recent years the media have increasingly sought—and been granted—access to pretrial *discovery* materials and proceedings. As Chapter One explains, during the discovery process each side is permitted to obtain information from the other through a variety of techniques including depositions (in which witnesses answer questions under oath, with the responses recorded by a court reporter) and written statements of various types. Often these discovery materials are newsworthy—and crucial to the success or failure of a lawsuit. These materials often become a part of the public record, available for anyone to read or copy.

There has also been debate about the circumstances under which courts should allow broadcasters to copy and air audio and videotapes that are submitted as evidence. For example, in 1986 the Ninth Circuit held that broadcasters have a limited right of access to taped evidence in the case of *Valley Broadcasting Co. v. U.S. District Court* (798 F.2d 1289). This case arose during the Las Vegas racketeering trial of reputed mafia kingpin Anthony "Tony the Ant" Spilotro, who was later murdered in a gangland-style execution in Chicago.

The trial judge refused to allow television station KVBC to copy taped evidence, but the appellate court ordered the judge to reconsider in light of KVBC's common law right of access to this material. (The court emphasized that Valley's reporters had *no* constitutional right to do anything more than attend the trial and copy a transcript of the evidence.)

The appellate court said there is a "strong presumption" that broadcasters are entitled to copy taped evidence unless a judge has "articulated facts" to show that the copying would jeopardize a defendant's right to a fair trial. The court said there was no risk of the evidence being destroyed during the copying because the court's tapes were only copies of the FBI's masters. Also, the court saw no more risk of jurors being prejudiced by seeing the taped evidence on television than by watching the normal news coverage of the trial.

In the late 1990s there were several more appellate court rulings on the extent to which there is a right of public access to court records under common law principles.

In 1998, the Ninth Circuit held that federal courts in that circuit, including those in nine western states, must follow specific guidelines to determine when the press and public are entitled to see sealed transcripts of closed court hearings and similar court records.

In a case involving alleged criminal wrongdoing by former Arizona Governor Fife Symington, the court said judges must provide some safeguards before sealing records in newsworthy cases: "If a court contemplates sealing a document or transcript, it must provide sufficient notice to the public and press to afford them the opportunity to object or offer alternatives," the court wrote in *Phoenix Newspapers v. U.S. District Court* (156 F.3d 940). "If objections are made, a hearing on the objections must be held as soon as possible," it added. The media objected to the sealing of transcripts of two hearings concerning alleged jury tampering during the ex-governor's trial. The appellate court held that there was no valid basis for the judge to keep these documents sealed after the trial. The public had a right to know that two jurors had received threatening telephone calls, something that could have influenced their decision to convict the former governor. (In a separate decision, the court later overturned Symington's conviction because of problems in jury handling at his trial.)

In another 1998 decision, the Ninth Circuit held that the public also had a right to see the psychiatric evaluation of the "Unabomber," Theodore Kaczynski. In *U.S. v. Kaczynski* (154 F.3d 930), the court held that the public's right to know outweighed Kaczynski's right of privacy. This decision was again based on common law principles, which require this balancing test to determine when court records should be open to the public. The court did not address another argument made by news organizations: that the press and public have a

First Amendment right of access to documents as significant as Kaczynski's psychiatric evaluation. (Kaczynski eventually pleaded guilty to charges of making and mailing letter bombs that killed several people over a period of years.)

An error in court records sealing resulted in a rare prior restraint on the media. In 2010, juice maker POM Wonderful was engaged in a bitter court battle with its former law firm in which the firm alleged that POM owed over $500,000 in legal fees generated during a standoff with a federal regulatory agency investigation. POM won a judge's order to seal court records; District of Columbia Superior Court Judge Judith Bartnoff sealed the records but they remained open by mistake, and a reporter for the *National Law Journal*, a legal newspaper, obtained them and prepared a story. The judge, on POM's request, issued a restraining order on July 23 against the paper to stop it from "publishing, posting, exhibiting, distributing, or selling any confidential documents or information ... that were obtained from documents in the Court docket."

ALM Media Properties, the owner of the *National Law Journal*, appealed the order to the D.C. Circuit on July 28, and major media companies joined together in an *amicus curiae* ("friend of the court") brief in support of ALM. Shortly after the brief was filed on July 30, POM's lawyers reversed themselves and asked the judge to lift the order, which she did—and media organizations were able to publish that it was the Federal Trade Commission investigating POM. The media breathed a sigh of relief. However, Judge Bartnoff seemed not to have minded issuing the gag order; the *Washington Post* quoted her as saying at the July 23 hearing, "If I am throwing 80 years of First Amendment jurisprudence on its head, so be it. None of that First Amendment jurisprudence, to my knowledge, is dealing with this issue." The FTC's investigation of POM Wonderful's assertions of health benefits in pomegranate juice is discussed in Chapter Thirteen.

The Oregon Supreme Court in 2012 allowed public access to 20,000 pages of "perversion files" kept by the Boy Scouts of America to keep sex offenders out of leadership roles. The Scouts had argued to keep the records sealed after they were used in a court case against a Scout leader accused of molesting a child. The state high court agreed that names of victims and those who made the accusations should be redacted (removed), but said that "the constitutional requirement of visibility in the administration of justice was important in the context of both civil and criminal justice (*Doe v. Corporation of the Presiding Bishop of the Church of Jesus Christ of Latter-Day Saints*, 2012 Ore. LEXIS 384).

How about access to records filed in support of requests for search warrants after the investigation is over? The Ninth Circuit said a qualified common law right of access applies, noting that such access is "important to the public's understanding of the function and operation of the judicial process and the criminal justice system and may operate as a curb on prosecutorial or judicial misconduct" (*U.S. v. The Business of the Custer Battlefield Museum and Store*, 658 F.3d 1188, 2011).

However, courts have found reasons to seal court records to which even some media organizations might not object. For example, in *U.S. v. Brice* (649 F.3d 793), the D.C. Circuit said that the records of two juvenile victims of Jaron Brice's underage prostitution scheme who were material witnesses in his conviction could be sealed. Brice requested that the records be unsealed, and the district court denied. In affirming the lower court, the appellate court assumed that material witness proceedings were generally considered to be public; however, in this case, "the public was not entitled to the records here, which contained 'substantial amounts of material of an especially personal and private nature relating to the medical, educational, and mental health progress' of the victims."

In short, the right of the press and the public to inspect court documents, obtain copies of videotaped evidence, and to attend courtroom proceedings has been often upheld since the Supreme Court put those rights in question with its *Gannett v. DePasquale* decision in 1979. Today a judge can deny public access to court documents and close courtroom proceedings only if it is clearly necessary to protect a defendant's right to a fair trial.

■ CAMERAS IN COURT

To the surprise of many Americans today, the kind of televised spectacle that unfolded in the O.J. Simpson murder trial could not have happened until recently: both television cameras and still photography were prohibited in almost all American courtrooms for many years, and those restrictions were not abolished until the 1980s.

Long before the Supreme Court addressed the fair trial-free press problem in the 1960s, there were controversies about the effect the media had on the decorum of a courtroom. This debate centered on the presence of cameras and broadcast equipment in court. An early case that dramatized the problem was the 1935 trial of Bruno Hauptmann, the alleged kidnapper and murderer of celebrated aviator Charles Lindbergh's young son. Although Hauptmann's trial did not take place until nearly two and a half years after the kidnapping, the courtroom was so jammed with reporters and photographers that it was often impossible to conduct orderly proceedings. There was a great deal of inflammatory publicity.

After Hauptmann was convicted and executed for the crime, a Special Committee on Cooperation between Press, Radio and Bar was established to recommend standards of publicity in judicial proceedings. In its final report, the committee said the Hauptmann trial was "the most spectacular and depressing example of improper publicity and professional misconduct ever presented to the people of the United States in a criminal trial."

At least partly in response to the Hauptmann trial, the American Bar Association in 1937 added Canon 35 to its recommended Canons of Judicial Ethics. That rule prohibited broadcasting and taking photographs in a courtroom: "The taking of photographs in the courtroom ... and the broadcasting of court proceedings are calculated to detract from the essential dignity of the proceedings, degrade the court and create misconceptions with respect thereto in the mind of the public and should not be permitted."

Canon 35 was later amended to prohibit television coverage specifically. In the early 1970s, it was revised again and incorporated into Rule 3A(7) of the ABA Code of Judicial Conduct, which replaced the Canons. At that point it permitted some television coverage of court proceedings, but only with the consent of all parties, and only then for use in educational institutions after all direct appeals were exhausted (which could be years later). Rule 3A(7) was rewritten to allow much more extensive television coverage, but before that happened, journalists fought a long battle for access to the nation's trial courtrooms.

These ABA rules, of course, were merely recommendations to the state and federal court systems; they were not mandatory. However, by the 1960s every state except Colorado and Texas had adopted rules forbidding most camera and broadcast coverage of court proceedings. And in 1946, radio broadcasts and photography were prohibited in federal courts by Rule 53 of the Federal Rules of Criminal Procedure. That rule was also later expanded to forbid television broadcasting and to prohibit photography or broadcasting in the "environs of the (federal) courtroom."

Stunned by these restrictions, broadcast journalists and photographers wondered why the First Amendment didn't protect their right to cover trials. The Supreme Court eventually ruled on these questions in a 1965 case, *Estes v. Texas* (381 U.S. 532). The case involved a Texas grain dealer with political connections, Billie Sol Estes. He was convicted of swindling a group of investors, but his conviction was reversed by the U.S. Supreme Court because two days of the preliminary hearing and part of the trial were televised under Texas' highly unusual court rules permitting it.

The television coverage of the pretrial hearing was obtrusive: there were bright lights, bulky cameras and cables trailing around the courtroom. Before the actual trial, the judge imposed some restrictions on the media, and the TV cameras were confined to a booth in the back of the room. However, it was still obvious to everyone in the courtroom that the cameras were there.

In reversing Estes' conviction, five justices said the television coverage had denied him a fair trial. Four justices agreed that the presence of television cameras inherently denied a defendant the right to a fair trial. The fifth member of the majority, Justice John Marshall Harlan, said it might be possible to televise ordinary trials—but not celebrated ones such as Estes'. However, the Court also predicted that future technical advances might make television cameras unobtrusive enough for use in courtrooms.

Admitting Cameras: Chandler v. Florida

By 1980, broadcast technology had indeed advanced. Thanks to solid-state electronics, cameras became much smaller and usable with far less lighting than was required in 1965. As a result, the rules began to change. A few more states began admitting still photographers and video crews into their courts. By 1980, about 10 states allowed broadcast coverage *even without the consent of the defendant,* something the *Estes* decision would not have permitted in major cases. Clearly, it was time for a new Supreme Court decision.

In 1981, the Supreme Court responded to the changing technology by changing the rules on courtroom television coverage. That happened in *Chandler v. Florida* (449 U.S. 560), a case in which two police officers were convicted of using their squad car and police radios in a burglary of a restaurant. At the time of their trial, Florida allowed television coverage of criminal trials on an experimental basis. Although the two officers objected, much of their trial was videotaped, and portions were shown on television. The two officers, Noel Chandler and Robert Granger, appealed their convictions, contending that the television coverage denied them a fair trial.

The Court ruled against Chandler and Granger. Voting 8-0, the justices held that the presence of television cameras does not inherently violate a defendant's constitutional right to a fair trial, although they left open the possibility that a defendant could show that his or her rights were violated in a specific case. Thus, the Court refused to overturn Florida's rules allowing television coverage of trials even without the defendant's consent. The court said that the states were free to adopt such rules if they wished.

Writing for the majority, Chief Justice Warren Burger said, "An absolute constitutional ban on broadcast coverage of trials cannot be justified simply because there is a danger that, in some cases, prejudicial broadcast accounts of pretrial and trial events may impair the ability of jurors to decide the issue of guilt or innocence uninfluenced by extraneous matter." But Burger's opinion made it clear that criminal defendants are entitled to protest their convictions if they can show that media coverage actually prejudiced the jury.

Chief Justice Burger cited the dramatic changes in broadcast technology between the 1960s and the 1980s. Burger made it clear that *Estes* had not prohibited all experimentation with cameras in the courtroom. He noted that Chandler and Granger had not shown that their right to a fair trial was actually jeopardized by the broadcast coverage.

As a result of the *Chandler* decision, the states that already allowed television coverage or still photography in their courtrooms were free to continue doing so, and a number of additional states authorized electronic and photographic courtroom coverage after that. Some of the states that previously permitted cameras in their courtrooms only with the consent of defendants dropped that requirement after the *Chandler* ruling was announced.

Obviously, the *Chandler* decision was a victory for the media, but it is important to remember what it did and did not say. It simply said there is no constitutional prohibition on cameras in the courtroom. It did *not* say the broadcast media have any special right of access to the nation's courts. Rather, *Chandler* said that the states are free to allow cameras in court if they choose to do so. Even then, when a particular defendant can show that media coverage denied him/her a fair trial, he/she is entitled to a new trial.

The response to the *Chandler* decision came quickly. In 1982 the American Bar Association recognized the new trend and revised Rule 3A(7), which previously urged the states to impose severe restrictions on broadcast and photographic coverage of criminal trials. As rewritten, the rule says the states may allow judges to permit photographic coverage if certain safeguards are met. It specifies that the coverage must be "consistent with the right of the parties to a fair trial" and must be handled so that cameras "will be unobtrusive, will not distract trial participants, and will not otherwise interfere with the administration of justice." However, this rule is still voluntary and not all states adhere to it.

By the 2000s, all 50 states were allowing television or still photographic coverage of some court proceedings. South Dakota became the 50th state to admit cameras when the state supreme court announced in 2001 that it would allow video and audio coverage of oral arguments. However, only 41 states allow camera coverage of criminal trials as opposed to appellate court proceedings, and a few of those permit cameras *only with the consent of the defendant,* something that is rarely granted. Several other states have other rules so restrictive that they effectively bar cameras from most trial courts. On the other hand, at least 35 states allow trial judges to admit cameras to their courts even if a defendant objects.

Cameras in Federal Courts

The last major holdout in admitting cameras has been the federal court system. However, the federal courts have been under increasing pressure from members of Congress as well as media representatives to open their doors to the electronic media. In 1990 U.S. Chief Justice William Rehnquist went on the record as "by no means averse to the idea" of allowing cameras in federal courts. Writing a letter to a member of Congress who was concerned about this question, Rehnquist took a position opposite to that of former Chief Justice Warren Burger, who once said cameras would be allowed in federal courts "over my dead body." At a 2006 Senate hearing, Justice David Souter used those same words in testimony opposing the use of cameras at the Supreme Court. Justice Anthony Kennedy said basically the same thing, but not in those words, in 2007 Congressional testimony.

On the other hand, Supreme Court justices have begun appearing in televised interviews much more frequently since John G. Roberts became chief justice. Even Antonin Scalia, who refused to allow media coverage of an event where he received an award for protecting freedom of speech in 2003, granted several media interviews in 2007 and 2008. Roberts has also discussed possible camera access to the Supreme Court with representatives of the Radio Television News Directors Association.

In 2012, two senators, the chair and ranking member of the Judiciary Committee, wrote a letter to the Supreme Court asking the justices to permit televising of the announcement of their decision on the Patient Protection and Affordable Care Act ("Obamacare"). Sens. Patrick Leahy (D-Vt.) and Charles Grassley (R-Ia.) wrote to Chief Justice Roberts, "Given the fundamental constitutional questions raised and the effects the decision will have, the Court should be aware of the great interest Americans have in the outcome of this case." A spring 2012 C-SPAN poll found that 95 percent of Americans believe the Court should be "more open and transparent"—but don't expect to see cameras rolling into the Supreme Court anytime soon.

The federal judiciary in 1991 began a three-year experiment allowing cameras in two U.S. (circuit) Courts of Appeals and six federal trial courts, but only civil trials and appellate proceedings, not criminal trials. During the experiment, the media had to use pooling arrangements: usually only one photographer or video crew was allowed in a courtroom. Also, the rules required photojournalists to wear "appropriate business attire" in court.

The federal experiment with cameras was extended through Dec. 31, 1994 by the U.S. Judicial Conference. However, the conference declined to extend the experiment beyond that date or to make it permanent. For a time, cameras were again barred from almost all federal court proceedings.

The Judicial Conference backpedaled a little in 1996, adopting rules under which each federal appellate court may decide for itself whether to admit cameras to *appellate proceedings*. The 1996 rules discouraged federal *trial courts* from admitting cameras even during civil cases, but they did not flatly forbid cameras except during criminal cases. By 1999 federal appellate courts in the Second Circuit in New York and the Ninth Circuit on the west coast voted to admit cameras in some cases, while the other federal circuits declined to do so.

In recent years Congress has considered—but never approved—legislation to open various federal courts to cameras. One bill to allow cameras in federal courts gained support when the American Bar Association endorsed the idea of having television cameras in courts to provide gavel-to-gavel coverage from the U.S. Supreme Court down to the local level. Advocates of greater electronic media access to federal courts were encouraged by the fact that the Supreme Court released audio tapes of oral arguments in *Bush v. Gore*—the case that ultimately determined the outcome of the 2000 presidential election. No one seriously suggested that the airing of those tapes caused any problem for the court. But it did allow millions of people to hear for themselves the arguments in this crucial Supreme Court case.

In 2007, the Judicial Conference approved a voluntary pilot program to allow federal courts to place audio recordings of court proceedings online. Judge Thomas F. Hogan, the conference's executive committee chair, said he expects many federal courts to participate. Hogan, the chief judge in the U.S. District Court in Washington, D.C., set up a media room with a closed-circuit video feed during the trial of former White House aide Lewis "Scooter" Libby. Hogan said he received no complaints about the television coverage of Libby's trial.

Rethinking Courtroom Cameras

The reaction to the Libby trial was in marked contrast to the reaction after O.J. Simpson's murder trial more than a decade earlier. After that televised trial, many lawyers and

**Focus on...
Perp walks**

It's a staple of many nightly newscasts: footage of a person accused of wrong-doing being walked in public in cuffs and orange prison jumpsuit. Critics have suggested that "perp walks" ("perp" is short for "perpetrator") might bias potential jurors against defendants, who are, of course, innocent until proven guilty.

In 2009 a federal judge upheld two New York media organizations' right to publish "perp walk" pictures of Long Island legislator Roger Corbin, charged with fraud. In response to Corbin's claim that publication of the photos constituted prejudicial publicity, Judge Arthur Spatt cited Supreme Court cases that forbid prior restraint and concluded, "The court is simply without authority to censor the press," finding it unlikely that news coverage would taint the jury pool in the heavily populated area (*U.S. v. Corbin*, 620 F. Supp. 2d 400, E.D.N.Y. 2009).

judges had second thoughts about admitting cameras to trial courts. Fortunately for the media, the Simpson case did not lead to wholesale changes in most states. In fact, in both Virginia and Georgia, measures to ban cameras were defeated after the Simpson trial. But the Simpson case clearly had an effect, especially in New York.

New York allowed cameras in its trial courts on an experimental basis in 1987, and the experiment was renewed several times. In 1995, the state legislature seemed ready to make the experiment permanent until the Simpson murder trial captured the nation's attention. Amidst that spectacle, the legislature balked and almost barred cameras altogether. But on the day before the third extension of the camera experiment was to expire in 1995, the legislature relented and voted to extend the experiment once again.

In 1997, a panel appointed by New York Governor George Pataki studied the issue extensively and recommended that cameras be allowed in the state's trial courts on a permanent basis. However, defense attorneys, victims' rights advocates and civil rights advocates formed the New York Fair Trial Coalition and began lobbying for a ban on courtroom cameras, calling the 10-year-long experiment "an abysmal failure." In mid-1997, the legislature allowed the experiment to end, thereby closing the state's trial courts to cameras. In 2005, New York's highest court ruled that the ban on cameras does not violate either the First Amendment or the state constitution (*Courtroom TV Network v. State of New York*, 5 N.Y.3d 222).

In spite of the official ban on cameras in New York trial courtrooms, New York judges have sometimes allowed cameras during especially newsworthy cases, including the trial in 2000 of four policemen charged with killing Amidou Diallo, an unarmed West African immigrant. The judge in that case ruled that the ban on cameras was unconstitutional, a holding that set no legal precedent but was encouraging to the media nonetheless.

If televising the Simpson murder trial had a major impact in places like New York, it also had some impact in California itself, where the state Judicial Council set up a task force to reconsider the question of cameras in the courtroom. The task force urged severe restrictions on cameras in California trial courts, including a ban on camera coverage of almost all pretrial proceedings. The Judicial Council rejected that proposal and retained a system in which it is up to the judge in each case to decide whether to admit cameras. However, judges were given strict new guidelines to follow in making this decision, and media lawyers predicted that the new guidelines would lead to cameras being barred more often. Among other things, the new rules forbid camera coverage of jury selection and proceedings that are closed to the public.

The Minnesota Supreme Court ordered in 2009 that a pilot project be set up to allow cameras in Minnesota courtrooms. The pilot disappointed critics as the court excluded a number of proceedings from camera coverage, including divorce and child custody, juvenile, child protection and paternity cases, civil commitment procedures and petitions for orders for protection. Only a few cases have been televised since the pilot started in July 2011.

In 2010, the Judicial Conference of the United States, the administrative body of the federal courts, approved a pilot project for up to three years to evaluate the effect of cameras in district courtrooms, as well as video recordings of civil proceedings and their publication. The courts will perform and be in charge of the recordings, which will be posted on a central website as well as on the local site. The pilot began in mid-July 2011 at 14 district courts, and so far almost 30 cases have been recorded. You can watch the videos at the central website, http://www.uscourts.gov/Multimedia/cameras.aspx.

Beyond Cameras: New Technologies in the Courtroom

Most judges focus their attention on print and broadcast access to courtrooms, but what about new technologies, like Twitter, commenting and blogging, and webcasting? Clearly, jurors should not use these technologies inappropriately; in 2010, the Judicial Conference endorsed model jury instructions for district courts to tell jurors that they may not use cell phones, computers or other such technologies in the court, during jury deliberations or outside the courthouse to discuss or research cases on which they are serving. But what about reporters or others using these technologies? The record is mixed.

A Colorado judge in 2009 allowed the use of Twitter, a micro-blogging tool where users can "tweet" short blurbs about their lives, and blogs in an infant-abuse trial. A *Wichita Eagle* reporter had already "tweeted" coverage of a capital murder trial in 2008. At least some judges view the new technology as similar to traditional reporting techniques, only faster.

But Twitter is still a sticky subject for many courts. The judge in the 2012 Chicago case of the murder of singer Jennifer Hudson's family banned Twitter from the courtroom (although there was a room just outside where reporters could tweet, it did not have an audio/video feed, just a rolling transcript) and reversed his ruling on allowing journalists to have cell phones after they kept ringing during testimony.

The Supreme Court has never been welcoming to technology; in 2012 the Marshal's Office shut down an attorney who was doing live tweets from the overflow room during the Patient Protection and Affordable Care Act ("Obamacare") oral arguments. The high court prohibits all outside technology to maintain judicial decorum, although oral arguments are recorded and made public.

A Tennessee criminal court addressed in 2009 the potential of comments posted on media organization websites to impair a defendant's Sixth Amendment rights. The court refused to order two news organizations to block those comments. Two murder defendants asked for orders disabling commenting functions on stories about their trial and requiring all posters on those sites to use their true names and addresses. The judge, in declining to grant the defendants' requests, applied the *Nebraska Press Association* test and said that while there was significant pretrial publicity, the court had already made other, less restrictive, attempts to control, and that disabling the ability of the public to comment on news stories would not prevent harm to the defendants, as people could post their thoughts elsewhere (*Tennessee v. Cobbins*, 37 Media L. Rep. 1749).

In fact, the Internet does not necessarily make the *Nebraska Press Association* test less workable, at least in Ohio. In 2010 the Ohio Supreme Court in *State ex rel. Toledo Blade Co.*

v. Henry Cty. Court of Common Pleas (925 N.E.2d 619) overturned a gag order on the media in the trial of the death of a child. The trial judge imposed the gag because he thought that the small jury pool could be tainted by pretrial publicity. Attorneys for the defendants had argued that the Internet made the *Nebraska Press Association* case no longer viable for determining the constitutionality of gag orders but offered no legal precedent to support that claim. The state high court declined to redraw the rules based on the form of media used.

But it's not all good news. New technologies in the courtroom were handed a defeat in 2009. The judge in Joel Tenenbaum's filesharing case (discussed in Chapter Six) had granted a request to allow the proceedings to be webcast by the Courtroom View Network, saying, "In many ways, this case is about the so-called Internet Generation—the generation that has grown up with computer technology in general, and the internet in particular, as commonplace. It is reportedly a generation that does not read newspapers or watch the evening news, but gets its information largely, if not almost exclusively, over the internet." She further noted that the public interest in this case would be best served by allowing the webcast (*Capitol Records Inc. v. Alaujan*, 593 F. Supp. 2d 319, E.D. Mass. 2009).

The recording companies objected, and the First Circuit sided with them, saying that the district court judge had no authority to make the webcasting decision. While the First Circuit noted that it was "mindful that emerging technologies eventually may change the way in which information—including information about court cases—historically has been imparted," it ruled that the district judge had incorrectly interpreted the relevant broadcast policies (*In re Sony BMG Music Entertainment*, 564 F.3d 1, 2009).

The Supreme Court in 2010 then declined to allow the Proposition 8 trial proceedings discussed in Chapter Five to be broadcast or streamed in real time to other courthouses. In *Hollingsworth v. Perry* (130 S. Ct. 705), the Court in a *per curiam* (unsigned) opinion dodged the general question about whether trials should or should not be broadcast.

In this case, the Court said, the lower court failed to follow proper procedures; it "attempted to change its rules at the eleventh hour to treat this case differently than other trials in the district." Justice Stephen Breyer, joined by three others, dissented, saying that the Court should have no standing to make such a determination: "This Court has no legal authority to address that larger policy question *except insofar as it implicates a question of law.*"

What about legal professionals' use of social media? The legal community has been somewhat slow to respond. The Florida Judicial Ethics Advisory Committee in 2009 said that judges may not "friend" attorneys on social networking sites who may appear before them, suggesting that this action may give the appearance of impropriety.

■ AN OVERVIEW OF MAJOR ISSUES

After several decades of controversy, the fair trial-free press problem is still with us, despite several Supreme Court cases holding that the First Amendment rights of the press and public cannot be ignored in an attempt to protect a defendant's Sixth Amendment rights. Celebrated cases, such as those involving O.J. Simpson, financial professionals like Jeffrey Skilling and politicians like Rod Blagojevich have underscored this problem.

The trend toward closed courtrooms was slowed considerably by the Supreme Court's *Richmond Newspapers v. Virginia*, *Globe Newspaper Co. v. Superior Court* and *Press-Enterprise v. Superior Court* decisions. However, courtroom closures remain a problem for the media in some states. Judges cite the threat of prejudicial publicity to justify closing the doors. But are they right? Do the media still tend to inflame public opinion in celebrated cases? Do the media have a right to cover crime news aggressively? Are the media sometimes *too* aggressive?

For years journalists have also been fighting for camera and video access to the nation's courtrooms—with some success. All states now permit cameras and broadcast equipment in some courts, although not necessarily in trial courts. That trend was encouraged by the Supreme Court's *Chandler v. Florida* decision, which said broadcast coverage of court proceedings is not inherently prejudicial to defendants.

The *Chandler* case didn't give the media any special right to take their equipment into the nation's courtrooms. The Supreme Court left it up to the *states* to decide when (and if) cameras will be admitted to their courtrooms, leading to policies that vary from state to state. Meanwhile, the battle for camera access to *federal* courts has been difficult for journalists and their supporters. Justice Elena Kagan said in her 2010 confirmation hearings that cameras in the high court would be "a great thing for the institution and a great thing for the American people." Will Chief Justice John Roberts allow cameras in the Supreme Court? Underlying all of this is a basic question: *should* the courts—especially trial courts—be open to cameras? How will the newest pilot project for cameras in federal courts change things? Although it is a good start, the fact that only about 30 cases so far have been recorded may validate critics' concerns about the slowness of the process. Is it reasonable, however, to expect a change so soon?

Fortunately for the media, another major fair trial-free press problem of an earlier era has largely disappeared. Thanks to *Nebraska Press Association v. Stuart*, "gag" orders have been imposed on the media only rarely in recent years. News sources in most celebrated cases are subjected to gag orders, but most trial judges now recognize that directly gagging the press is usually an unconstitutional prior restraint.

But those problems have been replaced by issues of new technology. How will the legal and judicial communities deal with situations rising from webcasting, social networking sites, public comments, and Twitter? Will courts adapt current rules and legal reasoning, or will judges find that they must or wish to create new ones?

Nevertheless, conflicts between the rights of a free press and the rights of those accused of crimes will surely continue as long as both the First and Sixth Amendments remain in effect. This is not a legal problem that is likely to be resolved soon—if ever.

Moreover, the fair trial-free press controversy has generated related legal problems, including the threat of contempt of court that arises when a judge demands—and a journalist declines to reveal—the source of information that was leaked to the press in violation of a gag order. The next chapter addresses these issues, detailing the growth of shield laws and the increasing use of contempt of court citations against reporters who refuse to reveal their sources in the years since judges began imposing gag orders on reporters' sources.

WHAT SHOULD I KNOW ABOUT MY STATE?

- What is my state's position on cameras in the courtroom: what kind of cases, what levels of court, what regulations must be followed?
- What is my state's court records policy and procedure? (See the Reporters Committee for Freedom of the Press' excellent "Open Government Guide" for a state-by-state comparison: http://www.rcfp.org/open-government-guide.)

SUMMARY

A SUMMARY
OF FAIR
TRIAL-FREE
PRESS
ISSUES

What Is the Problem?

The First Amendment guarantees freedom of the press—and that includes the right to cover crime news. However, a person charged with a crime has a Sixth Amendment right to a trial before an impartial jury—a jury made up of impartial persons who will base their decision solely on what they learn in court.

Why Shouldn't Jurors Learn About a Case in the Media?

Much information that may be published in the media will never be admitted into evidence in court and is not supposed to be considered by a jury.

Why Do the Courts Ignore Some of the Evidence?

A court may only hear evidence gathered by lawful means, not secured in violation of constitutional ban on illegal coerced confessions and illegal searches. And a jury is only supposed to decide whether a defendant is guilty as charged; information about a person's past is often irrelevant (but newsworthy).

What Has Been Done About This Problem?

The Supreme Court has urged trial judges to take steps to control inflammatory publicity, such as "gagging" participants in trials so they will not reveal prejudicial (and inadmissible) evidence to the media. However, the Court has also ruled that closing the courtroom is not usually the solution, saying that trials and pretrial proceedings should be open to the press and public unless the trial judge determines that a closed session is absolutely necessary to protect the defendant's rights. Many journalists oppose the judiciary's attempts to control publicity; they believe that these efforts interfere with the public's right to know about the administration of justice.

Are Cameras and Video Equipment Allowed in Court?

Many lawyers and judges question photographic and television coverage of the courts. They feel this may turn a dignified proceeding into a circus. However, the Supreme Court has ruled that the presence of cameras in court does not necessarily violate the right to a fair trial. All states allow cameras in some of their courtrooms, but not necessarily during criminal trials. Cameras have not generally been permitted in federal criminal courts.

What About New Technologies in the Courtroom?

There is inconsistency among courts and judges in allowing the use of technologies like social networks, Twitter and webcasting in trials or by judicial personnel.

8   *Newsgatherer's Privilege*

S ometimes journalists become participants instead of observers of the legal system. Journalists can be jailed and sued for refusing to identify confidential news sources—and they have also been sued for identifying confidential sources. Journalists have seen their newsrooms ransacked by law enforcement officials in search of evidence, and contempt of court—a legal threat that seemed to be disappearing at one time—has reappeared as a major problem for the news media.

In the past decade, journalists have faced subpoenas for newsgathering and confidential source information like never before. More aggressive attempts to compel journalists to turn over information to prosecutors and courts have resulted in unprecedented jailings and legal fines against journalists and news organizations. The three longest jail terms in American history for journalists refusing to turn over newsgathering material have all occurred since 2001: freelance writer Vanessa Leggett served 168 days in jail after being held in contempt for refusing to turn over notes about a murder investigation; *New York Times* reporter Judith Miller served 85 days until she decided to reveal the identity of a source who leaked the name of a CIA agent; and video blogger Josh Wolf spent 226 days in prison after he refused to turn over to the FBI videotapes of a street protest in San Francisco.

Also, following the Sept. 11 terrorist attacks, the government significantly cracked down on journalists using confidential sources to report on national security matters. The administrations of Presidents George W. Bush and Barack Obama approved subpoenas for dozens of journalists in cases where government officials were accused of illegally leaking information to reporters. During the first three years of the Obama administration, more government employees were prosecuted for illegal leaks to the press than all other presidential administrations combined. In June 2011, for example, former National Security Administration official Thomas Drake pleaded guilty to mishandling classified information after he allegedly told a *Baltimore Sun* reporter about possibly illegal government wiretapping. Drake narrowly avoided a trial on much more serious charges, including rare charges filed under the Espionage Act of 1919, which could have resulted in a more than 30-year prison sentence because the government didn't want to reveal classified information in open court.

Another journalist, James Risen of the *New York Times*, has been the subject of several subpoenas for information about who leaked to him details of the Iranian nuclear program for his book, *State of War: The Secret History of the CIA and the Bush Administration*. Oftentimes, to prove that a government employee leaked information to a journalist, the journalist's testimony is needed to prove the government's case.

Risen continues to fight to protect his sources in the courts. In 2011, he won the right not to testify during the trial of former CIA officer Jeffrey Sterling, who was indicted on charges that he disclosed top-secret information to Risen about a CIA effort to combat Iran's nuclear weapons program with erroneous weapon designs (*U.S. v. Sterling*, 818 F. Supp. 2d 945, 2011). Using the Fourth Circuit's balancing test, Judge Leonie Brinkema found that the government had not exhausted other means to obtain the information it sought and that it had a compelling interest in obtaining that information (only that "Risen's testimony will 'simplify the trial and clarify matters for the jury' and 'allow for an efficient presentation of the Government's case'"—not a good enough reason to compel the testimony). A criminal trial, Judge Brinkema wrote, is "not a free pass for the government to rifle through

reporter's or newsgatherer's privilege:
a limited right for reporters to keep sources and/or unpublished information confidential against subpoenas.

subpoena:
Latin for "under penalty;" an order to an individual to appear before a body at a particular time to give testimony.

contempt:
a judge's tool to keep order in his/her courtroom and to enforce his/her orders.

types of contempt:
direct contempt: an act that violates the decorum of the courtroom.

indirect contempt: an act outside the courtroom that disrespects the court.

criminal contempt: punishment for an act of disrespect to the court.

civil contempt: a coercive technique to encourage compliance with the court's order.

motion to quash:
request for a judge to dispose of a subpoena.

a reporter's notebook." The government has appealed the case to the Fourth Circuit, which heard oral arguments in May 2012.

Since colonial times, newspaper editors and journalists have advanced several arguments for why confidential sources are necessary to their role in informing the public about news. First, they argue that without the right to protect confidential sources, freedom of the press could be eviscerated, and thus they believe the First Amendment gives them a legal right to protect sources. Second, journalists contend that without confidential sources, many news stories could never be reported. It is commonplace for "whistleblowers" (people with inside information about wrongdoing in government or business) to come forward and talk to a reporter in secret, something they could not do without a pledge of confidentiality. If reporters had to reveal their sources, many people with important information would not talk to them out of fear of the recriminations that might result. Therefore, many journalists believe their moral and ethical responsibilities to protect sources are compelling that they would rather go to jail than break a promise of confidentiality.

On the other hand, prosecutors, lawyers and judges want all relevant information to be made available to the court, and they are increasingly using their contempt of court power to enforce orders requiring journalists to supply confidential information. Judges often feel that journalists are no different from other citizens and should comply with subpoenas. And if journalists choose to break a valid court order, many judges believe that journalists should face the consequences—jail and/or fines—just like any other lawbreaker.

The law for journalists is complex, as this chapter shows. First, there exists a limited constitutional and common law privilege in the federal courts, or at least in most appellate circuits. This *qualified federal reporter's privilege* is rooted in constitutional law, common law, and judicial rules. Additionally, federal administrative rules place additional limitations on subpoenas to journalists. Second, 49 states have some type of reporter's privilege that applies to actions state and local officials and state courts. While some of these laws are rooted in constitutional and common law, many are based in statutory law, known as *shield laws* (laws that sometimes excuse journalists from disclosing confidential information). In 2011, West Virginia became the 40th state to pass a shield law, following Kansas, Wisconsin, Texas and Hawaii in recent years. Because the patchwork of legal protections, it is possible for a journalist to be legally entitled to protect a source in state courts but not federal courts. Thus, it is important for journalists to know their legal rights and vulnerabilities when making promises of confidentiality.

■ TOOLS OF THE COURT

Judges, grand juries, lawyers, and legislative committees have the power to issue *subpoenas* in the legal system. As a general principle, the courts operate under the notion that *anyone* with relevant information to legal proceedings has a citizen's duty to cooperate. When individuals do not comply with valid subpoenas and court orders, they may be held in *contempt of court.* Journalists have often chosen to be held in contempt rather that reveal their sources as a matter of ethical principle. For much of American history, journalists held in contempt generally avoided harsh consequences in part because of the professional support they received for upholding journalism ethical principles. However, in recent years the consequences for journalists have become more severe.

Whether journalists have a privilege against testifying depends on the context and jurisdiction. The term *privilege,* as used in this chapter, means an exemption from a citizen's normal duty to testify when ordered to do so in court or in another official information-gathering proceeding. In earlier chapters, privilege has been used in a different sense. In libel law, for example, privilege is a defense, a concept that allows public officials to make defamatory statements while performing their duties without fear of a lawsuit—and allows the media to accurately report those statements without the risk of a libel judgment.

In this chapter, however, privilege means an exemption from having to testify about confidential matters. The privilege concept is an old one that developed under the English common law. Several kinds of privilege were recognized under the common law, including the husband-wife, doctor-patient, lawyer-client and priest-penitent privileges. Each of these was established to protect a relationship that needed to be kept confidential for socially important reasons. These privileges have numerous exceptions, but all still remain viable today, at least under some circumstances. A doctor or lawyer, for instance, cannot be compelled to testify in court about many of the confidential things a patient or client may reveal. Likewise, in many instances a priest (or other member of the clergy) cannot be forced to testify about the things he/she learns from a parishioner during a confession or pastoral counseling.

Quashing Subpoenas

Journalists and news organizations routinely get subpoenas for all sorts of information. Sometimes, police agencies or lawyers seek outtakes from broadcasters as part of an investigation or during the discovery process. Grand juries sometimes subpoena journalists for eyewitness testimony or to verify the contents of a news story. And sometimes, subpoenas seek the identity of a confidential source. According to one study in 2006, 7,000 subpoenas were issued to newspapers and broadcasters in the United States.

If a journalist is served with a subpoena for newsgathering information, they will often fight the subpoena in court by filing a *motion to quash.* A motion to quash the subpoena is a request for a judge to vacate the order and dispose of the subpoena. If the action occurs in a state court where a shield law provides journalists protections in the case, judges will regularly grant a motion to quash. In the federal courts, judges apply a complex balancing test to determine whether to quash a subpoena against a journalist.

According to one study by the Reporters Committee for Freedom of the Press, a state shield law was cited as the most common reason for the successful quashing of a journalist's subpoena. In other cases, subpoenas were regularly quashed because judges deemed they were overbroad, that the information sought was not necessary to the case, and that there were other ways to obtain the information that were less intrusive to the First Amendment.

Contempt of Court

Contempt of court is a very old—and very new—legal problem for journalists. Basically, it originated with the idea that a judge should be able to control the decorum of the courtroom, and should have the authority to summarily punish those who violate that decorum. American judges have had contempt powers ever since the founding of the republic, and English and colonial judges exercised the power considerably before that.

There are several different kinds of contempt of court, and the distinctions among them are sometimes crucial in cases involving the media. First, there is *direct contempt*, which involves an act that violates the decorum of the court or shows disrespect for the legal process. A citation for direct contempt usually results from either misconduct in or near the courtroom or from the refusal to obey a judge's order. A photographer who surreptitiously takes a picture in a courtroom where cameras are not permitted risks a citation for direct contempt of court. Similarly, a reporter who refuses to reveal a source of information when ordered to do so by a judge may be cited for direct contempt.

Contempt may be either criminal or civil in nature. *Criminal contempt*, as the name suggests, is a punishment for an act of disrespect for a court. That disrespect might be in the form of a photographer taking unauthorized pictures in court or a lawyer violating court rules in her zeal to win her case. In either instance, the offense would be an example of direct contempt of court and would lead to a criminal sanction. The punishment might be a fine or a jail sentence, or both.

Civil contempt, on the other hand, is not a punishment at all, although it may lead to a stay in jail. Civil contempt is a form of coercion: a person who is disobeying a court order is locked up until he or she decides it would be better to obey the court order. Thus, it can result in an indefinite sentence. The *contemnor* (the person cited for contempt of court) is free to leave any time—if he or she obeys the court order. But if this person stands on principle and steadfastly refuses to obey the order, the jail term could theoretically last for a lifetime in some states. Reporters who refuse to reveal their sources are often cited for civil contempt, and thus run the risk of an extended stay in jail if no compromise can be reached.

One thing particularly troubles many journalists about contempt of court: often the judge unilaterally defines the offense, determines that there has been a violation, tries and convicts the guilty party, and sets the sentence—all within a few minutes. Contempt citations may be appealed, and many involving journalists are, but the fact remains that judges have enormous power in this area. Unfortunately, that power is sometimes abused.

Nevertheless, a judge's contempt power has limits other than the recourse to a higher court. For example, if a criminal contempt sentence exceeds six months, the judge is not permitted to decide the case unilaterally—without a jury. The U.S. Supreme Court has ruled that there is a constitutional right to a jury trial in cases of "serious" criminal contempt, but not in "petty" cases—which the court has defined as cases involving jail sentences of six months or less (see *Bloom v. Illinois*, 391 U.S. 194, 1968; *Baldwin v. New York*, 399 U.S. 66, 1970). This constitutional limit doesn't necessarily affect civil contempt, which has no fixed term in many instances.

■ THE FIRST AMENDMENT AND REPORTER'S PRIVILEGE

While privileges have been recognized for hundreds of years, the idea of a journalist's privilege developed mostly in the twentieth century. The common law traditionally did not recognize journalists as among the people who could invoke privilege. Maryland adopted a *shield law* (a statutory law shielding a reporter from the duty to reveal sources of information) in 1896, but it was some 30 years before the next such law was enacted anywhere in the United States. By 2011, statutory shield laws had been enacted in 40 states and the District of Columbia. A number of other states have recognized a reporter's shield either by formal court rules or by precedent-setting court decisions. However, many journalists have argued that, even in the absence of a shield law, the First Amendment protects their right to keep their sources confidential.

An appellate court first ruled on the argument that the First Amendment constitutes a shield law in a 1958 libel decision, *Garland v. Torre* (259 F.2d 545). Columnist Marie Torre made some unflattering statements about actress Judy Garland and attributed them to an unnamed CBS network executive. Garland sued for libel and demanded the identity of the source during the pretrial discovery process. Torre refused to name her source and a federal trial court cited her for contempt. She appealed, and the U.S. Court of Appeals upheld the citation; Torre was sentenced to 10 days in jail.

In an opinion by Potter Stewart (later a Supreme Court justice) the appellate court conceded that this case required a difficult balancing of two rights, but the information sought went to the heart of Garland's claim, Stewart said. Thus, the reporter's right to keep a source confidential had to give way to the right of a court to require the disclosure of relevant information.

After that decision, the idea of a constitutional privilege for journalists remained in limbo for a decade. But a flood of contempt citations of journalists forced journalists to try again. In 1970 and 1971, three court rulings on the issue were appealed to the Supreme Court. In one of these cases a court recognized a constitutional privilege, while in the other two the lower courts declined to do so. To resolve this conflict, the Supreme Court agreed to hear the three cases together.

Branzburg v. Hayes

As a result of the split between appellate circuits, the Supreme Court consolidated the cases under *Branzburg v. Hayes* (408 U.S. 665), an important 1972 decision that denied the existence of a journalist's constitutional privilege in cases such as the ones before the Court. However, the ruling was confusing because the vote was 5-4, with only four justices rejecting a constitutional shield outright while another four (the dissenters) said there should be a qualified constitutional shield. A few years later, Justice Potter Stewart gave a speech in which he called the vote "four and a half to four and a half." The swing vote was provided by Justice Lewis Powell, who said the First Amendment should not excuse journalists from revealing their sources in these cases. However, Powell also suggested that the First Amendment might protect journalists' sources under some other circumstances.

The three cases that were consolidated in *Branzburg* involved widely varying circumstances, but all had one thing in common: reporters had refused to answer grand juries' questions about possible criminal activity they witnessed. The case where a court recognized

FIG. 40. Black Panther Convention, Lincoln Memorial, June 1970.

Library of Congress, Prints and Photographs Division, [LC-DIG-ppmsca-04303].

a constitutional shield, *U.S. v. Caldwell*, involved Earl Caldwell, an African-American reporter for the *New York Times*. Caldwell had interviewed leaders of the militant Black Panther movement. In California, a federal grand jury investigating militant groups subpoenaed Caldwell to testify and to bring along his notes and tapes.

Caldwell refused even to appear. Not only would testifying breach his confidential relationships with his news sources, he said, but merely appearing would undermine that confidential relationship. Since federal grand jury proceedings are secret, the Panthers might never know for sure whether he kept his promises of confidentiality if he appeared.

Caldwell and the *Times* asked a federal district court to *quash* (set aside) the grand jury subpoena. The court granted the request only in part, and Caldwell appealed. The Ninth Circuit ordered the subpoena quashed, ruling that Caldwell had a First Amendment right to keep his sources confidential. The U.S. government appealed to the Supreme Court.

In the second case of the *Branzburg* trilogy, *In re Pappas,* television journalist Paul Pappas was invited to a Black Panther headquarters in Massachusetts. He also promised not to disclose any information he was given in confidence. A county grand jury summoned him and asked what he had seen at Panther headquarters. He refused to answer many of the grand jury's questions, citing the First Amendment. The state Supreme Court rejected his argument and he appealed to the U.S. Supreme Court.

In the *Branzburg* case itself, *Louisville Courier-Journal* reporter Paul Branzburg observed two young men processing hashish and wrote a bylined story about it. The article included a tightly cropped photo of a pair of hands working with what the caption said was hashish. Later, Branzburg wrote an article about drug use in Frankfort, Kentucky. The article said he spent two weeks interviewing drug users. Branzburg was twice subpoenaed by grand juries, but he refused to testify, citing both a Kentucky shield law and the First Amendment. He challenged both subpoenas, but the Kentucky Court of Appeals ruled against him, declaring that neither the First Amendment nor the Kentucky shield law applied to his situation. The shield law, the court said, only applied to the identities of informants; it did not excuse a reporter from testifying about events he personally witnessed. Branzburg also appealed to the U.S. Supreme Court.

Consolidating the three cases, the majority said all three reporters had to comply with the grand jury subpoenas. Thus, the high court affirmed the lower court rulings in *Branzburg* and in *In re Pappas* while reversing the *Caldwell* decision. Four justices said flatly that a journalist has the same duty as any other citizen to testify when called upon to do so.

The majority's decision, written by Justice Byron White, framed the issue as this: "The sole issue before us is the obligation of reporters to respond to grand jury subpoenas as other citizens do and to answer questions relevant to an investigation into the commission of crime." Grand juries, Justice White wrote, have two primary functions in our society: to determine if probable cause exists to believe a crime has been committed, and to protect citizens from unfounded criminal prosecutions. Its investigative powers are necessarily broad, and the grand jury plays an important, constitutional role that outweighs any burden on newsgathering that might come from the occasional subpoena to reporters. Justice White said a rare subpoena to a journalist would only have an *incidental burden* on newsgathering. Interestingly, he concluded the decision by writing, "We do not question the significance of free speech, press or assembly to the country's welfare. Nor is it suggested that news gathering does not qualify for First Amendment protection; without some protection for seeking out the news, freedom of the press could be eviscerated."

Justice Lewis Powell, who provided the crucial fifth vote to reject a reporter's privilege in these cases, wrote an important concurrence that left open the possibility that the First Amendment might excuse a reporter from revealing confidential information under other circumstances. Powell said:

> The asserted claim to privilege should be judged on its facts by striking of a proper balance between freedom of the press and the obligation of all citizens to give relevant testimony with respect to criminal conduct. The balance of these vital constitutional and societal interests on a case-by-case basis accords with the tried and traditional way of adjudicating such questions.

Thus, Powell felt a balancing process was necessary, with a constitutional shield for journalists available in some cases. One dissenter (Justice Douglas) took the absolute position that no restriction on freedom of the press was constitutional, not even the requirement that reporters testify in a court. Justice Potter Stewart (joined by Brennan and Marshall) believed the First Amendment requires a qualified journalist's privilege. These three justices said that, to justify requiring a journalist to reveal his sources, the government should have to show:

1. That there is probable cause to believe the journalist has *clearly relevant information* regarding a specific probable violation of law;
2. That the *information cannot be obtained in some other way* that doesn't so heavily infringe on the First Amendment;
3. That there is a *compelling and overriding interest* in the information.

Even though Justice Stewart's three-part test appeared in a dissenting opinion, it has been used by many lower federal and state courts in deciding journalist's privilege cases. The *Branzburg* decision, it turns out, was not quite the defeat for the media that it first appeared to be. The high court refused to create a constitutional shield law, but five of the nine justices (the four dissenters plus Powell) did say that the Constitution gives journalists at least a limited right to withhold confidential information. Since then, a number of lower courts have undertaken the balancing process suggested by Powell, often ruling that journalists' confidential information is privileged in situations different from the ones that led to the *Branzburg* ruling (grand jury investigations). In so ruling, courts have often looked to the guidelines in the *Branzburg* dissent.

After Branzburg: *A Qualified Privilege Develops*

Immediately after *Branzburg*, news organizations feared that confidential sources would dry up. They first turned to Congress for help, lobbying for the passage of a federal shield law. Between 1972 and 1975, Congress debated dozens of qualified and absolutist proposals but failed to pass a law. But journalists began to see that the lower courts were beginning to interpret *Branzburg* in ways favorable to them. Perhaps foreshadowing things to come, only a few months after *Branzburg* a federal appellate court looked to the dissenting and concurring opinions rather than the opinion of the court to find a precedent. It would be the first of hundreds of lower court decisions to do so, in what makes *Branzburg* just a peculiar Supreme Court decision. The majority of federal appellate circuits now recognize a limited, or qualified, journalist's privilege and apply some version of Justice Stewart's three-part test to determine whether journalists can be compelled to testify. The circuits are split on several key issues, including how the strong the privilege is in criminal cases, whether it applies to both criminal and civil cases, and whether it applies to both confidential and non-confidential information.

The first case to interpret *Branzburg* beyond its majority decision came just months after the Court's decision. Late in 1972, the Second Circuit ruled that a case was sufficiently different from *Branzburg* to justify a different result. In *Baker v. F & F Investment* (470 F.2d 778), the court said a journalist has a constitutional right not to reveal his sources, at least under certain circumstances.

In *Baker*, the author of an article exposing the "blockbusting" practices of real estate agents (tactics calculated to panic white homeowners into selling out at low prices) was asked to reveal his source—but in a civil lawsuit between black home buyers and real estate firms. Since the source was in the real estate business, he could be subjected to harassment and economic harm if identified, the writer said. The appellate court allowed this writer to keep his source confidential, noting that unlike *Branzburg* (which involved grand jury investigations) this was a civil lawsuit to which the journalist was not a party. In this instance, the court said the First Amendment protected the author's right to keep his source confidential.

In the decades since *Branzburg* and *Baker*, courts have cited several rationales in addition to the constitutional argument for a reporter's privilege. Some federal courts have recognized a limited federal common law journalist's privilege within the Federal Rules of Criminal Procedure, the Federal Rules of Civil Procedure and the Federal Rules of Evidence. None of these rules actually mentions a reporter's privilege, but several federal courts have held that a qualified reporter's privilege is inherent in them. For instance, Rule 17(c) of the Federal Rules of Criminal Procedure authorizes courts to set aside subpoenas that are "unreasonable or oppressive." Rule 501 of the Federal Rules of Evidence recognizes the concept of evidentiary privileges. It doesn't specifically cite a reporter's privilege, but the Congressperson most responsible for drafting Rule 501 said: "The language of Rule 501 permits the courts to develop a privilege for newspaper people on a case-by-case basis."

Throughout the 1980s and 1990s, a number of federal appellate courts recognized a limited reporter's privilege on various grounds, including the First Amendment, the federal rules of procedure, federal common law or a combination of these. However, none of the federal courts recognized the sort of absolute privilege journalists wanted. Instead, the courts have weighed reporter's privilege claims against other considerations, often ruling that the privilege must give way—or at least that the media must let a judge examine the purportedly confidential information to determine whether it should be disclosed. In such cases, difficult confrontations between the press and the judiciary often result.

Criminal vs. Civil Proceedings

As a general rule, federal courts are more likely to recognize a privilege for journalists in the context of civil proceedings. In criminal cases, the privilege is often balanced against a defendant's Sixth Amendment rights to a fair trial or law enforcement needs to conduct a full investigation. And the privilege has rarely, if ever, been upheld in grand jury investigations.

In 1981, for example, the U.S. Court of Appeals for Washington, D.C., in 1981 endorsed a strong reporter's privilege in civil litigation. In *Zerilli v. Smith* (656 F.2d 705), U.S. Justice Department officials allegedly leaked wiretapped telephone conversations of Detroit underworld leaders to the *Detroit News*. Two reputed underworld figures sued the Justice Department and sought a court order requiring a reporter to reveal his sources.

The judge refused to issue such an order, and his decision was appealed. The appellate court affirmed the refusal, noting that the plaintiffs had not exhausted alternative means of securing the information. They had not queried Justice Department employees who had access to the tapes, for instance. In civil cases to which the reporter is not a party, a reporter is exempt from revealing his or her sources "in all but the most exceptional cases," the appellate court held. The court said that to overcome the reporter's privilege, a civil litigant must show that: (1) the lawsuit is not frivolous; (2) the information sought is crucial to the case; and (3) all alternative sources for the information have been exhausted.

Similarly, the Third Circuit affirmed a reporter's right to keep her sources confidential in a civil case, *Riley v. Chester* (612 F.2d 708, 1979). A police officer who was involved in a dispute with the local police chief made news by suing the chief. Then he subpoenaed a reporter to learn the source of a news story he considered unfavorable. However, the reporter, Geraldine Oliver of the *Delaware County* (Pa.) *Daily Times*, refused to identify the source at a court hearing. Oliver was cited for contempt, but the appellate court overturned the citation because the identity of the source was not relevant enough to the case to override the qualified reporter's privilege. The court said that three requirements had to be met before a reporter should be required to disclose confidential information: (1) the information had been sought elsewhere; (2) the information could not be obtained from other sources; and (3) the information was clearly relevant to the case.

Focus on...
A federal shield law

According to the Department of Justice, between 2001 and 2007, 65 journalists were subpoenaed in federal cases. Most journalists would agree that there is a need for a federal shield law. But so far none have passed.

One of the major criticisms of shield laws is their potential abuse in a media environment where anyone with a website or a blog can claim to be a journalist. It is problematic (and rife with constitutional concerns) to define what a journalist is.

So who counts as a journalist? One House version of the federal shield law used a "function" test: "a person who regularly gathers, prepares, collects, photographs, records, writes, edits, reports, or publishes news or information that concerns local, national, or international events or other matters of public interest for dissemination to the public for a substantial portion of the person's livelihood."

In a civil libel case, the First Circuit handed down yet another decision recognizing the existence of a journalist's privilege. In *Bruno & Stillman v. Globe Newspaper Co.* (633 F.2d 583, 1980), the court ruled on a dispute over pretrial discovery of a reporter's confidential sources by emphasizing the balancing of rights necessary in such cases. The court reaffirmed the existence of the privilege, but said the trial court had to balance the First Amendment interests involved against the plaintiff's need for the information. The case was remanded, with instructions for the trial judge to follow in deciding whether to order the newspaper involved (the *Boston Globe*) to disclose its sources for a series of stories criticizing the plaintiff's products (fishing boats).

The Fifth Circuit also recognized the existence of a reporter's privilege in 1980, in *Miller v. Transamerican Press* (709 F.2d 524). But in that case, the court said the privilege had to give way to a libel plaintiff's need for confidential information without which he could not prove actual malice. Thus, that appellate court allowed the discovery of a magazine's confidential sources. The case resulted from an article in *Overdrive* magazine (a specialty magazine for truck drivers) alleging mishandling of the Teamsters Union's Central States Pension Fund. The appellate court upheld a lower court ruling that the identity of a source for the article "went to the heart of the matter" in the libel suit, since the plaintiff could probably not prove actual malice without checking on what the source told the article's author.

In criminal cases, federal courts have sometimes recognized a qualified privilege, but in some cases rules that journalists must nonetheless testify. For example, the Third Circuit refused to uphold the reporter's privilege in another 1980 decision, *U.S. v. Criden* (633 F.2d 346). In that case, Jan Schaffer, a *Philadelphia Inquirer* reporter, refused to testify about her conversations with a U.S. attorney during the "Abscam" case, in which many public officials were charged with bribery. The U.S. attorney admitted the conversations had occurred, and Schaffer was eventually cited for contempt. The Third Circuit affirmed a contempt citation, noting that the issue here was not confidentiality (the source had already waived his right to confidentiality) but the conduct of the U.S. attorney in allegedly "leaking" word of the investigation to the press. In this criminal proceeding, the defendants were seeking a dismissal by alleging prosecutorial misconduct and sought Schaffer's testimony to show such misconduct. The appellate court ruled that the reporter's testimony was crucial to the case and thus affirmed the civil contempt citation. In so ruling, the court noted:

> When no countervailing constitutional concerns are at stake, it can be said that the privilege is absolute; when constitutional precepts collide, the absolute gives way to the qualified and a balancing process comes into play to determine its limits.

The Third Circuit then applied the three-part test it enunciated in *Riley* and found it satisfied. Thus, the court said the reporter's privilege had to yield to the defendants' Sixth Amendment right to a fair trial in this particular case.

In 1981 the U.S. Supreme Court refused to hear an appeal of the Third Circuit decision, in effect forcing Schaffer to choose between testifying and going to jail. However, all four of the Philadelphia "Abscam" defendants either were acquitted or had the charges against them dismissed. The contempt citation against Schaffer was dropped after she agreed to reveal whether she had in fact interviewed the U.S. attorney in the case, without revealing the content of the conversation. Nevertheless, the case was closed only because the defense attorneys said they no longer needed Schaffer's testimony—not because of any victory for the reporter's privilege.

Similarly, in 1980 the Third Circuit ruled against the producers of the CBS television program "60 Minutes" on a reporter's privilege issue. In *U.S. v. Cuthbertson* (630 F.2d 139), a federal judge in New Jersey ordered CBS to submit confidential materials to him for an in-chambers review. The judge hoped to determine whether the materials should be released to the defendants in a criminal case that stemmed from a "60 Minutes" story entitled "From Burgers to Bankruptcy." The story questioned the franchising practices of an East Coast fast-food chain, Wild Bill's Family Restaurants. A grand jury later indicted several Wild Bill's executives on various criminal charges. The executives subpoenaed CBS' outtakes and other unpublished information before their trial. The judge ordered CBS to provide much of the requested material for an in-chambers inspection. When CBS refused, the judge cited the network for contempt, and CBS appealed. The appellate court affirmed the judge's order. The judge would have to see the materials in order to adequately weigh the defendants' need for them against the network's qualified privilege to keep them confidential, the appellate court ruled. Thus, the appellate court affirmed the contempt citation against CBS. CBS asked the U.S. Supreme Court to review the lower courts' rulings, but the petition was denied. CBS reluctantly allowed the judge to review the requested materials.

Grand jury subpoenas remain the most difficult type of subpoena for journalists. Because *Branzburg* focused entirely on these types of subpoenas—and rejected them—the federal courts been hesitant to extended the qualified privilege to these types of subpoenas.

Perhaps no journalist who ever faced a subpoena for refusing to reveal confidential information started with less backing and ended up with more national recognition than Vanessa Leggett, who was jailed for 168 days in 2001 and 2002 for refusing to reveal her notes, tapes and confidential sources to a federal grand jury investigating a murder in Houston. Leggett, who spent several years investigating the murder of Houston socialite Doris Angleton, was not initially recognized as a journalist by some. Although she was writing a book about the murder, she had not yet signed a contract when she was subpoenaed. Nor did she have many previous publication credits, although she had won a writing award for early work on her book and she taught a college writing class. But as her case unfolded, it became clear that she was indeed a journalist—a newsgatherer intending to communicate a newsworthy story to the public.

Leggett spent many hours interviewing Roger Angleton, who was accused of murdering Doris Angleton, the estranged wife of his wealthy brother, Robert Angleton. Roger apparently confessed during his interviews with Leggett—and then committed suicide shortly before his trial. Prosecutors brought charges against Robert for allegedly arranging the murder but he was acquitted in state court.

When a federal grand jury began investigating the case, Leggett was served with a subpoena. She refused to comply, citing her need for confidentiality. She was cited for contempt and jailed in a federal detention center. When it became clear that she was prepared to stay in jail indefinitely to protect her notes, tapes and confidential sources, the local and national media rallied to her cause. A prominent Houston attorney for whom Leggett had worked as an investigator defended her, with support from attorneys representing news organizations, but both a federal judge and the Fifth Circuit rejected Leggett's First Amendment claims.

In an unpublished opinion that set no legal precedent, the Fifth Circuit refused to set aside her contempt citation, declaring that reporter's privilege does not apply to federal

Focus on...
Protecting "Deep Throat"

The most famous, and perhaps consequential, confidential source in modern American journalism was "Deep Throat." For more than 30 years, *Washington Post* reporters Bob Woodward and Carl Bernstein protected the identity of the notorious man who leaked damaging information about President Nixon and his administration during the Watergate investigation in the 1970s.

Coined "Deep Throat" by a managing editor of the *Post* in reference to a pornographic movie because the source spoke to the journalists clandestinely and only on "deep background," the source was pivotal in pointing the two rookie reporters in the right direction as they investigated a web of illegal and unethical activity by Nixon and his top aides. The reporters won a Pulitzer Prize for their reporting.

FIG. 41. President Nixon leaving the White House after his resignation, August 9, 1974.

Oliver F. Atkins, White House photographer.

In 2005, W. Mark Felt was identified as "Deep Throat" by his family near the end of his life as he was suffering from dementia. Felt had been the No. 2 man in the FBI during the Nixon years. In his book *The Secret Man: The Story of Watergate's Deep Throat*, published after Felt identified himself, Woodward wrote that he believed Deep Throat was motivated by a desire to make sure journalists continued to dig into conduct of the administration, which had been successful in a number of cover-ups. In the end, more than 30 administration officials had committed major crimes.

grand jury investigations—or even to criminal proceedings. The Supreme Court later declined to hear an appeal of this questionable decision; federal prosecutors argued that the case was moot because Leggett was out of jail by then. She was only released from jail because the grand jury adjourned in early 2002 without issuing any indictments. A second federal grand jury was convened later and did indict Robert Angleton, but without issuing a subpoena to Leggett. Soon Leggett's own story of personal courage was making national news. Among other honors, she received the prestigious PEN First Amendment Award in New York and signed her long-sought book contract.

Confidential vs. Non-Confidential Information

Many times, journalists are subpoenaed for *non-confidential* information rather than the identity of a confidential source. For example, broadcasters are particularly vulnerable to subpoenas for outtakes or unaired video. The federal courts have also wrestled with these types of cases and have issued disparate rulings. As a general rule, the federal courts have been less likely to protect this kind of information under the federal qualified privilege.

As more federal court decisions have helped to clarify the scope and limitations of the journalist's privilege, one other point has become increasingly clear: the privilege often does *not* apply to a journalist's *eyewitness observations*. When a journalist happens to be an eyewitness to an event or activity that leads to a federal lawsuit, the courts have consistently declined to excuse the reporter from testifying about what he or she saw and heard. For example, in *Dillon v. City and County of San Francisco* (748 F.Supp. 722, 1990), a federal court reviewed the history of federal case law on reporter's privilege and concluded there was no legal basis for excusing a television cameraman from testifying about a confrontation that he witnessed between a citizen and police officers. The court pointed out that if the citizen were suing the police in a state court instead of a federal court, the California shield law would apply to the case, and it might excuse the photographer from testifying. However, state shield laws do not normally apply in federal cases.

In 1999, the Second Circuit reaffirmed that reporter's privilege exists in that circuit, which is important for journalists because that circuit includes New York, the home of many major print and broadcast news organizations. Ruling in *Gonzales v. NBC* (194 F.3d 29), the court upheld the privilege after initially denying its existence—but then held that NBC did not qualify for it in this instance. The case resulted from a 1997 NBC *Dateline* story about alleged police misconduct against minorities in Louisiana. The story led to a lawsuit against the police by a Hispanic couple, and they sought outtakes from NBC. The appellate court eventually ruled that the outtakes were relevant to a significant issue in the case and were unavailable elsewhere—and ordered NBC to comply with a subpoena for the outtakes.

The Second Circuit relied on the reasoning in *Gonzales* in the 2011 case of *U.S. v. Treacy* (639 F.3d 32) and said that privilege claims in civil and criminal cases should be treated the same. A district court had limited the cross-examination of a journalist in the trial of James Treacy, former chief operating officer and president of Monster Worldwide, Inc., the online recruiting site, for securities fraud in which Treacy was convicted. The prosecution had subpoenaed a *Wall Street Journal* reporter to testify about statements made by Treacy in a *Journal* article. Treacy's attorneys were limited in their cross-examination of the reporter on privilege grounds, and Treacy argued that this limitation violated his constitutional right to confront his accuser.

The appellate court agreed that Treacy's rights were violated but that the error by the district court was harmless and did not affect the outcome of the trial. More importantly, however, for reporters, the court clearly rejected the notion that assertions of privilege in criminal trials should be treated more strictly than those in civil trials:

> We now hold that, in instances where a reporter is not protecting a confidential source or confidential materials, the showing required to overcome the journalist's privilege is the same in a criminal case as it is in a civil case—namely, the showing required by *Gonzales*—and that this is true whether the party seeking to overcome the privilege is the prosecution or the defense.

A New Era of Jail Threats

By the mid-2000s, the federal government was issuing subpoenas to journalists in record numbers, and many federal courts were backing away from the concept of reporter's privilege. One influential federal appeals court refused to recognize the privilege in a widely noted 2003 decision, *McKevitt v. Pallasch* (339 F.3d 530).

Richard A. Posner, a nationally known judge who has backed the news media in privacy cases (including *Desnick v. ABC*, discussed in Chapter Five) issued a ruling in *McKevitt* that shocked journalists. He rejected the idea of a reporter's privilege, saying, "We do not see why there need to be special criteria merely because the possessor of the documents or other evidence sought is a journalist."

Writing for a unanimous three-judge panel of the Seventh Circuit in Chicago, Posner issued his ruling *after* three journalists had already handed over tapes of interviews with an

American who infiltrated the "Real IRA," a militant Irish organization. Michael McKevitt, who allegedly planned terrorist acts as head of the Real IRA, was on trial in Dublin, Ireland. His lawyers wanted tapes of interviews with David Rupert, the American informant, to determine if they contradicted Rupert's testimony against McKevitt in an Irish court.

When Abdon Pallasch and other reporters were ordered to produce the tapes by a federal judge, they sought an emergency stay from the appellate court. After it was denied, they relinquished the tapes to avoid what their lawyers feared would be a bad legal precedent. But Judge Posner's court issued an opinion anyway, without requesting briefs or oral arguments. The court rejected a petition from 26 media organizations for an *en banc* rehearing.

Another federal appeals court reaffirmed the principle that reporter's privilege does not apply to federal grand jury investigations in a 2004 case that led to four month's home confinement for a television reporter. The First Circuit upheld a $1,000-a-day civil contempt penalty against Jim Taricani, a 30-year veteran reporter for WJAR-TV in Providence, R.I. Taricani obtained and WJAR aired a videotape of an undercover FBI investigation of alleged corruption by Providence city officials. Both federal prosecutors and defense lawyers in the corruption case were under a gag order forbidding them to reveal the tape to anyone. A federal judge ordered Taricani to identify his source. When he refused, the judge imposed the $1,000 daily fine.

Applying the *Branzburg* precedent, the federal appeals court ruled that reporter's privilege does not protect Taricani because the corruption case involved a federal grand jury proceeding—the specific situation in which the Supreme Court rejected the existence of a constitutional privilege for journalists (*In re Special Proceedings*, 373 F.3d 37).

WJAR eventually paid Taricani's fines, which had grown to $85,000. The federal judge then cited Taricani for criminal contempt and ordered him to serve four months of home confinement, saying he would have jailed Taricani but for the reporter's severely compromised immune system due to a heart transplant in 1996. During the confinement, which ended in early 2005, Taricani was forbidden to work or even to access the Internet. Ironically, Taricani's source, who turned out to be a defense lawyer, later identified himself, putting Taricani in the awkward position of protecting a source who no longer wanted protection—and putting a federal prosecutor in the questionable position of pursuing sanctions against a reporter after the identity of the source was known. Taricani's source was later convicted of perjury because he had denied being the source under oath before he confessed.

While Taricani was confined at home, another federal appeals court issued a ruling that eventually sent Judith Miller of the *New York Times* to jail for 85 days for refusing to reveal her sources during a federal investigation of a leak to the media of the name of an undercover CIA officer. In the same case, Matthew Cooper of *Time* magazine also faced jail until his source released him from his promise of confidentiality, leaving Cooper free to testify.

Syndicated columnist Robert Novak identified a woman named Valerie Plame as an undercover CIA operative. There was speculation that someone in the Bush administration had revealed her name as retribution for a newspaper article by her husband, retired diplomat Joseph C. Wilson, contradicting President George W. Bush's claim that Iraq had attempted to obtain materials for nuclear weapons in Africa. Miller, a Pulitzer Prize winner for her reporting about international terrorism, gathered information about the Plame incident, but she never published anything about it. She and Cooper received subpoenas from a special prosecutor investigating the possible leak of Plame's identity. When they refused to reveal their sources, they were cited for contempt of court.

In 2005 the federal appeals court in Washington rejected Miller's and Cooper's claims of reporter's privilege under the First Amendment (*In re Grand Jury Subpoena - Miller*, 397 F.3d 964). The court relied on the *Branzburg v. Hayes* decision in ruling that federal investigations such as these are beyond the scope of any journalistic privilege. The court declined to reconsider that decision *en banc* and the Supreme Court refused to hear an appeal.

Miller went to jail to protect the identity of her source. She was released when she agreed to testify before the grand jury investigating the leak of Plame's identity. Miller said her source specifically released her from her promise not to name him, both in a letter and a telephone call to her in jail. She then testified before the grand jury and identified the source as I. Lewis "Scooter" Libby, onetime top aide to Vice President Dick Cheney. Libby was indicted on several criminal charges by the grand jury and resigned from his White House post. In 2007 he was convicted of perjury and obstruction of justice and ordered to prison, but his prison sentence was commuted by President Bush. The basic charge against him was trying to cover up his role in identifying Plame as a CIA operative.

However, Miller became part of the story herself. Amid a growing controversy about her reporting methods, both among *New York Times* staffers and among media watchers elsewhere, Miller resigned from the *Times*. Among other things, the *Times'* senior editors questioned whether she misled them or at least failed to fully inform the *Times'* Washington Bureau chief about her dealings with Bush administration officials. Miller later made news when she joined a parade of other journalists in testifying at Libby's trial in 2007.

In 2005 the U.S. Court of Appeals in Washington also upheld contempt of court citations against four other journalists in *Wen Ho Lee v. Department of Justice* (413 F.3d 53), again denying an *en banc* rehearing. The appellate court again held that reporter's privilege did not apply, ruling that the sources' names were central to the case and could not be obtained elsewhere. The four included reporters for the Associated Press, CNN, the *Los Angeles Times* and the *New York Times*. They reported on the prosecution of nuclear scientist Wen Ho Lee. After 58 of 59 charges against him were dropped, he sued the federal government for invasion of privacy because information about his case was leaked to the press.

Fearing that four more reporters would be jailed, the news organizations in 2006 agreed to settle the case by paying Lee a total of $750,000. The federal government gave Lee another $895,000 to drop the case. By then the news organizations had also run up legal expenses of about $5 million to defend their reporters.

While these cases were unfolding, several other journalists faced—or served—jail time for refusing to reveal their sources or confidential information.

The *New York Times* was forced to give reporters' telephone records to federal authorities in another 2006 case, *New York Times Co. v. Gonzales* (459 F.3d 160). The case involved two reporters who didn't want to turn over their telephone records to avoid identifying their sources. One of the reporters was Judith Miller, who had just spent 85 days in jail for refusing to name her source in the Valerie Plame investigation. The Second Circuit voted 2-1 to reject the argument that reporter's privilege based on the First Amendment should allow the reporters to keep their phone records confidential. The Supreme Court rejected a request by the *Times* for an emergency stay of the appellate court's order.

In a grand jury investigation, prosecutors sought the reporters' phone records to identify their sources for stories about two U.S.-based Islamic charities that were under investigation for allegedly funding terrorist activities. Federal investigators said calls by the reporters to the charities seeking comments for a story alerted the charities about the government's plans to raid their facilities and freeze their assets. The reporters were not accused of any complicity with the two charities or of interfering with the federal investigation.

The court said the telephone records were vital to the grand jury investigation, but they also said that under some other circumstances, such as reporting about government misconduct, reporters would have a greater right to protect phone records that might help identify confidential sources.

Also in 2006, two *San Francisco Chronicle* reporters were ordered to serve 18 months in jail unless they identified their sources for stories about alleged steroid use by Barry Bonds and other famous athletes.

The two reporters, Mark Fainaru-Wada and Lance Williams, wrote "Game of Shadows," the book that revealed the activities of the Bay Area Laboratory Co-Operative (BALCO) steroid network. They also wrote about steroid use by athletes in a series of *Chronicle* stories.

The two reporters were released from their pending sentences in 2007 when a BALCO defense attorney admitted revealing secret grand jury testimony to them. In a plea bargain, the lawyer was convicted of contempt of court and other charges; the Justice Department then dropped its attempt to force the reporters to testify.

The effects of the string of negative precedents leaves an ominous legal situation for journalists. As Lucy Dalglish, the executive director of the Reporters Committee for Freedom of the Press told Professor Jason M. Shepard in his book, *Privileging the Press: Confidential Sources, Journalism Ethics and the First Amendment*, up until the 2000s, "journalists thought there'd be no problem in protecting a source, and if in a blue moon if they had to, if they were asked to reveal a source, they would gladly go to jail, and they were thinking of jail in terms of hours or days at most. Now we're in a completely different ball game."

A Federal Shield Law Fails Again

Alarmed at all of these cases, major news organizations once again sought a federal shield law that would protect journalists from contempt of court citations for refusing to reveal confidential information, just as they had after the *Branzburg* decision in 1972.

Immediately after the *Branzburg* Supreme Court decision, dozens of bills were introduced in Congress in an attempt to establish a federal statutory shield law. The majority opinion in *Branzburg* emphasized that Congress would be free to enact a shield law even though the high court declined to create one by judicial decree. However, Congress became hopelessly bogged down in the details of the proposed federal shield laws, and none was approved in the *Branzburg* era. Two of the major issues that troubled Congress both in the 1970s and recently were the problem of deciding who should be covered and the *"prescient witness"* question. A prescient witness is someone who actually witnesses a crime, such as reporter Branzburg. There was a strong feeling in Congress that someone like Branzburg should have to testify about the unlawful activity he witnessed. But others in Congress felt such an exception would fatally weaken a shield law. Moreover, Congress could never agree on the definition of a journalist. A shield law applicable only to mainstream journalists would have been politically acceptable, but it would have created serious First Amendment problems.

By the 2000s, another troublesome question was the status of Internet bloggers as journalists. After the string of negative precedents between 2001 and 2007, the media once again turned to Congress. In 2007, the House of Representatives overwhelmingly approved a federal shield law. The vote was 398-21, far more than sufficient to override a threatened presidential veto. At about the same time, a similar proposal was approved by the Senate

Judiciary Committee. The bill would have covered professional journalists but *not* bloggers or others who do not earn substantial money by their journalistic work. It would protect journalists from being required to reveal confidential information or the names of their sources under many circumstances. Courts would be able to set aside the shield and force journalists to provide certain information that might assist in solving crimes, prevent an act of terrorism or track down leaks of information that would endanger national security. It did not get a Senate vote and died when Congress adjourned.

The House again passed a federal shield law by voice vote, and in late 2009, the Free Flow of Information Act passed the Senate Judiciary Committee. It appeared poised for passage—more than 80 years after the first shield bill was introduced in Congress. The Department of Justice was not standing in the way: Attorney General Eric Holder has said that Justice can support a federal shield law if it does not interfere with efforts to protect national security or to discover the identities of those who leak classified information. And for the first time, the bill had the support of a president. But failure by the full Senate to pass the bill before the congressional session adjourned in late 2010 meant yet another failure.

Some commentators believe that a federal shield law will not come soon or easily. For example, William Lee, journalism professor at the University of Georgia, lamented in 2012 that "Congress has been unable to solve the problem of national security leaks in a manner that garners bipartisan support." Moreover, he claims, bloggers and citizen journalists create further complications for a federal shield law.

Do reporters still need a federal shield law? Journalists are regularly called to testify or be deposed in federal lawsuits, from which state shield laws cannot protect them. For example, David Ashenfelter, a *Detroit Free Press* reporter, was called in 2009 to be deposed in a Privacy Act lawsuit against the Department of Justice brought by former federal prosecutor Richard Convertino. Convertino sought information about confidential sources used by Ashenfelter in his reporting on an investigation into alleged misconduct by Convertino in a federal terrorism trial. The Sixth Circuit (*In re Ashenfelter*, 2009 U.S. App. LEXIS 29512) said that Ashenfelter had to testify; he had not made the case for an "extraordinary" situation that would warrant the court stepping in before the testimony.

When put on the stand in April 2009, Ashenfelter invoked his Fifth Amendment right against self-incrimination, saying that he himself could be liable if he revealed his sources, and U.S. District Judge Robert Cleland accepted that argument, so Ashenfelter was able to keep his sources confidential. (As this was a federal case, the Michigan shield law was of no help to Ashenfelter.)

State Rulings on the Constitutional Reporter's Privilege

In addition to the rulings by federal courts, a number of state supreme courts have recognized a journalist's privilege, based on First Amendment principles, even in the absence of a statutory shield law. For instance, in 1977 the Iowa Supreme Court recognized a qualified First Amendment privilege for reporters. In a libel case, *Winegard v. Oxberger* (258 N.W.2d 847), the court roughly followed Justice Stewart's three-part test in the *Branzburg* dissent, indicating that a reporter could refuse to reveal confidential information, at least in a civil proceeding, unless: (1) the information sought "goes to the heart of the matter" before the court; (2) other reasonable means of obtaining the information have been exhausted; and (3) the lawsuit in which the information is sought does not appear to be "patently frivolous." However, the Iowa Supreme Court weighed the case and decided that three-part test was met, so the reporter was not excused from revealing her sources for several stories about a protracted divorce case that led to a libel suit.

A number of other state courts have also found a constitutional basis for a journalist's privilege, sometimes even in criminal proceedings when a defendant contended the information was needed for his or her defense. In so doing, some state courts have ruled that a qualified reporter's privilege is inherent in their own state constitutions as well as the federal Constitution. The Wisconsin Supreme Court so ruled in a murder case (*Zelenka v. Wisconsin*, 266 N.W.2d 279, 1978), although the court emphasized that the journalist's right to withhold confidential information had to be balanced against the defendant's need for the information. The case stemmed from a drug-related murder, and the defendant sought the identity of the source for an underground newspaper story that claimed the victim had been cooperating with narcotics officers. The state Supreme Court said the defendant had not shown that the privileged information would have helped him in his defense. Thus, the court upheld the reporter's right to keep a source confidential.

In 1982, the New Hampshire Supreme Court ruled in much the same way in another murder case: *New Hampshire v. Siel* (8 Media L. Rep. 1265). In that case two student journalists at the University of New Hampshire refused to release documents that would have revealed their sources for a story about the murder victim's alleged drug dealings. The state Supreme Court affirmed a judge's ruling that the materials sought from the student journalists would not have affected the outcome of the case. Similarly, courts in many other states have recognized at least a limited reporter's privilege in the absence of a state shield law.

Although California has a strong shield law in its state constitution, the California Supreme Court has also ruled that the concept of reporter's privilege sometimes protects journalists in situations not covered by the shield law. In a 1984 decision, *Mitchell v. Superior Court* (37 C.3d 268), the court ordered a trial judge to reconsider an order requiring a small newspaper to reveal its sources during a libel lawsuit. The case began after the *Point Reyes Light* published a series of articles critical of the Synanon Foundation, a purported drug rehabilitation program. The newspaper won a Pulitzer Prize for the stories, but Synanon sued for libel and then demanded names of the paper's sources during pretrial discovery.

The California Supreme Court conceded that the shield law did not protect journalists from having to reveal their sources when defending a libel case. But Synanon had a very weak libel case—and apparently was pursuing the lawsuit solely to learn the names of whistleblowers within Synanon who had talked to reporters. The court said reporter's privilege should excuse journalists from revealing their sources when a libel case appears to be without merit or when the social importance of protecting the identities of sources outweighs a libel plaintiff's need for the information. This ruling was a major victory for journalists who believe they have an ethical duty to protect their news sources from reprisals.

On the other hand, some state supreme courts have flatly refused to recognize any reporter's privilege, even a qualified one. The Idaho Supreme Court, for instance, once refused to recognize any sort of First Amendment privilege for journalists, even in a civil libel suit (*Caldero v. Tribune Publishing*, 562 P.2d 791, 1977), although that court later moderated its stand on this issue in *Sierra Life v. Magic Valley Newspapers* (6 Media L. Rep. 1769, 1980), another libel case in which the plaintiff demanded the identity of confidential sources during pretrial discovery proceedings. The court acknowledged that a journalist's confidential information has to be shown to be *relevant* before it can be discovered and said the plaintiff had not shown that knowing the identity of the sources would help prove its libel case. Thus, while the Idaho Supreme Court afforded limited protection to journalists' sources in *Sierra Life*, Idaho journalists enjoy far less protection from indiscriminate discovery or subpoenas than do journalists in some states. In states such as Idaho, journalists need a statutory shield law far more than they do in states where the courts have given them more constitutional protection.

■ STATE SHIELD LAWS

Most states have now enacted statutory shield laws, but these laws vary widely in philosophy and approach. Moreover, some state shield laws have been significantly altered by judicial interpretation. The highest court in New Mexico once went so far as to overturn a statutory shield law as an unconstitutional encroachment on the information-seeking authority of the judiciary (see *Ammerman v. Hubbard Broadcasting*, 551 P.2d 1354, 1976), although the court later reversed its position. Another state (California) placed its shield law in the state constitution to make it safer from attacks on its constitutionality in the courts.

The following states adopted shield laws in the years shown here (listed in the order of adoption): Maryland (1896), New Jersey (1933), Alabama (1935), California (1935), Arkansas (1936), Kentucky (1936), Arizona (1937), Pennsylvania (1937), Indiana (1941), Montana (1943), Michigan (1949), Ohio (1953), Louisiana (1964), Alaska (1967), New Mexico (1967), Nevada (1967), New York (1970), Illinois (1971), Rhode Island (1971), Delaware (1973), Nebraska (1973), North Dakota (1973), Minnesota (1973), Oregon (1973), Tennessee (1973), Oklahoma (1974), Colorado (1990), Georgia (1990), South Carolina (1993), Florida (1998), North Carolina (1999), Connecticut (2006), Washington (2007), Maine (2008), Hawaii (2008), Texas (2009), Kansas (2010), Wisconsin (2010) and West Virginia (2011). Many of these statutes have been extensively revised since their original enactment and, as just noted, many have been heavily modified by judicial interpretation. In fact, almost every state by now provides some protection for journalists who need to protect confidential information, either via a shield law or court decisions recognizing some form of reporter's privilege. In several states, the highest court has recognized a reporter's privilege that is about as strong as most shield laws. For example, in 2008 the Utah Supreme Court adopted Rule 509 of the Utah Rules of Evidence, requiring all Utah courts to respect the right of journalists to keep unpublished information and the identity of their sources confidential in most circumstances. And in 2010, the Massachusetts high court protected the use of anonymous sources under the fair reporting privilege in a libel case, in a case discussed in Chapter Four (*Howell v. Enterprise Publishing Co.*, 455 Mass. 641).

Some state shield laws appear to be strong but have been weakened by court decisions. Others have been upheld and even strengthened by court decisions. Generally, shield laws fall into three groups: (1) absolute privilege laws, which seemingly excuse a reporter from ever revealing a news source or other confidential information in a governmental inquiry; (2) laws that only apply the privilege if information derived from the source is actually published or broadcast; and (3) qualified or limited privilege laws, which may have one or many exceptions, often allowing the courts to disregard them under certain circumstances.

The Courts and State Shield Laws

Sadly, the reality about shield laws is that many lawyers and judges don't like them. Judges sometimes find themselves dealing with reporters who possess important

FIG. 42. Attorney
General Eric Holder.

*Official portrait, U.S.
Department of Justice.*

information—information that might well affect the outcome of a case—but who simply refuse to fulfill what judges see as a civic responsibility by disclosing it. Some judges wonder how a court can seek the truth under those circumstances, and they view shield laws as obstacles to justice, laws made by people who are, after all, politicians. Shield laws, they feel, strip the courts of some of their authority to do an important job. Many judges seem perfectly willing to weigh a journalist's privilege against other interests; some are willing to create such a privilege judicially in the absence of a statutory law, as already explained. However, when a legislature makes the decision for them—and makes the privilege absolute under all circumstances—judges tend to look for loopholes.

Perhaps the sentiment of the legal establishment was best summarized many years ago by John Wigmore, the preeminent scholar on the law of evidence. Speaking in 1923 about the nation's first shield law, enacted in Maryland in 1896, he said: "the (Maryland) enactment, as detestable in substance as it is in form, will probably remain unique."

Wigmore's prediction was wrong, of course, but the sentiment has been shared by generations of lawyers and judges. For years judges have been whittling away at the older common law evidentiary privileges of spouses, doctors, lawyers and the clergy, and they have shown great ingenuity in interpreting the language of state shield laws to reduce their impact.

Probably the most notable example of a court decision overturning a shield law is *Ammerman v. Hubbard Broadcasting*, the New Mexico case cited earlier. In that decision the state supreme court said the legislature doesn't have the power, under the state constitution, to restrict a judge's authority in this way. Thus, the court simply invalidated the whole shield law by declaring it to be a *procedural* rule. The legislature has no authority to dictate procedural court rules to the judiciary, the court said.

However, amid outcries from journalists and their supporters, the New Mexico Supreme Court added a provision to the state's Rules of Court to replace the invalidated shield law. The new court rule (Rule 11-514) is similar to many newer state shield laws in its scope. Basically, Rule 11-514 excuses journalists from disclosing their sources' names and other confidential information unless: (1) the information is "material and relevant" to a pending case, (2) the information is not available elsewhere, (3) the information is crucial to the party seeking its disclosure, and (4) the information is so important that the need for it outweighs the "public interest in protecting the news media's confidential information and sources."

No other state's highest court has gone quite as far as New Mexico's did in overturning a statutory shield law, but several other courts have handed down decisions narrowing the scope of state shield laws or broadening their exceptions. For instance, New York courts repeatedly carved out judicial exceptions to that state's shield law in the early years after its enactment in 1970. By 1973, the courts had created a prescient witness exception and ruled that the law didn't apply unless a reporter had promised confidentiality to a source. They also ruled that the law didn't apply if the information came to a reporter unsolicited (see *WBAI-FM v. Proskin*, 344 N.Y.S.2d 393, 1973). In New York, more than a dozen reported court decisions have gone against journalists who were seeking to keep sources or information confidential under the state's shield law.

Responding to that trend, in 1990 the New York legislature effectively overruled many of these court decisions by strengthening the state shield law. As revised, the shield law protects not only the names of sources but also virtually all other unpublished information, including reporters' notes, film and video outtakes, and information that came to a reporter unsolicited. Such information need not be revealed by a journalist except if it is proven necessary in a criminal case and is unavailable elsewhere. But the privilege is still far from absolute: a New York federal court said in 2010 that a documentary filmmaker's outtakes must be turned over in response to a subpoena (*In re Application of Chevron Corp.*, 709 F. Supp. 2d 283). The court said that the outtakes did qualify for state shield law protection but that the burden to overcome that protection had been met.

Yet the New York shield law continues to provide protection in many cases. For example, former *Wall Street Journal* reporter Jesse Eisinger did not have to testify in a 2012 case brought by Janet and James Baker against Goldman Sachs for a failed investment venture (*Baker v. Goldman Sachs & Co.*, 669 F.3d 105, 2012). The Bakers wanted to subpoena Eisinger about two articles he had written about a company with whom the Bakers merged their company (and lost their investment when that company went bankrupt). Finding that the New York shield law provides an absolute privilege against reporters testifying about information obtained under an agreement of confidentiality, and a qualified privilege for information that is not published and not obtained under confidentiality, the Second Circuit said that the Bakers had not made sufficient arguments to overcome the privilege. In fact, the court said, if the Bakers succeeded, the outcome "would undermine the privilege created by New York's statutory shield law."

Across the continent in California, the pattern is much the same as in New York. State courts repeatedly narrowed the scope of a seemingly absolute shield law, even though the law itself was strengthened. First, an appellate court said the law simply didn't apply when a judge was trying to find out who violated a judicial "gag" order. The legislature doesn't have the authority to pass a law that makes it impossible for courts to investigate violations of their orders, the court held (*Farr v. Superior Court*, 22 C.A. 3d 60, 1971). Later, another California appellate court said the shield law didn't apply when the information might help exonerate someone charged with a crime, because the defendant's constitutional right to a fair trial was paramount. Thus, the reporter would be required to bring in the requested information for a judge's inspection in his chambers, with the judge entitled to release the information if he deemed it significant to the case (*CBS v. Superior Court*, 85 C.A.3d 241, 1978). In 1980 the people of California voted to place the shield law in the state Constitution, where it was somewhat safer from judicial modification.

The California Supreme Court created a significant exception to that state's shield law in 1990, ruling that it does not necessarily cover reporters with evidence that could help exonerate the accused. In *Delaney v. Superior Court* (50 C.3d 785), the court said the shield law ordinarily applies to eyewitness observations and other non-confidential information as well as confidential information in a journalist's possession. However, the court went on to say that the shield law does *not* apply when a judge determines that the information is crucial to the defendant in a criminal case: the defendant's fair-trial rights take priority and the journalist can be forced to testify—or jailed for contempt of court if he or she refuses.

On the other hand, the California Supreme Court later ruled that the *Delaney* principle does not apply to the prosecution. Prosecutors have no due-process right to circumvent the shield law and force journalists to testify or provide evidence in their possession (*Miller v. Superior Court,* 21 C.4th 883, 1999). As a result, the defense may be able to get around the shield law at times when prosecutors cannot, although at least one later case held that the prosecution must usually be afforded the right to cross-examine a journalist who testifies for the defense—or else the defense cannot use evidence obtained from the journalist.

The California Supreme Court has also ruled that in civil cases in which a journalist is not a party (i.e., the journalist is not suing anyone or being sued), the state shield law provides absolute protection from contempt of court citations (*New York Times Co. v. Superior Court,* 51 C.3d 453, 1990). In such civil cases, journalists are not legally required to reveal confidential information at all. However, if they do not, they may encounter certain legal problems, despite the existence of the shield law. For example, under California law a journalist may sometimes be sued for monetary damages by the losing party in a civil case if the journalist refuses to provide evidence that would help that party win the case.

In New Jersey, an equally large loophole was created in the state shield law by a state Supreme Court decision—but then the law was significantly strengthened. In the celebrated Myron Farber case, the court said the shield law must give way when a criminal defendant seeks evidence held by a journalist. At the very least, the journalist must submit the material to a judge, who is to make an in-chambers evaluation and decide whether to release the information (*In re Farber,* 394 A.2d 330, 1978).

Myron Farber's troubles were short-lived but still painful, both for Farber (who eventually spent 40 days in jail) and the *New York Times* (which was assessed $285,000 in fines). The case arose from stories Farber wrote for the *Times* in 1976, investigating a series of mysterious deaths at a New Jersey hospital 10 years earlier; the stories were largely responsible for the indictment of Dr. Mario Jascalevich for murder.

About halfway through the doctor's eight-month trial in 1978, Farber and the *New York Times* were subpoenaed to release information from interviews with witnesses at the trial. Farber and the *Times* refused and were cited for criminal and civil contempt. Farber was fined $1,000 and ordered jailed until he chose to provide the subpoenaed information. The *Times* was fined $100,000 plus $5,000 a day until the court order was obeyed.

Farber and the *Times* appealed the orders to the New Jersey Supreme Court, contending that both the First Amendment and the New Jersey shield law, a seemingly absolute one, protected them. The state Supreme Court denied their appeal, ruling that the shield law does not apply when a criminal defendant needs information from a journalist for his defense. The court ordered Farber and the *Times* to submit the requested material to the trial judge to examine in his chambers so the judge could decide whether the material was necessary to the defense or if it should be kept confidential.

Both Farber and the *Times* refused to comply. Farber went to jail and the *Times* continued paying $5,000 a day until the trial was concluded and the case was given to the jury, which quickly acquitted Dr. Jascalevich. After that, all contempt citations were dropped. Eventually the New Jersey shield law was strengthened and the governor pardoned both Farber and the *Times*, refunding the fines. Jascalevich later lost his license to practice medicine in New Jersey when the state's medical board found him guilty of malpractice.

In the aftermath of the *Farber* decision, both the New Jersey Legislature and the state Supreme Court acted to *strengthen* that state's shield law. In *Maressa v. New Jersey Monthly* (445 A.2d 376, 1982) and *Resorts International v. New Jersey Monthly* (445 A.2d 395, 1982), the New Jersey Supreme Court ruled that the shield law is virtually absolute in libel cases. In the *Maressa* ruling, the court said:

> Twice in recent sessions, the legislature has made evident its intent to preserve a far-reaching privilege in this state. And twice in recent terms, this court has construed the shield law to protect confidential information to the extent allowed by the United States and New Jersey Constitutions. Absent any countervailing constitutional right, the newsperson's statutory privilege not to disclose confidential information is absolute.

Another state in which the courts have strengthened a shield law is Pennsylvania, where the state Supreme Court significantly expanded the shield law's scope in *In re Taylor* (412 A.2d 32, 1963). The Pennsylvania law specifically protected only "sources of information," but the court interpreted that language to include notes and other unpublished materials, even if they did not reveal the news source. Moreover, Pennsylvania courts have liberally interpreted a phrase in the law that exempts reporters from revealing their sources "in any legal proceeding." "Any legal proceeding" really means what it says, these courts have ruled.

Furthermore, a federal court deciding a case that arose in Pennsylvania chose to observe the state shield law in *Steaks Unlimited v. Deaner* (623 F.2d 264, 1980). That decision is not surprising, inasmuch as federal courts are supposed to apply most types of state law in "diversity of citizenship" cases (i.e., cases decided in federal rather than state courts only because they involve citizens of two different states). The Pennsylvania shield law did not apply in the federal case from Pennsylvania discussed earlier (*Riley v. Chester*) because it was not a diversity case. *Riley* was a federal civil rights case. The same was true in the *Dillon v. San Francisco* case, where a federal court declined to follow the California shield law.

In Minnesota, the state shield law was severely narrowed by a 1996 Minnesota Supreme Court decision, *Minnesota v. Turner* (550 N.W.2d 622). In that case, the court held that the shield law protected only the names of news sources and not other confidential information such as reporters' unpublished notes. In response, the Minnesota media launched a coordinated campaign to persuade the legislature to strengthen the shield law—and the legislature did so in 1998. The amended version of the Minnesota shield law specifically protects confidential information as well as the names of sources. Like many shield laws in effect today, the revised Minnesota shield law requires journalists to disclose otherwise-confidential information if it is clearly relevant to a court case, cannot be obtained elsewhere, and is so important that there is a compelling and overriding interest requiring disclosure.

In Florida, which never had a statutory shield law until 1998, the provisions of the shield law are similar to those in the revised Minnesota law. In Florida, the shield law allows exceptions if the information sought is relevant, is unavailable elsewhere, and there is a compelling reason to force a reporter to testify.

■ WHO IS A JOURNALIST?

Among the most controversial aspects of the reporter's privilege today is whether, and under what circumstances, bloggers are considered journalists. But the question of "non-traditional" journalists has been a controversial of privilege lawsuits for decades. Even in *Branzburg*, the majority said defining who is a journalist for legal protections "would present practical and conceptual difficulties of a higher order. Sooner or later, it would be necessary to define those categories of newsmen who qualified for the privilege, a questionable procedure in light of the doctrine that liberty of the press is the right of the lonely pamphleteer who uses carbon paper or a mimeograph just as much as of the large metropolitan publisher who utilizes the latest photocomposition methods." Since 1972, dozens of "non-traditional" and "self-described" journalists have sought privilege protection. Under the federal qualified privilege, courts have examined how closely the individuals resemble traditional journalists. Under state laws, courts generally look to the definitional clauses of state statutes to determine whether someone qualifies for protection.

Under the Federal Qualified Privilege

Several federal cases established that investigative book authors and documentary filmmakers are sufficiently like traditional journalists to invoke the reporter's privilege.

For example, in *Silkwood v. Kerr-McGee* (563 F.2d 433, 1977), the Tenth Circuit recognized the reporter's privilege and said it applied to a documentary filmmaker. The court overturned a trial judge's order requiring the filmmaker to reveal his confidential information because the party seeking it (the Kerr-McGee Corporation) had not tried to secure it elsewhere first. In any future request for the filmmaker's (or any other journalist's) confidential information, the trial court was ordered to weigh: (1) the relevance and necessity of the information; (2) whether it went "to the heart of the matter;" (3) its possible availability elsewhere; and (4) the type of case involved. The *Silkwood* case attracted wide attention because Karen Silkwood was killed in an auto accident *en route* to testify to the Atomic Energy Commission about allegedly dangerous practices of Kerr-McGee. In this civil lawsuit her heirs and others charged the company with violating her civil rights.

An investigative book author was also granted privilege protection in the case of *Shoen v. Shoen* (5 F.3d 1289, 1993). The case began after author Ronald Watkins began doing research for *Birthright*, a book about the battle between Leonard Shoen, the U-Haul founder, and his sons Mark and Edward. During the feud, Eva Berg Shoen, the wife of a third son, was brutally murdered at the family's vacation home in Colorado. Before Watkins interviewed him for the book, Leonard was widely quoted in the media as saying the two sons with whom he was feuding were responsible for Eva's death. They sued their father for libel and subpoenaed Watkins, demanding the notes and tapes from his interviews with their father.

Watkins appealed the subpoena, and the Ninth Circuit ruled that an investigative *book author* such as Watkins could be protected by reporter's privilege. the court held that Watkins could not be forced to reveal his journalistic work product because the sons had not exhausted all other possible sources of the information they wanted. They had not even taken a deposition to obtain the information directly from their father before seeking it from Watkins. The appellate court said that a book author, like other newsgatherers, may invoke reporter's privilege under these circumstances. Like conventional news reporters, book authors have historically played an important role in bringing newsworthy events to light, the court noted.

Focus on...

Was Josh Wolf a journalist?

Josh Wolf claims to be the longest jailed journalist in American history for committing journalism. But is he? In 2005, the 22-year-old Wolf headed out to the streets of San Francisco to record an "anarchist" protest. The protest turned violent when a police officer was struck by a pipe and seriously injured. Demonstrators also attempted to set a police car afire. Wolf sold some of his footage to local television stations and posted some of it on his blog.

When Wolf refused to hand over all of his video to authorities or to testify before a federal grand jury, a judge found him in contempt and jailed him. The Ninth Circuit declined to decide whether or not Wolf was a journalist for purposes of privilege protection, but said that all citizens have a duty to comply with grand jury subpoenas—journalist or not.

In early 2007 Wolf was released from prison after 226 days when he agreed to post the video sought by authorities on his website and to answer two questions under oath: did he see the officer being struck, and did he see the attempted burning of the police car. He answered no to both questions. It turned out his video didn't show either incident.

FIG. 43. Josh Wolf, April 2006.

Wolf claimed that he was a citizen journalist who regularly blogged about local anarchists and thus was a journalist under the law. The Reporters Committee for Freedom of the Press agreed and helped pay his legal bills.

Photo by Enric Teller, cirne.com. Used with permission.

The sons then obtained a court-ordered deposition from their father and went after Watkins' notes and tapes again. Watkins again refused to cooperate and was cited for contempt of court. Just before Watkins was to be jailed for contempt, the Ninth Circuit intervened again. In *Shoen II* (*Shoen v. Shoen*, 48 F.3d 412, 1995), the court delivered another strong affirmation of the reporters' privilege concept. Here was a book author whose source was not confidential (everyone knew it was the elder Shoen). Nor did the source object to Watkins turning over his notes and tapes. Nonetheless, the court said a journalist could not be forced to turn over his research materials except as a last resort.

The court adopted a new three-part test for cases such as this one (i.e., cases involving a reporter who is not a party to a civil lawsuit, who has no confidential sources, and whose sources do not object to the disclosure of the information sought). Judge Jerome Farris said that in this kind of case the party seeking to overcome the journalistic privilege must show that the information is "unavailable despite exhaustion of all reasonable alternative sources," is not cumulative (i.e., repetitive) and is "clearly relevant to an important issue in the case." The court said Watkins should not be compelled to turn over his notes and tapes because the information they contained was not clearly relevant to the sons' libel case and also because the notes and tapes were cumulative, duplicating information the sons had already obtained elsewhere.

Two federal appellate decisions provide some guidance for when someone *does not* qualify for protection. In 1987, the Second Circuit Court of Appeals in *von Bulow v. von Bulow* (811 F.2d 836) ruled that Andrea Reynolds could not invoke the privilege after she received a subpoena for information she collected during the trial of Claus von Bulow, who was accused of poisoning his wife. Reynolds, who the court described as an "intimate friend" of Claus von Bulow, had collected investigative reports on von Bulow's children and had taken notes for a potential autobiography. In rejecting Reynolds' claim to be a journalist, the Court ruled that an individual needed to have an intent at the beginning of a newsgathering process to disseminate news publicly in order to qualify for privilege protection.

Similarly, in 1998 the Third Circuit rejected the privilege for a professional wrestling commentator. In *In re Madden (Titan Sports v. Turner Broadcasting)* (151 F3d. 125), Mark Madden, a professional wrestling commentator for World Championship Wrestling (WCW), was subpoenaed by a competing professional wrestling company, the World Wrestling Federation (WWF), in a lawsuit about unfair competition. Madden claimed that because he recorded a commentary for a 1-900 line for fans to call, he was a journalist and could avoid complying with a subpoena. The Third Circuit ruled that Madden was not a journalist because he was not engaged in investigative reporting, not gathering news, and did not possess an intent at the start of a newsgathering process to disseminate news to the public.

The four appellate court cases discussed above suggest that courts will look at an individual's purposes, processes and products to determine if they are journalists under the law.

One recent case suggests that courts might take into account an individual's adherence to basic journalistic standards. If individuals get too close to their sources or give up some of their editorial independence, they may be less likely to invoke the privilege. For example, in 2011 the Second Circuit ruled that a documentary filmmaker was not entitled to privilege protection because he had not established that he was an independent journalist while working on a film about alleged environmental damage in Ecuador caused by the Texaco Petroleum Company. At issue in *Chevron v. Berlinger* (629 F.3d 297) was whether award-winning documentary filmmaker Joseph Berlinger was essentially acting as a public relations tool to tell the story from the plaintiff's perspective and under their control, or if he was collecting information for the "purpose of independent reporting and commentary."

For three years, Berlinger followed the plaintiffs and their attorneys, accumulating more than 600 hours of video for his film *Crude*, released in 2009, which detailed the environmental damage and health effects allegedly caused by Texaco. Berlinger's outtakes had been subpoenaed as part of litigation in Ecuador, and the American courts were asked to compel the production of evidence for use in the foreign trial. The oil company believed the "outtakes" could show improper conduct on behalf of the plaintiffs' attorneys. While one issue in the case was the lower protection afforded to "outtakes" than confidential source information, another was whether the filmmaker was acting as an independent journalist or not. The district court emphasized the fact that Berlinger got the idea for the film after he was approached by the plaintiff's lawyers, and that Berlinger removed a scene from a first cut of the film because the plaintiffs' lawyers objected, as evidence that he lacked sufficient independence as a journalist. The Second Circuit focused on the supposed lack of *independence of the journalistic process* to uphold the district court's order.

State Statutory Construction

Under state law, the question of who is a journalist often requires courts use statutory construction approaches to determine applicability of the law. Some statutes have very broad definitions, such as the District of Columbia, which defines "news media" as "newspapers, magazines, journals, press associations, news agencies, wire services, radio, television, or any printed, photographic, mechanical, or electronic means of disseminating news and information to the public." Others are quite narrow, such as Georgia, which provides protection to individuals who disseminate "through a newspaper, book, magazine, or radio or television broadcast." The statutory definitions can be very important. For example, in 2005 in *Price v. Time* (416 F. 3d 1327), the Eleventh Circuit ruled that a reporter for *Sports Illustrated* could not invoke the privilege in a libel lawsuit because the Alabama statute only applied to "any newspaper, radio broadcasting station or television station"—not a magazine.

In recent years, bloggers have increasingly sought privilege protection. In one important case, a California appellate court ruled that bloggers for the "O'Grady's Powerpage" website qualified as journalists under California's shield law. A district court had upheld a subpoena against the bloggers, requiring them to reveal who leaked to them information about yet-to-be-released Apple Computer products. But the California Court of Appeals in *O'Grady v. Superior Court* (44 Cal. Rptr. 3d 72, 2006) said the bloggers and their website were sufficiently like traditional journalism to qualify them for protection. Because the bloggers regularly reported about Apple and were in the habit of "gathering and disseminating of news," the court said they met the statutory language that protects a person "connected with or employed" by a "newspaper, magazine or other periodical publication." The bloggers were more like online newspapers because their website posts "reflect a kind and degree of editorial control that makes them resemble a newspaper or magazine far more closely" than other online web sites. "In no relevant respect do they appear to differ from a reporter or editor for a traditional business-oriented periodical," the court wrote. The court emphasized that the bloggers employed traditional journalistic methods and values in their work, and the decision was the first decisive victory for bloggers invoking the reporter's privilege.

Not all bloggers or online writers will qualify for privilege protection. While the New Hampshire Supreme Court allowed the state reporter's privilege law to apply to an online website's attempts to protect an anonymous poster (*Mortgage Specialists Inc. v. Implode-Explode Heavy Industries Inc.*, discussed in Chapter Three), the New Jersey Supreme Court ruled otherwise. In the 2011 case of *Too Much Media LLC v. Hale* (206 N.J. 209), the New Jersey Supreme Court ruled that Shellee Hale must reveal the sources of information she posted on various website forums. Hale posted allegedly defamatory content about the owners of a web company that provides financial transaction software to online adult websites. She claimed she would be protected as a journalist under New Jersey's broad shield law. However, the state high court said that people who post on unmoderated web forums are not connected with the "news media." "Those forums allow people a chance to express their thoughts about matters of interest. But they are not the functional equivalent of the types of news media outlets outlined in the Shield Law," the court wrote.

In Oregon, a plaintiff was awarded $2.5 million when a judge found that a blogger was *not* entitled to protection under Oregon's shield law. Crystal Cox was critical of Obsidian Financial Group and its founder, Kevin Patrick, on her blog. In finding for the plaintiff, the judge wrote that the Oregon shield law did not cover bloggers, as Cox was not "affiliated with any newspaper, magazine, periodical, book, pamphlet, news service, wire service, news or feature syndicate, broadcast station or network, or cable television system" as defined by the state shield law. Moreover, the judge said, no First Amendment implications applied because Cox was not a media professional, the issues she blogged about were not of public interest, and Patrick and Obsidian Financial Group were not public figures (*Obsidian Finance Group, LLC v. Cox*, 40 Media L. Rep. 1084, 2011).

■ LAWSUITS BY NEWS SOURCES

Ordinarily, when journalists promise confidentiality to a news source, they will go to great lengths to keep that promise. But on rare occasions a reporter—or perhaps an editor—will decide that a source's name is so important to a story that the name must be used, despite the fact that the source was promised anonymity.

Such a situation led to a landmark Supreme Court decision in the 1991 case of *Cohen v. Cowles Media Co.* (501 U.S. 663). By a 5-4 vote, the Supreme Court ruled that the First Amendment does *not* protect the media from being sued by a news source if a promise of confidentiality is broken, regardless of the newsworthiness and relevance of the name to an important story.

The case began in 1982 when Dan Cohen, a public relations aide to the Republican candidate for governor of Minnesota, gave several reporters documents that revealed petty misdeeds many years earlier by the Democratic candidate for lieutenant governor (an arrest at a protest rally during the 1960s and a $6 shoplifting conviction that was later set aside). Cohen leaked the information to the press just before the election.

Although the reporters promised not to identify Cohen, the editors of the *Minneapolis Star Tribune* and *St. Paul Pioneer Press* decided to use his name. If they were to run the story anonymously, they felt they would be dealing an unfair last-minute blow to the Democrats. If they did not publish the story, they could be accused of a cover-up to aid the Democrats. Thus, they felt the fairest way to handle the story was to run it and identify the source as a Republican activist.

When Cohen's name was used, he was immediately fired. He sued for breach of contract, arguing that the promise of confidentiality was an enforceable contract under Minnesota law. A jury awarded him $200,000 in actual damages and $500,000 in punitive damages.

The two newspapers appealed, arguing that they should have a First Amendment right to publish truthful information about an event as newsworthy as an election—without risking a lawsuit afterward. The Minnesota Supreme Court agreed and overturned the entire jury verdict, ruling that the First Amendment indeed does protect the media from liability for publishing the name of the source for a clearly newsworthy story. The state court also ruled that Cohen could not sue for breach of contract under Minnesota law. However, the court said that a legal doctrine called *promissory estoppel* might allow Cohen to sue if the case were not barred by the First Amendment. In essence, *promissory estoppel* is a remedy for a person who does something in reliance on someone else's promise and is injured when that promise is broken, but who does not have a valid contract for some reason.

The U.S. Supreme Court overturned the Minnesota court's ruling. The high court said that *promissory estoppel* is a "generally applicable law" (i.e., a law that applies to everyone, not just the media). Generally applicable laws, the five-member majority said, apply to the media—despite the First Amendment. The First Amendment protects the media's right to publish truthful information, but only if it is lawfully obtained. Writing for the majority, Justice Byron White said Cohen's information was not lawfully obtained because of the broken promise of confidentiality:

> The press may not with impunity break and enter an office or dwelling to gather news. Neither does the First Amendment relieve a newspaper reporter of the

obligation shared by all citizens to respond to a grand jury subpoena and answer questions, even though the reporter might be required to reveal a confidential source.... (T)he First Amendment does not confer on the press a constitutional right to disregard promises that could otherwise be enforced under state law....

The four dissenting justices disagreed with that line of reasoning, arguing that the story in question was so newsworthy that the use of Cohen's name was justified: voters had the right to know that the Republican gubernatorial candidate's public relations person was leaking stories to the press about a Democratic candidate. In his first major dissenting opinion as a Supreme Court justice, David Souter argued strongly for more First Amendment protection than the majority was affording to the media. Souter wrote: "There can be no doubt that the fact of Cohen's identity expanded the universe of information relevant to the choice faced by Minnesota voters ...(and) the publication ...was thus of the sort quintessentially subject to strict First Amendment protection." Less than a year earlier, Justice Souter had replaced William Brennan, the author of *New York Times v. Sullivan* and many other key decisions upholding and expanding freedom of the press. Souter's dissenting opinion surely was one with which Brennan would agree.

The *Cohen* decision produced a variety of reactions among journalists. Many noted the irony of the press having to defend a lawsuit for *revealing* a source when reporters are much more likely to get into legal trouble for *not revealing* a source. And several media attorneys warned that the *Cohen* decision could encourage news sources who are unhappy with the way they appear in print or on television to sue the media, contending that they were promised confidentiality. Since most interviews between a reporter and a news source are private meetings between two people (with no witnesses available to corroborate either party's claims), such a lawsuit would end up being a credibility contest between the source and the journalist on the witness stand—with a jury acting as referees.

In the end, it will be up to each state to determine when news sources may sue the media for naming them. Some states may not allow such lawsuits except if there is a written contract promising confidentiality and it is breached (a remote possibility). Others may allow cases like this one to go to court on a promissory estoppel theory.

For Cohen, the lawsuit finally ended in 1992—10 years after it began—when the Minnesota Supreme Court reconsidered the matter and held that he was entitled to collect the $200,000 in actual damages but no punitive damages. The state court said the promissory estoppel doctrine did apply in Cohen's situation.

■ NEWSROOM SEARCHES

For a time a related legal problem produced some alarm among journalists: law enforcement searches of print and broadcast newsrooms. In a disturbing 1978 decision, the U.S. Supreme Court ruled that the First Amendment does not create any privilege that would protect the media from newsroom searches even if no journalist is suspected of a crime (*Zurcher v. Stanford Daily*, 436 U.S. 547).

The case began in 1971 when a large group of demonstrators occupied the Stanford University Hospital and were forcibly ejected by Santa Clara County (California) sheriff's deputies and Palo Alto police. The *Stanford Daily*, the student newspaper at Stanford University, covered the incident, which was marked by considerable violence. A number of persons, including several law enforcement officers, were injured. Two days later, the *Daily* ran a special edition with a number of photographs of the disturbance.

The Santa Clara County district attorney's office got a search warrant and four police officers searched the *Daily's* office in the presence of several staff members. No member of the staff was suspected of any involvement in the violence, but the police searched the offices for additional photographs or relevant information. They found none.

The *Daily* staff sued the local officials in a federal civil action, alleging violations of the First, Fourth and Fourteenth Amendments. Both the federal district court and the Ninth Circuit ruled in the student journalists' favor, but the Supreme Court reversed those rulings.

In a 5-3 decision, the Supreme Court said the Constitution does not prevent an unannounced search of a newspaper, even when no member of the staff is suspected of any crime. The court said that such a search is constitutional as long as the normal requirements of specificity and reasonableness are satisfied by the search warrant. Police would not be permitted to go rummaging through a newspaper's files indiscriminately, but if a warrant described specific evidence, the police could conduct a newsroom search in an attempt to obtain that evidence, the court ruled.

However, the Supreme Court made it clear that Congress or state legislatures could act to forbid newsroom searches; the high court merely said it wasn't going to forbid them judicially. Within days of the *Zurcher* decision, anti-newsroom search bills were introduced in a number of state legislatures and in Congress. Eventually at least eight states passed such laws: California, Connecticut, Illinois, Nebraska, New Jersey, Oregon, Texas and Washington.

The Privacy Protection Act of 1980

Congress also passed a comprehensive federal law limiting newsroom searches, the Privacy Protection Act of 1980. This far-reaching federal law effectively overruled *Zurcher*, outlawing most newsroom searches by federal, state and local law enforcement officials.

Under the Privacy Protection Act, law enforcement officials are prohibited from conducting searches and seizures involving "documentary materials" (photographs, tapes, films, etc.) held by newsgatherers except under very limited circumstances. The law allows searches and seizures only when: (1) the person holding the information is suspected of a crime; (2) there is reason to believe the materials must be seized immediately to prevent someone's death or serious injury; (3) there is reason to believe giving notice and seeking a subpoena would result in the materials being destroyed, changed or hidden; or (4) the materials were not produced as a result of a court order that has been affirmed on appeal.

The rules regarding a journalist's *work product* (e.g., notes and rough drafts) are even tougher. These materials cannot be seized except when the journalist is suspected of a crime or when necessary to prevent someone's death or bodily injury.

Anyone who is searched in violation of the Privacy Protection Act may sue the federal government and most state and local governments, but evidence secured in violation of the bill may nonetheless be used in court. The law also directed the U.S. Justice Department to prepare guidelines for searches by federal officers involving evidence held by someone not suspected of a crime but also not working in a First Amendment-related area such as a newsroom. Perhaps the major virtue of the Privacy Protection Act is that it usually requires law enforcement officials to get subpoenas instead of search warrants if they wish to obtain information from journalists.

Why is this distinction important? Search warrants are ordinarily authorized by judges unilaterally; the person who is the object of the search has no chance to argue against the issuance of the warrant. He or she first learns of the warrant's existence when law enforcement officers show up and enter the premises (by force, if necessary).

Subpoenas, on the other hand, are merely court orders directing someone to produce information. They can be challenged on legal grounds, and their issuance can be appealed. Granted, subpoenas are a major problem for journalists; some large newspapers and television stations have attorneys working nearly full time on the job of resisting subpoenas. Nevertheless, most journalists would much rather face a subpoena than have their offices raided by law enforcement officers armed with a search warrant.

The Privacy Protection Act is an improvement over the situation in which journalists found themselves after the *Zurcher* decision. However, many journalists wish the law had been made even tougher: evidence secured during illegal newsroom searches should not be admissible in court, they contend. In the area of newsroom searches, as in the broader area of reporter's privilege, the major legal problems are not completely resolved.

■ AN OVERVIEW OF MAJOR ISSUES

There is an inherent conflict between the need of journalists to protect their sources and other confidential information, on the one hand, and the need of the courts to obtain all relevant facts on the other. Judges believe they cannot mete out justice if they are denied access to crucial information. But journalists believe they must protect confidential information—for a number of socially important reasons.

Although a significant majority of states have shield laws, the courts have repeatedly carved out judicial exceptions to these laws, requiring reporters to disclose confidential information despite the seeming applicability of a shield law. In a number of states, the appellate courts have significantly weakened state shield laws by judicial interpretation. In response to that trend, the voters in one state (California) placed their shield law in the state constitution. But almost as soon as that happened, the courts began whittling away at this new constitutional shield law just as if it were still merely an act of the state legislature.

However, there is a countervailing trend in the development of the reporter's privilege: a surprising number of both federal and state courts have recognized the privilege judicially, even in the absence of a statutory shield law. In no fewer than seven states lacking shield laws, the state's highest court has taken this step.

Moreover, many federal courts have recognized a reporter's privilege as a matter of federal common law if not constitutional law. This judicially created reporter's privilege is by no means absolute: the courts are reserving the right to weigh the privilege against other factors, such as the relevance of the requested information and the court's need for it.

However, by the mid-2000s some federal courts were refusing to recognize any right of journalists to protect confidential information, and a number of journalists faced jail sentences. Record numbers of journalists were being issued federal subpoenas—65 between 2001 and 2007, by one count. And with a federal shield law having failed several times, the protections for reporters called to testify in federal cases are not as robust as they might be.

Reporters and judges both feel there are important ethical principles at stake in this area. Like fair trial-free press, this issue represents an inherent conflict between two important rights, both of which must be respected in a democratic society. And like fair trial-free press, this dilemma is not likely to be resolved soon.

WHAT SHOULD I KNOW ABOUT MY STATE?

SUMMARY

A SUMMARY OF NEWS- GATHERER'S PRIVILEGE

- Does my state have a shield law? What does it cover? What does it NOT cover?
- What does my state's common law say about reporter's privilege? What about my federal district court and circuit court? An excellent resource for all these questions: Reporters Committee for Freedom of the Press' "Privilege Compendium" at http://www.rcfp.org/privilege.

What Is Contempt of Court?

Judges may punish persons who show disrespect for a court or disobey a court order by citing them for contempt. When a journalist promises to keep information (like the identity of a news source) confidential, he/she has an ethical obligation to keep that promise, even if a court asks. Thus, an ethical journalist may risk a contempt citation—and perhaps a jail sentence. The Supreme Court has said that *promissory estoppel* applies to journalists, so if a journalist makes a promise, he/she must keep it.

What Is Reporter's Privilege?

Because many important stories could not be researched without promising confidentiality to key news sources, journalists believe they should have a right to keep their film outtakes, unpublished notes and sources' names confidential. Reporter's privilege is the concept that a newsgatherer has at least a limited right to withhold this information, even when asked to reveal it by a judge.

What Is a Shield Law?

A *shield law* is a statutory law that excuses journalists from revealing confidential information when asked to do so in court. About 37 states have such laws, but some of them have so many exceptions that they provide a reporter little protection from a contempt of court citation. Also, courts have sometimes declined to accept shield laws, ruling that they improperly abridge the judiciary's authority. There is currently no federal shield law.

Without a Shield Law, Does Reporter's Privilege Exist?

In *Branzburg v. Hayes*, a majority of the Supreme Court justices said a limited constitutional reporter's privilege exists under certain circumstances, but not under the circumstances that led to the *Branzburg* case (grand jury investigations where reporters allegedly knew of or witnessed unlawful activity). A number of federal and state courts have recognized a qualified privilege for reporters to withhold confidential information. This privilege usually does not apply if the information is clearly relevant and necessary to the case and is unavailable from other sources.

9 *Freedom of Information*

Of the various legal battles modern media organizations must fight, one of the most difficult and frustrating is the struggle for *freedom of information*. Without the freedom to gather the news, the freedom to publish is little more than a right to circulate undocumented opinions—a right to editorialize without any right to report the facts.

In recent years, the media have made significant gains in the battle for access to government meetings and records, but there have been defeats, especially since the events of Sept. 11, 2001. As governments have expanded in size, their sheer vastness has made it easy for them to conceal important information from public scrutiny. Moreover, the tendency of the federal government to keep secrets in the name of national security has grown drastically since World War II. Clinton administration officials estimated in 1995 that no fewer than 3.5 million documents a year were being declared secret for reasons of national security alone. The trend became more pronounced as the threat of terrorism grew after Sept. 11.

Almost no one would argue that governments should release information that could assist potential terrorists, but if democracy itself is to work, the public still must be well informed about the activities and policies of government. How can the people intelligently compare the policies of rival candidates unless there is freedom of information? Without freedom of information, how can the people evaluate government policy toward countries such as Iran, Iraq and North Korea, cited by President George W. Bush as an "axis of evil" in a speech about the threat of terrorism after Sept. 11?

Clearly, the need for national security must be balanced against the need for openness in government. The WikiLeaks saga of 2010 and 2011 dramatically demonstrates the clash between the government's desires to keep information secret and the public wishes to know the inner workings of war and diplomacy. And courts have heard increasing numbers of cases on FOIA and open records issues: in the 2010 term, in fact, the U.S. Supreme Court handed down decisions in no fewer than four cases with FOIA or state secrets implications.

The late-2000s recession and the federal government's bailouts of several large banks also resulted in at least one FOIA request. In *McKinley v. Board of Governors of the Federal Reserve System* (647 F.3d 331, 2011), the D.C. Circuit said that the Federal Reserve could withhold information obtained by the Board as part of the bailout offered to investment bank Bear Stearns under Exemption 5, inter- and intra-agency memos (discussed later).

Perhaps the threat of terrorism might justify secrecy about the inner workings of a nuclear power plant or a water treatment facility. But how can the voters know if the city budget is reasonable or the school board is following sound educational policies unless the public can know what those budgets and policies actually are and how they were determined?

Recognizing these needs, journalists and public interest groups have campaigned for openness in local, state and national government for years. That fight has produced dramatic improvements in public access to official records and proceedings. Today, all 50 states have laws requiring most agencies of state and local government to hold open meetings as well as laws guaranteeing public access to many government records. When World War II ended, only a few states had such laws.

Issues of open government and freedom of information were high on President Barack Obama's agenda in his first few months. On his first full day in office, Obama issued a memorandum on the Freedom of Information Act (FOIA) that called on agencies to "usher in a new era of open government." In 2009, Attorney General Eric Holder issued comprehensive new guidelines that direct all executive branch departments and agencies to apply a presumption of openness when dealing with FOIA requests. The attorney general's memo said that agencies should not withhold information simply because it would be legal to do so and should always consider whether they could make partial disclosures rather than withholding documents completely. And at the end of 2009, the director of the Open Government Directive issued a memo that said that departments would be expected "to take specific actions to implement the principles of transparency, participation, and collaboration" President Obama had announced his first day, and set deadlines for those actions.

But then the administration dragged its feet in releasing White House visitor logs. A federal district court said that White House visitor logs are properly considered agency records held by the Secret Service, not the White House itself, and subject to FOIA. Moreover, if there are national security or other exemptions that apply to some of the records, the Secret Service can isolate and exempt those records from disclosure; the agency cannot merely claim that the request is "unreasonably burdensome" to execute (*Judicial Watch, Inc. v. U.S. Secret Service*, 803 F. Supp. 2d 51, 2011). And in June 2009 the administrative exercised secrecy regarding the release of photos allegedly showing U.S. troops abusing Iraqi and Afghan prisoners during the Bush administration. Critics suggest that Obama's reversal on the photos flies in the face of his early commitments to openness in government.

The Second Circuit had ruled that the photos must be publicly disclosed under the Freedom of Information Act (*ACLU v. Department of Defense*, 543 F.3d 59). President Obama had initially said that the photos would be released after the Second Circuit's decision but then asked government attorneys to object to the court's order, saying that the release of the photos would "further inflame anti-American opinion" and "put our troops in greater danger," reversing himself.

FIG. 44. Lyndon B. Johnson.

Yoichi R. Okamoto, White House Press Office, January 9, 1969 via Wikimedia Commons.

Focus on...
LBJ and the FOIA

Lyndon Baines Johnson, the 36th president, signed the Freedom of Information Act on July 4, 1966. Johnson was no fan of the FOIA; he did not hold a signing ceremony and edited the signing speech written by his aide, Bill Moyers, to be more cautious.

Moyers had originally written: "This legislation springs from one of our most essential principles: a democracy works best when the people know what their government is doing. They must have access to the policies and rules by which department and agencies operate. Government officials should not be able to pull curtains of secrecy around decisions which can be revealed without injury to the public interest. Good government functions best in the full light of day."

LBJ's edits: "This legislation springs from one of our most essential principles: a democracy works best when the people have all the information that the security of the nation will permit." (The rest of the paragraph was cut.)

Moyers later said that LBJ "hated the thought of journalists rummaging in government closets and opening government files; hated them challenging the official view of reality."

The Obama administration asked the Second Circuit to cancel its decision ordering the release. The court complied, saying that the government did not immediately have to turn over photos but can have more time for other legal options. Then Congress passed a bill to prevent the release of controversial photos of alleged U.S. abuse of prisoners and detainees. Called the Detainee Photographic Records Protection Act of 2009, the act amended FOIA to bar from release any photograph "taken between September 11, 2001 and January 22, 2009 relating to the treatment of individuals engaged, captured, or detained after September 11, 2001, by the Armed Forces of the United States in operations outside of the United States." It was included in a Homeland Security appropriations bill and signed into law in 2009. In 2009 the Supreme Court vacated the Second Circuit opinion and sent the case back to the lower court for review under this law.

In a June 2009 *Newsweek* article, David Sobel, an attorney who litigates FOIA cases, said, "For a president who said he was going to bring unprecedented transparency to government, you would certainly expect more than the recycling of old Bush secrecy policies."

In 2012, the Second Circuit found that the government may withhold certain redactions dealing with the Central Intelligence Agency's use of waterboarding as an interrogation method because the information pertained to "a highly classified, active intelligence method" (*ACLU v. Dep't of Justice*, 2012 U.S. App. LEXIS 10213).

But there are some bright spots. In May 2009, the administration revealed Data.gov, whose purpose is "to increase public access to high value, machine readable datasets generated by the Executive Branch of the Federal Government." Departments were instructed to post at least three "high-value" datasets by January 2010.

On the federal level, millions of documents have been made public under the Freedom of Information Act since it was enacted in 1966. In addition, many federal agencies that once treasured the privilege of holding private meetings to shape their policies are subject to the 1976 Government in the Sunshine Act. That law has many loopholes, but at least it has opened some formerly closed meeting room doors.

How significant are these laws? The number of requests for information under the federal FOIA exceeded four million for the first time in 2004. It would take a book as long as this one just to summarize all of the FOIA lawsuits that have been filed. But is the information that is ferreted out of once-locked government files under FOIA really important?

Using the FOIA, researchers learned that the Central Intelligence Agency spied on Martin Luther King, Jr. and other pioneer civil rights leaders, and that longtime FBI Director J. Edgar Hoover used the FBI in efforts to discredit King. Other FOIA inquiries revealed government experiments with mind-controlling drugs that killed at least two persons in the 1950s. Meanwhile, still other researchers using the FOIA learned of Central Intelligence Agency (CIA) efforts to overthrow a government in Chile and to use journalists as foreign agents. The FOIA also forced the FBI to acknowledge—after waging a 20-year legal battle with a historian to keep the information secret—that it had spied on singer John Lennon.

Journalists also used the FOIA to expose the safety hazards posed by the Ford Pinto's gas tank, to help find out why the Hubble Space Telescope's mirror failed to work properly, and to alert citizens to the environmental hazards posed by the Department of Energy's nuclear weapons plants in several states. Many socially important and newsworthy government secrets have been uncovered because of the FOIA. The act was used to discover long-concealed health hazards caused by radiation and the dangers of Agent Orange to Vietnam War veterans. It was also used to unearth important details of America's unsavory role in the Bay of Pigs invasion of Cuba and President Nixon's plans for military action in Cambodia.

And after President Obama announced that Osama bin Laden had been killed in a military action at his compound in Abbottabad, Pakistan in May 2011, several media organizations filed FOIA requests for information on the raid. A district judge in 2012 (*Judicial Watch, Inc. v. Dep't of Defense*, 2012 U.S. Dist. LEXIS 58537) said that the Department of Defense did not have records containing video or photographs taken during or after the raid that ended with the death of Osama bin Laden requested by conservative government watchdog group Judicial Watch, but the Central Intelligence Agency did—and claimed exemptions against releasing any of them. Citing concerns that "extremist groups will seize upon these images as grist for their propaganda mill," the court said that it would not compel the release of the documents. But the judge seemed almost regretful, writing, "The Court is also mindful that many members of the public would likely desire to see images of this seminal event. Indeed, it makes sense that the more significant an event is to our nation—and the end of Bin Laden's reign of terror certainly ranks high—the more need the public has for full disclosure. Yet, it is not this Court's decision to make in the first instance." However, Judicial Watch was successful in obtaining documents in 2012 that included meetings between government agencies and Kathryn Bigelow, Academy Award-winning director of *The Hurt Locker*, and a screenwriter to provide the director information for a feature film.

The federal Freedom of Information Act is just one law among many intended to open closed doors and unlock secret files, although it is a very important one. This chapter summarizes these freedom of information laws, and then surveys other problems media organizations and the public encounter in their quests for information.

■ THE FEDERAL FREEDOM OF INFORMATION ACT

When Congress enacted the federal FOIA in 1966, its primary users were expected to be journalists. Certainly journalists who were alarmed at the growing trend toward government secrecy took the lead in lobbying for its passage. But ever since the FOIA was approved, its main users have been corporations, academic researchers and private individuals with a special interest in a particular topic. Most of those actually filing formal requests for information are lawyers representing private clients, not journalists representing the public interest. In fact, historians and other academicians file far more requests under the FOIA than journalists. FOIA requests take time, and journalists tend to need information too quickly to wait for a formal request to be honored by a slow-moving bureaucracy. Perhaps the authors of the FOIA were a little naive when they ordered government agencies to respond to FoI requests in 10 working days; critics have said that no government agency moves that quickly. Recognizing this fact, in 1996 Congress extended the time limit to 20 working days as part of a major FoI reform, which is discussed later.

What are the basic provisions of the FOIA? It declares that a vast number of records kept by administrative agencies of the federal government shall be open for public inspection, and that copies are to be provided at a reasonable cost. Unless these "agency records," as they are called, fall within one or more of nine specific exemptions, they must be opened to the public on request.

To facilitate this process, a 1974 amendment to the FOIA requires agencies to publish lists of their records and their fee schedules for making copies in response to FoI requests.

Fees may be waived or reduced when an agency feels that releasing a document would benefit the general public and not just one individual or company. That provision has caused some controversy, since it allows agencies to charge one requester more than another for the same information. The FBI once charged the major wire services $9,000 for material that it provided free to one writer whose work was a public service (in the FBI's opinion).

A requester need not justify a FOIA request, but those who convince an agency that they are serving the public interest have a big advantage at the agency's cash register. In 1986 Congress amended the FOIA to reduce the fees government agencies may charge news organizations and nonprofit educational or scientific institutions, while increasing the fees that commercial businesses must pay. Businesses must usually pay for the time government agencies spend searching for requested documents and reviewing them prior to their release. Journalists and nonprofit groups are usually excused from those charges altogether. Other non-commercial requesters may encounter different rules, depending on the agency they are dealing with. The Federal Communications Commission, for example, does not charge non-commercial requesters for the first two hours of search and review time or the first 100 pages released in response to a request. But after that, the meter starts running.

Although federal agencies may give a price break to journalists and nonprofit groups, they are not supposed to consider the identity or purpose of a requester in deciding whether to release a particular document. The U.S. Supreme Court once said this: "Because Congress clearly intended the FOIA to give any member of the public as much right to disclosure as one with a special interest in a particular document ... the identity of the requesting party has no bearing on the merits of his or her FOIA request" (*Department of Defense v. Federal Labor Relations Authority*, 510 U.S. 487, 1994).

In an effort to avoid complying with the law, federal agencies have sometimes claimed that honoring a certain FOIA request would be prohibitively expensive. The courts have generally not heeded that argument, instead compelling agencies to comply despite the alleged cost. For instance, in a 1980 decision (*Long v. Internal Revenue Service*, 596 F.2d 362), a federal appellate court held that the IRS had to supply requested information even if it would cost $160,000, as the IRS claimed.

For FoI purposes, the term "agency" is defined to include executive departments, military departments, government corporations, government-controlled corporations, other executive agencies and independent regulatory agencies. In short, it covers just about the entire federal government except for Congress and the courts.

Once an agency receives a formal request for a particular record, it is supposed to respond by either providing the record or denying the request (and explaining why it did so) within 20 working days. However, the courts have repeatedly excused government agencies from this time limit, ruling that the deadline is "directory" rather than "mandatory." Sometimes FOIA requests may take a year or more, although a federal appellate court has ruled that an eight-year delay was too long (*Fiduccia v. Department of Justice*, 185 F.3d 1035, 1999). The OPEN Government Act of 2007 ordered federal agencies that fail to meet the 20-day deadline to refund search and copying fees to noncommercial requesters.

If a request is denied, the requester has a right to appeal the denial, first through the agency's appeals procedures and then to the federal courts. Thousands of lawsuits have been filed in the federal courts under these provisions of the FOIA. As a result of amendments to the FOIA in 1974 and 1976, federal judges are empowered to review the requested documents in private in their chambers and then rule on the validity of an agency's decision

reverse FOIA suit:
a suit filed by a
company against a
government agency
to try to prevent the
agency from revealing
information.

**Glomar response (or
Glomarization):**
when an agency says
it can neither confirm
nor deny the existence
of records requested
under the FOIA.

Vaughn index:
in denials of FOIA
requests, a list that
must identify each
document the agency
withheld; the statu-
tory exemption(s)
under which it was
withheld; and how
disclosure would harm
the interests of the
exemption(s).

to deny the request. The judge must decide if the documents properly fall within one of the nine exceptions, thus justifying government secrecy. Briefly, the nine exceptions are:

1. Documents that have been properly classified as
   confidential or secret in the interest of national
   security or U.S. foreign policy;
2. Documents relating to "internal personnel rules and
   practices" of federal agencies;
3. Matters that are specifically exempted from public
   disclosure by some other statutory law;
4. Trade secrets and certain other financial and
   commercial information gathered by government
   agencies;
5. Interagency and intraagency memoranda that
   involve the internal decision-making process (e.g.,
   working papers and tentative drafts);
6. Personnel and medical files and similar documents
   that should be kept confidential to protect individual
   privacy;
7. Investigatory files compiled for law enforcement
   purposes, but only when the disclosure of such
   files would: (a) interfere with law enforcement;
   (b) deprive a person of a fair trial; (c) constitute
   an unwarranted invasion of personal privacy; (d)
   disclose a confidential source; (e) disclose investigative techniques and thereby permit someone to
   circumvent the law; or (f) endanger the life or safety
   of any individual;
8. Documents prepared by or used by agencies regulating banks and other financial institutions;
9. Oil and gas exploration data, including maps.

Obviously, many of these exceptions are so broad and all-
encompassing that they can be used to justify massive government
secrecy. In addition to the millions of government documents that
are classified for national security reasons, millions more are confidential for other reasons. The exceptions for law enforcement files
and internal memoranda, for example, have been widely used to
withhold information from the public.

Using the FOIA

Anyone seeking information under the FOIA should make it
clear in writing that he or she is making a FOIA request, perhaps
mentioning the act by its official citation: Title 5 of the United
States Code, Section 552 (or simply 5 U.S.C. 552). The request

should be as specific as possible, identifying the desired record exactly as the agency identifies it, and include how much the requester is willing to pay. Each agency publishes information about its record-keeping scheme in the *Federal Register*, available online and in many large libraries, to assist FOIA users in identifying the records they seek. Many agencies allow FOIA requests to be submitted online.

An FoI request should first be directed to the official designated to handle FoI requests within a particular agency. If that fails, the request should next go to the agency head, unless the agency has specified a different appeals procedure.

If that too fails, the requester has little recourse except to go to court—or perhaps cultivate "sources" within the agency who may be willing to "leak" the material surreptitiously.

If a request for information under the FOIA is denied, the person who made the request is supposed to receive a list of the documents being withheld with an explanation of the legal justification for withholding each document. This list is called a *Vaughn Index*, because a federal appellate court ruled that such an accounting is necessary in *Vaughn v. Rosen* (484 F.2d 820, 1973).

Under a policy adopted by the Bush administration after Sept. 11, federal agencies were directed to abandon a Clinton administration policy adopted in 1993 that required the release of information unless it is "reasonably foreseeable that disclosure would be harmful." Under the new policy, announced by Attorney General John Ashcroft on Oct. 12, 2001, government agencies are encouraged to keep information secret whenever there is a "sound legal basis" for doing so. This new directive cited the importance of "safeguarding national security, enhancing the effectiveness of law enforcement agencies, protecting sensitive business information and, not least, preserving personal privacy."

The new policy also said, "It is only through a well-informed citizenry that the leaders of our nation remain accountable to the governed and the American people can be assured that neither fraud nor government waste is concealed." But when requested information falls into a gray area where either openness or secrecy might be legally defensible, the new policy encouraged government officials to opt for secrecy by saying, "Any discretionary decision by your agency to disclose information protected under the FOIA should be made only after full and deliberate consideration of the institutional, commercial, and personal privacy interests that could be implicated by disclosure of the information."

The OPEN Government Act of 2007 reversed this presumption, directing government agencies to favor disclosure in gray areas, setting aside Ashcroft's post-Sept. 11 order.

President Bush issued another FoIA-related executive order in late 2005. This order directed federal agencies to create FoIA Service Centers and to designate executives to hear complaints about the performance of these service centers. Agencies were directed to post information about this on their websites. The order also directed agencies to reduce their backlogs of FOIA requests.

The Bush administration's FOIA directives did not rescind a second Clinton administration FoI policy, an executive order signed by President Clinton in 1995 that made major changes in the way federal agencies handle secret information. The executive order revised the rules under which agencies classify documents as secret for national security reasons. Among other things, the 1995 executive order requires agencies to declassify most documents after 25 years and make them available for public inspection. Agency heads such as the director of the CIA are permitted to make exceptions to the 25-year-disclosure rule, but only with the approval of a committee set up to review these exceptions.

The 1995 rule exempts CIA documents that would reveal the names of its "intelligence sources" as well as Defense Department documents relating to such things as war plans. While FoI attorneys pointed out that the 1995 policy still gives agencies such as the CIA and Pentagon wide latitude to keep secrets, several were quoted as saying it was a distinct improvement over the old system—a change that made millions of additional government documents accessible to the public under the FOIA. But even that left many advocates of open government concerned because the Bush administration in 2003 postponed the release of documents under the 1995 executive order, giving federal agencies an extra three years to determine which documents should be released and which should not.

For anyone who plans to use the FOIA, an extremely valuable resource is available from the Reporters Committee for Freedom of the Press on its website at http://www.rcfp.org/federal-open-government-guide. Titled *Federal Open Government Guide*, it includes government agency FoI directories and fee schedules, plus general instructions and samples of request letters, appeals letters, fee waiver requests and the legal documents needed to file a lawsuit. The organization's website (www.rcfp.org) is also an excellent source of information on FoI and other media law issues.

FOIA Lawsuits

If the time comes when an FOIA lawsuit is necessary, the act includes a provision allowing a court to require the government to pay the requester's attorney's fees and court costs if the lawsuit is successful. And if the court finds that agency personnel acted capriciously in denying the original request, the Civil Service Commission is required to hold a proceeding to decide if the government employees who denied the request should be disciplined.

Of the numerous lawsuits filed under the FOIA, a few should be summarized to illustrate the typical workings of the act and the role of the courts in interpreting it. The first exception (for national security) is a broad one that the courts have tended to uphold. In fact, judges have sometimes declined to even look at classified material in their chambers if an agency submits a convincing *affidavit* (a statement made under oath) to justify the need for keeping the document secret. However, other courts have ruled that documents must have been properly classified for the national security exception to apply. In a 1974 case (*Schaffer v. Kissinger*, 505 F.2d 389), the D.C. Circuit held that Red Cross reports on South Vietnamese prison camps had not been classified under proper procedures and thus had to be released.

Nevertheless, the national security exception remains a gigantic and very troublesome loophole in the FOIA. Numerous abuses of the national security classification system have been revealed over the years, among them instances where it was used to conceal corruption, government waste and bureaucratic bungling.

The Assassination Records Review Board, created by Congress in 1992 after years of protests about the federal government's insistence on keeping so many records about the assassination of John F. Kennedy secret, completed a lengthy review of classified records in 1998. The board concluded that the government had "needlessly and wastefully" withheld millions of records that did not need to be secret, and this secrecy "led the American public to believe that the government had something to hide" about the Kennedy assassination.

Another noteworthy illustration of the same point was the government's attempt to censor *The Progressive* magazine when it planned to publish an article on the hydrogen bomb, an article prepared from readily available public information. (That case is also discussed in Chapter Three.) It has been suggested more than once that foreign spies in America should spend their time reading popular newspapers and magazines, doing Google searches and browsing in public libraries rather than snooping around the Pentagon.

Nevertheless, the national security exception to the FOIA must be taken seriously because it allows the government to withhold many important documents from public inspection, thus concealing not only legitimate military and diplomatic secrets but also much information that should be public in a democracy. Since Sept. 11 the national security exception has evolved into a more generic homeland security exception that has been used to justify unprecedented secrecy, some critics have charged.

Among the other exceptions, several have stirred considerable controversy. The trade secrets and private business information exception, for instance, has prompted a number of double lawsuits with federal agencies caught in the middle. On one side, someone (often a competitor) is seeking information that may be covered by the trade secrets exception. On the other, the private company that originally submitted the information is suing to compel the government to keep the material confidential. The latter kind of lawsuit is called a *"reverse FOIA"* suit.

Here's an example of a reverse FOIA suit: A district court in Washington, D.C., granted summary judgment to the Federal Aviation Administration (FAA) in a case filed by the National Business Aviation Association to prevent the FAA from releasing a list of aircraft registration numbers to ProPublica, an investigative journalism website. The association argued that the records should be withheld under Exemption 4, covering trade secrets. The FAA said that the information must be released, and the court agreed (*National Business Aviation Association v. FAA and ProPublica*, 686 F. Supp. 2d 80, 2010). The list requested by ProPublica contained those aircraft that had elected to be on the FAA's "Block List" managed by the association; flights by aircraft on that list were kept secret from the public. A *USA TODAY* story on the data revealed that a televangelist, college boosters, the CEO of restaurant chain Hooters, and executives from American International Group (AIG) were among those who used the blocking service.

Of more interest to journalists and scholars, however, have been the exceptions for law enforcement information, internal personnel rules and internal working documents. The federal courts have shied away from compelling law enforcement agencies to disclose information that they contend is essential to their investigatory functions. However, the courts have been somewhat less inclined to let federal agencies broadly interpret the exception for internal agency materials. On a number of occasions, agency efforts to maintain internal confidentiality have failed.

One notable case of this sort is a 1976 Supreme Court decision, *Dept. of the Air Force v. Rose* (425 U.S. 352). That case arose when legal researchers sought records of honors and ethics code violation hearings at the Air Force Academy, with the names of alleged violators deleted. The Court ruled that where there is a genuine and significant public interest in an agency's policies, those policies should be disclosed unless their revelation would jeopardize an investigation or prosecution, noting the clear Congressional intent that such information be made public as long as no individual's personal privacy rights are threatened.

Federal agencies often cite personal privacy to justify secrecy, sometimes in absurd ways. The National Highway Traffic Safety Administration was widely criticized by journalists and safety advocates in the mid-2000s when it removed from its website the entire database of the exact locations of auto fatalities. When a safety advocate filed an FoI request to obtain the data, the request was denied on the ground that revealing where accidents occurred would

Focus on...
Exception 3 statutes

Exception 3 of the FOIA says that certain statutes may exempt information from release under FOIA. To qualify, a statute must either leave no discretion for release to the agency or must establish criteria for withholding, or refer to particular information to be withheld.

In 2010, the Department of Justice released a list of statutes that courts have over the years found to qualify as Exception 3 statutes. Some examples:

FIG. 45. Gavel and law book.

Author's collection.

- Immigration and Nationality Act: exempts "certain records pertaining to the issuance or refusal of visas to enter the United States;"
- Espionage Act: exempts "certain classified information pertaining to the communication intelligence and cryptographic devices of the United States or any foreign government;"
- Federal Victims' Protection and Rights Act: exempts "certain records containing identifying information pertaining to children involved in criminal proceedings;" and
- Social Security Act: exempts "death certificates and records pertaining to deaths provided to the Commissioner of Social Security."

invade the privacy of accident victims. Safety advocates pointed out that police agencies routinely disclose not only the locations of accidents but also the names of victims. NHTSA has accident location data nationwide, and it would be useful to those studying traffic safety to know which highways and intersections are most hazardous, but the database is a secret.

But the Supreme Court in 2011 declined to extend the privacy exemption to corporations. The Court reversed a Third Circuit decision extending personal privacy exceptions in FOIA to corporations. In *FCC v. AT&T, Inc.* (131 S. Ct. 1177), the Court said that Exemption 7(C), that exempts from release "records or information compiled for law enforcement purposes" that "could reasonably be expected to constitute an unwarranted invasion of personal privacy," did not apply to AT&T's records that were handed over to the Federal Communications Commission as part of an agency investigation on alleged overcharging. CompTel, a trade association of competitors, used the FOIA to request those records.

The Court unanimously said that the exemption did not extend to corporations. The term "personal," Chief Justice John Roberts said, was intended to apply to people only. "In fact, we often use the word 'personal' to mean precisely the opposite of business-related: We speak of personal expenses and business expenses, personal life and work life, personal opinion and a company's view," wrote Roberts, adding with a judicial wink, "We trust that AT&T will not take it personally."

Many other practical problems have become evident as federal agencies, information seekers and the courts have attempted to live under the FOIA. One of the most important of these problems is the fact that agencies can escape the law by either destroying or concealing sensitive records, and public officials can sometimes circumvent it by simply taking their records home with them. There may be no way for anyone outside an agency to prove that a given document ever existed, if the agency steadfastly maintains that it didn't.

Moreover, in a 1980 decision (*Kissinger v. Reporters Committee for Freedom of the Press*, 445 U.S. 136), the Supreme Court ruled that former Secretary of State Henry Kissinger could keep his diary of official telephone calls secret because he took the diary home with him, unless the government itself should compel him to return it. In response to Justice William Rehnquist's majority opinion, the dissenting justices warned that this ruling would give major government officials freedom to completely escape the reach of the FOIA by simply taking their important papers home.

In another major 1980 decision (*Forsham v. Harris*, 445 U.S. 169), the Supreme Court made it clear that private organizations doing research under government grants need not make their data public. The Court ruled that such research data simply doesn't fall within the definition of "agency records" and is thus not covered by the FOIA.

In 1982, the Supreme Court continued the trend toward a narrow interpretation of the FOIA, handing down two more decisions that restricted public access to government information under the act: *FBI v. Abramson* (456 U.S. 615) and *U.S. Department of State v. Washington Post* (456 U.S. 595).

In *Abramson*, the high court ruled that some of the information compiled by the Nixon administration about its critics was exempt from disclosure under the FOIA. The FBI had originally gathered the information for investigatory purposes, and the court said the information was covered by the law enforcement investigatory exception even though it was eventually recompiled and put to partisan political uses.

The *Abramson* decision produced two separate dissents. They said the majority was in effect amending the FOIA by its broad interpretation of the law enforcement investigatory exception and pointed out that the records were clearly not compiled in their present form for law enforcement purposes and therefore should not fall within the exception.

The *Washington Post* case expanded the scope of the exception for "personnel, medical and similar files." The Court held that records indicating whether an individual holds a U.S. passport are a "similar file" that falls within the exception if the individual's interest in privacy outweighs the public interest in disclosure.

The *Post* sought to find out if two Iranian nationals living in Iran were also U.S. citizens with American passports. The State Department refused to provide that information, contending that to provide it would "cause a real threat of physical harm" to both men. The *Post* sued under the FOIA. In deciding the case, a virtually unanimous Court said, "Although Exemption 6's language sheds little light on what Congress meant by "similar files," the legislative history indicates that Congress did not mean to limit Exemption 6 to a narrow class of files containing only a discrete kind of personal information, but that "similar files" was to have a broad rather than a narrow meaning." The justices remanded the case to determine if the privacy rights of the Iranians outweighed the public interest in disclosure.

Again considering privacy issues, the Supreme Court ruled in 1997 that a government agency's mailing list should not be disclosed under the FOIA (*Bibles v. Oregon Natural Desert Assn.*, 519 U.S. 355). The court balanced the public's right to know against the privacy rights of those on the list, and ruled that names on such a list should only be released when their disclosure would "shed light on an agency's performance of its statutory duties or otherwise let citizens know what their government is up to."

A 2004 Supreme Court decision expanded the privacy exception to the FOIA further, holding for the first time that a deceased person's relatives may invoke it. In *National Archives and Records Administration v. Favish* (541 U.S. 157), the court upheld a decision by the federal government to deny public access to photographs of the body of Vincent Foster, Jr., a Clinton administration official who committed suicide in 1993. His body was found in an area managed by the National Park Service. Attorney Allan Favish, who disputed the verdict of several investigative bodies that Foster's death was a suicide, sued under the FOIA for access to photos taken by the U.S. Park Police. The Supreme Court said the privacy rights of Foster's family outweighed the public interest in disclosure.

In 1985 the Supreme Court restricted the scope of the FOIA in another way, this time by excluding many Central Intelligence Agency (CIA) records from disclosure under the FOIA. In the case of *CIA v. Sims* (471 U.S. 159), the court ruled that the CIA may keep the identities of its sources of intelligence data secret even when national security is not involved. The case arose when the Ralph Nader Public Citizen Health Research Group sought the names of researchers and institutions that participated in a CIA project involving mind-altering drugs during the 1950s. The project required researchers to administer drugs that are now illegal to unwitting subjects. Some of the researchers and institutions agreed to have their names released, but many others refused—and the CIA withheld their names. The Nader organization then sued to obtain the names.

The FOIA has no specific exception to protect the identities of the CIA's sources. However, the blanket exception for information exempted from disclosure by another law (exception 3) has been used by the CIA to keep its sources secret. The law that established the CIA authorized the agency to keep its sources of information secret.

In ruling in favor of the CIA, the high court emphasized that intelligence work requires secrecy, and that the fear of being identified may lead intelligence sources to refuse to cooperate with the CIA. Thus, the court chose to liberally interpret the law allowing the CIA to keep its sources secret.

The Supreme Court drastically restricted public access to FBI records in a 1989 case, *U.S. Department of Justice v. Reporters Committee for Freedom of the Press* (489 U.S. 749). In one sweeping decision, the court ruled out public access under the FOIA to the FBI's criminal histories on at least 24 million people. These criminal histories—often called "rap sheets"—are computerized compilations of personal information from various sources, including state and local law enforcement agencies.

The Court's unanimous ruling created a vast across-the-board exception to the FOIA for records that might in any way affect personal privacy. Moreover, the court's language is so broad that it may apply to other government agencies and not just the FBI, severely limiting the FOIA's applicability to records about individual people.

Explaining the Court's decision, Justice John Paul Stevens wrote:

> [W]e hold as a categorical matter that a third party's request for law enforcement records or information about a private citizen can reasonably be expected to invade that citizen's privacy, and that when the request seeks no "official information" about a government agency, but merely records that the government happens to be storing, the invasion of privacy is "unwarranted."

The Supreme Court said in this far-reaching decision that there is a difference between records about the activities of a federal agency itself and records maintained by the agency about individuals, with individual records broadly exempted from the FOIA.

This ruling was widely assailed by journalists and others who pointed out that many of the most telling revelations about past government wrongdoing have come from records about individuals. The mere fact that the FBI is keeping records on some individuals not suspected of a crime may raise serious questions.

A few months later, the Supreme Court went still further, ruling that many documents obtained by the FBI from other government agencies are also exempt from disclosure. In a case called *John Doe Agency v. John Doe Corp.* (493 U.S. 146, 1989), the high court said the government could not be compelled to release certain documents concerning the Grumman Corp. because they were "compiled for law enforcement purposes." Grumman requested the documents from the Defense Contract Auditing Agency during a federal grand jury investigation of aerospace industry accounting practices. The auditing agency responded by turning the documents over to the FBI, which then refused to release copies under the FOIA exception for documents compiled for law enforcement purposes. The Court agreed that such documents should be exempt from disclosure.

Taken together, these 1989 rulings and several earlier Supreme Court decisions seem to be sending a message to the federal bureaucracy, and especially to the FBI: when in doubt, withhold information that is requested under the FOIA. The Court has repeatedly declared that the FoI exceptions "must be narrowly construed." But when faced with a specific request for government information, the Court continues to rule that the exceptions allow broad government secrecy.

However, the Supreme Court backpedaled a little in a 1993 decision, *U.S. Department of Justice v. Landano* (508 U.S. 165). In that case, the Court held that the exception for law enforcement records does not give the FBI an automatic right to refuse to release information that might identify a source. The Court acknowledged that ordinarily FBI informants' names should be kept confidential, but the justices said the FBI is not entitled to a legal presumption that this kind of information is *always* confidential. Instead, the FBI must consider such requests for information on a case-by-case basis.

Although many Supreme Court decisions interpreting the FOIA have involved the national security and law enforcement exceptions, the high court has interpreted a number of other provisions of the law. In 2001, for example, the Supreme Court unanimously ruled that the Bureau of Indian Affairs cannot keep its correspondence with Indian tribes confidential under the FoI exception for "inter-agency and intra-agency memorandums or letters." In *Department of the Interior v. Klamath Water Users Protective Association* (532 U.S. 1), the court said communications between the BIA and Indian tribes are not comparable to communications between government agencies and their paid private consultants, which were previously ruled confidential under this FoI exception.

In 2008, the Supreme Court upheld the right of those seeking information under the FOIA to pursue their requests even if the same agency recently turned down a request for the same information. In *Taylor v. Sturgell* (553 U.S. 880), the high court unanimously disavowed the doctrine of *virtual representation* under which a lower court had dismissed Brent Taylor's FoI appeal. In this case, Taylor, executive director of the Antique Aircraft Association, filed a request with the Federal Aviation Administration for plans for the F-45, an antique plane. A friend of Taylor's had previously requested the same plans from the FAA and had been turned down on the ground that they contained trade secrets and the manufacturer wanted to keep them confidential. When Taylor filed his request and got no response from the FAA, he sued. A lower court dismissed his claim, ruling that the earlier requester was Taylor's virtual representative and therefore Taylor was precluded from pursuing his case.

The Court did not order the plans Taylor sought to be released, but it did say that precluding Taylor's request because of the earlier one was improper. News organizations and government watchdogs backed Taylor, fearing that government agencies could use Taylor's case to dismiss requests by people seeking similar information for different reasons.

A federal appeals court said in 2009 that the Office of Administration, an organization that provides support and administrative services to the president, does not meet the definition of a federal agency under FOIA. The DC Circuit court said that the office "performs only operational and administrative tasks in support of the President and his staff and therefore, under our precedent, lacks substantial independent authority" (*Citizens for Responsibility and Ethics in Washington v. Office of Administration*, 566 F.3d 219). The fact that the office had been complying with FOIA requests for decades and had regulations in place for handling requests did not matter, said the court, because "past views have no bearing on the legal issue whether a unit is, in fact, an agency subject to FOIA."

But in another case the same year, the same appeals court said that documents withheld by the Office of Management and Budget (OMB) were *not* exempt from disclosure under FOIA. Public Citizen, a non-profit public interest organization, had requested OMB legislative and budgetary clearance policies, and OMB released some parts of 22 documents but *redacted* (blacked out) significant portions of those documents, saying they were exempt under Exemption 2 (internal documents) and Exemption 5 (pre-decisional/deliberative documents). The court said that the fact that the documents had never been outside the agency was not enough to render them exempt and that not all documents were deliberative enough in nature to justify the exemption. In 2010, the court re-issued the opinion (*Public Citizen v. Office of Management and Budget*, 598 F.3d 865). In fact, the court wrote that release of the documents was central to FOIA's mission: "[T]he documents at issue here lie at the core of what FOIA seeks to expose to public scrutiny. They explain how a powerful agency performing a central role in the functioning of the federal government carries out its responsibilities and interacts with other government agencies."

In 2010, the Electronic Frontier Foundation (EFF) brought suit against the Office of the Director of National Intelligence (ODNI), alleging that, under FOIA, the public has a right to information about telecommunications carriers' attempts to avoid liability for their roles in the government's surveillance activities post-Sept. 11 (*Elec. Frontier Found. v. Office of the Dir. of Nat'l Intelligence*, 595 F.3d 949). EFF requested communications between ODNI, members of Congress, and telecommunications firms regarding amendments to the Foreign Intelligence Surveillance Act (FISA) which would provide immunity to firms who assisted in the surveillance where it violated state or federal law. The court said that the carriers' lobbyists' identities must be revealed, citing an important public interest component:

> With knowledge of the lobbyists' identities, the public will be able to determine how the Executive Branch used advice from particular individuals and corporations in reaching its own policy decisions. Such information will allow the public to draw inferences comparing the various agents' influence in relation to each other and compared to the agents' or their corporate sponsors' political activity and contributions to either the President or key members of Congress.

Exemption 2 should not be divided into "high" and "low" standards, said the Supreme Court in 2011 in *Milner v. Dept. of the Navy* (131 S. Ct. 1259). Some circuits had divided internal information into two categories, "Low 2" and "High 2." Routine or trivial information is "Low 2," of low societal value, such as agency management or "housekeeping" information;

the Court has already held that there is no substantial public interest in its disclosure in *Dept. of the Air Force v. Rose* (discussed earlier). But it had not ruled on the "High 2" category, which includes more substantial matters, and the circuits were split in their applications of the exemption. At issue in *Milner* was the Ninth Circuit's decision that the Navy could keep secret documents that record locations of explosives stored near Port Townsend, Wash. Plaintiff Glen Scott Milner lived near this location. The Navy denied Milner's request under Exemption 2, the internal personnel rules and practices exemption; the district court agreed, and a divided Ninth Circuit affirmed.

The Supreme Court reversed on an 8-1 vote, saying that Exemption 2 pertains only to "records relating to employee relations and human resources issues." Justice Elena Kagan made the holding clear: "Our construction of the statutory language simply makes clear that Low 2 is all of 2 (and that High 2 is not 2 at all)".

Justice Kagan did not want the government to be able to use Exemption 2 as a fallback reason for record denial. There are other alternatives for the Department of Defense to keep the information confidential if it truly believes that is necessary, including Congressional action, she said. Justice Stephen Breyer dissented, saying that because the High 2/Low 2 distinction had been applied consistently for 30 years and seemed to be working for all involved, he would "let sleeping dogs lie."

Other FOIA Problems

Users of the FOIA also encounter other practical problems. One of them, as already noted, is the problem of delays in compliance. Many federal agencies have large backlogs of FoI requests. This poses a particular problem for journalists as opposed to other users of the FOIA. While a historian or a business enterprise may be prepared to wait a year or two for information, that kind of a delay is often fatal for a journalist working on a timely news story.

In 2010, the National Security Archive and George Washington University conducted a FOIA audit, funded by the Knight Foundation. In it, they found that "the Obama Administration—which the President pledged would be 'the most open and transparent administration in history'—has clearly stated a new policy direction for open government but has not conquered the challenge of communicating and enforcing that message throughout the Executive Branch." FOIA requests as old as 18 years linger in some agencies, few agencies have yet to make concrete changes in their FOIA policies to comply with the policy shift, and only four agencies showed both increases in information releases coupled with decreases in denials under FOIA.

Another problem with the FOIA can be high court costs and attorney's fees. Those who sue the government for the release of

redact:
to edit or black out sensitive parts of a document before its release; for examples of redacted documents, visit The John Lennon FBI Files website at www.lennonfbifiles.com.

"High 2" and "Low 2" categories:
categories that were used by some appeals courts to determine the importance of information under Exception 2 of the FOIA, eliminated by the Supreme Court in 2011.

virtual representation:
a doctrine where a non-party may be bound to the judgment in a previous case if certain factors are met.

qui tam:
from the Latin phrase *qui tam pro domino rege quam pro se ipso in hac parte sequitur,* meaning "[he] who sues in this matter for the king as for himself;" an action brought by a private person on behalf of the government, and the person may be awarded some of the damages if they are found.

FIG. 46. Joan Baez
sings at the Civil Rights
March on Washington,
D.C., August 28, 1963.

*National Archives, ARC
Identifier 542017/Local
Identifier 306-SSM-4C(53)3.
Item from Record Group
306: Records of the U.S.
Information Agency,
1900-1992.*

documents and "substantially prevail" in court are entitled to have the government pay their costs and attorney's fees. However, if the lawsuit is not successful, the document requester is likely to have a large legal bill to pay. The FOIA doesn't say anything about those who seek documents having to pay the government's expenses if they lose. However, the general rules governing federal appellate court proceedings say that the winner is entitled to recover court costs (but not lawyers' fees) from the loser in any lawsuit that reaches a federal appellate court.

On the basis of these rules, the U.S. Justice Department sought—and eventually won—an order from a federal appellate court requiring singer Joan Baez to pay $365 of the government's court costs in an FOIA appeal. Baez gained the release of about 1,500 pages of FBI records about her, but she sued to obtain additional files the government had kept secret. Although she lost, at first the appellate court refused to order her to pay the government's court costs. Then the court reconsidered and ruled that she had to pay (*Baez v. U.S. Justice Department*, 684 F.2d 999, 1982). This case was troubling to many civil libertarians, not because of the amount of money Baez was ordered to pay but because of the precedent it established.

Still another problem encountered by those who use the FOIA is the legally sanctioned censoring of documents. The act permits agencies to delete portions of documents that fall within an exception while releasing the remainder of the document. The result is sometimes a document with page after page of *"redactions"*— black or blank space, interrupted only by conjunctions and prepositions.

Perhaps the most serious FOIA problem of all is that the federal bureaucracy has made concerted efforts to weaken the FOIA time and again. Both the FBI and the CIA have lobbied Congress for a blanket exception from the act. Citing the cost of complying with FOIA requests and alleged breaches of national security, some officials argued that public access rights should be sharply curtailed. In 1982 Congress restricted access to information involving the CIA by passing the Intelligence Identities Protection Act. That law made it a crime to engage in a "pattern of activities" with the "intent to identify and expose covert agents." The law was apparently aimed at former CIA agents who reveal agency secrets—a troubling instance of prior censorship in and of itself.

Congress never gave the FBI and CIA the blanket exceptions they wanted. However, in 1986 Congress authorized the FBI and other federal law enforcement agencies to reject

FOIA requests without confirming or denying the existence of the requested documents. Previously, the FBI often had to disclose the existence of a document to justify not releasing it. That gave useful information to people who wanted to know if they were under FBI scrutiny. A *Glomar response* (or "Glomarization") is when an agency says it can neither confirm nor deny the existence of requested records. The name comes from a case in which the Central Intelligence Agency refused to confirm or deny ties to a submarine retrieval vessel named the Glomar Explorer, owned by Howard Hughes (*Phillippi v. CIA*, 546 F.2d 1009, 1976).

The Second Circuit allowed the National Security Agency to *Glomar* seven requests from attorneys who were trying to determine whether their phone calls with clients in Guantánamo Bay detention had been intercepted. After establishing that the *Glomar* response has been adopted in other circuits (precedents in the First, Seventh, Ninth, and D.C. Circuits), the Second Circuit said that it was also acceptable in its jurisdiction and moreover, could be applied to the requests in the case (*Wilner v. Nat'l Security Agency*, 592 F.3d 60, 2009).

However, the FBI was *not* permitted to Glomarize in response to a death-row inmate's request for information that he claimed might exonerate him in four murders for which he was convicted (*Roth v. Dep't of Justice*, 642 F.3d 1161, 2011). In denying the agency's response, the D.C. Circuit said that the public had an interest in knowing if the FBI held information that could substantiate the inmate's claims and that any privacy issues that the men that the inmate claimed were responsible for the deaths were outweighed by that interest. In fact, the court said, the inmate's death sentence "strengthens the public's interest in knowing whether the FBI's files contain information that could corroborate his claim of innocence."

The Supreme Court also limited the use of FOIA in actions under the False Claims Act (FCA). The FCA is a federal law, similar to whistleblowing statutes, that allows non-government workers to file *qui tam* (on behalf of the government) actions against federal contractors, alleging wrongdoing by those contractors, with the possibility of recovering a percentage of any damages. The act bars claims "based upon the public disclosure of allegations or transactions in a criminal, civil, or administrative hearing, in a congressional, administrative, or Government Accounting Office report, hearing, audit, or investigation, or from the news media." The question before the Supreme Court in a 2011 case, *Schindler Elevator Corp. v. U.S. ex rel. Kirk* (131 S. Ct. 1885), was this: "whether a federal agency's written response to a request for records under the Freedom of Information Act (FOIA), 5 U.S.C. §552, constitutes a 'report' within the meaning of the public disclosure bar." The Second Circuit said it didn't, but Supreme Court said it does—thus saying that FOIA requests could not be used to support *qui tam* cases under the FCA.

Justice Clarence Thomas wrote for a 5-3 majority that the government provided "no principled way to define 'report' to exclude FOIA responses without excluding other documents that are indisputably reports." In dissent, Justice Ruth Bader Ginsburg, joined by Justices Sonia Sotomayor and Stephen Breyer, expressed concern about the effect on whistleblowers. She wrote that the Court's opinion "severely limits whistleblowers' ability to substantiate their allegations before commencing suit" and called on Congress to remedy that.

In 2011 the Senate passed the "Faster FOIA" bill, which would establish a commission to make recommendations to Congress for legislation that would decrease response times.

Despite all of these difficulties, the FOIA remains a valuable tool for information gathering. This law has opened millions of files to public scrutiny, files that otherwise would have remained secret indefinitely.

The OPEN Government Act of 2007

In 2007 Congress approved and President George W. Bush signed a new law to make various changes in the FOIA, the OPEN Government Act of 2007. Politicians seem to love acronyms, and this one means "Openness Promotes Effectiveness in our National" Government Act of 2007. The new law reversed many of the Bush administration's efforts to increase government secrecy after the 2001 terrorist attacks. As noted earlier, it also restricted the scope of an order by then-Attorney General John Ashcroft directing federal agencies to resist requests for information under the Freedom of Information Act whenever there was a legal basis for doing so.

Among other things, the 2007 law brought nonproprietary information held by government contractors within the scope of the FOIA. The new measure required agencies to meet the 20-day deadline for responding to FoI requests or else refund search and duplication fees paid by noncommercial requesters. Also, agencies now have to explain instances where part of a document is redacted before it is released to a requester. In addition, the 2007 legislation set up a system for requesters to track the status of their queries and created an ombudsman in each agency to deal with disputes over information requests without litigation. The ombudsman heads the Office of Government Information Services, housed at the National Archives and Records Administration. In 2009, Miriam Nisbet, the director of the Information Society Division of the United Nations Educational, Scientific and Cultural Organization (UNESCO), since 2007, was appointed the first FOIA ombudsman.

A federal appeals court said that the OPEN Government Act does not apply retroactively, and a plaintiff cannot recover attorney's fees for a case settled in 2005 (*Summers v. Dept. of Justice*, 569 F.3d 500, 2009).

■ ELECTRONIC FREEDOM OF INFORMATION

The enormous growth of online communications and the Internet during the 1990s led to major changes in the way government agencies handle and disseminate information. And it led to changes in public perceptions about public records, creating new FoI problems.

On one hand, the Internet has made it much easier for governments to provide large amounts of information to the public. But on the other hand, it has led to unprecedented public demands for government secrecy: once a net surfer discovers a site that has personal information about individuals available online, thousands of others may learn about it in a few hours—and start demanding that the site be shut down. In many instances agencies have responded to these controversies by removing information from their online databases that was routinely available to the public in paper form for years. To the alarm of journalists, this has resulted in the loss of public access to newsworthy public information in many cases: the paper records may no longer exist, and the electronic version may be off limits to the public. And at the other extreme, many government agencies have put their public records out to bid, with the winning bidder given the right to *computerize* the records and *charge hefty fees for public access to once-free public records*. News organizations have fought battles from coast to coast over this shrinkage of public access to public records.

Electronic Freedom of Information Act Amendments

Responding to some of the new FoI problems and opportunities created by the Internet and the rapid growth of computer usage in and out of government, Congress extensively amended the FOIA in the Electronic Freedom of Information Act Amendments of 1996.

The Electronic FOIA Amendments were widely reported in the media as merely requiring government agencies to make their records available in electronic form—on the Internet, on CDs and DVDs or in other ways. However, the 1996 law did much more than that.

The Electronic FOIA changed the way federal agencies respond to FoI requests in three basic ways: (1) it required agencies to make it easier for the public to identify and access government records, (2) it facilitated the computerization of the FoI compliance process, and (3) it completely reformed the timetable and procedures that agencies must follow in responding to FoI requests.

To assist the public in accessing federal records, the 1996 law required agencies to provide detailed indexes and guides to explain what records are available and where they may be found. Also, the law divided government records that fall under the FOIA into three categories: those that must be published, those that must be made available in agency reading rooms or placed online even if no one makes a request, and those that must be made available when there is a request.

To computerize the FoI compliance process, the 1996 law required many agencies to set up "electronic reading rooms." Whereas those seeking government information previously had to go to an agency's headquarters in Washington and camp out in a "public reading room," in many instances the documents kept in those rooms are now online. As a result, anyone with a computer and Internet service can read the same documents at home. This one provision of the 1996 act alone vastly increased public access to federal records. In fact, it may have increased public access as much as the FOIA itself did 30 years earlier.

The Electronic FOIA Amendments also provided for other enhancements of the FoI process. In addition to flatly declaring that records kept in electronic form are fully covered by the FOIA, the law required agencies to provide materials in a variety of computer formats.

The 1996 act also seriously addressed the problem of redactions for the first time. When electronic records are *redacted* (i.e., blacked out), it is often impossible even to tell that this has happened. Entire sections can be deleted—with no paper trail to show where the deletions occurred. The 1996 law said that agencies must indicate where there have been redactions and how much was redacted where it is feasible to do so and where disclosing that information will not in itself reveal confidential information.

Finally, the 1996 act addressed the chronic problem of interminable delays. It gave agencies 20 working days instead of 10 to respond to FoI requests, but it also made major changes in what agencies must do if they will miss this deadline. For one, journalists and a few others were authorized to have their requests expedited in some instances. In addition, those whose requests are complex and may require considerable agency time are given an opportunity to scale back or simplify their requests in return for faster processing. And requesters who face delays are supposed to be notified and given an estimated compliance time. The 2007 law went even further on this point, setting up a tracking system for FoI requests.

Aside from the specific details in the Electronic FOIA Amendments, one of the most important innovations in this law was the requirement that agencies identify the information that is repeatedly requested and avoid wasting time processing duplicative requests over and over again. The law said that when an agency determines that particular information must be released under the FOIA—and is likely to be requested again—the agency must put that information where the public can access it routinely (usually without even filing a formal FoI request).

■ FOI LIMITATIONS

Executive Privilege

Ever since the days of George Washington and Thomas Jefferson, American presidents and sometimes others in the executive branch have asserted a right to withhold information from Congress and the courts under a concept called *executive privilege*. The legal foundation for executive privilege is vague; chief executives won the right to keep many of their working papers confidential because no one was really in a position to challenge that kind of secrecy.

Executive privilege has also been claimed by some executive officers of state and local governments. As it developed, the privilege generally covered not only military and diplomatic secrets but also many of the internal documents generated within the executive branch of government.

The executive orders issued by Presidents Harry Truman and Dwight D. Eisenhower in the 1950s to govern the rapidly growing national security classification system were justified by the concept of executive privilege. Those orders allowed military and diplomatic secrets to be classified on three levels: confidential, secret and top secret. Only those who had been granted an appropriate security clearance were to be given access to this information.

As the national security classification system grew, it became a complicated bureaucratic operation that annually locked up millions of documents, as mentioned earlier. The Pentagon Papers case (discussed in Chapter Three) illustrates the problems in this area. The case arose when several newspapers obtained copies of a secret report about the Vietnam War. The newspapers' editors felt the public should know about the conclusions reached in the Pentagon Papers. They believed these papers were classified not so much to protect national security as to conceal the diplomatic errors of several presidents and their administrations.

In resolving the case, the Supreme Court allowed the papers to be published but did not generally rule on the concept of executive privilege itself. The FOIA in effect recognized executive privilege by exempting from disclosure two kinds of information that executive privilege had covered: matters affecting national security and the internal working documents of federal agencies.

However, executive privilege was carried a step too far by the Nixon administration during the Watergate scandal, and the result was a U.S. Supreme Court decision that severely restricted its scope. As the scandal drifted nearer to the president himself, Nixon sought to invoke executive privilege to avoid releasing some very incriminating tape recordings to a court. The tapes included a number of conversations between Nixon and his aides, and Nixon realized how damaging some of them would be if made public. The Watergate special prosecutor contended that the tapes were needed in the prosecution of several Nixon aides.

Nixon's refusal to release the tapes, which he justified by citing executive privilege, was challenged by the special prosecutor, and the case reached the Supreme Court. In the resulting 1974 decision (*U.S. v. Nixon*, 418 U.S. 683), the scope of executive privilege was drastically curtailed. In a unanimous decision, the Supreme Court ruled that executive privilege is absolute only in connection with military and diplomatic information that must be kept secret to protect national security. In other areas, the high court said, the privilege has to be balanced against other interests, such as the obligation of every citizen (including the president) to step forward with evidence of a crime that may be in his possession. Like the reporter's privilege, executive privilege has its limits.

The Supreme Court ordered the president to release the Watergate tapes. That, of course, accelerated the chain of events that led to Nixon's resignation from the presidency later in 1974. The tapes revealed ever more incriminating evidence that Nixon and his top aides had conspired to cover up crimes that were planned in the White House.

Thus, executive privilege is a less formidable justification for government secrecy today than it once was. However, these new limitations on executive privilege are of little help to the press and public, since the FOIA still exempts so much of the information that was once kept secret under the justification of executive privilege.

Nevertheless, some of the internal government information that was once hidden by executive privilege is now available at least to the courts. And when such information is presented as evidence in court, it may become a part of the public record. The problem of public access to court records is discussed later in this chapter; Chapter Seven discusses courtroom closures to protect confidentiality.

The 1974 Privacy Act

Journalists and civil libertarians—normally allies on First Amendment issues—are often on opposite sides of one of the most troubling problems in the freedom of information area. When the public's right to know and the individual's right to personal privacy conflict, the two groups often sharply disagree. Organizations such as the American Civil Liberties Union (ACLU) argue strongly for laws assuring the secrecy of personal information collected by government agencies, even at the expense of journalists' access to information.

Congress attempted to deal with this problem by enacting the 1974 Privacy Act, the first comprehensive federal law intended to protect individuals from improper disclosure of personal information by government agencies. The Privacy Act was a response to the growing public alarm over the massive amount of personal information government agencies were placing in computerized data banks. Groups such as the ACLU argued that these data banks constituted a major threat to individual freedom. If the private information kept in these data banks were to fall into the wrong hands, flagrant abuses could occur. Journalists, on the other hand, feared that a strong privacy protection law would be misused by government officials as an excuse for needless secrecy. Bureaucrats could avoid public scrutiny of their own deeds (and misdeeds) in the name of protecting individual privacy.

As it was finally enacted, the 1974 Privacy Act (5 U.S.C. § 552a) represents something of a compromise on this issue. The act applies to all information contained in hundreds of government record-keeping systems, placing strict limits on the manner in which the records are used. The act forbids federal agencies to release personal data from these record-keeping systems, or even transfer it to another federal agency without the permission of the person the information concerns.

The Privacy Act grants private individuals certain rights to inspect their own records in government data banks, with provisions allowing them to correct errors they discover. In addition, federal officials who improperly release personal records may be sued for damages, attorney's fees and court costs.

The act includes a number of exceptions, allowing government agencies to release personal information without the affected person's permission for law enforcement purposes, for use by the census bureau and Congress itself, and for similar purposes. Significantly, the Privacy Act also allows the release of personal data that is defined as public information under the FOIA. The Privacy Act was written this way to minimize its effect on the FOIA.

As it turned out, the Privacy Act generally created only minor problems for most journalists, but problems nonetheless. One of the exceptions to the FOIA excludes "personnel and medical files and similar files the disclosure of which would constitute a clearly unwarranted invasion of personal privacy." That language is broad enough to give federal officials considerable leeway in deciding what personal information they must release under the FOIA, and what they may withhold. Furthermore, the Privacy Act tends to discourage officials from releasing information in borderline cases because of the disparity between the consequences of violating the two laws.

The FOIA allows those seeking information to sue officials who balk at releasing information, but only for attorney's fees and court costs. The Privacy Act, on the other hand, provides penalties for violations as well.

Thus, although the Privacy Act was written in such a way as to minimize restrictions on the release of information that would otherwise be accessible under the FOIA, it does discourage openness in some cases. An official who errs in the direction of disclosing too little information faces no monetary penalty and only a vague threat of disciplinary action under the FOIA; the official who errs in the direction of disclosing too much information faces monetary penalties under the Privacy Act.

Perhaps the most controversial data bank to which the Privacy Act provided personal access is the one maintained by the Federal Bureau of Investigation. One problem is that the FBI is often slow in releasing individual files, and when files are finally released they are often censored. (File censoring is permitted by the Privacy Act because these are, after all, law enforcement investigatory files.) Moreover, there are several exceptions that sometimes permit the FBI to refuse to disclose even the existence of personal records. But nonetheless, the act gives private persons their first opportunity to learn something about the records the FBI may be keeping on them.

(Note that the Privacy Act gives individuals a limited right to inspect *their own files*. The Supreme Court's 1989 decision in the *Department of Justice* case held that the FBI has an across-the-board right to refuse to release files about individuals to *other persons*. That decision does not affect the right of an individual to seek access to his or her own file.)

The FBI's handling of personal information under the Privacy Act has stirred criticism from both civil libertarians and journalists. On at least one occasion, the FBI piously refused to release to journalists any background information on a well-known murder suspect. However, the FBI did issue 15,000 "wanted" posters to post offices, and these posters contained much of the information journalists were seeking.

In 1988, Congress strengthened the Privacy Act by passing the Computer Matching and Privacy Protection Act. This law governs the transfer of information between government agencies' computer databases. A great deal of this information is transferred from one agency to another to cross-check whether individuals are entitled to government assistance they may be receiving. This law added a verification requirement to prevent individuals from losing their benefits through misidentification and other data-handling errors. It also established Data Integrity Boards in many federal agencies to oversee the use of computerized data-matching programs.

Several recent cases interpreted elements of the Privacy Act. Information must be part of "a system of records" to qualify for Privacy Act protection, said the D.C. Circuit (*Armstrong v. Geithner*, 608 F.3d 854, 2010). William Armstrong alleged that the Department of the Treasury violated the Privacy Act when it disclosed details of an investigation into his conduct. The district court found for the defendant, and the appeals court agreed.

One of Armstrong's co-workers filed an anonymous complaint against him, and that triggered an investigation by the Treasury Department. While under investigation, Armstrong found another job at the U.S. Department of Agriculture, but never got a chance to work there; he was fired after a series of anonymous letters warned USDA employees that it was a mistake to hire him. The anonymous complainant said that she did not get the information she wrote in the letters or the complaint from investigation materials or supervisors; "she insisted she had based the letters upon independent sources—the rumor mill, her original complaint, and her own observations, assumptions, and speculation." These, said the court, were not records in "a system of records" under the Privacy Act, so no violation occurred.

The Supreme Court found for the government in a 2012 Privacy Act decision, one in which the Ninth Circuit reversed and remanded a lower court's decision that granted summary judgment to the Federal Aviation Administration for a Privacy Act violation, even though the agency's release of information was found to be unlawful. The district court denied pilot Stanmore Cooper's claim because even though it found that the FAA had unlawfully shared information about his HIV-positive status with other agencies, he had not claimed "actual damages"—which the court determined were *pecuniary* (financial) damages—so he did not meet the burden under the Privacy Act.

The Ninth Circuit reversed, saying that although the term "actual damages" was unclear, in using it, "Congress clearly intended that when a federal agency intentionally or willfully fails to uphold its record-keeping obligations under the Act, and that failure proximately causes an adverse effect on the plaintiff, the plaintiff is entitled to recover for both pecuniary and nonpecuniary injuries." But in finding for the government, Justice Samuel Alito disagreed, saying, "Congress intended 'actual damages' in the Privacy Act to mean special damages for proven pecuniary loss." The opinion produced a blistering dissent from Justice Sonia Sotomayor, who said that the decision "cripples the act's core purpose of redressing and deterring violations of privacy interests" (*FAA v. Cooper*, No. 10-1024).

The "Buckley Amendment"

At the same time as the enactment of the 1974 Privacy Act and the 1974 amendments to the FOIA, Congress also approved the "Buckley Amendment," more formally known as the Family Education Rights and Privacy Act (20 U.S.C. 1232g). That federal law, which is sometimes identified by its initials (FERPA), is often confused with the more general 1974 Privacy Act, and in fact the two have similar provisions. The Buckley Amendment was so named because Sen. James Buckley of New York led the effort to add it to the 1974 Elementary and Secondary Education Act amendments, a major federal-aid-to-education bill.

The Buckley Amendment gives parents the right to see their children's school records and forbids the release of these school records to outside parties without the parents' consent. Similarly, it allows students over age 18 to see their own school records, and requires their consent before these records may be released to outside parties. School systems that fail to obey the Buckley Amendment may be denied federal funds. In 2002 the U.S. Supreme Court made it clear that the denial of federal funds is usually the sole remedy for noncompliance: students cannot use the Buckley Amendment to sue schools that divulge their personal information (*Gonzaga University v. Doe*, 536 U.S. 273). The Supreme Court also clarified another aspect of the Buckley Amendment in 2002, ruling that it does not preclude such everyday classroom practices as having students grade each others' quizzes (*Owasso*

Independent School District v. Falvo, 534 U.S. 426). The court said the law was intended by Congress only to cover permanent records maintained by teachers and other school employees.

The Buckley Amendment has had some impact on the news-gathering activities of the media, at times in absurd ways. Overzealous school officials have sometimes used it as an excuse to withhold newsworthy and non-sensitive information about students involved in athletics or other newsworthy extracurricular activities. But perhaps the Buckley Amendment's most serious effect on news-gathering has been to increase the secrecy of school disciplinary records. That has sometimes made it difficult to report on newsworthy disciplinary actions, such as those involving student athletes or political activists. Fearful of losing federal money, some school officials have tended to avoid risking any appearance of non-compliance with the Buckley Amendment.

Campus newspapers are sometimes accused of violating the Buckley Amendment by reporting on the academic eligibility of student athletes and government officers, who are usually required to maintain a certain grade average to be eligible for their positions. The college administrators responsible for making sure that student officers and athletes are eligible are not always diligent in checking grade records. As a result, investigative journalists sometimes learn that a particular student leader is academically ineligible—and publish that newsworthy fact. That inevitably brings charges that the campus newspaper has violated the Buckley Amendment by revealing student grades, which are supposed to be confidential.

Controversies of this type have occurred at numerous colleges—almost invariably because college officials do not understand what the Buckley Amendment really does and doesn't say. The Buckley Amendment says schools that have *ongoing policies* of not keeping grades confidential *are ineligible for federal funds*. It does not forbid student newspapers to publish student leaders' grades to prove that they are academically ineligible. Nor does it say that a college could lose its federal funds just because the campus newspaper reveals a few student leaders' grades in a clearly newsworthy story about their fitness to serve.

Campus officials often cite the Buckley Amendment as a basis for keeping reports of campus crimes secret. However, there has been a national movement in recent years to force officials to reveal campus crime rates and in some cases information about specific crimes.

In 1990 Congress enacted the Crime Awareness and Campus Security Act, requiring all colleges and universities receiving federal funds to issue annual reports of crime statistics as well as descriptions of security arrangements. The law requires the use of uniform crime reporting procedures so that students and their families can compare the crime rates at different institutions as a factor in choosing a college. It does not require campuses to open their police records to the press, however.

Congress also revised the Buckley Amendment to declare that "law enforcement unit" records on college campuses are not "educational records" that must be kept confidential. However, this revision of the Buckley Amendment stopped short of requiring campus officials to make information about specific crimes public. It merely declared that the Buckley Amendment does not require such information to be kept secret.

The 1990 Congressional action did not settle the matter, however. On many campuses, administrators continued to cite the Buckley Amendment as a basis for keeping campus records concerning specific crimes and court proceedings confidential.

Initially, several courts responded by ruling that the Buckley Amendment cannot be used to justify keeping campus crime records secret if they are supposed to be open under state law. For example, a federal judge so ruled in a pioneering lawsuit filed by Traci Bauer, editor of the Southwest Missouri University *Standard*, to compel the administration to open these records (*Bauer v. Kincaid*, 759 F. Supp. 575, 1991).

Soon other student editors filed similar lawsuits to force administrators to disclose campus crime or court information under state freedom of information laws. By 1997, both the Ohio Supreme Court and the Georgia Supreme Court had ruled that campus officials had to release information about campus crimes or court proceedings in spite of the Buckley Amendment (see *The Miami Student v. Miami University*, 680 N.E.2d 956, 1997; and *Red & Black Publishing Co. v. Board of Regents of the University of Georgia*, 427 S.E.2d 257, 1993). Both courts concluded that the Buckley Amendment does not apply to campus crime and court records. Note that these cases did not create any new legal right of access to university crime and court records; that is governed by state FoI laws. But if such records would otherwise be public under the applicable state law, these courts held that the Buckley Amendment does not override state laws and transform crime records into "educational records."

Congress entered this controversy by adding language to the 1998 reauthorization of the Higher Education Act declaring more emphatically that the Buckley Amendment cannot be used to justify secrecy about violent crimes and certain other crimes committed on campus. If this information would otherwise be made public (under a state open record law, for example), Congress declared that the Buckley Amendment does not change that.

Perhaps more important, the 1998 version of the Higher Education Act also included language requiring all colleges and universities receiving federal funds (including private schools with federally insured student loans) to create and maintain a log of criminal incidents reported to campus police or security department—and make this log public. This log must include the nature, date, time, general location and disposition of each complaint. The log must be made public within two business days, and new information that is later discovered about an incident must be added to the log and made public within two business days. There is an exception for information that would identify a victim or jeopardize an ongoing investigation. The 1998 law also strengthened the requirements in the legislation that colleges and universities must publish an annual report of campus crime statistics.

The campus crime law is officially known as the Jeanne Clery Disclosure of Campus Security Policy and Campus Crime Statistics Act. It is named in memory of a Lehigh University student who was unaware of recent crimes on her campus and who left her security door propped open, enabling an intruder to enter her room and murder her. Reports of campus crime that are filed as required by this law are sometimes called Clery Act reports.

Unfortunately for the student press, that is not the end of the story. In 1998 the U.S. Department of Education filed its own lawsuit in federal court to override the Ohio Supreme Court decision and force university officials in Ohio to keep campus crime information secret when an offense is handled through campus disciplinary proceedings. The Department of Education pointed out that the Ohio Public Records Act exempts from disclosure any record that state or federal law requires to be kept secret. Contending that the Buckley Amendment does cover campus disciplinary proceedings, federal officials obtained an injunction ordering university administrators not to release records pertaining to these proceedings. In 2002, the Sixth Circuit upheld that injunction, ruling that the Buckley Amendment requires campus disciplinary records and proceedings to be confidential (*U.S. v. Miami University*, 294 F.3d 797).

The *Miami University* decision did not affect the requirement that all colleges and universities disclose general information about campus crimes as well as the police log, but it did uphold the rule that campus disciplinary proceedings are confidential under the Buckley Amendment. Inasmuch as they are confidential under the Buckley Amendment, that also makes them confidential under the Ohio Public Records Act because that law exempts from disclosure anything that is secret under another state or federal law, the court concluded.

The Student Press Law Center has a detailed report for journalists about covering campus crime available on its website (www.splc.org).

The Federal Advisory Committee Act

Congress enacted the Federal Advisory Committee Act (FACA) in 1972 to try to control the growing use of secret advisory committees by the executive branch of government. It requires various non-government organizations that give advice to the government to hold open meetings and maintain public records. It covers a variety of advisory bodies—entities that include one or more persons who are *not* federal "officers" or "employees" and that give advice to the president or an agency in the executive branch of the federal government.

However, its usefulness was limited by a 1989 Supreme Court decision, *Public Citizen v. Department of Justice* (491 U.S. 440). The court ruled that Congress did not intend for the act to cover privately funded bodies such as the American Bar Association committee that reviews the qualifications of prospective federal judges. Thus, the ABA panel can continue to meet in secret and maintain secret records when it evaluates potential judges (including possible Supreme Court justices). The decision also means that many other private groups may meet secretly and make recommendations to government officials. The court did not overturn the Advisory Committee Act itself, but by ruling that the act does not apply to the ABA panel it may open the way for other groups to claim that they are exempt from the act's open-meeting and open-record provisions. This could curtail the public's right to know about many advisory group recommendations that shape federal government policy.

A highly publicized FACA case arose in 1993, when President Bill Clinton established a President's Task Force on National Health Care Reform and named his wife, Hillary Rodham Clinton, to head it. The Task Force, which almost always met in secret, consisted entirely of senior government officials—except for the First Lady, who held no official government position (nor could she under the Anti-Nepotism Act, the law forbidding federal officials to appoint close relatives to government positions). In *Association of American Physicians and Surgeons v. Hillary Rodham Clinton* (997 F.2d 898), a federal appellate court had to decide whether the task force was subject to FACA—and thus required to hold open meetings.

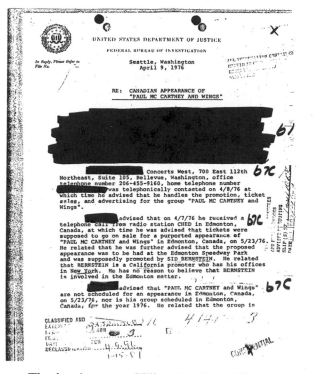

FIG. 47. Page from the FBI FOIA online reading room, showing redaction of information about a Paul McCartney and Wings concert in Edmonton, Canada in May 1976.

Federal Bureau of Investigation FOIA Reading Room, full file available at http://foia.fbi.gov/beatles/beatles_pt04.pdf.

The key issue was Hillary Rodham Clinton's status. If she did not qualify as a full-time federal "officer" or "employee," then FACA would apply to the task force (because one of its members would have been a private citizen, not a government official). But the court traced the history and status of "first ladies" and concluded that the first lady was the equivalent of a federal "officer" or "employee" even though she could not be paid or hold any official position while married to the president. As a result, her task force was not a private advisory body subject to FACA but instead an internal body within the Clinton administration, the court held. Therefore, it could meet in secret.

In 2005, the same appellate court ruled on the applicability of FACA to a task force set up by President Bush, and ruled that it was not subject to the advisory committee act. Bush in 2001 set up a body called the National Energy Policy Development Group, headed by Vice President Richard Cheney and composed entirely of members of the Bush Administration. However, the group invited a number of outsiders, including energy industry representatives, to attend meetings and offer advice. The task force was disbanded later that year.

In an *en banc* decision (with all judges participating, not just a panel of three), the U.S. Court of Appeals in Washington, D.C. decided *In re Cheney* (406 F.3d 723). The court said inviting outsiders to meetings did not make the energy task force a private advisory body subject to FACA. Writing for the court, Judge A. Raymond Randolph wrote, "The outsider might make an important presentation, he might be persuasive, the information he provides might affect the committee's judgment, but having neither a vote nor a veto over the advice the committee renders to the president, he is no more a member of the committee than the aides who accompany congressmen or cabinet officers to committee meetings."

Criminal History Information

For many working journalists, another serious obstacle in gathering information has been the effect of state and federal privacy laws on access to information about persons accused of crimes. In 1976, the federal Law Enforcement Assistance Administration (LEAA) issued a controversial set of guidelines intended to restrict the release of personal information by law enforcement agencies. The guidelines required state and local police agencies receiving federal aid to develop policies governing the release of information about persons arrested or charged with crimes. The guidelines were prompted at least in part by the LEAA's efforts to establish a new nationwide computerized law enforcement information network. LEAA officials feared that the vast amount of personal information available through this new system would lead to abuses such as the indiscriminate release of individual criminal history information (records of past arrests and convictions).

Originally, the LEAA guidelines were intended to seal all criminal history records in the interest of individual privacy. But those rules produced strenuous objections by journalists. In their final form, the guidelines did not specifically tell local police agencies what their information policies had to be, but they did require them to develop consistent policies.

As a result of the LEAA recommendations, some law enforcement agencies stopped releasing criminal history information to the press. Even current police blotter information that had traditionally been available was sometimes denied to the press. In many states, all records of arrests that do not lead to convictions—and even some records of arrests that do lead to convictions—are now sealed or simply destroyed. At least 47 states restrict access to criminal history "rap sheets" under some circumstances. (FBI rap sheets were addressed by the *Reporters Committee* case discussed earlier.)

Information-seeking journalists and open government advocates often disagree with civil liberties groups about this issue. Civil libertarians argue that a person should not be permanently stigmatized by public access to his or her police arrest record, particularly if the arrest does not lead to a conviction. When a record of an arrest has been legally *expunged* (erased), ACLU leaders are particularly emphatic in their contention that making information about it public is an injustice. Many journalists, on the other hand, feel that while closing these records does protect individual privacy, it also allows wholesale abuses by law enforcement agencies. To support that assertion, they cite the dangers to civil liberties inherent in secret arrests and secret police activities. Also, they argue that society needs protection from persons with criminal records. They cite instances when privacy laws prevented employers from discovering employees' criminal records, with the result that ex-convicts were placed where they could commit similar crimes again; for instance, a 1980 case in Texas where an employee of a mental institution raped a patient, and officials had been denied access to his criminal record (including a previous rape conviction) when they hired him.

This ongoing conflict will not soon be resolved. As Chapter Seven points out, there has been a long-term trend away from easy access to information about criminal suspects' past deeds, a trend prompted by the fair trial-free press dilemma at least as much as by the concern for personal privacy.

Federal Driver's Privacy Protection Act

With little debate or even publicity in the news media, Congress passed a law in 1994 that significantly curtailed access to motor vehicle registration records and driving records. The federal Driver's Privacy Protection Act (DPPA) was enacted as a part of the omnibus

1994 anti-crime bill. This law requires every state to close its motor vehicle registration and driving records to the press and public, although there is an exception allowing insurance companies and private investigators, among others, to retain access to these records. Any state may pass legislation to opt out of the across-the-board federal secrecy requirements as long as individuals may arrange to have their own records kept confidential.

The DPPA was enacted as a public safety measure. To justify the bill, Congress cited the 1989 murder of actress Rebecca Shaeffer by a fan. The fan obtained her address from a private investigator who had access to California Dept. of Motor Vehicles records. However, journalists who opposed the bill pointed out that this rationale makes no sense: private investigators are exempt from the new secrecy requirements.

To journalists, the DPPA represents the loss of a powerful investigative tool. Columnist Dan Lynch of the *Albany Times Union* pointed to numerous important stories developed by reporters using motor vehicle and driving records. For example, the media have checked driving records to learn that some airline pilots and the captain of the Exxon Valdez (the tanker that ran aground, causing a disastrous Alaskan oil spill), among others, had drunk driving convictions and should not have been placed in jobs where they could endanger public safety. Lynch also pointed out that in New York City the media began checking the driving records of people involved in fatal accidents—and reported that many of them had dozens of suspensions or revocations, but were still driving.

Several states challenged Congress' authority to tell them how to handle driving records, but in 2000 the U.S. Supreme Court upheld this controversial law. Ruling in *Reno v. Condon* (528 U.S. 141), the court upheld the right of Congress to use the commerce clause of the U.S. Constitution as a basis for requiring the states to keep these records secret.

In a unanimous ruling, the court deviated from a recent pattern of overturning federal laws regulating conduct by the states. This time, the court held that the principles of federalism were not violated by an act of Congress for several reasons. The court concluded that selling driver's license information to advertisers and insurers, which a number of states were doing, amounted to commercial activity by the states that could be regulated under the Constitution's commerce clause. By ruling as it did, the court reversed a decision by the Fourth Circuit, which had upheld a challenge to the DPPA by the state of South Carolina.

Even companies "stockpiling" driver data for future use is acceptable under DPPA, said the Eighth Circuit in 2011 in *Cook v. ACS State & Local Solutions, Inc.* (663 F.3d 989). Janice Cook, a Missouri driver, brought suit against several businesses who had obtained information under DPPA, and Cook alleged that the lack of immediate use of the data by these companies violated the DPPA. In denying the claim, the court said that DPPA "only requires that the information be obtained for a permissible purpose" and no mention was made in the law about when the information must be used.

Federal Contracts and State Secrets

In *Gen'l Dynamics Corp. v. U.S.* (131 S. Ct. 1900), the Supreme Court said in 2011 that in a long-running contract battle over a large defense contract, the sensitivity of national secrets meant that the case had to start over. The companies contracted with the Pentagon to develop a stealth bomber, and the government handed over sensitive information as part of the contract. When the project fell behind, the contract was cancelled, and the companies sued to recover costs. But the government said that the companies had sensitive information that was too risky to national security to come out in court, so they could not sue.

Justice Antonin Scalia wrote for a unanimous Court that the case was probably more important to the companies than in the development of any far-reaching or important contract law. However, Scalia said, "Both parties—the Government no less than petitioners—must have assumed the risk that state secrets would prevent the adjudication of claims of inadequate performance." Scalia did suggest that in the future, companies need to consider the ramifications of entering into government contracts that involve state secrets and negotiate appropriately: "They can negotiate, for example, the timing and amount of progress payments to account for the possibility that state secrets may ultimately render the contract unenforceable."

■ FEDERAL OPEN MEETING LEGISLATION

Another aspect of the struggle for freedom of information involves access to the meetings of government agencies. This is one of the oldest and most difficult information-gathering problems encountered by journalists. In theory, all public agencies should conduct the public's business openly, with citizens invited to listen in. But in practice many public officials find it tempting to make their decisions behind closed doors, announcing them in carefully worded press releases afterward. Obviously, if the press is to serve as a watchdog on behalf of the public, reporters must have a right to attend the meetings where public officials make their important decisions. To ensure this right, journalists have campaigned for open-meeting laws for many years—with some success.

In fact, at least 46 states already had open-meeting laws before Congress finally enacted such a law in 1976. That 1976 federal law, the Government in the Sunshine Act (5 U.S.C. 552b), requires about 50 administrative agencies to conduct some of their meetings in public. The policy-making boards and commissions of these agencies must meet at announced times and places, with the public generally invited to attend. However, closed sessions are still permitted for 10 different reasons; the legal officer of the agency must specify the basis for each closed meeting.

The first nine grounds for secret meetings closely parallel the nine FOIA exceptions, listed earlier in this chapter. They include such things as matters affecting national security, personnel matters, law enforcement investigations, discussions of trade secrets and the like. The tenth subject that may be discussed in a closed meeting is pending litigation and similar adjudicatory matters.

Whatever the reason for a closed meeting, the board or commission must vote to close a meeting before the public may be excluded, and the vote must be recorded. The agency must then keep accurate and complete records of what goes on during the closed meeting. In most instances, that record must be either a verbatim transcript or a tape recording of all proceedings. In some instances, however, detailed minutes are permitted instead.

When an agency holds a closed meeting, it must quickly publish the results of any votes, including a record of how each commissioner or board member voted.

Any person may initiate a lawsuit against an agency that appears to be violating the Government in the Sunshine Act, and federal district courts are authorized to issue injunctions ordering federal agencies to comply with the law. When a complaining party wins such a lawsuit, the federal court is authorized to require the federal government to pay his or her attorney's fees and court costs. However, the act contains no civil or criminal penalties for government officials who violate its provisions. In addition, the law specifically orders federal courts not to invalidate actions taken by agencies during illegal secret meetings. Thus, the federal open meeting law has virtually no "teeth" in it. As we shall see shortly, it is much weaker than many state open meeting laws in this respect.

Another major loophole in the Government in the Sunshine Act is that it does *not* prohibit government agencies from making major decisions by circulating private policy memoranda among commissioners. Some federal agencies decide many important matters by circulating memos and then merely announce their decisions at open meetings, which may occur only once a month or, in some instances, even less frequently. The Nuclear Regulatory Commission (NRC) and the Equal Employment Opportunity Commission (EEOC) have both been accused of using such tactics to evade the spirit of the Sunshine Act.

The Sunshine Act covers a number of well-known agencies in addition to the NRC and EEOC, including the Federal Communications Commission, Federal Trade Commission, Interstate Commerce Commission, Consumer Product Safety Commission, National Transportation Safety Board, Civil Service Commission, Securities and Exchange Commission, U.S. Postal Service board of governors and Federal Reserve Board. The act applies to the central policy-making board of each of these agencies but not to local or national staff meetings, even if those meetings involve important policy matters. Nor does it apply to cabinet-level departments or to some of the advisory bodies closest to the presidency, such as the National Security Council.

The Government in the Sunshine Act excludes most informal gatherings and unofficial meetings held by members of federal boards and commissions. In a 1984 decision, the U.S. Supreme Court ruled that it was proper for a majority of the members of the Federal Communications Commission to meet in private with communications leaders from other countries at an international conference. The court said the gathering in question was not a "meeting" and the international body itself was not an "agency" within the meaning of the law (*FCC v. ITT World Communications*, 466 U.S. 463).

In short, the federal open meeting law leaves much to be desired. It allows closed meetings for a wide variety of dubious reasons. Moreover, its enforcement provisions are notably weak, and it fails to cover many of the federal bodies that make the most important decisions. Nevertheless, it is a first step toward openness in the gigantic federal bureaucracy, a bureaucracy that once felt it had an absolute right to do the public's business in private without interference from meddlesome reporters or private citizens.

■ STATE OPEN MEETING AND RECORD LAWS

Although the federal FOIA and Government in the Sunshine Act are important, most journalists find their own state FoI laws even more relevant than the federal laws. On a daily basis, thousands of journalists rely on state open meeting and public record laws to provide access to many of their most important news sources.

But while state public record and open meeting laws are of paramount importance to many journalists, they vary enough that summarizing all of them in a national textbook isn't feasible. An online search will often lead to a website that summarizes the open meeting and public record laws of a particular state. The website of the Reporters Committee for Freedom of the Press (www.rcfp.org) is a good place to start. Its "Open Government Guide," available online, is searchable by state.

Most state open meeting and public record laws resemble the federal laws in some respects. In fact, many state open meeting laws were extensively revised in the late 1960s and

1970s—the era when the federal laws were enacted—and many new state laws were approved then, too. State open meeting laws typically apply to the agencies of both state and local government. Most require state boards and commissions, city councils, school boards and county governing boards to hold open meetings at regularly announced times and places. Any person is permitted to attend most of these open meetings, although some state laws have provisions authorizing public officials to remove anyone who creates a disturbance.

Virtually all state open meeting laws provide for closed or "executive" sessions. Most state laws spell out the circumstances under which these closed sessions are permitted, authorizing private meetings for matters affecting national security, personnel matters, discussions of pending lawsuits and usually various other subjects. Some states allow closed meetings for only a few reasons, while others allow them for many more.

An increasing number of state open meeting laws provide legal remedies for violations, allowing any citizen to sue the offending government body for an injunction to halt further illegal secret meetings. In addition, many state open meeting laws authorize the courts to invalidate actions taken at unlawful closed meetings, a provision the federal Government in the Sunshine Act lacks. Such provisions are important, because the possibility of having a major action overturned in court is a strong deterrent to holding secret meetings.

Another provision missing in the federal law—but present in many state open meeting laws—is criminal sanctions for knowing violations. In many states it is a misdemeanor for government officials to participate in a closed meeting if they know the subject at hand should be discussed only during an open meeting. However, criminal prosecutions remain rare because it is difficult to prove that a government body actually discussed an illegal subject behind closed doors and that the officials involved knew they were violating the law.

Nonetheless, sometimes prominent public officials are prosecuted for violating state open meeting laws. In 2003, for instance, a former president of the Florida State Senate was jailed for violating Florida's FoI law. The ex-senate president was serving as chair of the Escambia County Board of Commissioners when he was jailed for discussing redistricting with the county election supervisor by telephone while another county commissioner listened in, in violation of the law.

In some states, there is a state-level freedom of information commission that serves as a watchdog agency, enforcing the open meeting and public record laws. Other states have similar commissions, but without enforcement powers. And in others, enforcement is in the hands of the attorney general or local prosecuting attorneys. In some states—Ohio, for example—the courts can remove officials from office for violating the open meeting laws.

State Public Record Laws

Likewise, the provisions of public record laws vary widely around the country. All 50 states have laws in this area. Most state public records laws define the term "public records" broadly enough to encompass a wide variety of documents maintained by agencies of state and local government. And most such laws allow general public access to these records without requiring that the person inquiring demonstrate any special interest or "need to know."

State public record laws consistently exempt certain kinds of records from public disclosure, most often personnel records, law enforcement investigatory records and records of juvenile courts, adoptions, parole matters, etc.

Most state public record laws specifically provide for judicial review in instances where public access is denied, and about two-thirds of the states provide criminal sanctions for officials who improperly deny public access. About one-third of the states require government agencies to pay the attorneys' fees of those who successfully sue for access to public records.

In all 50 states the comprehensive public record laws supplement other provisions for public access to government records. Long before it was fashionable to enact comprehensive open records legislation, various records were open to the public under the common law, and many of these miscellaneous common law provisions for public access have also been codified. Records that were traditionally open under the common law include records of the ownership of private land, birth, marriage and death records, and various court records.

In some instances, lawmaking in this area has occurred by vote of the people. For example, the people of Washington state enacted a public record law by popular vote in 1972. California voters approved a constitutional amendment adding an "inalienable" right of privacy to Article I, Section 1 of the state constitution in 1974. In 1992, Florida voters approved a constitutional amendment creating a constitutional right of access to public records and meetings in Article I, Section 24 of the Florida Constitution. In 2002, Floridians voted three-to-one in favor of a constitutional amendment to strengthen this provision. Under the amendment, it takes a two-thirds vote of the state legislature to create new exceptions to the Florida FoI laws. In 2004, California voters approved a constitutional amendment that reaffirmed the state's open meeting and public records laws and wrote the right of public access into the state constitution. The amendment, approved by 83 percent of the voters, declared that the state's sunshine laws "shall be broadly construed" when they further "the people's right of access" and "narrowly construed" when they limit access. Almost immediately Gov. Arnold Schwarzenegger and 10 other state officials made their appointment calendars public. A 1991 California Supreme Court decision had said the governor's appointment calendar was confidential under a judicially created "deliberative process" exception to the California Public Records Act (*Times Mirror v. Superior Court*, 53 C.3d 1325).

In Florida, just before the voters strengthened the state's constitutional right of access in 2002, the state legislature created a new exception to the state's Public Records Act, exempting autopsy photographs from public disclosure. That exemption, which was called the Earnhardt Family Protection Act, was quickly passed and made retroactive when the news media sought death scene photographs of race driver Dale Earnhardt, who was killed during the 2001 Daytona 500. A Florida appeals court later upheld this change in Florida law (*Campus Communications Inc. v. Earnhardt*, 821 So.2d 388, 2002).

As on the federal level, state public record laws have had to be reconciled with privacy laws. Most states have privacy statutes that limit public access to personal information in state databases. These laws, sometimes given euphemistic titles such as "Information Practices Act," usually forbid state officials to release personal information without the individual's permission. Some of them go much further than the federal Privacy Act in sealing records that would otherwise be open under public records laws.

In 1999 the U.S. Supreme Court ruled on a case concerning access to public records under state law. In *Los Angeles Police Department v. United Reporting Publ'g Co.* (528 U.S. 32), the Court upheld a provision of the California Public Records Act forbidding the release of addresses of crime victims and persons arrested for a crime for commercial use.

The high court upheld California's right to release these addresses to non-commercial users while denying them to lawyers, insurance companies, drug counselors, driving schools and others who might use the information commercially. A provision of the California law requires law enforcement agencies to release such information to journalists, scholars and politicians, among others, while denying it to commercial users. The Court pointed out that a state is under no obligation to release such information to *anyone*, much less to *everyone*.

The Court seemed deeply divided over the rationale for this decision, although the 7-2 majority said the state law was not invalid on its face. However, it seemed to be inviting a future legal challenge based on the argument that the law is invalid as applied to companies such as United Reporting by denying them equal protection of the law.

The Supreme Court ruled on a state open records law in 2010, holding that petition signers do not have a constitutional right to keep their identities private, and state open record laws treating those signatures as public records are valid. In *Doe v. Reed* (130 S. Ct. 2811), an 8-1 majority said, "Disclosure of referendum petitions does not as a general matter violate the First Amendment." Washington passed a law that expanded the rights of registered domestic partners, include same-sex partners. A state political committee, Protect Marriage Washington, gathered petition signatures to place a referendum on the ballot challenging the domestic partnership law. Another group invoked the Washington Public Records Act (PRA) to obtain copies of the petition, which contained signers' personal information.

Chief Justice John Roberts wrote for the Court. He said that First Amendment review does apply to signatory information; that information is a political view or statement. He applied "exacting scrutiny" to the PRA challenge, which "requires a 'substantial relation' between the disclosure requirement and a 'sufficiently important' governmental interest." The state has an interest in combating election fraud and providing information to the electorate. Roberts agreed and noted that citizen participation in the verification process was clearly related to the interest. He also said that Protect Marriage Washington had not offered sufficient evidence that they would suffer harm if the information was disclosed; the organization had only offered concerns about what *might* happen. Roberts also noted that "the PRA is not a prohibition on speech, but instead a *disclosure* requirement." Thus no one is being forced not to speak by the PRA.

The lone dissenter, Justice Clarence Thomas, said that the disclosure requirement would chill citizens' willingness to participate in the political process. He also saw signatures as part of the freedom of association element of the First Amendment, which he believed was abridged here: "The loss of associational privacy that comes with disclosing referendum petitions to the general public under the PRA constitutes the same harm as to each signer of each referendum, regardless of the topic."

The Ninth Circuit in 2009 denied an attempt by same-sex marriage supporters to obtain campaign strategy documents from their opponents in the Proposition 8 trial in California, using the same notion of associational rights: "The freedom to associate with others for the common advancement of political beliefs and ideas lies at the heart of the First Amendment. Where, as here, discovery would have the practical effect of discouraging the exercise of First Amendment associational rights, the party seeking discovery must demonstrate a need for the information sufficiently compelling to outweigh the impact on those rights" (*Perry v. Schwarzenegger*, 591 F. 3d 1147). The group could not demonstrate such a need.

The Fifth Circuit, sitting *en banc*, upheld the Texas Open Meetings Act in 2010, dismissing as moot a challenge to it by two city council members. A three-judge panel of that circuit had said that the act's criminal provisions unconstitutionally chilled the First Amendment rights of city officials. The council members had been indicted by a grand jury for violating the open meetings act when they sent e-mails to a quorum of the city council discussing when to call a meeting to consider a contract. They were charged with holding an illegal closed meeting (the charge was later dropped).

The council members sued, alleging that their First Amendment rights had been chilled. The three-judge panel noted that "The First Amendment's protection of elected officials' speech is full, robust, and analogous to that afforded citizens in general" and said that the correct level of review was strict scrutiny (*Rangra v. Brown*, 566 F.3d 515). The court remanded the case back to the district court to apply strict scrutiny. The Fifth Circuit agreed to hear the case *en banc* but then dismissed it as moot, as the plaintiffs were no longer in office; one judge dissented, saying that the plaintiff could still face charges as a result of the case.

Lawsuits are filed in many states seeking public access to government officials' e-mails and text messages under state freedom of information laws. Some government officials claim they do not use e-mail in their official capacities. Others say they delete all e-mails daily or weekly and insist that there are no archived backup copies on their government-sponsored servers. In many states government officials' e-mail messages, like their "snail-mail" correspondence, are public records unless the subject matter falls within a specific exemption.

■ ACCESS TO OTHER PLACES AND PROCEEDINGS

Having a strong public records or open meeting statute solves some of a journalist's information-gathering problems, but in a number of circumstances these laws are of little help. For instance, public records laws rarely govern the release of court records, and open meeting laws do not guarantee access to either the courts or the scene of a news event. These laws are of little value when a journalist needs to cross police lines to reach the scene of a disaster. Nor are they of any assistance when a journalist wishes to cover a controversial criminal trial or visit a prison where inmates are allegedly mistreated.

In the absence of a statutory law assuring journalists access to these places and proceedings, is there any constitutional right of access to the news? In several cases involving access to prisons, the U.S. Supreme Court has said there is no such right.

The high court decided two such cases, *Saxbe v. Washington Post* (417 U.S. 843) and *Pell v. Procunier* (417 U.S. 817), the same day in 1974. The court said prison rules against interviewing individual prison inmates were not a violation of the First Amendment. The *Pell* case arose in California when a policy that gave journalists freedom to interview specific prisoners was eliminated. That happened after an escape attempt in which several persons were killed. Thereafter, the media were only allowed to interview inmates selected more or less at random, not the inmates they wished to interview. Prison officials contended that media interviews had made celebrities of certain prisoners and helped provoke the escape attempt. The *Saxbe* case challenged federal rules that prohibited media interviews with inmates.

The Supreme Court said these rules do not violate the constitutional rights of journalists since journalists have no special right of access to prisons. The court said neither journalists nor ordinary citizens have a right to freely visit prisons and interview inmates.

However, lower federal courts in California tried to avoid following this precedent, and the result was another Supreme Court ruling on prison access in 1978, *Houchins v. KQED* (438 U.S. 1). In that case, television journalists wanted to visit a portion of a jail where an inmate had committed suicide, a place where a psychiatrist said conditions were so bad that inmates could suffer psychological damage. Jail authorities denied access to the reporters and they sued, contending that prison conditions were a matter of legitimate public concern. A federal district court agreed, ordering authorities to let journalists see and photograph the controversial area of the jail. In the meantime, public tours of the jail had been initiated, but they did not include that area.

The Ninth Circuit affirmed the decision, but the Court reversed. Writing for the majority, Chief Justice Warren Burger reiterated the Court's view that journalists have no constitutional right of access to prisons. He acknowledged that prison conditions are a matter of public concern, but he said, in effect, that the subject is none of the media's business: "The media are not a substitute for or an adjunct of government, and like the courts, they are ill-equipped to deal with the problems of prison administration." Burger said that if journalists wanted to find out about prison conditions, they should interview former inmates, prisoners' lawyers, prison visitors and public officials. In short, he said, the press has no constitutional right of access to places not accessible to the general public.

The *Houchins* decision was alarming enough, but a year later the Supreme Court handed down *Gannett v. DePasquale* (discussed in Chapter Seven), allowing even pretrial courtroom proceedings to be closed to the press and public. However, during the 1980s the Court backed away from these denials of First Amendment protection for newsgathering activities. As noted in Chapter Seven, in *Richmond Newspapers v. Virginia* (the landmark 1980 decision holding that closed trials are not ordinarily permitted by the Constitution), the majority opinion included language suggesting that the Court recognized a First Amendment right to gather news. In a concurring opinion in the *Richmond Newspapers* case, Justice John Paul Stevens put it strongly: "Until today the court has accorded virtually absolute protection to the dissemination of ideas, but never before has it squarely held that the acquisition of newsworthy matter is entitled to any constitutional protection whatsoever."

Many journalists saw *Richmond Newspapers v. Virginia* as a great victory for the right to gather the news. However, the majority opinion was somewhat less enthusiastic on this point than Justice Stevens' concurring opinion, and subsequent court decisions have not extended the concept very far beyond its original application (access to courtrooms).

In the 2000s, many of these issues were debated again in connection with attempts by journalists to cover executions, including preliminary steps such as preparing an inmate for a lethal injection. As more and more states resumed capital punishment, this controversy grew—and ended up in court. A battle over the right of the news media to witness executions in California led to a series of federal court decisions that initially restricted access and then granted the media greater rights.

In 1998, the Ninth Circuit upheld a prison warden's restrictions on the viewing of executions in California. Under these restrictions, journalists did not get to see anything more than the inmate on a gurney, already sedated and perhaps unconscious, in the final moments before the official pronouncement of death. The court ruled that journalists have no special right to view an execution, and that these restrictions were reasonable. The court did suggest that there may be a First Amendment right, although a "severely limited" one, to witness capital punishment and ordered a lower court to reconsider whether the authorities' security concerns justified excluding the media (*California First Amendment Coalition v. Calderon*, 138 F.3d 1298). Then a federal judge ruled in 2001 that California prison authorities had not justified their refusal to allow the media to view the entire process.

The state again appealed, and this time the Ninth Circuit upheld the right of witnesses at California executions to observe the full process. In *California First Amendment Coalition v. Woodford* (299 F.3d 868, 2002), the court rejected the contention of prison authorities that witnesses should not be allowed to see the guards or medical technicians prepare the inmate for the lethal injection to protect the safety of the guards and technicians. If the guards and technicians were observed and identified by witnesses, they might face threats or acts of violence, prison officials contended. The court said this was an exaggerated response to prison safety concerns, noting that the anonymity of guards and technicians could be protected by having them wear surgical masks.

The Ninth Circuit scolded Idaho for failing to bring its execution rules into line in 2012 in *AP v. Otter* (2012 U.S. App. LEXIS 11746). Saying that the state "has had ample opportunity for the past decade to adopt an execution procedure that reflects this settled law," the court rejected all arguments the state offered to override the First Amendment presumption for the media to view executions in their entirety.

But the *en banc* Seventh Circuit upheld a ban on death row interviews requested by *prisoners* in *Hammer v. Ashcroft* (570 F.3d 798). Based on *Pell,* Judge Frank Easterbrook said that "the Bureau of Prisons could enforce a system-wide rule against personal or video interviews between prisoners and reporters"—even when, as in this case, it is the prisoner requesting the interview, not a member of the media. Dissenters claimed that the majority "glosses over facts regarding the application of the relevant policies, and concludes with the astonishing proposition that the government may limit a prisoner's access to the media based on its distaste for the anticipated content of the prisoner's speech."

Another access problem involves journalists' rights to cross police and fire lines to reach the scene of an accident or natural disaster. In virtually all states, journalists are afforded at least some special privileges of this kind, but they are usually treated as privileges, not rights. They can be denied by authorities. However, when law enforcement authorities grant access to some favored journalists while denying it to others, another problem arises. May authorities play favorites among journalists without violating the First Amendment?

In a case involving access to police press passes, the California Supreme Court once allowed such favoritism. The *Los Angeles Free Press,* an "underground" newspaper with a paid circulation of nearly 100,000 at the time, sought the same press pass privileges as were routinely granted to other newspapers and was turned down by local police, and that denial was upheld by the state high court in a 1970 decision, *Los Angeles Free Press v. City of Los Angeles* (9 C.3d 448). In so ruling, the court accepted the contention that the *Free Press* didn't regularly cover police beat news except when it involved social issues. Thus, the police said, the *Free Press* didn't have the same need for press credentials as more conventional newspapers.

A few years later, a federal appellate court ruled on a similar question involving the granting of White House press credentials. In that case (*Sherrill v. Knight,* 569 F.2d 124), the Secret Service had denied press credentials to two "underground" newspaper reporters on the grounds that they had been convicted of crimes. Ruling in 1978, the court refused to accept the Secret Service's argument that it had complete discretion in granting or denying White House press credentials; the agency had to establish procedures for granting press passes. Reporters must be told the reason for any denial and given an opportunity to reply.

Thus, these cases suggest that the police may grant information-gathering privileges to some journalists and not to others, but only if there are defensible guidelines to govern the awarding of these privileges. The decision cannot be arbitrary.

Access to Judicial Proceedings

Another problem of access to information has involved the nation's judiciary. As Chapter Seven indicates, there was a nationwide trend toward closed preliminary courtroom proceedings immediately after the Supreme Court's *Gannett v. DePasquale* decision.

For a time, preliminary hearings were routinely closed in many states when a judge felt that prejudicial publicity would result from an open hearing. Similarly, pretrial hearings on motions to suppress evidence were often closed, again to prevent publicity about evidence that may never be presented to a jury. However, since the Supreme Court's decision in the *Richmond Newspapers v. Virginia* case and several others that followed it, courtroom closures have become much less common—and less of a problem for journalists. The problem of closed courtrooms is discussed in Chapter Seven.

Another problem for journalists is access to *grand jury* proceedings. Grand juries are bodies that hear evidence and decide whether to charge persons with a crime. All major federal criminal prosecutions begin with a grand jury indictment, and many politically sensitive—and newsworthy—state cases are initiated this way. The Fifth Amendment to the U.S. Constitution requires grand jury indictments in major federal cases but not state cases.

Grand jury proceedings are almost always closed, in part to keep suspects from learning what is happening and fleeing before they can be charged and arrested. Grand jury transcripts (i.e., the official record of the grand jury proceeding) are also closed in most states, although some states make transcripts public after all of those charged with crimes are actually arrested. If no one is charged with a crime, the grand jury transcript remains sealed in most cases. And even in states that normally allow public access to the transcripts after all of those charged are arrested, courts may order the transcript sealed in newsworthy cases, such as those involving wrongdoing by public officials or celebrities.

If a grand jury transcript is sealed, there is little a journalist can do to learn its contents, aside from engaging in such investigative reporting techniques as inquiring of persons who were present at the closed proceedings. Judges sometimes object to that kind of newsgathering, but what grand juries do is often newsworthy.

Other records kept by the judiciary are usually open under an old common law tradition, but there are important exceptions. Much news can be gleaned from the filings that occur in both civil and criminal lawsuits. The complaints and responses filed by those involved in lawsuits are usually public, and they may reveal newsworthy details about individuals' and businesses' plans, finances and past deeds (or misdeeds). One thing to remember about these documents is that they may not be protected by the qualified privilege libel defense until they are acted upon by a judge; reporters must be especially careful about reporting potentially libelous information contained in newly filed court records.

Some court records that involve personal matters are sealed in many states. For instance, probation department reports that recommend either jail terms or probation for persons convicted of crimes may be kept secret because they contain very personal information.

In addition, certain entire categories of court information may be off limits to reporters. For example, juvenile court proceedings are almost always closed, and the records that result are usually confidential. However, the Ohio Supreme Court ruled in 2006 that judges have to hold a hearing and make findings of fact before closing even juvenile court proceedings (*State ex rel. Plain Dealer v. Floyd,* 855 N.E.2d 35). Some states also have laws requiring the confidentiality of proceedings and records involving rape victims.

Access to Private Organizations and Property

Everything we have discussed so far in this chapter involves access to government information. However, many newsworthy things happen in private business enterprises. For instance, when a corporation decides to open or close a plant, the economy of an entire city can be drastically altered. What right of access, if any, does a reporter have to investigate?

Unfortunately, the answer is often "none." Private businesses need not admit reporters to their policy-making board meetings, and private business records are rarely open for public inspection. However, there are ways private corporate information can be researched.

Perhaps most important, almost all corporations whose stock is publicly traded are subject to very specific disclosure requirements under federal securities laws. The federal Securities and Exchange Commission is responsible for enforcing two important Depression-era laws that require honesty and openness in the release of corporate information. These laws, the Securities Act of 1933 and the Securities Exchange Act of 1934, were passed to correct some of the abuses that led to the stock market collapse in 1929. The corporate takeover battles of the 1980s led to demands that these laws be made even stronger.

The Securities Act requires most corporations to file detailed reports on their management and business prospects with the SEC before they may offer their stock for public sale. The Securities Exchange Act requires publicly traded corporations to continue providing current information on their business and financial conditions even when they are not issuing new stock. A publicly held company cannot conceal either good news or bad news to defraud the investing public. Nor may a corporation's officers use what the securities laws call "insider information" to profit at the expense of unwary investors. For instance, when an oil company discovers a promising new field, its executives cannot quietly buy up a lot of stock at low prices before they publicly announce the discovery. And when a company is the target of a takeover bid (which often causes the value of its stock to increase), that fact must be disclosed in a timely manner.

As a result of these laws and the SEC's traditionally vigorous enforcement, major corporations must disclose a great deal of corporate information to the public. The 1934 Securities Exchange Act is no freedom of information law, but at least it does provide the press and public with more information about corporate doings than might otherwise be available. In compliance with these laws, major corporations provide a steady stream of news releases that are supposed to be frank and forthright in describing the company's business prospects.

When it comes to businesses that are operated as purely private entities (such as sole proprietorships, partnerships and non-publicly traded corporations), there are few legal requirements for the public release of information. Such companies may or may not adhere to an enlightened information policy on a voluntary basis.

However, even the smallest and most secrecy-prone private firm has to deal with federal, state and local governments, and its government filings can provide valuable information. The federal FOIA and virtually all state public records laws exempt trade secrets from disclosure, but private businesses must file a variety of other documents that an inquiring reporter may be able to see and copy. For instance, often a private land developer will file detailed reports and plans to win local approval for a new construction project, generating public records that an alert reporter can use to learn many details about what would otherwise be a hush-hush deal. In addition, when a private company is involved in litigation, it must often disclose information in court records that it would never otherwise release.

Another problem for journalists is the need to go onto private property to cover the news. When a disaster occurs on private property, for instance, journalists routinely go to the scene of the event along with law enforcement, fire and other emergency personnel. However, journalists have to be aware that they may be sued for trespassing or invasion of privacy for doing so. When there is no event as clearly newsworthy as a major disaster, the potential liability of reporters who trespass to get a story may be even greater. The growth of "tabloid television" aggravated these legal problems, which are discussed in Chapter Five.

■ PRACTICAL SUGGESTIONS FOR MEDIA PROFESSIONALS

The procedures for using the federal FOIA were discussed earlier, and the procedures under state public records laws are generally similar, but how does one gain access to a government meeting that is closed when it shouldn't be? In fact, how do you know for sure what is really happening behind closed doors?

The first step is to be absolutely sure what your rights are under the applicable open meeting law. Many journalists carry a copy of their state's open meeting and public records laws with them whenever they are on an assignment. When an agency you are covering goes into a closed session, insist on learning the specific legal basis for the closure. Make it clear that you understand the open meeting law too—and are prepared to assert your rights.

If a public agency still insists on going into a closed session when you doubt its legality, you have a dilemma. You should make it known that your employer is prepared to challenge any unlawful closed meeting in court, if in fact your employer will back you. If not, you have to decide if you are prepared to go it alone. Many state laws (and the federal Government in the Sunshine Act) provide for the government to pay your attorney's fees if you win, but if you lose, you may be out a lot of money. Moreover, you will probably have to spend a lot of money long before a court will award you any reimbursement of your attorney's fees.

There is, of course, a second problem: reporting what happens in a closed meeting. In many states and under the federal law, government bodies are required to keep either detailed minutes or a transcript of closed proceedings. Find out what the requirements are in your state, and make it clear you want to see the transcript or minutes at the earliest possible time. Failing that, many journalists simply wait out the closed meeting and interview some of the participants, perhaps double-checking by separately interviewing others who attended the meeting. And there are always whistleblowers, often with their own private agendas—but they can nevertheless provide useful information.

Today whistleblowing has become a global passion, thanks to websites like WikiLeaks, which provides a home for thousands of leaked government and corporate documents while protecting the anonymity of the sources. For a time in 2008, a federal judge issued an order shutting down WikiLeaks at the request of a Swiss bank—an unprecedented prior restraint. Later the judge recognized the First Amendment issues he had raised and set aside the order. Meanwhile, the order caused more people to view documents that had been little noticed on WikiLeaks when they appeared on "mirror" sites around the world. In 2011, after several large releases of government information on WikiLeaks, Congress and other agencies sent out memos to remind government workers that the information is still classified, even if it is public, that it should not be accessed by those without appropriate clearance.

■ AN OVERVIEW OF MAJOR ISSUES

Secrecy is an inherent part of the management style of so many government officials that no experienced journalist really expects the battle for freedom of information to end—ever. Although America has had federal and state FoI laws in effect for several decades, governments show no great enthusiasm for open meetings and records. Given the slightest excuse, many government agencies will close their files and lock their meeting-room doors. After Sept. 11, 2001, there was a major effort by federal officials to narrow FOIA's scope in the name of homeland security. Where should the line be drawn between national security and government openness? Should it be different due to the threat of international terrorism?

Raising even more concerns from open government advocates, the Department of Justice in 2011 had considered a revision to FOIA that would permit agencies to say records did not exist, even if they do, in response to FOIA requests that the agency wished to deny (the actual language said that the agency "will respond to the request as if the excluded records did not exist"). Bowing to public pressure and outrage from all sides of the political spectrum, the department dropped the proposed rule.

The growth of the Internet has triggered another challenge for the advocates of open government. Americans are demanding more protection for their personal information from government and corporate intrusion, but the public interest in WikiLeaks is undeniable. Is there a way to reconcile this with the need of journalists for access to information, even personal information? Should it be different when information is *online?*

A major goal of FoI advocates may be to reduce the number of exceptions to FoI laws while adding effective legal remedies for unlawful government secrecy—warding off bureaucrats' attempts to rid themselves of the onerous task of doing the public's business in public.

Like many other issues that are both legal and ethical, freedom of information is not a simple problem with simple solutions. In a democracy, the public has a right to know what government officials are doing and how they are spending taxpayers' money. The public watchdog function is one of the key roles of the press—and now of online media. All too often government misconduct is hidden in the guise of protecting national security or individual privacy—or any of a dozen other high-sounding excuses for secrecy. Nevertheless, there are times when public access to information creates troubling ethical questions.

Perhaps the media can best safeguard the public's right to know by aggressively fighting government secrecy, while at the same time exercising restraint in publishing information when the potential for private harm outweighs the potential for public good.

WHAT SHOULD I KNOW ABOUT MY STATE?	• What are my state's open meetings and records laws? • What do those laws protect, and what do they limit? • How have my state's open meetings and records laws been interpreted in state or federal courts? A great resource, noted in Chapter Seven: the Reporters Committee for Freedom of the Press' "Open Government Guide" found at http://www.rcfp.org/open-government-guide.

A SUMMARY OF FOI LAWS

SUMMARY

What Are Freedom of Information (FoI) Laws?

Taken as a group, FoI laws are state and federal statutory laws that permit public access to the documents generated by government agencies and to the meetings of government bodies. While granting general public access, virtually all such laws also contain numerous exceptions, limiting public access to meetings and records that deal with certain subjects.

What Is the Federal FOIA?

The federal FOIA is an act of Congress requiring many federal agencies to open their records for public inspection and copying. Government agencies must publish lists of their records to assist FOIA users in identifying the records they wish to see. Agencies now have 20 working days to respond to most FoI requests, but that deadline is often ignored. Information falling into any of nine specified categories is exempt from public disclosure.

How Does the Privacy Act Affect the FOIA?

Theoretically, the 1974 federal Privacy Act does not limit public access to government records. Instead, it allows an individual to inspect many of his/her own records in government data banks, and it protects personal records from misuse. However, its practical effect is to restrict access to much information about individuals that might otherwise be accessible to journalists.

What Is the Government in the Sunshine Act?

The Sunshine Act is a law requiring the governing boards of about 50 federal agencies to hold open meetings. These boards must announce their meetings in advance and must allow the public to attend unless certain confidential subject matter is being discussed.

Do the States Have FoI Laws?

All 50 states have laws requiring government agencies to hold open meetings and permitting some public access to government records. These laws generally apply to both state and local government agencies, but they usually limit or deny public access to meetings and records dealing with certain subjects, most commonly personnel matters (the hiring and firing of employees).

What Can a Citizen Do If an FoI Law Is Violated?

The federal FOIA and Sunshine Act both authorize private citizens to sue offending government agencies, with the agency required to pay a citizen's attorney fees and court costs if he/she wins the lawsuit. Many state laws have similar provisions.

10 *Obscenity and the Law*

There is no more controversial problem in First Amendment law than the conflict between free expression principles and the right of those who make or enforce the laws to set limits on sexual communications. The Supreme Court has made it clear that *legally obscene materials* are not protected by the First Amendment and may be suppressed by local, state or federal authorities. But if, on the other hand, a work is *not* obscene, it is constitutionally protected and may not be completely banned. Thus, it is essential to define obscenity—and yet that task has stymied the courts for many years.

The nation's highest court has had to intervene in this field repeatedly, sometimes reviewing specific works to decide if they are obscene on a case-by-case basis. It's an onerous and thankless task for a court whose other responsibilities are so lofty. In a moment of utter frustration, former Supreme Court Justice Potter Stewart once famously admitted he couldn't define obscenity, but added: "I know it when I see it."

Even if the Supreme Court has had trouble defining it, many people besides judges and professional pornographers need to know what is and isn't legally obscene. Print and broadcast journalists, cinematographers, photographers and advertising people, for instance, need to know the ground rules. Journalists are often accused of publishing something obscene when, in fact, the material falls nowhere near the legal definition of obscenity.

In 2006 Congress drastically increased the fines broadcasters must pay if they allow non-obscene but *indecent* words or conduct to slip into radio and television programming before 10 p.m. The Court has held that governments may not ban non-obscene material from most of the media even if it is indecent under the Federal Communications Commission's standards for *broadcasters*. But as Chapter Eleven explains, the FCC, acting under Congressional pressure, is aggressively cracking down on indecent material that would be completely legal in other media, including cable or satellite television, winning at least a partial victory at the Supreme Court in 2009—and, moreover, the Court passed up the opportunity to overturn the entire indecency regime in 2012 (discussed in Chapter Eleven).

In 1996, Congress passed the Communications Decency Act as part of the broader Telecommunications Act, banning not only obscenity but also indecent material on any part of the *Internet* accessible to minors. The Court overturned the main provisions of that law in a 1997 decision, *Reno v. ACLU* (521 U.S. 844), holding that the Internet is entitled to the same broad First Amendment protection as the print media.

The controversy about alleged indecency in cyberspace is only one part of a larger national debate over morality and alleged censorship in the arts. After several artists whose works were offensive to many won federal grants, Congress imposed restrictions on the content of works that are financially supported by the National Endowment for the Arts (NEA). Those who select grant recipients were directed to "take into consideration general standards of decency and respect for the diverse beliefs and values of the American people." NEA grant recipients were required to sign anti-obscenity pledges under this controversial 1990 legislation. The U.S. Supreme Court upheld these requirements in *National Endowment for the Arts v. Finley* (524 U.S. 569, 1998).

All 50 states have laws to control obscenity, and federal law prohibits both the importation and distribution of obscene works. In addition, federal law bans the use of minors—or adults appearing to be minors—in sexually explicit films, videos, photographs and computer-generated images. The ban on adults who appear to be minors has generated a

obscenity:
sexual material that gets no First Amendment protection.

Hicklin rule:
an early rule for determining obscenity in which isolated passages taken out of context were evaluated for their effect on the most susceptible members of society.

variable obscenity:
sexual material that is considered to be obscene on the basis of its appeal to minors, whether or not it would be obscene to adults.

heated controversy—and more lawsuits, as explained later. Federal law allows heavy fines and lengthy prison terms for violators of these laws. Also, the federal Racketeer Influenced and Corrupt Organizations Act (RICO) allows the seizure of the assets of businesses that deal in obscenity. Separate laws allow customs agents, among other federal officials, to seize and destroy obscene materials.

Many state laws make producing, performing or selling obscene works a crime and also allow their seizure. But when these state and federal laws are enforced, the result is often a conflict between individual liberty and society's purported right to dictate moral standards for everyone.

As the ultimate interpreter of the meaning of the First Amendment, the U.S. Supreme Court often must resolve these controversies over obscenity. But in the years since the Court first tried to define obscenity in 1957, its attempts to define what is—and isn't—legally obscene have sometimes caused more confusion than enlightenment. Given the difficulty of coming up with a legally sound definition of obscenity, many states and cities have looked for alternate ways to control the sale or exhibition of sexually oriented books, magazines and films. For example, many cities have attempted to zone adult businesses out of residential neighborhoods. And some communities have used nuisance laws against these businesses—with varying degrees of success.

This chapter traces the development of American obscenity law from its English and colonial roots to its current status.

■ EARLY PORNOGRAPHY BATTLES

In colonial America and Victorian England there were fervent but inconsistent efforts to eradicate literature that those in power considered obscene. As early as 1712, the Massachusetts colonial legislature passed a law that made it a crime to publish "any filthy, obscene, or profane song, pamphlet, libel or mock sermon."

Meanwhile, the English common law on obscenity was evolving through court decisions, and colonial courts and legislatures looked to the common law for guidance. The common law foreshadowed things to come in this field by failing to define obscenity and instead focusing on the alleged corruption of youth and threats to order.

By the mid-1800s, however, England and America were moving toward specific statutory laws aimed at obscene works. The Tariff Act of 1842 was the first federal law in America designed to restrict the flow of obscenity. It prohibited the "importation of all indecent and obscene prints, paintings, lithographs, engravings and transparencies." In 1857, it was expanded to include printed matter as well. The U.S. Post Office entered the field in 1865, when Congress enacted a law that made mailing obscene materials a crime.

Meanwhile, what was happening in England continued to shape American law. Lord Campbell's Act of 1857 and the first case tried under it produced a standard for obscenity that was followed in America as well as England for many years. Adopted as the Victorian period was beginning, the act prohibited obscene books and prints. It was tested in 1868 when a judge seized copies of an anti-Catholic pamphlet by a man named Henry Scott. Scott appealed to Benjamin Hicklin, recorder of London, and Hicklin ruled in Scott's favor. However, Britain's chief justice, Alexander Cockburn, reversed Hicklin's decision and ruled:

> The test of obscenity is whether the tendency of the matter charged as obscenity is to deprave and corrupt those whose minds are open to such immoral influences and into whose hands a publication of this sort may fall.

In short, Scott's work was held obscene because of how certain passages in the work might affect the most susceptible readers. And that concept came to be known as the "*Hicklin* Rule" because the case was named *Regina v. Hicklin* (L.R. 3 Q.B. 360, 1868).

The *Hicklin* Rule was enthusiastically adopted by American courts in the late 1800s and early 1900s. The *Hicklin* Rule allowed a work to be ruled obscene based on isolated passages taken out of context, and it defined obscenity in terms of its effect on the *most susceptible* members of society. As a result, all sorts of once-respected classical literature became suspect. The country was in the mood for a moral crusade.

It wasn't long until a crusader came along to meet the need. His name was Anthony Comstock, and he developed a following as he campaigned for morality. He and his supporters spent four months in 1873 lobbying Congress; the result was what came to be known as the Comstock Law, or more officially the federal Anti-Obscenity Act of 1873. This act went far beyond the 1865 law, giving the U.S. Post Office the power to banish from the mails any "obscene, lewd, lascivious, or filthy book, pamphlet, picture, paper, letter, writing, print, or other publication of an indecent character."

Conspicuously absent was any definition of obscenity; that would be left up to the people at the post office who would enforce the law. And who would that be?

None other than Anthony Comstock became the post office's special agent to ferret out obscenity and banish it from the mails. He pursued his new duties with a passion, and once boasted that he had "destroyed 160 tons of obscene literature."

Not content to bar dirty books from the mails, Comstock organized citizens groups to suppress "immoral" books even if they weren't mailed anywhere. Two of the most famous of these groups were the New York Society for the Suppression of Vice and the New England Watch and Ward Society.

These organizations cared little about the distinctions between great literature and pure pornography; anything "immoral" was fair game. Anthony Comstock and his followers made the word "Victorian" mean prudish. For 70 years, almost any sort of material depicting or referring to any kind of sex was likely to be censored.

What about the First Amendment? Apparently it never even occurred to the Victorians that freedom of the press included any protection at all for erotic expression. But somehow, both literature and human life survived—and the *Hicklin* Rule drifted out of style in the twentieth century.

■ CHANGING STANDARDS AFTER 1900

By 1920 times were changing, and so was the law. In that year a New York appellate judge ruled that a book must be evaluated as a whole rather than being banished because of isolated passages. Further, the judge said the opinions of qualified critics should be considered before a book is ruled obscene. That happened in *Halsey v. New York Society for the Suppression of Vice* (180 N.Y.S. 836).

Finally, in 1933 federal Judge John Woolsey refused to follow the most basic part of the *Hicklin* Rule, the idea that a work was to be judged by its effect on the most susceptible members of society. In reviewing James Joyce's classic work, *Ulysses*, he refused to follow the *Hicklin* Rule, under which he would have had to rule it obscene. He said a work must be judged by its effect "on a person with average sex instincts" rather than by its influence on the most corruptible members of society. Moreover, he said the work had to be judged as a whole, not by looking at isolated parts.

In 1934 the U.S. Court of Appeals upheld that decision (*One Book Entitled 'Ulysses' v. U.S.*, 72 F.2d 705). The appellate court—with Augustus and Learned Hand, two famous jurists who were cousins, in the majority—handed down a ruling that all but abolished the *Hicklin* Rule. The appellate court affirmed Judge Woolsey's view that the work should be judged as a whole and weighed by its effect on the average person.

The Landmark Roth Case

By the 1950s, many state and federal courts had abandoned the *Hicklin* Rule in favor of the more liberal one suggested in the *Ulysses* decision, but the U.S. Supreme Court had not attempted to write a definition of obscenity that would square with the First Amendment.

In 1957 the Supreme Court reviewed a series of obscenity prosecutions and finally dealt with this issue. In *Butler v. Michigan* (352 U.S. 380), the court overturned a Michigan law that prohibited the sale of any book that might incite minors to commit depraved acts or corrupt their morals. In so doing, the court said that states cannot quarantine "the general reading public against books not too rugged for grown men and women in order to shield juvenile innocence." If that were allowed, the court said, the result would be "to reduce the adult population of Michigan to reading what is only fit for children."

Thus, the Supreme Court had taken its first step toward the ultimate elimination of the *Hicklin* Rule: it had said material cannot be forbidden to adults just because it may be considered bad for children. Four months later, the Court handed down another obscenity decision, and this one has been viewed as the Court's landmark ruling in the field. The case was *Roth v. U.S.* (354 U.S. 476, 1957). Samuel Roth was convicted under federal law for mailing erotic materials and nude images that federal prosecutors alleged to be obscene. It was decided together with another case, *Alberts v. California*, in which David Alberts had been convicted of violating a California law against possessing obscene materials for sale.

The Supreme Court upheld both convictions, deciding that the laws under which they were convicted did not violate the Constitution. The Court specifically ruled that obscene materials are not protected by the First Amendment.

However, Justice William Brennan's majority opinion also adopted a definition of obscenity that some lower courts had been following in lieu of the *Hicklin* Rule. The court said that henceforth no state could ban sexually oriented materials as obscene unless they were legally obscene under this new definition. Using the new definition, a court determines

In the 1870s, Anthony Comstock began an anti-indecency crusade that encompassed not only sexual content but also birth control and abortion issues. In the early 1870s he raided Manhattan bookstores for their erotica, and in 1873 he joined the the New York Society for the Suppression of Vice.

Comstock used that position to lobby for the passage of the 1873 act for the "Suppression of Trade in, and Circulation of, Obscene Literature and Articles of Immoral Use," or the Comstock Act, which allowed for federal marshals to seize obscene materials from the mails, as well as any information about birth control. George Bernard Shaw coined the term "comstockery" to mean "moralistic censorship;" Comstock had targeted Shaw's play *Mrs. Warren's Profession* about prostitution.

In his 1883 book, *Traps for the Young*, Comstock instructed parents or anyone who has "the welfare of the rising generation at heart," to refuse to "patronize any person who exposes to public view or keeps for sale the vile and crime full illustrated papers of the day."

FIG. 48. The arrest of abortionist Ann Lohman (a.k.a. Madame Restell) by Anthony Comstock.

From the 23 February 1878 edition of the New York Illustrated Times, via Wikimedia Commons.

whether a work is obscene by asking "whether to the average person, applying contemporary community standards, the dominant theme of the material taken as a whole appeals to prurient interest."

Thus, the Supreme Court specifically disavowed the *Hicklin* test, partly because it permitted judging obscenity "by the effect of isolated passages upon the most susceptible persons." The *Hicklin* test violates the First Amendment, the court ruled. However, the courts that tried Roth and Alberts both used proper definitions of obscenity, so their convictions were affirmed. Still, *Roth* is a very important case because it officially adopted a new definition of obscenity and made it binding everywhere in America.

The *Roth* case produced the first of a series of dissenting opinions on obscenity law by Justices Hugo Black and William O. Douglas. These two jurists took an absolutist position about the First Amendment. They said the First Amendment protects even obscenity. Thus, they argued that criminal prosecutions based on the content of the materials—or the bad thoughts they allegedly inspire—should be unconstitutional.

For years these justices consistently maintained that obscenity laws are unconstitutional, a position free expression advocates heartily endorsed. However, on several occasions their absolutist stance created problems: it enabled the Court to reverse obscenity convictions but made it impossible for a majority of the justices to agree on the reason for the reversal. The result was a series of plurality decisions that left the nation unsure what the law really was.

Shortly after the *Roth* decision, the Supreme Court was called on to review a number of other cases involving sexually explicit material. Soon a trend began: the Court repeatedly overturned lower courts' determinations that various works were obscene. In 1958 and 1959 alone, the high court reversed obscenity rulings involving a collection of nudist and art student publications, a gay magazine and another magazine that included nudity. The Court also overturned a state statute prohibiting movies depicting adultery and reversed a ruling that held bookstore owners responsible for the content of all the books they offered for sale. These decisions represented a trend toward liberalism on obscenity. The justices continued to consider obscenity beyond the protection of the First Amendment, but fewer works were being adjudged obscene while more works were being given First Amendment protection.

Expanding the Roth Test

The *Roth* case was a landmark decision, and like many landmark decisions it left some questions unanswered. For instance, what is the definition of a community for "community standards"? Does it encompass a local area, or is it something larger than that? And what does it take to violate those community standards?

The Supreme Court addressed the latter issue in a 1962 decision, *Manual Enterprises v. Day* (370 U.S. 478). The case involved the Post Office's attempts to ban from the mail several magazines intended mainly for a gay audience. Although the majority opinion branded the magazines "dismally unpleasant, uncouth and tawdry," the Court said they were not obscene and thus upheld their right to use the U.S. mail. Under the federal obscenity law in force at the time, a work had to appeal to "prurient interest" and be "patently offensive" before it could be banned. The Court said these publications were not patently offensive. The Court also affirmed a position it had previously taken that mere nudity is not obscene.

That case left "community standards" undefined, but a 1964 Supreme Court decision, *Jacobellis v. Ohio* (378 U.S. 184), addressed that problem. Nico Jacobellis, a theater manager, was convicted of violating an Ohio law by showing an allegedly obscene French film, *Les Amants*. The court reversed Jacobellis' conviction, ruling the film non-obscene. It had been shown in about 100 cities, including at least two others in Ohio. Justice Brennan, writing for the Court's plurality, said the Constitution requires *national* standards on obscenity. "The federal Constitution would not permit the concept of obscenity to have a varying meaning from county to county or town to town," he said.

However, Brennan's reference to national standards attracted a strenuous protest from Chief Justice Earl Warren, who argued that local standards are precisely what was intended in *Roth*. "[C]ommunities throughout the nation are in fact diverse, and it must be remembered that, in cases such as this one, the Court is confronted with the task of reconciling conflicting rights of the diverse communities within our society and of individuals," Warren said. And it was in this case that Justice Potter Stewart made his famous quote: "I shall not today attempt further to define the kinds of material I understand to be [hard-core pornography]; and perhaps I could never succeed in intelligibly doing so. But I know it when I see it, and the motion picture involved in this case is not that."

As we shall see, Warren's view rather than Brennan's eventually prevailed, but for a decade judges assumed there should be *national* obscenity standards, with local juries obliged to follow them, no matter how much those standards differed from local sentiment.

"Fanny Hill" and "Social Value"

The constitutional law of obscenity was further expanded in 1966, when the Supreme Court ruled that a 200-year-old erotic work, *Memoirs of a Woman of Pleasure* (often called "Fanny Hill"), was not obscene. In *Memoirs v. Massachusetts* (383 U.S. 413), the Supreme Court was again unable to reach enough of a consensus for a majority opinion, but the plurality opinion authored by Justice Brennan suggested a three-part test for obscenity: the original *Roth* test, plus "patent offensiveness," and a requirement that the work be "utterly without redeeming social value."

In *Roth,* Brennan had said works that are obscene lack any "redeeming social importance," but the *Roth* decision did not specifically make the absence of "social importance" a part of the test for obscenity. However, lower courts began to consider that factor, and Brennan referred to it again in *Jacobellis.* Finally, in *Memoirs* Brennan said a liberalized version of the "redeeming social importance" concept was a constitutionally required part of the test for obscenity. He said a work could not be considered obscene if it had "social value." However, Brennan's opinion in *Memoirs* was still only a plurality opinion. Justices Black and Douglas continued to vote to overturn obscenity convictions—but on the rationale that the First Amendment protects even obscene materials.

But despite its lack of majority support on the Supreme Court, the "social value" test was very widely accepted after 1966. Like Brennan's concept of national standards, the "social value" test would eventually be abandoned by the Supreme Court, but for a time it made obscenity prosecutions extremely difficult. Proving that a work is "utterly without redeeming social value" is by no means easy. Almost any obscenity defendant could find an expert witness somewhere who would testify that the work in question has some sort of social value.

The *Memoirs* case involved what some might consider a classic bit of erotica. Written about 1749 by an Englishman named John Cleland (1709-1789), it is a first-person account of the activities of a high-class prostitute in London. The book attracted the censors of Massachusetts as early as 1821. By the 1960s, "Fanny Hill" had been translated into Braille, placed in the Library of Congress, and purchased by hundreds of other libraries. And yet, the Massachusetts attorney general tried to have it "banned in Boston" again, nearly 150 years after the first such effort. This final attempt to ban "Fanny Hill" in Boston failed, of course, when the nation's highest court ruled that the book was not legally obscene.

Alternatives to Proving Obscenity

After the *Memoirs* decision, the Supreme Court moved away from attempting to define obscenity and looked to other factors in deciding three important obscenity cases.

In *Ginzburg v. U.S.* (383 U.S. 463), the court upheld the federal obscenity conviction of a well-known pornographer, Ralph Ginzburg. In so ruling, the court avoided dealing with the question of whether the publications he was convicted of marketing were inherently obscene and instead took note of the way he promoted his works. The court said there was abundant evidence of pandering, "the business of purveying textual or graphic matter openly advertised to appeal to the erotic interest of their customers."

Ginzburg originally tried to mail his publications from Intercourse and Blue Ball, Pa., but the post offices in those small towns couldn't handle the volume, so he settled for Middlesex, N.J. The court concluded that those mailing points were selected only for the effect their names would have on his sales. Thus, the Court affirmed an obscenity conviction based on the conduct of the seller rather than the content of the works.

The next year, in *Redrup v. New York* (386 U.S. 767, 1967), the Supreme Court reversed three state obscenity convictions. In all three cases, a state court had assumed the material was "obscene in the constitutional sense," but the Court said those decisions were wrong. However, the justices could not agree on any one standard by which to judge obscenity.

As a result, the Court backed away from defining obscenity and simply listed three categories of marketing that might justify state prosecutions without any finding that the works themselves are obscene. The three were: (1) the sale of sexually titillating material to juveniles; (2) the distribution of such materials in a manner that is an assault on individual privacy because it is impossible for unwilling persons to avoid exposure to it; and (3) sales made in a "pandering" fashion.

The result of *Redrup*, apparently, was that only hard-core pornography could be banned. The court seemed to be extending constitutional protection to materials that, though possibly obscene, were neither pandered nor forced upon unwilling recipients. The impact of the *Redrup* decision is shown by the fact that it was cited as a basis for the reversal of 35 reported obscenity convictions in the next year and a half. Some of these reversals came in additional Supreme Court rulings that were decided without formal opinions, with others in decisions of lower state and federal courts.

The Supreme Court affirmed its suggestion in *Redrup* about obscenity and minors a year later in *Ginsberg v. New York* (390 U.S. 629, 1968). There, the Court upheld the conviction of Sam Ginsberg (not to be confused with Ralph Ginzburg) for violating a state law against selling to minors material defined to be obscene on the basis of its presumed effect on them. In affirming Ginsberg's conviction, the Court accepted the concept of "*variable obscenity*"—that is, "material defined to be obscene on the basis of its appeal to [minors] whether or not it would be obscene to adults." This concept is important in understanding the violent video-game law struck down by the Court in 2011 to be discussed in Chapter Eleven.

Thus, the sum effect of these three decisions is to allow obscenity prosecutions under special circumstances, even though it had become almost impossible to prove a work was legally obscene to adults.

The Warren Court's Finale

In 1969 the Supreme Court handed down the last major obscenity decision of the liberal Warren era (Chief Justice Warren retired later that year). But that last decision went a long way toward protecting the private possession of obscene matter from government scrutiny.

In *Stanley v. Georgia* (394 U.S. 557), the court overturned an obscenity conviction that resulted from a law enforcement "fishing expedition." Police searched Robert Eli Stanley's home in quest of bookmaking materials, but instead they found some possibly interesting films in a dresser drawer in his bedroom. They set up his movie projector, watched the films, and then arrested him for possessing obscene matter in violation of a Georgia law.

In the Court's majority opinion, Justice Thurgood Marshall said, "Whatever may be the justification for other statutes regulating obscenity, we do not think they reach into the privacy of one's home. If the First Amendment means anything, it means that a state has no business telling a man, sitting alone in his own house, what books he may read or what films he may watch." Marshall said, in effect, that there is a constitutional right to possess and use even obscene materials in the privacy of one's home. Also, Marshall wrote, the First Amendment protects the "right to receive information and ideas, regardless of their social worth."

However, the court warned that this ruling was not intended to abolish "*Roth* and the cases following that decision." This was a unique set of facts, and two years later the Supreme Court refused to extend *Stanley* to other situations. In the meantime, of course, Chief Justice Earl Warren had retired and the makeup of the court was shifting.

In two cases decided the same day in 1971, *U.S. v. Reidel* (402 U.S. 351) and *U.S. v. Thirty-Seven Photographs* (402 U.S. 363), the Court backed away from the *Stanley* principle. In *Reidel*, the court upheld the constitutionality of the federal obscenity law's ban on mailing obscene matter even to consenting adults, avoideding the "right to receive" concept from *Stanley*. In *Thirty-Seven Photographs*, the Court said customs officials could still seize obscene materials from a returning traveler's luggage, even if they were intended for private use.

Two years later, in *U.S. v. Twelve 200-foot Reels of Super 8mm Film* (413 U.S. 123, 1973), the Supreme Court was even more emphatic in saying the First Amendment does not give a private individual any right to bring allegedly obscene materials back from abroad. Once a person makes it home with his obscene materials he is safe, but if officials catch him en route, it is a different matter.

These decisions were widely criticized as inconsistent with the language of *Stanley*. The *Stanley* decision was only *distinguished* and not reversed, but it was obvious by 1973 that the Supreme Court's view of obscenity was changing. Richard Nixon had by then appointed four new justices to the Supreme Court, and he made it clear that one of the things he was looking for was justices who would crack down on pornography. A new and more conservative majority on obscenity matters was coalescing.

■ SETTING A NEW STANDARD

The new Supreme Court majority had an opportunity to make its own statement on obscenity law in 1973, and the result was a new landmark decision that revised much of what the Warren court had done, *Miller v. California* (413 U.S. 15). The four Nixon appointees and Justice Byron White made a five-justice majority, and Justice Brennan, long the author of important majority and plurality opinions on obscenity, began writing dissents.

In *Miller* and four other cases decided at the same time, the court revised the *Roth-Memoirs* test, abandoning the "redeeming social value" concept. The new majority also disavowed the idea of requiring nationally uniform "community standards," thereby freeing each state to adopt standards that might differ from those in other states—or even from one community to the next within a state. The *Miller* case arose when Marvin Miller conducted a mass mail campaign to sell "adult" material. Five of his brochures were sent to a Newport Beach, Calif., restaurant, and the recipients complained to police. Miller was convicted of violating California obscenity law and appealed to the U.S. Supreme Court.

The Court took the occasion to write a specific new test for obscenity. The new test said a work is obscene if:

1. An average person, applying contemporary community standards, would find that the work, taken as a whole, appeals to the *prurient interest*;
2. The work depicts or describes, in a *patently offensive* way, sexual conduct, and the applicable state law specifically defines what depictions or descriptions are prohibited; and
3. The work, taken as a whole, lacks *serious literary, artistic, political or scientific value*.

Thus, the Court reaffirmed the first two parts of the test set forth in *Memoirs*, although the community standards could now be local. Also, the term "patently offensive" would have to be defined in statutory law. However, the third part of the *Memoirs* test, the "redeeming social value" concept, was abandoned in favor of "serious literary, artistic, political or scientific value," something slightly easier to prove in a criminal proceeding.

It was still only a 5-4 decision, but the *Miller* decision marked the first time since 1957 that a majority of the Supreme Court had been able to agree on "concrete guidelines to isolate 'hard core' pornography from expression protected by the First Amendment."

In abandoning national standards, Chief Justice Warren Burger emphasized the diversity of the communities of America. "It is neither realistic nor constitutionally necessary to read the First Amendment as requiring that the people of Maine or Mississippi accept public depiction of conduct found tolerable in Las Vegas, or New York City," Burger said. One of the Court's goals in allowing the states to adopt local standards, certainly, was to reduce the workload of the federal courts. The Court had been asked to review hundreds of obscenity cases, and the justices felt obliged to accept far more of these cases than they would have preferred. But if the Court was seeking to get out of the obscenity business, it failed. In the years after *Miller,* the high court had to accept a number of additional obscenity cases.

Forum Shopping and Objective Standards

The Supreme Court answered another important question about the *Miller* decision some years later in *Pope v. Illinois* (481 U.S. 497, 1987). In this case the high court clarified the way the three-part *Miller* test must be applied in state obscenity prosecutions.

The *Pope* case involved a challenge to the validity of an Illinois obscenity conviction in which all three parts of the *Miller* test were measured against prevailing community standards. Although *Miller* had said either statewide or local community standards could be used to determine whether a given work was obscene, that was only one part of the test. An Illinois court used subjective community standards to determine all three parts, including the question of whether the work had serious value.

The Supreme Court held that the measurement of "serious ...value" was to be based on *objective standards.* The court said a *"reasonable man"* test should be used to determine whether a literary work has serious value. Expert witnesses could be summoned to testify as to the serious literary, artistic, political or scientific value, if any, of a work.

Writing for the Court, Justice Byron White said, "The proper inquiry is not whether an ordinary member of any given community would find literary, artistic, political, or scientific value in allegedly obscene material, but whether a reasonable person would find such value in the material taken as a whole." This hardly represented a major change in obscenity law: an objective standard is usually employed to determine whether questionable works have serious value. However, in this case the Court made it clear that the use of such a standard is required by the First Amendment. Without it, local communities could declare important literary works to be obscene by citing their own standards for seriousness. The result could be acts of censorship that would abridge First Amendment freedoms.

In so ruling, the Supreme Court was responding to its own experience with situations in which local juries did apply parochial standards in obscenity cases and rule a serious literary work to be obscene, forcing the appellate courts to intervene. That is precisely what happened in *Jenkins v. Georgia* (418 U.S. 153, 1974). A jury convicted Billy Jenkins, a theater manager, of violating the Georgia obscenity statute by showing an Academy Award-nominated R-rated film, *Carnal Knowledge.* The film had occasional scenes of nudity and non-explicit scenes suggesting that sexual intercourse occurred.

The case reached the Supreme Court, which said the film did not depict sex in a patently offensive way and was thus not outside the protection of the First Amendment. Local juries must consider all parts of the *Miller* test, including the "patent offensiveness" factor, in determining obscenity, the Court said.

But more to the point, perhaps, was the fact that this case forced the court to hedge on its commitment to local standards. If a jury in an isolated community somewhere decides a work that is considered a serious one everywhere else violates the local standards there, isn't that exactly what the court invited in *Miller*?

In the 1974 case of *Hamling v. U.S.* (418 U.S. 87), Justice Brennan dissented when the court affirmed a federal obscenity conviction, warning, "National distributors choosing to send their products in interstate travels will be forced to cope with the community standards of every hamlet into which their goods may wander."

For those who produced or appeared in nationally distributed books or films, this problem became a very serious one. For example, Harry Reems, male star of the widely known explicit movie *Deep Throat,* was prosecuted for violating federal obscenity laws in Memphis, Tenn. The movie was not made there, and it was apparently shown there only twice (before the theater was raided by police). But Reems was caught traveling through town and criminally prosecuted—although his movie had been shown legally in hundreds of cities by then.

Aside from the problem of varying "community standards," doesn't this sort of thing also raise issues of fundamental fairness? Is a publisher or actor afforded "due process of law" when forced to defend a lawsuit hundreds or thousands of miles from where he or she lives and works, just because a copy of the allegedly obscene material made its way there?

These questions were raised repeatedly as the Justice Department launched wave after wave of criminal actions against Los Angeles-based adult video producers by obtaining grand jury indictments in Florida, Oklahoma, Pennsylvania and Texas, not in Los Angeles.

In 2006 this issue was again controversial when the Supreme Court refused to review a federal appeals court decision allowing criminal prosecution in western Pennsylvania of a Los Angeles-based adult video producer. In *U.S. v. Extreme Associates* (431 F.3d 150), the circuit court rejected the company's argument that its customers had a privacy right to download videos from its website or receive them in the mail. This continued the Bush administration's promised return to aggressive obscenity enforcement after a 10-year hiatus. The Clinton administration generally did not make obscenity enforcement a priority. But in this case, a Los Angeles company faced a criminal trial in Pennsylvania because some of its allegedly obscene adult videos were received by customers there. In 2005, a Justice Department official told the Associated Press that 40 people and businesses had been convicted in pornography cases in the first four years of George W. Bush's presidency, with 20 more cases pending. For comparison, he said there were only four such prosecutions in eight years during the Clinton administration.

Even the Clinton administration was inconsistent about prosecuting obscenity cases in faraway venues. In 1993 it said that policy was being reconsidered. However, a year later the Justice Department filed criminal charges in Memphis against a couple who lived near San Francisco because they maintained pornographic computer images on a private bulletin board system at their home in California. An undercover federal agent in Tennessee signed up for access and paid a fee to obtain a password—and then downloaded enough images to persuade a jury in Memphis to convict them on federal obscenity charges. Their convictions were upheld on appeal in *U.S. v. Thomas* (74 F.3d 701, 1996).

Although federal prosecutors still engage in forum shopping at times, the lower courts everywhere must follow the Supreme Court's instructions in *Pope v. Illinois*: they must decide the "serious... value" part of the *Miller* test on the basis of an *objective* analysis of what is and isn't serious value. That cannot be determined by local community standards alone. This is why the Eleventh Circuit overturned a federal judge's determination that 2 Live Crew's album, "As Nasty As They Wanna Be," was obscene. In *Luke Records v. Navarro* (960 F.2d 134, 2002), the court noted that the judge based his determination of community standards in South Florida on his own experience in the community. And the sheriff who was seeking to have the album declared obscene offered no expert testimony that it lacked serious literary, artistic, political or scientific value. But the defense produced several experts on music, literature and African-American culture who testified that the album did indeed have serious value. In view of that, the court ruled that the sheriff had failed to prove that the 2 Live Crew album was legally obscene.

Pornography and Minors

While the courts were wrestling with the problems of community standards, another trend has been developing in obscenity law: a nationwide crackdown on the production and distribution of films and other works depicting minors in sexually explicit roles. By the early 1980s the federal government and at least 20 states had passed laws to ban the use of minors in such roles even if the work was not legally obscene.

In 1982, the Supreme Court ruled on the constitutionality of these laws in *New York v. Ferber* (458 U.S. 747). The Court carved out an exception to the normal rules on obscenity, upholding a New York law that permitted criminal prosecutions for those who produce or sell printed matter or movies in which minors perform sex acts, without proof of obscenity.

The Court ruled that states have the right to prohibit children from appearing in sexually explicit scenes regardless of the literary merit or non-obscene nature of the work. Where such a scene is needed for literary or artistic reasons, the court said "a person over the statutory age who looked younger could be utilized." The Court gave the states a relatively free hand to regulate the use of minors in sexually explicit roles.

In 1990, the Supreme Court again allowed the states to adopt more restrictive rules for minors than for adults. In *Osborne v. Ohio* (495 U.S. 103), the court carved out an exception to the *Stanley v. Georgia* ruling (discussed earlier). *Stanley* had created a right to possess even obscene books or movies in the privacy of one's own home without government interference. In *Osborne*, the Court said Ohio could prosecute a person for the mere private possession of sexually oriented materials in his own home *if the materials involved children*.

In a controversial 6-3 ruling, the Court rejected arguments that upholding the Ohio law could open the way for laws to punish parents who possessed nude photographs of their own children. The majority held that the Ohio law was not unconstitutionally broad or vague. (The Ohio law contained an exemption allowing parents to possess photographs of their own children.) Writing for the Court, Justice Byron White said the need to control child pornography was so "compelling" that the states were free to enact laws that might be unconstitutional under other circumstances.

What about sexually explicit videos starring an actor or actress who claimed to be an adult at the time the videos were made, but who turns out to have been under age? There have been several legal battles over that issue involving actress Traci Lords, who made a number of adult videos before she was 18, using false documents to misrepresent her age. The 1977 Protection of Children Against Sexual Exploitation Act seemingly made it a federal crime to produce or distribute sexually explicit materials involving minors, regardless of whether the producer or distributor knows that a performer is under 18. However, a federal appellate court ruled in

1988 that producers of videos could present evidence that they were deceived about a performer's age in their defense (*U.S. v. U.S. District Court*, 858 F.2d 534). And in 1994, the Supreme Court reinterpreted the 1977 law and ruled that it does not permit the criminal prosecution of anyone who does not know that a person appearing in an adult video is under age (*U.S. v. X-Citement Video Inc.*, 513 U.S. 64).

Congress offered prosecutors a way around the safeguards for film and video producers in the *X-Citement Video* decision by passing the *Child Pornography Prevention Act of 1996*. In sweeping terms, this law banned not only the use of minors in sexually explicit roles (even non-obscene ones) but also images that "*appear to depict a minor engaged in sexually explicit conduct.*" The law established stiff fines and prison sentences not only for producers of films, videos, photographs or computer-generated images that appear to depict a minor engaged in sexual activity but also for persons who merely possess such a film, video or image.

The Child Pornography Prevention Act was immediately challenged in court by civil libertarians, booksellers, photographers, adult film producers and others who said it could be used to prosecute anyone who possessed a copy of many mainstream movies, including not only *Taxi Driver* but also *The Exorcist*, *Dirty Dancing*, *Animal House* or *The Last Picture Show*, among many others.

Explaining the intent of the 1996 law, Sen. Orrin Hatch, R-Utah, its primary sponsor, said that computer-generated images are virtually impossible to distinguish from photographs, often making it difficult for law enforcement authorities to act against child pornography because no minor's face is identifiable. However, he said, computer images pose the same dangers as unretouched photographs of child pornography: they can be used to seduce children into sexual activity and to encourage pedophiles to prey on children.

In 2002 the U.S. Supreme Court overturned the provision of the Child Pornography Prevention Act that banned computer-generated images and other images that only "appear to" depict a minor engaged in a sex act. Ruling in *Ashcroft v. Free Speech Coalition* (535 U.S. 234), the Court voted 6-3 to overturn that part of the law.

Justice Anthony Kennedy agreed that the Child Pornography Prevention Act was overly broad and vague. Congress had tried to justify the ban on computer simulations on the ground that while no actual children were exploited in the creation of such images, real children could be harmed because the images could feed the prurient appetites of pedophiles. But Kennedy's majority opinion upheld a lower court's conclusion that the government had failed to show a link between computer-generated images and exploitation of children. This decision does not affect provisions of the Child Pornography Prevention Act and parallel state laws banning the creation, sale or mere possession of images of real children

---

Focus on...
Definitions for porn

While it's common to use the word "pornography" for any kind of sexual content, the legal system recognizes several levels of sexual materials with different levels of protection.

Obscenity gets no protection. Obscene material is material that a jury believes appeals to the prurient interest, contains patently offensive portrayals of sex, and has no serious literary, artistic, political or scientific value.

Indecency, discussed in Chapter Eleven, is a standard only for broadcast.

Child pornography need not meet the legal test for obscenity; as long as there are minors involved, it can generally be banned.

Finally, *pornography* is a generic term for sexual content that gets First Amendment protection. Some use the term *erotica* to describe artistic sexual material as opposed to the commercialized variety.

engaging in sex acts—those laws remain intact and have been upheld by numerous state and federal courts. It doesn't even affect provisions of the federal law that ban the use of computer-morphing techniques to alter images of real children to make it appear that they are engaged in sex acts. Nor does the decision limit the power of the authorities to prosecute those who produce, sell or possess computer-generated or other images that are legally obscene. The issue here was prosecutions based on images that are not legally obscene and do not involve the use of real children as models.

In 2003, Congress approved a new law designed to get around the *Free Speech Coalition* decision and again ban computer-generated child pornography. The new law prohibited the sale of materials represented to be child pornography, allowing prosecution of those who intend others to believe that the material offered is obscene child pornography—whether it is or not. Among other provisions, it also criminalized the use of child pornography by sexual predators to entice minors to engage in sexual activity or to appear in pornographic materials. Congress, which has come to love acronyms, called the new law the PROTECT Act ("Prosecutorial Remedies & Other Tools to end the Exploitation of Children Today" Act).

In 2008, the U.S. Supreme Court upheld the major feature of the PROTECT Act—the ban on offering material purported to be child pornography. In *U.S. v. Williams* (553 U.S. 285), the 7-2 majority put dealing in child pornography beyond the protection of the First Amendment. Writing for the majority, Justice Antonin Scalia said, "Child pornography harms and debases the most defenseless of our citizens.... We hold that offers to provide or requests to obtain child pornography are categorically excluded from the First Amendment."

The case restored the conviction of a man who told an FBI agent posing as a customer that he had photos of his own four-year-old daughter engaged in sex. Agents raided his home and found child pornography—but not the photos he had described. He was convicted but a federal appeals court overturned the conviction.

Justices David Souter and Ruth Bader Ginsburg dissented. Noting that the Justice Department prosecuted over 1,200 child pornography cases in 2006, Souter said, "Perhaps I am wrong, but without some demonstration that juries have been rendering exploitation of children unpunishable, there is no excuse for cutting back on the First Amendment."

In one case, *Commonwealth of Pennsylvania v. Diodoro* (970 A.2d 1100, 2009), the fact that someone had just searched for child pornography was sufficient for a conviction. The Pennsylvania Supreme Court asked whether searching for child pornography, following links to that pornography and having child pornography images in the computer *cache* (a temporary storage area where data is stored for fast access) counts as "knowing possession or control" of child pornography under Pennsylvania law and answered that it does. Anthony Diodoro had admitted searching for child pornography but said that simply having images in his computer cache was not sufficient to say that he actually "possessed" them. The court disagreed, saying that to interpret the law in the way Diodoro suggested would be to open up a giant loophole in the state child pornography law that the legislature did not intend.

But another state supreme court disagreed. The Oregon Supreme Court said that searching did *not* count as possession in Oregon in a 2011 case, *Oregon v. Barger* (247 P.3d 309). The defendant, Barry Barger, was convicted for possession of child pornography when investigators found eight child porn images in the cache of Barger's computer. Barger argued that the Oregon law required him to "possess" and "control" the images, and a finding that they were just in a temporary cache was not enough. The state high court agreed. Saying that Barger's acts of "obtaining" and "viewing" the images did not constitute "possession" and "control" of them, the court overturned the conviction: "we conclude that the acts at issue here—navigating to a website and bringing the images that the site contains to a computer screen—are not acts that the legislature intended to criminalize." Cases like this, that turn on the meaning of words like "possess" and "view," demonstrate the difficulty courts have in determining what statutes mean when applied, or what legislatures intended them to mean when they passed them.

Anime or *manga* (Japanese video and still comics) works that portray children engaged in sexual activities have been included in the PROTECT Act's prohibitions in several jurisdictions in the late 2000s. In *U.S. v. Whorley* (550 F.3d 326, 2008), the Fourth Circuit said that the PROTECT Act applies to cartoon depictions of child pornography that are deemed to be obscene. Dwight Whorley was arrested for using a state computer to download Japanese anime cartoons depicting children in sexual situations. The court said, "It is not a required element of any offense under this section that the minor depicted actually exist" and said that PROTECT "criminalizes receipt of '*a visual depiction of any kind*, including *a drawing, cartoon,* sculpture, or painting,' that '*depicts a minor engaging in sexually explicit conduct*' and is obscene." The court declined to rehear the case *en banc*.

Manga collector Christopher Handley pled guilty in 2009 under the PROTECT Act to "possessing obscene visual representations of the sexual abuse of children" when he received sexually explicit comic books containing illustrations of child sex abuse and bestiality in the mail. None of Handley's collection portrayed real children or adults; it was all cartoon depictions. A federal district court in Iowa had struck down parts of PROTECT in 2008 (*U.S. v. Handley*, 564 F.Supp.2d 996), saying that the sections of the PROTECT Act that "do not require that the material be deemed obscene" by a jury, but instead substitute standards set by Congress, are unconstitutional. But Handley still faced charges for possession of obscene material, and he pled guilty to avoid a higher sentence. In 2010, he received a sentence of six months in jail, followed by three years of supervised release and five years of probation.

Those convicted of child pornography distribution or possession have argued in recent years that their sentences were unreasonable—particularly those requiring computer or Internet bans—with mixed results. A sampling of the dozens of such cases each year: The Second Circuit agreed that a 240-month sentence was both inappropriately determined and substantively unreasonable (*U.S. v. Dorvee*, 604 F.3d 84, 2010). The Third Circuit upheld one ban on Internet access for a man convicted of child pornography and of enticing the molestation of a child (*U.S. v. Thielemann*, 575 F.3d 265, 2009) but overturned a lifetime ban on Internet usage as "plain error" (*U.S. v. Heckman*, 592 F.3d 400, 2010). The D.C. Circuit upheld a sentencing enhancement, saying that it was correctly applied when the defendant transferred child pornography with the knowledge that it will be viewed by a minor (*U.S. v. Love*, 593 F.3d 1, 2010), but the same court overturned a 30-year ban on computer use for another defendant, sending the case back to allow for the use of computers for work (*U.S. v. Russell*, 600 F.3d 631, 2010).

The Eleventh Circuit, however, vacated and remanded for re-sentencing the 240-month sentence of a man found to have shared child pornography through the use of filesharing application LimeWire. The law provides for a penalty enhancement "if the offense involves distribution of child pornography 'for the receipt, or expectation of receipt, of a thing of value,'" and the government did not show that the man had expected "a thing of value" for the distribution (*U.S. v. Vadnais*, 667 F.3d 1206, 2012).

But what about the use of public libraries by sex offenders? In *Doe v. City of Albuquerque* (667 F.3d 1111), the Tenth Circuit rejected a ban placed on a sex offender from entering a

FIG. 49. Dolls based on Japanese anime.

Alessino, "Pinky Street," November 9, 2008 via Flickr, Creative Commons attribution license.

public library, saying that the First Amendment right to receive information was denied to the man, and the total ban on entry was overbroad. Indeed, the court said, there were less restrictive ways to implement the city's desire to ensure children's safety, including "establishing designated hours during which sex offenders are permitted to use the libraries, requiring sex offenders to check into the libraries, or designating certain areas of the libraries for use by registered sex offenders."

■ OTHER FORMS OF CENSORSHIP

Postal Censorship

From Comstock to the *Blucher* case, many federal efforts to suppress allegedly obscene materials have centered on the postal service. However, postal censorship has its limits. A notable example is the time when the Post Office tried to censor *Esquire* magazine, which was then regarded as sexually oriented—but hardly hard-core pornography. The case began in 1943 when the postmaster general refused the magazine second-class mailing privileges.

A federal appellate court reversed that postal decision, and the Supreme Court agreed. Justice William O. Douglas, writing for the Court, said, "Congress has left the postmaster general with no power to prescribe standards for the literature or the art which a mailable periodical disseminates" (*Hannegan v. Esquire*, 327 U.S. 146, 1946).

After that adverse ruling, the postal service backed away from most efforts to censor popular publications, but it was given a new role in obscenity law enforcement in 1968. At that point Congress passed the Pandering Advertisement Act (39 U.S.C. 3008), a law allowing postal patrons to demand that their names be removed from objectionable mailing lists after they receive material they consider sexually offensive. The Post Office is required to force mailers to remove names from their lists in compliance with these requests. The Supreme Court upheld that law in 1970 in *Rowan v. Post Office* (397 U.S. 728). Congress strengthened the law in 1971, allowing postal customers to have their names removed from offensive mailing lists before the first objectionable item arrives in the mail.

The U.S. Post Office has also engaged in various other forms of censorship. For example, for many years it was unlawful to mail unsolicited advertisements for contraceptive devices.

However, *Bolger v. Youngs Drug Products Corp.*, a 1983 Supreme Court decision discussed in Chapter Thirteen, overturned those regulations on First Amendment grounds.

Films, Obscenity and Censorship

Motion pictures have created censorship problems ever since the cinema emerged as a form of entertainment and art. From the early days of magic lantern shows to the modern era of adult films, citizens' groups have demanded censorship to protect public morals. For years the movies were criticized for offering irrelevant escapism—and for being too relevant. From the 1920s until the 1960s, it was common for cities and states to operate film censorship boards that engaged in prior restraint of motion pictures, something that would have been unconstitutional if applied to almost any other communications medium. That practice ended gradually, as the Supreme Court extended more First Amendment protection to motion pictures. More recently, some newspapers have refused to carry ads for movies of which they disapproved, and cities have tried to zone offensive theaters out of town.

Meanwhile, of course, films of all kinds have appealed to the millions, often while local authorities were trying to shut them down. At one point in the 1970s, more than half a million Californians had paid to see the controversial adult film *Deep Throat* in Los Angeles County, while the authorities were censoring it and seizing copies whenever it was shown in neighboring Orange County.

But censorship crusades by no means began when the modern motion picture rating system was introduced and films were first given adults-only ratings in the 1960s. Amidst a furor, Ohio authorities censored a film and then won the Supreme Court's blessing in 1915. That case (*Mutual Film Corp. v. Industrial Commission of Ohio*, 236 U.S. 230) set a precedent that stood for 37 years: movies were *not* protected by the First Amendment, the Court said.

Justice Joseph McKenna, writing for a unanimous Supreme Court, said, "The exhibition of motion pictures is a business pure and simple." Thus, movies should not be regarded as part of the press. Instead, they were mere entertainment and did not purvey ideas or public opinion. Moreover, movies had a special capacity for evil, the court said.

The *Mutual Film* decision was both a cause and the result of mediocrity in the film industry. Because early films were often unsophisticated and lacking in artistic quality, the Supreme Court had no problem dismissing them as frivolous entertainment and not a vehicle for significant ideas. But at least in part because of the Supreme Court's ruling, American films remained a frivolous form of entertainment for many years.

It was not until 1952 that the Supreme Court finally said films were a vehicle for important ideas, and it took an Italian film to make the high court change its mind. New York authorities banned a Roberto Rossellini film called *The Miracle*, in which a peasant girl encounters a stranger she believes to be the Biblical Joseph and gives birth to a child she imagines to be the Christ child. The film was initially licensed for showing in New York, but religious leaders led by Cardinal Francis Spellman launched a major protest. In the face of this pressure, the film board reversed itself and prohibited further showings, declaring the film to be "sacrilegious." That decision was appealed, and in *Burstyn v. Wilson* (343 U.S. 495), the Supreme Court said for the first time that films are "a significant medium for the communication of ideas," and afforded them First Amendment protection. The Court said *The Miracle* could not be banned, but the ruling did not preclude later censorship of other films. Unfortunately, no specific guidelines for review boards were provided, and the licensing of films continued for another two decades in many states and cities.

Thus, several more film censorship cases followed. In *Times Film Corp. v. Chicago* (365 U.S. 43, 1961) the Supreme Court upheld the constitutionality of a film prior censorship system, but in 1965 in *Freedman v. Maryland* (380 U.S. 51) the court required film censors to observe procedural safeguards in reviewing films. In the meantime, however, both the Supreme Court and lower courts considered a number of other film censorship cases, often overruling specific instances of prior restraint.

Times Film involved a challenge to Chicago's licensing system by the producer of a movie that obviously would have been granted a license: a movie version of a Mozart opera. But Times Film refused to submit the film to the licensing board and instead challenged the system. The Supreme Court upheld the city's power to license films, finding films beyond the scope of the *Near v. Minnesota* ruling on prior censorship (see Chapter Three).

However, four years later in *Freedman v. Maryland,* the Supreme Court backed away from giving *carte blanche* to film censors. The case arose from a challenge to Baltimore's censorship system, which was much like Chicago's. As in the Chicago case, the film in question (*Revenge at Daybreak*) was not sexually explicit, but it still had to be licensed.

However, this time a movie exhibitor made a more convincing case: he argued that the procedures were unfair and slow. In fact, it could take so long to get a license, he argued, that everyone who wanted to see the film would have gone somewhere else to see it before it was legal to show it in Baltimore. The Supreme Court agreed and overturned the Maryland system because it lacked adequate procedural safeguards for movie exhibitors. The court said any licensing system would be required to: (1) operate very quickly; (2) assure prompt judicial review, with any final censorship order made only by the court; and (3) place the burden of proof on the censor rather than the film exhibitor.

Maryland rewrote its licensing procedures in an effort to comply with the *Freedman* decision, and in 1974 the Supreme Court affirmed a federal court ruling upholding the new procedures (*Star v. Preller*, 419 U.S. 956). The new procedures gave the censorship board five days to grant or deny a license. Denials had to be submitted to a court for review within three days, and an appeal of a court decision allowing censorship was given top priority on the appellate calendar. Also, the licensing board had the burden of proof to show that the film was obscene. However, Maryland eventually abandoned movie censorship altogether.

From a filmmaker's point of view, it was a good riddance. Local censorship boards were notorious for banning films that were by no means legally obscene but that merely offended the moral, religious or racial sentiments of the censors.

Meanwhile, the motion picture industry was attempting to ward off government control with vigorous self-regulation. Beginning in the 1920s, the Motion Picture Association of America maintained a tough code governing movie content, and a code committee exercised censorship powers over movies. Critics attributed the irrelevance and frivolity of early American movies more to the influence of this industry body than to direct government controls. In 1968 the MPAA shifted to a more permissive approach. Rather than attempting to censor movies, the MPAA introduced a rating system that would simply advise theatergoers about the content of each movie in advance. The rating system, with its ubiquitous G, PG, PG-13, R and NC-17 ratings, has largely accomplished its objective of protecting unwilling persons from offensive material while allowing others to see more explicit movies.

This rating system, however, has raised new questions. For example, participation in the rating system is voluntary, but the ratings are sometimes used as the basis for laws regulating the video business. Some states have considered laws that would forbid renting R or NC-17 rated

FIG. 50. Jack Valenti, head of the Motion Picture Association of America from 1966 to 2004, talks to a Hollywood audience at a military concert in his honor in Beverly Hills, Calif., 2000.

Department of Defense News, image available at the DOD website, http://www. defenselink.mil/dodcmsshare/ newsstoryPhoto/2000-12/ scr_200012045b_hr.jpg.

videos to minors, and Utah banned the showing of such movies on cable television. As Chapter Eleven explains, the Utah law was eventually overturned by the Supreme Court. If laws are to be enacted that base censorship decisions on these ratings, that means the MPAA—a private entity dominated by a few large film companies—is engaging in prior restraint without any constitutional safeguards for movie producers and exhibitors, much less for the general public.

This is particularly true because an unfavorable rating (or having to release a film with no rating at all) can be a financial disaster for a movie distributor. In fact, the rating system itself was revised in 1990 to eliminate the old X rating after several high-budget movies received the X rating. In the minds of many theater-goers, an X rating meant that the film was basically an adult film with hard-core pornographic scenes. Few newspapers would even accept advertising for X-rated films.

The MPAA revised the system after such movies as *Wild Orchid* and *Henry and June* were given X ratings. The association simply eliminated the X rating altogether and replaced it with NC-17 (no children under 17 admitted). Although critics of the movie industry contended that this was nothing more than a cosmetic change, the NC-17 designation lacked the stigma of the old X rating—and most newspapers began accepting ads for some NC-17 movies. Ironically, *Wild Orchid* and several other movies of that period that had initially been given X ratings were edited to qualify for R ratings before their release in mainstream theaters. (*Henry and June* was released with an NC-17 rating and was shown in many theaters that did not normally carry X-rated fare.)

The rating system continued to draw criticism for its arbitrariness in the 2000s. In 2007, the MPAA said it would allow movie makers appealing a rating to cite examples from other movies that were given a less restrictive rating. The MPAA also said it would post the rating standards and appeal procedures on its website.

Censorship of the Internet

Starting in the late 1990s, a new issue concerning censorship and pornography gained worldwide attention: the question of censoring pornographic or indecent messages and discussions on the Internet. As noted earlier, Title V of the Telecommunications Act of 1996 (known as the *Communications Decency Act of 1996*, or CDA) prohibited not only obscenity but also "indecent" or "patently offensive" material on any part of the Internet that is accessible to minors. Transmitting such material to a site on the Internet accessible to minors was declared to be a crime punishable by a $250,000 fine and two years in prison.

Amidst a worldwide online protest of government censorship of the Internet, several lawsuits were quickly filed to challenge this law, and two federal courts barred its enforcement in mid-1996. The Supreme Court heard an immediate appeal, and in 1997 the high court ruled that the key provisions of the Communications Decency Act were unconstitutional (*Reno v. ACLU*, 521 U.S. 844).

In a decision that was unanimous in most respects, the high court declared for the first time that the Internet is entitled to the *highest* level of First Amendment protection, like newspapers and books. The extension of full First Amendment protection to the Internet—in contrast to the more limited protection available to most of the electronic media—is perhaps the greatest victory the Supreme Court has given to free expression advocates in many years. Those who challenged the Communications Decency Act included a diverse list of organizations: the American Library Association, the American Civil Liberties Union, the Electronic Frontier Foundation, newspaper publishers, book publishers, writers' groups and large corporations such as Apple and Microsoft. They had expressed concern that the law was so broad and vague that it could be used to criminalize many Internet sites and prevent the discussion of topics such as abortion, breast cancer and AIDS prevention.

The Court agreed. All nine justices voted to overturn the act's provision banning the display of patently offensive material at any site where minors could see it. Seven of the nine also voted to overturn a section prohibiting the transmission of indecent material if minors could receive it. Justice John Paul Stevens wrote for the majority, "The interest in encouraging freedom of expression in a democratic society outweighs any theoretical but unproven benefit of censorship." Stevens also noted that on the Internet "any person with a phone line can become a town crier with a voice that resonates farther than it could from any soapbox" and that "the same individual can become a pamphleteer." Therefore, there is "no basis for qualifying the level of First Amendment scrutiny that should be applied to this medium."

Concurring in part and dissenting in part, Justice Sandra Day O'Connor, joined by Chief Justice William Rehnquist, said she too found much of the law to be unconstitutionally broad and vague. But she said she would uphold the part of the law that forbids the deliberate transmission of indecent material from an adult to minors—provided all of the recipients are minors. She likened the Communications Decency Act to a law requiring a bookstore owner to stop selling sexually oriented magazines to adults if a minor walks into the store.

The Court did not comment on the provisions of the Communications Decency Act banning obscene materials. In fact, those provisions were not even challenged in the *Reno v. ACLU* case. As explained earlier, if something is legally obscene, it is not protected by the First Amendment and may be barred from all media including books, magazines and newspapers. But many things that are offensive to many people are *not* obscene in a legal sense.

What is historic about this case is that it rejected the federal government's attempt to ban *non-obscene material* from the Internet if it is indecent or patently offensive and thereby make the Internet legally equivalent to the broadcast media, not the print media.

In 1999, the Supreme Court upheld a section of the Communications Decency Act banning obscene e-mail (*ApolloMedia Corp. v. Reno*, 526 U.S. 1061). In a one-sentence order, the Supreme Court affirmed a lower court ruling that interpreted the e-mail ban to apply *only* to obscenity and not to indecency.

In *Reno v. ACLU,* the Court also noted that there are other less intrusive means of protecting children from adult material on the Internet, including filtering software that can be installed on a computer to keep children from accessing adult sites. Internet filtering software soon became the focus of a new round of legislation and lawsuits. In 2000, Congress enacted a law called the *Children's Internet Protection Act.* It directed the Federal Communications Commission to adopt new rules under which libraries and schools must install Internet filtering software to be eligible for federal aid for web access. After the FCC complied with Congress' mandate, the American Library Association and civil liberties groups joined in a lawsuit challenging this new law. They contended that it violates the First Amendment by denying students and library patrons access to many non-obscene websites, including some that aren't even adult-oriented in their content.

In a widely anticipated 2003 decision, the U.S. Supreme Court upheld the Children's Internet Protection Act, ruling that it does not violate the First Amendment for Congress to impose conditions such as Internet filtering on grants awarded to libraries and schools (*U.S. v. American Library Association,* 539 U.S. 194).

Writing for the 6-3 majority, Chief Justice William Rehnquist called the filtering requirement "a valid exercise of Congress' spending power." He said, "Congress has wide latitude to attach conditions to the receipt of federal assistance to further its policy objectives." One key to that conclusion was the fact that the law does not prevent librarians from disabling the filtering at the request of any adult. Libraries are also free to maintain separate, non-federally funded computers that don't have the software installed. Dissenting, Justice John Paul Stevens, joined by Ruth Bader Ginsburg and David Souter, said the law amounts to legislative overkill—"a statutory blunderbuss that mandates this vast amount of overblocking" of constitutionally protected material on the Internet.

But the Washington Supreme Court in 2010 said that libraries could, in accordance with the First Amendment and the state constitution, *refuse* to disable their filters or unblock sites on an adult patron's request. Several patrons complained that some sites they thought were protected were blocked by the library's filters, and the library decided that it would not unblock the sites except when they were erroneously blocked because they did not fall into a prohibited categories (like pornography or spyware). The patrons said the filtering policy was overbroad. In *Bradburn v. North Central Reg'l Library Dist.* (231 P.3d 166), the state high court disagreed: the library's policy "is a standard for making determinations about what will be included in the collection available to [library] patrons." Thus, the policy is just a part of regular library decisions about what materials it will offer as part of its collection.

Even before the Children's Internet Protection Act was passed in an attempt to mandate library filtering, Congress attempted to get around the *Reno v. ACLU* Supreme Court decision in other ways. In 1998, Congress banned sexually explicit materials at Internet sites accessible to minors by passing the Child Online Protection Act (COPA). In this law, Congress avoided the indecency concept and attempted to ban material "harmful to minors"—and only from commercial websites that are accessible to minors. But this law still had not been allowed to go into effect a decade later.

COPA was immediately challenged by a new coalition of civil libertarians and others, and they made essentially the same argument as in the challenge to the Communications Decency Act: because it is so difficult to keep minors away from any Internet site, this would force sites to engage in self-censorship, denying adults access to constitutionally protected material. The challenge led to two U.S. Supreme Court decisions. Even after the second decision in 2004, the constitutionality of COPA was still uncertain.

Immediately after COPA was enacted in 1998, a federal judge issued an injunction to prevent it from going into effect until a trial could be held on the constitutional arguments raised by those challenging the law. Then in 2001, a federal appellate court in Philadelphia upheld the injunction, declaring that with today's technology there may be no constitutional way to deny minors access to objectionable websites.

The appellate court focused on the worldwide scope of the Internet in upholding the injunction against COPA, concluding, "the standard by which (the act) gauges whether material is harmful to minors is based on identifying contemporary community standards (which) essentially requires that every web publisher subject to the statute abide by the most restrictive and conservative state's community standards in order to avoid criminal liability."

The Supreme Court reversed the appellate court in 2002 and suggested that the use of community standards on the Internet does *not* violate the First Amendment. However, the Court left the injunction against enforcing the law intact until the lower court could reconsider First Amendment questions raised by those challenging the law. In its decision, *Ashcroft v. ACLU* (*"Ashcroft I,"* 535 U.S. 564), the Court voted 8-1 to allow community standards to be used to judge websites, although several justices issued opinions expressing concern about the potential for conservative communities to censor what surfers may view elsewhere.

In 2003, the federal appeals court in Philadelphia again ruled that COPA is unconstitutional because it makes it too difficult for adults to view materials protected by the First Amendment, including nonpornographic materials. The court said the law is invalid for several reasons, including its lack of a distinction between materials inappropriate for young children and for teenagers (*ACLU v. Ashcroft*, 322 F.3d 240).

The Supreme Court ruled on COPA again in 2004 (*Ashcroft v. ACLU*, *"Ashcroft II,"* 542 U.S. 656). The Court voted 5-4 to sustain the injunction until a lower court could again reconsider and perhaps hold a trial on the constitutional issues raised.

Justice Anthony Kennedy emphasized that the use of filtering software may be a less restrictive way to achieve Congress' objective of keeping harmful materials away from minors than censoring material at its source. "There is a potential (in COPA) for extraordinary harm and a serious chill upon protected speech," he wrote. Kennedy pointed out that Congress can only restrict adult materials on U.S.-based websites, while parents can use filtering software to keep their children from accessing adult material on websites anywhere in the world.

In 2007, Judge Lowell Reed Jr. in Philadelphia ruled that COPA is unconstitutional after conducting a month-long trial. He issued a permanent injunction barring the law's enforcement. Reed said filtering software is a more effective means of keeping pornography away from children, imposing less of a burden on First Amendment freedoms. Reed also noted that since the law was enacted in 1998, new issues have arisen that are not covered by COPA, including the presence of online predators on social networking sites that are exempt because COPA targets only commercial Internet publishers.

In *ACLU v. Mukasey* (534 F.3d 181), the Third Circuit affirmed the district court's injunction against COPA, saying that the district court had correctly found that filtering software was a less restrictive means of achieving the government's goals, and in January 2009 the Supreme Court declined to hear an appeal, ending COPA's 10-year saga of litigation. It remains to be seen what the FCC will say in its findings in response to the Child Safe Viewing Act (discussed in Chapter Eleven); we may see new laws attempting to protect children by regulating online sexual content.

As discussed earlier, in 2010 it was announced that the organization that manages the Internet domain name system would allow the sale of .xxx domains. Will this make it easier for censorial activity to take place, as alleged by some critics? That remains to be seen.

Censorship by Government Grant?

As noted earlier, in 1998 the Supreme Court ruled in *National Endowment for the Arts v. Finley* that it does not violate the First Amendment for those who award government grants for the arts to consider "general standards of decency and respect for the diverse beliefs and values of the American people." The Court was ruling on a challenge to standards Congress directed the National Endowment for the Arts (NEA) to adopt in 1990. The new rules were a reaction to a public outcry over the funding of several controversial artists by the NEA. Four performance artists who were initially denied federal grants under the new standards, including New York performance artist Karen Finley, challenged the rules.

In upholding the grant criteria, the Supreme Court overturned decisions by two lower federal courts that had held the rules to be an unconstitutional form of viewpoint discrimination. Writing for the Supreme Court, Justice Sandra Day O'Connor said, "Congress has wide latitude to set spending priorities." She noted that libraries routinely choose to spend tax dollars to buy certain books while rejecting others, including those considered indecent or unsuitable for children. She said that the grant system is not unconstitutional on its face. She also emphasized that the system could be implemented in a way that would be unconstitutional viewpoint discrimination, but there was no evidence of that before the Court.

Justice Antonin Scalia concurred and said, *"Avant-garde artistes such as respondents remain entirely free to pater les bourgeois;* they are merely deprived of the additional satisfaction of having the bourgeoisie taxed to pay for it." In essence, Scalia said, of course deciding who gets government arts grants involves viewpoint discrimination. But in this context that does not violate the First Amendment.

The lone dissenter, Justice David Souter, argued that the NEA criteria inevitably involve viewpoint discrimination that violates the First Amendment because the federal government has not justified it.

As a practical matter, the decision had little effect on the arts: the four artists who challenged the rules received grants early in the litigation, and the NEA no longer gives much money to individual artists. Instead, arts-oriented groups and organizations receive most of the grant money, and they are screened by panels of experts and community representatives.

■ MUNICIPAL PORNOGRAPHY REGULATION

Given the difficulty of defining obscenity and winning criminal convictions, many local governments have attempted to control adult-oriented businesses in other ways.

Nuisance Laws

One method used by local governments is to ask a court to declare an adult-oriented business a *public nuisance.* In such a civil action, a city may be able to win a court-ordered closure by meeting a lower standard of proof than is required in criminal cases.

However, the Supreme Court placed constitutional limits on this approach in a 1980 decision, *Vance v. Universal Amusement* (445 U.S. 308). The case involved a Texas nuisance law

Focus on...
A national obscenity standard for online content?

It's the Brennan/Warren argument brought online: should obscenity standards be national or local? In 2009, the Ninth Circuit in *U.S. v. Kilbride* (584 F.3d 1240) advocated a national obscenity standard. The defendants' bulk e-mail business contained some sexual ads, leading to a federal obscenity conviction. The court affirmed the convictions but, more importantly, said that a national standard "must be applied in regulating obscene speech on the Internet, including obscenity disseminated via e-mail," agreeing with five justices in *Ashcroft v. ACLU*, the Supreme Court's 2002 case dealing with the constitutionality of the Child Online Protection Act (COPA).

FIG. 51. "Rice and Barton's Big Gaiety Spectacular Extravaganza Co.," an 1890s burlesque show.

Library of Congress, Prints and Photographs Division, [LC-USZC2-1386].

However, the Eleventh Circuit, in an unpublished (non-precedential) opinion, disagreed. In *U.S. v. Little* (38 Media L. Rep. 1289), the court said that the traditional *Miller* test was appropriate for judging the obscenity of online trailers for explicit videos—explicitly declining to follow the Ninth Circuit's lead. That court said that to the extent that *Ashcroft* advocated a national obscenity standard, those statements were *dicta* (not the official ruling of the Court). Even though the Eleventh Circuit's decision was non-precedential, some believe that this split in the circuits makes it possible that the Supreme Court will take up the question.

that was construed to authorize closing down adult movie theaters merely because they had shown obscene films in the past. It was not necessary to prove that any film currently showing was obscene. The Court said the Texas law lacked adequate procedural safeguards to protect the movie exhibitor's rights and that it posed an unconstitutional prior restraint.

But the Court ruled in 1993 that federal officials have the legal authority to shut down a chain of adult businesses and seize its assets after a few items are ruled legally obscene. The 5-4 majority held that this is a *subsequent punishment* for the crime of selling obscene matter, not an unlawful *prior restraint* in violation of the First Amendment (*Alexander v. U.S.*, 509 U.S. 544). In this case, the Court majority upheld the right of federal agents to use the Racketeer Influenced and Corrupt Organizations (RICO) Act to seize the assets of adult book and video stores once some materials are ruled legally obscene. However, in a companion case on the same day, the justices ruled that such a forfeiture of assets could be so excessive as to violate the Eighth Amendment, which forbids cruel and unusual punishments and "excessive fines" (*Austin v. U.S.*, 509 U.S. 602). Based on that ruling, the high court sent *Alexander* back to a lower court to decide whether seizing 100,000 books and videos after only seven items were ruled obscene might constitute an excessive fine.

Women's Rights and Pornography

In the 1980s several cities considered laws that would control pornography in another way—by declaring that its existence violates the civil rights of women. Such a law was adopted in Indianapolis and later ruled unconstitutional. In effect, this law gave women the right to complain of civil rights violations when material that they found offensive was offered for sale at local stores or shown in local theaters. However, the American Civil Liberties Union and other groups protested that these laws flagrantly violated the First Amendment. If material not legally obscene under the *Miller* test is censored as a result of civil rights complaints, the result would be an unconstitutional denial of free expression, they contended.

In 1986, the Indianapolis law was ruled unconstitutional by the Supreme Court. In *Hudnut v. American Booksellers Association* (475 U.S. 1001), the high court affirmed a Seventh Circuit decision without issuing an opinion. In overturning the law on First Amendment grounds, the appellate court had pointed out that the law could be used to outlaw classic literary works such as Homer's *Iliad* because they depict women as "submissive objects for conquest and domination." Such works could be banned under the law regardless of their literary, artistic or political value. "The state may not ordain preferred viewpoints in this way," the court concluded.

Zoning, Decency Laws and Adult Businesses

Communities have also attempted to control adult-oriented businesses through zoning powers and public decency laws, and they have enjoyed some success. The use of zoning to control such businesses has been encouraged by several Supreme Court decisions, starting with a 1976 case, *Young v. American Mini-Theatres* (427 U.S. 50). That case arose in Detroit, where city officials attempted to limit the number of adult-oriented businesses that could exist in a given neighborhood. The Court said this was constitutionally permissible, even if the city didn't define obscenity with great precision, since the city wasn't forbidding adult materials altogether but simply controlling the time, place and manner of their distribution.

Encouraged by that ruling, hundreds of other American cities adopted zoning restrictions on adult businesses, sometimes zoning them out of town altogether. However, in 1981 the Supreme Court made it clear that communities could not use zoning to banish adult entertainment entirely without violating the First Amendment. That ruling came in *Schad v. Mt. Ephraim* (452 U.S. 61). In that case, the Supreme Court overturned a New Jersey community's ban on live entertainment as a violation of the First Amendment. Under its zoning powers, the city attempted to outlaw nude dancing and other forms of live entertainment. Overruling the local ordinance, the Court said that mere nudity does not make entertainment obscene. The majority said the city could ban all forms of entertainment (including motion picture theaters), but that local officials could not use their zoning powers to forbid nude dancing while allowing other forms of entertainment. The Court pointed out that this case was different from the Detroit case, in which adult-oriented businesses were dispersed around town and not banned altogether.

While the *Schad* decision held that nude dancing is not necessarily obscene, and therefore does have some First Amendment protection, a decade later the Supreme Court hedged a little in another case involving nude dancing, *Barnes v. Glen Theatre* (501 U.S. 560, 1991). The *Barnes* case was a challenge to Indiana's public decency law which, like similar laws in many cities and states, prohibits nudity in public places, including private business establishments such as bars. Based on *Schad* and other court decisions, authorities in most states assumed that these laws against public nudity did not apply to performances onstage or other activities in the performing arts. However, in *Barnes*, a divided Supreme Court upheld the application of a public decency law to nude dancing in a bar, although only three justices could agree on a legal rationale for doing so.

In essence, the three justices in the Court's main opinion in the *Barnes* case said that nude dancing, while marginally an expressive activity protected by the First Amendment, could be banned in a bar or other private establishment because the limitation on expressive activity

community standards:
local customs or norms that govern what is acceptable in sexual material.

zoning laws:
laws that regulate how land can be used.

secondary effects:
harmful side effects allegedly associated with adult businesses, such as increased crime, drugs, prostitution and lower property values.

was "incidental" to the state's larger goal of banning public nudity to prevent crime, protect public morals and the like. They seemed to feel that First Amendment freedoms were not seriously impaired here because all an erotic dancer had to do to avoid violating the law was to wear "pasties" and a "G-string," as Chief Justice William Rehnquist put it.

Justice Antonin Scalia concurred, but said he thought nude dancing should be completely beyond the protection of the First Amendment. Justice David Souter, on the other hand, also concurred in the Court's decision to uphold the Indiana law, but on narrower legal grounds. Unlike the other four justices who voted to uphold the anti-nudity law, Souter seemed to be drawing a line and saying he would not support a broader ban on nudity in the visual or performing arts. And the four dissenting justices (Byron White, Thurgood Marshall, Harry Blackmun and John Paul Stevens) would have overturned the public decency law as a violation of the First Amendment.

The *Barnes* ruling was widely assailed by advocates of full First Amendment protection for the performing arts, but praised by groups that favor restrictions on what they view as obscenity or indecency in the arts. However, the case did not signal any immediate change in broader applications of obscenity law to the performing arts because five justices (Souter plus four dissenters) were unwilling to support an across-the-board ban on nudity in the arts.

The Supreme Court ruled on nude dancing in private clubs again in 2000, again upholding a government's right to ban nude dancing in private clubs. In *City of Erie v. Pap's A.M.* (529 U.S. 277), the Court overturned a Pennsylvania Supreme Court decision that an Erie, Pa. ordinance violated the First Amendment. In a 6-3 decision, the Court said that Erie did not violate the First Amendment

FIG. 52. Adult bookstore marquee on Hollywood Blvd.

Rick S. Hall, "Preview Booths," March 16, 2010 via Flickr, Creative Commons attribution license.

when it banned nude dancing at a club called "Kandyland" and required performers to wear at least "pasties" and a "G-string."

Of the six justices in the majority, four said nude dancing is expressive activity that is entitled to some First Amendment protection. However, they concluded that *"secondary effects"*—neighborhood problems associated with nude dancing establishments such as crime and illegal drug use—justified the city's requirement that performers wear minimal clothing. As in the *Barnes* decision, the plurality stopped short of ruling that all nudity in the performing arts could be banned. Instead, they said only that Erie officials had adequately justified their ban on nude dancing in private clubs by showing its ill effects on the community.

Writing for the plurality and quoting portions of an earlier Supreme Court decision, Justice Sandra Day O'Connor said that although "society's interest in protecting this type of expression is of a wholly different, and lesser, magnitude than the interest in untrammeled political debate, and few of us would march our sons or daughters off to war to preserve the citizens' right to see specific anatomical areas exhibited at establishments like Kandyland," nude dancing is nonetheless entitled to some First Amendment protection.

The Fourth Circuit upheld Virginia's alcohol licensing scheme against an overbreadth challenge by a nightclub where the dancers wear only "pasties" and "G-strings" using intermediate scrutiny. In *Imaginary Images, Inc. v. Evans* (612 F. 3d 736), the appellate court said that "Virginia's policy regarding alcohol at erotic dancing locales is about as tame as one could imagine," allowing a lot of freedom in regards to the consumption of alcohol around erotic performances. Given this existing restraint, the court said, and the fact that in this case, "the political process has not sought to push the constitutional envelope and… lawmakers have responded conscientiously to prior opinions of this and other courts," the law was constitutional.

In short, it is constitutionally permissible for a city to ban nude dancing in private clubs based on a "secondary effects" rationale, and to ban all adult businesses in residential areas or near churches and schools. However, many courts have now ruled that a city cannot use its zoning powers to force all adult-oriented businesses to get out of town. To completely banish adult businesses, local officials would have to prove that each one is engaged in producing, exhibiting or selling legally obscene works. In some states, even that isn't enough: the most local authorities can do is to have each legally obscene work banned on a case-by-case basis—a very costly and cumbersome process.

On the other hand, in 1986 the Supreme Court had reaffirmed the right of local governments to use zoning ordinances to exclude adult theaters in all but remote areas, even if the practical result is to make it impossible for any adult business to make a profit.

In *Renton v. Playtime Theatres* (475 U.S. 41), the Court ruled 7-2 that the city of Renton, Wash. could prohibit adult businesses within 1,000 feet of any park, school, church or private residence. This meant that adult businesses could only operate in one isolated and largely vacant area of the city. The Court rejected arguments by adult business owners that this zoning policy would force them to locate only in an unprofitable "industrial wasteland." The Court said that as long as some sites are available for adult businesses, cities may prevent them from locating in most neighborhoods.

Writing for the Court, Justice William Rehnquist said that sexually explicit speech does not deserve as much constitutional protection as political speech. Therefore, stringent time, place and manner restrictions on adult businesses are constitutional even when similar restrictions on other kinds of speech might be unconstitutional. In essence, the court was recognizing a "hierarchy-of-speech" theory in which sexually explicit communications are near the bottom of the list. The Court also accepted Renton officials' argument that their zoning policy was needed to prevent urban decay, despite the fact that the fear of blight was based on the experiences of other cities and not on local experience. A lower court had overturned the Renton ordinance partly because the prediction of urban decay near adult businesses was not based on local experience.

In 2009 a divided Utah Supreme Court upheld a law taxing businesses whose employees provide services while nude or only partially clothed, saying the regulation was constitutional "as a content-neutral regulation of conduct that imposes *de minimis* [minimal] burdens on protected expression" (*Bushco v. Utah State Tax Commission*, 225 P.3d 153). And in 2012 the Third Circuit upheld a law requiring creators of sexual content to keep age records on performers (*Free Speech Coalition, Inc. v. Holder*, 677 F.3d 519). The court said the regulations were content neutral and thus subject to *intermediate scrutiny* (not content based, as the plaintiffs suggested). The law, said the court, clearly "clearly advance[s] a substantial governmental interest—protecting children from sexual exploitation by pornographers." But the court did remand the law to a lower court to allow the plaintiffs to make the case that the law was not sufficiently narrowly tailored.

In 1990, the Supreme Court decided three cases on local regulation of adult businesses, declaring that cities must provide procedural safeguards for adult businesses that they seek to regulate or ban (*FW/PBS Inc. v. City of Dallas*, 493 U.S. 215). Relying heavily on the 1965 film censorship case, *Freedman v. Maryland,* the Court overturned a Dallas, Texas, ordinance because it did not strictly limit the city's censorship powers and provide for a prompt judicial review of restrictions on adult businesses. But the Court reaffirmed the principle that local governments may regulate these businesses. Local officials may use zoning laws to isolate adult businesses in out-of-the-way places. However, if adult theaters and bookstores are to be banned altogether, their materials must be ruled legally obscene. A jury must find each book, magazine or movie obscene in a legal sense and not merely pornographic or indecent.

In 2002, the Supreme Court once again addressed the use of zoning to curb adult businesses without proving that the materials they offer are obscene. Ruling in *City of Los Angeles v. Alameda Books* (535 U.S. 425), the Court upheld key portions of a Los Angeles ordinance that prohibits adult stores from providing video viewing booths as well as selling books and videotapes if the combined business (an "adult superstore") causes more problems for the neighborhood than a video store or video viewing parlor would by itself. The Court voted 5-4 to allow cities to ban the combination of the two types of business at a single location, responding to the city's argument that a concentration of adult businesses in one place can cause more crime and urban blight than a single business would, and the sale of videotapes and providing a place for customers to view the tapes are really two different businesses. In 2011 the Ninth Circuit reversed a summary judgment by a district court in favor of Alameda Books, saying that the plaintiffs had not presented "actual and convincing" evidence "casting doubt" on the city's rationale for its rule (*Alameda Books v. City of Los Angeles*, 631 F.3d 1031).

Zoning ordinances have come under attack for lacking justification and vagueness. Indiana passed an ordinance in 2003 that said that any business that derives 25 percent or more of its revenue from adult products or devotes 25 percent or more of its space or inventory to such products would be considered an adult entertainment business, subject to additional licensing and restrictions on business hours. The city relied on the secondary effects doctrine. The ordinance was overturned in 2009 in *Annex Books v. City of Indianapolis* (581 F.3d 460). Judge Frank Easterbrook, writing for the Seventh Circuit, said that the city had provided no evidence to justify the ordinance: "Indianapolis has approached this case by assuming that any empirical study of morals offenses near any kind of adult establishment in any city justifies every possible kind of legal restriction in every city. That might be so if the rational-relation test governed, for then all a court need do is ask whether a sound justification of a law may be imagined." The court remanded the case for an evidentiary hearing.

But courts differ on issues of vagueness. Berlin, Conn., passed a zoning ordinance saying that adult-oriented stores, defined as having "a substantial or significant portion of its stock in trade in Adult Books, Adult Videos or Adult Novelties or any combination thereof," could not operate within 250 yards of residential areas. The Connecticut Supreme Court upheld the ordinance in 2008. A company alleged that the "substantial or significant portion" part of the ordinance was unconstitutionally vague, and a district court agreed. The Second Circuit reversed; even though only 12 percent of the company's stock consisted of adult materials, that was "substantial" enough (*VIP of Berlin v. Town of Berlin*, 593 F.3d 179, 2010).

The Second Circuit ruled in 2010 that when courts evaluate the constitutionality of zoning ordinances regarding adult businesses, alternative sites must be evaluated both at the time the ordinance is passed and at the time it is challenged. The town of Smithtown, N.Y., created a zoning ordinance for adult businesses, and at the time it was passed, there were plenty of places for adult businesses to relocate. However, by the time of the challenge, the rules had been changed—to the dismay of TJS, operating the Oasis Gentleman's Club. The court, holding for TJS, said that "the First Amendment does not allow courts to ignore post-enactment, extralegal changes and the impact they have on the sufficiency of alternative avenues of communication" (*TJS of New York, Inc. v. Town of Smithtown*, 598 F.3d 17).

Individual dancers do not have standing to challenge injunctions against their venues, said the Sixth Circuit in 2012. A nude dancer challenged the nudity laws of her Michigan township as a civil rights violation, but the court was unmoved. In *Ludwig v. Twp. of Van Buren* (2012 U.S. App. LEXIS 12511), the court said that Crystal Ludwig, a nude dancer at Garter Belt, a strip club, could not raise a separate claim against the injunction. The court said Ludwig was bound by the injunction when she "accepted her employment-like contractual arrangement with a corporation that was bound by a permanent injunction."

■ NEW TECHNOLOGIES AND SEXUAL CONTENT

As has historically been the case, it did not take long for new technologies like cell phones and social networking sites to face legal issues concerning sexual content—particularly in their use by minors.

Sexting ("sex" plus "texting"), the practice of sending and receiving sexually explicit pictures electronically, often between cell phones, has come under legal scrutiny, raising questions of whether teens who sext are engaging in illicit child pornography. Studies on the phenomenon have put the number of teens who have sexted nude or partially nude pictures of themselves as high as one in five. As was discussed in Chapter Five, the Supreme Court said that a city's review of an employee's sexting on his government pager was permitted (*City of Ontario v. Quon*). The Court did not use the term "sexting" for Jeff Quon's activities, but it did say that some of the messages were "sexually explicit."

In one highly controversial case, a county district attorney threatened to bring felony child pornography charges against three Pennsylvania teenagers who appeared partially nude in cell phone pictures unless the girls went on probation, paid a $100 program fee and completed an education and counseling program—an option several other teens had accepted. One of the two pictures at issue showed two girls from the waist up, wearing white bras, and the other showed a girl with a towel around her waist, her breasts exposed. The girls and their parents alleged that these images were not child pornography and were protected by the First Amendment.

The Third Circuit did not address all the First Amendment implications of sexting, but it did order the district attorney not to initiate criminal charges. It added that requiring the girls to participate in an education program where they would be forced to write about why sexting was wrong and address questions about "[w]hat it means to be a girl; sexual self-respect, [and] sexual identity" would be a violation of their First Amendment rights against compelled speech (*Miller v. Mitchell*, 598 F.3d 139).

In 2010, the Massachusetts legislature added both instant and text messages, e-mail and other electronic communications to its child pornography law, two months after the highest court in the state said that the current law did not include such activities, and it was up to the legislature, not the courts, to add them (*Commonwealth v. Zubiel*, 921 N.E.2d 78).

Some states have passed or are considering legislation that would reduce the penalty for minors caught sexting, either sending or receiving, to avoid having teenagers labeled sex offenders. Utah did so in 2009, reducing the penalty to a misdemeanor for minors (it remains a felony for those over the age of 18). Also in 2009, child pornography charges were dropped against a 14-year-old New Jersey girl for posting nude pictures of herself on MySpace. The teenager agreed to probation and an education and counseling program.

But, in 2011, a federal judge in Kentucky applied the law regarding sexual exploitation against minor children to 14-year-olds involved in a sexting scandal. In a scenario that is probably all too common in junior highs and high schools, an eighth-grade girl recorded a video of herself masturbating and sent it to the cell phone of a boy she liked because he told her he would not be her friend if she didn't. Despite promises to keep it to himself, he uploaded it to a computer, and it was posted online—causing her mental anguish.

The girl sued under the federal law against sexual exploitation of children, which applies to "any person who employs, uses, persuades, induces, entices, or coerces any minor to engage in…sexually explicit conduct for the purpose of producing any visual depiction of such conduct" if it crosses state lines (which makes it a federal case). The boy moved for dismissal. The judge, denying the motion to dismiss, said that the federal law applied even to minors, as there was nothing in the text of the law to say it didn't. The judge added that it was "not surprising that no federal precedent exists for a suit against a minor under these statutes, given the relatively recent rapid emergence of 'sexting' by minors. However, prosecutors have begun to charge minors under child pornography statutes." So the girl's action could proceed against the boy. Why wasn't she charged? She claimed to have been "induced" to make and send the video, and if she was successful in that claim, she would be a victim of child pornography, not a perpetrator (*Clark v. Roccanova*, 772 F. Supp. 2d 844).

Nor can defendants always hide behind their own digital creations. In *U.S. v. Schales* (546 F.3d 965, 2008), the Ninth Circuit said that images created by taking non-pornographic pictures of local minors and using photoediting software to paste those minors' faces onto images of child pornography that he downloaded from the Internet were included in PROTECT's prohibitions, saying that "the existence of an actual minor is unnecessary."

However, some were shocked when a California appeals court found that a man did *not* engage in child pornography when he used photo-editing software "to alter pornographic pictures of women he had collected from the Internet by replacing a woman's head with [his girlfriend's daughter's] head." The daughter, only 13 years old, also got drugs and alcohol from the man. The appeals court said that the California penal code's language ("the matter depicts a person under the age of 18 years personally engaging in or simulating sexual conduct") "requires a real child to have actually engaged in or simulated the sexual conduct depicted." The decision turned on the word "personally"—the court said that because the daughter did not personally engage in or simulate the conduct, as required by the penal code, but an image of her head was merely pasted onto another body, the man's conviction was overturned (*People v. Gerber*, 196 Cal. App. 4th 368, 2011).

■ AN OVERVIEW OF MAJOR ISSUES

The overriding issue about obscenity and the First Amendment today is a very old one: who should have the right to decide what is obscene in a diverse, democratic society? The rules governing allegedly obscene matter have undergone rapid change in the last few decades, but the underlying issue is not new. We have seen the spectacle of book-burnings throughout American history. We have even seen the *same book* banned in three centuries.

Is there a movement away from tolerance for erotic expression that marked the recent past? Criminal prosecution again awaits some of those who produce, sell or display sexually oriented books, movies, music and visual images, materials that some see as art and others regard as filth. In trying to strike a balance between First Amendment freedoms and moral standards, aren't we debating the same issues today that have been debated for centuries? Has anything really changed except the technology we use for the explicit depiction of sex?

Is Congress right to see new threats to morality in the new technologies? Should the global reach of the Internet make a difference? Should content be limited to words and images that will offend no one anywhere in the world? Should freedom in all countries be limited to what is acceptable in the most morally conservative countries? Can we really have *community standards* on the Internet, as the Supreme Court has suggested? And should adults be limited to materials suitable for the children who inevitably surf the net?

What about government grants for the arts or for library computers? Is it right for the government to set standards that include a "respect for the diverse beliefs and values of the American people?" Doesn't that inevitably constitute viewpoint discrimination? Is viewpoint discrimination wrong in this context?

Although the issues of censorship and freedom are not new, the explosion of digital communications technology has given them a new currency. Will we ever reach a consensus about the appropriate limits of erotic expression, if in fact there should be limits?

WHAT SHOULD I KNOW ABOUT MY STATE?

- What are my state's obscenity laws, and how have those laws been interpreted in the courts?
- How is my community zoned? Where, if they exist, are adult businesses permitted?
- What are my state's child pornography laws, and how have they been interpreted?
- What are my state's and community's public nuisance laws?
- Does my state have any laws that attempt to regulate what children see online?

A SUMMARY OF OBSCENITY AND THE LAW

Does the First Amendment Protect Obscenity?

The Supreme Court has consistently held that the First Amendment does *not* protect materials that are legally obscene, but it does protect materials that may be indecent or offensive but not legally obscene. If a work is legally obscene, it may be censored and its producer may be punished. If not, it is protected by the First Amendment and cannot be censored.

What Was the Hicklin Rule?

For many years, obscenity in both England and the United States was defined by the *Hicklin* Rule, which looked to *a work's effect on the most susceptible members of society* to determine if it was obscene. The *Hicklin* Rule classified a work as obscene even if only isolated passages were obscene, regardless of the merit of the work as a whole. This rule was abandoned after the *Ulysses* decision, in which a federal court ruled that James Joyce's classic work, taken as a whole, was not obscene to average persons.

What Was the Roth Test?

Handed down by the Supreme Court in 1957, the *Roth* test defined obscenity as "whether to the average person, applying contemporary community standards, the dominant theme of the material taken as a whole appeals to prurient interest." First Amendment protection was thus extended to works that might have been classified as obscene in an earlier era. During the 1960s, the Court expanded on *Roth*. For a time, it appeared "community standards" were national standards (which could happen again), and a work could not be censored unless it was "patently offensive" and "*utterly* without redeeming social value."

What Was the Miller v. California Decision?

In 1973, a new conservative majority on the Supreme Court redefined obscenity, abandoning both national standards and the "social value" test. Instead, the Supreme Court said a work is legally obscene if: (1) it meets the original *Roth* test; (2) it describes sexual conduct in a "patently offensive" way; and (3) taken as a whole, it lacks serious literary, artistic, political or scientific value. The court said that local community standards could vary, although works with serious value determined by objective standards cannot be censored anywhere.

May the Distribution of Non-Obscene Erotic Works Be Restricted?

Cities may use zoning laws to restrict adult businesses to certain areas. Also, minors may be forbidden to appear in or purchase non-obscene erotic works.

11 *Regulation of Electronic Media*

The legal status of the electronic media is unique. In addition to other legal problems that confront all media, broadcasters, cable systems and satellite television providers must deal with a federal agency whose specific task is to supervise and regulate them.

Like publishers, broadcasters may be sued for libel, invasion of privacy, or copyright infringement. Likewise, they share with other media the problems of advertising regulation, antitrust law and restrictions on their access to information. However, the electronic media must also contend with direct government regulation by the *Federal Communications Commission.* A broadcaster must get a license from the FCC before going on the air and must renew it periodically. Cable systems are not formally licensed by the FCC, but they are subject to various federal laws, FCC regulations and rules imposed by the local governments that grant their franchises. In between license or franchise renewals, broadcasters, cable and satellite operators must comply with hundreds of government regulations covering everything from the content of their programming to the technical quality of their signals. The print and Internet media face no comparable rules.

Furthermore, as some broadcasters and cable operators have learned, a license or franchise renewal is by no means automatic. RKO General fought a 20-year legal battle against government sanctions that nearly forced the company to forfeit 13 radio and television licenses worth perhaps a billion dollars on the open market. In the end, RKO lost its license to operate a television station in Boston—a license worth at least $150 million at the time—and was forced to sell a number of other stations at bargain basement prices.

RKO General was accused of serious wrongdoing: the government's actions against RKO General were not exactly unprovoked. But can you imagine the government ordering Google.com, or perhaps the *Boston Globe, New York Times* and *Los Angeles Times,* to shut down forever? Although that kind of thing happens in some countries, it would be unthinkable in America. And yet, it can happen to broadcasters.

How did the federal government acquire such life-and-death power over the broadcast industry? The answer lies in the nature of the *radio spectrum.* Only a limited number of frequencies are available, and the number of stations that may transmit at one time without causing interference is also limited. The idea that this justifies government regulation of broadcasting is called the *scarcity rationale.* Early in the twentieth century Congress relied on this rationale when it decreed that the entire radio spectrum would be used to serve *the public interest, convenience and necessity.* Congress was saying that those who were chosen to use the limited space available in the radio spectrum had a special obligation to the public.

As a result, the Federal Communications Commission was established to regulate broadcasting and other non-governmental uses of the radio spectrum. Over the years, the FCC assumed broad authority over the electronic media under the scarcity rationale. However, today there are many new technologies of mass communication, and the entire philosophy of broadcast regulation—including the scarcity rationale itself—has been re-examined by the FCC, Congress and the courts.

Although cable television systems use wires rather than the airwaves to deliver programming to their subscribers, the FCC has broad jurisdiction over cable systems too. Satellite radio and TV systems use the airwaves to deliver programming to their subscribers, and cable systems use the airwaves to receive the content that they send on to subscribers. And yet cable and satellite broadcasters are exempt from some of the rules that over-the-air broadcasters find most objectionable, such as the ban on "indecency" except late at night. Why the scarcity rationale justifies heavier government regulation of broadcasters than its fee-based competitors is one of the basic questions in broadcast regulation. How the FCC acquired its regulatory powers and how it exercises them are the major topics of this chapter.

For many years, the FCC tended to believe it was fulfilling its mandate if it issued licenses and wrote ever-more-complex rules to regulate the conduct of licensees. Sometimes the FCC saw itself as a super media critic, nudging and cajoling broadcasters to offer what FCC officials considered to be better programming and better public service. In 1961, early in John F. Kennedy's presidency, the newly appointed FCC chair, Newton Minow, made his famous "Vast Wasteland" speech at a large gathering of broadcasters. At a time when more than 90 percent of all viewers were watching just three television networks (ABC, CBS and NBC), Minow said all three were doing such a shoddy job that the government would intervene if network programming didn't improve.

By the 1980s, however, the FCC was taking a very different view of its mission as a regulator. Another FCC chair, Mark Fowler, called television "a toaster with pictures," and thus not in need of much government regulation. In that era the FCC took a series of controversial steps to deregulate the broadcast and cable industries, dropping rules that Fowler called "regulatory underbrush." Instead of trying to ensure public service through government regulation, the commission began looking to marketplace forces to achieve that goal. The FCC adopted the philosophy that competition is healthy, and that more competition equals better public service. But the agency still vacillates in its positions on regulation, abandoning some deregulatory moves of the 1980s and imposing new content controls on broadcasters—raising new questions about the First Amendment rights of the broadcast media.

In 1996, Congress approved the Telecommunications Act, the most comprehensive communications legislation enacted since 1934. Congress took major steps to foster new competition among broadcasters, cable systems, telephone companies and others who offer communications services. Many provisions of this law freed the communications industries from long-standing government rules and regulations. But Congress also endorsed new government controls on broadcast content, including the widely debated (but widely ignored) V-chip system to allow viewers to exclude sexually oriented or violent programming.

All of these new developments have created new problems, not only in the United States but also in other countries as the communications business has become an increasingly global enterprise. For that reason, the international regulation of mass communications has become increasingly important in recent years.

■ BROADCAST REGULATION: A GLOBAL VIEW

Although this fact is sometimes overlooked, some of the most basic decisions concerning broadcasting are made at the international level and not by the FCC. Radio and television signals freely cross international boundaries, and broadcasters cannot operate with blatant disregard for the interference they might cause in other countries.

For this reason, many basic issues in telecommunications policy are decided on a worldwide basis. By treaty, the International Telecommunications Union (ITU), headquartered in Geneva, Switzerland, has overall responsibility for international administration of radio and television matters (www.itu.net). Its approximately 190 member nations hold conferences to

FIG. 53. National Broadcasting Co., 30 Rockefeller Plaza, New York City. Radio broadcast in studio, 1945.

Library of Congress, Prints and Photographs Division, [LC-G613-T-48380].

discuss major international issues. Recent meetings have focused on topics such as global broadband, sustainability and information security.

Allocating frequencies is often a primary function of these international conferences. No nation may simply place its radio and television stations on whatever frequencies it wishes; frequency assignment policies must be set on a global basis to avoid incompatible uses. Each country is free to decide which station transmits on a given channel in the AM, FM or television bands, for instance, but the decision about how much of the spectrum is set aside for broadcasting (as opposed to other uses) is made on an international basis.

In addition to worldwide telecommunications policy-making, there is regional coordination. For communications purposes, the world is divided into three regions. Region I encompasses Europe, Africa and the countries of the former Soviet Union. Region II includes North and South America, and Region III covers Asia and the Pacific (except for the former Soviet states). The United States regularly meets with its neighbors at Region II conferences to agree on radio and television frequencies in this hemisphere. International cooperation is vital, particularly at a time when many nations are moving into new satellite broadcasting technologies. A single satellite positioned 22,000 miles above the equator can transmit a signal powerful enough to be received in an enormous area; a satellite transmitter may have a radio "footprint" that can cover half a continent, ignoring all boundary lines. Broadcasters and other users of the radio spectrum have always battled for more turf, but today more than ever before those battles are becoming volatile international feuds.

■ THE RADIO SPECTRUM

Most of these electronic turf wars occur, of course, because of one simple fact about the radio spectrum: there are not enough channels to go around, either in the United States or abroad. Everyone wants more frequencies. The FCC has launched a major effort to modernize its

AM:
"amplitude modulation," broadcast via radio carrier wave that works by varying its amplitude, changing the strength of the transmitted signal.

FM:
"frequency modulation," broadcast via radio carrier wave that works by varying the frequency rather than the amplitude.

Hertz (Hz):
a unit of measure, named for German physicist Heinrich Hertz, which is defined as the number of cycles per second, with one Hz meaning one cycle per second; a *kiloHertz* (kHz) is 1,000 Hertz, a *megaHertz* (mHz) is 1,000 kHz, and a *gigaHertz* (gHz) is 1,000 mHz.

VHF:
"very high frequency," ranging from 30 MHz to 300 mHz, commonly used for FM radio and TV broadcast.

UHF:
"ultra high frequency," ranging between 300 mHz and 3 gHz (3,000 mHz), commonly used for two-way radio systems and cordless telephones.

spectrum allocation policies—in the hope that room can be found for more broadcasters and for more non-broadcast users of the radio spectrum. Congress passed legislation to release part of the radio spectrum that was once reserved for federal government use in an effort to make room for new communications technologies—and to bring in additional revenue through spectrum auctions.

When FCC policy makers discuss the radio spectrum, they use technical jargon. It is hard to avoid running into terms such as "Hertz," "megaHertz," "AM," "FM," "VHF," "UHF," etc.

AM means *amplitude modulation*; it was the original means by which sound was superimposed on a radio signal. *FM* means *frequency modulation*, a newer method of putting sound on a radio signal. Each method has advantages. FM generally provides better sound quality and greater immunity to static.

A *Hertz* (abbreviated Hz) is a unit of measurement, just as a foot, a mile or a pound is a unit of measurement. However, a Hertz is a measurement of frequency in the radio spectrum. Every station is assigned to transmit on a certain frequency or "channel." That frequency is measured in Hertz. One Hertz equals one electrical cycle per second. One *kiloHertz* (kHz) is 1,000 Hertz; one *megaHertz* (mHz) is 1,000 kiloHertz, or one million Hertz. The term Hertz was chosen to honor Heinrich Hertz, a German scientist whose early research proved the existence of radio waves. Thus, the term Hertz is usually capitalized.

A station's frequency, expressed in kiloHertz or megaHertz, is its home address in the radio spectrum. For example, an AM radio station might operate on 1070 kHz (which is the same as 1.07 mHz). An FM station might operate on 94.7 mHz. Only one station can transmit on each frequency in a given geographic area; if two or more stations transmit on the same frequency, interference will result and neither station can be heard by many listeners. Therefore, each radio and television station has a unique frequency on which no one else may transmit in that station's service area. If two *co-channel* stations (i.e., two stations sharing the same frequency) are placed too close together, harmful interference will result.

Different types of stations have differing service areas. AM radio signals *propagate* (travel from the transmitting antenna to listeners' receivers) differently than FM radio or television signals. VHF (very high frequency) television signals propagate differently than UHF (ultra high frequency) signals. Because the loss of even a small amount of its service area can cost a station thousands of viewers (and millions of dollars in advertising revenue), mundane technical questions such as service area designations are hotly contested.

Further complicating matters for radio stations, an AM radio broadcaster's service area may be different at night than it is in the daytime. AM radio signals propagate mainly by *groundwave* during the day. That means signals literally travel along the surface of the earth. AM stations with high-power transmitters have a reliable groundwave range of roughly 100 miles, depending on the terrain. At night, local groundwave propagation still occurs, but AM radio signals also travel by *skywave propagation.* That means some of the transmitted energy travels out toward space and is reflected back to distant points on the earth by the ionosphere (the Earth's upper atmosphere). AM radio signals also travel out toward space during the daytime, but the ionosphere absorbs most of the energy and very little is reflected back during daylight hours.

As a result of this skywave propagation, high-powered AM radio stations can sometimes be heard well at distances of 700 miles or more at night. In the early days of radio this was a tremendous advantage because it allowed persons far away from any station to hear some radio broadcasts. However, as the spectrum filled up it became a major problem; one powerful station can interfere with all others over an enormous area. The FCC requires many AM radio stations either to reduce their power or go off the air altogether at night to prevent interference to distant stations. Today there are only a few dozen high-power *clear channel* stations on the AM dial, but those that remain are still authorized to serve a large geographic area at night by skywave propagation. The skywave phenomenon also explains why a very powerful radio transmitter in Cuba can cause interference all over North America.

The radio spectrum also includes many other frequencies, each with their own unique characteristics. Above the AM radio frequencies, there is a region called the *shortwave* spectrum, which runs from about 2 to 30 megaHertz (mHz). Some shortwave frequencies are usable for worldwide skywave propagation even during the daytime. Beginning in the 1920s, they were used for international "shortwave broadcasting" as well as other commercial, government and military communications where long distances had to be spanned. Long-distance telephone services used shortwave radio in the days before microwave technology and communications satellites were developed. Even today, more than a hundred nations do international shortwave broadcasting, although many shortwave broadcasters also stream their international programming over the Internet and do podcasting. On any given day or night, an American shortwave listener can hear such stations as Radio Moscow, Radio Australia, the British Broadcasting Corporation and our own Voice of America. Some, like the BBC and VOA, operate under government rules requiring that they practice objective journalism, but others do not. Almost all of these organizations broadcast in English (and many other languages), often on several different frequencies at once to cover different parts of the world, including areas where Internet access is limited.

Above the shortwave spectrum is the VHF region, spanning 30 to 300 megaHertz. At these frequencies, there is little skywave propagation, so a broadcaster's service area extends only a little beyond the visual horizon. Stations with antennas on high towers, buildings or mountaintops achieve much better coverage than those with less favorable antenna sites. VHF television stations (channels 2-13) and FM radio stations use these frequencies.

Above the VHF portion of the radio spectrum, there is also a TV broadcasting allocation in the ultra high frequency (UHF) region, which runs from 300 to 3,000 mHz. But even in this vast amount of space, the demand for channels has exceeded the supply. For example, the frequencies from 470 to 890 megaHertz were originally set aside for UHF television channels 14 through 83. However, that tied up so much of the spectrum that other users (such as two-way police, fire and business communications) ran out of room. The FCC finally took back channels 70 through 83 and reallocated them for various two-way radio services and other uses. In some cities, the FCC also reassigned channels 14 through 20 for these

FIG. 54. U.S. Broadcast Allocation Chart, from National Telecommunications and Information Administration, U.S. Department of Commerce, October 2003.

See it in full-color and much larger at http://www. ntia.doc.gov/files/ntia/ publications/2003-allochrt. pdf.

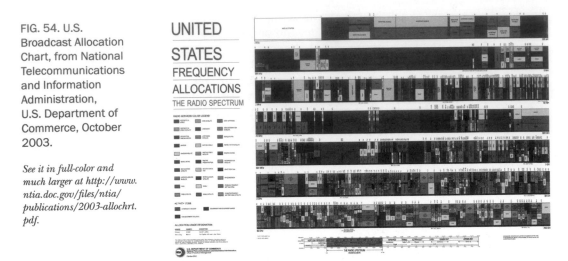

other services. In 2006, Congress passed legislation requiring broadcasters to go all-digital on Feb. 18, 2009 and relinquish channels 52 through 69 for public safety communications and for additional wireless broadband Internet services.

As we continue to go up in frequency, there is a great deal of spectrum in the microwave region (frequencies above 3,000 megaHertz). As the frequency is increased, the cost of equipment tends to go up and the reliable communication range on the Earth's surface declines. However, these frequencies are ideal for satellite and space communications as well as local, short-range wireless and cellphone communications. Satellite television takes a huge amount of the microwave spectrum. The broadcast spectrum is a limited resource, but sophisticated engineering can coax more space out of that resource. In 2008, the FCC unanimously approved rules for devices using spectrum that sits between broadcast TV channels. This unused space, about 300 545 U.S. 913 mHz to 400 mHz, is known as "white space." Because it can travel long distances and penetrate walls, it is best for wireless broadband services. The FCC called its move "a careful first step" to allow unlicensed devices in the white spaces and said it would be vigilant in protecting existing licenses from interference.

When radio broadcasting was in its infancy, the major rationale for government regulation was that there just wasn't enough room for everyone. Even though we've learned how to use hundreds of times more of the spectrum than we were using in the beginning, there still isn't enough room to accommodate everyone who would like to become an over-the-air broadcaster. And the demand for spectrum for non-broadcast services has become enormous. In recent years Congress has authorized the FCC to hold auctions to award licenses for many types of communications services. The radio spectrum, like so many of our other natural resources, is limited—and the demand greatly exceeds the supply.

■ THE BIRTH OF BROADCAST REGULATION

When the pioneers of radio were conducting their experiments at the start of the twentieth century, they had no idea they were developing a new mass communication medium. They were looking for a way to send Morse code messages from one point to another without telegraph wires.

The first serious users for radio communication (it was called "wireless" then) were the world's navies and commercial shipping lines. By the early 1900s, Europe and North America were criss-crossed with telegraph wires, so the early inventors saw only one obvious need for wireless communication: at sea.

The first major legislation governing radio in the United States, the Radio Act of 1912, recognized this reality. It did not anticipate the development of commercial radio broadcasting, but it did provide for the licensing of shipboard and shore stations, among other things.

The 1912 act was prompted in part by the sinking of the luxury liner *Titanic*. The fact that the *Titanic* had a wireless station was credited with saving hundreds of lives, but many more might have been saved had the wireless stations of that era been better organized. There was a ship much closer to the *Titanic* than the one that came to its rescue, but that ship's wireless operator was off duty when the disaster struck, so no one aboard knew what was happening. Consequently, the 1912 Act required all large ships to be equipped with wireless and to have operators on duty full time. Also, the act established qualifications for wireless operators, set technical standards for wireless stations, and reserved certain wavelengths for government use and for distress signals.

After World War I, radio broadcasting developed almost overnight and almost by accident. Westinghouse and other equipment manufacturers supported stations such as Dr. Frank Conrad's widely noted Pittsburgh station, KDKA, mainly to promote the sale of more equipment, not to establish a new mass medium of communications.

However, in 1921 and 1922 radio broadcasting suddenly caught on much as the Internet caught on in the 1990s. Hundreds of stations rushed in to fill the available space in what is now the AM broadcast band. By the mid-1920s, there were so many stations that conditions were, at best, chaotic. Interference, not all of it accidental, reached intolerable levels.

Although the 1912 Radio Act had authorized the Department of Commerce to license radio operators and stations, federal courts ruled that Secretary of Commerce Herbert Hoover had no authority to stop issuing licenses when the entire AM radio band was occupied. Nor did Hoover have the authority to tell broadcasters which frequencies to use. Some stations jumped from frequency to frequency in a frantic effort to avoid interference.

The AM broadcast band by 1926 or 1927 had layer upon layer of signals, with the louder ones covering up weaker ones and with signals suddenly disappearing and showing up elsewhere on the dial. In a move that some in the industry have regretted ever since, the nation's broadcasters demanded government action to bring order out of that chaos. For five consecutive years in the 1920s, national radio conferences were held to make these demands. Most industries dread government regulation; here was an industry *asking* for it.

Congress responded with the Radio Act of 1927, which set up a separate regulatory body for radio communications, the Federal Radio Commission. The FRC was composed of five commissioners, appointed by the president. Significantly, the FRC was given the authority to assign broadcasters to specific frequencies and to deny licenses when there was no room for additional stations. The FRC's staff was still housed within the Department of Commerce, but the commission had wide authority. The FRC quickly went to work creating order on the AM broadcast band. There were simply too many stations on the air, so the commission began gradually reducing the number. In deciding who should get a license, the FRC had several goals, including assuring that everyone in America could receive at least one radio station; providing service to as many persons as possible from as many diversified sources as possible; and providing outlets for local self-expression.

The FRC's authority was based on the Interstate Commerce Clause in the U.S. Constitution. For a time after the 1927 Radio Act was passed, some broadcasters contended that they were exempt from Federal Radio Commission regulation because their signals did not cross state lines. However, the FRC claimed jurisdiction over all broadcasters as *ancillary* to the regulation of interstate broadcasting: even purely local broadcasting could interfere with stations whose signals did cross state lines, the FRC said. The U.S. Supreme Court upheld the FRC on this point (*U.S. v. Nelson Brothers*, 289 U.S. 266, 1933).

Within a few years, the AM band was an orderly place, with each station assured an interference-free frequency, at least in its local area. The commission created several classes of stations to serve different purposes. First, certain powerful stations were designated as "clear channel" stations—stations that shared their frequencies with no one else anywhere in the country at night. These assignments went to stations that already had wide listening audiences and high-power transmitters. Their mission was to serve their metropolitan areas in the daytime and vast regions of the country at night.

Other stations were restricted to lower transmitter power and forced to share their frequencies with other broadcasters. At the bottom of the pecking order were daytime-only stations that had to leave the air at nightfall to make way for the clear channel giants.

Although the FRC was effective in achieving its major goals, it was replaced during President Franklin D. Roosevelt's "New Deal" administration. Roosevelt set out to systematically reorganize the federal government, and he felt the FRC should have both broader authority and a separate administrative staff. To effect those changes, the Communications Act of 1934 was passed, establishing the basic regulatory structure that exists today. The FRC was replaced by the Federal Communications Commission. The FCC was given a separate staff, making it a fully independent regulatory agency. In addition to radio broadcasting, its jurisdiction was extended to include long-distance telephone service as well as virtually all non-governmental uses of the radio spectrum.

The FCC was specifically forbidden to "censor" broadcasting, but it was given extensive authority to regulate broadcasters in other ways. The most important power given the FCC, of course, was the power to grant or deny licenses. Broadcasters were required to renew their licenses periodically, as they still must today. The FCC was authorized to assure that broadcasters served "the public interest, convenience and necessity," a mandate the FCC used as a basis for imposing various programming requirements on broadcasters.

Within a few years, the Federal Communications Commission moved far beyond its original role as a traffic cop of the airwaves. The commission began not only saying who could use what frequency, but also issuing detailed rules to govern broadcasters' content and business practices. When the FCC adopted a package of "Chain Broadcast Regulations," the major radio networks said the FCC had gone beyond its authority. The networks went to court to test the commission's right to make such rules. In a landmark 1943 decision, the Supreme Court relied on the scarcity rationale to uphold the FCC's authority. The Court said the agency was entitled to regulate broadcasting comprehensively, going far beyond its role as a traffic cop (*NBC v. U.S.*, 319 U.S. 190). That case (and other early court decisions) gave the FCC broad authority over all radio and television broadcasting as well as many other telecommunications services.

The FCC's authority is limited in certain respects. For example, the commission has little authority over government and military uses of the radio spectrum. A large part of the useful radio spectrum is reserved for federal government and military uses, including an enormous chunk of the VHF, UHF and microwave regions. Government uses of the spectrum are coordinated by the National Telecommunications and Information Administration (see the chart). Earlier, the authority now exercised by the NTIA was exercised by various executive offices. Although the FCC consults with the NTIA on many spectrum use matters, the NTIA has the final say over most federal government telecommunications.

Some critics of this two-headed system think it is not the ideal way to serve the public interest. If federal government and military radio users were subject to FCC jurisdiction, the radio spectrum would surely be allocated differently than it is now. Commercial users of the spectrum chronically face severe frequency congestion. And they sometimes look longingly over the electronic fence, as it were, to the uncrowded green pastures of radio space where a few government users lazily graze. In fact, they sometimes do more than just look: Congress recently enacted legislation to reallocate a large segment of the government's radio spectrum (a total of 200 MHz) for non-government uses. Much of this spectrum has been auctioned off to private companies for use in developing new communications technologies. These spectrum auctions bring in billions of dollars to the U.S. treasury: bidders are willing to pay high prices because so little spectrum is left to satisfy so many unmet needs. The best the FCC can hope to do is allocate scarce resources as fairly as possible, accommodating as many of the potential spectrum users as it can.

■ AN OVERVIEW OF THE FCC

The Federal Communications Commission's basic mandate has remained much the same ever since 1934, although the commission itself was reduced from seven members to five in 1982. The five commissioners serve as the agency's policy makers. They are appointed by the president with the consent of the Senate for five-year terms. Only three of the five members may come from one political party. President Barack Obama nominated Julius Genachowski as the chair of the FCC, and he was confirmed in mid-2009.

The commission has the power to adopt administrative regulations that have the force of law, so it is a lawmaking body. But it is a law enforcement and executive body as well. It makes judgmental decisions—often crucially important ones to broadcasters—in selecting among competing applicants for an available frequency. Moreover, it functions somewhat as a court would in weighing evidence in proceedings to penalize those who violate its rules. In short, the agency makes the rules, it enforces them, and it judges alleged violators.

However, the FCC's powers are limited. It must afford all parties who appear before it "due process of law" as required by the Fifth Amendment, and it must not violate the First Amendment—or any other part of the Constitution. Also, its jurisdiction is limited by the Communications Act of 1934, and its decisions may be appealed to the U.S. Courts of Appeals, and from there to the Supreme Court. On numerous occasions the federal courts have overturned decisions of the FCC.

When an FCC decision is appealed, the court must determine if the FCC exceeded its statutory authority or violated the Constitution, or if the agency "abused its discretion" by reaching a decision that was not justified by the facts.

FCC Procedures

As a rule-making body, the FCC must follow specific procedures, as must other federal administrative agencies such as the Federal Trade Commission (see Chapter Thirteen).

When the commissioners need information on a particular subject, they may issue a *Notice of Inquiry.* Then they will await responses from interested parties. Or they may propose new regulations by issuing a *Notice of Proposed Rulemaking.* These notices are published online on the FCC's website (located at www.fcc.gov) and in the *Federal Register,* a daily publication of the federal government that announces actions by many federal agencies. After a rule making proposal is announced, interested parties are invited to respond with comments. Then anyone who wishes may react to the comments by submitting "reply comments."

After receiving written comments, the commissioners may also conduct a hearing at which oral arguments are presented. Finally, the commissioners vote on the proposed rule. If it is approved, the new rule becomes a part of the agency's official regulations, which appear in Title 47 of the *Code of Federal Regulations.*

If you have a special interest in a particular FCC rule, you can look up both the rule and the commission's detailed statement about the rule on the FCC's website or in the *Federal Register,* which you will find in any well-equipped law library and many large city libraries. The website also includes other information about the agency and the issues it is considering.

Although the major policy decisions are made by the five commissioners, the bulk of the FCC's work is carried out by the agency's administrative staff. The agency does most of its work through "bureaus," each of which has a separate area of responsibility.

The *Media Bureau* is of primary concern to broadcasters and cable systems. It is responsible for licensing and supervising radio and television stations and cable television systems. It also handles many post-licensing matters concerning direct broadcast satellite systems. The bureau handles the paperwork of licensing and other administrative matters, referring only the most controversial questions to the commission itself. However, the commissioners and ultimately the federal courts often review the bureau's decisions.

The *Wireline Competition Bureau* regulates landline telephone and other "common carrier" communications. A common carrier is a utility-like operation that must serve everyone who seeks service and is prepared to pay for it. The states regulate these services within their boundaries through their public utilities commissions; the FCC regulates services and rates. Its stated goals include fostering competition and promoting fairness in these industries.

The *Wireless Telecommunications Bureau* handles most domestic wireless and two-way communications services, including cellular telephone and similar services, paging, public

FIG. 55. FCC commissioners, May 2012.

Official portrait, Federal Communications Commission.

From left to right: Jessica Rosenworcel, Robert McDowell, FCC chair Julius Genachowski, Mignon Clyburn, and Ajit Pai.

safety communications, and amateur radio. It licenses and regulates most kinds of private, non-broadcast radio operations.

The *International Bureau* licenses shortwave stations whose signals routinely cross international borders. In addition, it licenses satellite communications systems (which also transmit signals that often cross international boundaries), and handles much of the work required for U.S. participation in World Radio Conferences and other international activities.

The *Enforcement Bureau* enforces the FCC's regulations, supervising everything from broadcasters' compliance with technical standards to the enforcement of local telephone companies' compliance with regulations designed to foster competition.

The *Consumer & Governmental Affairs Bureau* handles all kinds of consumer-related matters, responding to inquiries from individual consumers as well as maintaining contacts with state and local governments and industry groups.

The FCC established a new *Public Safety and Homeland Security Bureau* in 2006. Its mandate is to improve communications during national emergencies such as Sept. 11 and during natural disasters such as hurricanes and earthquakes.

In addition to these specialized bureaus, the FCC has a central administrative staff, a science and technology office, a large legal staff and a plans and policies office, among other offices and divisions. Obviously, the FCC has vast responsibilities beyond the regulation of broadcasting. Only a small part of the FCC's regulatory energy is directed toward such high-profile activities as regulating the nation's television and radio stations.

■ BROADCAST LICENSING

Certainly the FCC's most intimidating power is its licensing authority, and particularly its power to revoke or refuse to renew an existing license that could be worth a fortune on the open market.

In recent years few areas of broadcast regulation have changed as rapidly as the licensing process. A series of court decisions and acts of Congress forced the FCC to revise long-standing procedures. For most of the history of broadcasting, the FCC decided who would get a broadcast license through elaborate procedures that involved *comparative hearings*—a process that could drag on for years or, in some instances, decades. Now the FCC is awarding new licenses by auctioning them off to the highest bidder and the comparative hearing process is disappearing into history.

Actually, the FCC has two different licensing procedures, one for new license applicants and another for renewals of existing licenses. For an applicant seeking a new license, the process starts with an elaborate procedure to determine if a frequency is available.

The FCC has a *table of allocations* that determines whether a frequency is available for a new station in a particular community. An applicant for a new license must either seek a channel that is already allocated to an area but is not in use or convince the FCC to make a new assignment. Both are longshots these days. Almost all existing channels are in use, and the FCC will not make a new assignment unless it can be shown that a new station would not interfere with any existing station. Every station has a defined service area in which it is protected from interference. The result: for most would-be station owners, there is no choice but to buy one from the present licensee—at a high price. But if there should be an available frequency, the FCC conducts an auction, with the license going to the winning bidder. Until recently, the FCC accepted applications for any available frequency and then sorted through the qualifications and promises of competing applicants, often holding a comparative hearing to decide who would get the license. The winner would then receive a construction permit and eventually a license.

All applicants had to file mountains of paperwork to show that they would serve the needs of their communities and to convince the FCC that they qualified for a license in terms of character, financial standing, technical capability, programming plans, non-discrimination in employment and non-ownership of conflicting media. Applicants had to be U.S. citizens. Most of these qualifications still apply, but the process of screening applicants is much simpler. Once applicants are qualified, in most cases they may participate in auctions.

One of the most controversial parts of the FCC's comparative hearings process was the agency's *preferences*. The FCC favored applicants who didn't own other broadcast stations and who promised "integration of ownership and management," which meant the applicant would actually run the station and not be an absentee owner.

The FCC was also concerned about those who applied but had no intention of operating a station. Speculators would apply to induce serious applicants to buy them out by paying large "settlements." In 1990, the FCC changed the rules to ban settlement payments that exceeded an applicant's "legitimate and prudent expenses" (which might include engineers' and attorneys' fees, for example).

Court Decisions on Licensing Preferences

For many years the commission gave a preference to minority group members and women in evaluating license applications, a step designed to help correct the traditional underrepresentation of women and minorities in broadcast ownership. That led to situations in which a woman or minority applicant was given a license in preference to white male applicants who believed they were better qualified—and were prepared to go to court to prove it. The resulting legal challenges to the preference system produced several controversial court decisions on broadcast licensing and affirmative action in general.

In 1990, the Supreme Court reaffirmed the minority preference rules in the case of *Metro Broadcasting v. FCC* (497 U.S. 547). The *Metro Broadcasting* case became a major test of federal government affirmative action policies in general, and the court surprised many broadcasters by voting 5-4 to uphold these minority preferences. A year earlier, the Supreme Court had ruled that many affirmative action policies of state and local governments were unconstitutional in *Richmond v. J.A. Croson Co.* (488 U.S. 469). In the *Richmond* case, the court ruled that state and local affirmative action policies, when challenged in court, had to be justified under a *compelling governmental interest* test. That test made it difficult to defend programs that favor one party over another on the basis of race.

But in the *Metro Broadcasting* case, Justice Byron White switched sides and provided the fifth vote to uphold the affirmative action policy on the ground that it was mandated by Congress and should not be judged against the tough *compelling government interest* standard. White was often reluctant to overrule government policies endorsed by Congress. As a result, the FCC's policy favoring license applicants who are minorities was upheld—for the time being. However, in 1995—only five years later—the Supreme Court took the unusual step of reversing the *Metro Broadcasting* decision, ruling that federal affirmative action programs must indeed be justified under the *compelling government interest* standard. The 1995 decision, *Adarand Constructors Inc. v. Peña* (515 U.S. 200), held that any federal program granting a preference to members of one race over another must be justified by proof that it is an appropriate remedy for a specific, provable instance of previous discrimination. And all race preference programs are subject to *strict judicial scrutiny*, the 5-4 majority in *Adarand* ruled.

Justice Sandra Day O'Connor, writing for the majority, quoted her own opinion in the *Croson* case, in which she said strict judicial scrutiny of racial preferences is needed "to smoke out illegitimate uses of race by assuring that the legislative body is pursuing a goal important enough to warrant use of a highly suspect tool."

For broadcasters, this decision had far-reaching consequences. The FCC soon dropped many of its preferences, including most bidding preferences in spectrum auctions. In some earlier auctions for non-broadcast spectrum, women and minorities had been given credits of up to 40 percent in the bidding, so that a bid of $6 million by a woman or minority group member would win the license over a bid of up to $10 million by a white male, for example. That preference was controversial because the whole point of spectrum auctions is to raise money to reduce the federal deficit. Under the rules announced after *Adarand*, many preferences were dropped, although some future auctions were open only to small businesses—but with the licenses going to the highest bidder, without regard to gender or ethnicity.

Several other parts of the FCC's comparative hearing and preference system were also rejected by court decisions or disallowed by Congress. Shortly before the Supreme Court reversed itself on federal affirmative action programs in 1995, Congress abolished the FCC's *tax certificate* program, in which those who sold broadcast stations or cable systems could avoid paying capital gains taxes on the sale if they sold to a company controlled by women or minorities. The rationale for this policy, like the rationale for the licensing preference, was to encourage more minorities and women to become station and cable system owners. When the Court upheld the minority preference in the *Metro Broadcasting* decision in 1990, it also upheld the tax certificate program in a companion case, *Astroline Communications v. Shurberg Broadcasting* (497 U.S. 547).

In 1995, however, there was widespread media publicity about several instances in which large, wealthy corporations were receiving multimillion dollar tax breaks under the tax certificate program. Legislation to eliminate the entire tax certificate program was passed by Congress and signed by President Clinton, cutting off that and other questionable deals.

Even before the Supreme Court created doubts about the validity of the minority preferences, the women's preference in broadcast licensing had been overturned by the U.S. Court of Appeals in Washington, D.C. In an opinion by Judge Clarence Thomas, now a Supreme Court justice, the appellate court voted 2-1 to declare the women's preference unconstitutional. The court ruled that the

Focus on...
The revolving door

Former FCC commissioner Meredith Attwell Baker came under attack when she resigned from the FCC in 2011, not for leaving the agency but for immediately taking an industry job as the top lobbyist for NBC.

Baker did nothing wrong, as long as she abides by the pledge she took that upon leaving the FCC: she cannot lobby anyone in the agency for two years. Still, some say, moves like hers increase public mistrust of government.

A *New York Times* editorial in May 2011, entitled "That Didn't Take Long," called for regulatory changes: "Congress should expand the definition of lobbying beyond face-to-face encounters to any effort to influence government decisions for their clients. It should also set tight caps on what former officials, including former lawmakers, can earn from lobbying before they must register as lobbyists.".

FCC had failed to prove the preference would really foster diversity of opinion or programming (*Lamprecht v. FCC*, 958 F.2d 382, 1992).

In 2008, the FCC adopted new rules to create preferences for small businesses in licensing, favoring businesses with annual revenue below $6.5 million in the case of radio and $13 million in television license proceedings. The FCC reasoned that these rules would foster broadcast ownership diversity without running afoul of the court decisions overturning preferences for women and minorities.

Court Decisions on the EEO Rules

In addition to the court decisions overturning preferences in broadcast licensing, the D.C. Circuit has twice rejected the FCC's attempts to enforce equal employment opportunity (EEO) requirements over and above those that apply to other businesses. After the two court decisions, the FCC implemented a third set of EEO rules in 2003.

Under the FCC's original EEO rules, each licensee was required to seek out women and minorities for its work force. For many years, the FCC required broadcasters to achieve at least 50 percent of "parity." For example, if 20 percent of the population of a station's service area was African-American, at least 10 percent of the station's workforce had to be African-American for the station to be in compliance.

In 1998, the U.S. Court of Appeals in Washington, D.C., overturned the FCC's entire EEO program in *Lutheran Church-Missouri Synod v. FCC* (141 F.3d 344). The decision resulted from the FCC's attempt to penalize two Lutheran Church-owned radio stations near St. Louis, Mo. for EEO violations and other alleged infractions. The church went to court, arguing that an FCC requirement to hire outside the church for all but on-air employees violated the First Amendment guarantees of freedom of religion. (This was an important issue because the percentage of church members falling into some minority categories was much lower than the percentage in the larger community.)

The FCC had long justified its EEO rules by arguing that even low-level employees such as secretaries, if drawn proportionately from all races and both genders, would influence a station's programming and make it better reflect the diversity of America. Under that rationale, the Lutherans argued, the government was in effect forcing religious stations to modify their message by hiring non-believers. A three-judge appellate panel agreed, overturning the EEO program as unconstitutional.

After this court decision it is still unlawful for a broadcaster to discriminate *against* women and minorities in hiring. But the FCC cannot legally penalize a broadcaster for failing to meet the numerical EEO requirements, which in effect had required broadcasters to hire a certain percentage of women and minorities even if better qualified white males applied. The FCC asked the court to reconsider the case, but it declined to do so.

The FCC ended the case by renewing the licenses of the two Lutheran-owned radio stations. In 2000, the agency adopted a second set of equal employment opportunity (EEO) rules to replace the rules that were declared unconstitutional in the *Lutheran Church* decision. These EEO rules required broadcasters (and cable and other "multichannel video" companies as well) to do broad outreach in an effort to recruit a diverse workforce. However, unlike the EEO rules that were rejected by the court, the second version of the EEO rules included no quotas.

Instead of requiring broadcasters to hire on the basis of race to meet specific quotas, the second rules required broadcasters either to engage in a series of outreach efforts specified by the FCC or to devise their own methods and then document what they did, and to file regular employment reports with the FCC. Addressing another concern of the court in the *Lutheran Church* case, the new rules permitted religious broadcasters to hire believers for all positions, not just on-air positions.

Even though the revised rules contained no hiring quotas, many broadcast attorneys were alarmed at the very complex outreach and reporting requirements. Many feared that broadcasters would have difficulty complying—and might never know if they are out of compliance until the FCC launched an enforcement action. Eventually the National Association of Broadcasters, joined by the state broadcasting associations in all 50 states, challenged the new EEO rules in a lawsuit in the federal appellate court in Washington, D.C.

In 2001, the D.C. Circuit overturned the FCC's revised EEO rules. In setting aside the new rules, the court rejected the FCC's requirement that broadcasters must create minority outreach programs and report the results to the FCC. Although the new rules did not include the numerical quotas that the court found to be unconstitutional in the FCC's original EEO rules, the court said the new minority recruiting rules were also unconstitutional: "The rule (the new recruiting requirement) does put official pressure upon broadcasters to recruit minority candidates, thus creating a race-based classification that is not narrowly tailored to support a compelling governmental interest and is therefore unconstitutional" (*MD/DC/DE Broadcasters Association v. FCC,* 236 F.3d 13).

The language in the *MD/DC/DE Broadcasters* decision is so sweeping that it left many legal observers wondering if any set of rules that requires broadcasters to recruit on the basis of race would be constitutional. The FCC asked the court to reconsider and reinstate the rules; the court denied that request.

The FCC then rewrote the rules a third time. The third set of EEO rules require broad outreach, but without the requirement to keep records of the race and gender of employees or interviewees. Under these rules, which went into effect in 2003, broadcasters as well as cable and satellite operators must widely publicize full-time job openings, participate in outreach options such as job fairs and internships and collect data that indicates where job notices were placed.

Although the latest rules do not require broadcasters to report the demographic makeup of their staffs, the FCC said it would consider requiring annual reports from licensees that would include that information. The plan to separate the collection of demographic data from the EEO outreach rules appeared to be intended to allow the FCC to continue tracking licensees' hiring practices by race and gender while insulating the EEO rules from judicial attack.

License Renewal Problems

Almost as soon as a station is licensed, it must begin preparing for the next crisis in the relationship between broadcaster and government: renewal time. At that point, the broadcaster is supposed to show good stewardship in the use of its assigned frequency.

For many years, most broadcasters assumed that once they had a license from the FCC, it was theirs indefinitely. A license to broadcast in a big city (not including station equipment or any of the other accoutrements of an established business) came to be worth millions of dollars. This is true despite the fact that a broadcast license is theoretically nothing more than an authorization to use a frequency for the license term. The 1934 Communications Act says a license *never* becomes a vested right. In fact, broadcasters have to sign an agreement acknowledging that their frequencies will remain public property indefinitely.

However, in actual practice the FCC virtually rubber-stamped most renewals for many years. To lose a license, one had to commit a serious crime or try to deceive the FCC (by falsifying a license application, for example). However, that changed somewhat in the 1960s and 1970s. Both the FCC and the courts began taking a new look at the licensing process. And the process changed again when the 1996 Telecommunications Act mandated new procedures for license renewals.

A key turning point in the 1960s was a federal court ruling, *Office of Communication of the United Church of Christ v. FCC* (359 F.2d 994, 1966; 425 F.2d 543, 1969). In that case, a public interest group requested a hearing to protest the renewal of a Mississippi television station's license on the ground that its programming evidenced blatant racial prejudice. The FCC refused to grant the group any standing to challenge the license renewal, but a federal appellate court ordered the FCC to hold a new hearing and allow the group to appear. Next, the FCC held such a hearing but placed the burden of proof on the citizen group. The federal court overruled the FCC again, declaring that the burden of proof should have been on the licensee to justify its performance. Then the court set aside the license renewal, and the station eventually lost the license.

After that decision, citizens' groups demanded and won standing to oppose a number of other license renewals, and sometimes rival applicants demanded a comparative hearing so they could attempt to show that they could make better use of the frequency. This was a new element in the renewal process; no longer could a broadcaster merely fill out the forms and rest assured that renewal would be a routine matter. The risk that an opponent might file a *petition to deny* a license renewal came to be a fact of life for broadcasters.

Further breaking the rubber-stamp tradition, the FCC shocked the broadcast industry by denying renewal to an incumbent television licensee in Boston in 1969. A rival group challenged the renewal of WHDH, and the FCC eventually decided the challenger could do a better job than the incumbent.

The policy of holding a comparative hearing when a renewal is challenged was not new, but the rules had so favored the incumbent licensee that challengers had little chance to win. If the incumbent licensee had provided even average service, that record was supposed to be given preference over the mere promises of a challenger. But in this case, the FCC ignored the broadcaster's record of average service and granted the license to a challenger who promised better things. In so ruling, the FCC noted that the incumbent licensee, also the owner of the Boston *Herald-Traveler* newspaper, had shown little interest in the active management of the television station. Really, the station was little more than a source of revenue for the newspaper. A federal appellate court affirmed the FCC decision in 1970 (*Greater Boston Television Corp. v. FCC*, 444 F.2d 841).

During the 1980s, the FCC simplified the renewal process and eliminated thousands of pages of paperwork—forms that some critics of the process said the FCC staff didn't have time to read anyway. However, a coalition of minority groups went to court to challenge the FCC's authority to eliminate the more detailed application forms. They said the shorter renewal form excused most broadcasters from having to show any record of public interest programming at all. But in a 1983 ruling, the U.S. Court of Appeals in Washington, D.C., upheld the simplified renewal process (*Black Citizens for a Fair Media v. FCC*, 719 F.2d 407). The court said occasional "audits" were sufficient to ensure that broadcasters would meet their obligations.

Congress and the FCC both acted to ease the license renewal burden for broadcasters several times in the 1980s and 1990s. In 1981, Congress lengthened license terms from three years to seven years for radio stations and from three years to five years for television stations. The 1996 Telecommunications Act took this a step further, directing the FCC to extend license terms to eight years for both radio and TV stations.

In 1989 the FCC took another step to limit the cost and uncertainty of license renewals. Recognizing that many challengers were filing a petition to deny a license renewal only in the hope of getting the licensee to pay a large settlement and not because of legitimate concerns about the station's performance, the FCC imposed strict limits on financial settlements of license renewal disputes. In the future, licensees would not be allowed to pay challengers more than their actual expenses as a settlement. (In 1990, the FCC adopted the same restriction on settlements among rivals for *new station licenses,* as explained earlier.)

Finally, the license renewal process was greatly simplified by Congress in the Telecommunications Act of 1996. Probably the most important change was the elimination of the comparative license renewal process.

Broadcast license renewals are now a two-step process in which the FCC first determines if the licensee is entitled to a renewal. Others may still oppose the license renewal, but the FCC considers only the renewal/nonrenewal question, not competing applications from others who might like to have the license. Only if the FCC should decide a licensee has committed such serious offenses as to be ineligible for a renewal does the second step occur. During that second step, the former licensee is denied a renewal, and other applications for the channel are accepted.

The 1996 Telecommunications Act also made other changes in the renewal process. Among other things, it required broadcasters to submit a summary of comments received from the public about violence in the station's programming. And it mandated a three-point evaluation of license renewals by the FCC. In reviewing each renewal application, the FCC was directed to make sure that the station: 1) has served the public interest, convenience and necessity; 2) has not committed any serious violation of the rules; and 3) has not committed a series of minor violations that constitute a "pattern of abuse."

How does a station show that it complies with all of the requirements to obtain a license renewal? "Stay tuned" may be the answer. In the mid-2000s, media activist groups at both ends of the political spectrum were challenging the renewals of radio and television licenses.

One of the most lengthy license non-renewal cases in the FCC's history unfolded in the 1970s and 1980s, when the commission decided to strip RKO General, once one of the nation's largest broadcasting corporations, of all of its stations, including major-market television stations in New York, Boston and Los Angeles. In 1980, the FCC acted to take away the three big-city licenses—and also made it clear that RKO's other radio and television licenses would be in jeopardy when they came up for renewal.

RKO claimed the three television licenses in question were worth at least $400 million and immediately appealed the FCC's decision. In 1981 the U.S. Court of Appeals affirmed the FCC's non-renewal of the Boston license (*RKO v. FCC,* 670 F.2d 215), and the Supreme Court declined to hear the case in April of 1982. Thus, RKO reluctantly went off the air in Boston and handed the channel over to a new licensee. The FCC forced RKO to divest itself of many other stations over the next 15 years.

The FCC served notice in 1999 that license non-renewal is still a viable option. In the first such action in a decade, the FCC voted in mid-1999 to deny a license renewal to a Miami, Fla. television station: WHTF(TV), owned by the Trinity Broadcasting Network.

The commission's majority ruled that the religious network was unqualified for a renewal because it misled the commission in the 1980s to get around the FCC's ownership limits. An FCC administrative law judge concluded that Trinity created a minority-front company to take advantage of higher ownership limits then in effect for minority-owned companies, and that Trinity later misled the FCC about its ongoing control over the minority company.

The commission earlier had held up license renewals for Trinity's entire network of 12 full-power and 300 low-power television stations while this issue was being adjudicated. In the 1999 vote, however, the FCC agreed to disregard Trinity's alleged deception in determining the network's eligibility to renew its other licenses.

However, Trinity appealed the loss of the Miami license to a federal appellate court, and the court reversed the FCC's decision in 2000 *(Trinity Broadcasting of Florida v. FCC*, 211 F.3d 618). The court concluded that the minority ownership and control regulations that Trinity allegedly violated were too vague to be the basis for a license revocation.

As a result, Trinity was allowed to keep its Miami license but still had to pay about $31 million to settle license renewal challenges that had been filed against several of its stations by private entities.

■ BROADCAST CONTENT REGULATION

Aside from its frequency allocation and licensing functions, the FCC's main job is to supervise the ongoing operations of its licensees. While a certain amount of that supervision involves technical matters—frequency stability, modulation percentage, power level, and such—a far greater concern to the public (and to most broadcasters themselves) is the FCC's rules governing *content*.

Although Section 326 of the 1934 Communications Act specifically forbids the FCC to "censor" broadcasters, over the years the commission has adopted a number of rules to regulate broadcast content. Also, both the 1934 Communications Act and the 1996 Telecommunications Act, among other federal laws, have provisions governing broadcast content.

One of the FCC's major goals for many years was to disentangle itself from content regulation. FCC regulators in the 1980s pointed out that no government agency has the authority to tell the print media how much of a specific kind of material to publish. Nor does any government agency have that kind of control over cable and satellite television or the Internet media. Why, the FCC asked, should broadcasters be second-class citizens when it comes to First Amendment freedoms? Some citizen groups responded to that question by arguing that broadcasters are given a government-sanctioned monopoly and should have to provide some mandatory public service in return. After all, the FCC does select just one broadcaster to operate on a given frequency in each community, denying that privilege to all others.

Whatever the pros and cons of deregulation, during the 1980s the FCC eliminated many of its rules governing broadcast content on the ground that they were inappropriate if not unconstitutional. By 2000, though, the FCC reversed its philosophy and started imposing new controls on broadcast content.

This section is about regulation and deregulation. A number of important restrictions on broadcast content are still in force or have recently been added—restrictions that do not apply to most other communications media. But other restrictions, including the Fairness

Doctrine, which was perhaps the most controversial content regulation of all, have been abolished.

The Law of Political Broadcasting

Probably the most important aspects of broadcast content regulation are the laws and rules concerning political broadcasting. The key provision is Section 315 of the Communications Act, often called the *Equal Time Rule* or "equal opportunity provision." It has been a part of the Communications Act ever since it was enacted in 1934. In addition to Section 315—which is an act of Congress and cannot be unilaterally rewritten by the FCC—there are many FCC rules that spell out the details of broadcasters' obligations during election campaigns. The FCC adopted a major revision of these rules in 1991.

Section 315 requires broadcasters to provide equal access to the airwaves to all legally qualified candidates for a given public office during election campaigns. It reads in part:

> If any licensee shall permit any person who is a legally qualified candidate for any public office to use a broadcasting station, he shall afford equal opportunities to all other such candidates for that office in the use of such broadcasting station....

The Equal Time Rule has a number of provisions, some of them troublesome for broadcasters. Section 315 specifically exempts *"bona fide"* newscasts, news interviews, news documentaries and, significantly, coverage of news events such as political conventions and debates between candidates. That means a broadcaster can cover news stories involving one candidate without having to include all other candidates.

In 1984, the FCC extended the exemption for news and public affairs programs to many talk shows, thus allowing them to host political candidates during election campaigns without having to give equal time to all other candidates for the same office. In its 1991 rewrite of the rules, the FCC expanded this provision by saying that Section 315 really only applies to "uses" of a station that are controlled, approved or sponsored by a candidate, such as political advertising.

Section 315 doesn't require broadcasters to give politicians free time for campaign advertising. Rather, it merely requires that all candidates be treated equally. If one is sold airtime for a certain fee, the Equal Time Rule merely requires that others be allowed to purchase equal time in the same part of the broadcast day for the same price. If the other candidates can't afford to buy the airtime, the station has no obligation to give them free time. But if one candidate is given free airtime, all other candidates for the same office must also be given free airtime.

The lack of a requirement that broadcasters give candidates free airtime is something that the FCC and the Clinton administration were anxious to change in the late 1990s. President Clinton and both of the men he appointed to head the FCC (Reed Hundt and William Kennard) frequently called on broadcasters to give major party candidates free airtime during their campaigns. The television networks and other leaders of the industry responded by pointing to the large amount of broadcast news programming that is already devoted to political campaigns. But that airtime is *controlled by broadcast journalists*, not the candidates. What the Clinton administration and the FCC were seeking was airtime for candidates to use as they please—without journalists controlling the format and asking potentially

There are several kinds of regulations that affect media organizations. All of them have the potential to alter what those media organizations can publish and what the public can consume.

Structural regulations regulate the relationships between media companies and deal with issues of ownership. Antitrust law is about managing structural regulations, and that will be covered in Chapter Twelve.

Content regulations regulate what is being said, whether to prevent, encourage, or demand certain kinds of speech. Much of what we've discussed in this book so far has dealt with content regulation.

Technical regulations, which don't often implicate First Amendment concerns, regulate how technology works; for example, regulations on radio transmitters that control radio frequency interference.

embarrassing questions. In effect, they were asking for *free advertising time* for political candidates.

Clinton mentioned this issue in his 1998 State of the Union message. The next day, FCC Chair Kennard said the FCC would propose rules concerning free airtime for political candidates. That produced a storm of criticism from Congressional Republicans. The FCC responded by issuing only a Notice of Inquiry to solicit public comments without actually proposing new rules that would require free airtime for politicians.

If Section 315 were the only applicable provision of the Communications Act, a station could comply with the Equal Time Rule by simply excluding all political advertising. That would, after all, be providing all candidates *equal* time—none. However, another provision of the Communications Act places an additional requirement on broadcasters. Section 312(a)(7) says broadcasters may have their licenses revoked if they fail to provide *reasonable access* to candidates *in federal elections*. ("Federal" means elections for the House and Senate as well as the presidency and vice presidency.) As a result, a broadcaster cannot avoid the Equal Time provision by simply turning away all federal candidates; they must be allowed to purchase some airtime for political advertising. But the 1991 revision of the rules makes it clear that broadcasters are not obligated to provide "reasonable access"—or any access at all—to candidates for state and local offices. Section 315 does require broadcasters to "afford reasonable opportunity for the discussion of conflicting views on issues of public importance," but the FCC has interpreted that to mean only that each station must cover the issues—not provide access to candidates for any particular non-federal office. However, if a station does sell airtime to a non-federal candidate, it must offer to sell equal time to other candidates for the same office.

During the 1980 presidential election campaign, the constitutionality of Section 312(a)(7) was tested in court. The Carter-Mondale presidential campaign asked to purchase 30 minutes of airtime on each network in late 1979, about a year before the election. All three networks refused to honor the request, despite the provisions of Section 312(a)(7). CBS offered only five minutes during prime time, while NBC and ABC flatly rejected the request. The FCC then ruled that the networks had failed to meet their obligation to provide federal candidates "reasonable access" under Section 312(a)(7).

The networks challenged the FCC's ruling in court, and that led to an important 1981 Supreme Court decision upholding the commission, *CBS v. FCC* (453 U.S. 367). Voting 6-3, the high court affirmed the FCC's authority under Section 312(a)(7) to order broadcasters to air federal candidates' political statements. The court upheld the FCC's determination that the campaign had begun, even though the general election was nearly a year away at the time the issue arose. Of course, the 1981 decision came too late to help the Carter-Mondale campaign, but it was a major victory for future candidates and a defeat for broadcasters.

The Supreme Court majority ruled that the First Amendment rights of candidates and the public outweighed the First Amendment rights of broadcasters in this particular context. Writing for the Court, Chief Justice Warren Burger pointed out that the FCC need not (and does not) honor all requests for airtime by federal office seekers, but Burger said the FCC was well within its statutory authority in ordering the networks to air the Carter-Mondale campaign statements in late 1979.

In fact, Burger noted that the FCC had set forth specific guidelines for broadcasters to follow in determining when candidates would have a right of access to the airwaves under Section 312(a)(7). In this case, the FCC was justified in concluding that the three major networks had violated those guidelines, Burger said.

Because the Equal Time Rule only requires equal treatment for candidates running in the *same election*, stations may sell advertising during a non-federal *primary election* only to those running for the Democratic and Republican nominations and not to those seeking minor party nominations. In the primary, the minor party candidates aren't actually running against the Democratic and Republican candidates. However, during the general election campaign all candidates for the same office must be allowed to buy comparable airtime at the same rates. A federal appellate court provided this interpretation of Section 315 in 1970 (*Kay v. FCC*, 443 F.2d 638). But remember that in federal elections, all candidates must be offered "reasonable access" to broadcast airtime if they can pay for it. And once a broadcaster sells (or gives) airtime to *any* candidate, federal, state or local, other candidates in the same election must be treated equally.

Under these rules, it has become commonplace for broadcasters to accept advertising from federal candidates and candidates for the most prominent state and local offices, while rejecting advertising from all candidates for less important state and local offices.

Politicians and Lowest Unit Charges

Still another aspect of the political broadcasting rules has become a bookkeeping nightmare for both broadcasters and candidates: the *lowest unit charge* provision in Section 315(b). This provision requires broadcasters to charge candidates the lowest rate that they charge their most favored commercial advertisers for advertising within the 45 days of a primary election and 60 days of a general election. Note that this provision applies to *all* candidates, not just federal candidates.

The lowest unit charge rule means the candidates get the rate charged the largest volume advertisers, even if that discounted rate isn't normally offered to one-time or short-term advertisers. Prior to the 45- and 60-day periods, candidates may be charged rates "comparable" to those charged other advertisers, which means that a candidate doesn't get the quantity discount then without buying enough advertising to qualify for it.

In its 1991 rewrite of the political broadcasting rules, the FCC went to great lengths to clarify the lowest unit charge rule. In addition to volume discounts, most stations offer lower rates for *preemptible* airtime (that is, an ad that can be dropped if someone else comes along later and offers to pay more for the same airtime). On the other hand, someone who purchases *non-preemptible fixed* airtime is guaranteed that the ad will air at a specific time—but that kind of advertising costs more. Many stations have found that they can maximize their advertising revenue by using this system.

The FCC conducted an audit of stations' political advertising sales practices in 1990, and learned that many politicians were actually paying more than commercial advertisers because they were compelled to buy non-preemptible fixed airtime instead of preemptible airtime. That was defeating the purpose of the lowest unit charge provision in Section 315(b). In fact, the FCC found that candidates often weren't even told that preemptible time was available at a lower cost.

To remedy these problems, the FCC's 1991 rewrite of the rules requires broadcasters to tell candidates about all of the rates and classes of airtime available, and to allow candidates to purchase the least expensive airtime offered to anyone. And if a candidate's ads are preempted (i.e., taken off the air to make time for an advertiser willing to pay a higher rate), the station must provide a "make good" (i.e., get the candidates' ads on the air at another time) before the election if it has provided "time-sensitive" make goods to any commercial advertiser in the previous year. Also, the FCC ordered broadcasters to apply the same rules to candidates as to their most favored commercial advertisers in establishing priorities for protection against preemption.

Given the complexity of the lowest unit charge rule, there have been numerous disputes—and lawsuits—between broadcasters and candidates over political advertising rates. A number of candidates have sued broadcasters in state courts, alleging that they were overcharged for advertising in violation of the lowest unit charge rule. Even these lawsuits turned out to be far more complex than anyone (even the lawyers) expected.

In response to the lawsuits alleging overcharges for political advertising, the FCC issued a declaration that the FCC itself has exclusive jurisdiction over lowest unit charge disputes. The courts do not have jurisdiction over this, the FCC declared. Then the Eleventh Circuit dismissed the FCC ruling as an "agency opinion" that does not prevent the courts from hearing lowest unit charge lawsuits (*Miller v. FCC*, 66 F.3d 1140, 1995). But a few months later the Ninth Circuit said the Eleventh Circuit was wrong: the FCC's declaration is valid and deprives the courts of jurisdiction over these cases (*Wilson v. A.H. Belo Corp.*, 87 F.3d 393). While the courts quarrel among themselves, political candidates who think they were overcharged can take their complaints to the FCC for certain, and maybe in some parts of the country the courts will hear their cases, too.

Because the lowest unit charge rule applies only to candidates and not *ballot propositions*, some broadcasters who reject advertising from all candidates for minor state and local offices are perfectly willing to accept advertising for state and local ballot propositions—but at higher ad rates than candidates pay.

Political Debates and Other Problem Areas

Another messy area under the Equal Time Rule has been candidates' debates. For many years, the rule was interpreted to require broadcasters who aired debates between the major candidates to give equal time to all minor candidates as well. The major networks said they could never afford the airtime to do that. In 1960, when John F. Kennedy and Richard Nixon held the first nationally televised presidential debates, Congress passed a law temporarily setting aside Section 315 so equal time would not have to be given to minor candidates.

In several subsequent presidential elections, no nationally televised debates occurred because Congress chose not to set aside Section 315 again. In 1964, for instance, the polls indicated that Lyndon Johnson was far ahead of his Republican challenger, Barry Goldwater. Johnson's strategists felt he had nothing to gain and a lot to lose if he debated

Goldwater, so the Democratic majority in Congress refused to set aside Section 315. For various reasons there were no nationally televised debates during the 1968 and 1972 campaigns, either.

However, in 1975 the FCC reinterpreted Section 315 to mean that a debate sponsored by a non-broadcast organization would be considered a bona fide news event, and hence exempt from the requirements of Section 315 (see *In re Aspen Institute and CBS,* 55 F.C.C.2d 697). That new interpretation, which came to be known as the *Aspen Rule,* was quickly challenged by Shirley Chisholm, a candidate in the 1976 presidential election, but a federal appellate court upheld the rule (*Chisholm v. FCC,* 538 F.2d 349, 1976).

Thus, in both 1976 and 1980, presidential debates were sponsored by the League of Women Voters and dutifully covered as *bona fide* news events by the networks. Had the debates been staged by a broadcaster or network, it would have been necessary to include (or give equal time to) perhaps 30 lesser-known candidates for president.

The FCC ruled in 1983 that broadcasters could sponsor debates directly instead of having them sponsored by third parties such as the League of Women Voters. At the same time, the FCC dropped rules that restricted the use of debates or segments of debates in news programs. The League of Women Voters challenged that reinterpretation of the rule, but lost in the U.S. Court of Appeals (*League of Women Voters v. FCC,* 731 F.2d 995, 1984).

Nevertheless, whether candidates' debates are sponsored by broadcasters or outside organizations, ethical questions arise when only certain candidates are invited to take part. Because of television's great influence, some would argue that any debate that excludes some candidates for an office violates the spirit if not the letter of the Equal Time provision. A particularly strong argument for this position can be made in state and local elections, where there may be only three or four candidates running (as opposed to the 30 or so who usually become legally qualified candidates in a presidential election).

FIG. 56. Robert M. ("Fighting Bob") La Follette, Sr. from Wisconsin, giving first radio campaign speech, September 1, 1924.

Library of Congress, Prints and Photographs Division, [LC-USZ62-42073].

The Supreme Court ruled on this aspect of the Equal Time Rule in a 1998 decision: *Arkansas Educational Television Commission v. Forbes* (523 U.S. 666). At issue was whether public television stations licensed to a government entity such as a state have a First Amendment obligation to include *all* candidates in a political debate—even the ones who have no realistic chance of winning.

By a 6-3 vote, the Supreme Court ruled that even government-owned television stations have *no* obligation to include all candidates in a debate. The majority held that government-run stations, like private ones, have the right to make news judgments about which candidates are viable enough to be included in a debate sponsored by the station.

Justice Anthony Kennedy, writing for the court, said that forcing public broadcasters to include all candidates "would result in less speech, not more" because debates simply could not be held if 20 or 30 different candidates for president had to be included in each debate.

However, Kennedy added that government-controlled stations have a special obligation to be "viewpoint neutral" in their standards for deciding which candidates to include in a debate, never excluding a prominent candidate because he or she might oppose abortion or affirmative action, for example.

Justices John Paul Stevens, David Souter and Ruth Bader Ginsburg dissented, arguing that for a government entity to exclude some candidates from a debate while including others "implicates constitutional concerns of the highest order." The dissenters were particularly troubled because the five Arkansas state-owned stations involved in this case did not have clear, objective criteria to be used in determining which candidates are viable enough to be included in debates.

This case was seen as particularly important for public broadcasters because about two-thirds of the nation's 350 public television stations are licensed to a state.

There are other ethical and legal problems in political broadcasting. For example, the fact that news events are excluded from the Equal Time Rule allows incumbents to get extensive media coverage without other candidates having any similar opportunity. When Senator Edward Kennedy was challenging Jimmy Carter for the 1980 Democratic presidential nomination, he asked the FCC to require the networks to give him equal time to reply to one of Carter's nationally televised news conferences. The FCC turned Kennedy down, and the D.C. circuit upheld that decision (*Kennedy for President Committee v. FCC*, 636 F.2d 432, 1980).

Showing the old movies of actors who become politicians (such as Arnold Schwarzenegger) poses a problem for broadcasters: the Equal Time Rule requires stations that air movies in which a candidate appears (even in a non-political dramatic role) to give equal time to other candidates for the same office if the movie is aired during the campaign period. A federal appellate court once upheld this interpretation of the rules (*In re Paulsen v. FCC*, 491 F.2d 887, 1974). The FCC's 1991 rewrite of the rules temporarily eliminated this problem, but the FCC later reinstated its earlier interpretation of Section 315.

Section 315 does not allow broadcasters to "censor" a political broadcast. If a candidate libels someone on the air, there is nothing the broadcaster can do to stop it. However, the Supreme Court has exempted broadcasters from any liability for defamatory remarks on such occasions (see *Farmers Educ. and Coop. Union v. WDAY*, discussed in Chapter Four).

This ban on censorship of political broadcasts also poses other dilemmas for broadcasters. For example, what happens if a candidate chooses to include language the broadcaster considers distasteful? Occasionally a candidate insists on including vulgar or offensive language in a political statement—language that a broadcaster could not ordinarily air without incurring the wrath of the FCC. In 1984, the FCC issued a statement declaring that despite Section 315 broadcasters can prevent a candidate from using language that is not normally permitted on the airwaves.

However, broadcasters sometimes must allow candidates to include material that offends some (or many) viewers. For example, in recent years a number of candidates who opposed abortions have included photographs of aborted fetuses in their advertising. Acting on the advice of the FCC, a number of stations refused to air these ads in prime time—even if an opposing candidate had advertised in prime time. In 1996, a federal appellate court held that this "channeling" of anti-abortion campaign ads to times when the audience is small violates the Equal Time Rule. The court said that political candidates have a special right of access, even if their ads are offensive (*Becker v. FCC*, 95 F.3d 75).

Other problems have arisen as broadcasters tried to apply the Equal Time Rule. For example, what happens when on-air broadcast employees run for public office? Suppose a deejay with a four-hour show runs for the city council. If he or she doesn't take a leave of absence, must all other candidates be given similar deejay shows? The FCC's traditional answer to that question has been yes: the station must either take the broadcaster-candidate off the air during the campaign period or give all other candidates equal time—for free. In *Branch v. FCC* (824 F.2d 37), the D.C. Circuit in 1987 upheld the FCC's interpretation of the rules. The Equal Time Rule means what it says, even if a candidate is also a broadcaster, the court held. The Supreme Court refused to review that decision.

Broadcasting, Ascertainment and Localism

By 2008, the FCC was restoring content regulation rules that were eliminated 25 years earlier, including some that many broadcasters viewed as among the most troubling government controls of all: the *ascertainment*-related rules. Those rules underscored the reality that broadcasters do not have the full First Amendment rights that protect other media from government control of their content.

Until 1984, over-the-air broadcasters (but not other electronic media outlets) had to do formal community ascertainment, a process of interviewing community leaders to solicit their opinions about issues they considered important to the community. Broadcasters were required to do programming to address those issues. This requirement led to programming about everything from local race relations to the need for a new sewage treatment plant—talk programming led by officials and experts even on radio stations that normally aired only music of a certain type. Those programs almost always had low ratings, driving away listeners and

Section 315:
also called the Equal Time Rule, the rule that requires broadcasters to provide equal access to the airwaves to all legally qualified candidates for a given public office during election campaigns; broadcasters cannot censor political messages.

Section 312:
the rule that requires broadcasters to provide reasonable access to candidates in federal elections.

lowest unit charge:
the requirement that broadcasters must charge candidates the lowest rate they charge their best advertisers for 45 days before a primary and 60 days before a general election.

viewers who had tuned in for a very different kind of programming. Ascertainment also involved filing voluminous reports with the FCC to justify license renewals. The FCC staff often didn't read this documentation, but it could be used in license renewal challenges to contend that a broadcaster wasn't serving its local community. The question really came down to whether stations would provide programming that their audience preferred or programming preferred by the government. The ascertainment-related rules were eliminated at least in part because of their First Amendment implications.

In 2007, the FCC adopted a new rule requiring television stations to complete and file a new "Standardized Television Disclosure" form every three months, outlining not only their ascertainment efforts but also reporting how much of their programming fell into various categories, such as local news programming, "civic affairs" programming, "electoral affairs" programming, locally produced "non-paid" religious programming and other programming that the FCC believed would meet community needs. The process set up *de facto* programming quotas. In 2008, the FCC followed up by issuing a long-anticipated Broadcast Localism Report. It proposed additional rules that would require radio and television broadcasters to set up community advisory boards and to do specific programming to meet various community needs as specified by the FCC.

These rules were a response to calls by media reform groups for a return to local programming of the sort required in the ascertainment era. But to many broadcasters, this seemed to be a major increase in government regulation of their content at a time when they were already losing viewers or listeners to cable and satellite media that are largely free of government content regulation and often do little local public affairs programming, opting instead for what the ratings indicate most viewers and listeners actually prefer.

Broadcasters report significant burdens as a result of these regulations. The forms are onerous to complete (it was estimated in 2009 that the documentation would require 400 hours a year to complete, or 10 full 40-hour working weeks), and setting up advisory boards and holding meetings added to the costs in time. As with the Fairness Doctrine, some conservative commentators have suggested that the localism policies could be used to stifle conservative talk radio by denying them licenses for failing to "serve the public interest," calling the localism rules a "back-door Fairness Doctrine."

FIG. 57. President Gerald Ford and Jimmy Carter on television during presidential debate in Philadelphia, Penn., September 23, 1976.

National Archives and Records Administration.

The Fairness Doctrine

Probably no rule that the FCC ever adopted has been as controversial as the Fairness Doctrine, established in 1949 and abolished in 1987. The Fairness Doctrine is relevant today because there have been repeated proposals in Congress to reinstate it. The most recent such legislation failed to pass in 2008. President Barack Obama has said he does not support its return, and conservative legislators have charged that the doctrine could be used to shut down conservative talk shows.

The Fairness Doctrine required commercial broadcasters to keep their public affairs programming reasonably balanced: when they covered one side of a controversial issue, they had to balance that presentation by seeking out and airing opposing viewpoints—even if they had to give representatives of opposing views free airtime. Many members of Congress, some public interest groups, and many others advocate restoring the Fairness Doctrine. On the other hand, most broadcasters (especially broadcast journalists) have vehemently opposed it as a violation of their First Amendment rights because it allowed government bureaucrats to second-guess their news judgments.

When the FCC abolished the Fairness Doctrine in 1987, that may have been the FCC's most controversial decision ever: the Democratic majority in Congress voted to overrule the FCC and put the Fairness Doctrine into statutory law, only to have President Reagan veto that legislation. In 1989, Congress again considered legislation to reinstate the Fairness Doctrine—and President George H.W. Bush made it clear that he, too, would veto any such legislation. But when Bill Clinton's victory in the 1992 presidential election gave the Democrats control of the White House as well as both houses of Congress, legislation to reinstate the Fairness Doctrine was again introduced.

Congress never passed Fairness Doctrine legislation during the 1992-94 period. When the Republicans gained control of both houses of Congress in 1994, there was little likelihood that the Fairness Doctrine would be reinstated by an act of Congress in that era.

Why do Democrats tend to favor the Fairness Doctrine while Republicans tend to oppose it? Until recent elections, Republicans and conservative causes consistently raised more money to buy airtime than Democrats and liberal causes. Perhaps it is not too much of an oversimplification to say that Democrats support the Fairness Doctrine while Republicans oppose it because it required broadcasters to give *free* airtime to liberal causes more often than conservative ones (because backers of conservative causes were more likely to have the money to *buy* airtime).

The Fairness Doctrine was always a vague, general policy. It led to relatively few disciplinary actions against broadcasters and almost no license non-renewals. One notable exception to that generalization involved a conservative religious radio station. The owner promised fairness to all religious faiths when he sought FCC permission to purchase the station, but then he followed a policy of presenting only one viewpoint. The license was not renewed, a decision a federal court upheld (*Brandywine-Main Line Radio v. FCC*, 473 F.2d 16, 1972).

However, most complaints of Fairness Doctrine violations were not even passed along to broadcasters by the FCC. The FCC received thousands of Fairness Doctrine complaints each year, and only a few resulted in an inquiry, let alone a formal action against the broadcaster.

Unlike the Equal Time Rule, which requires broadcasters to sell *equal* time to opposing candidates, the Fairness Doctrine never required minute-for-minute equality of access. Instead, it merely said broadcasters had to provide overall balance in their programming by presenting varied opinions on controversial issues sooner or later. A broadcaster could cover one side of an issue today and the other next week.

While the Fairness Doctrine was unpopular with broadcasters, many of whom felt it not only abridged their First Amendment rights but also stifled the coverage of controversial issues rather than fostering it, some consumer and media watchdog organizations saw it as the public's only hope of assuring that broadcasters would serve the public interest and not just their own private commercial interests.

Why, then, did the FCC abolish the Fairness Doctrine after 38 years?

In voting to abolish the Fairness Doctrine, each of the commissioners made speeches filled with rhetoric about freedom of the press. But their basic arguments for eliminating the Fairness Doctrine boiled down to these three:

First, the Fairness Doctrine gave government bureaucrats the right to second-guess the news judgments of broadcast journalists, opening the door for potentially dangerous violations of the First Amendment. No government agency has similar authority to supervise the editorial judgments of the print media.

Second, the Fairness Doctrine actually deterred instead of encouraging full news coverage: the fear of having to provide free airtime to a variety of dissenting groups led many broadcasters to avoid controversial stories, or at least to tone them down to avoid offending anyone. These tendencies were evidence of the "chilling effect" the Fairness Doctrine had on the First Amendment rights of broadcasters. (Under a corollary to the Fairness Doctrine called the Cullman Rule, broadcasters were required to give free airtime to opposing viewpoints if no one representing a particular viewpoint could afford to purchase airtime.)

Finally, some people argued that the scarcity rationale, which was traditionally used to justify broadcast content regulation by the government, was no longer relevant because of the large number of new program sources available to the public, including cable and other newer technologies.

In explaining the commission's 1987 decision to drop the Fairness Doctrine, Dennis Patrick, the FCC chair at the time, said, "Our action today should be cause for celebration, because by it we introduce the First Amendment into the 20th century. Because we believe it will serve the public interest, we seek to extend to the electronic press the same First Amendment guarantees that the print media have enjoyed since our country's inception."

The FCC's action in 1987 was almost anticlimactic: the commission had conducted a massive investigation of the Fairness Doctrine in 1984-85, an inquiry that produced documentation of numerous instances in which the Fairness Doctrine had a chilling effect on the free expression rights of broadcasters, stifling rather than encouraging the coverage of important issues.

After the Fairness Doctrine was repealed, several opposition groups decided to use a lawsuit that was already under way as a vehicle to challenge the FCC's right to abolish the doctrine. The case was *Syracuse Peace Council v. FCC* (867 F.2d 654), which began when WTVH-TV in Syracuse, N.Y. carried several commercials advocating the construction of a nuclear power plant. The FCC ruled that the broadcaster violated the Fairness Doctrine by refusing to provide airtime for the Peace Council to argue against the nuclear power plant.

The broadcaster appealed the FCC's ruling to federal court, and the court sent the case back to the FCC with specific instructions to consider its First Amendment implications. The FCC did—and abolished the Fairness Doctrine itself. Then the Syracuse Peace Council—backed by pro-Fairness Doctrine groups—went back to federal court, contending that the FCC had no right to abolish the Fairness Doctrine.

In 1989 the Court of Appeals ruled that the FCC had the authority to abolish the Fairness Doctrine. Later another federal appeals court agreed. In *Arkansas AFL-CIO v. FCC* (11 F.3d 1430, 1993), the Eighth Circuit issued an *en banc* ruling (a ruling by all judges serving on that court instead of the usual panel of three judges) that again reaffirmed the FCC's authority to abolish the Fairness Doctrine. The case stemmed from a request by labor unions and others that the FCC declare KARK-TV in Little Rock, Ark. guilty of failing to cover all sides fairly in a 1990 ballot referendum. The FCC said the station had no obligation to cover all sides because the Fairness Doctrine had been repealed. The court upheld the FCC's decision, but stopped short of ruling that the Fairness Doctrine, if reinstated, would violate the First Amendment.

If Congress were to pass Fairness Doctrine legislation, that would surely lead to a new court test of the doctrine's constitutionality—where the First Amendment implications would have to be squarely addressed. It remains to be seen whether the Fairness Doctrine will ever be reinstated, but the controversy surrounding it refuses to die. In 1996, still another challenge to the FCC's abandonment of the Fairness Doctrine was rejected by the Ninth Circuit (*Coalition for a Healthy California v. FCC*, 87 F.3d 383).

Shortly after the FCC eliminated the Fairness Doctrine in 1987, a coalition of media organizations asked the commission to clarify whether some related rules had also been abolished. The commission eventually declared, to the surprise of many, that the *Personal Attack Rule* remained in force, requiring broadcasters to continue notifying the victims of personal attacks (and in some instances, to give these persons free airtime for a reply). The FCC also reaffirmed its *Political Editorializing Rule*, which required broadcasters who endorse candidates to offer opponents free time to reply on the air.

The Radio-Television News Director's Association (RTNDA) challenged the constitutionality of the Personal Attack and Political Editorializing Rules in a lawsuit that was not resolved until 2000—13 years after the Fairness Doctrine itself was abolished and 20 years after the RTNDA first challenged these rules in court. In 1998, the FCC deadlocked 2-2 on a vote to abolish these two rules, with Chair William Kennard not voting because he worked on this issue as a lawyer for the National Association of Broadcasters in the early 1980s. Given the FCC's tie vote, a federal appellate court asked the two commissioners who voted against abolishing the rules to provide an explanation for their votes that the court could consider in ruling on the RTNDA's long-delayed legal challenge to the rules. More time passed, and the court eventually asked the FCC to eliminate the two rules or justify their continuing existence. Still another year passed with no formal response from the FCC, although the FCC did temporarily suspend the two rules for 60 days during the 2000 election.

The appellate court decided that wasn't enough. In late 2000 the court overturned the Personal Attack and Political Editorializing Rules. The court said that the two rules "interfere with the editorial judgment of professional journalists and entangle the government in day-to-day operations of the media." Ruling in the case of *Radio-Television News Directors Association v. FCC* (229 F.3d 269), the court issued a strongly worded opinion ordering the FCC to eliminate the rules permanently because it had failed to justify their continued existence.

Broadcast journalists praised the decision as a major victory for their First Amendment rights. They argued from the beginning that these rules forced them to avoid covering certain issues and therefore had a chilling effect on freedom of expression.

FCC Chair William Kennard said he was "disappointed" with the court's decision and said the FCC would monitor broadcasters' handling of controversial issues while studying "how best to ensure that the public receives balanced coverage." Michael Powell, who was named to replace Kennard as FCC chair by President George W. Bush in 2001, made it clear that he thought these two rules—and many of the FCC's other broadcast content controls—were contrary to the First Amendment. It was not the government's place to tell broadcasters what content they should carry, in his view.

Of course, nothing in the decision to abolish the Fairness Doctrine or the related rules affects the Equal Time provisions of the Communications Act (Section 315). Section 315 still requires broadcasters to offer all candidates for a given office equal opportunities to purchase airtime, as it has ever since the Communications Act was enacted in 1934.

The Supreme Court and the Fairness Doctrine

In the debate over the constitutionality of the Fairness Doctrine, both sides carefully reviewed the Supreme Court's few previous decisions on its constitutionality. In 1969, the high court upheld the Fairness Doctrine in the case of *Red Lion Broadcasting v. FCC* (395 U.S. 367). That case arose at the end of the 1964 presidential election when a radio evangelist named Billy James Hargis attacked Fred Cook, the author of a book that criticized Republican candidate Barry Goldwater. The attack was aired over Red Lion's radio station in Pennsylvania, and Cook demanded reply time under the Personal Attack Rule.

Red Lion replied by telling Cook, in effect, to buy an advertisement. Instead, Cook complained to the FCC, which ordered the station to give Cook reply time. Red Lion appealed, charging that it violated a broadcaster's First Amendment rights to be forced to provide airtime to someone like Cook.

The Supreme Court agreed with Red Lion that the case involved a First Amendment issue. However, the court said the First Amendment rights of the general public took precedence over the rights of broadcasters. Red Lion was ordered to give Cook time to reply to the personal attack.

In contrast, a few years later the Supreme Court said that the print media have no obligation whatever to give space to those with whom they disagree. In the landmark case of *Miami Herald v. Tornillo* (418 U.S. 241, 1974), the Supreme Court overturned a Florida law requiring newspapers to publish replies from political candidates who are personally attacked in print. The court said the print media have a First Amendment right to publish only one side of controversial issues and to attack people without granting them space for a reply, if they so choose. Thus, there cannot be a Fairness Doctrine or a Personal Attack Rule for the print media under the First Amendment.

Many broadcasters felt this disparity in editorial freedom made them second-class citizens under the First Amendment. Those who felt that way were encouraged in 1984 when the Supreme Court suggested that it was having second thoughts about the policies announced in the *Red Lion* decision.

In 1984, the Supreme Court addressed the First Amendment rights of public noncommercial radio and television stations—and suggested that it might be time to reconsider the constitutionality of the Fairness Doctrine itself. That happened in the case of *FCC v. League of Women Voters of California* (468 U.S. 364).

This case was a challenge to a Congressional ban on editorializing by public broadcasters, and the court said it violated the First Amendment. It was the first time the high court had ever overturned a federal content restriction on broadcasters on First Amendment grounds. And the court seemed to invite a review of the validity of many other broadcast content restrictions, including the Fairness Doctrine.

The Court rejected the arguments of those who felt public broadcasters should not carry editorials expressing their own views because they receive government funds. Congress had banned editorializing by stations receiving federal funds on the theory that if they editorialized these stations would feel obligated to support the government's policies. In effect, these stations could become propaganda organs for the government, Congress feared.

The Court disagreed with that rationale and said there were many ways public broadcasters could be insulated from political pressures that might influence their editorial policies without simply forbidding them to speak out on the issues.

Although the Supreme Court's decision came on a narrow 5-4 vote, the majority opinion was so sweeping that it raised doubts about the continuing validity of the entire range of broadcast content controls. Writing for the majority, Justice William J. Brennan included a footnote that said the Court might have been prepared to reexamine the scarcity rationale that has justified the restrictions on broadcast content. Brennan wrote:

> The prevailing rationale for broadcast regulation based on spectrum scarcity has come under increasing criticism in recent years. Critics, including the incumbent Chairman of the FCC, charge that with the advent of cable and satellite television technology, communities now have access to such a wide variety of stations that the scarcity doctrine is obsolete. We are not prepared, however, to reconsider our long-standing approach without some signal from Congress or the FCC that technological developments have advanced so far that revision of the system of broadcast regulation may be required.

That signal came within the next few years, of course, when the FCC abolished the Fairness Doctrine. Today, broadcasters have no obligation even to carry opposing viewpoints under most circumstances. Putting the final nail in the doctrine's coffin, FCC chair Julius Genachowski pledged to remove the Fairness Doctrine from the books so, as he told *Broadcasting & Cable* magazine, "that there can be no mistake that what has been a dead letter is truly dead." In August 2011, the FCC finally officially axed the Fairness Doctrine, along with 83 other rules that the agency believed were no longer necessary.

Banning Indecency on the Airwaves

The FCC's *Indecency Rule*, a controversial topic off and on for more than 40 years, is a major issue again in the 2000s. Indecency, never defined in a way that most broadcasters considered clear, involves the use of offensive language or images by broadcasters. The rule does *not* apply to cable and satellite television networks, nor to Internet webcasting and podcasting—all of which have greater First Amendment protection than over-the-air broadcasting.

The latest controversy was triggered by several incidents where celebrities were accused of violating the rules on national television. Perhaps most notably, singer Janet Jackson's halftime performance with Justin Timberlake during the 2004 Super Bowl included a brief breast-baring scene that sparked outrage in Washington and across the country.

Congress responded in 2006 by passing the Broadcast Decency Enforcement Act, a law that increased the maximum fines the FCC may impose on broadcasters by a factor of 10.

Now a single station can be fined $325,000 for one profane or indecent word or image, up to a maximum of $3 million for one program. If 100 stations carry the same network feed, they could be fined a total of $32.5 million for one word or $300 million for one program.

So what is indecency? For many years the FCC used a definition of indecency that the Supreme Court employed in a 1978 case, *FCC v. Pacifica Foundation* (438 U.S. 726):

> [Indecency is] language or material that, in context, depicts or describes, in terms patently offensive as measured by contemporary community standards for the broadcast medium, sexual or excretory activities or organs.

Under that definition, which has been given a variety of different interpretations over the years, frontal nudity and certain offensive words have been banned except during a *"safe harbor"* overnight between 10 p.m. and 6 a.m. Separate laws also ban profanity and legally obscene material on the air.

After rarely enforcing the indecency rule for many years, the FCC launched a crackdown in 1987, giving broadcasters a preview of what was to come in the early 2000s. The FCC started fining broadcasters for offensive language and content. That crackdown led to a series of court decisions and a major controversy involving broadcasters, citizens' groups, Congress and the FCC.

The longest-running target of the FCC's crackdown on alleged broadcast indecency has been Howard Stern's syndicated radio program. Stations that carried Stern's controversial show were hit with fines of about $2 million by the mid-1990s. Stations owned by Infinity Broadcasting alone were fined $1.7 million for indecency violations on Stern's show. In 2004, the nation's largest radio group, Clear Channel Communications, paid a fine of $1.75 million on top of an earlier $755,000 fine for alleged indecency in its programming, including Stern's show. Stern was then dropped by the six Clear Channel stations that carried him, and the giant radio group launched a broad effort to curb the language and visual images used on its radio and TV stations.

Meanwhile, other broadcasters felt the FCC's new wrath over indecency. NBC was condemned but not fined by the FCC for rock star Bono's use of the phrase "fucking brilliant" during a live telecast of the 2003 Golden Globe awards. The FCC overruled its own staff, which had ruled Bono's words non-indecent because they were not used in a sexual context. In so ruling, FCC Chair Michael Powell acknowledged that the FCC's enforcement policies were being changed in 2004. NBC apologized for the incident but emphasized that the rules in place in 2003 "did not subject broadcasters to strict liability for fleeting utterances in live broadcasts."

The Federal Communications Commission voted in September, 2004 to impose a $550,000 penalty on CBS for the breast-baring incident involving singer Janet Jackson during the 2004 Super Bowl halftime show. The fine was aimed at 20 CBS-owned stations, each of which faced what was then the maximum penalty, $27,500. At the time it was the largest fine ever imposed on television stations as opposed to often-fined radio stations.

Viacom, then the parent company of CBS, eventually paid the fine—and then challenged the FCC in federal court, seeking a refund. Although CBS apologized to viewers, Viacom officials said the incident did not meet the legal standard for a finding of broadcast indecency, which must include a determination that the broadcast was patently offensive.

In 2009, the Third Circuit threw out the $550,000 fine against CBS for the Jackson "wardrobe malfunction" in *CBS v. FCC* (535 F.3d 167), saying that the FCC had "strayed from its long-held approach of applying identical standards to words and images when reviewing complaints of indecency." The FCC appealed to the Supreme Court. After the Court ruled narrowly in favor of the FCC in the "fleeting expletive" indecency case, *FCC v. Fox Television*, it remanded the case back to the Third Circuit to evaluate in light of that decision (*FCC v. CBS Corp.*, 556 U.S. 1218, 2009). In 2011, the Third Circuit again vacated the FCC's fine against CBS for the "wardrobe malfunction," saying that the agency "failed to acknowledge that its order in this case reflected a policy change and improperly imposed a penalty on CBS for violating a previously unannounced policy" (*CBS Corp. v. FCC*, 663 F.3d 122). The court said that the FCC did not tighten its policies until *after* the Super Bowl broadcast.

The Supreme Court denied *cert* to hear an appeal, but Chief Justice John Roberts took the unusual step of issuing a two-page concurring opinion of the denial of *cert*, saying that he wasn't sure the Third Circuit had it right: the "fleeting expletive" policy was for words, and the FCC "never stated that the exception applied to fleeting *images* as well, and there was good reason to believe that it did not" (*FCC v. CBS Corp.*, No. 11-1240). Justice Ruth Bader Ginsburg also added a brief concurrence urging the FCC to revisit its indecency policy.

In 2004 Viacom had agreed to pay $3.5 million to settle a series of other indecency charges unrelated to the Janet Jackson case. Although many involved Howard Stern's show on Viacom's Infinity Broadcasting radio stations, the settlement also resolved indecency complaints that had been filed against such TV programs as *CSI* and *Big Brother*. In the settlement, Viacom also agreed to put a time delay on all live programming, discipline employees who violate FCC rules and hold classes on indecency compliance.

The FCC also announced fines totaling $1.18 million against Fox television stations for a sexually explicit episode of *Married by America*. Unlike the fines Viacom faced for the Janet Jackson incident, this sanction applied to all stations that carried the Fox feed, not just network-owned stations. Many Fox stations were challenging the fines, contending that they had no way to know in advance what the content of this unscripted reality show would be and that they merely passed through network programming.

In 2006, the FCC imposed more large indecency fines, including $3.6 million in fines of CBS stations for airing a partially obscured teen sex scene on "Without a Trace." The penalty was later reduced to $3.35 million when the FCC learned that some of the 100-plus stations that had been fined actually aired the show during the safe harbor after 10 p.m.

At the same time, the FCC fined broadcasters for a number of other programs. One college-owned station was fined for airing *Godfather and Sons*, a widely acclaimed PBS documentary on the blues as a musical genre. That prompted PBS to urge its stations to bleep all potentially offensive words in PBS programming, and even to obscure the faces of people who utter bleeped-out words.

In 2008, the FCC fined the ABC network $1.4 million for airing an episode of *NYPD Blue* that showed a woman's nude buttocks. ABC was fined because the scene was aired before the 10 p.m.-6 a.m. safe harbor in the Central and Mountain time zones. The FCC did not fine ABC for airing the show on the east and west coasts, where it was broadcast after 10 p.m. ABC said it would appeal the fines.

Obviously frustrated by the FCC's indecency crusade, Howard Stern abandoned traditional radio for Sirius, a fee-based satellite radio provider, in 2006. Because satellite radio is exempt from the FCC's indecency rule and other content-based regulations that have troubled him for years, Stern said government regulation has doomed over-the-air radio. "I think FM radio is dead," he said.

However, Stern's forecast may have been premature. In 2007 the Second Circuit overturned many of the FCC's recent indecency enforcement actions and ordered the agency to reconsider (*Fox Television Stations v. FCC*, 489 F.3d 444). Specifically, the court overturned the FCC's sanctions of the fleeting use of four-letter words during live broadcasts. This case did not involve the Janet Jackson/Justin Timberlake Super Bowl performance, although that episode was on everyone's mind as this litigation unfolded. A separate legal challenge to the FCC's $550,000 fine in that case was thrown out by the Third Circuit in 2009, and the Supreme Court finally closed the case in 2012.

In a strongly worded opinion in the *Fox* case, the appellate court condemned the FCC for changing its rules concerning spontaneous utterances without justifying the change. Tracing the history of indecency enforcement, the court noted that the FCC had not considered fleeting utterances to be indecent until recently—and still didn't seem to mind if they occurred during news broadcasts. The court was particularly troubled that the FCC allowed the airing of some movies with four-letter words, including *Saving Private Ryan,* while punishing broadcasters when a celebrity used the same words during a live awards show. The court didn't mention the fact that President Bush used one of the forbidden words during a major international conference in 2006. Fearing the FCC's wrath, most networks bleeped the President's word from their news coverage—an action with huge First Amendment implications.

FCC Chair Kevin Martin criticized the court for its 2007 decision, saying the decision "may have prohibited the commission from enforcing any restrictions on language." In a statement to the media, Martin repeatedly used the four-letter words that the FCC had fined broadcasters for airing—an apparent example of court-decision rage. The FCC appealed the decision to the Supreme Court, which has agreed to rule on the case, probably in 2009.

The decision was actually a narrow one, not addressing the basic First Amendment issues raised by Fox and other television networks. All the court really said was that the FCC had to reconsider cases where it penalized broadcasters for airing fleeting offensive utterances.

The other issue that the appellate court didn't decide was the reasonableness of punishing over-the-air broadcasters for the use of four-letter words when the same words are perfectly legal at all hours of the day and night on cable and satellite networks. At least 85 percent of U.S. households receive cable or satellite television.

The FCC won a narrow victory on appeal in the Supreme Court (*FCC v. Fox Television*, 556 U.S. 502, 2009). In one of the most highly anticipated decisions of the year, the Supreme Court reversed the Second Circuit's decision in favor of Fox and said that the FCC's "fleeting expletives" policy did not violate the Administrative Procedure Act (APA).

Justice Antonin Scalia wrote the opinion for the Court. He did not use any of the expletives at issue in the opinion, referring to them as the "F-word" and "S-word" or using asterisks in place of some of the letters (e.g., quoting Cher as saying "So f 'em"). He traced the development of FCC indecency policy and said that the FCC's changes in how it dealt with "fleeting expletives" were not arbitrary and capricious under the APA. The agency, said Scalia, "need not demonstrate to a court's satisfaction that the reasons for the new policy are *better* than the reasons for the old one; it suffices that the new policy is permissible under the statute, that there are good reasons for it, and that the agency *believes* it to be better." Moreover, he added, the Court would not apply a more stringent definition of the "arbitrary and capricious" standard to an agency whose actions implicated constitutional liberties.

In responding to a concern raised in Justice Stephen Breyer's dissent that the Court's decision would require small broadcasters to invest in expensive screening technology, and some of those broadcasters would be unable to afford such technology, Scalia took a swipe at Hollywood celebrities:

> We doubt, to begin with, that small-town broadcasters run a heightened risk of liability for indecent utterances. In programming that they originate, their down-home local guests probably employ vulgarity less than big-city folks; and small-town stations generally cannot afford or cannot attract foul-mouthed glitteratae from Hollywood. Their main exposure with regard to self-originated programming is live coverage of news and public affairs. But the Remand Order went out of its way to note that the case at hand did not involve "breaking news coverage," and that "it may be inequitable to hold a licensee responsible for airing offensive speech during live coverage of a public event"…

Justices John Paul Stevens, David Souter, Stephen Breyer, and Ruth Bader Ginsburg dissented. Stevens said that the FCC's initial views, formed in close proximity to Congressional mandates delegating the agency's actions, had worked fine for decades and should be presumed to be closest to what Congress wanted when it gave the agency authority to act. Ginsburg said that in her view, the change in policy exemplified arbitrary and capricious decision-making, and moreover, "there is no way to hide the long shadow the First Amendment casts over what the Commission has done."

Justice Anthony Kennedy concurred in part and dissented in part. While he agreed that the judgment against the FCC should be reversed, he also agreed with Breyer that under the APA the agency must explain its rejection of "the considerations that led it to adopt that initial policy."

Justice Clarence Thomas concurred in the outcome but, in an opinion that gives hope to those who dislike increased regulations on broadcasters, he said that he has grave concerns about the cases on which those regulations rest: *Red Lion Broadcasting v. FCC* and *FCC v. Pacifica Foundation*. He pointed to the changes in technology that have taken place since those decisions were handed down and explicitly invited a case where those precedents could be evaluated: "I am open to reconsideration of *Red Lion* and *Pacifica* in the proper case."

The Second Circuit heard oral arguments for the second time in January 2010 on the remand of the indecency case. The oral argument did not go smoothly for the FCC; thus, it was not much of a surprise when the Second Circuit in *Fox Television v. FCC* (613 F.3d 317) dropped its bombshell: the entire FCC indecency regime is unconstitutional, and it "violates the First Amendment because it

Focus on…
The Fairness Doctrine

Despite having been abolished in 1987, the Fairness Doctrine continues to make political news. The topic was so hot that Julius Genachowski was asked specifically by Sen. Kay Bailey Hutchison (R-Tex.) if indeed he opposed it during his FCC chair confirmation hearings. He said he did oppose it.

There is some doubt whether a new Fairness Doctrine would survive constitutional scrutiny a second time around. As Justice Thomas pointed out in *FCC v. Fox Broadcasting*, since the doctrine was found to be constitutional in *Red Lion*, the foundations for treating broadcasters differently than print media have started to crumble.

However, the question is now essentially moot, as Genachowski has stated that he will remove the Fairness Doctrine from the books. He is on record as saying it had the possibility to chill speech.

is unconstitutionally vague, creating a chilling effect that goes far beyond the fleeting expletives at issue here."

The media environment, the court said, has changed since the rules were enacted in 1978, and technology like the V-chip enables parents to exercise more control over children's television viewing. Moreover, the FCC's policy is vague: "For instance, while the FCC concluded that 'bullshit' in a 'NYPD Blue' episode was patently offensive, it concluded that 'dick' and 'dickhead' were not." Networks thus do not know what exactly will be deemed indecent under the standard. The FCC appealed to the Supreme Court, which granted *cert*.

But the Court dodged First Amendment questions about indecency in its 2012 decision (*FCC v. Fox Television Stations*, No. 10-1293). Instead, the Court relied on Fifth Amendment due process grounds to find the FCC's policies regarding fleeting expletives to be unconstitutionally vague. Justice Anthony Kennedy, writing for the majority, said, "The Commission failed to give Fox or ABC fair notice prior to the broadcasts in question that fleeting expletives and momentary nudity could be found actionably indecent. Therefore, the Commission's standards as applied to these broadcasts were vague, and the Commission's orders must be set aside." Justice Ruth Bader Ginsburg, concurring in the judgment, urged the reconsideration of Pacifica, agreeing with Justice Thomas in the 2009 Fox case.

The case is perhaps more notable for what it did *not* do. The justices, in addition to declining to review the First Amendment implications of the FCC's overall regulation of indecent speech, also did not review the FCC's current indecency policies. Nor did the Court close the door on a revised indecency policy or on judicial review of the current or revised policies, instead saying the FCC could "modify its current indecency policy in light of its determination of the public interest and applicable legal requirements."

Indecency is still very much on the agendas of both the government and the public. In 2008, Congress passed, and President George W. Bush signed, the Child Safe Viewing Act. The act requires the FCC to study advanced blocking technologies (as well as their availability and encouragement) that would help parents keep "indecent or objectionable" content from their children. These technologies could apply to a variety of electronic communication, including the Internet. The FCC called for comments and in 2009 reported that the consensus seemed to be that there was no one technology that would work across all platforms. Moreover, the FCC acknowledged "the need for greater education and media literacy for parents and more effective diffusion of information about the tools available to them."

Long before the current controversy over broadcast indecency began, the U.S. Supreme Court declared that indecent but non-obscene material could be banned from the airwaves during the daytime hours, even if the same material was legal in other media. In the 1978 *FCC v. Pacifica Foundation* case (cited earlier), the Court voted 5-4 to uphold a mild FCC sanction against Pacifica, a foundation that operates several noncommercial radio stations, including WBAI in New York City. WBAI aired a program on contemporary attitudes toward language, and it included a 12-minute monologue by comedian George Carlin entitled "Filthy Words." In it, Carlin named "the original seven words" that "you couldn't say on the public...airwaves" and ridiculed society's taboos about the words, "shit, piss, fuck, cunt, cocksucker, motherfucker and tits." The program was broadcast at 2:00 p.m., preceded by a warning that some of the content might be offensive to some persons. Those words, by the way, appeared in the official Supreme Court decision (unlike in the 2009 decision).

A man who said he and his son inadvertently stumbled on the monologue while listening to their car radio complained to the FCC, and the FCC eventually placed a warning notice in the station's license renewal file. The FCC did not find the language obscene but did decide it was "patently offensive" and indecent—and therefore inappropriate for the airwaves. Further such incidents could lead to a license non-renewal, the FCC said.

Pacifica Foundation appealed to the courts. The Supreme Court ruled that the language, though not legally obscene, was inappropriate for broadcasting, at least during the daytime. The Court said the words were indecent even if they might be constitutionally protected under other circumstances. Explaining its decision, the Court made an analogy to nuisance law and quoted an earlier decision defining a nuisance as "merely a right thing in the wrong place—like a pig in the parlor instead of the barnyard." Then the court concluded: "We simply hold that when the commission finds that a pig has entered the parlor, the exercise of its regulatory power does not depend on proof that the pig is obscene."

Although the FCC did not initially regard this Supreme Court decision as a mandate to enforce the rules against broadcast indecency aggressively, that changed later.

By the mid-1990s, the D.C. Circuit handed down four separate decisions on the FCC's post-*Pacifica* indecency enforcement. In the end, the court issued an en banc decision holding that the FCC, acting on orders from Congress, could ban indecency from the airwaves at all times except during a "safe harbor" period between 10 p.m. and 6 a.m.—hours when relatively few children are in the broadcast audience (*Action for Children's Television v. FCC*, 58 F.3d 654, 1995). The 7-4 majority held that there is a compelling government interest in protecting children from indecent material that justifies banning broadcast indecency from over-the-air stations during the daytime when many children are in the audience. Armed with that ruling, the FCC began its recent crackdown in 2004.

The FCC does not just fine stations for indecency; it can also levy fines for a station's refusal to respond to its requests for information. In 2010 it proposed a $25,000 fine against Fox TV Stations not because of its broadcast of a controversial episode of *American Dad*, but because the agency said Fox did not answer its questions about which stations actually broadcast the episode in question, which allegedly drew 100,000 indecency complaints.

Regulating Children's Programming

In addition to its rules on political broadcasting and indecency, the FCC has at various times enforced a number of other broadcast content regulations.

Programming and advertising aimed at children have been a prime example. After a controversy over children's television programming that lasted for more than 20 years, in 1996 the FCC adopted rules requiring all commercial television stations to offer at least three hours a week of regularly scheduled programming to meet the *educational and informational* needs of children. When a digital TV station airs multiple program streams, each stream must include three hours of children's programming per week.

Under the children's programming rules, each station must provide this special programming in segments at least 30 minutes in length between the hours of 7 a.m. and 10 p.m. The children's programming is not supposed to be preempted, even for news or sports events, more often than 10 percent of the time. This poses a problem for stations on the west coast, because major sports events in the east often begin before the traditional Saturday morning children's program block ends in the Pacific time zone.

The children's educational programming must be clearly identified as such on the air. Also, stations are required to notify program guides, indicating the appropriate age range for each program. In addition, each station must have a staff member who acts as a children's

FIG. 58. Federal Communications Commission logo.

Federal Communications Commission

Focus on...
Counting complaints

The FCC releases quarterly reports on the numbers of complaints it receives in many areas, including broadcast indecency. There are wild fluctuations in the numbers of complaints the FCC reports that it receives on a monthly basis, causing some commentators to suggest that the FCC should disclose more about where complaints are coming from.

An example: In January 2008, the FCC reported getting a whopping 108,919 indecency complaints, compared to just 10,825 in February 2008 and a mere 1,187 complaints in March 2008. The agency does say that these numbers may include duplicate complaints and those that don't contain enough information for action to be taken on them, but of course the FCC doesn't reveal who is sending the complaints.

It may be that there is just that much fluctuation depending on what is broadcast on TV and radio, but critics claim that activist groups, like the Los Angeles-based Parents Television Council, have a disproportionate impact on the process. PTC has on its website a complaint form that can be filled out, sometimes months or years after the initial broadcast, that will send a complaint to the FCC. A complainant would not even have had to have seen the broadcast. Some have called on the FCC to clarify its policies on accepting and reporting indecency complaints so the public can have a better understanding of complaint trends.

educational programming liaison, and each station must file quarterly reports with the FCC to explain how the children's programming requirements are being met.

The adoption of these rules followed an extended controversy in which advocacy groups argued that all television stations have a duty to provide educational programming for children. The networks and major station groups responded by pointing to the various programming and community services they were already providing that had educational value for children. Some pointed out that despite its widely praised quality, PBS educational programming has had low ratings. Given a choice, most viewers have voted with their remote control units for other kinds of programming.

The trade press and other First Amendment advocates expressed concerns about the implications of the mandatory children's programming requirements for other reasons. Here, they noted, is a government agency dictating program content, telling commercial broadcasters to provide the kind of children's programming that *the government thinks children should be watching*—and then to promote it to persuade viewers to watch what's good for them instead of the programming they might prefer to watch.

By the 2000s, the networks' concerns about mandatory children's programming were greater than ever. With several cable networks offering children's programming full time, major over-the-air networks saw ratings for their children's programming drop even lower.

The 1996 rules were by no means the first FCC initiative in this area. As early as 1974, the FCC issued a policy statement calling on broadcasters to discontinue certain practices, such as allowing children's show hosts to advertise products. The commission also urged broadcasters to voluntarily upgrade their children's programming.

Congress passed a law to regulate children's programming in 1990, the Children's Television Act. It limits advertising on children's shows to 12 minutes per hour on weekdays and

10.5 minutes per hour on weekends. This provision applies only to shows intended for children age 12 and younger. The law also requires broadcasters to prove at license renewal time that they have met the "educational and informational needs" of children age 16 and younger by airing programs *specifically designed for that purpose.* The limits on commercials also apply to cable television, including both cable network shows and locally produced programming.

The advertising limits have been enforced aggressively. The FCC has conducted a number of audits of station compliance, and stations carrying excessive advertising have often been fined. In one 1999 action, the FCC fined two jointly owned Illinois stations, WRSP-TV in Springfield and WCCU(TV) in Urbana, $110,000 for 304 violations of the limits between 1994 and 1996. Another station, WDBD(TV) in Jackson, Mississippi, was also fined $110,000 for 158 violations of the limits between 1993 and 1998. In 2004, the FCC hit two cable networks with large fines for carrying too many commercials during children's television programs. The FCC fined Nickelodeon $1 million and ABC Family $500,000. These fines seemed small in comparison to a record $24 million fine that Univision Communications agreed to pay in 2007. Univision, the United States' largest Spanish-language broadcaster, incurred the FCC's wrath by airing telenovelas to fulfill its obligation to carry three hours of children's educational programs a week. It apparently agreed to pay the fine to win FCC approval of the network's sale to an investor group in Los Angeles.

The Children's Television Act also established a National Endowment for Children's Television to support educational programs. In addition, Congress directed the FCC to address the problem of toy-based shows and determine if they were improper *program-length commercials* because they so clearly promoted toys based on the shows' characters—a concern that was being voiced again a decade later.

Acting in 1991, the FCC adopted new rules concerning toy-based shows in response to the Congressional mandate. The rules forbid commercials within a show (or within one minute on either side of the show) for toys based on characters in that show. And the rules forbid hosts of children's shows from doing commercials on the premise that young children cannot distinguish commercials from the non-commercial segments of the show. The commercials must be separated from non-commercial segments of children's shows. But the FCC declined to ban toy-based shows altogether, a decision that was widely criticized by groups advocating quality children's programming.

The FCC responded by issuing a new notice of proposed rulemaking concerning educational programming for children in 1995. That proposal led to the three-hour mandatory children's educational programming requirement the commission adopted a year later.

The FCC in 2010 issued a number of fines for violations of children's programming rules. The largest, for $70,000, was leveled against a Spokane station for showing on 86 occasions over nine months "a commercial for the Collector's Zone during the 'Yu-Gi-Oh!' 30-minute program" which contained a "very brief pictorial and aural reference to Yu-Gi-Oh! trading cards."

Regulating Violent Programming

Another controversy about government regulation of broadcast content involved television violence. The Telecommunications Act of 1996 required all television set manufacturers to include a so-called *V-chip* in all but the smallest television sets so parents could program their TV sets to block programming they didn't want their children to watch. The act also required the industry to come up with a "voluntary" rating system so programs with ratings for excessive violence or sexual content can be blocked by parents. Programs not rated as suitable for children were to carry an encoded signal to prevent television sets with the V-chip from receiving them unless parents (or whoever controls the TV set) enter the correct code to receive these shows. In 1998, the FCC adopted rules requiring manufacturers to include the V-chip system in all new TV sets by January, 2000, except for sets with screens smaller than 13 inches.

In mandating the V-chip system, Congress and the FCC were responding to a public outcry about the high rate of violent crime and pregnancy among teenagers in America. Congress apparently accepted the argument of many parents and others that at least part of the blame lies with violent and sexually oriented programming on television. The 1996 law gave the industry one year to come up with a "voluntary" rating system—or else the FCC would convene an advisory committee to set up the ratings.

Soon after the Telecommunications Act became law, the industry set up its own task force to develop a rating system for television shows, drawing on the experience of the Motion Picture Association of America with its rating system for movies. However, the original TV rating system did not provide the one thing that many groups critical of television programming wanted the most: program ratings specifically indicating violent or sexually oriented content or offensive language with letter ratings. Industry critics, backed by key members of Congress and the Clinton administration, demanded changes. In mid-1997, the industry agreed to modify the system, adding letters to designate violence, sexual content, suggestive dialogue, offensive language or fantasy violence. The rating is displayed in a corner of the screen at the beginning of each rated show.

Perhaps the most basic concern about the ratings and the V-chip system is whether it really works. "Unless a new V-chip television is going to come equipped with a pair of handcuffs, it won't stop kids from finding ways to watch forbidden shows," one network executive told the trade press after the 1996 law was passed.

In fact, one thing that delayed progress in developing V-chip technology was the difficulty of designing a programming system too complex for adolescents to figure out, but simple enough for most adults. Leaders of the Consumer Electronics Manufacturers Association predicted that many children and especially teen-agers would devise ways to get around the program blocking. When V-chip-equipped TV sets began appearing in stores in early 2000, merchants generally reported widespread consumer indifference to the V-chip system. In 2005, the broadcast industry began a campaign to make parents more familiar with the V-chip system, hoping to ward off additional government regulation of content. Despite that campaign, a nationwide survey by the nonpartisan Kaiser Family Foundation reported in 2007 that only 16 percent of parents said they had ever used the V-chip, although 71 percent of those who had used it found it to be "very useful." Complaints about violent programming continued. In 2007, the FCC issued a report on TV violence and urged Congress to authorize the agency to crack down on violent programming. The report didn't define violence or explain how these new regulations would comply with the First Amendment.

The Supreme Court granted *cert* in *Video Software Dealers Assn. v. Schwarzenegger* (556 F.3d 950), a Ninth Circuit case addressing whether a California law regulating the sale or rental of "violent" videogames to minors and imposing a labeling requirement was constitutional. The appellate court applied strict scrutiny and said that it was not. The state asked the court to use the "variable obscenity" (obscenity to minors) standard discussed in Chapter Ten, but the court rejected that approach, saying that the Supreme Court's obscenity standards have been limited to sexual, not violent, content. The state, the court added, had not provided evidence to demonstrate harm, and there were less restrictive means available to address the state's concerns. As for the labeling requirement, the court overturned it as well, noting that "[u]nless the Act can clearly and legally characterize a video game as 'violent' and not subject to First Amendment protections, the [label] does not convey factual information."

In this case, closely watched by videogame manufacturers and players, the Supreme Court in 2011 struck down the California law that prohibited the sale or rental of violent videogames to minors. In *Brown v. Entertainment Merchants Assoc.* (131 S. Ct. 2729) (the name changed when the governor of California changed), the Court by a 7-2 vote agreed with the Ninth Circuit and said that the law could not withstand strict scrutiny, and Congress and state legislatures could not pass laws that restrict this kind of speech.

Justice Antonin Scalia, writing for the majority, rejected the application of variable obscenity to violent videogames. The state, he wrote, "wishes to create a wholly new category of content-based regulation that is permissible only for speech directed at children"—and that is not acceptable. Nor does the state have "a free-floating power to restrict the ideas to which children may be exposed." In fact, Scalia noted, citing stories from Hansel and Gretel to Snow White to Homer's *Odyssey*, children are regularly exposed from childhood to violence and violent imagery. And the fact that the violence in videogames is unlike that in classical literature or fairy tales does not make it unprotected, said Scalia: "Reading Dante is unquestionably more cultured and intellectually edifying than playing Mortal Kombat. But these cultural and intellectual differences are not *constitutional* ones."

Basically, Scalia said, the law was both too narrow *and* too broad:

> As a means of protecting children from portrayals of violence, the legislation is seriously underinclusive, not only because it excludes portrayals other than video games, but also because it permits a parental or avuncular veto. And as a means of assisting concerned parents it is seriously overinclusive because it abridges the First Amendment rights of young people whose parents (and aunts and uncles) think violent video games are a harmless pastime. And the overbreadth in achieving one goal is not cured by the underbreadth in achieving the other. Legislation such as this, which is neither fish nor fowl, cannot survive strict scrutiny.

Justice Samuel Alito, joined by Chief Justice John Roberts, concurred in the outcome, but they thought that the law "fails to provide the fair notice that the Constitution requires" and would have overturned it on those grounds.

Justices Clarence Thomas and Stephen Breyer dissented. Thomas relied on the intent of the founders, claiming that history demonstrates that parents were expected to have full control over their children. "The practices and beliefs of the founding generation establish that 'the freedom of speech,' as originally understood, does not include a right to speak to minors (or a right of minors to access speech) without going through the minors' parents or guardians," he wrote. Breyer, while agreeing that videogames are expressive content deserving of First Amendment protection, would restrict access by those under 17 to videogames that are "highly realistic" and "violent." He also believed that the language of the statute was clear. "Why are the words 'kill,' 'maim,' and 'dismember' any more difficult to understand than the word 'nudity?'" he asked. Breyer also attached two lengthy appendices to the opinion containing citations of academic articles on the psychological harm that could result from playing violent videogames.

Regulating Format Changes

The FCC also has become involved in content regulation on some occasions when a radio station proposed to change a unique programming format. During the 1970s, the only classical music stations in several cities tried to abandon that format, spurring protests by classical music lovers. The FCC originally refrained from getting involved in these controversies. However, the federal courts began ordering the FCC to review format changes when a station abandoned a unique format and the change produced widespread protests. For instance, that happened in Atlanta (*Citizens Committee to Preserve the Voice of the Arts in Atlanta v. FCC*, 436 F.2d 263, 1970).

Then in 1974 the federal appellate court that serves Washington, D.C.—the court that has heard so many FCC appeals over the years—decided *Citizens Committee to Save WEFM v. FCC* (506 F.2d 246). The court, ruling *en banc*, ordered the FCC to hold a hearing whenever a unique format is being abandoned and a substantial number of persons object.

However, two years later, the FCC issued a policy statement calling for the court to reverse itself and let the commission stay out of such disputes. The FCC said "the public interest in diversity of entertainment formats is best served by unregulated competition among licensees." But the federal appellate court in Washington refused to back down, and the result was a Supreme Court decision on the FCC's proper role in broadcast format changes. Ruling in 1981, the Supreme Court affirmed the FCC's right to stay out of broadcast format disputes in *FCC v. WNCN Listeners Guild* (450 U.S. 582). The court said entertainment programming was within the broadcaster's discretion. The seven-justice majority wrote: "We decline to overturn the commission's policy statement, which prefers reliance on market forces to its own attempt to oversee format changes at the behest of disaffected listeners."

The Supreme Court decision was a major victory for the broadcast industry, which has strongly supported the FCC's moves to deregulate the field, but it was a defeat for classical music lovers and others who feared that minority tastes will not be served if all broadcasters are free to tailor their programming for the audiences that are most attractive to advertisers.

Other Content Regulations

For almost 25 years, broadcasters were subject to another content control that was always controversial and, some said, never successful: the *Prime Time Access Rule*. It was adopted by the FCC in 1971 and abolished in 1995. Under this rule, the ABC, NBC and CBS networks were generally limited to three hours of evening programming during the four-hour period from 7 to 11 p.m. Monday through Saturday (6 to 10 p.m. in the central and mountain time zones), with exceptions for news events and special occasions. The rule only applied in the 50 largest metropolitan areas.

The FCC's stated objective was to create new opportunities for local programming by limiting the portion of the evening hours the networks could lock up. But local network affiliates generally relied on syndicated programming such as "Wheel of Fortune" and "Jeopardy" to fill the non-network time instead of doing local public affairs programs. (A syndicated program is one produced independently and then sold directly to local stations rather than to a network.) In abolishing the rule, the FCC noted that ABC, NBC and CBS "no longer dominate the television marketplace." Eliminating the rule freed stations to choose whatever prime time programming they wished, including reruns of network shows that previously could be aired during the access period only by independent stations.

Among the other FCC regulations governing content are rules governing sponsorship identification. Broadcasters must identify the sponsors of ads and disclose the fact if some-one has paid for the airing of non-advertising material.

The sponsor identification regulations were at the center of a controversy in the mid-2000s. Broadcasters sometimes use *video news releases* (VNRs) that appear to be news stories but are actually produced by corporations or government agencies. There was widespread criticism when the White House Office of National Drug Control Policy distributed VNRs that looked like news stories with a narrator who identified herself as "Karen Ryan" and said she was "reporting." Some stations aired these releases without identifying their government origin. The FCC issued a public notice in 2005 warning that such practices violate the spon-sor i.d. rules. "VNRs are essentially prepackaged news stories, that may use actors to play reporters and include suggested scripts to introduce the stories," the notice said. "Listeners and viewers are entitled to know who seeks to persuade them... Whenever broadcast stations and cable operators air VNRs, licensees and operators generally must clearly disclose to members of their audiences the nature, source and sponsorship of the material," the notice added. The FCC also asked for assistance from the public in identifying "covert commercial pitches" (as Commissioner Jonathan S. Adelstein put it) in which a company pays for prod-uct placement in a TV show. The FCC reiterated that under the rules paid endorsements and product placements must be identified as such, something that often doesn't happen. In 2006 the FCC sent inquiries to 77 television stations that were accused by a watchdog group of airing VNRs without identifying their source.

The FCC also has another rule governing broadcast content: a restriction on over-the-air hoaxes. The rule was enacted in response to several widely publicized incidents in which radio stations reported fake events in the early 1990s. For example, a Los Angeles station aired a phony murder confession, a station in St. Louis reported during the Persian Gulf war that the United States was under nuclear attack, and a Virginia station reported that a large waste dump was about to explode. The potential dump explosion created a panic remi-niscent of the one caused by Orson Welles' classic "War of the Worlds" broadcast in 1938. (In a special Halloween broadcast on network radio, Orson Welles dramatized H.G. Wells' tale about an invasion of Earth by Martians. In Welles' program, music was interrupted by authentic-sounding news bulletins that terrified millions of people, especially near the Martians' purported landing site in New Jersey.)

The FCC responded to the more recent hoaxes by banning broadcast fabrications about crimes and catastrophes that "divert substantial public safety resources" or "cause substantial harm to public health and welfare."

Hoaxes raise troubling ethical questions, of course, but the FCC's response to these hoaxes again illustrates the limited First Amendment rights of broadcasters. Does any government agency have the right to forbid tabloid newspapers from publishing pure fabri-cations as news? Should the government be allowed to ban what it considers to be false stories in newspapers, or just on radio and television? Should hoaxes be banned in all of the media? When does a broadcast dramatization—a fictitious work—become a hoax and therefore illegal on the air?

Payola, the practice of record labels, promoters and others secretly paying radio deejays for putting certain songs on the air, was controversial more than 50 years ago. The FCC

V-chip:
mandatory television technology that allows parents to program their TVs to block objectionable content, like sex or violence, based on program ratings assigned by the networks.

Prime Time Access Rule:
an FCC regulation that restricted the amount of network programming that local TV stations owned by, or affiliated with, a network may air during in the evening.

Video news release:
a video version of a press release, created by public relations or advertising professionals to try to influence public opinion.

eventually rewrote the rules to outlaw it unless it is disclosed. But in the 2000s, the issue reappeared and triggered a new crackdown, led at first by then-New York Attorney General Eliot Spitzer, not the FCC.

One of Spitzer's targets, CBS Radio, agreed in 2006 to donate $2 million to nonprofit New York music programs to end Spitzer's investigation. Spitzer's office had evidence that CBS Radio employees accepted gifts from music labels to play songs that would not otherwise have been aired. Another target, Entercom Communications, agreed to a $4.45 million settlement. Spitzer, who later served as New York governor but resigned after a call-girl scandal, also won a total of $30 million in settlements from four leading record labels and passed along evidence of misconduct by other broadcasters to the Federal Communications Commission for its own investigation of alleged radio industry payola.

In 2007, four broadcast groups, Clear Channel, CBS Radio, Entercom Communications and Citadel Broadcasting, signed an FCC consent decree agreeing to pay $12.5 million in fines. While admitting no wrongdoing, the four broadcast groups promised that their 1,600-plus radio stations would not accept compensation for airing music without disclosing it and also agreed to provide more airtime for independent and local artists.

Another kind of content that has been restricted is advertising and other programming that promotes gambling. The advertising of gambling is restricted both by FCC regulations and by various state laws. However, government-run lotteries may advertise on local stations in their areas, and charitable lotteries are generally exempt from these restrictions, as are promotions and prize drawings by businesses other than casinos. Under the Charity Games Advertising Clarification Act of 1988, only casinos and others whose gambling is an end in itself are now forbidden to advertise *by federal law*. However, the 1988 act left the states free to restrict or ban lottery advertising even if the advertising would be legal under federal law.

What constitutes a lottery? A lottery exists any time the three *elements of a lottery* are present. They are: (1) a valuable prize; (2) determining the winner at least partly by chance; and (3) requiring participants to pay some "consideration" to enter the contest. To get around these rules, many businesses have set up drawings with the disclaimer, "no purchase necessary," to eliminate the consideration element and make their drawings legal to advertise. In many states, that is no longer necessary for businesses not primarily engaged in gambling.

What happens if one state has a state-run lottery, and broadcasters in an adjacent state wish to carry its advertising? The U.S. Supreme Court ruled on the question of out-of-state lottery advertising in 1993, and held that a broadcaster in a non-lottery state cannot carry ads for a nearby state's lottery if the state of licensing forbids lottery advertising, even if the station has a large audience in the state that has a lottery (*U.S. v. Edge Broadcasting*, 509 U.S. 418). The case involved WMYK-FM, a radio station licensed to a North Carolina town only three miles from the Virginia border. North Carolina has no state lottery and forbids lottery advertising. However, more than 90 percent of WMYK's listeners are in Virginia, which does have a state-sponsored lottery. Nevertheless, the Supreme Court upheld the laws under which the station was barred from carrying ads for the Virginia lottery. The court upheld North Carolina's right to ban lottery advertising on stations licensed in that state, and ruled that the federal law granting states the right to ban lottery advertising does not violate the First Amendment.

However, after the *Edge Broadcasting* decision, several courts, including the Supreme Court, took a more permissive view of casino gambling ads, if not government-run lottery advertising. In 1997, a federal appellate court held that the statutory laws and FCC regulations banning casino advertising violate the First Amendment rights of Nevada broadcasters. In *Valley Broadcasting v. U.S.* (107 F.3d 1328), the Ninth Circuit held that the many loopholes and exceptions in the ban on lottery advertising undermine the government's stated rationale for this restriction on broadcasters' freedom of speech. A few months later, a federal district court in New Jersey ruled similarly, overturning the ban on advertising by Atlantic City casinos (*Player's International v. U.S.*, 988 F.Supp. 497).

The U.S. Supreme Court then weighed in with its decision in *Greater New Orleans Broadcasting Association v. U.S.* (527 U.S. 173, 1999). The high court unanimously ruled that the federal government may not ban broadcast advertising for private casino gambling. This cleared the way for New Orleans broadcasters, and broadcasters in many other states, to carry casino gambling ads. The rationale of the decision, which is discussed in Chapter Thirteen, appears broad enough to allow stations in states that do not have casino gambling—but do not prohibit gambling advertising—to carry ads for casinos in other states.

After the Court's *Greater New Orleans* decision, the FCC issued a statement saying that broadcasters are indeed free to carry gambling ads anywhere that gambling is legal—but hedged about the rights of broadcasters in states that prohibit gambling. Nevertheless, the FCC stopped enforcing the lottery rule, leaving broadcasters free to carry advertising for out-of-state casinos if their state does not forbid gambling advertising. However, this does not supersede the *Edge Broadcasting* decision, which refused to legalize lottery advertising by broadcasters licensed to a state that has no state lottery and prohibits lottery advertising.

Broadcasters are subject to many other laws that govern advertising in general. For instance, the federal Truth-in-Lending Act requires the full disclosure of all credit terms if any of the terms of a loan are mentioned in an ad, as explained in Chapter Thirteen. Almost no one would quarrel with the wisdom of having laws requiring credit advertising to be truthful and complete. However, the required disclosures are sometimes so detailed that they cannot all be squeezed into a short broadcast advertisement.

In the late 1990s several other new federal controls on broadcast content were considered by the FCC. In addition to the new children's educational program requirements and the V-chip rules, in 1997 the FCC's then-chair, Reed Hundt, advocated the following: (1) a ban on hard liquor advertising on radio and television; (2) at least one minute of free public service announcements (PSAs) during prime time every night on each network; (3) free airtime for political candidates; (4) a new "family hour" from 8 to 9 p.m. each evening, with programming limited to material suitable for families with children; and (5) other public interest requirements that broadcasters would have to meet in return for their new digital licenses. Although Hundt's successor, William Kennard, did not pursue some of these initiatives with Hundt's fervor, Kennard did endorse the proposal for free airtime for political candidates, announcing in 1998 that the FCC would launch a new inquiry into this matter.

Meanwhile, a presidential Advisory Committee on Public Interest Obligations of Digital Television Broadcasters was created in 1997 to offer suggestions concerning Hundt's fifth proposal. This committee released 10 recommendations in 1998; most were quite general. One was that the FCC should adopt minimum public interest standards for digital broadcasters (without suggesting what they should be), while another was that the FCC should require broadcasters to report their public interest activities four times a year. The committee also said Congress should create a trust fund for public broadcasting and set aside a TV channel in each community for educational programming. And the commission urged the National Association of Broadcasters to adopt a new voluntary code of conduct to replace one that was eliminated to settle an antitrust lawsuit in the early 1980s. The NAB was developing a new code in the mid-2000s.

As for serving "the public interest," the FCC, Congress, and media advocacy groups debated what that should mean. Is it in the public interest for the government to require broadcasters to provide free airtime to political candidates? If so, should only major-party candidates get free airtime? What other things should broadcasters do to serve the public interest in the digital age? Should cable and satellite TV channels be held to the same standard? Who should decide what is in the public interest? Should it be Congress? The FCC? Broadcasters themselves? If government makes these decisions and tells broadcasters what to put on the air, where does the First Amendment fit into the equation?

■ CABLE TELEVISION REGULATION

Just as radio was the growth medium in the 1920s and television boomed in the 1950s, cable and cable-like technologies were the mass communications growth leaders in the 2000s. In 1980, about a quarter of all American homes were served by cable; by 2008, about 85 percent were served by cable, satellite or other subscription television services.

Cable began in the 1950s as something called "community antenna television" or CATV. In its early days, it was literally what its name implied: an elaborate antenna system serving a whole community. Because it offered little more than improved television reception, CATV first developed in rural areas far from the nearest television transmitters. By pooling their resources, the people of a community could afford a large antenna system and signal boosters to receive the weak signals from distant television stations. Each home was connected to this central receiving system via coaxial cable, a special kind of wire that will efficiently carry television signals a considerable distance.

When cable television got its start in the countryside, it had little appeal in big cities where reception was good. However, in the 1960s that began to change because of two trends. First, a growing number of people were forbidden to put up TV antennas at condominiums, apartment complexes and even some tracts of single family homes. Instead, they were offered cable hookups for a fee. But even more important, cable systems began offering a lot more than clear television reception: they began providing many additional channels of programming, including out-of-town "superstations," original made-for-cable programming and such special attractions as music videos, recent movies and sports events.

The History of Cable Regulation

Because cable systems do not actually transmit an over-the-air signal, they are not treated as users of the radio spectrum, and they need no FCC license to operate (although cable systems do receive programming via satellites that use the airwaves). Cable also has other advantages. For instance, the number of channels that may be offered via cable is limited mainly by the number of channels a television receiver or cable converter can cover. A local cable system can put programming on every one of those channels without interfering with other cable systems or over-the-air broadcasters.

Because of these factors, cable television was able to develop without much federal regulation—at first. However, by the late 1960s, broadcasters became alarmed at the growth of cable television systems. So did the producers of television programming, which cable operators picked up off the air at no charge—and then delivered to their subscribers for a fee. Two U.S. Supreme Court decisions held that cable operators did not have to pay copyright royalties for the material carried over their systems, since the court viewed CATV as nothing more than an adjunct of the television receiving function (see Chapter Six). The owners of copyrighted programming felt they were being deprived of a fair profit by these Supreme Court decisions, and Congress enacted the 1976 Copyright Act in part to remedy this situation. Cable systems now pay royalties for the copyrighted programming on non-local stations that they carry. Also, under the Cable Television Consumer Protection and Competition Act of 1992, they must pay, or at least obtain broadcasters' consent, to carry some local stations but not others, for reasons that are explained later.

As cable systems expanded and began carrying distant signals, broadcasters became alarmed about this new medium. If a cable system imported distant signals, that could mean economic losses for local broadcasters. At least some of the cable subscribers would watch distant stations instead of local ones, especially if a cable system offered subscribers high-budget stations based in large cities along with nearby low-budget stations. Also, of course, the added non-broadcast programming represented new competition for broadcasters, siphoning off part of their audience.

Given the embryonic status of CATV in the 1950s, the FCC had refused to assume jurisdiction over cable because CATV didn't involve a use of the spectrum and the commission had no specific statutory authority to regulate it. But by 1966 the FCC had changed its mind. To protect broadcasters and program producers, the FCC then issued regulations for cable television systems. The new regulations had many very technical provisions, but one of the most important was a strict limit on distant signal importation. For instance, cable systems were required to carry the nearest station affiliated with each network rather than more distant ones. The rules also spelled out the relationship between cable systems and local governments, which had been granting franchises (in effect, government-sanctioned monopolies) to CATV operators.

The FCC claimed the authority to make these rules by arguing that cable affected on-the-air broadcasters, and that regulation was necessary to carry out the commission's regulatory responsibilities to broadcasters. Legally, this was called "ancillary jurisdiction."

The FCC's cable rules were quickly challenged in court, and in 1968, the Supreme Court affirmed the FCC's authority to regulate cable television in *U.S. v. Southwestern Cable Co.* (392 U.S. 157). The high court found authority for the FCC's regulation of cable not only in the concept of ancillary jurisdiction but also in a provision of the Communications Act that places wire and telecommunications in general under FCC control.

Regulation, Deregulation and Reregulation

With the Supreme Court's blessing, the FCC repeatedly expanded its cable rules, placing more and more restrictions on cable systems. Many cable operators felt these rules were intended to protect the FCC's major clientele, the over-the-air broadcasters, not to promote the public interest. By the early 1970s, cable systems were required to do these things: (1) provide local public and government access channels if they had more than 3,500 subscribers; (2) originate a minimum amount of local programming, again if they had 3,500 subscribers; (3) refrain from importing distant signals or "leapfrogging" over the nearest network affiliate in providing each network's programming (these were called the "non-duplication" and "signal carriage" requirements); and (4) respect syndication agreements by not carrying a distant station's syndicated shows if a local station had exclusive rights to the show.

In addition, each system had to get sort of a *de facto* license called a "certificate of compliance" from the FCC before it could conclude its franchise agreement with local government officials, and cable systems had to comply with most of the other requirements imposed on broadcasters, such as the Equal Time Rule, the Fairness Doctrine and equal employment opportunity policies.

Faced with these comprehensive (and costly) federal regulations, a cable system again challenged the FCC's authority to issue such orders. But in 1972 the Supreme Court voted 5-4 to affirm the commission's program origination requirements (*U.S. v. Midwest Video Corp.*, 406 U.S. 649). Ironically, the FCC had dropped many of its access and programming requirements during this lawsuit and did not immediately reinstate them afterward, although cable systems were still required to provide equipment to those who wanted to do programming on such public access channels as remained available.

During most of the 1970s the FCC continued to regulate cable systems heavily in an effort to keep them from doing anything to upset the commission's policy of defining television service in terms of local markets. In 1976, the commission issued new rules on public access and also required cable systems with over 3,500 subscribers to eventually provide at least 20 channels.

However, Midwest Video, the company that lost the narrow 1972 Supreme Court decision, again challenged the commission's rulemaking authority. This time, Midwest Video won. In 1979 the Supreme Court overturned the FCC's new public access and channel capacity requirements (*FCC v. Midwest Video*, 440 U.S. 689). The court said these rules, in effect, made common carriers of cable systems, placing them under obligations the Communications Act forbids the FCC to impose on broadcasters. Moreover, the court said the rules went far beyond what was reasonably ancillary to the FCC's lawful responsibilities in broadcast regulation. In effect, the Supreme Court told the FCC to go back to Congress and get the specific authority to do these things if they were really in the public interest:

> The Commission may not regulate cable systems as common carriers, just as it
> may not impose such obligations on television broadcasters. We think author-
> ity to compel cable operators to provide common carriage of public originated
> transmissions must come specifically from Congress.

While this Supreme Court decision overturned the FCC's nationwide rules requiring cable systems to provide public access, that did not mark the end of public access. First of all, some cable systems continued to provide public access channels on a voluntary basis. In addition, Congress passed legislation in 1984 that reinstated many public access requirements.

After its setback in the second *Midwest Video* decision, the FCC decided it was time to undertake a major deregulation of the cable industry. As noted earlier, cable operators had long argued that the FCC's rules were more intended to protect broadcasters by stunting the growth of cable than to serve the public interest.

The FCC heeded the cable systems' arguments and deregulated cable in 1980. The FCC abandoned the restrictions on distant signal importation. This allowed cable systems to offer their subscribers a much wider choice of programming—but at the expense of small-market television stations, some of whose viewers preferred to watch metropolitan stations via cable.

In 1980, the FCC also deleted the *Syndicated Exclusivity Rule* (or "Syndex"), but only temporarily. The Syndex rule required cable systems to black out syndicated programs shown by distant stations (including "superstations") when a local station had an exclusive agreement to show the program.

In deciding to drop the Syndex rule, the FCC noted that the syndication rules were intended to protect producers when they had no copyright protection from cable systems. With cable systems by then required to pay copyright royalties for distant signals, the FCC majority felt the rules were obsolete. Charles D. Ferris, the commission chair at the time, said the FCC action "removed the regulatory debris of a previous decade."

Ironically, this "regulatory debris" made a comeback a few years later: the FCC voted to restore the Syndicated Exclusivity Rule in 1988. Eliminating Syndex was unpopular with many broadcasters and program producers in 1980; that decision was infamous to these groups by 1988. (Note that the Syndex rule is different from the "Fin-Syn" rule—the Financial Interest and Syndication Rule. Until it was abolished, the latter curtailed network syndication rights and program production; it is discussed in Chapter Twelve.)

When it restored the Syndex rule, the FCC noted that much of the programming of superstations consisted of reruns of old network programs also carried on local stations. "Instead of a rule of reruns, which is what we have now, I think we can, through Syndex rules, better achieve program diversity that will appeal to differing viewer preferences," said FCC Chair Dennis Patrick.

The new Syndex rule differed from the old one in several respects. For one thing, it permitted superstations to negotiate exclusive national syndication rights contracts. Under such a contract, only the superstation could carry a certain show. No local station would then be able to obtain rights to that show. The new rule also exempted cable systems with fewer than 1,000 subscribers and cable systems that carry "distant" stations from nearby towns when viewers can pick up the signals off the air with a good antenna.

The new Syndex rule took effect in 1990. Several cable system owners and superstations challenged the new Syndex rule in court, but in *United Video v. FCC* (890 F.2d 1173), the U.S. Court of Appeals held that the FCC had the legal authority to reimpose this rule.

In 1984, the Supreme Court ruled on another of the FCC's cable regulations, sharply curtailing the power of local governments to regulate cable content when the local rules conflict with the FCC's rules. In *Capital Cities Cable Inc. v. Crisp* (467 U.S. 691), the court overturned an Oklahoma law that prohibited cable systems from carrying advertising for wine and hard liquor, even if the advertising in question was legal where it originated. (Although the Oklahoma law banned wine and hard liquor advertising on that state's television stations, stations in several nearby states were allowed to carry it.)

The Oklahoma law directly conflicted with the federal must-carry rules then in effect, which required cable systems to carry nearby television stations without altering the content of their broadcasts. Several cable systems near other states' borders were required by FCC regulations to carry television signals from out of state, including their alcoholic beverage advertising. As a result, Oklahoma cable operators were in a classic Catch-22 situation. If they obeyed the federal must-carry rules and carried alcoholic beverage advertising, they faced prosecution under Oklahoma law. If they obeyed the state law and blacked out such ads, they risked punishment for violating federal regulations.

The high court resolved this conflict by ruling decisively in favor of the federal rules. The court said that the FCC, like Congress, clearly has the authority to preempt state and local laws that conflict with federal purposes. In essence, the court said cable content was a federal matter, not subject to local rules that conflict with federal policies.

However, the court did not rule that state laws forbidding liquor advertising are inherently in violation of the First Amendment, although both broadcasters and cable operators had urged the court to reach that conclusion. Rather, the high court based its decision to overturn the Oklahoma law solely on the concept of federal preemption, not the First Amendment. Thus, a state may still forbid alcoholic beverage advertising as long as the state law does not conflict with any federal law.

But the *Capital Cities* decision did make it clear that state and local governments may not impose rules on cable systems that conflict with federal rules.

In 1988, the Supreme Court ruled on another aspect of the right of the FCC—and local governments—to regulate cable television. The court held in *City of New York v. FCC* (486 U.S. 57) that local governments could not impose more strict technical requirements on cable systems than those established by the FCC. The FCC had adopted standards for such things as signal quality and had prohibited local governments from setting different standards. The idea was to allow the cable industry to operate under uniform national standards rather than standards that might vary from town to town.

New York argued that the FCC's standards were too low and that a city should be free to set higher standards than the FCC's. The Supreme Court ruled that the FCC had the right to set uniform national standards and to prevent any city from establishing different standards.

The FCC extended for five years a prohibition against exclusive contracts between cable operators and cable networks. Several cable companies petitioned for a review of the statute. In *Cablevision Sys. Corp. v. FCC* (597 F.3d 1306, 2010) the D.C. Circuit denied their petition, saying that the FCC did not exceed its authority in extending the prohibition, and the decision to do so was not arbitrary and capricious. The companies' First Amendment claims also failed, the court said, as the FCC met the intermediate scrutiny standard applied by the court (a statute is upheld if "it furthers an important or substantial governmental interest; if the governmental interest is unrelated to the suppression of free expression; and if the incidental restriction on alleged First Amendment freedoms is no greater than is essential to the furtherance of that interest").

Cable Television Legislation

Even before *Capital Cities*, local governments and cable operators were lobbying in Congress, seeking a clarification of the roles of federal, state and local governments in regulating cable. As local governments saw their right to regulate cable being eroded by the Supreme Court and the FCC, their leaders decided they needed cable legislation from Congress—even if it wasn't exactly the kind of legislation they had originally hoped for. They worked out a compromise with the cable industry; the two rival groups jointly endorsed an amended version of a cable bill that had been bogged down in Congress for two years. Called the Cable Communications Policy Act of 1984, it was enacted late in that year.

In this legislation Congress further curtailed the right of local governments to regulate cable systems. The law deregulated many cable subscription fees after a two-year transition period wherever cable systems had "effective competition," which meant merely that there had to be three local television stations that viewers could watch without cable, if they had a good antenna. In addition, the 1984 law barred local governments from charging franchise fees in excess of five percent of a cable system's gross revenues. In return for this rate deregulation, the law authorized many local governments to require public access, government and educational channels—something the second *Midwest Video* Supreme Court decision had prohibited in the absence of an act of Congress.

The Cable Communications Policy Act affirmed the right of local governments to award franchises, but it also protected cable operators from arbitrary franchise nonrenewals. The law also excluded telephone companies from the cable business except in rural areas (a provision that was eventually overturned by the 1996 Telecommunications Act), and it prohibited TV stations from owning cable systems in their service areas (although the FCC can grant waivers of these restrictions). And the law required cable operators to wire their entire franchise service areas, not just the most affluent neighborhoods where the potential for profit might be greatest.

CATV:
"community antenna television," an antenna system serving a whole community.

must-carry rule:
a Cable Act provision that required cable systems to carry local broadcast channels, held to be content-neutral and necessary for the survival of over-the-air broadcast stations.

FIG. 59. Anderson Cooper.

Joe Seer / Shutterstock.com.

Focus on...
Equal time provisions for "infotainment" shows?

As more television shows straddle the line between news and entertainment (like Jon Stewart and Stephen Colbert), how will the equal time rules for political broadcasting apply to these shows? Such a question was asked about CNN's talk show "Anderson," featuring Anderson Cooper. The producers filed a request for a decision from the FCC about whether the show was exempt from the Section 315 equal time rules.

In 2011, the FCC said, in a nutshell, that yes, parts of "Anderson" could be considered a news show: "Based on the record before us, we conclude that the news interview segments of 'Anderson' qualify for the bona fide news interview exemption under Section 315(a)(2) because they are regularly scheduled; their producers control them; and the producers' decisions on format, content, and participants are based on newsworthiness and not on an intention to advance or harm an individual's candidacy."

The 1984 act left the cable industry free to grow with minimal government regulation. However, the FCC, Congress and local governments began hearing many complaints about poor service and skyrocketing rates charged by cable systems under deregulation. Critics began calling cable an "unregulated monopoly," because in most areas there was only one cable system, leaving consumers with no real choice if they wanted any of the non-broadcast programming that became available. Without either competition or government regulation of their rates, many cable systems were free to do just about whatever they wanted, and consumers were the losers, critics charged.

In addition to rapidly rising subscription fees, another thing that concerned many consumers was the manner in which the fees were apportioned between the basic tier of cable service and premium tiers. In many places, the basic tier included little more than broadcast signals (which consumers with antennas could receive for free), but it carried a high monthly fee. On the other hand, the premium cable channels, which consumers generally could not get anywhere else, were offered for only a small additional charge. The fees were not proportional to the cost of the programming to cable systems, critics said.

By 1992, the complaints about cable's rates and service were so widespread that Congress reregulated the industry, enacting the Cable Television Consumer Protection and Competition Act of 1992. The bill was passed just before the 1992 election, and then-President George H.W. Bush vetoed it. Congress mustered a two-thirds majority to override the veto, something that had never before happened during his presidency. Perhaps that indicated the degree to which Congress was hearing from angry constituents about the cable industry's alleged misdeeds. In a single act of Congress, the entire regulatory structure of the cable industry was revised. The law made sweeping changes in cable regulation—and in the relationship between the broadcast and cable industries. The era of cable deregulation was over—for the moment, at least. These are some of the highlights of the 1992 Cable Act:

Rate regulation - Local governments were empowered to reregulate basic cable rates everywhere except where there is "effective competition," which was defined as 50 percent of the households in an area having a choice between two cable or cable-like services, with the smaller of the two having a 15 percent or higher market share.

Rate rollbacks—The FCC was directed to adopt rules to reduce cable rates substantially. In 1993, the FCC adopted rules intended to reduce most cable systems' rates by about 10 percent, but the rules were so complex and voluminous that virtually everyone was confused. The full text of the rate regulations exceeded 500 pages in length! The rate rollbacks were expected to save consumers about $1.5 billion per year, but in some communities rates actually went up, not down. In 1994, the FCC adopted extensive amendments to its rate rollback rules. The result was additional rate reductions that averaged about seven percent, although the actual reduction still varied widely from one community to the next. The FCC exempted very small cable systems from some of the rate regulations. Many of these rate regulations were repealed in early 1999 under provisions of the 1996 Telecommunications Act.

Proportional rates—Cable systems were directed to charge rates that were proportional to their costs for various kinds of programming, and to fairly apportion the cost of the system itself among the various basic and premium channels.

Service standards—The FCC was directed to establish minimum service standards. Cable systems were told to have someone on duty to answer the telephone and respond to customers' complaints about poor reception, for example.

Nondiscriminatory program access for cable's competitors—The FCC was directed to adopt rules under which wireless and other non-cable video delivery systems would have fair access to the popular cable networks at a reasonable price.

Must-carry/retransmission consent—In perhaps the most important single aspect of the 1992 Act, each television station was given the right to choose either "must-carry" or "retransmission consent." If a station selected "must-carry," all cable systems in its service area were then required to carry that station (although no cable system was to be required to set aside more than one-third of its channel capacity for commercial television stations). However, the station would receive no payment for the mandatory carriage of its signal by cable systems. On the other hand, each station could also choose "retransmission consent." Then local cable systems were not allowed to carry that station's signal without obtaining permission and, presumably, some form of payment to the station.

All stations were required to notify their local cable systems of their choice by mid-1993, and most large stations opted for retransmission consent. Then the serious negotiations began, with both sides well aware that if a station and a local cable system could not agree on a price, the cable system would be free to drop the station. In the end, virtually all television stations agreed to accept some form of non-cash compensation for carriage of their signals by cable systems. For the most part, the cable industry simply refused to pay for broadcast signals, and broadcasters found that they lacked sufficient bargaining power to win major concessions from cable companies. What broadcasters got in lieu of cash payments from cable systems was a variety of other kinds of compensation for the right to retransmit broadcasters' signals. Several major networks and broadcast station groups gained new cable channels. ABC, NBC and Fox got cable channels in this way. Some stations and smaller groups got free advertising or promotional time on the cable. CBS held out for cash payments for retransmission consent—and got nothing in the 1993 negotiations, although it did in later rounds (retransmission consent agreements have to be renegotiated every few years). By the mid-2000s, more broadcasters were successful in negotiating for cash payments from cable systems for retransmission consent.

Channel repositioning—Cable systems were ordered not to reposition television stations that select the must-carry option to a different channel than their on-air channel without the station's consent. In addition to their on-air channel, stations were given the right to choose a channel they occupied on the cable system as of certain earlier dates. (One of broadcasters' major complaints had been that it was impossible to advertise their programming and urge viewers to watch "channel two," for instance, if their signal was moved to various other channels by cable systems in their service area).

In addition to these highlights, the 1992 act included other provisions. Altogether, the FCC was required to write regulations governing no fewer than 28 different provisions of the new law. The new rules were so complex that both the cable industry and its critics predicted that it could take decades to straighten out all of the details of the 1992 Cable Act.

Faced with the prospect of such a massive reregulation, the cable industry filed numerous different lawsuits in an attempt to keep the 1992 law from going into effect. However, most of these lawsuits were not successful. By far the most important court test of the 1992 Cable Act came in *Turner Broadcasting System v. FCC*, a case that produced two Supreme Court decisions, one in 1994 (512 U.S. 622) and another in 1997 (520 U.S. 180). In the 1994 ruling, the high court voted 5-4 to uphold the authority of Congress to authorize the FCC to impose must-carry requirements on cable systems. In so ruling, the court chose not to follow several earlier decisions of lower federal courts that had said previous must-carry rules violated the First Amendment rights of cable operators.

The Supreme Court noted that cable operators often have a monopoly of the primary television delivery system in a community. If a cable system with monopoly power should drop a television station, that could deny the station access to the majority of the viewers it is licensed by the FCC to serve. The high court said that the government's goal of fostering universal, over-the-air television service for the entire public was sufficiently important to justify requiring cable operators to carry local TV stations, even if it meant deleting other, made-for-cable programming.

In the 1994 case, the Court sent the case back to a lower court to reconsider whether cable systems that drop local TV stations really do threaten their ability to serve the public.

The Supreme Court reconsidered the *Turner Broadcasting* case in 1997 and again voted 5-4 to uphold the must-carry rules. In the meantime a lower court had amassed considerable evidence that without must-carry, many local stations would indeed lose up to two-thirds of their potential audience. And some stations would probably go bankrupt as a result. On this basis, the high court's majority concluded that must-carry was necessary to fulfill the government's objectives of assuring the survival of free local broadcast television and fostering competition in the TV programming marketplace. On the other hand, the burden this imposed on most cable operators was found to be minimal. Thus, the must-carry requirement was not an undue restriction on cable operators' First Amendment freedoms, the Court held in its 1997 ruling.

As a result of the *Turner Broadcasting* decision, the must-carry provision of the 1992 Cable Act remains in effect, requiring all but the smallest cable systems to carry local TV stations.

The must-carry provision was in the courts again in 2009 in *Cablevision Sys. Corp. v. FCC* (570 F.3d 83) (not the same case as the exclusive contracts case, although they share a name). The case arose out of a dispute between a broadcast television station and a cable system. The FCC ruled that Cablevision could not exclude WRNN, a station licensed in Kingston, N.Y., from its Long Island cable systems. Cablevision appealed, and the Second Circuit upheld the FCC's order. Cablevision appealed to the Supreme Court, asking the Court to reconsider whether the must-carry provision was still necessary in this media environment's increased competition, creating a stir among both consumer advocates and cable companies and stations. However, the Court declined to hear the appeal, leaving the must-carry rule in place—for now.

Meanwhile, many other lawsuits challenging various other provisions of the 1992 Cable Act were combined, and in an important decision in 1995, the D.C. Circuit rejected most of the cable industry's claims. In *Time Warner Entertainment v. FCC* (56 F.3d 151) the court upheld the FCC's rate rollbacks, which averaged 17 percent over two years.

The appellate court also upheld the FCC's authority under the Cable Act to regulate rates in both the basic tier of service (which usually includes local TV stations) plus the "enhanced basic" tier (which often includes such channels as CNN, ESPN and MTV). The court said it was reasonable for the FCC to regulate both to prevent cable systems from moving popular programming from tier to tier to escape rate regulation. Perhaps most important, the appellate court rejected the cable industry's basic argument: that many of these rules violate cable operators' First Amendment rights.

Another controversial issue was largely resolved in 1993 when several leading cable program providers settled antitrust lawsuits by agreeing to sell their programming to non-cable video services such as direct broadcast satellite (DBS) systems.

Can the FCC make rules to limit anti-competitive practices in cable under the Cable Act of 1992? Yes, in some cases, said the D.C. Circuit in 2011 (*Cablevision Sys. Corp. v. FCC*, 649 F.3d 695). The FCC had created new rules to extend anti-competitive programming restrictions applied to satellite programming to cable programming, and cable companies objected. The court said that the Cable Act gave the FCC authority to promote public interest and increased competition, and that the new regulations were reasonable exercises of the act's goals. The court also rejected the claim that the rules violated the First Amendment by burdening the speech of cable companies. In applying intermediate scrutiny, the court said that the FCC "has no obligation to establish that vertically integrated cable companies retain a stranglehold on competition nationally or that all withholding of terrestrially delivered programming negatively affects competition."

What will be the definition of a cable company? Broadcasters and cable companies are watching Internet start-ups closely, as these new companies have the potential to significantly impact how television is delivered to American consumers. The FCC is reviewing *multichannel video programming distributors* (MVPDs), which may affect the ways in which online programming is regulated, particularly regarding retransmission rights. These MVPDs often operate without the restrictions or rights accorded to cable or satellite providers. Courts are being asked to consider whether new companies like ivi and Aereo are cable companies. ivi retransmits over-the-air broadcasts from channels like ABC and Fox but without paying retransmission fees. It claims to be operating legally because of a loophole under which cable and satellite companies can retransmit this programming as long as they pay copyright fees as mandated by Section 111 of the Copyright Act—which ivi has applied to do. A federal district court refused to consider ivi a cable company, saying, "No technology … has been allowed to take advantage of Section 111 to retransmit copyrighted programming to a national audience while not complying with the rules and regulations of the FCC and without consent of the copyright holder" (*WPIX, Inc. v. ivi, Inc.*, 765 F. Supp. 2d 594, 2011). ivi appealed to the Second Circuit, which heard arguments in 2012.

Aereo, on the other hand, uses tiny antennae, the size of a dime, to bring local over-the-air broadcasting to its customers for a monthly fee. It argues that, rather than ivi's national reach, it focuses on the local consumer, merely making the free broadcasts available legally using individual antennae. Aereo has won its first battle in the courts against the broadcasters (*WNET v. Aereo, Inc.*, 2012 U.S. Dist. LEXIS 70749). A federal district judge threw out an unfair competition claim, saying it was pre-empted by the Copyright Act. However, two copyright claims are still pending.

Cable Franchises and the First Amendment

The cable franchising process, in which local governments authorize a cable system to wire a community, crossing public streets in the process, has been the subject of a number of legal battles that raised First Amendment issues.

In *City of Los Angeles v. Preferred Communications* (476 U.S. 488, 1986), the Supreme Court partially upheld a U.S. Court of Appeals ruling that the local government franchising process may violate the First Amendment rights of cable operators as "electronic publishers." In so ruling, the Court accepted an argument that cable operators had been making for years— that their First Amendment rights cannot be arbitrarily abridged by local governments.

Preferred Communications announced that it wanted to provide cable service in a portion of Los Angeles where another company already held an exclusive franchise from the city. Preferred challenged the city's right to grant one company the exclusive right to communicate by cable while denying that right to all others.

Preferred Communications argued that because the utility poles could carry several sets of television cables, the grant of a cable monopoly was comparable to the city council choosing one newspaper to serve the city and then denying distribution rights to all other newspapers. In essence, Preferred Communications was arguing that utility poles, like city sidewalks, are a First Amendment forum where local authorities must permit rival communicators to deliver their messages.

That argument had been made before without much success, but this time an appellate court accepted it, ruling that cable systems are engaged in a form of communication that deserves essentially the same First Amendment protection as newspapers and magazines.

In its 1986 decision, the Supreme Court refused to go as far as the Court of Appeals did. In an opinion by Justice William Rehnquist, the court agreed that cable systems "plainly implicate First Amendment interests." However, Rehnquist refused to equate cable's First Amendment rights with those of newspaper publishers. Instead, he said cable's rights had to be balanced against "competing social interests," perhaps including a city's desire to award exclusive franchises.

The Supreme Court sent the *Preferred* case back to a trial court to reconsider. In 1990, a federal judge in Los Angeles ruled that the utility poles in Los Angeles could indeed support more than one set of cables. Therefore, the Los Angeles policy of allowing only one cable system to operate in a particular area is a violation of the First Amendment, the court ruled. Also, the judge overturned Los Angeles' requirement that cable systems provide public access channels and meet minimum technical standards. Those rules, too, violate the First Amendment rights of cable operators, the court ruled. As a result of the *Preferred Communications* case, in many instances it is now possible for new systems to go into business in competition with existing cable operators, with or without the city's blessing. However, the cost of establishing a new system is so high that it has happened in only a few cities. On the other hand, telephone company-based TV service has grown rapidly during the 2000s, offering many more consumers another choice.

Banning Indecency on Cable

The cable industry has won several more First Amendment victories in lawsuits challenging government attempts to ban indecent but non-obscene adult programming on cable channels.

In 1987 the Supreme Court ruled that cable systems cannot be forbidden to carry indecent programming by state or local governments. In *Wilkinson v. Jones* (480 U.S. 926, affirming 800 F.2d 989), the Supreme Court upheld a lower court ruling that Utah's state Cable Decency Act is unconstitutional. The high court did not issue its own opinion or even hold oral arguments on the case. Nevertheless, by affirming a lower appellate court's decision, the Court gave this case the weight of a Supreme Court decision.

The Utah law that was invalidated had forbidden nudity or sex acts on cable systems except between midnight and 7 a.m. In overturning the law, the Court of Appeals had said, "The scope of the language (in the Utah law) is so uncertain as to chill legitimate expression in a way that the (Constitution's) overbreadth doctrine forbids."

In 1996, the Supreme Court again addressed the question of sexually oriented programming on cable in *Denver Area Educational Telecommunications Consortium v. FCC*, 518 U.S. 727). In this case, the Court ruled on the constitutionality of three provisions of the 1992 Cable Act concerning "patently offensive" sexually oriented programming on cable access channels. The high court upheld Section 10(a) of the 1992 Act, which said cable operators may ban patently offensive material on commercial leased access channels if they choose to do so. The court said this provision does not violate the First Amendment; it leaves cable operators free to carry such programs or reject them, just as cable operators have a First Amendment right to carry or reject other cable programming.

However, the Court overturned Section 10(b) and Section 10(c) of the 1992 Cable Act, ruling that both violate the First Amendment. Section 10(b) required cable operators who choose to carry patently offensive material on a leased access channel to segregate it on a single channel and block that channel to everyone except subscribers who specifically ask to receive it 30 days in advance. The court said this was an excessive burden on First Amendment freedoms: it would not allow a viewer to decide spontaneously to watch a specific program; nor would it protect subscribers who feared having their names appear on a list of persons who had requested to receive a "sex channel."

The Supreme Court also ruled that cable operators cannot censor sexually oriented programming on public access, educational and government channels, as Section 10(c) of the 1992 law required. The court said these channels have traditionally been a public forum, not subject to censorship.

The Communications Decency Act, which is a section of the 1996 Telecommunications Act, went further in regulating adult programming on cable, requiring cable systems that carry sexually explicit adult channels either to scramble them completely or carry them only between 10 p.m. and 6 a.m.

Complete scrambling is not technically feasible for some older cable systems because of "signal bleed" (which allows some non-subscribers to see a fuzzy picture or hear muffled audio in spite of the scrambling). That meant adult channels could only broadcast during the late-night hours under this law. Playboy Entertainment sued, alleging a First Amendment violation. A three-judge federal court ruled that the scrambling requirement violates the First Amendment. The court concluded that providing an additional blocking device to any household that requests one (which is permitted under another provision of the Telecommunications Act) is a less restrictive alternative to the daytime blackout requirement as a way to deal with signal bleed.

The federal government appealed, leading to still another Supreme Court decision and another decisive First Amendment victory for cable in 2000: *U.S. v. Playboy Entertainment Group* (529 U.S. 803). In this case, the high court voted 5-4 to allow adult cable programming in the daytime even if a cable system cannot prevent all signal bleed. The Court's 5-4 majority said the provision allowing any subscriber who wants it to request an additional blocking device is sufficient to enable parents to keep their children from watching adult programming on a fuzzy, partially scrambled screen. The Court noted that fewer than one percent of cable subscribers had requested the additional device, despite the widespread mailing of notices of its availability, indicating minimal parental concern about signal bleed.

The majority said it was a violation of the First Amendment for government to deny non-obscene adult programming to millions of daytime viewers who want it when the extra blocking device is a less-restrictive alternative to government censorship for those who do not want even a fuzzy, partially scrambled picture arriving in their homes. Writing for the Court, Justice Anthony Kennedy said, "This case involves speech alone; and even where speech is indecent and enters the home, the objective of shielding children does not suffice to support a blanket ban if the protection can be accomplished by a less restrictive alternative." Kennedy also said parents reacted to this problem "with a collective yawn."

Meanwhile, many cable systems offered new "family tiers" that excluded channels carrying programs not considered suitable for young children. Another controversial idea was to require cable systems to offer *à la carte* pricing. That would allow subscribers to choose only those channels they actually want instead of packages of channels.

Consumers have long wanted the ability to purchase individual cable channels instead of the bundles traditionally offered by cable companies. But is such bundling unlawful? The Ninth Circuit said no, at least not under antitrust law. The court rejected consumer allegations that cable companies' bundling of multi-channel packages was a violation of Section 1 of the Sherman Antitrust Act (*Brantley v. NBC Universal*, discussed in Chapter Twelve).

Cable and Digital Recording

In 2009, the question was asked whether a remote-storage digital video recorder (RS-DVR) system, a cross between DVRs and video-on-demand services which stores programs on drives maintained not by consumers but by a cable company for retrieval on demand, violates the Copyright Act by infringing exclusive rights of reproduction and public performance. The Second Circuit said no (*Cartoon Network and CNN v. CSC Holdings*, 536 F.3d 121). While the *Sony* Betamax case discussed in Chapter Six addresses the time shifting issue from the perspective of consumers using their own equipment to save programming, this case deals with cable companies storing copyrighted content.

CSC's system splits the delivery of a cable program into two streams when it comes in, one that is delivered to the consumer immediately, and a second stream with a buffer that evaluates whether any customer has asked to record the program. If yes, the data is sent to that customer's hard disk. If no, the buffer is discarded.

The Second Circuit said that making a "copy" has two elements: "the work must be embodied in a medium, i.e., placed in a medium such that it can be perceived, reproduced, etc., from that medium (the 'embodiment requirement'), and it must remain thus embodied 'for a period of more than transitory duration' (the 'duration requirement')."

The court said that the buffer, which could hold no more than 1.2 seconds of programming at a time before being overwritten, was sufficiently transitory so as not to fulfill the "duration element" of the test. The Supreme Court declined to hear an appeal.

■ NEW ELECTRONIC MEDIA TECHNOLOGIES

A number of promising new electronic communications technologies have appeared in recent years. Some seem destined to fundamentally alter media consumption patterns. Others have failed to win consumer acceptance, becoming boondoggles that produced nothing but billion-dollar losses for investors.

Cable, of course, is hardly a new technology. But its emergence as the fastest growing video delivery system of the 1980s contributed to disappointing early failures of direct broadcast satellites (DBS) and some other new technologies. By the early 2000s, though, a new generation of satellite television services became viable competitors to cable while other new technologies such as the Internet and digital television (DTV) gained prominence.

Digital and High-Definition Television

After years of research, planning and debate, in 1997 the FCC acted to authorize the transition to digital television in the United States.

Under the FCC's rules, each existing full-power television station was assigned a new channel for DTV. The FCC ordered network-owned and network-affiliated stations in the largest markets to begin digital broadcasting in 1999, with stations in smaller markets required to go digital in 2000 and 2001. For various reasons, many stations were unable to meet those deadlines. By 2005, though, most television stations had launched their DTV channels, although only about 15 percent of American households owned digital television receivers then.

That posed a major problem. The federal government needed to retrieve some of the old analog TV channels and sell them to new users, including police and fire authorities who desperately need more channels. Wireless broadband Internet service providers also need some of those channels if they are to provide a viable alternative to cable and telephone company-based Internet service. Recognizing these needs, Congress decreed that broadcasters must go all-digital, shutting off their analog broadcasts on February 18, 2009.

Cable and satellite systems provided digital converter boxes to subscribers who own only analog TV sets—for a fee. However, an estimated 70 million analog TV sets are not hooked to a cable or satellite service. That includes second or third TV sets in many homes with subscription TV service. Nearly 20 percent of American homes have no cable or satellite service at all. Without converters or new digital TV sets, those households would lose their television service in 2009. Congress allocated about $1.5 billion to subsidize the purchase of digital converter boxes for those homes.

Meanwhile, the FCC adopted rules requiring TV manufacturers to include digital capability in all new TV sets, starting in March 2007. That means TV sets had to have built-in digital tuners and not merely be "digital ready" (which means they will receive digital programming only with an external converter). The converter boxes don't allow the reception of true high-definition television (HDTV) signals on analog TV sets. The signals are converted back to standard definition.

The digital transition was postponed from February 18 to June 12, 2009 by the DTV Delay Act; FCC commissioners and President Obama all supported the delay. Demand for coupons to defray the costs of digital converters had been high and had exceeded the funding provided; millions were left on waiting lists. The Short-term Analog Flash and Emergency Readiness Act (SAFER) allowed about 120 full-power stations in 87 markets to maintain analog "nightlight" service for 30 days to provide emergency service and information about the analog shutdown.

How smoothly did it go? The FCC in a June 13, 2009, press release, the day after 971 stations' analog signals "went dark," reported almost 700,000 calls from June 8 through 12 to its helpline. On the day of the transition, the FCC put 4,000 agents on telephone support. Although he was pleased how the transition had gone, acting FCC Chairman Michael Copps added, "But our job is far from over. This transition is not a one-day affair."

Under the FCC's rules for digital TV, each station may broadcast *high-definition television* (HDTV) on its digital channel or instead deliver four or five lower quality programs simultaneously on subchannels within the digital channel. Many broadcasters are carrying multiple signals most of the broadcast day, providing more programming choices than ever before, but without the long-promised picture quality of HDTV. Some plan to lease some of their subchannels or to broadcast radio programming instead of TV on some of the subchannels.

The FCC also adopted a rule requiring cable systems to carry the full digital signal of each local TV station, even if that consists of several standard-definition subchannels instead of one HDTV channel. During a transition period, cable systems were also required to carry many TV stations in an analog format for viewers unable to receive digital signals.

An additional problem for many small market and public television stations is still the challenge of paying for the digital transition. Going digital requires new studio equipment, new transmitters and often new towers. Industry executives have estimated that switching to digital is costing the average station $8 to $12 million, with an additional cost of about $100 million each for the major networks. In 2008, Congress was considering legislation to subsidize the digital transition for many smaller stations, including low-power stations.

Cable-Telephone-Internet Convergence

Perhaps no part of the Telecommunications Act of 1996 had a greater long-range impact on the American way of life than the provisions designed to open all of the communications industries to new competition. Among other things, this law allows telephone companies ("telcos") and cable systems to enter each others' businesses and preempts many state and local regulations that stood in the way.

Even before the 1996 law was enacted, a number of states had taken steps toward allowing cable companies to offer telephone service, and vice versa. The FCC had also taken some preliminary steps in that direction, too. But Congress declared that wide-open competition is to be the norm. This means:

- Local phone companies are allowed to offer video programming, even in their own telephone service areas.
- Local phone companies may offer Internet access and television programming.
- Local phone companies may offer long-distance telephone service.
- Cable systems may offer local telephone service and broadband (high-speed) Internet access.
- Local phone companies are free to manufacture telephone equipment, something they were largely prevented from doing under the court order that broke up the nationwide AT&T monopoly.

To facilitate all of these changes in the communications business, the 1996 act overruled a variety of federal, state and local regulations and industry practices that might stand in the way. In 2002 the Supreme Court upheld the rules giving cable systems access to utility poles at low cost, even if the cable system is using the poles to deliver high-speed Internet access instead of television (*Nat'l Cable & Telecommunications Assn. v. Gulf Power Co.,* 534 U.S. 327).

In addition to all of these provisions, the 1996 act included a vast array of provisions designed to foster competition and prevent anticompetitive business practices. The various companies are not allowed to "cross-subsidize" their new businesses with revenue from their established businesses in which they enjoy a near monopoly. And technical standards must not be set up by entities such as the research arm of the local phone companies in a manner that gives the phone companies a competitive advantage.

By the 2000s, millions of American households had dropped traditional telephone service for service offered by cable companies or over the Internet. Meanwhile, major telcos were setting up their own broadband delivery systems to make their television and Internet services competitive with those offered by cable companies.

Direct Broadcast Satellites

The number-one high-tech disappointment of the 1980s was the direct broadcast satellite (DBS) business. A decade later, DBS had become a dramatic success story—boosted by government regulators as a needed source of competition for cable.

Billed in the early 1980s as the television technology of the future, DBS at first was a dismal failure. All of the original DBS companies bailed out, victims of technical, financial and marketing problems that began almost as soon as DBS was first proposed as a serious medium of mass communication. All of the firms that were originally awarded licenses for direct satellite broadcasting dropped their plans in the face of prohibitive costs and serious questions about the economic potential of the service. Several would-be satellite program providers were forced to absorb multi-million dollar losses in the process. It was not until much later that DBS became a viable medium.

The concept underlying DBS is fairly simple, although the technology to accomplish it is complex and expensive. A number of satellites are positioned above the equator at an altitude of 22,300 miles. At that altitude each satellite would orbit the earth at a speed that exactly matches the Earth's rotation speed. The result: each satellite appears to remain stationary over one point on the Earth's surface, not moving at all. Such a satellite is said to be *geosynchronous.* This allows receiving dish antennas to be locked in position, permanently pointed at a satellite. If communications satellites were not geosynchronous, very costly tracking hardware

high-definition television: a digitally broadcast system with higher resolution than traditional television systems; the use of digital video compression means that less bandwidth is used than for analog broadcasts.

and software would have to be used to keep every dish antenna pointed at a satellite that appeared to be moving around the sky.

Once a geosynchronous satellite is in orbit, transmitting stations on the ground send up signals on an "uplink" frequency. The satellite receives these signals and retransmits them back to earth on a "downlink," which is usually a different frequency.

Geosynchronous communications satellites are not new. Virtually all major cable systems, broadcasters, wire services and newspapers have used these satellites for years to relay programming or information. However, the early communications satellites operated with such low transmitter power that a very sensitive (and therefore large) dish antenna was required to receive the signal. Perhaps one reason the DBS ventures of the early 1980s failed is because consumers had to have large dish antennas in their yards (or on their roofs) to receive the satellite signals. Early satellite dishes were typically about 10 feet in diameter (and ugly, in the opinion of many homeowners' associations, local governments and neighbors).

What is new about DBS today is that there is a new generation of satellites with more powerful transmitters operating on higher frequencies, allowing good reception with dish antennas only two or three feet in diameter—small enough to be mounted inconspicuously in a window, on a balcony or in an out-of-sight corner of the roof.

While the DBS ventures of the 1980s all failed, several major players in the communications business launched new DBS systems in the 1990s; the DBS industry had a combined total of more than 20 million subscribers by 2008—enough to have a major impact on the fortunes of cable companies.

DirecTV and EchoStar, the leading DBS providers, gained many new subscribers in 1999 and 2000 after Congress passed the Satellite Television Home Viewers Act, allowing satellite systems to carry local television stations, including those offering network programming. Before then, DBS providers were barred from carrying the major broadcast networks except in "white areas" far enough from any city to be out of range of over-the-air TV stations. This law amended the Copyright Act to allow this; it is discussed in Chapter Six.

Under the 1996 Telecommunications Act, the FCC took other steps to help DBS systems provide viable competition to cable. For instance, the FCC overruled local zoning and deed restrictions that prohibited the small dish antennas needed for DBS. The FCC adopted rules requiring local governments, homeowners' associations and landlords to allow not only dish antennas but also TV antennas for those who wanted to receive free TV broadcasts over the air. The FCC rule governing apartments allows tenants to put antennas on balconies and other private areas but not on roofs or outside walls.

Other Technologies

Perhaps the new video delivery technology that has captured the public imagination more than any other is Internet, iPod, iPad and other tablets and cell phone-based television broadcasting. Many television broadcasters are moving aggressively to add streaming to their existing websites so they can do full-blown broadcasting using these new technologies. They are well aware that other industries (including newspaper publishers, among others) are also moving rapidly toward video streaming on the Internet. More and more consumers are getting video programming via the Internet and cellphones. This kind of convergence may force policy-makers to rewrite all of their definitions of broadcasting and publishing. Broadcasters and newspaper or magazine publishers are becoming direct competitors on the Internet, all offering interactive (two-way) broadcasting and video on demand. Many in

FIG. 60. Syncom, the first geosynchronous satellite, 1963.

NASA Images.

the industry are saying the *iPodization* of television is inevitable. The major networks offer programming directly to iPod viewers, an arrangement that could short-circuit local broadcasters and undercut their audience (and advertising) base.

But will these technologies survive legal actions by content providers? In 2011, Time Warner Cable released an app for the iPad that allowed users to stream its cable channels on the device, a move that is being challenged in court by cable companies.

A technology that is sometimes labeled as "new" is *low-power television (LPTV)*. LPTV is really nothing more than a new kind of conventional television broadcasting that was introduced during the 1980s. The FCC acted in 1982 to allow "mini-stations" to serve small towns and localized areas in larger cities. The idea was that these stations would transmit with low power and would operate efficiently with low overhead and bring TV service to communities that had little or no local service. To help them do that, the FCC freed LPTV stations of many regulations that apply to full-power stations. LPTV stations are authorized to serve a radius of 10-15 miles from their transmitter sites. In the 1990s, more than 2,200 LPTV stations were on the air or under construction.

However, by 2000 LPTV faced a threat from digital television: new interference from high-power digital stations. In some communities LPTV stations were forced to change to less desirable channels, accept new interference, or even curtail their operations to avoid causing interference to new digital television stations, which have legal priority over LPTV stations. Eventually LPTV stations were given some protection from the new DTV stations, but only LPTV stations that were broadcasting at least 18 hours a day, with three hours of local programming, were given this protection. Only about 400 of the 2,200 LPTV stations meet these standards.

Another new communications technology is digital audio broadcasting, formally known as the *Digital Audio Radio Service (DARS)*. DARS offers more than 100 channels of high-quality sound, delivered to consumers by satellites for a fee of $10-$15 a month. This service provides mainly nationwide programming rather than local programming.

Four companies applied for digital audio broadcasting licenses. The FCC set aside frequencies in the UHF spectrum for satellite radio and adopted rules for the new service.

In 1997, DARS spectrum auctions were held. The two winning bidders offered a total of $173 million for their spectrum. The two companies, XM and Sirius, launched their services in 2001. XM had more than 9 million subscribers by early 2008, while Sirius had 8.3 million. Some industry analysts were predicting the two satellite radio firms would have as many as 35 million subscribers by 2010.

In 2008, the FCC approved a proposal by Sirius and XM to merge into a single entity. The merger was approved earlier by the Justice Department, but it was vehemently opposed by local radio broadcasters and consumer groups, partly because the original FCC authorization of digital satellite radio included a ban on the two companies ever merging.

Hoping to compete with the new satellite-delivered digital radio services, over-the-air radio broadcasters in 2002 won FCC permission to launch "in-band on-channel" (IBOC) digital broadcasting. This allows AM and FM broadcasters to offer CD-quality sound to those equipped to receive it. By 2006, about 600 radio stations were broadcasting digital multi-channel programming, but the least expensive radios that could receive the digital signals were still selling for about $200.

In 2000 the FCC created another kind of broadcasting: *low-power FM (LPFM) radio*. Recognizing that most existing radio stations are owned by large corporations, the FCC began licensing very low-power stations to serve local communities or small areas within larger communities. This plan, which was strenuously opposed by commercial and public broadcasters, is discussed further in the section on broadcast ownership in Chapter Twelve.

Perhaps the oldest "new" technology of all is AM radio broadcasting. Long dismissed as an outdated technology that could not deliver good sound quality, old-fashioned analog AM radio may make a comeback, with the backing of the broadcast industry and the FCC. The FCC allocated 10 new channels for AM radio just above 1600 kHz, where the AM band ended almost from the beginning of AM broadcasting.

In addition, the commission set a higher standard for audio quality on the new channels, and set up a priority system for awarding frequencies to existing stations, with a preference for a few daytime-only stations in large cities so they could broadcast full time and for stations that had interference problems on their previous channels.

■ INTERNET TECHNOLOGIES AND CHALLENGES

In the 2000s, it has become increasing clear how essential Internet access is to all sectors of society. As a result, state and federal government sought to expand access to (and exercise control over) Internet services, and businesses saw huge money-making opportunities. The year 2010 saw a court case that forced the FCC to scramble to find authority to regulation the technology of the online environment. The FCC also offered a plan to attempt to ensure that all American have access to high-speed Internet access at affordable prices.

Broadband
President Barack Obama promised access to fast, affordable broadband (high-speed Internet access) as part of his campaign. The FCC in 2005 summarized its Broadcast Policy Statement in four maxims: Internet consumers are entitled to "any lawful content, any lawful application, any lawful device, any provider." Congress in 2009 directed the FCC to come up with a broadband plan to ensure that all Americans have access to broadband capabilities. In 2010, the FCC did so—its 376-page plan, called "Connecting America" (available at

broadband.gov) notes that nearly 100 million Americans do not have broadband at home and lays out an ambitious plan to remedy that.

The plan is four-fold: establishing policies for competition; ensuring efficient allocation and use of government resources; creating incentives for adopting broadband; and setting standards to maximize use. The major long-term goal in the plan is: "At least 100 million U.S. homes should have affordable access to actual download speeds of at least 100 megabits per second and actual upload speeds of at least 50 megabits per second." Other goals include leading the world in broadband innovation, assisting with affordability, ensuring faster speeds for public institutions like schools and hospitals, and making certain that first responders have access to a fast, interoperable national network.

Who will pay for this bonanza? No one, the FCC says; it will be paid for by spectrum auctions: "Given the plan's goal of freeing 500 megahertz of spectrum, future wireless auctions mean the overall plan will be revenue neutral, if not revenue positive." The plan generated controversy when it was released; the *New York Times* reported that telecom agencies, television stations, and rural Internet providers were expressing concern. All agreed that the goals were laudable but, as one analyst put it, "the devil is always in the details."

Net Neutrality

Currently, all websites are delivered on an equal basis; if you go to Amazon.com, your webpage is delivered just as fast as if you go to the White House's website (whitehouse.gov) or the *New York Times* (nytimes.com) or a social networking site like Facebook or MySpace. This is *net neutrality*, the concept that all traffic that passes through the Internet should be treated equally, became a hot political and social topic in the late 2000s. Concerns arose when Internet service providers began considering methods of service wherein they could charge more for faster access to certain sites or types of data, in effect creating a two- (or more) tiered Internet. Critics alleged that this was just a way for providers to make money by selling premier services.

The FCC supports net neutrality and acted as though it had the authority to mandate it. However, in 2010 the D.C. Circuit said that not only was there no express authority for the FCC to regulate net neutrality, there was no authority in the ancillary powers granted to the FCC by the Communications Act of 1934, either. This was a huge setback for the FCC and a significant win for Comcast, a broadband provider.

Comcast had blocked or delayed traffic from BitTorrent sites, which take up a lot of bandwidth, arguing that such measures were necessary to manage network capacity. The FCC issued an order against Comcast, saying that its actions contravened federal broadband policy. Comcast had already stopped these actions but filed suit anyway, alleging that the FCC had no authority to regulate in this area.

The D.C. Circuit overturned the order, saying that the FCC had "failed to tie its assertion of ancillary authority over Comcast's Internet service to any 'statutorily mandated responsibility'" (*Comcast Corp. v. FCC*, 600 F.3d 642).

In response, FCC chair Julius Genachowski issued a statement called "The Third Way" in which he proposed a hybrid structure for broadband which he said would give the FCC enough power to regulate net neutrality without overreaching. Under this approach, the FCC would "recognize the transmission component of broadband access service—and only this component—as a telecommunications service" and "apply only a handful of provisions of Title II [common carriers] that, prior to the Comcast decision,

net neutrality:
a policy that prevents restrictions on the delivery of online content or websites, under the idea that all traffic that flows through the Internet should be treated the same.

were widely believed to be within the Commission's purview for broadband."

Then the FCC in 2010 adopted new rules, called "The Free and Open Internet," that required more transparency from Internet service providers, forbid Internet service providers like telephone and cable companies (called "fixed-line" providers) from preventing access to their competitors or to certain websites, and mandated more relaxed rules for wireless providers. Under the rules, consumers who are heavy users can be charged more.

Verizon quickly challenged the new rules in the same court (but not the same three judges) that decided the 2010 Comcast case saying that the FCC had no regulatory authority here. Verizon said, "We are deeply concerned by the FCC's assertion of broad authority for sweeping new regulation of broadband networks and the Internet itself. We believe this assertion of authority goes well beyond any authority provided by Congress, and creates uncertainty for the communications industry, innovators, investors and consumers." MetroPCS also sued. But the D.C. Circuit dismissed their claims, saying that they were too early (*Verizon v. FCC*, 2011 U.S. App. LEXIS 6908).

The rules were published in the Federal Register and went into effect in 2011, and Verizon and other companies promptly filed suit; the D.C. Circuit consolidated the cases into one case, including a suit brought by advocacy group Free Press, alleging that wireless broadband should be treated no differently than wired. The case is unlikely to be argued before 2013. In 2012, the FCC announced the formation of an Open Internet Advisory Committee, as called for by its own rules, and its members include representatives from Comcast and AT&T as well as from Netflix and the Disney Company and a number of law and technology professors (it will be chaired by Harvard law professor Jonathan Zittrain).

But the issue hasn't left the public radar: in 2012 the CEO of movie streaming company Netflix, Reed Hastings, accused Comcast of violating net neutrality principles when the cable company exempted its own Xfinity app (video streaming over Xbox 360) data use from its 250GB monthly data cap—making it far more attractive for Comcast users to use its service rather than Hulu or Netflix, whose data usage would count against the monthly cap. Senator Al Franken (D-Minn.) took notice and sent a letter to the FCC urging the agency to investigate: "Even if this [action] does not amount to a technical violation, it certainly raises serious questions about how Comcast will favor its own content and services to the detriment of its competitors." The FCC responded that Comcast wasn't in violation because Xfinity does not stream over the open Internet.

Computer Fraud and Abuse Act

As many of these technologies use not only the Internet but personal computers of many kinds, laws have been developed to punish those who would use the technology for illicit gain or bad intentions. One such law is the Computer Fraud and Abuse Act (CFAA), passed in 1986 but currently the focus of several appellate courts. The act says essentially that whoever uses a "protected computer" for a variety of reasons like damaging a computer or information, trafficking in passwords, or compromising confidentiality can be criminally punished.

The *en banc* Ninth Circuit limited the reach of the CFAA, also the act used to prosecute Lori Drew in the Megan Meier cyberbullying case (*U.S. v. Drew*, 259 F.R.D. 449, 2009). In *U.S. v. Nosal* (676 F.3d 854, 2012), the court said that the act could be used to prosecute many Americans who engage in harmless but unauthorized computer use at work. David Nosal, who worked for Korn/Ferry, an executive search firm, asked several colleagues to help him start a competing firm; those colleagues used their passwords to log into a confidential source database and give that contact information to Nosal. The court said that the language of the CFAA was focused on access to that material, which Nosal's colleagues were permitted to do, not the use of that material. The always-quotable chief judge of the Ninth Circuit, Alex Kozinski, said that to interpret the law more broadly would open up a lot of harmless activities many engage in at work to criminal prosecution:

> Basing criminal liability on violations of private computer use policies can transform whole categories of otherwise innocuous behavior into federal crimes simply because a computer is involved. Employees who call family members from their work phones will become criminals if they send an email instead. Employees can sneak in the sports section of the *New York Times* to read at work, but they'd better not visit ESPN.com. And sudoku enthusiasts should stick to the printed puzzles, because visiting www.dailysudoku.com from their work computers might give them more than enough time to hone their sudoku skills behind bars.

The dissenters pointedly noted that the case was not about sudoku or ESPN, but rather "stealing an employer's valuable information to set up a competing business with the purloined data." Given that several circuit courts (the Fifth, Seventh and Eleventh) have weighed in with different, broader interpretations of the CFAA, some have suggested that the issue is ripe for a Supreme Court review.

◼ AN OVERVIEW OF MAJOR ISSUES

The electronic media face enormous legal, economic and policy questions today. We may be in the midst of a communications revolution even more far-reaching than the one that brought us television 60 years ago. With cable or satellite TV in about 85 percent of all American homes, and with digital television, Internet-based television, satellite radio and podcasting all here, many of the old rules of broadcast law and economics are obsolete. The day when three major television networks could dominate home entertainment in America is past. In 1979, ABC, CBS and NBC commanded 91 percent of the prime time television audience. By 2008, the original "big three" networks' share of the prime time audience was usually far below 50 percent and steadily declining. Fox, a latecomer to network broadcasting, often had a larger audience than any of the "big three." Cable and satellite networks also were winning a large share of the audience.

Recognizing these trends, the Federal Communications Commission has tried several different approaches to broadcast regulation in recent years. Some would say the FCC has moved in fits and starts, taking a zig-zag route toward no discernable destination.

In the early years of television, the FCC attempted to promote the public interest by adopting the Fairness Doctrine and other content controls. Then an FCC chair started calling the old rules "regulatory debris" and launched a broad deregulation of electronic communications. The FCC looked mainly to the marketplace for answers, while attempting to provide a "level playing field" for broadcasters, cable and other audio and video delivery systems. Then starting in the 1990s, the FCC adopted or considered a series of new content controls, raising new questions about the degree to which the First Amendment should protect the electronic media.

Perhaps the most fundamental question is this: should the federal government regulate broadcast content? When then-FCC Chair Newton Minow called network television a "vast wasteland" in 1961, he clearly believed the government had the power—and the obligation—to regulate content to improve it (based on his and other government officials' views of what content was good and bad for the American public). By the 1980s, another FCC chair was saying television is merely "a toaster with pictures," and thus not in need of much federal regulation.

Is either of these views right in a country with a First Amendment as well as a tradition of requiring broadcasters to serve the public interest, as that is defined by the government?

Are the FCC's rules, new and old, really "regulatory debris?" Is deregulation a good idea? What about abolishing a rule like the Fairness Doctrine? Should broadcasters be as free as newspaper publishers are to cover the news as they see it? Or should the government decide how not only broadcasters but also other media cover the issues of the day? Should the government even decide what is in the public interest?

Should television be "friendly to kids," as another FCC chair suggested? Does the federal government know what is best for the nation's children—or adults, for that matter? If so, is it right for over-the-air broadcasting to be singled out for government controls that do not apply to other media? And do these content controls really work? Can parents armed with a TV set and a V-chip programming device really keep their kids from seeing the TV shows that their friends are watching? Will many even try? Should Congress authorize the FCC to restrict TV violence? Would such regulations violate the First Amendment?

Should there be different indecency rules for over-the-air television than there are for satellite and cable channels? Do most viewers really know when they have clicked from an over-the-air channel to a cable channel? Do the rules protect children from language and images that they would never hear or see anywhere else? Does it make sense to protect children by banning words that are routinely used at most schools and in most neighborhoods?

Cable has seen regulation, deregulation, reregulation—and then more deregulation. During the 1990s the FCC adopted the most complex regulatory scheme cable has ever faced in America. The question that remains, of course, is whether the public really won or lost under this regulatory regimen. The cable industry said that with the rate rollbacks, retransmission consent fees and other new costs, there would be little money left for new programming and technology. Broadcasters and public interest groups, on the other hand, pointed to a litany of alleged abuses by cable systems during the cable industry's "unregu-lated monopoly" era. "They had it coming," some said of the tough rules cable faced.

In the new millennium, are we in an era of deregulation or reregulation? The answer might depend on whether one is talking about content controls or something else. There has been a major effort to clear the way for new multi-channel media "voices."

Promoting localism is again a key goal in the FCC's regulation of broadcasting. Broad-casters may wonder why they need the government's help in choosing their programming, while other media systems are free to make their own decisions based on what the ratings services say the audience prefers.

In all of this, has anybody really answered the big question: will all of the new audio and video services and new proposals for government regulation of content really give us better programming or just another "vast wasteland?" Is programming to address the perceived need of community leaders for new infrastructure really better programming than "Ameri-can Idol" or live sports coverage?

Where does the Internet fit into this equation? The Internet's broad First Amendment protection may lead to new questions—and new absurdities. Is it okay to have a four-letter word or an explicit depiction of sex on television if it arrived via the Internet but not okay if it arrived via over-the-air television (or cable, if Congress bans indecency on cable)? What if children view or hear programs containing four-letter words on their iPods?

It is clear that one of the federal government's goals in the 2000s is to help Americans get information online. How should this goal be accomplished? Should the FCC have the authority to regulate the Internet, including how Internet traffic is managed, or should there be a new agency created—or no regulator at all?

What about the traditional scarcity justification for broadcast regulation? Is it still valid in this multichannel world? The primary factor limiting the introduction of new video programming services today is the economic saturation of the marketplace, not the physi-cal saturation of the radio spectrum. Is the fact that the FCC receives more applications for licenses than it can accommodate still the overriding consideration today, given the alterna-tives to traditional broadcasting that now exist? Over-the-air broadcasting is just one of many systems available to those who wish to disseminate video programming to consumers.

At this point the same economic factors that limit the number of newspapers also set the limits on television-like services. Either industry could add numerous additional outlets—if the marketplace would support them. True, a broadcaster must have a government license while a newspaper publisher does not, but that hardly seems to be the issue: new television-like services are appearing all over the landscape while major newspapers are failing.

With audio and video streaming on the Internet, anyone can be a "broadcaster" now—no government license is needed. Is the scarcity rationale still viable?

WHAT SHOULD I KNOW ABOUT MY STATE?	• Much of this law is federal law. • How are my local broadcast stations complying with localism reporting standards? • What cable franchises are in my area? What arrangements do they have with the cities?

SUMMARY

A SUMMARY
OF
ELECTRONIC
MEDIA
REGULATION

Why Do Broadcasters Have Special Laws to Follow?

Broadcasters do not own their frequencies; spectrum is a valuable and limited resource; Congress declared that those given the privilege of using it must serve *the public interest, convenience, and necessity.* Broadcasters obtain licenses from the Federal Communications Commission, the agency charged with regulating the electronic media. License renewal challenges by citizens' groups and others have become more commonplace than they once were, but non-renewals are still rare.

What Are the Major Rules Governing Broadcast Content?

The *Fairness Doctrine* was an FCC policy that for nearly 40 years required broadcasters to provide overall balance in their programming. It was abolished in 1987, to the dismay of Congress and some public interest groups but to the delight of broadcasters who objected to government officials second-guessing their judgments. Despite calls to bring the Fairness Doctrine back, current FCC commissioners and chairs oppose it. The *Equal Time Rule,* on the other hand, is a provision of the Communications Act that requires broadcasters to sell comparable airtime to political candidates at similar rates; it has not been abolished. Television stations are also required to carry three hours per week of children's educational programming, and broadcasters are required to serve the public interest, as that is defined by the FCC, in various other ways.

What is Indecency?

Indecency is a standard of law applied to sexual content broadcast on over-the-air television or radio (not cable or satellite TV or radio). The FCC may regulate indecent content that is broadcast during the hours of 6:00 a.m. and 10:00 p.m., when children are most likely to be in the audience. The agency may punish "fleeting expletives" if they take place during that time.

How Is Cable Television Regulated?

Cable television systems need no FCC license, since they do not broadcast over the air. However, they are subject to many FCC rules because their operations affect on-the-air broadcasting. Cable was deregulated during the 1980s, but in 1992 Congress reregulated cable. The 1992 law mandated subscription rate reductions and must-carry or retransmission consent requirements to protect local television stations. Cable systems also must have *franchise agreements,* which give cities and counties some control over cable systems. The 1996 Telecommunications Act has repealed some rate reductions and other rules established by the 1992 law.

12 *Media Ownership Issues*

Does it matter who owns America's media? Does the public win or lose when one corporation owns many newspapers, magazines, movie and television studios, Internet services, radio stations, television stations, networks and cable systems—or a combination? Ever since William Randolph Hearst and the Scripps family built the nation's first newspaper chains more than a century ago, these have been controversial questions.

Media critics often regard the ongoing trend toward centralized ownership of the media as a threat to journalistic freedom—and the public interest. Regardless of how well intentioned the management of a large media conglomerate may be, central ownership deprives the media of the independence that is so vital in a democracy, critics say. But others say the growing concentration of ownership of the traditional media is inevitable if they are to survive in the highly competitive new media marketplace, in which all traditional media— newspapers and over-the-air broadcasters alike—are losing readers, listeners, viewers and advertisers to new, largely unregulated competitors. Like other businesses, media companies can achieve economies of scale by combining operations. For example, a company that owns eight radio stations in one city can sell advertising, do programming and handle station engineering more efficiently than eight individually owned stations. Some industry analysts say the older media must merge and cut costs or many traditional media voices will be silenced by economic realities.

However, even the defenders of multimedia ownership concede that abuses have occurred, and government agencies have sometimes tried to correct these abuses. The Antitrust Division of the U.S. Justice Department, for instance, has often acted against anticompetitive business practices in the media. And at times the Federal Communications Commission has limited both chain ownership in broadcasting and cross-ownership of print and broadcast media. At other times, however, both Justice and the FCC have acquiesced when large multimedia conglomerates merged with other equally large corporations. Sometimes the FCC has even set aside its own rules to facilitate these mergers. And Congress relaxed many media ownership restrictions in the Telecommunications Act of 1996, adopting the philosophy that companies should be free to grow and compete with other growing companies, all of whom are free to enter each other's areas of business. The 1996 law not only abolished many ownership restrictions, it also directed the FCC to review the remaining restrictions every few years to determine which ones can be eliminated.

The FCC acted on this Congressional mandate in 2003 by abolishing or liberalizing many long-standing ownership restrictions on a controversial 3-2 vote. By 2004, Congress had vetoed a portion of the FCC's ownership deregulation and a federal appeals court had halted implementation of many other aspects of the deregulation, ordering the FCC to reconsider many of the actions it took a year earlier (*Prometheus Radio Project v. FCC*, 373 F.3d 372). After the Supreme Court declined to review that decision, the FCC in 2007 announced a new, scaled-back liberalization of its ownership rules, prompting still more lawsuits and a new attempt to overrule the FCC in Congress.

In 2009, new Department of Justice antitrust head Christine Varney in her first speech asserted that the Obama administration would be much more aggressive on antitrust violations than its predecessor. She said that she planned to "go 'back to the basics" and evaluate single-firm conduct against...tried and true standards that set forth clear limitations on how monopoly firms are permitted to behave."

Never have questions of communications media ownership and business practices been more controversial than they are now, with almost daily news accounts of mergers, ownership rule changes and antitrust lawsuits.

■ AN OVERVIEW OF ANTITRUST LAW

Serious government regulation of monopolistic business practices in America began with the *Sherman Antitrust Act*, enacted in 1890 to combat rampant abuses in the post-Civil War era of industrialization. The act is the nation's pioneering antitrust law; it forbids a wide variety of "contracts, combinations ...or conspiracies in restraint of trade or commerce."

In 1914 the *Clayton Act* was adopted, forbidding certain other business practices and expanding the federal government's antitrust enforcement powers. This law was strengthened in 1950 by the addition of the Celler-Kefauver Act, which prohibits one company from buying out a competitor where the result is more monopoly and less competition. Thus, business ownership as well as business practices have come under federal regulation.

Of the many business practices banned by these antitrust laws, a few should be specifically noted. For instance, *price fixing* and *profit pooling* are prohibited. That means it is generally unlawful for competing companies to enter an agreement either to charge non-competitive prices or share profits. Rival companies are supposed to keep each others' prices low by competing. They're not supposed to conspire to avoid price competition.

In addition, many *mergers, tying arrangements* and *boycotts* are illegal. A merger is an arrangement in which two businesses combine. Mergers are illegal when they substantially reduce competition, to the detriment of consumers or other businesses. Before a merger of large companies can occur, federal officials must review and approve the transaction.

A tying arrangement forces customers to buy something they may not want to get something they do want and cannot readily get elsewhere. Boycotts take many forms, but one common type is a refusal to do business with a person or a company as a means of coercing that person (or company) to do something he or she wouldn't otherwise be willing to do.

These business practices may or may not violate the law, depending on the specific facts of a particular case. In some antitrust cases, the courts apply the *rule of reason*, weighing the specific facts to determine whether a violation has occurred. This may involve a very complex economic analysis, often involving close judgment calls. In other cases, the *per se rule* applies: some business practices are so egregiously unlawful as to be *per se* antitrust violations.

Federal antitrust laws establish three different kinds of legal actions to be used against businesses that engage in anti-competitive practices: (1) criminal prosecutions by the U.S. government to punish wrongdoers; (2) civil actions by the U.S. government to halt monopolistic business practices; and (3) civil actions for *treble damages* by private individuals or other businesses that may have been injured by these practices. Treble damages means the victim of monopolistic business practices is entitled to recover three times his or her actual losses. This very strong remedy is intended to discourage violations of the antitrust laws.

All of these are provisions of *federal* antitrust laws. They apply to businesses engaged in interstate commerce and to local businesses whose activities in some way affect interstate commerce. The U.S. Justice Department's Antitrust Division is primarily responsible for enforcing these laws. However, where purely local businesses are involved, the jurisdiction over antitrust matters falls to the 50 states, all of which have at least some laws prohibiting

FIG. 61. Antitrust cartoon showing the oil trust trampling on "common people" and police, about 1901.

Library of Congress, Prints and Photographs Division, [LC-USZ62-63122].

monopolistic business practices within their borders. Also, *state* officials may sue to enforce the *federal* antitrust laws. For example, in 1990 the Supreme Court held that a state may sue to halt a merger between competing companies, even if the merger was already approved by the federal government (*California v. American Stores*, 495 U.S. 271).

In a unanimous non-media decision, the Supreme Court in 2010 said that the National Football League does not function as a "single entity" when granting a company an exclusive apparel license and therefore violated the Sherman Antitrust Act in doing so (*American Needle, Inc. v. National Football League*, 130 S. Ct. 2201). The NFL granted Reebok the exclusive right to manufacture hats, and when American Needle lost its contract with the NFL, it sued, claiming that the NFL teams were conspiring in restraint of trade. The Seventh Circuit agreed, but the Supreme Court reversed. Joint action, said the Court, is not the only way to promote football. Justice John Paul Stevens wrote that "defining the product as 'NFL football' puts the cart before the horse. Of course, the NFL produces NFL football, but that does not mean that cooperation amongst NFL teams is immune from [Sherman Act] scrutiny." The case was remanded.

In recent years, a number of American companies have also learned that antitrust enforcement isn't just a matter of satisfying federal and state regulators in the U.S. The European Union has a policy-making commission with the power to overrule mergers and acquisitions that will have an adverse effect on competition in Europe. More than one merger that won regulatory approval in the United States has been rejected by European authorities. With the globalization of trade, no large American company can ignore European regulators and complete a merger or acquisition that has been disapproved in Europe.

The Microsoft Antitrust Case

Public attention was focused on antitrust law in the 2000s more than at any time in recent history because of the *U.S. v. Microsoft Corp.* case. The U.S. Justice Department and 18 states jointly sued Microsoft, alleging a variety of unlawful business practices by the giant software company. Judge Thomas Penfield Jackson, who presided at the original trial, first determined that Microsoft in fact had a monopoly of personal computer operating systems with Windows. He then ruled that, as a matter of law, many of Microsoft's business practices were antitrust violations. For example, he ruled that Microsoft engaged in unlawful *tying arrangements*, improperly tying the Windows operating system with its Internet browser, Internet Explorer, to the detriment of Netscape, a competing browser. He also found that Microsoft charged computer makers more for Windows if they included competing application software than if they included only Microsoft products, and that Microsoft had its software engineers go to a lot of trouble to make Microsoft applications run better than competing applications under Windows—an effort to use the company's operating system monopoly to increase its market share in the applications business. He also ruled that several other Microsoft business practices were unlawful.

Judge Jackson then issued orders to remedy these violations. Among other things, he ordered Microsoft broken up into two companies, one to develop and market the Windows operating system and another to do everything else Microsoft was doing. He also ordered Microsoft to sell the Windows operating system to all large computer makers for the same price, regardless of whether they included competing applications with their computers.

Judge Jackson then certified the case for a direct appeal to the U.S. Supreme Court on an expedited schedule. Microsoft opposed not only the judge's decision and his proposed remedies but also the direct appeal to the Supreme Court. The Supreme Court rejected the direct appeal, sending the case to the U.S. Court of Appeals in Washington, D.C.

In 2001, the appellate court unanimously overturned Jackson's proposed remedies, including the breakup of Microsoft. The court also disqualified Jackson from hearing the next round of proceedings in the case because he made inflammatory statements to the media several times. While the appellate court acknowledged that there was no evidence of "actual bias" by Jackson, the court said his comments would cause an "informed observer" to "question his impartiality."

However, the appellate court upheld Jackson's finding that "the company behaved anti-competitively... and that those actions contributed to the maintenance of its monopoly power" and also broke the law in other ways. So the case was sent back to the trial court to reconsider several issues, including appropriate remedies for Microsoft's antitrust violations, but with a different judge presiding (*U.S. v. Microsoft Corp.*, 253 F.3d 34).

The case was then assigned to Judge Colleen Kollar-Kotelly. Before she could rule on the questions left unresolved after the appellate court decision, the U.S. Justice Department and nine of the 18 states agreed to settle the case. Judge Kollar-Kotelly then ordered a 60-day public comment period on the settlement, as required in antitrust cases. An unprecedented 30,000 written comments were filed with the court, mostly objecting to the settlement.

The nine states that didn't join in the settlement asked for added sanctions to remedy Microsoft's antitrust violations. Judge Kollar-Kotelly eventually approved the settlement, granting only a few of the holdout states' demands—most notably by ordering Microsoft to disclose some sensitive technologies to its rivals much earlier than the company and the Justice Department had proposed.

Seven of the nine holdout states did not appeal, but Massachusetts, under Attorney General Thomas Reilly, pursued the case. West Virginia at first joined Massachusetts in an appeal but then settled with Microsoft in mid-2003, accepting about $20 million in computer hardware and software for its schools in return for dropping out of the appeal.

In mid-2004, the U.S. Court of Appeals in Washington, D.C. ruled against Massachusetts and upheld the settlement in *Commonwealth of Massachusetts v. Microsoft Corp.* (373 F.3d 1199). The unanimous six-judge panel praised the settlement as "well done," declaring it to be in the public interest. The court rejected Massachusetts' request that Microsoft be required to remove parts of Windows and reveal more of its code to competitors, saying such a move might help competitors but would not help consumers. "Such drastic fragmentation would likely harm consumers," the court wrote. The court also rejected an appeal by a computer trade association that opposed Microsoft.

Judge Kollar-Kotelly retained jurisdiction until at least 2011 to monitor Microsoft's compliance with the terms of the settlement and made it clear there would be ongoing judicial scrutiny of the company's business practices. But she granted only a small part of what the nine states had sought in addition to the changes in Microsoft's business practices covered by the settlement.

Meanwhile, Microsoft agreed to settle a group of private antitrust lawsuits by promising to give about $1 billion worth of software and refurbished hardware to schools in low-income areas, a proposal that drew criticism because the cost to Microsoft for making extra copies of its software and giving away out-of-date hardware would be minimal—and hardly an adequate sanction for Microsoft's monopolistic behavior toward its competitors. A federal judge rejected this settlement as inadequate, a move that forced Microsoft to renegotiate the deal. In 2004, Microsoft agreed to pay $1.1 billion in California to settle antitrust claims from an estimated 14 million customers. Microsoft also settled an antitrust lawsuit filed in Minnesota for about $175 million, an Iowa lawsuit for $180 million and one filed in Vermont for $9.7 million. In other states, Microsoft settled for large but often undisclosed sums.

In the mid-2000s Microsoft settled several other large antitrust lawsuits. The company agreed to pay AOL Time Warner $750 million to drop a lawsuit alleging that unlawful business practices by Microsoft led to the demise of Netscape as a rival to Microsoft's Internet Explorer web browser. Then the company paid about $2 billion to settle lawsuits with Sun Microsystems, $761 million to settle with RealNetworks, $536 million to settle with Novell Inc. and $425 million to settle a lawsuit filed by a Silicon Valley high-tech security firm. Microsoft also struck a deal with the Computer & Communications Industry Association in which the association pledged not to appeal Microsoft's settlement with the federal government to the Supreme Court.

While Microsoft was fighting multiple antitrust battles in U.S. courts, it was also fighting antitrust litigation in the European Union. In 2004, the European Commission, a regulatory arm of the EU, found Microsoft guilty of anti-competitive and monopolistic business practices in Europe, fining the company about $600 million and ordering changes in the way Windows is packaged and sold there. The EU forced Microsoft to stop bundling the Windows operating system with its media player to allow other media software producers to compete more effectively. When Microsoft then launched the unbundled version of Windows as "Windows XP Reduced Media Edition," EU regulators acted quickly to halt the use of that name. In 2005, EU regulators also told Microsoft to make more information available to competing makers of networking software.

In 2008, the European Commission fined Microsoft an additional $1.39 billion for failing to comply with its earlier antitrust orders, bringing to $2.63 billion the total fines imposed on Microsoft by European regulators. Microsoft once again appealed, further extending this protracted legal battle with astronomical financial consequences.

Microsoft continued to have antitrust troubles with the European Union in 2009. The company decided that Windows 7 will be shipped to the EU market in fall 2009 without Internet Explorer 8 to avoid EU charges that it was unlawfully tying the browser to the operating system. Some critics allege that this move will not be enough to satisfy EU regulators, who have already fined Microsoft billions in various fines.

In May 2011, the Microsoft saga in the U.S. finally ended with the expiration of the consent decree. The *Seattle Times*, in a retrospective of the investigation, noted that Microsoft would have no celebrations at the conclusion of the historic episode, but the company said in a press release, "Our experience has changed us and shaped how we view our responsibility to the industry. We are pleased to bring this matter to successful resolution, and we are excited to keep delivering great products and services for our partners and customers."

■ THE FIRST AMENDMENT AND ANTITRUST LAW

For about 150 years, Congress and the Department of Justice assumed that they had no right to regulate the business practices of the media because of the First Amendment, but that changed in the New Deal era. The economic depression of the 1930s, the formation of a labor union for journalists, and the Roosevelt administration's willingness to challenge business practices that earlier administrations ignored all contributed to new scrutiny of the media. By 1945, the U.S. Supreme Court had twice ruled that the business practices of the media were very much within the government's purview. Both of these pioneering cases involved the Associated Press, the nation's largest news wire service.

The U.S. Supreme Court ruled that the First Amendment does not exempt the media from regulations that apply to other industries in a 1937 case involving labor laws, *AP v. National Labor Relations Board* (301 U.S. 130). The case arose when an Associated Press writer was fired for engaging in union organizing activities on behalf of the American Newspaper Guild. The guild complained to the NLRB, which found the AP guilty of an unfair labor practice. The wire service appealed the NLRB ruling, and the Supreme Court affirmed it, brushing aside the AP's argument that union activity was a threat to the agency's editorial freedom. The Court said that the National Labor Relations Act "permits a discharge for any reason other than union activity or agitation for collective bargaining with employees."

Later in the opinion, the Court added:

> The business of the Associated Press is not immune from regulation because it
> is an agency of the press. The publisher of a newspaper has no special immunity
> from the application of general laws. He has no special privilege to invade the
> rights and liberties of others.

A few years later, the Supreme Court again ruled against the AP's claims of a First Amendment exemption from government regulation in a landmark case involving antitrust law, *Associated Press v. U.S.* (326 U.S. 1, 1945).

This case arose when the *Chicago Sun's* application for AP membership was vetoed by its primary competitor, the *Chicago Tribune.* Under the AP's bylaws, each member was given what amounted to blackball privileges to prevent competitors from joining the wire service and gaining access to its worldwide news coverage. This policy had been in effect for nearly 100 years, but when it was used by such a prominent newspaper to blackball a well-known competitor, it invited government scrutiny.

The U.S. Justice Department challenged the exclusion of the *Chicago Sun* from AP membership as a violation of federal antitrust laws. The Justice Department pointed out that it was very easy for newspapers that did not directly compete with an AP member to join the organization. However, any potential competitor of an AP member was forced not only to get past the competitor's potential veto but also to pay a very large sum of money to join. Without joining the organization, a paper could not get AP news, since it was also against the bylaws to provide AP news to a non-member.

The case reached the Supreme Court, which ruled that these bylaw provisions indeed violated antitrust law. The high court emphasized that the First Amendment does not exempt the media from obeying laws regulating business practices: "The fact that the publisher handles news while others (engaged in business) handle goods does not...afford the publisher a peculiar constitutional sanctuary in which he can with impunity violate laws regarding his business practices."

Moreover, the Court said, what the AP was doing amounted to a denial of the freedom to publish for many would-be members. Its bylaws, far from furthering the goal of freedom of the press, actually inhibited freedom of the press:

> Freedom to publish is guaranteed by the Constitution, but freedom to combine to keep others from publishing is not. Freedom of the press from governmental interference under the First Amendment does not sanction repression of that freedom by private interests.

After the Supreme Court had twice ruled against the Associated Press on questions involving the government's right to regulate its business practices, the Justice Department brought actions against a number of newspaper publishers who appeared to be violating federal antitrust laws.

■ NEWSPAPER ANTITRUST CASES

Two antitrust cases involving newspapers reached the U.S. Supreme Court during the 1950s and several others were decided by lower federal courts.

antitrust:
prohibitions of agreements or practices that restrict trade and competition between companies, and bans on anti-competitive practices that lead to a company's dominant position.

joint operating agreement (JOA):
two or more companies combine some operations to share costs and reduce expenses; in newspapers, the companies combine their advertising and business departments and operate separate editorial departments.

The first of these cases involved a newspaper accused of refusing to accept advertising from anyone who placed advertising with a local radio station. The case, *Lorain Journal Company v. U.S.* (342 U.S. 143, 1951), resulted in a unanimous Supreme Court ruling in favor of the government and against the publisher. Because the paper reached almost every home in its market area, its threat to refuse advertising from those who advertised on the radio station was a viable one: many merchants needed to advertise in the paper because there was no other way to reach a lot of their customers.

Defending its policies in court, the newspaper cited not only the First Amendment but also the well-recognized principle that a publisher has a right to refuse advertising. The Supreme Court dismissed these arguments, pointing out that antitrust law creates an exception to the publisher's right to refuse advertising. When the refusal to accept advertising is based on a desire to monopolize commerce, that right must give way to the right of other businesses to be free of monopolistic competition, the court said. A lower court injunction against the paper's business practices was affirmed, as was an unusual and slightly humiliating order that the newspaper publish a notice of the ruling every week for six months.

However, a newspaper publisher fared better in another antitrust lawsuit that reached the Supreme Court in the 1950s, *Times-Picayune v. U.S.* (345 U.S. 594, 1953). In that case, the Justice Department challenged a tying arrangement in which an advertiser had to buy space in an evening paper, the *New Orleans States*, in order to get space in the same company's morning paper, the *New Orleans Times-Picayune*. A competing evening paper, the *New Orleans Item*, was the alleged victim in this tying arrangement.

When the case reached the Supreme Court, the justices voted 5-4 in the Times-Picayune Company's favor. The majority sympathized with the Justice Department's contention that this was a tying arrangement. However, the court said there was insufficient evidence of injury to the other paper to justify an antitrust action in this particular instance. This was true because the *Item* was profitable. In addition, the *Item* was gaining in ad revenue and actually carrying more advertising than its evening competitor, the Times-Picayune Company's *States*. The Supreme Court majority refused to view the *Times-Picayune* as a sufficiently "dominant" product for the tying arrangement to be unlawful. In short, the Justice Department failed to prove its case. Only a few years later the *Item* did fall upon hard times and was taken over by the Times-Picayune Company, forming the *New Orleans States-Item*.

Still another antitrust action against a newspaper arose in the 1950s, one that is remembered because it illustrates all three kinds of antitrust lawsuits permitted under federal law. The Eighth Circuit case, *Kansas City Star v. U.S.* (240 F.2d 643, 1957), resulted from a variety of questionable practices by the employee-owned Star Corporation, the publisher of Kansas City's only morning and evening daily newspapers and also owner of the leading network-affiliated radio and television stations in town. (A competing daily paper had gone bankrupt before these lawsuits were completed.)

The company engaged in several monopolistic practices. For example, advertisers and subscribers had to buy a combination ad or subscription in both the morning *Times* and afternoon *Star* to get either one. You couldn't advertise in (or subscribe to) just one. In addition, some advertisers who also bought space in the competing paper before it failed were threatened with the cancellation of their ads in the Star-owned papers. Also, some advertisers were forced to buy ads in the *Times* and *Star* to get advertising on the company's radio and TV stations. In one case, a business partly owned by a major league baseball player was threatened with a blackout of news about the player on the sports pages if the business didn't discontinue its advertising in the competing paper.

Overall, it was a flagrant example of abuses by an ownership that wielded too much influence in one city. Critics of the situation suggested that being employee-owned doesn't necessarily make a newspaper more ethical than it might be if controlled by a huge out-of-town chain. Other observers saw irony in the fact that a newspaper founded by one of the most public-spirited publishers of the late 1800s—William Rockhill Nelson—would stoop to these depths. The *Star* gained its position of dominance because of Nelson's commitment to his community, only to abuse its power after the founder's death in 1915.

Whatever the *Kansas City Star's* distinguished past, the Justice Department took an unsentimental look at the present and filed both criminal and civil antitrust lawsuits. The Justice Department sought criminal sanctions against the corporation and some of its executives in addition to a civil order to halt the unlawful practices. A federal court of appeals affirmed criminal convictions of the corporation and the advertising manager in 1957. The company settled the civil suit by agreeing to sell off its radio and TV stations and to stop forcing advertisers to buy space in both papers to get space in either one.

Meanwhile, a variety of private treble damage civil suits were filed against the embattled company, which eventually settled most of these lawsuits. An interesting footnote to this complex litigation is that, some two decades later, the employee owners sold the Star Corporation to Capital Cities Communications, ending one of the last large-scale experiments with employee ownership in American journalism. The *Star* later became a Knight Ridder newspaper and then a McClatchy paper when that chain purchased Knight Ridder in 2006.

An antitrust lawsuit of another sort resulted in the mid-1960s when the Times Mirror Corporation, publisher of the *Los Angeles Times,* purchased one of the last family-owned daily newspapers in Southern California, the *San Bernardino Sun-Telegram.* The Justice Department sued to force Times-Mirror to resell the *Sun* on the ground that its purchase by Times-Mirror substantially lessened competition in San Bernardino County. The city of San Bernardino is about 60 miles east of downtown Los Angeles.

In a federal district court proceeding, the Justice Department showed that the only real competition the Sun Company had in much of that huge county came from the *Times.* Moreover, several other papers in the county either ceased daily publication or were sold to chains at about the same time. The court ruled that the *Sun's* purchase violated federal antitrust law and ordered Times-Mirror to resell the paper. The judge's decision was affirmed without opinion by the U.S. Supreme Court in 1968 (*Times-Mirror v. U.S.,* 390 U.S. 712).

In compliance with this decision, Times-Mirror sold the Sun Company to the Gannett Corporation, a large newspaper chain then headquartered in New York. While Gannett owned far more newspapers than Times-Mirror, it had none in Southern California then. Therefore, this sale did not violate the law against acquisitions that lessen competition.

This entire sequence of events disturbed observers of Southern California journalism for two reasons. First, in the name of preventing monopolies, the Justice Department forced an absentee owner 60 miles away to sell out to an absentee owner 2,500 miles away. Moreover, at that time Times-Mirror also owned the *Orange Coast Daily Pilot,* another suburban daily even closer to Los Angeles and even more directly in competition with the *Times* than the *San Bernardino Sun.* Certainly Times-Mirror's track record with the *Daily Pilot* had been a good one in terms of both community service and ethical business practices. Perhaps the

Justice Department would have opposed Times-Mirror's acquisition of the *Daily Pilot* too, had it not happened before such acquisitions were given close government scrutiny.

Nevertheless, antitrust law is clear on this point: it's perfectly legal to buy newspapers in various markets all over America, but it isn't legal to buy nearby newspapers in *overlapping* markets. The fact that a management close to home may be better able to meet community needs than one thousands of miles away complicates the ethical issues here, but it doesn't change the law. On the other hand, the Justice Department has a lot of discretion in these matters. In recent years there have been other media takeovers, mergers and buyouts that would appear to be violations of antitrust law at least as flagrant as the *Los Angeles Times'* purchase of the *San Bernardino Sun.* The 1980s and 1990s were an era of deregulation and government acquiescence to mergers; deals that might not have been allowed by the country's antitrust guardians in the 1960s or 1970s were sometimes approved more recently.

However, during the Clinton era that approach to antitrust enforcement appeared to change. In 1995, the Justice Department went to court to halt the sale of the *Northwest Arkansas Times* in Fayetteville to a group with ownership ties to Donrey Media, the publisher of a competing paper in a nearby town, *The Morning News of Northwest Arkansas.* The Justice Department explained its action by issuing a news release that said, "Unless this transaction is blocked, the vigorous competition that has existed between these two newspapers for readers and advertisers will be substantially reduced or eliminated. That means the citizens of Fayetteville and Springdale will pay higher prices for their newspapers, and local businesses will pay higher advertising rates."

A federal judge agreed with the Justice Department's position and ordered the sale rescinded in mid-1995. A Justice Department spokeswoman said this marked the first time in 13 years that the agency had sued to halt a newspaper merger. The *Northwest Arkansas Times* was later sold to a company that did not own any nearby newspapers.

■ JOINT OPERATING AGREEMENTS

The late 1960s also produced another Supreme Court decision on antitrust law that disturbed many publishers. The case, *Citizen Publishing Co. v. U.S.* (394 U.S. 131, 1969), stemmed from a *joint operating agreement* ("JOA"), a kind of cooperative arrangement between once-competing newspapers that had become commonplace. Under a joint operating agreement, two newspaper publishers in the same town merge many of their business and printing operations but maintain separate editorial staffs so the two papers retain separate identities. The objective, of course, is to cut costs by only maintaining one expensive newspaper printing plant, for instance, instead of two. Obviously, it works best if one of the papers is a morning paper and the other an afternoon paper, so scheduling conflicts can be minimized. These arrangements often also include joint advertising sales, with advertisers offered a package deal and a discount if they place ads in both papers.

Such an agreement had existed between the *Tucson Daily Citizen* and the *Arizona Daily Star* since 1940. Not only did it involve a merger of production, advertising and circulation operations of the two papers, but it also involved profit pooling. In the mid-1960s, the *Star* appeared to be in financial difficulty, but a purchase offer from a large newspaper chain was rejected. Shortly later, the owners of the *Citizen* organized a new company and bought the *Star.* As a result of this series of events, the once-independent editorial staff of the *Star* found itself working for the owners of the *Citizen.*

The U.S. Justice Department challenged not only the change of ownership but the entire JOA as a violation of antitrust law. The case reached the Supreme Court in 1969, and the Court agreed that much of this cooperative arrangement was illegal. Justice William O. Douglas said the only defense for acquisition of the *Star* by the *Citizen* was the *Failing Company Doctrine*, which allows a company to buy out a competitor on the brink of bankruptcy. The rationale for this judicially created exception to antitrust law is that the rival company's failure would lessen competition anyway. However, Douglas said the Failing Company Doctrine didn't apply here because neither paper was failing at the time the JOA was initiated. The decision was shocking to publishers all over America because JOAs were then in effect in 22 cities, involving 44 daily newspapers. If this decision were left intact, many other JOAs would also be illegal. Publishers said many of the participating newspapers would be forced to shut down because they could not afford to operate a complete business and printing facility on their own.

The American Newspaper Publishers Association, the major trade organization for the industry, went to work lobbying for a change in antitrust laws to legalize joint operating agreements. Congress obliged in 1970 with the *Newspaper Preservation Act*. Basically, this law legalized the 22 existing joint operating agreements, including the one in Tucson. In effect, Congress revised the law to overrule the Supreme Court's interpretation of it.

In addition to protecting the existing JOAs, the Newspaper Preservation Act authorized the Justice Department to approve new agreements when it could be shown that at least one of the newspapers involved would fail without a JOA. The Newspaper Preservation Act was opposed by the Justice Department, which contended it would allow publishers to enter anti-competitive arrangements even when they could survive on their own. Publishers of small newspapers also opposed it, fearing that the large papers in their area would offer joint advertising packages so attractive the smaller papers would be squeezed out of the marketplace. Also, labor unions opposed the act because it authorized consolidations that would certainly eliminate jobs. Nevertheless, the act quickly moved through Congress and was signed by President Nixon.

Once enacted, the Newspaper Preservation Act was challenged on constitutional grounds by a small San Francisco newspaper, the *Bay Guardian*. This muckraking alternative paper contended that the joint operating agreement between the *San Francisco Chronicle* and *San Francisco Examiner* resulted in an unconstitutional infringement of its First Amendment rights by encouraging a monopoly that made it difficult for other papers to operate.

In a 1972 decision, a federal district judge rejected the *Guardian*'s arguments, affirming the constitutionality of the Newspaper Preservation Act (*Bay Guardian Co. v. Chronicle Publishing Co.*, 344 F.Supp. 1155). However, the lawsuit against the San Francisco papers continued on other grounds and was eventually settled for an amount in excess of $1 million. Ironically, almost 30 years later Hearst sold the *Examiner*, purchased the rival *Chronicle*, and won an antitrust lawsuit challenging that transaction.

In the years since its enactment, the Newspaper Preservation Act hasn't exactly produced an avalanche of applications for new joint operating agreements. In fact, the Justice Department approved only two agreements during the the law's first 10 years on the books, although a third pair of newspapers entered an agreement prior to receiving Justice approval.

The first application for a new JOA came in 1974, when the well-entrenched *Anchorage* (Alaska) *Times* and "failing" *Anchorage Daily News* asked permission to merge their non-editorial operations. The agreement was approved, but it did not help the *Daily News*: its circulation slipped to 12,000 (compared to 46,000 for the *Times*). Finally, the *Daily News* withdrew from the agreement, sued the *Times,* and sold a controlling interest to C. K. McClatchy, then the head of the fast-growing McClatchy chain in California. Taking over in 1979, McClatchy poured money into the *Daily News,* modernizing its operation. The editor, Katherine Fanning, who later became the first woman to be editor of a national newspaper (the *Christian Science Monitor*), upgraded the *Daily News* editorial product enough that it won a Pulitzer Prize. By 1980, its circulation was up to 30,000, while the Times had slipped to 44,000. And by 1990, the roles were completely reversed—it was the once-dominant *Times* that was a "failing newspaper."

In an ironic turn of events, the *Times* ceased publication in 1992—after the *Daily News* agreed to carry some of the conservative columns and editorials from the *Times* in addition to its own for 10 years.

In 1979 the Justice Department approved another JOA, this one involving the "failing" *Cincinnati Post,* owned by the large Scripps-Howard chain, and the *Cincinnati Enquirer,* which was purchased during the approval process by the even bigger Gannett chain. Critics of the whole process wondered whether the *Post* was really failing or if perhaps two large chains simply saw a good way to cut their costs and enhance their long-term profit possibilities.

Meanwhile, a strange sequence of events unfolded in Chattanooga, Tenn., in 1980. The "failing" *Chattanooga Times* entered into a JOA with the *Chattanooga News-Free Press* without first securing the government's permission as required by the Newspaper Preservation Act. The two papers asked for Justice Department approval of their merger, but while the government was considering the issue, the *Times* abruptly fired 102 production employees, shut down its printing press, and in effect merged its printing operations with those of its crosstown competitor. After some embarrassing moments during which the publishers were chastised for their impatience, the Justice Department approved the Chattanooga JOA.

Later Newspaper Combinations

One of the longest and most bitter battles ever fought over a joint operating agreement occurred in Seattle. The financially troubled *Seattle Post-Intelligencer* ("the *P-I*") and the *Seattle*

FIG. 62. Sen. John Sherman from Ohio, between 1865 and 1880.

Library of Congress, Prints and Photographs Division, [LC-DIG-cwpbh-04797].

Focus on...
The Sherman Antitrust Act of 1890

The Sherman Act was passed in 1890 to permit the federal government to act against *trusts,* or arrangements that consolidate industry power under one controlling board. It was named for Sen. John Sherman (R-Ohio). The act has two sections. The first section focuses on the means of attempting to gain a monopoly, and the second examines the end results of potential monopolies.

Section One has three parts:
    (1) an agreement
    (2) that unreasonably restrains competition and
    (3) that affects interstate commerce.

Section Two has two parts:
    (1) the possession of monopoly power and
    (2) the willful acquisition or maintenance of that power other than by having a superior product or good business sense, or by accident (innocent monopolies are legal).

Times sought government permission to merge their non-editorial operations in 1981, sharing printing and business operations and publishing a joint Sunday edition. But that was just the beginning of the story.

By the early 2000s the *Seattle Times* was trying to end the agreement, a move that could cause the still-troubled *P-I* to fail. The *Times* cited a provision in the original agreement allowing either party to withdraw after three consecutive years of losses, something that occurred in the 2000s, according to the *Times*. Hearst Corp., owner of the *P-I*, challenged the *Times'* calculations, particularly because a long labor dispute had caused some of the losses. Hearst sued to keep the agreement in effect. In 2005 the Washington Supreme Court ruled for the *Times*, eliminating a major hurdle in the *Times'* effort to pull out of the agreement (*Hearst Communications Inc. v. Seattle Times Co.*, 115 P.3d 262). Two years later, Hearst and the *Times* agreed to settle their ongoing legal battles with the *Times* paying Hearst $24 million to cancel key provisions of their joint operating agreement while both pledged to continue publishing in Seattle—for the time being.

The 1981 merger plan drew protests from suburban newspaper publishers, major retail advertisers and employee groups, who contended the merger would result in price-fixing, excessively high ad rates, a decline in the quality of both papers and needless employee layoffs. Nevertheless, the plan was approved by Attorney General William French Smith in 1982. However, foes of the merger sued to prevent the agreement from going into effect. They argued that Hearst had not been willing either to sell the *P-I* or make changes to improve its balance sheet. In a 1983 decision, the Ninth Circuit allowed the merger. The court held that it is not necessary to offer a failing newspaper for sale to justify a joint operating agreement. The Ninth Circuit said Hearst had adequately shown that new management would not be successful in maintaining the paper as an independent entity. Therefore, the Justice Department's decision approving the merger was valid (*Committee for an Independent P-I v. Hearst Corp.*, 704 F.2d 467).

In its decision—a key ruling on the right of two newspapers to merge under the Newspaper Preservation Act—the court said that when there is sufficient evidence that a paper will probably fail under any ownership, the owner need not sell the paper to qualify for a JOA.

Another legal battle over a joint operating agreement occurred in the late 1980s in Detroit, one of the few American cities that still had two truly competitive daily newspapers under independent ownership and control. In fact, it would have been hard to find another city with two competing papers as evenly matched in circulation and news coverage as the *Detroit News* and the *Detroit Free Press*.

The era of vigorous competition between the two—a Detroit tradition for a century—ended in a joint operating agreement in 1988. The *News*, which had just been purchased by Gannett, and the *Free Press*, owned by the Knight Ridder chain, received the approval of Attorney General Edwin Meese to enter a JOA just before Meese left office. That cleared the way for the merger of all but the news departments of two of the largest and strongest newspapers ever to enter into such an agreement.

Just before the two papers were to be merged, a federal appellate court ordered the merger delayed pending an appeal of the legality of the joint operating agreement. A coalition opposing the merger, Michigan Citizens for an Independent Press, challenged the merger on the ground that neither paper was actually in danger of failing. The group contended that the two large newspaper chains had orchestrated a circulation war between the two papers that was certain to cause both to lose money—purely in an effort to justify a joint operating agreement.

Nevertheless, in *Michigan Citizens for an Independent Press v. Thornburgh* (868 F.2d 1285, *aff'd* 493 U.S. 38), the federal court ruled that the Justice Department had adequate legal grounds to approve the merger. The U.S. Supreme Court affirmed that ruling on a 4-4 vote with Justice Byron White not participating, thereby freeing the two Detroit newspapers to merge in 1989. (When the Supreme Court is equally divided, the lower court ruling is automatically affirmed.) The Detroit collaboration ended in 2005, when the Gannett Co., Knight Ridder and MediaNews Group reshuffled the ownership of Detroit's two daily newspapers.

Gannett, still the largest U.S. newspaper chain, agreed to take control of the *Detroit Free Press* from Knight Ridder, while selling the *Detroit News* to MediaNews Group. Knight Ridder and Gannett swapped ownership of several smaller daily newspapers in other cities as a part of the same deal. Gannett and MediaNews Group then announced that they would form a new partnership, if not an actual joint operating agreement, to handle the business operations of the two Detroit newspapers.

Only a few months later, Knight Ridder, under pressure from stockholders who thought breaking up the company would increase the value of its stock, announced its own dissolution. The McClatchy group, a newspaper chain based in Sacramento, Calif., purchased Knight Ridder. McClatchy then sold 12 of Knight Ridder's 32 daily newspapers to others, keeping the 20 papers that some market analysts called "the cream of the crop." Among the papers McClatchy re-sold were the *Philadelphia Inquirer* and *Philadelphia Daily News*, plus the *San Jose Mercury News* and several other San Francisco Bay area newspapers. MediaNews Group acquired most of the Bay Area papers in a complex deal with Hearst, publisher of the *San Francisco Chronicle*. That gave MediaNews Group almost complete ownership of Bay Area newspapers surrounding the *Chronicle*, while Hearst acquired several newspapers in other areas. MediaNews Group has a reputation for buying up newspapers in adjacent towns and then cutting costs by merging many of their operations. The Hearst-MediaNews deal was challenged in a private antitrust lawsuit, but that was settled in 2007 on undisclosed terms.

McClatchy, known for the journalistic excellence of its newspapers, already owned the *Sacramento Bee* and the *Minneapolis Star Tribune*, among other newspapers. It kept the *Miami Herald, Kansas City Star, Fort Worth Star Telegram* and 17 other papers it acquired from Knight Ridder. McClatchy later sold the *Star Tribune* to a private equity investment company.

The Justice Department's Antitrust Division has also approved a few more joint operating agreements, including one involving the *Las Vegas Sun* and *Las Vegas Review-Journal*, and another involving the *York* (Pa.) *Daily Record* and the *York Dispatch*. The Las Vegas combination led to a bizarre only-in-Las-Vegas deal in 2005: the prosperous Libertarian-leaning *Review-Journal* agreed to place the politically liberal, advertising-poor *Sun* inside its own newspaper—as an insert. So subscribers get one newspaper wrapped around its competitor.

Another new joint operating agreement was announced in 2000 when the *Denver Post* and the *Rocky Mountain News*, rivals for more than 100 years, said they would merge all but their news departments. In 2009, the *Rocky Mountain News* closed.

Two Charleston, W.V., newspapers agreed to restructure their JOA in 2010 and take steps to increase competition to avoid antitrust violations in a case dating from 2008 (*U.S. v. Daily Gazette Company and MediaNews Group, Inc.*, 567 F. Supp. 2d 859). The *Charleston Gazette* and the *Charleston Daily Mail* entered into a JOA in 1958 but continued to be competitive in coverage and circulation.

In 2004 the *Daily Mail* was sold to the *Gazette*, which reduced staff and began to market the paper less competitively so it could be closed; in a competitive impact statement, the judge accused the company of "plann[ing] to deliberately transform a financially healthy and stable *Daily Mail* into a failing newspaper and close it far earlier than the market would have otherwise dictated." In 2010, the Daily Gazette Company settled with the Department of Justice. The previous owner of the *Daily Mail* will retain an option to re-purchase 20 percent of the paper, maintain management seats, and choose its editorial content. The *Daily Gazette* will need Justice permission to stop publishing the *Daily Mail.*

By the early 2000s, the idea that joint operating agreements could save "failing" news-papers was widely questioned. While these agreements undoubtedly have saved some newspapers from oblivion (or at least postponed their demise), it was becoming clear that metropolitan daily newspapers are an endangered species, with or without joint operating agreements. Since the Newspaper Preservation Act was enacted in 1970, more than 160 daily newspapers in the United States have stopped publishing and many more will surely fail as circulation (and with it, advertising revenue) continues to plummet in the Internet era. In 2012, only six cities have newspapers with JOAs: Charleston, W.V.; Detroit, Mich., Ft. Wayne, Ind.; Las Vegas, Nev.; Salt Lake City, Utah; and York, Pa.

■ BROADCAST MEDIA OWNERSHIP ISSUES

Few aspects of communications law have been as controversial and volatile as the questions of ownership and control of the electronic media. Congress, the FCC, the Justice Department and the courts all devoted endless hours to these issues before the FCC adopted a controversial deregulation of its broadcast ownership rules in 2003 and a federal appeals court ordered the FCC to reconsider in 2004, leading the agency to adopt a more modest plan in 2007.

The Telecommunications Act of 1996 requires that the FCC conduct a review of its media ownership rules every four years. The FCC issued a Notice of Inquiry in May 2010 as the start of its 2010 quadrennial regulatory review of broadcast ownership rules—the fifth one since the Telecommunications Act was passed. It is particularly interested in five ownership issues: the Local Television Ownership Cap, limiting owners to two stations in markets with at least eight competitors; the Local Radio Ownership Cap, limiting owners to eight stations in the largest markets; the Newspaper-Broadcast Cross-Ownership Rule, forbidding cross-ownership of broadcast stations and newspapers without a waiver; the Radio-Television Cross-Ownership Rule, limiting the number of radio and television stations owned by a single company in one market; and the Dual Network Rule, prohibiting common ownership of any of the top four television stations. The FCC also seeks comment on structural analysis and other issues, particularly the impact of digital technologies, in pursuit of its policy goals of localism, competition, and diversity.

Broadcast ownership has been controversial almost from the beginning of broadcasting. Just before the U.S. Justice Department challenged the Associated Press' exclusionary practices in the early 1940s, the Federal Communications Commission was taking a tough look at the way the networks (especially NBC) dominated radio broadcasting in America. Originally, the FCC had little authority over antitrust matters, but as part of its licensing process the commission has always been empowered to consider all factors that affect the "public interest, convenience and necessity." Thus, the FCC has the right to scrutinize the business practices and ownership patterns of broadcast licensees.

By the late 1930s, the FCC didn't like what it saw in radio broadcasting. About 97 percent of all night-time transmitter wattage was controlled by three networks, with the vast majority of the most powerful stations affiliated with either the National Broadcasting Company or the Columbia Broadcasting System. In fact, NBC operated two different networks, both of which had affiliates in many major cities.

Even more disturbing, the networks imposed strict contractual controls on their affiliates. For instance, network affiliates were not permitted to carry any programming from another network. Moreover, affiliates were locked into five-year contracts with the networks—something the FCC found alarming in view of the fact that broadcasters were then issued licenses for only three years at a time. And the networks tied up virtually all of their affiliates' prime time programming. In addition, affiliates' rights to reject network programs were limited.

To end these abuses, the FCC issued a set of rules known as the *Chain Broadcasting Regulations* in 1941. These rules prohibited many of the questionable network practices. One provision was intended to force NBC to sell one of its two networks. NBC quickly took the FCC to court, charging that these new rules exceeded the FCC's authority and violated the First Amendment.

In *NBC v. U.S.* (319 U.S. 190), an important 1943 case that foreshadowed the *Associated Press v. U.S.* decision, the Supreme Court ruled against NBC on all grounds. The court said the First Amendment does not exempt broadcasters from government regulation of their business practices. Moreover, the court said, the FCC could properly issue rules to curb monopolistic network policies, despite the fact that enforcement of antitrust laws is beyond the commission's authority. After this decision NBC had no choice but to sell one of its networks, so the "Blue" network—the one that NBC executives considered the weaker of the two—was sold later in 1943. That network became known as the American Broadcasting Company two years later, joining CBS and NBC to form the big three of broadcasting that dominated the industry for decades. The other radio network of the 1930s, the Mutual Broadcasting System, included a large number of affiliates, but most of them were in smaller markets. Mutual remained only a minor force in broadcasting.

Broadcast Ownership Restrictions

The FCC has adopted a variety of restrictions on broadcast ownership over the years to prevent monopoly control of the airwaves. All of these rules have been intended to supplement the antitrust laws, which also forbid anti-competitive business practices by broadcasters. However, the FCC's philosophy about this has varied greatly. The FCC first adopted tough restrictions on the number of stations one individual or company could own and then abandoned many of those rules, little by little. The FCC and Congress had already loosened many ownership restrictions even before the FCC's 2003 deregulation of the ownership rules and the 2004 federal appeals court ruling overturning most of the 2003 FCC action (*Prometheus Radio Project v. FCC*, 373 F.3d 372).

In the Telecommunications Act of 1996, Congress ordered the FCC to liberalize some of its oldest broadcast ownership rules. The 1996 law also directed the FCC to conduct comprehensive reviews of its remaining ownership restrictions every two years (later every four years) and to eliminate rules no longer needed. Those reviews, plus several court decisions overturning other FCC rules, led to the 2003 and 2007 FCC deregulation actions.

For many years no individual or company could own more than seven television stations, seven AM radio stations and seven FM radio stations nationwide. That rule was sometimes called the *Rule of Sevens*. In 1984, the FCC changed the number to 12 of each, thus creating the *Rule of Twelves*. The FCC liberalized the radio station ownership rules again in 1992, increasing the limit to 18 AM and 18 FM stations under one ownership. That limit was increased to 20 AM and 20 FM stations in 1994, with minority-controlled companies permitted to own up to 23 AM and 23 FM stations. The television station limit was left at 12 in 1992.

Congress abolished these limits by passing the 1996 Telecommunications Act, leaving *no* limit on the number of radio or television stations one company may own nationwide. However, the 1996 law did retain a limit on the percent of the nation's television households one company's stations could reach, but that limit was also liberalized. Under the rules in effect between 1984 and 1996, one company could own stations that reached no more than 25 percent of the nation's television households. The limit was increased to 35 percent by the 1996 act. In its 2003 deregulation, the FCC further liberalized the limit, allowing any one company to own stations that reach up to 45 percent of the nation's television households. In 2004, Congress responded to a public outcry over the FCC's 45 percent cap, substituting a 39 percent ceiling in its place.

Note that all of these limits—the original 25 percent cap, the 35 percent limit, the FCC's proposed 45 percent ceiling, and the 39 percent cap adopted by Congress in 2004—apply only to stations owned by a company; the limits do not apply to *affiliates*. Each of the major networks has affiliates that reach virtually *all* television households. Each network also has *network-owned and operated stations,* most of them in large cities. The limits apply only to these network-owned stations and to large groups of stations owned by other companies.

All of these TV ownership limits have included a "UHF discount" provision: only half of the households in a metropolitan area are counted toward the limit if a company owns a UHF station rather than a VHF station there. (UHF is defined as channel 14 or higher.) Thus, under the present 39 percent cap, one company could conceivably own stations that reach 78 percent of all television households if it owned only UHF stations. The rationale for this provision is that UHF stations have poorer coverage and draw smaller audiences. The UHF discount is one of several FCC rules designed to encourage UHF station ownership. Critics say the UHF discount no longer makes sense in a day when most viewers get their television via cable or satellite, not over the air. There is little or no difference in VHF and UHF signal quality when the signal is relayed via cable or satellite. In an apparent concession to these realities, the FCC in 2003 said the UHF discount will not be used for calculations of the number of households served by stations owned by the four largest networks once the transition to digital television is complete.

The FCC liberalized the old 35 percent limit in 2003 partly because of a federal appeals court decision questioning the old limit. The U.S. Court of Appeals in Washington, D.C., in 2002 ordered the FCC either to eliminate or better justify the 35 percent cap. In *Fox Television Stations v. FCC* (280 F.3d. 1027) the court also overturned an FCC rule forbidding one company to own both a TV station and a cable system in the same market.

The FCC also had another restriction on cable system ownership: a rule saying that no company could own cable systems serving more than 30 percent of all subscription TV households nationwide. The U.S. Court of Appeals in Washington overturned that restriction in 2001 (*Time Warner Entertainment Co. v. FCC,* 240 F.3d 1126). In 2007, the FCC reinstated the 30 percent cable limit.

The same federal appellate court undermined still another aspect of the FCC's television ownership rules in a 2002 decision. Ruling in *Sinclair Broadcast Group v. FCC* (284 F.3d 148), the court rejected the FCC's justification for its television Duopoly Rule. The Duopoly

Rule, rewritten in 1999, allowed one company to own two television stations in the same market if there were eight competing "voices," which the FCC defined as television stations under eight different ownerships even after one company buys a second station. The court rejected this definition of "voices" as arbitrary and capricious because it ignored other media outlets such as newspapers, radio stations and cable television.

In its 2003 deregulation, the FCC tried to respond to all of these court decisions—and inspired another adverse court decision in the process.

Although there is no longer a nationwide limit on the number of radio stations that one company may own, there are still local limits, and the FCC did not further liberalize them in 2003. In metropolitan areas having 45 or more radio stations (counting both AM and FM stations), one company may own up to eight stations, although no more than five of them may be AM stations or FM stations. (This rule prevents any one company from owning eight FM stations or eight AM stations in one market.) In markets having 30 to 44 stations, the limit is seven stations; no more than four of them may be either AM or FM. In markets with 15-29 stations, the limit is six stations, of which no more than four may be either AM or FM. In markets with fewer than 15 stations, one company may own no more than five stations or half of the total stations in the market, and no more than three may be either AM or FM. There is an exception for markets with three stations: one company may own two of them if the two are an AM-FM combination.

The FCC made minor changes in the local radio ownership rules in 2003. The definition of a local market was rewritten to close a loophole that allowed a single company to own all of the radio stations in a relatively small city. In some cases an FCC-defined market included enough surrounding towns with radio stations that one company could own all of the stations in a given city without violating the ownership formula. In an attempt to close that loophole, the FCC decided to use market definitions developed by the Arbitron rating service in place of its former definitions based on signal coverage areas. Another issue was that the old rules did not count stations in Canada and Mexico, even if they could be heard well in U.S. cities near the border. A company could get around the limits by taking control of foreign stations in addition to buying as many stations as the law allows in a U.S. border city. The 2003 rules largely closed that loophole.

The FCC's 2003 deregulation was especially controversial because the 1996 Telecommunication Act's liberalization of local radio ownership restrictions (and its elimination of the nationwide radio ownership limit) led to major changes in radio broadcasting. Several large radio station groups quickly expanded, buying many stations—and driving up the selling price of radio stations in the process. By the late 2000s, Clear Channel Communications had grown from a small Texas company with a handful of radio stations to a giant national corporation with more than 1,200 stations (about 10 percent of all American radio stations).

Many new owners of station groups combined various aspects of their stations' operations. For example, it became commonplace for station groups to program several stations jointly, manage them jointly, and sell advertising for them jointly. A company can now purchase several small stations surrounding a big city and do regional programming, including some simulcasting on the various stations. This allows a company to buy inexpensive small stations and compete with the giant metropolitan stations, encouraging listeners to tune in to whichever of the jointly programmed stations is loudest in their area. Critics say that something is lost in this equation, though: there is less local service to the small suburban towns that the individual stations once served exclusively.

Critics also charged that something else is lost when a large company buys up local media outlets: news programming. The FCC itself conducted a study that reached this conclusion in 2004, but the study was not released publicly until whistleblowers revealed its existence two years later. The study showed that locally owned stations, on average, had more local news programming than stations owned by large outside corporations.

The U.S. Justice Department has also monitored the growth in corporate ownership of broadcasting. In several cases where a late-1990s radio consolidation fully complied with the FCC's rules and the 1996 Telecommunications Act, the Justice Department refused to approve the deal because it would have left one company with what antitrust officials felt was excessive economic power in a particular market. Even if a merger complies with the FCC's rules, it has to comply with antitrust law as well.

The FCC's ownership rules also address another phenomenon in broadcasting: the use of time brokerage or *local marketing agreements (LMAs)* in which a station owner gives someone else the right to program the station. Like owning multiple stations in the same market, LMAs are attractive to station owners because of the cost savings possible if one station's staff can program and sell advertising for two or more stations. The ownership rules say that a station operated under an LMA is treated as if the person or firm in control of the station actually owns it. Therefore, a company that programs stations under an LMA in a given city may not be allowed to own as many stations there. The FCC did not rewrite this rule in 2003.

Over the years the FCC also adopted a variety of rules restricting cross-ownerships. *Cross-ownership* is a situation in which one individual or company owns more than one kind of communications medium, usually in one market. The most notable of these rules is the newspaper-broadcast cross-ownership rule.

The FCC adopted the *newspaper-broadcast cross-ownership rule* in 1975. It banned new cross-ownerships between newspapers and television stations in the same market. The FCC allowed a number of companies that already owned both a newspaper and a television station in the same market to keep both until one or the other is sold.

From the beginning, this rule stirred criticism from all sides. Both broadcasters and newspaper publishers attacked the ban on new cross-media combinations. Consumer groups, meanwhile, attacked the FCC for not insisting on the breakup of more existing cross-ownerships.

When the resulting case, *FCC v. National Citizens Committee for Broadcasting* (436 U.S. 775, 1978), reached the Supreme Court, the court unanimously affirmed the FCC's cross-ownership rule, thus satisfying neither group of critics. The court said the FCC had acted within its authority and had based its rule on appropriate grounds.

Since 1975, the FCC has granted only a few waivers to let multimedia owners get around the rule and acquire both a newspaper and a TV station in the same market. (The rule also banned radio-newspaper cross-ownerships, but waivers of that restriction became routine in the 1990s.) In 1998 the FCC reluctantly granted the Tribune Company a waiver to own a Miami, Fla. television and a newspaper in nearby Fort Lauderdale, and then said future waivers would be granted only rarely. However, the FCC backpedaled on this point after a biennial review of ownership rules in 2000, saying it would consider more waivers, especially in large markets with many media voices. Apparently Tribune was counting on getting more waivers in 2000 when it took control of Times-Mirror Corp., publisher of both the *Los Angeles Times* and *Newsday* in New York. Tribune owns television stations in both markets. Tribune also was fighting to preserve another cross-ownership—in Hartford, Connecticut, where it owned two television stations and the *Hartford Courant*, the leading newspaper. The FCC granted Tribune a temporary waiver but refused to make it permanent while the cross-ownership rule is being reconsidered again.

Acting on an accelerated timetable in 2007, the FCC approved a new plan to deregulate the long-controversial newspaper-TV cross-ownership rules. On a partisan 3-2 majority, the FCC modified the rules to allow one company to acquire both a newspaper and a TV station in the nation's 20 largest markets, provided the station is not one of the top four in the market in terms of revenue and also provided there are still eight different media "voices" (TV stations or newspapers) after the merger.

The new rules, written and pushed through the commission by FCC Chair Kevin Martin, would allow newspaper-broadcast combinations in smaller markets if the merger involves a failing newspaper or would result in at least seven hours per week of local news programming on a station that was not previously airing local news. Martin justified the liberalized rules by pointing to the widespread financial woes of the newspaper industry, which has experienced declining advertising revenue and readership in the Internet era. Many local TV stations have also seen viewership decline in recent years, a reality that led the FCC to liberalize its Duopoly Rule to allow one company to own more than one TV station in larger metropolitan areas. That rule was relaxed in the 1990s.

The new rules were widely assailed by critics of corporate media ownership who said the rules would inevitably reduce the number of independent media voices.

The FCC's 2007 deregulation granted the Tribune Corporation a permanent waiver in Chicago because the company owned both WGN-TV and the *Chicago Tribune* long before cross-ownership was banned in 1975. It had acquired both newspapers and TV stations in other markets under previous waivers or loopholes in the ownership restrictions. The 2007 deregulation granted Tribune new (but temporary) waivers in New York, Los Angeles, Hartford and South Florida.

However, in 2011, in the most recent installment of the *Prometheus* cases, the Third Circuit again rejected the rule relaxations on newspaper-broadcast combinations, and it upheld other local broadcasting ownership restrictions retained by the FCC. Saying that the FCC had not given appropriate notice for comments on the change in rules, the court added that the procedures followed by the commission in this rule change were "highly irregular." Thus, the court said, "we have little choice but to conclude that the FCC did not ... fulfill its 'obligation to make its views known to the public in a concrete and focused form so as to make criticism or formulation of alternatives possible'" (*Prometheus Radio Project v. FCC*, 652 F.3d 431). The court also told the FCC to do a better job evaluating its rules for their impact on diversity in media ownership. Public interest groups hailed the decision as a win—as a spokesperson for the advocacy group Media Access Project said, "This decision is a vindication of the public's right to have a diverse media environment."

Demonstrating what can be done to cut costs when one company owns both a newspaper and a television station in the same market, in 2008 Tribune combined the offices of WSFL-TV, its Miami TV station, and the *South Florida Sun Sentinel*, merging advertising, business and content-producing operations of the jointly owned newspaper and TV station. In a way, Tribune was coming full circle by doing this. During the 1920s, the *Chicago Tribune* sponsored a pioneering radio station, WGN (the call sign was derived from the *Tribune's* slogan, "World's Greatest Newspaper") with heavy involvement of newspaper staffers and financial subsidies from the newspaper of more than $1 million during WGN's first 15 years on the air.

Like many early radio station owners, the Tribune company did not see radio as a commercially viable business but wanted a high-profile radio station for other reasons.

Combining the offices of two TV stations in the same market, as opposed to combining a newspaper and a TV station, has become commonplace since the FCC legalized owning two TV stations in the same market by amending its television *Duopoly Rule* in 1999. In 2003, the agency further liberalized its television Duopoly Rule to allow one company to own up to three stations in the largest markets instead of two, and to own two stations in some smaller markets where no company could own more than one station under the previous rules. This was a response to the federal appeals court's *Sinclair Broadcasting* decision in 2002. The FCC's 2003 rules would have allowed a company to own three TV stations in any market with 18 or more stations, or two in any market with five or more stations.

Most of the 2003 ownership rule changes (but not the 39 percent limit on the number of television households one company may serve, which was imposed by Congress after the FCC raised the cap to 45 percent) were questioned by the Third Circuit in its 2004 *Prometheus* decision. The Philadelphia-based court's 2-1 majority did not actually overturn many of the rules, but it did tell the FCC either to rescind the liberalized rules or better justify them. The FCC then reconsidered and adopted its 2007 deregulation, but did not authorize a single company to own three TV stations in the same market this time. The *Prometheus* ruling drew a strenuous dissent from Chief Judge Anthony Scirica, who accused his colleagues of substituting their views for those of the FCC on public policy issues within the FCC's jurisdiction.

As many listeners switch to largely unregulated web-based or satellite radio services and viewers opt for cable, satellite and web-based television, the larger question the FCC and the traditional media themselves must address is how to compete in this new world.

But cable is not immune from antitrust actions. In another case that implicated the Administrative Procedure Act (the same one discussed in Chapter Eleven in the Fox "fleeting expletives" case), a federal appeals court in 2009 said that there would be no exclusive cable rights for cable companies in apartment buildings they wire—ending exclusive agreements allowing companies to get exclusive rights to provide service to all residents in a complex by wiring multi-unit buildings. The DC Circuit upheld the FCC's banning of these deals and said pre-existing deals like them could not be enforced, and said that the FCC did not violate the APA, and in fact had appropriately "balanced benefits against harms and expressly determined that applying the rule to existing contracts was worth its costs" (*National Cable & Telecommunications Assoc. v. FCC*, 567 F.3d 659).

In *Brantley v. NBC Universal, Inc.* (675 F.3d 1192, 2012), the Ninth Circuit said that cable companies' grouping popular channels with less popular ones into packages did not violate Section 1 of the Sherman Antitrust Act. While "tying" of products together may have antitrust implications, particularly if the tying "impose[s] restraints on competition in the market for a tied product," such tying must actually injure competition. But, said the court, "plaintiffs here have not alleged in their complaint how competition (rather than consumers) is injured by the widespread practice of packaging low- and high-demand channels."

And, in 2012, the U.S. Supreme Court granted *cert* on a case reviewing the Third Circuit's ruling on whether cable customers could file suit as a class against alleged antitrust violations in Comcast's pricing schemes in Philadelphia (*Behrend v. Comcast Corp.*, 655 F.3d 182). While not an actual antitrust case, this case could establish how consumers can sue large media corporations for actions in restraint of trade. The Court will hear the case next Term.

Low-Power Radio: An Alternative?

While large corporations were buying more and more stations during the 1990s, the FCC approved a plan to foster grassroots ownership of local radio stations. In 1998, FCC Chair William Kennard called for a study of a proposal to allow *microradio* stations, extremely low power locally owned stations that would serve a small community or a small area of a larger city. The proposal was seen as a response to the growing popularity of "pirate" radio stations that were simply going on the air without a license.

At a time when some companies own hundreds of radio stations, it has not been easy for an individual to obtain a radio license: the few new licenses that are available are being auctioned off at high prices, and existing stations also sell for enormous sums of money. In recent years, more and more people who feel they have something to say and nowhere to say it have built bootleg radio stations to broadcast a few hours a day—until being caught by the FCC. FCC officials said they shut down nearly 100 pirate radio stations during 1997 alone. In 2006, the number busted by the FCC was closer to 200. To do that, the commission assigned a large part of its enforcement staff to that effort.

A driving force behind the pirate radio movement was a station calling itself "Free Radio Berkeley" in California. When the FCC sought a court order to shut that station down, the station's lawyer argued that the lack of any provision for low-power radio broadcasting violated the First Amendment. A federal court at first refused to order Free Radio Berkeley off the air; it took the FCC two years to persuade the court to issue a permanent injunction against this pirate station. By the time the court finally did so in mid-1998, Free Radio Berkeley was legendary on the Internet: imitators were springing up all over the country, with the help of free advice—and transmitter "kits"—from Free Radio Berkeley's founder, Stephen Dunifer. In 2012, he was still running workshops to teach unlicensed broadcasters how to set up their stations and get on the air (see www.freeradio.org).

Apparently believing that this indicated a need for low-power, minimally regulated radio stations to serve local communities, Kennard said the FCC would consider licensing such stations. The whole idea was bitterly opposed by many commercial and public broadcasters concerned about interference problems (and perhaps competition) from the new stations. Many broadcasters feared that, once authorized, low-power radio stations would be impossible for the FCC to control. Such stations would show up all over the radio dial on channels not authorized for them, broadcasters predicted.

Despite these concerns, in 2000 the FCC created the low-power FM radio service. In an effort to open up the airwaves to local community groups who are largely excluded from corporate-owned broadcasting, the FCC approved two classes of LPFM radio stations with maximum power levels of 10 watts and 100 watts. The new 10-watt and 100-watt stations will be heard well over a radius of 1-2 miles and 3.5 miles, respectively.

LPFM stations must be noncommercial. Owners of existing radio and television stations, cable systems and newspapers are not eligible for these licenses. The licenses are granted only to local residents. The FCC's intent is for these stations to have some production facilities and staff present in the community. To make room for LPFM stations, the FCC relaxed the mileage separation rules that protect broadcasters from interference. However, amidst an outcry from existing broadcasters, Congress intervened, attaching a provision to a large federal spending bill that restricted the new low-power FM radio stations mainly to smaller markets where they can operate without violating the FCC's original mileage separation rules. Congress later relaxed the restrictions on LPFM licensing a little.

However, by then another problem stood in the way of licensing local LPFM stations. The FCC in 2003 had opened an application window for FM *translator* stations, and 13,000 applications were submitted. Translators are low-power stations originally intended to rebroadcast a nearby station into a local community where it cannot be received well, often due to mountainous terrain. But translators and LPFM stations share the same frequencies. If these translator applications were to be granted, there would be no room left for LPFM stations in large cities. In 2005 the FCC stopped issuing new translator licenses after local broadcasting advocacy groups pointed out that three organizations in one town in Idaho had been granted about 100 translator licenses for communities all over the country and resold them to religious broadcasters who intended to build new national networks instead of doing local programming in each community.

By 2006, another problem had emerged. Of the initial 255 LPFM stations authorized in 2000, only a handful were on the air with regular programming, raising questions about the viability of LPFM as a form of local broadcasting in a day when unlicensed webcasting and podcasting are booming. Yet by 2012 over 800 LPFM licenses had been issued.

The Financial Interest and Syndication Rule

Another ownership restriction that has been eliminated is the long-controversial *Financial Interest and Syndication Rule* (often simply called the *"Fin-Syn" rule*). It was adopted in 1970 and was controversial from its inception until it was eliminated in several stages during the 1990s. The Fin-Syn rule limited the right of the three then-dominant networks to produce and syndicate their own entertainment programming. Because the syndication rights to network television shows are worth billions of dollars, there has been an ongoing power struggle between the networks and Hollywood's program producers, and the Fin-Syn rule has seen almost as many revisions and court challenges as the ownership rules.

The original 1970 Fin-Syn rule curtailed the in-house production of entertainment programming by the major networks. It prohibited the networks from acquiring a financial interest in the independently produced shows they aired. Also, the rule barred the networks from controlling and profiting from the syndication of "reruns" of network shows. The idea was to allow the independent program producers to keep the profits from off-network syndication. The FCC believed the networks had so much leverage that they would never allow independent producers to control syndication rights without a federal rule requiring it.

The independent producers argued that they made little or no profit from the networks' initial use of their shows because the networks' payments barely covered production costs. The producers said they earned most of their profits by syndicating the shows to local stations for use as reruns. Thus, the producers said they needed the Financial Interest and Syndication Rule to keep the networks out of the syndication business.

Under this rule, many of Hollywood's independent producers prospered during the 1970s and 1980s. But by the 1990s, ABC, CBS and NBC were no longer dominant. Their share of the television audience had dropped from above 90 percent to something less than 50 percent. More viewers were watching made-for-cable programming, independent stations and new broadcast networks, especially Fox.

It was clear that the three leading networks did not have the economic clout or the stranglehold on the audience that they once had. The FCC responded to the changing economic picture by eliminating the Fin-Syn rule in a series of steps between 1991 and 1995. By 2000, the effect of abolishing the Fin-Syn rule had become clear: of 37 new series chosen for the fall, 2000 season by ABC, CBS and NBC, 24 were either owned or co-owned by the host network, according to reports in the trade press. In 2003 independent producers were lobbying for a new Fin-Syn rule, contending that they were finding it almost impossible to get their programming on the networks without such a rule. Opponents, in turn, pointed out that there are far more networks today than there were when Fin-Syn was in force.

■ MASS MEDIA MERGERS AND ANTITRUST LAW

The last two decades have been times of unprecedented corporate mergers and acquisitions. With federal regulators clearly taking a relaxed attitude toward antitrust enforcement during much of this period, corporate America became engulfed in high-stakes consolidations. There were numerous takeovers and buyouts of media corporations, often raising antitrust questions that might have led to enforcement actions by the federal government in an earlier time. All three of the oldest television networks were purchased or merged in recent years. General Electric took control of NBC, Westinghouse purchased CBS and Walt Disney Co. purchased Capital Cities/ABC. The Westinghouse-CBS combination also merged with Infinity Broadcasting to create one of the nation's largest and most powerful radio groups (second in size only to the radio empire created by Clear Channel Communications).

In 1999 CBS announced still another megamerger: it joined up with Viacom in a merger under the Viacom name, bringing together CBS, Westinghouse, Infinity, Paramount Pictures, MTV, Nickelodeon, 35 television stations, about 163 radio stations, Blockbuster, several major production companies, two broadcast networks (CBS and UPN) and several other cable networks—all under single ownership. The FCC said that it would modify its rules to allow the two networks to be operated jointly under common ownership and completed that action in 2001, allowing each of the largest networks to own a smaller network.

However, megamergers don't always last: in 2005 Viacom was spun off from what became CBS Corporation. The new Viacom took several cable networks including MTV plus Paramount Pictures, leaving CBS with the broadcast networks, radio and TV stations and Paramount's television production company, among other assets.

Meanwhile, Time Warner, itself a media conglomerate created by a previous high-stakes merger, took control of Turner Broadcast System, Ted Turner's media conglomerate. And in 2000 America Online, the leading Internet service provider and owner of Netscape after a previous merger, announced that it would take control of the entire Time Warner empire in a deal originally valued at an incredible $181 *billion*. By the time the merger was completed, its value was reduced to $99 billion due to the rapid decline in the value of technology stocks in late 2000. Even so, a merger of that magnitude triggered widespread concern within the federal government, among public interest groups and elsewhere, especially after Time Warner blacked out ABC programming for 36 hours during a compensation dispute with Disney in 2000. The AOL Time Warner merger won final government approval in early 2001, a year after the merger was announced. To win regulatory approval, Time Warner had to make a number of concessions, including agreeing to open its broadband network to AOL's competitors. By 2008, AOL's business had dwindled to a fraction of what it was during the glory days of dial-up Internet access, and Time Warner also decided to spin off its cable systems into a separate company to focus on program production and publishing.

In 2009 Time Warner announced plans to spin off AOL. The online service had been losing revenue and profits for years, and Time Warner said it was planning to focus on its core businesses in television and film production, television networks and publishing.

The FCC by then had declared that cable systems are not "telecommunications services" and therefore do not have to open their broadband networks to competitors. In 2005, the U.S. Supreme Court upheld that FCC ruling in *National Cable & Telecommunications Association v. Brand X Internet Services* (545 U.S. 967), allowing cable systems to exclude competitors from their networks. Consumer groups and non-cable Internet service providers argued that giving cable a monopoly would drive up prices. They pointed out that broadband Internet service is much more expensive and less prevalent in the U.S. than in many other countries. The high court's 6-3 majority ruled as it did in part on the rationale that cable companies have invested heavily in broadband and should be able to reap profits from that investment.

Telephone companies, whose DSL services are cable's main broadband competition, said they would seek the same right to exclude competitors from their lines that cable won at the Supreme Court. New broadband services, such as wireless and "broadband over power lines" (BPL), face other regulatory and technical hurdles that prevent them from offering an alternative for consumers in the near future. By 2005 at least 14 states had passed laws to prevent cities from offering broadband services, further limiting competition.

Other big mergers stirred controversy during the 2000s. In 2004 GE, the parent of NBC, won government permission to merge with Vivendi Universal, creating a conglomerate with two television networks, numerous cable channels, theme parks, studios and television stations as well as GE's vast worldwide network of non-media businesses that range from financial services to jet aircraft engine manufacturing.

Other communications-related industries were altered by large mergers in recent years. In 1996 SBC Communications, the parent of Southwestern Bell, acquired Pacific Telesis, the parent of Pacific Bell, for about $17 billion, in the first-ever merger of two "Baby Bells," the regional telephone companies that were once part of AT&T. Three years later, SBC won regulatory approval to purchase still another Baby Bell, Chicago-based Ameritech Corp. for $61 billion. Then in 2005 SBC took over AT&T, its own former parent company, at a time when AT&T was near bankruptcy. In 2006, SBC (now calling itself AT&T) acquired Bell-South in an $86 billion deal that created a new AT&T nearly as large as the one dissolved in an antitrust lawsuit more than 20 years earlier. Meanwhile, Bell Atlantic and Nynex, two other giant regional phone companies, announced their own merger.

Other media mergers attracted attention and stirred controversy in the 2000s. In one of the most controversial such moves, News Corp., parent company of the Fox Television Network, the 20th Century Fox movie studio, 35 TV stations, MySpace.com, and many other media properties, took control of Dow Jones & Co., publisher of the *Wall Street Journal.* Although the deal included a provision guaranteeing the editorial independence of the *Journal,* it troubled critics of media consolidation more than most mergers because of the newspaper's long-cultivated national reputation for excellence.

The FCC permitted the merger in 2008 of XM Satellite Radio and Sirius Satellite Radio, subject to several conditions, including a 36-month price cap, *à la carte* subscription packages (including a family-friendly option), and the issuance of interoperable radio receivers within nine months.

In 2011, the FCC and Department of Justice approved the merger of Comcast and NBC Universal, creating a $30 billion company. The FCC announced in a press release

Fin-Syn rule:
short for "Financial Interest and Syndication," a rule that prohibited networks to have a financial interest in the television programs they aired and to create in-house syndication.

that Comcast had committed to "increase local news coverage to viewers; expand children's programming; enhance the diversity of programming available to Spanish-speaking viewers; offer broadband services to low-income Americans at reduced monthly prices; and provide high-speed broadband to schools, libraries and underserved communities, among other public benefits." While the FCC and Justice officials said the merger would serve the public interest, critics allege that the merger gives the new company unprecedented consolidated media power. Nor were FCC commissioners unanimous in their endorsement. Michael Copps, a Democrat, dissented, saying, "Comcast's acquisition of NBC Universal is a transaction like no other that has come before this commission—ever. It reaches into virtually every corner of our media and digital landscapes ... And it confers too much power in one company's hands."

How did the antitrust laws affect all of these big-ticket mergers and buyouts? The Hart-Scott-Rodino Antitrust Improvements Act of 1976 requires prior government approval for all large corporate mergers and acquisitions. Both the Justice Department and the Federal Trade Commission must be notified before the merger can occur. And when a merger involves broadcast properties, FCC approval of license transfers is required as well.

For the most part, these mergers drew few protests from the antitrust lawyers at the Justice Department, and the FCC routinely issued waivers of some cross-ownership rules, allowing many deals to go through. Eventually many of the merged companies had to sell some of their newly acquired properties to comply with the rules. And in some cases the Justice Department has refused to approve mergers that fully complied with the FCC's rules and the Telecommunications Act. For example, in 1996 Justice challenged a merger that would have given one company (American Radio Systems Corp.) control of eight radio stations in Rochester, N.Y.— the maximum number permitted by the FCC's ownership rules. Justice officials pointed out that the company would control 64 percent of the radio advertising revenue in the Rochester market. Moreover, the company would have six of Rochester's eight most powerful radio signals. The Justice Department refused to approve the consolidation until the company sold three of its eight stations.

Much the same thing happened in the Cincinnati market, where a 1996 merger would have given Jacor Communications control of a 53 percent market share of radio advertising. Jacor had to sell a highly rated station to get Justice's blessing for its merger.

In explaining these actions, Justice Department officials said they were looking at many factors to determine whether proposed mergers were pro-competitive or anti-competitive. Factors that could make a merger anti-competitive might include an excessive radio advertising market share, dominance of a popular format (e.g., owning all of the album-oriented rock stations in a market), owning too many of the most powerful stations in a market, or even dominance in a certain age group that was highly desired by advertisers.

Perhaps the bottom line with all of these mergers and takeovers is that the FCC, the FTC and the Justice Department all have broad discretion in deciding when to let two big companies join forces and when to play hardball with them.

In 2010 the FTC and the Department of Justice issued new joint Guidelines for horizontal mergers—mergers of companies that are actual or potential competitors. The basic message of the Guidelines, the agencies said, "is that mergers should not be permitted to create, enhance, or entrench market power or to facilitate its exercise." The document provided a blueprint on how the agencies will evaluate mergers to determine whether market power is affected, outlining types and sources of evidence that will be examined, and supplied hypothetical cases and their outcomes. The agencies also committed to "avoiding unnecessary interference with mergers that are either competitively beneficial or neutral."

The FTC further elaborated on its evaluation process in prepared remarks given to the House Subcommittee on Courts and Competition Policy in September 2010:

> Using the fact-specific approach laid out in the Guidelines, the Commission uses its extensive experience and applies a range of analytical tools to the evidence to evaluate the likely competitive effects of a merger. As part of this process, we ask: will this merger reduce competition in the future, or will new or existing competitors emerge to challenge the merged firm so that customers will receive the benefits of competition going forward?

Antitrust and the Internet

Given how much mass media has moved online, it is no surprise that many of the most recent antitrust battles have focused on online competition and commerce. Big names like Google and Apple are having to appear before Congress and the courts to defend their business models and trade practices against antitrust claims.

A consumers' group won the right to pursue antitrust claims against Verisign, a major domain name registrar, for its actions in the .com domain name market. In *Coalition for ICANN Transparency Inc. v. Verisign* (567 F.3d 1084), the Ninth Circuit in 2009 reversed a district court's dismissal of antitrust claims against Verisign. The court said that the coalition had successfully argued that Verisign may be engaging in predatory pricing in the .com top-level domain and trying to monopolize the market for domain names that are expiring.

Since 2001, Verisign has managed the databases of registered .com and .net domain names, contracting with the Internet Corporation for Assigned Names and Numbers (ICANN) to do so. The court said that "Verisign and ICANN had the intent to impose terms for pricing and price increases that restrained trade," thus violating Section 1 of the Sherman Act. Verisign also violated Section Two of the Sherman Act, the court said, by trying "to control ICANN's operations in its own favor." The case was remanded to the district court.

What about agreements on how much to charge for music online? The Second Circuit vacated a district court's dismissal in 2010 of an antitrust case alleging that major recording companies, including Sony and Vivendi, conspired to fix the prices and terms under which their music would be sold over the Internet (*Starr v. Sony BMG Music*, 592 F.3d 314). The court said the antitrust claim did not fail to meet the Sherman Act's requirements. Plaintiffs had argued that there was evidence of illegal conspiracy, including the charging of "unreasonably high prices" for music and the similarity of the companies' copyright restriction plans. The court remanded the case to determine if there was a Sherman Antitrust Act violation.

In 2011, several government bodies began antitrust investigations against Google. A Senate antitrust panel held hearings into allegations that Google's search results favor its own commercial ventures over others. Jeffrey Katz, the CEO of shopping site Nextag, testified, "When you search for 'running shoes' or 'digital camera,' Google transforms itself from an independent search engine to a commerce site. But that is not what happens when you type in a search for, say, 'kidney dialysis.'" Several senators sent a letter after the hearing to the FTC to encourage it to investigate the search company for antitrust violations. The FTC was already considering whether Google prevents smart phone companies that use its Android operating system from using other, competing systems. The agency in 2012 hired an outside attorney for this investigation, a move that the *New York Times* reported might signal the FTC's plans to take the matter to court.

A trial date in June 2013 has been set for an antitrust case brought by the government against Apple and several book publishers accused of electronic book ("eBook") price-fixing. The Justice Department had brought suit against Apple in April 2012, alleging that it had worked with five publishers to set eBook prices as early as 2010. Three of those publishers already settled with Justice, but two (Macmillan and Penguin Group) are fighting the charges. But all five publishers and Apple could not get a federal judge to dismiss a class action suit against them by eBook consumers, alleging price-fixing collusion. Judge Denise Cote, in harsh language against Apple, said that the company "did not try to earn money off of eBooks by competing with other retailers in an open market; rather, Apple 'accomplished this goal by [helping] the suppliers to collude, rather than to compete independently'" (*In re Elec. Books Antitrust Litig.*, 2012 U.S. Dist. LEXIS 68058).

■ AN OVERVIEW OF MAJOR ISSUES

At a time when the nation's giant media corporations are maneuvering for bigger shares of the communications marketplace, there are major unresolved issues in media ownership and antitrust law. Recent times have seen massive media consolidation without much intervention by the Justice Department, which is supposed to act under the antitrust laws to prevent mergers and consolidations that lessen competition. At other times, relatively small mergers have received considerable scrutiny at the Justice Department.

Just what sort of merger is "anti-competitive" rather than "pro-competitive"? Does it really lessen competition when one company owns program production facilities, hundreds of broadcast stations, cable systems, television networks, national magazines and newspapers? What about foreign ownership of American communications companies? The FCC has rules limiting foreign ownership of broadcast stations, but not Hollywood production companies. Does foreign ownership in Hollywood have any implications for the public interest? Should the limits on foreign ownership of radio and television stations be liberalized?

What about private equity investment firms—money managers with billions of dollars from pension funds and wealthy individuals to invest—buying media companies that were once publicly owned? For companies that once had their stock traded on Wall Street, with all of the public disclosure requirements that entails, this was a return to the days of doing business behind closed doors. In 2007 alone four of the largest station groups (Tribune, Clear

Channel, Univision and Ion) announced plans to be acquired by private equity investors. Is that in the public interest?

The FCC's 2003 and 2007 deregulations of broadcast ownership restrictions were highly controversial—in Congress and across the country. Did the FCC go too far in letting one network (or other media company) own TV stations that reach 45 percent of the nation's television households instead of 35 percent? Did Congress do the right thing by cutting the ceiling back to 39 percent? What about the 2007 liberalization of newspaper-television cross-ownership restrictions? Is it a good thing for a newspaper publisher to be able to buy a local television station and combine news operations—or for one company to own three television stations instead of two in the largest markets? Given Congress' mandate to the FCC to conduct regular reviews of the ownership restrictions, and given a series of earlier court decisions overturning various restrictions, did the FCC have a choice? Do the traditional ownership restrictions make sense in a marketplace that offers so many new choices in home entertainment programming? Are there lessons to be learned from what happened after the national radio ownership limits were eliminated by the 1996 Telecommunications Act?

The Internet has created new questions about monopolization and collusion. In the 2005 *Brand X* decision, cable systems won the Supreme Court's authorization to exclude competitors from broadband cable networks. Telephone companies are seeking the same regulatory treatment so they can exclude competitors from their DSL systems. Other would-be broadband competitors face serious obstacles, leaving U.S. consumers with limited choices and high prices for broadband service compared to consumers in many other countries. Because cable and the telcos have invested heavily to set up broadband services, their investors expect the highest return possible, but where does that leave consumers?

The influence of investors has also raised other issues. Wall Street likes profitability and the potential for growth. The 2006 dismantling of Knight Ridder, once the second largest newspaper chain in America, was largely the result of stockholder pressure. Like other newspaper companies, Knight Ridder didn't offer strong growth prospects even though the company remained profitable in the 2000s. Wall Street analysts thought—perhaps correctly—that the individual newspapers might be worth more than the company as a whole. Similar considerations may have played a role in the split of CBS and Viacom into two companies. The combined company had seen its stock price stagnate, and the spinoff created a company expected to grow rapidly (the new Viacom) and a company composed of older, slower-growth businesses (CBS). Does Wall Street have too much influence on the media? But is ownership by private equity firms better?

Questions like these will affect all of our lives. Fortunes may be made and lost, and the public interest may be served or disserved, as private industry and government regulators struggle to find answers.

WHAT SHOULD I KNOW ABOUT MY STATE?	• What are my state's applications of federal antitrust laws? • What antitrust laws does my state have? • Are any of the newspapers in my area in a joint operating agreement? What are the terms? • Who owns the media organizations in my city or county?

A SUMMARY OF OWNERSHIP ISSUES

Do Antitrust Laws Apply to the Media?

Yes. For many years, publishers argued that the First Amendment exempted them from antitrust laws, but the Supreme Court ruled otherwise in 1945. Antitrust laws forbid price fixing, profit pooling, tying arrangements, boycotts and certain other coercive business practices. Also, mergers that substantially reduce competition are unlawful.

What Is a Joint Operating Agreement, or JOA?

Under a JOA, two competing newspapers merge their business, advertising and printing operations while maintaining separate editorial staffs. Some publishers say they could not stay in business without such arrangements. The Supreme Court once ruled that a joint operating agreement violated antitrust laws, but then Congress passed the Newspaper Preservation Act, legalizing existing agreements and setting up a procedure for the approval of new ones.

What Is Cross-Ownership?

Cross-ownership occurs when one party owns a combination of newspapers, broadcast properties and/or cable systems in the same metropolitan market area. Under FCC rules that were upheld by the Supreme Court, new newspaper-broadcast cross-ownerships were forbidden for many years. In 2003 the FCC dropped many of these restrictions; a federal appellate court ordered the FCC to reconsider in 2004, and the agency released new rules in 2007.

What Are the Broadcast Ownership Restrictions?

Under the Telecommunications Act of 1996, there is no limit to the number of radio or television stations one company may own nationally. However, no company may own more than two television stations or eight radio stations in a large metropolitan area. In smaller markets the number of stations a company may own is correspondingly lower. No company may own television stations that reach more than 39 percent of the nation's television households under a 2004 act of Congress.

How Will the New Technologies Affect Media Ownership?

As new technologies such as fiber optics, satellite communication, digital television and high-speed Internet access develop, the print and electronic media are converging, and the corporations behind these technologies are merging, with each seeking to offer as many communication services as possible.

13 *Advertising and the Law*

Like broadcasting, the advertising industry has specialized legal problems not shared by other mass communications industries. In addition to the legal problems other communicators face, advertisers—like broadcasters—have a federal agency assigned to look after them: advertisers have to get along with the Federal Trade Commission. Advertisers must also deal with other federal agencies and state-level advertising regulators, sometimes including officials of multiple states or multiple federal agencies working together.

Marketing and advertising cases are becoming increasingly expensive in current years; in 2009, the *New York Times* reported that Pfizer, a pharmaceutical company, agreed to pay $2.3 *billion* in a civil and criminal settlement with the Department of Justice over its marketing of the painkiller Bextra. It is the largest health care fraud settlement and the largest criminal fine ever, said the *Times.* "The whole culture of Pfizer is driven by sales, and if you didn't sell drugs illegally, you were not seen as a team player," said a former Pfizer sales representative, whose whistleblowing complaints drove the investigation.

The Department of Justice fined Merck nearly $322 million for an illegal marketing campaign involving the painkiller Vioxx in 2012. Merck had marketed Vioxx for rheumatoid arthritis before the Food and Drug Administration had approved it for such use. This "off-label" marketing is a violation of the Food, Drug, and Cosmetic Act, which states that a drug cannot be marketed for a use before the FDA says it's safe and effective for that use.

Advertisers have fought many legal battles in recent years and have even won a few, including several U.S. Supreme Court decisions that extended substantial First Amendment protection to commercial speech.

■ THE FIRST AMENDMENT AND ADVERTISING

For many years, the prevailing rule was that advertising had no First Amendment protection. If a particular expression of fact or opinion could be dismissed as *commercial speech,* it could be arbitrarily suppressed by law. The *Commercial Speech Doctrine,* as it came to be known, simply said advertisers were at the mercy of every arm of government, without the guarantees of freedom the Constitution afforded to most other kinds of speech and publishing.

That has all changed, starting in 1975. The U.S. Supreme Court handed down a series of decisions between 1975 and 1980 that established substantial First Amendment protection for commercial speech. During the 1980s, the Supreme Court wavered at times, sometimes upholding government restrictions on advertising in decisions that seemed inconsistent with the cases from the 1970s. But in the 1990s, the Supreme Court again strongly reaffirmed the First Amendment protection of commercial speech. In 1996, the high court handed down a decision on liquor price advertising that was so broad it appeared to give commercial speech *almost* the same First Amendment protection as noncommercial speech.

This line of cases is one of the best examples of American law growing through judicial precedent to be found anywhere in the mass communications field.

The starting point for this summary is a 1942 Supreme Court decision that denied First Amendment protection to commercial speech, a landmark ruling that stood for many years. That case is *Valentine v. Chrestensen* (316 U.S. 52). It stemmed from a bizarre situation. Just before World War II, a man named F.J. Chrestensen acquired a surplus U.S. Navy submarine and tried to dock it at a city-owned wharf in New York City. City authorities wouldn't let him, so he had to arrange for other dock facilities. Next, he started advertising guided tours of the submarine, but city officials wouldn't let him distribute his handbills on city streets because an anti-litter ordinance banned all but political leaflets. So he added a note criticizing city officials for refusing him dockage to the back of the handbill. Then he took the city to court for denying his right to distribute literature. The Supreme Court had just ruled in favor of that right in the first of the Jehovah's Witness cases (see Chapter Three).

When his case reached the Supreme Court, Chrestensen was in for a surprise. The high court said his back-of-the-handbill political statement was really a ruse to justify a purely commercial advertisement. And that was different from the Jehovah's Witness cases. Where purely commercial advertising is involved, the First Amendment does not apply, the Court ruled. For many years, *Valentine* was regarded as the prevailing precedent on commercial speech. In fact, when the landmark *New York Times v. Sullivan* libel decision was announced in 1964, the Court went to some trouble to explain why the *Valentine* rule didn't apply (the *Sullivan* libel suit was based on an advertisement). The Court said the ad involved in the *Sullivan* case was an idea ad supporting the civil rights movement, not an ad for a purely commercial product or service as in *Valentine*. Thus, the *Valentine* rule still denied First Amendment protection to commercial advertising for another decade, despite *New York Times v. Sullivan*.

In 1973, the Supreme Court again denied First Amendment protection to commercial advertising, this time in a case involving the "help wanted" ads in a large newspaper. In *Pittsburgh Press v. Pittsburgh Commission on Human Relations* (413 U.S. 376), the Human Relations Commission ordered the newspaper to stop classifying its employment ads as "Jobs—Male Interest" and "Jobs—Female Interest." The newspaper contended that there were editorial judgments inherent in the decision to classify job openings that way, and that those judgments were protected by the First Amendment.

The Court disagreed, ruling that the classified ads are not only commercial speech but commercial speech promoting an illegal form of discrimination as well. The court had no difficulty in ruling that whatever First Amendment considerations might be involved were secondary to the city's right to outlaw advertising for an illegal commercial activity.

FIG. 63. Patent medicine ad for Merchant's Gargling Oil, about 1873.

Library of Congress, Prints and Photographs Division, [LC-USZ62-48534].

An interesting follow-up note to this case is that in 1979 the Pennsylvania Supreme Court ruled against the Human Relations Commission when it tried to stop the *Pittsburgh Press* from accepting "help wanted" ads from individuals who wished to indicate their age, sex, race or religion in the ad. The commission objected to such language as "salesman age 30," "born-again Christian seeks work in Christian business," or "white woman seeks domestic work." The state high court said the job seeker had a First Amendment right to communicate such information as this, even though an employer isn't supposed to consider these factors. The U.S. Supreme Court declined to review this second *Pittsburgh Press* decision. Despite this decision, most federal and state laws governing housing and employment discrimination forbid advertising that expresses a preference for applicants of a particular race, gender, family status or sexual orientation.

What if an online service that carries thousands or millions of ads fails to screen out every ad that could promote illegal discrimination—or doesn't do any screening at all? Is the online service liable, or only the advertiser? In 2008 two federal appeals courts ruled on that issue and reached opposite conclusions—in cases involving famous online services: Craigslist.org and Roommates.com.

The Seventh Circuit ruled that Craigslist.org is not the publisher of the ads posted on its site and therefore cannot be held accountable for their content. The court said Craigslist is not comparable to a newspaper that publishes classified ads. Ruling in *Chicago Lawyers' Committee for Civil Rights Under Law v. Craigslist* (519 F.3d 666), the court said Section 230 of the Communications Decency Act exempts Craigslist from liability for ads posted by others. Although the court did not say Internet providers have complete protection from all liability for materials on their sites, the court did say Internet providers are exempt from liability for posting unscreened third-party content.

When this case was litigated, 30 million people were posting ads on Craigslist every month. Craigslist reported in 2009 that the number rose to 50 million in the U.S. alone.

The court said the lawyers' group that brought the case is free to sue individuals who post illegal ads—or to urge federal prosecutors to go after those whose Craigslist ads violate the Fair Housing Act or other laws. But Craigslist is protected by Section 230. The court said, in essence, that Craigslist cannot be expected to review millions of ads every month to spot ads that advocate an illegal act any more than a telephone company can screen every call or UPS and Fedex can screen every package for illegal content. As anyone who has surfed Craigslist for long knows, there are not only ads that could promote housing discrimination but also ads offering all sorts of services that may not be legal. Craigslist has taken many steps to curb such ads, including warnings to those who post ads and invitations for users to flag illegal ads. But if an illegal message is posted in spite of all that, Craigslist is not responsible for its content, according to this Seventh Circuit decision.

However, soon after the *Craigslist* decision an 11-judge *en banc* panel of the Ninth Circuit reached a different conclusion in a case involving Roommates.com. Ruling in *Fair Housing Council of San Fernando Valley v. Roommates.com* (521 F.3d 1157, 2008), the court said Roommates crossed the line and lost Section 230 immunity because it requires those who want to place ads to create a "profile" by answering specific questions about their gender, family status and sexual orientation. Doing that screening makes Roommates an "information content provider" and not a mere conduit for content created by others. The 8-3 majority in this hotly contested case said Roommates' profile questions made this case different and caused Roommates to lose its Section 230 immunity. The majority opinion said

Roommates would not lose its immunity if all it did was to allow advertisers to post a message in a comment box without any structuring by the service.

The dissenting judges in *Roommates* pointed out that no court had yet determined any of the profiles to be actual advocacy of unlawful housing discrimination. Most fair housing laws exempt individuals' choices of roommates from discrimination complaints. It's not usually illegal to rule out prospective roommates who would share your residence based on their age, gender, family status or sexual orientation. A single, 21-year-old female can choose to share her home only with other young women who have no children, as opposed to older men who want to move in with their children, for example. Even private individuals who rent out up to three single-family homes are exempt from most fair housing laws. So the question raised in the *Roommates* case comes down to whether it is right to penalize an Internet provider for allowing ads that may or may not promote illegal housing discrimination.

Given two federal appeals court decisions that reached opposite conclusions about the liability of Internet services for possible fair housing violations by their users, perhaps the Supreme Court will someday rule on this issue.

Craigslist did responde to pressure from several states' attorneys general when a masseuse was killed in Boston in 2009 after being lured to a hotel by a medical student who found her on Craigslist. The alleged killer had met his victim when she had advertised in Craigslist's "erotic services" category. Craigslist was asked by the attorneys general to remove the ads, and it complied, eliminating its "erotic services" category and creating a new "adult services" category. The attorneys general had labeled the category "nothing more than an Internet brothel." But that change fared no better; in response to another letter from the attorneys general in 2010, Craigslist also closed down its entire adult services section.

Early Victories for Commercial Speech

Only two years after the original *Pittsburgh Press* decision, the Supreme Court handed down the first of its major decisions extending First Amendment protection to commercial speech (*Bigelow v. Virginia*, 421 U.S. 809, 1975). The case began in 1971 when Jeffrey Bigelow published an ad in *The Virginia Weekly* for an abortion service in New York, where abortions had just been legalized. The Supreme Court's *Roe v. Wade* decision, which held that abortions could not be banned in any state, did not occur until 1973. Both abortions and abortion advertising were illegal in Virginia in 1971.

Bigelow was prosecuted for violating the Virginia law. He appealed his conviction; the U.S. Supreme Court used his case to rewrite the Commercial Speech Doctrine. The high court emphasized that the service in question was not illegal where it was offered, and said the readers had a First Amendment right to receive this information. The court distinguished this case from *Pittsburgh Press* by pointing out that the commercial activity in question in the *Pittsburgh* case was illegal. But above all, the Supreme Court in *Bigelow* declared that this message did not lose the First Amendment protection it would otherwise enjoy merely because it appeared in the form of an advertisement. The high court said that in the future there would have to be a *compelling state interest* to justify laws prohibiting any form of commercial speech that has a legitimate purpose.

A year later the Supreme Court took another giant step toward protecting commercial speech under the First Amendment. In *Virginia State Board of Pharmacy v. Virginia Citizens Consumer Council* (425 U.S. 748, 1976), the Supreme Court overturned Virginia's state law against advertising the prices of drugs. Many other states had similar prohibitions on drug price advertising, but the Supreme Court again emphasized the First Amendment right of consumers to receive information as it overturned the state regulations.

Again, the Court said the information in question was protected by the First Amendment despite its commercial nature. At that point, it seemed clear that the old *Valentine* doctrine was dead: commercial speech did have constitutional protection. However, while the Court recognized the importance of price advertising to the free enterprise system, it also emphasized that this ruling in no way affected the right of governments to control false and misleading advertising.

In 1977, the Supreme Court handed down several more decisions strengthening the First Amendment protection of commercial speech. First, in *Linmark Associates v. Willingboro* (431 U.S. 85), the Supreme Court said homeowners have a First Amendment right to place "for sale" signs in front of their homes. The town of Willingboro, N.J. had outlawed "for sale" signs at a time when the area's racial composition was changing. There was considerable "white flight" and city officials wanted to discourage panic selling by white homeowners. One way to do this, the city felt, was to keep it from appearing that entire neighborhoods were for sale. A real estate firm challenged the constitutionality of the ordinance.

In defending the ordinance, city officials pointed to the social importance of racial integration and the evils of "white flight." Also, they said, homeowners who really need to sell their homes have other ways to advertise (by listing their homes with real estate agents or using newspaper classified ads, for instance). Nevertheless, the Supreme Court ruled against the city. In an opinion written by Justice Thurgood Marshall, the majority said the city could not constitutionally deprive its residents of the information that a "for sale" sign offers. "If the dissemination of this information can be restricted, then every locality in the country can suppress any facts that reflect poorly on the locality," Marshall wrote.

Although the *Linmark* decision held that homeowners have a First Amendment right to put up "for sale" signs, many cities continued to restrict real estate signs. For example, some towns allowed "for sale" signs but banned "sold" signs on the theory that the presence of a lot of "sold" signs would also send the message that many homeowners are leaving.

In addition to *Linmark*, in 1977 the Supreme Court handed down a commercial speech decision that was not at all surprising in view of its ruling in *Bigelow v. Virginia*. In *Carey v. Population Services International* (431 U.S. 678, 1977), the court overturned a variety of New York laws that restricted advertising of contraceptive devices. Even though these devices were legal in New York, state laws prohibited advertising, in-store displays and even sales of these products except by licensed pharmacists. Even pharmacists could not sell these devices to anyone younger than age 16. The Court found First Amendment violations in these laws and said there was no compelling state interest to justify them, as required in *Bigelow*.

The Central Hudson Test

In 1980, the Supreme Court established a new legal test that has been used ever since then to determine the validity of government restrictions on commercial speech. That happened in the case of *Central Hudson Gas and Electric v. Public Service Commission of New York* (447 U.S. 557). The *Central Hudson* case challenged rules adopted by the New York Public Service Commission in 1977 in an effort to promote conservation and discourage energy use. Among other things, the commission prohibited advertising by utilities that might encourage consumption of utility services rather than conservation. The Central Hudson Gas and Electric Company challenged this wide-ranging regulation of its advertising. The company lost in the New York Court of Appeals, which ruled that the ban was justified because the need to conserve energy outweighed the slight free speech issue involved.

The U.S. Supreme Court reversed the New York court, holding that the ban on promotional advertising would have only a "highly speculative" effect on energy consumption or utility rates, and that a total ban on such advertising was going too far. If there was any doubt by this time, the court said commercial speech is constitutionally protected if it concerns "lawful activity" and is not misleading or fraudulent.

If commercial speech is constitutionally protected, how can the courts determine if a particular government restriction is proper under the First Amendment? In the *Central Hudson* case the Supreme Court said courts should evaluate government restrictions on advertising under these four criteria:

1. whether the expression is *protected by the First Amendment* (if it involves deception or unlawful activities, it is not protected by the First Amendment and may be banned without considering this test);
2. whether the *governmental interest that justifies the restrictions is substantial;*
3. whether the regulation *directly advances the governmental interest* in question;
4. whether the regulation is *more broad than needed* to fulfill the governmental interest.

This test has been cited in hundreds of cases since it was handed down in 1980 in the *Central Hudson* case, as both state and federal courts have had to rule on a variety of government restrictions on advertising. At the same time as its *Central Hudson* decision, the high court ruled on a separate case involving *noncommercial corporate speech,* as opposed to commercial speech. The court established a different test for judging the constitutionality of government restrictions on that type of speech. This topic is discussed later in the chapter.

Lawyers' Advertising as Commercial Speech

The Supreme Court has repeatedly addressed the First Amendment rights of lawyers and other professionals who advertise—and who are subject to special rules restricting their right to do so. The Court first dealt with lawyer advertising in 1977, handing down one of its most far-reaching commercial speech decisions: *Bates v. Arizona State Bar* (433 U.S. 350).

That case overturned Arizona's ban on advertising by lawyers, a rule similar to those found in nearly every other state. The case involved a legal clinic run by two young lawyers. The lawyers were disciplined by the State Bar for advertising the prices of routine legal services, prices that were far below the "going rate" charged by other lawyers.

In ruling against the state bar, the Supreme Court again emphasized the First Amendment right of consumers to receive commercial information. The court said advertising by lawyers (and presumably other professionals) could not be prohibited unless it was misleading or fraudulent. However, the Court expressed reservations about ads that say something about the quality of the services offered ("we're the best lawyers in town"), because such ads could well be misleading.

That warning about misleading advertising by professionals foreshadowed two more Supreme Court rulings, *Ohralik v. Ohio State Bar Association* (436 U.S. 447, 1978) and *Friedman v. Rogers* (440 U.S. 1, 1979). In *Ohralik,* the Supreme Court affirmed sanctions against a lawyer for soliciting new clients in a manner that is sometimes called "ambulance chasing."

The Court said the First Amendment does not prevent a state bar association from adopting rules against that sort of conduct. In *Friedman*, the Court went a step further, upholding a Texas ban on the use of trade names by optometrists. The Court said a trade name could be misleading and that it did not provide consumers important information—as did the commercial advertising in question in earlier cases—and could be misleading because there could be a change of optometrists (and thus a change in the quality of service offered) without the name changing. Therefore, a state is not violating the First Amendment when it requires an optometrist to practice under his own name rather than a trade name, the Court ruled. This case was viewed as a slight retreat by some, and critics pointed out that it was customary and completely legal for law firms, for instance, to continue to use the names of the founding partners long after their deaths. Isn't such a name really a trade name at some point? Wouldn't that also be misleading? The Court didn't address that issue.

The Supreme Court also decided a number of other commercial speech cases involving advertising or solicitations by attorneys: *In re R.M.J.* (455 U.S. 191, 1982), *Zauderer v. Office of Disciplinary Counsel* (471 U.S. 626, 1985), *Shapero v. Kentucky Bar Association* (486 U.S. 466, 1988), *Peel v. Attorney Registration and Disciplinary Commission* (496 U.S. 91, 1990), *Ibanez v. Florida Department of Professional and Business Regulation* (512 U.S. 136, 1994) and *Florida Bar v. Went For It Inc.* (515 U.S. 618, 1995). Perhaps the fact that the Supreme Court has handed down so many rulings on lawyer advertising not only illustrates how deeply divided the legal community is on this issue, but also that lawyers tend to file lawsuits.

The case of *In re R.M.J.* involved regulations that severely restricted lawyers' advertising in Missouri. The rules allowed lawyers to use only certain words to describe the kinds of law that they practiced, and the approved words were in legalese, not layman's terms. A lawyer could not advertise that he or she handled personal injury or real estate cases, for instance. An unnamed lawyer violated these rules and was disciplined. The Supreme Court overturned the disciplinary action, holding that the attorney's advertising was protected by the First Amendment. However, the Court again re-emphasized the point that only nondeceptive advertising—by lawyers or anybody else—is protected by the First Amendment.

The *Zauderer* case began when Philip Zauderer, a Columbus, Ohio, lawyer, was disciplined for publishing newspaper ads that contained a drawing of the Dalkon Shield contraceptive, which has been linked to miscarriages, injuries and possibly cancer. Zauderer's ads said that he was representing numerous women in lawsuits against the manufacturer of the Dalkon Shield and would be willing to take more cases involving the controversial device.

The Supreme Court voted 5-3 to strike down Ohio's ban on the use of illustrations in lawyers' advertising. The Court said, in essence, that bar associations could require lawyers' ads to be truthful and little more. As it had in earlier commercial speech cases, the Court said in the *Zauderer* case that consumers had a right to receive the message that local authorities wanted to suppress, and that the advertiser had a right to communicate it.

The Court did uphold Ohio's right to discipline Zauderer for aspects of his advertising, however. For example, his ads promised that women who filed Dalkon Shield lawsuits would not have to pay any lawyer's fees if they lost, since he was handling the cases on a contingent-fee basis. However, women who lost their cases were still obligated to pay certain court costs, and the disciplinary committee penalized Zauderer for failing to explain that in his ads.

In 1988 the Supreme Court's *Shapero v. Kentucky Bar Association* decision overturned restrictions on targeted direct-mail solicitations by lawyers. Kentucky and about 20 other states barred lawyers from mailing solicitations to people who might have a specific need for a lawyer (in this case, people facing the loss of their homes through foreclosures).

The Supreme Court again ruled in favor of advertising by attorneys in a 1990 case, *Peel v. Attorney Registration and Disciplinary Commission*. In this case, the Court said Illinois could not prevent lawyers from advertising the fact that they are certified specialists in a particular legal specialty. In a 5-4 decision, a divided Court held that such advertising could be false or misleading under some circumstances. However, a majority also agreed that an across-the-board ban on all such advertising even when it is truthful went too far.

In 1994, the Court followed that decision by ruling that the Florida Board of Accountancy could not prevent accountants who are also lawyers from advertising that fact. In *Ibanez v. Florida Department of Professional and Business Regulation*, the Court held that Silvia Ibanez, who was a certified financial planner as well as a lawyer and an accountant, could advertise these credentials on her business cards and in her yellow pages listing. To deny her that right would be an improper restriction on commercial speech, the Court held.

On the other hand, a year later the Supreme Court upheld another Florida rule that prohibits lawyers from soliciting business with targeted mailings to accident or disaster victims within 30 days of the incident. In *Florida Bar v. Went For It Inc.*, the Court said it was not a violation of the First Amendment for Florida to forbid such solicitations because the state has a substantial government interest in "protecting the privacy and tranquility of personal injury victims and their loved ones against intrusive, unsolicited contact by lawyers," Justice Sandra Day O'Connor said in the majority opinion.

The Second Circuit, in *Alexander v. Cahill* (598 F.3d 79, 2010), affirmed a district court's ruling overturning New York's rules on attorney advertising, alleging that they could be enforced arbitrarily and discriminatorily, and they violated the First Amendment because they prohibited protected speech. The rules barred "testimonials from clients relating to pending matters, portrayals of judges or fictitious law firms, attention-getting techniques unrelated to attorney competence, and trade names or nicknames that imply an ability to get results." The court applied the *Central Hudson* test and said the rules failed the last two parts; the state had failed to show that consumers were misled, and the rules covered more speech than necessary. The court let stand the prohibition on fictitious law firm names.

Appeals courts have also upheld a Wisconsin state bar rule on the use of bar association fees to fund public image campaigns (*Kingstad v. State Bar of Wisconsin*, 622 F.3d 708, 2010, in the Seventh Circuit), a Texas state law that prohibits solicitation for legal services to accident victims for 30 days after the accident because the law met the standards under *Central Hudson* (*McKinley v. Abbott*, 643 F.3d 403, 2011, in the Fifth Circuit), and, also using *Central Hudson*, parts of the Louisiana Rules of Professional Conduct that forbid attorneys from promising results, using pictures of non-clients and depicting them as clients, and using "a nickname, moniker, motto or trade name that states or implies an ability to obtain results in a matter" (*Public Citizen v. La. Attorney Discipline Bd.*, 632 F.3d 212, 2010, also in the Fifth Circuit; the court upheld parts of the rules that forbid testimonials to past success, portrayals of judges or juries, and font size and other formatting regulations on ads).

The 1980s: Hedging on Commercial Speech

The Supreme Court has ruled on commercial speech rights in several other contexts, with mixed results. In 1981 the Court ruled on the right of local governments to outlaw roadside billboards in *Metromedia v. San Diego* (453 U.S. 490). The court overturned a San

Diego city ordinance banning both political and commercial billboard messages. However, the court was deeply divided in deciding the case, and Justice William Rehnquist called the decision a "virtual Tower of Babel from which no definitive principles can be drawn."

Nevertheless, a majority of the justices did agree that San Diego's billboard ban was too broad because it banned all billboards containing political messages as well as purely commercial ones. The Court left open the possibility that a narrower ordinance forbidding only commercial but not political billboards would be constitutionally permissible. But beyond that, the five different opinions seemed to shed more confusion than light.

The Ninth Circuit used the *Metromedia* case as precedent in a 2009 decision that upheld a Los Angeles ordinance restricting billboards but allowing bus shelter advertising. The facts in *Metro Lights v. Los Angeles* (551 F.3d 898) were, according to Judge Diarmuid O'Scannlain, "virtually identical" to those in the *Metromedia* case, and the same outcome was "compelled" by *Metromedia*. Metro Lights had asked the court to distinguish the *Metromedia* case by suggesting that the billboard ordinance was content based, but the court was not convinced. Moreover, Los Angeles is permitted to value one kind of commercial speech over others. Both cases featured a ban on billboards and an exception for bus shelters and transit stops "enacted to promote traffic safety and aesthetics."

In 1984, the Supreme Court again addressed the constitutionality of a local ordinance restricting political signs, but this time the court decided that such an ordinance did not violate the First Amendment. In *Members of the Los Angeles City Council v. Taxpayers for Vincent* (466 U.S. 789), the court said the city of Los Angeles has the right to ban political posters on public property. The Court ruled that forbidding posters on city-owned utility poles and buildings was not an excessive restriction on First Amendment freedoms.

The Court said this decision was not inconsistent with the *Metromedia v. San Diego* decision, in which a ban on all billboards (including those on private property with the owner's consent) was overturned as a First Amendment violation. In contrast, the Los Angeles ordinance only prohibited attaching posters to public property, not placing signs and billboards on private property. In upholding the ordinance, the Court said a city has the right to prevent the "visual assault on the citizens...presented by an accumulation of signs posted on public property."

What about political signs on private property rather than public property? As Chapter Three explains, the Supreme Court has ruled that a city may not ban all signs on private property conveying political messages (see *City of Ladue v. Gilleo*, 512 U.S. 43).

In view of the earlier commercial speech rulings, the Supreme Court surprised no one when it decided *Bolger v. Youngs Drug Products Corp.* (463 U.S. 60) in 1983. The court overturned the post office's ban on mailing unsolicited ads for contraceptive devices. The court said such a ban denies consumers access to important information that the public has a constitutional right to receive. In the majority opinion, Justice Thurgood Marshall emphasized the importance of family planning and the prevention of venereal disease as social issues, and said the post office had not adequately justified the ban on mailing this material.

Unfortunately, Supreme Court decisions are often not as consistent and predictable as the commercial speech cases of the late 1970s and early 1980s seemed to be. In 1986, there was a surprise awaiting those who thought they understood the Commercial Speech Doctrine. In *Posadas de Puerto Rico Associates v. Tourism Company of Puerto Rico* (478 U.S. 328, 1986), the court announced one of its most widely noted and controversial decisions on commercial speech. The court *upheld* Puerto Rico's Games of Chance Act of 1948, which legalized casino gambling on the island but barred casinos from advertising locally, while allowing casino advertising aimed at tourists. The law was challenged by Posadas, a Texas-based partnership that operated the Condado Holiday Inn Hotel and Sands Casino. The Tourism Company, a public corporation responsible for enforcing the island's gambling law, twice fined Posadas for advertising locally, and the casino operator eventually challenged the constitutionality of the Puerto Rican law. The local "advertising" included such things as matchbook covers and elevator signs that used the forbidden word "casino."

The high court's majority opinion—written by Justice William Rehnquist—not only affirmed the Puerto Rican law but also mentioned alcoholic beverages and cigarettes as products whose advertising could be further restricted without violating the First Amendment. The court said, in essence, that advertising of anything "deemed harmful" enjoys less First Amendment protection than other advertising, even if the product itself is legal. Ironically, a decade later the Supreme Court would reconsider that idea and hand down a series of decisions *upholding* the First Amendment rights of alcohol, gambling and tobacco advertisers—again illustrating the uncertainties in this area of law.

In defending their law restricting gambling ads, Puerto Rican officials said the law was designed to attract tourist dollars while minimizing the harmful effects of gambling on the health, safety and welfare of Puerto Ricans. They cited "the disruption of moral and cultural patterns, the increase in local crime, the fostering of prostitution, the development of corruption and the infiltration of organized crime" as evils that the ban on local casino advertising was designed to minimize.

The Supreme Court's 5-4 majority agreed that these were substantial government purposes—substantial enough to justify restrictions on commercial speech.

The ruling attracted strenuous dissents from four justices, including William Brennan, who said the Puerto Rican law was intended to "suppress the dissemination of truthful information about entirely lawful activity merely to keep its residents ignorant." And Justice John Paul Stevens contended that the law violates the First Amendment by discriminating among the media. "I do not understand why (the Court) is willing to uphold a Puerto Rico regulation that applies one standard to the *New York Times* and another to the *San Juan Star*." The *Posadas* ruling was clearly a setback for the advertising, broadcasting and newspaper publishing industries, all of whom filed briefs urging the court to overturn the Puerto Rican law.

The Court followed up the *Posadas* decision with another ruling that upheld restrictions on commercial speech in 1989, *State University of New York v. Fox* (492 U.S. 469). In this case, the court upheld the SUNY system's rules restricting commercial activities on campus. The rules forbid using campus facilities for many types of selling; a cookware salesperson was arrested for refusing to leave a dormitory on the SUNY Cortland campus where she was conducting a "Tupperware party" in violation of the rules.

The Court not only upheld the SUNY rules but also used the case to declare that governments need not use the "least restrictive means" to regulate commercial speech. If political speech is involved, the least restrictive means test still applies, but the Court's 6-3 majority held that governments have more leeway in regulating commercial speech under the First Amendment. The majority said that the *Central Hudson* test is satisfied if there is a "reasonable fit" between a government's purpose and the restrictions on commercial speech that are adopted to help achieve that purpose.

Dissenting, Justice Harry Blackmun (joined by William J. Brennan and Thurgood Marshall) objected to this rewriting of the law: "The majority holds that "least-restrictive

FIG. 64. Supreme
Court Justice Harry
Blackmun, official
Supreme Court portrait,
1976.

*Library of Congress, Prints
and Photographs Division,
[LC-USZ62-60137].*

means" analysis does not apply to commercial speech cases, a holding it is able to reach only by recasting a good bit of contrary language in our past cases."

The *SUNY* decision continued the Supreme Court's movement away from upholding commercial speech rights in close cases. For a time in the late 1980s, the court appeared to be retreating from the sweeping protection it extended to commercial speech in the 1970s. But a very different trend emerged in the 1990s.

The 1990s: Expanding Commercial Speech Rights

The Supreme Court reaffirmed and expanded the constitutional protection of commercial speech during the 1990s, beginning with a 1993 case involving advertising circulars. By 1996, there could be no doubt that truthful commercial speech about lawful activities enjoys substantial protection from government censorship.

In the 1993 case, *Cincinnati v. Discovery Network* (507 U.S. 410), the court said the city of Cincinnati could not flatly ban newsracks for commercial literature while allowing newspaper vending machines. As explained in the section on newsrack ordinances in Chapter Three, city officials had ordered publishers of free magazines that were predominantly advertising to remove 62 newsracks from city property while allowing about 2,000 newspaper stands to remain in place.

In a 6-3 ruling, the Court said the city had not provided a reasonable basis for this action. Citing the *SUNY* case, the court emphasized that, even though commercial speech does not enjoy the same level of protection as noncommercial speech, it cannot be arbitrarily banned. The court again said a government that bans commercial speech must show a "reasonable fit" between a legitimate government purpose (such as safety or aesthetics) and the action taken. The majority was clearly troubled when the city tried to defend its action by talking about visual blight and litter—at a time when it was acting against only the 62 newsracks for free magazines, not the 2,000 newspaper stands. The court said the city had seriously underestimated the value of commercial speech under the First Amendment.

While the *Cincinnati* case was a strong affirmation of the First Amendment rights of commercial speech, the majority stopped short of giving it full protection. The Court reaffirmed that a government may restrict commercial speech when there is a "reasonable fit" between the restriction and the government's legitimate goals. This is a far lower standard than a government must meet to justify censoring noncommercial speech on the basis of its content. Moreover, shortly after handing down the *Cincinnati* decision, the Court announced a decision in which restrictions on commercial speech were upheld: *U.S. v. Edge Broadcasting* (509 U.S. 418). In this case, the court upheld laws that prohibited a North Carolina radio station from advertising Virginia's state-sponsored lottery, even though more than 90 percent of the station's listeners were in Virginia. The court said North Carolina had a legitimate governmental interest in discouraging its citizens from gambling and held that the state's ban on lottery advertising advanced that interest, even though it also prevented many listeners in Virginia from hearing ads for their own state's government-sponsored lottery.

However, in 1999 the Supreme Court ruled that the ban on broadcast advertising of gambling cannot be enforced against broadcasters in states where such gambling is legal. The high court unanimously overturned the ban on First Amendment grounds in *Greater New Orleans Broadcasting Association v. U.S.* (527 U.S. 173). The Court reversed a lower court decision upholding the ban against New Orleans broadcasters, who wanted to carry advertising for local casinos.

Writing for the Court, Justice John Paul Stevens said the federal law in question fails to meet two parts of the commercial speech test set forth in the *Central Hudson* case. Noting that there are exceptions to the ban on gambling advertising for Indian-owned casinos and state-run lotteries, Stevens said the law has so many loopholes that it does not materially advance the government's claimed interest in reducing compulsive gambling.

"The operation of Section 1304 (the ban on casino advertising) and its attendant regulatory regime is so pierced by exemptions and inconsistencies that the government cannot hope to exonerate it," Stevens wrote. He said the government "cannot overcome the presumption that the speaker and the audience, not the government, should be left to assess the value of accurate and nonmisleading information about lawful conduct. Had the government adopted a more coherent policy, or accommodated the rights of speakers in states that have legalized the underlying conduct, this might be a different case," he concluded.

Two years earlier, the Ninth Circuit ruled in a Nevada case that the ban on gambling advertising violates the First Amendment (*Valley Broadcasting v. U.S.*, 107 F.3d 1328). That decision left broadcasters free to carry gambling ads in the western states in the Ninth Circuit. Now broadcasters in other parts of the country are free to carry casino gambling ads. The language of the *Greater New Orleans* Supreme Court decision suggested that even broadcasters in non-gambling states may carry casino gambling ads as long as there is no state law that forbids gambling advertising. In fact, after this Supreme Court decision, the FCC stopped enforcing its restrictions on gambling except in the situation that led to the *Edge Broadcasting* decision: a radio or television station in a non-lottery state still cannot advertise another state's lottery in violation of the law in the state where it is licensed.

Cigarettes, Alcohol and the First Amendment

To the amazement of those who remember the Supreme Court's language in *Posadas de Puerto Rico* about the low status of advertising for products and services "deemed harmful," the court has decisively upheld not only gambling advertising but also tobacco and alcoholic beverage advertising in recent years.

In 1995, the Supreme Court overturned the beer labeling rules enforced by the Bureau of Alcohol, Tobacco and Firearms in the Treasury Department. In *Rubin v. Coors Brewing Co.* (514 U.S. 476), the Court unanimously ruled that there is a First Amendment right to disclose the alcohol content of beer on the label, something that federal law and ATF policies prohibited. Writing for the Court, Justice Clarence Thomas acknowledged that the government had a substantial interest in curbing beer "strength wars." However, he said the ban was overly broad because there are other ways the government could prevent brewers from promoting their products by emphasizing high alcohol strength. Explaining the Court's decision, Thomas said, "Here (Coors) seeks to disclose only truthful, verifiable and nonmisleading factual information concerning alcohol content."

If the *Coors Brewing* case in 1995 was a victory for those who engage in commercial speech and a defeat for government regulators, the Supreme Court went even further in affirming the First Amendment protection of commercial speech in a 1996 ruling that also involved alcoholic beverages: *44 Liquormart v. Rhode Island* (517 U.S. 484).

In a case hailed by many in the advertising industry as a decisive victory, the Court unanimously ruled that Rhode Island cannot ban liquor price advertising. All nine justices agreed that even the 21st Amendment, which repealed nationwide Prohibition but allowed individual states to ban alcoholic beverages, does not allow the states to legalize alcoholic beverages and then ban their advertising. The 21st Amendment, the Court held, does not override the First Amendment.

Although all nine justices voted to overturn Rhode Island's ban on liquor price advertising, the justices were divided in their reasoning. There was no single majority opinion of the Court. But the conclusion was clear enough. At least seven of the nine justices either disavowed the *Posadas de Puerto Rico* decision or "distinguished" it (which means they said it does not apply to this situation while not voting to overturn it). Justice John Paul Stevens wrote the plurality opinion. When a government bans a type of advertising instead of just regulating it, he wrote, courts must exercise "special care" in applying the *Central Hudson* test. Stevens and the three other justices who joined in all or part of his opinion wanted to extend broad First Amendment protection to commercial speech—perhaps protection as broad as that afforded to noncommercial speech.

Justice Clarence Thomas went even further: he said the *Central Hudson* criteria need not be considered because restrictions on commercial speech such as these are *per se* unconstitutional. Thomas added, "All attempts to dissuade legal choices by citizens by keeping them ignorant are impermissible." Justice Stevens' plurality opinion was only a bit more restrained: "The First Amendment directs us to be especially skeptical of regulations that seek to keep people in the dark for what the government perceives to be their own good."

Four justices joined in an opinion by Sandra Day O'Connor which agreed that the Rhode Island ban on liquor price advertising was unconstitutional, but only because the ban failed to satisfy the *Central Hudson* test. O'Connor said there was no "reasonable fit" between the ban and the state's stated goal: discouraging alcohol consumption by keeping liquor prices high. One thing that clearly troubled several justices was the across-the-board nature of the Rhode Island law: it left open no alternate channels of communication for businesses that want to advertise liquor prices.

Given the four different opinions, *44 Liquormart* was not as clear an affirmation of the First Amendment status of commercial speech as it might have been. Nonetheless, commercial speech has come a long way since 1942—when the Supreme Court said it had no First Amendment protection at all.

In 2001, the Court ruled that the regulation of cigarette advertising is federally preempted under the Federal Cigarette Labeling and Advertising Act, thereby invalidating hundreds of state and local laws banning or restricting tobacco ads. In *Lorillard Tobacco Co. v. Reilly* (533 U.S. 525), a case challenging restrictions on tobacco advertising in Massachusetts, the court ruled by a 5-4 vote that many of the state's regulations violated the First Amendment as well as being federally preempted.

Writing for the Court, Justice Sandra Day O'Connor said the states may not single out cigarette advertising for special restrictions. She said the states may still use their zoning powers to regulate all advertising, but they cannot target cigarette advertising without intruding into a federally preempted area.

This case marked the second time in about a year that the Supreme Court overturned a government attempt to regulate cigarette advertising or marketing. In 2000, the court said the Food and Drug Administration lacked the authority to curb cigarette marketing by regulating tobacco as a drug (in *FDA v. Brown & Williamson Tobacco*, which is discussed later). Neither ruling involved the Federal Trade Commission's authority to regulate cigarette advertising.

The *Lorillard* case was a challenge to Massachusetts regulations forbidding tobacco ads within 1,000 feet of any school, park or public playground and requiring retailers to post point-of-sale advertising at least five feet off the floor, out of the immediate sight of young children. The court overturned those rules, and in the process swept away state and local restrictions on cigarette ads in many other states by holding that the regulation of cigarette advertising is federally preempted.

The Court also ruled that Massachusetts' restrictions on outdoor and point-of-sale advertising for cigars and smokeless tobacco, which are *not* federally preempted, are invalid because they violate the First Amendment. As the court did in overturning Rhode Island's ban on alcoholic beverage price advertising in *44 Liquormart* and the federal ban on broadcast ads for casino gambling in *Greater New Orleans Broadcasting*, the court once again refused to allow a "vice exception" to the First Amendment—abandoning the rationale used to justify Puerto Rico's ban on local advertising by casinos in the *Posadas de Puerto Rico* case.

FIG. 65. "Gentlemens' Delight" tobacco advertisement, 1870s.

Library of Congress, Prints and Photographs Division, [LC-USZ62-79320].

In a concurring opinion joined by Justices Antonin Scalia and Anthony Kennedy, Justice Clarence Thomas was again the Court's most outspoken defender of "vice advertising." "Harmful products, (like) harmful ideas, are protected by the First Amendment," he wrote. He objected to the Court's "uncertain course" on commercial speech, with "much of the uncertainty being generated by the malleability of the four-part balancing test of *Central Hudson*." Justice O'Connor's majority opinion was more reserved, but it also said Massachusetts was violating the First Amendment as well as the federal labeling law because the rules were overly broad: the 1,000-foot buffer zone meant tobacco ads were banned virtually everywhere in the major cities. She cited *Reno v. ACLU*, the case in which the court rejected a ban on indecency on the Internet because it denied adults their First Amendment rights in the name of protecting children (see Chapter Ten), and said the same principle applies to tobacco advertising. "Protecting children from harmful materials...does not justify an unnecessarily broad suppression of speech addressed to adults," she wrote.

The result: unless anti-smoking groups can persuade Congress to end the federal preemption, tobacco advertising will be governed by federal law—and by the industry's 1998 settlement of a massive lawsuit by 46 states. In the $206 billion settlement, the industry voluntarily agreed to discontinue billboard advertising, stop using cartoon characters or otherwise targeting underage smokers and to bankroll an anti-smoking billboard campaign. That settlement was not affected by the *Lorillard Tobacco* decision.

The Federal Cigarette Labeling and Advertising Act forbids only broadcast advertising of cigarettes while requiring health warnings in ads and on cigarette packages. If the federal law or FTC regulations were to be expanded to further curtail tobacco advertising, that, too, could raise First Amendment issues, given the court's recent rulings on "vice" advertising. Taken together, the *Greater New Orleans* case on gambling, the *Coors* and *44 Liquormart* cases on alcoholic beverages and the *Lorillard Tobacco* decision on cigarette advertising illustrate just how far the court has come since its *Posadas de Puerto Rico* decision in 1986.

The U.S. Supreme Court in 2007 allowed the states to entertain some lawsuits involving tobacco marketing. In *Watson v. Philip Morris* (551 U.S. 142), the court allowed consumer groups to pursue class action lawsuits in state courts to litigate their claims that tobacco companies falsely marketed "light" cigarettes as safer than other cigarettes. Philip Morris had argued that these cases could only be heard in federal courts because tobacco companies were testing cigarettes using methods approved by the FTC—and using those testing methods made the companies federal agents. The court didn't buy that argument.

Nevertheless, most state regulation of tobacco advertising is now federally preempted. The California Supreme Court emphasized that point in a 2007 decision dismissing class-action lawsuits by smokers who said they took up the habit as minors because of the tobacco industry's marketing. The court unanimously rejected the smokers' lawsuits because they couldn't prove that any particular ads were misleading and targeted exclusively to children, factors that might have allowed them to sue under various state laws and avoid the federal preemption problem (*In re Tobacco Cases II*, 41 C.4th 1257). The state high court relied on the U.S. Supreme Court's *Lorillard Tobacco* decision in reaching this conclusion.

Forced Advertising and the First Amendment

Still another advertising issue involving First Amendment rights was addressed in three U.S. Supreme Court decisions and several lower court cases in the late 1990s and the early 2000s: mandatory assessments imposed on growers to pay for generic advertising of farm products. Some growers object to state and federal laws that force them to pay for advertising campaigns to which they object, preferring instead to advertise the unique qualities of their own products.

The U.S. Supreme Court in 2005 upheld *government-sponsored* advertising and marketing programs for which farmers and ranchers must pay. Ruling in *Johanns v. Livestock Marketing Association* (544 U.S. 550), the court's 6-3 majority said that a beef advertising program created by an act of Congress does not violate the First Amendment. Beef producers are assessed $1 per head of cattle to pay for advertising.

Writing for the Court, Justice Antonin Scalia said, "Compelled support of government— even those programs of government one does not approve—is of course perfectly constitutional, as every taxpayer must attest."

The key to the *Johanns* decision is that the program was government-sponsored. It may resolve other challenges to mandatory advertising programs that were making their way through the courts. These challenges were encouraged when the Supreme Court earlier overturned a mandatory advertising program for mushrooms.

Ruling in 2001, the Supreme Court held that the mushroom advertising program violated the First Amendment. Ruling in *U.S. v. United Foods Inc.* (533 U.S. 405), the Court overturned a federal program that required all mushroom growers to pay for generic advertising. However, the program was not actually run by a government agency. United Foods, a Tennessee mushroom grower, objected, preferring to do its own advertising that emphasized the quality of its mushrooms as opposed to those grown elsewhere.

Writing for the Court, Justice Anthony Kennedy said that the advertising assessments constituted "compelled speech." He traced the history of prior cases involving such issues as government agencies forcing all workers to pay union dues used for political purposes in concluding that coerced speech is just as unconstitutional as a government ban on speech.

The *United Foods* decision was surprising to some because four years earlier the Supreme Court had upheld a California state program that required all growers to pay for generic product advertising (*Glickman v. Wileman Brothers & Elliot Inc.*, 521 U.S. 457). Justice Kennedy distinguished the 2001 decision from *Glickman* by pointing out that the growers in the earlier case were part of an association that had a *government-sponsored regulatory marketing scheme.* No such arrangement existed in the mushroom industry, he pointed out.

Another factor about *Glickman* is that the California Supreme Court found a way to get around it. In a follow-up to *Glickman,* the California court ruled that there may be a right under the state constitution to opt out of certain forced advertising programs even when there isn't under the federal constitution (*Gerawan Farming v. Lyons,* 24 C.4th 468, 2000). The California court said the state constitution guarantees broader free expression rights than the First Amendment, particularly in the area of commercial speech.

The Ninth Circuit found that a requirement that grape growers pay assessments levied by the California Table Grape Commission for generic advertising did not violate the First Amendment (*Delano Farms v. California Table Grape Commission,* 586 F.3d 1219, 2010). Several growers alleged that the law "harmfully equate[d] all table grapes, by virtue of the 'generic' advertisements." The court found that the ads were government speech and the First Amendment does not apply: "Because the Commission's activities are effectively controlled by the State of California, also rendering them government speech…the Commission's advertising activities are government speech and thus beyond the restraints of the First Amendment."

The *en banc* Ninth Circuit certified a question to the California Supreme Court about a compelled speech issue. In *Beeman v. Anthem Prescription Management, LLC* (2012 U.S. App. LEXIS 11392), the federal appellate court asked the California Supreme Court to answer the question of whether "California Civil Code section 2527 compel[s] speech in violation of article I, section 2 of the California Constitution," because the statute "requires drug claims processors to generate studies about pharmacy pricing, summarize the results and disseminate the information to their clients."

Advertising Prostitution

In what may be one of the only court decisions to address the issue, the Ninth Circuit in 2010 reversed a district court's decision that Nevada's regulations on prostitution advertising violated the First Amendment (*Coyote Publishing Inc. v. Miller*, 598 F.3d 592). The court applied a *Central Hudson* analysis and found that the state has a substantial interest in limiting "the commodification of human sexuality."

The restrictions on advertising advanced that interest in that "[i]ncreased advertising of commercial sex throughout the state of Nevada would increase the extent to which sex is presented to the public as a commodity for sale." Finally, the court said that the regulations did not burden more speech than necessary; they were regionally tailored to match the places in Nevada where prostitution is legal. The Supreme Court denied *cert.*

Focus on...
The Colbert SuperPAC

FIG. 66. Stephen Colbert at the Peabody Awards.

Anders Krusburg/Peabody Awards. 71st Annual Peabody Awards, Waldorf-Astoria Hotel, May 21, 2012 via Flickr, Creative Commons attribution license.

SuperPACs, under current law, may raise unlimited amounts of money from corporations, unions, and wealthy individuals to advertise for political causes and candidates. When Stephen Colbert announced he would form a SuperPAC named "Americans for a Better Tomorrow, Tomorrow," he may have raised eyebrows. But, said the Federal Elections Committee, Colbert was well within his legal rights to do so. In an advisory opinion in 2012, the FEC said, "The Commission concludes that Mr. Colbert may establish and operate the Committee, which plans to solicit and accept contributions in unlimited amounts for the purpose of making independent expenditures from individuals, political committees, labor organizations, and corporations..."

When Colbert decided to run for the President of the United States of South Carolina, though, he had to turn over control of his SuperPAC to someone else. Jon Stewart stepped in to take the reins. Both said that there would be no coordination, not even, as Stewart said, "a series of Morse-code blinks to convey information with each other on our respective shows." Colbert's SuperPAC demonstrates the impact of *Citizens United* on campaign fundraising. As of Jan. 30, 2012, the PAC had raised $1,023,121.24, according to FEC filings.

Want to contribute, or just want a smile? Check out http://www.colbertsuperpac.com.

commercial speech doctrine:
a limited level of First Amendment protection awarded to advertisements or speech that is intended to sell goods or services.

corporate speech doctrine:
corporations are considered entities entitled to some First Amendment protection; restrictions on that speech are acceptable only if one of the following are met: (1) the restriction is a "precisely drawn means of serving a compelling state interest;" (2) the restriction is required to fulfill a "significant government interest" and regulates only time, place and manner, leaving open "ample alternate channels for communication;" or (3) the restriction is narrowly drawn and only applies to speech under a few special circumstances where disruption of government activities must be avoided.

■ CORPORATE FREEDOM OF SPEECH

While the Supreme Court was extending some First Amendment protection to commercial speech, the court also began to protect another kind of speech: *noncommercial corporate speech.* The court took a major step in this direction in 1978, ruling that corporations also have First Amendment rights. In *First National Bank v. Bellotti* (435 U.S. 765), the Court overturned a Massachusetts law that forbade corporate advertising for or against ballot measures except when such a measure might "materially affect" a company's business. In reaching this conclusion, the Court emphasized the importance of a free flow of information, even when some of that information comes from corporations rather than individuals.

Massachusetts tried to defend its ban on corporate political advertising by arguing that corporations have so much money they could drown out other viewpoints if allowed to advertise. However, there was no evidence presented to prove that, and the court wasn't persuaded. Another problem with the Massachusetts law was that it allowed corporations engaged in mass communications (newspapers, television stations, etc.) to say anything they pleased on political issues, but that freedom was denied to other corporations. The Supreme Court said that, if anything, banks and other financial institutions might be better informed on economic issues than the media.

Thus, *First National Bank v. Bellotti* was a major victory for corporate advertising. It didn't guarantee corporations any special right of access when the media refuse to accept their issue-oriented advertising (a problem discussed later in this chapter), but it did say that, where the media are willing to accept advertising from corporations, a state cannot prohibit it just because it comes from a company instead of an individual or a campaign committee.

As explained earlier, when the Supreme Court decided the *Central Hudson* case in 1980 (affirming the right of utility companies to advertise for more business, even if the advertising might encourage energy use rather than conservation) the court also handed down an important decision on noncommercial corporate speech: *Consolidated Edison v. Public Service Commission of New York* (447 U.S. 530). In that case, the Court said the New York Public Service Commission could not prevent utility companies from sending their customers inserts with their bills that discussed "political matters" or "controversial issues of public policy."

Like the *Central Hudson* case, *Consolidated Edison* challenged rules adopted by the New York Public Service Commission in 1977. In this case, New York's highest court had held that the ban on inserts with bills was a reasonable regulation of the time, place and manner of speech.

The U.S. Supreme Court reversed the New York court on that point, ruling that the ban on bill inserts was an excessive restriction of corporations' First Amendment rights.

This was a major victory for the First Amendment rights of corporations. Unlike the *First National Bank* decision, which came on a narrow 5-4 vote, this case was decided by a 7-2 majority—with seven justices voting to uphold the right of corporations to speak out on the issues of the day. In addition, the court set forth legal guidelines that can be used to determine whether future restrictions on corporate speech are valid.

The Court noted the distinction between commercial advertising, in which a company seeks to promote sales of a product or service, and noncommercial corporate speech, in which a company expresses its views on controversial issues. When a government attempts to restrict noncommercial corporate speech as opposed to commercial speech, the Supreme Court established a more stringent test than the one applied to the regulation of commercial speech in the *Central Hudson* case. When noncommercial corporate speech is involved, government restrictions are justified only if *one* of these three conditions is met: (1) the restriction in question is a "precisely drawn means of serving a compelling state interest;" (2) the restriction is required to fulfill a "significant government interest" and merely regulates time, place and manner, leaving open "ample alternate channels for communication;" or (3) there is a narrowly drawn restriction on speech under a few circumstances where disruption of government activities must be avoided, such as a military base.

In 1986, the Supreme Court again reaffirmed that corporations have First Amendment rights in *Pacific Gas & Electric Company v. Public Utilities Commission of California* (475 U.S. 1). In this case, the Public Utilities Commission (PUC) had ordered PG&E, a large utility company, to insert a utility watchdog group's materials with consumers' utility bills in place of the company's own newsletter four times a year. The court held that the PUC order violated the First Amendment rights of the utility company. Four justices joined in a plurality opinion that said the company's newsletter "receives the full protection of the First Amendment." They said forcing the company to insert an outside group's material in place of its own is unconstitutional.

A fifth justice (Thurgood Marshall) agreed that the PUC could not force a utility company to insert notices from outside groups with utility bills, but he also said that corporate communications should not enjoy full First Amendment protection. And three other justices dissented, saying they would have allowed the PUC to require utility companies to insert a watchdog group's materials with utility bills.

This was, in short, a mixed victory for corporate First Amendment rights, delivered by a deeply divided Supreme Court. And corporate speech rights fared no better in a 1990 Supreme Court decision, *Austin v. Michigan Chamber of Commerce* (494 U.S. 652). In this case, the Court affirmed a Michigan law that prohibited contributions to political candidates from the general treasury of a company or private association, while allowing contributions from special-purpose funds. The majority declared that this type of restriction on corporate speech does not violate the First Amendment, at least in part because it does allow corporations to endorse or oppose candidates through separate funds or political action committees. The Court did *not* reverse its earlier rulings on corporate freedom of speech in this case. This case does, nonetheless, represent a limitation on the First Amendment rights of corporations and private associations.

The distinction between commercial speech and noncommercial corporate speech may have been blurred in a case the Supreme Court agreed to hear and then dismissed in 2003,

Nike v. Kasky (539 U.S. 654). In that case, Nike, a manufacturer of shoes and athletic apparel, responded to criticism of working conditions at its overseas factories by issuing press releases, letters to the editor and other corporate messages addressing the charges.

Nike was then sued by consumer activist Marc Kasky under California's false advertising law, disputing the truthfulness of the company's statements on this issue. A California appellate court held that Nike's statements were protected by the First Amendment and were not commercial speech. The California Supreme Court reversed that ruling and held that Nike's messages really were commercial speech because they were aimed in part at consumers who might buy more of the company's products if they believed the company's statements about working conditions at its factories. In *Kasky v. Nike Inc.* (27 C.4th 939, 2002), a 4-3 majority of the state Supreme Court ruled that the company's statements were not entitled to First Amendment protection and were instead subject to the false advertising law. Thus, Kasky would have a right to take his claims to trial. Justice Ming W. Chin protested in a dissenting opinion, saying that restricting only one side (Nike) in a public debate, while leaving Nike's critics free to say whatever they please, is manifestly unfair. "Handicapping one side in this important worldwide debate is both ill-considered and unconstitutional," Chin said.

The Supreme Court agreed to hear the *Nike* case but then dismissed it on the final day of the 2002-2003 term, apparently because a majority of justices decided the case should go to trial before being considered by the high court. That led to a dissent by Justice Stephen Breyer, joined by Sandra Day O'Connor, arguing that even postponing a ruling on this case would have a chilling effect on the First Amendment rights of other corporations that wish to speak out on controversial issues. Eventually Nike settled with Kasky, agreeing to pay about $1.5 million to a workers' rights group to monitor conditions in overseas factories.

What does this mean? It means that there is still a hierarchy of First Amendment protection, depending on the nature and source of the message. Commercial advertising still enjoys less constitutional protection than idea-oriented or "editorial" advertising and similar forms of noncommercial corporate speech. But even noncommercial corporate speech enjoys something less than complete First Amendment protection, and the distinction between commercial speech and noncommercial speech is becoming less clear in the 2000s.

Federal Political Advertising Restrictions

The year 2010 saw a significant shakeup in campaign finance law. But the Court's decision in the controversial *Citizens United v. FEC* case did not arise in a vacuum. The Supreme Court has been considering campaign funding issues for decades.

The First Amendment protection of corporate speech was a key factor in a 2007 Supreme Court decision that upheld the right of corporations, labor unions and other entities to do issue advertising on television mentioning a candidate by name, free of campaign spending limits. In *Federal Election Commission v. Wisconsin Right to Life* (551 U.S. 449), the court overturned a portion of the Bipartisan Campaign Reform Act (BCRA, and popularly called the McCain-Feingold Act) that prohibited issue advertising mentioning a federal candidate by name within 30 days of a primary election or within 60 days of a general election.

Congress enacted the McCain-Feingold Act in 2002 to curb abuses of "soft money" (unlimited, unregulated contributions by wealthy individuals, corporations, unions and other entities to political parties as opposed to specific candidates). One of its provisions was a ban on the use of soft money to fund "issue advertising" that may be heavily partisan and aimed at specific candidates. Earlier federal laws and similar laws in most states already limited the amount of money any individual or any entity may donate to a specific candidate.

Under McCain-Feingold, money spent on television advertising referring to a "clearly identified candidate" is treated as a campaign contribution, subject to the limits on such contributions. However, those restrictions do not apply to more general issue ads that do not refer to candidates, and in the 2004 election large contributions flowed into the coffers of independent organizations that were getting around the law by bankrolling advertising that did not name any candidate.

In 2003, the Supreme Court had upheld much of the McCain-Feingold Act, including key provisions affecting political advertising on television (*McConnell v. FEC*, 540 U.S. 93). The Court said then that the act was not unconstitutional on its face. Parts of *McConnell* were overturned in *Citizens United*, discussed below.

However, in 2007 a new 5-4 majority on the Supreme Court overturned the restriction on issue advertising that names candidates in *FEC v. Wisconsin Right to Life* (551 U.S. 449). The court held that entities spending this unregulated money have a First Amendment right to mention candidates in their issue advertising, even late in a campaign. The court's lead opinion by Chief Justice John G. Roberts made a distinction between legitimate issue ads that mention a candidate and other ads that are "susceptible of no reasonable interpretation other than as an appeal to vote for or against a specific candidate." The latter fall within the McCain-Feingold Act's restrictions on "electioneering communications." Applying the test from the *Bellotti* case to this kind of issue advertising, the court said corporate funding of ads that are really campaign ads can still be restricted, while the funding of ads that address an issue but mention a candidate is protected by the First Amendment.

What's the difference between issue advertising and electioneering communications? In the *Wisconsin* case, the Right to Life group wanted to air ads urging citizens to contact the state's two U.S. senators and ask them to allow a Senate vote on several nominees for federal judgeships. One of the senators, Russell Feingold (who co-sponsored the McCain-Feingold Act), was running for re-election. The ads didn't specifically urge voters to support or oppose Feingold, but a lower court said the ads could be banned as electioneering communications. The Supreme Court majority disagreed and said such ads are constitutionally protected, even during an election campaign.

The 2007 decision did not affect the other major provision of the McCain-Feingold Act, its limit on fund-raising for campaign advertising by political parties and political action committees. That part of the law is still valid.

In 2008, the Supreme Court voted 5-4 to overturn another feature of McCain-Feingold: a "millionaires amendment" that allowed those running against a wealthy candidate who was spending a lot of his/her own money to exceed the normal contribution limits. The majority said this violates the First Amendment right of candidates to use personal funds by burdening them with otherwise unlawful excess gifts to opponents (*Davis v. Federal Election Commission*, 554 U.S. 724).

The Federal Election Commission, which enforces the McCain-Feingold Act, issued regulations in 2006 that treat the Internet far differently than broadcasting, largely exempting many Internet postings from campaign advertising rules. In general, the FEC only regulates messages on the Internet if they are actually paid advertising or paid fund-raising messages for a candidate. Other messages such as YouTube videos can be posted anonymously without even their production cost being treated as a campaign contribution.

FIG. 67. Secretary of State Hillary Rodham Clinton talking to President Barack Obama, aboard Air Force One, April 2009.

Official White House Photo by Pete Souza, April 28, 2009 via Flickr.

The Supreme Court considered whether a film should be considered to be an "electioneering communication" in 2009 and 2010 in *Citizens United v. FEC* (130 S. Ct. 876). Citizens United, a conservative Virginia non-profit group, created a film entitled *Hillary: The Movie,* a critical examination of then-Democratic presidential hopeful Senator Hillary Rodham Clinton. The group wanted to show the film and ads promoting it, which included interviews and footage of Senator Clinton at public appearances, during the election season. Citizens United argued that the film was not "electioneering communication" because it did not expressly recommend a vote against Clinton, but the district court said the film could not be interpreted as anything other than an encouragement to vote against her.

In a rare and surprising move, the Court did not issue an opinion in the *Citizens United* case in the 2008 term in which it heard oral arguments; instead, it reheard the case in September 2009, a month before the new term started. In one of the most eagerly-awaited speech cases of the year, the Court shifted its perspective on campaign finance speech and regulation. It overturned two of its own precedents (parts of *McConnell* and all of *Austin v. Michigan Chamber of Commerce,* discussed in Chapter Thirteen) and ruled that limits on corporate spending for political advertisements violated basic First Amendment principles that supply citizens and corporations with a fundamental right to engage in political speech. Justice Anthony Kennedy, writing for the Court, said that the movie could *only* be considered to be corporately funded "electioneering communications" prohibited by a provision in McCain-Feingold. However, that provision was an unconstitutional infringement of the First Amendment rights that corporations share with citizens. In declining to decide the case narrowly and without overturning McCain-Feingold, Kennedy wrote:

> We decline to adopt an interpretation that requires intricate case-by-case determinations to verify whether political speech is banned, especially if we are convinced that, in the end, this corporation has a constitutional right to speak on this subject. ...[T]he Court cannot resolve this case on a narrower ground without chilling political speech, speech that is central to the meaning and purpose of the First Amendment.

In a bitter dissent read from the bench, Justice John Paul Stevens soundly rejected the notion that corporations should have the same speech rights as people. "Corporations," he said, "have no consciences, no beliefs, no feelings, no thoughts, no desires." Speech funded by corporations has a great potential to drown out speech by citizens, he said, adding that citizens who believe that their government is controlled by corporations are unlikely to be engaged in the civic process:

> When citizens turn on their televisions and radios before an election and hear only corporate electioneering, they may lose faith in their capacity, as citizens, to influence public policy. A Government captured by corporate interests, they may come to believe, will be neither responsive to their needs nor willing to give their views a fair hearing. The predictable result is cynicism and disenchantment: an increased perception that large spenders "'call the tune'" and a reduced "willingness of voters to take part in democratic governance."

The *Citizens United* case has already begun to have repercussions in campaign finance law. The Colorado Supreme Court struck down a state constitutional amendment limiting labor unions' abilities to contribute to political candidates. Amendment 54, which passed by a narrow margin, made it illegal for companies or unions with government contracts that total more than $100,000 to contribute to candidates for state or local office (*Dallman v. Ritter*, 225 P.3d 610, 2010).

A First Amendment challenge to the McCain-Feingold soft money provisions limiting contributions was raised by state and national Republican party committees in *Republican Nat'l Committee v. FEC* (698 F. Supp. 2d 150, 2010). The D.C. Circuit rejected the arguments by the committees that the limits were unconstitutional, saying that it had no authority as a lower court to overturn a Supreme Court decision on whether such contributions to national parties were banned. The Supreme Court affirmed the decision without hearing oral arguments in June 2010.

In 2010, the D.C. Circuit overturned an FEC rule that non-profit organizations who expressly advocate for certain candidates rather than just for issues are limited in how much money they can spend on those candidates (*SpeechNow.org v. FEC*, 599 F.3d 686). SpeechNow is a non-profit, tax-exempt organization of five individuals that formed to advocate for candidates who support free speech rights. The FEC had told the group that it must register as a political committee and be bound by those expenditure limits ($5,000 per donor). Pointing out that the Court in *Citizens United* held that "the government has *no* anti-corruption interest in limiting independent expenditures," the appeals court overturned the rule. The FEC said it did not plan to appeal.

Prior to the release of the *Citizens United* decision, the D.C. Circuit issued *EMILY's List v. FEC* (581 F.3d 1, 2009) in which it nullified a $5,000 annual cap imposed by the FEC on individual giving to non-profit organizations. The rule was enacted after the 2004 presidential election in which many individuals flooded non-profit organizations with donations to support political ads and get-out-the-vote initiatives.

EMILY's List, a non-profit abortion-rights group that supports pro-choice female Democratic candidates, challenged the rule as a First Amendment violation. The court agreed that the regulations contravened the Court's jurisprudence: "[T]he First Amendment, as the Court has construed it, safeguards the right of citizens to band together and pool their resources as an unincorporated group or non-profit organization in order to express their views about policy issues and candidates for public office." The FEC declined to appeal.

An amendment to the federal elections act, the DISCLOSE ("Democracy is Strengthened by Casting Light on Spending in Elections") Act passed the House in 2010. The DISCLOSE Act, proposed to combat what some members of Congress saw as the dangerous ramifications of the Court's decision in *Citizens United*, would require the head of the organization funding a political advertisement to appear on-camera (some call this the "stand by your ad" requirement) and would also require all corporations and advocacy groups to create campaign accounts to which donations of over $1,000 would be reported to the FEC, as well as expenditures from those accounts. The bill failed to advance in the Senate.

The *Citizens United* case significantly changed the campaign finance arena. The whole legal area is in flux as cities and states try to figure out whether their existing campaign finance regulations are constitutional in the wake of the Court's holding.

There have been many cases heard in many courts since *Citizens United* was handed down in early 2010. For example, in a Washington case, the Ninth Circuit said that, based on *Citizens United*, the state's disclosure law, which "enables the public to 'follow the money' with respect to campaigns and lobbying," did not violate the First Amendment (*Human Life of Wash. v. Brumsickle*, 624 F.3d 990, 2010). The Ninth Circuit said that the City of Long Beach's anti-corruption rule that was intended to "reduce the influence of large contributors with a specific financial stake in matters before the City Council" had been narrowed by *Citizens United* to cover "*quid pro quo* corruption only, as opposed to money spent to obtain 'influence over or access to elected officials.'" (*Long Beach Area Chamber of Commerce v. City of Long Beach*, 603 F.3d 684, 2010). The Ninth Circuit also upheld a injunction on San Diego's campaign finance regulations that restricted fundraising and spending of independent politicial committees under *Citizens United* and *Buckley v. Valeo*; the court noted, almost with a sigh, that "the district court properly applied the applicable preliminary injunction standard in the context of the presently discernible rules governing campaign finance restrictions" (*Thalheimer v. City of San Diego*, 645 F.3d 1109, 2011). But the Eighth Circuit upheld a Minnesota law that prohibited direct contributions to candidates and their affiliated entities (*Minn. Citizens Concerned for Life v. Swanson*, 640 F.3d 304, 2011).

But the U.S. Supreme Court was not through with campaign finance. In its first such decision since *Citizens United*, a divided Supreme Court overturned the Ninth Circuit and struck down an Arizona law providing escalating matching funds to candidates who accept public financing. In *Ariz. Free Enterprise Club's Freedom Club PAC v. Bennett* (131 S. Ct. 2806), the Court reversed the Ninth Circuit's holding that the matching funds system was only a minimal burden and justified based on the desire to reduce *quid pro quo* corruption.

The Arizona matching funds law allowed candidates for state office who accept public financing to receive additional funds from the state—roughly dollar-for-dollar for those spent by opposing privately financed candidates, and dollar-for-dollar for those spent by independent groups supporting privately funded candidates. Relying on *Davis v. FEC*, the Court said that the state's justification of leveling the playing field was not sufficient to justify the matching scheme. Writing for the majority, Chief Justice John Roberts said, "'Leveling the playing field' can sound like a good thing. But in a democracy, campaigning for office is not a game. It is a critically important form of speech. The First Amendment embodies our choice as a Nation that, when it comes to such speech, the guiding principle is freedom—the 'unfettered interchange of ideas'—not whatever the State may view as fair."

Justice Elena Kagan, joined by Justices Ruth Bader Ginsburg, Stephen Breyer, and Sonia Sotomayor, dissented: "The First Amendment's core purpose is to foster a healthy, vibrant political system full of robust discussion and debate," she wrote, adding that "the Act promotes the values underlying both the First Amendment and our entire Constitution by enhancing the 'opportunity for free political discussion to the end that government may be responsive to the will of the people.'"

Rejecting the majority's claim that the matching scheme restricts speech, Kagan wrote, "What the law does—all the law does—is fund more speech."

Citizens United continues to have a significant impact on the campaign finance world. In 2011 and 2012, no fewer than six circuits decided cases that turned on the Court's decision in *Citizens United.* An example: the Seventh Circuit in *Wisconsin Right to Life Political Action Committee v. Barland* (664 F.3d 139, 2011) overturned a Wisconsin law limiting the amount that individuals could contribute to state and local candidates, political parties, and political committees to $10,000 a year, writing, "*Citizens United* held that independent expenditures do not pose a threat of actual or apparent *quid pro quo* corruption, which is the only governmental interest strong enough to justify restrictions on political speech. Accordingly, applying the $10,000 aggregate annual cap to contributions made to organizations engaged only in independent spending for political speech violates the First Amendment."

Critics continue to allege that the ruling was an open invitation for corruption and huge expenditures by corporations, but the Court signaled in 2012 that it wasn't ready to revisit the case. A divided Montana Supreme Court in *Western Trad. P'ship, Inc. v. Attorney General of Montana* (363 Mont. 220) said that Citizens United didn't apply to a 1912 state law that restricted spending on political campaigns. Calling the *Citizens United* opinion a "crabbed view of corruption," the state supreme court said that the Montana law wasn't affected by *Citizens United* because of the state's history and the differences between Montana's law and McCain-Feingold, overturned by Citizens United. Even one of the dissenters said that Citizens United was "smoke and mirrors" but believed that the court was bound to follow the dictates of a constitutional ruling by the Supreme Court.

The U.S. Supreme Court issued a one-page *per curiam* (unsigned) opinion without oral argument in 2012, *American Trad. P'ship, Inc. v. Bullock* (No. 11-1179), stating that *Citizens United* did indeed apply to the Montana law, and the state had not advanced any meaningful distinctions to demonstrate why it should not. Four justices dissented. Justice Breyer, writing for himself and Justices Ginsburg, Sotomayor and Kagan, wrote, "Montana's experience, like considerable experience elsewhere since the Court's decision in *Citizens United,* casts grave doubt on the Court's supposition that independent expenditures do not corrupt or appear to do so."

Focus on...
Miami Herald v. Tornillo, 418 U.S. 241 (1974)

Jerome Barron, who argued for access in the *Tornillo* case, claimed that media had become so large and monopolistic that it was difficult to access them.

The Court was not unsympathetic. Chief Justice Burger quoted Justice William O. Douglas on the dangers of monopoly ownership: "Where one paper has a monopoly in an area, it seldom presents two sides of an issue. It too often hammers away on one ideological or political line, using its monopoly position not to educate people, not to promote debate, but to inculcate in its readers one philosophy, one attitude—and to make money."

But that wasn't enough. Noting its sensitivity to "whether a restriction or requirement constituted the compulsion exerted by government on a newspaper to print that which it would not otherwise print," the Court rejected Barron's position.

The current state of campaign finance jurisprudence is perhaps best summarized by D.C. Circuit judge Brett Kavanaugh, who led off the decision in the 2010 *Republican Nat'l Committee* case with this summary:

> The Supreme Court's First Amendment jurisprudence establishes several principles regarding the regulation of campaign finance. First, Congress may impose some limits on contributions to federal candidates and political parties because of the *quid pro quo* corruption or appearance of *quid pro quo* corruption that can be associated with such contributions. Second, Congress may not limit expenditures by candidates and political parties. And third, Congress may not limit non-connected entities—including individuals, unincorporated associations, nonprofit organizations, labor unions, and for-profit corporations—from spending or raising money to support the election or defeat of candidates.

Perhaps if Judge Kavanaugh rewrote this summary in 2012, he would add that the Court is also suspicious of funding matching schemes that are justified as states' attempts to level the campaign playing field. And he might suggest that we won't soon see a revisiting of *Citizens United.*

The Court also in 2012 ruled that fee-paying non-union member workers cannot be forced to pay dues to support causes with which they don't agree. In *Knox v. SEIU* (No. 10-1121), the justices said that the First Amendment does not permit a union to make a special assessment without notice and the consent of those it affects. "To respect the limits of the First Amendment, the union should have sent out a new notice allowing nonmembers to opt in to the special fee rather than requiring them to opt out," the Court said.

■ ADVERTISING AND MEDIA ACCESS

Is there a constitutional right to place an ad in the media? Or may an advertiser buy space (or time, in the case of broadcasting) only if those who control the media are willing to accept the ad? To put it another way, is there any right of access to newspapers or radio and television stations?

The answer to these questions has traditionally been straightforward: there is *no* right of access to the print media for advertising purposes, and only a *limited* right of access to the broadcast media, mainly for political advertising. Even so, under certain unusual circumstances, a right to advertise may exist—particularly if the rejected advertiser can show that the refusal to place his/her material fell within a pattern of unfair or monopolistic business practices. Also, under certain circumstances government-sponsored media cannot deny public access.

Courts have repeatedly ruled that newspapers have no obligation to carry anyone's commercial advertising. Several appellate decisions were setbacks for advocates of public access to the press, but an even greater defeat came in 1974, when the U.S. Supreme Court handed down its landmark decision on access to the print media. The decision, *Miami Herald v. Tornillo* (418 U.S. 241), overturned a Florida state law creating a limited right of access.

The case arose when Pat Tornillo, a Miami teacher's union leader, ran for the state legislature. The *Miami Herald* twice editorially attacked Tornillo. Tornillo demanded space for a reply. The law seemed to be on his side when he made this demand: Florida had a right-of-reply law requiring newspapers to publish replies when they editorially attacked candidates for office. The *Herald* turned Tornillo down and he sued, invoking the Florida law. The state Supreme Court ruled in his favor, and the newspaper appealed to the U.S. Supreme Court. The Supreme Court unanimously reversed the Florida ruling, affirming the newspaper's First Amendment right to control its content without government interference. Thus, the Court invalidated Florida's right-of-reply law.

Writing for the Court, Chief Justice Warren Burger said, "A responsible press is an undoubtedly desirable goal, but press responsibility is not mandated by the Constitution and like many other virtues it cannot be legislated." The First Amendment simply does not permit a government to tell a newspaper publisher what to print and what not to print, he noted. Of course, this case involved a state's attempt to dictate editorial content rather than advertising, but the decision affirmed the publisher's right to control the content of his entire publication; the ruling was not limited to the news side. In the years since *Tornillo,* courts have continued to reject any right of access to the editorial and advertising columns of newspapers and magazines except when there was evidence of unfair or monopolistic business practices.

What sort of monopolistic business practices would cause a court to force a newspaper to accept unwanted advertising? A good example is provided by a series of lawsuits challenging the classified advertising policies of the *Providence Journal* and *Providence Evening Bulletin.* These papers did not accept ads from rental referral services, a policy they defended as necessary to prevent fraud.

In a complex series of lawsuits, several rental referral services challenged this policy. They claimed it violated federal antitrust laws because the Providence papers enjoyed a virtual monopoly in their market and were, in fact, competitors of the rental services (both newspaper ads and rental referral services help people find housing).

At first the federal courts upheld the Providence papers' policies as reasonable anti-fraud measures: they said the referral service challenging the policies was guilty of deceptive practices. However, in 1983 a federal appellate court ruled that there was no evidence of fraud by another referral service. The court said the papers were violating antitrust laws by denying advertising space to this would-be competitor. However, by then this referral service had gone out of business, and a federal judge awarded just $3 as token damages. (See *Home Placement Service v. Providence Journal,* 682 F.2d 274, 1982.)

The point: a newspaper that enjoys a virtual monopoly in its service area (as many papers do) risks an antitrust lawsuit if it denies advertising space to someone whose business might be viewed as being in competition with the paper. However, aside from potential antitrust situations, both print and broadcast media are generally free to reject advertising if they wish. As Chapter Eleven explains, however, there are circumstances when broadcasters must accept advertising that the print media are free to reject. For example, broadcasters must accept political advertising in federal elections under Section 312(a)(7) of the Communications Act. Newspapers and magazines, on the other hand, may turn down all political ads or even accept ads for one candidate and not others.

Under some other circumstances, though, advertisers may feel they have more access to print than to the broadcast media. Many broadcasters voluntarily exclude ads espousing controversial ideas. A number of major corporations have attempted to place issue-oriented ads on television, only to be rebuffed. Several of them, notably Mobil Oil and the Kaiser

Corporation, have purchased newspaper and magazine ads to protest their denial of advertising space in the electronic media. For whatever practical reasons, the print media have been much more willing to carry idea ads than broadcasters, although neither medium is ordinarily under any legal obligation to do so.

The print media are also more receptive to some other kinds of ads. For example, many broadcasters voluntarily reject hard liquor ads, and federal law has prohibited broadcast advertising of cigarettes since 1971. The print media routinely carry ads for these products.

Access to Government-Sponsored Media

Another exception to the rule that there is no mandatory access to the media involves government-run communications media. Under some circumstances government-sponsored media have an obligation to be *viewpoint-neutral*, and that may involve accepting advertising that the staff might prefer to reject.

Starting in the 1960s, several state and federal courts recognized a limited right to advertise on city buses. When state action is involved, as it is with these media, courts sometimes ruled that the authorities were constitutionally required to accept controversial advertising. For example, a federal court in New York and a state court in California both prohibited public transportation systems from flatly denying space to advertisers whose ideas they disliked. (See *Kissinger v. New York City Transit Authority*, 274 F.Supp. 438, and *Wirta v. Alameda-Contra Costa Transit District*, 68 C.2d 51.)

However, the idea that there should be any general right of access to state-run media was dealt a severe blow by another U.S. Supreme Court ruling, *Lehman v. Shaker Heights* (418 U.S. 298). In that 1974 decision, handed down the same day as the *Tornillo* ruling, the Supreme Court denied a political candidate's appeal for access to the advertising space on a city-run bus line. The bus line's policy was to accept only commercial ads, not political ads, and the Supreme Court denied that the First Amendment creates any right to advertise even on government-run media such as this. Although the Supreme Court has repeatedly said city streets and parks, for instance, are "public forums" protected by the First Amendment, it refused to rule that ad space on city-run buses is automatically a public forum.

On the other hand, if a state-run communications medium rejects one candidate's ads while accepting others, the person whose ads are rejected may still have a case under the Fourteenth Amendment's "equal protection" clause, the court said. But in the *Lehman* case, all political ads were rejected; there was no discrimination, and the advertising acceptance policies were *viewpoint-neutral*.

As a result of the *Lehman* decision, courts in recent years have usually refused to order access to ad space even in government-run media, as long as those in charge follow their advertising acceptance policies consistently.

However, the problem of public access to a state-run communications medium sometimes takes a different perspective when the management creates a public forum by accepting some political and social issue ads, while rejecting ads from those whose ideas it dislikes. A federal appellate court so ruled in a case involving the Washington, D.C. public transit system. In *Lebron v. Washington Metropolitan Area Transit Authority* (749 F.2d 893, 1984), the court held that transit officials could not reject a photo montage critical of the Reagan administration by artist Michael Lebron after accepting a variety of other political ads.

In 1998, a federal appellate court reached the same conclusion when a public transit system rejected anti-abortion ads after accepting other ads concerning sex and family planning. In *Christ's Bride Ministries v. Southeastern Pennsylvania Transportation Authority* (148 F.3d 242), the court held that the transit system had created a public forum by its ad acceptance policies. Therefore, the court ruled that the transit system violated the First Amendment by rejecting an ad in which an anti-abortion group wanted to say, "Women Who Choose Abortion Suffer More & Deadlier Breast Cancer."

On the other hand, if a government medium consistently accepts only commercial advertising and does not create a public forum for political and social issue ads, it can reject such ads. In *Children of the Rosary v. City of Phoenix* (154 F.3d 972), another 1998 decision, a federal appellate court upheld the right of a city-run bus system in Phoenix, Ariz. to reject anti-abortion advertising because the buses consistently carried only commercial advertising.

It is not easy to reconcile all of the varying court decisions involving the right to advertise in state-run media, but the prevailing rule since *Lehman* seems to be that there is no such right unless an agency of government accepts some ads of a certain type and then arbitrarily rejects other similar ads.

In 1995, the Supreme Court called new attention to this issue by ruling that Amtrak is a government agency for First Amendment purposes in *Lebron v. National Railroad Passenger Corp.* (513 U.S. 374)—another case involving artist Michael Lebron. Thus, when Amtrak rejected Lebron's proposal to purchase space for a political ad on "The Spectacular," a large billboard in New York City's Penn Station (controlled by Amtrak), that raised a First Amendment issue. The case was remanded to a lower court to conduct a First Amendment analysis and determine whether Amtrak as a government agency had any obligation to accept the billboard display. The proposed display combined a photo montage and text to attack the family that owns the Coors Brewing Co. for their support of conservative political causes.

A federal appellate court reconsidered the case and said Amtrak's status as a government agency didn't change anything. In a brief opinion, the court concluded that the First Amendment was not violated because Amtrak had never accepted any political advertising for The Spectacular—and had no obligation to do so in the future. Therefore, Amtrak had the right to reject Lebron's display (*Lebron v. National Railroad Passenger Corp.*, 74 F.3d 371, 1995). As noted earlier, the Supreme Court ruled in *Lehman v. Shaker Heights* that even government-run media can reject political advertising as long as they do so consistently.

Two billboard regulations were before the courts in 2010, and both were upheld. New York has billboard zoning regulations that prohibit the placement of billboards that do not advertise an on-premise business within 200 feet and within sight of major roads. Clear Channel Outdoor challenged those rules as an unconstitutional restriction on commercial speech. The Second Circuit applied the *Central Hudson* test and found that the regulation advanced the state's interest in public safety and aesthetics without burdening too much speech (*Clear Channel Outdoor, Inc. v. City of New York*, 594 F.3d 94).

Los Angeles' billboard regulations similarly ban signs located within 2,000 feet of and viewed primarily from freeways or on-/off-ramps; the rules also prohibit "supergraphics," multi-story vinyl ads that span across buildings. A supergraphics company brought suit, alleging that the regulations were unconstitutional (*World Wide Rush, LLC v. City of Los Angeles*, 606 F.3d 676), especially since the city bent its own rules to allow signs at several locations. The court said that these exceptions were intended to advance the city's interests in safety and beauty, and the city has the authority to create both the regulations and the exceptions, noting that "The First Amendment is not implicated by the City Council's exercise of legislative judgment in these circumstances."

■ FEDERAL ADVERTISING REGULATION

Beyond the issues of advertising access and commercial speech, advertising law is a field dominated by the Federal Trade Commission and, to an increasing degree, other federal agencies as well as state and local regulatory agencies.

Unquestionably, the FTC is the most important single regulatory agency for advertisers. Created by the Federal Trade Commission Act in 1914, this independent federal agency is responsible for overseeing many kinds of business activities in America. The 1914 act said: "Unfair methods of competition in commerce are hereby declared unlawful; the Commission is hereby empowered and directed to prevent persons, partnerships, or corporations from using unfair methods of competition in commerce."

The FTC's initial mandate was to prevent unfair business practices—but only for the protection of other businesses. It was not at first given the job of protecting consumers from fraudulent business practices.

Perhaps this was because of a very old tradition in American advertising. The prevailing attitude was *caveat emptor* (roughly translated, "let the buyer beware"). For several centuries, that meant advertisers were free to flagrantly exaggerate the merits of their products. Newspapers in the 1800s were full of fraudulent advertising, most notably ads for patent medicines. These medicines were trumpeted as cures for everything from colds to cancer, although many of them had no medicinal value at all.

The consumer who was deceived by this false advertising had few legal remedies under the common law; the only remedies available involved complicated lawsuits that were difficult to win. Most victims of advertising fraud had no choice but to accept their losses and vow not to be fooled again.

However, the FTC quickly made false advertising one of its main concerns. By the 1920s, the majority of its enforcement actions involved advertising. The FTC contended that false advertising was unfair to other businesses. For instance, in a famous case that went all the way to the Supreme Court, the FTC challenged a company that advertised clothing as "natural wool" when it was really only 10 percent wool. In *FTC v. Winsted Hosiery Co.* (258 U.S. 483, 1922), the court agreed that false advertising is a form of unfair competition, since it diverts customers from honest merchants' products to those of dishonest competitors.

However, a few years later the Supreme Court curtailed the FTC's crusade against false advertising by ruling that the agency had no authority to act on behalf of consumers in the absence of evidence that the false advertising was unfair to a competing business. That happened in 1931, in *FTC v. Raladam* (283 U.S. 643).

As a result, the FTC's powers were sharply reduced, but only temporarily. In two other cases during the 1930s, the Supreme Court upheld FTC actions against deceptive selling tactics (*FTC v. R.F. Keppel & Brother,* 291 U.S. 304, and *FTC v. Standard Education Society,* 302 U.S. 112). And in 1938, Congress enacted the *Wheeler-Lea Amendment,* authorizing the FTC to act against "unfair or deceptive acts or practices" that might mislead the consumer. Wheeler-Lea also expanded the FTC's enforcement powers.

The FTC operated under this enabling legislation until 1975, when its powers were again expanded by the *Magnuson-Moss Act.* That law specifically empowered the commission to act against fraudulent practices all the way down to the local level. No longer would it be limited to practices involving interstate commerce as it had been; instead, the FTC could pursue businesses that merely "affected" interstate commerce. In addition, Magnuson-Moss authorized the FTC to issue "Trade Regulation Rules," orders carrying the force of law that govern business practices in entire industries.

Under these broad new powers, the commission entered an unprecedented period of activism in the late 1970s, but some of its actions so angered many business leaders that they prevailed upon Congress to hold up the FTC's budget until the agency changed its policies. As a result, in 1980 the agency briefly had to lock its doors and cease all operations. Finally, it was given an operating budget, but with severe restrictions on its authority, in the Federal Trade Commission Improvements Act of 1980. The 1980s saw a much tamer FTC in action, pursuing advertising fraud with far less enthusiasm than was true a decade earlier. By the 2000s, though, the FTC returned to a more aggressive posture in enforcing advertising rules.

FTC Enforcement Tools

The Federal Trade Commission, like the Federal Communications Commission, is an independent regulatory agency. It is governed by a five-member commission, with an administrative staff of more than 1,000 persons. The five commissioners are appointed by the president with Senate ratification.

How does the FTC go about the task of enforcing the rules against deceptive advertising? First, the FTC uses a three-part analysis to determine if a particular advertisement is deceptive: 1) Identify each affirmative claim or material omission and ask the advertiser to document what the ad says; 2) determine whether the claim could mislead a typical consumer acting reasonably; and 3) determine whether the claim is "material" (i.e., is it likely to affect purchasing decisions?). In deciding this, the FTC looks at the "net impression" created by an advertisement.

How does the FTC even locate advertising messages that may be deceptive? In addition to relying on complaints from consumers and competitors, the FTC does a lot of its own monitoring of the traditional media and, increasingly, the Internet. Once what appears to be a widespread problem is identified, the FTC may conduct a *sweep*: a simultaneous law enforcement action targeting numerous businesses of a certain kind in a particular region. Often the FTC staff works closely with a state's attorney general in these actions. Investigators may "test shop" many businesses—or systematically surf the Internet for a particular type of advertising that is under investigation. These sweeps often yield dramatic results— and send a message to others that the FTC is out there looking for false or misleading advertising.

Once the FTC decides an advertising message is unlawful and that formal action is warranted, the commission may use a variety of enforcement tools. Although most involve legal actions, the FTC's most effective means of controlling fraudulent advertising is

indemnification clause:
a clause in a contract that says that one party will hold the other harmless for any damages incurred.

Magnuson-Moss Act:
the federal law that covers product warranties and allows the FTC to act against fraudulent practices wherever they occur.

often publicity. Since an advertiser's purpose is to persuade a segment of the public to buy or believe something, one of the worst things that can happen to an advertiser is to have the same media that carry the ads also publish news stories reporting that a government agency thinks the ads are false.

But beyond the clout of its press releases, the FTC has a variety of enforcement powers. The agency often acts on the basis of complaints from consumers or other businesses, but whatever the source of a complaint, the first step in an enforcement action is usually for the FTC to notify an advertiser that it considers his or her ads deceptive or misleading. The advertiser may be provided a copy of a proposed *cease and desist order*, along with supporting documents. Rather than face the lengthy and costly proceedings that lead to the issuance of such a decree, the advertiser may well choose to sign a *consent agreement*, agreeing to discontinue the challenged advertising without admitting any wrongdoing.

Even though this is an informal way to settle an FTC complaint, the consent agreement is placed in the public record. There is usually a 60-day period for public comment on it, after which the FTC may issue a *consent order*, which carries the force of law.

In some cases, the FTC is willing to let an advertiser merely sign an affidavit called an *assurance of voluntary compliance*. But under either this procedure or the more official consent order, the FTC usually negotiates with the advertiser to reach a settlement. The agency prefers to avoid its more formal proceedings when possible, not only to save staff time but also to halt the misleading advertising quickly enough to protect the public. A typical advertising campaign runs for only a few months; the entire campaign may be over long before the FTC can complete its formal proceedings.

However, if the advertiser refuses to sign a consent order, the agency may initiate formal proceedings. Those proceedings involve bringing the advertiser before an administrative

---

Focus on...
"Hillary: The Movie"

The *Citizens United* case turned on whether federal campaign finance laws applied to a critical feature-length film about Sen. Hillary Clinton by a conservative non-profit organization intended to be shown in theaters and on-demand to cable subscribers. The Supreme Court ultimately overruled some of its earlier jurisprudence and held that there could be no limits on independent political spending by corporations. The decision brought firestorms of controversy over whether the speech of ordinary citizens would be diluted by huge expenditures by large companies, or whether instead this was a huge win for free speech.

But what about the movie itself? Clinton appears in archive footage, and conservative commentators like Ann Coulter, Bay Buchanan and Newt Gingrich were featured. Justice Anthony Kennedy, who wrote the majority opinion in *Citizens United*, summed it up best: "The movie, in essence, is a feature-length negative advertisement that urges viewers to vote against Senator Clinton for President. In light of historical footage, interviews with persons critical of her, and voiceover narration, the film would be understood by most viewers as an extended criticism of Senator Clinton's character and her fitness for the office of the Presidency."

FIG. 68. Hillary: The Movie DVD.

Author's collection.

law judge, who will hear both the commission's and the advertiser's arguments and issue a ruling. The commission has the right to review the judge's decision, and may issue a formal cease and desist order, which the advertiser may then appeal to a federal appellate court. Because these are civil proceedings, the defending advertiser isn't afforded the full rights available in criminal trials. For instance, an administrative law judge may decide the FTC is wrong and the challenged ads are perfectly legal. In a criminal trial, that would be an acquittal and would end the proceeding. But here, the FTC can rule that the ads are illegal and issue a decree anyway, ignoring the judge's findings. The advertiser has no recourse then, except to appeal the FTC decision to a federal appellate court.

Once a consent order or cease and desist order is in effect, the advertiser faces large civil penalties—sometimes $10,000 a day or more—for violating its terms.

In addition to these enforcement tools, the FTC uses several other procedures. For example, the FTC can bring a legal action against an advertiser in a federal district court, avoiding the delays inherent in the handling of cease and desist orders.

Another option is for the FTC to publish purely advisory *Guides*. These pamphlets tell advertisers how the FTC interprets the law on a given point, such as the use of testimonials in advertising or product pricing. Violating a *Guide* is not a violation of law, but *Guides* are valuable to advertisers because they provide insight into the FTC's current thinking on various advertising practices. Another similar FTC action is to issue *Advisory Opinions*. Like *Guides*, they are voluntary, but they differ in that they are issued in response to inquiries from advertisers rather than on the commission's own initiative.

A similar policy guideline—but carrying the force of law—is called a *Trade Regulation Rule*, or "TRR." These rules generally apply to an entire industry, requiring certain specific advertising practices and forbidding others. The liberal use of TRRs was largely responsible for the Congressional action to limit the FTC's authority in 1980.

During the 1970s the FTC also launched another major effort to control advertising fraud, this one through an *Advertising Substantiation Program*. In this program, the FTC required certain industries to document all claims in their ads, something that produced voluminous and highly technical reports in some cases.

Two more of the FTC's more controversial approaches to enforcement have been *Affirmative Disclosure Orders* **and** *corrective advertising*. Affirmative disclosure involves requiring the advertiser to reveal the negative as well as the positive aspects of a product. In a pioneering case of this sort, a federal appellate court upheld an FTC order aimed at the makers of Geritol. Geritol was advertised as a "tired blood" cure for the elderly, and the manufacturer was ordered to reveal that it did little to help people with certain kinds of anemia (*J.B. Williams Co. v. FTC*, 381 F.2d 884, 1967). The FTC required hundreds of advertisers to reveal similarly negative facts about their products after this decision.

Many advertisers found these requirements onerous and embarrassing, but corrective advertising angered the business community even more. Probably the most famous FTC corrective advertising order was one aimed at Warner-Lambert Company, maker of Listerine mouthwash. For nearly a century, Listerine had been advertised as a cure for colds and sore throats, a claim that medical research did not support.

The FTC ordered Warner-Lambert not only to spend $10 million on advertisements admitting that Listerine would not cure sore throats, but also to preface the correction with the phrase, "Contrary to prior advertising." Warner-Lambert appealed the FTC ruling, but the federal appellate court affirmed the corrective order—although it did agree that saying "contrary to prior advertising" was too much penance. Warner-Lambert was allowed to run its corrective ads without that confession of past sins (*Warner-Lambert Co. v. FTC*, 562 F.2d 749, 1977). The Supreme Court denied *cert.*

The FTC has issued a number of other corrective advertising orders, including one that required the makers of STP oil additive to publish ads telling the public its claims that STP would reduce auto oil consumption were based on unreliable road tests.

The FTC again required a petroleum company to do corrective advertising in 1997. The Exxon Corporation settled an FTC complaint by agreeing to run television ads informing consumers that its most expensive premium grade of gasoline does not keep engines cleaner or reduce maintenance costs. Exxon previously aired ads claiming its Exxon 93 Supreme gasoline "has the power to drive down maintenance costs" and "keeps your engine cleaner." In fact, all grades of Exxon gasoline contained the same engine-cleaning additives, which are similar to those in many other brands of gasoline, the FTC noted. While agreeing to do corrective advertising in 18 major markets, Exxon did not admit any wrongdoing in connection with its previous advertising.

The FTC ordered corrective advertising in another field in 1999, directing the manufacturer of Doan's back-pain medicine to spend $8 million on ads including the words, "Although Doan's is an effective pain reliever, there is no evidence that Doan's is more effective than other pain relievers for back pain." The FTC took this action because Doan's manufacturer, Novartis, and its predecessor, Ciba-Geigy Corp., spent about $65 million over a 20-year period on advertising claiming that Doan's was better for back pain than other pain relievers, a claim that could not be substantiated.

In 2000, the Bayer Corporation agreed to spend $1 million on consumer education to settle FTC charges that it made unsubstantiated claims in its aspirin ads. Bayer ads said that aspirin will prevent heart attacks and strokes without explaining that some persons may not benefit or may actually be harmed by an aspirin regimen. Bayer agreed to give free brochures to consumers to correct its advertising, and to do print ads to tell consumers of the availability of these brochures.

Other Examples of Enforcement Actions

In addition to cases involving various forms of penance by advertisers, the FTC has acted against thousands of advertising campaigns that the agency considered to be false, misleading or deceptive. A few examples illustrate the FTC's approach to advertising regulation.

Perhaps the best-known FTC case for many years, in part because it produced a U.S. Supreme Court decision, was the "sandpaper shave case," *FTC v. Colgate-Palmolive Co.* (380 U.S. 374, 1965). In one of the most famous television ads of the era, Colgate-Palmolive Rapid Shave was shown shaving the sand off sandpaper. The only problem was that what the viewer really saw was sand being scraped off a transparent plastic sheet. The FTC contended that this was deceptive and ordered the ads halted. Colgate-Palmolive chose to fight the order and set out to prove that the sand really could be shaved off a sheet of sandpaper. The company did it, but it took a little longer in real life than in the ads: about 90 minutes.

The Supreme Court eventually upheld the FTC's conclusion that the ad was deceptive. In so ruling, the Court did not say that *all* television mockups are deceptive. But, the Court said, mockups that are central to the point of the ad or enhance the product are deceptive. A common industry practice was to use mashed potatoes in place of ice cream because of the heat generated by television lighting. The Court used that mockup to explain its point. Perhaps showing actors eating ice cream that was really mashed potatoes would not be deceptive if the point of the ad was to promote something else, but it would be deceptive if the point was to sell the ice cream by showing its rich texture and full color, the Court said.

In the years since *Colgate-Palmolive*, the FTC has acted against a variety of advertising practices. The FTC has gone after advertisers who used a number of other mockups, mockups that hardly seem as deceptive as the Rapid Shave commercial. In one Lever Brothers commercial for All detergent, an actor was shown standing in a huge washing machine with a stain on his shirt. The water rose to his neck and then receded—and the stain vanished. The FTC said it was deceptive, since the whole process couldn't really happen that fast.

On another occasion, the FTC went after the makers of Prestone Anti-Freeze for a commercial showing the "magnetic film" in Prestone protecting a strip of metal from acid. The FTC objected because the acid used in the demonstration was not the same kind encountered in auto radiators and because certain other test conditions didn't duplicate what really happens in a car.

Often the FTC has based its complaints on ads that were literally true but nonetheless deceiving. As early as 1950 the commission acted against a cigarette manufacturer for advertising that a study found its brand lower in tar and nicotine than others tested. That was true, but the study also concluded that all brands tested were dangerously high in tar and nicotine. The ads were literally true but still misleading, the FTC said.

The FTC has also challenged advertising claims that were controversial and dealt with issues on which there was scientific disagreement. In 1974, the commission filed a complaint and sought an injunction against the National Commission on Egg Nutrition for publishing ads that said, "there is no scientific evidence that eating eggs increases the risk of heart and circulatory disease." A federal appellate court upheld the FTC's action to halt this advertising claim, although the court overruled an FTC order requiring future egg ads to say the health issue was controversial and that experts differed.

The FTC has also expressed interest in misleading testimonials, requiring that celebrities who endorse products actually use them, and that "experts" who give endorsements must really be experts. Moreover, the claims users make in endorsements must in fact be verifiably true. A grass-roots or "plain folks" ad cannot have someone saying he gets 50 miles per gallon from his Guzzlemobile Diesel when tests indicate it won't deliver over 40. In fact, an ad in which "Mrs. Holly Hollingsworth" of "Guzzle Gulch, Nevada" endorses a product must actually show Mrs. Hollingsworth, not an actress portraying Mrs. Hollingsworth.

In 1978, the commission acted against entertainer Pat Boone for what the FTC considered to be a misleading endorsement of a skin-care product. The FTC accused the manufacturer, the advertising agency and Boone of participating in false and misleading advertising. The FTC charged that the product would not cure acne as the ad implied it would. The commission sought a $5,000 penalty from Boone, and he signed a consent order agreeing to pay the $5,000 into a fund to compensate customers who were misled by the ad.

This action, the first to hold a celebrity accountable for a misleading endorsement, was a major shock to other celebrities who endorse products. After the Boone incident, virtually all celebrities demanded *indemnification clauses* in their endorsement contracts. (Indemnification means the advertiser must pay any penalty the celebrity may incur because of the ad.)

Nevertheless, several other well-known celebrities have faced sanctions for endorsements. Actors George Hamilton and Lloyd Bridges were sued in the late 1980s for appearing in ads endorsing an investment plan that turned out to be fraudulent. After the plan's promoters went bankrupt and investors lost millions of dollars, both actors settled the lawsuits by paying undisclosed sums to those who lost money by investing in the plan.

If a celebrity is not aware of the falsity of an endorsement, he or she may escape liability. The FTC launched an enforcement action against former baseball star Steve Garvey and Enforma Natural Products for false weight-loss claims in infomercials and other advertising. Enforma had income of at least $100 million from sales of its products between 1998 and 2000 and Enforma eventually paid $10 million in penalties for making false claims about its products. However, a federal court rejected the FTC's action against Garvey, ruling that because he and his wife had tried the products and actually lost weight, he was unaware of the falsity of the scripts he read. In 2004, the FTC appealed that decision and the Ninth Circuit upheld the ruling in Garvey's favor (*FTC v. Garvey*, 383 F.3d 891).

Like testimonials, comparison advertising has attracted the FTC's attention. Traditionally, advertisers have hesitated to criticize each other's products, partly out of fear of lawsuits and partly because industry self-regulation codes discouraged the practice. But in 1979, the FTC issued a policy statement demanding that the advertising industry and broadcasters drop their restrictions on comparative ads and calling on advertisers to compare their products "objectively" against competing brands by name.

If the 1970s saw the FTC push aggressively into new areas such as advertising substantiation, corrective advertising and comparative advertising, the 1980s were an era of retrenchment. In fact, in the mid-1980s there was growing uncertainty about the FTC's basic rules defining what constitutes deceptive advertising. In 1983, FTC Chair James Miller released an "enforcement policy statement" that said the commission would henceforth only regard advertising as deceptive if it harmed a hypothetical "reasonable consumer." However, it was not clear what legal significance this new statement would carry, and it was widely criticized in Congress as inadequate to protect the public from false and misleading advertising.

By the 1990s, the FTC was again aggressively pursuing advertisers who were allegedly guilty of misleading consumers. For example, in 1993 the commission launched a highly publicized effort to stop five of the nation's largest commercial diet programs from engaging in deceptive advertising. The FTC accused the five of making unsubstantiated weight-loss claims and disseminating consumer testimonials that did not represent the typical experiences of consumers who used these programs. The FTC said the weight-loss firms had to include in their advertising disclaimers such as: "For many dieters, weight loss is temporary," or "This result is not typical. You may be less successful."

Three of the five firms signed consent decrees agreeing to comply with the FTC's demands. The other two, Jenny Craig and Weight Watchers, engaged in protracted legal battles against the FTC. Weight Watchers won at least a minor victory against the FTC in 1994 when a federal appellate court ruled that the company had the right to sue the FTC to challenge the agency's enforcement policies for the weight-loss industry. Weight Watchers charged that the FTC was changing its rules governing weight-loss advertising on a case-by-case basis instead of conducting a formal rulemaking proceeding to change its rules (*Weight Watchers International v. FTC*, 47 F.3d 990).

At almost the same time as its actions against weight-loss programs and the Eskimo Pie Corp., the FTC sought a $2.4 million civil penalty against General Nutrition Inc., the operator of about 1,500 GNC stores. GNC was accused of violating previous consent orders by making unsubstantiated claims about various health-oriented products. GNC eventually signed a consent decree in which it agreed to pay the $2.4 million penalty and stop making unsubstantiated health claims for its products.

In 2002 the FTC launched a new initiative against misleading weight-loss claims. This time, it called on the media to reject both conventional advertising and infomercials that include implausible claims of miracle weight loss. The FTC released guidelines for the media to follow in evaluating such claims. That caused several media and First Amendment lawyers to protest, citing the right of the media to publish advertising without first evaluating the accuracy of each ad.

In 2007, the FTC fined the makers of four other weight-loss products a total of $25 million. The FTC accused the four, Xenadrine EFX, CortiSlim, One-A-Day WeightSmart and TrimSpa, of false and misleading advertising.

The FTC continues to be concerned about false weight loss claims. In 2011, the agency upheld a $37.6 million award against Kevin Trudeau for disobeying settlement agreements on advertising the content of his book, *The Weight Loss Cure "They" Don't Want You to Know About*. Trudeau argued that the fine should not be calculated against the amount of consumer loss, but the Seventh Circuit disagreed. Moreover, the court added, "The government is not impotent to protect consumers—nor is the court powerless to enforce its orders—by imposing narrowly tailored restrictions on commercial speech" (*Trudeau v. FTC*, 662 F.3d 947). The FTC may not be able to catch every phony weight-loss advertiser, but more established advertisers may face costly penalties even for advertising that could be misleading but isn't false. In 1999, the Mazda Corporation agreed to pay $5.25 million in fines and civil penalties alleged violations of an earlier FTC order requiring the car maker to disclose the terms of its car and truck leases in its print and television advertising. Among other things, the FTC concluded that the disclosures were in small and unreadable print, offset by distracting images and sounds, and on screen for too short a time.

The FTC has taken other initiatives in the area of obesity and weight loss. The agency issued a report in 2006 urging the food industry to better address the problem of childhood obesity. Although voluntary, the guidelines could lead to new regulations. Among other things, the FTC urged advertisers to make sure foods advertised to children meet minimum nutritional standards. The FTC also called for marketing that better educates consumers about nutrition and fitness.

POM Wonderful markets pomegranate juice, and many of its advertisements make claims on the juice's health benefits. But an administrative judge said that without substantiation, POM cannot claim that its juice cures anything. The judge wrote a 345-page decision saying POM ads would result in some reasonable consumers believing that drinking POM "treats, prevents or reduces the risk of heart disease," or treats prostate cancer or erectile dysfunction (*In the Matter of POM Wonderful LLC*, No. 9344, May 2012)—when, in fact, there is no data to suggest that. POM has said it will appeal.

The FTC is also cracking down on mobile apps claiming health benefits. For example, in 2012 the agency said that claims that apps "AcneApp" and "Acne Pwner," which its owners claimed would cure acne with pulses of light from a smart phone, would actually cure acne were unsubstantiated. The FTC fined the companies, marking the first time that the agency targeted health claims in the mobile app market.

But the FTC also provides a website to help consumers navigate the sometimes-complex world of health and weight loss products and services. Check out http://www.ftc.gov/bcp/edu/microsites/whocares/index.shtml.

FTC Actions Against "Unfair" Practices

The FTC has increasingly looked beyond advertising that was merely deceptive or misleading and began to act against ads it considered unfair even though they were truthful, starting in the 1970s. Critics came to call this policy the *Unfairness Doctrine*, an obvious reference to the Federal Communications Commission's old Fairness Doctrine in broadcasting.

The FTC's definition of what it considers unfair advertising was summarized in a 1994 policy statement. An advertisement is unfair if it: (1) causes or is likely to cause substantial consumer injury; (2) which is not reasonably avoidable by consumers themselves; and (3) is not outweighed by countervailing benefits to consumers or competition.

The FTC's authority to act against ads that are merely "unfair" was affirmed by the U.S. Supreme Court in a 1972 decision, *FTC v. Sperry Hutchinson Co.* (405 U.S. 233). The court said the FTC has the power to act against "business practices which have an unfair impact on consumers, regardless of whether the practice is deceptive ...or anti-competitive in the traditional sense." After that ruling, the FTC initiated a series of controversial actions against "unfair" advertising. In 1979, for instance, the commission responded to bicycle ads in which it felt unsafe riding habits were shown by ordering the advertiser to distribute public service ads on bicycle safety.

The FTC also used its authority during this era to issue Trade Regulation Rules to ban allegedly unfair practices in a variety of industries. These campaigns stirred bitter opposition among businesses and eventually in Congress.

For example, in 1978 the commission initiated a very controversial proposal to severely restrict television advertising aimed at children. The proposed restrictions would have completely banned advertising aimed at young children and prohibited ads for sugared food products targeted to older children. At one point before the commission voted on the matter, the FTC chair at the time, Michael Pertschuk, made public statements on the issue that were so prejudicial that national organizations in advertising sought—and won—a court order prohibiting him from voting on the matter. The order was reversed by a federal appellate court, but industry leaders never trusted him again.

The FTC also proposed rules forcing funeral directors to list all their prices and service options, as well as rules requiring used car dealers to inspect the cars they sell and post a list of mechanical problems on each car. On other occasions, the commission acted to break up Sunkist Growers, an agricultural cooperative, and launched campaigns against various trademarks, seeking to take them from their owners and have them declared generic words. The FTC also issued rules requiring trade and vocational schools to provide a great deal of information to incoming students, and let them withdraw with a prorated tuition refund during their programs.

The FTC's policy on corrective advertising angered the advertising profession. The extensive use of the Unfairness Doctrine against advertisers intensified that feeling, as did the move to ban children's television advertising. Pertschuk's public pronouncements further united the business community. Finally, the rules aimed at morticians, used car dealers, the Sunkist cooperative and trade schools were the FTC's undoing.

Responding to nationwide protests about the FTC's regulatory zeal, Congress refused to appropriate a budget for the agency in 1980 and then enacted the restrictive Federal Trade Commission Improvements Act. This law extended the FTC's funding for three more years, but at a high price. It temporarily prohibited the FTC from acting against advertising that is only "unfair" but not deceptive or misleading. Responding in part to the industry's complaints and in part to the Court's rulings extending First Amendment protection to advertising, Congress declared that FTC actions should not be aimed at truthful advertising.

In addition, the 1980 act halted the FTC proceeding on children's television until the commission published a new specific proposal aimed only at "deceptive" advertising, and ordered the FTC to publish the text of every proposed new rule at the start of the rule making proceeding. The FTC eventually terminated its study of advertising aimed at children in 1981 without taking any action.

The 1980 act specifically set aside the FTC's actions involving morticians and agricultural cooperatives such as Sunkist Growers (although the FTC later adopted extensive regulations concerning advertising by morticians). Moreover, the commission was ordered to give Congress advance notice of new proposed rules. The 1980 law also declared that Congress would have the power to veto future FTC regulations. Finally, the FTC was ordered to reduce the paperwork burden it had imposed on businesses and to stop trying to invalidate businesses' trademarks.

Taken as a whole, these revisions constituted a substantial curtailment of the FTC's power. Business interests lobbied heavily in Congress to harness the FTC; their campaign happened to fit in with the mood of the times. Certainly popular distaste for government regulation was a factor in Ronald Reagan's decisive victory in the 1980 presidential election. In the years that followed, Congress repeatedly debated the merits of the Unfairness Doctrine—and eventually allowed the FTC to act against unfair advertising again.

Congress exercised its power to veto FTC regulations in 1982, overturning the FTC's long-awaited rules requiring auto dealers to disclose known defects in used cars. However, later that year a federal appellate court ruled that Congress did not have the right to give itself this veto power. In 1983, the Supreme Court agreed, ruling in an unrelated case: *Immigration and Naturalization Service v. Chadha* (462 U.S. 919). With that one ruling, the high court invalidated some 200 different laws that gave Congress the power to veto actions taken by agencies in the executive branch of the federal government.

The proper role of the Federal Trade Commission has been a subject of ongoing Congressional debate ever since. By the early 1990s the FTC had abandoned the non-regulatory posture it assumed during the 1980s, and Janet Steiger, the FTC chair in the first Bush administration, declared that henceforth the FTC would take a more aggressive posture in

FIG. 69. Camel cigarette advertisement In Times Square, 1943.

Library of Congress, Prints and Photographs Division, [LC-USW3-018258-D].

enforcing the advertising laws. She said the FTC wanted to eliminate the public perception that the agency was no longer interested in fighting false and misleading advertising.

The FTC followed through. By 2000, the FTC was nearly as aggressive as it had been in the 1970s, launching hundreds of regulatory actions against advertisers every year. The agency was especially targeting advertisers who made questionable environmental claims and false, misleading or unfair advertising that might appear on the Internet.

Earlier, the FTC had released industry-wide regulations to prevent false or misleading "green" or environmental advertising claims. Among other things, the new rules require those who claim a product has "recycled content" to document the amount that really is made from recycled materials. The rules also prohibit the use of terms such as "ozone safe" or "ozone friendly" if the product contains any ozone-depleting chemical, and they ban the use of terms such as "biodegradable" to describe products that will not degrade quickly when buried in a landfill.

The FTC, "Joe Camel" and Cigarette Advertising

One of the most controversial advertising campaigns in American history involved "Joe Camel," R.J. Reynolds' cartoon character used to promote the Camel cigarette brand. "Old Joe," or "Smokin' Joe," as his fans sometimes called him, first appeared in European advertising for Camel cigarettes during the 1970s. A massive "Old Joe Camel" campaign was launched in the United States in 1988—and drew immediate fire from critics of the tobacco industry. Their main claim: "Old Joe" unfairly targeted underage smokers.

Before the controversy ended, the entire tobacco industry was fighting new restrictions on cigarette advertising from coast to coast—restrictions that ultimately led to a Supreme Court decision overturning state and local laws regulating cigarette ads: *Lorillard Tobacco Co. v. Reilly* (discussed earlier).

During the mid-1990s, the FTC spent several years trying to decide how to deal with cigarette advertising, and particularly how to handle "Old Joe Camel." In 1994, the FTC voted 3-2 not to pursue an unfair advertising complaint against "Old Joe." But three years later, the FTC voted 3-2 to reverse itself and bring legal action to halt the "Old Joe" campaign.

This strange case began after the attorneys general of 27 states jointly asked the FTC to halt the ads, contending that the "Old Joe" campaign resulted in a huge increase in smoking among teenagers. Joined by various public health and consumer groups, they cited large statistical increases in overall smoking rates among teenagers, and pointed out that Camel's market share among underage smokers increased enormously after the "Old Joe" campaign began. They argued that this cartoon camel—this "debonair dromedary"—was enormously appealing to teenagers. In refusing to halt the "Old Joe" ad campaign in 1994, a deeply divided FTC decided that R.J. Reynolds was targeting young adults rather than teenagers and that, in any case, the company had a First Amendment right to use this cartoon character. In reaching that conclusion, the FTC's 3-2 majority rejected the recommendation of its own staff, which contended that "Old Joe" did encourage underage smoking. For its part, R.J. Reynolds vehemently denied that the "Old Joe" campaign targeted teenagers, despite its stunning success with that segment of the market.

Soon after the 1994 FTC vote, *Advertising Age*, a leading advertising industry trade publication, took the unusual step of urging R.J. Reynolds to discontinue the "Old Joe" campaign in spite of the company's victory at the FTC. The influential trade journal said this step would be wise because "Old Joe" provided an easy target for antismoking groups that want to ban all cigarette advertising. A week later, R.J. Reynolds' president replied in a letter to the editor, refusing to halt the campaign.

By 1997, however, the public mood had changed. Cigarette manufacturers were on the defensive everywhere. And there was far more evidence that cigarette makers had indeed set out to target teenagers. The FTC then reconsidered the "Old Joe" issue and voted 3-2 (with two new commissioners in the majority) to launch a legal action designed to banish "Old Joe" as an unfair advertising image that improperly targeted underage smokers. The FTC not only voted to ban "Old Joe" but to order R.J. Reynolds to run a corrective advertising campaign to combat underage smoking.

Meanwhile, R.J. Reynolds faced many other legal problems stemming from the "Old Joe" campaign. For example, in 1994 the California Supreme Court ruled that individual citizens could sue R.J. Reynolds for targeting minors with the "Old Joe" campaign on the ground that it encouraged them to violate state laws against underage smoking. In *Mangini v. R.J. Reynolds Tobacco Co.* (7 C.4th 1057), the state court said lawsuits based on cigarette advertising were not then federally preempted under the Federal Cigarette Labeling and Advertising Act. The California court said that, while this federal law does preempt most state regulation of cigarette advertising, it does not prevent lawsuits against advertising that would encourage "illegal smoking by youths." Although the U.S. Supreme Court later ruled in the *Lorillard Tobacco* case that regulating cigarette advertising is usually federally preempted, the high court declined to review the California court's ruling at that point, clearing the way for the *Mangini* case to go to trial. When that happened, R.J. Reynolds began negotiating with representatives of antismoking activist Janet Mangini, the lead plaintiff, and various government agencies that joined in the lawsuit.

In 1997, R.J. Reynolds settled the *Mangini* case, agreeing to halt the "Old Joe Camel" ad campaign permanently in the United States. Although Reynolds had announced the end of the "Old Joe" campaign earlier, its demise was made a part of this settlement, along with a large cash payment to fund anti-smoking advertising aimed at teenagers.

The FTC ultimately dropped its civil lawsuit against R.J. Reynolds after the tobacco industry reached its landmark $206 billion settlement with 46 states. The industry agreed to end billboard advertising, to stop using cartoon characters and to refrain from targeting underage smokers. The industry also agreed to compensate the states for some health costs associated with cigarette smoking. (The other four states—Mississippi, Texas, Florida and Minnesota—reached a separate $40 billion settlement with the tobacco industry earlier.)

Despite the tobacco industry's promises, the Federal Trade Commission reported in 2001 that the industry had dramatically increased its overall spending for advertising and marketing after the settlement. At about the same time, five states jointly sued R.J. Reynolds for allegedly breaching the terms of the settlement, accusing Reynolds of being the worst offender in the industry in marketing to young people.

In 2003, a global anti-tobacco-advertising treaty backed by the World Health Organization was approved in Geneva, Switzerland by delegates from 40 nations. By 2005, 57 nations had ratified the treaty, but not the United States. Under this treaty, all signing countries are required to ban tobacco advertising and event sponsorships within five years. In keeping with this agreement, the European Union has now banned most print as well as broadcast advertising of tobacco products. Even if the U.S. eventually signs it, the treaty has a loophole that may prevent its full implementation here. One provision says each country must implement the treaty "in accordance with its constitution." A complete ban on cigarette advertising might not square with the First Amendment.

In *Altria Group v. Good* (555 U.S. 70), the Supreme Court in 2008 addressed whether the Federal Cigarette Labeling and Advertising Act preempts state law deceptive practice claims in connection with the advertising of cigarettes as "light" or containing "lower tar and nicotine." The Court said it did not: Neither the Labeling Act's preemption provision nor the Federal Trade Commission's actions in this field preempt a state-law fraud claim.

Other Federal Regulators

Although the Federal Trade Commission has the primary responsibility for regulating advertising on the federal level, a number of other federal agencies also have responsibilities in this general area.

Under the Food, Drug and Cosmetic Act of 1938, the Food and Drug Administration is responsible for assuring the purity and safety of foods, drugs and cosmetics. One of the FDA's major duties is to act against false and fraudulent packaging and labeling practices. In this respect, its duties overlap those of the FTC, which is empowered to act against false food, drug and cosmetic advertising. The two agencies generally cooperate in sharing their regulatory responsibilities. Product labeling or advertising that raises environmental issues may also be regulated by the Environmental Protection Agency. In 1994, the FDA and FTC agreed to use the same definitions in evaluating claims made in food advertising.

The FDA plays an important role in regulating prescription drug advertising. In 1997 the FDA issued new guidelines that made it easier for drug makers to target the general public with their advertising. Until then, prescription drug advertising mainly targeted medical professionals. After 1997 prescription drug advertising became the fastest-growing kind of consumer advertising. Prescription drug ads must be submitted to the FDA for review when they appear in the media but not beforehand. By the 2000s, direct-to-consumer drug advertising had become a $4 billion business, and critics charged that drug makers were too heavily promoting the advantages of their products without adequately emphasizing risks and side effects. Congress later considered but did not pass legislation that would have forbidden direct-to-consumer drug advertising during a waiting period after a drug receives FDA approval, giving drug makers more time to discover unexpected side effects. The legislation also would have required FDA approval of drug advertising in advance.

In 2008, Merck & Co., a leading drug manufacturer, agreed to pay $58 million to settle lawsuits filed by 29 states and the District of Columbia alleging that its ads for Vioxx, a painkiller, underplayed the drug's health risks. It turned out that the drug doubles the risk of heart attacks and strokes. Merck was also negotiating a much larger settlement ($4.85 billion) of thousands of lawsuits by individuals who alleged that they suffered health problems after using Vioxx. In the settlement with the states, the company also agreed to submit future TV commercials for its drugs to the FDA for prior review before airing them.

Responding to criticism of direct-to-consumer drug advertising, the Pharmaceuticals Research and Manufacturers Association adopted voluntary advertising guidelines that went into effect in 2006. The guidelines say that all new direct-to-consumer television advertising should be submitted to the FDA before it is aired, and that ads should provide a balanced presentation of benefits and risks associated with each drug.

The FDA has also taken steps to regulate tobacco as a drug—and to severely restrict cigarette advertising. The FDA adopted rules in the 1990s, backed by the Clinton administration, to limit cigarette advertising on billboards and in most magazines to plain black type, without illustrations. The FDA also ordered tobacco companies to stop sponsoring sporting events and concerts in the name of their tobacco brands (although they could still sponsor events using their corporate names). In addition, the FDA acted to ban cigarette vending machines and to require the tobacco industry to fund a $150 million educational campaign to discourage teenagers from smoking. The campaign was to include heavy use of television.

Most of the FDA's tobacco rules never went into effect: they were immediately challenged in federal court. In 2000, the U.S. Supreme Court ruled that the Food and Drug Administration lacked the statutory authority to regulate tobacco as a drug. In *FDA v. Brown & Williamson Tobacco* (529 U.S. 120), the Court overturned a number of the FDA's restrictions on cigarette marketing.

The Court did not rule out the possibility of future Congressional action to give the FDA the authority to regulate tobacco as a drug. Instead, the court merely said the FDA had no such authority under existing federal law. Unless Congress changes the law, the FDA cannot enforce its regulations that restrict minors' access to cigarettes, among other things.

The 5-4 majority traced the legislative history of the acts of Congress governing the FDA and concluded that Congress never intended to authorize the FDA to regulate tobacco as a drug. In fact, the FDA itself denied that it had the authority to regulate tobacco for many years before it announced the new restrictions on tobacco marketing in 1996.

This Supreme Court decision did not affect the voluntary agreement of the tobacco industry to curtail its advertising as part of its settlement of lawsuits filed by the states: that agreement still stands. Nor did this case affect the Federal Trade Commission's authority to regulate cigarette advertising. In fact, this Supreme Court decision didn't even directly affect most of the FDA's restrictions on cigarette advertising, as opposed to other aspects of cigarette marketing. In a separate action, a federal court earlier overturned the advertising portions of the FDA's rules. In *Beahm v. Food and Drug Administration* (966 F.Supp. 1374), a judge ruled that those rules exceeded the FDA's statutory authority.

Then, in 2009, Congress passed the Family Smoking Prevention and Tobacco Control Act, granting the Food and Drug Administration the authority to regulate tobacco advertising and creating a tobacco control center within the FDA. The act bans flavored cigarettes (excluding menthol). It also limits advertising aimed toward young smokers and regulates the size of warning labels and the use of terms like "light," "mild" or "low."

The act was challenged on First Amendment grounds in early 2010 by five tobacco companies in *Commonwealth Brands, Inc. v. U.S.* (678 F. Supp. 2d 512), targeting the increased warning label size and requirements on package design. A federal district court agreed in part, saying that the package design requirements were problematic, and the tobacco companies "are clearly right when they say that images of packages of their products, simple brand symbols, and some uses of color communicate important commercial information about their products, i.e., what the product is and who makes it." The government did not explain how restricting those symbols or colors would achieve its goals. But the tobacco companies lost on their warning label challenge.

The FDA announced in 2011 that new cigarette packaging laws would be imposed, starting in 2012, and that the design would contain "color graphic images depicting the negative health consequences of smoking; these images were proposed to accompany the nine new textual warning statements" outlined in the Tobacco Control Act. These warnings include such statements as "WARNING: Tobacco smoke can harm your children" and "WARNING:

The NAD is seeing more cases than in years past, the *Dallas Morning-News* reported in 2009—presumably by companies seeking to avoid expensive litigation.

As an example, Wal-Mart pulled ads that claimed that shoppers could save $700 a year on groceries by shopping at Wal-Mart after a Texas supermarket chain challenged the claim at the NAD.

Wal-Mart said that the statement was qualified by the term "on average" but the NAD disagreed: "The use of the phrase 'on average' does not temper the overriding message that the viewer—wherever he or she is located—can expect to obtain these savings."

Wal-Mart agreed to pull the ad but said that it believed the ad was substantiated by a 2008 study from which it obtained the $700 number. The NAD did say that Wal-Mart's use of the catch-phrase "unbeatable prices" was acceptable.

Cigarettes cause fatal lung disease." The images will take up more of the package than current warnings do; the agency said that this change was in response to studies demonstrating that larger warnings would confer greater health benefits than the existing ones.

In 2012, the Sixth Circuit in *Discount Tobacco City & Lottery v. U.S.* (2012 U.S. App. LEXIS 11820) upheld most of the Act, including provisions that placed restrictions on the marketing of some tobacco products, bans on event sponsorship, branding of non-tobacco merchandise and free samples, and the packaging space allotment, as well as the color graphic label requirements. "Ample evidence establishes that current warnings do not effectively inform consumers of the health risks of tobacco use and that consumers do not understand these risks," said the court, and thus the Act was an appropriate use of government power to combat consumer deception. But a federal judge overturned the graphic labels as unconstitutional (*R.J. Reynolds v. FDA*, 40 Media L. Rep. 1473, 2012). Rather than the government's stated goal of educating consumers, the court said, "[t]he Government's reliance on the graphic images—which were chosen based on their ability to provoke emotion, a criterion that does not address whether the graphic images affect consumers' knowledge of smoking risks—coupled with the toll free number, further supports the conclusion that the Government's actual purpose is to convince consumers that they should 'QUIT NOW.'" Moreover, plaintiffs had shown a number of ways the government could achieve its goals without burdening tobacco companies' speech rights, so the law was not narrowly tailored. The government has appealed.

The legal battle over cigarette advertising has overshadowed other regulatory actions by the Food and Drug Administration—actions that may be on firmer legal footing. For years, the FDA has refused to let the makers of dietary supplements claim that their products will cure or even treat the symptoms of diseases. These products, used by millions of Americans and sold almost everywhere, represent a $6 billion business. Medications designed to treat specific illnesses must undergo rigorous testing; these dietary supplements are usually sold without any government-supervised testing to prove their effectiveness. In 2000, the FDA loosened its restrictions on dietary supplements, announcing that they can claim to treat symptoms of "common conditions" that are considered "passages of life" such as morning sickness in pregnancy or memory loss. These products still cannot be advertised as treatments for specific diseases without full testing and documentation, the FDA said.

The FDA suffered another setback in 2002. The U.S. Supreme Court overturned a federal law prohibiting the advertising of compounded prescription drugs. Acting in the case of *Thompson v. Western States Medical Center* (535 U.S. 357), the Court voted 5-4 to invalidate a provision of the 1997 Food and Drug Administration Modernization Act that banned compounded drug advertising. Compounded drugs are combinations of prescription drugs prepared by pharmacists to meet the special needs of patients at the request of doctors. Under federal law, drugs may be compounded without the normal testing that is required of new drugs as long as the compounded drug is not advertised.

Explaining the Court's rejection of this law as unconstitutional, Justice Sandra Day O'Connor wrote, "If the First Amendment means anything, it means that regulating speech must be a last—not first—resort. Yet here it seems to have been the first strategy the government thought to try." In making this observation, Justice O'Connor was evaluating the ban on compounded drug advertising under the classic *Central Hudson* test of the validity of government restrictions on commercial speech. She pointed out that there are several ways the federal government could achieve its stated goal—to prevent the mass production and widespread sale of compounded drugs that have not undergone the normal testing required of new drugs—without banning advertising. Thus, she wrote, this ban on advertising failed to meet the final part of the *Central Hudson* test: the ban was more extensive than necessary to achieve the government's goal.

Other federal agencies have the authority to regulate various aspects of advertising. The Federal Communications Commission has some authority in the advertising area, although much of it is indirect, derived from the FCC's licensing powers. For many years the FCC had specific guidelines that limited the amount of advertising a broadcaster could carry without risking special scrutiny at license renewal time. Those guidelines were eventually deleted as part of a comprehensive deregulation package. The FCC still has the right to consider the quantity and quality of advertising when it renews broadcast licenses, but there are no longer any specific quotas for broadcasters to follow except in the case of advertising in children's programs. In practice, most broadcasters carry less advertising than the old FCC guidelines permitted, anyway.

The FCC also has several other rules that affect broadcast advertising, perhaps the most notable being regulations requiring sponsorship identification. And Congress got into the regulatory act with the FCC in 2011 with the passage of the Commercial Advertisement Loudness Mitigation Act, or CALM Act, which requires the FCC to make compliance with the document "Recommended Practice: Techniques for Establishing and Maintaining Audio Loudness for Digital Television" mandatory—to ensure that commercials aren't louder than regular television. The CALM Act will go into effect on December 13, 2012.

Another federal agency with authority over some advertising is the Securities and Exchange Commission. The SEC is responsible for preventing the release of incomplete or fraudulent information about corporations whose stock is publicly traded. Thus, the SEC has responsibility for advertising regarding offerings of stock and certain other investment advertising. The agency exercises its authority by acting mainly against the corporation whose advertising is judged false, often by canceling stock offerings. It requires those who advertise stock offerings to make it clear that a media ad is neither an offer to sell nor a solicitation of an offer to buy, since media ads don't lend themselves to the highly detailed reporting of corporate information that is required. That information is provided in a prospectus.

Still another federal agency with authority over advertising is the Bureau of Alcohol, Tobacco and Firearms, which regulates alcoholic beverage labeling and advertising, among other things. The bureau has stirred controversy in recent years by sometimes refusing to allow winemakers to make health claims (even claims they could document) or to use reproductions of paintings by noted artists that included nudity in wine labels or advertising. Although the bureau has the authority to ban "obscene and indecent" wine ads, critics have accused its staff of acting arbitrarily in some of these situations.

Wine labels and advertising were at the center of another dispute in the mid-2000s. European vintners strenuously object to U.S. winemakers calling their products "Champagne," "Burgundy" or "Chablis." All are European geographic designations. Eventually U.S. and European negotiators joined in a World Trade Organization agreement that allows existing U.S. wines carrying those designations to be sold in Europe, while no new U.S. wines bearing those names can be exported to Europe. This cuts both ways: in 2007, Napa Valley, Calif. vintners won an agreement from the European Union that wines bearing the Napa name cannot be sold in Europe if the grapes are grown anywhere but the Napa region. This is not exactly a minor issue: Americans spend about $2.3 billion on European wines every year, while Europeans buy about $1 billion in American wines, almost all from California.

Napa Valley vintners have fought a separate wine label war against other California winemakers, eventually securing a state law that forbids the use of the "Napa" label on wines made from grapes grown in other parts of California. The restriction on the word Napa was upheld by the California Supreme Court in litigation aimed at Bronco Wine Co., which had purchased several trademarks that included Napa or Napa Valley names (see *Bronco Wine Co. v. Jolly*, 33 C.4th 943, 2004). Bronco even opened the largest wine production facility in Napa—to process grapes grown elsewhere. Bronco has a following for its low-cost wines, including "Two Buck Chuck," the Bronco-owned Charles Shaw label.

Another restriction on advertising is included in the federal Truth-in-Lending Act. "Regulation Z," adopted by the Federal Reserve Board to implement this act, requires advertisers to disclose a number of details about credit arrangements if the terms are mentioned at all in an ad. For instance, any quotation of an interest rate must include a declaration of the "annual percentage rate" (APR). Similarly, an ad that quotes a down payment or monthly payment must also disclose additional details of the financing: you cannot merely say a particular car sells for "$1000 down and $400 a month" without disclosing the other terms and the APR. Real estate and auto ads often fail to comply with Regulation Z, and the FTC occasionally launches well-publicized campaigns to force advertisers to obey the law.

Federal Lawsuits for Damages

Still another sanction for false advertising was created by Section 43(a) of the federal trademark law, the Lanham Act (discussed in Chapter Six). Under the Lanham Act's advertising fraud provisions, companies may file civil lawsuits against competitors whose advertising is false and detrimental to their business. Significantly, the Lanham Act now permits courts to award *treble damages* (i.e., three times the actual monetary damages) in these private false-advertising lawsuits. And the victims of false advertising may also win injunctions—court orders to halt the advertising.

A number of courts have awarded damages in federal false advertising lawsuits under the Lanham Act. A large advertising fraud judgment—$40 million—was affirmed by the U.S. Court of Appeals in *U-Haul International v. Jartran* (793 F.2d 1034, 1986). In that case, Jartran entered the move-yourself market with an aggressive advertising campaign, and U-Haul (Jartran's main competitor) sued. The court held that some of Jartran's claims were false and detrimental to U-Haul's business. The huge damage award was based on a projection of

U-Haul's lost profits ($20 million) plus the amount of money Jartran spent on false advertising (another $20 million).

The Lanham Act allows substantial damage awards not only against advertisers but also against *advertising agencies,* according to a 1992 federal court decision. In *The Gillette Co. v. Wilkinson Sword Inc.,* an unpublished decision of a federal district court in New York, the Friedman Benjamin advertising agency was ordered to pay almost $1 million in damages to The Gillette Co. for preparing ads that falsely claimed Wilkinson's shaving system provided a shave six times smoother than Gillette's.

Few advertising fraud cases filed under the Lanham Act have drawn more media attention than the "pizza wars" case, *Pizza Hut Inc. v. Papa John's Int'l Inc.* (227 F.3d 489, 2000). Papa John's ran an advertising campaign with the theme, "Better Ingredients, Better Pizza" and with follow-up ads comparing specific ingredients in its pizza and competitors' pizza. Pizza Hut sued, alleging that Papa John's ads were deceptive and intended to mislead customers. After a trial jury ruled in Pizza Hut's favor, Papa John's appealed. A federal appellate court overturned the verdict, ruling that Pizza Hut failed to prove that consumers were actually deceived sufficiently that their purchasing decisions were affected by Papa John's advertising claims, which the Court called "typical puffery." Proof not only that consumers were deceived, but also that the deception affected their purchasing decisions, is an element of a Lanham Act advertising fraud case. The Supreme Court declined to review this case in 2001. What is *puffery?* Puffery includes exaggerated claims that a reasonable consumer would not rely on or claims of product superiority so vague or subjective that consumers will generally recognize the claim as an exaggeration.

There are limitations to the Lanham Act's power, however. The Seventh Circuit said in 2010 in *Stayart v. Yahoo* (623 F.3d 436) that users cannot use the Lanham Act to sue search engines just because their names happen to pop up next to sponsored ads for objectionable products when typed in as searches. Beverly Stayart filed several unsuccessful district court cases alleging that the search engines should be liable for linking her name randomly to products of which she doesn't approve. She tried a number of different approaches, and the Seventh Circuit case was a Lanham Act challenge.

Stayart typed her name into Yahoo's search engine, and the results shocked her: "links to online pharmaceutical companies, links to pornographic websites, and links that directed her to other websites promoting sexual escapades." She sued Yahoo, alleging violations of the Lanham Act in Yahoo's associating her name with products she didn't endorse.

The court said Stayart did not have standing to sue because she didn't have a commercial interest in her name, a standard required by the Lanham Act. The act "is a private remedy for a commercial plaintiff who meets the burden of proving that its commercial interests have been harmed by a competitor."

■ STATE ADVERTISING REGULATION

Virtually all states also have laws empowering their officials to act against advertising fraud. At least 45 states have adopted various versions of what has been known as the "Printer's Ink Statute," an advertising fraud law first proposed in *Printer's Ink* magazine in 1911.

The statute makes advertising fraud a crime, giving state and local prosecutors the responsibility for enforcement. Because it is a criminal law that must be enforced by officials who often feel they have more serious crimes to worry about, enforcement has traditionally been lax. Recognizing the shortcomings of this law, most of the states have enacted other laws giving consumers and competitors civil remedies in instances of advertising fraud: victims of false advertising generally may sue for damages under state law as well as the federal Lanham Act. In addition, some states have given local and state prosecutors civil enforcement responsibilities much like those the FTC Act gave to the Federal Trade Commission. In a few other states, separate agencies have enforcement responsibilities.

Filling a Regulatory Vacuum

During the 1980s the Federal Trade Commission scaled back its efforts to prevent false or misleading advertising. Hamstrung by crippling budget cuts and commissioners who wanted the agency to tread softly in its enforcement efforts for philosophical reasons, the FTC came to be viewed as a paper tiger by many advertisers.

However, the chief legal officers in the 50 states launched a coordinated effort to step into this regulatory vacuum. In most states, the attorney general is charged with enforcing state advertising fraud laws; the attorneys general found that by acting together they could wield just about as much clout as the Federal Trade Commission did in earlier times.

Acting jointly through the National Association of Attorneys General (NAAG), the attorneys general adopted national guidelines for airline advertising in 1988 in an attempt to eliminate questionable airline advertising practices. Then NAAG went after what its members viewed as deceptive advertising by auto rental agencies: in 1989 NAAG adopted guidelines for policing ads by auto rental agencies. The 50 states were, in effect, putting national advertisers on notice that there are still nationwide rules to prevent advertising fraud—even if the FTC is no longer willing or able to enforce its own rules vigorously in every instance.

This coordinated effort to set up national standards for advertising truthfulness in the absence of FTC action was led by the attorneys general of California, New York, Texas and several other large states. The national rules governing auto rental advertising were announced in Washington, D.C., saying the NAAG's airline advertising guidelines led to a dramatic decline in deceptive advertising in that industry. At the same time, it was announced that the uniform national rules would tell car rental agencies clearly what is acceptable and unacceptable in their advertising.

By 1990, NAAG members had launched several other crackdowns on allegedly deceptive advertising. For example, they challenged dessert-maker Sara Lee for marketing as "Lite Classics" food items with no reduction in calories. They went after the Kraft Co. for marketing "Cheez Whiz" as cheese when it included ingredients not found in cheese. (The company agreed to call the product a "cheese food.") And they forced the Mobil Chemical Co. to stop selling Hefty trash bags as biodegradable when they would not biodegrade for many, many years in a typical trash disposal site. They also acted against cereal makers Kellogg and General Mills for making allegedly false health claims.

However, the state attorneys suffered a major setback in 1992 when the U.S. Supreme Court ruled that under the Airline Deregulation Act of 1978 only the U.S. Department of Transportation may regulate airline advertising (*Morales v. TWA*, 504 U.S. 374). In effect, the court said that in the absence of federal regulation, the airlines are free to do as they please in their advertising.

Writing for a 5-3 majority, Justice Antonin Scalia pointed out that the deregulation act prohibited the states from enforcing any laws "relating to rates, routes or services" of the airlines. Scalia concluded that advertising is "related" to fares; therefore, he said, only the federal government may regulate airline advertising.

That is *not* true in most other industries, though. This ruling had no effect on the other coordinated attacks on deceptive advertising by state attorneys general. The new pressure from the states has surely caused some advertisers to long for the old days when they only had to worry about one federal agency. Now they could be forced to defend themselves against advertising fraud charges in up to 50 different state legal actions at one time. Most advertisers feel that they have no choice but to follow the guidelines adopted by the 50 attorneys general. Ironically, soon after NAAG got its advertising regulation system going, the FTC itself became more aggressive in regulating advertising. For advertisers, the result could be more regulation than ever, with both NAAG and a revitalized FTC acting against allegedly false, misleading and unfair advertising practices.

Other State Regulations on Advertising

In a win for data mining companies, states may not regulate how prescribing data is used without meeting heightened scrutiny, said the Supreme Court in 2011. Several states had laws that banned using information gathered from pharmacies about doctors' prescribing history for the purposes of increasing drug sales. The practice, called "detailing," has pharmaceutical sales representatives meet individually with physicians to promote their wares, armed with data from pharmacies about prescribing histories. The First Circuit upheld these laws in New Hampshire law and Maine, but the Second Circuit overturned the Vermont law. The Supreme Court granted *cert* in the Vermont case to settle the matter. In *Sorrell v. IMS Health* (131 S. Ct. 2653), the Court said by a 6-3 vote that pharmaceutical marketing speech was protected by the First Amendment, and laws that regulate this speech must undergo heightened scrutiny which the Vermont law failed to meet in this case.

Justice Anthony Kennedy noted that Vermont had not alleged that the detailing information was false or misleading, so the law was simply premised on "a difference of opinion." He wrote for the Court:

> The State may not burden the speech of others in order to tilt public debate in a preferred direction. "The commercial marketplace, like other spheres of our social and cultural life, provides a forum where ideas and information flourish. Some of the ideas and information are vital, some of slight worth. But the general rule is that the speaker and the audience, not the government, assess the value of the information presented."

Justice Stephen Breyer, joined by Justices Ruth Bader Ginsburg and Elena Kagan, dissented. They would have found that the regulation of detailing was connected to an important government interest in regulating commercial speech and would have upheld the Vermont law, which would have survived a *Central Hudson* analysis.

Breyer wrote, "It (the Vermont law) deprives pharmaceutical and data-mining companies of data, collected pursuant to the government's regulatory mandate, that could help pharmaceutical companies create better sales messages. In my view, this effect on expression is inextricably related to a lawful governmental effort to regulate a commercial enterprise."

In *Int'l Dairy Foods Assoc. v. Boggs* (622 F.3d 628, 2010), the Sixth Circuit determined that Ohio's law prohibiting the labeling of milk from cows not treated with rBST (recombinant bovine somatotropin, also known as recombinant bovine growth hormone (rbGH)) with labels like "rBST free," "antibiotic-free" and "pesticide-free" was unconstitutional. The two kinds of milk were different, the court said, disagreeing with the FDA on the issue. After first finding that the labeling was not misleading, the court looked at the other parts of the *Central Hudson* test and noted that the Ohio law does not directly advance the state's interest and is more extensive than necessary. rBST has yet to be found in regular milk, the state argued; therefore, the statement "rBST free" is misleading and should be banned. But, said the court, there was another way: The claim 'rbST free,' when used in conjunction with an appropriate disclaimer, could assure consumers that the substance is definitively not in milk so labeled while also advising them that it has yet to be detected in conventional milk." Thus, since the rule burdens more speech than necessary, it must be struck down.

■ SELF-REGULATION

Another important influence on the content of advertising is self-regulation, the voluntary methods the advertising industry and the media have developed to prevent the release of false and distasteful advertising.

In 1971, four major advertising and business groups united to form an organization known as the National Advertising Review Council (NARC). The council is a cooperative venture of the American Association of Advertising Agencies, the American Advertising Federation, the Association of National Advertisers and the Council of Better Business Bureaus. NARC is housed at the Council of Better Business Bureaus, which has a staff-level National Advertising Division and a Children's Advertising Review Unit to do much of the administrative work of handling truth-in-advertising issues. Decisions may be appealed to a voluntary appeals body, the National Advertising Review Board.

With representation from national advertisers and advertising agencies as well as non-industry or public representatives, NARC accepts complaints about advertising and asks advertisers to substantiate their ad claims. The council asks advertisers to change their ads if they cannot be substantiated. If they refuse, the council is authorized to present its findings to a suitable government enforcement agency, but that is almost never necessary.

Although NARC's main tools are persuasion and peer pressure, it has dealt with hundreds of questionable advertisements and represents an excellent example of an industry endeavoring to keep its own house in order without government involvement.

For many years, the National Association of Broadcasters maintained similar voluntary codes for radio and television advertising and programming practices. Broadcasters who subscribed to these codes were allowed to display a "seal of good practice." At one time about 4,500 television and radio broadcasters were code subscribers.

The NAB codes set limits on the number of commercials broadcasters were to carry and also set standards for the content of both advertising and non-advertising materials. The NAB "Code Authority" and "Code Board" enforced these rules, although their only real enforcement power was to prevent violators from using the "seal of good practice."

However, in 1979 the U.S. Justice Department filed an antitrust lawsuit against the NAB, charging that the codes constituted a restraint of trade. By placing limits on the number of commercials and the amount of commercial time that would be permitted, the NAB codes artificially forced up ad rates, the government contended.

After losing the case in federal district court, the NAB signed a consent decree in 1982, agreeing to drop many of the provisions of the television code. To avoid any further potential antitrust liability, the NAB then decided to eliminate its codes altogether and to disband the Code Authority and Code Board. Thus, the broadcast industry's first major attempt at self-regulation fell victim to a government antitrust lawsuit. In the mid-2000s, the NAB was developing a new voluntary code.

In the print media, there is no industry-wide code of advertising practices. Various organizations have adopted codes of ethics, but they generally deal with editorial matters, not advertising. However, many major newspapers have their own policies on advertising acceptability, and these policies are very influential. The *New York Times* not only has an advertising acceptability policy but also a department that reviews ads prior to publication. That department independently checks advertising claims and bars future ads from those found to have violated the company's standards. The *New York Times* prohibits ads considered in bad taste and attacks on individuals or competing products, among others.

In 2011, the FTC announced that it would again review the voluntary rules (for the fourth time in 12 years) that alcoholic beverage advertisers use, and it is likely that social media advertising will be among the areas on which the agency will focus its attention.

■ ADVERTISING ON THE INTERNET

The explosive growth of Internet advertising led to a variety of government initiatives to regulate that advertising.

One major regulatory effort began in response to a public outcry: Congress passed a law to curb "spam," or unsolicited advertising by bulk e-mail. The technology of e-mail makes it easy to build an enormous mailing list—and to send a deluge of messages to everyone on that list. An advertiser can send messages to millions of e-mail addresses almost instantly and at virtually no cost. It was inevitable that such a powerful technology would be abused.

The federal *CAN-SPAM Act*, which went into effect in 2004, banned unsolicited commercial e-mail, preempting state anti-spam laws that were in some cases stricter than the federal law. The CAN-SPAM Act forbids sending unsolicited e-mail after any recipient has asked a spammer to discontinue it. It requires commercial e-mail to include a valid postal address, opt-out information and a reply mechanism. Spammers are required to remove opt-outs from their lists within 10 days. Violators may face both criminal and civil penalties. CAN-SPAM is still another Congressional acronym. The full name is "Controlling the Assault of Non-Solicited Pornography and Marketing Act."

The problem, of course, is that most spammers conceal their identity and provide no valid sender's address that would facilitate consumer opt-outs. Recognizing this problem, the federal CAN-SPAM Act forbids "spoofing," the practice of concealing a message's origin by using someone else's e-mail address. Like the ban on spam itself, the ban on spoofing has proven almost impossible to enforce.

The federal anti-spam law asked the Federal Trade Commission to consider developing a do-not-spam registry patterned after its largely successful do-not-call registry aimed at unsolicited telemarketing. In mid-2004, the FTC declined to set up a do-not-spam registry. The commissioners, voting unanimously, ruled that such a registry would do more harm than good because spammers would send even more unwanted e-mail to every address on the list. The FTC did launch well-publicized enforcement actions against a few spammers who could be tracked down, including four Detroit area residents who were sending out millions of messages to sell a fraudulent weight-loss patch. The FTC said the four were earning about $100,000 a month by selling the useless patches to consumers who responded to the spam messages. The FTC also said the four had caused innocent persons to receive thousands of complaints and sometimes to have their e-mail addresses blacklisted because the four were spoofing others' addresses.

Unfortunately for consumers, for every spammer that the FTC manages to catch, there are surely dozens of others who escape detection. In 2005, a year after the federal CAN-SPAM Act went into effect, Microsoft estimated that about 80 percent of all e-mail is spam, up from 50 to 60 percent before the law went into effect. Microsoft and other computer companies were working on technology-based solutions to the problem.

Questions were immediately raised about the constitutionality of the federal CAN-SPAM Act. However, courts have generally upheld state anti-spam laws. In 2001 the Washington Supreme Court upheld that state's anti-spam law in a case where a bulk e-mailer had been sending up to one million pieces of unsolicited e-mail a week promoting a $40 package he called, "How to profit from the Internet." The court declared that the Washington anti-spam law did not violate either the First Amendment or the interstate commerce clause of the U.S. Constitution (*Washington v. Heckel*, 24 P.3d 404). In 2002, an appellate court also upheld California's anti-spam law (*Ferguson v. Friendfinders*, 94 C.A.4th 1255).

A mass e-mailer did not run afoul of California law when it sent its e-mails from multiple domain names to avoid e-mail spam filters, said the California Supreme Court (*Kleffman v. Vonage Holdings*, 551 F.3d 847, 2010). The California law prohibits falsifying or misrepresenting header information, so as long as all e-mails contain correct header information, the law does not prohibit them—even though this technique tricks spam filters into thinking that the information comes from different sources.

But not all spammers are so fortunate: in 2010 Florida announced a $2.9 million settlement with ModernAd Media, LLC, after finding it in violation of the federal CAN-SPAM Act, which also prohibits misleading headers. ModernAd Media must now "disclose and prominently display all necessary information on internet-based advertisements necessary so consumers can make informed decisions before they agree to purchase products or participate in trial offers," according to the Florida attorney general's press release.

A plaintiff in 2010 got creative in his ongoing fight against spam: rather than relying on CAN-SPAM or state laws, he sued a domain name registrar—but failed. In *Balsam v. Tucows Inc.* (627 F.3d 1158), the Ninth Circuit rejected Daniel Balsam's attempt to hold Tucows, a domain name registrar, liable for refusing to provide a spammer's identity without a court order. Balsam claimed to have gotten over a thousand spam e-mails from an adult website. He sued the company under California's anti-spam law and got a default judgment of $1,125,000. There was only one problem: who could he collect it from? The company who owned the domain name ("adultactioncam.com") had opted into Tucow's privacy policy, so Balsam could not find out the name of the owner. He then demanded that Tucows turn over the name or be forced to pay the judgment itself.

Tucows, to be a registrar, had to agree to ICANN's (Internet Corporation for Assigned Names and Numbers) Registration Accreditation Agreement (RAA), which requires registrars to "accept liability for harm caused by wrongful use of the Registered Name, unless it promptly discloses the identity of the licensee to a party providing the Registered Name Holder reasonable evidence of actionable harm." In other words, Balsam claimed that Tucows would have to assume liability for the harm caused to Balsam if it did not give up the name of the person who owned the spamming website. But the court said Balsam was wrong: "Contrary to Balsam's arguments, nothing supports his claim that the parties to the RAA intended to benefit, or confer any rights upon, Balsam or any other third party."

The Ninth Circuit also dealt a blow to text message spam in 2009 in *Satterfield v. Simon & Schuster* (569 F.3d 946). Laci Satterfield sued Simon & Schuster for sending an unsolicited text message advertisement for a new Stephen King book to her son's cell phone. She claimed that the message violated the Telephone Consumer Protection Act because they were sent through an automatic telephone dialing system; Simon & Schuster said that there was no auto-dial system, no "calls" as defined by the law actually took place, and Satterfield agreed to the ads when she joined a ringtone download service.

The Ninth Circuit disagreed. The court said it was unclear whether an auto-dial system was used, a text message could reasonably be considered a call under FCC rules ("to communicate with or try to get into communication with a person by telephone"), and that no permission was given. The case was remanded.

Consumer advocates have also been concerned about outright fraud in advertising on websites. The FTC has launched a series of sweeps that targeted fraudulent e-commerce. One of the FTC's chief concerns was false, misleading or unfair health claims on the Internet: by 1999 the FTC had notified the owners of several hundred sites that their health claims could violate federal law. In a 1999 announcement, the FTC said about one-fourth of the sites that received such notices over a two-year period removed the questionable claims or shut down their websites altogether without any further federal enforcement action. The FTC said it was considering various options to deal with the others, including legal actions to halt false or misleading advertising.

In 2001, the FTC responded to Sept. 11 by going after websites that were exploiting the fear of terrorism by making false claims about cures for various diseases. The FTC warned operators of about 40 websites to remove claims that dietary supplements can cure anthrax or smallpox and also went after operators of websites claiming that products such as zinc mineral oil can cure anthrax. Sites offering gas masks, protective suits, mail sterilizers and products to detect the presence of anthrax also were warned to drop deceptive claims.

The Federal Trade Commission also took another step to combat false and misleading Internet advertising: the FTC added a section to its own website (www.ftc.gov) addressing the issue. The report has links to examples and mock ads that illustrate the FTC's suggestions for Internet advertising. While the information available on this site is only the FTC's opinion and is not legally binding, it is dangerous for any advertiser to ignore the FTC's published guidelines. In fact, the FTC's report, entitled "Dot Com Disclosures," also has links to many of the FTC's advisory *Guides* concerning advertising of various types of products and services, which should be of special interest to advertisers in the affected areas. In 2012, however, the agency was revisiting that report to update it.

A 2009 report from the FTC entitled "Self-Regulatory Principles For Online Behavioral Advertising" caused some to believe that the FTC was planning to increase its scrutiny of *online behavioral advertising*—defined by the FTC as "the practice of tracking an individual's online activities in order to deliver advertising tailored to the individual's interests."

In its report, the FTC offered four principles that the advertising industry should evaluate in crafting a self-regulatory plan for online behavioral advertising that look somewhat similar to those proposed for data privacy: transparency: "meaningful disclosures to consumers about the practice and choice about whether to allow the practice;" security: "reasonable data security measures so that behavioral data does not fall into the wrong hands, and ... retain data only as long as necessary for legitimate business or law enforcement needs; consent: "before a company uses behavioral data in a manner that is materially different from promises made when the company collected the data" and affirmative express consent for sensitive data: "for example, data about children, health, or finances..." It is clear that the FTC is interested in *opt-in* strategies, where consumers must *actively agree* to events before they occur, rather than *opt-out* ones, in which they must tell companies to *stop* doing something.

In essence, the FTC's position is that all of the consumer safeguards that apply in other kinds of advertising also apply online. That means all of the normal rules concerning deceptive and unfair practices must be observed by Internet advertisers. Internet advertisers must be prepared to substantiate their claims. And advertisers must make "clear and conspicuous" affirmative disclosures in many instances.

Also in 2009, the FTC said it would start evaluating bloggers and their endorsements and advertisements. The FTC's *Guides for the Use of Endorsements and Testimonials in Advertising*, or "Endorsement Guides," allow the agency to pursue both bloggers and companies that give them freebies or otherwise compensate them for reviews for false claims or failure to disclose conflicts of interest. What counts as an "endorsement?" The FTC defines endorsements as "any advertising message...that consumers are likely to believe reflects the opinions, beliefs, findings, or experiences of a party other than the sponsoring advertiser, even if the views expressed by that party are identical to those of the sponsoring advertiser."

The *Guide* raised several concerns. Critics expressed fears that the FTC may start investigating bloggers who do reviews without any compensation or freebies. They also pointed out the likely futility of trying to monitor hundreds of thousands of blogs, with new ones appearing daily. The FTC said it was primarily concerned about those who receive money for blogging positive reviews or who have an undisclosed marketing arrangement with a company. Google's sale of trademarks as keyword search terms also implicates Lanham Act concerns, as discussed in Chapter Six (*Rescuecom v. Google* and *Rosetta Stone v. Google*).

The first fine leveled under the new endorsement rules came in 2011 when the FTC fined a company that sold guitar lesson materials online $250,000 for deceptively advertising its products through online affiliates who posed as just ordinary customers or as independent reviewers. Legacy Learning Systems Inc., based in Nashville, did not reveal, as the *Guides* mandate, the fact that the online affiliates "received in exchange for substantial commissions on the sale of each product resulting from referrals"—resulting in sales of more than $5 million for Legacy.

What about employers' use of social media to screen potential employees? In the first case by the Federal Trade Commission to address this issue, data broker Spokeo settled for $800,000 on charges that it violated the Fair Credit Reporting Act. Although Spokeo did notify users on its site that the information was not to be used in violation of the act, the FTC said it "failed to revoke access to or otherwise ensure that existing users...did not use the company's website or information for [Fair Credit Reporting Act]-covered purposes" (*U.S. v. Spokeo, Inc.*, CV-12-05001, 2012).

■ AN OVERVIEW OF MAJOR ISSUES

As America undergoes a new revolution in communications technology, major questions about advertising and media economics are unanswered. In view of cable and satellite television, plus the declining market share of free, advertiser-supported broadcasting, is it certain that advertising will remain the dominant source of revenue for the media? What will happen if it isn't? Millions of people now devote a lot of their television-viewing time to advertising-free video programming such as movies on DVDs or DVRs. New technology makes it easier than ever for consumers to "zap" commercials that cost advertisers millions of dollars to put on the air. Will advertisers always be willing to pay the bills?

Criticism of cigarette advertising has been intense in recent years, but should there be an across-the-board ban on this advertising? There have been many other government efforts to regulate or forbid cigarette advertising. Does this really violate the First Amendment rights of tobacco companies, as the Supreme Court said in its *Lorillard Tobacco* decision? Are restrictions on cigarette ads an appropriate response to the problem of teen smoking? What about the proposed cigarette packaging regulations, with their dramatic images of death and disease? Will these survive constitutional scrutiny?

What role should Congress and the courts play in advertising regulation? Will the courts continue the trend, begun in 1975, toward constitutional protection for commercial speech? Or will the courts again say a message is protected only if its creator is in the business of selling ideas rather than products and services? Do the Supreme Court's *44 Liquormart, Greater New Orleans* and *Lorillard Tobacco* decisions mark the beginning of a new era of protection for commercial speech, even speech promoting a "vice?"

What about the high court's decision not to rule on the *Nike* case in 2003? Was Justice Breyer right when, in dissenting from the dismissal of Nike's appeal, he said even letting such a case go to trial will have a chilling effect on other corporations that wish to express their views on controversial issues?

What of the FTC's varying zeal in enforcing the law? If the FTC fails to aggressively enforce its rules forbidding false and misleading advertising, should other bodies step in? Will Congress step in and forbid advertising for some "harmful" products or services? Also, what role will self-regulation play in the future of advertising?

What of the trend toward enormous damage awards in false advertising lawsuits under the Lanham Act? Should the threat of *treble damages* for advertising fraud change the way advertising claims are verified before a campaign begins? Are these awards a threat to the freedom to engage in robust advertising?

And what about political advertising and campaign finance regulations? In the wake of the highly controversial and far-reaching *Citizens United* case, the Supreme Court has cast doubt on the constitutionality of many state and local regulations on campaign finance.

In short, are we moving into an era of new freedom for advertisers, or perhaps a new era of heavy government regulation of advertising?

WHAT SHOULD I KNOW ABOUT MY STATE?	• What are my state's advertising fraud and consumer protection laws? • How have those laws been interpreted to regulate advertising in my state? • What are my state's campaign finance laws? How will they fare under *Citizens United?*

SUMMARY

A SUMMARY OF ADVERTISING AND THE LAW

Is Advertising Protected by the First Amendment?

Until 1975, *commercial speech* was not generally protected by the First Amendment. However, since then the Supreme Court has extended some constitutional protection to commercial speech and greater protection to noncommercial corporate speech. While advertising has its own body of law, the general rules of media law, like libel and copyright, also apply to advertising.

Do Advertisers Have a Right of Access to the Media?

Generally, there is no right of access to the media. A publisher or broadcaster may accept or reject advertising at will, unless the acceptances and rejections fall into a pattern of unfair or monopolistic business practices. However, broadcasters (but not other media) must sell advertising to federal election candidates, and sometimes state-owned media are required to grant advertising access.

Who Regulates Advertising Content and Why?

The primary federal agency that regulates advertising is the Federal Trade Commission. To protect the public from false and misleading advertising, the FTC has a Congressional mandate to monitor advertising and act against practices it considers improper. The FTC's authority extends to all U.S. media, including online. It has several enforcement tools, including informal letters of compliance, consent decrees and formal cease and desist orders. The FTC may require substantiation of an advertising claim, and it may order corrective advertising if an ad has been particularly false or misleading. It issues formal trade regulation rules and advisory guides addressing specific advertising content.

Does Anyone Else Regulate Advertising?

Other federal agencies have authority over certain kinds of advertising. All 50 states have statutory laws prohibiting fraudulent business practices; some states vigorously enforce them against false advertisers, but some are less diligent. The National Association of Attorneys General has coordinated multistate legal actions against allegedly fraudulent advertising.

Does the Advertising Industry Self-Regulate?

The advertising industry has an elaborate system of self-regulation. The National Advertising Division (NAD), part of the Better Business Bureau, works with national advertisers to ensure that advertising meets regulatory standards and is fair. Decisions of the NAD can be appealed to the National Advertising Review Board.

14 *Freedom of the Student Press*

Almost all student media—no matter how well edited or produced—eventually face the wrath of administrators who don't like something in print, online or on the air. Official reactions vary from telephone calls or irate memos to outright censorship.

Although the student press has been censored for as long as there have been student newspapers, instances of censorship appear to rise and decline in cycles. Until the 1960s, administrative censorship seemed almost routine on many high school and college campuses. And when it happened, the staffs and their faculty advisers could do little about it.

The student protest era of the late 1960s changed that—for a while. Students in that period were unwilling to limit their expression to editorials bemoaning the lack of school spirit or urging students to keep the campus clean. Instead, many high school and college newspapers focused on issues such as war and peace, civil rights and later drug use, sexual orientation and other sensitive issues. Amazingly, many of them got away with it, creating a legacy of First Amendment protection that stood up in court for many years.

However, the trend was clearly away from campus press freedom by the 1980s, 1990s and 2000s—at least at the high school level. Many student editors then were less concerned about the great issues of the day than their predecessors had been. Perhaps the Supreme Court was responding to the mood of the times when it severely curtailed the freedom of high school journalists in 1988 and lower courts began hedging in some cases involving college students as well.

The Court first extended First Amendment protection to students in 1969; at least 125 other decisions followed that precedent, overruling administrative censorship of student publications and other campus expression. In case after case in the Vietnam war era, the courts ruled that public school and college administrators could not arbitrarily censor student expression. Whenever an instance of censorship involved state action (i.e., an act by a government employee such as a public school principal or college dean), the courts held that the First Amendment and other constitutional safeguards applied. At private institutions, though, school officials are not government officials; the courts have rarely found state action in their conduct. That creates a different problem, discussed later.

In the 1980s, the law came full circle: lower courts began wavering in their support of campus freedom, and then the Supreme Court handed down its famous (some would say infamous) *Hazelwood School District v. Kuhlmeier* ruling (484 U.S. 260, 1988), which held that the official student newspapers at high schools are *not* ordinarily protected by the First Amendment. The Court said in a footnote that it was not deciding in that case whether the same is true at the college level. In fact, the *Hazelwood* decision didn't even give administrators a free hand to censor official high school newspapers where there is a state law or local school policy forbidding administrative censorship. Nevertheless, the *Hazelwood* case signaled a clear reversal of the trend in court rulings on student press freedom. In 2005, a controversial federal appellate court decision held that *Hazelwood* applies to subsidized student media at the college level (*Hosty v. Carter*, 412 F.3d 731).

There are hundreds of confrontations between administrators and student journalists every year. Although many of these incidents involve blatant prior restraint that may not be legal even today, these acts of censorship often go unchallenged because no one has the money, the inclination or the legal resources to haul campus officials into court. This chapter discusses cases that *did* make it to court and produced legal precedents.

■ EARLY SUPREME COURT DECISIONS

In many areas of media law, the basic principles can be traced to a few landmark Supreme Court decisions, and student press freedom is one of those areas. In 1969, the Court ruled on the case of *Tinker v. Des Moines Independent Community School District* (393 U.S. 503), often called the "black armbands case." The case arose when John and Mary Beth Tinker, ages 15 and 13, and a 16-year-old friend were suspended for wearing black armbands at school as a symbolic protest of the Vietnam War. The Des Moines school principals had heard of the pending protest and hurriedly adopted a rule against wearing armbands on campus.

The suspension was challenged on First Amendment grounds. Two lower courts upheld the school officials' action, but the Supreme Court reversed, declaring the act symbolic speech, protected by the First Amendment. Justice Abe Fortas, writing for the Court, said:

> First Amendment rights, applied in the light of the special characteristics of the school environment, are available to teachers and students. It can hardly be argued that either students or teachers shed their constitutional rights to freedom of speech or expression at the schoolhouse gate.

The Court noted that the three students did nothing to disrupt the educational process. The court said, "In our system, state-operated schools may not be enclaves of totalitarianism. School officials do not possess absolute authority over their students."

However, the Court did make it clear that the rights of students were not "co-extensive" with the rights of adults off campus. The court said freedom could be suppressed when its exercise interferes with the rights of others or "would materially and substantially interfere with the requirements of appropriate discipline in the operation of the school."

Two More Supreme Court Rulings

During the early 1970s, the U.S. Supreme Court addressed the First Amendment status of college students in two noteworthy cases; both expanded students' rights on campus.

In the first of these cases, a chapter of the Students for a Democratic Society, a national student organization known for its militancy, sought official recognition as a campus group at Central Connecticut State College, and was turned down because of SDS' national reputation for disruptive tactics. Without official status, the group could not use campus facilities for meetings and other functions. The group sued, and in *Healy v. James* (408 U.S. 169, 1972), the Supreme Court said the local group couldn't be denied campus privileges merely because of the national organization's reputation. Public colleges "are not enclaves immune from the sweep of the First Amendment," the court said, ruling that the college president's decision abridged the students' constitutional rights.

A year later, in *Papish v. University of Missouri Curators* (410 U.S. 670), the high court overruled the expulsion of Barbara Papish, a graduate student and editor of the *Free Press*. Papish had previously angered university officials by distributing her paper when high school students and their parents were on campus, but when she published an issue they regarded as particularly indecent, they took action. The edition that led to the expulsion had a political cartoon depicting a policeman raping the Statue of Liberty and the Goddess of Justice, and a headline entitled, "Mother Fucker Acquitted."

The Supreme Court ruled that neither the cartoon nor the headline was obscene. Nor did Papish's activities "materially and substantially" interfere with campus order, the court said. The Court ordered Papish reinstated unless her expulsion could be justified on academic grounds, citing *Healy*: "We think *Healy* makes it clear that the dissemination of ideas—no matter how offensive to good taste—on a state university campus may not be shut off in the name alone of 'conventions of decency.'"

■ THE SUPREME COURT CHANGES THE RULES

By the late 1980s it was clear that the mood of the country had changed. The student protest era was over, and most school officials were determined to reassert their authority. The Supreme Court decided it was time to help the authorities do precisely that.

In its first rulings on the First Amendment rights of students since the heyday of the student protest movement, the Supreme Court sharply curtailed students' constitutional rights. Even before the landmark *Hazelwood* decision, the court began chipping away at students' First Amendment rights.

Ruling in 1986 in the case of *Bethel School District v. Fraser* (478 U.S. 675), the Supreme Court held that a Washington state high school student could be disciplined for delivering a speech containing sexual innuendoes, even though the speech contained no four-letter words and was clearly not obscene in a legal sense. Nor did the speech threaten to disruption the educational process.

The *Fraser* case began in 1983 when Matthew Fraser gave a speech at a Bethel High School assembly to endorse a friend's candidacy for a student body office. A state champion public speaker, Fraser avoided obscenity in the nominating speech, but he thoroughly amused those students who understood his innuendoes.

However, school administrators didn't think it was funny: they suspended Fraser for two days and removed his name from a list of candidates in a student election to select a graduation speaker. Fraser won the graduation speaker election on a write-in vote and school officials permitted him to speak at his graduation—but only after he filed the lawsuit that led to the Supreme Court decision.

The lower courts ruled that school officials had violated Fraser's First Amendment rights by suspending him, but the Supreme Court disagreed. Writing for a 7-2 majority, Chief Justice Warren Burger said, "The schools, as instruments of the state, may determine that the essential lessons of civil, mature conduct cannot be conveyed in a school that tolerates lewd, indecent, or offensive speech and conduct such as that indulged in by this confused boy." Burger took pains to distinguish this case from the landmark *Tinker v. Community School District* decision, in which the Supreme Court had strongly affirmed the First Amendment rights of students nearly 20 years earlier. Burger said this case was different because "the penalties imposed in this case were unrelated to any political viewpoint." In *Tinker*, students were punished for wearing black armbands to protest the Vietnam war.

It does not follow, Burger added, "that simply because the use of an offensive form of expression may not be prohibited to adults making what the speaker considers a political point, that the same latitude must be permitted to children in a public school." Significantly, the Court declined to use a *Tinker* analysis, which would have asked whether Fraser's speech was disruptive or violated others' rights—the two grounds for censorship in *Tinker*.

Having ruled against Matthew Fraser, the Supreme Court had little difficulty disposing of the *Hazelwood School District v. Kuhlmeier* case two years later. The Court ruled against the editors of *The Spectrum*, the student newspaper at Hazelwood East High School in Missouri. Their principal censored two articles they planned to publish: a story about teenage pregnancy that quoted students who had become pregnant, and an article in which students explained how their parents' divorces had affected them. None of the students' real names were used in the stories.

The Supreme Court held in a 5-3 decision that the principal was entitled to censor the articles even though they neither violated the rights of other students nor threatened to cause a campus disruption (the landmark *Tinker* ruling had permitted campus censorship for only these two reasons). Writing for the Court, Justice Byron White said, "We hold that educators do not offend the First Amendment by exercising editorial control over the style and content of student speech in school-sponsored expressive activities so long as their actions are reasonably related to legitimate pedagogical concerns."

White said school officials never intended for this student newspaper to be an open forum for student opinion like the "underground" and off-campus newspapers involved in so many earlier court decisions that upheld students' rights. Instead, White concluded, school officials "reserved the forum (i.e., the school newspaper) for its intended purpose, as a supervised learning experience for journalism students. Accordingly, school officials were entitled to regulate the contents of (the) *Spectrum* in any reasonable manner." White's majority opinion added:, "A school need not tolerate student speech that is inconsistent with its basic educational mission, even though the government could not censor similar speech outside the school...." How can the *Hazelwood* ruling be reconciled with the Court's strong affirmation of student rights in the original *Tinker* decision? White explained:

> The question whether the First Amendment requires a school to tolerate particular student speech—the question we addressed in *Tinker*—is different from the question whether the First Amendment requires a school affirmatively to promote particular student speech. The former question addresses educators' ability to silence a student's personal expression that happens to occur on the school premises. The latter question concerns educators' authority over school-sponsored publications, theatrical productions, and other expressive activities that students, parents, and members of the public might reasonably perceive to bear the imprimatur of the school.

Justice William Brennan wrote a dissenting opinion in which he and two other justices who often took liberal positions on First Amendment issues (Thurgood Marshall and Harry Blackmun) condemned the message the majority was sending to students:

> The young men and women of Hazelwood East expected a civics lesson, but not the one the Court teaches them today.... Such unthinking contempt for individual rights is intolerable from any state official. It is particularly insidious from one to whom the public entrusts the task of inculcating in its youth an appreciation for the cherished democratic liberties that our Constitution guarantees.

Nevertheless, the precedent from the *Hazelwood* case is clear: the First Amendment does not ordinarily protect official student newspapers (and other school-sponsored activities,

FIG. 70. The original "Bong Hits" banner at the Newseum, Washington, D.C.

Public domain image by Mlschafer, via Wikimedia Commons.

such as drama productions) from administrative control. However, this does not necessarily mean that school newspapers have no protection at all from administrative censorship: the Supreme Court ruling did not invalidate state laws and local policies that protect the free-press rights of student journalists. All the Court really said was that, in the absence of any other rules barring administrative censorship, the First Amendment does not protect student newspapers from such censorship.

The legislatures in about 20 states have considered laws that would extend some protection from administrative censorship to high school journalists. At least seven states—Arkansas, California, Colorado, Iowa, Kansas, Massachusetts and Oregon—now have such laws. Oregon's law, enacted in 2007, almost failed in the state Senate, passing on a 16-14 vote only after it was weakened. It was the first to cover both high school and college media in a single bill, but to win Senate approval the bill's sponsors had to delete a provision declaring the student media to be public forums and also a provision protecting media advisers from retaliatory dismissals. In 2007, Illinois enacted a law protecting the freedom of college but not high school student media. It is discussed later.

California's high school student press law, the nation's first, was enacted in 1977, long before the *Hazelwood* decision. This law—Education Code Section 48907—prohibits administrative censorship of school newspapers unless the content is obscene, libelous or likely to cause disruptive or unlawful acts. A California appellate court specifically ruled that Section 48907 remains valid after the *Hazelwood* decision (see *Leeb v. DeLong*, 198 C.A.3d 47, 1988).

In 2007—almost 20 years after *Hazelwood*—another California appellate court interpreted Section 48907 broadly enough to protect a student journalist who published an anti-immigrant column in a high school newspaper (*Smith v. Novato Unified School District*, 150 C.A.4th 1439). Administrators tried to justify censoring the paper by *predicting* that the column might cause a disturbance. The court said, "A school may not prohibit student speech simply because it presents controversial ideas and opponents of the speech are likely to cause a disruption. Schools may only prohibit speech that incites disruption, either because it specifically calls for a disturbance or because the manner of expression (as opposed to the content of the ideas) is so inflammatory that the speech itself provokes the disturbance."

While the *Hazelwood* decision applies only to official school-sponsored activities, students who express controversial views in unofficial newspapers or in other ways may be punished by methods that do not involve direct prior restraint—as Matthew Fraser was, with the Supreme

Court's blessing. Students who feel strongly enough about an issue to go to the trouble of publishing an unofficial newspaper or tract often end up including offensive language as well as political rhetoric. Under the *Fraser* precedent, school officials may justify punishing them on the basis of the language alone.

Under the *Tinker* rule, school officials were allowed to abridge students' First Amendment rights only when the exercise of those rights might disrupt the orderly educational process or violate the rights of others. Under the *Hazelwood* rule, no threat of a disruption is needed to justify censorship. Instead, the First Amendment no longer prevents school officials from restricting students' rights whenever there is a violation of what school officials consider to be the proper standards of good taste and decency for students.

That point was underscored in a 2007 U.S. Supreme Court decision that upheld a high school principal's seizure of a banner with the slogan, "Bong Hits 4 Jesus." Ruling in *Morse v. Frederick* (551 U.S. 393), a 5-4 decision with several concurring and dissenting opinions, the court said because the message on the banner could be interpreted as advocating illegal drug use, it was not protected by the First Amendment. In an opinion by Chief Justice John G. Roberts, the court again declined to use a *Tinker* analysis. Although there was no disruption of the educational process and no evidence of a violation of the rights of others (the two circumstances when *Tinker* allowed student speech to be suppressed), the apparent advocacy of drug use was enough to justify censorship, Roberts said.

Joseph Frederick, then a student at Juneau-Douglas (Alaska) High School, was suspended for 10 days for displaying his "Bong Hits 4 Jesus" banner across the street from the school as the Olympic Torch Relay was passing by—in what he acknowledged was an attempt to get on national television. The torch relay was an event leading up to the Winter Olympics in Salt Lake City in 2002. Principal Deborah Morse crossed the street, confronted Frederick, crumpled the banner and suspended him. He sued, alleging a violation of his First Amendment rights and seeking money damages from Morse. School officials did not claim that displaying the banner disrupted the torch relay or school activities, but they said it interfered with the school's goal of promoting a drug-free environment.

Reversing a ruling of the Ninth Circuit, the Supreme Court said Frederick's "Bong Hits" message had no First Amendment protection. The court conceded that Frederick or anyone else would have the right to display that banner off campus, but the court said Frederick was surrounded by other students and faculty at a school "social event or class trip" across the street from the school during school hours.

Emphasizing the limited scope of this decision, two of the five-member majority, Justices Samuel Alito and Anthony Kennedy, filed a concurring opinion in which they said they voted with Roberts only because the issue was drug use. They emphasized that the decision would not allow any restriction on political or social advocacy by students. Justice Stephen Breyer said he would have ruled in favor of the principal only because he thought she shouldn't face monetary damages for a decision she had to make on the spur of the moment. Breyer favored avoiding the First Amendment issue altogether. In dissent, three other justices argued strongly that Frederick's banner should be protected by the First Amendment. "That the court believes such a silly message can be proscribed as advocacy [of drug use] underscores the novelty of its position, and suggests that the principle it articulates has no stopping point," Justice John Paul Stevens wrote in dissent.

Student speech decisions continue to be a mixed bag. For example, in three Eighth Circuit cases in 2008 and 2009, there were several outcomes.

Black armbands made a return to the courts in 2008, and in the circuit in which *Tinker* originated. In *Lowry v. Watson Chapel School District* (540 F.3d 752), the Eighth Circuit upheld students' rights to wear protest armbands. Arkansas student Chris Lowry and others wore black armbands to protest a school dress code and were disciplined. The facts in *Lowry* were nearly identical to those in the *Tinker* case, but administrators tried to distinguish by saying that the issue was not the Vietnam war but merely a dress code. The court was not convinced: "In both cases, a school district punished students based on their non-disruptive protest of a government policy." The Supreme Court declined to hear the district's appeal.

In *Riehm v. Engelking* (538 F.3d 952, 2008), the Eighth Circuit affirmed the dismissal of a case brought against school officials and Cook County, Minn., by high school student David Riehm and his mother, Colleen. Riehm had written several essays that his English teacher found both frightening and offensive and that resulted in Riehm's psychiatric evaluation. The court dismissed the case against the county for insufficient evidence and found one of the essays to be a true threat and thus unprotected.

In the final Eighth Circuit case, *B.W.A. v. Farmington R-7 School District* (554 F.3d 734, 2009). B.W.A., a minor, wore clothing to school featuring the Confederate flag and was suspended. He filed a civil rights claim, asserting that his First Amendment rights had been violated. The Eighth Circuit said that "schools may act proactively to prohibit race-related violence." The court, in dismissing the student's case against the Missouri school district, added that "the school's ban on the flag was reasonably related to a substantial disruption, did not amount to viewpoint discrimination, and did not violate the First Amendment."

■ COLLEGIATE FALLOUT FROM HAZELWOOD

The *Fraser* and *Hazelwood* cases had far-reaching implications for the legal rights of students, implications that extended well beyond a student's right to publish news stories about divorce and pregnancy or to give a speech containing a few sexual innuendoes. *Hazelwood's* impact has been felt even at the college level. While a footnote in *Hazelwood* said the court was not ruling on the status of student publications at the college level, a U.S. Supreme Court decision such as that one inevitably has an impact on courts that rule on the scope of First Amendment freedoms on college campuses. In recent years, several federal appeals courts have held that *Hazelwood* does apply to college students, although other courts have disagreed.

A year after the *Hazelwood* decision, a federal appellate court said that if student activities (including campus newspapers) are

---

Focus on...
The "bong hits" case

The Supreme Court's majority opinion in *Morse v. Frederick* was that the message on Joseph Frederick's banner was advocacy of drug use and therefore acceptable for school officials to censor. But other justices had interesting things to say in their concurring and dissenting opinions.

Justice Clarence Thomas concurred and would overturn *Tinker* too: "As originally understood, the Constitution does not afford students a right to free speech in public schools."

But Justice John Paul Stevens issued a scathing commentary on the majority's view of the banner's meaning: "To the extent the Court independently finds that "BONG HiTS 4 JESUS" objectively amounts to the advocacy of illegal drug use—in other words, that it can most reasonably be interpreted as such—that conclusion practically refutes itself. This is a nonsense message, not advocacy."

part of the curriculum, they may not enjoy full First Amendment protection (*Alabama Student Party v. Student Gov't Assn.*, 867 F.2d 1344, 1989).

However, in the 2000s federal courts ruled both ways on this issue. In 2001, the Sixth Circuit decisively supported the First Amendment rights of the college media in *Kincaid v. Gibson* (236 F.3d 342). The court, ruling *en banc*, held that Kentucky State University officials violated the First Amendment by impounding all copies of the KSU yearbook in 1994.

Earlier, a three-judge panel of that court ruled that KSU administrators did not violate the First Amendment because the yearbook was not a public forum protected by the First Amendment. Campus officials objected to the yearbook for several reasons, including its color (purple), the lack of captions for many of the photographs, and the inclusion of considerable off-campus material.

In the later ruling, the judges held that the KSU *Thorobred* yearbook was a limited public forum and could not be arbitrarily censored by administrators. Significantly, the court ruled that the U.S. Supreme Court's *Hazelwood* decision does not apply to student publications at the college level, at least in this particular instance. The eight-judge majority even said campus media that are nonpublic forums cannot be censored if the censorship is not *viewpoint-neutral.*

To reach its conclusion that the yearbook was a limited forum entitled to substantial First Amendment protection, the majority analyzed KSU's written policy governing the yearbook, the actual practice of the university in overseeing it, the nature of the yearbook as an expressive activity and the campus context.

After the *en banc* decision, KSU officials settled the case by agreeing to pay $5,000 to each of the two students who had brought the lawsuit plus $60,000 in attorney's fees. KSU also agreed to release the impounded yearbooks and attempt to distribute them to the students who were entitled to receive them seven years earlier.

On the other hand, in 2005 the Seventh Circuit rejected the Sixth Circuit's reasoning and applied *Hazelwood* to college students in *Hosty v. Carter* (cited earlier). In another *en banc* decision, the court voted 7-4 to overturn an earlier decision by a three-judge panel of the Seventh Circuit and to limit the First Amendment rights of student journalists in that circuit (which covers Illinois, Indiana and Wisconsin).

In *Hosty,* Patricia Carter, the dean of student affairs at Governors State University near Chicago, had ordered the printer of the student newspaper, *The Innovator,* not to publish future issues until she had a chance to review and approve the copy. Margaret Hosty and other newspaper staffers sued, alleging that this prior administrative review violated the First Amendment. Initially, the three-judge panel agreed, holding that the *Hazelwood* principle does not apply at the college level. The court also ruled that the law on this point is so clear that Carter could be held personally liable and forced to pay damages for violating the students' First Amendment rights.

Then the three-judge panel's decision was withdrawn and the *en banc* panel ruled that Carter had qualified immunity from being personally liable because the law does not clearly support the students' position. In fact, the majority said that student freedom must be analyzed under *Hazelwood*. The court said: "We hold, therefore, that *Hazelwood* framework applies to subsidized student newspapers at colleges as well as elementary and secondary schools." Under that standard, administrative censorship is not barred by the First Amendment. The majority opinion, written by Judge Frank Easterbrook, also said, "There is no sharp difference between high school and college newspapers," alluding to the fact that some are financially subsidized or produced by journalism classes, or both. *The Innovator* was subsidized but not produced by a class.

However, the court also said that a student newspaper could be a "designated public forum." If it is, it would be protected by the First Amendment. In 2006, the U.S. Supreme Court declined to review the *Hosty* decision.

The *Hosty* case prompted strong reactions across the country. It was widely condemned by journalism educators and First Amendment advocates. The Student Press Law Center, which filed an *amicus curiae* brief ("friend of the court," a legal brief supporting a position) supporting the students in *Hosty,* issued a statement downplaying the significance of the case for student newspapers. The SPLC said many newspapers would qualify as public forums, although *Hosty* could curtail other forms of student expression. The SPLC also emphasized the point that *Hosty* is a binding legal precedent in only three states.

While federal circuit court decisions are binding only within the particular circuit, such rulings carrying considerable legal weight in other circuits. In fact, many of the earlier federal appellate court decisions upholding student press freedom have been widely cited outside the particular circuits in which they originated.

Christine Helwick, the general counsel for the 400,000-student California State University system, issued a memo to campus presidents in 2005 that discussed the impact of *Hosty* in California. She said the case suggested that they may have "more latitude than previously believed to censor the content of subsidized student newspapers."

That may have been true, but not for long. In 2006 the California legislature enacted a new law forbidding administrative censorship of student newspapers at public colleges and universities in the state. The law amended Section 66301 of the state's Education Code, a general free-expression law, to include this language: "Nothing in this section shall be construed to authorize any prior restraint of student speech or the student press."

The Illinois legislature passed a similar law, the College Campus Press Act, in 2007 taking direct aim at *Hosty* in the state where the case arose. The Illinois law declares that all campus media at public colleges and universities are public forums. Then it says: "Campus media, whether campus-sponsored or noncampus-sponsored, is not subject to prior review by public officials of a state-sponsored institution of higher learning... Collegiate student editors of campus media are responsible for determining the news, opinions, feature content and advertising content of campus media. This section does not prevent a collegiate media adviser from teaching professional standards of grammar and journalism to collegiate student journalists. A collegiate media adviser must not be terminated, transferred, removed, otherwise disciplined or retaliated against for refusing to suppress protected free expression rights of collegiate student journalists and of collegiate student editors..." The Illinois law also protects public colleges from lawsuits based on the content of student media.

In *Moore v. Watson* (2012 U.S. Dist. LEXIS 33167), the Illinois College Campus Press Act was found to protect campus newspapers from administrative censorship. Chicago State University's paper *Tempo's* editor-in-chief George Providence and adviser Gerian Moore brought suit against the university because administration had fired Moore and caused Providence to withdraw. Providence alleged that the university administrators had forced him "to submit newspaper copy for prepublication review, delayed the paper's publication, imposed restrictions on interviews with University staff, withdrew funding for the paper, and locked Providence out of the newspaper office." Relying both on the Campus Press Act and the Constitution, the judge said that Providence should be readmitted to school and

Moore be reinstated, because the university "are barred by the First Amendment from taking 'adverse action against the student newspaper, including engaging in conduct designed to chill the speech contained in future editions, on the basis of the views expressed in the publication unless such action served a compelling government interest.'"

In 2008, California adopted the Journalism Teacher Protection Act, which applies to both high school and college advisers. It amends several sections of the Education Code, and it says that "an employee shall not be dismissed, suspended, disciplined, reassigned, transferred, or otherwise retaliated against for acting to protect a pupil engaged in the conduct authorized under this section, or conduct that is protected by the First Amendment to the United States Constitution or Section 2 of Article I of the California Constitution."

The law was passed as a reaction to an increased number of instances in California where administrators pressure, and sometimes retaliate against, advisers over student speech. Under the law, students also do not lose their right to sue for censorship or retaliation they experienced while in school when they graduate.

Distribution of Off-campus Newspapers

May an *off-campus* newspaper be distributed on campus if the administration objects? Several court decisions have addressed that issue, including *Hays County Guardian v. Supple* (969 F.2d 111, 1992). A federal appellate court held that administrators at Southwest Texas State University could not use a rule against commercial solicitation on campus to severely restrict the distribution of a free, advertiser-supported community newspaper.

Focus on...
"Boobies" in school

You've probably seen them on the street or on campus: brightly colored silicone bracelet with slogans on them, made popular by Lance Armstrong's "LiveStrong" campaign for cancer research.

An organization named Keep A Breast (keep-a-breast.org) created a series of bracelets to support breast health and cancer prevention and early detection. These bracelets were emblazoned with the phrases "I ♥ Boobies"

FIG. 71. "I ♥ Boobies" bracelets.

Author's collection.

and "Keep A Breast." They became popular with students at colleges, high schools, junior highs and even grade schools—sometimes running afoul of dress codes that forbid sexual references.

Some students decided to fight back—with mixed results. A Pennsylvania court supported two girls who wore the bracelets. Citing *Tinker* and *Fraser*, the judge wrote: "The bracelets are intended to be and they can reasonably be viewed as speech designed to raise awareness of breast cancer and to reduce stigma associated with openly discussing breast health" (*B.H. v Easton Area Sch. Dist.*, 827 F. Supp. 2d 392, 2011). But a federal judge in Wisconsin refused to allow the bracelets, saying, "It is reasonable for school officials to conclude that this phrase is vulgar and inconsistent with their goal of fostering respectful discourse by encouraging students to use 'correct anatomical terminology' for human body parts" (*K.J. v. Sauk Center Sch. Dist.*, 3:11-cv-00622-bbc, 2012). The Easton school district appealed the Pennsylvania case to the Third Circuit, which heard oral arguments in April 2012. Stay tuned.

The court noted that campus officials allowed unfettered distribution of the official student newspaper (which contained advertising) as well as literature that did not include advertising. The court noted that ads in a newspaper do not reduce its First Amendment protection. The campus had the characteristics of a public forum—where the distribution of newspapers could not be arbitrarily restricted. College officials could adopt reasonable time, place and manner regulations, but they could not enforce distribution rules so restrictive that they severely curtailed a community newspaper's ability to reach students.

Campus Newspaper Theft

In recent years a new problem has plagued many college newspapers: large-scale newspaper thefts that in some cases were condoned if not encouraged by campus administrators. By 2006, there had been incidents on at least 200 campuses in which someone or some group systematically removed the entire press run of a newspaper from the newsracks. Sometimes the act was a protest against a specific story or the newspaper's editorial policies in general, but on other occasions there was no discernible reason for the theft. In some cases, campus police acted to halt newspaper thefts and to apprehend those who cleaned out the newsracks. But on other campuses administrators ordered the police *not* to act and openly sided with the thieves. Since most campus papers are free for the taking, some administrators refused to accept that taking the entire press run was even a wrongful act, despite the fact that the cost of printing replacement copies runs into hundreds or thousands of dollars.

The Student Press Law Center responded to this problem by suggesting that campus newspapers include a statement saying individual copies are free, but multiple copies carry a substantial charge. This at least makes it more clear that taking the entire press run is theft. However, even that has not worked on some campuses: some administrators have decreed that such a statement would constitute the imposition of an illegal new student fee.

On many college campuses, administrators are well aware that they cannot directly censor the student media without risking a lawsuit and a lot of bad publicity. But with a wink and a nod, they can certainly encourage someone else to do the dirty work for them by rounding up all the copies of an offending newspaper.

In 2003, a federal appeals court held that off-duty sheriff's deputies who purchased all available copies of a newspaper from newsracks and stores may have violated the publisher's federally protected rights in *Rossignol v. Voorhaar* (316 F.3d 516). While this case didn't involve a student newspaper, it did offer a possible legal remedy for large-scale newspaper theft by employees at a public college or university. In this case, the appellate court said the deputies, who systematically bought all copies of a newspaper critical of the local sheriff and his allies on the eve of an election, may have violated a federal civil rights law. A federal judge later ruled that the deputies violated the publisher's First Amendment rights and were not immune to liability under the civil rights law.

In 2007 the California legislature passed the California Newspaper Theft Law, making it a misdemeanor to take more than 25 copies of a free paper with the intent of recycling or selling the papers, stopping others from reading it, or harming a business competitor.

Campus Advertising and the First Amendment

Another troubling question on some campuses is whether the campus media have the right to accept controversial advertising: what happens if the administration or state officials order a campus newspaper to reject alcoholic beverage advertising, for example?

Alternately, what happens if the staff decides on its own not to accept a certain kind of advertising?

This question has been litigated for 40 years. In the 1960s federal courts in New York and Wisconsin overturned state-supported school and college administrators' efforts to keep student newspapers from accepting ads that espoused controversial ideas. Some of the same issues were raised in the 1970s when a federal appellate court rejected an appeal for access to the ad columns of the Mississippi State University newspaper in *Mississippi Gay Alliance v. Goudelock* (536 F.2d 1073, 1976). The Gay Alliance wanted to place an announcement of its services and was turned down by the staff. The court said this case was different from previous public school advertising access cases because here the staff, as opposed to the administration, rejected the ad. Hence, there was no state action in this decision to reject advertising from a gay organization. But in addition, the court said previous court decisions had given the editors final say over the content anyway.

The Third Circuit overturned a Pennsylvania law banning alcoholic beverage advertising in campus media as a violation of the First Amendment. In 2004, the court ruled in favor of *The Pitt News*, the student newspaper at the University of Pittsburgh (*Pitt News v. Pappert*, 379 F.3d 96). In a decision written by Samuel Alito, now a Supreme Court justice, the appellate court noted that *The Pitt News*, a financially independent, advertiser-supported newspaper, derived a significant part of its revenue from alcoholic beverage advertising before the state barred alcoholic beverage advertisers from placing ads in campus media in 1996. After that, several off-campus publications distributed on campus alongside *The Pitt News* continued to carry alcohol ads, but not *The Pitt News*. Because of the obvious financial implications of this state law, *The Pitt News* challenged its constitutionality.

At first, the courts had sided with the state. In 2000, the Third Circuit declined to overturn the law because the ban applied only to advertisers, leaving the newspaper free to say whatever it wanted about alcoholic beverages or the establishments that serve them, as long the paper didn't get paid (*Pitt News v. Fisher*, 215 F.3d 354). In that case, the court relied on the *Central Hudson* test (see Chapter Thirteen) to uphold the law as a restriction on commercial speech.

The Pitt News pursued the case further and eventually prevailed when the Third Circuit heard a later appeal and accepted the argument that because the policy financially burdened the campus newspaper while benefiting its off-campus competitors, it singled out one medium of communication as opposed to others for disfavored treatment. Citing classic Supreme Court decisions on newspaper taxation such as *Grosjean v. American Press* and *Minneapolis Star & Tribune v. Minnesota Commissioner of Revenue* (discussed in

Chapter Three), Judge Alito wrote: "If the government were free to suppress disfavored speech by preventing potential speakers from being paid, there would not be much left of the First Amendment."

But the Fourth Circuit upheld a state ban on some kinds of alcohol advertising in college newspapers in 2010 in *Educational Media Company at Virginia Tech v. Swecker* (602 F.3d 583). Ignoring the Third Circuit's decision in the *Pitt News* case, the court used a *Central Hudson* analysis and acknowledged that the state has a substantial interest in reducing student drinking that is met by reducing alcohol advertising in student media, which, the court pointed out, "'college student publications' primarily target college students and play an inimitable role on campus" and establishments that sell alcohol want to advertise there. The ban is not complete, the court noted, because it targets only certain types of alcohol ads, allows ads associated with restaurants, and "only applies to 'college student publications'—campus publications targeted at students under twenty-one." The dissenting judge would have invalidated the law using the *Pitt News* analysis.

Campus Fees, Campus Groups and Student Freedom

In 1995, the U.S. Supreme Court ruled on another aspect of student press freedom: the right of a religious student group to receive university printing subsidies if other groups receive such subsidies. In *Rosenberger v. Rector and Visitors of the University of Virginia* (515 U.S. 819), the high court ruled that the University of Virginia had to pay for the printing of a Christian student newspaper from its Student Activities Fund if it paid for the printing of other student groups' newspapers. In so ruling, the 5-4 majority held that the First Amendment's *establishment clause* (which has been interpreted to forbid government sponsorship of religious activities such as prayers in public schools) does not require a public university to withhold support from a religious student newspaper when it supports other publications produced by student organizations.

Writing for the majority, Justice Anthony Kennedy said the university was engaged in *viewpoint discrimination* in violation of the free expression provisions of the First Amendment because it favored student newspapers expressing certain viewpoints over others. The viewpoint discrimination in the university's action was "a denial of the right of free speech and would risk fostering a pervasive bias or hostility to religion, which could undermine the very neutrality (toward religion) the Establishment Clause requires," Kennedy wrote.

The Supreme Court ruled on a related case concerning student fees at universities in 2000. This time the court held that a public university may grant money derived from mandatory student fees to controversial organizations as long as the money is available to various groups on a *viewpoint-neutral* basis. Ruling in *Board of Regents v. Southworth* (529 U.S. 217), the court rejected a challenge by conservative students to the University of Wisconsin's practice of awarding student fee money to groups with which these students disagreed.

Writing for a unanimous court this time, Justice Kennedy said that it does not violate the First Amendment for student fee monies to be given to groups that espouse controversial viewpoints. Although this does force students to pay fees that go to groups with which they may disagree, Kennedy said this is not unconstitutional as long as the fee-granting process is open to a wide variety of organizations with divergent viewpoints. This is different from a situation where students (or government employees) might be forced to pay fees to support only one specific viewpoint, Kennedy said. The court has held that government workers may not be forced to pay dues that support a union's political activities, for instance. In contrast, here the mandatory student fee money was given to many different groups with varying viewpoints—not just to a group representing one viewpoint.

The Supreme Court ordered a lower court to make sure that the fee-granting system at Wisconsin really is viewpoint-neutral before reaching a final decision on this case. This case differs from the *University of Virginia* case in that the student-fee-awarding policy there was *not* viewpoint-neutral: student fee money was denied to campus publications produced by religious groups while being awarded to groups producing non-religious publications.

In 2010, the Supreme Court supported a public law school's decision to deny a religious student organization official campus status because the bylaws of the organization did not comply with the university's non-discrimination policy, which included a provision that students could not be denied membership in organizations based on religion or sexual orientation (*Christian Legal Society v. Martinez*, 130 S. Ct. 2971). The Christian Legal Society required its members to sign a "Statement of Faith" and agree to adhere to other religious tenets. This violated Hastings Law School's "all-comers" policy that allows open eligibility for student group membership.

The Ninth Circuit upheld the law school's decision, and the Court agreed. Writing for a 5-4 Court, Justice Ruth Bader Ginsburg said that "[c]ompliance with Hastings' all-comers policy...is a reasonable, viewpoint-neutral condition on access to the student-organization forum." She said that the policy was reasonable and content-/viewpoint-neutral: "It is, after all, hard to imagine a more viewpoint-neutral policy than one requiring *all* student groups to accept *all* comers." She also said that the policy was "all the more creditworthy" because it allowed law students "substantial alternative channels" for communication.

In dissent, Justice Samuel Alito, writing for himself and Justices Antonin Scalia, Clarence Thomas, and Chief Justice John Roberts, said that the policy was not viewpoint-neutral, adding, "Brushing aside inconvenient precedent, the Court arms public educational institutions with a handy weapon for suppressing the speech of unpopular groups—groups to which, as Hastings candidly puts it, these institutions 'do not wish to...lend their name[s].'"

The Ninth Circuit said that the *Christian Legal Society* decision required it to uphold the non-discrimination policy of San Diego State University as content- and viewpoint-neutral. Thus, a religious fraternity and sorority, having been denied official standing by San Diego State, could not claim that the rule was unconstitutional. However, the court did say that it may be that the policy was not fairly applied and remanded the case to determine if it was (*Alpha Delta Chi v. Reed*, 648 F.3d 790, 2011). The Supreme Court denied *cert.*

Other College First Amendment Questions

By the early 2000s, a number of courts had upheld the First Amendment rights of students and others on college campuses in several other contexts. For example, in 2001 the Seventh Circuit upheld the right of students to present a controversial play at the Fort Wayne campus of Indiana University-Purdue University in *Linnemeir v. Board of Trustees of Purdue University* (260 F.3d 757). The play, *Corpus Christi,* depicts a Christ-like figure as a gay man and has language that is offensive to many Christians. A group of residents sued to halt the student performance, contending that by allowing a presentation of anti-Christian material, the university was violating the First Amendment's establishment of religion clause, which requires separation of church and state.

The appellate court rejected that argument and allowed the play to be presented, ruling that to stop the play would violate the students' First Amendment free-expression rights.

Writing for the court, Judge Richard A. Posner said, "The contention that the First Amendment forbids a state university to provide a venue for the expression of views antagonistic to conventional Christian beliefs is absurd. It would imply that teachers in state universities could not teach important works by Voltaire, Hobbes, Hume, Darwin, Mill, Marx, Nietzsche, Freud, Yates... and countless other staples of Western culture."

But the Ninth Circuit ruled in 2001 that a college violated the First Amendment by prohibiting the expression of Christian beliefs on campus. In *Orin v. Barclay* (272 F.3d 1207), the court said Olympic Community College in Bremerton, Wash., violated the free speech rights and free exercise of religion rights of anti-abortion demonstrators by forbidding them to discuss the religious basis for their beliefs. College officials imposed conditions on two anti-abortion protesters, including a ban on "religious worship or instruction." The judge said, "Having created a forum for the demonstrators' expression, [the dean of students] could not, consistent with the dictates of the First Amendment, limit their expression to secular content."

The Ninth Circuit again addressed First Amendment rights on campus in a 2007 case involving campaign spending limits in student elections, *Flint v. Dennison* (488 F.3d 816). The court upheld a $100 spending limit in elections at the University of Montana and allowed the university to deny office to a student who overspent the limit. In off-campus elections, such limits on direct spending by candidates are unconstitutional (*Buckley v. Valeo*, 424 U.S. 1, 1976). However, the court said student elections are only a limited public forum, so the First Amendment doesn't fully apply.

The First Amendment also doesn't necessarily protect faculty advisers of student media. Nor does it necessarily give students standing to sue on behalf of a reassigned or terminated adviser. In 2007, the Tenth Circuit so ruled in dismissing as moot an appeal by former student editors after their faculty adviser was reassigned to other duties at Kansas State University. In *Lane v. Simon* (495 F.3d 1182), the court said the case had to be dismissed because the plaintiffs, former editors of the KSU *Collegian*, had graduated. In a brief opinion that focused on the mootness issue, the three-judge panel cited two earlier cases in which a student's graduation rendered her/his constitutional rights claims moot.

Former *Collegian* editors Katie Lane and Sarah Rice alleged that the reassignment of their faculty adviser, Ron Johnson, violated their First Amendment rights. Johnson was initially a party to the lawsuit, but his case was dismissed by a district court judge and he did not appeal. The district judge ruled that Johnson's First Amendment rights were not violated because he didn't engage in any activities protected by the First Amendment, such as editing the news. Like many advisers, he exercised no control over the newspaper's content.

The two student editors appealed, but the court said the entire case should be dismissed because the students had graduated: "Plaintiffs have not formally sued in a representative capacity, and there has been no effort on anyone's part to substitute current editors as parties. ...*Amici* urge us to confer third-party standing to plaintiffs on behalf of current and future *Collegian* editors. Given that Johnson did not appeal, and neither the publisher nor the present editors have joined in this litigation, we cannot countenance this type of end-run around the general requirement that parties raise their own claims..." The Student Press Law Center and others joined the case as *amicus curiae* ("friend of the court").

Although this ruling makes it more difficult for students to litigate cases like this one, at least in the Tenth Circuit, the editors faced difficult hurdles to begin with. In this appeal two former editors were claiming that the reassignment of their adviser violated their rights even after they graduated. But they served out their terms as editors without any incidents of administrative censorship, they faced no disciplinary action, and they graduated as planned.

Many colleges have areas set aside for protests, often established during the Vietnam era. But not all "free speech zones" are acceptable. The University of Cincinnati had a zone that was only 0.1 percent of its campus and required 10 days' notice before its use; students attempting to gather signatures for a petition were unable to do so effectively because of the low traffic near the small area. A federal judge said that other open areas of campus were considered to be public fora, and the 10-day notice requirement was vague and overbroad. Moreover, she wrote, "the University has simply offered no explanation of its compelling interest in restricting all demonstrations, rallies, and protests from all but one designated public forum on campus" (*Univ. of Cincinnati Chapter of Young Am. for Liberty v. Williams*, 2012 U.S. Dist. LEXIS 80967).

■ HIGH SCHOOL CASES AFTER HAZELWOOD

At the high school level, the *Hazelwood* decision clearly opened the way for widespread administrative censorship where no local law or policy forbids it. In 1989, a federal appellate court held that administrators may also control the content of the advertising in high school newspapers, yearbooks and athletic event programs. In *Planned Parenthood v. Clark Co. School District* (887 F.2d 935), the court upheld a decision by school officials to forbid advertising by Planned Parenthood clinics in Las Vegas school publications. The court declared that under the *Hazelwood* precedent, school officials could ban advertising as well as editorial content concerning "potentially sensitive topics, such as those related to teenage sexual activity."

However, if school officials choose not to control advertising in school publications but instead leave decisions about advertising entirely up to the student staff, there is no state action involved in a school newspaper or yearbook's rejection of a controversial ad. The students are then free to accept or reject advertising, as a federal appellate court ruled in *Yeo v. Town of Lexington* (141 F.3d 241, 1997).

In this case, the First Circuit ruled that student editors at Lexington High School in Massachusetts could reject advocacy advertising, in this case an ad from a group advocating sexual abstinence. The court said there was a clear record that the students and not school officials were in complete control of the school newspaper and yearbook, and that they made the decision to reject the ad on their own. Because there was no state action involved here, there was no right of access to the student newspaper and yearbook.

Even the broad sweep of the *Hazelwood* decision has limits: there are still circumstances under which school officials may violate the First Amendment by censoring a student newspaper. In 1994, the New Jersey Supreme Court overruled an act of administrative censorship of an official school newspaper at a *junior high school*—on First Amendment grounds. In *Desilets v. Clearview Regional Board of Education* (647 A.2d 150), the state Supreme Court held that the principal of Clearview Junior High School did not have sufficient grounds to censor two movie reviews that were written by Brien Desilets, then an eighth grader, for publication in the *Pioneer Press,* the school's official student newspaper. The reviews concerned *Mississippi Burning* and *Rain Man,* both R-rated films. Although the principal later conceded that he had no objection to the content of either review, he said he removed them from the school paper because of the movies' R ratings. School officials did not want to encourage junior high students to see R-rated movies, he said.

In the lawsuit that followed, the Appellate Division of the Superior Court of New Jersey held that this act of administrative censorship violated the First Amendment *in spite of the Hazelwood precedent,* and the New Jersey Supreme Court ultimately agreed. The principal and superintendent attempted to justify the censorship under the school board's policy on school publications by arguing that reviews of R-rated movies fell within the category of "material which advocated the use or advertised the availability of any substance believed to constitute a danger to student health." But nothing in either review said anything about any "substance" that could affect "student health." Nor is either movie about such subjects. School officials even conceded that a Clearview teacher who discussed *Mississippi Burning* in class and encouraged students to see it had done nothing improper.

The court distinguished this case from *Hazelwood,* rejecting the idea that school officials had a legitimate pedagogical reason for discouraging students to see R-rated movies when the rating system itself leaves that decision up to parents and when R-rated movies had been discussed in at least one class at that school—with the apparent blessing of school officials.

The New Jersey Supreme Court emphasized that the school officials involved in this case had no adequate policy governing issues such as the content of the school newspaper. The court chastised the state commissioner of education for failing to assure that the schools had clear policies on such matters. The court did not hold that there is a First Amendment right of student newspapers to publish reviews of R-rated movies. Nor did the court challenge the basic holding of *Hazelwood*—that school officials can control the content of official school publications when they have valid pedagogical reasons for doing so. What the New Jersey Supreme court did say was that, given the lack of a sound policy, school officials did not have a valid basis for censoring this particular newspaper.

Unofficial Newspapers: Still Free

Only 10 months after the *Hazelwood* ruling, a U.S. Court of Appeals reiterated the principle that school officials still may not arbitrarily censor unofficial student publications. In *Burch v. Barker* (861 F.2d 1149, 1988), the appellate court overturned a Renton, Wash., school district policy requiring prior administrative review of all student-produced publications.

A group of students produced an unofficial newspaper called *Bad Astra* and distributed about 350 copies at a senior class barbecue at Lindbergh High School. A parent placed copies in faculty mailboxes as well. While the newspaper was generally critical of school officials, it contained no material that could be considered profane, obscene, defamatory or commercial, the court concluded.

Although Brian Barker, the school principal, said he did not object to the content of the newspaper, he placed letters of reprimand in five students' files because they circulated the paper without seeking prior administrative approval. But the court ruled that the school policy requiring prior review of all student publications was overbroad and therefore violated the students' First Amendment rights. To require such across-the-board administrative approval amounts to an improper prior restraint, the court said.

In overruling the school district policy, the court declared that this situation was not comparable to the *Hazelwood* case because the policy here applied to *all* unofficial publications—not just official publications as in the *Hazelwood* case. School officials cannot engage in wholesale prior censorship of unofficial publications without violating the First Amendment, the court ruled.

While the *Burch* case reaffirmed the principle that non-school-sponsored publications cannot be censored arbitrarily, it would not preclude administrative sanctions if a particular publication contained offensive content. In fact, the *Burch* decision emphasized that while a sweeping policy of prior restraint is unconstitutional, school officials remain free to punish students afterward if they distribute offensive or disruptive materials.

Unofficial and Off-Campus Websites: Not Always Free, But Sometimes

With the growth of the Internet, a new student press freedom issue has arisen: the censorship of *off-campus* student websites, such as those on social network sites, accompanied by on-campus disciplinary action against the students. This raises serious First Amendment questions. In 2002, the Pennsylvania Supreme Court upheld disciplinary action against an eighth grader for an off-campus website that contained "derogatory, profane, offensive and threatening comments" about a teacher and the school principal. The court said there was a sufficient connection to the school because students viewed the website on a campus computer and it created an actual and substantial disruption (*J.S. v. Bethlehem Area School District*, 807 A.2d 847).

Starting in 2011, federal appellate courts started to hear these cases, with mixed results. In *Doninger v. Niehoff* (642 F.3d 334, 2011), the Second Circuit addressed both on- and off-campus speech acts. Avery Doninger, a student at Lewis S. Mills High School in Burlington, Conn., wrote a blog post expressing her distress at the fact that a battle-of-the-bands festival called Jamfest would not be held in the school auditorium on the scheduled date because a school official who operated the sound equipment would not be available (students could reschedule or move the event to the cafeteria).

Doninger went home and sent out a mass e-mail from a parent's official school account that encouraged people to contact the school and complain to get Jamfest back on schedule in the auditorium, despite a school policy that prohibited the use of these e-mail accounts this way. The next day, the principal, Karissa Niehoff, said that the superintendent was so upset by the e-mails she got that Jamfest would be cancelled, and maybe if the students behaved, it would be brought back. That night Doninger wrote on her public LiveJournal blog site, calling the administrators "douchebags" and encouraging more support on behalf of the Jamfest event.

Then, when Doninger went into the administrative office to accept her nomination for senior class secretary, the principal told her that she could not run for the position because of the blog post. When elections for student government occurred, several students made T-shirts with "Team Avery" and "Support LSM Freedom of Speech" printed on them and wore them to the school assembly where candidate speeches were to take place. School administrators caught these students before they entered and made them remove the shirts. Doninger had such a shirt in her backpack but did not wear it to the assembly.

The Second Circuit said that it was not clearly established that punishing Doninger for her blog and making the students remove their "Team Avery" T-shirts would violate their First Amendment rights. The court said that based on the facts, it was "reasonably foreseeable that Doninger's post would reach school property and have disruptive consequences there." But the court did not reach the actual First Amendment question of whether the speech should have been protected—it only addressed whether administrators knew they were abridging Doninger's rights by punishing her for the blog, and said that the law was still unsettled, so they could not have known. As for the T-shirts, the court said the same thing: the law is unsettled, so administrators could not have known that they were violating student speech rights. The court said that if the principal made a mistake, it was a reasonable one—hardly a ringing endorsement of student free expression rights.

Two cases handed down by the same federal appellate court on the same day in 2010 reached contradictory conclusions. Two different three-judge panels of the Third Circuit examined cases in which high school students had created false and offensive MySpace profiles for their principals on non-school computers. But in 2011, the Third Circuit clarified its position on off-campus student speech when it reheard both cases *en banc.*

In *Layshock v. Hermitage School District* (593 F.3d 249), the court upheld a district court's decision in favor of student Justin Layshock. The court said that its decision was based on the fact that the student created the profile off-campus, and the profile did not disrupt the school—even though the profile suggested that the principal did drugs and shoplifted. The Third Circuit agreed with the district court that the school could not "establish[] a sufficient nexus between Justin's speech and a substantial disruption of the school environment."

But on the other hand, a different panel upheld a district court's decision against middle school student J.S. (not the same one in the Pennsylvania case) for the vulgar profile she created of her principal in *J.S. v. Blue Mountain School District* (593 F.3d 286), alleging that he was a sex addict and pedophile. The court said that the speech was not protected because the school had good reason to believe that the profile would cause school disruption.

The panel in *J.S.* distinguished its holding from that in *Layshock* by pointing out that the disruption issue was key: "Unlike the instant case, the school district in *Layshock* did not argue on appeal that there was, under *Tinker,* a nexus between the student's speech and a substantial disruption of the school environment." The cases were re-argued before the Third Circuit sitting *en banc* in 2010, the first time this issue had been heard by an *en banc* appellate court. The court again issued the opinions on the same day in June 2011. In both opinions the court made it clear that schools must exercise caution before attempting to regulate off-campus student speech.

In *Layshock* (650 F.3d 205), the court said, "It would be an unseemly and dangerous precedent to allow the state, in the guise of school authorities, to reach into a child's home and control his/her actions there to the same extent that it can control that child when he/she participates in school sponsored activities." Nor was the mere fact that the speech could be and was accessed on campus enough to establish the school district's jurisdiction to punish Layshock. But the court dodged a direct answer on whether that would always be the case—it just said that in this case, it was not. The Supreme Court denied *cert.*

In *J.S.* (650 F.3d 915), the court said that there was no disruption in school caused by the fake MySpace profile, and students couldn't even see the page in school because school computers blocked the MySpace website. In addition, the profile was so juvenile and outrageous that no one would take it seriously (the profile said things like "it's your oh so wonderful, hairy, expressionless, sex addict, fagass, put on this world with a small dick PRINCIPAL[.] I have come to myspace so i can pervert the minds of other principal's [sic] to be just like me"). Moreover, the court said, the student created it as a joke, did not identify the principal by name, and made it private so that only she and her friends could see it.

Comparing the *Tinker* case facts to this case, the court said, "If *Tinker's* black armbands—an ostentatious reminder of the highly emotional and controversial subject of the Vietnam war—could not 'reasonably have led school authorities to forecast substantial disruption of or material interference with school activities,' neither can J.S.'s profile, despite the unfortunate humiliation it caused for [the principal]." Because, the court said, neither it nor the

Supreme Court had ever permitted schools to punish students for speech that took place off-campus, was not sponsored by the school, and did not cause substantial disruption, the court declined to do so here.

A concurring opinion by Judge D. Brooks Smith that is highly protective of off-campus speech drew the agreement of four other judges. Judge Smith gave a good example of why off-campus speech cannot be targeted by school officials:

> Suppose a high school student, while at home after school hours, were to write a blog entry defending gay marriage. Suppose further that several of the student's classmates got wind of the entry, took issue with it, and caused a significant disturbance at school. While the school could clearly punish the students who acted disruptively, if *Tinker* were held to apply to off-campus speech, the school could also punish the student whose blog entry brought about the disruption. That cannot be, nor is it, the law.

But six dissenting judges said that the majority "allows a student to target a school official and his family with malicious and unfounded accusations about their character in vulgar, obscene, and personal language" and leaves officials powerless to punish offenders and make students accountable for their actions.

But private social media use is still contentious and problematic for schools, particularly when it's students targeting other students. Kara Kowalski, a senior at Musselman High School in Berkeley County, W.V., was suspended from school for five days for creating a MySpace page called "S.A.S.H.," which she said stood for "Students Against Sluts Herpes" and was targeted against another student. In ruling that Kowalski could be so disciplined, the Fourth Circuit said that she "used the Internet to orchestrate a targeted attack on a classmate, and did so in a manner that was sufficiently connected to the school environment as to implicate the School District's recognized authority to discipline speech which 'materially and substantially interfere[s] with the requirements of appropriate discipline in the operation of the school and collid[es] with the rights of others'" (*Kowalski v. Berkeley County Schools*, 652 F.3d 565, 2011).

Other Issues

Dress codes, often passed in elementary and high schools to avoid issues like gang affiliation or classroom distraction and to promote safety and harmony, are increasingly the subject of lawsuits. A recent example comes from the Fifth Circuit in *Palmer v. Waxahachie Independent School District* (579 F.3d 502). Paul Palmer, a Texas high school student, wore a t-shirt to school supporting John Edwards for president in 2008. He was ordered to remove it because it contained printed words which did not support the school, its instructional goals, or school spirit. The district revamped its dress code, and Palmer submitted three shirts for approval: the original Edwards t-shirt plus a polo shirt with the same message and a t-shirt that contained "Freedom of Speech" on the front and the text of the First Amendment on the back. The school rejected the shirts.

The court said the rule was content-neutral because it did not target any particular kind of speech even though the code allowed certain expression, saying, "The District was in no way attempting to suppress any student's expression through its dress code—a critical fact based on earlier student speech cases—so the dress code is content-neutral." The court then applied intermediate scrutiny, under which the code passed. The circuits are split on the level of scrutiny to be applied to student speech cases, but the Supreme Court declined to hear an appeal.

Moreover, courts have been supportive of administrative decisions that involve students making violent comments, writing violent essays or notes, or wishing violence upon others. An example from many in recent years: in *Cuff v. Valley Cent. Sch. Dist.* (677 F.3d 109, 2012), a fifth-grade student drew a picture of an astronaut and expressed a desire to blow up the school with teachers inside. Another student saw the drawing and brought it to a teacher's attention; the fifth-grader was suspended. In upholding the suspension, the Second Circuit said that the student's history of violence, as well as concerns of his teachers, suggested that there might be disruption to normal school activities as a result of this drawing, and that *Tinker* only required a showing of "facts which might reasonably have led school authorities to forecast substantial disruption of or material interference with school activities," not that such disruption actually occurred. Other courts, said the Second Circuit, "have allowed wide leeway to school administrators disciplining students for writings or other conduct threatening violence." Another example: *Riehm v. Engelking*, discussed earlier.

■ FREEDOM AT PRIVATE SCHOOLS

This chapter has been devoted to freedom of expression at public schools and colleges. What about private institutions? At private schools, the general rule is that freedom only exists if school officials find it in their interest to grant it: in the absence of *state action,* the First Amendment does not apply. When a private university newspaper is censored or its editors are fired, normally the worst the administration need fear is bad public relations. The school may face condemnation by professional media and journalistic organizations, but there is usually little chance for the aggrieved students to win a lawsuit.

This problem was well illustrated by a 1980 incident at Baylor University, a Baptist church-related institution in Waco, Texas. *Playboy* magazine was doing a photo feature on "Girls of the Southwest Conference," and a *Playboy* photographer was coming to town. University President Abner McCall warned that any Baylor student who posed nude for *Playboy* would be punished (and presumably expelled). The Baylor newspaper, the *Lariat,* editorially said that Baylor students should be free to make up their own minds about whether to pose. Then McCall told the *Lariat* editors not to cover the growing *Playboy* controversy. The editors rejected that blatant censorship, and several were fired. Shortly, more staff members and two journalism professors resigned in protest. One faculty member who resigned was abruptly ordered to leave Baylor in mid-semester. Before it was over, the Baylor incident stirred a national controversy, but the *Lariat* staff had no legal recourse. They were out.

Although the issues that provoke censorship aren't often as spectacular as the one at Baylor, censorship incidents are not unusual at private universities.

During the era of student activism, many lawsuits were filed alleging constitutional violations by private institutions, but the courts consistently ruled in favor of school officials—except in a very few cases where state action could be shown.

To establish state action, it must be shown that a government is deeply involved not only in funding the institution but also in its management. In separate cases (neither involving student press freedom), state action has been shown at two major private universities in Pennsylvania: Pittsburgh and Temple. However, in both instances Pennsylvania had entered agreements with school officials in which the state provided major funding in return for substantial reductions in tuition for Pennsylvania residents. Moreover, the state was given the power to appoint one-third of each institution's governing board. (See *Isaacs v. Temple University*, 385 F.Supp. 473, 1974; and *Braden v. Pittsburgh University*, 552 F.2d 948, 1977.)

Aside from the two Pennsylvania cases, court decisions establishing state action at private schools are hard to find. A New York court once issued a memorandum opinion in connection with a settlement of a student discipline lawsuit against Hofstra University. The opinion discussed the procedural rights of students, but didn't address the basic issue of whether state action was present (*Ryan v. Hofstra*, 324 N.Y.S.2d 964, 1971). On the other hand, a number of court decisions have held that state action does not exist at various private universities. For instance, in *Furumoto v. Lyman* (362 F.Supp. 1267, 1973), a court failed to find state action at Stanford University, despite massive federal grants and a state charter.

In 1982, the Supreme Court may have settled the question of state action at private educational institutions. In *Rendell-Baker v. Kohn* (457 U.S. 830), the Court ruled that state action was not present at a private high school for students with special problems, even though the school received 90 percent of its revenue from government funds. In a 7-2 ruling, the Court made it very unlikely that state action can be shown at a purely private school or college.

Thus, the conclusion seems clear: in the absence of an arrangement like those at Temple and Pittsburgh, there's no state action, and private school administrators may therefore ignore the First Amendment. There is, however, one other possible recourse. Some scholars have suggested that the common law principles of private association law be applied to student rights cases. A private association must operate in accordance with its own bylaws. When it fails to do that, its members may turn to the courts for help. That principle has not often been used by students, but it could be, given a university policy that guarantees freedom of the press and a clear violation of that policy. Perhaps in an appropriate case a court would follow this reasoning and recognize that private university students have some rights, at least when the institution has adopted a policy that says they do.

But that doesn't mean that there aren't workarounds for students at private schools. Student journalists at a private college dealt with censorship by administrators in a very creative way in 2011. When told they could not publish a story about a professor who had allegedly used exotic dancers at an off-campus symposium on the front page "above the fold" where it could be seen in campus newsracks, the editors decided to leave the top half of the front page totally blank except for the words "See below the fold" in small type—where, of course, the full story ran. The editors at the LaSalle University *Collegian* then ran an editorial explaining why they did what they did.

■ PRACTICAL CONSIDERATIONS

So far, we've talked about student press freedom mostly in terms of lawsuits and the First Amendment. Because this chapter will certainly be read for guidance by students facing threats of censorship, a few practical observations are in order.

First, it should be emphasized that it is sometimes necessary to fight for constitutional rights—in court, if necessary. School administrators often ignore the First Amendment until forced to recognize that it exists. Student newspapers are censored every year without anyone doing anything about it.

It is unfortunate but true that winning one's constitutional rights can be expensive and time-consuming. If you are censored, you may have some tough choices to make. Ask yourself some questions. Is the censorship really unlawful? High school administrators now have wide latitude to control the content of official student newspapers unless there is a state law or local policy forbidding censorship. College administrators have less latitude in controlling the student press, although that could change as a result of recent court decisions.

Also, how important is the item you've been told you can't publish? How would a judge react to it? Justice Oliver Wendell Holmes' legal maxim, "hard cases make bad law," applies here. Don't pursue a case that invites a bad legal precedent, one that could be used to deny freedom to students elsewhere. A well-documented story about malfeasance by the college administration is one thing; a column that uses four-letter words gratuitously is another.

After weighing these questions, there are some specific steps to take if you have a case worth pursuing. First, go through all available channels. Consult your faculty adviser if you have one. If there is a publications policy board, take the case there. Only if all internal remedies fail is it time to consider a lawsuit.

But if you reach that point, weigh your options again. Is there a local attorney willing to represent you on a low-cost basis? The American Civil Liberties Union has represented students in numerous First Amendment cases. The Student Press Law Center in Washington may also be able to offer advice—or help you find an attorney. If legal help isn't available, compromise may again be in order. But if, on the other hand, you really have a good case and a good lawyer, perhaps your name will someday appear in law books like this one.

■ AN OVERVIEW OF MAJOR ISSUES

The question of student press freedom is a miniature version of many other questions addressed in this book. In trying to answer this question, the Supreme Court and federal appellate courts extended First Amendment rights to students at public high schools and colleges—and then began to curtail those rights.

Underlying these legal principles there are questions on which there is no consensus. To what extent should students be protected by the First Amendment? When are prior restraints justified at a public school or college? Should the rules differ at high schools and colleges? Why should the rules be different for private schools? Should underground newspapers be treated differently than official ones?

If the rationale for extending First Amendment rights to students is the concept of state action, doesn't that run afoul of the idea that the *taxpayers* should have the final say about what goes on at a public school? Aren't school board members the democratically elected representatives of the people? Isn't the school principal the school board's surrogate, charged with doing the public's bidding? In effect, the Supreme Court has ruled that the principal has the powers of a publisher, to exercise control at will.

In other areas of law, the courts have often ruled that the First Amendment sets strict limits on government actions that deprive individuals of their rights, public opinion notwithstanding. To some degree, at least, those limits apply to school officials. In the end, perhaps the most basic question in student press law is this: should the schools be a microcosm of society at large, or should they be insulated places with stricter rules and fewer constitutional safeguards?

WHAT SHOULD I KNOW ABOUT MY STATE?

SUMMARY

A SUMMARY OF STUDENT PRESS LAW

- Does my state have any protections for student speech and press? Are they statutes, common law, or both, and what do they say? (Be sure to check out the Student Press Law Center's website at www.splc.org for help or support.)
- What does my school or campus policy say about student speech and press rights?
- How has my federal circuit handled student free speech and press issues?

Does the First Amendment Apply to Students?

In *Tinker v. Des Moines Ind. School District*, the Supreme Court extended First Amendment protection to students attending public schools. But the Supreme Court said high school students' rights on campus are not as extensive as those normally available off campus. Students' freedom of expression may be limited when necessary to protect the rights of others and to maintain an orderly educational process. The courts have generally extended somewhat broader First Amendment rights to college students.

Are Student Publications Constitutionally Protected?

Federal courts have consistently held that unofficial or "underground" high school publications are protected by the First Amendment and may not be arbitrarily censored by school administrators. The courts have sometimes refused to allow censorship even when such a publication included earthy language or controversial subject matter.

Where Do High School Journalists Stand Now?

In *Hazelwood School District v. Kuhlmeier* the Court said the First Amendment does not prevent administrators from censoring official high school newspapers. The Court said there is a difference between the free speech activities that public school officials must *tolerate* (as in *Tinker*) and the kind of speech the First Amendment requires them to sponsor by permitting it in official publications or at school activities. However, these decisions do not override state laws and local policies that forbid administrative censorship in some states.

Are Private Schools Treated Differently?

The legal rationale for extending First Amendment protection to students was that public school officials' acts constitute *state action*. The First Amendment prohibits the denial of free expression rights by governments, not by private entities. Unless a private school official's conduct constitutes state action (which it rarely does), the First Amendment is inapplicable.

Selected Excerpts from the Law

The First Amendment
Congress shall make no law respecting an establishment of religion, or prohibiting the free exercise thereof; or *abridging the freedom of speech or of the press*; or the right of the people peaceably to assemble, and to petition the Government for a redress of grievances. (ratified 1791)

The Fourth Amendment
The right of the people to be secure in their persons, houses, papers, and effects, against unreasonable searches and seizures, shall not be violated, and no Warrants shall issue, but upon probable cause, supported by Oath or affirmation, and particularly describing the place to be searched, and the persons or things to be seized. (ratified 1791)

The Sixth Amendment
In all criminal prosecutions, the accused shall enjoy the right to a speedy and public trial, *by an impartial jury* of the State and district wherein the crime shall have been committed... (ratified 1791)

The Fourteenth Amendment
...No state shall make or enforce any law which shall abridge the privileges or immunities of citizens of the United States; *nor shall any state deprive any person of life, liberty or property, without due process of law*; nor deny to any person within its jurisdiction the equal protection of the laws.... (ratified 1868)

Section 326 of the Communications Act
Nothing in this Act shall be understood or construed to give the (Federal Communications) Commission the power of censorship over the radio communications or signals transmitted by any radio station, and no regulation or condition shall be promulgated or fixed by the Commission which shall interfere with the right of free speech by means of radio communication.

Section 1464 of the U.S. Criminal Code
Whoever utters any obscene, indecent, or profane language by means of radio communication shall be fined under this title or imprisoned not more than two years, or both.

Index